CW00394610

THE OXFORD HANDBO

POLITICAL
BEHAVIOR

THE OXFORD HANDBOOKS OF POLITICAL SCIENCE

GENERAL EDITOR: ROBERT E. GOODIN

The *Oxford Handbooks of Political Science* is a ten-volume set of reference books offering authoritative and engaging critical overviews of all the main branches of political science.

The series as a whole is under the General Editorship of Robert E. Goodin, with each volume being edited by a distinguished international group of specialists in their respective fields:

POLITICAL THEORY
John S. Dryzek, Bonnie Honig & Anne Phillips

POLITICAL INSTITUTIONS
R. A. W. Rhodes, Sarah A. Binder & Bert A. Rockman

POLITICAL BEHAVIOR
Russell J. Dalton & Hans-Dieter Klingemann

COMPARATIVE POLITICS
Carles Boix & Susan C. Stokes

LAW & POLITICS
Keith E. Whittington, R. Daniel Kelemen & Gregory A. Caldeira

PUBLIC POLICY
Michael Moran, Martin Rein & Robert E. Goodin

POLITICAL ECONOMY
Barry R. Weingast & Donald A. Wittman

INTERNATIONAL RELATIONS
Christian Reus-Smit & Duncan Snidal

CONTEXTUAL POLITICAL ANALYSIS
Robert E. Goodin & Charles Tilly

POLITICAL METHODOLOGY
Janet M. Box-Steffensmeier, Henry E. Brady & David Collier

This series aspires to shape the discipline, not just to report on it. Like the Goodin–Klingemann *New Handbook of Political Science* upon which the series builds, each of these volumes will combine critical commentaries on where the field has been together with positive suggestions as to where it ought to be heading.

THE OXFORD HANDBOOK OF

POLITICAL BEHAVIOR

Edited by

RUSSELL J. DALTON

and

HANS-DIETER KLINGEMANN

OXFORD

UNIVERSITY PRESS

OXFORD
UNIVERSITY PRESS

Great Clarendon Street, Oxford OX2 6DP

Oxford University Press is a department of the University of Oxford.
It furthers the University's objective of excellence in research, scholarship,
and education by publishing worldwide in

Oxford New York

Auckland Cape Town Dar es Salaam Hong Kong Karachi
Kuala Lumpur Madrid Melbourne Mexico City Nairobi
New Delhi Shanghai Taipei Toronto

With offices in

Argentina Austria Brazil Chile Czech Republic France Greece
Guatemala Hungary Italy Japan Poland Portugal Singapore
South Korea Switzerland Thailand Turkey Ukraine Vietnam

Oxford is a registered trade mark of Oxford University Press
in the UK and in certain other countries

Published in the United States
by Oxford University Press Inc., New York

© The several contributors 2007

The moral rights of the authors have been asserted
Database right Oxford University Press (maker)

First published 2007
First published in paperback 2009

All rights reserved. No part of this publication may be reproduced,
stored in a retrieval system, or transmitted, in any form or by any means,
without the prior permission in writing of Oxford University Press,
or as expressly permitted by law, or under terms agreed with the appropriate
reprographics rights organization. Enquiries concerning reproduction
outside the scope of the above should be sent to the Rights Department,
Oxford University Press, at the address above

You must not circulate this book in any other binding or cover
and you must impose the same condition on any acquirer

British Library Cataloguing in Publication Data

Data available

Library of Congress Cataloging in Publication Data

Oxford handbook of political behavior / edited by Russell J. Dalton and Hans-Dieter Klingemann.
p. cm. — (Oxford handbooks of political science)
ISBN 978-0-19-927012-5 (alk. paper)
1. Political psychology. 2. Political behavior. 3. Political sociology.
I. Dalton, Russell J. II. Klingemann, Hans-Dieter.
JA74.5.093 2007
306.2—dc22 2007003074

Typeset by SPI Publisher Services, Pondicherry, India
Printed and bound by
CPI Group (UK) Ltd, Croydon, CR0 4YY

ISBN 978-0-19-927012-5 (Hbk.)
978-0-19-956601-3 (Pbk.)

9 10 8

To Angus Campbell,
Warren E. Miller,
Philip E. Converse,
and Donald Stokes,
the founders of our field.

PREFACE

There are few areas in political science where scholarly knowledge has made greater progress in the past two generations than the field of political behavior. From Aristotle's time until the 1950s, the description and explanation of public opinion was based on the impressions of political "experts." We could not systematically study what citizens actually believed, how they acted, or why they voted for one party rather than another.

The advent of systematic, scientific public opinion surveys dramatically changed our knowledge of the average citizen. We see this advance in contemporary politics. Where once politicians guessed what the public favored, they can now monitor public policy preferences through a plethora of public opinion surveys. Campaigns were once idiosyncratic processes, with campaign managers acting with limited information. Now, there is a sophisticated knowledge of how voters think and act. One suspects that a campaign from the 1950s would not be able to compete with a modern campaign that has the benefit of this knowledge. Our understanding of political participation and political attitudes is similarly enriched.

This Handbook documents our current knowledge about citizen attitudes and actions that resulted from this behavioral revolution. Moreover, the revolution is continuing. Initially, surveys of public opinion were limited to only a few, affluent democracies. In the past decade, research has expanded to a near global scale. We are now able to compare how citizens in Berlin compare to those in Benin, how voting in San Francisco compares to voting in San Salvador.

The goal of this Handbook is to introduce the reader to the key concepts in our field, the empirical evidence that scholars have collected, and the remaining research questions that still face us. We have organized sections to reflect the major themes in the field, and invited the leading scholars in each area to summarize the research literature. In addition, for each section we asked a leading figure to write a final chapter in the section that discusses the broad topics and remaining research questions in the field. We want to thank all of the authors for their exceptional contributions to this volume. We learned a great deal about the state of political behavior research, and we trust the reader will also learn a great deal from this collection.

In a project this large, we also have accumulated a list of people who supported this effort. Robert Goodin collaborated with Hans-Dieter Klingemann on the *New Handbook of Political Science* that planted the seed for this series, and Goodin oversaw the expanded Handbook series. We appreciate Bob's advice and support. Dominic Byatt at Oxford University Press championed this Handbook series and has been an ideal editor and supporter. The Center for the Study of Democracy at the University of California, Irvine, and the Wissenschaftszentrum Berlin für Sozialforschung generously provided support for the completion of this project. Liz Schiller helped us prepare the manuscript for submission, a major undertaking for a book of this size. Tanya Dean at Oxford University Press expertly guided the Handbook through the production process.

A successful research program answers significant research questions, and inevitably generates new questions. We think the reader will see both traits in the collection of political behavior articles that follows.

Russell J. Dalton & Hans-Dieter Klingemann
Irvine & Berlin

Contents

PART IV   POLITICAL VALUES

PART V   NEW DEBATES IN POLITICAL
BEHAVIOR

PART VI   POLITICAL PARTICIPATION

PART VII   DOES PUBLIC OPINION MATTER?

PART VIII   THE METHODOLOGY OF COMPARATIVE POLITICAL BEHAVIOR RESEARCH

ABOUT THE CONTRIBUTORS

Christopher J. Anderson is Professor of Government at Cornell University.

André Blais is Professor of Political Science at the Université de Montréal and holds a Canada Research Chair in Electoral Studies.

Jean Blondel is Professorial Fellow at the European University Institute, Florence and Visiting Professor at the University of Siena.

Philip E. Converse is Distinguished Professor-Emeritus, the University of Michigan, and Director-Emeritus, Center for Advanced Study in the Behavioral Sciences, Stanford, California.

John Curtice is Professor of Politics at Strathclyde University, Glasgow.

Russell J. Dalton is Professor of Political Science at the University of California, Irvine.

Kevin Deegan-Krause is Associate Professor of Political Science at Wayne State University.

Richard C. Eichenberg is Associate Professor of Political Science at Tufts University.

Yilmaz Esmer is Professor of Political Science and International Relations at Bogazici University, Istanbul.

Dieter Fuchs is Professor of Political Science at the University of Stuttgart.

James L. Gibson is Sidney W. Souers Professor of Government, Washington University in St. Louis and Fellow, Centre for Comparative and International Politics, Stellenbosch University, South Africa.

Loek Halman is Associate Professor of Sociology at Tilburg University.

Anthony Heath is Professor of Sociology at the University of Oxford and a Professorial Fellow of Nuffield College.

Ursula Hoffman-Lange is Professor of Political Science at the University of Bamberg.

Sören Holmberg is Professor of Political Science and Election Research at Göteborg University.

Robert Huckfeldt is Distinguished Professor of Political Science at the University of California, Davis.

Ronald Inglehart is Professor of Political Science at the University of Michigan.

Takashi Inoguchi is Professor Emeritus, University of Tokyo and Professor of Political Science, Chuo University, Tokyo.

M. Kent Jennings is Professor of Political Science at the University of California, Santa Barbara, and Professor Emeritus at the University of Michigan.

Max Kaase is Professor Emeritus of Political Science at the University of Mannheim.

Miki Caul Kittilson is Assistant Professor of Political Science at Arizona State University.

Hans-Dieter Klingemann is Professor of Political Science and former Director of the research unit Institutions and Social Change at the Social Science Research Centre, Berlin.

Oddbjørn Knutsen is Professor of Political Science at the University of Oslo.

Ruud Koopmans is Professor of Sociology at the Free University of Amsterdam.

James H. Kuklinski is Professor of Political Science at the University of Illinois.

Staffan Kumlin is Hans Meijer Pro Futura Fellow at Göteborg University and the Swedish Collegium for Advanced Study in the Social Sciences.

Matthew S. Levendusky is Post-doctoral Associate at Yale University.

Michael S. Lewis-Beck is F. Wendell Miller Distinguished Professor of Political Science at the University of Iowa.

Peter Mair is Professor of Comparative Politics at the European University Institute, Florence, and at Leiden University.

Michael Margolis is Professor of Political Science at the University of Cincinnati.

Ian McAllister is Professor of Political Science at the Australian National University, Canberra.

Ferdinand Müller-Rommel is Professor of Comparative Politics at the University of Lüneburg.

Diana C. Mutz is Samuel A. Stouffer Professor of Political Science and Communication at the University of Pennsylvania and serves as Director of the Institute for the Study of Citizens and Politics at the Annenberg Public Policy Center.

Kenneth Newton is Professor of Comparative Politics at the University of Southampton and Visiting Research Fellow at the Social Science Research Center, Berlin.

Pippa Norris is Director of Democratic Governance at the United Nations Development Programme in New York and the Maguire Lecturer in Comparative Politics at Harvard University.

Mark Peffley is Professor of Political Science at the University of Kentucky.

Thorleif Pettersson is Professor of Sociology of Religion at Uppsala University.

Buddy Peyton is a Graduate Student at the University of Illinois.

Robert Rohrschneider is Professor of Political Science at Indiana University.

Richard Rose is Director of the Centre for the Study of Public Policy at the University of Aberdeen.

Dieter Rucht is Professor of Sociology and Co-director of the research group "Civil Society, Citizenship and Political Mobilization in Europe" at the Social Science Research Center, Berlin.

Shamit Saggar is Professor of Political Science at the University of Sussex and non-executive chairman of the Law Society Consumer Board.

Susan E. Scarrow is Associate Professor of Political Science at the University of Houston.

Rüdiger Schmitt-Beck is Professor of Political Science at the University of Duisburg-Essen.

Holli A. Semetko is Professor of Political Science at Emory University.

Doh Chull Shin is Professor of Political Science at the University of Missouri and holds the chair in Korean studies.

Paul M. Sniderman is Fairleigh S. Dickinson Jr. Professor in Public Policy at Stanford University.

Stuart N. Soroka is Associate Professor of Political Science at McGill University.

Mary Stegmaier is Assistant Dean in the College of Arts and Sciences and Lecturer in the Departments of Politics and Economics at the University of Virginia.

James Stimson is Raymond Dawson Distinguished Bicentennial Professor at the University of North Carolina at Chapel Hill.

Dietlind Stolle is Associate Professor of Political Science at McGill University.

Jacques Thomassen is Professor of Political Science at the University of Twente.

Jan W. van Deth is Professor of Political Science and International Comparative Research at the University of Mannheim.

Christian Welzel is Professor of Political Science at the Jacobs University Bremen (JUB).

Bernhard Weßels is Senior Researcher at the Social Science Research Center Berlin and a Lecturer in Political Science at the Freie Universität Berlin.

Christopher Wlezien is Professor of Political Science and Faculty Affiliate in the Institute for Public Affairs at Temple University, Philadelphia.

Edmund Wnuk-Lipiński is Rector of Collegium Civitas, Warsaw, and Chairman of the Academic Board in the Institute of Political Studies, Polish Academy of Sciences, Warsaw.

PART I

INTRODUCTION

CHAPTER 1

CITIZENS AND POLITICAL BEHAVIOR

RUSSELL J. DALTON
HANS-DIETER KLINGEMANN

ONE might claim that the wellspring of politics flows from the attitudes and behaviors of the ordinary citizen, and that the institutions of a democratic political process should be structured to respond to the citizenry. This claim has stimulated debates about the abilities of the public and the quality of citizen participation that began with Aristotle and Socrates and continue in the pages of contemporary political science journals.

The continuation of these debates over centuries might suggest that research has made little progress in addressing these questions. We will argue, however, that in the past generation the field of comparative political behavior has made tremendous progress in describing the attitudes and behavior of publics, and the citizens' role within the political process. We summarize the current debates in six areas of political behavior: the sophistication of mass publics, modernization processes, political values, voting choice, political participation, and representation.

The expanding collection of public opinion data is one of the major accomplishments in comparative political behavior over the past several decades (see Kittilson chapter; Heath, Fisher, and Smith 2005). *The Civic Culture* (Almond and Verba 1963) marked a dramatic step forward in comparative research by studying the publics in five nations; for a considerable period such cross-national studies remained quite rare. Today, in addition to ad hoc comparative surveys, several institutionalized or semi-institutionalized cross-national surveys are repeated regularly, some with a near-global scope. The European Commission sponsors the Eurobarometer surveys in the member states of the European Union. A New Europe Barometer, Latinobarometer, Afrobarometer, East Asian Barometer, and Asiabarometer survey citizens in these regions. Separate research consortiums regularly conduct the European Values Study (EVS), the International Social Survey Program (ISSP), the European Social Survey (ESS), and the Comparative Study of Electoral Systems (CSES). The largest number of nations is included in the World Values Surveys (WVS), conducted in four waves since 1981 with a fifth wave launched in 2005–7. In short, over the past few decades comparative political behavior has become a very "data-rich" field of research.

A second theme is the transformation of political behavior that has occurred simultaneously with the rapid expansion of empirical knowledge. Political behavior in advanced industrial democracies has shifted in fundamental ways during the latter half of the twentieth century. A dramatic process of social and political modernization has also transformed much of the developing world. The Third Wave of democratization has reformed the political systems and the citizenry in the new democracies of central and eastern Europe, Asia, Africa, and Latin America.

These new developments provide distinctive opportunities to test old theories, expand the boundaries of knowledge, and develop new theories. We normally observe political systems in a state of equilibrium, when stability and incremental change dominate our findings. Now we can examine questions of political change and adaptation that often go to the heart of theoretical interests, but which we could seldom observe directly in earlier times.

This essay summarizes some of the debates that are currently most visible in the scholarly literature and which preoccupy many of the articles in this Handbook.

1 MASS BELIEF SYSTEMS
AND COMMUNICATION

One of the enduring debates of political behavior research involves basic questions about the public's political abilities—the public's level of knowledge, understanding, and interest in political matters. For voters to make meaningful decisions, they must understand the options the polity faces. Citizens must have a sufficient knowledge of the workings of the political system if they intend to influence and control the actions of their representatives. Almond and Verba (1963), for example, considered cognition important in defining a political culture, and Dahl (1989, 307–08) stressed the quality of the political debate as a precondition to arrive at what he has called "enlightened understanding."

Debates about the political abilities of the public remain one of the major controversies in political behavior research as discussed in several of this volume's chapters. The early empirical surveys found that the public's political sophistication fell short of theoretical ideal (Campbell et al. 1960; Converse 1964; Butler and Stokes 1969). For most citizens, political interest and involvement barely seemed to extend beyond casting an occasional vote in national elections. Furthermore, people apparently brought very little understanding to their participation in politics. It was not clear that voting decisions were based on rational evaluations of candidates, parties, and their issue positions.

This image of the uninformed and unsophisticated voter began to reshape the view of the citizenry and democratic politics. Some experts argued that if the bulk of the public is unsophisticated, it is better for democracy that people remain politically uninvolved. And if this was beneficial to democracy, other scholars were anxious to argue the pitfalls of too excessive political mobilization and the benefits of political order in less developed nations (Huntington 1968).

This debate has continued until the present, as summarized in the chapter by Kuklinski and Peyton. A revisionist approach argues that contemporary publics have greater political sophistication than early research presumed, because either measurement was flawed or sophistication has increased as a consequence of social modernization. Other researchers argued that the sophistication of voters is significantly affected by the political environment, and the initial studies of the American public in the quiet 1950s discounted the public's engagement. This contextual explanation of political sophistication was further supported by cross-national studies indicating that sophistication varies sharply across nations, with the relatively non-ideological American system displaying one of the least ideological publics (Klingemann 1979; Stacy and Segura 1997). Moreover, research on information cues argues that the sophistication citizens need to come to a meaningful choice in politics are heavily overstated. Quite naturally, citizens economize their investment in the information they need to come to meaningful decisions and most of them are able to optimize this investment in ways that keep democracies working (Lau and Redlawsk 2006; Lupia and McCubbins 1998). People in western democracies now live in an information rich environment.

In contrast, other research claims that political information and engagement remains limited in western democracies (Delli Carpini and Keeter 1991; Wattenberg 2006). Some scholars claim that the situation is actually deteriorating, and modernization atomizes and alienates citizens, and further disengages them from politics (Putnam 2000). Indeed, one recent book argues that people are disinterested in politics and just do not want to be bothered with the responsibilities of democratic citizenship (Hibbing and Theiss-Morse 2002).

In short, one school of research argues the glass is half empty, and going down—the opposite school argues the glass is half full, and going up. This political science prestidigitation in action—to have both things happen at once—is often based on analyses of the same public opinion surveys. As many of the chapters in this volume demonstrate, the resolution of this question has fundamental implications for how we think about political behavior and the citizens' role in the democratic process. For instance, if one thinks that the instruments of referenda and initiatives should be strictly limited or expanded, heavily depends on one's view of the citizens' civic competence (Kriesi 2005).

In this introduction, we want to suggest a different way of thinking about this question. Previous research often reaches different conclusions because it asks different questions, and has different standards of evaluating available evidence. Rather than asking if voters meet the ideal expectations of democratic theorists, which has often been the implicit standard, it might be more productive to observe that people are regularly making political choices and ask how these choices are actually made. Bowler and Donovan (1998: 30 f.) aptly put it this way: "Voters, to use an analogy, may know very little about the workings of the internal combustion engine, but they do know how to drive. And while we might say that early voting studies focused on voter ignorance of the engine, the newer studies pay more attention to the ability to drive." Thus, many of the chapters in this volume (such as Mutz, Huckfeldt, and Sniderman and Levendusky) ask the pragmatic question of how people make life decisions— including who to vote for in the next election or in a referendum. The answer is often that they use information shortcuts, cues, emotions, heuristics and other methods to reach reasonable choices, and reasonable choices when structured by institutions and cumulated across the electorate lead to democratic choice (Surowiecki 2004).

This continuing debate is a source of vitality in political behavior research, because it focuses attention on the question of what democracy expects of its citizens and whether these expectations are met. In addition, this debate has reshaped our understanding of how people actually make their political choices (e.g. Popkin 1991; Zaller 1992; Lupia and McCubbins 1998). The lofty ideals of classic democratic theory presumed a rational decision-making process by a fully informed electorate. Even given more positive judgments about the political sophistication of contemporary electorates, most voters (and even some political scientists) still fall short of the standards of classic democratic theory. However, we now understand that this maximalist definition of the prerequisites for informed decision making is unnecessary. Instead, we should look at whether citizens can manage the complexities of politics and make reasonable decisions given their political interests and positions. Empirical research is emphasizing a satisficing approach to decision making in which models ask what are the pragmatic ways that individuals actually make their political choices.

2 MODERNIZATION AND DEMOCRATIZATION

One of the most powerful social science concepts to emerge in political behavior research—and one central to the study of citizen attitudes and behavior—is the concept of political culture. Almond and Verba's (1963) seminal study, *The Civic*

Culture, contended that the institutions and patterns of action in a political system are closely linked to the political culture of the nation. The culture, in turn, is shaped by the historical, economic and social conditions of a nation. Cultural studies are especially important in the study of democratization, as analysts try to identify the cultural requisites of democracy (Almond and Verba 1963; Eckstein 1966; Pye and Verba 1965).

Despite the heuristic and interpretive power of the concept of political culture, there are recurring questions about the precision and predictive power of the concept (Laitin 1995). Kaase (1983), for instance, said that measuring political culture is like "trying to nail jello to the wall." That is, the concept lacked precision and often became a subjective, stereotypic description of a nation rather than an empirically measurable concept. Some analysts saw political culture in virtually every feature of political life, others viewed it merely as a residual category that explained what remained unexplainable by other means. Even more problematic was the uneven evidence of culture's causal effect.

Several recent studies have prompted a renaissance of political culture research and the link between modernization and political behavior. Inglehart demonstrated the congruence between broad political attitudes and democratic stability for twenty-two nations in the 1981 World Values Survey (Inglehart 1990). Putnam's (1993) study of regional governments in Italy provided even more impressive testimony in support of cultural theory. Putnam demonstrated that the cultural traditions of a region—roughly contrasting the cooperative political style of the North to the more hierarchic tradition of the South—were a potent predictor of the performance of contemporary governments. These studies generated counter findings, and a new research debate emerged (e.g. Inglehart 1997; Reisinger 1995; Jackman and Miller 1996).

Moreover, the democratization wave of the 1990s focused attention on the nexus between modernization and political culture. To what extent did political change in central and eastern Europe arise from gradual changes in the political culture? More important politically, to what extent can the prospects for democracy be judged by their public's support for democratic politics? Public opinion surveys probed Russian public opinion on this issue, finding surprisingly high levels of support for basic democratic principles in the former Soviet Union (Miller, Reistinger, and Hesli 1993; Gibson, Duch, and Tedin 1992; Zimmerman 2002). Researchers mapped the political culture of other central and eastern European nations, examining the role of political culture in prompting the transitions and the consolidation of democracy (Rose, Haerpfer, and Mishler 1998; Rohrschneider 1999; Klingemann, Fuchs, and Zielonka 2006). Rather than the apathy or hostility that greeted democracy after transitions from right-wing authoritarian states, the cultural legacy of communism in central and eastern Europe appears to be much different. Several of the chapters in this book map these differences and the research issues that still remain.

An equally rich series of studies is emerging for Asia, Africa, Latin America, and other developing regions. Despite the potential effects of conservative Confucian traditions and the government's hesitant support for democracy in many nations, the cultural foundations of democracy also are well-developed in many Asian societies

(Dalton and Shin 2006). Perhaps the most exciting evidence comes from studies of the People's Republic of China. Even in this hostile environment, there is surprising support for an array of democratic principles (Tang 2005; Shin in this volume). Similarly, the Afrobarometer studies provide the first systematic comparisons of public opinion on this continent, and the nature of political behavior in these developing nations (Bratton, Mattes, and Gyimah-Boadi 2004). The Latinobarometers examine the political culture across Latin America (Lagos 1997). The breadth of support for democracy visible across a range of international survey projects—even in less than hospitable environments—is a surprising finding from this new wave of research, and suggests that the aspirations for freedom, equality, and democratic rights is a common human value. One might question whether these opinions are sufficiently ingrained to constitute an enduring political culture in many developing nations, but even abstract endorsements of democratic norms are a positive sign about the prospects for democratic reform (van Beek 2005).

This research has also stimulated new debates on the broad course of human development. On the one hand, new versions of the social modernization thesis suggest a common pattern of social and political change as nations develop economically. This is most clearly seen in the chapters by Inglehart and Welzel in this volume and their joint book (Inglehart and Welzel 2005). On the other hand, others claim that historical experiences and national traditions produce different patterns of cultural development and distinct cultural regions—which may produce new sources of regional conflict (see Inogouchi in this volume). While this debate is ongoing, its very existence illustrates how the broadening of systematic opinion research to developing nations has renewed old debates about the courses and consequences of political culture.

As questions about political culture have grown in relevance for the democratizing nations, important cultural changes have also emerged within the advanced industrial democracies. Inglehart's (1977, 1990) thesis of postmaterial value change maintains that the socioeconomic forces transforming western industrial societies are creating a new phase of human development. As affluent democracies have addressed many of the traditional "material" social goals, such as economic well-being and security, other political values are increasing attention toward new "postmaterial" goals of self-expression, personal freedom, social equality, self-fulfillment, and improving the quality of life. Inglehart's postmaterial thesis has gained considerable attention because of its potentially broad relevance to the politics of advanced industrial societies, although this thesis has also generated much scholarly debate (van Deth and Scarborough 1995).

Other studies examine whether a key element of a democratic political culture is changing in advanced industrial democracies: citizen orientations toward government. Almond and Verba (1963) maintained that democracy was based on a supportive public that endorsed a democratic system even in times of tumult. In the United States and many west European democracies, however, citizens are now less trustful of politicians, political parties and democratic institutions (Dalton 2004; Pharr and Putnam 2000; Norris 1999; Nye, Zelikow, and King 1997). When coupled with evidence of changing orientations toward partisan politics and changing patterns of political participation (see below), this suggests that the ideals of a democratic political culture are changing among western publics.

In summary, the study of modernization and democratization illustrates the two themes of this book. First, research has made great progress in developing the empirical evidence that describes the political values for most nations in the world. Where once scientific empirical evidence of citizen orientations was quite thin and primarily limited to the large western democracies, we now have rich evidence of how citizens think and act across nearly the entire globe. The growing empirical evidence has also reinforced the importance of key theoretical concepts that were developed during the early behavioral revolution. For example, Eckstein's (1966) concept of cultural congruence has provided a valuable framework for examining the interaction between citizen values and political processes. We now have a much richer and sounder theoretical and empirical knowledge about what are the significant attributes of a political culture (Fuchs in this volume).

Second, as the empirical evidence has grown, it is also apparent that we are living through a period of substantial political change—in both the advanced industrial democracies and the developing nations. This pattern presents several challenges for researchers. Normally, political institutions and the basic principles of a regime are constant; thus it is difficult to study the interaction between institutional and cultural change. However, the recent shifts in regime form in many nations create new opportunities to study the relationship between culture and institutional choices—and how congruence is established. Changing political norms enable us to study political culture as a dynamic process. Attempts to test theories of cultural change or theories on the non-political origins of political culture are fertile research fields during this unusual period of political change.

Finally, the democratization process and changing democratic expectations in the West raise other questions. There is not just one "civic culture" that is congruent with the working of a democratic system. Experience suggests that there are a variety of democratic cultures, as well as ways to define culture, that require mapping and further study. Just as the institutionalists have drawn our attention to the variations in the structure of the democratic politics and the implications of these differences (Rhodes, Binder and Rockman 2006), we need to develop a comparable understanding of how citizen norms can create and sustain alternative democratic forms (Fuchs and Klingemann 2002).

3 DEBATES ON POLITICAL BEHAVIOR

One of the central roles of citizens in democracies and other political systems is to make decisions about political matters. In democracies, this involves decisions about which parties or candidates to support in an election, as well as decisions about which issue positions to hold, how to participate in politics, and so forth. In other political systems, the choices are different, but the task of making a choice remains. In an authoritarian system, the choice might be between making an openly affirmative statement to a government declaration, remaining silent about it or subtly or even openly criticizing it. In any case, citizens make choices when political issues are brought to their attention, whether in an autocratic or democratic system.

In democratic systems electoral choices are at the center of the political process. Thus, the study of electoral choice has quite naturally been a core theme in political behavior research, and past research has produced dramatic advances in our knowledge about how voters reach their decisions. Early electoral research presumed that many voters were ill prepared to deal with the complexities of politics; thus voters relied on shortcuts—such as group cues or affective partisan loyalties—to simplify political decision making and guide their individual behavior (Lazarsfeld, Berelson, and McPhee 1954; Campbell et al. 1960; Lipset and Rokkan 1967). This approach also stressed the underlying stability of party competition because people supposedly based their political decisions on enduring social cleavages, and stable party-voter alignments were a focus of research.

During the 1980s, this model of stable cleavage-based or partisanship-based voting first came under challenge. Within a decade the dominant question changed from explaining the persistence of electoral politics to explaining electoral change (Dalton, Flanagan, and Beck 1984). Decreases in class and religious divisions were a first prominent indicator that electoral politics was changing. Franklin and his colleagues (1992) found that a set of social characteristics (including social class, education, income, religiosity, region, and gender) had a decreasing impact on partisan preferences in western democracies over time. Nieuwbeerta (1995) similarly found a general erosion of class voting across twenty democracies. Franklin concluded with the new "conventional wisdom" of comparative electoral research: "One thing that has by now become quite apparent is that almost all of the countries we have studied show a decline...in the ability of social cleavages to structure individual voting choice" (Franklin et al. 1992: 385).

One of the major findings from the last generation of electoral research holds that social position no longer determines political positions as it did when social alignments were solidly frozen (see the chapters by Knutsen, and Esmer & Pettersson in this volume; cf. Evans 1999; Heath, Jowell, and Curtice 2001). In many western democracies, the declining influence of group cleavages on electoral choice is paralleled by a weakening of affective party attachment that was the basis of the Michigan model of electoral choice. In nearly all the advanced industrial democracies for which long-term survey data are now available, partisan ties have weakened over the past generation (Dalton and Wattenberg 2000). Similarly, there has been a decrease in party-line voting and an increase in partisan volatility, split-ticket voting, and other phenomena showing that fewer citizens are voting according to a party line or group-determined lines (Thomassen 2005).

The decline of long-term predispositions based on social position or partisanship should shift the basis of electoral behavior research to short-term factors, such as candidate image and issue opinions (see chapters by Lewis-Beck and Stegmaier, and Deegan-Krause). Thus, recent research is focusing on whether the new electoral order includes a shift toward candidate-centered voting choice (McAllister in this volume; Wattenberg 1991; Aarts, Blais, and Schmitt 2005). Furthermore, there are signs of a growing personalization of political campaigns in western democracies: photo opportunities, personalized interviews, walkabouts, and televised candidate debates are becoming standard electoral fare.

The decline in long-term influences on the vote also increases the potential for issue voting (Franklin et al. 1992; Evans and Norris 1999; Dalton 2006). While there appears to be a consensus that issue voting has become more important, there is less consensus on a theoretical framework for understanding the role of issues in contemporary political behavior. A large part of the literature continues to work within the social-psychological approach, examining how specific issues affect party choice in specific elections, or how issue beliefs are formed. Other scholars focus on the systemic level, examining how aggregate electoral outcomes can be predicted by the issue stances of the parties. In a sense, this part of the research literature reminds us of the story of the blind men and the elephant: several different research groups are making progress in explaining their part of the pachyderm, but there is not a holistic vision of the role of issues for contemporary electoral choice.

For advanced industrial democracies, the increase in candidate and issue voting has an uncertain potential for the nature of the democratic electoral process. It is unclear whether these changes will improve or weaken the "quality" of the democratic process and the representation of the public's political interests. Public opinion is becoming more fluid and less predictable. This uncertainty forces parties and candidates to be more sensitive to public opinion, at least the opinions of those who vote. Motivated issue voters are more likely to have their voices heard, even if they are not accepted. Furthermore, the ability of politicians to have unmediated communications with voters can strengthen the link between politicians and the people. To some extent, the individualization of electoral choice revives earlier images of the informed voter that we once found in classic democratic theory: if voters rely less on group cues, they base their choices more on their own judgment. Models of rational choice that seemed to rest on implausible assumptions in previous times have thus gained in credibility.

At the same time, there is a potential dark side to these new patterns in electoral politics. The rise of single-issue politics handicaps a society's ability to deal with political issues that transcend specific interests and the negotiation of trade-offs. In addition, elites who cater to issue publics can leave the electorally inactive disenfranchised. Too great an interest in a single issue, or too much emphasis on recent performance, can produce a narrow definition of rationality that is as harmful to democracy as "frozen" social cleavages. In addition, direct unmediated contact between politicians and citizens opens the potential for demagoguery and political extremism. Both extreme right-wing and left-wing political movements probably benefit from this new political environment, at least in the short term. At the same time as the electorate is less stable on the basis of established party alignments, it is also more susceptible to potential media manipulation.

In summary, comparative electoral studies have made major advances in our understanding of political behavior. This has in no way settled old debates. It has invigorated them. But they take place on a firmer base of evidence. This is another area in which research began with limited empirical evidence—national election studies were still quite rare in the 1960s and comparable cross-national analyses were exceedingly rare. Today, this literature on electoral behavior represents one of the largest fields of political behavior research. Moreover, as the empirical evidence has accumulated, it has become more apparent that the nature of electoral behavior is changing in advanced industrial democracies. The current research challenge is to define the nature of the new electoral order that is emerging.

3.1 Electoral Choice in Emerging Democracies

There is an apparent similarity between the portrait of voting choice we have just described and the situation in emerging democracies in central and eastern Europe, Asia, Africa, and Latin America. Emerging party systems are unlikely to rest on stable group-based cleavages, especially when the democratic transition has occurred quite rapidly, as in central and eastern Europe. Thus, studies of new democracies in Latin America and central and eastern Europe emphasize the high level of electoral volatility and fluidity in these party systems (Berglund, Hellén, and Aarebrot 1998; Mainwaring 1999; Mainwaring and Zoco 2007). Similarly, new electorates are unlikely to have long-term party attachments that might guide their behavior. Thus, with the exception of important socio-cultural cleavages, such as ethnicity, electoral choice in many new democracies may involve the same short-term factors—candidate images and issue positions—that are emphasized in the electoral politics of advanced industrial democracies (e.g. Colton 2000; Rose, White, and McAllister 1997; Barnes and Simon 1998; Tucker 2005; Deegan-Krause in this volume). Indeed, there is a seeming preoccupation with the issue of economic voting in these transitional systems, and less attention to full models of electoral choice (for positive examples see Tworzecki 2003; Tucker 2002).

The new democratic systems of central and eastern Europe, Asia, Africa, and Latin America, for instance, face the task of developing a relatively stable and institutionalized basis of party competition. Without more structure, it is difficult for citizens to learn about the policy choices available to them, and translate this into meaningful electoral choices. Without more structure, it is difficult to ensure accountability in the democratic process. This situation presents the unique opportunity to study this process to examine how new party attachments take root, the relationships between social groups and parties form, party images develop, and citizens learn the process of representative democracy. However, the creation of party systems in the world of global television, greater knowledge about electoral politics (from the elite and public levels), and fundamentally different electorates are unlikely to follow the pattern of earlier democratization periods. Thus, a major question is whether new democracies will develop a system of liberal-democratic responsible party government and electoral choice, and what are the consequences if they do not.

To answer these questions will require a dynamic perspective on the processes of electoral change. It is frankly too soon to determine how political scientists will respond to these challenges. There has already been an impressive development to improve the empirical base of research in these new democracies—a development that took decades in most of the western democracies. There are many encouraging signs and impressive empirical studies emanating from central and eastern Europe, Asia, Africa, and Latin America but the evolutionary process is still uncertain.

4 Political Participation

Democratic or not, all polities expect some public involvement in the political process, if only to obey political orders. Thus, one section of the Handbook focuses on political activity. Democracy, however, expects more active involvement than a non-democratic order because democracy is designed to aggregate public preferences into binding collective decisions. Necessarily this requires an active citizenry, because it is through interest articulation, information, and deliberation that public preferences can be identified, shaped and transformed into collective decisions that are considered as legitimate. Autocratic regimes also engage the public in the political process, although this primarily served as a means to indoctrinate the public to conform to decisions that elites have made. But even the control capacities of autocratic regimes are limited so that it has to somehow address what the citizenry wants and needs.

The major empirical advance in this field has documented the levels of participation across nations and highlighted distinctions between different modes of political action. Verba and his colleagues (Verba, Nie, and Kim 1978; Verba, Schlozman, and Brady 1995) demonstrated that various forms of action differ in their political implications, and in the factors that stimulate individuals to act. This was extended by others to include the growth of unconventional political action that occurred since the 1960s (Barnes, Kaase, et al. 1979; Jennings, van Deth, et al. 1990). This theoretical framework of participation modes is the common foundation of participation research.

Having identified the modes of action, researchers sought to explain patterns of participation. This was once an area intensely debated by rationalist and social-psychological theories of political behavior. The rationalist approach framed decisions to participate in simple cost-benefit terms, best represented in Olson's (1965) *Logic of Collective Action*. The charm of parsimony made this an attractive theoretical approach, but this parsimony created oversimplifications, false research paradoxes and actually limited our understanding of citizen action. More productive is the social-psychological model that stresses the influence of personal resources, attitudes, and institutional structures in explaining patterns of action (e.g. Verba, Nie, and Kim 1978; Verba, Schlozman, and Brady 1995).

For the past several years, the most intense debate has focused on whether the level of political participation is systematically changing in western democracies. As supporting evidence, the longstanding "paradox of participation" has noted that turnout in the United States has decreased since the 1960s, even though educational levels and the affluence of the nation have dramatically increased (Brody 1978; Rosenstone and Hansen 1993).

Putnam (2000) provocatively argued that declining turnout is part of a broader trend that has us "bowling alone." Putnam claimed that social engagement is dropping in advanced industrial societies as a result of societal changes, such as changing labor patterns among women, rising television usage, urban sprawl, and the decline of traditional social institutions. These trends have supposedly led to a decline in social capital—the skills and values that facilitate democratic participation—and thereby to declines in the citizenry's participation in politics.

The study of social capital and the changes in the patterns of participation in contemporary democracies has been one of the most fertile areas of research for the past decade, as described in several chapters in this volume. On the one side is clear cross-national evidence of declining turnout in advanced industrial democracies (Blais 2000; Wattenberg 2002; Franklin 2004). Other measures of partisan activity, such as party membership, also show clear downward trends in most nations (Scarrow 2000). This might be seen as part of a more general downturn in civic engagement because church attendance, union membership, and the engagement in several types of traditional voluntary associations and collective activities are declining. On the other side is a growing body of evidence that new forms of civic and political action—such as contacting, direct action, contentious politics, self-help groups, local initiatives, donations—are counterbalancing the decline in electoral participation and other traditional forms of civic engagement (Zukin et al. 2006; Pattie, Seyd, and Whiteley 2004; Cain, Dalton, and Scarrow 2003; Costa and Kahn 2001). In addition, social group membership and the formation of social capital seem to be increasing in many advanced industrial democracies, making the US an atypical case (Stolle in this volume; Putnam 2002). Moreover, modernization processes seem to change the ways in which people interact and engage in the public sphere, transforming the character of social capital instead of eliminating it altogether: loyalist forms of elite-guided engagement go down but spontaneous forms of self-driven engagement go up (Norris 2002; chapters by Rucht and Koopmans in this volume).

This controversy touches the very vitality of the democratic process, and the resolution of the controversy is as yet unclear. The evidence of decreasing group involvement of the old type and declining social capital of the traditional form is strongest for the United States, but this might not indicate a general erosion of civic engagement and social capital. It might simply reflect a transformation of the ways in which citizens relate to each other and their communities. If one includes new forms of interaction and engagement, participation levels and the various methods of political action are generally expanding in most advanced industrial societies—even while participation in the traditional form of party membership and electoral politics is decreasing. New forms of engagement and participation expand political participation beyond the boundaries of what it was conventionally viewed to be. These tendencies reflect a great flexibility of democracies, allowing forms of participation to adapt to changing societal conditions. The new style of citizen participation places more control over political activity in the hands of the citizenry as well as increasing public pressure on political elites.

However, the expanding repertoire of action also may raise potential problems. For example, the changing nature of political participation can increase inequalities in political involvement, which would bias the democratic process in ways that conflict with the ideal of "one (wo)man one vote" (Verba, Schlozman, and Brady 1995; Cain, Dalton, and Scarrow 2003; Parry, Moyser, and Day 1992). New forms of direct action are even more dependent on the skills and resources represented by social status, and thus may increase the participation gap between lower-status groups and higher-status individuals. These new forms of participation also create new challenges for aggregating diverse political demands into coherent government policy. Ironically, overall increases in political involvement may mask a growing social-status bias in citizen participation and influence, which runs counter to democratic ideals.

The challenge for established democracies is to expand further the opportunities for citizens to participate in the political process and meaningfully structure the decisions affecting their lives. To meet this challenge means ensuring an equality of political rights and opportunities that will be even more difficult to guarantee with these new participation forms. However, a socially biased use of expanded political opportunities should not blame the opportunities but should blame the policies that fail to alleviate the social bias, such as unequal access to education and other social benefits that influence the citizens' resources to participate in politics.

4.1 Participation in Emerging Democracies

The questions involving political participation are obviously different in emerging democracies and non-democratic nations. In new democracies the challenge is to engage the citizenry in meaningful participation after years of ritualized engagement or actual prohibitions on participation. In some cases this experience is a mirror-image of old democracies: in old democracies citizens are moving from conventional to unconventional politics, in new democracies citizens often toppled authoritarian regimes by revolutionary upheavals and have now to learn the routines of conventional participation.

Election turnout was often fairly high in the immediate post-transition elections in Eastern Europe, but has subsequently declined in most nations. Similarly, party activity has atrophied as democratic institutions have developed (Barnes and Simon 1998; van Biezen 2003). And while there was a popular lore claiming that a robust underground civil society prompted the democratization trend in eastern Europe, post-transition research finds that social engagement is now limited

(Howard 2003). Many east Europeans had engaged in unconventional politics during the democratic transitions of the late 1980s and early 1990s, but these forms of action diminished after the transition in a kind of "post-honeymoon" effect (Inglehart and Catterberg 2003). Consequently, eastern Europe still faces the challenge of integrating citizens into democratic politics and nurturing an understanding of the democratic process.

The challenges of citizen participation are, of course, even greater in non-democratic nations. The advance of survey research has provided some unique insights into participation patterns in these environments. Shi's study of political participation in Beijing (1997), for example, found that there was much more extensive public involvement than expected. Furthermore, political participation can occur in more varied forms in political systems where citizen input is not tolerated and encouraged through institutionalized channels (also see Jennings 1997). Similarly, Bratton and his colleagues (2004) find a surprisingly robust range of political activity across a set of African nations. If this occurs in these two settings, then we might expect a greater role for the citizen even in transitional political systems.

The desire to participate in the decisions affecting one's life is common across the globe, but political institutions can shape whether these desires are expressed and how (Inglehart and Welzel 2005). Possessing the skills and resources to be politically active is an equally important factor. Research is now identifying how these two forces combine to shape the patterns of citizen action.

5 Does Public Opinion Matter

Another section of this Handbook addresses the topic of the impact of public opinion on policy makers and governments—which is the ultimate question in the study of public opinion within a democracy. To what extent do the views of policy makers and the outputs of government policy reflect the preferences that the public itself prefers?

The indirect effect of public opinion in a democracy, mediated through representative institutions, has created questions about the congruence of mass–elite outcomes, and the factors that affect this intermediation process. However, systematically studying this process has had a difficult research history, despite the theoretical and political importance of the topic.

The first empirical study of representation was the famous Miller–Stokes study of representation in America (Miller and Stokes 1963). This model and research approach were soon expanded to a host of other advanced industrial democracies (Barnes 1977; Converse and Pierce 1986; Thomassen 1994). This research examined some of the most important questions in research on democracy, but the findings were limited. The theoretical model developed in the United States did not travel well to other democracies. In addition, the resources required to conduct parallel studies of the citizenry and political elites were exceptional. Thus, in the fifty years since the original Miller–Stokes study, their full research project has not been replicated in the United States.

Other studies in the United States have examined elements of the representation process; for instance, comparing the congruence between mass and elite opinions in the aggregate or the dynamics of mass opinion change (Erikson, McKuen, and Stimson 2002; Stimson 2004). Researchers have also examined the congruence between public policy preferences and the outcomes of government (Page and Shapiro 1992). Gradually, this research has also spread to other western democracies, often adopted to national institutions or the structure of representation (Miller et al. 1999; Schmitt and Thomassen 1999). One important branch of this approach compares programmatic profiles of political parties and political preferences of their followers. Most of the findings produced thus far seem to indicate that in terms of left–right orientations parties have not lost their capacity to represent and mobilize citizen support for public policies (Klingemann et al. 1994; Budge et al. 2001; Klingemann et al. 2006).

The contributions in this Handbook engage these important research questions. Wlezien and Soroka examine the congruence between mass policy preferences and the policy outputs of government. Blondel and Müeller-Rommel review the research on political elites, and their perspectives of mass politics, political representation, and their role within the democratic process. Weßels summarizes the collective findings of the series of representation studies that have been conducted to date, and provides an insightful cross-national comparison of how institutions shape the representation process. Stimson's chapter adds a broader view of what we have learned, and the research questions that remain.

In one sense, this represents one of the areas with the greatest theoretical and empirical potential to understand the functioning of the democratic process through the mass–elite relationship. But it also remains one of the most challenging areas to study and compare across nations. But gradually we are developing a better understanding of how the democratic process actually functions, which yields a positive view of the vitality of the process.

6 CHANGING PUBLICS: A CONCLUSION

We have just lived through what are arguably the most significant political events of our lifetimes: the collapse of the Soviet Empire and the global democratization wave of the 1990s. As advanced industrial societies are evolving into a new form of democratic politics, we are witnessing the initial development of democracy in a new set of nations. The democratization waves in central and eastern Europe, Asia, and Africa touch at the very core of many of our most basic questions about the nature of citizen politics and the working of the political process. Normally we study democratic systems that are roughly at equilibrium and speculate on how this equilibrium was created (or how it changes in minor ways). Moreover, during the earlier waves of democratic transition the tools of empirical social science were not available to study political behavior directly. The current democratization wave thus provides a virtually unique opportunity to address questions on identity formation, the creation of political cultures (and possibly how cultural inheritances are changed), the establishment of an initial calculus of voting, and the dynamic processes linking political norms and behavior. These questions represent some of the fundamental research issues of our time. The answers will not only explain what has occurred during this democratization wave, but may aid us in better understanding the basic principles of how citizens function within the political process. There has never been a richer opportunity to study the choices of citizens across regime forms and between old and new democracies. The conditions to arrive at a theory of how citizens come to political choices depending on different political settings, and how these choices affect the settings has never been better than today.

In each of these areas discussed in this chapter, research can be described in two terms. First, there has been a fundamental expansion of our empirical knowledge over the past generation of research. Until quite recently, a single national survey provided the basis for discussing the characteristics of citizen behavior; and such evidence was frequently limited to the larger advanced industrial democracies. Indeed, there were large parts of the world where our understanding of the citizenry, their attitudes, and behavior were based solely on the insights of political observers— which can be as fallible as the observer. Contemporary comparative research is now more likely to draw on cross-national and cross-temporal comparisons. Research has developed the foundations for the scientific study of the topic.

Second, we have noted the ironic development that our expanding empirical evidence has occurred during a time when many basic features of citizen attitudes and behaviors are changing in ways that make modeling citizen politics more complex. In part, these trends reflect the tremendous social and political changes that have occurred in the world during the past generation. Modernization has transformed living conditions throughout the world, altered the skills and values of contemporary publics, and offered new technological advances that change the relationship between citizens and elites. Perhaps, this is the most interesting object worthy of study. For never before in history has the interaction between elites and people been shifted so much to the side of the people.

The global wave of democratization in the 1990s has dramatically increased the role of the citizenry in many of the new democracies in central and eastern Europe, Asia, Latin America, and Africa. This latter development makes our task as scholars of the citizen more relevant than ever before, but also more difficult. Even as our research skills and empirical evidence have expanded, the phenomena we study have been evolving—something that physicists and chemists do not have to deal with.

These changes produce uncertainty about what new styles of political decision making, or what new forms of political participation are developing. In addition, the nature of citizen politics is becoming more complex—or through our research we are now realizing that greater complexity exists. This produces a real irony: even though we have greater scientific knowledge, our ability to predict and explain political behavior may actually be decreasing in some areas. For instance, we know much more about electoral behavior than we did in the 1950s, but simple socio-demographic models that were successful in predicting electoral behavior in the 1960s are much less potent in explaining contemporary voting behavior. So we have gained greater certainty about the uncertainty of voter decisions.

Finally, if we step back from the individual chapters and their findings, we see broad outlines of what we think are some of the most productive areas for future research. Several aspects of research design offer exciting potential for the future. For instance, most studies are derived from random surveys of individuals. This design focuses our attention on individuals as autonomous political actors and theories emphasizing the individualization of politics. However, people exist in a social, economic, and political context that also influences their political behavior. For example, limited political knowledge can be overcome by asking spouses, friends, or neighbors (Huckfeldt in this volume; Gunther, Montero, and Puhle 2006). Even more important, characteristics of the political context can alter the processes shaping citizen attitudes and behavior, such as exposure to supportive or dissonant information (Huckfeldt et al. 2004; Mutz 2006). Equally exciting are new research opportunities to study how the institutional structure of a polity interacts with citizen behavior (e.g. Anderson et al. 2005). Thus, studying this complex of social and political interactions should yield new insights into how political behavior is shaped.

Another innovation is the introduction of experiments and quasi-experiments to our research tools. For example, Sniderman's (Sniderman and Piazza 1993; Sniderman et al. 2000) experiments in studying racial attitudes and prejudice illustrate how experiments and creative questionnaire design can provide unobtrusive measures of sensitive topics. Such experiments also partially address one of the weaknesses of cross-section public opinion survey by providing leverage to study causality by manipulating choices presented to survey respondents, and analyzing how opinions change. This innovation has tremendous potential that should be utilized more in future research (Lau and Redlawsk 2006).

An even more dramatic sign of the development of political behavior research is the increasing complexity of research designs. Once, a single national sample was the basis of extensive research because such evidence was still rare. However, as our knowledge has increased and our theories have become more complex, this calls for more complex research designs. Election studies, for instance, need to study individuals in context, including multiple and converging data collections: social context, media content, party actions, and other elements of the total process. Doing more of what we did in the past—more questions, more surveys, larger sample sizes—is not likely to generate the theoretical or empirical insights necessary to move the research field forward. Complex theories and complex processes require more complex research designs.

We also believe that research will engage a new set of theoretical issues as the field moves forward. It is more difficult to briefly outline the forefront for research, because theoretical questions are more diverse than the methodological innovations we have just outlined. However, several areas of potential inquiry stand out for their potential. While most research has focused on single nations, and typically western democracies, the global expansion of research means that issues of social modernization and cross-national development are likely to be especially fruitful areas of study. This is a case were we have been theory rich, and information poor—and now these theories will be tested, and undoubtedly new models developed in their place. Similarly, past theorizing has focused on explaining systems and behavior in equilibrium. Theories of political change seem an especially fruitful area for inquiry giving the dynamic nature of contemporary politics.

Finally, one should not forget that because of the sheer number of countries for which survey data are available, we are for the first time in the situation to move to the aggregate level of analyses, conducting statistically significant tests of the basic assumption underlying all research into mass belief systems: that variation in these belief systems has a true impact on a society's level of democracy. Aggregate-level analyses of the correlates of democracy was usually left to political economists who could more easily correlate socioeconomic indicators to levels of democracy. But we can now test their models against political culture, examining if socioeconomic factors or features of political culture have a stronger impact on democracy. As recent studies show (Inglehart and Welzel 2005), features of political culture have as strong an impact on levels of democracy as socioeconomic factors.

The goal of this Handbook is to introduce the readers to the research we have accumulated in each of these areas, and the research questions that remain. We came away from this project with tremendous respect for what has been achieved since the onset of modern comparative research. At the same time, answering one question generates new questions, and the essays in this Handbook are full of new areas for study that will deepen our knowledge in key areas of political behavior.

References

AARTS, K., BLAIS, A., and SCHMITT, H. eds. 2005. *Political Leaders and Democratic Elections*. Oxford: Oxford University Press.

ALMOND, G., and VERBA, S. 1963. *The Civic Culture*. Princeton: Princeton University Press.

—— —— eds. 1980. *The Civic Culture Revisited*. Boston: Little Brown.

ANDERSON, C. et al. 2005. *Losers' Consent: Elections and Democratic Legitimacy*. New York: Oxford University Press, 2005.

BARNES, S. 1977. *Representation in Italy*. Chicago: University of Chicago Press.

—— and SIMON, J. eds. 1998. *The Postcommunist Citizen*. Budapest: Erasmus Foundation.

—— KAASE, M., et al. 1979. *Political Action*. Beverly Hills, Calif.: Sage.

BARTOLINI, S., and MAIR, P. 1990. *Identity, Competition, and Electoral Availability: The Stability of European Electorates, 1885–1985*. Cambridge: Cambridge University Press.

BEAN, C. 1993. The electoral influence of party leader images in Australia and New Zealand. *Comparative Political Studies*, 26: 111–32.

BERELSON, B., LAZARSFELD, P. and McPHEE, W. 1954. *Voting*. Chicago: University of Chicago Press.

BERGLUND, S., HELLÉN, T., and AAREBROT, F. eds. 1998. *The Handbook of Political Change in Eastern Europe*. Cheltenham: Edward Elgar.

BLAIS, A. 2000. *To Vote or not to Vote: The Merits and Limits of Rational Choice Theory*. Pittsburgh: University of Pittsburgh Press.

BOWLER, S., and DONOVAN, T. 1998. *Demanding Choices: Opinion, Voting, and Direct Democracy*. Ann Arbor: University of Michigan Press.

BRATTON, M., MATTES, R., and GYIMAH-BOADI, E. 2004. *Public Opinion, Democracy, and Market Reform in Africa*. Cambridge: Cambridge University Press.

BRODY, R. 1978. The puzzle of political participation in America. In *The New American Political System*, ed. S. Beer. Washington, DC: American Enterprise Institute.

BUDGE, I., and FARLIE, D. 1983. *Explaining and Predicting Elections: Issue Effects and Party Strategies in Twenty-three Democracies*. London: Allen & Unwin.

—— et al. 2001. *Mapping Policy Preferences: Estimates for Parties, Electors, and Governments 1945–1998*. Oxford: Oxford University Press..

BUTLER, D., and STOKES, D. 1969. *Political Change in Britain*. New York: St Martin's.

CAIN, B., DALTON, R., and SCARROW, S. eds. 2003. *Democracy Transformed? Expanding Political Opportunities in Advanced industrial Democracies*. Oxford: Oxford University Press.

CAMPBELL, A., CONVERSE, P. MILLER, W., and STOKES, D. 1960. *The American voter*. New York: Wiley.

COLTON, T. 2000. *Transitional Citizens: Voters and What Influences Them in the New Russia*. Cambridge, Mass.: Harvard University Press.

CONVERSE, P. 1964. The nature of belief systems in mass publics. pp. 206–61 in *Ideology and Discontent*, ed. D. Apter. New York: Free Press.

—— and PIERCE, R. 1986. *Representation in France*. Cambridge, Mass.: Harvard University Press.

COSTA, D., and KAHN, M. 2001. Understanding the decline in social capital, 1952–1998. Cambridge: National Bureau of Economic Research, Working Paper NO 8295.

CREPAZ, M. 1990. The impact of party polarization and postmaterialism on voter turnout. *European Journal of Political Research*, 18: 183–205.

DAHL, R. A. 1989. *Democracy and its Critics*. New Haven: Yale University Press.

DALTON, R. 2004. *Democratic Challenges, Democratic Choices*. Oxford: Oxford University Press.

—— 2006. *Citizen Politics: Public Opinion and Political Parties in Advanced Industrial Democracies*, 4th edn. Washington, DC: CQ Press.

——, FLANAGAN, S., and BECK, P. eds. 1984. *Electoral Change in Advanced Industrial Democracies*. Princeton: Princeton University Press.

—— and SHIN, D. eds. 2006. *Citizens, Democracy and Markets around the Pacific Rim*. Oxford: Oxford University Press.

—— and WATTENBERG, M. eds. 2000. *Parties without Partisans: Political Change in Advanced Industrial Democracies*. Oxford: Oxford University Press.

DELLI CARPINI, M., and KEETER, S. 1991. *What Americans Know about Politics and Why it Matters*. New Haven: Yale University Press.

DOWNS, A. 1957. *An Economic Theory of Democracy.* New York: Harper.

ECKSTEIN, H. 1966. *Division and Cohesion in Democracy.* Princeton: Princeton University Press.

ERIKSON, R., MACKUEN, M., and STIMSON, J. 2002. *The Macro Polity.* New York: Cambridge University Press.

EVANS, G. ed. 1999. *The End of Class Politics? Class Voting in Comparative Perspective.* Oxford: Oxford University Press.

—— and NORRIS, P. eds. 1999. *Critical Elections: British Parties and Voters in Long-Term Perspective.* Thousand Oaks, Calif.: Sage.

—— and WHITEFIELD, S. 1995. The politics and economics of democratic commitment. *British Journal of Political Science,* 25: 485–514.

FINIFTER, A., and MICKIEWICZ, E. 1992. Redefining the political system of the USSR. *American Political Science Review,* 86: 857–74.

FRANKLIN, M. 2004. *Voter Turnout and the Dynamics of Electoral Competition in Established Democracies since 1945.* New York: Cambridge University Press.

—— MACKIE, T., and VALEN, H. ed. 1992. *Electoral Change: Responses to Evolving Social and Attitudinal Structures in Western Countries.* New York: Cambridge University Press.

FUCHS, D., and KLINGEMANN, H. 2002. Eastward enlargement of the European Union and the identity of Europe. pp. 58–80 in *The Enlarged European Union: Diversity and Adaptation,* ed. P. Mair and J. Zielonka. London: Frank Cass.

GIBSON, J., DUCH, R., and TEDIN, K. 1992. Democratic values and the transformation of the Soviet Union. *Journal of Politics,* 54: 329–71.

GUNTHER, R., RAMÓN MONTERO, J., and PUHLE, H. eds. 2006. *Electoral Intermediation, Values, and Political Support in Old and New Democracies.* Oxford: Oxford University Press.

HALL, P. 1999. Social capital in Britain. *British Journal of Political Science* 29: 417–61.

HEATH, A., FISHER, S., and SMITH, S. 2005. The globalization of public opinion research. *Annual Review of Political Science,* 8: 297–333.

—— JOWELL, R. and CURTICE, J. 2001. *The Rise of New Labour: Party Policies and Voter Choices.* Oxford: Oxford University Press.

HIBBING, J., and THEISS-MORSE, E. 2002. *Stealth Democracy: Americans' Beliefs about how Government Should Work.* New York: Cambridge University Press.

HOWARD, M. 2003. *The Weakness of Civil Society in Post-communist Europe.* New York: Cambridge University Press.

HUCKFELDT, R., DALTON, R., and BECK, P. 1998. Ambiguity, distorted messages, and environmental effects on political communication. *Journal of Politics,* 60: 996–1030.

—— et al. 2004. *Political Disagreement: The Survival of Diverse Opinions within Communication Networks.* New York: Cambridge University Press.

HUNTINGTON, S. 1968. *Political Order in Changing Societies.* New Haven: Yale University Press.

—— 1996. *The Clash of Civilizations and the Remaking of World Order.* New York: Simon & Schuster.

INGLEHART, R. 1977. *The Silent Revolution.* Princeton: Princeton University Press.

—— 1990. *Culture Shift in Advanced Industrial Society.* Princeton: Princeton University Press.

—— 1997. *Modernization and Postmodernization.* Ann Arbor: University of Michigan.

—— and CATTERBERG, G. 2003. Trends in political action: the development trend and the post-honeymoon decline. Ch. 1 in *Islam, Gender, Culture, and Democracy,* ed. R. Inglehart. Willowdale: de Sitter.

—— and WELZEL, C. 2005. *Modernization, Cultural Change, and Democracy: The Human Development Sequence.* Cambridge: Cambridge University Press.

IVERSON, T. 1994. The logics of electoral politics: spatial, directional and mobilization effects. *Comparative Political Studies,* 27: 155–89.

JACKMAN, R., and MILLER, R. 1995. Voter turnout in the industrial democracies during the 1980s. *Comparative Political Studies,* 27: 467–92.

—— —— 1996. A renaissance of political culture *American Journal of Political Science,* 40: 697–716.

JENNINGS, M. 1997. Political participation in the Chinese countryside. *American Political Science Review,* 91: 361–72.

—— van DETH, J., et al. 1990. *Continuities in Political Action.* Berlin: deGruyter.

KAASE, M. 1983. Sinn oder Unsinn des Konzepts "Politische Kultur" für die vergleichende Politikforschung. In *Wahlen und politisches System,* ed. M. Kaase and H. Klingemann. Opladen: Westdeutscher Verlag.

—— and NEWTON, K. eds. 1995. *Beliefs in Government* Oxford: Oxford University Press.

KLINGEMANN, H. 1979. Measuring ideological conceptualization. Pp. 215–54 in *Political Action,* ed. S. Barnes, M. Kaase, et al. Beverly Hills, Calif.: Sage Publications.

—— and FUCHS, D. eds. 1995. *Citizens and the State.* Oxford: Oxford University Press.

—— and ZIELONKA, J. eds. 2006. *Democracy and Political Culture in Eastern Europe.* London: Routledge.

—— et al. 1994. *Parties, Policies, and Democracy.* Boulder, Colo.: Westview Press.

—— VOLKENS, A. BARA, J., BUDGE, I., and MACDONALD, M. 2006. *Mapping Policy Preference II.* Oxford: Oxford University Press.

KNUTSEN, O. 1987. The impact of structural and ideological cleavages on West European democracies. *British Journal of Political Science,* 18: 323–52.

KRIESI, H. 2005. *Direct Democratic Choice: The Swiss Experience.* Lanham, Md.: Lexington Books.

LAGOS, M. 1997. Latin America's smiling mask. *Journal of Democracy,* 8: 125–38.

LAITIN, D. 1995. The "Civic Culture" at thirty. *American Political Science Review,* 89: 168–73.

—— 1998. *Identity in Formation: The Russian-Speaking Populations in the Near Abroad.* Ithaca, NY: Cornell University Press.

LAU, R., and REDLAWSK, D. 2006. *How Voters Decide: Information Processing during Election Campaigns.* New York: Cambridge University Press.

LAZARSFELD, P. F., BERELSON, B., and MCPHEE, W. N. 1954. *Voting.* Chicago: University of Chicago Press.

LIPSET, S., and ROKKAN, S. eds. 1967. *Party Systems and Voter Alignments.* New York: Free Press.

LUPIA, A., and MCCUBBINS, M. 1998. *The Democratic Dilemma: Can Citizens Learn what They Need to Know?* Cambridge: Cambridge University Press.

MAINWARING, S. 1999. *Rethinking Party Systems in the Third Wave of Democratization: The Case of Brazil.* Stanford University Press.

—— and ZOCO, E. 2007. The stabilization of interparty competition: Electoral volatility in old and new democracies, *Party Politics.*

MERRILL, S., and GROFMAN, B. 1999. *A Unified Theory of Voting: Directional and Proximity Spatial Models.* Cambridge: Cambridge University Press.

MILLER, A., REISINGER, W., and HESLI, V. eds. 1993. *Public Opinion and Regime Change: The New Politics of Post-Soviet Societies.* Boulder, Colo.: Westview.

MILLER, W., and SHANKS, M. 1996. *The New American Voter.* Cambridge, Mass.: Harvard University Press.

MILLER, W., and SHANKS, M., and STOKES, D. 1963. Constituency influence in Congress. *American Political Science Review*, 57: 45–56.

MILLER, W. et al. 1999. *Policy Representation in Western Democracies*. Oxford: Oxford University Press.

MULLER, E., and SELIGSON, M. 1994. Civil culture and democracy. *American Political Science Review*, 88: 635–52.

MUTZ, D. 2006. *Hearing the Other Side: Deliberative versus Participatory Democracy*. New York: Cambridge University Press.

NIE, N., VERBA, S., and PETROCIK, J. 1976. *The Changing American Voter*. Cambridge, Mass.: Harvard University Press.

NIEUWBEERTA, P. 1995. *The Democratic Class Struggle in Twenty Countries, 1945–1990*. Amsterdam: Thesis Publishers.

NORRIS, P. ed. 1999. *Critical Citizens: Global Support for Democratic Government*. Oxford: Oxford University Press.

——— 2002. *Democratic Phoenix: Reinventing Political Activism*. Cambridge: Cambridge University Press.

NYE, J., ZELIKOW, P., and KING, D. eds. 1997. *Why Americans Mistrust Government*. Cambridge, Mass.: Harvard University Press.

OLSON, M. 1965. *The Logic of Collective Action*. Cambridge, Mass.: Harvard University Press.

PAGE, B., and SHAPIRO, R. 1992. *The Rational Public: Fifty years of Trends in Americans' Policy Preferences*. Chicago: University of Chicago Press.

PARRY, G., MOYSER, G., and DAY, N. 1992. *Political Participation and Democracy in Britain*. Cambridge: Cambridge University Press.

PATTIE, C., SEYD, P., and WHITELEY, P. 2004. *Citizenship in Britain: Values, Participation and Democracy*. New York: Cambridge University Press.

PHARR, S., and PUTNAM, R. eds. 2000. *Discontented Democracies: What's Wrong with the Trilateral Democracies*. Princeton: Princeton University Press.

POPKIN, S. 1991. *The Reasoning Voter*. Chicago: University of Chicago Press.

POWELL, G. 2000. *Elections as Instruments of Democracy*. New Haven: Yale University Press.

PUTNAM, R. 1993. *Making Democracy Work*. Princeton: Princeton University Press.

——— 2000. *Bowling Alone: The Collapse and Revival of American Community*. New York: Simon & Schuster.

——— ed. 2002. *Democracies in Flux: The Evolution of Social Capital in Contemporary Society*. Oxford: Oxford University Press.

PYE, L., and VERBA, S. eds. 1965. *Political Culture and Political Development*. Princeton: Princeton University Press.

REISINGER, W. 1995. The renaissance of a rubric: political culture as concept and theory. *International Journal of Public Opinion Research*, 7: 328–52.

REMMER, K. 1991. The political economy of elections in Latin America. *American Political Science Review* 87: 393–407.

RHODES, R., BINDER, S., and ROCKMAN, B. 2006. *The Oxford Handbook of Political Institutions*. Oxford: Oxford University Press.

ROHRSCHNEIDER, R. 1999. *Learning Democracy: Democratic and Economic Values in Unified Germany*. Oxford: Oxford University Press.

ROSE, R., HAERPFER, C., and MISHLER, W. 1998. *Democracy and its Alternatives: Understanding Post–communist Societies*. Baltimore: Johns Hopkins University Press.

——— and MISHLER, W. 1998. Negative and positive party identification in post-communist countries. *Electoral Studies*, 17: 217–34.

——— WHITE, S., and MCALLISTER, I. 1997. *How Russia Votes*. Chatham, NJ: Chatham House.

ROSENSTONE, S., and HANSEN, J. 1993. *Mobilization, Participation, and American Democracy.* New York: Macmillan.

SCARROW, S. 2000. Parties without members? Pp. 79–102 in *Parties without Partisans*, ed. R. Dalton and M. Wattenberg. Oxford: Oxford University Press.

SCHMITT, H., and THOMASSEN, J. eds. 1999. *Political Representation and Legitimacy in the European Union.* Oxford: Oxford University Press.

SELIGSON, M., and BOOTH, J. 1993. Political culture and regime type: Nicaragua and Costa Rica. *Journal of Politics*, 55: 777–92.

SHI, T. 1997. *Political Participation in Beijing.* Cambridge, Mass.: Harvard University Press.

SHIN, D. 1999. *Mass Politics and Culture in Democratizing Korea.* Cambridge: Cambridge University Press.

SNIDERMAN, P., BRODY, R., and KUKLINSKI, J. 1984. Policy reasoning and political values. *American Journal of Political Science*, 28: 74–94.

—— BRODY, R., and TETLOCK, P. 1991. *Reasoning and Choice.* New York: Cambridge University Press.

—— and PIAZZA, T. 1993. *The Scar of Race.* Cambridge, Mass.: Harvard University Press.

—— et al. 2000. *The Outsider: Prejudice and Politics in Italy.* Princeton: Princeton University Press.

STACY, G., and SEGURA, G. 1997. Cross-national variation in the political sophistication of individuals: capability or choice? *Journal of Politics*, 59: 126–47.

STIMSON, J. 2004. *Tides of Consent: How Public Opinion Shapes American Politics.* New York: Cambridge University Press.

SUROWIECKI, J. 2004. *The Wisdom of Crowds: Why the Many Are Smarter than the Few and How Collective Wisdom Shapes Business, Economies, Societies and Nations.* New York: Doubleday.

TANG, W. 2005. *Public Opinion and Political Change in China.* Stanford, Calif.: Stanford University Press.

THOMASSEN, J. 1994. Empirical research into political representation. Pp. 237–64 in *Elections at Home and Abroad*, ed. M. K. Jennings and T. Mann. Ann Arbor: University of Michigan Press.

—— ed. 2005. *The European Voter: A Comparative Study of Modern Democracies.* Oxford: Oxford University Press.

TUCKER, J. 2002. The first decade of post-communist elections and voting: what have we studied, and how have we studied it? *American Review of Political Science*, 5: 271–304.

—— 2005. *Regional Economic Voting.* New York: Cambridge University Press.

TWORZECKI, H. 2003. *Learning to Choose: Electoral Politics in East-Central Europe.* Stanford, Calif.: Stanford University Press.

VAN BEEK, U. 2005. *Democracy under Construction: Patterns from Four Continents.* Bloomfield Hills & Opladen: Barbara Budrich.

VAN BIEZEN, I. 2003. *Political Parties and New Democracies: Party Organization in Southern and East-Central Europe.* London: Palgrave.

VAN DETH, J., and SCARBOROUGH, E. eds. 1995. *The Impact of Values.* Oxford: Oxford University Press.

VERBA, S., NIE, N., and KIM, J. 1978. *Participation and Political Equality.* Cambridge: Cambridge University Press.

—— SCHLOZMAN, K., and BRADY, H. 1995. *Voice and Political Equality.* Cambridge, Mass.: Harvard University Press.

WATTENBERG, M. 1991. *The Rise of Candidate Centered Politics.* Cambridge, Mass.: Harvard University Press.

WATTENBERG, M. 2002. *Where Have All the Voters Gone?* Cambridge, Mass.: Harvard University Press.

—— 2006. *Is Voting for Young People?* New York: Longman.

WEIL, F. 1989. The sources and structure of legitimation in Western democracies. *American Sociological Review*, 54: 682–706.

ZALLER, J. 1992. *The Nature and Origins of Mass Opinion.* Cambridge: Cambridge University Press.

ZIMMERMAN, W. 2002. *The Russian People and Foreign Policy: Russian Elite and Mass Perspectives, 1993–2000.* Princeton: Princeton University Press.

ZUKIN, C., KEETER, S., ANDOLINA, M., JENKINS, K., and DELLI CARPINI, M. 2006. *A New Engagement? Political Participation, Civic Life, and the Changing American Citizen.* New York: Oxford University Press.

PART II

MASS BELIEF
SYSTEMS AND
COMMUNICATION

CHAPTER 2

....

POLITICAL
SOCIALIZATION

....

M. KENT JENNINGS

THE evolution and development of political socialization as a distinct area of scholarship has been recently chronicled and evaluated in several places, though not always under the formal name of political socialization (e.g. Renshon 2003; Sapiro 2004; Sears and Levy 2003). That being the case, I will move fairly quickly into what I see as major turning points and recent developments. First, however, it is important to address the issue of the so-called bull and bear markets of political socialization research. As shall be demonstrated, we have recently re-entered the bull market.

It would be a mistake, though, to say that an interest in political socialization disappeared for any great length of time. True, only a few publications devoted explicitly to pre-adults appeared between the mid-1970s and the early 1990s. The concepts and findings from earlier research had, however, thoroughly penetrated the discipline of political science and had become embedded in a number of subfields, including public opinion, electoral behavior, political culture, and political movements. Some evidence along those lines comes from an examination of political science journal abstracts, which reveal a fairly steady mention of political socialization at an average rate of nearly twenty per year between 1972 and 1996 (Sapiro 2004). In addition, there has been a very active research committee on political socialization and education within the International Political Science Association for the past quarter-century.

That said, there is no question that the pace of scholarly inquiries has increased since the early 1990s. Before turning to that resurgence, I will address the fact that very few inquiries deal with children.

1 THE LOSS OF CHILDHOOD

Early work in the United States was based on collecting primary data from school-age children (e.g. Easton and Dennis 1969, Greenstein 1965). These investigations emphasized the content and progression of political learning over the childhood years. They also noted the positive and relatively benign processes and outcomes of political socialization. Strong inferences were drawn about the systemic consequences of such positive orientations.

Ironically, however, these studies did not set the tone for future research in their focus on pre-adolescents. Subsequent scholarship has only occasionally dealt with children. Outcroppings have appeared, such as a three-wave study that did include pre-teenagers and which demonstrated the remarkable impact of political campaigning on information and partisan crystallization and the important role played by media exposure (Sears and Valentino 1997; Valentino and Sears 1998). Even these reports, however, are based on data collected in 1980–1.

Three reasons can be advanced for the virtual disappearance of childhood studies. First, political scientists are not very interested in children. As pithily overstated by Torney-Purta, "most psychologists have to be convinced that anything happening *after age 12* makes a difference, whereas political scientists have to be convinced that anything happening *before age 18* makes a difference" (Torney-Purta 2005, 471, emphasis in the original). A second reason is that the cohorts represented by the children with such benign views of politics in mid-century America were the very same ones that manifested dramatic displays of social and political unrest and rebellion a decade later. Rightly or wrongly, some observers took this to mean that the socialization lessons of childhood could be easily undone. Third, and relatedly, replications of the early studies in the wake of critical events in the United States, including the Watergate scandal of the early 1970s, revealed how quickly children could alter their views about politics (e.g. Dennis and Webster 1975).

Sapiro (2004) makes a spirited argument for a return to the study of childhood. She argues that advances in development psychology have challenged the cognitive incompetence arguments, that social categorization and identity processes are now a more central part of our understanding about political socialization and are crucial building blocks for the child, and that emerging consensus on what constitutes political competencies provide normative guidelines for evaluating socialization outcomes for children. Nevertheless, studies of children have been rare. Rather, attention has focused on adolescents, young adults, and beyond. In what follows I take up several developments that have helped fuel a scholarly resurgence in political socialization research in recent years.

2 THE IMPACT OF REAL WORLD EVENTS

Just as the student protest movement in western countries in the 1960s and early 1970s ushered in a raft of studies highly relevant to the field,[1] so too have external events in the 1980s and 1990s fostered fresh research. Two secular developments have been pivotal.

2.1 Declining Civic Virtue in Western Democracies

One impetus consists of the apparent decline in social capital, civic virtue, and traditional political engagement said to characterize upcoming cohorts in many western societies. Prompted by such trends, a variety of institutions and researchers have turned to the question of the education and training of the young. Most of these projects deal with adolescents and young adults.

The research can be divided into three main areas, one of which is the formal curriculum. As a corrective to the early conclusion by Langton and Jennings (1968) regarding the inefficacy of exposure to civics courses in the United States, Niemi and Junn (1998) concluded that the impact was considerably more than trivial.[2] Other research indicates that particular styles of teaching about government and politics are more effective than others (e.g. Andolina et al. 2003), findings also reported in an international study (Torney-Purta 2002). By their very nature, most such inquiries are short term panels or one-time assessments, thus limiting a longer-term evaluation.

A second line of research concerns the impact of participating in extracurricular and voluntary associations during adolescence. Here the evidence is more convincing, partly due to the availability of better data. Cross-sectional surveys (Andolina et al. 2003) short-term panel studies (Campbell 2006; Smith 1999), long-term panels (Stolle and Hooghe 2004; Jennings and Stoker 2004) and retrospective accounts (Verba, Schlozman, and Brady 1995, 416–60) show the salutary consequences of student government and voluntary association membership on adult levels of civic engagement and political participation. Adolescents engaging in such activities seem to acquire skills and predispositions that yield returns, which may vary by time and site, as they wend their way through life.

Community service programs (usually at the secondary school level) that in various ways combine community outreach with classroom instruction constitute a third focus of research. The rationale for such programs is to develop participatory skills and an interest and concern about the general welfare. Such programs encompass a wide range by site, duration, and format, and some are much more politically charged than others. Early evaluations of such programs produced mixed results

---

[1] I omit that considerable literature due to its dated appearance.

[2] This finding has been undermined by the revelation that the effects appeared predominantly among students currently enrolled in a civics class (Green 2000).

(Galston 2001), partly because of weak study designs. More carefully designed recent studies are more promising. One such inquiry employed a quasi-experimental approach and demonstrated that high school students who were required to serve but had initially been less inclined to do so became more likely than others to contemplate future political engagement and also became more interested in politics and increased their understanding thereof (Metz and Youniss 2005). A large cross-sectional study of American high schoolers revealed widely varying practices and that service appeared to increase their levels of political interest, knowledge, and skills but had little impact on political tolerance (Niemi, Hepburn, and Chapman 2000).

2.2 A Changing World Order

A second development consists of the Cold War winding down coupled with the emergence of transitional and new democracies around the globe. A changing world order has provided a natural laboratory for examining the processes and outcomes of political socialization. Perhaps equally important from a research standpoint, the opening up of these societies has also made it politically and practically possible to undertake relevant research.

These events have often led to studies of efforts by the new regimes to instill in pre-adults, especially via the educational system, the norms of democracy and, in some instances, marketplace economics (Slomczynski and Shabad 1998). Well-designed research in such disparate settings as post-apartheid South Africa (Finkel and Ernst 2005), post-Communist Poland (Slomczynski and Shabad 1998), democratizing Argentina (Morduchowicz et al. 1996), and recovering Bosnia and Herzegovina (Soule 2003) point toward the ability of a carefully constructed and seriously implemented civics curriculum to elevate levels of political comprehension and, somewhat less so, a variety of democratic values. A survey of three established and four transitioning democracies revealed moderate to high rates of volunteer work, especially among females, although the impact of such work on feelings of civic commitment ranged from nil to substantial and varied according to gender (Flanagan et al. 1998).

A changing world order has also led to investigations of basic political norms and their correlates in a number of diverse settings. For example, Finchilescu and Dawes (1998) portrayed the differential responses of adolescents to regime change in South Africa according to race/ethnicity, age, and location. A survey of high schoolers in Hungary, Bulgaria, and the Czech Republic revealed gender, age, and country differences in perceptions of economic disparity and the value of individual initiative (Macek et al. 1998).

Although not necessarily associated with a changing world order, studies of the impact of particular and ongoing events have also made a mark. Included here are studies of Catholic and Protestant children in strife-torn Northern Ireland (e.g. Whyte 1998). Israeli adolescent responses to the Rabin assassination and terror attacks revealed differences according to political orientation, gender, and to the events themselves (Raviv et al. 2000). An unusual project uncovered substantial links between stressful political life events and psychological distress among South African adolescents, regardless of race and also among Israeli and Palestinian youth (Slone, Kaminer, and Durrheim 2000). Using intensive research methods, Coles (1986) paints poignant portraits of children trying to cope with stressful situations in a number of countries.

3 RENEWED INTEREST IN THE DYNAMICS OF SOCIALIZATION

As noted earlier the question of persistence seemed to bedevil the study of children, though surely in part because of the cognitive and experiential limitations of childhood. Partly in reaction to that quandary the focus of most socialization inquiries shifted to what happens in the adolescent and young adulthood years and to how that plays out over time. Such a shift rests to some degree on the platform of the impressionable years model of political learning, which posits considerable fluctuation in political orientations during the adolescent and young adult years, followed by a period of modest to strong crystallization, and then by *relative* stability from thereon.[3] While the model thus postulates persistence and the possible emergence of Mannheim-like generations and generation units (Mannheim 1927), it by no means excludes the working of subsequent life cycle and widespread period effects.

Expanding and richer databases have helped promote the renewed interest in the dynamics of socialization. Panel studies that begin prior to adulthood and track people over an extended period of time are ideal for assessing these models and for tracing the continuities and discontinuities in political orientations. Such projects are inherently difficult. Two very long-term American studies of small, select populations, most notably the Bennington College project that began in the 1930s (Alwin, Cohen, and Newcomb 1991), and the Terman gifted children project that began in the 1940s (Sears and Funk 1999) continue to be mined even as the participants fade from view. Both inquiries support the impressionable years model and reveal the kinds of orientations that are likely to persist and, equally significant, how they are applied in later life.

A third long-term project in the United States with broader coverage is the four-wave multi-generation "student-parent socialization project," which has at its core a national sample of the 1965 class of high seniors. Results bearing on dynamics from this study support the formative years hypothesis and also help reveal how orientations acquired during those years have fed into the increasing degree of

---

[3] A competing model, mid-life stability, is similar except that it predicts a tapering off of stability in the later years.

partisan polarization in the American public (Jennings and Stoker 2005). Other results from that project show the impact of early-acquired civic norms on subsequent voting rates (Campbell 2006), the importance of social class stability in affecting political participation (Walsh, Jennings, and Stoker 2004), the durability of protesters as a generation unit (Jennings 2002), and how marriage can affect behaviors and attitudes brought into the marriage (Stoker and Jennings 1995, 2005).

Short-term panel data sets are becoming more frequent, as noted in the earlier citation of Smith (1999). Illustratively, as part of a survey of xenophobia among seventh to tenth graders in East and West Berlin, Boehnkje, Hagen, and Hefler (1998) found higher levels in the later years and among East Berliners and those not in the university bound track. Another German study uncovered four different types of development in political orientations over a seven-year period (Krampen 2000). A survey of Dutch adolescents and young adults indicated that the relationship between moral reasoning and attitudes about political cultural issues increased with age and education (Raaijmakers, Verbogt, and Vollebergh 1998). Working with American data based on two-year panel periods Campbell (2006, ch. 6) demonstrated that volunteering while in high school predicts volunteering and voting turnout, though not more demanding political activities, in young adulthood.

Short and long-term panel studies, while invaluable, will probably continue to be relatively infrequent. Another data source for capturing dynamic aspects of political socialization will, on the other hand, continue to expand. Replicated surveys of youthful samples, such as the Monitoring the Future project in the United States, will provide grist for the mill of replacement cohort analysis (e.g. Rahn and Transue 1998). Such studies obviously do not permit tracing out the long-term pathways of cohorts, whereas replicated studies of adult cross-section samples do. Although longitudinal data of this sort have been available for some time, the passage of time has resulted in an impressive collection data sets in many countries. Here I refer to such projects as ongoing national election studies, General Social Surveys, regional "barometer" surveys, and the World Values Surveys.

Extended longitudinal surveys permit such diverse projects as determining the cross-national generational basis of value change (e.g. Abramson and Inglehart 1995), identifying the lingering generational differences in appraisals of new and old regimes in post-Soviet Russia (Mishler and Rose 2005) and East Germany (Finkel, Humphries, and Opp 2001), charting the gradual rather than abrupt changes prompted by cohort replacement in the Netherlands (van den Broek 1999), whether the American cohorts coming of age in the 1960s constitute a distinctive political generation (Davis 2004), and the seeming uniqueness of America's long civic generation (Putnam 2000). Investigations of this sort implicitly or explicitly employ the impressionable years model of political socialization.

Although longitudinal data are optimal for observing possible generation (and other) effects, the use of clever designs, novel instrumentation, and deep substantive knowledge as applied to one-shot surveys can also be productive. Tessler, Konold, and Reif (2004), for example, capitalize on the discrete historical eras of Algeria to show the singularity of one era in shaping political views. Verba,

Schlozman, and Burns (2005) demonstrate that African-Americans coming of age during the civil rights movement recalled a more politically stimulating home environment than did other African-Americans and also went on to record higher levels of political participation.

In a quite different vein, the possible persistence of orientations derived from the impressionable years has also been studied from the standpoint of collective memories. Adult survey respondents in a wide range of countries have been asked to recall and reflect upon significant national events within the past half-century. Their answers proved to reflect disproportionately the events that occurred during their adolescent to young adulthood years (e.g. Jennings and Zhang 2005; Schuman, Akiyama, and Knäuper 1998; Schuman and Rodgers 2004; and Schuman, Vinitzky, and Vindour 2003). Thus long after the event itself, the imprint remains, a critical test of the impressionable years thesis.

4 A NEW EMPHASIS ON CONTEXTUAL EFFECTS

From the outset the study of political socialization has been dominated by sample survey methodology, using either fixed or more flexible instrumentation. Partly because survey research has been the method of choice, research attention has typically focused on individuals and their attributes as units of analysis. More recently there has been a decided turn toward building in the relevant contextual features that attend the socialization process. In doing so, socialization inquiries are joining a growing stream of political behavior research.

4.1 Within-country Studies

The theoretical and substantive importance of contextual features in the political socialization process has been recognized from the outset of systematic study. Nevertheless, most of the early survey work devoted specifically to pre-adults paid little attention to larger contextual effects. That situation is changing. Illustratively, Conover and Searing (2000) have engaged in intensive studies of a small number of vividly contrasting secondary school communities in the United States (and Great Britain). Young adolescents constitute the focus of the analysis, but information about their context is generated by interviews with their parents, teachers, and community leaders, and ordinary citizens, and observational and aggregate level data, thus providing rich contextual information. Based on their American study, they concluded that civic engagement and civic education were more closely tied to the practice of citizenship in certain types of communities than others.

Small-scale studies such as the one just described provide an intimate, process-oriented look at contextual effects, but are limited in terms of generalization. They also suffer from an inability to specify the effects of particular contextual levels over and above or interacting with individual characteristics of those being socialized. Political socialization inquiries have recently begun to employ multi-level models in an effort to specify and understand the contribution of contextual features. Multi-level modeling is often preferred with nested designs, frequently present in socialization studies, because the observations at different levels are not independent.

Two recent reports of adolescents in the United States exemplify the trend. Both move beyond using individual student and familial characteristics as determinants of socialization outcomes by employing features of the communities and schools in which the students are "nested." One study utilized census and electoral data to characterize the school catchment areas and hence the sociopolitical contexts in which the students lived (Gimpel, Lay, and Schuknecht 2003). Their results indicate that sociopolitical diversity elevated information holding and participation while homogeneous and uncompetitive environments dampened various indicators of civic engagement. Another conclusion is that the local partisan context has more impact on adolescents in the minority than those in the majority party (Gimpel and Lay 2005).

A second report, based on a variety of American cross-sectional and panel surveys, tested two theories of voting motivation—to protect one's interests or to fulfill a sense of duty (Campbell 2006). Again, community and school contextual features are built into the analysis and treated in a multi-level fashion. A major conclusion is that more homogeneous secondary school environments appeared to foster anticipated and actual participation based on a sense of civic duty whereas more heterogeneous contexts encouraged participation based on more instrumental goals.

As noted earlier, the accumulation of extended timed series survey data has encouraged the application of socialization perspectives to the longitudinal analysis of birth cohorts. An analytic problem here is that the passage of time is an aggregate, not individual-level datum. In a strong sense, time constitutes a context and a different analytic level. That being so, it is argued that multi-level models should be used rather than conventional multivariate approaches such as ordinary least squares regression.

In one of the first applications of this reasoning, Mishler and Rose (2005) analyze fourteen waves of the New Russia Barometer surveys conducted between 1992 and 2005. The impact of time (qua secular change or period effects), which was quite significant in their report, is clearly delineated by applying multi-level modeling. They use this and other results from the study to advance a thesis dubbed a lifetime learning model. This model represents a melding of cultural theory, which is heavily laced with pre-adult socialization processes, and institutionalist theory, which argues for contemporaneous learning and adaptability by adults as they respond to changing circumstances. Given the ever-expanding base of country-specific longitudinal surveys, it seems very likely that time will be more formally treated as a context and that multi-level models will be used in tracing out generation, life cycle, and historical effects as part of the larger political socialization project.

4.2 Cross-national Studies

By their very nature cross-national investigations lend themselves to searching for contextual effects with respect to political socialization. Indeed, the very concept of a civic culture in Almond and Verba's classic work (1963) was predicated in part on the existence of different socialization contexts across their five-nation study. Until recently, such efforts have been confined to a small number of countries.

Perhaps the most systematic efforts to assess contextual effects in small N inquiries are the attempts to assess the impact of party systems on the transmission of partisanship and political ideology from parent to child.[4] Working with parent–child pair data from a number of countries and responding in part to the earlier work by Converse and Dupeux (1962), Percheron and Jennings (1981) argued that some party systems facilitated the transmission of a general left–right ideology in addition to or instead of attachment to particular parties. Subsequently, Westholm and Niemi (1992) amended this proposal by showing that there were both direct and indirect effects of parental partisanship *and* ideology and that these varied systematically with the nature of the party system. More recently, Ventura (2001) added an Israeli data set to the mix and made a case for the political bloc as the subject of transmission in Israel, and Nieuwbeerta and Wittebrood (1995) noted the complications afforded by the presence of the strong and diverse Dutch multi-party system. In all these instances, substantial knowledge about the context provided by the party system helped in understanding the magnitude and nature of parent to child transmission.

As with the single country studies, more advanced statistical techniques for analyzing the impact of context are also beginning to emerge in cross-national studies. Currently, the best prospects for comparative multi-level modeling as applied to pre-adults come from the IEA Civic Education Study, conducted under the auspices of the International Association for the Evaluation of Educational Achievement. This project consists of self-administered questionnaire data, and auxiliary information about the schools and teachers, gathered from around 90,000 young adolescents in twenty-eight countries and about 50,000 somewhat older ones in twelve countries (Torney-Purta et al. 2001). The clustering of student respondents by civic education classroom within each sampled school lends itself to multi-level modeling at the classroom, school, and country level. Multi-level analysis based on this project is just now beginning to appear.[5]

A more plentiful and growing source of data for large N assessments of contextual effects rests in the substantial number of longitudinal, cross-national studies of adult populations. As noted earlier, these replications are particularly, though not solely, important from a socialization perspective in terms of demonstrating cohort effects, whether these be due to compositional changes or to "experiential" processes of a Mannheimian sort. Depending upon the nesting properties of the research design,

---

[4] Some reports emerging from the 28-nation IEA Civic Education project also take a small N approach (e.g. Torney-Purta, Barber, and Richardson 2004).

[5] Campbell (2006, ch. 5) used the United States portion of the project.

there may be one or more contextual levels. By now there are a sizeable number of such projects in various stages of longitudinality and containing varying amounts of comparable measures.

5 REVISITING THE ROLE OF THE FAMILY

From the earliest scholarly inquiries on through to the present time the role of the family as a prime agent of socialization has occupied an important place in the literature. By inference it was assumed that the family, mainly parents, played a predominant role given the child's early and prolonged exposure to the family on the one hand, and the relative degree of continuity observed in political cultures on the other hand. Such reasoning was predicated on the basis of social learning theories (direct modeling, cue giving, and reinforcement processes within the family) or the impact of factors associated with various social and economic characteristics of the family—the social milieu pathway (Dalton 1982).

It was not until the advent of study designs that included independent information from both parents and children that more specific tests of propositions about the reproduction of parental political characteristics in their offspring could be conducted. As noted in the preceding section, many of these studies continue to focus on partisanship and ideology and have enriched our understanding of parental influence. In that respect social learning in the form of the direct transmission model seems to work reasonably well and varies in rather predictable ways according to systemic characteristics. With respect to a number of other orientations, the model often proved to be wanting in early studies (e.g. Allerbeck, Jennings, and Rosenmayr 1979; Jennings and Niemi 1968), and thereby generated some skepticism about direct parental influence. More nuanced assessments have demonstrated, however, that topic salience and perceptual accuracy enhance remarkably the likelihood of reproductive fidelity (e.g. Tedin 1974; Westholm 1999) and that taking measurement error into account also increases the similarity between parent and child (Dalton 1980). It also turns out that the transmission model tends to be generally more robust than a model using family social traits as predictors of offspring political traits (Glass, Bengston, and Dunham 1986; Jennings 1984; and US Department of Education 1999, 45–56).

Two intriguing questions about parental influence require complex designs: how enduring is parental influence and are there differences in parental impact across generations? These questions have been addressed using the American long-term, multi-generation "student-parent socialization project" initially based on a national sample of high school seniors and their parents (Jennings, Stoker, and Bowers 2005). As for the first question, parent–child correspondence is at its zenith *before* the child leaves home, drops substantially as the child moves through young adulthood, and levels off subsequently. One key factor affecting sustained parental impact is parental attitudinal stability on the political topic at hand; another factor is parental politicization level. As for the second question about intergenerational differences in parental influence, the answer is one of continuity. Congruence between the erstwhile high school seniors and their *offspring* as of 1997 closely matched that between the seniors and their *parents* in 1965, this being so despite vast changes in the social and political landscape over time.

Family influence continues to be assessed by introducing family socioeconomic and political characteristics into the analysis, most especially in the absence of direct measures of parental characteristics. Thus many of the civic engagement studies referenced above utilize family-level estimates obtained from youthful respondents either as independent or control variables. The reliability of such respondent reports ranges widely, with more confidence being placed in reports about concrete, objective traits. As Tedin noted some time ago (1976), perceptions about all but the most potent of parental political attitudes are fraught with error.

Cross-section studies of adults also continue to utilize reports about the family of origin as a way of understanding adult orientations. Illustratively, in one imaginative inquiry Miller and Sears (1986) demonstrated that the continuity of demographic features from the family of origin to one's adult years had a strong bearing on levels of social tolerance. Addressing a traditional topic with a rich data set, Verba, Schlozman, and Burns (2005) showed that more parental education increases the likelihood of later offspring political participation not only by providing a richer political environment in the home but also by enhancing the educational attainments of their offspring which are, in turn, related to participation.

6 FOREGONE ALTERNATIVES AND NEW OPPORTUNITIES

I close this chapter with a brief comment about what might have been and what might yet be. A missed opportunity concerns the large influx of immigrants into a number of countries over the past few decades. Not only did this present a chance to study the socialization processes and outcomes regarding pre-adults, but it also represented a unique opportunity to analyze the resocialization of adults. Some relevant work, often flying under the conceptual banner of integration and differentiation, has appeared (e.g. Cain, Kiewiet, and Uhlaner 1991; de la Garza et al. 1992; Bowlen, Nicholson, and Segura 2006). For the most part, however, systematic inquiries with a focus on socialization as such have been lacking.[6] Part of the difficulty is that ordinary

---

[6] Here, as elsewhere, my restriction to the English-language literature has undoubtedly excluded some pertinent contributions.

probability samples of pre-adult and adult populations usually do not include enough distinctive immigrant groups for analytic purposes. More purposive sampling schemes such as that employed by Gimpel, Lay, and Schuknecht (2003) are in order. The window of opportunity has shrunk in many places, but ample space remains for innovative research.

A possible new research direction has been recently advanced, one which joins a stream of research linking the social sciences and behavioral genetics. Alford, Funk, and Hibbing (2005) use data from twin studies in the United States to argue that genetics plays a more than trivial role in the construction of political orientations. At this early stage it is difficult to predict the future of this innovation. Still, it brings a provocative addition to the political socialization literature and links the subfield to emergent trends in the discipline.

REFERENCES

ABRAMSON, P., and INGLEHART, R. I. 1995. *Value Change in Global Perspective*. Ann Arbor: University of Michigan Press.

ALFORD, J. R., FUNK, C. L., and HIBBING, J. R. 2005. Are political orientations genetically transmitted? *American Political Science Review*, 99: 153–67.

ALLERBECK, K., JENNINGS, M. K., and ROSENMAYR, L. 1979. Generations and families: political action. Pp. 487–522 in *Political Action: Mass Participation in Five Western Democracies*, ed. S. Barnes and M. Kaase. Beverly Hills, Calif.: Sage.

ALMOND, G., and VERBA, S. 1963. *The Civic Culture: Political Attitudes and Democracy in Five Nations*. Princeton: Princeton University Press.

ALWIN, D. F., COHEN, R. L., and NEWCOMB, T. M. 1991. *Political Attitudes over The Life Span: The Bennington Women after Fifty Years*. Madison: University of Wisconsin Press.

ANDOLINA, M. W., JENKINS, K., ZUKIN, C., and KEETER, S. 2003. Habits from home, lessons from school: influence on youth civic engagement. *PS: Political Science and Politics*, 36: 275–80.

BOEHNKE, K., HAGEN, J., and HEFLER, G. 1998. On the development of xenophobia in Germany: the Adolescent Years. *Journal of Social Issues*, 54: 585–602.

BOWLER, S., NICHOLSON, S. P., and SEGURA, G. M. 2006. Earthquakes and Aftershocks: Race, democracy, and partisan change. *American Journal of Political Science*, 50: 146–59.

CAIN, B. E., KIEWIET, R., and UHLANER, C. J. 1991. The Acquisition of Partisanship by Latinos and Asian Americans. *American Journal of Political Science*, 35: 390–422.

CAMPBELL, D. 2006. *Why We Vote: How Schools and Communities Shape our Civic Life*. Princeton: Princeton University Press.

COLES, R. 1986. *The Political Lives of Children*. Boston: Houghton Mifflin

CONOVER, P., and SEARING, D. 2000. A political socialization perspective. Pp. 91–124 in *Rediscovering the Democratic Purposes of Education*, ed. L. M. McDonnell, P. M. Timpane, and R. Benjamin. Lawrence, Kan.: University Press of Kansas.

CONVERSE, P. E., and DUPEUX, G. 1962. Politicization of the French electorate in France and the United States. *Public Opinion Quarterly*, 26: 1–23.

DALTON, R. 1980. Reassessing parental socialization: indicator unreliability versus generational transfer. *American Political Science Review*, 74: 421–31.

—— 1982. The pathways of parental socialization. *American Politics Quarterly*, 10: 139–57.

DAVIS, J. A. 2004. Did growing up in the 1960s leave a permanent mark on attitudes and values: evidence from the General Social Survey. *Public Opinion Quarterly*, 68: 161–83.

DE LA GARZA, R. O., DESIPIO, L., GARCIA, C., GARCIA, J., and FALCON, F. 1992. *Latino Voices: Mexican, Puerto Rican, and Cuban Perspectives on American Politics.* Boulder, Colo.: Westview Press.

DENNIS, J., and WEBSTER, C. 1975. Children's images of the President, in 1962 and 1974. *American Politics Quarterly*, 3. 386–405.

EASTON, D., and DENNIS, J. 1969. *Children in the Political System.* New York: McGraw Hill.

FINCHILESCU, G., and DAWES, A. 1998. Catapulted into democracy: South African adolescents' sociopolitical orientations following rapid social change. *Journal of Social Issues*, 54: 563–83.

FINKEL, S. E., and ERNST, H. R. 2005. Civic education in post–Apartheid South Africa: alternative paths to the development of political knowledge and democratic values. *Political Psychology*, 26: 333–64.

—— HUMPHRIES, S., and OPP, K.-D. 2001. Socialist values and the development of democratic support in the former East Germany. *International Political Science Review*, 22: 339–61.

FLANAGAN, C., BOWES, J. M., JONSON, B., CSAPO, B., and SHEBLANOVA, E. 1998. Ties that bind: correlates of adolescents' civic commitments in seven countries. *Journal of Social Issues*, 54: 457–75.

GALSTON, W. A. 2001. Political knowledge, political engagement, and civic education. *Annual Review of Political Science*, 4: 217–34.

GIMPEL, J. G., and LAY, J. C. 2005. Party identification, local partisan contexts, and the acquisition of participatory attitudes. Pp. 209–27 in *The Social Logic of Politics*, ed. A. S. Zuckerman. Philadelphia: Temple University Press.

—— —— and SCHUKNECHT, J. E. 2003. *Cultivating Democracy: Civic Environments and Political Socialization in America.* Washington, DC: Brookings Institution.

GLASS, J., BENGSTON, V. L., and DUNHAM, C. C. 1986. Attitude similarity in three generation families: socialization, status inheritance, or reciprocal influence? *American Sociological Review*, 51: 685–98.

GREEN, J. P. 2000. Review of R. G. Niemi and J. Junn, *Civic Education. Social Science Quarterly*, 81: 696–97.

GREENSTEIN, F. I. 1965. *Children and Politics.* New Haven: Yale University Press.

JENNINGS, M. K. 1984. The intergenerational transfer of political ideology in eight western nations. *European Journal of Political Research*, 12: 261–76.

—— 2002. Generation units and the student protest movement in the United States: an intra– and intergenerational analysis. *Political Psychology*, 23: 303–24.

—— and NIEMI, R. G. 1968. The transmission of political values from parent to child. *American Political Science Review*, 62: 169–84.

—— and STOKER, L. 2004. Social trust and civic engagement across time and generations. *Acta Politica*, 39: 342–79.

—— —— 2005. Aging, generations, and the development of partisan polarization in the United States. Unpublished paper.

—— —— and BOWERS, J. 2005. Politics across generations: family transmission reexamined. Unpublished paper.

—— and ZHANG, N. 2005. Generations, political status, and collective memories in the Chinese countryside. *Journal of Politics*, 67: 1164–89.

KRAMPEN, G. 2000. Transition of adolescent political action orientations to voting behavior in early adulthood in view of a social-cognitive action model of personality. *Political Psychology*, 21: 277–97.

LANGTON, K., and JENNINGS, M. K. 1968. Political socialization and the high school civics curriculum. *American Political Science Review*, 62: 852–67.

MACEK, P., FLANAGAN, C., GALLAY, L., KOSTRON, L., BOTCHEVA, L., and CSAPO, R. 1998. Postcommunist societies in times of transition: perceptions of change among adolescents in Central and Eastern Europe. *Journal of Social Issues*, 54: 547–61.

MANNHEIM, K. [1927] 1952. The problem of generations. Pp. 276–320 in *Essays on the Sociology of Knowledge*, ed. P. Keckemeti. London: Routledge & Kegan Paul.

METZ, E., and YOUNISS, J. 2005. Longitudinal gains in civic development through school–based required service. *Political Psychology*, 26: 413–38.

MILLER, S. D., and SEARS, D. O. 1986. Stability and change in social tolerance: a test of the persistnece hypothesis. *American Journal of Political Science*, 30: 215–35.

MISHLER, W., and ROSE, R. 2005. Generations, aging, and time: patterns of political learning during Russia's transformation. Paper prepared for 3rd ECPR General Conference, Budapest.

MORDUCHOWICZ, R., CATTERBERG, E., NIEMI, R., and BELL, F. 1996. Teaching political science knowledge and democratic values in a new democracy: an Argentine experiment. *Comparative Politics*, 28: 465–76.

NIEMI, R. G., HEPBURN, M. A., and CHAPMAN, C. 2000. Community service by high school students: A cure for civic ills? *Political Behavior*, 22: 45–69.

—— and JUNN, J. 1998. *Civic Education: What Makes Students Learn*. New Haven: Yale University Press.

—— and WESTHOLM, A. 1992. Political institutions and political socialization: a cross-national study. *Comparative Politics*, 25: 25–41.

NIEUWBEERTA, P., and WITTEBROOD, K. 1995. Intergenerational transmission of political party preference in the Netherlands. *Social Science Research*, 24: 242–61.

PERCHERON, A., and JENNINGS, M. K. 1981. Political continuities in french families: a new perspective on an old controversy. *Comparative Politics*, 13: 421–36.

PUTNAM, R. 2000. *Bowling Alone: The Collapse and Revival of American Community*. New York: Simon & Schuster.

RAAIJMAKERS, QUIINTEN, A. W., VERBOGT, T. F. M. A., and VOLLEBERGH, W. A. M. 1998. Moral reasoning and political beliefs of Dutch adolescents and young adults. *Journal of Social Issues*, 54: 531–46.

RAHN, W. M., and TRANSUE, J. E. 1998. Social trust and value change: the decline of social capital in American youth, 1976–1995. *Political Psychology*, 19: 545–65.

RAVIV, A., SADEH, A., RAVIV, A., SILBERSTEIN, O., and DIVER, O. 2000. Young Israelis' reactions to national trauma: the Rabin assassination and terror attacks. *Political Psychology*, 21: 299–322.

RENSHON, S. 2003. Political socialization in a divided society and dangerous world. Pp. 427–56, in *Encyclopedia of Government and Politics*, vol. i, 2nd edn., ed. M. Hawkesworth, and M. Kogan. London: Routledge.

SAPIRO, V. 2004. Not your parents' political socialization: introduction for a new generation. *Annual Review of Political Science*, 7: 1–23.

SCHUMAN, H., AKIYAMA, H., and KNÄUPER, B. 1998. Collective memories of Germans and Japanese about the past half-century. *Memory*, 6: 427–54.

—— and RODGERS, W. 2004. Cohorts, chronology, and collective memories. *Public Opinion Quarterly*, 68: 217–54.

—— VINITZKY, V., and VINDOUR, A. D. 2003. Keeping the past alive: memories of Israeli Jews at the turn of the century. *Sociological Forum*, 18: 103–39.

SEARS, D. O., and FUNK, C. 1999. Evidence of the long-term persistence of adults' political predispositions. *Journal of Politics*, 61: 1–28.

—— and LEVY, S. 2003. Childhood and adult political development. Pp. 60–109 in *Oxford Handbook of Political Psychology*, ed. D. O. Sears, L. Huddy, and R. Jervis. Oxford: Oxford University Press.

—— and VALENTINO, N. A. 1997. Politics matters: political events as catalysts for preadult socialization. *American Political Science Review*, 91: 45–65.

SLOMCZYNKSI, K., and SHABAD, G. 1998. Can support for democracy and the market be learned in school? A natural experiment in post-communist Poland. *Political Psychology*, 19: 749–79.

SLONE, M., KAMINER, E., and DURRHEIM, K. 2000. The contribution of political life events to psychological distress among South African adolescents. *Political Psychology*, 21: 465–88.

SMITH, E. 1999. The effects of investments in the social capital of youth on political and civic behavior in young adulthood. *Political Psychology*, 20: 553–80.

SOULE, S. 2003. The crucible of democracy: civic education in Bosnia and Herzegovina. Unpublished dissertation, University of California, Santa Barbara.

STOKER, L., and JENNINGS, M. K. 1995. Life cycle transitions and political participation: the case of marriage. *American Political Science Review*, 89: 421–36.

—— —— 2005. Political similarity and influence between husbands and wives. Pp. 51–74 in *The Social Logic of Politics*, ed. A. S. Zuckerman. Philadelphia: Temple University Press.

STOLLE, D., and HOOGHE, M. 2004. The roots of social capital: attitudinal and network mechanisms in the relation between youth and adult indicators of social capital. *Acta Politica*, 39: 422–41.

TEDIN, K. L. 1974. The influence of parents on the political attitudes of adolescents. *American Political Science Review*, 68: 1579–92.

—— 1976. On the reliability of reported political attitudes. *American Journal of Political Science*, 20: 117–24.

TESSLER, M., KONOLD, C., and REIF, M. 2004. Political generations in developing countries: evidence and insights from Algeria. *Public Opinion Quarterly*, 68: 184–216.

TORNEY–PURTA, J. 2002. The school's role in developing civic engagement: a study of adolescents in twenty-eight countries. *Applied Developmental Science*, 6: 202–11.

—— 2005. Adolescents' political socialization in changing contexts. *Political Psychology*, 25: 465–78.

—— BARBER, C. H., and RICHARDSON, W. K. 2004. Trust in government-related institutions and political engagement among adolescents in six countries. *Acta Politica*, 39: 380–406.

—— LEHMAN, R., OSWALD, H., and SCHULZ, W. 2001. Citizenship and education in twenty-eight countries: civic knowledge and engagement at age fourteen. Amsterdam: IEA. www.wam.umd.edu/~iea

US Department of Education, National Center for Education Statistics. 1999. *The Civic Development of 9th-Through 12th-Grade Students in the United States:1996*, NCES 1999–131, by R. G. Niemi and C. Chapman. Washington, DC.

VALENTINO, N., and SEARS, D. O. 1998. Event-driven political socialization and the preadult socialization of partisanship. *Political Behavior*, 20: 127–54.

VAN DEN BROEK, A. 1999. Does differential cohort socialization matter? The impact of cohort replacement and the presence of intergenerational differences in the Netherlands. *Political Psychology*, 20: 501–23.

VENTURA, R. 2001. Family political socialization in multiparty systems. *Comparative Political Studies*, 34: 666–91.

VERBA, S., SCHLOZMAN, K. L., and BRADY, H. E. 1995. *Voice and Equality: Civic Voluntarism in American Politics*. Cambridge, Mass.: Harvard University Press.

—— and BURNS, N. 2005. Family ties: understanding the intergenerational transmission of political participation. Pp. 95–114 in *The Social Logic of Politics*, ed. A. S. Zuckerman. Philadelphia: Temple University Press.

WALSH, C. W., JENNINGS, M. K., and STOKER, L. 2004. The effects of social class identification on participatory orientations toward government. *British Journal of Political Science*, 34 (June 2004), 469–95.

WESTHOLM, A. 1999. The perceptual pathway: tracing the mechanisms of political value transfer across generations. *Political Psychology*, 20: 525–52.

—— and NIEMI, R. G. 1992. Political institutions and political socialization. *Comparative Politics*, 25: 25–41.

WHYTE, J. 1998. Political socialization in a divided society: the case of Northern Ireland. Pp. 156–77 in *International Perspectives on Community Service and Political Engagement*, ed. M. Yates and J. Youniss. Cambridge: Cambridge University Press.

CHAPTER 3

....

BELIEF SYSTEMS AND POLITICAL DECISION MAKING

....

JAMES H. KUKLINSKI
BUDDY PEYTON

Buoyed by forty years of systematic research, political scientists should be able to tell a coherent story about citizens and politics. How much do citizens know about politics? Do they understand left–right ideology, and do they think in ideological terms? Do they hold meaningful attitudes on current issues? Do they update their beliefs and attitudes in response to changing conditions?

To a commendable extent, political scientists have met the expectation. Most, if asked, would tell a story much like the following: A sizeable segment of the adult population knows little about politics. Failing to understand the left–right context that structures debates among their elected representatives, they cannot adequately assess those debates or the policy proposals that generate them. When asked, these same citizens express policy preferences. These preferences wobble randomly over time, however, suggesting that most respondents fail to hold real opinions, but, to please the interviewers, answer the survey questions anyway. The relative few, in contrast, understand the contours of politics, hold firm beliefs and attitudes, and generally get things right.

This story has a familiar ring, and for good reason. Converse (1964) first told it more than four decades ago, and scholars have been retelling it ever since. It is as though each new generation of scholars repeats the story as a rite of passage into the community of public opinion researchers. Its staying power is a testament to the impressive quality of Converse's writing, argument, and evidence.

However, three revisions of the original story now exist. The "downbeat" revision questions the performance of Converse's exalted few, showing that these highly partisan individuals undertake a variety of arguably unreasonable mental gymnastics to retain their existing political attitudes. Ironically, their very understanding of politics provides the know-how necessary to perform the gymnastics. The "really downbeat" revision tells a story in which all citizens lack true political attitudes. At its limit, this revision tells a story of inevitability in which all citizens lack complete and coherent political beliefs and preferences.

The "upbeat" revision takes Converse in the opposite direction. In it, proportionately far more than 12 percent of US citizens know the basics of politics. They rationally update their beliefs and preferences in response to changing conditions. They also use general principles—core values and political ideology, for example—to inform their (real) attitudes and to make reasonably good choices and judgments. Moreover, citizens in some European countries display especially high levels of political knowledge, suggesting that political contexts can enhance citizen performance independently of individual capabilities and motivations.

The discussion in this chapter proceeds as follows. We first review and summarize the original story, as told in Converse's "The Nature of Mass Belief Systems" (1964) and elsewhere (Converse 1970, 2000; Converse and Markus 1979). Discussions of the three revised stories and the studies that gird them follow. The final, most important section of this chapter first addresses the validity of the three revisions, as we portrayed them. This concern arises because the revisionist stories stem from integrating the literature in a particular way, with which others might disagree.[1] The remainder of the section proposes that the public opinion literature has become schizophrenic. Some of the four stories contradict each other. In most cases, these contradictions arise because scholars act as though they are oblivious to the implications of others' research. This is most evident in but not limited to the case of upbeat revisionists, who favorably cite Converse's original study and then ignore the implications of his substantive conclusions.

1 THE ORIGINAL STORY

Converse began with the notion of political belief systems, which are integrated mental structures in which the component elements logically fit together. For most countries, he argued, the left–right character of elite discourse defines the logic (also see chapter by Mair in this volume). Political ideology serves as the glue that constrains and integrates political belief systems.

---

[1] For example, we paid little attention to publication chronology when identifying the three revisions.

Taking advantage of a 1956–58–60 American National Election panel study (ANES), Converse set out to determine how well US citizens understand left–right ideology. He employed several strategies. Most notably and most widely cited, he coded respondents' open-ended answers to 1956 questions asking them to express what they liked and disliked about the two parties and their 1956 presidential candidates. Using a generous coding scheme, Converse found that he could label only 12 percent of all respondents as either ideologues or near-ideologues, which is to say that they referred to the parties and candidates in left–right terms.[2] In other words, little more than one of ten Americans *actively used* ideological modes of thought.

The 1960 wave of the panel asked respondents whether they *recognized* one party as more liberal or conservative than the other. If they answered in the affirmative, they were first asked which party seemed the more conservative and then asked, "What do you have in mind when you say that the Republicans (Democrats) are more conservative than the Democrats (Republicans)?" If respondents said they did not see a difference, they were asked whether they wanted to guess whether people generally consider Democrats or Republicans as more conservative.[3] If the individual guessed, then he or she received a follow-up question asking what people had in mind when they called one or the other party more conservative. Twenty-nine percent refused to answer either closed-ended question. Another 8 percent tried to answer the closed-ended question but then could not answer the open-ended follow-up. About half of all respondents gave a right answer to both the closed- and open-ended questions. But only about 15 percent of all respondents, even in the presence of explicit priming, answered the open-ended questions in a way that reflected a broad understanding of liberal-conservative ideology, at least by Converse's standard.[4]

Converse also examined the inter-item correlations among responses to policy preference questions and found them to vary from weak to non-existent. People who took a liberal position on one issue did not necessarily take a liberal position on another. Equivalent correlations among a sample of incumbents and challengers running for the 85th Congress were markedly higher, underlining the greater ideological consistency among this elite group.[5]

On every front Converse considered, the evidence told the same story: most people show little understanding of ideological politics. He identified issue publics, small numbers of people who had become knowledgeable about a specific issue or two, but the overall level of understanding left much to be desired. The relatively few who understood left–right politics tended to be better educated, more interested in politics, and generally more similar to the politicians who represented them.

---

[2] Converse used the 1956 wave of the panel study for this analysis.

[3] The researchers asked this question to separate those who did not see a difference from those who saw a difference but cynically believed it was meaningless.

[4] A sizeable number of respondents correctly identified Republicans as more conservative than Democrats and then, when asked what they meant, spoke largely in spend-save terms. Converse distinguishes them from those who gave answers comparable to the ones his ideologues and near-ideologues gave in the 1956 wave.

[5] Achen (1975) and Erikson (1979) raise important measurement concerns that we do not pursue here.

In principle, people could fail to grasp liberal-conservative ideology and still hold meaningful attitudes. To explore this possibility, Converse traced respondents' across-time opinions on a single issue, power and housing, using the 1956-58-60 ANES panel study. The item read as follows: "The government should leave things like electrical power and housing for private businessmen to handle." He chose this issue because it represented a limiting case: neither politicians nor anyone else discussed power and housing during the four-year period and thus those who expressed real opinions on it should not have changed them (Converse 1970). Many people indicated they lacked an opinion, a finding that fell by the wayside in subsequent critiques and discussions of Converse. Among those who answered the (agree-disagree) item, most appeared to answer randomly. Only a small proportion—about 20 percent—held stable attitudes across all three time periods. Converse did not report—presumably the small number of cases prevented him—whether those who held fixed opinions across time included the 12 percent whom he had labeled ideologues or near ideologues.

Sensitive to the possibility that the 1956-58-60 results stemmed from the choice of issues and the time frame of the study, Converse and Markus (1979; also see Converse 2000) revisited the issue instability thesis using the 1972–74–76 ANES panel study. They found, once again, that partisan identification changed relatively little across time. But just as Converse found earlier, issue preferences generally lacked stability. This time, however, there were exceptions: preferences remained highly stable on abortion, busing, and legalization of marijuana, what Converse and Markus called the new moral issues. Moreover, the four-year continuity coefficient on the seven-point ideology scale was a relatively high .56, suggesting that many people remain ideologically consistent across time. This finding seemingly challenged Converse's original conclusion that only a relative few people understand ideology. The authors explained the size of the continuity coefficient on two grounds: first, 35 percent or more of the respondents failed to place themselves on two successive administrations of the scale, and thus did not enter into the calculation of the continuity coefficient; second, substantial numbers of the remaining respondents placed themselves at the center of the scale, presumably because they did not understand left–right ideology. Converse and Pierce (1986) reported similar findings among French citizens. Unlike the earlier American studies, the France study included a two-wave elite panel. Moreover, the elite and mass panels used identical questions, which allowed the researchers to speak more confidently than Converse could earlier to the mass–elite differences.

Among Converse's many contributions, establishing a criterion by which to determine whether people hold true attitudes arguably stands as the most important. Before he wrote, a researcher would (reasonably) assume that respondents' one-time answers represented their real preferences. That assumption will not do, Converse showed. The key is whether respondents express essentially the same preferences *over time*. Only when they do can the researcher legitimately construe a stated preference *at any one point in time* as real. We will return to this insight later.

2 THE DOWNBEAT REVISION

Converse did not explicitly state that the relatively few citizens who understand politics and hold real attitudes carry the day for democratic governance; presumably he thought so. Others have carried the notion forward in one fashion or another. Luskin (1990, 331) states boldly that in a representative democracy "only a small proportion of the population can participate in politics to the fullest." In his mind, these are Converse's relative few. When Althaus (1998, 2003) and Bartels (1996) conduct simulations to determine whether the less informed would hold the same policy preferences as the more informed if they possessed more information, they assume that the more knowledgeable set the standard; they hold the right opinions. But do informed citizens warrant an exalted status in democratic governance? Recent evidence suggests that they might not.

At the time Converse wrote, the dominant psychological theories were cognitive-motivational, emphasizing in particular the individual's desire to maintain belief-attitude consistency. Trained as a social psychologist, he knew those theories well. For reasons only Converse knows, he chose to emphasize cognition over motivation in "Mass Belief Systems."[6] During the two decades following its publication, psychology and political psychology did the same, turning to cognition-dominated theories of information processing. Only recently have researchers in both fields begun, once again, to account for the effects of motivation.

Why is this history important? Once political scientists began to consider how motivations affect citizen decision making, they generated findings that shifted attention from the many who do not understand politics to the relatively few who do. Precisely because they understand politics, it appears, these relatively few are able to employ an array of mental gymnastics to maintain their existing beliefs and attitudes.

Under normal circumstances, when the political environment is not constantly bombarding citizens with belief-challenging arguments and information, these individuals often hold factually wrong beliefs that reinforce their existing attitudes. In other words, they can easily believe what they want to believe, and do. For example, Nadeau and Niemi (1995; Nadeau, Niemi, and Levine 1993) found that respondents who saw Hispanics as a source of crime were more inclined to overestimate their size than those who did not. The well educated and politically astute were especially vulnerable to such bias.

So what happens when politically sophisticated people hear an argument or receive factual information that challenges their political preferences? Do they adjust their beliefs and attitudes accordingly? Taber and Lodge (2006) conducted experiments in which they asked subjects to evaluate arguments about various

---

[6] Only Converse knows for sure, but finding an almost complete lack of attitude consistency within the context of existing psychological research probably surprised him.

policies. They found that subjects evaluate attitudinally congruent arguments as stronger than attitudinally incongruent arguments; counter-argue contrary arguments and uncritically accept supporting arguments; and seek out confirmatory evidence. These mental processes, in turn, lead to attitude polarization, that is, a strengthening of the original attitudes. More relevant here, strongly partisan and politically astute respondents show an especially strong proclivity to rely on these processes.

Similarly, in unusually high information environments where challenging facts persist, these attentive and knowledgeable individuals ultimately change their beliefs; but then they find means to retain their political attitudes. Panel studies conducted over the duration of the Iraq war found that strong Republicans maintained their support for the war, despite worsening conditions, by interpreting existing conditions and predicting future ones to their advantage. They construed US troop casualties as less severe than, for example, weak Republicans did, and also predicted lower levels of future casualties. And when the Bush administration itself acknowledged that weapons of mass destruction probably did not exist in Iraq, politically astute Republicans attributed their absence to one of two factors: they had been moved to another country or Saddam had destroyed them just prior to the US invasion (Gaines et al. 2006).[7]

One might justifiably argue that much of this evidence reflects healthy skepticism on the part of the relative few; politically sophisticated people should resist change. However, at some point this resistance is no longer reasonable. In Taber and Lodge's words (2006, 22), "skepticism becomes bias when it becomes unreasonably resistant to change and especially when it leads one to avoid information . . . . And polarization seems to us difficult to square with a normatively acceptable model (especially since the supporters and opponents in [a] policy debate will *diverge* after processing exactly the same information)" (original italics). They might have added that these mental gymnastics greatly reduce the capacity of the citizenry to provide democratic intelligence, that is, to let policy makers know whether existing policies are failing or succeeding.

The downbeat revision, then, differs qualitatively from Converse's. The difference lies not with who knows what about the general contours of politics; on this, the two tales converge. Nor does it lie with the politically uninformed; in both instances, they play a limited role in democratic governance. Rather, it lies with the performance of the politically knowledgeable; in the story recounted here, they often fail to hold accurate factual beliefs, and they devote most of their mental energies to maintaining their attitudes, often unreasonably. In short, they fail to provide the guidance of which they otherwise would be capable.

---

[7] Related evidence comes from Luskin and Fishkin's research on deliberative polls (1998). They found that deliberations effected attitude change among participants. Follow-up surveys conducted several weeks after the deliberations found that most people, and certainly the politically knowledgeable, returned to their original policy positions, even though they continued to know more than they did before the experience.

3 THE REALLY DOWNBEAT REVISION

Converse concluded that relatively few people understand ideological politics and hold true attitudes. The downward revision, by introducing motivation, raises questions about the performance of these few. It generates an unsettling question: does democratic governance lack a compelling rationale?

In the really downbeat revision, this question takes on added meaning. It reveals a citizenry whose answers to survey questions about politics and policy reflect the considerations that happen to come to mind. In turn, which considerations come to mind depends on the political communications the individual recently received. These "top-of-the head" answers imply that while people might express "opinions" at any moment, they are not fixed and thus not true. This verdict applies to all citizens, not just the less informed.[8]

Political scientists will immediately recognize this story; John Zaller developed it in his widely read and acclaimed *The Nature and Origins of Mass Opinion* (1992), which builds more directly on Converse than any other single study. He develops a formal model based on axioms, which he summarizes as follows (1992, 51): "Opinion statements, as conceived in my four-axiom model, are the outcome of a process in which people *receive* new information, decide whether to *accept* it, and then *sample* at the moment of answering questions. For convenience, therefore, I will refer to this process as the Receive-Accept-Sample, or RAS, model." People's attention to politics determines whether they receive information, and their ideological predispositions and, more generally, core values shape whether they accept it.

Zaller offers varied evidence in support of his model. He undertakes a survey experiment in which he asked half of the respondents a series of standard National Election Study questions on aid to blacks, federal job guarantees, and the proper level of government services. The other half received the same questions, but right after they answered the items they were asked to stop and think about the ideas that went through their minds as they answered. He shows that which ideas, or considerations, come to mind strongly shapes the attitudes that respondents express. More important, he shows that these considerations vary across time, and thus so do people's expressed attitudes.

The other data consist of American National Election Surveys combined with coded *New York Times* news stories. In an impressive set of empirical analyses, Zaller shows that when politicians and other political activists agree on an issue—support for a US invasion, for example—citizens think as one. When elites polarize, citizens do also.

[8] In a word, people experience ambivalence, a concept that Hochschild (1981) first introduced in her study of citizens' attitudes toward equality. Hochschild conducted lengthy open-ended interviews with 28 individuals to uncover the ambivalence. Other studies of political ambivalence, all based on survey data, include Alvarez and Brehm (2002), Basinger and Levine (2005), Grant and Rudolph (2003), Lavine and Steenbergen (2005), and Rudolph (2005). None of these authors goes as far as Zaller to derive the implications of ambivalence for the nature and role of public opinion in democratic societies. On the other hand, Zaller, unlike others, does not view ambivalence in terms of value or attitude conflict. We thank Tom Rudolph for this astute observation.

Attentive citizens, who are strongly disposed in one ideological direction or the other, show the greatest polarization. That is because these individuals simply echo what their preferred party leaders say.

Bartels takes the implications of Zaller's work to a more extreme conclusion than Zaller did. In a chapter of a book dedicated to Converse, Bartels (2003) distinguishes between attitudes and preferences (a distinction that we have not made in our discussion). He argues that people hold attitudes—psychological tendencies—but not preferences—definite and particular expressions. Borrowing heavily from the Tversky–Kahneman research on framing effects (1982, 1986; also see Iyengar 1987, 1990; Quattrone and Tversky 1988; but see Druckman 2001, Druckman and Nelson 2003), as well as Zaller, Bartels concludes that the political environment strongly shapes how these psychological tendencies become manifested. He concludes:

[T]he common view of political scientists seems to be that the signs of "casual and shallow" thinking that Converse took as evidence of non-attitudes may characterize some of the people some of the time, or even most of the people most of the time, but are by no means endemic. My own reading of the evidence is more pessimistic. At least if "attitudes" are taken to mean logically consistent summary evaluations of any conceivable political object . . . then it seems clear to me that even splendidly well informed, attentive citizens will routinely flunk the test. (2003, 63)

[T]he evidence already in hand provides rather modest grounds for imagining that the context dependence of political attitudes . . . is simply a result of ignorance, inattention, or bias, to be remedied by more careful thought or unfettered deliberation. For the moment, at least, it seems to me that we must probably accede to [the] conclusion that the context dependence of preferences is an unavoidable consequence of basic cognitive and evaluative processes. (64)

The fundamental shortcomings of the human thought process, especially when exacerbated by the nature of competitive politics, preclude the kind of democracy that normative theories prescribe. Citing Riker (1982, 244), Bartels reaches this grand conclusion (2003, 74): "'popular rule' is impossible but . . . citizens can exercise 'an intermittent, sometime random, even perverse, popular veto' on the machinations of political elites." This is a far more excitable conclusion than Converse's!

4 THE UPBEAT REVISION

Until now, the discussion has progressed toward increasingly more downbeat conclusions about the nature of public opinion and citizen performance. Not all research has moved in this direction. To the contrary, an accumulation of research reaches far more upbeat conclusions than Converse reached. Because many scholars have contributed to it, and often from different perspectives, the upbeat revision is less cohesive and self-evident than the other two revisions. It is every bit as important.

Thirty-two years after "Mass Belief Systems," Delli Carpini and Keeter (1996) undertook the single most comprehensive analysis of political knowledge and information. The authors did not limit their definition of political knowledge to ideological understanding, asking instead what US citizens know with respect to the rules of the game, the currently important political actors, and the substance of domestic and foreign affairs. They take advantage of a large number of existing surveys, as well as their own, to determine the percentages of the respondents who provide the right answers to (mostly) closed-ended survey questions. Warning that "it is meaningless to talk about how much the 'public' knows about politics" (269) given the unequal distribution of knowledge across citizens and across specific survey items, they nevertheless conclude that "more than a small fraction of the public is reasonably well informed about politics—informed enough to meet high standards of good citizenship" (269). Although Delli Carpini and Keeter do not explicitly define "more than a small fraction," they clearly mean it to include far more than 12 percent of the citizenry. In other words, they find a notably more knowledgeable citizenry than Converse did. The authors also report that levels of political knowledge among US citizens did not change over the past fifty years, which eliminates a handy explanation of the discrepancy between their and Converse's conclusions.

Not only does the upbeat version find a relatively informed citizenry, it also finds citizens that act as Bayesian rational updaters when new information comes their way (Gerber and Green 1998; Green, Palmquist, and Schickler 2004). For example, Democrats, Republicans, and Independents alike update their beliefs about the economy and their approval ratings of presidents. If the economy worsens, for example, people say the economy is weakening. Moreover, they update their beliefs in the same, expected direction and to the same extent.[9]

The preceding works portray a citizenry who ground their beliefs and attitudes in reality, implying that people hold true beliefs and attitudes. Many other studies, far too many to recite here, convey the same message. Kinder and Winter (2001) used the 1992 National Election Study to explore the black-white divide on racial and social welfare issues. They identified significant attitudinal differences across the two races on most of the attitudinal items, all in line with what one would expect. In every instance, African Americans expressed more liberal opinions, overall, than whites did. In the 1992 presidential election, of those favoring aid to minorities 69 percent voted for Bill Clinton while only 17 percent voted for George Bush; of those favoring national health care 61 percent voted for Clinton while 20 percent voted for Bush; and of those opposing the death penalty, 70 percent voted for Clinton and 19 percent voted for Bush (Erikson and Tedin 1995). These dramatic differences shout loudly: people hold meaningful political attitudes.

Moreover, they effectively draw on their core values and political ideologies when forming their attitudes and candidate evaluations. Feldman (1988) shows that how much people valued the work ethic and equality of opportunity shaped their evaluations of Ronald Reagan as president. Those who strongly favored equality of

---

[9] Note how this conclusion, which is derived from survey data, conflicts with Taber and Lodge's experimental studies of motivation and attitude maintenance, which we cited earlier (also see Bartels 2000). We will return to this conflict, as well as to others, in the next section.

opportunity, for example, supported liberal government policy more than those who opposed it. These assessments of government policy, in turn, shaped how favorably people evaluated Reagan's positions. Those who expressed support for the work ethic held more positive images of Reagan than those who did not.[10] Equally compelling, Hurwitz and Peffley (1987) demonstrate that people use a hierarchically structured belief system to form foreign policy preferences. Core values such as ethnocentrism and moral beliefs about killing serve as the foundation. In-between these core values and specific foreign policy preferences are what Hurwitz and Peffley call postures. Functioning as mediators, they include themes such as whether the government should pursue an isolationist policy, and whether the government should adopt an aggressive stance in its relationships with other countries. Hurwitz and Peffley demonstrate that ordinary citizens, even those who know little about foreign policy, draw on this hierarchically structured belief system to infer specific preferences.

Others working in the upbeat perspective show, seemingly in contradiction to Converse, that citizens use their self-proclaimed ideologies to make appropriate candidate choices and evaluations. For example, Levitin and Miller (1979) find that some Democrats called themselves conservatives and some Republicans called them- selves liberals in the 1972 and 1976 presidential elections. Using the 1972–6 panel data, they also show that the individual-level ideological continuity correlation is .65, compared to .80 for partisan identification. Ideological self-placement looks remark- ably stable across time. Most significantly, ideology and partisan identification independently shape the vote; far more liberal than conservative Democrats support Democratic candidates, and so on. In a follow-up and more thorough study that covers all elections from the 1950s through the 1990s, Miller and Shanks (1996) argue that enduring ideological predispositions play a major role in shaping voters' reac- tions to election campaigns and their presidential choices.

Let us pause and summarize the upbeat version as we have stated it thus far. Substantial informational gaps exist between the most and least informed. Never- theless, a sizeable majority of citizens grasps at least some of the basic political contours. Even more impressively, people appear to update their factual beliefs consistently with changed conditions. They notice, for example, when the economy falters or improves. They hold real attitudes. African Americans consistently take more liberal policy positions than whites, for example; and those who hold liberal attitudes show markedly greater support for Democratic presidents. In addition, citizens use their core values and political ideologies to derive "the right" policy preferences and choose "the right" candidates.[11]

---

[10] A third value, support for the free enterprise system, had no effect.

[11] Despite its importance to the public opinion literature, we do not discuss the use of political heuristics. That research asks how citizens can make reasonable decisions even when they lack informa- tion (Brady and Sniderman 1985; Mondak 1993a, 1993b; Sniderman, Brody, and Tetlock 1991; Mutz 1998). This chapter focuses more narrowly on what citizens know (or don't know) and how they use whatever knowledge they possess. We also skip the collective opinion literature (MacKuen, Erikson, and Stimson 1989 and Nardulli 2005), some of which finds salvation in aggregation (Page and Shapiro 1982; but see Althaus 1998).

Cross-national studies also contribute, albeit indirectly, to the upbeat revision. Early research, some of it by Converse himself (Converse and Dupeux 1962; Converse and Pierce 1986), reported low levels of issue constraint and ideological understanding (Butler and Stokes 1969) among French and British citizens. A later and more comprehensive study of five countries—Austria, Britain, Germany, the Netherlands, and the United States—essentially replicated Converse's original analysis, including the accounting of non-responses, and identified higher levels of ideological understanding, overall, suggesting an over-time increase in comprehension (Klingemann 1979a, 1979b).[12] Dalton (2002) attributes this change in comprehension to increased education levels and the greater availability of mediated political information.

Moreover, Klingemann (1979a, 1979b; also see Dalton 2002) found that the level of ideological sophistication varied across the five countries. German and Dutch citizens showed more understanding of left–right ideology than citizens in the United States and Great Britain. This finding suggests that characteristics of political systems—the structure of the party system, the availability of ideologically based information, and so forth—shape how much citizens know about ideological politics. In an attempt to answer this question more directly, Gordon and Segura (1997) studied more than 11,000 respondents in twelve countries. They found country-level factors to have the larger effects and to account for more of the variance in political sophistication than individual-level characteristics. For example, people who lived in countries with national proportional representation and multiparty systems did better at placing parties on a left–right scale, all else equal, than those who did not. Institutions can enhance (or inhibit) what people know about politics, quite independently of their own motivations and capabilities.[13]

5 AN ARGUABLY SCHIZOPHRENIC LITERATURE

The preceding discussion has covered much territory: from Converse's original and widely cited story to three revisions of it. Two of the three revisions reach more pessimistic conclusions about citizens and public opinion than Converse did, the other a more optimistic conclusion. Such variability in scholars' evaluations raises two questions: Is the research enterprise schizophrenic? In any event, how could scholars reach such differing conclusions? We will address these matters below. First, however, do the three revisions represent valid characterizations of the literature?

---

[12] This finding appears to contradict Delli Carpini and Keeter's, which we cited earlier.

[13] In a replication of the Gordon and Segura study, Peyton (2006) uses hierarchical linear modeling to show that system- and individual-level characteristics interact. For example, some system characteristics reduce the information gap between the more and less educated.

This would be a readily answerable question if a single, right characterization served as the standard. Of course, it does not; if it did, we would not be entertaining the question. Scholars do not always agree on how to characterize a single study, let alone on how to integrate many studies. Chronology sometimes serves as the basis for integration, but the three revisions do not follow a single chronology, from oldest to most recent. If the four stories followed a natural evolution from, say, Converse to the upbeat version, only a chronological ordering would do. That is not the case.

Instead, therefore, the constructions of the revisions reflect a conscious effort to identify distinct and markedly different stories. The first two revisions—the downbeat and really downbeat revisions—emerge from relatively small bodies of literature that most students of public opinion would acknowledge as well-defined research programs (albeit by more than a single author or group of coauthors). Political motivation anchors the first program, ambivalence and its implications the second. The upbeat revision draws on more highly disparate literatures, to be sure, but that alone does not undermine its validity as a characterization. Improper interpretation of those literatures is another matter. We made every effort to remain faithful to them. In the end, we leave it to others to demonstrate the errors of our way.

Right or wrong, the integration of the literature into Converse's original story and three revisions reveals a dismayingly high number of contradictions. Converse and the really downbeat revision disagree on the existence of true attitudes among the few who understand politics. Converse and the upbeat revision differ fundamentally and consistently in their conclusions about citizens' capabilities. The downbeat and really downbeat revisions differ in their conclusions about the existence of true political attitudes among the politically astute. The upbeat revision takes political attitudes for granted while the really downbeat revision asserts that such attitudes do not exist. There are other inconsistencies.

Do these conflicts and contradictions reflect a truly schizophrenic literature, or are they no more than the kinds of across-study differences that every field experiences? The remainder of this section takes a closer look at selected contradictions to determine how they arose and how deeply they go. To anticipate: it looks like schizophrenia to us.

Converse's twin conclusions that few citizens understand political ideology and few hold true attitudes serve as natural starting points. An implication follows from each conclusion. The lack-of-ideological-understanding conclusion produces the following implication and its corollary:

Scholars should rarely and cautiously use closed-ended measures of ideology in their analyses. They will likely interpret statistically significant relationships between such measures and other measures of interest as applying to all of their respondents when in fact the relationships probably arise from multiple causal processes. The posited effects of ideology will hold for a small, genuinely ideological set of the sample, while the ideology measure is, for the remaining respondents, a noisy reading of something distinct from ideological understanding that is also related to vote or policy preference.

Similarly, since Converse demonstrated a lack of issue stability among Americans in two different studies and on a wide range of issues, the working assumption must be that, except on a few moral issues, most people do not hold true political attitudes. Thus the second implication and its corollary:

Unless scholars demonstrate, with panel data, that people hold stable and thus real attitudes, they should rarely and cautiously use cross-sectional attitude measures in their analyses. They will likely interpret statistically significant relationships between such measures and other measures of interest as indicating that all of their respondents hold true attitudes when in fact only a small percentage do. For the remainder, the attitude measures are a noisy reading of something distinct from true attitudes that is also related to the other measures of interest.

Finally, Converse (1990, 2000) has often decried the large percentages who do not answer the survey items. From his perspective, this group is not solely a nuisance to be cast aside as quickly as possible; it comprises an important part of the story about the nature of public opinion in American politics. Thus a third implication:

If scholars seek a balanced and not overly-optimistic judgment about the nature of public opinion, they must take non-respondents into account.[14]

If Converse reached the right conclusions, and we derived the right implications, then many of the studies included in the upbeat version begin to look problematic. Students of public opinion routinely use the closed-ended, seven-point ideology scales that the ANES inserted after Converse first wrote. The scales run from extremely liberal to extremely conservative. In any American National Election Study, somewhere between 20 and 30 percent of the survey respondents fail to answer the question (a point to which we return below). This leaves 70 to 80 percent who do answer it. But if Converse's original 12 percent estimate of those who understand left–right ideology is about right, then one conclusion follows: somewhere between 58 percent (70 percent–12 percent) and 68 percent (80 percent–12 percent) of ANES respondents answer the closed-ended ideology questions without understanding ideology itself.

In turn, conclusions that ideologies drive candidate evaluations, such as Levitin and Miller's, take on a mysterious quality. Precisely what do the significant regression coefficients represent? Do they indicate that *all*, or at least *most*, of the respondents draw on their ideologies? That is the conclusion researchers normally draw. However, it does not comport with Converse's original portrayal of American citizens.

In 1985, Knight replicated Converse's open-ended analysis using the 1980 ANES. She found essentially the same distribution that Converse found, although ideologues, defined to include Converse's ideologues and near-ideologues, now comprised 22 percent of the sample. They were better educated, more interested in politics, and more politically knowledgeable than others. Even more telling, Knight then analyzed candidate evaluation as a function of partisan identification, ideological self-label, and a set of issue preferences within each of Converse's four groups (ideologue, group benefit, nature of the times, and no issue content). Her finding could not have been stronger: only among Converse's ideologues did ideological self-label, as

---

[14] Converse has never stated these implications, which are ours alone, and he might not agree with them.

measured by the seven-point scale, shape presidential candidate evaluations; and among this group, self-proclaimed ideology packed a wallop. Among the other groups, it failed to reach statistical significance. Knight concludes that "the effects of ideology are qualitatively different among (Converse's) ideologues, and do not penetrate far beyond this level.... The ideology glass is ... brimming among ideologues and nearly empty among all other citizens" (1985, 851). In other words, her findings imply that a small percentage of all respondents produced the relationship between self-described ideologies and candidate evaluations that Levitin and Miller reported. For the remainder, it reflects something other than a true ideological connection.

In fairness, Levitin and Miller cite Converse's findings early in their article, acknowledging the controversy over the "appropriateness of the criteria and the methods used to define and measure the prevalence of ideological thought" (1979, 751). They proceed to use the closed-ended measure nevertheless, on the grounds that they construe ideology much like partisan identification: as a filter or predisposition on which people can draw, perhaps, in many cases, without understanding what it really means. By defining political ideology as a predisposition and not as understanding, Miller and Levitin consciously distinguish their conception from of Converse's. But notice that the literature now suffers from an equally serious problem: the use of an identical label, political ideology, to represent different ideas. The tradeoff hardly represents intellectual progress.

What, then, about cross-sectional measures of political attitudes? From Converse's perspective, cross-sectional data cannot distinguish real from not-real attitudes. Nevertheless, scholars use cross-sectional measures, anyway. In other words, these studies assume precisely what Converse's analysis of attitude stability implies they could not assume: one-time responses represent true attitudes.

Consider a concrete cross-sectional item: government guarantee of a job. Converse and Markus (1979) uncovered considerable attitude instability on it. Most people, apparently, do not hold true attitudes about job guarantees. Nevertheless, Kinder and Winter (2001), in a study we noted earlier, use this and other cross-sectional attitude items to explore the black–white divide on racial and social welfare issues. They identified significant attitudinal differences across the two races on most of the items, including government job guarantee. So did Converse and Markus overstate the attitude instability on this item? Did pure chance work in Kinder and Winter's favor?[15] The choice is clear: Converse and Markus are right, in which case Kinder and Winter should justify their use of the government guarantee item, or Converse (and Markus) is wrong, in which case someone must present evidence in support of the claim. Pending a resolution, the term schizophrenia does not grossly misrepresent the current state of affairs.

Note that Levitin and Miller report the number of missing cases, while Kinder and Winter do not. The latter authors, unfortunately, not the former, represent current

---

[15] Quite possibly the authors justified their neglect of Converse and Markus in their own minds, but they never explicated the reasoning. Probably three-quarters of all public opinion studies conducted over the past 40 years resemble Kinder and Winter. We could have chosen any one of them, although Kinder serves a useful purpose: he is one of the leading public opinion scholars in political science who has often praised the quality of Converse's work.

practice. Substantively, neither study acknowledges these missing cases when reaching a final verdict about citizen performance. From Converse's perspective, this omission seriously distorts the story.

But could Converse have overstated his conclusions? Or do his conclusions no longer apply with the same force they did in 1964? Scholars have suggested both possibilities. A decade after Converse wrote, Marcus, Tabb, and Sullivan (1974) argued that open-ended questions measure verbal skills more than they measure political understanding; and that measures of issue constraint ignore individual rationales that would justify the low constraint. Moreover, Converse imposed a very high standard. For example, he categorized people who discussed liberal and conservative in spend-save terms as not really understanding left–right ideology. Yet political observers frequently portray ideological politics in these very terms. No one, furthermore, has convincingly argued that open-ended questions more validly measure political understanding than closed-ended questions. Not surprising, the latter reveal a more fully informed citizenry (Delli Carpini and Keeter 1996). Finally, Kinder (2003) argues that relatively many people now hold true attitudes, especially on burning social issues. Converse and Marcus (1979) themselves reported evidence supporting Kinder's claim. Today's world does not resemble the world of the early 1960s.

Overall, however, different research choices seem to explain the divergence of Converse and the upbeat revision. These include: the use of open-ended versus closed-ended questions; different interpretations of positive associations between ideological self-labels and other variables of interest; assumptions about the validity and meaning of cross-sectional attitude measures; and the incorporation of non-responses into the final story about citizen performance. That Converse wrote first, of course, does not make him right. To date, however, those who have contributed to the upbeat revision have not yet fully confronted these differences and then justified their practices.

Similar contradictions appear when comparing Converse with the really downbeat version, represented by Zaller's *The Nature and Origins of Mass Opinion* (1992) and, later, Bartels' elaboration. Recall that ideological orientation and attitude change, along with political awareness, form the core of Zaller's top-of-the-head model of the survey response. That ideological orientation serves as a key component of Zaller's model immediately raises the possibility that his research violates two of the implications identified above: scholars should rarely and cautiously use closed-ended measures of ideology and they should take missing data into account when reaching their final portrayals (especially given the large number of missing cases on the ideology measures). That he used cross-sectional attitude measures raises the possibility that Zaller also violated the third implication: scholars should rarely and cautiously use cross-sectional measures of attitude. On the other hand, Zaller developed his model and conducted his empirical analysis with the utmost care, and constantly with an eye on Converse.

Lamenting the lack of domain–specific measures of political values, Zaller makes a case for using measures of general left–right orientations (1992, 27). Operationally, these measures tap people's predispositions to accept or resist the political communications they receive from their environments. In Zaller's words:

At some points in this study I will describe individuals as "liberal" or "conservative." In so doing, I will *never* (his emphasis) mean to imply that the people so designated are necessarily full-fledged, doctrinaire ideologues of the left or right. I will mean only that the people tend to be closer to one or the other pole of the constellation of associated liberal-conservative values. (Ideology is an indicator) of *predispositions* (his emphasis) to accept or reject particular political communications. (1992, 27–8)

Zaller could not be more explicit about his conception of ideology, which echoes Levitin and Miller's.

He measures left–right orientations in various ways, depending on data availability. Sometimes he includes the seven-point ideology item, sometimes not. Often he uses cross-sectional attitude measures—attitudes toward government services and government job guarantees, for example. These are among the very items on which Converse and Markus (1979) found people to lack true attitudes. Most intriguing, Zaller measures people's 1956 ideological orientations by constructing domestic and foreign policy scales. Some of the items comprising the scales are those Converse originally used to show a lack of issue constraint!

Zaller, like just about every scholar who uses responses to closed-ended questions, also violates the third implication. Although he diligently reports the number of cases, he does not given the proportion of respondents who were excluded from the analyses because they failed to answer one or more questions. Nor does he consider the implications of the missing cases, which approach 30 percent on occasions, for his overall story. In other words, he reaches his conclusions using only part of the data base that Converse uses.

To be clear: we are not criticizing Zaller's outstanding work. Many we included view *The Nature and Origins of Mass Opinion* as the most important statement on public opinion since Converse himself. But this only underlines the depth of the schizophrenia. In taking Converse to new heights, Zaller, of all authors, appears to violate all three implications of his work!

Finally, the downbeat and really downbeat revisions both portray citizens in a darker light than Converse did, and yet offer diametrically opposed views of Converse's ideologues and near-ideologues. In the downbeat version, these citizens dig their heels in the ground and tenaciously protect their existing political beliefs and attitudes. Political attitudes are not only real; they are, for the most part, immovable. But in the really downbeat version, these same individuals do not hold true attitudes.[16] That is because their expressed attitudes at any point in time reflect the considerations that recent political debate and discussion bring to mind. To be sure, these politically knowledgeable people do not form their attitudes randomly, but this is a far cry from holding rock-solid attitudes.

This contradiction, one of the most striking, might not be as severe as it appears. Sniderman, Tetlock, and Elms (2001) find that political attitudes depend on a combination of political predispositions and particular situations. In their "probable

---

[16] We do not distinguish between attitudes and preferences, even though Bartels' argument centers on that distinction. We try, nevertheless, to be true to the spirit of his argument, which is to say that we equate attitudes with Bartels' preferences.

cause" experiment, for example, they find that both self-labeled liberals and conservatives call a police search for drugs more reasonable when told the suspects were using bad language than when told they were well dressed. This is the situational component. Across both situations, liberals take a more lenient position than conservatives. This is the pre-dispositional component. And thus the conclusion: although contextual changes can cause attitudes to look unstable, it is a big leap to call them meaningless, as the pre-dispositional component shows. Whether Sniderman et al. fully reconcile the downbeat and really-downbeat revisions is debatable. They do offer hope of reconciling at least some of the contradictions.

The term schizophrenic, as applied to human beings, refers to an extreme personality disorder. Does public opinion research suffer an equivalent disorder? Unfortunately, in our view, it does. Mounting additional empirical studies will probably exacerbate, not eliminate the problem. Perhaps it is time to pause and take stock of the enterprise.

6 CONCLUDING COMMENT

This chapter began with the observation that political scientists have been able to tell a coherent story about citizens and public opinion. That story came directly and fully from Converse. In light of the three revisions, however, this observation no longer holds. As inevitably happens following the publication of a simple, profound, and generally crystal-clear statement on a scholarly topic, subsequent work muddied the waters. Simple became complicated; subtle changes in concept definition and measurement accumulated into increasingly larger departures from the original ideas; and scholars changed the criteria by which to judge citizen performance. An abundance of riches generated by forty years of additional research has, ironically, led from crystal-clear to schizophrenic. Crystal-clear does not mean right, just as schizophrenic does not imply wasted efforts. At this very moment, however, students of public opinion could not tell the proverbial person on the street a simple and comprehensible story about citizens and public opinion. Unless, that is, they want to say, simply, that most people don't understand the contours of politics and most don't hold true political attitudes. Life was much easier when there was only Converse!

REFERENCES

ACHEN, C. 1975. Mass political attitudes and the survey response. *American Political Science Review*, 69: 1218–23.

ALTHAUS, S. 1998. Information effects in collective preferences. *American Political Science Review*, 92: 545–58.

ALTHAUS, S. 2003. *Collective Preferences in Democratic Politics: Opinion Surveys and the Will of the People.* New York: Cambridge University Press.

ALVAREZ, R., and BREHM, J. 2002. *Hard Choices, Easy Answers.* Princeton: Princeton Univesity Press.

BARTELS, L. 1996. Uninformed votes: information effects in presidential elections, *American Journal of Political Science,* 40: 194–230.

—— 2000. Partisanship and voting behavior, 1952–1996. *American Journal of Political Science,* 44: 35–50.

—— 2003. Democracy with attitudes. Pp. 48–82 in *Electoral Democracy,* ed. M. MacKuen and G. Rabinowitz. Ann Arbor: University of Michigan Press.

BASINGER, S., and LAVINE, H. 2005. Ambivalence, information, and electoral choice. *American Political Science Review,* 99: 169–84.

BRADY, H., and SNIDERMAN, P. 1985. Attitude attribution: a group basis for political reasoning, *The American Political Science Review,* 79: 1061–78.

BUTLER, D., and STOKES, D. 1969. *Political Change in Britain,* 2nd edn. New York: St Martin's Press.

CONVERSE, P. 1962. Politicization of the electorate in France and the United States. *Public Opinion Quarterly,* 26: 1–23.

—— 1964. The nature of belief systems in mass publics. Pp. 206–61 in *Ideology and Discontent,* ed. D. Apter. New York: Free Press.

—— 1970. Attitudes and non-attitudes: continuation of a dialogue. Pp. 168–89 in *The Quantitative Analysis of Social Problems,* ed. E. Tufte. Reading, Mass.: Addison-Wesley.

—— 1990. Popular representation and the distribution of information. Pp. 369–88 in *Information and Democratic Processes,* ed. J. A. Ferejohn and J. H. Kuklinski. Chicago: University of Illinois Press.

—— 2000. Assessing the capacity of mass electorates. *Annual Review of Political Science,* 3: 331–53.

—— and DUPEAX, G. 1962 Politicization of the electorate in France and the United States. Pp. 269–91 in *Elections and the Political Order,* ed. A. Campbell, P. E. Converse, W. E. Miller, and D. E. Stokes. New York: John Wiley & Sons.

—— and MARKUS, G. 1979. Plus ça change . . . : the new CPS Election Study Panel. *American Political Science Review,* 73: 32–49.

—— and PIERCE, R. 1986. *Political Representation in France.* Cambridge, Mass.: Harvard University Press.

DALTON, R. 2002. *Citizen Politics: Public Opinion and Political Parties in Advanced Industrial Democracies,* 3rd edn. New York: Seventh Bridges Press.

DELLI CARPINI, M., and KEETER, S. 1996. *What Americans Know about Politics and Why it Matters.* New Haven: Yale University Press.

DRUCKMAN, J. 2001. The implications of framing effects for citizen competence. *Political Behavior,* 23: 225–56.

—— and NELSON, K. 2003. Framing and deliberation: how citizens' conversations limit elite influence. *American Journal of Political Science,* 47: 729–45.

ERIKSON, R. 1979. The SRC Panel Data and mass political attitudes. *British Journal of Political Science,* 9: 89–114.

—— and TEDIN, K. 1995. *American Public Opinion,* 5th edn. New York: Allyn & Bacon.

FELDMAN, S. 1988. Structure and consistency in public opinion: the role of core beliefs and values. *American Journal of Political Science,* 32: 416–40.

GAINES, B., KUKLINSKI, J., PEYTON, B., and QUIRK, P. 2006. The rational public: partisans, facts, and the Iraq War. Working paper.

GERBER, A., and GREEN, D. 1998. Rational learning and partisan attitudes. *American Journal of Political Science,* 42: 794–818.

GORDON, S., and SEGURA, G. 1997. Cross-national variation in the political sophistication of individuals: capability or choice? *Journal of Politics*, 59: 126–47.

GRANT, J., and RUDOLPH, T. 2003. Value conflict, group affect, and the issue of campaign finance. *American Journal of Political Science*, 47: 453–69.

GREEN, D., PALMQUIST, B., and SCHICKLER, E. 2004. *Partisan Hearts and Minds: Political Parties and the Social Identities of Voters*. New Haven: Yale University Press.

HOCHSCHILD, J. 1981. *What's Fair: American Beliefs about Distributive Justice*. Cambridge, Mass.: Harvard University Press.

HURWITZ, J., and PEFFLEY, M. 1987. The means and ends of foreign policy as determinants of presidential support. *American Journal of Political Science*, 31: 236–58.

IYENGAR, S. 1987. Television news and citizens' explanations of national affairs. *American Political Science Review*, 81: 815–32.

—— 1990. Framing responsibility for political issues: the case of poverty. *Political Behavior* 12: 19–40.

KINDER, D. 1983. Diversity and complexity in American public opinion. In *Political Science: The State of the Discipline*, ed. Ada W. Finifter. Washington, DC: American Political Science Association.

—— 2003. Belief systems after Converse. In *Electoral Democracy*, ed. M. MacKuen and G. Rabinowitz. Ann Arbor: University of Michigan Press.

—— and WINTER, N. 2001. Exploring the racial divide: blacks, whites, and opinion on national policy. *American Journal of Political Science*, 45: 439–56.

KLINGEMANN, H. 1979*a*. Measuring ideological conceptualizations. In *Political Action*, ed. S. Barnes, Max Kasse, et al. Beverly Hills, Calif.: Sage Publications.

—— 1979*b*. The background of ideological conceptualizations. In *Political Action*, ed. S. Barnes, Max Kasse, et al. Beverly Hills, Calif.: Sage Publications.

—— 1979*c*. Ideological conceptualization and political action. In *Political Action*, ed. S. Barnes, Max Kasse, et al. Beverly Hills, Calif.: Sage Publications.

KNIGHT, K. 1985. Ideology in the 1980 election: ideological sophistication does matter, *Journal of Politics*, 47: 828–53.

LAVINE, H., and STEENBERGEN, M. 2005. Group ambivalence and electoral decision making. In *Ambivalence, Politics, and Public Policy*, ed. S. Craig and M. Martinez. New York: Palgrave-Macmillan.

LEVITIN, T., and MILLER, W. 1979. Ideological interpretations of presidential elections. *American Political Science Review*, 73: 751–71.

LUSKIN, R. 1990. Explaining political sophistication. *Political Behavior*, 12: 331–61.

—— and FISHKIN, J. 1998. Deliberative polling, public opinion, and democracy: the case of the national issues convention, paper presented at the American Association for Public Opinion Research Annual Meeting, Saint Louis, Mo., May 14–17, 1998.

MACKUEN, M., ERIKSON, R., and STIMSON, J. 1989. Macropartisanship. *American Political Science Review*, 83: 1125–42.

MARCUS, G., TABB, D., and SULLIVAN, J. 1974. The application of individual differences scaling to the measurement of political ideologies. *American Journal of Political Science*, 18: 405–20.

MILLER, W., and SHANKS, J. 1996. *The New American Voter*. Cambridge, Mass.: Harvard University Press.

MONDAK, J. 1993*a*. Source cues and policy approval: the cognitive dynamics of public support for the Reagan agenda. *American Journal of Political Science*, 37: 186–212.

MONDAK, J. 1993*b*. Public opinion and heuristic processing of source cues. *Political Behavior*, 15: 167–92.

MUTZ, D. 1998. *Impersonal Influence: How Perceptions of Mass Collectives Affect Political Attitudes.* New York: Cambridge University Press.

NADEAU, R., and NIEMI, R. 1995. Educated guesses: the process of answering factual knowledge questions in surveys. *Public Opinion Quarterly,* 59: 323–46.

—— —— and LEVINE, J. 1993. Innumeracy about minority populations. *Public Opinion Quarterly,* 57: 332–47.

NARDULLI, P. 2005. *Popular Efficacy in the Democratic Era: A Re-examination of Electoral Accountability in the U.S., 1828–2000.* Princeton: Princeton University Press.

PAGE, B., and SHAPIRO, R. 1982. Changes in Americans' Policy Preferences, 1935–1979. *Public Opinion Quarterly,* 46: 24–42.

PEYTON, B. 2006. Revisiting cross-national Sophistication. Working paper.

QUATTRONE, G., and TVERSKY, A. 1988. Contrasting rational and psychological analyses of political choice. *American Political Science Review,* 82: 719–36.

RIKER, W. 1982. *Liberalism against Populism: A Confrontation between the Theory of Democracy and the Theory of Social Choice.* San Francisco: Freeman.

RUDOLPH, T. 2005. Group attachment and the reduction of value-driven ambivalence. *Political Psychology,* 26: 905–28.

SNIDERMAN, P., BRODY, R., and TETLOCK, P. 1991. *Reasoning and Choice: Explorations in Political Psychology.* New York: Cambridge University Press.

—— TETLOCK, P., and ELMS, L. 2001. Public opinion and democratic politics: the problem of non-attitudes and social construction of political judgement. In *Citizens and Politics: Perspectives From Political Psychology,* ed. J. Kuklinski. New York: Cambridge University Press.

TABER, C., and LODGE, M. 2006. Motivated skepticism in the evaluation of political beliefs. *American Journal of Political Science,* 50(3): 755–69.

TVERSKY, A., and KAHNEMAN, D. 1982. The framing of decisions and the psychology of choice. In *Question Framing and Response Consistency,* ed. R. Hogarth. San Francisco: Jossey-Bass.

—— —— 1986. Rational choice and the framing of decisions. *Journal of Business* 59: 251–78.

ZALLER, J. 1992. *The Nature and Origins of Mass Opinion,* Cambridge: Cambridge University Press.

CHAPTER 4

ELITE BELIEFS AND THE THEORY OF DEMOCRATIC ELITISM

MARK PEFFLEY
ROBERT ROHRSCHNEIDER

EARLY studies of public opinion revealed a number of startling and wholly unfavorable comparisons between mass belief systems and those of elites, variously defined. In a series of landmark studies, one analyst after another documented the decidedly impoverished state of political sophistication of public opinion when compared to elites, particularly in the US: remarkably low levels of political information, a lack of ideological thinking, little "constraint" among various policy attitudes (e.g. Converse 1964), and a disturbing lack of commitment to basic democratic principles such as political tolerance and minority rights (e.g. Stouffer 1955; McClosky 1964; Prothro and Grigg 1960). The only silver lining in these early studies was the comparatively high level of sophistication and democratic virtue discovered among activists and elites. Elite political attitudes were not just based on a vaster store of information and expertise, but were highly structured by ideologies and were firmly anchored to an ongoing commitment to democratic principles and institutions. These findings, coming as they did from a number of different quarters, appeared to confirm a central claim of the theory of democratic elitism: political elites and activists were the "carriers of the democratic creed" who protected the democratic order from an unsophisticated and often undemocratic public.

These scholars also said a great deal about both the sources and the benefits of the superior quality of elite beliefs in democratic politics. Elites are more sophisticated, it was argued, because they have all the advantages on their side: they are better educated, better socialized into the give-and-take of democratic politics, possess a disproportionate degree of expertise, and are recruited from the most able socioeconomic strata. There are also sizeable benefits that presumably spring from sophisticated elite beliefs. Elite communication is greatly facilitated because reliance on a common ideology provides a powerful and efficient heuristic for making sense of the confusing buzz of information in the political world. Elite discourse thus helps to structure political debate so that publics can adopt elite "packages" of ideas—to know "what goes with what," even if they do not know why (Converse 1964). Moreover, if a consensus exists among elites in their support for democratic values, such values are likely to be transmitted to the public at large, or at least to its more politically active elements (McClosky 1964; McClosky and Zaller 1984).

The claims of elitists have been the focus of a protracted debate in the political behavior literature for the last fifty years. This chapter does not review the entire body of elite studies; fortunately, others in this volume cover various aspects of elite research (Blondel and Mueller-Rommel; Hoffman-Lange) and masses (Kuklinski and Peyton; Mutz; Gibson) that are beyond the scope of our review. Instead, we focus on empirical evidence for four of the more controversial pillars of the democratic elitism thesis defined by the early studies (e.g. Converse 1964; McClosky 1964; Prothro and Grigg 1960): (1) an elite consensus exists in their support for and commitment to democratic values (the consensus-pillar), (2) elites' democratic attitudes are highly structured (constraint pillar), (3) elites are substantially more democratic than the mass public (the mass–elite pillar), and (4) act as reliable guardians of democracy, protecting democratic institutions from an unsophisticated and intolerant public (the guardianship pillar).

In addition, our review gives particular weight to survey studies comparing elite and mass opinions in cross-national contexts, for such studies help to overcome one of the more serious limitations of the early research: the near-exclusive focus on mature democracies, in general, and the US, in particular. As shall become clear, as one moves beyond the US, the pillars of democratic elitism become increasingly questionable propositions. A central concern of this review article is to assess the extent to which the pillars of the elitism thesis hold up when viewing the evidence from a cross-national perspective.

Accordingly, this chapter assesses the claims of the elitists by evaluating empirical evidence from three bodies of research. First, we examine the growing body of elite research on political tolerance, both in the US and abroad, which provides the most direct evidence about how committed elites are to democratic values compared to mass publics. Second, we explore analyses of elite beliefs in new democratic institutions—either at the national or the supra-national level (e.g. the European Union)—to determine whether political elites support the norms of newly established democratic institutions. In the concluding section, in addition to providing a final assessment of theory and research, we consider recent elite studies that shed light on our central question. What does the available evidence tell us about the quality of elite decision making at the beginning of the twenty-first century?

1 THE LONG-TERM SOURCES OF ELITE BELIEFS

What factors shape elite beliefs? Most analyses would point to their socialization as an important source of elite attitudes. The fundamental idea of the socialization approach is that the exposure of political elites to the operating procedures of a regime develops the values that underlie that institutional framework. The confluence of pre-adult socialization, adult political learning, and the selective recruitment of individuals with desirable traits contribute to the emergence of mass–elite differences in political beliefs (Putnam 1973, 1976; Searing 1971).

At the beginning of elites' socialization is their exposure to a range of sources that all members of a polity are exposed to, mostly through parents and peers, but also religious institutions, mass media, or friendship networks (Putnam 1976). These forces operate both at the national and supranational level. For instance, Euro-elites' prior national experience shapes their preferences on integration, such that commission officials "from political systems in which political authority is concentrated . . . believe that national institutions are capable of effective control. . . . The political system that is most conducive to these preferences is that of a large, unitary, state" (Hooghe 2001, 116). This research suggests that earlier elite learning constitutes a powerful influence on elite beliefs.

In addition, political elites are disproportionately exposed to the norms of a regime and thus have more opportunities to internalize regime norms than ordinary citizens (Putnam 1973; Aberbach, Putnam, and Rockman 1981; Rohrschneider 1999). Selective recruitment, in turn, entails that individuals with regime-conforming characteristics are selected for leadership positions in the first place (Sullivan et al. 1993). Elite research therefore uniformly finds that individuals with higher education or with system-conforming values are more likely to advance to positions of prominence than individuals who lack these attributes. Finally, *political* elites are, if anything, strategic actors. They take into account short-term factors such as the performance of a regime, or the personal benefits they derive from a specific set of institutions (Hooghe 2001). It is thus not only the long-term effects of socialization on elite attitudes that must be accounted for, but also elites' more short-term self-interest that should predict their political belief systems. Only a combination of socialization and self-interest factors is likely to provide a fuller understanding of how elites behave the way they do—and whether they are likely to act as defenders of the democratic creed.

Given the varied range of sources that contribute to the learning of elite beliefs, it is difficult, perhaps even impossible, to pinpoint the unique contribution of each process. However, if as numerous studies demonstrate, elite socialization shapes elite attitudes, these studies cast some doubt on the consensus and guardianship pillar of democratic elitism especially in new democracies. For we cannot assume that political elites are the standard bearers of the democratic creed in previously authoritarian nations where democratic learning could not have occurred. Indeed, the notion that education serves as a source not only of enlightenment but also of indoctrination led some analysts to suggest several decades ago that one must consider the undemocratic circumstances under which elites came to be educated: if elites are educated in an authoritarian context, they may actually be more reluctant to endorse democratic values (Klingemann 1966). Thus, once we move outside the realm of mature democracies, socialization arguments raise the disquieting possibility that post-authoritarian elites may not endorse democratic values and beliefs to the same degree that their US counterparts do.

Let us examine the available evidence in light of this implication. We begin by reviewing research on political tolerance which speaks directly to the four tenets of democratic elitism. Subsequently, we review the emerging literature on elite beliefs in other value domains and countries.

2 POLITICAL TOLERANCE RESEARCH

More than any other area, research comparing levels and sources of political tolerance (defined as a willingness to allow the expression of ideas that one opposes) of masses and elites has provided one of the most focused assessments of the elitist theory of democracy. The seminal studies of Stouffer (1955) and McClosky (1964), who found dramatically higher levels of political tolerance among elites than masses, provided much of the initial empirical support for democratic elitism. In his landmark survey study of political tolerance in the US during the McCarthy "Red Scare" era, Stouffer (1955) uncovered a large gap between masses and elites (defined as leaders of local political and community organizations) in their tolerance of left-wing groups (mainly communists). McClosky (1964) also found that political elites (delegates to the 1956 Democratic and Republican conventions) were more committed to democratic norms and values than the mass public. Findings from these and other studies (e.g. Prothro and Grigg 1960) laid the groundwork for the elitist theory of democracy by suggesting that democracies were only likely to endure if elites—acting as "guardians of democracy" and "carriers of the democratic creed"—protected the regime from an intolerant public.

Other survey studies of political tolerance helped to establish democratic elitism as the conventional wisdom. Nunn, Crocket, and Williams (1978) replicated Stouffer's survey in the 1970s and concluded that mass–elite differences in levels of political tolerance are attributable to the selective recruitment of elites from higher socio-economic strata. In addition, McClosky and Brill (1983, 243) concluded that elites in their surveys were more supportive of democratic values because they were better positioned to learn such complex norms than ordinary citizens. Not only are elites more likely to be exposed to libertarian principles and the practical lessons of applying such principles to "actual (and often puzzling) cases," but elites are more likely to possess the motivation and "knowledge, enlightenment, and openness to alternative modes of thought and conduct that are not often found among the mass public." The conventional wisdom encapsulated in democratic elitism thus reversed the traditional roles of citizens checking elites in classical democratic theory. As McClosky and Brill (1983, 434) argued, we should "take comfort from the fact, as Stouffer did, that community leaders who are more tolerant than the general public are likely to exercise a disproportionate influence over public policy." This literature, in short, helped to establish the first pillar of the elitism thesis—elites are fundamentally unified behind democratic values.

In the late 1980s and early 1990s, however, the elitist theory of democracy as applied to political tolerance came under sustained attack by tolerance researchers whose findings in the US and abroad raised serious questions about the wisdom of relying on elites to serve as guardians of democracy. One of the more trenchant critiques of democratic elitism comes from Sniderman and his colleagues' (1989, 1991, 1996) Charter Rights study in Canada. This project consisted of a large mass sample and a sample of political elites from the legislative, executive and judicial branches of government. The authors found that even in mature democracies like Canada the differences across elites of different political parties often eclipse average mass–elite differences in levels of political tolerance. Across an array of civil liberties controversies, Sniderman and his colleagues found that elites from more than one Canadian political party were less tolerant than the public overall.

In addition, Sniderman et al. (1989) extended this insight to the US, where they re-examined McClosky and Brill's (1983) findings to show that, in similar fashion, whereas McClosky and Brill compare only the average levels of mass–elite differences in political tolerance, breaking down both groups by ideology demonstrates that conservative elites in the US were less tolerant than conservative citizens and were markedly less tolerant than liberal citizens. Thus, in both Canada and the US, comparisons between elites and masses overall may be misleading. Rather, it matters which elites are in power and which elites make policy. To draw another example from western Europe, when extremist right-wing or xenophobic parties emerge, they are led by non-democratic elites. The general point is that there may be significant differences across parties regarding the extent to which political elites support the democratic creed. In short, the consensus pillar may not apply to all elites.

One could add that it also makes a difference which values (or groups) in controversies over liberties are in conflict. Sniderman et al. (1996) find that when elites and citizens are presented with arguments designed to talk them out of their initial opinion on tolerance, elites are just as likely to switch positions as citizens. Even more disturbing, elites (and citizens) who initially adopt a tolerant position are more likely to change their views than those who initially adopt an intolerant position (cf. Barnum and Sullivan 1989; Gibson 1998; Peffley et al. 2001).

Sniderman et al. (1991, 363) conclude that "there is less than compelling evidence that political elites, merely by virtue of being elites, are distinctively reliable guardians of civil liberties. There is marked divergence within elites by party; indeed, so much so that what counts is not whether elites or ordinary citizens, but rather which elites, make civil liberties policy." Clearly, political learning at the elite level involves exposure not simply to the values of the larger culture but also to the norms of particular groups, which may or may not be tolerant. In short, democratic elitism assumes that the decisive contrast is between masses and elites, thus ignoring which elites prevail. But the electoral system chooses among competing sets of elites, not a mythical average. It thus matters which elites are compared to mass publics when evaluating the validity of the first (consensus) and third (mass–elite differences) pillars of the elitism thesis.

The consensus pillar of elitist theory encounters the greatest resistance from studies of political tolerance outside the US and other English-speaking countries (e.g. Great Britain, New Zealand). As several scholars have pointed out, if elitist theory claims that elites are more inclined to learn the dominant norms of the system than the masses, then elites from formerly non-democratic regimes or in newly emerging democracies may provide a much weaker commitment to demo-cratic values and practices (e.g. Klingemann 1966; Gibson and Duch 1991). Obvi-ously, to test this proposition one needs cross-national surveys conducted in countries where elites have been exposed to different regime norms and democratic practices.

Rohrschneider's (1996, 1999) study of political tolerance among members of the united Berlin Parliament shortly after the fall of the Berlin Wall and unification offers one of the more stringent tests of this proposition. This study gains analytical leverage from a naturally occurring quasi-experimental design where a major differ-ence between eastern and western MPs is the different institutional-level learning experiences to which they were exposed before unification. Thus, any differences between eastern and western MPs can be attributed to institutional learning. Rohrschneider's findings underline the importance of institutional learning when it comes to extending civil liberties to offensive groups. On the one hand, MPs from former East and West Germany showed similar levels of support for *general* values of democracy, presumably because citizens in previously authoritarian systems devel-oped a preference for western democratic values through a variety of sources (e.g. access to western television, contacts with the West, etc.). On the other hand, eastern elites were much less likely to connect their support for democratic values to specific applications of tolerance of least-liked groups. Thus, despite their higher socioeconomic status, elites provide a shaky foundation for tolerance if their insti-tutional learning experiences encourage intolerance.

The preceding studies raise serious questions about the consensus and mass–elite pillars, especially in non-western countries and in circumstances of high threat and objection to offensive groups. Under more "normal" conditions of moderate levels of threat, however, many studies continue to find that while mainstream elites often equivocate in their support for democratic values, they are still more tolerant than mass publics. In short, the third pillar of the democratic elitism thesis may still hold up, at least under certain conditions. Just why this is the case is the subject of a rare four-nation (Britain, Israel, New Zealand, and the United States) study of the sources of the gap in tolerance between citizens and national legislators by investigators whose prior work critiqued various aspects of elitist theory (Sullivan et al. 1993). After extensive analysis, Sullivan and his colleagues determined that two explanations account for mass–elite differences in levels of tolerance: (1) "the *selective recruitment* of Members of Parliament, Knesset and Congress from among those in the electorate whose demographic, ideological and personality characteristics predispose them to be tolerant" (italics added, 51), and (2) the transforming adult *political* socialization experiences associated with becoming a political leader and governing that affect political tolerance over and above the impact of individual-level, personal characteristics, such as the necessity of having to compromise with one's opponents and the responsibility of having actually to govern.

We should stress, however, as the authors acknowledge, there are likely to be many exceptions to the conditions under which either selective recruitment or political socialization operate to generate higher levels of political tolerance among elites than among masses. First, as we discussed above, many elites are less tolerant than the masses on several civil liberties issues. Second, Sullivan et al. are obviously referring to the socializing experiences of political leaders operating in a democratic system, not a more authoritarian system or a younger, emerging democracy where liberal norms are less consensual and less internalized among elites (cf. Shamir 1991).

In addition, elite socialization toward tolerance may only lead to a sober second thought when elites perceive that the threat from dissident groups is below a certain threshold. As others have noted, the elite-mass gap in tolerance occurs primarily when the target group in question is not perceived by elites to pose a serious threat to the democratic order—e.g. communists and the KKK in the 1970s in the US or non-extremist groups elsewhere. In contrast to such "easy" tests of tolerance, when political elites perceive a high level of threat from dissident groups, the gap between elite and mass tolerance shrinks considerably. In such cases, neither elite individual characteristics nor political socialization are sufficient to impel elites to substantially greater tolerance levels than ordinary citizens. Thus, when confronted with extremist groups perceived to be highly threatening, political leaders in Israel, Germany, Canada, and local elites in the US in the 1950s were *not* dramatically more likely to engage in a sober second thought than were ordinary citizens.

One final caveat noted by Barnum and Sullivan (1989) and others (e.g. Gibson and Bingham 1985), is that most studies, with the exception of Stouffer, have defined elites rather narrowly as members of national legislatures. Local-level officials (e.g. police, permit-granting officials, local elected officials, lower court judges) who are in a position to restrict political freedom are not necessarily more tolerant—or even *as* tolerant—as members of the public (cf. Gibson 1988; Shamir 1991; McClosky and Brill 1983; Barnum 1982).

All in all, tolerance research seriously questions the universality of the first component of the elitism thesis (elites are consensually unified). It also provides considerable evidence that the constraint and mass–elite pillars emerge principally when specific conditions are present (e.g. stable democratic institutions, low or moderate levels of threat from groups). Overall, however, the third pillar of greater elite than mass tolerance receives perhaps more consistent support across a range of contexts, but even here various contingencies and caveats apply.

A final limitation of elitist theory in the context of tolerance research is that it assumes that elite *attitudes* translate into *behavior*. Evidence for the first three attitudinal pillars is often taken as support for the fourth, guardianship pillar, which stresses the behavior of political elites in protecting democracy from an intolerant public. Most elite research, however, does not provide direct evidence of how elites act because it focuses almost exclusively on the attitudes of elites (and masses), paying little attention to the correspondence between elites' attitudes and their role in the policy-making process when deciding to either tolerate unpopular groups or repress them. Do elites actively prevent repression, as elitist theories assume? Do they discourage the mobilization of mass intolerance against offensive groups? Or do political elites act like politicians, bending to political calculations when it is expedient to promote the repression of unpopular groups, regardless of their expressed attitudes? In other words, to what extent do elites act as guardians of democracy, as elitist theory claims (i.e. the guardianship pillar)?

We find disquieting answers in the few studies that examine the role of elites in *making* tolerance policy. Gibson's (1988) study of the political repression of communists during the McCarthy era in the American states explored the degree to which tolerance of communists among masses or elites (aggregated from Stouffer's surveys) were better able to explain the number of state laws passed to repress communists during the late 1940s and early 1950s. In an ingenious use of the original Stouffer data, Gibson's intriguing "whodunit" analysis of the independent effects of mass and elite attitudes on state policies points the finger more at elites than ordinary citizens. Though masses may have been willing accomplices, contrary to elite theory, there is ample evidence that elites played a defining role in the McCarthy Era, not as guardians of democracy, but as a mobilizing force for political repression in the states.

Michal Shamir's (1991) study of political tolerance in Israel casts further doubt on the proposition that political elites act as reliable guardians of democracy. By surveying elites and masses during a time when the Israeli Knesset considered banning extremist groups who won seats in the legislature,[1] Shamir's study challenges elitist theory on three major counts. First, in contrast to elitist theory, her national survey of Israeli Knesset members and citizens found that the former was just as intolerant as the latter. Second, she found that elite discourse and policy making on the important question of banning political groups was influenced more by the Members' ad hoc political calculations than their attitudes. Shamir documented that Members voted to ban groups as a result of political calculations

---

[1] After the 1984 elections, the Knesset considered banning one extremist group on the right (Kash, an extremist, anti-Arab right-wing group) and another on the left (the Progressive List for Peace, an extreme left-wing party espousing the views of Palestinian nationalism).

and coalition building. *Competing elites did not restrain each other's intolerance toward particular groups but rather cooperated in limiting a broader array of groups.* Third, as in the McCarthy Era in the US, elites were not guardians of democracy but initiated various efforts to mobilize intolerance among the public, which was largely a passive observer and not the source of repressive policy.

Once again, evidence for elitist theory is at its weakest in situations of high threat and objection to offensive groups. On the one hand, it could be argued that the findings of these two studies are most worrisome because the guardianship role of elites is most critical for preserving civil liberties when threat *is* high from unpopular groups. On the other hand, elites may nevertheless play an important guardianship role when threat is below a certain threshold and the political risks of protecting unpopular groups are not viewed as prohibitive.

3 Elite Attitudes in Other Value Domains

If we extend our purview to other democratic values besides tolerance, we again find that support for the pillars of the elitism thesis is dependent on context, especially when we move outside of the realm of advanced industrial democracies. Let us begin with the good news. The few studies of democratic values of elites show that elites in western Europe support liberal democratic ideals (Putnam 1973; Aberbach Putnam, and Rockman 1981; Rohrschneider 1994), while other forms of democracy, such as socialist models, receive little support. At the general, abstract level then, western European elites are indeed strong supporters of liberal democratic forms of governance, consistent with the consensus pillar.[2]

The news becomes more grim as the focus shifts beyond the stable democracies of the West and the evidence supporting the consensus pillar is much weaker. A series of mass–elite comparisons in Russia and the Ukraine by Miller, Hesli, and Reisinger, for example, indicates that elites who were elected after the collapse of socialism base their understanding of the term "democracy" to a considerable degree on liberal ideals of political freedoms, the rule of law, and political participation and are fairly supportive of market reforms, despite their socialist upbringing (Miller et al. 1997, 1995; Reisinger et al. 1996). At the same time, however, there are substantial differences within the elite sector, depending on whether elites are political or bureaucratic, or whether they reside in rural or urban areas. In a similar vein, a study of local Chinese elites shows that elites are quite divided over civil liberties: local Communist

---

[2] We are somewhat tentative in our assessment, given the few numbers of studies which directly examine elite conceptions of democracies.

party members are much less likely to favor democratic procedures than activists favoring institutional change (Chen 1999). Thus, just as Sniderman et al. (1996) argued in the context of civil liberties in Canada and the US, whether we find support for the consensus pillar depends critically on which elites are being examined.

Furthermore, there is only weak support for the mass–elite pillar of the elitism thesis. On the one hand, mass publics are more likely than elites to mention social egalitarian protections of democracies. This suggests that elites are more committed to the liberal democratic creed than mass publics. On the other hand, "the differences are not huge" (Miller, Hesli, and Reisinger 1997, 178). A general pattern is that, just as Rohrschneider (1999) found for Germany, post-authoritarian elites are *relatively* more committed to democratic principles than mass publics. At the same time however, political elites are not necessarily consensually unified behind democratic principles; neither are mass–elite differences as substantial as one finds in western Europe. We therefore conclude that the consensus and mass–elite pillars of the democratic elitism thesis are not fully supported in a post-authoritarian context, certainly not to the degree that the elitism thesis presumes.

Regarding the constraint pillar, we find similarly mixed evidence in the research literature about elite beliefs. In western Europe, political elites and political activists exhibit much higher levels of constraint than ordinary publics (Converse and Pierce 1986). Similarly, political elites display a considerable degree of attitudinal consistency across a range of democratic attitudes, such as liberal democratic rights, perceptions of conflict, and pluralist party competition (Putnam 1973). In contrast, politically elites in new democracies lack this structure. For instance, Miller, Heslie, and Reisinger find that the interconnections between democratic beliefs at the elite level is rather low, sometimes no higher than that of mass publics. They argue that the lower constraint results from the lack of consistency in the information environment in fledgling democracies that "lack institutions and arrangements that enhance predictability in procedures, stable party alignments, and representational account-ability" (Miller, Heslie, and Reisinger 1995, 22–3). A virtually identical conclusion emerges in a study of political elites and citizens in Beijing (Chen 1999). Overall, the implications of these analyses are sobering: when moving outside the realm of mature democracies it is not just the content of elite beliefs that falls short of the elitism thesis; it is their structure as well.

In summary, our discussion and evidence about elite beliefs seriously complicates the pillars of the democratic elitism thesis. We may not assume, without any systematic empirical study, that elites even in mature democracies are consensually unified behind the democratic creed. And we certainly may not assume that elites in new regimes are the defenders of the creed. The second pillar is also problematic: the belief systems of elites in new democracies are often surprisingly unstructured. Stronger support for the democratic elitism argument emerges for the third, mass–elite pillar: to the degree that mass and elite beliefs are compared, studies reveal across the board that elites are more democratic than mass publics, although once again these differences are often not very large.

4 STRATEGIC SOURCES OF ELITE BELIEFS

While our discussion up to this point has emphasized (regime) socialization as a foundation for elites' commitment to democratic values, research demonstrates a substantial variation in the degree to which different elites in the same country support democratic values. This suggests to us that elites do not simply enact the values they acquired during the socialization process, but are also strategic actors who consider a range of short-term calculations when deciding whether to support a democratic regime. These short-term factors include a variety of considerations, from the economic performance of regimes to elites' national interests when evaluating European integration. Theoretically, it is important to recognize that elites evaluate institutions based not only on their long-standing predispositions, but also from the standpoint of their personal and policy goals. Political elites are naturally drawn to governing structures that efficiently produce desirable policy outputs (Putnam, Leonardi, and Nanetti 1993) and that give them access to decision-making processes (Highley and Gunther 1992).

The importance to elites of good governmental performance was demonstrated by Robert Putnam and his collaborators in their study of Italian elites (1993). Their ingenious analysis shows that when malfunctioning institutions are replaced with institutions that perform better, the same politicians become more supportive of those institutions. This evidence squares with a large literature on the tendency for countries experiencing more economic success to foster democratic stability in the long-term (e.g. Lipset 1959; Przeworski 1991), a linkage that requires greater support of successfully performing democratic institutions from political elites (and publics). The important point here is that elites' preferences for specific institutions cannot be divorced from their desire for institutions that perform adequately. As Miller, Heslie, and Reisinger argue: "if [citizens] believe that the present regime is not fulfilling their expectations of that ideal democracy, then they will be less supportive of the current attempts at democratization" (1997, 185). In other words, elites may reject a democratic regime for performance-related reasons, not just because they lack a commitment to democratic values.

A second factor that may enter the strategic calculations of elites, and subsequently influence the content of elite beliefs about democratic processes, is that political elites have access to the decision-making institutions of a system. Some newly designed regimes exclude minority elites—for instance, along religious, ideological, or ethnic lines—and this usually reduces their willingness to accept democratic structures. For this reason, a number of analysts suggest that during democratic transitions so-called "pact-making" elites must include all relevant elite sectors (Highley and Gunther 1992) in order to encourage most elites to accept new democratic institutions. These tactical considerations also become apparent in Hooghe's analysis of bureaucrats in the European commission: material incentives do shape their institutional preferences (Hooghe 2005).

In summary, these studies strongly suggest that short-term political calculations influence elites' willingness to endorse democratic institutions. This may overcome some of the deficits in democratic socialization—if the performance of new regimes is favorable. In other words, elites may become defenders of the democratic creed even if initially they are not strongly committed to democratic values. If, however, new democracies fail to perform adequately or elites are barred from access to decision-making institutions, they may be unwilling to support democratic regimes even if they hold the right kind of beliefs. Thus, the short-term calculations of politicians may lead them away from being the guarantors of democracies, just as research on political tolerance suggests (see Gibson 1988; Shamir 1991).

5 CONCLUSION

We conclude with the following assertions. First, the consensus pillar of the democratic elitism thesis cannot be assumed to be universally true. While elites may support democratic beliefs, there is sufficient evidence to suggest that there are so many exception to this "rule" that it should not be taken for granted. Second, as a general rule, elite beliefs tend to be more structured than mass beliefs. However, we also found evidence that the constraint pillar must be seriously qualified in new democracies since we encounter so many exceptions that it is questionable that this pillar applies to non-democracies. Third, perhaps the strongest support emerges for the mass–elite pillar. To the degree that differences between the two levels emerge, political elites are clearly more democratic than ordinary publics. We do note, however, that this statement is relative: in conditions of high threat and in many non-western democracies, the gap between masses and elites in their commitment to democratic principles shrinks considerably. Fourth, the few studies that examine the behavior of elites in carrying out their guardianship role raise serious questions about whether elected elites are reliable guardians under conditions of high threat.

All in all, then, studies of elite belief systems have made some progress in articulating and examining the various components of elite theory. However, in order to make further advances we would like to see not just *more* studies of elite attitudes, but research designs that take advantage of recent advances in mass survey technology. The conventional cross-sectional survey is the predominant form of elite survey and is perfectly suitable for assessing the consensus of elite values and making static comparisons with mass samples. But, as others have pointed out, it is poorly equipped to assess the dynamics of political reasoning or the strength of respondents' commitment to various ideals. Mass surveys on political tolerance, for example, now routinely incorporate a variety of survey experiments that can be used to assess how pliable one's initial responses are in the face of persuasive appeals and changes in critical features of civil liberties vignettes. While this technology has been employed in a handful of elite studies (e.g. Sniderman et al. 1991), there obviously needs to be more, especially in order to assess the degree to which elites equivocate in their commitment to democratic principles under different political conditions.

In addition, there need to be more longitudinal studies of elite attitudes in countries where critical features of the political environment are changing in order to assess the *dynamics* of political learning and socialization of elites. We would like to know, for instance, whether elites in newly democratizing regimes adjust their values as a result of their experience with democratic politics. To our knowledge, only one study interviews the same political elites at two different time points in order to examine whether political attitudes change after a regime transition (Rohrschneider 1999). There are a host of unresolved issues that can be addressed with panel data, such as the stability of elite attitudes, the extent to which elites reject democracies when the performance of institution fails, or, as mentioned in the previous paragraph, how pliable elite attitudes are.

We conclude, however, by pointing to an important area where we know surprisingly little about elite beliefs: what is the quality of the elites' actual decisions? We discussed some evidence, based on tolerance research, which questions whether political elites actually protect civil liberties when they make policy decisions (Gibson 1988; Shamir 1991). Overall, however, there is a surprising shortage of studies that directly examine the actual behavior of elites, particularly the short term, strategic factors and the foibles of human judgment that prompt elites to depart from their role of expert decision makers and defenders of the democratic creed.

The exception is Philip Tetlock's work investigating the responsiveness of real experts' beliefs to counterfactual information. Tetlock presents evidence that shows that, for a variety of reasons, experts often render decisions that are often no better than those an amateur observer of policy issues would have made (Tetlock 1999, 2005). He presents persuasive evidence that a number of mechanisms lead policy makers astray, in particular their prior commitment to a policy position that leads them to stick to a position even if it turns out to be incorrect, and their inability to incorporate new, discrepant information.

All in all, then, perhaps one poignant way to highlight the central conclusion of this chapter is to say that elites may be our best bet in securing democratic rights and civil liberties—but they are far from being a safe bet.

References

ABERBACH, J., PUTNAM, R., and ROCKMAN, B. 1981. *Bureaucrats and Politicians in Western Democracies.* Cambridge, Mass.: Harvard University Press.

BARNUM, D. G. 1982. Decision making in a constitutional democracy: policy formation in the Skokie free speech controversy. *The Journal of Politics,* 44: 480–508.

—— and SULLIVAN, J. 1989. Attitudinal Tolerance and Political Freedom in Britain. *British Journal of Political Science,* 19: 136–46.

CHEN, J. 1999. Comparing mass and elite subjective orientations in urban China. *Public Opinion Quarterly*, 63 (2): 193–219.

CONVERSE, P. 1964. The nature of mass belief systems in mass publics. Pp. 207–27 in *Ideology and Discontent*, ed. D. E. Apter. London: Free Press.

—— and PIERCE, R. 1986. *Political Representation in France*. Cambridge, Mass.: Belknap Press of Harvard University Press.

GIBSON, J. 1988. Political intolerance and political repression during the McCarthy Red Scare. *American Political Science Review*, 82: 511–29.

—— 1998. A sober second thought: an experiment in persuading Russians to tolerate. *American Journal of Political Science*, 42: 819–50.

—— and BINGHAM, R. 1985. *Civil Liberties and Nazis: The Skokie Free Speech Controversy*. New York: Praeger.

—— and DUCH, R. 1991. Elitist theory and political tolerance in Western Europe. *Political Behavior*, 13: 191–212.

HIGHLEY, J., and GUNTHER, R. 1992. *Elites and Democratic Consolidation in Latin America and Southern Europe*. New York: Cambridge University Press.

HOOGHE, L. 2001. *The European Commission and the Integration of Europe*. Cambridge: Cambridge University Press.

—— 2005. Several roads lead to international norms, but few via international socialization: a case study of the European Commission. *International Organization*, 59: 861–98.

KLINGEMANN, H. 1966. Keine Saeulen der Demokratie: Ueber die Haltung der Gebildeten zur NPD. *Akut*, 19 (29/30): 6–9.

LIPSET, S. M. 1959. *Political Man*. Baltimore: Johns Hopkins University Press.

McCLOSKY, H. 1964. Consensus and ideology in American politics. *American Political Science Review*, 58: 361–82.

—— and A. BRILL. 1983. *Dimensions of Tolerance: What Americans Think About Civil Liberties*. New York: Russell Sage Foundation.

—— and ZALLER, J. 1984. *The American Ethos: Public Attitudes toward Capitalism and Democracy*. Cambridge, Mass.: Harvard University Press.

MILLER, A., HESLI, V., et al. 1997. Conception of Democracy among Mass and Elites in Post-Soviet Societies. *British Journal of Political Science*, 27: 157–90.

—— —— and REISINGER, W. 1995. Comparing citizen and elite belief systems in post-Soviet Russia and Ukraine. *Public Opinion Quarterly*, 59: 1–40.

—— —— —— 1997. Concepts of democracy among mass and elite in post-Soviet societies. *British Journal of Political Science*, 27 (2): 157–90.

NUNN, C., CROCKETT, H. Jr., and WILLIAMS, J. Jr. 1978. *Tolerance for Nonconformity*. San Francisco: Jossey- Bass Publishers.

PEFFLEY, M., KNIGGE, P., and HURWITZ, J. 2001. A multiple values model of political tolerance. *Political Research Quarterly*, 54: 379–406.

—— and ROHRSCHNEIDER, R. 2003. Democratization and political tolerance in seventeen countries: a multi-level model of democratic learning. *Political Research Quarterly*, 56: 243–57.

—— and SIGELMAN, L. 1989. Intolerance of communists during the McCarthy era: a general model. *Western Political Quarterly*, 43: 93–111.

PROTHRO, J. W., and GRIGG, C. W. 1960. Fundamental principles of democracy: bases of agreement and disagreement. *The Journal of Politics*, 22: 276–94.

PRZEWORSKI, A. 1991. *Democracy and the Market: Political and Economic Reforms in Eastern Europe and Latin America*. New York: Cambridge University Press.

PUTNAM, R. D. 1973. *The Beliefs of Politicians: Ideology, Conflict, and Democracy in Britain and Italy*. New Haven: Yale University Press.

—— 1976. *The Comparative Study of Political Elites*. Englewood Cliffs, NJ: Prentice-Hall.

—— LEONARDI, R., and NANETTI, R. 1993. *Making democracy work: civic traditions in modern Italy*. Princeton: Princeton University Press.

REISINGER, W., MELVILLE, A., MILLER, A. and HESLI, V. 1996. Mass and elite political outlooks in post-Soviet Russia: how congruent? *Political Research Quarterly*, 49: 77–101.

ROHRSCHNEIDER, R. 1994. Report from the laboratory: the influence of institutions on political elites' democratic values. *American Political Science Review*, 88 (4): 927–41.

—— 1996. Institutional learning versus value diffusion: the evolution of democratic values among parliamentarians in Eastern and Western Germany. *Journal of Politics*, 68: 442–66.

—— 1999. *Learning Democracy: Democratic and Economic Values in Unified Germany*. Oxford University Press.

SEARING, D. 1971. Two theories of elite consensus: tests with West German data. *American Journal of Political Science*, 15 (3): 442–74.

SHAMIR, M. 1991. Political intolerance among masses and elites in Israel: a reevaluation of the elitist theory of democracy. *Journal of Politics*, 53: 1018–43.

SNIDERMAN, P. M., BRODY, R. A., et al. 1991. *Reasoning and Choice: Explorations in Political Psychology*. Cambridge: Cambridge University Press.

—— FLETCHER, J., RUSSELL, P. H., TETLOCK, P. E., and GAINES, B. J. 1991. The fallacy of democratic elitism: elite competition and commitment to civil liberties. *British Journal of Political Science*, 21: 349–70.

—— —— —— —— 1996. *The Clash of Rights: Liberty, Equality, and Legitimacy in Pluralist Democracy*. New Haven: Yale University Press.

—— TETLOCK, P., GLASER, J., GREEN, D., and HOUT, M. 1989. Principled tolerance and the American mass public. *British Journal of Political Science*, 19: 25–45.

STOUFFER, S. 1955. *Communism, Conformity and Civil Liberties*. New York: Doubleday.

SULLIVAN, J., WALSH, P., SHAMIR, M., BARNUM, D., and GIBSON, J. 1993. Why politicians are more tolerant: selective recruitment and socialization among political elites in Britain, Israel, New Zealand and the United States. *British Journal of Political Science*, 23 (January): 51–76.

TETLOCK, P. 1999. Theory-driven reasoning about plausilbe pasts and probable futures in world politics: are we prisoners of our pre-conceptions? *American Journal of Political Science*, 43 (2): 335–66.

—— 2005. *Expert Political Judgment: How Good Is It? How Can We Know?* Princeton: Princeton University Press.

CHAPTER 5

POLITICAL PSYCHOLOGY AND CHOICE

DIANA C. MUTZ

POLITICAL psychology is, at heart, concerned with the characteristics of individuals and of situations that are most conducive to a successful political system. For most political psychologists whose work is reviewed in this chapter, the ideal political system is a western-style democracy, with individual rights and responsibilities for self-governance, combined with varying degrees of protection of minority interests. For these reasons, the kinds of citizen choices that are most valued and most widely studied are ones that reflect these emphases. They include, but are not limited to, high levels of political information, active political participation, fair-minded evaluation of political alternatives, and so forth.

Given the sheer volume of work in this burgeoning area, I cannot hope to do a thorough review of the many contributions of political psychology in recent years. Moreover, another recent volume in this same series, the *Oxford Handbook of Political Psychology*, does an admirable job in summarizing the many developments in this field (see Sears, Huddy, and Jervis 2003). Thus, I have chosen to highlight three of the more recent trends and most promising new areas of investigation in political psychology that have emerged over the last few decades. I explore these particular themes not only because they are recent, but also because they hold some promise of changing, in some fundamental way, how we think about political psychology.

This chapter begins with an overview of the recent emphasis on the importance of emotion in understanding political choices. Next, I turn to research dealing with the ability of citizens to process information in an unbiased fashion. This category includes studies of motivated reasoning and selectivity, as well as research on the effects of partisanship and ideology on the processing of information. Third, I highlight the contributions of methodological innovations to our understanding of political psychology. While no one method is a cure-all, recent advances in the field of neuroscience are opening up new approaches with the potential to help us better understand the black box psychological processing of political stimuli.

Finally, I conclude by reflecting upon political psychologists' emphasis on the importance of information, cognition, and rationality in research over past decades, examining rationality's use as a standard (both empirical and normative) for judging the quality of decision-making processes. It is ironic that political psychology so often defines itself in opposition to rational choice approaches, and yet its standard for normative judgments is virtually the same.

1 THE ROLE OF EMOTION
IN POLITICAL CHOICE

Over the last few decades, political psychologists have enriched our understanding of choice by incorporating emotion into models that were formerly almost exclusively cognitive in describing political decision-making processes. In order to describe the progress (and lack thereof) in this domain, it is useful to first discuss several terms that are used more or less interchangeably within contemporary political psychology, including mood, affect, feeling, and emotion. As Kuklinski (2001) has noted, the study of these concepts within political psychology is still in its infancy, and "[we] do not always adopt the same conception of identically labeled psychological phenomena." As a result, it is less clear than one might think what is and is not known about the role of emotion in political behavior. I begin by sorting through some of the most frequently used terms and operationalizations, and then turn to the difficulty of differentiating emotions from other phenomena.

Within political psychology, the term *affect* often is used to describe whether an individual likes or dislikes some political object, or whether it is positively or negatively valenced, or "affectively charged," to use a popular terminology. Common measurement techniques such as feeling thermometers or Likert scales are used to ascertain an individual's positive or negative evaluation of some political person, policy, or object.

Unfortunately, this operationalization of affect is often difficult or impossible to distinguish from political judgments and opinions more generally. Few doubt that affect influences political attitudes and the processing of political information, but as it is usually measured by political scientists, such positive or negative judgments need not necessarily result from emotional reactions. After all, one may feel positively or negatively toward a political object for reasons that are wholly cognitive in nature.

It has long been acknowledged, for example, that the strongest predictor of candidate choice in the American National Election Studies (ANES) comes from the feeling thermometer ratings of presidential candidates (see e.g. Bartels 1988). Such measures are often referred to as indicators of affect toward the candidates, and yet this evidence is a weak basis on which to claim that emotion plays an important role in political choice. Thermometer ratings may instead represent running tallies of respondents' likes and dislikes about the candidate over time, which is a far cry from the kind of visceral reaction to a political event that the study of emotion promises to help us understand.

Just as like or dislike for political objects and measures drawn from feeling thermometers should not be considered synonymous with emotion, another seemingly related concept— mood—is also frequently conflated with emotion. Whereas emotions tend to be fleetingly experienced in response to a specific stimulus, and then dissipate, mood refers to a much longer-lasting phenomenon. Moods are also less focused in their target than are emotional reactions (see Bless 2001).

Because of the inconsistent use of terms in the study of emotion and politics, and because of highly variable operationalizations of those same terms, it is difficult to draw a clear line between research on political attitudes and studies of political emotion. Researchers have proposed a variety of theories of emotion over the last century, but almost all define emotion in terms of physiological arousal, which is often (though not necessarily) combined with a cognitive label of some kind. To be consistent with most psychologists' definitions, political emotion should involve some kind of negative and/or positive reaction to a political object, along with a concurrent experience of arousal. This visceral reaction may occur below the level of conscious recognition, and is relatively automatic, that is, it need not be mediated by cognition.

Conceptually, emotions also are different from attitudes in that emotional reactions are relatively short-lived and highly focused. Perhaps because emotion involves well-known physiological symptoms, it is often assumed that people must know it when they feel it. But emotions need not be particularly pronounced or obvious to the person experiencing them. Although the natural tendency in studies of emotion and politics is to treat the political object that evokes the emotion as if it were the sole cause, the kind of cognitive label that people give to emotion is determined at least in part by cues present in the environment at the time. Likewise, when arousal is artificially induced unbeknownst to experimental subjects, they will nonetheless report experiencing an emotion and attribute it to something even though it was not the actual cause of their arousal.

A great deal of research within political science has focused on particular types of emotions, such as anxiety, anger, fear, or enthusiasm. This focus most likely results from the steady supply of self-report measures of these emotions in the ANES and other election surveys. Others have focused more on the extent to which emotional arousal occurs, without respect to the subspecies of emotion being experienced. Both approaches are relevant so far as they lead to an understanding of how emotions are involved in political attitudes and behavior. Unfortunately, the traditional survey method has made it difficult to disentangle the experience of emotional arousal from the cognitive assessment of the object and the labeling of the specific emotion.

To date, the most prominent theory tying emotion to political psychology is Marcus, Neuman, and MacKuen's (2000) theory of affective intelligence, which posits that affect ultimately serves to make citizens more sophisticated. When anxious about how things are going in the political world, this generalized anxiety drives a search for more information, and for better use of existing information resources. Thus greater political "intelligence" is induced by emotion, at least this specific variety. Drawing on ANES data, Marcus and colleagues argue that general-ized anxiety about politics causes people to engage in more effortful information gathering and processing. As a result, they are less likely to rely on default heuristics such as party identification in informing their vote preferences, and more likely to seek out and rely on substantive information. According to their formulation, emotion plays an indirect role in promoting more effortful processing by motivating citizens to seek out and use more information. In other words, emotion is the driving force behind a process that ultimately improves the quality of political decision making. More specifically, Marcus and colleagues argue that a specific positive emotion—enthusiasm—elicits greater participation, whereas the negative emotion labeled anxiety elicits an information search.

The theory of affective intelligence has undoubtedly played an important role in renewing consideration of emotion in a field that has been heavily cognitive through-out its brief history. Perhaps even more importantly, this work has brought about reconsideration of the normative perspective on emotion that is common to most political psychology. Much of political theory has disdained the role of emotion in political decision making and, until recently, political psychologists have largely followed suit. Psychologists have recognized the important role emotion plays in intelligent functioning, and how cognition alone leads to serious dysfunction. Political psychologists have been slower to take up the defense of emotion as a pot-entially positive force in political decision making.

The theory of affective intelligence is not without its critics. Although few argue with the general logic of the theoretical framework, nor that emotions may serve useful (as well as potentially harmful) purposes in the political world, the empirical evidence supporting affective intelligence has been criticized as limited and inconclusive. For one, evidence is limited to retrospective self-reports of emotional reactions. Evidence of affective intelligence hinges on the validity of survey questions asking respondents to tell the interviewer whether a given political figure has ever made them feel angry, afraid, anxious, enthusiastic, and so forth. While such measures have face validity, studies outside the political realm raise doubt that they provide accurate recall of previously experienced emotions. Without the presence of the emotion-inducing event or object, such reports tend to be heavily mediated by cognitions (Breckler 1984). Likewise, induced emotion is quite different from semantically activated reports of emotion. As Niedenthal and colleagues (2003, 327) suggest, "affect infusion ... requires that the perceptual aspects of an emotion are experienced, not merely the semantic aspects."

In a related critique, Ladd and Lenz (2004) point out that while the theory of affective intelligence suggests that a *generalized* anxiety among members of the electorate drives greater engagement and the search for more information, empirical evidence is based on whether anxiety is reported to have been produced *by specific candidates*. Thus it is not a general emotional state that is operationally tapped in examinations of affective intelligence, but rather how one feels about a candidate or candidates. Using ANES data, Ladd and Lenz show, not surprisingly, that candidate preference and vote choice are related to comparative emotions toward the two candidates. The extent that one candidate produces more anxiety than another is strongly related to candidate preference. They argue that those reporting anxiety may, indeed, be more engaged, but only spuriously so, either because intensely held preferences drive both anxiety and engagement, or because political engagement leads to still stronger reactions to the campaign. As Ladd and Lenz note, the results seen thus far are consistent with evidence of affective intelligence, but they do not rule out other possible interpretations.

Clearly, some doubt exists regarding the specifics of affective intelligence, but few doubt that politics can be emotion provoking, nor that emotion matters to the political choices that people make. Although affective intelligence focuses our attention on the benefits of emotion for political behavior, emotion is also widely acknowledged to be potentially manipulative. As Brader and Corrigan (2005, 1) point out in their study of the emotional content of political advertisements, "The full significance of emotions for politics comes not because emotions influence the political behavior of citizens, but rather because political actors know that they do and try to capitalize on the power of emotions to achieve their goals." Most consultants believe in the importance of emotional appeals, though these lay theories have not been validated by empirical evidence (e.g. Kaid and Johnston 2001).

Methodologically, political scientists find it difficult to study emotion as distinct from cognition. Survey data alone cannot make a strong case for emotions as a cause of most politically relevant outcomes (e.g. Glaser and Salovey 1998; Isbell and Ottati 2002). But even in experimental settings, efforts to manipulate emotion without changing the informational content of messages prove quite difficult. For example, in two experiments on the role of emotion in political advertising, Brader (2005) compares the reactions of subjects exposed to ads that include emotional cues for enthusiasm and fear to those that do not. Operationally, he does this by comparing a relatively negative script to a similar one that includes evocatively fearful images and music, and a relatively positive ad to one that includes enthusiastic music and images. He suggests that imagery and music are critical to emotional appeals, whereas verbal content is processed in highly cognitive ways. While there is some evidence that pictures are particularly good at inducing emotional responses relative to words, like most scholars, Brader relied on the post hoc report of emotion.

It would be fairly simple to interpret the results of Brader's study if one could validate that information is entirely contained within the verbal content of communications, whereas changing the visual content and music alters only emotions. As psychological studies suggest, some words carry far more emotional content than others do, just as some pictures do (see Lang, Bradley, and Cuthbert 1997). But just as a picture is often said to be worth a thousand words, there is no clear way to change images and music within a presentation without also changing the information that viewers are given, and the context in which they are interpreting it. Within psychology, many researchers use standardized sets of words and pictures that allow them to roughly equate stimuli as strongly or weakly positive, negative or neutral in the emotions they elicit. But standardized stimuli like these have yet to be developed for political psychology. Moreover, to do so would be quite difficult. Whereas smiling babies and cute bunnies are consensually regarded as producers of positive affect in the psychology lab, George Bush could be one person's positive stimulus and another's strong negative one.

How else might researchers manipulate emotion without inadvertently changing other variables in their designs? In one study, subliminal cues were used to induce emotional reactions without viewer awareness and thus also without changing the visual or verbal information of which subjects were cognitively aware (see Weber, Lodge, and Taber 2005). This approach has the advantage of holding information constant, but it probably also mutes the potential effects that emotion might have relative to real world examples of emotion-inducing messages.

Furthermore, even if one does not seek to manipulate emotion, but instead measures it as an outcome, our usual methodological toolbox is limited in what it has to offer. The heavy reliance on emotion as reported by subjects after the fact casts serious doubts on the appropriate interpretation of many studies. If, as many psychologists suggest, affect is most often experienced extremely quickly and often in the absence of conscious cognitive awareness (see Zajonc 1980; Bargh and Chartrand 1999), then the usual approaches to measurement will not do. People only become aware of their emotions if they are very strong emotions, and most directed at the political world probably do not reach that level. As Alford and colleagues (2005, 20) summarize, "Emotion produces choices and behavior without much in the way of controlled cognitive deliberation that is introspectively transparent." Even if one trusts self-reports, there is the additional hurdle of getting subjects to accurately recall felt emotions. Civettini and Redlawsk (2005) find that when affect is reported immediately after a stimulus, and then recalled later in the same experiment, there are nonetheless high levels of error in their self-reports.

All of this is problematic for what we political scientists ask of our survey respondents and experimental subjects. There is no easy solution, but it seems doubtful that post hoc self-reports of emotion will continue to be defensible as the standard measure of emotional response. If political psychologists are convinced—as we seem to be—that automatic, preconscious emotional reactions precede and shape the kind of subsequent cognitive processing that transpires, then there is little choice but to pursue alternative approaches. If we are to further an understanding of emotion and politics that is more than simply a repackaging of studies of political cognition, then we need to sort out our terminological inconsistencies and improve methods of measurement. Despite progress, we know far too little about the extent to which emotions are involved in political judgment. At best we can say that we have studied the effects of some emotions that citizens are aware of and can label, and can respond to in some purposive way. But that points to a huge limitation on current knowledge.

2 THE PSYCHOLOGY OF BIASED PROCESSING

Because of the ever-increasing range of choice offered to citizens and consumers, one of the most active areas of political psychology research is the study of whether people are biased versus fair-minded processors of political information. Do people assimilate information in a rational way, or do they raise the bar for convincing evidence when new information contradicts their existing views? Are they simply rational updaters who take new information and add it to their existing mix in order to formulate a new opinion? Or are they selective in what they expose themselves to and to what extent they revise their views accordingly?

This research is triggered in part by renewed interest in parties and partisanship in American elections. The early research suggesting that partisanship was declining in the 1970s gave way to a consensus of "renewal" in the 1980s and 1990s (Fiorina 2002). The strength of the statistical relationship between party identification and vote choice rose continuously from 1972 to 1996, but this new consensus diffused relatively slowly throughout the discipline (see Bartels 2002). In addition, even widespread acceptance of the increased strength of this relationship has not necessarily meant that everyone agrees that party identification is now a stronger predictor of vote choice. As Fiorina (2002) points out, if party identification now works in concert with other determinants of vote choice that once predicted in opposite directions or not at all, then there may be good reason to call this new consensus into question.

More recently, Levendusky (2005) showed that party identification and ideology are much more tightly aligned now than in the 1970s. Whereas party ID and ideology were once largely orthogonal, liberals are now predominantly Democrats and conservatives are predominantly Republicans. This sorting process, he argues, has occurred as a result of elite polarization. When elites are ideologically polarized and send homogeneous signals about what it means to be a Democrat/Liberal and a Republican/Conservative, then the electorate "sorts" themselves into more consistent categories, largely by changing ideology to align with party identification.

Interestingly, what it means precisely to "identify" with a political party remains an unanswered question. Party identification is easily the most widely used concept in all of political psychology if not political science, but it has been reified to such an extent that its meaning is seldom questioned, except in comparative contexts. Moreover, the extent to which people in various countries will self-identify with a party hinges precariously on how the question is asked. In a study comparing a variety of approaches to asking about party attachments in Canada, the US, and Britain, Blais and colleagues (2001) found that the extent of these publics willing to adopt these labels went from 76 percent to 48 percent, based on a minor change in the wording of the question.

Despite some skepticism about the newfound power of partisanship in the United States electorate, the strengthening of this statistical relationship has spawned a resurgence of interest in the extent to which partisanship biases the processing of political information. Whereas twenty-five years ago one was more likely to read about partisanship in the academic journals as a source of high levels of political knowledge, mobilization, and attitude consistency, many contemporary political psychologists study partisanship as a source of bias in the processing of political information. Political parties have been at the root of the debate over biased assimilation from the very beginning of election research. As Angus Campbell and colleagues (1960, 133) argued, "Identification with a party raises a perceptual screen through which an individual tends to see what is favorable to his partisan orientation." The theme of partisan resistance to new information persists in contemporary models of the vote, and it is argued to cause people to selectively consume information and/or selectively interpret the implications and importance of new information, so that it does not threaten their existing views.

Interest in selective perception and selective exposure has been with us since the earliest election studies (e.g. Lazarsfeld, Berelson, and Gaudet 1944), but only recently have these basic ideas taken root in more complex models of information processing. Selectivity and biased processing represent one of the most active areas of research in recent political psychology. As the number of avenues for obtaining political information has increased, political psychologists want to know whether citizens select sources that are more likely to reinforce their existing views. Further, to what extent is new information interpreted and processed so as to reinforce existing beliefs, and to what extent are citizens responsive to new information?

One prominent example of the emphasis on motivated reasoning is Lodge, Taber, and colleagues' work suggesting that all political concepts are affectively charged as positive or negative, and that this information is stored in long-term memory (see e.g. Taber, Lodge, and Glathar 2001; Lodge and Taber 2005). New information is not necessarily retained, but it is used to update the affective tags that are attached to these concepts in memory. When asked for an evaluation of a political concept, citizens are said to recall the affective tally attached to the concept. Feelings serve as a summary of information that is no longer accessible in memory. This model represents a relatively rational approach to choice, though not necessarily in the Bayesian sense of rational updating.

However, as Lodge, Taber, and colleagues (e.g. Taber, Lodge, and Glathar 2001) have pointed out, an accurate model of political reasoning must take into account that it is often motivated by goals other than accuracy. In their motivated reasoning model, the online tally is not simply an unbiased account of previously encountered information. Instead, directional goals continually alter the processing and integration of new information into the tally. To the extent that the goal is to maintain one's prior beliefs (as opposed to pursuing accuracy), people may ignore or devalue contrary information. They may also seek evidence selectively, biasing the considerations they draw from memory, exercising different levels of scrutiny for disconfirming evidence, and/or altering the weights attached to different criteria in a way that is less threatening to the prior belief. According to this model, directional goals "emerge spontaneously as the affective tags associated with elements of the problem represented in long-term memory are brought into working memory (hot cognition)."

According to this model, the direction and strength of affect toward a political person or idea will cause most citizens to be "biased reasoners" who fail to treat new evidence fairly: "Most citizens most of the time will be decidedly 'partisan' in what and how they think about and reason about political leaders, groups, events, and issues" (185). Interestingly, advocates of this model suggest that it is neither wholly a vice nor a virtue. On the one hand, an online tally provides a better summary of one's past evaluations than preferences based on the recollection of specific pros and cons that happen to come to mind at any given point in time. The online model thus implies that choices are based on more information than is evident in assessments of knowledge made at the time of the decision. On the other hand, that same affective tally biases the processing of subsequent information, and is, in that sense, normatively undesirable.

Lau and Redlawsk (2006) have constructed a closely related model of motivated reasoning based on behavioral decision theory. In their model of the vote choice, they focus on the process of decision making and how individual motivations influence the extent to which voters choose correctly. They begin by accepting the notion that pre-existing preferences bias subsequent assimilation of information, but they attempt to determine where such motivations enter into this process. Using an interactive information board/computer screen that allows people to seek out information in order to make decisions, they suggest that bias enters into information gathering and processing at many points along the way to decision-making. Surprisingly, voters who use a classically rational decision-making process, that is, one involving a deep and balanced information search, "were in many circumstances less likely to make a correct decision compared to voters using an intuitive or fast and frugal strategy" (Lau and Redlawsk 2005, 23). Barker and Hansen (2005) likewise question whether more information and deeper cognitive processing is the answer to what ails citizens. They found that subjects who engaged in systematic cognitive processing had weaker and less consistent attitudes than subjects in a control group.

Two recent studies stake out the ground on both sides of this important debate over whether citizens ultimately make good use of information. Gerber and Green (1999) use aggregate opinion data to argue that selectivity and perceptual bias are actually *not* the norm when citizens take in new information. Using over-time aggregate data, they argue that Republicans, Democrats, and Independents all basically change their views in the same direction and to the same extent as a result of new information. Based on an analysis of presidential approval among Republicans, Democrats, and Independents, Gerber and Green (1999, 205) conclude that all three groups tend to go up and down together over time: "Only the faintest traces of selective perception are evidence from partisan tends in presidential approval. All three partisan groups move together—sometimes markedly—as party fortunes change." They applaud this pattern as rational in both the colloquial and Bayesian sense of the term. In other words, citizens appear to demonstrate Bayesian learning, with all groups making equally good use of new information as it comes along. If people were truly biased processors, they argue, their views would not move in parallel in response to ongoing political events.

If Gerber and Green's claim is correct, it has far-reaching consequences for some of the most widely believed tenets of mass political behavior. Partisanship, in this view, is simply a running tally of information and judgments that have occurred over time. It summarizes information efficiently but has no influence on choice independent of the information and value judgments that it encapsulates. This conceptualization stands in sharp contrast to the traditional idea of partisanship as a driving force in how people perceive, interpret, and respond to the political world. According to Gerber and Green, information is key to understanding the political fortunes of candidates and policies, and the public responds roughly as if it were updating its views accordingly.

For most political psychologists, Gerber and Green's conclusion is shocking if not implausible. How could so many studies, laboratory and otherwise, demonstrate findings of resistance to counter-attitudinal information, particularly in the context of political views that have been relatively stable throughout a person's lifetime? If prior views do, in fact, bias the processing of new information, one would expect this pattern to be observable in the realm of political decision making if it happens at all.

Interestingly, using the same standard model of Bayesian updating as the basis for his conclusion, Bartels (2000) suggests that biased processing is alive and well in the American public, with partisanship as its driving force. Bartels suggests that when oppositional partisan groups adjust their views in the same direction and to roughly the same extent over time, it is anything but evidence of Bayesian learning.

To help explain the basis for this difference of opinion, Figure 5.1 illustrates the same kind of over-time evidence that convinced Gerber and Green that political psychologists' assumptions about biased processing were greatly exaggerated. As new information becomes available to all three groups—say, for example, news that the economy has improved—all three partisan groups move toward higher levels of presidential approval. The trendlines in Figure 5.1 exemplify this parallel movement in presidential approval, though obviously from groups that began with very differ-ent attitudes toward a Republican president in this hypothetical example. Downturns due to bad news such as economic decline would cause all three groups' approval levels to plummet, as they do in this illustration between 1985 and 1988.

In contrast, Figure 5.2 provides an illustration of what Bartels thinks Bayesian learning should look like in over-time public opinion data. As new information becomes available—perhaps news that the economy has worsened—the three groups of partisans update their presidential approval ratings in light of their initial views.

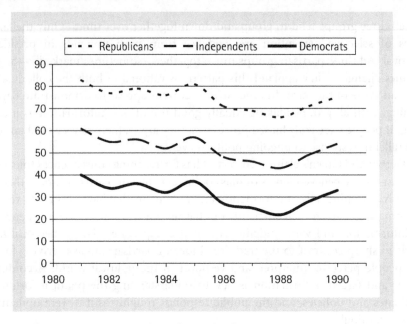

Fig. 5.1 Gerber/Green representation of Bayesian learning

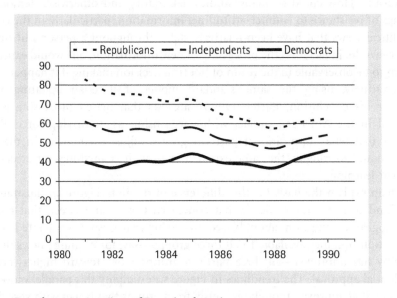

Fig. 5.2 Bartels representation of Bayesian learning

In contrast to the Gerber/Green expectation, downward movement of approval due to negative information is not even across all groups, but is more pronounced in groups that begin with higher levels of approval. This occurs in a Bayesian model because the new information is more significant to the extent that it contradicts initial expectations. So, for example, in Figure 5.2 the decline in approval between

1981 and 1982 produces a shallower slope for Democrats, whose expectations for the Republican president were quite low to begin with. For Republicans, negative information of this kind is more of a surprise given their generally positive expectations, thus the extent of impact is greater for this group as shown by the steeper downward slope between 1981 and 1982. Most importantly, the net effect of Bayesian updating is some convergence of opinion. Whether the news is positive or negative, the three lines ultimately move closer and closer together over time. And even when the new information that citizens must incorporate is outside the range of expectation—better than even what the most supportive expect, or worse than what the most oppositional political group expects—the differential change in light of expectations should still bring the groups closer together if they are processing via Bayesian learning.

Thus Bartels suggests that we should not find real data that mimics Figure 5.1 particularly reassuring in its implications. It substantiates, rather than refutes, the hypothesis of biased processing. Moreover, Bartels's conclusion comports with the bulk of evidence in political psychology—that is, that partisans are indeed biased assimilators and that patterns of Bayesian convergence such as what is illustrated in Figure 5.2 are uncommon.

Neither model, however, takes us through the full range of possibilities for how citizens respond to new political information. Thus far we have discussed these models in terms of events and information with clear positive or negative implications that all citizens would share. News that pollution levels have increased, or that unemployment is down, for example, would be received as negative and positive news, respectively, by all citizens. But new information about position issues as opposed to valence issues could easily create polarization within a Bayesian framework. For instance, if the "new information" about the president is that he vetoed a gun control bill, then Republicans should move in the more positive direction, if at all, and Democrats in a more negative direction. In this scenario, Bayesian learners should, quite rationally, polarize.

Whatever their differences, biased processing models are typical of contemporary political psychology in that they share an underlying skepticism that information is the cure for all that ails the quality of political decisions. If people are not passive recipients of information, but rather active choosers, interpreters, and rationalizers, then the limitations of information become apparent.

We are, in one sense, at an early stage in research that models biased processing, still sorting out what qualifies as evidence and what does not. To understand this process more fully in the future, researchers must unpack the process of biased assimilation in order to understand how bias occurs in the selection of information sources, the credibility granted to those sources, the discounting of information, and the relative weights given to new information in updating preferences. These are all separate mechanisms by which new information could differentially affect partisan groups based on their initial predispositions.

3 BEYOND SELF-REPORT: NEW SOURCES
OF THEORY AND EVIDENCE

Methodologically, political psychology has been criticized for relying too heavily on cross-sectional survey data (e.g. Krosnick 2002). Although this criticism seems valid with regard to much of the past work in this subfield, a greater level of methodological pluralism is difficult to find in any other subfield within political science. Burgeoning pluralism is evident in the kinds of methods political psychologists use as well as in the types of measures they now employ to operationalize key concepts.

In comparing early research in political psychology with today's studies, there is a striking difference in the extent to which political psychologists trust self-reports as a means of getting at the black box processes involved in formulating political choices. For example, when authors of classics such as *The People's Choice* wanted to know why people voted the way they did, they simply asked them. In contrast, the consensus view today is that the reasons people offer for their decisions "are better understood as justifications of a decision that has already been made" (12). (See also Lau 1982; McGraw 2000; Rahn, Krosnick, and Breuning 1994.)

For better or worse, humans appear to have little ability to introspect about the actual causes of their attitudes and actions. Nonetheless, they are disturbingly facile at rationalizing the choices and actions that they make. I say "disturbing" because as social scientists, we may be led on many a wild goose chase by people's abilities to rationalize their emotions and choices. In addition, it is disturbing to lose the comfort of believing that there is an accessible, transparent logic to individuals' political choices.

A dramatic example of the need to be skeptical of self-report and introspective accounts of behavior is illustrated by Wegner (2002) in a study in which electrical stimulation was used unbeknownst to experimental subjects to force them to react involuntarily by standing up. Despite the fact that their decision to stand was completely outside of their control, a large percentage reported a logical reason why they did so. Our brains are apparently compelled to offer deliberate, conscious reasons for our actions, but these rationalizations may have little to do with what actually happens. If we cannot understand the origins of our decision to sit or stand, how can we possibly understand the origins of a far more complex decision such as a vote choice?

What options do intrepid explorers of the black box psychological processes underlying political choices have to turn to? The good news is that the methodological repertoire for political psychology has undoubtedly expanded over the past fifty years. In addition to the survey data that served as the initial springboard for interest in the psychology of political choices, scholars now make regular use of laboratory experiments as well.

But the expansion in methodologies has not been exclusively toward imitating the internal validity of psychologists' laboratory studies. In addition, experimental designs embedded within surveys provide researchers with new insights into understanding the basis of sensitive and socially undesirable political opinions and behaviors such as non-voting (see Holbrook and Krosnick 2005) and negative attitudes toward racial minorities (Sniderman et al. 1991). What is more, field experiments have been brought back into the methodological mix as well, primarily by Green and his associates (see e.g. Green and Gerber 2002). Still others study the psychology of political decision making in the context of real world political choices, as Glaser (2002) did in his study of the effects of ballot structure on the outcome of school bond initiatives.

Recognizing that so much of what political psychologists want to know may transcend the realm of self-report or even self-awareness, scholars also increasingly pursue measures that do not require research participants' conscious awareness or introspection. Response times in answering questions, for example, are used to better understand respondents' associations between positive or negative attributes and racial groups. In the most sophisticated applications of these techniques, researchers use complex designs to understand the associative links that facilitate attitudes.

The two most widely used paradigms for evaluating implicit (as contrasted with explicit) attitudes, are the "implicit association test" (IAT; see Greenwald, McGhee, and Schwartz 1998), and the "bona fide pipeline" (BFP; see Fazio et al. 1995). The IAT measures the strength of an association between two target categories (e.g. black and white) and two attributes (e.g. good and bad) by having people categorize examples of the target and attribute categories at the same time. So, for example, respondents would be presented with a test stimulus (e.g. a picture of a flower), and asked to sort what they observe into one category if it is either Black or good, or a second category if the object is either White or bad. The speed with which they perform this task across a number of stimuli is then compared to the speed with which they perform the same task with the two groups switched so that they sort objects into either a Black/bad category or a White/good category. In this particular example, negative attitudes toward Blacks would be assessed by comparing response latencies on the Black-bad and White-good trials to the Black-good and White-bad trials. Interestingly, even when one knows how the test works and is aware of what is being measured, it is still next to impossible for respondents to falsify results by trying to respond more quickly to some pairings than others.

The BFP also measures implicit attitudes, but in this case a prime such as a Black or White face is presented before an adjective is shown. In this case, negative associations with Blacks would be demonstrated by faster latencies when Black faces and negative adjectives are shown, and slower latencies for Black faces followed by positive adjectives relative to the same latencies after the presentation of White faces.

Both techniques avoid the perils of self-report and solve social desirability biases. In studies of racial attitudes, they also predict race-related behaviors (Fazio and Olson 2003). Although these are controversial measures of racial prejudice and of negative attitudes toward groups (see e.g. Arkes and Tetlock 2004), they are uncontroversial as indicators of the associations that people maintain, whether they act on them or not. One might well ask whether they are really necessary to political psychology outside of a few particularly sensitive topics such as race. The answer to this question remains to be seen, but as political psychologists increasingly seek understandings of phenomena outside the realm of conscious awareness, techniques of this kind will undoubtedly become increasingly valuable.

Finally, another set of methods involving psycho-physiological approaches to political attitudes and behaviors has opened up new possibilities as political psychologists begin to see how social neuroscience and psycho-physiological measurement techniques may be useful for understanding political attitudes and behavior. Technological advances in our ability to observe physiological evidence of the processes underlying political choice have drawn a small group of scholars to incorporate the tools of neuroscience into their work. Although a thorough review of studies that employ psycho-physiological and social neuroscience approaches is beyond the scope of this chapter, a special issue of *Political Psychology* published in 2003 (Volume 24: 4) provides useful examples of how social neuroscience is increasingly incorporated into political psychology. Given the field's focus on understanding real world political events, these techniques are not likely to replace traditional methods within political psychology, but they are a very promising means of augmenting our limited access to people's internal states.

Recently political psychologists also have begun to draw on evolutionary psychology as a basis for understanding reactions to the political world. For example, Alford, Funk, and Hibbing (2005) use the results of twin studies to distinguish the environmental determinants of political attitudes from their inherited traits. They conclude that attitudes toward a wide variety of political issues, as well as affect toward the major parties, is significantly influenced by genetic predisposition. Likewise, Sidanius and colleagues' theory about the role of gender in social dominance orientation is rooted in evolutionary psychology. Mutz and Reeves (2005) also draw on evolutionary psychology to understand viewers' reactions to incivility in televised political discourse.

To be sure, the potential applications of these approaches to political choice are in their infancy, but they appear relevant to some of the very same questions political psychologists have been trying to answer for years. For example, brain imaging studies demonstrate that activity in one area of the brain can bias what goes on elsewhere in the brain, thus bolstering conclusions about biased processing. Moreover, there appears to be no centralized location in the brain for integrating information and making choices (see Alford, Hibbing, and Smith 2005). Thus there is unlikely to be any one calculus for political decision making.

To date, very little of this evidence is directed toward answering the kinds of questions that plague political psychology, but the implications are clear. For example, McClure et al. (2004) show that judgments made about immediate versus delayed gratification activate different areas of the brain. As Alford and colleagues explain, "the time element stimulated different parts of the brain that are associated with different functions. Specifically, the possibility of immediate gratification seems to activate the emotional part of the brain, but when immediate gratification is not an option, the more reflective and cognitive part of the brain is activated." As political scientists ponder how promises of tax cuts influence choice relative to long-term promises to protect the environment, such findings may well become applicable.

4 INFORMATION AS THE GOLD STANDARD

It is a profoundly erroneous truism . . . that we should cultivate the habit of thinking about what we are doing. The precise opposite is the case. Civilization advances by extending the number of operations which we can perform without thinking about them. Operations of thought are like cavalry charges in a battle—they are strictly limited in number, they require fresh horses, and must only be made at decisive moments. (Alfred North Whitehead, 1911)

If an extraterrestrial took a cursory glance at the books published in political psychology over the past fifteen years, she would come away with the impression that what we earth people value in our citizens is information, reason, and rationality. Consider, for example, Ferejohn and Kuklinski's *Information and Democratic Processes* (1990), Popkin's *The Reasoning Voter* (1991), Sniderman, Brody, and Tetlock's *Reasoning and Choice* (1991), Lupia, McCubbins, and Popkin's *Elements of Reason: Cognition, Choice, and the Bounds of Rationality* (2000), Page and Shapiro's (1992) *The Rational Public,* and so forth. These books do not concur on all matters, but the desirability of rational, well-informed political choices resonates throughout all of these volumes.

A closer look would reveal that the bulk of studies concur that people do not have loads of information about politics—indeed, far from it. But this closer examination would nonetheless suggest that most political psychologists *wish* citizens had perfect information, and think the political process would be far better off if citizens could at least better approximate this goal. As Kuklinski (2002) has suggested, rational choice assumes citizens are even-handed processors of information, while political psychology tends to assume (and to find) that they are not, though it nonetheless argues that they should be.

In this respect, Whitehead's statement above may seem an anathema from the perspective of political psychology. What could be more sacred than the idea that good citizens should put a great deal of thought into the political choices they make? Are we, indeed, depleting citizens' resources by asking them to make too many political decisions? Or are we reaching the wrong conclusions by assuming that the best decisions are ones made based on the most information? It is worth remembering that the well-educated citizen was not always the gold standard in politics.

Contemporary political psychology is beginning to question whether a classic rational decision-making process is truly what political psychology should pursue as its gold standard. In all three of the areas discussed in this chapter, political psychologists are reconsidering the emphasis on information and cognition as the root of ideal political choice. Studies of emotion and politics suggest that emotion is equally, if not more, important to political choice than cognition, and they question whether that is necessarily a bad thing. Studies of information processing suggest that information is severely limited in its capacity to improve political choice given the extent of biased processing; moreover, rational decision making does not necessarily mean better choices. As new approaches to measurement are applied to political choice, they further suggest that much of human decision making—political or otherwise—may be driven by processes of which citizens are not aware.

Taken together, these trends suggest that one of the most long-lasting premises of political decision making—that information gathering, thinking, and reasoning make for superior political decisions relative to visceral, subconscious reactions—is being called into question. Whereas political psychologists in the past have thought of citizens as information processors, they are rapidly becoming seen as less purposeful and as having less conscious control over their preferences. Whether such a representation of citizen choice is more accurate than the citizen as rational processor and/or more normatively desirable remains to be seen. In an era when voters are being asked to make more individual political choices than ever before, the horses may indeed need rest.

REFERENCES

ALFORD, J., FUNK, C., and HIBBING, J. 2005. Are political orientations Genetically Transmitted? *American Political Science Review,* 99: 153–67.

—— HIBBING, J., and SMITH, K. 2005. The challenge evolutionary biology poses for rational choice. Paper presented at the Annual Meeting of the American Political Science Association, Washington, DC.

ARKES, H., and TETLOCK, P. 2004. Attributions of implicit prejudice, or "would Jesse Jackson 'fail' the implicit association test?" *Psychological Inquiry,* 15(4): 257–78.

BARGH, J., and CHARTRAND, T. 1999. The unbearable automaticity of being. *American Psychologist,* 54: 462–79.

BARKER, D., and HANSEN, S. 2005. All things considered: systematic cognitive processing and electoral decision making. *Journal of Politics,* 67 (2).

BARTELS, L. 1988. *Presidential Primaries and the Dynamics of Public Choice.* Princeton: Princeton University Press.

—— 2000. Partisanship and voting behavior, 1952–1996. *American Journal of Political Science,* 44: 35–50.

—— 2002. Beyond the running tally: partisan bias in political perceptions. *Political Behavior* 24: 117–50.

BLAIS, A., GIDENGIL, E., NADEAU, R., and NEVITTE, N. 2001. Measuring party identification: Britain, Canada and the United States. *Political Behavior,* 23 (1): 5–22.

BLESS, H. 2001. The consequences of mood on the processing of social information. Pp. 391–412 in *Blackwell Handbook of Sociology: Individual Processes*, ed. A. Tesser and N. Schwartz Malden, Mass.: Blackwell Publishers.

BRADER, T. 2005. Striking a responsive chord: how political ads motivate and persuade voters by appealing to emotions. *American Journal of Political Science*, 49: 388–405.

—— and CORRIGAN, B. 2005. Emotional cues and campaign dynamics in political advertising. Paper presented at the Annual Meeting of the American Political Science Association, Washington, DC.

BRECKLER, S. 1984. Empirical validation of affect, behavior and cognition as distinct components of attitude. *Journal of Personality and Social Psychology*, 47: 1191–205.

CACIOPPO, J., and VISSER, P. 2003. Political psychology and social neuroscience: strange bedfellows or comrades in arms? *Political Psychology*, 24: 647–56.

CAMPBELL, A., CONVERSE, P., MILLER, W., and STOKES, D. 1960. *The American Voter*. New York: Wiley.

CIVETTINI, A., and REDLAWSK, D. 2005. A feeling person's game: affect and voter information processing and learning in a campaign. Presented at the Annual Meeting of the American Political Science Association, Washington, DC.

FAZIO, R. H., JACKSON, J. R., DUNTON, B. C., and WILLIAMS, C. J. 1995. Variability in automatic activation as an obtrusive measure of racial attitudes: a bona fide pipeline? *Journal of Personality and Social Psychology*, 69: 1013–27.

—— and OLSON, M. A. 2003. Implicit measures in social cognition research: their meaning and use. *Annual Review of Psychology*, 54: 297–327.

FEREJOHN, J., and KUKLINSKI, J. 1990. *Information and Democratic Processes*. Urabana, Ill.: University of Illinois Press.

FIORINA, M. 2002. Parties and partisanship: a 40-year retrospective. *Political Behavior*, 24: 93–115.

GERBER, A., and GREEN, D. 1999. Misperceptions about perceptual bias. *Annual Review of Political Science*, 2: 189–210.

GLASER, J. 2002. White Voters, Black Schools: Structuring Racial Choices with a Checklist Ballot. *American Journal of Political Science*, 46 (1): 35–46.

—— and SALOVEY, P. 1998. Affect in electoral politics. *Personality and Social Psychology Review* 2 (3): 156–72.

GREEN, D., and GERBER, A. 2002. Reclaiming the experimental tradition in political science. Pp. 805–32 in *Political Science: The State of the Discipline*, ed. H. V. Milner and I. Katznelson, 3rd edn. New York: W. W. Norton & Co.

GREENWALD, A. G., McGHEE, D., and SCHWARTZ, J. L. K. 1998. Measuring individual differences in cognition: the implicit association task. *Journal of Personality and Social Psychology*, 74: 1469–80.

HOLBROOK, A., and KROSNICK, J. 2005. Vote over-reporting: testing the social desirability hypothesis in telephone and internet surveys. Paper presented at the 2005 Conference of the American Association for Public Opinion Research. Miami.

ISBELL, L., and OTTATI, V. 2002. The emotional voter. Pp. 55–74 in *The Social Psychology of Politics*, ed. V. C. Ottati, S. Tindale, et al. New York: Kluwer.

KAID, L., and JOHNSTON, A. 2001. *Videostyle in Presidential Campaigns*. Westport, Conn.: Praeger.

KROSNICK, J. 2002. Is political psychology sufficiently psychological? Distinguishing political psychology from psychological political science. Pp. 187–216 in Kuklinski 2002*b*.

KUKLINSKI, J. ed. 2001. *Citizens and Politics: Perspectives from Political Psychology*. New York: Cambridge University Press.

KUKLINSKI, J. ed. 2002. *Thinking about Political Psychology.* New York: Cambridge University Press.

LADD, J., and LENZ, G. 2004. Emotions and voting behavior: a critique. Paper presented at the annual meeting of the Midwest Political Science Association, Chicago.

LANG, P. S., BRADLEY, L. M., and CUTHBERT, B. N. 1997. International Affective Picture System (IAPS): technical manual and affective ratings. NIMH Center for the Study of Emotion and Attention, retrieved on January 30, 2006 from **www.unifesp.br/dpsicobio/adap/instructions.pdf**

LAU, R. R. 1982. Negativity in political perception. *Political Behavior,* 4: 353–78.

—— and REDLAWSK, D. 2005. Toward a procedurally plausible model of the vote choice: decision strategies, information processing, and correct voting. Paper presented at the annual meeting of the American Political Science Association, Washington, DC.

—— —— 2006. *How Voters Decide: Information Processing during Election Campaigns.* New York: Cambridge University Press.

LAZARSFELD, P., BERELSON, B., and GAUDET, H. 1944. *The People's Choice.* New York: Duell, Sloan & Pearce.

LEVENDUSKY, M. 2005. Sorting, not polarization: understanding the dynamics of mass partisan change. Midwest Political Science Association Meetings, Chicago.

LODGE, M., and TABER, C. 2005. Implicit affect for candidates, parties and issues: an experimental test of the hot cognition hypothesis. *Political Psychology.*

LUPIA, A., McCUBBINS, M., and POPKIN, S. eds. 2000. *Elements of Reason: Cognition, Choice, and the Bounds of Rationality.* New York: Cambridge University Press.

McCLURE, S., LAIBSON, D., LOEWENSTEIN, G., and COHEN, J. 2004. Separate neural systems value immediate and delayed monetary rewards. *Science* 306: 503–7.

McGRAW, K. M. 2000. Contributions of the cognitive approach to political psychology. *Political Psychology,* 21: 805–32.

MARCUS, G., NEUMAN, W. and MacKUEN, M. 2000. *Affective Intelligence and Political Judgment.* Chicago: University of Chicago Press.

MUTZ, D. C., and REEVES, B. 2005. The new videomalaise: effects of televised incivility on political trust. *American Political Science Review,* 99 (1): 1–15.

NIEDENTHAL, P. M., ROHMAN, A., DALLE, N. 2003. What is primed by emotion concepts and emotion words? Pp. 307–33 in *The Psychology of Evaluation: Affective Processes in Cognition and Emotion,* ed. J. Musch and K. C. Klauer. Mahwah, NJ: Erlbaum.

OLSON, M. and FAZIO, R. H. 2003. Relations between implicit measures of prejudice: what are we measuring? *Psychological Science* 14 (6): 636–9.

PAGE, B., and SHAPIRO, R. 1992. *The Rational Public: Fifty Years of Trends in Americans' Policy Preferences.* Chicago: University of Chicago Press.

POPKIN, S. 1991. *The Reasoning Voter: Communication and Persuasion in Presidential Campaigns.* Chicago: University of Chicago Press.

RAHN, W., KROSNICK, J., and BREUNING, M. 1994. Rationalization and derivation process in survey studies of political candidate evaluation. *American Journal of Political Science,* 38: 582–600.

SEARS, D., HUDDY, L., and JERVIS, R. 2003. The psychologies underlying political psychology. Pp. 3–16 in *Oxford Handbook of Political Psychology,* ed. D. Sears, L. Huddy, and R. Jervis. Oxford: Oxford University Press.

SIDANIUS, J., and PRATTO, F. 2001. *Social Dominance: An Intergroup Theory of Social Hierarchy and Oppression.* Cambridge: Cambridge University Press.

SNIDERMAN, P., BRODY, R., and TETLOCK, P. 1991. *Reasoning and Choice: Explorations in Political Psychology.* New York: Cambridge.

—— PIAZZA, T., TETLOCK, P., and KENDRICK, A. 1991. The new racism. *American Journal of Political Science,* 35: 423–47.

TABER, C., LODGE, M., and GLATHAR, J. 2001. The motivated construction of political judgments. In 2001. *Citizens and Politics: Perspectives from Political Psychology*, ed. J. H. Kuklinski. New York: Cambridge University Press.

WEBER, C., LODGE, M., and TABER, C. 2005. Subliminal priming and political campaigns: the impact of subliminally presented affective primes on campaign ad evaluations. Paper presented to the annual meetings of the American Political Science Association, Washington, DC, September.

WEGNER, D. 2002. *The Illusion of Conscious Will*. Cambridge, Mass.: MIT Press.

WHITEHEAD, A. 1911. *An Introduction to Mathematics*. New York: Holt.

ZAJONC, R. 1980. Feeling and thinking: preferences need no inferences. *American Psychologist*, 35: 151–75.

CHAPTER 6

INFORMATION, PERSUASION, AND POLITICAL COMMUNICATION NETWORKS

ROBERT HUCKFELDT

CITIZENSHIP takes on meaning through processes of communication, persuasion, and conflict that occur among interdependent citizens. Opinions, choices, and patterns of engagement do not arise as the inevitable consequences of individual characteristics, national crises, or news media coverage. Neither do they arise as the necessary results of an individual's location within particular groups and environments. Rather, interdependent individuals arrive at choices and decisions as interactive participants in a socially imbedded process that depends on networks of communication among and between individuals within particular settings (Granovetter 1985; Zuckerman 2005).

This view of the citizen's role in democratic politics is anchored in some of the earliest and most influential empirical treatments of elections and campaigns—studies recognizing that the group basis of politics plays an important role, not only for politicians and activists, but for ordinary citizens as well (Lazarsfeld, Berelson, and Gaudet 1948; Berelson, Lazarsfeld, and McPhee 1954; Campbell et al. 1960, 1966). Indeed, in his economic theory of democracy, Downs (1957) provides an efficiency motivation for this view, arguing that citizens quite sensibly make use of socially supplied information in their efforts to reduce the costs of political information. By relying on the advice of politically expert associates whose political biases are similar to their own, Downs argues that individuals are able to offload the costs of collecting, analyzing, and evaluating political information.[1]

Network theories of citizenship are inspired by these early insights regarding the importance of communities, groups, and political information exchanges among and between individuals. At the same time, network theories rely on a conceptual apparatus that moves beyond the traditional definitions of primary groups, organizations, and societal groups to define networks in terms of the relationships that exist among individuals—within and beyond the boundaries of traditionally defined groups. The introduction of communication networks into the study of democratic politics provides new insights on individuals and groups at multiple levels of analysis, thereby providing a direct assault on a range of micro-macro problems that confront political analysis (Eulau 1986).

This chapter provides a survey and interpretation of the contributions made by network theories to the study of citizens and democratic politics. This overview begins by locating network research within the rich substantive and theoretical tradition of individually and group-based studies of public opinion and electoral politics. The chapter then addresses a series of methodological issues in the study of political information networks. Finally, attention turns to the particular substantive and theoretical insights generated in the study of communication and persuasion among citizens; the persistence and consequence of political disagreement and heterogeneity within communication networks; citizenship capacity, social capital, and the diffusion of political expertise among citizens; communication networks and collective action; and the roles of groups and networks in modern politics.

1 POLITICAL SCIENCE ROOTS

The importance of social imbeddedness and interdependence among citizens is in many ways old news to most political scientists. Some of the earliest and most influential treatments of political behavior and citizenship addressed patterns of communication, persuasion, disagreement, and conflict that occur among and between citizens. The Columbia studies focused on patterns of communication and influence in their early election studies in Elmira, New York, and Erie County, Ohio (Lazarsfeld, Berelson, and Gaudet 1948; Berelson, Lazarsfeld, and McPhee 1954). In *Southern Politics*, V. O. Key (1949) identified white racial antagonism as an inherently political response most likely to occur when black racial concentrations threatened white hegemony in local politics. Warren Miller (1956) demonstrated the political

---

[1] Calvert's (1985) analysis suggests that rational citizens might also seek out political information from other citizens with whom they disagree.

disadvantages of minority status by examining the plight of partisan minorities within counties. Butler and Stokes (1974) argued that British voting behavior within social classes was contingent on the class composition of local constituencies.[2]

These early lessons are easily forgotten, particularly in the face of the dominant data collection technologies used to study political behavior and public opinion—most surveys produce information on socially independent individuals. At the same time, creative sampling designs have made it possible to aggregate individual survey responses at the level of politically meaningful geographic units, producing measures of central tendency and dispersion for opinions that are geographically organized. Important progress in the contextual analysis of political behavior continues to be accomplished by combining survey data at the level of individuals either with aggregate census and voting data or with survey data aggregated according to the spatial boundaries within which survey respondents are located (Segal and Meyer 1974; Wright 1976; Cho 2003; Pattie and Johnston 1999; Peffley and Rohrschneider 2003).[3]

Network studies can be seen as a particular species within a larger genus—as one type of a contextual analysis of politics (Knoke 1990). Eulau (1986) and Przeworski and Teune (1970) define contextual factors in terms of the aggregation of individual characteristics that affect individuals through processes of social interaction. Hence, contexts are created through the particular composition of the individuals who make up some group or aggregate population. Network studies *diverge* from contextual studies in their effort to incorporate a direct mapping for the particular patterns of recurrent interaction among actors. Absent direct measures on patterns of communication, neither the individual measures nor their associated aggregate versions directly address the specifics of communication and persuasion among the individuals who make up the aggregates.

2 NETWORKS, ECOLOGICAL FALLACIES, INDIVIDUALISTIC FALLACIES

What difference does all this make? Ignoring individual interdependence creates the potential for misspecifying the effects of *both* the individual *and* the aggregate factors that underlie political behavior. Assume for the moment that a positive association exists between contexts and networks—that people who reside in Democratic settings, for example, are more likely to encounter Democrats within their networks of political communication (Huckfeldt 1986). If various forms of political behavior are, in turn, contingent on an individual's location within networks of political communication, the likelihood of engaging in a behavior—holding an opinion,

---

[2] For reviews of the historical literature, see Books and Prysby (1991), Huckfeldt (1986), Huckfeldt and Sprague (1995).

[3] For discussions of related methodological issues see Boyd and Iversen (1979), Bryk and Raudenbush (1992), and Steenbergen and Jones (2002).

voting for a candidate, putting up a political yard sign—is apt to vary across these various contextual units of aggregation. Thus, aggregate analyses that ignore important patterns of interdependence enhance the risk of producing ecological fallacies (Achen and Shively 1995; Goodman 1953, 1959; King 1997; Przeworski 1974; Sprague 1976).

The corollary individualistic fallacy is just as important: an individual-level analysis that ignores patterns of interdependence runs the risk of mistakenly specifying the relationships between individual characteristics and individual behavior (Huckfeldt and Sprague 1995, 28–32). Indeed, both individualistic and ecological fallacies suffer from the same problem—the stated or unstated assumption that individual characteristics and attributes translate directly into likelihoods of opinions and behaviors independently of the networks and contexts within which individuals are imbedded. Individualistic fallacies are based on individual-level data, and ecological fallacies on aggregate data, but both ignore the implications that arise due to patterns of individual interdependence located in time, place, and setting.

In a straightforward, intriguing, and historically important analysis, Herbert Tingsten (1963) demonstrated that working-class residents of Stockholm were more likely to vote if they lived in working-class neighborhoods. One might construct a number of hypothesized explanations for this pattern. Perhaps the socialist parties were more likely to concentrate their mobilization efforts in working-class districts. Perhaps working-class neighborhoods made it more likely that working-class residents would interact with other workers, thereby encouraging political identities as workers and supporters of the working class. Canache (1996), Langton and Rapoport (1975), Putnam (1966), and others consider similar explanations for patterns of partisan behavior in Honduras, in Santiago, in American counties, and elsewhere. In all these instances, patterns of concrete social relations leading to distinctive patterns of political communication are responsible for producing environmentally contingent patterns of political behavior. And these environmental contingencies on individual behavior are precisely the circumstances that give rise both to ecological and to individualistic fallacies.

How common are these problems? Is the Tingsten result a rare case? The literature produces an abundance of examples in which individual political behavior occurs at the intersection between individual predispositions and various forms of social interaction and communication. For example, in their analysis of education and citizenship, Nie, Junn, and Stehlik-Barry (1996) argue that individual educational achievement stimulates political participation, but that participation is depressed by individual levels of education that lag behind the educational levels of others in the environment. In these various bodies of work, the authors point toward complex forms of interdependence among actors that can be directly addressed by imbedding the individuals within networks of interaction and communication. Replacing aggregate analyses with individual-level analyses is not a solution to the problems addressed by these studies—it would simply replace a misspecified aggregate model with a misspecified individual-level model. The first instance produces an ecological fallacy, the second produces an individualistic fallacy, and both arise due to unspecified patterns of interdependence among political actors.

3 Surveys and the Measurement of Social Networks

During the 1940s and 1950s, an important series of scholarly efforts fundamentally altered the intellectual terrain for studies of voting, elections, participation, and public opinion (Lazarsfeld, Berelson, and Gaudet 1948; Berelson, Lazarsfeld, and McPhee 1954; Campbell et al. 1960, 1966). The ensuing revolution in the study of democratic politics institutionalized the innovation of the modern sample survey as the fundamental tool for studying electoral politics, not only in the United States but worldwide. The question that naturally arose was, how does one incorporate studies of communication networks into a study design which intentionally and necessarily randomly samples individuals who are independent of one another?

The answer to this question was less than straightforward. Some of the earliest and most analytically powerful implementations of network research involved complete enumerations of the relationships within well-defined populations (e.g. monasteries, churches, organizations). That is, the presence or absence of particular relationships are documented between each and every dyad within a population, and these relationships are, in turn, analyzed using a range of powerful analytic techniques (Wasserman and Faust 1994; White 1970). These analytic techniques are very useful to many political science research settings, and they are more likely to be employed successfully within a range of substantive applications involving interaction among political elites, within policy-making systems, and within and among courts and legislatures (Heinz et al. 1993; Knoke et al. 1996; Lauman and Pappi 1976; Lubell and Scholz 2001; Schneider et al. 2003; Fowler 2006). At the same time, their applicability is typically less straightforward in the context of the large populations that provide the primary object of study for scholars concerned with studies of mass behavior:[4] public opinion, participation, voting, and legal compliance (see Roch, Scholz, and McGraw 2000). Within this intellectual domain, contextual measures of population composition were often treated as an acceptable alternative measurement device. The problem with this practice is that it obscures the very real differences between contexts and networks in the study of voting, elections, and public opinion (Huckfeldt and Sprague 1995).

One solution to the problem came in the form of social network batteries, name generators, and the conception of egocentric networks, all of which are implemented in the context of a traditionally defined sample survey. An early implementation of such a strategy took place in the 1966 Detroit Area Study, directed by Edward Laumann (1973). Rather than conceiving a network in terms of the pattern of relationships defined by a space, place, or group, the egocentric network is defined in terms of the relationships that connect to a particular individual, measured through a battery of survey questions in which respondents name and then describe their personal networks (see Burt 1986; Marsden 1987).

---

[4] For an interesting example to the contrary see Watts and Strogatz (1998) and Fowler (2005b).

The particular form and wording of network name generators vary across different efforts, but a respondent to a survey might typically be asked to identify the first names of the people with whom she discussed the events of the past election campaign.[5] After identifying some number of names, the interviewer asks the respondent a battery of questions about each of the identified discussants: the nature of the relationship between the respondent and the discussant, the reported frequency of interaction with each discussant, the reported frequency of political discussion, the relationships among the discussants, the respondents' perceptions of the discussants' opinions and viewpoints, as well as the respondents' perceptions regarding the frequency of disagreement with each of the discussants.

Some studies add a snowball component to the sampling design in which interviews are conducted with the discussion partners who have been identified by the main respondents to the initial survey. These second stage surveys are useful for several purposes. They provide reciprocity measures, as well as verification regarding the main respondent's ability to identify the discussants' preferences accurately. The snowball survey also provides measures of preference intensity for the discussant— the self-reported strength or extremity of discussant opinions. These intensity measures, in turn, create an opportunity to study the factors that enhance and impede the effectiveness of communication among and between citizens, as well as factors that enhance discussant influence.

Moreover, snowball surveys provide measures of engagement, participation, and political expertise for discussants within a political communication network. These measures make it possible to consider the value added problem in democratic politics—the extent to which communication among and between citizens helps to enhance the capacity of individual citizens, as well as the capacity of the electorate as a whole (Huckfeldt, Ikeda, and Pappi 2000; Huckfeldt 2001). In these and other ways, social network batteries coupled with snowball surveys of the main respondents' self-identified political networks provide naturally occurring *laboratories* for the investigation of political persuasion and communication processes among and between citizens.

4 THE RELATIONSHIP BETWEEN CONTEXTS AND NETWORKS

The line of demarcation between contexts and networks has sometimes been fuzzy in political science research. Part of the difficulty has been rooted in the perception that contexts are simply a poor person's measure of networks. That is, lacking the ability

---

[5] This particular name generator was used in the 1984 South Bend study (Huckfeldt and Sprague 1995). For analyses of alternative name generators see Huckfeldt et al. (1998*b*) and Straits (2000).

to produce a detailed mapping of the networks within which survey respondents are imbedded, analysts have often employed a random mixing assumption that provides a simple substitution of contexts for networks. The problem with this conceptual confusion is that networks are *not* a simple and direct translation of the contexts and opportunities for social interaction that surround an actor. Rather, networks are formed at the complex intersection between individual preference, individual engagement, and individual location within particular contexts. Hence, important differences exist between the networks and contexts of political behavior (Huckfeldt and Sprague 1995).

A primary difference relates to issues of endogeneity and exogeneity in the construction of contexts and networks. Even if an individual resides in a Democratic neighborhood in a Democratic city in a Democratic state, and even if she works at a workplace dominated by Democrats, she may still manage to find Republicans with whom to eat lunch (Finifter 1974). One can think in terms of a mobile context defined in terms of the "life space" that is occupied by a particular individual (Eulau 1986). This abstract life space might be created in response to the numerous locations of the individual in time, space, and social structure, thereby including all the opportunities that an individual has for social interaction. Conceived in such a manner, networks must be seen as being endogeneous both to individual preference and to the contexts where individuals are located.

If individuals reside in contexts composed entirely of Republicans, their discussions will take place with Republicans unless they decide to forgo political conversation. At the same time, individuals in heterogeneous contexts do not simply roll over and accept whatever the context happens to provide. They impose their own preferences as constraints on the search process. In this way, the construction of communication networks within the boundaries of social contexts can be seen as a problem of supply and demand—as individuals desiring to find acceptable associates in a context that sets constraints on supply.

5 Network Construction, Self-selection, and the Intersection of Stochastic Processes

Both supply *and* demand are usefully seen as inherently stochastic processes— processes that reflect probabilities related to particular combinations of individuals, individual characteristics, contexts, small- and large-scale population concentrations, and opportunities for social interaction. Supply is stochastic because the constraints imposed by the compositional properties of a particular context are inevitably probabilistic. The individual selection of discussion partners is stochastic because potential discussants carry along with them a bundle of characteristics, and a single discussion partner serves a variety of purposes. Hence, the construction of political communication networks occurs within the constraints of supply that are imposed by particular contexts, guided by the selection principles of the individuals who are engaged in constructing the networks, and the resulting communication networks thereby occur at the stochastic intersection of two inherently stochastic processes (Boudon 1986). At the same time, a number of formulations and empirical applications suggest that supply looms large in the production of these networks (Coleman 1964, ch. 16; Huckfeldt 1986; Huckfeldt and Sprague 1995).

In this context, the argument that individuals are influenced through political communication with other individuals is inherently vulnerable to a self-selection counter-argument (Achen and Shively 1995). According to this argument, for example, strong supporters of the Japanese Liberal Democratic Party often choose to live in LDP neighborhoods, to be employed at workplaces full of LDP supporters, and to talk about politics with other supporters of the LDP. If a study finds that individuals who work in LDP workplaces are more likely to talk politics with supporters of the LDP, a sometimes difficult-to-answer counter-argument might be that LDP supporters choose *both* to work at LDP work places *and* to associate with other LDP supporters. Hence, by implication, the relationship between the context and the network is spurious—exposure both to networks and to workplaces might be influenced by individual choice.

One response to this problem is to consider the relationships between contexts and networks in a setting where contextual self-selection is an unlikely option. Conceive an advanced democracy as a (very large) context, where the likelihood of self-selection on political grounds is very low. Based on this level of measurement, several efforts consider the likelihood that party supporters will encounter disagreement within their political communication networks as a function of the party's level of support in the electoral politics of the country as a whole. In a study based on Germany in the 1990 election, Japan in the 1993 election, and the United States in the 1992 election, respondents who support one of the major parties are much more likely to report agreement than supporters of the minor parties and candidates (Huckfeldt, Ikeda, and Pappi 2005; also see Ikeda and Huckfeldt 2001). American Democrats are less likely to report disagreement than Perot voters; Japanese LDP voters are less likely to report disagreement than the supporters of the Sakigake—a minor party that no longer exists; German Christian Democrats are less likely to report disagreement than supporters of the Green Party; and so on.

It is equally important to emphasize that each party's supporters report levels of agreement within their networks that surpass random mixing expectations. The moral is *not* that individuals fail to exercise discretion in the construction of political communication networks. Once again, political communication networks are created at the intersection of individual choice and environmental supply, and neither individual-level factors nor aggregate factors can provide a full explanation for network construction.

6 PERSUASION AND COMMUNICATION EFFECTIVENESS AMONG CITIZENS

The laboratories created by the snowball surveys provide the opportunity to assess factors affecting persuasion and communication effectiveness among citizens. In general, main respondents are better able to recognize preferences accurately if they share the preferences. These results complement an important stream of research related to the false consensus effect—an effect in which the individual perceptions of the preferences held by others are biased toward agreement (Fabrigar and Krosnick 1995). One explanation for this false consensus bias builds on cognitive dissonance theory—people find disagreement to be disturbing and they misinterpret the messages sent by the discussant (Festinger 1957). Another explanation is conflict avoidance—individuals avoid conflictive conversations thereby obscuring the communication of disagreement (MacKuen 1990).

Although these are plausible and often compelling arguments for misperception in many contexts, several persistent patterns make these explanations less than fully satisfying in the context of political communication networks. First, not only are main respondents less likely to perceive a discussant's viewpoints accurately if they disagree with the discussant, but they are also less likely to perceive a discussant's viewpoints accurately if they believe that other individuals in the network hold a preference that is different from that reported by the particular discussant. Hence, in making a judgment about another individual's preference, individuals may be generalizing on the basis of their own immediate circumstances—they may be reaching the judgment on the basis of prior information taken from the environment. For example, if the main respondent is voting Democratic, and she believes that all her other associates are voting Democratic, she may miss the fact that one of them is actually voting Republican. In this context, it is important for political scientists to remember that relatively few citizens wear their preferences as lapel pins, and preferences are often socially ambiguous, even in networks explicitly identified to be political. Hence, respondents are likely to form judgments based on prior expectations that arise through recurrent patterns of social interaction (Huckfeldt et al. 1998a).

Moreover, while the *accuracy* of respondent perceptions is compromised by disagreement, either between the respondent and the discussant or between the particular discussant and the more generalized network, these same forms of disagreement do not compromise the *confidence* of the respondent in his perceptions of the discussant's preferences, or in the *accessibility* of these perceptions, measured in terms of response latencies or response times (Huckfeldt, Johnson, and Sprague 2004). In short, there is little evidence to suggest that individuals are uncomfortable or unwilling to acknowledge disagreement.[6] Finally, while these communication

---

[6] There is, however, evidence to suggest that the manner in which disagreement is managed varies across different national settings. See Ikeda and Huckfeldt (2001); Huckfeldt, Ikeda, and Pappi (2005).

biases produced by disagreement are theoretically important, we should not miss the forest for the trees—overall levels of accuracy within the communication networks are quite high, even in the face of disagreement.

Why might individuals be relatively well equipped to confront disagreement politically? First, citizens who are less engaged by politics may be less troubled by disagreement. Second, the inherently subjective nature of politics and political preferences may make it easier for one individual to comprehend why disagreement might occur (Ross, Bierbrauer, and Hoffman 1976). Finally, some evidence suggests that citizens who encounter divergent preferences within their communication networks are less likely to feel that the preferences are extreme or unreasonable (Huckfeldt et al. 2005).

Many of the same factors that affect the accuracy of communication also affect persuasiveness. In particular, discussants are more likely to be influential if their preferences are widely shared within the larger networks within which respondents are located (Huckfeldt, Johnson, and Sprague 2004). In other words, an individual who communicates a widely shared preference is both more likely to be correctly understood, as well as being more likely to be influential. In this way, the realization of influence and persuasion within dyads is itself autoregressive, depending on the distribution of opinion within the larger network of which the dyad is only one part (Huckfeldt et al. 1998a; also see McPhee 1963).

The effectiveness and persuasiveness of political communication among citizens also depend, in very profound ways, on the particular preferences and characteristics of the messenger. Citizens with strong, unambiguous preferences are more likely to be correctly perceived, and they are, correspondingly, more likely to be influential. In contrast, there is little evidence to suggest that citizens with strong preferences are unable to perceive the preferences that are communicated by others. Hence, it is not that individuals with strong preferences are incapable of recognizing disagreement when they encounter it—citizens with strong preferences are excellent messengers, and their ability to perceive the messages of others is not compromised (Huckfeldt, Johnson, and Sprague 2004).

7 THE PERSISTENCE AND CONSEQUENCE OF NETWORK HETEROGENEITY

Important bodies of work point toward individuals withdrawing from political engagement as a consequence of disagreement (Lazarsfeld, Berelson, and Gaudet 1948; Berelson, Lazarsfeld, and McPhee 1954). Other important work points to the problematic capacity of maintaining disagreement within a population as the stable equilibrium outcome of a dynamic communication process (Abelson 1979; Axelrod 1997; Marsden and Friedkin 1994). But if disagreement produces a political angst that leads to a withdrawal from civic life on the part of individual citizens, or if political diversity is inevitably eliminated as a consequence of communication among citizens, we are left in a difficult situation with respect to the capacity of citizens for the give-and-take that undergirds democratic politics.

Recent analyses have reconsidered the factors that create and sustain political heterogeneity within communication networks. The presence of disagreement within political communication networks has generated some debate, however, with Mutz (2006) arguing that Huckfeldt, Johnson, and Sprague (2004) overstate levels of disagreement. Direct evidence with respect to this issue has accumulated over more than twenty years, most recently in the 2000 National Election Study. Among those respondents interviewed after the election who identify at least one discussant, only 41 percent of the Gore voters perceive that all their discussion partners support Gore, with 36.7 percent naming at least one discussant who supports Bush; only 47 percent of the Bush supporters perceive that all their discussion partners support Bush, with 35.5 percent naming at least one discussant who supports Gore (Huckfeldt, Mendez, and Osborn 2004). Comparable levels of disagreement are demonstrated in other studies (Huckfeldt, Ikeda, and Pappi 2005; Huckfeldt and Sprague 1995; and Huckfeldt, Johnson, and Sprague 2004). Moreover, individuals located within networks of increasing size—in Germany, Japan, and the United States—are dramatically less likely to report homogeneous agreement within their networks (Huckfeldt, Ikeda, and Pappi 2005).

All these studies consistently demonstrate strong evidence of clustering—Republicans are more likely to talk politics with Republicans, Social Democrats with Social Democrats, Komeito supporters with Komeito supporters, and so on. We would expect nothing less. To the contrary, these studies demonstrate that patterns of *both* agreement *and* disagreement can be profitably understood within complex processes of communication and persuasion.

7.1 How does heterogeneity persist?

Huckfeldt, Johnson, and Sprague (2004) adopt an agent-based, computational strategy to address the conditions that give rise to persistent heterogeneity within communication networks. Drawing on the work of Abelson (1979) and Axelrod (1997), their analysis constructs a series of simulations that are motivated by a range of empirical analyses. Building on survey analyses, these simulations suggest that diverse preferences are more likely to survive in circumstances where the consequences of political communication and influence between two individuals depend on the distribution of preferences across the individuals' larger networks of communication. In this way, communication and influence are autoregressive—the probability of agreement within a dyad depends on the incidence of the particular opinion or viewpoint within the larger network of communication.

These agent-based models incorporate an inherently non-linear representation of communication and influence within and among these micro-environments, thereby producing complex, non-deterministic outcomes. In higher-density networks, where everyone communicates with everyone else, autoregressive patterns of influence can be expected to reinforce tendencies toward homogeneity. In contrast, autoregressive mechanisms can be expected to sustain opinion diversity within lower-density networks—networks where an individual is less likely to communicate with the associates of her own associates. In these lower-density networks, patterns of communication are often characterized both by structural holes (Burt 1992) that create communication gaps between networks, as well as by the influential individuals who bridge these gaps (Granovetter 1973). Disagreement is more likely to be sustained in these circumstances because disagreeing individuals frequently receive support for their preferences elsewhere in their communication networks, from individuals who are not connected to the source of disagreement (Huckfeldt, Johnson, and Sprague 2004).

The implications for democratic politics are quite important. If election campaigns only serve to recreate a pre-existent political homogeneity within social groups, then the collective deliberations of democratic citizens are divorced from the dramas and events of politics. Alternatively, to the extent that citizens participate in a process that includes disagreement as well as persuasion, the systematic processes of communication that occur within these networks become crucial to democratic outcomes, even though the direction and magnitude of the effects may be both complex and indeterminate (Boudon 1986).

7.2 What are the consequences of heterogeneity?

The consequences of network heterogeneity and the experience of political disagreement have stimulated a number of research efforts, and a consensus has not yet emerged regarding the political effects of disagreement. Huckfeldt, Johnson, and Sprague (2004) argue that political heterogeneity is more likely to persist within larger, more extensive communication networks. Network size, in turn, is predicted by some of the same factors that predict political involvement and engagement. Individuals with higher levels of education and more extensive organizational involvements are more likely to reside in larger communication networks. Hence, the same individuals who are able to draw on larger reserves of social capital are also more likely to be politically active and engaged (Lake and Huckfeldt 1998), as well as to experience a more diverse mixture of political opinions and viewpoints within their networks of political communication. These analyses and others (Huckfeldt, Ikeda, and Pappi 2005; Huckfeldt and Mendez 2004) find little evidence to suggest that political disagreement and diversity within communication networks produce politically disabling consequences in terms of political participation. Indeed, Kotler-Berkowitz (2005) finds that increased diversity within networks serves to stimulate higher levels of political participation.

Mutz (2002a, 2002b) and Mutz and Martin (2001) have also examined the consequences of disagreement within communication networks. Their analyses are generally less optimistic regarding the democratic potential of communication across the boundaries of political preference, in part based on a finding that political heterogeneity (cross-cutting cleavages) tends to depress participation (Mutz 2002a), and in part based on an argument that homogeneity is widespread within communication networks (Mutz and Martin 2001). At the same time, much of the divergence in these various results is a matter of emphasis and expectation, and the various studies share a great deal in common. For example, Mutz (2002a) points toward the ambivalence producing consequences of political heterogeneity within patterns of political communication among citizens—a theme that is also pursued in the work of Visser and Mirabile (2004), Huckfeldt and Sprague (2000), and Huckfeldt, Mendez, and Osborn (2004).[7]

From a somewhat different vantage point, both Mutz (2002b) and Gibson (1992) focus on network heterogeneity effects on political tolerance. As Gibson (1992: 350) demonstrates, "(w)hy people differ in their levels of intolerance—and with what consequences—cannot be well understood by conceptualizing the individual in social isolation." He shows that homogeneous peer groups, less tolerant spouses, and less tolerant communities place limits on the freedom perceived by individual citizens. Hence, it would appear that normative commitments to tolerance and democratic ideals are likely to be short-lived unless they are reinforced through application in naturally occurring contexts of political communication. (For a complementary analysis, see Gibson's (2001) analysis of networks and civil society in Russia.) Similarly, Mutz (2002a) shows that higher levels of political disagreement within networks correspond to modestly higher levels of tolerance on the part of individuals. Findings such as these would seem to suggest that the likelihood of a political system characterized by high levels of tolerance is reduced to the extent that political tolerance depends on individually based normative commitments disembodied from recurrent patterns of social interaction and political communication.

Baker, Ames, and Renno (2006) provide a compelling analysis of the role played by heterogeneity and disagreement within political communication networks. In their study of the 2002 Brazilian election, they argue that network theories of political behavior have been evaluated in an unfriendly laboratory—the laboratory of the American political environment. In American politics, as in most mature democracies, political parties are highly institutionalized and play an important role in structuring voter choice. In contrast, political parties are underdeveloped in many new democracies, politics is more fluid and volatile, and political communication networks thereby become correspondingly more important. Their focus on heterogeneity and disagreement within networks and contexts is particularly important to their resulting analysis, and the authors shed light on the ways in which volatility is produced and then resolved during the campaign. They argue that deliberation among citizens was crucial to the outcome of the election, and that political communication networks enhanced the civic capacity of both individual citizens and the electorate. In an interesting and complementary analysis, Ikeda et al. (2005) compare partisanship effects and network effects on preference stability in Japan.

Finally, Druckman and Nelson (2003) show that some patterns of persuasion among citizens make it more difficult for citizens to be manipulated by elites. In a

---

[7] For more examples of scholarly disagreement regarding the extent of citizen disagreement, see Gimpel and Lay (2005) and Anderson and Paskeviciute (2005).

novel framing experiment, they show that subjects who discuss an issue within groups marked by diverse opinions are more likely to be immune to issue framing by elites. In this way, the exposure to diverse opinions through processes of social interaction and communication serve to inoculate public opinion against elite imposed frames, and hence interdependent citizens imbedded in heterogeneous networks of opinion are better able to exercise judgments that are independent of elite manipulation.

8 Citizenship Capacity, Social Capital, and the Diffusion of Political Expertise

Network studies of political communication and persuasion provide a theoretical, analytical response to the human limitations of the citizen in democratic politics. If citizens arrived at decisions independently—as self-contained, fully informed actors—their choices might be explained wholly as a consequence of their own devices. Political decision-making could be understood as the product of individual priorities and the alternatives available to particular individuals. The problem is that individual citizens possess neither full information, nor a biased sample of full information, nor the well-formed attitudes and belief systems that would have guided their choices in a coherent manner (Converse 1964). Moreover, seen from the vantage point of an economic theory of political decision-making (Downs 1957), the high costs of becoming informed, coupled with the minimal likelihood of casting a decisive vote, call into question an expectation that rational citizens would invest in the acquisition of information.

This problem—the problem of citizenship capacity—lies at the core of democratic politics, and its analytic implications are quite profound (Gibson 2001). Citizens operate in a complex political environment characterized by inherent uncertainty, and the task of citizenship might well be characterized as reaching decisions and judgments under uncertainty (Tversky and Kahneman 1973). Indeed, the recognition of this challenge has transformed the study of citizens and politics, leading to important new directions in scholarship aimed at identifying the methods and means whereby citizens confront these challenges (Sniderman 1993, Popkin 1991). Important contributions have been generated by cognitive research regarding attitudes, attitude strength, and the use of heuristics in processing political information and reaching decisions (Petty and Krosnick 1995; Lodge and Taber 2000; Sniderman, Brody, and Tetlock 1991).

The study of political communication provides a very direct means to incorporate social capital within the study of public opinion (Ikeda and Richey 2005). A primary benefit that derives from social capital relates to the information that people access through networks of social relationships. These informational benefits are directly related to public opinion because citizens are able to rely on one another for information and guidance in politics. Absent social networks, individuals would be forced to bear the acquisition and processing costs of political information on their own (Downs 1957). In this way, social capital that is accessed through networks of communication produces important efficiencies in the creation of informed public opinion (Coleman 1988).

Ignoring the informational potential of social communication has contributed to an underestimation of the knowledge, information, and sophistication that underlie public opinion, both in terms of individual and aggregate opinion holding (Page and Shapiro 1992; Erikson, MacKuen, and Stimson 2002). The inescapable fact is that individuals often perform quite poorly in providing adequate responses to survey questions regarding basic political knowledge, in providing well-thought-out rationales for their preferences and opinions, and even in providing thoughtful and stable responses to questions that solicit their opinions (Converse 1964; Delli Carpini and Keeter 1996; Sniderman 1993).

At the same time, individuals report more frequent political discussion with other individuals whom they believe know more about politics. Just as important, the descriptive adequacy of their judgments regarding the political expertise of others has been empirically confirmed (Huckfeldt 2001). Hence, political interdependence among citizens helps to explain why public opinion in the aggregate is more sophisticated than the opinions held by the average citizen.

The precise mechanism that leads individuals to depend more heavily on the political experts in their midst is less clear. One explanation is that people use "knowledge proxies" (Lupia 2005, 1992)—they rely on individuals whom they believe to be trustworthy and knowledgeable. Such an explanation fits in quite well with Downs's (1957) original arguments regarding the role of social communication as a cost-saving device for becoming informed. Another explanation for the social diffusion of political expertise is based on an unintentional, agent-based formulation (Axelrod 1997). It is not that individuals consciously look for trustworthy political experts in their midst, but rather that political experts tend to be the politically engaged citizens. Citizens talk with their expert associates more frequently because these particular associates (the experts) are endlessly talking about politics! In this way, the experts' opinions become important in the collective deliberations of democracy because their preferences are self-weighted by their own motivation and engagement.

9 NETWORKS AND COLLECTIVE ACTION

Communication networks are not only important in terms of information transmission and persuasion, but also in terms of mobilizing collective action. Much of the collective action literature has been in response to strategic behavior related to collective action problems (Olson 1966). Unless and until group leadership is able to resolve the free rider problem, groups cannot successfully form to achieve group goals (Salisbury 1969; Chong 1991). As Axelrod (1986) and others have demonstrated, collective action problems are often susceptible to solution in the context of repeated games—in the context of recurrent patterns of relationships among the actors who are seeking to organize a collective effort. Hence, one might argue that solutions to collective action problems can be seen as occurring within networks of relationships among strategic actors who use the information they acquire through repeated interactions to facilitate group efforts.

This insight is carried forward in the work of Yamagishi and Yamagishi (1994), who recognize the importance of networks and network relationships to cooperation and trust in group efforts in their comparison of Japan and the United States. Other efforts recognize the importance of covenants and sanctions to collective action problems (Ostrom, Walker, and Gardner 1992), thereby building on the networks of dyadic exchanges that underlie the creation of collective action. Lubell and Scholz (2001) show that cooperation is more likely to occur in contexts marked by higher levels of reciprocity, and hence it appears that expectations of cooperative behavior are conditioned by past experiences in broader networks of strategic interaction. Possibilities of altruistic punishment (Fehr and Gächter 2002; Fowler 2005a) incorporate the socially contingent nature of cooperation, even in networks where relationships are unlikely to be long-lived. More recently, Ahn, Isaac, and Salmon (2005) explore the endogeneity of groups in collective action settings relative to a dynamic, strategic pattern of network formation that is contingent on individual histories of cooperative behavior.

These bodies of work are intriguing on methodological as well as substantive grounds. By moving network research into the setting of the small group experimental laboratory, an opportunity is created to study the evolution of networks subject to particular experimental manipulations—manipulations that include variations in institutional arrangements. As we have seen, one limitation of the egocentric network technologies is that they are not able fully to exploit the analytic power of network research (Wasserman and Faust 1994). By pursuing the study of networks in the context of experimental research, the way is paved to exploit more fully the analytic utility of social network methodologies, not only relative to collective action and cooperation, but also with respect to communication and persuasion. Indeed, these efforts are serving to reinvigorate the vision of small group research in political science envisioned by Verba (1961) nearly fifty years ago.

10 NETWORKS AND THE ROLE OF GROUPS IN MODERN POLITICS

In conclusion, social networks provide an opportunity for political scientists to rediscover one part of the group basis of politics—to rethink and reconceptualize the role of groups in mass politics and public opinion. At the end of the Second

World War, when survey research and the empirical study of public opinion were in their infancies, nominal membership in many groups carried enormous political meaning. To say that an American voter was an Italian-American, or a Polish-American, or a German-American, or a white southerner, or a union member indicated a great deal about the voter's politics. Similarly, to say that a European voter was a union member, or a Catholic, or a Protestant similarly transmitted a great deal of information about the voter's location in politics and social structure. The political meaning attached to many of these groups has disappeared or been transformed, while other new groups—e.g. Christian fundamentalists, Green voters—have emerged (Kohler 2005; Levine, Carmines, and Huckfeldt 1997; Pappi 2001). Why have the strength and vitality of these patterns diminished over time? Why have other patterns emerged?

The meaning of group membership has always been anchored in patterns of association and interaction—in the networks within which individuals are imbedded. To say that a group is no longer politically meaningful is really to say that a nominal group no longer serves to define and demarcate patterns of social interaction and communication, because it is through these networks that communication and persuasion occur. In this way, studying public opinion within the context of communication networks creates an opportunity to reintroduce the study of groups in political analysis.

A danger related to conceiving groups in terms of networks is the failure to imbed dyads within larger networks of communication (Mendelberg 2005). This danger is especially pronounced in the context of egocentric networks, where it is perhaps natural—although often misleading—to focus attention on the information exchanges that occur between two individuals. These dyadic exchanges take on heightened levels of significance when they are viewed as contingent on an individual's full range of contacts, and one lesson to be derived from Baker, Ames, and Renno (2006), Lubell and Scholz (2001), and Huckfeldt, Johnson, and Sprague (2004) is that every dyad within a network must be viewed in the context of all the other dyads within the network.[8] In short, individuals, dyads, and networks must be analytically decomposed and reassembled to gain insight into the group basis of politics among citizens.

An important issue with respect to networks and the definition and vitality of groups is the spatial distribution of ties within and among various groups (Gimpel and Schuknecht 2003). In an earlier era, an individual's place of residence played a central role in constructing spatial boundaries on the distribution of communication networks (Fuchs 1955). In the modern era, freeways, subways, cell phones, and telecommuting have produced diffuse networks of interaction and communication. Hence, for some people, the spatial boundaries on communication have been dramatically attenuated, thereby producing an important line of inquiry related to the spatial diffusion of group ties (Baybeck and Huckfeldt 2002). The spatially diffuse nature of communication links is not only important in terms of the spatial

---

[8] As Stoker and Jennings (2005) and Zuckerman, Fitzgerald, and Dasovic (2005) show, this is even true for marital dyads.

attenuation of particular dyads, but also for the relative density of networks, for patterns of weak ties (Granovetter 1973) and structural holes (Burt 1992) within networks, and hence for the spread of political information and opinion in time and space, as well as within and beyond the boundaries of traditionally defined groups.

Finally, reported declines in the levels of social capital (Putnam 2000) often focus on the demise of many traditionally defined groups and organizations. Without denying the important implications that attend the disintegration of any form of social and political organization, it is also important to focus attention on the continuing reformulation that underlies the patterns of association serving as the basis for democratic politics (Pappi 2001; Mondak and Mutz 1997, 2001; Mutz and Mondak 2006). An alternative perspective to the decline of social capital argument is that social organization and social interdependence are endemic to any society, and absent a politically repressive regime (Mondak and Gearing 1998), communication among citizens becomes an irrepressible element of any democratic society. Thus, Tocqueville's (1969) insights regarding the importance of voluntary association to the new American republic are valid for any democratic political system, and a central task of political science is to locate the influential patterns of association and communication that are realized in particular places and times.

References

ABELSON, R. 1979. Social clusters and opinion clusters. Pp. 239–56 in *Perspectives on Social Network Research*, ed. P. W. Holland and S. Leinhardt. New York: Academic Press.

ACHEN, C., and SHIVELY, W. 1995. *Cross-level Inference.* Chicago: University of Chicago Press.

AHN, T. K., ISAAC, R., and SALMON, T. 2005. Endogenous group formation. Florida State University: working paper.

ANDERSON, C., and PASKEVICIUTE, A. 2005. Macro-politics and micro-behavior: mainstream politics and the frequency of political discussion in contemporary democracies. Pp. 228–48 in *The Social Logic of Politics*, ed. A. Zuckerman. Philadelphia: Temple University Press.

AXELROD, R. 1986. An evolutionary approach to norms. *American Political Science Review*, 80: 1095–111.

—— 1997. The dissemination of culture: a model with local convergence and global polarization. *Journal of Conflict Resolution*, 41: 203–26.

BAKER, A., AMES, B., and RENNO, L. 2006. Social context and voter volatility in new democracies: networks and neighborhoods in Brazil's 2002 elections. *American Journal of Political Science*, 50: 382–99.

BAYBECK, B., and HUCKFELDT, R. 2002. Urban contexts, spatially dispersed networks, and the diffusion of political information. *Political Geography*, 21: 195–220.

BERELSON, B., LAZARSFELD, P., and McPHEE, W. 1954. *Voting: A Study of Opinion Formation in a Presidential Election.* Chicago: University of Chicago Press.

BOOKS, J., and PRYSBY, C. 1991. *Political Behavior and the Local Context.* New York: Praeger.

BOUDON, R. 1986. *Theories of Social Change.* University of California Press.

BOYD, L. H., and IVERSEN, G. R. 1979. *Contextual Analysis.* Belmont, Calif.: Wadsworth Publishing.

BRYK, A., and RAUDENBUSH, S. 1992. *Hierarchical Linear Models.* Newbury Park, Calif.: Sage.

BURT, R. 1986. A note on sociometric order in the General Social Survey network data. *Social Networks,* 8: 149–74.

—— 1992. *Structural Holes.* Cambridge, Mass.: Harvard University Press.

BUTLER, D., and STOKES, D. 1974. *Political Change in Britain.* New York: St Martin's Press.

CALVERT, R. 1985. The value of biased information: a rational choice model of political advice. *Journal of Politics,* 47: 530–55.

CAMPBELL, A., CONVERSE, P., MILLER, W., and STOKES, D. 1960. *The American Voter.* New York: Wiley.

—— —— —— —— 1966. *Elections and the Political Order.* New York: Wiley.

CANACHE, D. 1996. Looking out my back door: the neighborhood context and perceptions of relative deprivation. *Political Research Quarterly,* 49: 547–71.

CHO, W. 2003. Contagion effects and ethnic contribution networks. *American Journal of Political Science,* 47: 368–87.

CHONG, D. 1991. *Collective Action and the Civil Rights Movement.* Chicago: University of Chicago Press.

COLEMAN, J. 1964. *An Introduction to Mathematical Sociology.* New York: Free Press

—— 1988. Social capital in the creation of human capital. *American Journal of Sociology,* 94: S95–S120.

CONVERSE, P. 1964. The nature of belief systems in mass publics. Pp. 206–61 in *Ideology and Discontent,* ed. D. Apter. New York: Free Press, 206–61.

DELLI CARPINI, M., and KEETER, S. 1996. *What Americans Know about Politics and Why It Matters.* New Haven: Yale University Press.

DENNIS, C. 1991. *Collective Action and the Civil Rights Movement.* Chicago: University of Chicago Press.

DOWNS, A. 1957. *An Economic Theory of Democracy.* New York: Harper & Row.

DRUCKMAN, J., and NELSON, K. 2003. Framing and deliberation: how citizens' conversations limit elite influence. *American Journal of Political Science,* 47: 728–44.

ERIKSON, R., MACKUEN, M., and STIMSON, J. 2002. *The Macro Polity.* New York: Cambridge University Press.

EULAU, H. 1986. *Politics, Self, and Society: A Theme and Variations.* Cambridge, Mass.: Harvard University Press.

FABRIGAR, L., and KROSNICK, J. 1995. Attitude importance and the false consensus Effect. *Personality and Social Psychology Bulletin,* 21: 468–79.

FEHR, E., and GÄCHTER, S. 2002. *Altruistic punishment in humans.* Nature, 415: 137–40.

FESTINGER, L. 1957. *A Theory of Cognitive Dissonance.* Palo Alto, Calif.: Stanford University Press.

FINIFTER, A. 1974. The friendship group as a protective environment for political deviants. *American Political Science Review,* 68: 607–25.

FOWLER, J. 2005a. Altruistic punishment and the origin of cooperation. *Proceedings of the National Academy of Sciences,* 102: 7047–9.

—— 2005b. Turnout in a small world. Pp. 269–87 in *The Social Logic of Politics,* ed. A. Zuckerman. Philadelphia: Temple University Press.

—— Connecting the Congress: A Study of Cosponsorship Networks. *Political Analysis,* 14: 456–87.

FUCHS, L. 1955. American Jews and the presidential vote. *American Political Science Review,* 49: 385–401.

GIBSON, J. 1992. The political consequences of intolerance: cultural conformity and political freedom. *American Political Science Review,* 86: 338–56.

—— 2001. Social networks, civil society, and the prospects for consolidating Russia's demo-cratic transition. *American Journal of Political Science*, 45: 51–69.

GIMPEL, J., and LAY, J. 2005. Party identification, local partisan contexts, and the acquisition of participatory attitudes. Pp. 209–27 in *The Social Logic of Politics*, ed. A. Zuckerman. Philadelphia: Temple University Press.

—— and SCHUKNECHT, J. 2003. *Patchwork Nation*. Ann Arbor: University of Michigan Press.

GOODMAN, L. 1953. Ecological regressions and the behavior of individuals. *American Sociological Review*, 18: 663–6.

—— 1959. Some alternatives to ecological correlation. *American Journal of Sociology*, 64: 610–24.

GRANOVETTER, M. 1973. The strength of weak ties. *American Journal of Sociology*, 78: 1360–80.

—— 1985. Economic action and social structure: the problem of embeddedness. *American Journal of Sociology*, 91: 481–510.

HEINZ, J., LAUMANN, E., NELSON, R., and SALISBURY, R. 1993. *The Hollow Core: Private Interests in National Policy Making*. Cambridge, Mass.: Harvard University Press.

HUCKFELDT, R. 1986. *Politics in Context*. New York: Agathon.

—— 2001. The social communication of political expertise. *American Journal of Political Science*, 45: 425–38.

—— IKEDA, K., and PAPPI, F. 2000. Political expertise, interdependent citizens, and the value added problem in democratic politics. *Japanese Journal of Political Science*, 1: 171–95.

—— —— —— 2005. Patterns of disagreement in democratic politics: comparing Germany, Japan, and the United States. *American Journal of Political Science*, 49: 497–514.

—— JOHNSON, P., and SPRAGUE, J. 2004. *Political Disagreement*. New York: Cambridge University Press.

—— and MENDEZ, J. 2004. Managing political heterogeneity: persistent disagreement within communication networks. Prepared for delivery at the annual meeting of the Midwest Political Science Association, April 2004.

—— —— and OSBORN, T. 2004. Disagreement, ambivalence, and engagement: the political consequences of heterogeneous networks. *Political Psychology*, 26: 65–96.

—— and SPRAGUE, J. 1995. *Citizens, Politics, and Social Communication*. New York: Cambridge University Press.

—— —— 2000. Political consequences of inconsistency: the accessibility and stability of abortion attitudes. *Political Psychology*, 21: 57–79.

—— BECK, P., DALTON, R., LEVINE, J., and MORGAN, W. 1998a. Ambiguity, distorted messages, and nested environmental effects on political communication. *Journal of Politics*, 60: 996–1030.

—— LEVINE, J., MORGAN, W., and SPRAGUE, J. 1998b. Election campaigns, social communication, and the accessibility of perceived discussant preference. *Political Behavior*, 20: 263–94.

—— CARMINES, E., MONDAK, J., PALMER, C. 2005. Blue states, red states, and the problem of polarization in the American electorate. Presented at the annual convention of the American Political Science Association, Washington, DC.

IKEDA, K., and HUCKFELDT, R. 2001. Political communication and disagreement among citizens in Japan and the United States. *Political Behavior*, 23: 23–52.

—— and RICHEY, S. 2005. Japanese network capital: the impact of social networks on Japanese political participation. *Political Behavior*, 27: 239–60.

—— LIU, J., AIDA, M., and WILSON, M. 2005. Dynamics of interpersonal political environment and party identification: longitudinal studies of voting in Japan and New Zealand. *Political Psychology*, 26: 517–42.

KEY, V. O., Jr. 1949. Southern politics in state and nation. New York: Knopf. Reissued by University of Tennessee Press in 1984.

KING, G. 1997. A solution to the ecological inference problem. Princeton: Princeton University Press.

KNOKE, D. 1990. *Political Networks*. New York: Cambridge University Press.

—— PAPPI, F., BROADBENT, J., and TSUJINAKA, Y. 1996. *Comparing Policy Networks*. Cambridge: Cambridge University Press.

KOHLER, U. 2005. Changing class locations and partisanship in Germany. Pp. 117–31 in *The Social Logic of Politics*, ed. A. S. Zuckerman. Philadelphia: Temple University Press.

KOTLER-BERKOWITZ, L. 2005. Friends and politics: linking diverse friendship networks to political participation. Pp. 152–70 in *The Social Logic of Politics*, ed. A. Zuckerman. Philadelphia: Temple University Press.

LAKE, R., and HUCKFELDT, R. 1998. Social networks, social capital, and political participation. *Political Psychology*, 19: 567–84.

LANGTON, K., and RAPOPORT, R. 1975. Social structure, social context, and partisan mobilization: urban workers in Chile. *Comparative Political Studies*, 8: 318–44.

LAUMANN, E. 1973. *Bonds of Pluralism*. New York: Wiley

—— and PAPPI, F. 1976. *Networks of Collective Action: A Perspective on Community Influence Systems*. New York: Academic Press.

LAZARSFELD, P., BERELSON, B., and GAUDET, H. 1948. *The People's Choice*. New York: Columbia University Press.

LEVINE, J., CARMINES, E., and HUCKFELDT, R. 1997. The rise of ideology in the post-New Deal party system, 1972–92. *American Politics Quarterly*, 25: 19–34.

LODGE, M., and TABER, C. 2000. Three steps toward a theory of motivated reasoning. Pp. 183–213 in *Elements of Reason: Understanding and Expanding the Limits of Rationality*, ed. A. Lupia, M. McCubbins, and S. Popkin. Cambridge: Cambridge University Press.

LUBELL, M., and SCHOLZ, J. 2001. Cooperation, reciprocity, and the collective action heuristic. *American Journal of Political Science*, 45: 160–78.

LUPIA, A. 1992. Busy voters, agenda control, and the power of information. *American Political Science Review*, 86: 390–403.

—— 2005. Deliberation, elitism, and the challenges inherent in assessing civic competence. Presented at the annual meeting of the International Society of Political Psychology, Toronto, July 2005.

MACKUEN, M. 1990. Speaking of politics: individual conversational choice, public opinion, and the prospects for deliberative democracy. Pp. 59–99 in *Information and Democratic Processes*, ed. J. Ferejohn and J. Kuklinski. Urbana: University of Illinois Press.

MCPHEE, W., with SMITH, R., and FERGUSON, J. 1963. A theory of informal social influence. Pp. 74–203 in W. McPhee, *Formal Theories of Mass Behavior*. New York: Free Press.

MARSDEN, P. 1987. Core discussion networks of Americans. *American Sociological Review*, 52: 122–31.

—— and FRIEDKIN, N. 1994. Network studies of social influence. Pp. 3–25 in *Advances in Social Network Analysis*, ed. S. Wasserman and J. Galaskiewicz. Thousand Oaks, Calif.: Sage Publications, 3–25.

MENDELBERG, T. 2005. Bringing the group back into political psychology: Erik H. Erikson Early Career Award address. *Political Psychology*, 26: 637–50.

MILLER, W. 1956. One party politics and the voter. *American Political Science Review*, 50: 707–25.

MONDAK, J., and GEARING, A. 1998. Civic engagement in a postcommunist state. *Political Psychology*, 19: 615–37.

—— and MUTZ, D. 1997. What's so great about League bowling? Presented at the annual meeting of the Midwest Political Science Association.

—— —— 2001. Involuntary association: how the workplace contributes to American civic life. Presented at the annual meeting of the Midwest Political Science Association.

Mutz, D. 2002a. The consequences of cross-cutting networks for political participation. *American Journal of Political Science*, 46: 838–55.

—— 2002b. Cross-cutting social networks: testing democratic theory in practice. *American Political Science Review*, 96: 111–26.

—— 2006. *Hearing the Other Side: Deliberative versus Participatory Democracy.* New York: Cambridge University Press.

—— and Martin, P. 2001. Facilitating communication across lines of political difference: the role of mass media. *American Political Science Review*, 95: 97–114.

—— and Mondak, J. 2006. The workplace as a context for cross-cutting political discourse. *Journal of Politics*, 1: 140–55.

Nie, N., Junn, J., and Stehlik-Berry, K. 1996. *Education and Democratic Citizenship in America.* Chicago: University of Chicago Press.

Olson, M. 1965. *The Logic of Collective Action.* Cambridge, Mass.: Harvard University Press.

Ostrom, E., Walker, J., and Gardner, R. 1992. Covenants with and without a sword: self-governance is possible. *American Political Science Review*, 86: 404–17.

Page, B., and Shapiro, R. 1992. *The Rational Public.* Chicago: University of Chicago.

Pappi, F. 2001. Soziale Netzwerke. Pp. 605–16 in *Handwoerterbuch zur Gesellschaft Deutschlands*, ed B. Schaefers and W. Zapf. Opladen: Leske & Budrich.

Pattie, C., and Johnston, R. 1999. Context, conversation and conviction: social networks and voting in the 1992 British General Election. *Political Studies*, 47: 877–89.

Peffley, M., and Rohrschneider, R. 2003. Democratization and political tolerance: a multi-level model of democatic learning in seventeen nations. *Political Research Quarterly*, 56: 243–57.

Petty, R., and Krosnick, J. ed. 1995. *Attitude Strength.* Hillsdale, NJ: Erlbaum.

Popkin, S. 1991. *The Reasoning Voter.* Chicago: University of Chicago Press.

Przeworski, A. 1974. Contextual models of political behavior. *Political Methodology*, 1: 27–61.

—— and Teune, H. 1970. *The Logic of Comparative Social Inquiry.* New York: Wiley.

Putnam, R. 1966. Political attitudes and the local community. *American Political Science Review*, 60: 640–54.

—— 2000. *Bowling Alone: The Collapse and Revival of American Community.* New York: Simon & Schuster.

Roch, C., Scholz, J., and McGraw, K. 2000. Social networks and citizen responses to legal change. *American Journal of Political Science*, 44: 777–91.

Ross, L., Bierbrauer, G., and Hoffman, S. 1976. The role of attribution processes in conformity and dissent. *American Psychologist*, 31: 148–57.

Salisbury, R. 1969. An exchange theory of interest groups. *Midwest Journal of Political Science*, 13: 1–32.

Schneider, M., Scholz, J., Lubell, M., Mindruta, D., and Edwardsen, M. 2003. Building consensual institutions: networks and the National Estuary Program. *American Journal of Political Science*, 47: 143–58.

Segal, D., and Meyer, M. 1974. The social context of political partisanship. Pp. 217–32 in *Social Ecology*, ed. M. Dogan and S. Rokkan. Cambridge, Mass.: MIT Press.

Sniderman, P. 1993. The new look in public opinion research. Pp. 281–303 in *Political Science: The State of the Discipline II*, ed. A. Finifter. Washington, DC: American Political Science Association.

—— Brody, R., and Tetlock, P. 1991. *Reasoning and Choice: Explorations in Political Psychology.* New York: Cambridge University Press.

SPRAGUE, J. 1976. Estimating a Boudon type contextual model: some practical and theoretical problems of measurement. *Political Methodology*, 3: 333–53.

STEENBERGEN, M., and JONES, B. 2002. Modeling multilevel data structures. *American Journal of Political Science*, 46: 218–37.

STOKER, L., and JENNINGS, M. 2005. Political similarity and influence between husbands and wives. Pp. 51–74 in *The Social Logic of Politics*, ed. A. Zuckerman. Philadelphia: Temple University Press.

STRAITS, B. 2000. Ego's important discussants or significant people: an experiment in varying the wording of personal network name generators. *Social Networks*, 22: 123–40.

TINGSTEN, H. 1963. *Political Behavior*, trans Vilgot Hammarling. Totowa, NJ: Bedminster. Originally published in 1937.

TOCQUEVILLE, A. 1969. *Democracy in America*, trans George Lawrence, ed. J. P. Mayer. New York: Harper & Row. Originally published in 1835, 1840.

TVERSKY, A., and KAHNEMAN, D. 1974. Judgment under uncertainty: heuristics and biases. *Science*, 185: 1124–31.

VERBA, S. 1961. *Small Groups and Political Behavior*. Princeton: Princeton University Press.

VISSER, P., and MIRABILE, R. 2004. Attitudes in the social context: the impact of social network composition on individual-level attitude strength. *Journal of Personality and Social Psychology*, 87: 779–95.

WASSERMAN, S., and FAUST, K. 1994. *Social Network Analysis*. New York: Cambridge University Press.

WATTS, D., and STROGATZ, S. 1998. Collective dynamics of "small world" networks. *Nature*, 393: 440–2.

WHITE, H. 1970. *Chains of Opportunity: System Models of Mobility in Organizations*. Cambridge, Mass.: Harvard University Press.

WRIGHT, G. 1976. Community structure and voter decision making in the south. *Public Opinion Quarterly*, 40: 201–15.

YAMAGISHI, T., and YAMAGISHI, M. 1994. Trust and commitment in the United States and Japan. *Motivation and Emotion*, 18: 129–66.

ZUCKERMAN, A. 2005. Returning to the social logic of politics. Pp. 3–21 in *The Social Logic of Politics*, ed. A. Zuckerman. Philadelphia: Temple University Press.

—— FITZGERALD, J., and DASOVIC, J. 2005. Do couples support the same political parties? Sometimes: evidence from British and German Household Panel Surveys. Pp. 75–94 in *The Social Logic of Politics*, ed. A. Zuckerman. Philadelphia: Temple University Press.

CHAPTER 7

POLITICAL COMMUNICATION

HOLLI A. SEMETKO

THE global political communications landscape and opportunities for political communication research continue to be shaped by developments in new technology. The cable and satellite revolutions of the 1970s and 1980s brought the delivery of many channels as well as more opportunities for citizens to turn away from televised political information entirely (Entman 1983). Coverage of the war in Vietnam during the 1960s and early 1970s (Hallin 1986) was much slower than the live news coverage that became routine in the early 1990s when CNN established itself as a global brand while reporting the first Gulf War (Bennett and Paletz 1994). With the arrival of the internet in the 1990s, the new opportunities for political communication and political communication research provided by the availability of new and old media sources online continue to evolve in surprising ways. Unheard of in the late 1990s, political blogging is now a major online industry (Crampton 2004). Certain blogs have become the primary news venue for many of the politically sophisticated, and create opportunities for political communicators in politics and the media to challenge traditional news media in a variety of previously unimagined ways (Oates, Owen, and Gibson 2006). Social movements that interact with mass media in predictable ways (Gamson and Wolfsfeld 1993) are helped by the internet to mobilize support outside routine channels (Bennett and Entman 2001; Norris 2002). The internet is also used by terrorists to go live in making their mark on the global media agenda (Norris, Just, and Kern 2003).

With the ability to transmit information instantaneously around the globe and bring attention to the latest catastrophe or issue, new media technology brings governments and citizens potentially closer together than ever before while at the same time providing greater opportunity to drive them apart (Davis and Owen 1998; Shah, Kwak, and Holbert 2001). Despite global media abundance, citizens in advanced industrial societies have become "distrustful of politicians, skeptical about democratic institutions and disillusioned about how the democratic process functions" (Dalton 2004, 1). While citizens in some low- income "societies in transition" have found ways to use the internet to promote open society, the dramatic changes in Russia over the past two decades show just how quickly a whiff of press freedom can pass (Mickiewicz 1988, 1999). Although the expansion of the European Union to twenty-five member states has brought about major gains and freedom of expression is the norm, most citizens around the world still live in societies without freedom of the press. Most citizens of the world do not experience the media abundance brought by new technology. The global reality is in fact a stark digital divide, both between information rich and poor countries and among publics within those countries (Norris 2001). Political communication and political communication research is not unaffected by this digital divide.

With this global and technological backdrop in mind, this chapter begins with a discussion of research on public opinion, political attitudes, and political communication before turning to political communication research methods in the contexts of new media and convergence. The key concepts of agenda-setting, priming, and framing are then discussed briefly, as well as the state of comparative political communication research. The micro-level effects of media use are discussed along with the macro-level consequences of changes in media environments, using examples from recent parliamentary elections in Europe. In conclusion I discuss opportunities for political communication research in the future.

1 Public Opinion, Political Attitudes, and Political Communication Contexts

Philip Converse's (1962, 1964) seminal research on attitude stability argued that the opinions or beliefs of most Americans display no consistent pattern (also see chapters by Kuklinski and Peyton; Converse). Analysis of American National Election Study (ANES) panel data from 1956, 1958, and 1960 show that so many individuals changed their minds on policy issues it seemed as if answers were given at random. For most people, policy attitudes were *non-attitudes*. Shifts in public opinion were largely explained by a lack of knowledge, interest, and ideology which led to a randomness of opinions on policy-related questions. Another view on what moves public opinion is based on a "rational public" whose opinions are moved by information in a way that displays a rational consistency between policy preferences and values (Page and Shapiro 1992), based on analysis of aggregate public opinion in the US. This perspective does not necessarily contradict Converse because individual-level random changes could appear stable at the aggregate level. Taken together, the two examples help us to think about one of the central problems in public opinion research from a political communication perspective: There is a tension between the individual level and the aggregate level, and many studies focus on one or another and employ only a single methodological approach that often ignores information-related variables. Coping with *non-attitudes* is a continuing challenge for survey researchers (Neijens 2004).

Writing in the early 1960s, Converse (1964) predicted that those with low levels of exposure to news and information, interest in politics, political knowledge, would change their views only randomly or not at all, while those with high levels would remain stable or display systematic change, and those in between would be the most open to influence from the information environment. Three decades later, Zaller (1992) argued that the relationship between attitude change and political awareness is non-linear, and demonstrated that those with moderate levels of knowledge are most likely to be influenced by information. He also claimed that the degree of elite consensus on an issue matters. Different levels of attention to politics and different political values among citizens, along with variation over time in the intensity of oppositional messages in the media, interact to explain both aggregate-level opinion shifts and individual-level changes over time.

Does the information in the media diminish or enhance the role of personal influence or the experience of one's personal networks in the formation of political attitudes? Mutz (1994) argued that the media, by reporting people's experiences and linking them to those of others, help people to make sense of their own personal experience as part of a large societal trend and by doing so potentially affect political opinions, political preferences, and decisions about whether or not to take political action. In *Impersonal Influence*, Mutz (1998) demonstrates the important role played by the media in shaping perceptions of societal-level trends and developments, and how these play a particularly important role in influencing political attitudes.

2 METHODS AND THE NEW MEDIA CONTEXT OF CONVERGENCE

The internet had not yet arrived when the major steps were taken to institutionalize and promote political communication scholarship in the 1980s and early 1990s. Scholars looked back to the pioneering work of sociologist and survey researcher Paul Lazarsfeld (1901–76), a founder of the field of communications research and pioneer in studying the role and impact of media in elections (Lazarsfeld, Berelson, and Gaudet 1944) in recognizing the foundations and importance of political communication research. It is probably not too much of a generalization to say that the body of political communication scholarship is primarily focused on political messages and their connection with and impact upon public opinion, and the institutions that contribute to producing political information.[1] The news media are described as one such political institution (Cook 1998; Schudson 2002).

Political communication research sheds light on how national news environments and the types of information available to most citizens have developed over time. In the US, for example, between 1960 and the early 1990s, US presidential campaign news became more negative and judgmental, less descriptive and less policy oriented, and more preoccupied with opinion polls and candidates' personalities, and these characteristics of campaign news were also evident in the coverage of the first year of the Clinton presidency (Patterson 1994). In comparison with American election news on television, British television coverage of general elections was more voluminous, more issue and policy focused, and less negative (Semetko et al. 1991), and these cross-national differences were largely explained by media and political system characteristics.

Despite the fact that Germany has comparatively higher rates of newspaper readership than many other European Union (EU) countries and comparatively higher rates of internet use, most Germans, like citizens in other EU countries name television news as the primary source of information about politics at election time. In contrast to the US and UK, German television offers more in the way of political and election-related programming available during prime time in the final weeks of the campaign. During the 2005 British general election, for example, the country's flagship main evening news programs (BBC and ITV or Channel 3) after some years of public discussion (Semetko 2000), had finally evacuated prime time to make room for entertainment programming. Audience demographics for early evening news programs in Britain in 2005 reveal quite different profiles from main evening news programs that were pushed beyond prime time into late night slots (after 10:00 pm) when audiences were much smaller and predominantly male.

In contrast to Britain, the overall decline in the visibility of newscasts in Germany from the mid-1980s through the mid-1990s appears considerably stronger for the private channels; prime time still holds a place for news on the public service channels (Pfetsch 1996). Flagship main evening news programs on Germany's two leading public service channels (ARD at 8:00 pm, ZDF at 7:00 pm) as well as the two most widely watched privately owned channels (RTL at 6:30 pm, SAT.1 at 6:45 pm) are experiencing relatively stable audience ratings and market shares, with some fluctuation. Each of these channels carries paid advertising, though the former two are governed by the public service broadcasting ethos, while RTL and SAT.1 are privately owned and operated. Even during the final phase of a highly competitive election campaign, each of these programs devotes not insubstantial portions of

---

[1] There is a great deal of political communication scholarship on rhetorical analysis of public speech in election campaigns, which draws on the classic elements of persuasion (Jamieson 1984, 1988, 1992, 1997).

the time to world events and foreign news. German news reporters and editors for these programs also continue to report on routine political news during the final weeks of an election campaign without actually mentioning the election in some of the news stories that feature the incumbent political leaders. In contrast, British and US reporters are much more likely to explicitly link every mention of a politician in the news to the ongoing election campaign in those countries (Semetko 1996). This tendency among German reporters to discuss routine political news at election time helps to explain the "Kanzlerbonus" or a visibility bonus for the incumbent Chancellor in German television news, and "Regierungsbonus" or a visibility bonus for the incumbent party or parties of government (Semetko and Schoenbach 1994), although the degree of the bonus has fluctuated considerably from one election to the next and even disappeared entirely in highly competitive races.

Research suggests that television news in Germany is less preoccupied with issues and matters of policy, and more attentive to the personalities and personal qualities of political leaders and their electoral chances. Comparing television news coverage during the elections in 1983, 1990, and 1998, Donsbach and Büttner (2005) report a clear tendency towards "tabloidization" as evidenced by a decline in policy news, an increase in personalization in the news, and the use of shorter stories or sequences. The trend was more pronounced on the two aforementioned private channels, but public broadcaster ZDF also appeared to be moving in this direction. These channels carry the daily news programs that the average German turns to in order to follow the major events of importance in the world each day. A host of new German all news channels have emerged in recent years, along with many sports and entertainment outlets.

With the rise of *infotainment* (Brants and Neijens 1998; Moy et al. 2004), and with market developments in the press and television and the general decline in audiences for news in traditional outlets (Hamilton 2003), the traditional starting point for political communication research—the news, its contents and uses by citizens—is no longer so easily captured in a research design. News appears in places other than traditional news programs (Baum 2002, 2003) and in traditional news programs, political reporting appears to be in decline. Political messages in the news exist in both the presence and absence of public affairs reporting. The growth in reporters assigned to report live and often local crime-related news and the increasing emphasis on personalized street crime news stories, for example, may not be considered to be political reporting, but it may have real political consequences for the ways in which citizens evaluate their national political leader (Valentino 1999).

A key part of the current research debate hinges on the issue of access. Access to space and time for reporters wanting to make it into the news agenda each day: Crime reporters, for example, may compete with political reporters for space in the news program or the newspaper. Access to news and information in general among the majority in most countries who do not claim to be highly interested in politics: Those who are less politically interested or aware, for example, may prefer to turn to one of the many entertainment options available in which "soft news" on important issues may appear without deeper context. Baum (2003) argues, for example, that "soft news," exemplified by the ways foreign affairs issues are discussed in entertainment programs, is an effective venue for delivering information about such issues to the audiences with less political interest. And access to news via the internet: internet use remains concentrated among the higher educated, higher-income groups in wealthier societies. For many young adults, under 30, news in conventional formats on television and in the press is passé and for the most part irrelevant to their daily lives. Instead, online sources, talk radio, and entertainment programming are the more popular sources of information on major events.

While the politically interested may be intensely following their favorite pre-selected topics in specialized channels or online and in blogs, the less interested and those not connected to the internet have less opportunity to partake in the campaign. Yet it is precisely those less interested who are in need of information to make up their minds, and who need to be informed about the importance of casting their vote. Lazarsfeld's words in *The People's Choice* come to mind: "the people who already knew how they were going to vote read and listened to more campaign material than the people who still did not know how they would vote. The group which the campaign manager is presumably most eager to reach—the as yet undecided—is the very group which is less likely to read or listen to this propaganda."

Much research focuses on the uses and effects of political communication in a campaign context (see, for example, Patterson and McClure 1976; Patterson, 1980, 1994, 2002 which are seminal studies on the US case), and reveals the importance of the campaign information environment on turnout and vote choice. Referendums are a more recent focus for political communication research. Referendums in the EU's various national and local contexts may play a major role in furthering or hindering the process of European integration. Research on national referendums in European contexts reveals a potentially more important role for the news media to play in influencing vote choice than in general election campaigns, because of the lack of clear cues from political parties in many referendums, due to the ways in which national party systems often fracture among the "Yes" and "No" camps, sometimes splitting parties and coalition partners. Editorial decisions taken by journalists, to bring one or another personality into the news, or to frame the referendum issue by focusing on one or another "subtopic" of the issue, may considerably alter the campaign agendas of the two opposing camps in unanticipated ways, and ultimately help to tip the balance towards one outcome (de Vreese and Semetko 2004a, 2004b).

Several political communication studies focused directly on the effects of news on public opinion, drawing primarily on traditional research methods such as analysis of cross-sectional survey data, panel survey designs, focus groups, and lab-based experiments (see Gamson 1992; Neuman, Just, and Crigler 1992; Iyengar and Kinder 1987, Iyengar 1991). Others focus on how the news agenda was formed and the role of news sources in shaping the news agenda, the characteristics of election news content and the role of journalists and political actors in shaping that content, and how that compares over time or cross-nationally (see, for example, Blumler and Gurevitch 1995; Cook 1998; Entman 2004).

One of the key characteristics of media convergence is an emphasis on visuals, which we may expect more of, in relation to text, in the media of the future. Doris Graber's (2001) research demonstrates the vital role played by visuals in political learning, and the retention and understanding of political information. As television and the internet become more graphic and visual than text driven, these will become more important sources for political learning. There are implications for the "unsophisticated" who differ from sophisticated television viewers in handling complex messages that require "complex processing at both the verbal and audiovisual levels" (Graber 2001: 35).

3 SURVEYS, EXPERIMENTS, TECHNOLOGY, AND THE INTERNET

Surveys based on random representative samples provide an opportunity to generalize findings to the public as a whole, and polls have been a main source of data for political communication research (Althaus 2003). One of the challenges faced by political communication researchers has been in the quality and number of survey questions available to provide insight into media use,[2] and the difficulties with measuring exposure (Price and Neijens 1997). The research on media effects puts forth broadly conflicting explanations: media use diminishes knowledge and involvement and contributes to demobilization and political cynicism, media use contributes to learning and political involvement, trust, efficacy, and mobilization. Aarts and Semetko (2003) demonstrate that conclusions about the "virtuous" relationship between media use and public opinion are misplaced (Norris 2000). Instead, they find evidence in support of a dual effects hypothesis among a national electorate in a long-standing European democracy, with positive (or negative) effects on knowledge, efficacy, and turnout linked to the structure of the audience for television news.[3] There is also evidence that European voters can be both cynical and engaged in electoral processes, particularly in reference to recent referendum campaigns (de Vreese and Semetko 2004a).

---

[2] This is most apparent in the time-series for the American National Election Study (ANES) in which two questions, one on exposure to news, and one on attention to news, were often asked. This provided a model for many other national election studies around the world, though ANES has occasionally devoted major portions of pilot and standard studies to political communication related questions. An elaborate set of media exposure questions was first developed in the context of the 1998 Dutch National Election Study (DNES) to gain insight into the debate over the relationship between media use and political cognition, attitudes, and mobilization.

[3] These relationships remain significant when controlled for political interest, age, education and other types of media exposure. Aarts and Semetko (2003) also address a problem central to media effects research, the problem of endogeneity. Lacking panel data, they use two-stage least squares (2SLS) with a statistic to test for endogeneity to address these concerns. This strengthens their conclusions because it largely rules out self-selection.

Experiments provide control over the source of influence, though traditionally the comparatively small samples provide a stumbling block to generalizing effects to the public. Despite the careful execution and compelling findings in two of the seminal studies in political communication research based on experiments (see Iyengar and Kinder 1990; Cappella and Jamieson 1997), the authors themselves note that while experiments are high in internal validity, they rank low in comparison with surveys on external validity.

The internet adds an entirely new research dimension to Harold Lasswell's (1948) model based on the question: "Who says what to whom and with what effect?" The changing technology arena and growth of the internet produce a wealth of research opportunities for political communication scholars. Experiments (and surveys) can now be conducted online, reducing the costs per participant and providing an opportunity for faster fieldwork in response to public events and crises, and with much larger experimental samples. Iyengar (2005) believes that this is the method of choice for experimental researchers now and in the future. The drawback at present is the unrepresentative character of internet users, who tend to be more educated, white, and male, in comparison with the general public. The internet itself also provides a new venue for research as scholars develop the role of the internet in organizing social movements and global campaigns on such issues as corporate social responsibility, the environment, and human rights (Bennett and Entman 2001; also see chapter by Margolis).

As cable and satellite technology in the US now make it possible to identify the (political) advertising broadcast at the (constituency) target level, researchers have gone beyond panel and cross-sectional survey data and experimental studies of media and communication effects, to investigate the links between the two. Research on political advertising examines the content and framing of the message and experimental tests of effects (Kaid and Holz-Bacha 2006), the negative character of advertising (APSR 1999), and negative campaigning and the consequences for political mobilization (Kahn and Kenney 1999). The new technology now available in the US to capture targeted advertising and to identify its audience adds a new dimension to the investigation of the effects of television advertising in election campaigns (Freedman and Goldstein 1999; Goldstein and Freedman 2002). Coupled with greater knowledge about media contents and uses during election campaigns, survey researchers have linked media content and information sources in modeling political attitudes, preferences, and behavior in unprecedented ways in the past decade (Banducci and Semetko 2003).

Political communication has also become more central to national election studies over the past two decades, as they have evolved from an almost exclusive preoccupation with party identification and long-term structural predictors of vote choice, to a range of public opinion-related dependent variables such as evaluations of the importance of issues, parties and leaders, general political attitudes such as trust in institutions and political efficacy, short-term influences on political participation and turnout, and concern about the spillover of campaign effects on attitudes into routine periods.

4 Key Concepts in Political Communication Research

Agenda setting, priming, and framing are key concepts in political communication research. The debate over whether and how these concepts, processes, or theories, in terms of effects on audiences, are actually related (Scheufele 2000), is not addressed here. I briefly review developments in agenda-setting, priming, and framing research.

4.1 Agenda Setting

The agenda-setting hypothesis suggests that the media play a major role in shaping the issue priorities of citizens, simply by choosing to give priority in the news to some stories rather than others. Research testing the agenda-setting hypothesis has drawn primarily on two sources of data: content analysis to establish the most important issues in the news and public opinion captured in cross-sectional surveys, time-series, panel studies, and experiments. Over the past few decades, hundreds of studies have found support for the hypothesis of media agenda-setting effects (for reviews, see McCombs 2004; McCombs, Einsiedel, and Weaver 1991; McCombs and Shaw 1993; Rogers, Dearing, and Bregman 1993). At the same time, however, searching for agenda-setting effects does not always lead to finding them. General elections in the UK in the 1980s and 1990s provided more than one example in which media agendas and audience agendas failed to coincide (see e.g. Miller et al. 1990; Norris et al. 1999), for example.

The agenda-setting hypothesis holds that the most prominent issues in the news are also the issues that become the most important in public opinion. McCombs and Shaw (1972) first applied the concept in a community study of media agenda setting in the 1968 US presidential campaign, comparing the rank order of issues in the news with those in public opinion and found a strong and significant correlation between the campaign agenda in the media and the public agenda. The study set forth the hypothesis that agenda setting is a process that is led by the news media.

A year-long panel study in the 1976 US presidential election identified the relative strengths of television and the newspapers in agenda setting and established that these effects vary over time, and established the causal link from media to public agendas (Weaver et al. 1981). A multi-wave panel study of the same 1976 campaign also showed that newspapers were more important than TV news for political learning and concluded that the more the issue was reported in the press the more low interest readers learned about the issue (Patterson 1980, 159).

Iyengar and Kinder (1987, 12) studied agenda setting with members of the general public within a controlled experimental setting in a routine (non-campaign period).

Their experiments and time-series analyses provided further substantial support for the agenda-setting hypothesis and concluded: "By attending to some problems and ignoring others, television news shapes the American public's political priorities. These effects appear to be neither momentary, as our experimental results indicate, nor permanent, as our time-series results reveal" (Iyengar and Kinder 1987, 33).

The type of issue may condition media power to influence public agendas. Real-world indicators may enhance or diminish the media message. "Unobtrusive" issues—such as foreign affairs issues with which viewers have little or no direct experience—are more susceptible to agenda setting (Baum 2002). One's civic agenda (his or her view of the most important issues or problems facing the community) may be quite different from one's personal agenda (his or her opinion about the most important problems he or she faces). Less support for the agenda-setting hypothesis is found when one's personal agenda is the focus of research (McLeod, Becker, and Byrnes 1974).

4.2 Priming

In a study of citizens' responses to Watergate, it was found that those with a "high need for orientation about politics" actually learn what issues "to use in evaluating certain candidates and parties, not just during political campaigns, but also in the longer period between campaigns (Weaver, McCombs, and Spellman 1975, 471). This process came to be described as *priming*. Earlier seminal studies also found evidence of the media's role in shaping the standards by which citizens evaluate political leaders and candidates (Patterson 1980; Patterson and McClure 1976; Protess and McCombs 1991; Weaver et al. 1981).

Social psychologists Fiske and Taylor (1984) defined priming broadly as the effects of prior context on the interpretation and retrieval of information. Iyengar and Kinder (1987) and Krosnick and Kinder (1990) defined priming more specifically as changes in the standards used by the public to evaluate political leaders, and found support for the priming hypothesis in their experiments (see also Krosnick and Brannon 1993; Miller and Krosnick 2000).

Peter (2002) critically assesses more than thirty studies from the fields of psychology, communication, and political science that deal explicitly with *media priming*, and provides a valuable theoretical contribution. Roskos-Ewoldsen, Klinger, and Roskos-Ewoldsen (2002) provide a meta-analysis of the priming literature that incorporates the research in the areas of violence as well as politics questions whether media priming actually shares characteristic common to the priming studied by cognitive and social psychologists. An important question for future media and psychological priming research is whether stronger priming effects result from more intense media primes. Together, these two studies illustrate the need to further distinguish priming effects from what has been described as that which is "chronically accessible" (see e.g. Lau 1989), both theoretically and operationally (see also Domke, Shah, and Wackman 1998).[4]

4.3 Framing

Framing focuses on the relationship between issues in the news and the public perceptions of these issues. The concept of framing "expands beyond agenda-setting research into *what* people talk or think about by examining *how* they think and talk about issues in the news" (Pan and Kosicki 1993, 70; see also Pan and Kosicki 2001; and Jasperson et al. 1998).

The process of framing refers to selecting "some aspects of a perceived reality" to enhance their salience "in such a way as to promote a particular problem definition, causal interpretation, moral evaluation, and/or treatment recommendation" (Entman 1993, 53). Framing effects have been defined as "changes in judgment engendered by subtle alterations in the definition of judgment or choice of problems" (Iyengar 1987, 816) or "one in which salient attributes of a message (its organization, selection of content, or thematic structure) render particular thoughts applicable, resulting in their activation and use in evaluations" (Price, Tewkesbury, and Powers 1997, 486).

Over the past three decades, our understanding of frames and framing effects has been advanced considerably by research that has often focused on the US context (for recent reviews and examples see Reese et al. 2001 and Shah et al. 2004). Research on framing has also advanced theoretically and methodologically with research in contemporary European contexts such as national media reporting on the European Union and European parliamentary elections (de Vreese et al. 2005), political campaigning in cross-national comparative electoral contexts in Europe (Esser and D'Angelo 2003), political reporting on protest and conflict in the Middle East (Wolfsfeld 1997, 2004), and news reporting on political scandals and its consequences (Canel and Sanders 2005).

Studies on how the news agenda is formed distinguish times of peace and prosperity when the press is more likely to be critical and reflexive from times of war and conflict when the press is more likely to reflect the national interest (Hallin 1986). The term "indexing" is used to describe how the national debate in the news tends to be found in the range of views held by public officials, in other words, "controversy and debate in media content conform to the contours of debate found among political elites whom journalists regard as decisive in the outcomes of the issues in the news" (Livingston and Bennett 2003: 366). News is thus indexed or pegged to official input. Entman (2004) shows, however, that even though the White House dominates the US news, it does not always control the way in which the news story is framed and thus, journalists, by criticizing the President and the Administration, are not always to be found indexing

---

[4] Complex interactions between knowledge, exposure, and interest led Krosnick and Brannon (1993) to revise the conclusion of Krosnick and Kinder (1990) on the knowledge and attentiveness (exposure and interest) groups most likely to be primed and the sign or direction of the priming effects of these variables. There is also some evidence to suggest that priming effects may occur across the board and may not always be mediated by levels of political involvement (see also Peter 2002).

their articles to official input. Entman (2004) instead proposes a "cascading" model of elite influence on public opinion via the media.

5 Political Communication in the Context of Media and Political Systems

Cross-national comparative political communication research has been the focus a number of notable volumes over the past two decades. These include some that focus on the development of theory (Blumler, McLeod, and Rosengren 1992); as well as more general overviews of the comparative field (Bennett and Entman 1994; Esser and Pfetsch 2004); and such topics as political communication in elections in France or Britain and the US (Kaid, Gerstle, and Sanders 1991; Semetko et al. 1991), and in modern democracies more generally (Swanson and Mancini 1996, Asard and Bennett 1997); as well as political communication in the context of politics in Israel and Palestine (Wolfsfeld 1997, 2004), Latin America (Waisbord 2000) and the expanding European Union (de Vreese 2002; Peter 2003).

Hallin and Mancini (2004) set forth an analytical framework to guide the comparative analysis of media systems and the study of political communication within those systems. They describe the Mediterranean "polarlized pluralist" model, the North Central European or "democratic corporatist" model, and the North Atlantic or "liberal" model. The theoretical insights into the forces and limits of homogenization also provide food for thought on the challenges presented in studying the influences on and effects of popular transnational media. Arabic-language Al-Jazeera is just one example of a transnational television network that claims to be objective in offering two sides to every issue, though analysis of its advertising, current affairs and news programming on the subject of the veil identifies the channel's religious agenda (Cherribi 2006).

5.1 Campaigns and Mobilization

One would expect media coverage to be greater in elections that are more salient, in races that are more competitive and when campaign expenditure is greater. Citizen engagement in these campaigns also can be expected to be greater. In one of the first studies to examine the impact of media coverage on European elections, Blumler et al. (1983) also argue that turnout in the 1979 European parliamentary elections was higher in countries in which there appeared to be more active campaigns: greater visibility and more partisan coverage of the election was associated with higher turnout.

Research on the uses and influence of the news media in comparison with other campaign activities in the 1999 European parliamentary election campaigns in all fifteen EU member countries examined two main aspects of campaign coverage that may influence citizen engagement in election campaigns—the visibility of the campaign and the tone of coverage. A visible campaign may mobilize voting by increasing the perceived benefits of voting. Traditionally party activities are seen as mobilizing efforts that encourage turnout, but a high visibility campaign in the news is also likely to bring it to the attention of potential voters and not necessarily dependent upon a party's on-the-ground activities. The tone of coverage may also play a mobilizing role. The evidence is mixed on the impact of negative advertising and it is not at all clear that it always demobilizes (Lau et al. 1999; Ansolabehere, Iyengar, and Simon 1999). Negative news may contribute to cynicism, but negative information tends to be more easily remembered and thus more effective at enhancing citizens' overall information levels. Kahn and Kenney (1999) show, for example, that it is only one form of negative campaigning that demobilizes—"mudslinging."

The "second order" nature of European parliamentary elections has been widely discussed (van der Eijk and Franklin 1996). In the minds of voters, parties and possibly candidates, these elections do not carry the same weight as national elections, and the task of engaging voters in the election is in many ways more difficult than in national elections. The European parliamentary election campaign may be more hard fought when parties are in disagreement over the future of Europe and research shows that anti-EU parties do have an influence on the amount of coverage the campaign receives and in mobilizing engagement in the campaign (Banducci and Semetko 2003). In the 1999 European parliamentary election campaign, for example, coverage was in fact more visible on both public and commercial channels in countries in which there was an active anti-EU party, one or more parties that by definition campaign against furthering European integration. Those parties, despite being against the EU, stood candidates for election to the European Parliament on an anti-EU platform. Countries with anti-EU parties devoted more TV news to the campaign, on both public and private channels, and a greater portion of the public news program was devoted to the campaign in comparison with private news programs in those countries.

For an election campaign that receives comparatively little attention in the news not only in comparison with national election campaigns (Semetko, de Vreese, and Peter 2000), but also in comparison with coverage devoted to other regular EU events such as the Summit meetings of EU heads of state (Semetko, van der Brug, and Valkenburg 2003, Semetko and Valkenburg 2000), or extraordinary events such as the launch of the euro (de Vreese, Peter, and Semetko 2001), as well as EU referendums, campaign news, and routine political news (Peter, Semetko, and de Vreese 2003; Peter, Lauf, and Semetko 2004), it is not surprising that the European level of government has comparatively less importance in the public mind. Reporting on the EU is not easy, not only because the visuals are often dull and bureaucratic, but also because the news organizations themselves experience real constraints when reporting on the EU.

The 1999 study examining different forms of engagement in the campaign found that strong anti-EU party campaigning in a country is associated with more news coverage about the election campaign in that country, but also negatively associated with citizens' interest in the campaign, as well as passive and active engagement: The more neutral or positive the tone of the news, the more it diminishes the negative effect of an anti-EU party on citizen engagement in the campaign. Citizens who spend more days watching public television are more likely to be actively engaged while days spent viewing television news on private stations had no significant effect on active engagement (Banducci and Semetko 2003). This pattern fits with that found in national elections in the Netherlands, where the consequences of an electorate divided by their information choices appear to be real differences in levels of engagement and knowledge (Aarts and Semetko 2003).

With the enlargement of the European Union (EU) from fifteen to twenty-five member states in May 2004, Europe grew by an equivalent number of national media and political systems which share some characteristics but not others, making European parliamentary election campaigns an especially fertile ground for cross-national comparative political communication research. Building public engagement with the development of the European level of governance is viewed by many EU staff and legislators in Brussels as a problem of political communication. The term "new" Europe emerged to describe the ten new member states in central Europe and "old" Europe came to describe the prior fifteen member states. And this distinction proved useful in comparing the contents and effects of European parliamentary election campaign communication among many member states in 1999 and 2004. The average visibility of the election campaigns in the news increased slightly from 1999 to 2004 in the old member states, and on average the campaigns were more visible in the new member states than the old. "Old" and "new" states also differed in the evaluation of the EU—news in the old member states on average was more negative towards the EU, with a mixed pattern emerging in the new member states (de Vreese et al. 2005, 2006). More visible European parliamentary election campaigns lead to greater participation or turn-out in those elections (Banducci and Semetko 2003).

6 CONCLUSION

As technology, communications and the internet have made it possible for news to be instantaneously transmitted and received around the globe, political communication research has also shifted from a preoccupation with local and national contexts to increasingly include international and comparative contexts. Despite the increasing prevalence of transnational audiences and interested publics around the globs, media systems, like party and political systems, continue to remain largely nationally bounded. An understanding of media and political systems, and their evolution and current form, is a necessary precursor for teaching and doing political communication research. Political communication scholars who come together at various professional meetings are often experts in their own national and regional contexts, making comparative political communication research challenging and exciting.

A new direction in political communication research involves other forms of technology to investigate cognitive processing of information. New technology in the form of functional magnetic resonance imaging (fMRI) is being used to study why Democrats and Republicans can hear the same information but reach opposite conclusions (Westen et al. in press). Physiological research of this kind, and the role played by emotions in political information processing, may become especially relevant to our future understanding of framing effects.

As we look into the future, the historically seminal concept of selective exposure may become central again in media abundant societies (Mutz 2001); selective exposure refers to selecting media that reflect one's political predispositions. But the media still hold an advantage over one's personal friends or networks, in the ability to expose one to views different from one's own. Mutz and Martin (2001, 97) put it this way: "individuals are exposed to far more dissimilar political views via news media than through interpersonal political discussants. The media advantage is rooted in the relative difficulty of selectively exposing oneself to those sources of information, as well as the lesser desire to do so, given the impersonal nature of mass media."

The concept of selective exposure nevertheless may further our understanding of the problem of access to digital information resources, including the digital divide within "media rich" societies. There are many poor countries on the other side of the digital divide, struggling to jump into the global economy while at the same time combating serious infrastructure, education, and health problems. Political communication research in those "media poor" societies will take the form of addressing the role of communication and information in addressing these societal problems.

References

AARTS, K., and SEMETKO, H. A. 2003. The divided electorate: effects of media use on political involvement. *Journal of Politics*, 65 (3): 759–84.

ALTHAUS, S. L. 2003. *Collective Preferences in Democratic Politics: Opinion Surveys and the Will of the People.* New York: Cambridge University Press.

ANSOLABEHERE, S., IYENGAR, S., and SIMON, A. 1999. Replicating experiments using aggregate and survey data: the case of negative advertising and turnout. *American Political Science Review*, 93 (4): 901–10.

APSR 1999. Special *American Political Science Review* issue devoted to advertising, 93 (4).

ASARD, E., and BENNETT, W. L. 1997. *Democracy and the Marketplace of Ideas: Communication and Government in Sweden and the United States.* Cambridge: Cambridge University Press.

BANDUCCI, S. A., and SEMETKO, H. A. 2003. Media and mobilization in the 1999 European parliamentary election. Pp. 189–204 in *Europe, Parliament and the Media*, ed. M. Bond. London: Federal Trust.

BAUM, M. 2002. Sex, lies and war: how soft news brings foreign policy to the inattentive public. *American Political Science Review,* 96 (1): 91–109.

—— 2003. *Soft News Goes to War: Public Opinion and American Foreign Policy in the New Media Age.* Princeton: Princeton University Press.

BENNETT, L., and ENTMAN, R. M. eds. 2001. *Mediated Politics: Communication in the Future of Democracy.* New York: Cambridge University Press.

—— and PALETZ, D. L. eds. 1994. *Taken by Storm: The Media, Public Opinion, and U.S. Foreign Policy in the Gulf War.* Chicago: University of Chicago Press.

BLUMLER, J. G. ed. 1983. *Communicating to Voters. Television in the First European Parliamentary Elections.* London: Sage.

—— and GUREVITCH, M. 1995. *The Crisis of Public Communication.* London: Routledge.

—— McLEOD, J., and ROSENGREN, K. E. (1992). *Comparatively Speaking.* Newbury Park, Calif.: Sage.

BRANTS, K., and NEIJENS, P. 1998. The Infotainment of politics. *Political Communication,* 15 (2): 149–64.

CANEL, M. J., and SANDERS, K. 2005. *Morality Tales: Political Scandals and the Media in Britain and Spain in the 1990s.* Creskill, NJ: Hampton Press.

CAPPELLA, J. N., and JAMIESON, K. H. eds. 1997. *Spiral of Cynicism: The Press and the Public Good.* New York: Oxford University Press.

CHERRIBI, S. 2006. From Baghdad to Paris: Al-Jazeera and the veil. *Harvard Journal of Press/Politics,* 11 (2): 121–38.

CONVERSE, P. E. 1962. Information flow and stability of partisan attitudes. *Public Opinion Quarterly,* 26 (4): 578–99.

—— 1964. Nature of belief systems in mass publics. Pp. 206–61 in *Ideology and Discontent,* ed. D. Apter. New York: Free Press.

COOK, T. E. 1998. *Governing with the News: The News Media as a Political Institution.* Chicago: University of Chicago Press.

CRAMPTON, J. W. 2004. *The Political Mapping of Cyberspace.* Chicago: University of Chicago Press.

DALTON, R. 2004. *Democratic Challenges, Democratic Choices: The Erosion of Political Support in Advanced Industrial Democracies.* New York: Oxford University Press.

DAVIS, R., and OWEN, D. 1998. *New Media and American Politics.* New York: Oxford University Press.

DE VREESE, C. H. 2002. *Framing Europe: Television News and European Integration.* Amsterdam: Aksant.

—— PETER, J., and H. A. SEMETKO. 2001. Framing politics at the launch of the euro: a cross-national comparative study of frames in the news. *Political Communication,* 18 (2): 107–22.

—— and SEMETKO, H. A. 2004*a. Political Campaigning in Referendums: Framing the Referendum Issue.* London: Routledge.

—— —— 2004*b.* News matters: influences on the vote in a referendum campaign. *European Journal of Political Research,* 43: 699–722.

—— BANDUCCI, S. A., SEMETKO, H. A., and BOOMGAARDEN, H. G. 2005. "Offline": the 2004 EP elections on television news in the enlarged Europe. *Information Polity,* 10 (3): 177–88.

—— —— —— —— 2006. The news coverage of the 2004 European Parliamentary election campaign in 25 countries. *European Union Politics,* 7 (4).

DOMKE, D., SHAH, D. V., and WACKMAN, D. B. 1998. Media priming effects: accessibility, association, and activation. *International Journal of Public Opinion Research,* 10 (1): 51–74.

DONSBACH, W., and BÜTTNER, K. 2005. Boulevardisierungstrend in deutschen Fernsehnachrichten. *Publizistik,* 50 (1): 21–38.

ENTMAN, R. B. 1983. *Democracy without Citizens: Media and the Decay of American Politics*. Oxford: Oxford University Press.

—— 1993. Framing: toward clarification of a fractured paradigm. *Journal of Communication*, 43: 51–8.

—— 2004. *Projections of Power: Framing News, Public Opinion, and U.S. Foreign Policy*. Chicago: University of Chicago Press.

ESSER, F., and D'ANGELO, P. 2003. Framing the press and the publicity process: a content analysis of metacoverage in campaign 2000 network news. *American Behavioral Scientist*, 46 (5): 617–41.

—— and PFETSCH, B. eds. 2004. *Comparing Political Communication: Theories, Cases, and Challenges*. Cambridge: Cambridge University Press.

FISKE, S. T., and TAYLOR, S. E. 1984. *Social Cognition*. Reading, Mass.: Addison-Wesley.

FREEDMAN, P., and GOLDSTEIN, K. 1999. Measuring media exposure and the effects of negative campaign ads. *American Journal of Political Science*, 43 (4): 1189–208.

GAMSON, W. A. 1992. *Talking Politics*. New York: Cambridge University Press.

—— and WOLFSFELD, G. 1993. Movements and media as interacting systems. *Annals of the American Academy of Political and Social Science*, 528: 114–25.

GOLDSTEIN, K. M., and FREEDMAN, P. 2002. Campaign advertising and voter turnout: new evidence for a stimulation effect. *Journal of Politics*, 64 (3): 721–40.

GRABER, D. A. 1988. *Processing the News: How People Tame the Information Tide*, 2nd edn. White Plains: Longman.

—— 2001. *Processing Politics: Learning from Television in the Internet Age*. Chicago: University of Chicago Press.

—— 2005. Political communication faces the 21st century. *Journal of Communication*, 55 (3): 479–507. (With the assistance of James M. Smith.)

HALLIN, D. C. 1986. *The Uncensored War: The Media and Vietnam*. Los Angeles: University of California Press.

—— and MANCINI, P. 2004. *Comparing Media Systems. Three Models of Media and Politics*. Cambridge: Cambridge University Press.

HAMILTON, J. T. 2003. *All the News That's Fit to Sell: How the Market Transforms Information into News*. Princeton: Princeton University Press.

HERR, P. J. 2002. The impact of campaign appearances on the 1996 election. *Journal of Politics*, 64 (3): 904–16.

IYENGAR, S. 1987. Television news and citizens' explanations of national affairs. *American Political Science Review*, 81 (3): 815–32.

—— 1991. *Is anyone responsible?* Chicago: Chicago University Press.

—— 2005. The state of the field report. *Political Communication Report*, 15 (3).

—— and KINDER, D. R. (1987). *News that matters*. Chicago: University of Chicago Press.

JACKSON, R. A. 1996. A reassessment of voter mobilization. *Political Research Quarterly*, 49 (2): 331–50.

JAMIESON, K. H. 1984. *Packaging the Presidency: A History and Criticism of Presidential Advertising*. New York: Oxford University Press.

—— 1988. *Eloquence in an Electronic Age*. New York: Oxford University Press.

—— 1992. *Dirty Politics: Deception, Distraction, and Democracy*. New York: Oxford University Press.

JASPERSON, A. E., SHAH, D. V., WATTS, M., FABER, R. J., and FAN, D. P. 1998. Framing the public agenda: media effects on the importance of the federal budget deficit. *Political Communication*, 15: 205–24.

KAHN, K. F., and KENNEY, P. J. 1999. Do negative campaigns mobilize or suppress turnout? Clarifying the relationship between negativity and participation. *American Political Science Review*, 93 (4): 877–89.

KAID, L. L., GERSTLE, J., and SANDERS, K. R. eds. 1991. *Mediated Politics in Two Cultures: Presidential Campaigning in the United States and France.* New York: Praeger.

—— and HOLZ-BACHA, C. 2006. *The Sage Handbook of Political Advertising.* New York: Sage.

KATZ, E., and LAZARSFELD, P. F. eds. 1955. *Personal Influence: The Part Played by People in the Flow of Mass Communications.* Glencoe, Ill: Free Press.

KROSNICK, J. A., and BRANNON, L. A. 1993. The impact of the Gulf War on the ingredients of presidential evaluations: multidimensional effects of political involvement. *American Political Science Review*, 87: 963–75.

—— and KINDER, D. R. 1990. Altering the foundations of support for the President through priming. *American Political Science Review*, 8: 497–512.

LASSWELL, H. D. 1948. *The Analysis of Political Behavior: An Empirical Approach.* London: K. Paul, Trench, Trubner & Co.

LAU, R. R. 1989. Individual and contextual influences on group identification. *Social Psychology Quarterly*, 52 (3): 220–31.

—— SIGELMAN, L., HELDMAN, C., and BABBIT, P. 1999. The effects of negative political advertisements: a meta-analytical assessment. *American Political Science Review*, 93 (4): 851–76.

LAZARSFELD, P. F., BERELSON, B., and GAUDET, H. 1944. *The People's Choice.* New York: Columbia University Press.

LIVINGSTON, S., and BENNETT, W. L. 2003. Gatekeeping, indexing, and live event news: is technology altering the construction of news? *Political Communication*, 20 (4): 363–80.

McCOMBS, M. E. 2004. *Advances in Agenda-Setting.* Austin, Tex.: University of Texas Press.

—— EINSIEDEL, E., and WEAVER, D. 1991. *Contemporary Public Opinion: Issues and the News.* Hillsdale, NJ: Lawrence Erlbaum.

—— and SHAW, D. L. 1972. The agenda-setting function of mass media. *Public Opinion Quarterly*, 36: 176–87.

—— —— 1993. The evolution of agenda-setting theory: 25 years in the marketplace of ideas. *Journal of Communication*, 43 (2): 58–66.

McLEOD, J. M., BECKER, L. B., and BYRNES, J. E. 1974. Another look at the agenda-setting function of the press. *Communication Research*, 1: 3–33.

MICKIEWICZ, E. 1988. *Split Signals: Television and Politics in the Soviet Union.* New York: Oxford University Press.

—— 1999. *Changing Channels: Television and the Struggle for Power in Russia.* New York: Oxford University Press.

MILLER, J. M., and KROSNICK, J. A. 2000. News media impact on the ingredients of Presidential evaluations: politically knowledgeable citizens are guided by a trusted source. *American Journal of Political Science*, 44: 301–15.

MILLER, W. L., CLARKE, H. D., HARROP, M., LeDUC, L., and WHITELEY, P. F. 1990. *How Voters Change: The 1987 British Election Campaign in Perspective.* Oxford: Clarendon.

MOY, P., McCLUSKEY, M. R., McCOY, K., and SPRATT, M. 2004. Political correlates of local news media use. *Journal of Communication*, 54: 532–46.

MUTZ, D. C. 1994. Contextualizing personal experience: the role of mass media. *Journal of Politics*, 56 (3): 689–714.

—— 1998. *Impersonal Influence: How Perceptions of Mass Collectives Affect Political Attitudes.* Cambridge: Cambridge University Press.

—— 2001. The future of political communication research: reflections on the occasion of Steve Chaffee's retirement from Stanford University. *Political Communication*, 18 (2): 231–6.

—— and MARTIN, P. S. 2001. Facilitating communication across lines of political difference: the role of mass media. *American Political Science Review*, 95 (1): 97–114.

NEIJENS, P. C. 2004. Coping with the non-attitudes phenomenon: a survey research approach. Pp. 295–313 in *Studies in Public Opinion: Attitudes, Nonattitudes, Measurement Error and Change*, ed. W. E. Saris and P. Sniderman. Princeton: Princeton University Press.

NEUMAN, W. R., JUST, M. R., and CRIGLER, A. N. 1992. *Common Knowledge. News and the Construction of Political Meaning*. Chicago: University of Chicago Press.

NORRIS, P. 2000. *A Virtuous Circle? Political Communications in Post-Industrial Democracies*. Cambridge: Cambridge University Press.

—— 2001. *Digital Divide? Civic Engagement, Information Poverty and the Internet in Democratic Societies*. New York: Cambridge University Press.

—— 2002. *Democratic Phoenix: Reinventing Political Activism*. New York: Cambridge University Press.

—— JUST, M., and KERN M. eds. 2003. *Framing Terrorism: The News Media, the Government and the Public*. New York: Routledge.

—— CURTICE, J., SANDERS, D. SCAMMELL, M., and SEMETKO, H. A. 1999. *On Message: Communicating the Campaign*. London: Sage.

OATES, S., OWEN, D., and GIBSON, R. 2006. *The Internet and Politics: Citizens, Voters and Activists*. London: Routledge.

PAGE, B. I., and SHAPIRO, R. Y. 1992. *The Rational Public: Fifty Years of Trends in Americans' Policy Preferences*. Chicago: University of Chicago Press.

PAN, Z., and KOSICKI, G. 1993. Framing analysis: an approach to news discourse. *Political Communication*, 10: 59–79.

—— —— 2001. Framing as a strategic action in public deliberation. Pp. 35–66 in *Framing Public Life*, ed. S. D. Reese, O. H. Gandy, and A. E. Grant. Mahwah, NJ: Lawrence Erlbaum.

PATTERSON, T. E. 1980. *The Mass Media Election: How Americans Choose their President*. New York: Praeger.

—— 1994. *Out of Order*. New York: Vintage.

—— 2002. *The Vanishing Voter: Public Involvement in an Age of Uncertainty*. New York: Alfred A. Knopf Publishers.

—— and MCCLURE, R. D. 1976. *The Unseeing Eye: The Myth of Television Power in National Elections*. New York: Putnam.

PETER, J. 2002. Medien-Priming—Grundlagen, Befunde und Forschungstendenzen [Media priming: foundations, results and research tendencies]. *Publizistik*, 47: 21–44.

—— 2003. Country characteristics as contingent conditions of agenda setting: the moderating influence of polarized elite opinion. *Communication Research*, 30: 683–712.

—— LAUF, E., and SEMETKO, H. A. 2004. Television coverage of the 1999 European Parliamentary Elections. *Political Communication*, 21 (4): 415–33.

—— SEMETKO, H. A., and DE VREESE, C. H. 2003. EU politics on television news: a cross-national comparative study. *European Union Politics*, 4: 305–27.

PFETSCH, B. 1996. Convergence through privatization? Changing media environments and televised politics in Germany. *European Journal of Communication*, 8 (3): 425–50.

PRICE, V., and NEIJENS, P. 1997. Opinion quality in public opinion research. *International Journal of Public Opinion Research*, 9 (4): 336–60.

—— TEWKSBURY, D., and POWERS, E. 1997. Switching trains of thought: the impact of news frames on readers' cognitive responses. *Communication Research*, 24: 481–506.

PROTESS, D., and McCOMBS, M. eds. 1991. *Agenda setting: Readings on media, public opinion, and policymaking*. Hillsdale, NJ: Lawrence Erlbaum.

REESE, S. D., GANDY, O. H., and GRANT, A. E. eds. 2001. *Framing Public Life: Perspectives on Media and our Understanding of the Social World*. Mahwah, NJ: Lawrence Erlbaum.

ROGERS, E. M., DEARING, J. W., and BREGMAN, D. 1993. The anatomy of agenda-setting research. *Journal of Communication*, 43 (2): 68–84.

ROSKOS-EWOLDSEN, D. R., KLINGER, M. R., and ROSKOS-EWOLDSEN, B. 2002. Media priming: a meta-analysis. Pp. 53–80 in *Meta-analysis of Media Effects*, ed. J. B. Bryant and A. R. Carveth. Mahwah, NJ: Lawrence Erlbaum.

SCHEUFELE, D. 2000. Agenda-setting, priming, and framing revisited: another look at cognitive effects of political communication. *Mass Communication and Society*, 3: 297–316.

SCHUDSON, M. 2002. The news media as political institutions. *Annual Review of Political Science*, 5: 249–69.

SEMETKO, H. A. 1996. Political balance on television: campaigns in the US, Britain and Germany. *Harvard International Journal of Press/Politics*, 1 (1): 51–71.

—— 2000. Great Britain: the end of the News at Ten and the changing news environment. Pp. 343–74 in *Democracy and the Media: A Comparative Perspective*, ed. R. Gunther and A. Mughan. Cambridge: Cambridge University Press.

—— DE VREESE, C., and J. PETER. 2000. Europeanised politics—Europeanised media? The impact of European integration on political communication. *West European Politics*, 23 (4): 121–40.

—— and SCHOENBACH, K. 1994. *Germany's "Unity" Election: Voters and the Media*. Cresskill, NJ: Hampton Press.

—— and VALKENBURG, P. M. 2000. Framing European politics: a content analysis of press and television news. *Journal of Communication*, 50 (2): 93–109.

—— VAN DER BRUG, W., and VALKENBURG, P. M. 2003. The influence of political events on attitudes towards the European Union. *British Journal of Political Science*, 33: 621–34.

—— BLUMLER, J. G., GUREVITCH, M., and WEAVER, D. H. 1991. *The Formation of Campaign Agendas*. Creskill, NJ: Lawrence Erlbaum.

SHAH, D. V., KWAK, N., and HOLBERT, R. L. 2001. "Connecting" and "disconnecting" with civic life: patterns of internet use and the production of social capital. *Political Communication*, 18 (2): 141–62.

—— —— SCHMIERBACH, M., and ZUBRIC, J. 2004. The interplay of news frames on cognitive complexity. *Human Communication Research*, 30 (1): 102–20.

SWANSON, D. L., and MANCINI, P. 1996. *Politics, Media and Modern Democracy: An International Study of Innovations in Electoral Campaigning and their Consequences*. Westport, Conn.: Praeger.

VALENTINO, N. A. 1999. Crime news and the priming of racial attitudes during evaluations of the President. *Public Opinion Quarterly*, 63 (3): 293–320.

VAN DER EIJK, C., and FRANKLIN, M. N. 1996. *Choosing Europe? The European Electorate and National Politics in the Face of Union*. Ann Arbor: University of Michigan Press.

WAISBORD, S. 2000. *Watchdog Journalism in South America: News, Accountability, and Democracy*. New York: Columbia University Press.

WATTENBERG, M., and BRIANS, C. L. 1996. Campaign issue knowledge and salience: comparing reception from TV commercials, TV news, and newspapers. *American Journal of Political Science*, 40 (1): 172–93.

—— —— 1999. Negative campaign advertising: demobilizer or mobilizer? *American Political Science Review*, 93 (4): 891–900.

WEAVER, D., GRABER, D. A., McCOMBS, M. E., and EYAL, C. H. 1981. *Media Agenda-Setting in a Presidential Election.* New York: Praeger.

—— McCOMBS, M. E., and SPELLMAN, C. 1975. Watergate and the media: a case study of agenda-setting. *American Politics Quarterly*, 3: 458–72.

WESTEN, D., KILTS, C., BLAGOV, P., HARENSKI, K., and HAMANN, S. (in press). The neural basis of motivated reasoning: an fMRI study of emotional constraints on political judgment during the U.S. Presidential election of 2004. *Journal of Cognitive Neuroscience.*

WOLFSFELD, G. 1997. *Media and Political Conflict: News from the Middle East.* New York: Cambridge University Press.

—— 2004. *Media and the Path to Peace.* New York: Cambridge University Press.

ZALLER, J. 1992. *The Nature and Origin of Mass Opinion.* New York: Cambridge University Press.

CHAPTER 8

....

PERSPECTIVES ON MASS BELIEF SYSTEMS AND COMMUNICATION

....

PHILIP E. CONVERSE

THE ethics of full disclosure require me to begin with an explanation. In the course of the past three years or so I agreed to prepare some comments on two different sets of papers, both of which had some bearing on my essay, "The Nature of Belief Systems in Mass Publics" (Converse 1964). Both sets of papers were commissioned from all-star casts, but with little overlap of authors at the prospectus stage and, as best I can see, none at all in the final count. I did not closely associate these two assignments in my own mind, in part because several years intervened between my agreement to participate in each. It was also true that the missions seemed quite different. My "other" assignment here involves an issue of the journal *Critical Review*, where about ten essays have been commissioned to address the question as to how views of the quality of mass democratic process may have evolved in the research community since my essay four decades ago. Moreover, this journal issue will contain a reprinting in totum of the Belief Systems paper itself, since the original parent volume has been out of print for many years. However, the dissimilarity of these two assignments has faded rapidly with the discovery that both of these deadlines for me have come to rest in the same month. Ethics of a different sort require that I do two distinct essays, albeit on highly overlapping subject matters. Yet ethics of still a third sort require that I refrain from contradicting myself on any matters of substance!

1 BELIEF SYSTEMS AND POLITICAL ATTITUDES

It turns out that several Handbook essays here bear on the Belief Systems piece. Indeed one of them, by Kuklinski and Peyton, has something more closely resembling a "shadow dialogue" with me than anything in my other assignment. This I naturally find irresistible, and shall begin exactly here. Space is too limited for a full dialogue, but I want to address (1) the topic of ideology in the classic sense and (2) the question of "real" political attitudes in the vast majority of the electorate.

1.1 Ideology

The authors, in discussing the "upbeat" persuasion among "revisionists," cite several findings from Levitin-Miller (1979), one of the most striking of which is the continuity correlation for the seven-point ideology scale as measured over the 1972–6 National Election Studies (NES) panel. This coefficient is reported as .65, or admittedly less than the same coefficient for party identification, given as .80, but which can claim to be "nearly as stable" as party identification, long established as the most stable attitude by far in these US election studies. That is, the stability of ideology is over four-fifths as large as the vaunted stability of partisansanship (.65/.80=.8125). This bears absolutely no resemblance to our findings on ideology, particularly in 1960, where we also measured ideological self-placement, although not on the later seven-point scale, which begs for comparison with the seven-point scale for party identification. Either there was a gigantic leap forward in ideological sensitivity of the mass electorate during the 1960s, or something is dreadfully wrong with the stability comparison these figures invite. Guess which? It takes but a moment's examination to see why this .65–.80 comparison is hopelessly misleading on the face of it, for a whole congeries of reasons piled one on the other. Let us count the ways.

To start slowly, one learns in elementary statistics that for the kind of ratio statement about relative stability invited by the .65–.80 comparison, one must first square the raw coefficients, to get into the currency of "shared variance" that supports more meaningful ratio comparisons. These corrected values for party and ideology are .64 and .4225, respectively, so that suddenly ideology is not over four-fifths as stable as party, but less than two-thirds as stable (.66).

The next correction is of a different sort, and may not be a correction at all. A year ago, I had reason to examine the continuity correlations, where available, for party and ideology seven-point scales in all NES four-year panels (1956–60, 1972–6, 2000–4). Since a seven-point ideology scale had not yet been devised at the time of the first panel, and the repetition in the third panel is marred by an experiment attempting to force people to choose some substantive position, the 1972–6 data on ideology stand alone. And for both party and ideology, my 1972 numbers differ from those cited. The four-year party coefficient for 1972–6 is .789 (although .813 in the first panel and .849 in the third). If an average were taken for the first two panels (not a silly maneuver under the circumstances), it would be almost exactly .80. Perhaps this was done. However, my continuity value for ideology in the middle panel is .564, not the .65 cited. Again taking the squares of my numbers, ideology is barely more than half as stable as party identification (.511). Since there is no quick way to prove which numbers are correct, I shall proceed with this accounting on two separate tracks, using both continuity estimates as a base, divided into "my numbers" vs. "theirs."

Now we have not yet begun to get serious about making this comparison. The problem is that the party variable and the ideology variable are at opposing extremes where "missing data" are concerned, just as Kuklinski and Peyton point out. For party identification, almost everybody can locate themselves on the scale. In this period less than 1.5 percent of the total sample fails to choose a position on the seven-point party scale, claiming in one way or another to be "apolitical." This variable routinely has fewer missing data than any other attitude measures in these election studies. The opposite is typically true for the ideology seven-point scale: it has more missing data than any other attitude measure in the study. In the 1972 and 1976 applications defining our ideology continuity correlations, an average of almost 25 percent of respondents are missing data because they prefer the option that they "haven't thought much about this." More than another 6 percent of the sample report that they don't know where they would fit on the scale, bringing the manifest "missing data" to more than 30 percent of the sample, or over twenty times the bulk of missing data on the party identification variable. Thus the two continuity correlations are thoroughly beyond simple comparison.

We can, however, establish comparability if we use the total-sample data for both variables. For example, in the party case we observe a .789 continuity correlation for 98.5 percent of the sample. How do we characterize the residual missing-data 1.5 percent of the sample in continuity correlation terms? Well, since these residual cases cannot relate themselves to the party continuum, we can impute a continuity correlation of $r=.000$ to them. Putting the two pieces together, we find a new and appropriately-reduced continuity correlation for party of. 777 (for my numbers), or. 788 (for theirs). We can do exactly the same for the ideology continuum, getting a total-sample value of $r=.392$ (my numbers) or .452 for theirs. Taking the squares again on both variables, we have ideology at. 154 and party at .604 (my numbers) or ideology at .204 vs. party at .621 (their numbers).

We are not yet finished, however, as there is likely to be more hidden missing data on the ideology variable that has no counterpart on the party variable. This suspicion arises with respect to a huge peak of self-locations exactly at the midpoint (#4) of the substantive 1–7 continuum. This peak is more heavily populated than either of the three substantive locations on one side of it added together, or on the other. When we did such a measurement in France we found the same effect, although it stuck out even more in that case because respondents were asked to place themselves on a scale from 0 to 100, and the parallel huge mode was located exactly at the 50-point mark (Converse and Pierce 1986). In this French case, the second most popular location was the manifest missing-data category. We also followed up the self-location question in France with a request for what kind of policy positions were called "left" vs. "right." Of course the large contingent who did not locate themselves had very little to say about meaning of the terms. But the large contingent who chose the "50" location also had about as little to say as well. This tipped us off to the fact that there were two response strategies for persons who did not comprehend the continuum enough to relate to it personally. They could suffer the embarrassment of confessing they could not relate to these ideological terms; or they could dodge such embarrassment by locating themselves at the only neutral point in sight (the 50-mark). Hence these locations—the two most popular choices by a wide margin in the US as well as France—are both saturated with missing data. Of course we could hardly argue that *no* persons at the midpoint in either country actually understood the continuum: middle-of-the-roadism is a very intelligible substantive choice. However, we are convinced that most of these midpoint-dwellers are simply more covert missing data, where understanding of the continuum in more crisp policy terms is concerned.

Given the ambiguity, we shall not finish our accounting by moving all midpoint dwellers to missing data. We shall very conservatively assume that a good half of them are also missing data, in the 1972–6 case, and not try to cope with the fact that some emptying at the midpoint would restore a little zip to any continuity correlation. Proceeding as before, we find that the recalculated ideology continuity coefficient (r^2) is in no way over four-fifths as stable as party identification, but more like one-fifth as stable (their numbers) or one-tenth as stable (ours). This is a very familiar neighborhood for an ideology measure, and one which relieves us of any need to account for a huge surge of ideological comprehension in the US during the 1960s. For total samples, the difference between cross-time stability for party identification and ideology is as night and day.

On the other hand, it can also be demonstrated that if we commission a highly compound variable from NES data that summarizes most available clues as to respondent information levels and involvement in politics, then the rate of gain in stability of ideological self-placements as we climb the deciles from bottom to top is considerably greater than the same display for party identification stability. In one sense, this would have to be true, given the wretched zero starting point for stability at the lowest levels of "sophistication." But what is interesting is that this rate of gain for ideology is sharp enough as to approach convergence from below with the stability shown for party identification at the highest levels of sophistication. And hence a significant role for ideological self-placement in predicting vote outcomes, bringing joy to Kuklinski–Peyton "upbeat revisionists," need not clash in any way with the situation that I was describing years before, especially when one-third to one-half of the "total sample" (the whole electorate)—and generally the less informed and interested—fail to vote in any case, and thus are missing data for vote predictions as well.

1.2 Holders of "Real" Attitudes

Kuklinski and Peyton stress how few people in the electorate I consider to hold any "real political attitudes." This is a rather loose reference, in the sense that no specific percentages are mentioned, and just how one could tell a "real" attitude from an unreal one is not covered. But it is easy to get the impression that "few" means some small fraction like the famous 12–15 per cent numbers that I do cite in the Belief Systems essay where active use of ideological frames of reference are concerned.

Now Kuklinski–Peyton hardly stand alone in this reading of the essay. In fact, I think a majority of critics have read the essay the same way, and I have always found it painful and perplexing. The next chance I had to write at length again about these matters I noted that while I stood by my observations of low information and labile policy opinions, I said it would be unwise to push these results too far. "They are frequently misinterpreted as saying that not much of anybody has public opinions about much of anything. This is a disastrous misconstruction, for it fits no data at all" (Converse 1975, 83). It would be hard to speak much more plainly on the subject.

Granted that many may have missed this sequel on the subject, I have remained puzzled at how the original essay could have been read in this fashion as well, short of some desperate need for straw men and caricature. So for this round I have reread the whole essay for the first time in over thiry years. I looked for sentences and passages that seem thoroughly incompatible with such an alleged point of view on my part, that I could cite in a short footnote of exculpation. I had a goodly harvest of these before I arrived, late in the essay, at the description of one of the weakest "levels of conceptualization" that I was coding from open-ended comments on the parties and the candidates in the presidential election. To achieve a level *at least* this low, I had to detect some significant trace of a policy issue concern being expressed by the respondent. And it turned out that 78 percent of the sample brought at least one such policy opinion into their remarks. What could be more obvious empirical proof in the essay itself that I nowhere was claiming that "few" in the electorate held any "real" political attitudes, much less policy ones? So at this point I stopped the list I was compiling.

Of course, this does not solve the question as to "how real is 'real'?" And here I must confess that still later in the essay I found a passage of four or five lines that I could see might be construed as such a claim, especially if "real" meant "replicable-over-time." This passage reported my analysis of the trophy "power and housing" issue, where the high prevalence of "as-if-random" response patterns could be documented. I did point out right there that the power and housing issue was unique across a battery of such issue items, and was the most esoteric item in the battery, as witnessed by a surplus of "don't know" responses. But I also commented that while the other issue items failed to fit the diagnostic model, it would be safe to assume that some lower fraction of "as-if-random" response could be expected elsewhere. Even this hardly fits the attribution that I felt few real political attitudes existed in the mass public; but I can grant it might represent the seed for such a reading, as might the parallel treatment in the "Non-Attitudes" paper (Converse 1970).

Actually, I would like to expand somewhat on this point, and regret that I did not do so in the original essay. It is obvious that inquiry into the complex matters covered by social science requires multiple methods to approach, since any given method of attack is likely to achieve some illumination but be blinded to other facets of the situation. (The values of a multi-method approach are reflected in most of the subjects tackled in this Handbook section, as we shall see.)

In the belief systems case, the advent of survey research gave a precious first view of belief systems in the public as a totality. Most survey research, however, is given over to "closed" questions, limiting the respondent to multiple-choice answers specified by the researcher. "Open-ended" questions, while liberating for respondents, are very time-consuming and likely to produce disparities that end up being uncodable. I was always grateful that in our election-study shop we invested in at least some open-ended questions. Without these, I would not have felt equipped to make some of the generalizations about belief systems that I ultimately did, with coding schemes like the "levels of conceptualization." But even this luxury was only partial.

In the same general period, Robert Lane (1962) had conducted an elegant "clinical" study of beliefs, interviewing subjects at considerable length as to their assessments of the political world around them. As his study and mine came to be read, I was often challenged in my implications that there were many important political topics about which people seemed to have little reaction. I had read the Lane report, and felt very little conflict in our accounts. This was because my study was really focused upon the degree of interconnectedness of political attitudes; and one constant complaint of Lane's was the frequency with which his informants failed to make rather elementary connections between cognate attitudes they expressed: "morselizing," he called it. Given the clinical interview setting, he was free to explore more intensively these points of disconnection, which he found very recalcitrant, even under coaching. I later published comments on the hue and cry about Lane finding lots more attitudes than my "method" detected (Converse 1975). I sent Lane a copy in advance, and he agreed wholeheartedly that we were describing the same reality, albeit from somewhat different starting points. So I granted the critics that there were real methods differences here. I proposed that closed questions were akin to fishing with a spear or a rifle; while the Lane method was fishing with a net. It is obvious which method will discover the more fish, which is why I am chary of statements about the absolute paucity of stray "fish in the pond," as opposed to statements about the paucity of links between whatever number of fish turn up with either method.

In this spirit, I disavow any reading of the Belief Systems essay that concludes that most citizens lack political attitudes. I think there is a limited stratum—10 percent? 20 percent?—with a very sparse complement of such attitudes, mostly because of an aversion to the whole subject of politics. We are reminded of the David Butler interview with a lady in England who, when asked if she would vote in the upcoming election, said "Heavens, no. It would only encourage them" (the political classes). After all, this by itself counts as a "political attitude," and probably a very replicable one for the holder, although perhaps lonely in that department. Actually, political attitudes abound: they simply tend to have narrow reach and idiosyncratic construction.

My discussion on issue publics in general, and political attitudes about visible social groupings in particular, testifies to my awareness of lots of "real" attitudes out there, although it is hardly a beginning of a typology of such.

1.3 The Theory of Democratic Elitism

Rohrschneider and Pefley address one spur of the elite-mass gradient in political sophistication, involving the presumption that politically "enlightened" elites are the guardians of democratic values, including political tolerance and minority rights. They argue a major corrective, not to the existence of large mass–elite differences in political cognitions, but to an early assumption based on data from well-rooted democracies, that reigning elites are necessarily imbued with such liberal democratic values. As comparative elite research has come to include a much larger range of countries, it is clear that "eliteness" by itself hardly ensures any deep installation of democratic values, and this corrective is certainly demanded by the deep history of most nation-states. Socialization into more autocratic past political practices can trump other forces on behavior at the elite level, as has been demonstrated in several of the newer democracies of Eastern Europe, and various fledgling democracies in less economically developed countries as well.

1.4 Political Socialization

Kent Jennings in this Handbook also discusses an increased emphasis within socialization research on "contextual effects." These are effects of the broader context that are often neglected in research. Some of these are within-country factors. While an attribute like party identification is seen as an entirely personal matter, I remember our delight in the discovery that although the effects were limited, party identifications were significantly stronger in those states where election laws presumed the normality of such identifications, as in requiring a statement of party preference in registering to vote (in order to avoid cross-party voting in party primaries), than in states where there was no such requirement (Campbell et al. 1960).

Of course such effects are likely to be writ even larger between countries with contrasting regimes, in exactly the ways that Rohrschneider and Pefley argue. Jennings goes on to point out that these effects are of great moment for a growing number of long-term democracies which are now recipients of large populations immigrating from countries with very different political traditions. There has been little research on either the political socialization of children from these immigrant families, or for that matter, the *resocialization* of the adult migrant generation. He argues that both are major lost opportunities, and I shall shortly add another to this important socialization list.

In part because the whole paradigm for socialization studies presumes that early inputs from formal education and informal experience affect views of the political world downstream, this field has been blessed with an unusual number of relatively long-term panel studies. Jennings reports a renewal of interest in the dynamics of socialization, which to date have in a general way supported the fundamental formative-years hypothesis, with an increasing scientific purchase on details to flesh out the picture.

1.5 Political Psychology

Diane Mutz reviews three developments in research in political psychology. One is a growing emphasis on emotions in the formation of political choices. From my own background in social psychology and the study of attitudes, I had always considered that we were working squarely at the intersection of cognition and emotion. After all, the reigning definition of an attitude was "affect organized around an object." But "affect" is thin gruel, relative to the full palette of emotions psychologists study, and Mutz waves off sums of plus and minus valences, or "thermometer scores," as not having much to do with real emotions, although the latter are admittedly difficult to study reliably. A second trend moves more to the cognitive side and examines the "biassed processing" of information. Some work in the area is of long standing, including the predispositions set by parisan identifications, or the study of selective exposure to information sources. More recent work debates such topics as the degree to which viewers of the political scene update their assessments in ways that fit the Bayesian paradigm. The third development carries us to the multi-method approaches mentioned above, to escape too heavy reliance on survey data. Here the possibilities are numerous and exciting, all the way from tighter laboratory studies of physiological states to exploration of neuroscience and brain imaging as a further window on both political emotions and aspects of information processing.

2 POLITICAL COMMUNICATION

Although it is only one large rivulet in the complex study of political communication, concern over levels of information in the electorate has stimulated interest in communication patterns from almost the outset of survey-based studies of the electorate. Paul Lazarsfeld at Columbia was a founder of communications research as a serious discipline; and his research group conducted the earliest serious presidential election studies starting in 1940. This group rapidly came to sense the weight of numbers of citizens who paid little attention to politics, and came to imagine that the success of democratic forms must rest on a kind of trickle-down process whereby the inattentive headed into elections must pick up cues from more attentive "opinion leaders." This theory was examined most completely in Berelson, Lazarsfeld, and McPhee (1954) and Katz and Lazarsfeld (1955).

In the Belief Systems essay I attempted one large-bore test of this hypothesis. In a system where the Republican Party catered to big business and the rich, while the Democrats tendered more to representing labor unions, minorities, and the working class, it seemed likely that the politically attentive would have little trouble voting their class interests. But the inattentive would have more trouble, unless the system was saturated with well-informed opinion leaders, available to provide cues. My dependendent variable was the correlation of class position and vote within "sophistication" levels based on the "levels of conceptualization" variable, from ideologues, through "group benefit" folks, then those most attentive to the "nature of the times", and finally those who betrayed no policy issue awareness at all, in their open-ended discussions of the political scene. Now one can argue that in a system perfectly lubricated by opinion leaders, with the individual sophistication multiplied downward through interpersonal communication, the degree of class voting would even out across attentiveness groupings (Converse 1964, 232, figure 1). Of course it does not, with strong and monotonic differences in class voting from top to bottom within these levels for male voters. (On the other hand, this gradient, while steep, might have been steeper still if there had been no "opinion leader" effect at all!)

The same table includes a parallel display for female voters. This is of more interest than might appear, and for two reasons. First, the suffrage had only been granted by Constitutional amendment to women in 1920. Thus there was a large cohort of women who were born too early to be socialized into political attentiveness in the Jennings sense. Indeed, one problem interviewers had interviewing housewives as late as the 1950s and 1960s was the frequent complaint "why are you asking *me* these questions? You should come back and talk to the Mister." The sharpness of this gender division of labor where politics was concerned is easy to lose sight of by modern times. Second, separating the women made sense because the considerable majority of them were indeed housewives. The older half of these housewives had grown up not expecting to follow politics, yet they had been eligible to vote for over a half-dozen presidential elections. What better test of the opinion leader theory, given a Most Accessible Opinion Leader, right in one's own household? But the women separately showed lower levels of class voting generally than the men, and less coherently as a function of levels of conceptualization.

2.1 Communication Nets

Our two Handbook chapters on political communication, by Huckfeldt and Semetko, bring us fast forward through forty years of research on the subject, and with a clear division of labor in the coverage. Huckfeldt's chapter focuses on studies of interpersonal communication networks, which elaborate marvelously on the limited "opinion leader" beginnings. Such work presumes that individual citizen decisions reflect in some considerable degree their owners' participation in a socially embedded process involving many connections through which interpersonal influence can flow. My own household is highly familiar with the simplest and most brazen version of such flow, whereby at the approach of each local election we consult with varying friends who pay attention to city council, the school board, the library board, judicial candidates, and the like. The Huckfeldt treatment spreads over a much larger canvas where influence may well be more subtle and less election-bound, but the importance of the network can hardly be questioned, however easily it may become lost from view in surveys of randomly selected individuals. Network studies in the grand manner tend to be large, expensive and complex, although the chapter is helpful with suggestions as to how some evidence of the communication context can be established even for more atomistic sample surveys. One halfway house involves a "snowball component" whereby discussion partners are elicited for some members of the main sample and independently interviewed about about own views and exchanged views.

One of the network variables which has emerged as central in recent years is the homogeneity or heterogeneity of opinion characterizing any given network, which may of course vary over time. One simple theory would argue that a network which is relatively stable might be expected to drift toward greater homogeneity over its life course. As it turns out, however, there are circumstances where network heterogeneity is more persistent than meets the eye. Among these are "lower-density" networks, where there are weak ties with individuals less likely to communicate directly with most or all other member of the net. Debates are also flourishing as to whether or not network heterogeneity increases either political participation or political tolerance. One intriguing recent finding is that political discussions in heterogeneous groups not only increase member political information, but also help to inoculate participants against elite trickery in "framing" policy debates in certain self-serving ways.

2.2 Communication Channels

Semetko covers a wide range of other more institutionalized or mainly one-way channels of communication to the citizen. She begins with a vivid reminder of how radically this scene has evolved on a global level, due to technologies that are in high revolution on almost an annual pace, as exemplified by developments like political blogging, unheard of a relatively few years ago, but already a major industry for political communication; or on the other hand, the rapid decline of the major evening TV news broadcasts. It is not easy to conduct research with political communication in such flux. Nonetheless, review is provided of a variety of research efforts, both survey and experiment based, to study the impact of news on public opinion and election outcomes. As Semetko points out, experimental approaches allow for control, but are by the same token weaker on external validity. The flowering of the internet also opens the door to conducting less costly experiments and surveys online, although internet users are far from being representative of the population.

In a particularly impressive section, Semetko discusses three key concepts which have become central in political communication research, because of repeated demonstrations of their potency in communication effects. These include (1) *agenda-setting*, achieved by the media through choices as to what news to select; (2) *priming*, or contributions by the media in suggesting standards for evaluation of political leaders and parties; and (3) *framing*, whereby certain facets of a situation or problem are rendered more salient to underscore a desired definition or interpretation of what is at stake. The power of all three of these ploys has been frequently demonstrated in media research; but the same phenomena are of course in the toolkits of campaign strategists and leadership *spinmeisters*. They would seem to deserve equal study within political psychology under the rubric of problems in individual information processing. (Or perhaps the dynamics and correlates of gullibility are too obvious for serious examination.) A different approach is represented by functional magnetic resonance imaging (rMRI) to see if it can help untangle why Democrats and Republicans can reach opposite conclusions when given the same information.

3   CONCLUSION

3.1 The Evolution of Belief Systems in Modern Electorates

I am often asked how durable I think the bleak portrait of the electorate I turned up in the 1950–60 period has been. My own empirical base for judgment is very limited, as I shifted to other pursuits after the election studies were appropriately put under more collective management around 1970. My casual view has been that there was nowhere to go but up, toward greater average voter competence, probably driven by the advance of education and functional literacy. As Kuklinski and Peyton point out, I was around long enough to appreciate some increased "muscle tone" in policy attitudes, although this seemed more a function of various moral issues brought to the surface by the culture wars of the 1960s than much change in more conventional issues of who gets what when and how.

When we had first decided to do some large election studies in France in the later 1960s, I was very eager to see what the French population looked like ideologically, and for a simple reason. The great multiplicity of French parties meant that it was hard to tell who was who without a scorecard. And the French press covered this blooming, buzzing party scene in fine degrees on the measuring stick of the left–right continuum, one great inheritance of the Revolution. So I fully expected to find a French electorate much more versed in the ballyhooed ideological yardstick. I was greatly disappointed: the French were not notably more agile in understanding "left" and "right" than US citizens were for the for the much less frequently-used terms "liberal" and "conservative." I came to realize that the public education system below elite levels in France was quite limited by US standards; there was still a large peasant population with limited literacy; and so on. But it also seemed true that the size of the party system was itself a special barrier to comprehension. We asked citizens how they felt about the actual number of parties, as well as what they would see the ideal French party system to have. Most preferred a smaller system, including a serious number who wanted only two parties. As one woman put it: "there should be only two parties: just enough to express all the nuances of opinion."

While advancing education no doubt is putting upward pressure on the competence of the US electorate, we should not forget another source, which I have mentioned above. This is the fact that in the period of the 1960 portrait there was still a significant reservoir of adult women in the sample who were socialized before female suffrage was approved, and hence who often considered "real" political attitudes to be a male prerogative. This cohort has now departed the scene, and it would seem that this fact in itself should raise average political awareness in some degree. Progress does occur!

Meanwhile by far our best marker for empirical updating of the portrait for the US electorate is Kathleen Knight's replication of the "levels of conceptualization" coding from open-ended materials in the 1980 National Election Study (1985). This enterprise did show significant improvement, by comparison with the 1956-based original. However, this improvement was of a special front-loaded sort. The small original fraction of ideologues and near-ideologues was on toward doubled, a quarter of a century later. Otherwise, however, the rest of the distribution seemed pretty much the same, once a tenth or so of the sample had been promoted out of it. Undoubtedly, if we were to know that progress is to be focused anywhere along the distribution, this is the most helpful point for it to be centered. Kuklinski and Peyton also cite more recent replications in a number of European countries (Klingeman 1979; Dalton 2002). These latter findings mesh nicely with Knight's work, and it is fair to suppose that they stem from advancing education, although it is worth remembering that in Europe as well as the United States, the earlier period involved cohorts of older women interviewed because they were eligible to vote, but who had grown up in a world where women did not do such a thing, and following politics was exclusively the male side of the division of labor. Indeed, in some countries where female suffrage was achieved later, these transitional cohorts of females would figure to have been larger in the 1950s and 1960s than they were in the United States.

What broader sense is to be made of these gains limited largely to the top end of the pyramid? Surely a significant portion of these advances reflect not only the dissipation of the female suffrage lag but, more importantly, marked advances in education all around. We should also include here the ever-growing supply of political communications from all sides and multiplying technologies. But why would these macrochanges not register across the spectrum? It almost seems as though there must be some counterforces, equally "macro," which limit these changes. Here it is useful to remember that the portrait is not a resultant of cognitive or information forces alone. Of comparable weight, we may presume, are motivational forces wrapped up in the trite term "political interest." And with this in mind, the modernizing world does not want for counterforces.

Perhaps it is myth in some degree, but in stereotypes of nineteenth-century US democracy, politics (both local and national) was about the best spectator sport in town. Now the potent distractions are in our faces from all directions: the celebrity culture, popular music, "reality" TV along with endless "unreal" forms, and so on. Including most notably, perhaps, spectator sports galore. And by now, spectator sports not merely in the conventional sense, but sports where ingenuity now invites a level of direct participation on the part of bystanders themselves, which can easily consume more private hours per month than fans could hope to scrape out of mere spectating. I speak of the development of "fantasy sports," built around professional baseball, football, and basketball, whereby fans compete to assemble artifactual teams of stars at auction, with the success of each mythic team depending on the relative aggregated performance of that set of athletes in that season's real sports action. We lack data on the number of hours spent nationally on this new form of amateur sports participation. But we do know, for example, that the amount of money changing hands nationally is up in the billions of dollars per year for fantasy *baseball* alone, dwarfing the amounts necessary to run a full 162-game season for some thirty teams of actual professional baseball players whose achievements dictate the outcomes of the "amateur" fantasy competition. In short, there is a vast and growing number of other interesting ways to spend one's time in our "modernized" societies to compete with politics-watching. This fact alone can mean that some persons in the lower levels of political interest might be increasingly distracted from following politics, despite enjoying gains in formal education.

The vistas for further research on the nature of belief systems range from the simple and obvious to more complex ways of increasing our understanding of what the reality is in these regards, and how it is evolving in modern democracies. At the simple end is continued monitoring from established benchmarks. For example, another quarter-century is approaching since the Knight update of the original Belief Systems paper. The raw data are still being collected, in reasonably comparable forms, putting a new half-century benchmark within reach. The main pitfall here would be drifts in the coding of open-ended material, in the direction of stricter or looser standards, which could look like secular change even if constancy were to prevail.

It is tempting to think of a "simpler and safer" monitoring of information levels, after the fashion of Delli Carpini and Keeter (1996). The problem here for long-term comparisons is that much political information is highly situational: recognition of public figures below the very top (the president), for example, ebbs and flows in the short term, and one would be rather hard pressed to design two information tests that would be *really* equivalent twenty years apart, save for items that represent lasting verities such as lengths of terms of various officials.

I have long found it useful to think of electorates in terms of two basic dimensions that in real life are largely orthogonal. One dimension is made up of all the "positioning" variables, most notably involving partisanship and all the policy preference variables. This dimension is cross-cut by one that registers information about and involvement in the political world, positions aside. Whatever one calls this dimension—political attentiveness, sophistication, etc.—it varies in natural electorates from very close to zero up to enormous heights. It is this variable we would like to measure for purposes of assessing long-term change. Most political surveys try to tap a large number of positioning variables, but tend to be woefully weak on the second dimension. A direct question about interest in politics is a good start, but near major elections it has a situational component which is not interesting variance. Other "knowledge" questions, such as recognition of the local congressman, produce a measure which has a lot of its working variance tied up in whether the respondent lives in a highly competitive district or not; or a district whose boundaries coincide with news watersheds, neither of which even pretends to differentiate attentive from inattentive neighbors.

No single item can make the needed discriminations here while sidestepping a lot of irrelevant variance. One item, however, once regularly asked in the US National Election Studies (ANES), is:

Some people seem to follow what is going on in government and public affairs most of the time, whether there's an election going on or not. Others are not that interested. Would you say you follow what's going on in government and public affairs most of the time, some of the time, only now and then, hardly any at all?

Response distributions on this item in the current period are excellent, with almost no missing data. The modal response across the four categories—"some of the time"—is only a little over one-third of the sample, and the smallest response— "hardly at all"—still attracts about one in seven. Correlations of this item with other cognate variables, such as information levels on one hand, or emotional involvement in politics on the other, are routinely higher than those between purer information levels or purer involvement measures. Its main defect is that it is not hinged to any objective frequencies, leaving it more open for "social-desirability" fudgings upward.

Nevertheless, if I were on a desert isle with only one variable to look at to assess long-term secular change in the political capacity of electorates, I think this is the item I would choose. However, more generic items of this kind need to be established in honor of my second basic dimension of democratic political life, to establish still more robust readings of trends in these matters, not to mention comparisons across electorates.

REFERENCES

BERELSON, B. R., LAZARSFELD, P. F., and McPHEE, W. F. 1954. *Voting*. Chicago: University of Chicago Press.

CAMPBELL, A. CONVERSE, P. E., MILLER, W. E. and STOKES, D. 1960. *The American Voter*. New York: John Wiley & Sons.

CONVERSE, P. E. 1964. The nature of belief systems in mass publics. Pp. 206–61 in *Ideology and Discontent*, ed. D. E. Apter. New York: Free Press of Glencoe.

—— 1970. Attitudes and non-attitudes: continuation of a dialogue. Pp. 168–89 in *The Quantitative Analysis of Social Problems*, ed. E. R. Tufte. Reading, Mass.: Addison-Wesley Publishers.

CONVERSE, P. E. 1975. Public opinion and voting behavior. Pp. 75–100 in F. Greenstein and N. Polsby, *Handbook of Political Science*, ed. F. Greenstein and N. Polsby, Reading, Mass.: Addison-Wesley.

—— and PIERCE, R. 1986. *Political Representation in France.* Cambridge, Mass.: Belknap Press of Harvard University Press.

DALTON, R. J. 2002. *Citizen Politics: Public Opinion and Political Parties in Advanced Industrial Democracies,* 3rd edn. New York: Seven Bridges Press.

DELLI CARPINI, M. X., and KEETER, S. 1996. *What Americans Know about Politics and Why It Matters.* New Haven: Yale University Press.

KATZ, E., and LAZARSFELD, P. F. 1955. *Personal Influence: The Part Played by People in the Flow of Mass Communications.* New York: Free Press.

KLINGEMANN, H.-D. 1979. Measuring ideological conceptualizations. Pp. 215–54 in *Political Action,* ed. Samuel Barnes. Beverly Hills, Calif.: Sage Publications.

LANE, R. E. 1962. *Political Ideology: Why the Common Man Believes What He Does.* New York: Free Press.

LEVITIN, T., and MILLER, W. E. 1979. Ideological interpretations of presidential elections. *American Political Science Review,* 73: 751–71.

PART III

MODERNIZATION AND SOCIAL CHANGE

CHAPTER 9

THE POLITICAL CULTURE PARADIGM

DIETER FUCHS

ALMOND and Verba's (1963) epoch-making study, *The Civic Culture*, has inspired an abundance of succeeding studies and has made the concept of political culture one of the most important concepts of empirical political research. According to Eckstein (1988, 789) the political culture approach can be considered as "one of the two still viable general approaches to political theory and explanation . . . the other still being political rational choice theory". In the competition of the two opposing approaches rational choice, which goes back to Downs's *Economic Theory of Democracy* (1957), has continuously gained in relevance. In the late 1970s and the early 1980s, rational choice became the leading approach in political science and political culture decisively lost in relevance. However, since the end of the 1980s the concept of political culture has experienced a remarkable revival (Inglehart 1988; Almond 1993; Reisinger 1995). There are several reasons for this revival.

First, phenomena such as the fortification of Islamic fundamentalism as well as the extraordinary success in modernization in many East Asian countries cannot be explained without accounting for cultural factors (Inglehart 1988). Second, Putnam's (1993) *Making Democracy Work*, which has almost gained the status of a classic, has unravelled a previous neglected dimension of political culture research. Putnam emphasizes the significance of republican virtues of a civic community, such as cooperation and solidarity, for a functioning democracy. Third, the collapse of the communist system in central and eastern Europe and the implementation of democracy in the region have culture as one of the key explanatory factors.

Considering the fact that the first and the second waves of democratization were followed by reverse waves (Huntington 1993), the stability of these democracies in the third wave of democratization is questioned once again. Many authors consider the development of a political culture that is congruent with the institutional structure as a prerequisite for the consolidation of the new democracies in the region (Linz and Stepan 1996; Rose, Mishler, and Haerpfer 1998; Diamond 1999; Merkel 1999).

Along with the new interest in the concept of political culture, the "old" points of criticism reappear (Barry 1970; Rogowski 1976; Dittmer 1977; Lijphart 1980; Pateman 1980; Kaase 1983). Recent studies of political culture partially readdressed and partly even aggravate these points of criticism (Lane 1992; Street 1994; Laitin 1995; Reisinger 1995; Jackman and Miller 1996a, 1996b). Some of the most important points of criticism will be addressed in the following analysis.

Given the enormous amount of literature on political culture, I would like to identify the elements that I examine here. This analysis will not offer an extensive critique of the concept of political culture (cf. Pye 1968; Kavanagh 1972; Rosenbaum 1975; and especially Patrick 1984). Neither will it deal with a survey of the most important empirical findings of political culture research (c.f. van Deth and Scarborough 1995; Klingemann and Fuchs 1995; Pollack et al. 2003; Dalton 2004, 2005). The objective of my analysis is first to explicate the core elements of the concept of political culture—which is rarely presented because of the complexity of the research area. Second, I specify and differentiate the concept by taking into account important points of criticism, new problems and perspectives. These objectives should contribute to theoretically clarifying the concept.

The analysis is conducted in four steps. The first step determines the paradigmatic core of political culture. This is followed by a suggestion of incorporating civic community or rather political community into the concept of political culture according to Putnam. The third step discusses the problems of aggregation and causality, which entails strategic implications for the concept of political culture. Finally, I draw up summary conclusions and some considerations on future research perspectives.

1 THE PARADIGMATIC CORE OF POLITICAL CULTURE

There are two possibilities in defining the characteristic features of the concept of political culture. To start with, one can focus on the concrete studies that are part of the political culture approach. The second possibility focuses on Almond and Verba, who are the founding fathers of empirical research of political culture. In my judgment, there is no reasonable alternative to the latter approach.

Political culture research is characterized by an enormous diversity of studies on political attitudes. However, the theoretical status of a particular attitude and its explanatory value often remain ambiguous. Both are mostly borrowed from *The Civic Culture* (Almond and Verba 1963) and this usually implicitly. Thus, political culture presents itself as collective term or a "rubric" (Reisinger 1995), which is analytically imprecise and hence has limited explanatory value. These two deficits appear in all criticisms regarding the concept. Yet, *The Civic Culture* has abetted this in two ways. First, it provides a very broad definition of political culture: namely, subjective orientations to politics. Second, the authors chose public-opinion surveys for the generation of the data set of *The Civic Culture*. This data collection method allows for a relatively simple analysis of individual attitudes. On the premise of their definition and the given instrument, the original concept of political culture is nevertheless only explored on its surface.

The following analysis tries to encompass the core of the paradigm (Kuhn 1996) and the research program (Lakatos 1970) respectively. Such a core is provided by the assumptions that cannot be abandoned unless the whole research design becomes obsolete. Such assumptions have been formulated in the introduction and the conclusion of *The Civic Culture* and Almond (1980) and Verba (1980) have further clarified these.

The underlying question of *The Civic Culture* relates to the persistence of democratic regimes. Herein rests the first and most pivotal assumption of the research program:

(1) A crucial factor for the persistence of a democratic regime is a political culture that is in congruence with the regime structure. Formulating this causal-analytically, democratic culture is a determinant for the persistence of a democratic regime.

What is more, three further assumptions relate to the notion of political culture:

(2) The political culture of a country essentially derives from the attitudes of the citizens.

(3) The attitudes that are relevant for the political culture are those that have been internalized through socialization processes and are of a profound and enduring nature. Usually such attitudes are referred to as value orientations (Kluckhohn 1951; van Deth and Scarbrough 1995; Gerhards 2005).

(4) Political culture is a macro-phenomenon. Only if it is considered a macro-phenomenon can it feasibly influence the macro-phenomenon of regime persistence.

The second, third, and fourth assumptions result in a fifth assumption:

(5) The political culture of a country must be construed by the aggregation of micro-data. The distribution of important attitudes of the citizens describes the operationalization of political culture as a macro-phenomenon.

Although the reference point of *The Civic Culture* is democracies, the scope of the political culture concept is not restricted to democratic regimes. The assumption that a regime that wants to remain persistent in the long run, requires a political culture that is in congruency with the institutional structure, can be generally applied to all regime types. To enhance clarity and simplicity, I will restrict the following analysis to democracies.

The second and third assumptions postulate that the political culture of a country is essentially based on the attitudes of its citizens. However, thus far we have not explicitly presented the attitudes being considered. Hence, the question regarding the content of political culture arises.

2 THE CONTENT OF POLITICAL CULTURE

There exists an extensive discussion on the concept of culture in the areas of anthropology and sociology (Keesing 1974; Peterson 1979; Gerhards 2005). Almond and Verba do not define their concept of political culture as a specification of the general culture concept against this research background. They merely refer to the ambiguities and the diffuseness of the discussion and then they immediately pinpoint political culture: "We employ the concept of culture in only one of its meanings: that of psychological orientation toward social objects" (Almond and Verba 1963, 13). Political culture "thus refers to the specifically political orientations" (Almond and Verba 1963, 12). Accordingly, the introduction of *The Civic Culture* defines political culture with the help of a matrix that establishes four classes (system as general object, input objects, output objects, self as object), and three attitudinal modes (cognition, affect, evaluation). However, the matrix insufficiently meets the utility criteria of the limitation and unambiguousness of the content. Although this definition limits the spectrum of possible attitudes, it is still too broad to provide viable grounds for analysis. Furthermore, the theoretical relevance of the individual attitudes remains unsettled in *The Civic Culture*. With regard to the matrix, critics have called the concept a catch-all term—which may be everything and yet mean nothing at all.

The founding fathers of the concept have reacted in two ways. First, political culture is subdivided into system culture, process culture, and policy culture (Almond and Powell 1978). System culture is the culture that is essential for the persistence of a democratic regime. Subsequently Almond (1980, 28; 1990, 153) defines system culture according to Easton (1965, 1975) as follows:

The system culture of a nation would consist of the distributions of attitudes toward the national community, the regime, and the authorities, to use David Easton's formulation. These would include the sense of national identity, attitudes toward the legitimacy of the regime and its various institutions, and attitudes toward the legitimacy and effectiveness of the incumbents of the various political roles.

Therewith, Easton's theory with its differentiation of the three objects and the corresponding attitudes was integrated into the concept of political culture. In the following, I shall draw on his theory in a modified form, as a starting point for further precision in the concept. This modification distinguishes between three hierarchically ranked levels of democracy and the specification of causal relationships between these levels (Fuchs 1999, 2002).

According to Easton (1965, 193) a regime encompasses three elements: "values (goals and principles), norms, and structure of authority." My modification extracts values from the regime and postulates that values are considered a theoretical dimension themselves (Fuchs 1999, 2002; similarly Dalton 2004). Thus, the regime is only determined by its institutional structure and hence it is analytically clarified. This corresponds with the ideas of neo-institutionalism (Levi 1996; Crawford and Ostrom 1995; Rothstein 1996). Moreover, this also corresponds with a later analysis by Easton (1990) *The Analysis of Political Structure*, in which he assigns behavioral norms and behavioral expectations not to structure but rather to the culture of a political system.

A further distinction between the institutional structure of a regime and the individual institutions is not necessary. The individual institutions are only relevant for the persistence of the democratic regime, if it is assumed that they are distinct from the regime as a whole. This, however, could be postulated for parliament in a representative democracy, but parliament only functions in relation to the government. And both institutions act within a frame of legal norms safeguarded by an independent judiciary. Therefore, the regime of a country can only be described through its institutional setting. Regime support, which is important for persistence, directly points at the institutional setting. Easton (1965) has alluded to this before, which becomes apparent in his definition of regime.

I distinguish between three objects of a political system and the attitudes aiming at them (commitment to democratic values, support of the democratic regime of the country, support of the political authorities). These can be structured hierarchically (Figure 9.1).

This hierarchical arrangement has several analytic advantages. First, as Easton (1965, 1975) has already suggested, but yet not fully established, the causal relationships between the three attitudes can be postulated. On the one hand, there is an *overflow of value orientations* on hierarchically lower objects. Easton (1975, 451) has termed the result of this overflow on the regime as *legitimacy*: "[Legitimacy] reflects the fact that in some vague or explicit way [a person] sees these objects as conforming to his own moral principles, his own sense of what is right and proper in the political sphere." On the other hand, there is a *generalizsation of experiences* concerning the actions taken by political authorities and the resulting outcomes on hierarchically higher objects. Easton (1975, 448) refers to the effect of these generalizations on the regime as *trust*. For Easton, legitimacy and trust are two types of diffuse regime support. The causal direction in every particular case, however, is an empirical question. Yet, it can be assumed that the causal direction moves top down (transfer) in fully established democracies, whereas it moves upwards (generalization) in newly established democracies (Mishler and Rose 2002).

A second advantage is the fact that each of the three hierarchically structured attitudes has different consequences for the political system. Support of the

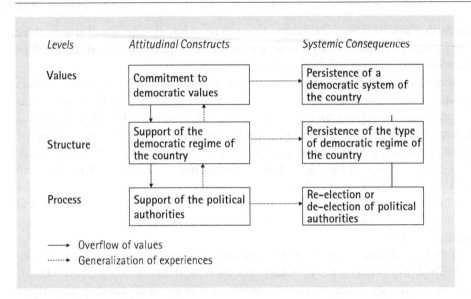

Fig. 9.1 Model of system culture

government holding office—the most important category of political authorities—has direct effects on its re-election or de-election. The support of a regime of a country affects the persistence of the regime. Additionally, the commitment to democratic values is pivotal for the question of whether the populace prefers a democracy or another type of rule.

A third advantage is closely linked to the differentiation between the democratic regime of a country and the commitment to democratic values. One of the criticisms of *The Civic Culture* is its orientation toward the Anglo-Saxon democratic experience (Brown 1977; Kaase 1983). Due to this, democracy as the normatively desired system of government was equated with a certain type of institutional setting. This equation might have been justified at the times when *The Civic Culture* was written. In the meanwhile, this became outdated by the ongoing discussion on the advantages and disadvantages of different normative models of democracy. Thus, a conceptual differentiation between the support of democratic rule and the support of the institutional setting of the country is needed. This allows for the possibility that citizens prefer democratic rule but not the present type of democracy in their country. In this way a pressure arises to reform and improve the democracy in a country (Fuchs and Roller 1998; Fuchs 1999). This idea underlies the concept of the "critical citizen," which has been formulated in recent analyses (Klingemann 1999; Norris 1999; Fuchs and Roller 2006). According to the conceptualization, political culture refers to two dependent variables: first, the persistence of democratic regimes in general and second, the persistence of a democratic regime within a certain country. With regard to the persistence of the democratic regime in general, the relevant attitude is the commitment to democratic values. In view of the persistence of a democratic regime within a country, the relevant attitude is the support of the regime. According to Easton, this support can be split into legitimacy and trust. Consequentially, the concept of political culture is reduced to a rather scarce content, and the problem of integrating the many individual-level orientations into a coherent concept is also reduced (Reisinger 1995).

3 COMMITMENT TO DEMOCRACY

The relevant attitudes for the persistence of the democracy in a country are the commitments to democratic values (cf. Figure 9.1). Among these the commitment to democracy is the most pivotal attitude of all. The stronger this commitment is, the more likely is the persistence and vice versa. Due to the significance of this attitude, I will present the distribution of the commitment to democracy for a selected set of countries and then discuss these shortly.

The crucial question is, how this commitment to democracy can be measured. Especially in new democracies, where the perception and evaluation of democracy is still ambiguous, as citizens tend to mix it with autocratic elements (Rose and Mishler 1994; Shin 1999). This problem can be reduced if attitudes towards democracy are systematically combined in an index with attitudes towards autocracy. Table 9.1 lists those respondents who have answered two questions on democracy clearly positively and two questions on autocracy clearly negatively, and labels them as *solid democrats*. Those respondents who believe that democracy is not better than autocracy or even prefer autocracy to democracy are labelled *non-democrats*. All other respondents are called *weak democrats*.

The countries listed in Table 9.1 are limited to those countries which have been considered "free" by Freedom House (2006). As the percentages of the three types show, there are remarkable differences between the regions and even within the regions themselves. The extent of *solid democrats* is relatively high in western and southern Europe and comparatively low in eastern Europe, Latin America, and Asia. Exceptions must be made in these summary estimations for Finland (western Europe) and Portugal (southern Europe). In both countries less than 30 percent are solid democrats. In the case of Asia, Japan is the exception and Argentina is South America's exceptional case. In both countries more than 25 percent are solid democrats.

In total there are eight countries, in which the extent of *non-democrats* overweighs the extent of *solid democrats*: Latvia, Lithuania, Romania, the Ukraine, Chile, Mexico, India, and Indonesia. As a criterion for the consolidation of a democracy it can be plausibly postulated that at least the majority of citizens support democracy and consider democracy as "the only game in town" (Linz and Stepan 1996; Diamond 1999; Fuchs and Roller 2006). According to this criterion democracy in these eight countries is certainly not yet consolidated. Above all in Lithuania and Ukraine

Table 9.1 Commitment to democracy (%)

Region	Non-democrats	Weak democrats	Solid democrats
Western Europe			
Austria	3.1	36.7	60.2
Belgium	7.6	53.9	38.4
Denmark	0.9	31.4	67.7
Finland	11.4	59.4	29.2
France	8.5	50.2	41.3
Germany	3.0	41.2	55.9
Iceland	1.3	39.4	59.3
Ireland	8.5	51.5	40.0
Italy	4.7	49.1	46.1
Luxembourg	8.5	57.5	33.9
The Netherlands	3.5	59.4	37.1
Sweden	4.7	45.9	49.5
Great Britain	12.3	41.9	45.9
mean	6.0	47.5	46.5
Southern Europe			
Greece	4.0	27.0	69.0
Malta	6.0	44.2	49.8
Portugal	10.9	67.8	21.3
Spain	7.4	60.7	31.8
mean	7.1	49.9	43.0
Central Europe			
Croatia	2.7	58.9	38.4
Czech Republic	4.5	56.6	38.9
Hungary	10.3	62.9	26.8
Poland	15.2	65.9	18.9
Slovakia	14.0	61.3	24.7
Slovenia	8.3	61.1	30.6
mean	9.2	61.1	29.7
Eastern Europe			
Bulgaria	15.9	61.5	22.6
Estonia	6.7	76.8	16.4
Latvia	13.0	77.5	9.5
Lithuania	12.5	75.1	12.3
Romania	31.0	53.6	15.4
Ukraine	20.1	71.9	8.0
mean	16.5	69.4	14.0
North America			
Canada	9.2	49.1	41.7
USA	12.6	58	29.4
mean	10.9	53.6	35.6

(Continued)

Table 9.1 (*Continued*)

Region	Non-democrats	Weak democrats	Solid democrats
Latin America			
Argentina	14.9	55.7	29.4
Chile	25.5	50.4	24.1
Mexico	34.7	58.7	6.5
Peru	13.6	72.7	13.7
mean	22.2	59.4	18.4
Asia			
India	20.5	63.7	15.7
Indonesia	33.3	66.6	0.1
Japan	4.6	67	28.5
South Korea	10.1	77.2	12.7
mean	17.1	68.6	14.3
South Africa	19.0	52.5	28.4

Source: World Values Survey / European Values Survey, 1999–2002.

(Europe), in Mexico (Latin America), and Indonesia (Asia) the number of *non-democrats* decisively exceeds that of the *solid democrats*.

The countries listed in Table 9.1 have been unambiguously considered democracies by Freedom House (2006). Yet the listed percentages for the commitment to democracy show that the implementation of democratic institutions must not necessarily entail corresponding attitudes of the citizens. This is also the case for countries such as Mexico and India, where democracy already exists for a long time. According to the paradigm of political culture, the reverse should be assumed if it is the attitudes towards the regime which affect the persistence of the regime.

4 POLITICAL CULTURE AND POLITICAL COMMUNITY

Almond defined system culture with reference to Easton's theory. As a result, this definition contains the attitudes towards the political community. Taking Easton (1965, 177) into account, the political community constitutes one of the three objects of a political system. Easton (1965, 177) defines it through a division of labor among the members of a community. Thus, this establishes a relation among the citizens. Easton further states that the theoretical relevance of the political community is the ability to produce and impose generally binding decisions for the society. The prerequisites for producing binding decisions for a community are the willingness of the members to agree to such a division of labor in order to regulate common affairs. The particular type of political system, which produces and implements binding decisions, is not relevant.

The paradigm of political culture, however, does not consider any type of political system, but focuses on democracy. This means that the division of labor among the citizens is not arbitrary. Rather, it is regulated by democratic values and norms and these establish a certain relation between the citizens. *The Civic Culture* addresses this aspect in Chapter IX, "Social relations and civic co-operation." Almond (1980, 28) later assigned this dimension to the category of process culture which consists of the "attitudes toward the self in politics . . . and attitudes toward other political actors (e.g. trust, co-operative competence, hostility)." Yet, this is merely a terminological categorization.

Recently, the aspect of political community was systematically developed as a theory of its own by Putnam (1993) in *Making Democracy Work*. As the title states, this study establishes an entirely new perspective than *The Civic Culture*. The reference point no longer is the persistence of democracies, but the functioning of democracies. Hence, democracies are assumed to be given, and the normative and practically relevant question considers their quality. The normative criterion for the assessment of liberal democracies is the governance of the political process through the demands raised by the citizens. This regulation occurs to the extent that institutions and authorities act responsively to these public demands and implement these as policies (Dahl 1971). Putnam (1993, 9) expresses his democratic standards: "A high-performance democratic institution must be both responsive and effective: sensitive to the demands of its constituents and effective in using limited resources to address those demands." His study focuses on the prerequisites of responsiveness and effectiveness as the criteria of democratic performance: "what are the conditions for creating strong, responsive, effective representative institutions?" (Putnam 1993, 6). The answer lies in the generation of a vibrant civic community. He operationalizes his question by constructing an "index of democratic performance" as the dependent variable and an "index of civic community" as the explanatory variable. In his empirical analysis of twenty Italian regions Putnam (1993, 98) discovers a very strong correlation of $r = .92$ between the two indices. This is not actual empirical proof for a causal effect of civic community on institutional performance, but at least this provides empirical evidence in support of this assumption. However, for my purpose, the theoretical logic of the assumed causal connection is more important than the discussion of the empirical finding.

Putnam elaborates this theoretical logic within his concept of social capital. Social capital encompasses the three characteristics: social trust, norms, and networks of civic engagement (Putnam 1993, 167; also see chapter in this volume by Stolle). In the context of social capital, Putnam restricts norms to generalized reciprocity (when he discusses civic community he furthermore names political equality, solidarity, and tolerance). These three characteristics are not all located on the same level, but they are involved in a causal and dynamic relation. If one disregards the feedback relation for one instance, then the dependent variable of the model of social capital is social trust. Social trust is influenced by the norm of generalized reciprocity and the active engagement in voluntary associations (Putnam 1993, 171). This active engagement in voluntary associations enhances the norm of generalized reciprocity. The networks of civic engagement constitute another dimension than the other two components of social capital: they are the socio-structural base for the development of such civic norms as the generalized reciprocity as well as social trust (Newton 2001; Gabriel et al. 2002).

Putnam focuses less on the internal structure of the characteristics of social capital, and more on the effect on institutional performance and therefore on the functioning of democracy. Putnam sees this as a dual-level process. On the first level, social trust enables cooperation of the citizens for mutual benefits (Putnam 1993, 171). Likewise, this cooperation improves the articulation of the citizens' common demands toward political authorities. The postulated effect of social capital on cooperation and institutional performance, however, is scarcely elaborated on and less persuasively justified than the internal interrelation of social capital (Levi 1996). Thus, a need for further theoretical clarification exists.

Putnam's study has been evaluated in very different ways. Laitin (1995, 171) describes it as a "stunning breakthrough in political culture research." In contrast, Jackman and Miller (1996a), Levi (1996), and Tarrow (1996) are far more critical of it. Critics are particularly concerned with Putnam's empirical analyses and evidence for his theoretical assumptions. Jackman and Miller (1996a), for instance, question the value of the one-dimensionality of institutional performance; they reach completely different results when they analyze individual components of institutional performance. Yet, more important is the criticism of the validity of both indices. The institutional performance measures policy performance (Tarrow 1996) and not democratic performance (Roller 2005). That these policies apply to Putnam's own democratic standards—responsiveness and effectiveness—can at best be implied. A comparable level of doubt exists for the explanatory variables. The civic community is described by Putnam—besides networks of civic engagement—through attitudes (civic norms, social trust), but the index of civic community encompasses no attitudes, such as civic norms and social trust. If the validity of both variables is doubted, the strong correlation between them cannot be interpreted as empirical evidence for the theoretically postulated effect of civic community on democratic performance.

These criticisms raise the question of whether Putnam's study truly represents progress in the field of political culture research. As I see it, the study is innovative first in terms of the question addressing the quality of democracies and second, in its fundamental theoretical assumption that the civic community is a decisive determinant for this quality.

The problem of the persistence of democratic regimes was appropriate and fruitful in the light of the breakdown of European democracies between the two world wars and the competition between communism and democracy after the Second World War. Following the breakdown of communism, however, democracy won out as the only legitimate type of rule on a near-global scale. Therefore, a change of perspective is necessary. This refers to the quality of existing democracies. Dahl (1989) demonstrated convincingly that establishing a democracy is not an "either/or"-question, to be answered only once. From a certain level onwards, a level from which a political system can be considered a democracy, the raising of the quality of this democracy to reach an ideal level is considerable and desirable. Putnam's research introduced this hotly debated topic in normative democratic theory into political culture research, and therein lays one of his innovations.

Another innovation is based on the postulation that the civic community above all is responsible for the quality of democracy. This idea is also developed in studies pertaining to many different disciplines of political science. Amongst them are the history of political thought (Tocqueville 1992), Republicanism (Taylor 1989), the theory of deliberative democracy (Habermas 1992; Bohman 2000), and the concept of civil society (Cohen and Arato 1992). In political culture research, this idea has only played a significant role since Putnam. As such, Putnam has prepared a more systematic linkage of normative and empirical research than was the case until then.

Putnam's civic community is a complex phenomenon, not to be entirely accommodated by political culture. On the one hand, it encompasses a socio-structural as well as a behavioral dimension. The socio-structural component consists of networks of voluntary associations and the behavioral components of active engagement in these voluntary associations. On the other hand, it encompasses an attitudinal dimension. This dimension consists of those norms and values that govern the political interactions and cooperation of citizens. On the premise that political culture is formed from attitudes and the analytical clarity of the concept is not further diluted, the attitudinal dimension of civic community can only be understood as a component of political culture. Civic norms and values such as social trust, political tolerance and generalized reciprocity are then cultural predictors for citizens' cooperative behaviour for the expression and implementation of their demands.

As a consequence of this discussion on the issue of Putnam's study, the core of the research program of *The Civic Culture* needs to be extended by a sixth assumption:

(6) The civic norms and values underlying the cooperation of the citizens are significant determinants for the functioning of a democracy. The normative criteria for its functioning are the responsiveness and effectiveness of the political institutions on the demands of the citizens.

5 THE PROBLEM OF AGGREGATION

To this day, political culture research predominantly consists of analyses on the micro-level of citizens. This is justified by the extent to which the relevance of the attitudes is theoretically explained and the central assumptions of the paradigm of political culture are applied. These assumptions maintain that political culture as a macro-phenomenon affects the persistence and quality of democracies. With regard to these assumptions, there is a severe conceptual problem as well as a considerable deficit in research. This section discusses this conceptual problem and the following section addresses the deficit in research.

The conceptual problem lies in the fact that political culture originates from the micro-level where its data is collected and yet it is a macro-phenomenon: "Political culture is the property of a collectivity...Individuals have beliefs, values and attitudes but they do not have cultures" (Elkins and Simeon 1979, 129). The aggregation of individual attitudes is the means used to transfer from the micro-level of the citizens to the macro-level of the collectivity. Various authors have criticized this mechanism of aggregation (Scheuch 1968; Pye 1972; Kaase 1983; Patrick 1984; Reisinger 1995; Seligson 2002). Reisinger (1995, 339) pinpointed the problem: "The challenge is to overcome the 'individualist fallacy'—the fallacy of deriving conclusions about a higher level of aggregation from data on individuals *without a theoretical rationale that links the two levels.*" One can object that it is not the individual attitudes that constitute the political culture of a collectivity but the distribution of these attitudes. According to Pye (1972, 293), however, this is only "a more sophisticated vision that macro-systems are no more than extrapolations of micro-systems."

The political culture paradigm has not overcome this problem of aggregation. However, the exploration of certain alternatives is a step towards a solution. The aggregation mechanism subsumes that the data of individual attitudes are collected through representative random samples. This aggregation implies that each individual receives an equal amount of weight in the whole data set. In how far is this justified? It is generally known that one of the most significant characteristics of the western civilization is the value of the individual. This is legally codified by the constitutions of most countries and is expressed in the equal weight of each citizen in the political system. Dahl (1989, 97) goes a step further and makes a "strong principle of equality" the starting point for the development of his criteria for an ideal democracy. To the extent that this value is implemented in the political system, this aggregation mechanism is appropriate. Thus, it can be implied that the distribution of the equally weighted attitudes of the citizens can also affect on the dependent variable of political culture.

Nevertheless, individualism as a basic and unequivocal value cannot be claimed for other civilizations (Lerner 1958; Huntington 1996; Eisenstadt 2000). In many Asian countries, the community ranks higher than the individual. Additionally, many of these Asian communities are particularly hierarchically structured, which results in the elite having a much stronger influence on the attitudes and behaviour of the average citizen than in the case of individualistic and egalitarian western communities. Thus, this can cast doubt on whether the representative random samples—which rests their value on the equal weight of each respondent—can be regarded as applicable. Insofar as elite surveys may be an alternative data source, this must be discussed elsewhere. Thus, we can assume that aggregation relying on the equal treatment of individual attitudes is justified in western communities.

The problem of aggregation is linked to two further problems. The first addresses the number of attitudes that need to be aggregated to thoroughly describe the political culture of a collectivity. This problem can be solved by assuming that for the dependent variable only one attitude is relevant. For the persistence of democracy in general and for that of an individual nation, the theoretically most probable attitudes would be the commitment to democracy as a value and the support of democracy in the particular country. It is not by chance that these attitudes have gained prominence in political culture research (Dalton 2004; Fuchs and Roller 2006). Nonetheless, if we assume that political culture is an amalgamation of several attitudes, the situation becomes more complicated. As a consequence, a pattern must be detected through the aggregation of attitudes. Fuchs and Klingemann (2002) have recently undertaken such a venture based on theoretical considerations and the method of a discriminant analysis. Yet, this was restricted to a descriptive analysis of a comparison of countries.

The other problem lies in the definition of a collectivity. Political culture is only conceivable as a characteristic of a collectivity. This, however, requires that the collectivity form a meaningful entity and not just an artificial construction. In today's nation-state democracies, the relevant collectivity is formally and unambiguously defined as the total of all individuals residing in state territory who have the legal status of citizens. Citizenship enables drawing clear borders between those who belong to the collectivity and those who do not. The collectivity of citizens elects its representatives, who are responsible for the people. This collectivity is the ultimate sovereign power and the persistence and quality of a democracy relates to it and depends on it. In Western communities with historically grown collectivities (national communities), the citizens subjectively perceive themselves as members of the collectivity. Thus, the collectivities of Western democracies are both formally and subjectively defined. They form a meaningful entity to which a political culture can be accounted. How far this also holds for postnational and supranational communities is another question, because these are problematic due to the unclear borders and the lack of historically grown commonalities. Only if it we assume that a collectivity exists to which a political culture can be assigned, can we raise the question of the causal effects of political culture.

6 THE QUESTION OF CAUSALITY

Thus far, political culture research has concentrated on analyses at the micro-level. At this level, the dependent variables are the political attitudes and behavior of the citizens, although political behavior cannot be accounted to the narrower concept of political culture. However, on a broader scale, studies with political behaviour as dependent variable can be allocated to the paradigm for two reasons: first because political behaviour can be explained through political attitudes, and second because they can function as an intervening variable between political attitudes and their systemic consequences. I shall focus on the attitudes as a substrate of political culture in the following.

The question of causality is relatively unproblematic on the micro-level of attitudes. Based on a given theoretical perspective, one attitude is defined as the dependent variable and one attempts to explain it with the help of additional attitudes. If, for example, the theoretical reference point is the persistence of democracies, then regime support could be the relevant dependent variable. If the quality of democracies is the theoretical reference point, social trust could be a meaningful option as a dependent variable. In the meantime, a plethora of studies has empirically analyzed the determinants for regime support. Since Putnam's investigation (1993), the number of studies explaining social trust has soared exponentially (cf. Gabriel et al. 2002; Hooghe and Stolle 2003; Newton chapter in this volume). To specifically determine the explanatory variable, the concept of political culture merely provides overall reference points. *The Civic Culture* (1963) postulates that the basic attitudes of political culture are internalized through processes of socialization. Yet, in a later analysis, Almond (1990) does not exclude the effects of experiences made with the institutional mechanisms and performance. This knowledge, however, does not provide sufficient instruction for the specification of empirically testable causal models. Therefore, theories from other approaches, such as system theoretical, institutionalist, or social psychological approaches, can be taken into consideration. These approaches serve to compensate the theoretical deficit on the micro-level.

Regardless of the question of which relevant attitudes are explained, such causal analyses remain *within* political culture. The theoretical relevance of attitudinal analyses results from the assumed effect of political culture on the persistence and quality of democracies. To verify this assumption and provide with it a paradigmatic supposition of the political culture concept, the persistence and quality of democracies must be defined as dependent variables and explained *through* political culture. This implies a transfer from the micro- to the macro-level.

There is limited research regarding such analyses on the macro-level. This stems from the lack of a necessary database, which must fulfil two criteria. First, it must contain random samples for an adequate amount of countries in order to conduct the analysis. Second, these samples must contain theoretically relevant variables of political culture. The World Values Survey, first carried out in 1981 and most recently in 1999–2002, meets this criterion. In terms of the paradigm of political culture, the potential for analysis of the World Values Survey has only been exploited by Inglehart and his counterparts so far (Inglehart 1997; Inglehart and Baker 2000; Inglehart and Welzel 2005, 2006). These studies provide empirical evidence of a correlation between political culture and institutional variables.

The persistence of democracies is operationalized in two of these studies with the durability of democracies (Inglehart 1997; Inglehart and Welzel 2005). Presuming that this is a valid measurement of the construct, the question of causality remains unanswered. One of the central points of criticism of the concept of political culture was addressed by Barry (1970): the problem of what is cause and what is effect. According to Barry (1970), the causal direction of political institutions on political culture is just as viable in reverse. The unanswered question of cause and effect on the macro-level cannot be solved with a regression analysis that uses the durability of democracy as the dependent variable. However, the durability of democracies can just as plausibly serve as an explanatory variable, which can be further specified and tested in terms of the explanation of political culture. As long as this empirical ambiguity exists, research relies on additional historical evidence for the location of a postulated causal direction. Yet, these bear a high plausibility (Almond 1980).

The question of causality is less complex if the dependent variable is the quality of democracy. The cases for analysis could be contemporary democracies and the World Values Survey could be used as the database for the survey of political culture. The standards of the quality of democracy are the responsiveness and effectiveness of political institutions among others. The responsiveness can be measured through the congruency between the demands of the citizens—data collected through representative random samples—and the party and governmental platforms (Klingemann 1995). Many OECD countries have a sufficient amount of macro-data to measure effectiveness. An example for the explanation of differences in the effectiveness in OECD countries is provided in a survey by Roller (2005). This investigation does not include cultural variables as predictors, but rather institutional, partisan, and socioeconomic variables. However, Roller's model for analysis can easily be supplemented by cultural variables. This would make it possible to empirically detect the relative explanatory value of the different categories of predictors for political effectiveness and, in a further step, compare different theoretical approaches.

Another possibility to measure the quality of democracies is the degree to which a civil society exists. This can be operationalized through the level of active membership of citizens in voluntary associations and the participation of citizens in activities of these voluntary associations. However, the vitality of the civil society as a democratic standard must be justified normatively beforehand. In liberal democracies, for instance, this democratic standard is not self-evident. Habermas (1992), for example, argued for this justification in his theory of deliberative democracy. Thus, civil society attains a double status in the paradigm of political culture. First, it is a dependent variable, as far as it is a democratic standard itself. Second, it is an explanatory variable, to the extent that it is congruent with the theory of Putnam (1993), where the dependent explanatory variable is the responsiveness and effectiveness of democratic institutions.

The deficit in theory of the concept of political culture that has already been described on the micro-level also applies to the macro-level. It concerns the persistence of democracies as well as the quality of democracies as explanatory variables. Regarding the quality of democracies, Putnam (1993) states that the aggregated social trust of the public affects institutional performance. This occurs because social trust improves cooperation for the articulation of the demands by the citizens. We have already discussed the need for theoretical clarification for the explanation of the chain of cause and effect postulated by Putnam.

Various arguments support a causal effect of the aggregated regime support on the persistence of the regime. In a liberal democracy with a competitive party system, a regime change is almost unimaginable, as long as the majority of citizens support the regime. For a stable democracy, Diamond (1999) argues that at least two-thirds of the citizens must support democracy. Taking into account that each ballot weighs equally, anti-system parties face no realistic chance of changing a regime when they represent such a small minority.

The explanation of the effect of political culture on the persistence and quality of democracies is not a theoretical explanation, rather a consideration of plausibility. Although Almond (1980) states that "political culture is not a theory" and concludes that "the explanatory power of political culture variables is an empirical question, open to hypothesis and testing." To reasonably specify a hypothesis, a theory is required and this theory is not provided by the political culture concept. In the light of established standards of scientific philosophy, the criticism of a deficit in theory must also be maintained on the macro-level. However, every research paradigm can only be judged adequately in comparison to competing paradigms. This competing paradigm is the political-economy approach located on the macro-level. Yet, it cannot suggest more than considerations of plausibility for the empirical evidence that is presented (Lipset 1993, 2000; Przeworski et al. 1996). On the macro-level, a fundamental deficit in theory exists and the question arises how this trouble spot can be solved in further research.

7 SUMMARY AND PROSPECTS

The renaissance of the concept of political culture has been accompanied by a series of evaluations, some of which were rather critical. Some of these evaluations carefully examine the renaissance and on the basis of designated standards of philosophy of science, they conclude that merely a "renaissance of a rubric" (Reisinger 1995) can be detected or political culture is simply a "degenerate research program" (Laitin 1995). In contrast to this, I would like to introduce two objections and two specifications of the question of political culture. This will be followed by an elaboration of core assumptions of the concept. This discussion serves to identify reference points for a positive heuristic of the political culture paradigm. According to Lakatos (1970), a positive heuristic is a criterion for a progressive research program.

The first objection essentially focuses on the reference point for the evaluation of the political culture concept. Many critics refer to the broad number of studies that describe themselves or are attributed to the political culture approach. One can reasonably doubt how many of these studies represent the concept of political culture, beyond their analyses of political attitudes. The impression of political culture being a rubric is closely linked to this observation. Consequently, we underestimate the theoretical potential for the development of the concept that derives from *The Civic Culture*. Almond (1980, 1990, 1993; Almond and Powell 1978) has hinted at this potential in various publications succeeding *The Civic Culture*. This essay has attempted to further clarify theoretical and analytical aspects.

On the one hand, I suggest differentiating the political system in three objects that are in hierarchical order. I have also postulated causal relationships between the attitudes that refer to these three objects. On the other hand, I have integrated Putnam's (1993) theory into the concept of political culture. Putnam's study has been proclaimed a "progressive research program" by Laitin (1995)—in contrast to political culture research as a whole—and perceived as a breakthrough. Through this integration, the concept of political culture accesses a relevant question: the quality and the functioning of contemporary democracies. This integration simultaneously has the result that the question of political culture is expanded beyond the persistence of regimes. Accordingly, this achieves a broad scope for possible analyses within the frame of political culture, and this is one of the criteria for a positive heuristic, which Laitin has demanded.

The second objection refers to the evaluation standards. The utility of a research program cannot be evaluated absolutely, but merely in comparison to the competing research design. Laitin (1995, 168) realizes that "any social science research program" would have difficulties in fulfilling the criteria. The competing research program is rational choice (Eckstein 1988; Reisinger 1995) and on the macro-level a political-economy approach. The latter is often linked to the rational choice paradigm.

Once the standards of philosophy of science are applied, the rational choice paradigm is also put under severe criticism (Friedman 1996). Green and Shapiro (1994) even state that there are *Pathologies of Rational Choice Theory*. One of these pathologies, the paradox of voting, has been refuted within the rational choice paradigm by Brennan and Lomasky (1993) with their concept of expressive voting. This concept contains orientations that are closely related to value orientations. Thus, the borderline to the political culture approach is blurred. I do not want to continue to elaborate on the contents of this discussion, rather I would like to state once more: the supremacy of the paradigm in comparison to others cannot be merely theoretically explained, but requires systematic and empirical comparisons in terms of its descriptive and explanatory potential. These systematic comparisons have not been addressed thus far and their implementation can be considered a positive heuristic for further research.

The question of *The Civic Culture* deals with the persistence of democracies. This is specified in transformation research. This approach describes the consolidation of democracies as the third phase of the system change, after liberalization and democratization (O'Donnell, Schmitter, and Whitehead 1986; di Palma 1990). A newly established democracy is consolidated to the extent to which the relevant actors have internalized democracy and its values (Linz and Stepan 1996; Diamond 1999). This complies with the essential idea of political culture: a persistent democracy requires the congruency of structure and culture. Transformation research has developed a theoretically sensible chronology and realizes that the development process has reached its final ideal if *all actors* have internalized democratic values (see chapter in this volume by Shin; Klingemann, Fuchs, and Zielonka 2006).

A further specification consists in the differentiation between the category of persistence and the attitudinal constructs that are assigned to it (cf. Figure 9.1). This is based on the premise that many different legitimate forms of democracy exist. Accordingly, one must differentiate between the persistence of democracy in general and the persistence of democracy that has been institutionalized in a certain country. For the political culture of a country this means that the citizens can prefer another type of democracy to the one that exists in their country, but in general they will still want to maintain democracy as such. Provided that the concept has been differentiated as mentioned above, the political culture research can tie with the discussion on different normative models of democracy (Fuchs 2002; Fuchs and Klingemann 2002).

I would like to conclude my discussion with two further considerations, which could result in a modification of core assumptions of the paradigm of political culture. One of the considerations refers to the broadening of the scope of the paradigm to countries that have either autocratic regimes or are regimes in the democratization process. These countries, which are no longer democratic or not yet democratic, are referred to as defect democracies (Diamond 1999; Merkel et al. 2003). The core assumption that the political culture is the essential prerequisite for the persistence and the change of a regime can also apply to these regimes. The inherently postulated effect that culture has on structure is presumably stretched on a longer time span in defect democracies than in functioning democracies. It seems implausible for autocracies and defect democracies that a regime may be persistent if its culture is incongruent with its structure. However, it is questionable whether the influential bearers of the political culture in these regimes are average citizens or whether they are elites. Considering the latter premise, the political culture, that is relevant for both regime persistence or regime change, cannot merely be constituted by the aggregation of attitudes through representative random samples but also through elite surveys.

The second consideration refers to the question of the bearers of political culture. In the research program that derives from *The Civic Culture* the bearers of political culture are the citizenry. Many theoretical studies (cf. Huntington 1996; Eisenstadt 2000) are based on the assumption that cultures have developed in the long run. This assumption also underlies the empirical analyses by Inglehart and Baker (2000) and Fuchs and Klingemann (2002). Both studies presuppose that the enduring culture has an effect on the current value orientations of the citizens. An analysis of those long-run cultures cannot replace the analysis of currently existing cultures. It can merely supplement the analysis. The persistence and the change of a regime may only be influenced through the actions of the citizens. Direct predictors for action are the attitudes that citizens possess at present. The attitudes are developed through processes of socialization and the socialization agencies (especially educational institutions and their actors) bear the influence of the culture that has developed in the long run.

The assumption that a culture that has developed in the long run can only be fruitful in social science if the specific bearer can be identified. Such bearers could be collective actors such as political parties, but most of all political institutions (Gerhards 2005). The culture in these institutions is manifested in the texts and the value orientations in these texts. I would like to name only two examples. One example, which is particularly relevant for political institutions, is the constitution. Constitutions enshrine principles and values that underlie a certain type of rule. The second example refers to the internalization of these principles and values, which is carried out in the process of socialization in educational institutions. Their culture can be described by analyses based on schoolbooks, curricula, or related texts.

Both the interrelation of elite culture and mass culture as well as the influence of culture in the long run on the contemporary culture can be empirically analyzed. These, however, require relatively complex research designs. The specification and implementation of these research designs constitutes another positive heuristic of the research program of political culture.

REFERENCES

ALMOND, G. 1980. The intellectual history of the civic culture concept. Pp. 1–33 in *The Civic Culture Revisited*, ed. G. A. Almond and S. Verba. Boston: Little, Brown & Company.

—— 1990. The study of political culture. Pp. 138–69 in *A Discipline Divided*, ed. G. A. Almond. Newbury Park: Sage Publications.

—— 1993. Foreword: the return to political culture. Pp. ix–xii in *Political Culture and Democracy in Developing Countries*, ed. L. Diamond. Boulder, Colo.: Lynne Rienner.

—— and POWELL, B. 1978. *Comparative Politics. System, Process, and Policy*. Boston: Little, Brown & Company.

—— and VERBA, S. 1963. *The Civic Culture: Political Attitudes and Democracy in Five Nations*. Princeton: Princeton University Press.

BARRY, B. 1970. *Sociologists, Economists, and Democracy*. London: Macmillan.

BOHMAN, J. 2000. *Public Deliberation. Pluralism, Complexity and Democracy*. Cambridge: MIT Press.

BRENNAN, G., and LOMASKY, L. 1993. *Democracy and Decision: The Pure Theory of Electoral Preference*. Cambridge: Cambridge University Press.

BROWN, A. 1977. Introduction. Pp. 1–24 in *Political Culture and Political Change in Communist States*, ed. A. Brown and J. Gray. London: Macmillan.

COHEN, J., and ARATO, A. 1992. *Civil Society and Political Theory*. Cambridge: MIT Press.

CRAWFORD, S., and OSTROM, E. 1995. A grammar of institutions. *American Political Science Review*, 89: 582–600.

DAHL, R. A. 1971. *Polyarchy. Participation and Opposition*. New Haven: Yale University Press.

—— 1989. *Democracy and its Critics*. New Haven: Yale University Press.

DALTON, R. J. 2004. *Democratic Challenges: Democratic Choices*. Oxford: Oxford University Press.

—— 2005. *Citizen Politics: Public Opinion and Political Parties in Advanced Industrial Democracies,* 4th edn. Washington, DC: CQ Press.

DETH, J. VAN, and SCARBOROUGH, E. eds. 1995. *The Impact of Values.* Oxford: Oxford University Press.

DIAMOND, L. J. 1999. *Developing Democracy: Toward Consolidation.* Baltimore: Johns Hopkins University Press.

DITTMER, L. 1977. Political culture and political symbolism: towards a theoretical synthesis *World Politics,* 29: 552–83.

DOWNS, A. 1957. *Economic Theory of Democracy.* New York: Harper & Row.

EASTON, D. 1965. *A Systems Analysis of Political Life.* Chicago: University of Chicago Press.

—— 1975. A re-assessment of the concept of political support. *British Journal of Political Science,* 5: 435–57.

—— 1990. *The Analysis of Political Structure.* New York: Routledge.

ECKSTEIN, H. 1988. A culturalist theory of political change. *American Political Science Review,* 82: 789–804.

EISENSTADT, S. N. 2000. *Die Vielfalt der Moderne.* Weilerswist: Velbrück Wissenschaft.

ELKINS, D. J., and SIMEON, R. 1979. A cause in search of its effects, or what does political culture explain. *Comparative Politics,* 11: 127–45.

FREEDOM HOUSE. 2006. *The Annual Survey of Political Rights and Civil Liberties,* **www.freedomhouse.org**

FRIEDMAN, J. 1996. *The Rational Choice Controversy.* New Haven: Yale University Press.

FUCHS, D. 1999. The democratic culture of unified Germany. Pp. 123–45 in *Critical Citizens: Global Support for Democratic Governance.* ed. P. Norris. Oxford: Oxford University Press.

—— 2002. Das Konzept der politischen Kultur: Die Fortsetzung einer Kontroverse in konstruktiver Absicht. Pp. 27–49 in *Bürger und Demokratie in Ost und West: Studien zur politischen Kultur und zum politischen Prozess,* ed. D. Fuchs, E. Roller, and B. Wessels. Wiesbaden: Westdeutscher Verlag.

—— and KLINGEMANN, H.-D. 2002. Eastward enlargement of the European Union and the identity of Europe. *West European Politics,* 25 (2): 19–54.

—— and ROLLER, E. 1998. Cultural conditions of the transformation to liberal democracies in Central and Eastern Europe. Pp. 25–77 in *Post-Communist Citizen,* ed. S. H. Barnes and J. Simon, Budapest: Erasmus Foundation and Hungarian Academy of Sciences.

—— and ROLLER, E. 2006. Learned democracy? The support of democracy in Central and Eastern European countries, *International Journal of Sociology,* 36, 3: 70–96.

GABRIEL, O. W., KUNZ V., ROßTEUTSCHER, S., and DETH, J. VAN 2002. *Sozialkapital und Demokratie: Zivilgesellschaftliche Ressourcen im Vergleich.* Vienna: WSV-Universitätsverlag.

GERHARDS, J. 2005. *Kulturelle Unterschiede in der Europäischen Union.* Wiesbaden: Verlag für Sozialwissenschaften.

GREEN, D. P., and SHAPIRO, I. 1994. *Pathologies of Rational Choice Theory: A Critique of Applications in Political Science.* New Haven: Yale University Press.

HABERMAS, J. 1992. *Faktizität und Geltung.* Frankfurt: Suhrkamp. English Publication: Habermas, J. 1996. *Between Facts and Norms,* trans W. Rehg. Cambridge: MIT Press.

HOOGHE, M., and STOLLE, D. 2003. *Social Capital: Civil Society and Institutions in Comparative Perspective.* New York: Palgrave.

HUNTINGTON, S. P. 1993. *The Third Wave: Democratization in the Late Twentieth Century.* New Haven: University of Oklahoma Press.

—— 1996. *The Clash of Civilizations and the Remaking of World Order.* New York: Simon & Schuster.

INGLEHART, R. 1988. The renaissance of political culture. *American Political Science Review*, 82: 1203–30.

—— 1997. *Modernization and Postmodernization: Cultural, Economic, and Political Change in 43 Societies*. Princeton: Princeton University Press.

—— and BAKER, W. E. 2000. Modernization, cultural change, and the persistence of traditional values. *American Sociological Review*, 65: 19–51.

—— and WELZEL, C. 2005. Political culture and democracy: analyzing cross-level linkages. *Comparative Politics*, 36: 61–79.

—— —— 2005. *Modernization, Cultural Change, and Democracy: The Human Development Sequence*. Cambridge: Cambridge University Press.

JACKMAN, R. W., and MILLER, R. A. 1996a. A renaissance of political culture? *American Journal of Political Science*, 40: 632–59.

—— —— 1996b. The poverty of political culture. *American Journal of Political Science*, 40: 697–716.

KAASE, M. 1983. Sinn oder Unsinn des Konzepts "Politische Kultur" für die Vergleichende Politikforschung, oder auch: Der Versuch, einen Pudding an die Wand zu nageln. Pp. 144–71 in *Wahlen und politisches System: Analysen aus Anlaß der Bundestagswahl 1980*, ed. M. Kaase and H.-D. Klingemann. Opladen: Westdeutscher Verlag.

KAVANAGH, D. 1972. *Political Culture*. London: Macmillan.

KEESING, R. 1974. Theories of culture. *Annual Review of Anthropology*, 3: 73–97.

KLINGEMANN, H.-D. 1995. Party positions and voter orientations. Pp. 183–205 in *Citizens and the State*, ed. H.-D. Klingemann and D. Fuchs. Oxford: Oxford University Press.

—— 1999. Mapping political support in the 1990s: a global analysis. Pp. 31–56 in *Critical Citizens: Global Support for Democratic Governance*. ed. P. Norris. Oxford: Oxford University Press.

—— and FUCHS, D. eds. 1995. *Citizens and the State*. Oxford: Oxford University Press 1995.

—— —— and ZIELONKA, J. eds. 2006. Democracy and political culture in Eastern Europe. London: Routledge.

KLUCKHOHN, C. 1951. Values and value orientations in the theory of action. Pp. 388–433 in *Toward a General Theory of Action*, ed. T. Parsons and E. Shils. Cambridge, Mass.: Harvard University Press.

KUHN, T. 1996. *The Structure of Scientific Revolutions*. 3rd edn. Chicago: University of Chicago Press.

LAITIN, D. 1995. The Civic Culture at thirty. *American Political Science Review*, 89: 168–73.

LAKATOS, I. 1970. Falsification and the methodology of scientific research programmes. Pp. 91–196 in *Criticism and the Growth of Knowledge*, ed. I. Lakatos and A. Musgrave. Cambridge: Cambridge University Press.

LANE, R. 1992. Political culture: residual category or general theory? *Comparative Political Studies*, 25: 362–87.

LERNER, D. 1958. *The Passing of Traditional Society: Modernizing the Middle East*. Glencoe, Ill.: Free Press.

LEVI, M. 1996. Social and unsocial capital: a review essay of Robert Putnam's "Making Democracy Work". *Politics and Society*, 24: 45–55.

LIJPHART, A. 1980. The structure of inference. Pp. 37–56 in *The Civic Culture Revisited*, ed. G. A. Almond and S. Verba. Boston: Little Brown.

LINZ, J., and STEPAN, A. 1996. *Problems of Democratic Transition and Consolidation. Southern Europe, South America, and Post-Communist Europe*. Baltimore: Johns Hopkins University Press.

LIPSET, S. M. 1993. The social requisites of democracy revisited. *American Sociological Review*, 59: 1–22.

—— 2000. Conditions for democracy. Pp. 393–410 in *Zur Zukunft der Demokratie im Zeitalter der Globalisierung: WZB Jahrbuch 2000*, ed. H.-D. Klingemann and F. Neidhardt. Berlin: Edition Sigma.

MERKEL, W. 1999. *Systemtransformation: Eine Einführung in die Theorie und Empirie der Transformationsforschung*. Opladen: Leske & Budrich.

—— PUHLE, H. J., CROISSANT, A., EICHER, C., and THIERY, P. 2003. *Defekte Demokratie Band 1: Theorie*. Opladen: Leske & Budrich.

MISHLER, W., and ROSE, R. 2002. Learning and re-learning regime support: the dynamics of post-communist regimes. *European Journal of Political Research*, 41: 5–36.

NEWTON, K. 2001. Social capital and democracy. Pp. 225–34 in *Beyond Tocqueville: Civil Society and the Social Capital Debate in Comparative Perspective*, ed. B. E. Edwards, M. W. Foley, and M. Diani. Hanover, NH: University of New England Press.

NORRIS, P. 1999. *Critical Citizens: Global Support for Democratic Governance*. Oxford: Oxford University Press.

O'DONNELL G., SCHMITTER P. C., and WHITEHEAD, L. 1986. *Transition from Authoritarian Rule: Comparative Perspectives*. Baltimore: Johns Hopkins University Press.

PALMA, G. DI 1990. *To Craft Democracies*. Berkeley: University of California Press.

PATEMAN, C. 1980. The civic culture: a philosophic critique. Pp. 57–102 in *The Civic Culture Revisited*, ed. G. A. Almond and S. Verba. Newbury Park, Calif.: Sage Publications.

PATRICK, G. 1984. Political culture. Pp. 265–314 in *Social Science Concepts: A Systematic Analysis*, ed. G. Sartori. Beverly Hills, Calif.: Sage Publications.

PETERSON, R. A. 1979. Revitalizing the culture concept. *Annual Review of Sociology*, 5: 137–66.

POLLAK, D., JACOBS, J., MÜLLER, O., and PICKEL, G. 2003. *Political Culture in Post-Communist Europe: Attitudes in New Democracies*. Aldershot: Ashgate.

PRZEWORSKI, A., ALVAREZ M., CHEIBUB J. A., and LIMONGI, F. 1996. What makes democracies endure? *Journal of Democracy*, 7: 39–55.

PUTNAM, R. 1993. *Making Democracy Work*. Princeton: Princeton University Press.

PYE, L. W. 1968. Political culture. Pp. 218–25 in *International Encyclopedia of Social Sciences 12*, ed. D. L. Sills. New York: Macmillan.

—— 1972. Culture and political science: problems in the evaluation of the concept of political culture. *Social Science Quarterly*, 53: 285–96.

REISINGER, W. 1995. The renaissance of a rubric: political culture as concept and theory. *International Journal of Public Opinion Research*, 7: 328–52.

ROGOWSKI, R. 1976. *Rational Legitimacy*. Princeton: Princeton University Press.

ROLLER, E. 2005. *The Performance of Democracies: Political Institutions and Public Policy*. Oxford: Oxford University Press.

ROSE, R., and MISHLER, W. 1994. Mass reaction to regime change in Eastern Europe, *British Journal of Political Science*, 24: 159–82.

—— —— and HAEPFER, C. 1998. *Democracy and Its Alternatives: Understanding Post-Communist Societies*. Oxford: Polity Press and Baltimore: Johns Hopkins University Press.

ROSENBAUM, W. A. 1975. *Political Culture*. New York: Praeger.

ROTHSTEIN, B. 1996. Political institutions: an overview. Pp. 133–66 in *A New Handbook of Political Science*, ed. R. E. Goodin and H.-D. Klingemann. Oxford: Oxford University Press.

SCHEUCH, E. K. 1968. The cross-cultural use of sample surveys: problems of comparability. Pp. 176–209 in *Comparative Research across Cultures and Nations*, ed. S. Rokkan. Paris: Mouton.

SELIGSON, M. A. 2002. The renaissance of political culture or the renaissance of the ecological fallacy? *Comparative Politics*, 34: 273–92.

SHIN, D. C. 1999. *Mass Politics and Culture in Democratizing Korea*. New York: Cambridge University Press.

STREET, J. 1994. Review article: Political Culture—from Civic Culture to Mass Culture. *British Journal of Political Science*, 24: 95–114.

TARROW, S. 1996. Making social science work across space and time: a critical reflection on Robert Putnam's Making Democracy Work. *American Political Science Review*, 90: 389–97.

TAYLOR, C. 1989. Cross-purposes: the liberal-communitarian debate. Pp. 103–30 in *Liberalism and the Moral Life*, ed. N. Rosenblum. Cambridge: MIT Press.

TOCQUEVILLE, A. DE 1992. *Democracy in America*, ed. J. P. Mayer, trans. G. Lawrence. New York: Harper & Row.

VERBA, S. 1980. On revisiting The Civic Culture: a personal postscript. Pp. 394–410 in *The Civic Culture Revisited*, ed. G. A. Almond and S. Verba. Boston: Little Brown.

CHAPTER 10

INDIVIDUAL MODERNITY

CHRISTIAN WELZEL

THE concept of Individual Modernity deals with the psychological characteristics that are supposed to become dominant among individuals as societies move through the far-ranging socioeconomic transformations known as *modernization*. Thus, the concept individual modernity is a specific version of modernization theory focusing on the subjective dimension of modernization. Because individual modernity is addressing psychological orientations that are assumed to become ever more dominant, it is directly related to theories of cultural change or value change, such as the theory of postmaterialism or the theory of rising emancipative values. As a psychological concept, individual modernity overlaps with the concepts of the "democratic character" and "open-mindedness" or "personality strength." The subsequent sections try to outline important aspects of these connections.

1 THE INDIVIDUAL MODERNITY SCALE

The term individual modernity has been introduced by Alex Inkeles (1969, 1978, 1983) who invented a scale of "overall modernity" (OM scale) to measure specifically modern psychological orientations among individuals. Unlike standard modernization theory, which concentrates on objective socioeconomic transformations, the concept of individual modernity is focusing on the psychological effects of modernization on people. It is searching for the "sociocultural aspects of development" (Inkeles 1978, 49). Accordingly, this theory operates at the micro-level.

Neutrally formulated, individual modernity comprises all orientations that become dominant psychological traits as modernization processes, such as industrialization and urbanization, transform the living conditions of individuals. It is assumed that the orientations of modern individuals become lasting personality traits, meaning that the *modal type of personality* changes in the wake of modernization, creating a "new man" who changes the cultural outlook of entire societies. Thus, collective changes of individual-level psychological attributes accumulate to cultural changes at the societal level, reshaping a society's prevailing psychological constitution. Looking at the concrete attitudes and orientations that constitute individual modernity, Inkeles (1978, 49) identified:

(1) an open attitude to new experience (open-mindedness);
(2) allegiance to secular authority (secularism);
(3) a positivist belief in scientific progress (positivism);
(4) a strong achievement orientation (meritocratism);
(5) a rational attitude towards careful planning (rationalism);
(6) a participant attitude to politics and community affairs (activism);
(7) a super-local identification with the nation (nationalism).

As modernization advances, ever more persons will be characterized by these orientations, making populations more open-minded and more secular, positivist, rational, activist, and achievement oriented.

2 INDIVIDUAL MODERNITY AND THE CIVIC CULTURE

Inkeles emphasized that the "modern personality" is not necessarily a "democratic personality." In this point he explicitly declared disagreement with Almond and Verba's (1963) civic culture approach:

Those familiar with the Civic Culture will recognize these traits as very similar to those delineated by Almond and Verba as defining the model of a democratic citizen. According to them the citizen of a democratic polity is expected . . . to stress activity, involvement, rationality. . . . But I hold that exactly the same qualities are appropriate to . . . the citizen of a one-party dictatorship such as that found in the Soviet Union. . . . It seems, therefore, that Almond and Verba have labeled as specifically "democratic" something which is a more general requirement placed upon the citizen of a modern state, whether democratic or otherwise. (Inkeles 1969, 255)

Inkeles's attempt to set his approach apart from Almond and Verba was partly misleading, for these authors, too, emphasized the distinction between "democratic" and "modern" qualities. In fact Almond and Verba (1963, 5) claimed that what they consider as the psychological underpinnings of a democratic order—the civic culture—"is not a modern culture, but one that combines modernity with tradition." More appropriately, Inkeles would have distanced himself from Harold D. Lasswell (1951) who indeed described a set of orientations similar to Inkeles' "modern personality" as the hallmark of a "democratic personality." Almond and Verba for their part dissociated their civic culture approach from Lasswell's democratic personality approach arguing that "Lasswell's democratic qualities are not specifically *political* [italics in the original] attitudes and feelings, and they may actually be encountered in great frequency in societies that are not democratic in structure" (Almond and Verba 1963, 10). Like Inkeles, Almond and Verba denied the democratic quality of such orientations as open-mindedness and self-esteem, which Lasswell considered as inherently democratic. Almond and Verba were interested in a civic culture that helps sustain a democratic political order. They believed that such a culture is not built on general psychological orientations towards life and people but consists of specifically political orientations that confer legitimacy to given institutions and the political system at large. Accordingly, satisfaction with democracy and commitment to democratic procedures are of more direct relevance to the stability and florescence of democratic regimes than such personality attributes as self-esteem and open-mindedness (Almond and Verba 1963, 15).

Still, there is a connection between the two approaches. For example, Almond and Verba place strong emphasis on "subjective competence" (i.e. the feeling of individual competence) as an orientation that democratic citizens need because democratic systems require active participation in politics and because active participation is only pursued by people who feel sufficiently competent in political matters. In this light a linkage between Almond and Verba's subjective competence (also conceptualized as "internal efficacy") and Lasswell's self-esteem is intuitively plausible: logically, people who have more self-esteem than others have most likely also stronger feelings of competence. Sniderman's (1975) research has demonstrated that this linkage indeed exists.

3 Two Variants of Modernity: Democratic and Totalitarian

Almond and Verba's notion reflects the prevailing view of modernization in the 1960s and 1970s when one saw open-minded attitudes linked with modernization but not with democracy. For not all modern mass polities have been democratic ones. Sniderman (1975, 220) summarizes this view when speculating that the same psychological qualities that distinguish a democrat in the United States may well characterize a communist in Soviet Russia; for insofar as the linkage between personality and political ideology is a matter of social learning, then high self-esteem...ought to drive individuals towards accepting the norms of their political culture, whatever those be.

This presumes that each political order is equally capable to instill in its people the values that sustain it. In other words, both democratic and totalitarian orders have the capacity to cope with modernization and with the open-minded orientations coming along with modernization.

Early on modernization was supposed to bring social mobilization and mass inclusion into politics (Deutsch 1963). But leading scholars such as Huntington (1968) emphasized that social mobilization and mass political involvement does not necessarily lead to capitalist western democracy. In line with Moore (1966) many social scientists considered the Soviet type of communist dictatorship as another variant of modernization. The fact that the Soviet model was totalitarian has not been seen as a contradiction to modernization. Quite the contrary, totalitarianism itself has been considered as a genuinely modern configuration of the state (Friedrich and Brzezinski 1965). In the same vein, Loewenstein (1957) and O'Donnell (1973) theorized about specifically modern forms of authoritarianism (for a revival of the idea of modern autocracies see de Mesquita and Downs 2005). Consequently, modern psychological orientations have not at all been seen as identical to democratic orientations. Modern orientations have been considered as compatible with any type of modern political order, be it democratic or not. Among the few scholars disagreeing with this view already in the 1960s was Parsons (1964). He reasoned that, because modernization has an inherently logical tendency to democratic freedom, all attempts to nurture modernization without democratization are doomed to fail. Parsons explicitly predicted the failure of the Soviet system for exactly this reason, prophesying that this system will either internally democratize or break down, for lack of democratic legitimacy will limit the capacity of the Soviet system to mobilize resources in competition with western democracy.

4 DEMOCRATIC PERSONALITY AND OPEN-MINDEDNESS

These contrasting view points raise the question "Are modern orientations equivalent to democratic orientations or not?" This question is so fundamental that it seems worthwhile to look back at what Lasswell himself described as the psychological attributes of a democratic personality. Unlike Almond and Verba, Lasswell saw an inherent democratic quality in people's orientations towards life and people in general, thinking that these general world-views manifest a deep-seated predisposition to authoritarian or democratic orders. Lasswell listed the following orientations towards life and people as the ones establishing a fundamental predis-position in favor of democratic orders (1951, 495–503):

(1) an "open ego," which means an "inclusive" attitude to others (inclusiveness);
(2) a "multi-valued" orientation that can cope with ambiguity (versatility);
(3) "confidence in human potentialities" (humanism);
(4) "self-esteem;" and
(5) "freedom from anxiety."

These building blocs are hierarchically ordered. At the origin is freedom from anxiety or the absence of threat perceptions. People who are free from anxiety do not have to fear failure; instead, they can consider their own failures as a source of learning. This nurtures self-esteem. Likewise, people who are free from anxiety do not have to fear that other people differ from them; instead, diversity among people can be considered as a source of stimulation. This nurtures humanism. Versatility and inclusiveness then develop as natural corollaries of self-esteem and humanism. This view is strongly influenced by Erich Fromm's (1942) insight that self-respect and respecting others are two flipsides of the same coin: a generally philanthropic attitude. By the same token, contempt for other people is often an indication of low self-respect.

There is considerable overlap between Lasswell's democratic qualities and what Rokeach (1960, 71–9) described as "open belief systems" or its opposite, "closed belief systems." Rokeach measured open- versus closed-mindedness by a "dogmatism scale" whose dogmatic pole includes the following (among other things): a strong belief into authority; intolerance of diversity; fatalism; low self-esteem; and threat perceptions. Again, threat perceptions are seen as the root of the whole syndrome, closing people's mind in making them intolerant and obsessed with ingroup favor-itism (to this point see the work of Monroe 1996). The closed type of belief systems in turn is very similar to Adorno's concept of the "authoritarian personality" (Adorno et al. 1950). In light of these conceptual overlaps it seems plausible to consider the two polarities between closed and open beliefs, on one hand, and between authoritarian and democratic orientations, on the other hand, as largely synonymous. Thus, closed beliefs can be equated with authoritarian orientations and open beliefs with demo-cratic orientations, with many possible mixtures in the gray area between the two extreme ends on this continuum.

Given that an individual's location on the continuum between authoritarian (closed) and democratic (open) beliefs is assumed to be rooted in threat perceptions, one has a theory at hand to predict under which conditions populations might change their prevalent orientation from one pole of the continuum to the other. Accordingly, one would assume that disasters that are perceived as existential threats, such as economic shocks, terrorism, collective violence, wars, or natural cata-strophes, make people more closed-minded, leading them to accept authoritarian solutions of given problems. Vice versa, if people experience freedom from anxiety through sustained periods of affluence, peace, and security, they open their mind, adopting the orientations that lead them to reject unlimited and uncontrolled authority, whether religious or political.

Beyond the attention of political scientists, cross-cultural psychologists (Triandis 1995, 60) have described the closed/authoritarian versus open/democratic polarity in terms of "conformism versus individualism," postulating an inherent linkage between the prevalence of conformist orientations and dictatorial systems and the prevalence of individualistic orientations and democratic systems (see also Rokeach 1973).

5 Open-Mindedness and Personality Strength

There is no question in psychology that self-esteem and open-mindedness are attributes indicating personality strength, mental health, subjective well-being, and even human development (Ryan and Deci 2000). But are these orientations modern in the sense that they emerge in the course of modernization? Or isn't it so that modernization causes psychopathological effects, mass depression, and alienation? Attempting to answer this question, Inkeles and Diamond (1980) analyzed a set of open-minded orientations, including "anti-authoritarianism, efficacy, satisfaction, participation, trust, benevolence, optimism." All of these orientations have been found to be more widespread in economically more advanced societies. A nation's overall level of economic development showed an independent effect on the strength of these attitudes, even controlling for people's individual characteristics. Accordingly, it seems after all indeed justified to equate open-minded orientations with modern orientations.

But what about the democraticness of open-minded orientations? We have learned that Inkeles and others rejected Lasswell's claim that these orientations are of an inherently democratic nature. However, research by Rosenberg (1956), Rokeach (1973), and Sniderman (1975, 217) suggests that self-esteem and open-mindedness strengthen commitment to democratic norms:

In any event, individual differences in self-esteem evidently exercise a profound influence over attitudes to politics.... Then, too, low self-esteem weakens commitment to the norms of democratic politics and strengthens susceptibility to the varieties of extremist politics. There is, then, much to recommend to the basic insight of such scholars as Mannheim and Lasswell who perceived the connection between the character of men and the kind of society they favor. (Sniderman 1975, 222)

From this point of view one would disagree with Inkeles, maintaining that modern and democratic psychological attributes are not so categorically different; and one would disagree with Almond and Verba, insisting that general psychological orientations, even though they are not directly related to political questions, do involve dispositions to political orders. However, this claim could not be analyzed until recently, because its investigation requires data about the beliefs of people in societies of a wide range of political orders. On a broad basis, such data became available only recently with the World Values Surveys.

6 THE UNIVERSALITY OF PSYCHOLOGICAL ORIENTATIONS

Cross-cultural research in the tradition of Inkeles showed little interest in specifically democratic orientations; the intention was to explore universally modern orientations that are to be found in all types of modern mass polities, be they democratic or not. Following Max Weber, Inkeles conceptualized modernization in terms of processes that were also going on in non-democratic societies, including industrialization, urbanization, bureaucratization, rationalization, secularization, and expanding education. Accordingly, Inkeles assumed that modern attitudes emerge primarily within contexts shaped by these forces. Empirically, Inkeles could indeed demonstrate that participative, innovative, secular, and rational orientations had been more pronounced among people working in industrial factories, people having attended a university, and people with more exposure to modern mass media. This has been shown in surveys among people from culturally diverse societies, including third world countries, supporting the claim that psychological changes toward individual modernity are not culture specific but universal among people exposed to similar socioeconomic forces.

The question of the universality of basic psychological orientations has been a guiding question in cross-cultural psychology and value research. Based on Rokeach's (1973) work on the nature of human beliefs, Shalom Schwartz (2003) attempted to map the universal structure of human values based on data from student-teacher samples from societies around the world. He could indeed demonstrate the existence of a "value circle" that structures the value orientations of people in any society along two universal conflicting principles: (*a*) one representing a polarity between values of self-enhancement and self-transcendence (which could well be understood as *egocentric versus altruistic values*); and (*b*) another representing a polarity between values of self-direction/stimulation versus conformity/security (often understood as *individualism versus collectivism*).

The existence of this universal structure does not foreclose that people in different societies emphasize opposite poles in the value structure. Quite the contrary, much of the research in cross-cultural psychology has been emphasizing the distinction between "individualistic" and "collectivist" cultures, showing that, even if one controls for an individual's personal background, culture shows an independent impact, leaving a more individualistic or collectivist imprint on people (Hofstede 1980; Triandis 1995; Markus, Kitayama, and Heiman 1996; Kuehnen and Oyserman 2002). However, studies in cross-cultural psychology are static in the sense that they treat culture simply as a given that is not itself exposed to changes by socioeconomic forces. Collective changes in psychological orientations from one pole to the other are not studied in this branch of research, for culture is conceptualized as a constant. Theories of value change take an opposite view.

7 THEORIES OF MODERN VALUE CHANGE

Inkeles's concept of individual modernity assumes a psychological dynamic: fundamental changes in people's orientations are supposed to occur as societies modernize. Under the notion of "value change," the dynamic aspect of changing psychological orientations among modern mass publics has been most extensively researched by Inglehart (1977, 1990). His theory of postmaterialistic value change has a number of points in common with Inkeles' personality approach. It starts from psychological assumptions and states that people's orientations are shaped in a sustained way by socioeconomic forces. This is plausible under the premise that socioeconomic forces change people's basic living conditions and that people's value orientations reflect their living conditions (or the experiences deriving from them). Under these premises Inglehart provides a more explicit theory about the mechanism by which socioeconomic forces change people's psychological orientations (see Inglehart chapter in this volume).

Starting from Abraham Maslow's (1954) pyramid of human needs, Inglehart assumes that psychological orientations are hierarchically ordered, such that lower-ordered needs must be fulfilled first before higher-ordered needs can emerge. Lower-ordered needs are *physiological* survival needs. Inglehart labels them "materialist" because their satisfaction requires the proliferation of material products such as food, shelter, and all kinds of commodities and technical equipment. Higher-ordered needs are *psychological* self-actualization needs. Inglehart calls them "postmaterialistic" because in order to satisfy them, non-material achievements such as political freedom are needed. Another facet of Inglehart's theory is based on the concept of formative socialization. It is conventional wisdom in lifespan psychology (Maier and Vaupel 2003) that experiences one makes during adolescence have a more lasting imprint on one's orientation in life than later experiences. Thus, experiences in one's formative years lead to the crystallization of relatively stable personality attributes (see also Easton and Dennis 1969).

Combining the formative experiences-thesis with the need hierarchy-thesis, one comes to the conclusion that socioeconomic development, if it happens, leads to a gradual replacement of materialist value priorities with postmaterialist priorities and that this process is driven by the younger cohorts replacing the older ones in the course of generational population replacement.

Accordingly, if socioeconomic conditions improve fundamentally from one generation to the next, the younger generation that is growing up under the improved conditions will experience the satisfaction of its material needs. Material need-satisfaction will become the new generation's formative experience so that its members take it for granted, opening their minds to higher-ordered concerns. Thus the new generation will feel the need of postmaterialistic achievements, placing more emphasis on environmental protection, meaning of life, and self-determination. The older generation will also experience more affluence but its formative experiences will leave on it a lasting imprint, such that the older generation continues to prioritize materialistic goals over postmaterialistic ones. Consequently, the affluence-driven value change from materialistic to postmaterialistic values will advance only as the older generation dies out.

According to Inglehart, individual modernity is reflected in postmaterialism. Postmaterialists have a post-economic preference structure in which concerns of the material living standard are replaced by lifestyle concerns about the ecological, cultural, and political quality of life. Inglehart's theory is correct in a number of fundamental points. But it can be refined or at least sharpened in three major aspects (for recent discussion see Clarke et al. 1999; Davis and Davenport 1999; Inglehart and Abramson 1999).

8 Continuing Salience of Economic Orientations

First, one does not need to be a survey expert to realize that post-economic issues have not at all replaced economic ones on the agenda of postindustrial societies. Electoral campaigns are still fought around economic issues and economic issues continue to dominate most voters' concerns. Since twenty years there is nothing that concerns voters in Western Europe more than mass unemployment, the increase of a low-wage sector, welfare state retrenchment and public austerity. Also, today's youth is in no way less consumption oriented than earlier generations (Deutsche Shell 2002). Postmaterialist values do also not hinder consumption needs to emerge on a higher level of sophistication. The highest need on Maslow's hierarchy, self-actualization, can be defined in rather hedonic terms, that is, in terms of luxury lifestyles and exotic experiences that require a lot of money to afford them, still making people concerned about their salaries and other material benefits. Put differently, material needs do not end after the first step in Maslow's ladder; they evolve the whole way up to the highest step. True, there are primary material needs: the sheer survival needs of food and shelter. But material survival needs are succeeded by more sophisticated secondary and tertiary material needs. Again, if a society reaches higher layers in the Maslowian pyramid of need satisfaction, material needs do not vanish; they become more sophisticated. Inglehart himself does most likely not deny this. But his writings have too often taken to the extreme to mean that materialistic preferences are replaced with postmaterialistic ones. This needs some clarification.

A first qualification of the postmaterialism thesis is that postmaterialist values do not simply *replace* materialist ones. Instead, postmaterialistic values are *added to* still existing materialistic values. Thus, there is not so much a replacement as a widening of people's value repertory, which allows people to change priorities according to circumstances (Klein and Poetschke 2000). Evidence from the Eurobarometer illustrated in Figure 10.1 shows that, even though over the past thirty years there has been a sharp decline in the proportion of "pure" materialists, the proportion of "pure" postmaterialists did not increase to the same extent as pure materialists diminished.

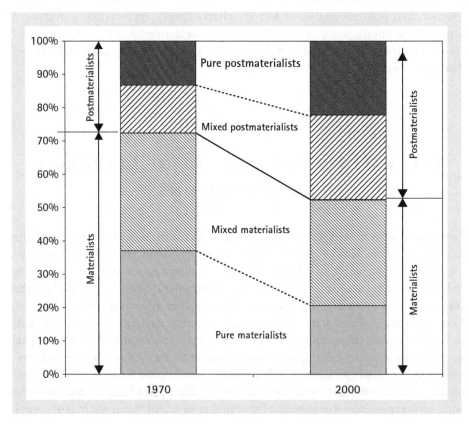

Fig. 10.1 Change in materialist–postmaterialist priorities in 5 EU-countries

Source: Data for France, Germany (West), Italy, Belgium, the Netherlands (samples equally weighed). Data from 1970 are from Eurobarometer, data for 2000 from World Values Survey 1999–2001.

A considerable portion of the decrease of pure materialists has been compensated by an increase of "mixed" materialists and postmaterialists. Only the "pure" form of materialism diminishes while materialism as such continues to exist—in combination with postmaterialism (as the prevalence of mixed types clearly illustrates). This value change is better described as a postmaterialist expansion rather than replacement of values.

9 LIBERAL RATHER THAN POSTMATERIALIST VALUES

Second, time-series evidence for a long-term increase in postmaterialist values is only available for the liberal items "freedom of speech" and "giving more say" but not for ecological items such as "making our countryside more beautiful" or idealistic items such as "having a society in which ideas count more than money." The term postmaterialism, however, is only useful as long as it is needed as an umbrella term to summarize a variety of conceptually distinct orientations, including liberal, ecological, and idealistic orientations. As long as available evidence for value changes is limited to liberal orientations only, it is more specific to call them just what they are: liberty aspirations. This term also represents more precisely these orientations' major thrust: civil and political freedom. In line with this reasoning, Welzel (2006) demonstrates that keeping the liberal components of postmaterialism separate is essential to discover attitudinal effects on democratic institutions. A positive attitudinal effect on the development of democracy is only demonstrable for liberty aspirations but not for the other components of postmaterialism. For this reason, Welzel (2006) follows Brint (1984) and Flanagan (1987) who prefer to label these attitudes as liberty aspirations rather than postmaterialist orientations. Subsequent paragraphs follow this use of the term as well.

10 ECONOMIC SECURITY AND INDIVIDUAL AUTONOMY

Still another argument supports this point. Following Lasswell (1951), Maslow (1954), and Rokeach (1960) it is quite plausible that such an open-minded orientation as liberty aspirations emerges from freedom of anxiety, that is, under less pressing and more permissive and comfortable existential conditions. The theory of postmaterialism goes along with this argument but presumes that *economic security* is the single most important aspect in making existential conditions more permissive.

This interpretation is not easy to reconcile with the fact that the post-1968 generation, which has been socialized under the oil-shocks and a continuing welfare state crises, experienced much lower levels of job security and much less secure social benefits than the baby-boomers, but still continues to show more strongly liberal orientations than previous generations, as Figure 10.2 illustrates.[1] According to the theory of formative years, the post-1968 generations should show less liberal values, if economic security is the major factor in making existential conditions more permissive. But they continue to show greater liberty aspirations. This raises doubts against economic security as the sole driving force behind liberty aspirations.

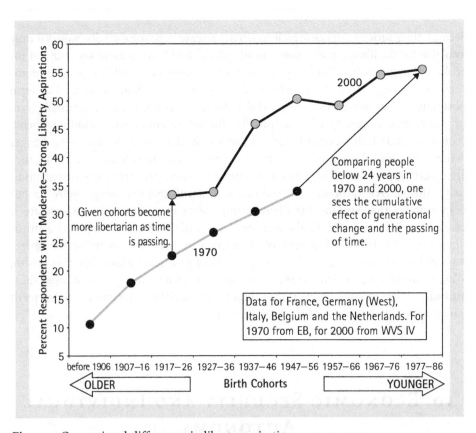

Fig. 10.2 Generational differences in liberty aspirations over 30 years

---

[1] Liberty aspirations are measured on a 0–3 ordinal index based on the libertarian items "protecting freedom of speech" and "giving people more say in important government decisions." These items are included in Inglehart's most widely used materialism-postmaterialism battery, which asks respondents to choose a first and second priority from four items (the other two items being "maintaining order in the nation" and "fighting rising prices"). Respondents are scored 0 on the liberty aspiration index if they attribute neither first nor second priority to any of the two liberty items. They are scored 1 if they attribute

An alternative to the experience of economic security as the source of liberty aspirations is the experience of individual autonomy. This experience continues indeed to grow as the individualization thesis suggests (Beck 2002), even though economic security declined since the 1970s. Thus, the continuing increase of liberty aspirations among succeeding cohorts in Western publics is more plausibly explained by a corresponding increase of individual autonomy than by a corresponding increase of economic security (for such an increase simply does not exist).

Evidence to this point is provided by the World Values Survey (using either the pooled data set or a sub-sample containing postindustrial societies only). If one accepts income as an indicator of economic security and level of education[2] as an indicator of individual autonomy (or intellectual autonomy which is a basic aspect of individual autonomy), then individual autonomy has a greater impact on individual-level liberty aspirations than economic security because education correlates at $r=.17$ while income correlates at $r=.11$ with liberty aspirations. But what about *perceived* economic security and *perceived* individual autonomy? Taking financial satisfaction as an indicator of perceived economic security and perceived control over life as an indicator of perceived autonomy, autonomy is more important than security because life control correlates at $r=.07$ with liberty aspirations, whereas financial satisfaction correlates even negatively, at $r=-.02$, with liberty aspirations. In multivariate regression the relative weight of these effects remains the same: education is a better predictor of liberty aspirations than income, and perceived control over one's life is a better predictor than financial satisfaction.

The evidence is even clearer at the aggregate level. For that matter I use per capita GDP as a measure of economic security and the size of the service sector in percent of the workforce as a proxy for individualization, the reason being that postindustrial service economies nurture the social complexity that makes individuals more autonomous in shaping their connections to others. Using measures of these two variables from 1990 to predict national percentages of people showing moderate to strong liberty aspirations in the mid-1990s ($N=65$), the effect of service sector size is definitely stronger and more significant (beta $=.60$ significant at the .000-level) than

---

second priority to one of these items, 2 if they attribute first priority to one of these items and 3 if both first and second priorities are attributed to these items. The percentage of people with moderate-strong liberty aspirations shown in Figures 10.2 and 10.3 indicates the percentage of respondents scoring 2 or 3 on the liberty aspiration index (which is equivalent to adding up mixed and pure postmaterialists in Inglehart's terminology). Note that Inglehart and Welzel (2005) use a more extended version of this index that ranges from 0 to 5 as they include priorities on the item "giving people more say on how things are done in their jobs and community." This item, however, is included in another battery that has not been used as widely and is therefore not available for extensive time-series analyses.

  [2] One might argue that level of education is also an indicator of economic security during one's formative years because people from better socioeconomic backgrounds are usually the ones obtaining higher education. This argument is plausible to the extent that there is a match between an individual's attained level of education and his or her parents' socioeconomic status. No question, this match exists. But it is far from being perfect (fortunately). Correlations are usually in a range of .20 to .30, meaning that some 5 to 10 percent in an individual's education attainment can be attributed to economic security in people's formative years. Education is also a means of upward mobility to escape the less privileged socioeconomic status of one's parents. Hence, one cannot simply take education as a proxy for economic security in formative years.

the effect of per capita GDP (beta = .27, significant at the .02-level). Again, the increase of individual autonomy (as a consequence of individualization) seems to be as important, if not more important, in giving rise to liberty aspirations as economic security.

11   PRE-INDUSTRIAL FREEHOLDER SOCIETIES AND RICH OIL-EXPORTING SOCIETIES

This is plausible from still another perspective. Usually economic security and individual autonomy are closely intertwined but sometimes these two experiences can fall apart. The cases in which this happens are rare but illustrative. One such rare case is rich oil-exporting countries of today; another one is freeholder societies of pre-industrial times.

For decades, publics of the super-rich oil-exporting countries, such as Bahrain or the Emirates, have been economically more secure than any other in the world. But they did not show any sign of strong liberty aspirations among their publics, even though they provided generous welfare benefits for the population at large. The reason for this perplexing phenomenon could be that individualization is not far advanced in these societies. Despite material affluence, these societies are still shaped by traditional social patterns. A rent-seeking economy based on the exploitation of natural resources does not have the same modernizing effect as a knowledge economy, even if exploiting oil makes it rich (Boix 2003). By contrast, pre-industrial freeholder and merchant societies, such as those in North America, England, the Low Countries, and Switzerland in the eighteenth century, were far from rich by today's standards. People have not been economically secure in absence of a welfare state that takes care of the most existential risks. But as owners of their land and as free agents on the market, they experienced a considerable degree of individual autonomy. Not coincidentally, exactly these meritocratic middle-class societies have shown strong indications of mass liberty aspirations when freeholders and town dwellers demanded civil rights and "no taxation without representation" in the liberal revolutions of the seventeenth and eighteenth centuries.

Individual autonomy seems to be as important to liberty aspirations as economic security. The experience of autonomy in pursuing one's daily activities is essential to nurture a basic sense of human agency, which makes people receptive to the idea of civil and political freedom, leading them to question unlimited and uncontrolled authority. This is not to say that economic security is unimportant. Quite the contrary, as the next section will show, economic security is important in promoting liberty aspirations. But its effect should be considered in connection with individual autonomy.

12 VALUE CHANGE THROUGH GENERATIONAL SHIFTS AND PERIODIC FLUCTUATIONS

The theory of postmaterialism needs additional qualification in a third aspect. There are tremendous periodic shifts between weaker and stronger liberty aspirations, depending on current inflation rates. Eurobarometer data illustrated in Figure 10.3 show an amazing coincidence between fluctuations in the consumer price index and liberty aspirations, such that higher inflation rates bring less emphasis on liberty, whereas lower inflation rates bring more emphasis on liberty.[3] These shifts are so pronounced that they are not easily reconcilable with the thesis that liberty aspirations are a stable personality

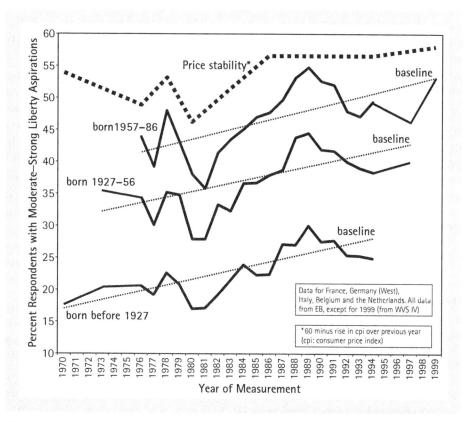

Fig. 10.3 Periodic fluctuations and stable cohort differences in liberty aspirations

---

[3] I can assure that the pattern shown in Figure 10.3 is not an artifact of the crude generational categorizations. A more fine-grained differentiation, using nine instead of three cohort categories, shows exactly the same pattern (see Inglehart and Welzel 2005, 106) but makes the graph nearly unreadable.

attribute. If this were the case, they must not be that sensitive to fluctuations in the economic cycle.

The finding of huge situational fluctuations confirms "regulatory focus theory" in psychology (Foerster, Higgins, and Idson 1998). This theory does not consider people's psychological orientation as a stable personality attribute but as situation shaped. Based on experimental evidence it is argued that people switch into a "prevention orientation" focusing on avoidance and security in pressing situations, whereas they switch into a "promotion orientation" focusing on achievement and unfolding in more permissive situations. Depending on the situation, all people—irrespective of personality characteristics—can be brought into a prevention or a promotion focus. The cyclical fluctuations in liberty aspirations can be interpreted as reflecting exactly this mechanism. Higher inflation means an economically more pressing situation, leading people to adopt a less liberal orientation in prioritizing economic security (i.e. a prevention focus). Conversely, lower inflation rates imply an economically more permissive situation leading people to switch to a more liberal orientation in preferring freedom of expression (i.e. a promotion focus).

Yet, it would be premature to give up the idea of stable personality attributes altogether. For the same evidence showing strong situational fluctuations in liberty aspirations also shows stable generational differences in liberty aspirations. The generational differences in liberty aspirations remain constant throughout every up and down of the inflation cycle, with each new generation fluctuating on a higher level of liberty aspirations than the previous one. Thus, although people's priorities fluctuate, they fluctuate around different generational *baselines*, the baselines themselves being rather stable. These generational baselines reflect the existential experiences in people's formative years, such that generations having made more pressing formative experiences fluctuate around a less liberal baseline; whereas generations having made more permissive existential experiences in their formative years fluctuate around a more liberal baseline. A cohort's baseline is a stable personality attribute but situational adjustments around the given baseline are nevertheless possible.

This is a fundamental insight into the logic of collective changes in psychological orientations. People's psychological orientations reflect both current circumstances *and* formative experiences. And both follow the same existential logic, pointing to three effects, each of which is observable in Figure 10.3:

(1) More pressing existential experiences in formative years anchor people's orientation-baseline at less liberal priorities; more permissive existential experiences in formative years anchor their orientation-baseline at more liberal priorities. As each new generation of people in western Europe has been socialized into more favorable existential conditions than the previous one, the orientation-baselines are anchored at more liberal priorities with each new generation (although the size of the increase diminishes in recent generations).

(2) Because existential conditions continued to be more permissive, the cohorts' given baselines themselves are slowly moving upward toward more liberal

priorities. This effect is in flat contradiction to the life-cycle thesis, which tells us that people become more conservative and less liberal as they age.

(3) Irrespective of the location of the orientation-baseline, fluctuations in current existential conditions lead to fluctuations of people's priorities around their baseline, with more pressing current conditions causing downward fluctuations toward less liberal priorities and more permissive current circumstances leading to more liberal priorities.[4]

Again, these three effects—stable baseline differences between generations, upwardly directed baselines over the long-run, and short-term fluctuations around the baselines—all follow the same existential logic: Diminishing external constraints on autonomous choice make people more liberty oriented.

13 Two Sets of Modern Values: Rational Values and Emancipative Values

As Inglehart and Welzel (2005) illustrate, liberty aspirations are the central component in a broader set of values, which they call self-expression values or emancipative values. Besides (1) an esteem of human freedom reflected in liberty aspirations, this fivefold syndrome includes: (2) an esteem of political self-expression reflected in participating in elite-challenging actions such as petitions; (3) an esteem of nonconformity reflected in a tolerance of homosexuality; (4) an esteem of other people reflected in generalized interpersonal trust; and (5) a sense of being at peace with oneself reflected in high levels of life satisfaction. It is clear that this syndrome of emancipative values is perfectly compatible with Lasswell's focus on self-esteem and esteeming others as the ingredients of a democratic personality.

Inglehart and Welzel demonstrate that emancipative values are a modern set of values in the sense that these values emerge in the wake of major socioeconomic transformations. Thus, one can consider the syndrome of emancipative values as a more recent elaboration of individual modernity. But emancipative values have to be set apart from another distinct set of values that also matures in the course of modernization: secular-rational values (henceforth: rational values). Both types of values, rational and emancipative ones, arise with modernization but do it to different

---

[4] Note that the (perceived) pressing versus permissive existential conditions are not only a matter of economic circumstances. It is also a matter of physical security. Thus, increasing crime rates, threats through political violence, civil war, or terrorism can also be perceived as pressing conditions that decrease the priority on liberty concerns. Hence, it is conceivable that the threat of international terror or the perceived threat of immigration shift the publics' emphasis toward less libertarian values.

degrees in different phases of modernization. Rational values emerge most powerfully during the industrial phase of modernization. The bureaucratizing, centralizing, and standardizing tendencies of industrialization give rise to a mechanical worldview that nurtures rational values. By contrast, emancipative values emerge most powerfully during the postindustrial phase of modernization. The de-standardizing and individualizing tendencies of postindustrialization give rise to a human-centric worldview that nurtures emancipative values.

14 Rational Values: Modern but not Democratic

Both sets of values have tremendous implications for people's authority orientations, bringing wide-ranging consequences for the power structure of political orders. Rational values legitimate authority in tying it to public consent (or its pretence), bringing mass involvement into politics and universal suffrage. This does not necessarily lead to democracy. Rational authority is instead perfectly compatible with an authoritarian power structure. Accordingly, Inglehart and Welzel demonstrate that industrialization goes together with rational values but societies with strongly rational values do not show a specific affinity to democratic systems of governance. Thus, the early emphasis on the distinction between modern values and democratic values is correct—as long as we restrict modern values to rational values.

15 Emancipative Values: Modern and Democratic

With emancipative values we come to a different conclusion. Emancipative values do not legitimate authority; they question it. With rational values, authority that is external to individuals, enshrined in extra-individual bodies such as the state, remains fully legitimate. In sharp contrast, emancipative values internalize authority into the self, seeing nothing more dignified than the decision-making freedom of the individual human being and the equality of all human beings in this decision-making freedom. This emancipative thrust is inherently inconsistent with unlimited or uncontrolled authority, however efficient and rational, making any sort of authoritarian system unsustainable when emancipative values emerge.

Indeed, as Inglehart and Welzel show, there is a stunning .90 correlation between the spread of emancipative values in a society and its level of democracy across a worldwide sample of 74 nations. Further, more widespread emancipative values make democracies more, not less, efficacious. This is reflected in the fact that the spread of emancipative values is closely correlated with all five of the World Bank's "good governance" indicators (Welzel, Inglehart, and Deutsch 2005). These values make publics self-assertive, defiant, and troublesome for decision makers. But exactly this means healthy pressures to keep elites honest, accountable, and responsive to what people want. Anyway, the distinction between modern values and democratic values vanishes when we focus on emancipative values, which are both modern and democratic.

16 CONCLUSION

These insights provide a late confirmation of Lasswell's approach. This is not only true because emancipative values come very close to what Lasswell described as the democratic character. Also, emancipative values do not contain any explicit reference to political regimes but nevertheless, as Inglehart and Welzel demonstrate extensively, show a much stronger impact on political orders than any regime-related attitude—disconfirming the premise of Almond and Verba that only specifically political attitudes are relevant for political regimes. In fact, psychological orientations towards life and people in general are more relevant.

In conclusion, the essence of emerging emancipative values lies in the fact that they are both modern and democratic. As Inglehart and Welzel argue, the emergence of these values transforms modernization into a process of human development that makes existing polities ever more people-centered, fueling such tendencies as consumer protection, gender equality or same sex marriage. In any event, the syndrome of emancipative values can be seen as a measure of both individual modernity and individual democraticness. The frequency of this orientation among populations is very closely associated with a society's democratic performance. In that sense, democracy is more than just a political regime. It is a way of life anchored in an emancipatory world-view.

REFERENCES

ADORNO, T., FRANKEL-BRUNSWICK, E., LEVINSON, D., and NEVITT SANFORD, R. 1950. *The Authoritarian Personality*. New York: Harper.
ALMOND, G., and VERBA, S. 1963. *The Civic Culture*. Princeton: Princeton University Press.

BECK, U. 2002. Losing the traditional: individualization and "precarious freedoms". Pp. 1–21 in *Individualization*, ed. V. Beck and E. Beck-Gernsheim. London: Sage.

BOIX, C. 2003. *Democracy and Redistribution*. New York: Cambridge University Press.

BRINT, S. 1984. New class and cumulative trend explanations of the liberal political attitudes of professionals. *American Journal of Sociology*, 90 (1): 30–71.

CLARKE, H., KORNBERG, A., MCINTYRE, C., BAUER-KAASE, P., and KAASE, M. 1999. The effect of economic priorities on the measurement of value change. *American Political Science Review*, 93: 637–47.

DAVIS, D., and DAVENPORT, C. 1999. Assessing the validity of the postmaterialism index. *American Political Science Review*, 93: 649–64.

DE MESQUITA, B. B., and DOWNS, G. W. 2005. Development and democracy. *Foreign Affairs*, Sept./Oct.

DEUTSCH, K. 1963. *The Nerves of Government*. New York: Free Press.

DEUTSCHE SHELL, ed. 2002. *Jugend 2002: 14. Shell Jugendstudie* [Youth 2002: 14. Shell Youth Study]. Frankfurt am Main: Fischer.

EASTON, D., and DENNIS, J. 1969. *Children in the Political System*. New York: McGraw Hill.

FLANAGAN, S. 1987. Value change in industrial society. *American Political Science Review*, 81 (4): 1303–19.

FOERSTER, J., HIGGINS, E., and IDSON, L. 1998. Approach and avoidance strength during goal attainment: regulatory focus and the "goal looms larger" effect. *Journal of Personality and Social Psychology* 75: 1115–31.

FRIEDRICH, C., and BRZEZINSKI, Z. 1965. *Totalitarian Dictatorship and Autocracy*, 2nd edn. Cambridge: Cambridge University Press.

FROMM, E. 1942. *The Fear of Freedom*. London: Routledge.

HOFSTEDE, G. 1980. *Culture's Consequences: Intentional Differences in Work-related Values*. Beverly Hills, Calif.: Sage.

HUNTINGTON, S. 1968. *Political Order in Changing Societies*. New Haven: Yale University Press.

INGLEHART, R. 1977. *The Silent Revolution*. Princeton: Princeton University Press.

—— 1990. *Culture Shift*. Princeton: Princeton University Press.

—— and ABRAMSON, P. 1999. Measuring postmaterialism. *American Political Science Review*, 93: 665–77.

—— and WELZEL, C. 2005. *Modernization, Cultural Change and Democracy: The Human Development Sequence*. New York: Cambridge University Press.

INKELES, A. 1969. Participant citizenship in six developing countries. *American Political Science Review*, 63: 112–41.

—— 1978. National differences in individual modernity. *Comparative Studies in Sociology*, 1: 47–72.

—— 1983. *Exploring Individual Modernity*. New York: Columbia University Press.

—— and DIAMOND, L. 1980. Personal development and national development: a cross-national perspective. Pp. 73–110 in *The Quality of Life: Comparative Studies*, ed. A. Szalai and F. Andrews. London: Sage.

KLEIN, M., and POETSCHKE, M. 2000. Gibt es einen Wertewandel hin zum "reinen" Post-materialismus? [Is there a value change toward "pure" postmaterialism?]. *Zeitschrift für Soziologie*, 29: 202–16.

KUEHNEN, U., and OYSERMANN, D. 2002. Thinking about the self influences thinking in general: cognitive consequences of salient self-concept. *Journal of Experimental Social Psychology*, 38: 492–9.

LASSWELL, H. 1951. *Democratic Character*. Glencoe, Ill.: The Free Press.

Loewenstein, K. 1957. *Political Power and the Governmental Process*. Chicago: University of Chicago Press.

Maier, H., and Vaupel, J. 2003. Age differences in cultural efficiency. Pp. 59–78 in *Understanding Human Development*, ed. U. Standinger and U. Lindenberger Boston: Kluwer.

Markus, H., Kitayama, S., and Heiman, R. J. 1996. Culture and basic psychological principles. Pp. 857–913 in *Social Psychology: Handbook of Basic Principles*, ed. E. T. Higgins and A. W. Kruglanski. New York: Guilford.

Maslow, A. 1988 [1954]. *Motivation and Personality*, 3rd edn. New York: Harper & Row.

Monroe, K. 1996. *The Heart of Altruism*. Princeton: Princeton University Press.

Moore, B. 1966. *The Social Origins of Democracy and Dictatorship: Lord and Peasant in the Making of the Modern World*. Boston: Beacon Press.

O'Donnell, G. 1973. *Modernization and Bureaucratic Authoritarianism*. Berkeley: California University Press.

Parsons, T. 1964. Evolutionary universals in society. *American Sociological Review*, 29: 339–57.

Rokeach, M. 1960. *The Open and the Closed Mind*. New York: Basic Books.

—— 1973. *The Nature of Human Values*. New York: The Free Press.

Rosenberg, M. 1956. Misanthropy and political ideology. *American Sociological Review*, 21: 690–5.

Ryan, R., and Deci, E. 2000. Self-determination theory and the facilitation of intrinsic motivation, social development, and well-being. *American Psychologist*, 55: 68–78.

Sen, A. 1999. *Development as Freedom*. New York: Alfred Knopf.

Schwartz, S. 2003. Mapping and interpreting cultural differences around the world. Pp. 43–73 in *Comparing Cultures, Dimensions of Culture in a Comparative Perspective*, ed. H. Vinken, J. Soeters, and P. Ester. Leiden: Brill.

Sniderman, P. 1975. *Personality and Democratic Politics*. Berkeley: University of California Press.

Triandis, H. 1995. *Individualism and Collectivism*. Boulder, Colo.: Westview Press.

Vanhanen, T. ed. 1997. *Prospects of Democracy: A Study of 172 Countries*. London: Routledge.

Welzel, C. 2006. Democratization as an emancipative process: the neglected role of mass motivations. *European Journal of Political Research* 45 (4): 871–96.

—— Inglehart, R., and Deutsch, F. 2005. Social capital, voluntary associations, and collective action: which aspects of social capital have the greatest "civic" payoff? *Journal of Civil Society* 1 (2): 121–46.

—— —— and Klingemann, H. 2003. The theory of human development: a cross-cultural analysis. *European Journal of Political Research*, 42 (2): 341–80.

CHAPTER 11

LEFT–RIGHT ORIENTATIONS

PETER MAIR

THE most basic rule of comparison is that it requires shared standards and common terms of reference. This is true for comparisons among individuals, among groups, among nations, and over time. In practice, this means that comparisons at any of these levels must use concepts that can travel and that mean more or less the same thing in all of the different settings that are compared. It also follows that the more extensive the comparison—that is, the more units that are involved and the greater the range of settings in which they are found—the more abstract is likely to be the concept that is employed in the comparison (Sartori 1970). It is largely for these reasons that left–right orientations, and the search for placements along a left–right dimension, have proved such an enduring element in comparative political analysis.

Ever since the seminal work of Downs (1957), students of political behavior and party strategy have become accustomed to think of party competition and voter alignments in unidimensional left–right terms. This was the spatial model that Downs had adapted from theoretical arguments originally developed by Hotelling (1929) and Smithies (1941) to account for the relationship between the location of competing stores on a high street (or ice-cream vendors on a beach) and the behaviour of their customers. In fact, the initial unidimensional scale that Downs adapted to his own theory of democracy, like those used by Hotelling and Smithies, ran from left to right simply in typographical terms, and Downs linked it to left and right in an ideological or substantive sense only when he added the assumption that all political questions could be treated as having a bearing on one crucial question or

* I would like to thank Zsolt Enyedi and Joost van Spanje for their help in preparing this chapter. The usual disclaimer applies.

issue: "how much government intervention in the economy should there be?" (Downs 1957, 116). This was then further specified through the assumption that the left end of the dimension represented full government control of the economy, while the right end represented a completely free market, and that every interval from extreme left (o) to extreme right (100) denoted the percentage of the economy that an actor at that point preferred to remain in private hands. This, for Downs, offered the opportunity to rank parties according to their views on the issue of government control "in a way that might be nearly universally recognized as accurate" (1957, 116) and hence that approximated to the real world situation.

At the same time, he also admitted to a lack of realism in the approach, in that a number of extreme right-wing parties were fascist, and hence opposed to the free market, thereby inclining towards the extreme left position on this single dimension, while most other parties were in practice "leftish on some issues and rightish on others" (1957, 116) and did not have a single or unequivocal position on the scale. Moreover, while it made a lot of sense to posit the notion of a single dimension—a single street or a beachfront—when dealing with stores and their customers, it was much less intuitively meaningful to speak of a single dimension when dealing with a virtual political reality (Sartori 1976, 326). On the other hand, by staying with a single dimension, and by identifying this dimension with a left–right "ideological" scale, it certainly became much easier to model party strategy and voter behaviour and to test the assumptions in a wide variety of different settings—that is, to travel. This capacity to abstract and generalize on the basis of the left–right dimension has always remained a key element in the appeal of these particular terms of reference and has stimulated an ever growing interest in the spatial theory of electoral competition (Ferejohn 1995; Benoit and Laver 2006).

The distinction between left and right, and the widespread use in scholarly analyses of the left–right dimension, has been usefully described as a "shorthand" device—something that "provides a general orientation toward a society's political leaders, ideologies and parties" and that thereby facilitates comparisons through space and time (Inglehart and Sidjanski 1976, 225). In other words, although parties and their policies may change and develop, the notion of left and right affords a more abstract standard which can be applied more or less uniformly in different settings and periods. This was a construct which, as Inglehart and Sidjanski went on to state, "simplifie[d] a complex reality and generate[d] a handy set of decision-rules" which could then be posited for use by voters as a standard that facilitated choice between parties as well as the switching between parties, and for use by leaders of coalition-seeking parties as a standard against which to line up potential allies. It was also a division which, when Inglehart and Sidjanski were making these arguments, appeared to be acquiring even more weight and utility. As Inglehart and Kingemann (1976, 243) noted in another contribution to the same collection of essays, the concepts of left and right were even then "taking on new life and new meaning for Western publics."

Left–right terms of reference, and the classifications which they entailed, have not always been accepted by parties themselves, however—or at least not by all parties. Some parties have obviously had no problem with deliberately aligning themselves in left–right terms, or in expressly pushing for the formation of broad left-wing or broad right-wing alliances. In other cases, however, the classification can sometimes be rejected out of hand. In 1984, Jonathan Porritt, then a leading member of the emerging British Green party, was very clear in asserting that his new movement stood outside the left–right divide: "We profoundly disagree with the politics of the right and its underlying ideology of capitalism; we profoundly disagree with the politics of the left and its adherence, in varying degrees, to the ideology of commun-ism. That leaves us little choice but to disagree, perhaps less profoundly, with the politics of the center and its ideological potpourri of socialized capitalism" (Porritt 1984, 43).[1] Yet other parties that accepted the terms sought to place themselves in the center, consciously rejecting a position on either the left or the right. Such was the case with the former agrarian parties of Scandinavia, for example, each of which was redefined as a Centre party in the wake of a series of organizational and program-matic reforms in the 1950s and 1960s (Daalder 1984; see also Hazan 1997).

Moreover, the appeal of the left–right dimension is also somewhat imbalanced. Although a reasonably large group of parties seem happy to use the term "left" in their titles, and although even more parties employ some version of the term "center," it is relatively difficult to find parties which are willing to use the label "right." That is, while parties may be located on the right, they are reluctant to associate themselves specifically with the label. One exception is the small Right Block in the Czech Republic, which polled 0.6 percent in the parliamentary elections of 2002, and the now defunct Czech Right, although the comprehensive handbook edited by Szajkowski (2005) does include references to various coalitions which also admit to being on the right, including the "Rightist Opposition—Industrialists, New Rights" in Georgia, the ephemeral "Union of Right-Wing Forces" in Romania, and the "Union of Rightist Forces" in Russia. It should also be noted that the literal translation of the prominent Norwegian party Høyre is also "the Right," even though it is now usually given as "Conservative."[2]

1 THE ACCEPTABILITY OF LEFT AND RIGHT

At a minimum, the left–right division appears to offer both sense and shape to an otherwise complex political reality. This is true in the first place for voters, who appear to have the capacity to locate themselves and the parties within these terms of reference. And it is true for scholars, who, since Downs (1957), have employed versions of the left–right dimension to classify parties and governments, and who

---

[1] In the same vein, both American and German Greens sometimes adopted the slogan "Neither Left nor Right but Forward," a phrase that was also later taken up by Charles Kennedy, then leader of the British Liberal Democrats.

[2] Høyre initially mobilised in the late nineteenth century in opposition to Venstre, a party name which literally translates as "the Left."

used these data to predict voter utilities, policy performance, and coalitional behavior. It also appears true for the parties themselves, whose programs and policies are susceptible to interpretation and analysis in left–right terms. Let us briefly look at these three—voters, researchers, and parties—in turn.

Already in 1973, according to data from the then newly established nine-country European Community survey, some 83 percent of European voters could locate themselves on a left–right scale, ranging from a low of 73 percent in Belgium to a high of 93 percent in West Germany. Most of these voters could also locate the parties in their systems along this same dimension (Inglehart and Klingemann 1976). Thirty years later, according to data from the European Social Survey of 2004, an average of 88 per cent of respondents in more than twenty countries could place themselves in left–right terms, although in this case also the variation across countries is quite pronounced (see Table 11.1). More than one-third of Portuguese respondents were unable or unwilling to define themselves in left–right terms, for example, as were more than one-fifth Greek respondents. By contrast, very few of the respondents in the Nordic countries demurred.

These data also demonstrate the broad acceptability of the left–right distinction in the newer post-communist democracies. In this case, unsurprisingly, the degree of incapacity or unwillingness of respondents to locate themselves in left–right terms is higher than in western Europe, and it is also more or less consistent across the four cases involved. But even here, the acceptability rate in 2004 is more than 75 percent, and in none of the four post-communist cases does the level fall as low as that recorded in Portugal. In the earlier round of the ESS survey in 2002–3 the acceptability rate was even higher, at around 83 percent. In European politics, in sum, the division between left and right is sufficiently meaningful to allow the vast majority of voters to recognize themselves within these terms.

This appears to be less true beyond Europe, however, and certainly when we travel beyond the world of the established European and Anglo-American democracies. The detailed World Values Survey figures reported in Dalton (2006), and which are drawn from surveys in 1999–2002, reveal a handful of countries where the percentage of respondents willing to locate themselves in left–right terms falls below 50 percent—- Algeria and Columbia (where only 46 percent of the public placed themselves on a left–right scale), Jordan (36 percent), Morocco (27 percent), and Pakistan (12 percent). As Dalton notes, the acceptability and/or understanding of the left–right dimension seems particularly weak in Arab states, although it is interesting to note that in two largely Muslim states outside the Arab world, Turkey and Indonesia, some 93 and 82 percent of respondents respectively did locate themselves in left–right terms. Despite some exceptions, levels of self-placement were also relatively low in the former republics of the Soviet Union. All of this suggests that there is probably a reasonably pronounced cultural bias in the acceptability for these terms, a bias that may be compounded by a lack of experience with democratic political competition.

There is less of a problem when it comes to the use of the terms by observers and analysts. For example, the first expert study of party positions in the early 1970s asked respondents to identify up to three dimensions of competition in a number of countries, to indicate which of these could be regarded as primary and which

Table 11.1 Proportion of respondents unable or unwilling
to place themselves on a left–right scale, 2002–2004

	2002–2003	2004
Austria	14.0	14.8
Belgium	14.0	9.5
Denmark	7.1	6.5
Finland	5.4	4.6
France	6.8	na
Germany	7.5	10.4
Greece	23.2	18.9
Ireland	17.5	na
Italy	22.4	na
Luxembourg	23.5	17.6
The Netherlands	4.4	na
Norway	2.3	2.2
Portugal	19.5	34.1
Spain	19.1	14.9
Sweden	5.4	4.9
Switzerland	8.2	8.2
United Kingdom	10.2	10.4
Czech Republic	10.2	18.4
Estonia	na	24.3
Hungary	17.1	na
Poland	17.3	20.1
Slovenia	21.3	28.3
Western Europe (mean)	12.4	12.1
Eastern Europe (mean)	16.5	22.8

Source: European Social Survey I and II.

auxiliary, and to locate parties along these dimensions (Morgan 1976). As Morgan reported (1976, 454), slightly more than half of all the scales listed by the scholars were versions of the "left–right" scale, including more than 75 percent of the so-called primary scales. In other words, among expert observers, the left–right dimension proved to be "indisputably the most common scale referent in every country and over the entire time for which [the] data are valid" (Morgan 1976, 454). Almost twenty years later, in an extensive survey of expert placements of parties in forty-two polities, depicting the principal political conflict in terms of left and right—also the default option—was the preferred option of some 80 percent of the expert respondents, while a further 5.5 percent opted for the essentially comparable terms "progressive" and "conservative." Indeed, among the forty-two polities covered in the survey, it was only in South Korea that a majority of experts preferred not to use the terms left and right (Huber and Inglehart 1995, 81). Parties were also clearly located in left–right terms by respondents in the Castles-Mair expert survey of European party systems in 1982 (Castles and Mair 1984), as well as by the respondents in the expert survey on attitudes to European integration conducted by Marks and his colleagues in 1999, and which probed positions on what was termed an "economic left–right" dimension (see Hooghe, Marks, and Wilson 2002). The most recent expert survey that covers this ground recorded successful expert codings of party positions on the left–right scale in 47 polities across the world, with in this case almost none among the more than 1,500 experts who were polled finding it impossible to apply the left–right terms of reference (Benoit and Laver 2006).[3]

Finally, the terms have emerged as the single most pervasive political division identified in a series of wide-ranging cross-national analyses of party programmes and election platforms (see, *inter alia*, Budge, Hearl and Robertson 1987; Laver and Budge 1992; Klingemann, Hofferbert, and Budge 1994; Budge et al. 2001). Much of the dimensional analyses from this research program inevitably concerns nation-specific oppositions. When framed in more abstract terms, however, and when generalized to more conventional ideological terms, most of these oppositions center around one version or another of the left–right divide. As the original authors of the study put it, a content analysis of the party programmes reveals that in almost all countries "some form of Left–Right dimension dominates competition at the level of the parties" (Budge and Robertson 1987, 94). Indeed, in a later analysis of the same cross-national data, the left–right scale was assumed to be the core dimension of policy positions alignment, and it was chosen a priori as the basis of a common scale for the parties in the different systems (Laver and Budge 1992, 25–6). As van der Eijk and Oppenhuis (1988, 29) once noted in a quite different analysis of mass political ideology, such a degree of shared cross-national meaning is itself evidence of "the common foundation of substantive political ideas from which left–right positions and ideological labels derive their meaning" (see also Mair 1997, 24–31).

2 THE REFERENTS OF LEFT AND RIGHT

But while the terms of reference may be widely shared, it is not clear that a genuinely common foundation exists. That is, while European or Anglo-American voters,

---

[3] The experts were asked to "locate each party on a general left–right dimension, taking all aspects of party policy into account." An earlier and more limited version of this recent expert survey did not include a general left–right scale as such, but instead sought to disaggregate the dimension into separate measures of party policy towards public finances, public ownership, social policy, and foreign policy (see Benoit and Laver 2006: Appendix A; Laver and Hunt 1992: 39).

observers, and even political actors themselves may be happy to use the terms left and right, it is not always that they all share the same meaning of the terms.[4]

On the one hand, the distinction between left and right is clearly overdetermined. Already in 1979, for example, Klingemann noted the quite pronounced variation both across countries and within countries in the way the distinction was interpreted by the public. Citing data from the eight-nation Political Action survey, he pointed out that many respondents were unable to give any meaning to the terms, while others reversed their meaning; some had a more ideological understanding, while others read it simply in partisan terms; and some associated the distinction with particular social groups, while in others it stimulated a moral or affective response (Klingemann 1979, 230–1). A few years later, in an analysis of the same eight-nation data and the 1976 Eurobarometer data, Sani and Sartori (1983, 310–9) showed how left–right orientations tapped into, and correlated strongly with, attitudes towards inequality, change, and the Cold War divide, as well as towards religion, the clergy, big business, and the police. Elsewhere, Evans (1993) found a close relationship between the politics of gender and left–right positioning, suggesting that this newly politicized divide was becoming absorbed within the older terms of reference. This was also soon the case with Green politics, for despite initially seeking to forge a dimension of competition quite removed from conventional left–right oppositions, the Green alternative quickly became associated with the broad coalition of the center–left, both in the perceptions of voters as well as in terms of the strategy followed by the parties (e.g. Inglehart 1987; Mair 2002). In sum, a lot of quite different oppositions appear to feed into and determine left–right identification and positioning—turning it into a sort of "super issue" (van der Eijk et al. 2005, 167; Knutsen 1995).

On the other hand, the distinction between left and right is also indeterminate and highly fluid. As is well known, the distinction first came into common usage in the early period of the French Revolution, and referred to the seating arrangements in the Legislative Assembly of 1791, in which those more sympathetic to the monarchy sat on the right, while those more opposed to the monarchy sat on the left. That is, the distinction referred to a position rather than to an identity. Thereafter the use of terms spread more widely (Ignazi 2003, 4–19; Lukes 2003; Benoit and Laver 2006) and, though most usually linked to the division between more radical and more conservative positions, the sets of actors with which it was associated, and hence also the ideological profiles, inevitably shifted. As once left-wing groups were challenged by even more radical opponents, they became more closely identified with the center and right, while their new left-wing rivals, in turn, were sometimes later pushed towards the center by the mobilization of still more radical groups. In other words, although the terms left and right entered ever more common usage, their referents slowly changed as the political spectrum as a whole shifted in a more radical direction through the nineteenth and twentieth centuries. Thus the once left-wing "Venstre," which opposed the more right-wing "Høyre" in late nineteenth-century Norway (see above), was itself pushed to the right following the mobilization of the Norwegian

---

[4] Beyond these territories, of course, meanings differ even more dramatically (e.g. Dalton 2006).

Labor party in the early part of the twentieth century, while the Labor party in its turn was pushed to the right following the emergence of the smaller Socialist Left party (*venstreparti*) in the late 1970s. The development of the left-right dimension over time has in this sense proved comparable to a sandbank, in which a shifting tide uncovered ever more ground on the left, while slowly washing away the space on the right, often leading to a convergence among those conservative forces who still sought to maintain their positions on ever narrower ground.

This shift in meanings has always made it difficult to pin down a substantive and enduring policy division that corresponds to left and right positioning. In a brief but wide-ranging theoretical analysis, Bobbio (1996) attempted to narrow the range of meanings by linking the left-right divide to the more concrete distinction between equality and inequality, associating the left with a demand for greater social equality, and the right with the demand for—or at least an acceptance of—greater inequality (see also Lukes 2003). Lipset and his colleagues also emphasized this association in an early analysis of the psychology of voting: "By left we shall mean advocating social change in the direction of greater equality—political, economic or social; by right we shall mean . . . opposing change towards greater equality" (quoted by Fuchs and Klingemann 1990, 224). Fuchs and Klingemann's own work on the popular understanding of the terms in three democracies, by contrast, suggested that there was a huge variety of meanings associated with notions of left and right, ranging from those linked to more abstract values or ideologies to those linked to specific parties and groups, even though in many cases this variety was reducible to oppositions revolving around the core class divide.

The most stable denotation for the left-right divide has come through its long-term association with the class conflict. Even in this case, however, the association is also unbalanced. For while the term "left" is easily associated with a specific class and with a broad set of political alternatives, the term "right" is far less clearly delineated. "Left" in this case, as in Bartolini's (2000, 10) usage, for example, is tied to "a specific set of ideas and political and social organizations stemming from the Industrial Revolution" and refers to the programmes, ideology, and political values of a distinct group of socialist and communist parties. That is, we use historical or sociological referents, rather than, as in Bobbio's case, a theoretical or philosophical referent: the left is the class left. Beyond this boundary, however, the distinctions become more clouded. The right, or what remains beyond the left, is varied, and includes secular as well as religious groups, and more liberal as well as more conservative orientations. Indeed, if the right extends across the full space that is left vacant by the left, and if identified by default, then it runs the entire gamut from moderate liberalism through to orthodox fascism, and defies organizational, sociological, or programmatic specification. For this reason, various scholars have sought to distinguish an independent center lying between left and right (e.g. Daalder 1984). Others, however, most notably Duverger (1954, 215) have argued that the center as such cannot exist, and that it is simply a meeting place between the moderates of the left and those of the right.

If the left can be pinned down to the class left, and to an identity that is shared by traditional socialist and communist parties, it then follows that the left-right dimension is closely linked to socialist vs. non-socialist (again, the default definition) preferences on economic and welfare policies—the core concerns of that class left (see also Knutsen 1995). Issues that fall outside this limited set of preferences may well be found to correlate with the left–right dimension—attitudes to gender, to the police, to the international order, and so on—but they would not be seen to form an intrinsic element of that dimension. Budge and Robertson's (1987, 394–5) analysis of party programmes and election statements also reached this conclusion, finding that the left–right dimension was primarily concerned with "economic policy-conflicts—government regulation of the economy through direct controls or takeover... as opposed to free enterprise, individual freedom, incentives and economic orthodoxy." The point was also reinforced by the expert survey of Huber and Inglehart (1995, tables 3 and 4), who found that in twenty-five of the forty-two countries surveyed, the left–right divide was seen as revolving principally around issues relating to the economy or to class conflict. Outside Europe, however, as Dalton (2006) observes, and particularly in Asia and Africa, economic divisions can prove relatively independent of left–right divisions, and this again suggests that the linkage visible in Europe is a product of a particular pattern of party political mobilization. In other words, left and right often take on and maintain the particular meanings that proved dominant when mass politics was first institutionalized (see also Fuchs and Klingemann 1990, 233).

3 Blurring Left and Right

All of this suggests that we can come close to a stable set of referents, both in terms of actors and in terms of policy preferences, albeit one that is more clearly specified at the left end of the dimension than at the right end, and that proves more coherent in the European context than elsewhere. But, much as proved to be the case with the seating arrangements in the original French *Assemblé*, even this way of conceiving differences between left and right has been recently subject to change and has been undermined by a series of separate developments: first, by the emergence of a new ideological left in many western democracies that has sometimes little to do with the traditional alternatives; second, by the gradual waning of policy opposition between the traditional left and the traditional right, and their increasing convergence on a consensual centre; third, by the changing character of the party alternatives on both left and right, and by their increased emphasis on office-seeking rather than policy-seeking goals; fourth, by the somewhat confounding patterns shown in the new alignments that have emerged in post-communist Europe, in which some of the more conventional positioning associated with left and right has been turned on its head; and finally, by the rise of ostensibly right-wing populist parties which, at the same time, promote the defence of values traditionally associated with the liberal left. Let us look at these more closely.

The first important development in this regard is the growth of a distinct "ideo-logical" left since the late 1960s, which has little in common either organizationally or sociologically with the traditional class left. Although initially emerging as an offshoot of established communist and social democratic parties, this new left was boosted and effectively transformed by the student protests in 1968, and gradually grew into a cluster of radical, postmaterialist, and often green political parties. This network remained quite removed from the conventional working-class organizations that dominated the class left. Kitschelt (1988, 195) has usefully defined this group as "left-libertarian," with political goals which "conform neither to traditional conser-vative nor to socialist programs, but link libertarian commitments to individual autonomy and popular participation, with a leftist concern for equality." The group is not particularly strong, as such, and usually polls no more than 10 percent of the vote in a number of advanced industrial democracies (Mair 2002). But its own distinct profile, both programmatically and electorally, and the force of the compe-tition that it has waged with conventional parties of the left, has undermined the promulgation of class appeals more generally.

With time, this new left drifted closer to traditional social-democratic parties in both a programmatic and a strategic sense. Green and new left parties now either remain independent and compete on their own, or they join forces with elements of the traditional left. Indeed, to date, despite various attempts to woo their support, these new parties have never aligned themselves with either center or right parties, and have entered executive office through coalition with the left in several established party systems. This results in the emergence of a broad left that proves more powerful in electoral terms—as witnessed by the electoral successes of the broad left in Italy in 1996 and 2006, in France in 1997, and in Germany in 1998—but that is much less distinct in ideological or social-structural terms. Indeed, the broadening of the term "left," on the one hand, and the general decline in the cohesiveness of social-structural identities, on the other, have probably accounted for the generally weak levels of association between social background and left–right orientations in recent years (see van der Eijk, Schmitt, and Binder 2005).

The second key development that has undermined the traditional distinctiveness of the left is the narrowing of the differences between left and right, and the increasing convergence on a shared or consensual center. Two related factors are involved. First, the combination of the end of the Cold War, the victory of democ-racy, and the absence of any serious contemporary alternative to the market economy inevitably leads parties on both left and right to share more and more of their policy priorities. As Perry Anderson (2000, 17) has put it, in this new post-1989 world, "there are no longer any significant oppositions—that is, systematic rival outlooks—within the thought-world of the West; and scarcely any on a world-scale either." This clearly has impacted on the capacity of the left to maintain a distinct profile. Second, the constraints imposed by globalization and, within Europe, by Europeanization, limit the room for maneuver previously enjoyed by many governments, such that the range of national options becomes increasingly limited, with governments more or less obliged to pursue certain policies and desist from others. This is true for governments of both the left and the right, with the result that it becomes less and less easy to distinguish such governments according to their partisan colors.

Given the limited options which they face, and given the extent to which decisions are also increasingly externalized to nonmajoritarian agencies or to European or other international decision-making institutions, governments tend to become national governments, with party government in policy terms becoming ever less marked. To be sure, these are contested assertions, and a number of recent contributions to the policy literature emphasize the continuing capacity of governments to shape the domestic order (see, for example, Scharpf and Schmidt 2000; Glatzer and Rueschemeyer 2005). Increasingly, however, it seems that it is primarily in the details that partisanship, like the devil, can be found, as well as in the legacies of the past. On the bigger stage, and increasingly so, as well as when heading towards an internationally more competitive future, options are clearly being foreclosed (Iversen 2005). Moreover, while the policies pursued at the national level in one polity may continue to differ from those pursued in another polity, thus limiting convergence between nations, there is often little option within each nation but to pursue an agreed domestic strategy. In this sense also, partisanship may count for little. As Dalton (2006) notes, certainly in the case of most of the advanced post-industrial democracies, it is now the large moderate center that dominates.

The third key development that undermines the meaning of left and right is the change in the character of the parties themselves—the shift towards more presidential as opposed to party-governmental decision making, the emergence of cartelized party systems, and the professionalization of political leadership more generally (Katz and Mair 1995, 2002; Poguntke and Webb 2005). This promotes the prioritizing of office-seeking as opposed to policy-seeking electoral strategies, and leads to a style of competition that is more closely engaged with issues of political management and efficiency rather than with substantive political or ideological oppositions. In this case, it is more difficult for left and right to distinguish themselves, in that the key binary dividing line becomes increasingly that of government vs. opposition, regardless of the partisan hue of either. Left and right orientations may still play a role at the mass level in this sort of politics, but their effect is likely to prove much less structured and more contingent (see also van der Eijk, Schmitt, and Binder 2005).

The fourth key development is the character of the emerging alignments in the new party systems of post-communist Europe. At one level, these new alignments clearly echo the more traditional left–right divides found in the older European democracies—that is, issues involving support for the welfare state, for social protection, and for the rights of workers tend to be promoted by socialist parties, and resisted, or at least downplayed, by more centrist or conservative actors. At another level, however, and particularly on issues relating to the advancement of reform, traditional patterns are sometimes reversed. Socialist parties—usually post-communist parties—take on the role of defending the remnants of the traditional power structure, and liberal and "conservative" actors promote the more radical reformist strategies. In other words, while divisions between left and right coincide with those between socialist and liberal on the economy and on equality, they tend to confound that division on issues of democracy and political reform. In this latter case, the right adopts the more radical stance. In some cases, moreover, the latter division predominates, in that economic issues play a secondary role in competition. This has been particularly the case during the early years of democracy among the former Soviet Republics, where support for the status quo and for communism was perceived to be a right-wing position (Weßels and Klingemann 1998, 7–8). In this case, then, the normal referents are turned on their head, with the right linked to a reform program which, in the West European context, would normally be associated with the left. As Markowski (1997, 223) has suggested, "the fact that the left is identified with 'change' and 'equality' does not square with the East European reality. In fact, most of the impulses for change are associated with *reducing* equality."

The final development is of much more recent origin, and involves the emergence in a number of western democracies of ostensibly right-wing populist parties that appeal to traditional liberal—and hence, left-leaning—values. The most prominent example is that of the Dutch Pim Fortuyn List (LPF), which took off in a sudden electoral surge just before the election 2002. In many ways, this was a conventional right-wing populist party—advocating quite simple solutions to often complex problems, and basing much of its initial appeal on attacking the established political class. Its initial appeal also included anti-immigrant views, however, and was strongly critical of Islamic culture, and it was this latter part of its strategy that was grounded on, and justified by a defense of the sort of liberal values that are usually promoted most strongly by the ideological left—that is, the party stressed the need to protect the rights of women and of gays, and urged a clear separation of church and state (Akkerman 2005). Here too, then, traditional left–right positions become confused, and hence less meaningful, a problem that is compounded by the tendency of elements within the contemporary left to support some of the more conservative elements within the pro-Islamic coalition (see Lappin 2006). On these particular issues, traditional leftist anti-imperialism is almost wholly reduced to anti-Americanism, such that the conventional positions of the liberal left and the conservative right are sometimes reversed.

4 THE RESILIENCE OF LEFT AND RIGHT

But while all five of these developments may weaken or confuse the meaning and referents of the left–right division, it still remains the most widely used shorthand term that is applied in the comparison of voters, parties, and leaders—across both space and time. There remain two major reasons for this. The first is that it continues to offer the best default option, for even if the left–right dimension has lost much of its substance and potency, it remains unchallenged by any potentially competing set of referents. One possible and influential alternative has been the materialist–postmaterialist dimension which, as initially described by Inglehart (1977; 1984, and chapter in this volume), was seen to cut straight across the conventional left–right divide. This new dimension had a strong generational bias, and was tied to the wider process of cognitive mobilization, so it seemed to have the potential to surpass left–right orientations as a dominant determinant of political behavior in the advanced democracies. At the same time, however, rather than moving away from the left–right imagery, Inglehart explicitly retained the older terms of reference, suggesting that the nature of the policies and support groups of the traditional left–right divide were simply changing, and that a fading "economic left–right" opposition was being replaced by a newly emerging "non-economic left–right" opposition.

In other words, although the rise of postmaterialism tended to "neutralize" the class divide, the effect was not so much to create a wholly new dimension but rather to reshape and redefine an existing divide. Indeed, in one of his most sustained analyses of the relationship between the new politics and the traditional left–right opposition, Inglehart (1984, 68–9) concluded that the most likely future scenario would be the synthesis of both sets of concerns into a new and more inclusive dimension, in that support for postmaterialism on its own could prove self-defeating.[5] Kitschelt's (1995) more recent attempt to specify an alternative scale has also been presented in terms of a "new politics" dimension, one that polarizes libertarian and authoritarian values and cuts across the traditional left–right economic divide (see also Talshir 2005). Here too, however, it seems that the actors and voters that might be seen to have carved out a distinct position on this dimension also become at least partially absorbed by a more inclusive left–right opposition, with left-libertarian parties often casting in their lot with the more traditional but also adaptable left alternatives, and with the liberal right sometimes moving in a more authoritarian direction in order to head off new and more radical challenges (Akkerman 2005). Most recently, this new dimension has been highlighted once again as a possible explanation for differential party positions towards European integration (Hooghe et al. 2002), though whether it can retain its autonomy in this regard is still open to question.

The second reason why left–right continues to be used as a shorthand term is that despite its various ambiguities, it continues to work. That is, predictions based on the left–right proximity of parties have proved relatively accurate in accounting for differential patterns of coalition formation (e.g. Laver and Budge 1992); analyses based on measuring the left–right balance of incumbent governments have proved reasonably robust in accounting for differential policy outcomes (e.g. Klingemann, Hofferbert, and Budge 1994); and, perhaps most importantly in this context, models based on the left–right positioning of parties and voters have proved steadily successful in accounting for

---

[5] This seems to have happened in practice. As Inglehart's (1987, 1299) own data later revealed, by the mid-1980s a large majority of postmaterialists had fallen in with the left. In 1970, for example, some 40 percent of the group had been supporting parties of the center and right; fifteen years later, some 75 percent were voting for the left. By the end of the century, moreover, those Green parties that had entered into government had done so in coalition with their social democratic rivals. See also Dalton (2006) who cites global figures to conclude that "postmaterialists are disproportionately Leftist, and this is the pattern in advanced industrial democracies, Latin America, Asian democracies, and Arab nations."

electoral choice and electoral change. In other words, the left–right divide, albeit not always uniformly specified, continues to serve as a powerful device in both national and cross-national explanations of political behavior, both at mass and elite levels.

What is also interesting here is that notions of "left" and "right," however variously defined, appear to retain an independent electoral appeal over above the particular appeal generated by the individual parties that are seen to be a constitutive part of that left and right. In terms of individual voting preferences, for example, van der Eijk and Niemöller (1983) broke new ground in showing how voters in multi-party systems can maintain multiple party identifications arrayed within either the left or the right, and how these only rarely cut across this principal divide. A similar behavioral stickiness is visible at the aggregate level, in that the bulk of aggregate electoral volatility that can be measured in post-war Europe has occurred inside the traditional class left bloc and inside the center and right, and only a relatively small amount of aggregate electoral instability can be accounted for by transfers across the left–right class cleavage boundary (Bartolini and Mair 1990). In other words, at least within the European context, voter choice is often limited and constrained not just by party preference, but also by a more general sense of identification with left or right—whether this be motivated by economic considerations, or by identities based on culture, religion, or whatever. As Sani and Sartori (1983, 314) conclude, "the left–right yardstick mirrors fairly well the voters' stands on some of the major conflict domains and echoes most of the voters' feeling towards significant political objects."

5 CONCLUSION

It has often been remarked of institutions that if they are to remain the same, as Tancred remarks in *Il Gattopardo*, then they have to change. This also captures the essence of the left–right orientations. Indeed, it is precisely because of the flexibility of the left–right dimension—or what Gordon Smith (1989) has referred to as its "plasticity"—and the ability of the terms left and right to accommodate new issues and new patterns of competition, that the terms themselves have proved so enduring. Left and right, from their beginning in the French *Assemblé*, as now, are above all *positions* rather than identities, and they are variously occupied by parties, by voters, and by leaders. For a long century, running from the early mobilization of the first working-class parties in the latter nineteenth century through to the beginning of the 1980s, the left position was principally occupied by, and took as its primary referent, the class left—socialist parties and later communist parties, and their more or less shared programs and ideology. In politics, the left was essentially the class left, and the right was everybody else.

By the beginning of the 1980s, however, that dominant association had begun to wane, first as a result of the mobilization of a newer and younger ideological left from the 1960s onwards, and later, at the end of the 1980s, as a result of the failure of the communist alternative and the global acceptance of the market economy. Yet, as Inglehart (1984) remarked, this did not mark the erosion in the importance of the left–right dimension as such; rather it involved a recasting of its referents, often away from class-specific issues towards a more generalized advocacy of equality.

Even this latter element is now being undermined, however. This is partly as a result of the post-communist experience, in which the left, and reformism more generally, sometimes came to mean an assault on traditional equality policies and structures, and partly as a result of the new populist mobilization, in which ostensibly right-wing parties have taken on the defense of left-leaning liberal values, while a number of forces on the left appear to be vocal in defense of more conservative positions. Should this new confusion continue, then the general utility of the left–right dimension is bound to be questioned. Scholars have favored the left–right dimension since, as noted above, it offers a means of simplifying and comparing multi-layered realities. For voters, as Fuchs and Klingemann (1990, 233) have noted, the left–right schema offered something in both structure and substance that facilitated efficient communication and orientation, particularly in complex political environments. If, however, it appears that this shorthand device is itself becoming more complex and opaque, then it may no longer serve the purposes for which it was initially devised.

References

AKKERMAN, T. 2005. Anti-immigration parties and the defence of liberal values: the exceptional case of the List Pim Fortuyn. *Journal of Political Ideologies*, 10 (3): 337–54.

ANDERSON, P. 2000. Editorial: Renewals. *New Left Review*, 2 (1): 5–24.

BARTOLINI, S. 2000. *The Political Mobilization of the European Left, 1860–1980: The Class Cleavage*. Cambridge: Cambridge University Press.

—— and MAIR, P. 1990. *Identity, Competition and Electoral Availability: The Stabilization of European Electorates 1885–1985*. Cambridge: Cambridge University Press.

BENOIT, K., and LAVER, M. 2006. *Party Policy in Modern Democracies*. London: Routledge.

BOBBIO, N. 1996. *Left and Right: The Significance of a Political Distinction*. Cambridge: Polity.

BUDGE, I., and ROBERTSON, D. 1987. Do parties differ, and how? Comparative discriminant and factor analyses. Pp. 387–416 in *Ideology, Strategy and Party Change: Spatial Analyses of Post-war Election Programmes in Nineteen Democracies*, ed. I. Budge, D. Hearl, and D. Robertson. Cambridge: Cambridge University Press.

—— HEARL, D. and ROBERTSON, D. eds. 1987. *Ideology, Strategy and Party Change: Spatial Analyses of Post-war Election Programmes in Nineteen Democracies*. Cambridge: Cambridge University Press.

—— KLINGEMANN, H., VOLKENS, A., BARA, J., and TANNEBAUM, E. 2001. *Mapping Policy Preferences: Estimates for Parties, Electors and Governments 1945–1998*. Oxford: Oxford University Press.

CASTLES, F., and MAIR, P. 1984. Left–right political scales: some expert judgements. *European Journal of Political Research*, 12 (1): 83–8.

DAALDER, H. 1984. In search of the centre of European party systems. *American Political Science Review*, 78 (1): 92–109.

DALTON, R. 2006. Social modernization and the end of ideology debate: patterns of ideological polarization. *Japanese Journal of Political Science*, 7 (1): 1–22.

DOWNS, A. 1957. *An Economic Theory of Democracy*. New York: Harper & Row.

DUVERGER, M. 1954. *Political Parties: Their Organization and Activities in the Modern State*. London: Methuen.

EIJK, C. VAN DER, and NIEMÖLLER, K. 1983. *Electoral Change in the Netherlands*. Amsterdam: CT Press.

—— and OPPENHUIS, E. 1988. Ideological domains and party systems in Western Europe. Paper presented to the XIV World Congress of IPSA, Washington, DC.

—— SCHMITT, H., and BINDER, T. 2005. Left-right orientations and party choice. Pp. 167–91 in *The European Voter*, ed. J. Thomassen. Oxford: Oxford University Press.

EVANS, G. 1993. Is gender on the "new agenda"? *European Journal of Political Research*, 24 (2): 135–58.

FEREJOHN, J. 1995. The spatial model and elections. Pp. 107–24 in *Information, Participation, and Choice*, ed. B. Grofman. Ann Arbor: University of Michigan Press.

FUCHS, D., and KLINGEMANN, H. 1990. The left–right schema. Pp. 203–34 in *Continuities in Political Action: A Longitudinal Study of Political Orientations in Three Western Democracies*, ed. M. Jennings et al. Berlin: de Gruyter.

GLATZER, M., and RUESCHEMEYER, D. eds. 2005. *Globalization and the Future of the Welfare State*. Pittsburgh: Pittsburgh University Press.

HAZAN, R. 1997. *Centre Parties: Polarization and Competition in European Parliamentary Democracies*. London: Pinter.

HOOGHE, L., MARKS, G., and WILSON, C. 2002. Does left/right structure party positions on European integration? *Comparative Political Studies*, 35 (8): 965–89.

HOTELLING, H. 1929. Stability in competition. *Economic Journal*, 39 (1): 41–57.

HUBER, J., and INGLEHART, R. 1995. Expert interpretations of party space and party location in 42 societies. *Party Politics*, 1 (1): 73–111.

IGNAZI, P. 2003. *Extreme Right Parties in Western Europe*. Oxford: Oxford University Press.

INGLEHART, R. 1977. *The Silent Revolution: Changing Values and Political Styles among Western Publics*. Princeton: Princeton University Press.

—— 1984. The changing structure of political cleavages in western society. Pp. 25–69 in *Electoral Change in Advanced Industrial Democracies: Realignment or Dealignment?*, ed. R. Dalton, S. Flanagan, and P. Beck. Princeton: Princeton University Press.

—— 1987. Value change in industrial societies. *American Political Science Review*, 81 (4): 1289–303.

—— and KLINGEMANN, H. 1976. Party identification, ideological preference and the left–right dimension among western mass publics. Pp. 243–73 in *Party Identification and Beyond*, ed. I. Budge, I. Crewe, and D. Farlie. New York: Wiley.

—— and SIDJANSKI, D. 1976. The left, the right, the establishment and the Swiss electorate. Pp. 215–42 in *Party Identification and Beyond*, ed. I. Budge, I. Crewe, and D. Farlie. New York: Wiley.

IVERSEN, T. 2005. *Capitalism, Democracy, and Welfare*. Cambridge: Cambridge University Press.

KATZ, R., and MAIR, P. 1995. Changing models of party organization and party democracy: the emergence of the cartel party. *Party Politics*, 1 (1): 5–28.

—— —— 2002. The ascendancy of the party in public office: party organizational change in twentieth-century democracies. Pp. 113–35 in *Political Parties. Old Concepts and New Challenges*, ed. R. Gunther, J. R. Montero, and J. Linz. Oxford: Oxford University Press.

KITSCHELT, H. 1988 Left-libertarian parties: explaining innovation in competitive party systems. *World Politics*, 40 (2): 194–234.

—— with McCANN, A. 1995. *The Radical Right in Western Europe: A Comparative Analysis.* Ann Arbor: University of Michigan Press.

KLINGEMANN, H. 1979. Measuring ideological conceptualizations. Pp. 215–54 in *Political Action: Mass Participation in Five Western Democracies*, ed. S. Barnes et al. London: Sage.

—— HOFFERBERT, R. and BUDGE, I. 1994. *Parties, Policies, and Democracy.* Boulder, Colo.: Westview Press.

KNUTSEN, O. 1995. Left–right materialist value orientations. Pp. 160–96 in *The Impact of Values*, ed. J. van Deth and E. Scarbrough. Oxford: Oxford University Press.

LAPPIN, S. 2006. How class disappeared from Western publics. *Dissent*, Winter.

LAVER, M., and BUDGE, I. eds. 1992. *Party Policy and Government Coalitions.* Basingstoke: Macmillan.

—— and HUNT, W. 1992. *Policy and Party Competition.* London: Routledge.

LUKES, S. 2003. Epilogue: the grand dichotomy of the twentieth century. Pp. 602–26 in *The Cambridge History of Twentieth-Century Political Thought*, ed. T. Ball and R. Bellamy. Cambridge: Cambridge University Press.

MAIR, P. 1997. *Party System Change: Approaches and Interpretations.* Oxford: Oxford University Press.

—— 2002. The green challenge and political competition: how typical is the German experience? Pp. 99–16 in *Continuity and Change in German Politics: Beyond the Politics of centrality? A Festschrift for Gordon Smith*, ed. S. Padgett and T. Poguntke. London: Cass.

MARKOWSKI, R. 1997. Political parties and ideological spaces in East Central Europe. *Communist and Post-Communist Studies*, 30 (3): 221–54.

MORGAN, M. 1976. The modelling of government coalition formations: a policy-based approach with interval measurement. Ann Arbor: University of Michigan Ph.D. Thesis.

POGUNTKE, T., and WEBB, P. eds. 2005. *The Presidentialization of Politics: A Comparative Study of Modern Democracies.* Oxford: Oxford University Press.

PORRITT, J. 1984. *Seeing Green: The Politics of Ecology Explained.* Oxford: Blackwell.

SANI, G., and SARTORI, G. 1983. Polarization, fragmentation and competition in western democracies. Pp. 307–340 in *Western European Party Systems*, ed. H. Daalder and P. Mair. London: Sage.

SARTORI, G. 1970. Concept misformation in comparative politics. *American Political Science Review*, 64 (4): 1033–53.

—— 1976. *Parties and Party Systems: A Framework for Analysis.* Cambridge: Cambridge University Press.

SCHARPF, F., and SCHMIDT, V. eds. 2000. *Welfare and Work in the Open Economy*, vol. i. Oxford: Oxford University Press.

SMITH, G. 1989. A system perspective on party system change. *Journal of Theoretical Politics*, 1 (3): 349–64.

SMITHIES, A. 1941. Optimum location in spatial competition. *Journal of Political Economy*, 49 (3): 423–39.

SZAJKOWSKI, B. ed. 2005. *Political Parties of the World*, 6th edition. Edinburgh: John Harper Publishing.

TALSHIR, G. 2005. Knowing right from left: the politics of identity between the radical left and far right. *Journal of Political Ideologies*, 10 (3): 311–35.

WEßELS, B., and KLINGEMANN, H. 1998. Transformation and the prerequisites of democratic opposition in Central and Eastern Europe. Pp. 1–34 in *The Postcommunist Citizen*, ed. S. Barnes and J. Simon. Budapest: Erasmus Foundation.

CHAPTER 12

POSTMATERIALIST VALUES AND THE SHIFT FROM SURVIVAL TO SELF-EXPRESSION VALUES

RONALD INGLEHART

THROUGHOUT most of history, survival has been uncertain for the vast majority of the population. But the remarkable economic growth of the era after the Second World War, together with the rise of the welfare state, brought fundamentally new conditions in advanced industrial societies. The post-war birth cohorts spent their formative years under levels of prosperity that were unprecedented in human history, and the welfare state reinforced the feeling that survival was secure, producing an intergenerational value change that is gradually transforming the politics and cultural norms of advanced industrial societies.

The best-documented evidence of value change is the shift from materialist to postmaterialist priorities (Inglehart 1977, 1990). Postmaterialist values emerge as people shift from giving top priority to "materialist" values such as economic and physical security, toward increasing emphasis on "postmaterialist" priorities such as autonomy, self-expression and the quality of life. This shift is linked with changing existential conditions—above all, the change from growing up with the feeling that survival is precarious, to growing up with the feeling that survival can be taken for granted. A massive body of evidence gathered from 1970 to the present demonstrates that an intergenerational shift from materialist to postmaterialist priorities has been occurring (Inglehart and Welzel 2005). But this is only one aspect of a broader cultural shift from survival values to self-expression values, which is bringing new political issues to the center of the stage and motivating new political movements.

This theory of intergenerational value change is based on two key hypotheses (Inglehart 1981):

(1) *A Scarcity Hypothesis.* Virtually everyone aspires to freedom and autonomy, but people's priorities reflect their socioeconomic conditions: they tend to place the highest value on the most pressing needs. Material sustenance and physical security are immediately linked with survival, and when they are scarce people give top priority to these "materialistic" goals; but under conditions of prosperity, people become more likely to emphasize "postmaterialist" goals such as belonging, esteem, and esthetic and intellectual satisfaction.

(2) *A Socialization Hypothesis.* The relationship between material scarcity and value priorities is not one of immediate adjustment: to a large extent, one's basic values reflect the conditions that prevailed during one's pre-adult years and these values change mainly through intergenerational population replacement. Although older generations tend to transmit their values to their children, if one's first-hand experience is inconsistent with one's cultural heritage, it can gradually erode.

The scarcity hypothesis is similar to the principle of diminishing marginal utility. It reflects the basic distinction between the material needs for physical survival and safety, and non-material needs such as those for self-expression and esthetic satisfaction.

During the past several decades, advanced industrial societies have diverged strikingly from the prevailing historical pattern: most of their population has *not* grown up under conditions of hunger and economic insecurity. This has led to a gradual shift in which needs for belonging, esteem and intellectual and self-expression have become more prominent. The scarcity hypothesis implies that prolonged periods of high prosperity will tend to encourage the spread of postmaterialist values—and enduring economic decline will have the opposite effect.

But there is no one-to-one relationship between socioeconomic development and the prevalence of postmaterialist values, for these values reflect one's subjective sense of security, and not simply one's objective economic level. One's subjective sense of security is shaped by a society's social welfare institutions as well as its mean level of income, and is also influenced by the general sense of security prevailing in one's society. Furthermore, people's basic value priorities do not change over night: the scarcity hypothesis must be interpreted in connection with the socialization hypothesis.

One of the most pervasive concepts in social science is that one's basic personality structure crystallizes by the time one reaches adulthood: early socialization carries greater weight than later socialization. A large body of evidence indicates that people's basic values are largely fixed when they reach adulthood, and change relatively little thereafter (Rokeach 1968, 1973; Inglehart 1977, 1997; also see chapter on socialization by Jennings in this Handbook). If so, we would expect to find substantial differences between the values of the young and the old in societies that have experienced a rising sense of security. People are most likely to adopt those values that are consistent with what they have experienced first-hand during their formative years. This implies that intergenerational value change will occur if younger generations grow up under different conditions from those that shaped earlier generations—so that the values of the entire society will gradually change through intergenerational replacement.

These two hypotheses generate several predictions concerning value change. First, while the scarcity hypothesis implies that prosperity is conducive to the spread of postmaterialist values, the socialization hypothesis implies that fundamental value change takes place gradually; to a large extent, it occurs as younger generations replace older ones in the adult population. After an extended period of rising economic and physical security, one would expect to find substantial differences between the value priorities of older and younger groups, since they would have been shaped by different experiences in their formative years. But a sizeable time lag would occur between economic changes and their political effects. Ten or fifteen years after an era of prosperity began, the birth cohorts that had spent their formative years in prosperity would begin to enter the electorate.

Per capita income and educational levels are among the best readily available indicators of the conditions leading to the shift from materialist to postmaterialist goals, but the theoretically crucial factor is not per capita income itself, but one's sense of existential security—which means that the impact of economic and physical security is mediated by the given society's social security system. Thus, we would not expect to find particularly high levels of postmaterialism in Kuwait: it should rank higher than Yemen or other low-income countries, but income equality and governmental effectiveness are low in the oil-exporting Gulf states, which means that many of their people didn't grow up taking survival for granted.

Several decades ago, Inglehart (1971) found dramatic age differences in the proportions of people emphasizing materialist and postmaterialist values, respectively, among the publics of six western countries. To measure these values, he asked people to say which goals they considered most important for their country to seek, choosing between such things as economic growth, fighting rising prices, maintaining order, and the fight against crime (which tap materialist priorities); and freedom of speech, giving people more say in important government decisions, more say on the job, and a society where ideas count (which tap postmaterialist priorities). Representative national surveys revealed huge differences between the values of young and old in all of these societies. Among those aged 65 and older, people with materialist value priorities outnumbered those with postmaterialist value priorities by more than 12:1. But as one moved from older to younger cohorts, the balance gradually shifted toward a diminishing proportion of materialists and a growing proportion of people with postmaterialist values. Among the youngest cohort (those from 18 to 25 years old in 1970) postmaterialists outnumbered the materialists.

But do these age differences reflect life-cycle effects or birth cohort effects? With data from just one time point, there is no way of knowing—and the two interpretations have very different implications. The life-cycle reading implies that the young will become increasingly materialist as they age, so that by the time they are 65 years old they will have become just as materialist as the 65 year olds were in 1970—which means that the society as a whole won't change at all. The cohort-effects interpretation implies that the younger cohorts will remain relatively postmaterialist over time—and that as they replace the older, more materialist cohorts, the prevailing values of the society *will* change, becoming increasingly postmaterialist.

Cohort analysis provides the only conclusive way to determine whether age differences reflect life cycle effects or intergenerational change based on cohort effects. In order to do so, one needs (1) survey data covering a sizeable time period; (2) surveys carried out at numerous time points, enabling one to distinguish period effects from life-cycle and cohort effects; and (3) large numbers of respondents in each survey—because breaking the sample down into six or seven birth cohorts, the sampling error margin rises to the point where noise starts to drown out the signal.

Building on earlier cohort analyses, Inglehart and Welzel (2005, chapter 4) present a cohort analysis that follows given birth cohorts over three decades, taking advantage of the fact that the Euro-barometer surveys asked the materialist/postmaterialist battery of questions almost every year, from 1970 to 2000, in all six of the countries first surveyed in 1970. Figure 12.1 shows the results, using the pooled data from Britain, France, West Germany, Italy, Belgium, and the Netherlands. Each cohort's position at a given time is calculated by subtracting the percentage of materialists in that cohort from the percentage of postmaterialists. Thus, at the zero point on the vertical axis, the two groups are equally numerous. The proportion of postmaterialists increases as one moves up; the proportion of materialists increases as one moves down. If the age differences reflected a life-cycle effect, then each of the cohort lines would gradually move downward, toward the materialist pole, as one moves from left to right across Figure 12.1, tracing the years from 1970 to 2000. The vertical scale of this figure shows the percentage of postmaterialists, minus the percentage of materialists—with zero indicating the point where the two types are equally numerous. If cohort effects are present, the pattern will not be diagonal but horizontal, with each birth cohort remaining about as postmaterialist at the end of the time series as it was at the start.

But we also need to take period effects into account. Our theory implies that short-term effects such as a major recession will tend to push all cohorts downward in response to current conditions; but with recovery, they will return to their former level, so that in the long run they will remain about as postmaterialist as they were at the start. Over short periods, a short-term fluctuation or period effect that pushed all the cohorts downward could give the mistaken impression that the age differences merely reflected life-cycle effects. The causes and implications of period effects have been debated extensively. The main arguments are summed up in Clarke and Dutt (1991), Duch and Taylor (1993), Clarke et al. (1999), Abramson and Inglehart (1994), and Inglehart and Abramson (1999).

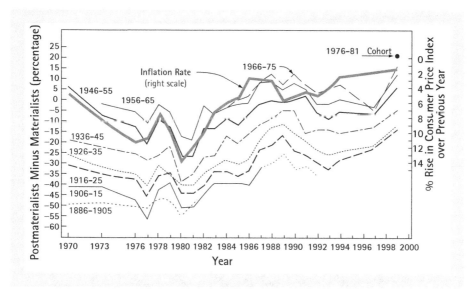

Fig. 12.1 Cohort analysis with inflation rate superimposed (using inverted scale on right): % Postmaterialists minus % materialists in six West European societies, 1970–1999

Source: Inglehart and Welzel 2005: 101. Based on combined weighted sample of European Community surveys carried out in West Germany, France, Britain, Italy, the Netherlands, and Belgium, in given years, using the 4-item Materialist/Postmaterialist values index.

Because we have data from numerous time points, we can see that period effects clearly *are* present in the years from 1970 to 2000 (they reflect current economic conditions, particularly inflation levels: note how closely the period effects in Figure 12.1 track inflation rates). But these period effects have no lasting impact: the younger cohorts remain relatively postmaterialist at every time point, despite short-term fluctuations, and at the end of three decades, each cohort is no more materialist than it was at the start (in fact, most of them are *less* so). There is no evidence whatever of life-cycle effects—by 2000, it has become apparent that the age-related differences that were found in 1970 reflect lasting cohort differences.

This implies that as the younger, less materialist cohorts, replace the older ones in the adult population, each society should shift from materialist toward postmaterialist values. This is precisely what happened. Figure 12.2 shows the net shift from 1970 to 2000 among the six publics we have just analyzed, plus three societies that were first surveyed in 1972 and 1973. In every country, we find a substantial net shift toward postmaterialist values—so much so that they now have more postmaterialists than materialists.

The vertical scale of this figure again shows the percentage of postmaterialists, minus the percentage of materialists—with the zero point indicating the point at which materialists and postmaterialists are equally numerous. In the early 1970s, materialists heavily outnumbered postmaterialists in all nine of these countries, all of which fell well below the zero point. For example, in the earliest US survey, materialists outnumbered postmaterialists by 24 percentage points; in West Germany, they outnumbered postmaterialists by 34 points. During the three decades following 1970,

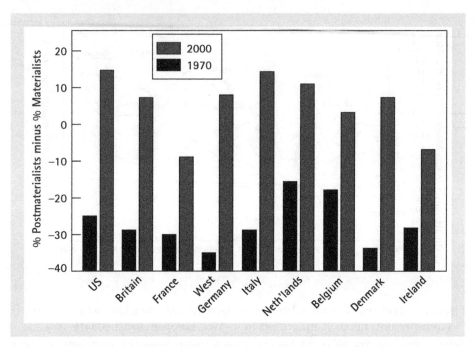

Fig. 12.2 The shift toward postmaterialist values among the publics of Nine Western societies, 1970–2000

Source: Inglehart and Welzel 2005: 103.

a major shift occurred: by the 1999–2001 surveys, postmaterialists had become more numerous than materialists in all nine countries. The American public shifted from having about three times as many materialists as postmaterialists, to having 2.5 times as many postmaterialists as materialists. Despite substantial short-term fluctuations, the predicted shift toward postmaterialist values took place.

The intergenerational value change thesis predicts a shift from materialist toward postmaterialist values among the populations of these societies. Empirical evidence gathered over a period of three decades supports this prediction: the large and persistent differences that we find between older and younger birth cohorts seem to reflect a process of intergenerational value change.

1 Controversies over the Value Change Thesis

During the years since the thesis of a postmaterialist shift was first published, scores of critiques have appeared. The early ones argued that the age differences found in 1970 simply reflected life-cycle effects: each cohort would grow more materialistic as it aged, so we should expect no net shift in prevailing values (Boeltken and Jagodzinski 1985). In the light of the evidence gathered during the next three decades, these claims have disappeared: the predicted erosion of postmaterialism that should have resulted from life-cycle effects, didn't happen: people did not become more materialist as they aged.

Other critics have claimed that materialism/postmaterialism is a one-dimensional model of human values—implying that this dimension is the *only* dimension that exists (e.g. Flanagan 1982, 1987; Braithwaite, Makkai, and Pittelkow 1996, etc). This sets up a straw man that is easily refuted, since human values are obviously multidimensional. The materialist/postmaterialist dimension clearly isn't the only dimension that exists— as is evident from my early work (Inglehart 1977), which examined the relationship between the materialist/postmaterialist dimension and other values dimensions. In *Political Action* I examined its relationship to ten other dimensions based on the Rokeach terminal values (Inglehart 1979, 314–18). And numerous publications have analyzed the relationships between the materialist/postmaterialist values dimension and various other value dimensions involving religion, politics, work motivations, gender equality, sexual norms, attitudes toward authority, and other orientations (e.g. Inglehart 1990; Inglehart and Abramson 1999; Inglehart and Norris 2003; Norris and Inglehart 2004; Dalton 2006; Nevitte 1996).

I *do* claim that a conceptually coherent and empirically demonstrable materialist/ postmaterialist values dimension exists, with materialist values at one pole, post-materialist values at the opposite pole, and the various mixed types at intermediate points on this dimension. Although this dimension can be broken down into its components, reflecting relative emphasis on economic and physical security, it does constitute a coherent single dimension: The underlying theory holds that those who experienced relatively high levels of economic and physical insecurity during their formative years tend to give top priority to materialist values; but that the economic miracles of the post-war era, combined with the welfare state, have given rise to increasing numbers of people who take economic and physical security for granted and tend to give top priority to self-expression and the quality of life. The central point is that, by focusing on one clearly defined dimension, it is possible to generate theoretical explanations and predictions that can be empirically tested.

Because the variables that tap this dimension are not correlated at the 1.0 level, it is possible to break it down into its subcomponents: using principal components factor analysis, one obtains a clear materialist/postmaterialist dimension in almost every society that has been tested (Abramson and Inglehart 1995, 101–14); but using varimax rotation, one can break this dimension down into two component dimen-sions. It is perfectly legitimate to do so: the approach one uses depends on one's theoretical perspective. In this case, our theory implies that those who give top priority to economic security (tapped by such items as "fight rising prices," and "economic growth") will also tend to give top priority to physical security (tapped by such items as "maintain order" and "the fight against crime"); and will give relatively low priority to the various postmaterialist goals. Empirically, they do—as is reflected in the fact that all of the materialist items show negative polarity on the materialist/ postmaterialist principal component dimension. Nevertheless, the items designed to tap material security are less strongly correlated with the items designed to tap physical security than they are with each other, and by using varimax rotation one can split them into two distinct factors (Flanagan 1982, 1987; Inglehart, 1987).

If one is specifically concerned with people's emphasis on physical security, it makes sense to do so. Or, moving in the opposite direction, if one's theoretical concerns deal with the much broader concept of modern versus traditional values, one can use the materialist/postmaterialist values battery as an indicator of this dimension: for empirically, these values prove to be a strong indicator of one's orientations concerning gender equality, tolerance of outgroups, political activism, environmental activism, interpersonal trust, and a number of additional orientations that have been labeled "self-expression values."

2 Postmaterialist Values: One Component of a Broader Dimension of Cultural Change

Postmaterialism itself is only one aspect of a still broader process of cultural change that is reshaping the political outlook, religious orientations, gender roles, and sexual mores of advanced industrial society (Inglehart 1990, 1997; Inglehart and Welzel 2005; Welzel chapter in this volume). The emerging orientations place less emphasis on traditional cultural norms, especially those that limit individual self-expression.

In order to identify the main dimensions of cross-cultural variance, Inglehart and Welzel carried out a factor analysis of each society's mean level on scores of variables, replicating the analysis in Inglehart and Baker (2000).[1] The two most significant dimensions that emerged reflected, first, a polarization between *traditional* and *secular-rational* values and, second, a polarization between *survival* and *self-expression* values.

Traditional values place strong emphasis on religion, respect for authority, and have relatively low levels of tolerance for abortion and divorce and have relatively high levels of national pride. *Secular-rational* values have the opposite characteristics. Agrarian societies tend to emphasize traditional values; industrializing societies tend to emphasize secular-rational values.

The second major dimension of cross-cultural variation is linked with the transition from industrial society to post-industrial societies—which brings a polarization between *survival* and *self-expression* values. The polarization between materialist and postmaterialist values is a sensitive indicator of this dimension—showing an extremely high loading on the broader dimension, as Table 12.1 demonstrates. For the same conditions that give rise to postmaterialist values, are also conducive to self-expression values. But self-

---

[1] For details on how these factor analyses were carried out, at both the individual and societal levels, see Inglehart and Baker (2000).

Table 12.1 Orientations linked with survival vs. self-expression values

Item	Correlation
SURVIVAL VALUES emphasize the following:	
Materialist/Postmaterialist Values	.87
Men make better political leaders than women	86
R. is not highly satisfied with life	.84
A woman has to have children to be fulfilled	.83
R. rejects foreigners, homosexuals, and people with AIDS as neighbors	.81
R. has not and would not sign a petition	.80
R. is not very happy	.79
R. favors more emphasis on the development of technology	.78
Homosexuality is never justifiable	.78
R. has not recycled something to protect the environment	.76
R. has not attended a meeting or signed a petition to protect the environment	.75
A good income and safe job are more important than a feeling of accomplishment and working with people you like	.74
R. does not rate own health as very good	.73
A child needs a home with both a father and a mother in order to grow up happily	.73
When jobs are scarce, a man has more right to a job than a woman	.69
A university education is more important for a boy than for a girl	.67
Government should ensure that everyone is provided for	.69
Hard work is one of the most important things to teach a child	.65
Imagination is not of the most important things to teach a child	.62
Tolerance is not of the most important things to teach a child	.62
Leisure is not very important in life	.61
Scientific discoveries will help, rather than harm, humanity	.60
Friends are not very important in life	.56
You have to be very careful about trusting people	.56
R. has not and would not join a boycott	.56
R. is relatively favorable to state ownership of business and industry	.54
SELF–EXPRESSION VALUES take opposite position on all of above	

Note: The original polarities vary; the above statements show how each item relates to this values index.

expression values encompass a number of issues that go well beyond the items tapped by postmaterialist values. For example, self-expression values reflect mass polarization over such issues as whether "When jobs are scarce, men have more right to a job than women;" or whether "Men make better political leaders than women" (which is almost as sensitive an indicator of self-expression values as postmaterialist values). This emphasis on gender equality is part of a broader syndrome of tolerance of outgroups, including foreigners, gays, and lesbians. Self-expression values give high priority to environmental protection, tolerance of diversity, and rising demands for participation in decision making in economic and political life.

The shift from survival values to self-expression values also includes a shift in child-rearing values, from emphasis on hard work toward emphasis on imagination and tolerance as important values to teach a child. Societies that rank high on self-expression values also tend to rank high on interpersonal trust and have relatively high levels of subjective well-being. This produces an environment of trust and tolerance, in which people place a relatively high value on individual freedom and self-expression, and have activist political orientations—the attributes that the political culture literature defines as crucial to democracy.

A major component of rise of self-expression values is a shift away from deference to all forms of external authority. Submission to authority has high costs: the individual's personal goals must be subordinated to those of an external entity. Under conditions of insecurity, people are generally willing to do so. Under threat of invasion, internal disorder, or economic collapse, people eagerly seek strong authority figures that can protect them from danger.

Conversely, conditions of prosperity and security are conducive to tolerance of diversity in general and democracy in particular. This helps explain a long-established finding: rich societies are much likelier to be democratic than poor ones. One contributing factor is that the authoritarian reaction is strongest under conditions of insecurity.

Since humans values are multidimensional, it is easy to find attitudes that are unrelated to the materialist/postmaterialist dimension. Davis and Davenport (1999) did so, arguing that this invalidated this measure. In reply, Inglehart and Abramson (1999) pointed out that the value change thesis predicts that postmaterialist values will predict other attitudes insofar as they are shaped by the degree to which one perceives survival as secure or insecure—but there is no theoretical reason to expect that postmaterialist values would predict *all* other attitudes. They then demonstrated that these values do predict a large number of orientations, reflecting the fact that whether one takes survival for granted or views it as precarious, does indeed shape a major component of one's world-view—as Table 12.1 also illustrates.

Originally skeptical of the postmaterialist value change thesis, Lafferty (1975) had published an article questioning whether the materialist/postmaterialist dimension tapped any deep-rooted orientation. He then carried out a survey designed to test this dimension's validity in the Norwegian context. After analyzing the findings, Lafferty and Knutsen (1985) concluded that postmaterialism tapped a highly constrained ideological dimension that occupies a central position in the world-view of the Norwegian public.

The rise of self-expression values reflects an intergenerational change in a wide variety of basic social norms, from cultural norms linked with ensuring survival of the species, to norms linked with the pursuit of individual well-being. For example, postmaterialists and the young are markedly more tolerant of homosexuality than are materialists and the old. And they are far more permissive than materialists in their attitudes toward abortion, divorce, extramarital affairs, prostitution, and euthanasia. Economic accumulation for the sake of economic security was the central goal of industrial society. Ironically, their attainment set in motion a process of gradual cultural change that has made these goals less central—and is now bringing a rejection of the hierarchical institutions that helped attain them.

3 Intergenerational Value Change in Economically Advanced and Low-Income Societies

Inglehart and Welzel (2005) analyze the shift from survival to self-expression values observed across four waves of the Values Surveys. They find that rich post-industrial societies show large intergenerational differences, with the younger cohorts generally placing much stronger emphasis on self-expression values than do the older cohorts. By contrast, low-income societies that have not experienced substantial economic growth during the past five decades do not display intergenerational differences—younger and older cohorts are about equally likely to display traditional values. This suggests that these intergenerational differences reflect historical changes, rather than anything inherent in the human life cycle. This interpretation is reinforced by the fact that, when we follow a given birth cohort's value orientations over time, they do *not* become more traditional or survival oriented as they age, as the life-cycle interpretation implies. Instead, the generational differences are an enduring attribute of given cohorts, which seem to reflect the different formative conditions they experienced as each cohort grew up under increasingly secure conditions.

Under some circumstances, one might argue that these age-linked differences simply reflect life-cycle effects, not intergenerational change—claiming that people have an inherent tendency to place increasing emphasis on survival values as they age. If such a life-cycle effect existed, the younger cohorts would place more emphasis on self-expression values than the older cohorts in *any* society. But this claim is untenable in the present case—for these intergenerational differences are found in developed societies, but not in low-income societies. There is no inherent tendency for people to emphasize survival values more strongly as they age. Likewise, there is no universal tendency for the young to emphasize self-expression values more strongly than the old. Such intergenerational differences emerge when a society has attained high levels of socioeconomic development. The generational differences found in developed societies seem to reflect long-term socioeconomic changes, rather than life-cycle effects.

The evidence suggests that a process of intergenerational value change has been taking place during the past six decades—though it is only indirect evidence. In order to demonstrate directly that long-term cultural changes are occurring, we would need evidence from surveys that had measured these values in both rich and poor countries throughout the past sixty or seventy years. Such data are not available and will not be available for several decades. Nevertheless, the time-series data that are now available show changes toward self-expression values in virtually all high-income societies—but not in low-income societies. We do not find a universal shift toward secular-rational and self-expression values, such as might result from some universal process of cultural diffusion or the internet. These cultural changes are linked with socioeconomic development, and are *not* occurring where it is absent.

The evidence suggests that major cultural changes are occurring through an intergenerational value shift linked with the fact that the younger birth cohorts have grown up under higher levels of existential security than those that shaped the formative years of the older cohorts.

4 CHANGING POLITICAL ALIGNMENTS

Decades ago (Inglehart 1977, 5 and chapter 7) I argued that the shift from materialist to postmaterialist values would bring a decline of social class voting and the rise of political conflict based on quality of life issues. The value change hypothesis implies that as intergenerational shift takes place, we should witness a shift from social class-based politics, centered on distribution of property and private or state ownership of the means of production, toward increasing emphasis on the physical and social quality of life and on self-expression. This value shift implies the rise of new political movements and parties, and the emergence of an increasingly elite-challenging public. As it happened, in subsequent decades class conflict ceased to dominate politics, as the women's movement, the environmentalist movement, the gay liberation movement, and other movements based on lifestyle rather than class, became increasingly prominent.

An oversimplified reading of this theory claims that it predicts the disappearance of economic issues—a straw man that is easily refuted by pointing out that economic issues still matter. The argument that postmaterialist issues would totally replace materialist ones never appears in any of my writings and is explicitly denied in several places. For example, a methodological debate about the use of rankings vs. ratings to measure value priorities (Bean and Papadakis 1994; Inglehart 1994; cf. Inglehart 1990) showed that because almost everyone likes economic security *and* physical security *and* freedom of speech *and* having more say in decisions, unless one uses forced-choice rankings, people will tend to give high ratings to *all* of these goals. But, although almost everyone places a positive value on all twelve of the items used to measure materialist vs. postmaterialist goals, materialists and postmaterialists consistently give them different *priorities*—a fact that emerges clearly when they are ranked.

I never claimed that postmaterialists do not need to eat: they obviously do. On the contrary, I pointed out that they have higher levels of consumption than materialists and (like virtually everyone) they like having high incomes. What I did claim, however, is that postmaterialists give a lower *priority* to high incomes than do materialists—and that is true, as is demonstrated by the fact that job motivations show a dramatic shift from emphasis on a high income and safe jobs, to emphasis on interesting work and working with people you like, as one moves from materialist to postmaterialist values (Inglehart 1977, 56).

An emerging emphasis on quality of life issues has been superimposed on the older, class-based cleavages of industrial society. From the mid-nineteenth century to the mid-twentieth century, politics was dominated by class conflict over the distribution of income and the ownership of industry. In recent decades, social class voting has declined and now shares the stage with newer postmaterialist issues that emphasize lifestyle issues and environmental protection.

The rise of postmaterialism does not mean that materialistic issues and concerns will vanish. Conflicts about how to secure prosperity and sustainable economic development will always be important political issues. Moreover, the publics in post-industrial societies have developed more sophisticated forms of consumerism, materialism, and hedonism. But these new forms of materialism have been shaped by the rise of postmaterialist values. New forms of consumption no longer function mainly to indicate people's economic class. Increasingly, they are used to express people's personal taste and lifestyle. This emphasis on self-expression is an inherent feature of postmaterialism, which is the central component of self-expression values.

The evidence makes it clear that the intergenerational value differences found in post-industrial societies do *not* reflect life-cycle effects. As Figure 12.1 demonstrated, given birth cohorts did not become more materialistic as they aged. Inglehart and Welzel (2005) demonstrate that this also holds true of the shift from survival to self-expression values. Analyzing data from all of the post-industrial societies that were surveyed in both the first (1981) and the fourth (2000) waves of the Values Surveys,[2] they find that from the start of this time series, younger birth cohorts placed more emphasis on self-expression values than older cohorts did, and given birth cohorts did not move away from self-expression values toward survival values as they aged from 1980 to 2000. Throughout this period, younger birth cohorts continued to place more emphasis on self-expression values than older ones. And although each of the birth cohorts aged by twenty years during the period covered by the Values surveys, none of them placed less emphasis on self-expression in 2000 than it did in 1981—as would have happened if these age differences reflected life-cycle effects.

If people's values are indeed shifting from materialist to postmaterialist priorities, the implications are far-reaching. The main axis of political conflict should gradually shift from class-based issues such as income redistribution and state ownership of industry, toward increasing emphasis on quality of life issues. New types of political movements

---

[2] These countries include Belgium, Canada, Denmark, Finland, France, Great Britain, Germany (West), Ireland, Italy, Japan, the Netherlands, Spain, Sweden, and the US.

and parties should emerge to champion these issues. And social class voting should erode, as the constituency supporting change shifts from its traditional working base to include postmaterialists from relatively secure middle-class backgrounds.

As predicted, social class voting has declined in most advanced industrial societies; in the last two US presidential elections, for example, the vote polarized much more strongly on lifestyle issues such as abortion and same-sex marriage than on social class, which had declined to the point where it had very little impact on voting.

The impact of changing values goes far beyond these changes in electoral behavior. The central issues of political conflict have shifted, with the rise of environmentalist movements, the women's movement, gay liberation, and other lifestyle movements. As Berry (1999) argues, postmaterialist values are motivating consumer, environmental, civil rights, and civil liberties groups to mount an increasingly effective challenge to corporate power. As Nevitte (1996) demonstrates, the rise of postmaterialist values is producing less deferential, increasingly elite-challenging publics. And as Gibson and Duch (1994) show, emerging postmaterialist values played a key role in the emergence and survival of democracy in the Soviet Union. Materialist/postmaterialist values are just one indicator of a much broader cultural shift from survival values to self-expression values that is bringing changing values concerning gender roles, sexual orientation, work, religion, and child-rearing.

One particularly important and non-obvious aspect of these values is their close linkage with the rise of gender equality. In the post-industrial phase of development, a trend towards gender equality becomes a central aspect of modernization (Inglehart and Norris 2003, 29–48). This transformation of established gender roles is linked with rising self-expression values, bringing increasing tolerance of human diversity and anti-discrimination movements on many fronts. This shift reflects the degree to which societal conditions allow people to develop their potential for choice (Anand and Sen 2000). Even today, women are confronted with societal disadvantages that make it more difficult for them than for men to develop their talents in careers outside the household. They have been socialized to accept these role limitations until very recently in history.

But history has recently taken a fundamentally new direction. In post-industrial societies, women no longer accept their traditional role limitations, and female empowerment has moved to a high place on the political agenda. Gender equality has become a central element in the definition of human development, for it is an essential aspect of human equality, like civil and political liberties and human rights. Never before in the history of civilization have women enjoyed more equality and more freedom in choosing their education, their careers, their partners, and their lifestyles than in contemporary post-industrial societies. This change is recent. Although it can be traced back to the introduction of female suffrage in some countries after the First World War, female empowerment only recently became a pervasive trend. It is reflected in a massive tendency toward increasing female representation in national parliaments and in a shift towards gender equality that is closely linked with the rising emphasis on self-expression values.

The United Nations Development Program has developed a "gender empowerment measure" that taps female representation in parliaments, in management positions and

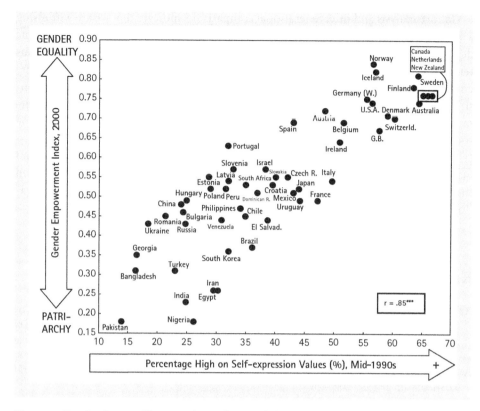

Fig. 12.3 Emphasis on self-expression values and the scope of gender empowerment

in administrative functions as well as gender equality in salaries. As Figure 12.3 demonstrates, emphasis on self-expression values (correlated at the $r = .82$ level with postmaterialist values) is strongly linked with the extent to which a given society actually approaches gender equality in political and social life.

As Inglehart and Welzel (2005) demonstrate, another major consequence of the shift toward postmaterialist values, and the broader shift toward self-expression values is conducive to good governance and the spread and flourishing of democratic institutions.

5 CONCLUSION

Intergenerational value changes reflect historic changes in a society's existential conditions. Far from being universal, these changes are found only in societies in which the younger generations have experienced substantially different formative conditions from those that shaped older generations.

Cohort analysis and intergenerational comparisons indicate that we are witnessing a gradual process of intergenerational value change linked with socioeconomic development, reflecting the fact that increasingly favorable existential conditions tend to make people less dependent on religion, and lead them to place increasing emphasis on self-expression. These findings reinforce the evidence that demonstrated that the publics of rich societies are much more likely to emphasize secular-rational values and self-expression values, than are the publics of low-income societies. A huge body of evidence, analyzed by three different approaches— (1) comparisons of rich and poor countries; (2) generational comparisons; and (3) time-series evidence from the past two decades—all points to the conclusion that major cultural changes are occurring, and they reflect a process of intergenerational change, linked with rising levels of existential security.

References

ABRAMSON, P., and INGLEHART, R. 1994. Education, security and postmaterialism: a comment on Duch and Taylor's "Postmaterialism and the Economic Condition." *American Journal of Political Science*, 38: 797–814.

—— —— 1995. *Value Change in Global Perspective*. Ann Arbor: University of Michigan Press.

ANAND, S., and SEN, A. 2000. Human development and economic sustainability. *World Development*, 28 (12): 2029–49.

BARNES, S. H., KAASE, M., et al. 1979. *Political Action: Mass Participation in Five Western Democracies*. Beverly Hills, Calif.: Sage.

BEAN, C., and PAPADAKIS, E. 1994. Polarized priorities or flexible alternatives? Dimensionality in Inglehart's materialism-postmaterialism scale. *International Journal of Public Opinion Research*, 6: 264–88.

BERRY, J. M. 1999. *New Liberalism: The Rising Power of Citizen Groups*. Washington, DC: The Brookings Institution.

BOELTKEN, F., and JAGODZINSKI, W. 1985. In an atmosphere of insecurity: postmaterialism in the European Community, 1970 to 1980. *Comparative Political Studies*, 17: 453–84.

BRAITHWAITE, V., MAKKAI, T., and PITTELKOW, Y. 1996. Inglehart's materialism-postmaterialism concept: clarifying the dimensionality debate through Rokeach's model of social values. *Journal of Applied Social Psychology*, 26: 1536–55.

CLARKE, H., and DUTT, N. 1991. Measuring value change in western industrialized societies: the impact of unemployment. *American Political Science Review*, 85: 905–20.

—— et al. 1999. The effect of economic performance on the measurement of value change: new experimental evidence. *American Political Science Review*, 93: 637–48.

DALTON, R. 2006 *Citizen Politics: Public Opinion and Parties in Advanced Industrial Democracies*, Washington, DC: CQ Press.

DAVIS, D., and DAVENPORT, C. 1999. Assessing the validity of the postmaterialism index. *American Political Science Review*, 93: 649–64.

DUCH, R. M., and TAYLOR, M. A. 1993. Postmaterialism and the economic condition. *American Journal of Political Science*, 37: 747–79.

—— —— 1994. A reply to Abramson and Inglehart's "Education, Security and Postmaterialism." *American Journal of Political Science*, 38: 815–24.

FLANAGAN, S. 1982. Measuring value change in advanced industrial societies: Inglehart's silent revolution from the perspective of Japanese findings. *Comparative Political Studies*, 14: 403–44.

—— 1987. Controversy: value change in industrial societies. *American Political Science Review*, 81 (4): 1303–19.

GIBSON, J., and DUCH, R. M. 1994. Postmaterialism and the emerging Soviet democracy. *Political Research Quarterly*, 475–39.

IKE, N. 1973. Economic growth and intergenerational change in Japan, *American Political Science Review*, 67: 1194–203.

INGLEHART, R. 1971. The silent revolution in Europe: intergenerational change in post-industrial societies. *American Political Science Review*, 65 (4): 991–1017.

—— 1977. *The Silent Revolution: Changing Values and Political Styles among Western Publics*. Princeton: Princeton University Press.

—— 1979. Value priorities and socioeconomic change. Ch. 11. in Barnes, Kaase et al. 1979.

—— 1981. Post-materialism in an environment of insecurity. *American Political Science Review*, 75 (4): 880–900.

—— 1987. Controversy: value change in industrial society. *American Political Science Review*, 81 (4): 1289–303.

—— 1990. *Culture Shift in Advanced Industrial Society*. Princeton: Princeton University Press.

—— 1994. Comment: polarized priorities or flexible alternatives? Dimensionality in Inglehart's postmaterialism scale. *International Journal of Public Opinion Research*, 6 (3): 289–92.

—— 1997. *Modernization and Postmodernization: Cultural, Economic and Political Change in 43 Societies*. Princeton: Princeton University Press, 1997.

—— and ABRAMSON, P. 1994. Economic security and value change. *American Political Science Review* (June), 336–54.

—— —— 1999. Measuring postmaterialism. *American Political Science Review* (September), 665–77.

—— and BAKER, W. 2000. Modernization, cultural change and the persistence of traditional values. *American Sociological Review* (February), 19–51.

—— and NORRIS, P. 2003. *Rising Tide: Gender Equality in Global Perspective*. Cambridge: Cambridge University Press.

—— and WELZEL, C. 2005. *Modernization, Cultural Change and Democracy*. New York: Cambridge University Press.

LAFFERTY, W. M. 1975. Basic needs and political values: some perspectives from Norway's silent revolution. *Acta Sociologica*, 19: 117–36.

—— and KNUTSEN, O. 1985. Postmaterialism in a social democratic state: an analysis of the distinctness and congruity of the Inglehart value syndrome in Norway. *Comparative Political Studies*, 17: 411–30.

MUELLER-ROMMEL, F. ed. 1989. *New Politics in Western Europe: The Rise and Success of Green Parties and Alternative Lists*. Boulder, Colo.: Westview Press.

NEVITTE, N. 1996. *The Decline of Deference: Canadian Value Change in Cross-national Perspective*. Peterborough, Ont.: Broadview Press.

NORRIS, P., and INGLEHART, R. 2004. *Sacred and Secular: Reexamining the Secularization Thesis*. New York: Cambridge University Press.

ROHRSCHNEIDER, R. 1990. The roots of public opinion toward new social movements: an empirical test of competing hypotheses. *American Journal of Political Science*, 34: 1–30.

ROKEACH, M. 1968. *Beliefs, Attitudes and Values*. San Francisco: Jossey-Bass.

—— 1973. *The Nature of Human Values*. New York: Free Press.

SCARBROUGH, E. 1995. Materialist and postmaterialist value orientations. Ch. 5 in Van Deth and Scarbrough 1995.

VAN DETH, J., and SCARBROUGH, E. eds. 1995. *The Impact of Values*. Oxford: Oxford University Press.

CHAPTER 13

CLASH OF VALUES ACROSS CIVILIZATIONS

TAKASHI INOGUCHI

SHORTLY after the end of the Cold War, Francis Fukuyama (1997) published his influential book, *The End of History and the Last Man*. He argued that the competition between capitalist democracy and socialist dictatorship ended with the victory of the former. Thus, history has ended in a single capitalist, democratic model. Supporting this point, the number of democracies has steadily increased since the 1970s. In December 2005, Freedom House (2005) reported that the number of democracies had grown to 122 with three new entrants, Burundi, Liberia, and Central Africa added to the list.

Similarly, economic development has continued. In 1992, O'Brien (1992) argued that financial services have been globally integrated due to the dramatic progress in computer technology that enables instantaneous financial transactions wherever one is located. Indeed, the amount of trade has been steadily rising for years. Especially noteworthy is the astronomical increase in currency trading since 1985 when the G5 countries (France, West Germany, Japan, the United States, and the United Kingdom) concluded the Plaza Accord. Prior to 1985, the amount of trade in goods and services surpassed the amount of trade in currency. Since 1986, currency trading has become 50 to 100 times as large as the trade in goods and services.

* For the very helpful comments on an earlier draft of this chapter, I thank Matthew Carlson, Russell Dalton, Hans-Dieter Klingemann, and Doh Chull Shin. I am grateful for the support from the Ministry of Education, Culture, Sports, Science, and Technology for the three grants I received, project numbers 11102001 (1999–2003), 15203005 (2002–2004), and 17002002 (2005–2009).

Worldwide democratization and financial integration illustrate the gigantic trans-formations of the past several decades (Held et al. 2003). Citizen values also reflect these societal changes. By values, I mean a set of preferred beliefs and norms, principles and practices deemed important by individual citizens. It is normal that the values held by citizens differ from one person to another. One thesis holds that these trends in democratization and economic development converge in a single model of the development of human values (see the chapters by Inglehart and Welzel, for example).

The counter position to the convergence argument is Samuel Huntington's (1996) provocative *Clash of Civilizations* thesis. When such factors as history, religion, language, and other cultural differences play a prominent role in value formation, they produce what Huntington calls the clash of civilizations. Huntington argues that some distinctive civilizations have developed sufficiently tightly knit and tenaciously held beliefs and norms that some of these sets are inherently incompatible with each other. Assuming the decomposability of those civilizational entities, he further argues that the Islamic and Chinese civilizations are more likely to pose difficult moments when the Atlantic civilization of the West finds it difficult to tolerate and accommodate.

Needless to say, I am not presupposing that there is a clash of civilizations as Huntington (1996) has argued. Instead, I present some illustrative examples of how key value dimensions compare across global regions, which seem to have civiliza-tional colorings in appearance and by implications. By civilization, I mean a subset of the humankind that forms a long endurable set of similarly waving and synergistic-ally vibrating brains and hearts. For the sake of simplicity, I do not use the term subcivilization to refer to entities, such as Islamic nations or Christian nations, but I use the term civilizations to refer to such subgroupings as well.

The substantive topics used in this chapter follow what Jean Blondel and Takashi Inoguchi (2006) state are the key dimensions of citizens' political culture: *identity, trust, and satisfaction.* "Political culture" refers to a set of beliefs and norms, prin-ciples, and practices that are political, that is, those pertaining to authority and coercion, and freedom. By identity, I mean something that one voluntarily uses to represent oneself symbolically. Trust involves the degree of confidence placed in and comfort attached to persons and institutions. By satisfaction, I mean the degree of gratification one gets from the state of affairs, be they income, life, health, marriage, the environment, politics, or neighborhood.

I conceptualize identity, trust, and satisfaction as integral to citizens' political culture. My point is perhaps understood more clearly once these three components are related to political regimes. Identity, trust, and satisfaction at the level of regimes are called identity, legitimacy, and efficacy, as exemplified in the democracy literature by authors such as Lipset (1981), Dahl (2000), and Pye (1988). Moreover, these dimensions overlap with many of the value factors that Huntington cited in his clash of civilizations hypothesis.

Because identity, trust, and satisfaction are integral parts of citizens' political culture and because political culture constitutes one of the core pillars of civilizations, I organize the substantive topics in this chapter accordingly. They are (*a*) the basic value configuration of the world, (*b*) religiosity, (*c*) regional identity, (*d*) social capital, (*e*) the role of government, (*f*) globalization and confidence in democratic institutions, and (*g*) happiness.

1 THE BASIC VALUE CONFIGURATION OF THE WORLD

Based on the World Value Surveys, Inglehart and Welzel (2005) have put forward one of the boldest representations of the macro-pattern of human values (also see Inglehart chapter and Welzel chapter in this Handbook). They use the World Values Survey, which spans the last three decades, to identify two key dimensions of values: (1) survival versus self-expression and (2) traditionalism versus secularism. Survival means the preoccupation about physical, sociological, and psychological security in its structural and acute forms. Survival values are preferred primarily in nations with low per capita income or where economic developmental momentum has not yet dissipated. This survival preoccupation is sometimes called materialism. Self-expression means the preference to not suppress the desires of heart and mind, body and brain. The emphasis on self-expression is sometimes called postmaterialism. Self-expressive values are preferred largely in those nations with high per capita income.

Traditionalism means the adherence to principles and practices that are taken for granted and routinized in society. Secularism means the separation of the sacred from the sphere of public domain. It means both religious freedom to individuals and the non-contagion of religion within the public space of society. These two key dimensions are derived from analyses of a large set of questions about values taken from approximately sixty societies around the world. These two dimensions tell us that the basic configuration of values is the competition between survival values and self-expressive values and the competition between traditionalism and secularism.[1]

In terms of crude geographical demarcation, Africa, the Middle East, South and Central Asia, the Caribbean and South America, and central and eastern Europe are trying to develop beyond survival values, whereas western Europe, the developed nations of East Asia, and North America are pulled toward self-expressive values. The first key dimension of values approximately divides between the South and the North, the developing versus the developed world. Along the second dimension lies one group that consists of Africa, the Americas, and most of the rest of the world with the exception of western Europe and East Asia that constitute the other

---

[1] Researchers have identified a few other such dimensions as the primordial ones: individualism versus collectivism (Hofstede 2000), nationalism versus cosmopolitanism, humanism versus materialism (Lane 2000), and left versus right (see Mair in this volume).

group in this dimension of values. In other words, west Europeans and maritime East Asians remain solidly secular and rational and increasingly self-expressive, whereas Americans remain more traditional in making religion more salient. Yet Americans are self-expressive. This does not vindicate the validity of the clash of civilizations thesis as Huntington (1996) claims. Rather west Europeans, maritime East Asians, and North Americans show a convergence of values on the first dimension.

Another striking feature in the Inglehart and Welzel world map is that the United States is a mild outlier among the other advanced industrial democracies. The United States has a large percentage of population who possess a high level of religiosity and those who are preoccupied with daily survival in comparison to the other G8 countries. Western Europeans and East Asians are far less religious and increasingly are more concerned with lifestyle, a pursuit that goes beyond daily survival. One illustration of the schism between Americans and west Europeans is their divergence on how to conceive international law in terms of the use of force and universal norms such as human rights (Isernia 2001) in the lead up to the Iraq War of 2003.

American fundamentalism and unilateralism are the two phrases applied to these visibly outlying features of Americans in the developed world. Thus, what Huntington (1996) calls the Atlantic civilization reveals an Atlantic schism a decade after the *Clash of Civilizations* was published. The Atlantic schism remains essentially unresolved even after the Iraq War of 2003, leaving the Atlantic relations like a frosty marriage.

2 MULTIDIMENSIONAL RELIGIOSITY

Since Karl Marx called religion the opium of the masses and Max Weber hailed the *Entzauberung* a step toward secularization and rationalization, two landmarks of modernity, most social scientists have played down the role of religion in discussions of the public space as distinguished from private space. Social scientists have long neglected the relationship of religion with politics, and this topic has been recently addressed by a number of important studies (Norris and Inglehart 2004; Jelen and Wilcox 2002; Varshney 2002; Lijphart 1979).

Steven Reed (2006) presented an iconoclastic study that tried to remedy what is called the western-centric and Christian-centric bias in this area of research. For instance, the World Values Survey asks: "How important is God in your life?" The survey also asks: "Apart from weddings, funerals, and christenings, how often do you attend religious services?" Reed (2006) instead uses the AsiaBarometer Survey that asks the following questions: "How often do you pray or mediate?" and "Which of the following activities do you think a religious person or group should be involved in?" Clearly, the latter questions attempt to be free from western and Christian biases often identified in many survey questions. Reed reaches two remarkable findings. First, traditions across religions are not so different from one another that they cannot be fruitfully compared. This makes these more neutral questions very attract-ive for cross-cultural comparisons. The AsiaBarometer Survey of 2005 studied fourteen countries in South and Central Asia, and many of these countries include a good number of Muslims, Hindus, Buddhists (Mahayana and Hinayana), Chris-tians (Catholic and other Christians), and a small number of believers from other religions. These religious groups are productively compared with remarkable eye-opening findings. Huber (2005) analyzed the link between beliefs and decisions to participate in religious services to see whether religious groups influence social policy in such areas as abortion.

Second, religiosity is not a unidimensional phenomenon; Reed (2006) examined two dimensions of private piety and community participation. As soon as we view religiosity as multidimensional, the time-honored distinction between secularization and sacralization must be questioned. The (clashing) values across multiple civiliza-tions appears precisely because Asia contains many major civilizations: Christian, Islamic, Hindu, Buddhist, and Confucian that have different expressions of their religious traditions.

This subject of multidimensional religiosity is a new subject. New angles have been raised and new survey data based on such new angles await more in-depth analysis. Only with such new data and new in-depth analysis can one discuss the implications of the clash of civilization thesis. Yet with even a meager amount of the current data, one can get the impression that the clash of civilization thesis is overexaggerated.

3 Forging Regional Identity

Another way in which civilization lines might be defined is by identification with a region or a civilization. By identity, I mean something that respondents use to represent themselves symbolically. National identity is an identity based on nationality. Regional identity is derived from attachments to a larger region beyond the nation-state that might reflect an attachment to a civilization as "Asian," "European," or "Islamic." Even without value differences, identities can differentiate regions and their publics.

For instance, European integrationists have made the inculcation of a European identity a priority since 1945 (Sinnott and Niedermayer 1995). Similarly, researchers examining East Asian integration often think about Asian identity. In other words, how much do citizens value national identity versus transnational identities? In building a sense of regional community, one needs to develop a sufficiently strong sense of identity to a regional community that includes shared interests, common institutions, and a joint shouldering of risks and burdens.[2] Huntington's clash of

---

[2] The identity question asked to respondents in some Asian countries is: "People often think about themselves in terms of nationality. If you are asked to think about yourself beyond such an identity,

civilization thesis makes conflicting statements about such geographic identities. At one point, the loss of national attachments is a cause of concern, at another point the development of cross-national regional identities is a source of concern.

Certainly, the clearest example of the development of regional identities has been Europe, and specifically the member states of the European Union. Eichenberg and Dalton (1993) examined public support for regional integration in Europe in terms of economic performance, political salience, and role in international relations. Noteworthy is their use of pooled cross-sectional and time-series analysis (also see Eichenberg in this volume; Gabel 1998). Sinnott and Niedermayer (1995) focused on policy, subsidiary, and legitimacy to measure regional identities that accommodate internationalized governance in Europe. Rosamond (1999) examined the impact of globalization on nurturing European identities. The consensus of this research is that new regional attachments are developing among west European publics because of the European integration process.

With an eye to wider European integration, east Europeans focus on democratic identity. Instead of focusing on ethnic, religious, or some other identities, empirical research also focuses on democratic identity, which is a prerequisite for accession to the European Union (Klingemann and Hofferbert 1999; Berglund 2003). Richard Rose and his associates (New Democracies Barometer and New Europe Barometer) have shown that the question "reject all the non-democratic alternatives" most clearly reveals the support for regime principles (Berglund 2003). Klingemann and Hofferbert (1999) have shown that, to reveal democratic satisfaction, the estimate of the conditions of individual human rights is the best indicator. In Central Asia, the issue of identities is unsettling. While ethnic and clan-based identities are clearly strong and distrust among different groups pose formidable barriers, state-building efforts have not been proceeding smoothly in a democratic fashion. Thus, calls for unitary state-building efforts and democratizing efforts do not seem to go together in the same direction (Collins 2006; Kasenova 2006).

Surprisingly, the AsiaBarometer Surveys indicate that some regional identities also exist in Asia (Inoguchi et al. 2005, 2006). In most of the ASEAN Plus Three countries, "Asian" identities are not weak. Cambodia and the Philippines are the most regionalist, judging from the large percentage of the respondents who choose the "Asian" option to the identity question (see note 2) in both countries. This regional identity is dismally weak in China (5%), India (15%), and Japan (26%). In between are those areas heavily inhabited by Muslim and ethnic Chinese populations: Indonesia, India, and Malaysia. Ethnic Chinese populations are also in China and Taiwan (of course) and Singapore and Malaysia. If one thinks about the sixteen countries that participated in the East Asian Summit Declaration in December 2005, this picture does not change because India's regional identity is the weakest of the three big countries. In general, pan-Asian regional identities are modest among Asian publics.

---

which would be your choice? (*a*) Asian, (*b*) Don't identify with any transnational group, (*c*) Other transnational identity (if yes, please state it), or (*d*) Don't know."

The three major countries in the region—India, China, and Japan—differ in their reasons for a weak regional identity. India tends to think that regional governance is India's task along with some regional organizations such as the South Asian Regional Cooperation forum. It is a bit like the United States thinking that global governance is the task of the United States and that the United States is the world's government (Mandelbaum 2006). China tends to think that the ASEAN Plus Three, with the exception of Japan, are more or less "respectful" to China and its rise. Thus, China seems to envisage its traditional tributary system as restored.[3] In the case of Japan, it is ambivalent about Asia. It is a bit like Britain and its relationship to the European continent. Both view the continent as a source of troubles and headaches, and believe that some distance is the most healthy approach, although functional interactions and friendly relations are of the utmost importance. Thus, the Japanese tend to think first as an industrial democracy of the G8 and a good ally of the United States and only secondarily as a country of Asia in Asia. Reflective of the weak regional identity of the Japanese is their "don't know" response to the regional question that registers a high of 30 percent.

The other two Oceanic countries, Australia and New Zealand, do not place much emphasis on an Asian identity. Even though their populations of Asian origins are on the slow increase, these nations do not discuss their multicultural heritages. In the previous Keating-led Labour administration, Australia was viewed as part of Asia, but in the current Howard-led Conservative administration, the dominant view is that Australia is not part of Asia in terms of civilization, although functionally it is in terms of mining, services, and other Australian niches. New Zealand more or less concurs with Australia, although its niches in Asia are different.

Regional identities in other parts of the world have not been examined as closely as they have in Europe. However, the Latinobarometer found that, shortly after their launching in 1995, all the regional groups for economic integration—the NAFTA, the Andean Pact, and Mercosur—had a good degree of awareness among the population of Latin America (Latinobarometer 1997). The presupposition underlying the survey on regional economic integration does not have much to do with identity. Yet a decade-long deepening of globalization has ironically prompted many Latin American countries to the identity issue through populist agitations and protectionist temptations like Venezuela, Bolivia, Brazil, and Chile.

In summary, Huntington was worried about the development of strong regional/civilizational blocs that would structure world politics in this century. He was especially concerned about the emergence of such regional blocs in the developing world. Ironically, the strongest evidence of such regional identities occurs within the European Union. The existence of such regional identities outside of the European

---

[3] As early as 1818, Emperor Jiaqing of the Qing dynasty registered that China is associated with two types of countries. The first type called tributary countries included Vietnam, Korea, and England. The second type called mutually trading countries included the Netherlands, France, and Japan (Inoguchi 2005b). King George III of England sent emissaries laden with gifts to China's Emperor Qianlong in 1793, requesting him to open the ports and the country. As understood by the Chinese Emperor, England acknowledged its tributary status to China.

Union is still limited, and the long and extensive process that was required to develop such transnational identities in Europe suggests that such regional identities will be slow to develop in other global regions.

4 CIVILIZATIONAL DIVIDES IN SOCIAL CAPITAL

Another possible civilization variable is the concept of social capital. Dietlind Stolle (in this volume) examines three major definitions of social capital: Coleman's (1990) "structure of relations between persons and among persons," Nan Lin's (2001) definition as "an investment in social relations with an expected return in the marketplace," and Robert Putnam's (1993, 2000a) "norms of generalized reciprocity, trust and networks of civic engagement" horizontally organized. Central to all three definitions is the concept of trust in others as a key element of social relations.

Francis Fukuyama (1997) foresaw that the primary divide in the contemporary world would be between high-trust and low-trust societies. Because capitalist democracy has become the increasingly universal and global way to organize human activities, attention would focus on how to conduct global economic and political management in a capitalist democratic fashion. In capitalist business transactions as well as democratic political games, high trust makes an enormous difference. If trust is high, business transactions are more certain, faster, and less costly. If trust is low, business transactions are more uncertain, slower, and more costly. Similarly, if trust is high in democratic politics, the games of politics are more calmly deliberated, more pragmatically conducted, and more rationally managed. If trust is low in democratic politics, politics are less calmly deliberated, more confrontationally conducted, and less rationally managed. The divide grows as global capitalist integration deepens. Moreover, the divide expands as democratic diffusion prevails over the globe.

Fukuyama predicted that high-trust societies would produce more wealth and sustain deeper democracy over the longer term. In his scheme of things, the United States, Britain, and Japan belong to the former type, whereas China, France, and Russia belong to the latter type. The former produces capitalism of a higher order, whereas the latter produces capitalism of a lower order. To illustrate why Japan is of high trust and China is of low trust, Fukuyama looked at the way that sons are adopted in Japanese and Chinese families. What would people do if their children were all female and they owned a business? The Japanese are more inclined to choose an adopted son from those they employ in their business, whereas Chinese business families are more inclined to stick to the bloodline. Fukuyama's reasoning is that the Japanese are of less narrow trust, whereas Chinese companies are of more narrow trust. Japanese families are less tightly organized but more pragmatically extendable by placing confidence in those chosen employees from one's own business company.

Global data from the World Values Survey paints a different picture of social trust. Newton (in this volume) shows that a simple East/West or North/South divide does not fully describe cross-national patterns of social trust. For instance, in contrast to Fukuyama's claim, social trust is high in China and Vietnam, and lower in some west European nations. Social trust is also noticeably lower in most east European nations or less developed African nations. In global terms, however, a clear positive relationship exists between levels of social trust and political or economic development.

Yamagishi (1998) put forward another divide in terms of bonding and bridging social capital. His cross-cultural experimental scheme contrasted how Americans and Japanese interact in the context of the prisoner's dilemma in order to see how players trust or distrust their respective adversary. By bonding social capital, he meant that social capital cements trust already there in terms of sociological and other attributes such as a common school tie or a shared lineage link. By bridging social capital, he meant that social capital forges trust and builds confidence among those who encounter each other for the first time. Yamagishi found that Americans tend to be social capital bridgers, whereas the Japanese tend to be social capital bonders. In other words, Americans use initial encounters with strangers to bring them into their expanding networks, whereas Japanese use initial encounters with strangers to determine whether they belong to a similar social circle and to consolidate the bond. Putnam (1997) also contrasted Americans and Japanese by characterizing the key features of their social capital. American social capital is generally non-discriminately friendly at the first stage with the potential for deeper ties developing after a face-to-face meeting. In a good contrast, Japanese social capital tends to be generally discriminately friendly at the first stage, followed by attempts to cement deeper trust if social attributes converge. Putnam describes American social capital as general and broad, whereas Japanese social capital is particularistic and narrow.

In an Asian context, Inoguchi (2005a) used the AsiaBarometer Survey to demonstrate that social capital is conceptualized along the three dimensions of interpersonal relationship, merit-based utility, and system-linked harmony (cf. Pye 1988). It is interesting that Asia has generated and accommodated five of the eight civilizations that Huntington identified, that is, Islamic, Hindu, Chinese, Japanese, and Christian. By focusing on Asia alone, it is possible to fruitfully discuss the potential clash of values within and across civilizations. No less importantly, when social capital is linked with different sets of values, this can create instances of incongruence and disharmony when these societies have transactions and interactions. First, being sociable and trustful is an indispensable component of social capital. It concerns whether people are good-natured or bad-natured. Second, social capital is closely tied to how much benefit is expected when you trust someone with whom you share a certain amount of risk. It is based on merit. It is utilitarian. Third, social capital is broadly embedded with the social system. It needs to have a similar wavelength with the ideological, institutional, and cultural framework of the social system. Along these three dimensions, Asian civic cultures are clustered in terms of quasi-civilizational landmarks, namely, (*a*) Japan and Korea; (*b*) Sri Lanka, India, Uzbekistan, and Myanmar; (*c*) Malaysia and Singapore; (*d*) China and Vietnam; and (*e*) the

Philippines and Thailand. The first cluster is Confucian developmental capitalist. The second cluster is former British colonialist-cum-Hinayana Buddhist-Hindu-Islamic. The third cluster is former British colonialist-cum-developmental author-itarianist. The fourth cluster is Confucian communist-cum-capitalist. The fifth is Third-Wave democracy capitalist. The three dimensions are derived from a set of questions on social capital incorporated in the 2003 AsiaBarometer Survey (Inoguchi et al. 2005).

In summary, there is a remarkable clustering of civic cultures based on social-capital-related questions in the AsiaBarometer Survey. On this level, at least, it appears that civilization patterns may be evident.

5 THE ATLANTIC SCHISM IN THE ROLE OF GOVERNMENT

Gosta Esping-Anderson (1990) has paradigmatically identified different worlds among advanced capitalist democracies in terms of the different values attached to the role of government. He identified three ideological camps: social democratic (Nordic), conservative (continental Europe and Japan), and liberal (Great Britain and the United States). Borre and Scarborough (1995) found similar patterns across west European democracies. Although these differences are not quite across civiliza-tions, they have civilizational colorings. After all, capitalism has many civilizational origins even among what Huntington terms the Atlantic civilization.

The role citizens assign to the government in the three public policy areas—old age pensions, health benefits, and unemployment insurance—roughly parallels the Atlantic schism as revealed by more recent opinions toward America's war against Iraq. Using three survey sources—the World Values Survey, the Eurobarometer Survey, and the International Social Survey Program—Mehrtens (2005) confirmed the value foundations of the three capitalisms of Esping-Anderson. He concluded that the public opinion bases of the three capitalisms are mildly strong, particularly between the first two ideological camps of the social democrats and the conservatives (including Japan) and the third camp, the liberals (Australia, Canada, Ireland, New Zealand, Great Britain, and the United States).

Broadening the scope of examination of welfare state attitudes, Staffan Kumlin (in this volume) identifies three areas that promise deeper analysis of welfare state attitudes, that is, general political values, specific policy preferences, and perform-ance evaluations. An impressive list of findings about them has been presented with such factors as social class, self-interest, social justice, and policy feedback causally linked to welfare state attitudes as found mostly in western industrial democracies.

There is less evidence on public opinion toward the role of government outside the western democracies. In comparing nine countries in western Europe and nine countries in East and Southeast Asia, Inoguchi and Wilson (forthcoming) find that Asians expect the government to play strong roles in the provision of welfare and employment just like Europeans and that Asians are no less inclined to give priority to economic growth at the expense of the environment.

In sum, the question of whether there are clear regional/civilizational differences in these orientations toward government must be answered with the combination of strong empirical evidence and mild skepticism of some of the clichés such as Asian values.

6 Globalization and Confidence in Democracy

Democracy, in general, and confidence in democracy, in particular, have been discussed and examined primarily in the context of nation-states at the domestic level (Klingemann and Fuchs 1997; Klingemann 1999; Norris 1999, 2002; and Dalton 2004; see Shin in this volume). However, the momentous tide of globalization (Held et al. 2003) has introduced a new dimension to democracy research, and support for democracy represents a basic cultural divide in Huntington's model.

The deepening of globalization seems to affect how researchers conceptualize democracy. Globalization fragments the national economy throughout the world. Those units with competitive niches rise whereas those units without such niches decline. All the former unite. Globalization reintegrates those units with competitive niches (Rosenau 2003). The fragmenting effects on democratic governance have led some, such as Guehennot (1999), to argue that globalization undermines the foundation of democracy by fragmenting the national electorates and bringing external global market forces to bear on how territorially bounded democracy functions. Guehennot has gone so far as to declare that democracy will end, hence his title, *La Fin de la democratie*. Comparing the democratic choice leaders made out of authoritarianism in Latin America in earlier times and more recently, O'Donnell and Schmitter (1986) argued that the sound assessment and judgment of leaders of democratization make a difference.

This mode of explanation sounds very much like that of rational choice theory. Its key words are uncertainty, choice, and key individual actors. O'Donnell and Schmitter claimed that instead of focusing on plantation landlords, the military, foreign capital, and the working class, the focus should be on the calculus of leaders placed under extraordinary uncertainty in judging the prospects for democracy. Their mode of explanation has been altered dramatically. In the past, they argued that certain socioeconomically distinguished classes represented themselves in choosing the course of the nation whether they were the military, the working class, the fledgling national middle class, foreign capital, or the plantation owners. In trying to explain the transition to democracy and the subsequent return to authoritarianism and dictatorship, O'Donnell and Schmitter had adopted the sociological class explanation. Now, their explanation is the individualistic rational choice explanation.

In contrast, my suspicion focuses on the deepening of globalization, which has made it more difficult for authors such as O'Donnell and Schmitter to adhere to Moore's (1966) model that sees socioeconomic development leading to democratization. This new scholarly approach is more at ease with the individualistic explanations of Acemoglu and Robinson (2005) presumably because the electorates are more atomized into less cohesive groups, which weakens and sometimes eliminates traditional class distinctions. In other words, one attaches increasingly less value to sociologically defined classes like industrial capitalists, plantation owners, workers, or rentiers.

As long as globalization undermines or sustains democracy and those values democracy embodies and enriches, it matters greatly. An empirical question arises: Does globalization promote democratic consolidation? Alternatively, does globalization reduce the effectiveness of democracy? The former argues that with globalization, especially with its increased capital mobility, democracy will be consolidated because it reduces the threat of the elites. The latter argues, as Guehennot does, that the greater capital mobility reduces the scope of collective choice in a democracy.

I formulate (2004) the relationship between globalization and confidence in democratic institutions as follows: the primary independent variables affecting the confidence in domestic institutions are (1) satisfaction with life and politics; (2) beliefs in civic duties, political apathy, antipathy toward politics and beliefs in free competition, government intervention, and government inefficiency; and (3) globalization as experienced in daily life in the contexts of the workplace, family and friends, TV news and entertainment, and other life experiences. The analyses demonstrated that satisfaction with life and with politics and beliefs in politics and the market both affect popular confidence in institutions. Globalization as experienced in daily life situations also exerts a significant negative influence on popular confidence in institutions. Especially noteworthy is the result that globalization tends to undermine the popular confidence in the civil service and the military, the two institutions that serve the state. Those who experience the impact of globalization through the workplace and the internet have greater confidence in domestic institutions such as parliament, law enforcement and the court, and big business. That is, those who experience globalization through their workplace and the internet are adapters to globalization, and are comfortable doing business and appreciate the order and stability maintained by law enforcement and the courts. In contrast, those who experience globalization through family and friends, through TV news and entertainment, and through employment tend to look down on the values of domestic institutions.

In general these findings imply that globalization has diverse effects on nations and individuals, depending on how they are linked to the international system. Sometimes globalization may reinforce trust in national institutions, and, at other times, it will have a negative effect.

7 IN PURSUIT OF HAPPINESS

John Stuart Mill wrote, "Those only are happy, who have their minds fixed on some object other than their own happiness; on the happiness of others, on the improvement of mankind, even on some art or pursuit, followed not as a means, but as itself an ideal end. Aiming thus at something else, they find happiness by the way" (Mill 1989, 117–18). This was a traditional way of looking at happiness before the Enlightenment according to McMahon (2006). The important thing was "being good" rather than "feeling good," but this changed with the Enlightenment. Influenced by the Enlightenment, the American Founding Fathers made the pursuit of happiness man's "unalienable right." Perhaps partially because of this legacy, Americans are compelled to think in terms of happiness. Hirschmann (1970) wrote about two Jewish friends who met each other in New York after a long period of not meeting: The one from Germany asked the other living in New York, "How are you?" The New Yorker responded, "I am happy; aber bin ich nicht so gluecklich." Needless to say, not only the Enlightenment, but also the American exceptionalism factor has crept in here (Lipset 1997).

Researchers often raise the question on happiness and its "causes:" Why do some rich people tend to be unhappy despite their high income level, whereas some poor people are happy in spite of their low income level? Does not a high income make one happy? In examining various surveys on happiness and sometimes a little less elusively satisfaction, one often encounters this puzzling question.

In examining the satisfaction level of some Asian countries, Inoguchi and Hotta (2006) discovered that the higher the level of religiosity the higher satisfaction, *ceteris paribus*. Those countries with high percentages of religious Muslim, Hindu, or Hinayana Buddhist populations tend to select the "happy" response, such as India, Uzbekistan, and Myanmar, somewhat irrespective of other seemingly important factors such as income level. Similarly, Inoguchi and Hotta (2006) showed that the higher the per capita income level, the lower the level of satisfaction. High-income countries in Asia—like Japan, South Korea, Taiwan, Hong Kong, and Singapore—tend to select the "not very happy" response for whatever reasons.

This pattern is broadly congruent with the global relationship between GNP per capita and survival and well-being (Inglehart and Welzel 2005 468–9; Veenhoven 2006). It appears that the impact of income on happiness declines as gross national product per capita goes up. Beyond a certain threshold of economic development, lifestyle seems to determine the degree of happiness. In learning from the history of happiness as recounted by McMahon (2006), one can only speculate whether religion might not be an opium for the masses, as Karl Marx argued some 150 years ago and as Max Weber argued about the *Entzauberung* a century ago. How much this-worldly value one accords to religion has changed the popular conception of happiness dramatically. In tandem with the diminishing space of other-worldly happiness, the popular conception of happiness has become more vulnerable to the turbulence of this-worldly life (cf. Lane 2000).

One must hasten to note, however, that asking about happiness or satisfaction in an authoritarian regime is slightly tricky. When internal security is strict and effective, then respondents tend to answer with their personal safety in mind. If the question about happiness or satisfaction is taken as an indicator of respondents' satisfaction with the regime, then they must play safe. In other words, they tend to express more happiness or satisfaction than they truly feel.[4] Although this scenario is obvious, it is very important to be reminded that the response of happiness and satisfaction has a lot to do with the degree of freedom the regime accords to a society. The AsiaBarometer Survey serves as an ample reminder of the need to be alert to this methodological and interpretive pitfall of survey data in societies that are not quite liberal nor democratic.[5]

8 CONCLUSION

Values held by citizens are inherently diverse. The clash of values is ubiquitous and observed across civilizations. The clash of values also results in adaptation through times. This chapter has surveyed such a clash of values across civilizations highlighting topics such as the cultural map of the world, religiosity, regional identity, social capital, conceptions on the role of government, globalization and confidence in democratic institutions, and happiness, as revealed mostly in survey data.

The above discussion seems to give empirical and conceptual credence to the title of this chapter (and its key argument), the clash of values across civilizations—not the clash of civilizations. What we have is the human civilization, under which there are subcivilizations such as those identified by Huntington (1996). Furthermore, such subcivilizations do not necessarily clash with each other. The clash takes place at the individual level. When not properly combined nor serendipitously contextualized, some values give rise to the enormous degree of incongruence and disharmony. They give the semblance of civilizational clashes. However, certain structural conditions

---

[4] The AsiaBarometer Surveys have not had problems conducting surveys in non-democratic regimes in Asia. Our strategy is simple: If national teams find an unaccomodatable question, they delete them but retain the rest. This principle does work. If you ask about confidence in institutions in some countries, you might be able to ask the question only when you delete a certain number of institutions. For example, in Myanmar the military regime is not interested in respondents being asked about their confidence in the military. Similarly, in Brunei the constitution stipulates that the King is the sole political actor, therefore, asking about respondents' confidence in institutions other than the monarch would be very awkward. What emerges from the AsiaBarometer Surveys is a clear picture of the relationship between freedom and confidence in government. In simple terms, the less freedom, the higher the confidence in government, *ceteris paribus*.

[5] Gallup international's Ijaz Gilani (2006) seems to be liable to this pitfall in measuring democracy score by taking an avarage of percentages of respondents who were positive about the following two questions: (1) elections in my country are held freely and fairly and (2) the rule in my country is by the will of the people.

and contingencies need to be identified and examined before we can rush to conclusions about the clash of civilizations.

Nevertheless, a clash of values is empirically identified through survey data. The mildly outlying position of the United States among the G8 countries in the Inglehart and Welzel cultural map of the world seems to give some credence to the Russian argument that the United States is the Neo-Bolsheviks of the twenty-first century, exporting democracy and free market ideologies to the rest of the world. The links between global forces and westernization is a complex topic.

Although the clash-of-civilizations literature has focused on religiosity, we have questioned even the existence of these differences. The AsiaBarometer Survey reveals that different religions can be effectively compared when questions are correctly formulated, and that more comparable patterns across regions appear. Differences exist, but perhaps not as dramatic as prior research has suggested.

The evidence on regional identities also tends to weaken the evidence of broad civilization differences. Regional identities have developed within the European Union. However, the potential drivers of community formation in Asia—China, India, and Japan—have citizens who tend to be the least regionally oriented in terms of their identities. Regional identities are also weak in other parts of the developing world.

A set of social capital questions as asked in the AsiaBarometer Survey has revealed the striking divergence of religious, cultural, and different colonial-historically inculcated conceptions of social capital in ten Asian societies. How people accord similar and dissimilar roles to the government, especially on social welfare, has some ideological and cultural origin among advanced individual democracies, that is, social democratic, conservative, and liberal. How the tide of globalization may alter the map of ideology and policy remains to be empirically and vigorously explored. Of all the subjects examined here, research has devoted the least attention to how globalization affects citizens' confidence in institutions. Asia-Europe Survey data suggest that globalization slightly decreases the confidence in domestic democratic institutions.

Happiness is elusive in the post-Enlightenment society in which the pursuit of happiness in this world is "legitimized" and exposed to the turbulence of this-worldly life. Those who focus on the pursuit of other-worldly happiness seem to respond to the happiness questions most affirmatively.

In conclusion, it may be appropriate to speculate here about the prospects for a culture clash in the future. The culture clash in regional identity may be rising. In tandem with the tide of globalization, the drive to regionalize economies has been on the steady rise in many parts of the world (Katzenstein 2005). Regional identities have been hampered by "big power chauvinism" in regions as well as by both narrower and broader identities. In addition, the culture clash in religiosity may be on the rise. As the physical movement of people has become more frequent and ubiquitous, the culture clash is increasing because people are intermixing more than in the past. At the same time, it seems people, more often than not, discover some modus operandi about religion and an ensuing clash. The culture clash in social capital may be increasing also. Business transactions have increased dramatically, which brings more people into contact. Accordingly, culture clashes arise in terms of how business partners and adversaries conceptualize risks. The government's role in social policy is increasingly affected by the tide of globalization despite the tenacity of historically, culturally, and ideologically held beliefs on the role of government. Globalization accelerates the need to make a decision on whether to enhance social safety nets or not, which is bound to initiate culture clashes as well. The culture clash in confidence in democracy is also on the rise. After all, globalization fragments the electorates, organizations, and neighborhoods. Globalization seems to dilute the cohesion and efficacy of democracy as organized in the nation-states. It seems, therefore, at least in the shorter term to be on the rise. The culture clash in happiness is also growing in relation to how one conceptualizes this world and the one after death. As long as other-worldly happiness is retained in one's religious belief, which is often manifested in lower-income societies, one does not bother too much with the turbulence of this-worldly life. Hence the often seen paradox of finding that some low-income societies are full of happy people.

After all, public values are like the DNA of world citizens. Even when the clash of values is empirically observed, one cannot rush to the conclusion about the clash of civilizations. The diversity of values within civilizations is immense. Furthermore, the malleability of values cannot be underestimated as scientific research on the long-term malleability of the DNA has shown. In addition, perhaps most importantly, the clash of values across civilizations takes place only on the given structure and framework that citizens are placed at a certain point in history. Hence, the need is great to be empirically solid and culturally and contextually sensitive in carrying out research in the areas I have addressed in this chapter.

REFERENCES

ACEMOGLU, D., and ROBINSON, J. 2005. *Economic Origins of Dictatorship and Democracy.* Cambridge: Cambridge University Press.

ALMOND, G., and VERBA, S. 1963. *The Civic Culture.* Princeton: Princeton University Press.

BERGLUND, S. 2003. Prospects for the consolidation of democracy in east central Europe. *Japanese Journal of Political Science,* 4(2): 191–213.

BLONDEL, J., and INOGUCHI, T. 2006. *Political Cultures in Asia and Europe,* London: Routledge.

BORRE, O. and SCARBOROUGH, E. eds. 1995. *The Scope of Government.* Oxford: Oxford University Press.

BRATTON, M., MATTES, R., and GYIMAH-BOACH, E. 2006. *Public Opinion, Democracy, and Market Return in Africa.* Cambridge: Cambridge University Press.

COLEMAN, J. 1990. *Foundations of Social Theory,* Cambridge, Mass.: Belknap Press.

COLLINS, K. 2006. *Clan Politics and Regime Transition in Central Asia.* New York: Cambridge University Press.

DAHL, R. 2000. *On Democracy.* New Haven: Yale University Press.

DALTON, R. 2004. *Democratic Challenges, Democratic Choices.* Cambridge: Cambridge University Press.

DALTON, R., and ONG, N. 2005. Authority orientations and democratic attitudes: a test of the "Asian values" hypothesis. *Japanese Journal of Political Science*, 6 (2): 211–31.

The Economist. 2006. Books and arts. January 12: 82–3.

EICHENBERG, R., and DALTON, R. 1993. Europeans and the European Community: the dynamics of public support for European integration. *International Organization*, 47 (4): 507–34.

ESPING-ANDERSON, G. 1990. *The Three Worlds of Welfare Capitalism*. Princeton: Princeton University Press.

FREEDOM HOUSE. 2005. *Freedom in the World 2005*. New York: Freedom House.

FUKUYAMA, F. 1997. *The End of History and the Last Man*. New York: Free Press.

—— 1995. *Trust: Social Virtues and the Creation of Prosperity*. New York: Free Press.

GABEL, M. 1998. *Interests and Integration*. Ann Arbor: University of Michigan Press.

GILANI, I. S. 2006. The global verdict on democracy: admiration for the norm, disillusionment with the practice. Pp. 37–60 in *Voice of the People, 2006*, ed. Gallup International. London: Gallup International.

GUEHENNOT, J. M. 1999. *La Fin de la democratie*. Paris: Flammarion.

HELD, DAVID et al. 2003. *Global Transformations*. London: Polity.

HIRSCHMANN, A. 1970. *Exit, Voice, and Loyalty*. Cambridge, Mass.: Harvard University Press.

HOFSTEDE, G. 2003. *Culture's Consequence: Comparing Values, Behaviors, Institutions and Organizations across Nations*. Beverly Hills, Calif.: Sage publications.

HUBER, J. D. 2005. Religious belief, religious participation, social policy attitudes across countries. Department of Political Science, Columbia University.

HUNTINGTON, S. 1991. *The Third Wave*. Norman: University of Oklahoma Press.

—— 1996. *The Clash of Civilizations and the Remaking of World Order*. New York: Simon & Schuster.

INGLEHART, R. 1977. *The Silent Revolution*. Princeton: Princeton University Press.

—— 1990. *Culture Shift in Advanced Industrial Society*. Princeton: Princeton University Press.

—— 1997. *Modernization and Postmodernization*. Princeton: Princeton University Press.

—— and WELZEL, C. 2005. *Modernization, Cultural Change and Democracy*. Cambridge: Cambridge University Press.

INOGUCHI, T. 2000. Broadening the basis of social capital in Japan. Pp. 358–92, 481–9 in *Democracies in Flux*, ed. R. Putnam. New York: Oxford University Press.

—— 2004 Globalization wa yoi governance o motarashite iruka (Does globalization bring about good governance?). *Nempo seijigaku* (Annals of Political Science), 199–227.

—— 2005a. Social capital in ten Asian societies. *Japanese Journal of Political Science*, 5(1): 197–211.

—— 2005b. Cong Riben de jiaodu toushi zhongguode minzuzhuyi (Penetrating into Chinese nationalism from a Japanese perspective). *Shijie jingji yu zhengzhi* (World Economics and Politics), 11: 49–50.

—— and HOTTA, Z. 2006. Quantifying satisfaction. Ch. 14 in *Human Beliefs and Values in Striding Asia*, ed. T. Inoguchi. Tokyo: Akashi shoten.

INOGUCHI, T., and WILSON, S. forthcoming. Globalization and policy evaluation in Europe and Asia. Book manuscript chapter.

—— et al. eds. 2005. *Values and Life Styles in Urban Asia: A Cross-Cultural Analysis and Sourcebook Based on the AsiaBarometer Survey of 2003*. Mexico City: Siglo Editores XXI.

—— et al. eds. 2006. *Human Beliefs and Values in Striding Asia: East Asia in Focus: Country Profiles, Thematic Analyses and Sourcebook Based on the AsiaBarometer Survey of 2004*. Tokyo: Akashi shoten.

ISERNIA, P. 2001. *Public Opinion and the International Use of Force*. London: Taylor & Francis.

JELEN, T., and WILCOX, C. eds. 2002. *Religion and Politics in Comparative Perspective.* Cambridge: Cambridge University Press.

KAGAN, R. 2003. *Of Paradise and Power: America and Europe in the New World Order,* New York: Alfred A. Knopf.

KASENOVA, N. 2006. Book review of Kathleen Collins, "Clan Politics and Regime Transition in Central Asia." *Japanese Journal of Political Science,* 7 (3): 311–13.

KATZENSTEIN, P. 2005. *A World of Regions: Asia and Europe in the American Imperium,* Ithaca, NY: Cornell University Press.

KLINGEMANN, H. 1999. Mapping political support in the 1990s. Ch. 2 in *Critical Citizens,* ed. P. Norris. Oxford: Oxford University Press.

—— and FUCHS, D. eds. 1997. *Citizens and the State.* Oxford: Oxford University Press.

—— and HOFFERBERT, R. 1999. Remembering the bad old days: human rights, economic conditions, and democratic performance in transitional regimes. *European Journal of Political Research.* 36: 155–74.

LANE, R. 2000. *The Loss of Happiness in Market Democracies.* New Haven: Yale University Press.

LATINOBAROMETRO (1997) Latinobarometro 1997–press release. Santiago, Chile: Latinobarometro.

LIJPHART, A. 1979. Religion vs. linguistic vs. class voting: the 'crucial experiment' comparing Belguim, Canada, South Africa and Switzerland. *American Political Science Review,* 73: 442–58.

LIN, N. 2001. *Social Capital: A Theory of Social Structure and Action.* Cambridge: Cambridge University Press.

LIPSET, S. 1981. *Political Man: The Social Basis of Politics.* Baltimore: Johns Hopkins University Press.

—— 1997. *American Exceptionalism: A Double-Edged Sword.* New York: Norton.

McMAHON, D. 2006. *Happiness: A History.* New York: Atlantic Monthly Press.

MANDELBAUM, M. 2006. *The Case for Goliath: How America Acts as the World's Government in the 21st Century.* New York: Public Affairs.

MEHRTENS, F. 2005. Three worlds of public opinion? Values, variation, and the effect on social policy. *International Journal of Public Opinion Research,* 16 (2): 115–43.

MILL, J. S. 1989. Autobiography, ed. J. M. Robson. London: Penguin.

MOORE, B. 1966. *The Social Origins of Democracy and Dictatorship.* Boston: Beacon Press.

NEWTON, K. 2001. Trust, social capital, civil society, and democracy. *International Political Science Review,* 22: 201–14.

NORRIS, P. ed. 1999. *Critical Citizens.* Oxford: Oxford University Press.

—— 2002. *Democratic Phoenix.* Cambridge: Cambridge University Press.

—— and INGLEHART, R. 2004. *Sacred and Secular.* Cambridge: Cambridge University Press.

O'BRIEN, R. 1992. *Global Financial Integration: The End of Geography.* New York: Council on Foreign Relations Press.

O'DONNELL, G., and SCHMITTER, P. 1986. Tentative conclusions about uncertain democracies. Pp. 1–78 in *Transitions from Authoritarian Rule,* ed. G. O'Donnell, P. Schmitter, and L. Whitehead. Baltimore: Johns Hopkins University Press.

PUTNAM, R. 1993. *Making Democracy Work.* Princeton: Princeton University Press.

—— 1997. Comments on the draft of the Inoguchi Chapter for *Democracies in Flux.* New York: Oxford University Press.

—— ed. 2000a. *Democracy in Flux.* New York: Oxford University Press.

—— 2000b. *Bowling Alone: The Collapse and Revival of American Community.* New York: Simon & Schuster.

PYE, L. 1979. *Communications and Political Development.* Princeton: Princeton University Press.

PYE, L. 1988. *Asian Power and Politics*. Cambridge, Mass.: Harvard University Press.

REED, S. 2006. Religiosity in Asia: a preliminary analysis of the 2005 AsiaBarometer, *The AsiaBarometer Project*. Tokyo: Chuo University.

ROSAMOND, B. 1999. Discourses of globalization and the social construction of European identities. *Journal of European Public Policy*, 6 (4): 652–68.

ROSE, R., MISHLER, W., and HAERPFER, C. 1998. *Democracy and Its Alternatives*. Oxford: Polity Press.

ROSENAU, J. 2003. *Distant Proximities: Dynamics beyond Globalization*. Cambridge: Cambridge University Press.

SINNOTT, R. 2006. Political culture and democratic consolidation in East and Southeast Asia. Ch. 1 in *Democratization, Governance and Regionalism in East and Southeast Asia*, ed. I. Marsh. London: Routledge.

—— and NIEDERMAYER, O. 1995. *Public Opinion and Internationalized Governance: Beliefs in Government*. New York: Oxford University Press.

TWIGG, J., and SCHECTER, K. ed. 2003. *Social Capital and Social Cohesion in Post-Guilt Russia*. New York: M. E. Sharpe.

VARSHNEY, A. 2002. *Ethnic Conflict and Civic Life: Hindus and Muslims in India*. New Haven: Yale University Press.

VEENHOVEN, R. 2006. *World Database of Happiness, Distributional Findings in Nations*. Rotterdam: Erasmus University. Available at: **www.worlddatabaseofhappiness.eur.nl**

YAMAGISHI, T. 1998. *Shinrai no kozo* (The Structure of Trust). Tokyo: University of Tokyo.

CHAPTER 14

....

DEMOCRATIZATION: PERSPECTIVES FROM GLOBAL CITIZENRIES

....

DOH CHULL SHIN

WE live in a monumental era for the advancement of democracy. Invented so long ago in ancient Greece, democracy has spread around the globe for the first time ever during the past three decades. In all regions of the globe, democracy has emerged as the political system most preferred by the mass citizenry (Gallup-International 2005). Even economically poor and culturally traditional societies, once viewed as inhospitable to democratic development now demand that free elections and other democratic institutions supplant undemocratic or personal forms of rule (Karatnycky and Ackerman 2005). Growing demands from ordinary citizens along with increased pressures and inducements from international communities have made democratization a global phenomenon (Carothers 1999).

This phenomenon has given scholars and policy makers new insights into what constitutes a functional democracy. A political system can become institutionally democratic with the installation of competitive elections and multiple political

* The author wishes to thank Michael Bratton of the Afrobarometer, Yun-han Chu of the East Asia Barometer, Marta Lagos of the Latinobarometer, and Richard Rose of the New Europe Barometer for collecting and sharing the public opinion data reported in this chapter. He also wishes to thank Wonbin Cho and Neil Munro for analyzing the data, and Byong-Kuen Jhee, Ibrahim Ozdamar, Rollin Tusalem, and Jason Wells for research assistance. He gratefully acknowledges thoughtful comments and suggestions from Michael Bratton, Russell Dalton, Hans-Dieter Klingemann, and Jack van der Slik.

parties. These institutions alone, however, do not make a fully functioning democratic political system. As Rose and his associates (1998, 8) aptly point out, these institutions constitute nothing more than "the hardware" of representative democracy. To operate the institutional hardware, a democratic political system requires the "software" that is congruent with the various hardware components (Almond and Verba 1963; Eckstein 1966). Both the scholarly community and policy circles widely recognize that what ordinary citizens think about democracy and its institutions is a key component of such software. Many experts, therefore, regard the mass citizenry's unconditional embrace of democracy as "the only game in town" as the hallmark of democratic consolidation (Bratton and Mattes 2001; Diamond 1999; Linz 1990; Rose 2001).

This chapter seeks to unravel the perspectives of ordinary citizens as they experience the introduction of democracy to their daily lives. How do these citizens take part in the process of transforming authoritarian rule into democracy? Does their active participation in this process contribute to the survival and growth of their new democratic regime? How broadly and deeply do they support democracy as both a political ideal and a reality? How does their level of support or demand for democracy compare with the level its institutions supply? Empirically, this chapter addresses these and related questions with accumulations of factual and public opinion data. Key sources are Freedom House and four regional barometer projects monitoring democratization in Africa, East Asia, Latin America, and New Europe. Our analysis highlights regional differences in institutional and cultural dynamics by comparing citizens' reactions to democratic change across these regions.

First this chapter explicates the notion of democratization and clarifies a number of key conceptual issues. Next it examines the evolution of the current wave of global democratization, which Huntington (1991) popularized as the third wave. Thirdly, it examines how citizen involvement in democratic regime change has affected the survival and growth of new democracies. Next comes the large part of the chapter, which compares, interregionally, the breadth, strength, depth of popular commitment to democracy by considering both pro-democratic and anti-authoritarian orientations among mass citizenries. Finally, the chapter compares the levels of popular demands for and institutional supplies of democracy, and explores the problems of and prospects for the democratic consolidation of countries currently in transition.

1 THE NOTION OF DEMOCRATIZATION

What constitutes democratization? In general, it refers to the movement to democracy. The existing literature on third-wave democracies generally agrees that democratization is a highly complex transformation involving a political system and its citizens. (Boix and Stokes 2003; Bunce 2000, 2003; Doorenspleet 2000; Geddes

1999; Karl 2005; McFaul 2002; Rose and Shin 2001; Shin 1994). Specifically, it refers to the process of transforming an authoritarian political system into a democratic system in which people influence government and government responds positively to their demands. The phenomenon, therefore, has multiple dimensions as democracy competes with its alternatives. The process of democratization has many stages with several analytically distinct steps that are empirically overlapping. The process also has multi-directions because one step of democratic development does not necessarily lead to a particular higher stage.

In the logic of causal sequence, the stages of democratization may run from the decay and disintegration of an old authoritarian regime and the emergence of a new democratic system, through the consolidation of that democratic regime, to its maturity (Dahl 1971; Shin 1994). In reality, however, the process of democratization has often failed to advance sequentially from the first to the last stage. As Puddington and Piano (2005) and Marshall and Gurr (2005) have documented, some new democracies disappear soon after they emerge, while others erode as much as they consolidate. As a result, many new democracies remain less than fully democratic even decades after the establishment of democratic institutions. For this reason, they are variously described as *electoral, incomplete, illiberal, broken-back,* or *delegative* democracies or the mixed or hybrid regimes of *competitive authoritarianism, fleckless pluralism,* or *dominant power politics* (Carothers 2002; Diamond 1999, 2002; Levitsky and Way 2002; O'Donnell 1994; Rose and Shin 2001; Zakaria 2003).

The same literature views democratization as a multifaceted phenomenon. Institutionally, it involves a transition from authoritarian rule to a political system that allows ordinary citizens to participate on a regular basis and compete in the election of political leaders. Substantively, it involves a process in which electoral and other institutions consolidate and become increasingly responsive to the preferences of the citizenry. Culturally, it is a process in which ordinary citizens dissociate themselves from the values and practices of authoritarian politics and embrace democracy as "the only game in town." As Dahl (2000), Karl (2000), and Linz and Stepan (1996) note, the process of democratizing a political system involves much more than the installation of representative institutions and promulgation of a democratic constitution.

Democratization is a multi-level phenomenon; on one level, the transformation must take place in individual citizens, and on another level, it must take place in the political regime that rules them. At the regime level, democratization refers to the extent to which authoritarian structures and procedures transform into democratic ones, and in the process, become responsive and accountable to the preferences of the mass citizenry (Dahl 1971; UNDP 2005). At the citizenry level, the extent to which average citizens detach themselves from the virtues of authoritarianism and become convinced of democracy's superiority constitutes democratic change.

Finally, we shall view democratization as a dynamic process of ongoing interactions between individual citizens and institutions of their democratic regime. Congruence theory suggests that the more the current institutional supply of democracy exceeds what citizens demand, the less likely democracy is to expand.

Conversely, the more cultural demand for democracy exceeds what institutions supply, the more likely is democracy to advance. When the institutional supply meets cultural demand, further democratization is unlikely (Inglehart and Welzel 2005; Mattes and Bratton 2003; Rose and Shin 2001).

2 INSTITUTIONAL DEMOCRATIZATION

Scholars dubbed the surge in democracy that occurred over the last three decades of the twentieth century the "third wave" of democratization (Huntington 1991; Diamond 2003). Powerful forces of the democracy movement spread from one region to another like a rushing wave. It emerged in southern Europe and has spread, in sequence, to other regions around the globe (O'Loughlin et al. 1998).

2.1 Diffusion

In the mid-1970s, the third wave of democratization first broke out in Portugal and Spain, where right-wing dictatorships had held power for decades; the democratic transition came to Greece in 1974.[1] From 1979 to 1985, Argentina, Bolivia, Brazil, Ecuador, Peru, and Uruguay successively underwent the democratic transition from military rule. In Chile, the democratic transition proceeded more slowly and emerged in 1989 after years of peaceful civic resistance movements against authoritarian rule. In June 2000, Vincente Fox's presidential victory in Mexico, the most populous Spanish speaking country in the world, marked the end of seven decades of single-party rule and a new era of democracy in the region (Hagopian and Mainwaring 2005).

In the mid-1980s when most military dictatorships in Latin America were overthrown, the third-wave of democratization reached the shores of East Asia (Croissant 2004). It first toppled the civilian dictatorship of Ferdinand Marcos in the Philippines in February 1986; massive "people's power" movements forced him to flee to Hawaii. Nearly three decades of military rule ended and in December 1987 the direct popular election of a president fully restored civilian rule in South Korea. In the same year, after nearly four decades of one-party dictatorship, Taiwan began to gradually democratize. It lifted martial law and established institutional democracy by holding its first direct presidential election in 1996. In 1990, Mongolia, one of the poorest and remotest countries in the world, abandoned its 60-year-old communist one-party system and held competitive multi-party elections to choose a president. And in 1992, Thailand re-emerged as a democracy when it rid itself of military rule. During this

---

[1] The existing literature is not in agreement over the inception of the third-wave democratization. According to Inglehart and Welzel (2005, 177) and Marshall and Gurr (2005, 16), a global shift from autocratic regimes to democracy began in the late 1980s, not in the mid-1970s.

time, three very poor countries in Asia—Bangladesh, Nepal, and Pakistan—became democracies.

By the end of the 1980s, the electoral and other democratic institutions were operative in all or much of three regions of the world—southern Europe, Latin America, and Asia. The other three regions of Eastern Europe, Africa, and the Middle East still remained resistant to the winds of democratization. In eastern Europe, the fall of the Berlin Wall in 1989 marked the end of one-party communist dictatorships and the rapid transitions to democratic rule based on competitive multi-party systems followed. In less than a year after the fall of the Berlin Wall, competitive and free elections took place to install democratic political systems in Bulgaria, the Czech Republic, Hungary, Poland, Romania, and Slovakia. The collapse of the Soviet Union in 1991 created fifteen states in the Baltic region and Central Asia. Seven of them emerged as democracies (Goehring and Schnetzer 2005; McFaul 2005; Rose, Mishler, and Haerpfer 1998).

In the early 1990s when the long history of communist dictatorships was ending in eastern Europe, the third wave of democratization began to roll in Africa, a vast region where only three countries were known as democratic states. In February 1990, the apartheid regime of South Africa released Nelson Mandela from prison and launched the slow process of ending racial oligarchy in response to years of economic sanctions from the democratic world. The March 1991 election in Benin marked the first example of peaceful transition of power in mainland Africa. In 1994, South Africa adopted one of the most democratic constitutions in the world and held competitive elections to create the most vigorous democracy in the region. In ensuing years, other countries allowed opposition forces to organize and compete in the electoral process under intense pressures from international aid agencies. By the standards of western democracies, electoral competitions in many countries were highly limited. Nonetheless, by 2001, fourteen countries had met the minimum conditions of democracy (Bratton, Mattes, and Gyimah-Boadi 2005, 17; Marshall and Gurr 2005, 42).

By the end of the last millennium, the Middle East was the only region hardly touched by the global wave of democratization. After the collapse of consociational democracy in Lebanon in 1975, Israel remained the sole democracy in the region. Although contested legislative elections were occasionally held in Algeria, Egypt, Jordan, Kuwait, Lebanon, and Morocco in the past decade, the head of the government in these and other Middle Eastern countries remained unelected until early this year. On January 9, 2005, Mahmoud Abbas was elected as the president of the Palestinian Authority, having defeated five other candidates. Two months later, millions of Lebanese people took to the streets to protest against Syria's military presence in their country in what became known as "the Cedar Revolution." Their protests drove the occupying Syrian troops out of Lebanon and disbanded the pro-Syrian government. In September 2005, a multi-candidate presidential election was held in Egypt for the first time in the country's history. These developments indicate that even the Middle East, the region known as the last bastion of autocratic rule, is not impervious to democracy's third wave (*Economist* 2005).

2.2 Breadth and Depth

In policy circles democracy is too often equated with the holding of free and competitive multi-party elections (Carothers 2002). The electoral conception of democracy, however, does not provide a full account of the process that transforms age-old authoritarian institutions into democratically functioning ones. This conception provides only a minimalist account because it deals merely with the process of elections and overlooks additional important institutions of democracy. It is formalistic or superficial because it fails to consider how democratically or undemocratically these institutions actually perform. It also provides a static account of institutional democratization because it ignores interactions between various democratic institutions between each round of elections.

To overcome these limitations of the formal and minimalist conceptions of electoral democracy, scholars have proposed a number of alternative conceptions, using terms such as *complete democracy, liberal democracy,* and *full democracy* (Collier and Levitsky 1997; Schedler and Sarsfield 2004). All such alternative notions extend beyond the elements of electoral democracy to matters of accountability, constitutionalism, pluralism, and the separation of powers. Electoral democracy advances to liberal democracy when the law constrains political authority while protecting individual citizens so that they can exercise political rights and civil liberties (Diamond 1999; O'Donnell 2004; Zakaria 2003). Incomplete democracy becomes complete when the institutions of elections, accountability, civil society, and the rule of law all have a firm hold (Linz and Stepan 1996; Rose and Shin 2001).

Freedom House annually monitors the electoral and liberal domains of institutional democratization. In 2004, Freedom House (2006) rated 122 of 192 independent countries (64%) as electoral democracies because their last major national elections met the international standard for being free, fair, competitive, regular, and open to all segments of the mass citizenry regardless of their cultural, ethnic, and socio-economic backgrounds. However, not all these electoral democracies are liberal countries (free countries) because some have elected leaders with serious problems regarding the rule of law, corruption, and human rights. Out of the 122 electoral democracies, 89 (73%) are rated as free, liberal democracies and 33 (27%) as partly free, illiberal democracies.[2] Note that liberal democracies outnumber illiberal democracies by nearly 3 to 1. Nonetheless, liberal democracies govern fewer than half (46%) the population of independent states in today's world after more than three decades of rapid democratization.

According to the data compiled by Freedom House in 2005, 23 of 48 countries in sub-Saharan Africa meet the minimum criteria of democracy and 11 of these 20 countries meet the definition of liberal democracy. Of 39 countries in East Asia and the Pacific, 7 are electoral democracies and 16 are liberal democracies. In eastern

---

[2] Freedom House annually rates every country on a seven-point scale that measures the extent to which the mass citizenry is guaranteed political rights and civil liberties. The mean score of 2.5 or lower on the seven-point scale is considered indicative of being advanced to liberal democracy.

Europe and central Asia, 4 of 27 countries are electoral democracies and 13 are liberal democracies. In western and central Europe, 24 of 25 countries are liberal democracies; the only country rated as an electoral democracy is Turkey. In America and the Caribbean, 9 of 35 countries are electoral democracies and 24 are liberal democracies. Of 18 countries in North Africa and the Middle East, only one country—Israel—is a liberal democracy.

To characterize democratization in regional terms, western and central Europe ranks first with 100 percent of countries earning a rating of at least an electoral democracy, followed by America and the Caribbean (94%), Eastern Europe and Central Asia (63%), East Asia and the Pacific (59%), sub-Saharan Africa (48%), and North Africa and the Middle East (6%). In achieving liberal democracies, western and central Europe ranks, once again, first with 96 percent and America and the Caribbean is a distant second with 69 percent. Eastern Europe and central Asia with 48 percent and East Asia with 41 percent rank, respectively, third and fourth, followed by sub-Saharan Africa (23%) and the Middle East and North Africa (6%).

2.3 Trends

Democracy even in its minimal, electoral form was highly unpopular among world governments when the third wave of democratization began three decades ago. A count by Freedom House (2006) revealed only 41 democracies among 150 independent states in 1974. Democracies, heavily concentrated in the regions of western Europe and North America, accounted for 27 percent of the states. In 2004, 122 of 192 independent countries (64%) were democracies.

Notably, the percentage of democratic states more than doubled from 27 to 62 percent during the three decades of the third wave. Most advances in democratization came during the first two decades (1974–94) when the percentage of democratic states rose sharply from 27 to 64 percent. During the last ten years, the percentage changed only slightly from 60 to 64 percent. During the same period, however, the percentage of liberal democratic states has risen modestly from 39 to 46 percent. These findings suggest that the first two decades of the third wave were, by and large, the period of electoral democratization, and the last decade was a period of advancement to liberal democratization.

A recent analysis of the Polity IV data by Marshall and Gurr (2005, 16) confirms Freedom House's finding that democracy has expanded more in a single generation than it had since its invention in Greece more than two and a half millenniums ago (see also UNDP 2002). Unlike the data compiled by Freedom House, the Polity data deal with the extent of both democracy and autocracy in the governance of independent states. According to that analysis, a dramatic global shift from autocratic regimes to democracy began by the late 1980s and continued through the 1990s. By 1977, there were 35 democracies, 16 mixed regimes, and 89 autocracies. In early 2005, there were 88 democracies, 44 mixed regimes, and only 29 autocracies. Over the last two and a half decades, the number of democracies has more than doubled while autocracies have dwindled to one-third their number. Evidently, we live in the historically unprecedented period of global shifts toward democracy.

3 Ordinary Citizens as Democratizers

Transitions from authoritarian rule have not always brought about democracies. According to the Polity IV Data, as many as twenty-one countries experienced re-authorization between 1997–2003.[3] Why have some transitions from autocratic rule reverted back to non-democracies while others remain democracies? Why have some new democracies turned into liberal democracies while others have not? Has the participation of the mass citizenry in the democratization process shaped the dynamics and trajectories of the process? Previously, answers to these questions have been hard to find because although there is a large body of the empirical literature examining the role of civil society in democratic transitions (Alagappa 2004; Fukuyama 2001; Newton 2001; Norris 2002), very little of this literature has examined the role civil society plays in advancing electoral or formal democracies into liberal democracies (Bermeo 2003; Collier 1999). A recent study by Freedom House (Karatnycky and Ackerman 2005) represents the first systematic research endeavor linking the success or failure of liberal democratization to non-violent civic activism.

To determine the importance of citizens' involvement in democratic reform, this Freedom House study analyzed the political dynamics of sixty-seven countries that had undergone transitions from authoritarian rule over the last three decades. Specifically, it analyzed the relationships between the mode of civic involvement in democratic regime change and the post-transition state of freedom, that is, the degrees of political rights and civil liberties citizens of these transition countries were experiencing in 2005, many years after the democratic transition.

The analysis reveals that transitions from authoritarian rule do not always lead to greater freedom. Of the 67 countries categorized, 52 percent are now Free, while 34 percent are Partly Free and 14 percent are Not Free. In 91 percent of the countries that become Free, their transitions were driven by civic forces alone or in combination with power holders. The corresponding figures for the groups of Partly Free and Not Free countries are, respectively, 60 percent and 44 percent. While 64 percent of transitions driven by civic forces become Free, only 14 percent of transitions driven solely by ruling elites become Free. The incidence of becoming Free post-transition is five times higher for the former than the latter.

---

[3] These countries are: Armenia, Belarus, Dominican Republic, Fuji, Gambia, Ghana, Haiti, Honduras, Lesotho, Malawi, Nepal, Niger, Nigeria, Pakistan, Peru, Russia, Solomon Islands, Sri Lanka, Sudan, Turkey, and Zambia.

To examine the impact of civic activism on liberal democratization, we reanalyzed the same data compiled by the Freedom House staff. Among the 50 countries whose transitions were driven by non-violent civic forces, 64 percent have turned into liberal democracies and 18 percent into non-democracies. Among the 14 countries where ruling elites drove the transition from authoritarian rule, only 14 percent have become liberal democracies and 50 percent have returned to non-democracies. When the transitions were driven by strong civic coalitions, not just civic coalitions, 75 percent of them became liberal democracies and only 6 percent emerged as non-democracies. When the transitions to democracy were made without the active and peaceful involvement of civic coalitions, 59 percent of them turned into non-democracies and 18 percent into liberal democracies (see Figure 14.1).

To put it differently, the likelihood that a transition from authoritarian rule would lead to liberal democracy was over four times higher for transitions supported by strong and non-violent civic coalitions than for those unsupported by any civic organizations at all. Conversely, the incidence of change to non-democracy is nearly ten times higher for the latter than the former. These findings suggest that the success or failure of liberal democratization depends largely on the role the mass citizenry

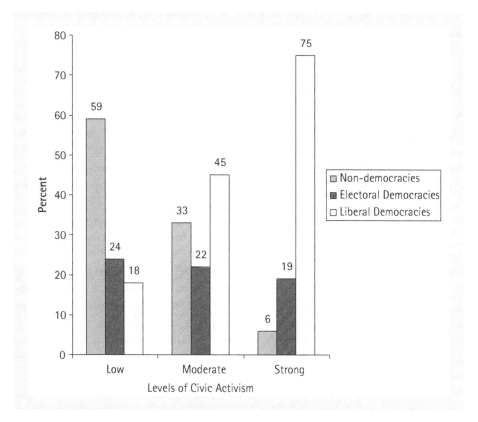

Fig. 14.1 The distribution of regimes by levels of civic activism
Source: Karatnycky and Ackerman (2005).

plays during the transition. The more vigorous, cohesive, and peaceful civil society is, the likelier the progress toward full democracy; the less vigorous and cohesive and more violent civil society is, the more common is the reversal to non-democratic rule.

4 CULTURAL DEMOCRATIZATION

Clearly, in the current wave of global democratization, civil society does sustain change toward full democracy. Active and cohesive civil society forces do successfully transform authoritarian regimes into electoral democracies and electoral democracies into liberal democracies. Absent these forces, many democratizing countries remain mixed regimes or revert back to non-democratic rule. An important question, then, is, why do some of these countries fail to develop a civil society that advances democratization on a continuing basis? In the literature on third-wave democracies, the answer consistently lies in the country's political culture (Bernhard 1993; Fukuyama 2001; Putnam 1993; Tarrow 1998).

4.1 Support for Democracy

Political culture refers to a variety of political attitudes, beliefs, and values, such as efficacy, tolerance, and trust. These attitudes, beliefs, and values all affect citizen conceptions of and involvement in civic life as well as political life. Yet, one is clearly more fundamental than the rest: the attitude that democracy is more preferable than any of its alternatives (Diamond 1999; Linz and Stepan 1996; Rose, Mishler, and Haerpfer 1998).

There are several specific reasons why democratization can advance when ordinary citizens embrace democracy as "the only game in town." Democracy, unlike other forms of government, is government by *demos* (the people) and thus cannot be foisted upon an unwilling people for any extended period of time. As government by the people, democracy depends principally on their support for its survival and effective performance (Mishler and Rose 1999). Only those committed to democracy as the best form of government are likely to reject anti-democratic movements to overthrow the new democratic regime, especially during a serious crisis (Dalton 2004; Inglehart 1990, 1997). Moreover, when citizens confer legitimacy on a newly installed democratic regime, it can make decisions and commit resources without resort to coercion. Therefore, there is a growing consensus in the literature on third-wave democracies that democratization is incomplete until an overwhelming majority of the mass citizenry offers unqualified and unconditional support for democracy (Fukuyama 1995; Diamond 1999; Linz and Stepan 1996).

4.1.1 *Conceptualization*

What constitutes support for democracy? In the literature on democratic political culture there is a general agreement that popular support for democracy especially in new democracies is a highly complex and dynamic phenomenon with multiple dimensions and layers (Dalton 2004; Klingemann 1999; Shin 1999). Democratic support is a multi-layered or multi-level phenomenon because citizens simultan cously comprehend democracy both an ideal political system and as a political system-in-practice. It is a multidimensional phenomenon because it involves the acceptance of democratic decision making as well as the rejection of democracy's alternatives.

To ordinary citizens who lived most of their lives under authoritarian rule, democracy at one level represents the political ideals or values to which they aspire. At another level, democracy refers to a political regime-in-practice and the actual workings of its institutions, which govern their daily lives (Dahl 1971; Mueller 1999; Rose, Shin, and Munro 1999). Popular support for democracy, therefore, needs to be differentiated into two broad categories: normative and practical. The normative or idealist level is concerned with democracy-in-principle as an abstract ideal. The practical or realist level is concerned with the various aspects of democracy-in-practice, including regime structure, political institutions, and political processes.

At the first level support for democracy refers largely to a psychologically loose attachment citizens have to the positive symbols of democracy. Democratic support at the second level refers to favorable evaluations of the structure and behavior of the existing regime (Easton 1965). As empirical research has recently revealed, there is a significant gulf between these two levels of democratic support (Klingemann 1999; Mishler and Rose 2001; Norris 1999). To offer a comprehensive and balanced account of democratic support, therefore, we must consider both levels of support, normative and practical.

Moreover, democratic support especially among citizens of new democracies involves more than favorable orientations to democratic ideals and practices. Citizens with little experience and limited sophistication about democratic politics may be uncertain whether democracy or dictatorship offers satisfying solutions to the many problems facing their societies. Under such uncertainty, citizens who are democratic novices often embrace both democratic and authoritarian political propensities concurrently (Lagos 1997, 2001; Rose and Mishler 1994; Shin 1999). Consequently, the acceptance of democracy does not necessarily cause rejection of authoritarianism or vice versa.

4.1.2 *Measurement*

For two decades, many scholars and research institutes conducted public opinion surveys in democratizing countries. Gallup-International Voice of the People Project, the Pew Global Attitudes Project, UNDP program on Democracy and Citizenship, the World Values Survey, and many other national and international surveys monitored and sought to unravel the dynamics of citizen reactions to democratic change.

They have compared the patterns and sources of those reactions cross-nationally, cross-regionally, and even globally (Camp 2001; Evans and Whitefield 1995; Gibson 1996; Gibson and Gouws 2005; McDonough, Barnes, and Pina 1998; Reisinger et al. 1994).[4]

Among the most systematic endeavors to unravel the dynamics of mass reactions to democratic change are four regional democracy barometers: the New Europe Barometer, the Latinobarometer, the Afrobarometer, and the East Asia Barometer. These barometer surveys ask a variety of structured and unstructured questions to ascertain—directly and indirectly—how the citizens of democratizing countries conceive, perceive, and evaluate democracy as a political system.[5] We selected a subset of items from their latest surveys, described below, to compare the levels and patterns of citizen support for democracy across Africa, East Asia, Europe, and Latin America.[6]

4.2 Normative Support: Democracy as an Ideal Political System

Numerous survey-based studies document that democracy as an ideal political system has achieved overwhelming mass approval throughout the world and become "virtually the only political model with global appeal" (Inglehart 2003, 52). In the last two waves of the World Values Surveys, for example, "a clear majority of the population in virtually every society endorses a democratic political system" (Inglehart and Welzel 2005, 264). Even in the Islamic Middle East, Confucian East Asia, and the former Soviet Union, large majorities are favorably oriented to democracy-in-principle (Dalton and Ong 2006; Gibson, Duch, and Tedin 1992; Park and Shin 2005; Pew Research Center 2003; Tessler 2002). According to the 2005 Voice of the People surveys conducted in sixty-five countries by Gallup-International (2005) between May and July 2005, "8 out of 10 global citizens believe that in spite of its limitations, democracy is the best form of government, almost 10 percent more than in 2004." Undoubtedly, the ideals of democracy attract an ever-increasing number of ordinary citizens.

Yet knowing ordinary citizens view democracy-in-principle favorably does not tell us just how democratic they would like their own political system to be. To address

---

[4] For comprehensive reviews of these surveys, see Norris (2004); Heath, Fisher, and Smith (2005).

[5] Critical reviewers of the overt and other approaches to the measurement of democratic support can be found in Inglehart (2003), Mishler and Rose (2001), and Schedler and Sarsfield (2004).

[6] The second round of the Afrobarometer surveys was conducted in 16 countries between May 2002 and November 2003. The first wave of the East Asia Barometer surveys was conducted in 5 countries from May 2001 through December 2002. The 2004 annual Latinobarometer surveys were conducted in 18 countries between May and June of the year. The seventh New Europe Barometer surveys were conducted in 13 countries from October 2004 to February 2005. Further information about these surveys is available from their websites: www.afrobarometer.org, www.eastasiabarometer.org, www.latinobarometro.org, and www.cspp.strath.ac.uk. It should be noted that the 15 countries in Afrobrometer Round 2 do not represent sub-Saharan Africa as a whole. Nor do the 5 East Asian countries reported in this study represent East Asia as a whole.

this never previously studied question, the East Asia and New European Barometers asked respondents to express their desire on a ten-point scale for which 1 means complete dictatorship and 10 means complete democracy. Scores of 6 and above on this scale indicate general support for democracy as a normative phenomenon, and scores of 9 and 10 indicate full support for it. On this scale, the five East Asian and the thirteen New European countries average, respectively, 8.3 and 8.0, the scores that indicate that although the citizens generally support democracy, they do not want to live in a complete or nearly complete democracy.

For each of the East Asian and New European countries, Table 14.1 reports percentages expressing general and full support for democracy as an ideal political system. In all East Asian and New European countries, majorities up to 97 percent do generally support democracy as an ideal system. Full supporters, however, constitute majorities in three of five East Asian countries and six of thirteen New European countries. Only in one country in each region—Thailand in East Asia and Hungary in Europe—did more than two-thirds of the population fully support democracy-in-principle. In most countries in both regions, large majorities have yet to become fully attached to democracy even as a normative phenomenon. As Inglehart (2003, 52) points out, many citizens seem only to give "lip service to democracy."

4.3 Practical Support: Democracy as a Political System-in-Practice

To what extent do the mass publics in new democracies endorse democracy as the best form of government in their country? To date, numerous public opinion surveys have attempted to measure public support for democracy-in-practice by tapping either citizen satisfaction with the performance of the existing regime or the perceptions of its relative preferability to undemocratic alternatives. Because this satisfaction approach is based on the dubious assumption that all citizens recognize the current regime as a democracy, it does not necessarily tap support for democracy-in-practice (Mishler and Rose 2001, 306; see Cnache, Mandak, and Seligson 2001). The professed preferences for democracy over its alternatives are generally considered a more valid measure of practical democratic support. Using this to measure the legitimacy of democracy, the levels of empirical democratic support in consolidated democracies like Spain and other western European countries varied between 70 and 92 percent in the late 1990s and the early 2000s (Diamond 2001; Torcal 2002).

To measure support for democracy-in-practice, all four regional barometers asked: "With which of the following statements do you agree most? (1) Democracy is always preferable to any other kind of government. (2) Under certain situations, a dictatorship is preferable. (3) For people like me, it does not matter whether we have a democratic government or non-democratic government." The respondents who rate democracy as always preferable to its undemocratic alternatives are deemed to endorse its legitimacy as democracy-in-practice (Diamond 1999; Linz and Stepan 1996).

Table 14.1 Orientations toward democracy and its alternatives

Region	Democratic desire	Democratic preference (%)	Authoritarian opposition (%)	Auth. dem. sup. (demand) (%)	Dem. exp. (supply) (%)	Comparison
East Asia						
Korea	95(31)	49	71	40	20	posi.
Mongolia	94(58)	55	43	30	36	negi.
Philippines	89(54)	65	40	29	40	negi.
Taiwan	88(35)	43	60	30	51	negi.
Thailand	97(82)	84	47	41	72	negi.
(mean)	93(52)	59	52	35	44	negi.
New Europe						
Czech Rep.	83(45)	54	75	45	31	posi.
Estonia	86(40)	44	72	38	23	posi.
Hungary	93(67)	61	75	56	20	posi.
Latvia	82(44)	55	62	39	8	posi.
Lithuania	87(52)	65	70	51	30	posi.
Poland	86(56)	37	50	25	16	posi.
Slovakia	79(41)	47	65	39	20	posi.
Slovenia	87(56)	59	74	50	19	posi.
Bulgaria	73(47)	50	52	36	12	posi.
Romania	90(63)	59	70	48	13	posi.
Ukraine	86(54)	59	51	37	11	posi.
Belarus	84(42)	51	26	16	10	posi.
Russia	56(31)	25	42	11	18	negi.
(mean)	82(49)	51	60	38	18	posi.
Africa						
Botswana	—	66	64	48	59	negi.
Cape Verde	—	66	65	47	41	posi.
Ghana	—	52	74	42	46	cong.
Kenya	—	80	80	67	76	negi.
Lesotho	—	50	63	36	48	negi.
Malawi	—	64	66	48	38	posi.
Mali	—	71	56	47	63	negi.
Mozambique	—	54	36	23	67	negi.
Namibia	—	54	37	24	60	negi.
Nigeria	—	68	62	48	32	posi.
Senegal	—	75	67	54	58	cong.
S. Africa	—	57	62	39	47	negi.
Tanzania	—	65	66	45	63	negi.
Uganda	—	75	59	44	54	negi.
Zambia	—	70	79	58	48	posi.
Zimbabwe	—	48	65	35	37	cong.
(mean)	—	63	63	44	52	negi.
Latin America						
Argentina	—	65	22	18	23	cong.
Bolivia	—	45	28	15	13	cong.

(Continued)

Table 14.1 (*Continued*)

Region	Democratic desire	Democratic preference (%)	Authoritarian opposition (%)	Auth. dem. sup. (demand) (%)	Dem. exp. (supply) (%)	Comparison
Brazil	–	41	32	18	23	cong.
Chile	–	57	16	12	37	negi.
Colombia	–	46	17	9	22	negi.
Costa Rica	–	67	15	9	44	negi.
Dominican Rep.	–	65	23	16	30	negi.
Ecuador	–	46	30	14	18	cong.
El Salvador	–	50	8	4	21	negi.
Guatemala	–	35	10	3	13	negi.
Honduras	–	46	11	5	20	negi.
Mexico	–	53	35	17	24	negi.
Nicaragua	–	39	24	9	13	cong.
Panama	–	64	20	13	25	negi.
Paraguay	–	39	10	9	18	negi.
Peru	–	45	14	7	11	cong.
Uruguay	–	78	49	45	48	cong.
Venezuela	–	74	31	25	36	negi.
(mean)	–	53	23	14	25	negi.

Note: Figures in parentheses are percentages of full supporters for democracy.

Keys: Auth. dem. sup.: authentic democratic support
  Dem. exp.: democratic experience
  cong.: congruence
  negi.: negative incongruence
  posi.: positive incongruence

Sources: The Afrobarometer II; the East Asia Barometer I; the Latinobarometer 2004; the New Europe Barometer VII.

Table 14.1 shows that majorities or near majorities of the adult population in all 16 African countries embrace democracy as always preferable to its alternatives in their country. The table also shows similar levels of democratic support in 4 of 5 East Asian countries (80%), 9 of 13 New European countries (69%), and 10 of 18 Latin American countries (56%). In terms of regional mean ratings, Africa registers the highest level of support with 63 percent. This region is followed by East Asia (59%), Latin America (53%), and New Europe (51%). In terms of how widely the extent to which citizens support democracy varies within each region, Africa and Latin America score, respectively, the lowest (32% points) and highest (43% points) degrees of variation. With the highest percentage of empirical democratic supporters and the least uneven distribution of these supporters within the region, Africa stands out from the rest of the democratizing world. Even in Africa, however, only six countries reached the two-third level, which Diamond (1999, 179) characterizes as "a minimum threshold of mass support for democracy in a consolidated regime."

4.4 Authentic Support: Committed Democrats

Citizens of new democracies had life experience with undemocratic rule prior to democratic regime change. Doubtless many of them remain attached to the age-old authoritarian mindset. In view of the importance of early life socialization (Mishler and Rose 2002), the professed preferences for democracy among these citizens cannot be equated with unconditional or unwavering support for it (Dalton 1994; Finifter and Mickiewicz 1992; Hahn 1991; Inglehart 1997; Mishler and Rose 2001). To measure such authentic support, we take into account both pro-democratic and anti-authoritarian orientations, as done in previous research (Bratton, Mattes, and Gyimah-Boadi 2005; Diamond 2001; Lagos 2001; Shin and Wells 2005).

Table 14.1 reports percentages of respondents who reject the various forms of authoritarian rule including military rule, strongman rule, and one-party dictatorship.[7] Opponents of authoritarian rule constitute substantial majorities of the citizenry in Africa (63%) and New Europe (60%) and a bare majority in East Asia (52%). In Latin America, they constitute a small minority of less than one-quarter (23%). Evidently, more citizens of Africa and New Europe oppose a reversal to authoritarian rule than citizens in East Asia and Latin America.

For each region, we now compare the distribution of democratic supporters and authoritarian opponents and ascertain its particular pathway to cultural democratization among the mass citizenry. In African countries as a whole, democratic supporters and authoritarian opponents are equally numerous (63%). In East Asia, democratic supporters outnumber authoritarian opponents by 7 percentage points (59% versus 52%). In Latin America, the former outnumber the latter by a larger margin of 30 percentage points (53% versus 23%). In New Europe, by striking contrast, the latter outnumber the former by 9 percentage points (60% versus 51%).

These contrasting patterns of attitudinal distribution suggest three distinct pathways to cultural democratization: (1) embracing democracy and rejecting authoritarian rule simultaneously; (2) embracing democracy before rejecting authoritarianism; and (3) rejecting authoritarianism before embracing democracy. Apparently, Africa falls into the first pattern of simultaneous democratization, East Asia and Latin America fall into the second pattern of embracing democracy first, and New Europe fits the third pattern of first rejecting authoritarianism.

To distinguish authentic support for democracy from other types of regime support, we now consider both practical support for democracy and opposition to authoritarian rule. We consider support for democracy authentic when ordinary citizens show they view democracy as the only political game by endorsing it always and rejecting its undemocratic alternatives fully (Bratton, Mattes, and Gyimah-Boadi 2005, 91; Shin and Wells 2005, 99). We can differentiate this type of democratic support from non-authentic or prototype, democratic regime support that is mixed with authoritarian orientations.

---

[7] The Latinobarometer asked a pair of questions about military rule and strongman rule to tap anti-authoritarianism.

Considering all the countries in each region together reveals no region has yet reached the 50 percent level of authentic support. Yet, mean levels of authentic support vary considerably; 14 percent in Latin America, 35 percent in East Asia, 38 percent in New Europe, and 44 percent in Africa. In no country in Latin America and East Asia does half the population or more respond as authentic democrats who are likely to support greater democracy. In Africa and New Europe, on the other hand, there are three countries that have already reached this level of authentic support for democracy.

While large majorities of four-fifths of East Asian and New Europeans are favorably attached to democracy as an ideal political system, small minorities of less than two-fifths are fully committed to it as a political enterprise. These findings confirm earlier research: popular support for democracy in third-wave democracies is broad in scope but shallow in depth (Bratton 2002; Gibson 1996; Shin and Wells 2005). They also accord with Inglehart's (2003, 51) claim that "overt lip service to democracy is almost universal today."

5 CITIZEN DEMAND VERSUS INSTITUTIONAL SUPPLY

An incomplete democracy will likely become complete only if people demand that their political leaders supply the essentials of democracy (Rose, Mishler, and Haerpfer 1998, 200). Accordingly, democratic progress in all four regions requires significant increases in the current levels of authentic support for democratic rule. Without increasing support or demand, these countries are likely to remain incomplete democracies (Rose and Shin 2001; see also Mattes and Bratton 2003; Rose, Munro, and Mishler 2004).

The movement toward more or less democracy, however, does not depend on the level of democratic demand from the citizenry alone; it also depends on the relationship between citizen demand and institutional supply. According to Inglehart and Welzel (2005, 187), "shifts toward more or less democracy follow the logic of reducing the incongruence between citizen demand and institutional supply of democracy." The more citizen demand for democracy outstrips what institutions supply, the more likely are political systems to move toward more democracy. When citizens demand less democracy than institutions supply, political systems are likely to stagnate or move toward less democracy. When popular demand exceeds institutional supply, positive incongruence occurs for further democratic development. When the latter exceeds the former, negative incongruence occurs for democratic decay.

5.1 Citizen Demand

During the current wave of democratization, we found in all four regions that many citizens do not view democracy as the best political system for their country. Even among those who prefer it to its alternatives, a minority embraces democracy unconditionally, while a majority is only committed to it "superficially" or "expediently." Between these two types of authentic and non-authentic supporters, we assume that it is the former who are leaders in cultural democratization. It is also reasonable to assume that leaders, not laggards, demand more democracy to complete the process of democratization. Authentic mass support for democracy takes expression as cultural or popular demand for democracy (Mattes and Bratton 2003).

5.2 Institutional Supply

People demand more democracy when what their institutions supply falls short of meeting their desires. It is likely that the experienced level of democracy, not the actual level of democracy, shapes popular demand for greater democracy. To measure the experienced level of democracy supplied by institutions, we chose a pair of questions from regional barometers. The East Asia and New Europe Barometers asked respondents to place their current political system on a scale for which 1 means complete dictatorship and 10 means complete democracy. Scores of 8 and higher on this scale are considered indicative of experiencing an adequate level of democracy.

All 5 East Asian countries received ratings above the scale's midpoint of 5.5 and are rated as democracies. In New Europe, only 6 of 13 countries are rated as democracies. In 2 of 5 East Asian countries, majorities of the citizenry rate the current level of institutional supply as adequate. On the other hand, in none of the 13 countries in New Europe does a majority judge the current system in an equally positive light. Obviously, Europeans perceive less democratic progress than East Asians do. Despite this difference, however, there is a general agreement that their political systems are far less than complete democracies.

In Africa and Latin America, citizens rated their new political systems with one of four verbal categories: (1) full democracy; (2) a democracy with minor problems; (3) a democracy with major problems; and (4) not a democracy. Responses in the first two categories indicate an adequate supply of democracy (Mattes and Bratton 2003). In as many as half the African countries, majorities rate their democracy as either a full democracy or a democracy only with minor problems. In striking contrast, the majority in no Latin American country rated its democracy as either a full democracy or a democracy with minor problems. In the eyes of citizens, more democratic advances appear to have been achieved in Africa than in Latin America.

When all the countries in each region are considered together, Africa is the only region in which a majority (52%) reports experiencing an adequate level of democracy. It is followed by East Asia (44%), Latin America (25%), and New Europe (18%). Why do Africans and East Asians rate their democracies much more positively than their peers in Latin America and New Europe? Do they do so because they are not capable enough to distinguish incomplete democratization from complete democratization? To explore these questions, Figure 14.2 compares across the regions the percentages reporting the experience of complete or full democracy. As expected, those who mistake the existing limited democratic rule for a full democracy and prematurely recognize the completion of democratization in their country are from three to over five times more numerous in Africa and East Asia than in Latin America and New Europe. Evidently, Africans and East Asians are far less cognitively sophisticated in knowledge about democratic politics than their peers in Latin America and New Europe.[8]

We next compare the levels of citizen demand and institutional supply of democracy across regions to determine whether democratic supply and demand are congruent or incongruent. To measure the extent of congruence in cultural and institutional democratization, we calculate a percentage differential index (PDI) by subtracting the percentage experiencing democracy adequately—democratic supply—from that of those who are unconditionally committed to democratic rule—democratic demand. Scores of this PDI can range from −100 to +100. Negative scores indicate the incidence of negative incongruence in which democracy is

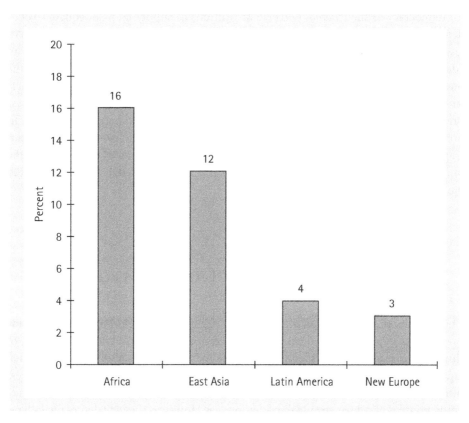

Fig. 14.2 Regional differences in experiencing complete or full democracy
Sources: see Table 14.1.

---

[8] The African and Asian country samples are not representative of their respective continents as a whole. For this reason, our cross-continental comparisons may not be highly accurate.

perceived as oversupplied (overdemocratization). Positive scores indicate the incidence of positive incongruence in which democracy is perceived as undersupplied
(underdemocratization). Because PDI scores of plus or minus 5 points indicate little
gulp between supply and demand, we interpret these as evidence of congruence rather
than incongruence in the levels of institutional and cultural democratization.

The last column of Table 14.1 shows 9 of 16 countries in Africa in negative
incongruence, 4 countries in positive incongruence, and 3 countries in congruence.
In East Asia, 4 of 5 countries are in negative congruence while 1 country is in positive
incongruence. In Latin America, 11 of 18 countries are in negative congruence and
7 countries in congruence. In New Europe, 12 of 13 countries are in positive incongruence and only 1 country, Russia, is in negative incongruence. Negative congruence
prevails in three of the four regions—Africa, East Asia, and Latin America while
positive congruence prevails in only one region, post-communist Europe.

According to the congruence theory of democratization, new democracies in
Africa, East Asia, and Latin America confront the problem of low popular demand
for democracy as their *demos* perceive institutions as supplying an adequate level of
democracy. Countries in New Europe, on the other hand, tend to face the problem of
low institutional supply as their *demos* perceive institutions as failing to supply an
adequate level of democracy. Between these two problems of democratization, the
one featuring a lack of popular demand for more democracy poses a greater obstacle
to successful democratization because this problem likely will stall the process
prematurely and discourage elites from supplying any more necessary reform. To
prevent a premature end to democratization or escape from "a low-level equilibrium
trap," citizens of new democracies have to do more than embrace "democracy as the
only game in town." They have to be sophisticated in knowledge about the limited
nature of the current democratic regime.

6 SUMMARY AND CONCLUSIONS

The current, third wave of democratization began in southern Europe in the mid-
1970s. This chapter has sought to provide a comprehensive and balanced account of
this wave by examining perspectives from the mass citizenries about its institutional
and cultural dynamics and their congruence. We found considerable global progress
during the three decades expanding the family of democratic countries and broadening popular affect for the ideals of democracy. However, the new democracies have
achieved relatively little progress in dissociating the mass citizenry from the age-old
habits of authoritarianism. In most of these countries today, only small minorities
are unconditionally committed to democratic politics. Even these committed democrats are not always cognitively capable of distinguishing limited democratic rule
from complete or full democracy. As a result, many new democracies are trapped in a

low-level congruence or negative incongruence between citizen demand and institutional supply of democracy.

To escape from this trap, third-wave democracies need an increasing number of authentic democrats who not only embrace democracy but also reject its alternatives. To advance toward full democracy, moreover, they need to multiply the number of authentic democrats who are cognitively sophisticated about the practices of democratic politics (Dahl 1992; Shin, Park, and Jang 2005). Without substantially increasing the existing level of democratic citizenship among the mass citizenry, these nascent democracies are likely to persist as incomplete or broken-back democracies. In this regard, we should note that the embrace of democracy as "the only game in town" is a first step, not a last step, toward the democratization of mass citizenries.

REFERENCES

ALAGAPPA, M. 2004. *Civil Society and Political Change in Asia: Expanding and Contracting Democratic Space.* Stanford, Calif.: Stanford University Press.

ALMOND, G., and VERBA, S. 1963. *The Civic Culture: Political Attitudes in Five Western Democracies.* Princeton: Princeton University Press.

BERMEO, N. 2003. *Ordinary People in Extraordinary Times: The Citizenry and the Breakdown of Democracy.* Princeton: Princeton University Press.

BERNHARD, M. 1993. Civil society and democratic transitions in east central Europe. *Political Science Quarterly,* 108: 307–26.

BOIX, C., and STOKES, S. 2003. Endogenous democratization, *World Politics,* 55 (4): 517–49.

BRATTON, M. 2002. Wide but shallow: popular support for democracy in Africa. Afrobarometer Working Paper 19.

—— and MATTES, R. 2001. Support for democracy in Africa: intrinsic or instrumental? *British Journal of Political Science,* 31 (3): 447–74.

—— MATTES, R., and GYIMAH-BOADI, E. 2005. *Public Opinion, Democracy, and Market Reform in Africa.* New York: Cambridge University Press.

BUNCE, V. 2000. Comparative democratization: big and bounded generalizations, *Comparative Political Studies,* 33 (6): 703–34.

—— 2003. Rethinking recent democratization: lessons from the postcommunist experience. *World Politics,* 55 (2): 167–92.

CAMP, R. ed. 2001. Citizen views of democracy in Latin America. Pittsburgh: University of Pittsburgh Press.

CAROTHERS, T. 1999. *Aiding Democracy Abroad: The Learning Curve.* Washington, DC: Carnegie Endowment for International Peace.

—— 2002. The end of the transition paradigm. *Journal of Democracy,* 13 (1): 5–21.

CNACHE, D., MANDAK, J., and SELIGSON, M. 2001. Meaning and measurement in cross-national research on satisfaction with democracy. *Public Opinion Quarterly,* 65: 506–28.

COLLIER, D., and LEVITSKY, S. 1997. Democracy with adjectives: conceptual innovation in comparative research. *World Politics,* 49 (3): 430–51.

COLLIER, R. 1999. *Paths toward Democracy.* New York: Cambridge University Press.

CROISSANT, A. 2004. From transition to defective democracy: mapping Asian democratization. *Democratization,* 11 (5): 156–78.

DAHL, R. 1971. *Polyarchy: Participation and Opposition.* New Haven: Yale University Press.

—— 1992. The problem of civic competence. *Journal of Democracy,* 3 (4): 45–59.

—— 2000. *On Democracy: A Citizen's Guide.* New Haven: Yale University Press.

DALTON, R. 1994. Communists and democrats: democratic attitudes in the two germanies. *British Journal of Political Science,* 24: 469–93.

—— 2004. *Democratic Challenges, Democratic Choices: Political Support in Advanced Industrial Societies.* Oxford: Oxford University Press.

—— and ONG, N. 2006. Authority orientations and democratic attitudes. Ch. 5 in Dalton and Shin 2006.

DALTON, R., and SHIN, D. ed. 2006. *Citizens, Democracy and Markets around the Pacific Rim.* Oxford: Oxford University Press.

DIAMOND, L. 1999. *Developing Democracy: Toward Consolidation.* New Haven: Yale University Press.

—— 2001. How people view democracy: findings from public opinion surveys in four regions. **http://democracy.stanford.edu/Seminar/Diamond** 2001.

—— 2002. Thinking about hybrid regimes. *Journal of Democracy,* 13 (2): 21–35.

—— 2003. Universal democracy. *Policy Review,* 119: 3–25.

DOORENSPLEET, R. 2000. Reassessing the three waves of democratization. *World Politics,* 52: 384–406.

EASTON, D. 1965. *A System Analysis of Political Life.* New York: Wiley.

Economist. 2005. Tentative steps down the road to democracy. *Economist,* September 9.

ECKSTEIN, H. 1966. *A Theory of Stable Democracy.* Princeton: Princeton University Press.

EVANS, G., and WHITEFIELD, S. 1995. The politics and economics of democratic commitment. *British Journal of Political Science,* 28: 485–514.

FINIFTER, A., and MICKIEWICZ, E. 1992. Redefining the Political System of the USSR: Mass Support for Political Change. *American Political Science Review,* 86: 857–74.

FREEDOM HOUSE. 2006. *The Annual Survey of Political Rights and Civil Liberties.* **www.freedomhouse.org**

FUKUYAMA, F. 1995. The primacy of culture. *Journal of Democracy,* 6 (1): 7–14.

—— 2001. Social capital, civil society, and development. *Third World Quarterly* 22 (1): 7–28.

GALLUP-INTERNATIONAL. 2005. Voice of the people 2005. **http://extranet.gallup-international. com/uploads/internet/VOP2005_Democracy%20FINAL.pdf**

GEDDES, B. 1999. What do we know about democratization after twenty years? *Annual Review of Political Science,* 2: 115–44.

GIBSON, J. 1996. A mile wide but an inch deep (?). *American Journal of Political Science,* 40 (2): 396–420.

—— DUCH, R., and TEDIN, K. 1992. Democratic values and the transformation of the Soviet Union. *Journal of Politics,* 54 (2): 329–71.

—— and GOUWS, A. 2005. *Overcoming Intolerance in South Africa.* New York: Oxford University Press.

GOEHRING, J., and SCHNETZER, A. 2005. *Nations in Transit 2005: Democratization in East Central Europe and Eurasia.* Lanham, Md.: Rowman & Littlefield.

HAGOPIAN, F., and MAINWARING, S. 2005. *The Third Wave of Democratization in Latin America.* New York: Cambridge University Press.

HAHN, J. 1991. Continuity and change in Russian political culture. *British Journal of Political Science,* 21: 393–421.

HEATH, A., FISHER, S., and SMITH, S. 2005. The globalization of public opinion research. *Annual Review of Political Science,* 8: 297–331.

HUNTINGTON, S. 1991. *The Third Wave: Democratization in the Late Twentieth Century.* Norman: University of Oklahoma Press.

INGLEHART, R. 1990. *Culture Shifts in Advanced Industrial Society.* Princeton: Princeton University Press.

—— 1997. *Modernization and Postmodernization.* Princeton: Princeton University Press.

—— 2003. How Solid is Mass Support Democracy—And How Can We Measure It? *PS: Political Science and Politics,* 36 (1): 51–7.

—— and WEITZEL, C. 2005. *Modernization, Cultural Change, and Democracy.* New York: Cambridge University Press.

KARATNYCKY, A., and ACKERMAN, P. 2005. How freedom is won: from civic resistance to durable democracy. **www.freedomhouse.org**.

KARL, T. 2000. Electoralism. In *The International Encyclopedia of Elections,* ed. R. Rose et al. Washington, DC: Congressional Quarterly Press.

—— 2005. From Democracy to democratization and back. Stanford University, Center for Democracy, Development, and the Rule of Law Working Paper No. 45.

KLINGEMANN, H. 1999. Mapping political support in the 1990s: a global analysis. Pp. 31–56 in *Critical Citizens: Global Support for Democratic Governance,* ed. P. Norris. Oxford: Oxford University Press.

LAGOS, M. 1997. Latin America's smiling mask. *Journal of Democracy,* 8 (3): 125–38.

—— 2001. Between stability and crisis in Latin America, *Journal of Democracy,* 12 (1): 137–45.

LEVITSKY, S., and WAY, L. 2002. The rise of competitive authoritarianism. *Journal of Democracy,* 13 (2): 51–65.

LINZ, J. 1990. Transitions to democracy. *Washington Quarterly,* 13: 143–62.

—— and STEPAN, A. 1996. *Problems of Democratic Transition and Consolidation.* Baltimore: Johns Hopkins University Press.

MARSHALL, M., and GURR, T. 2005. Peace and conflict. Center for International Development and Conflict Management, University of Maryland.

MATTES, R., and BRATTON, M. 2003. Learning about democracy in Africa: awareness, performance, and experience. Afrobarometer Working Paper No. 31.

McDONOUGH, P., BARNES, S., and PINA, A. L. 1998. *The Cultural Dynamics of Democratization in Spain.* Ithaca, NY: Cornell University Press.

McFAUL, M. 2002. The fourth wave of democracy and dictatorship. *World Politics,* 54 (2): 212–44.

—— 2005. Transitions from postcommunism. *Journal of Democracy,* 16 (3): 5–19.

MISHLER, W., and ROSE, R. 1999. Five years after the fall. Pp. 78–99 in *Critical Citizens,* ed. P. Norris. Oxford: Oxford University Press.

—— —— 2001. Political support for incomplete democracies. *International Political Science Review,* 22 (4): 303–20.

—— —— 2002. Learning and relearning democracy. *European Journal of Political Research,* 41: 5–36.

MUELLER, J. 1999. *Capitalism, Democracy, and Ralph's Pretty Good Grocery.* Princeton: Princeton University Press.

NORRIS, P. ed. 1999. *Critical Citizens.* Oxford: Oxford University Press.

—— 2002. *Democratic Phoenix: Reinventing Political Activism.* Cambridge: Cambridge University Press.

—— 2004. From the civic culture to the Afrobarometer. Presented at the annual meeting of the American Political Science Association, Chicago.

NEWTON, K. 2001. Trust, social capital, civil society, and democracy. *International Political Science Review,* 22 (2): 201–14.

O'DONNELL, G. 1994. Delegative democracy. *Journal of Democracy,* 5 (1): 55–69.

O'DONNELL, G. 2004. Why the rule of law matters. *Journal of Democracy*, 15 (4): 5–19.

O'LOUGHLIN, J. et al. 1998. The diffusion of democracy, 1946–2004. *Annals of the Association of American Geographers*, 88 (4): 545–74.

PARK, C., and SHIN, D. C. 2005. Do Asian values deter popular support for democracy? *Asian Survey* (forthcoming).

PEW RESEARCH CENTER 2003. Views of a changing world 2003, http://people- press.org/ reports/display.php3?ReportID=185

PUDDINGTON, A., and PIANO, A. 2005. Worrisome signs, modest shifts: the 2004 Freedom House Survey, *Journal of Democracy*, 16 (1): 103–8.

PUTNAM, R., with LEONARDI, R., and NANETTI, R. 1993. *Making Democracy Work: Civic Traditions in Modern Italy*. Princeton: Princeton University Press.

REISINGER, W., MILLER, A., HESLI, V., and MAHER, K. Political values in Russia, *British Journal of Political Science*, 45: 183–223.

ROSE, R. 2001. A diverging Europe. *Journal of Democracy*, 12 (1): 93–106.

—— and MISHLER, W. 1994. Mass reaction to regime change in Eastern Europe. *British Journal of Political Science*, 24: 159–82.

—— —— and HAERPFER, C. 1998. *Democracy and its alternatives*. Baltimore: Johns Hopkins University Press.

—— MUNRO, N., and MISHLER, W. 2004. Resigned acceptance of an incomplete democracy: Russia's political equilibrium. *Post-Soviet Affairs*, 20 (3): 195–218.

—— and SHIN, D. C. 2001. Democratization backwards: the problem of third-wave democracies. *British Journal of Political Science*, 31 (2): 331–75.

ROSE, R., and MUNRO, N. 1999. Tensions between the democratic idea and reality: South Korea. Ch. 7 in *Critical Citizens: Global Support for Democratic Governance*, ed. P. Norris. Oxford: Oxford University Press.

SCHEDLER, A., and SARSFIELD, R. 2004. Democrats with adjectives. Afrobarometer Working Paper No. 45.

SHIN, D. C. 1994. On the third wave of democratization: a synthesis and evaluation of recent theory and research. *World Politics*, 47 (1): 136–70.

—— 1999. *Mass Politics and Culture in Democratizing Korea*. New York: Cambridge University Press.

—— PARK, C., and JANG, J. 2005. Assessing the shifting qualities of democratic citizenship: the case of South Korea. *Democratization*, 12 (2): 202–22.

—— and WELLS, J. 2005. Is democracy the only game in town? *Journal of Democracy*, 16 (2): 88–101.

TARROW, S. 1998. *Power in Movement: Social Movements and Contentious Politics*. Cambridge: Cambridge University Press.

TESSLER, M. 2002. Islam and democracy in the Middle East. *Comparative Politics*, 34 (3): 337–54.

TORCAL, M. 2002. Support for democracy and the "consolidation effect" in new democracies. Unpublished manuscript.

UNITED NATIONS DEVELOPMENT PROGRAMME. 2002. *Human Development Report 2002: Deepening Democracy in a Fragmented World*. New York: Oxford University Press.

—— 2005. *Democracy in Latin America: Toward a Citizens' Democracy*. Peru: Santillana Publishing Co.

ZAKARIA, F. 2003. *The Future of Freedom: Illiberal Democracy at Home and Abroad*. New York: W. W. Norton.

CHAPTER 15

....

PERSPECTIVES ON POLITICAL BEHAVIOR IN TIME AND SPACE

....

RICHARD ROSE

MODERNIZATION involves a radical transformation of a society, the shift from a traditional agricultural society to an educated industrial or post-industrial society (Bell 1974; Lerner 1958). Transformation on this scale does not happen very often, and in low-income or developing countries it is only starting or partially achieved. Because its effect is pervasive, modernization presents a challenge to established social, economic, and political institutions. The political outcome may be a democratic regime, a totalitarian regime, or a series of changes between democratic and undemocratic regimes (Finer 1997, 1474 ff.; see also Shin's chapter in this volume).

The study of political behavior is typically concerned with individual behavior in societies in which modern, and above all democratic political institutions are taken for granted. While there are major studies of what happens to individuals in modernizing or low-income societies (see e.g. Pye 1962; Inkeles 1983; Scott 1985; Welzel in this volume), and in totalitarian regimes (Shlapentokh 2001), the primary focus is on stable modern societies. The typical method of research is conducting a survey that produces quantified data. Instead of inferring national values from the writings of philosophers, surveys seek to identify the content and distribution of

* This chapter was prepared by the author as a contribution to a study of diverging paths of post-communist countries across time and space, financed by the British Economic & Social Research Council (RES-000-12-0193).

political behavior and values within a representative cross-section of the national population. Surveys can produce more reliable evidence than compilations of anecdotes and press cuttings or diary entries. Using survey data avoids the ecological fallacy of drawing inferences about individuals from aggregate data, such as election results, or from such reified terms as national history and traditions (Robinson 1950).

Even though the typical political behavior article focuses on a single country at a single point in time, it is often presented within a universalistic framework outside time and space. Among modern political scientists, Aaron Wildavsky was especially distinctive in emphasizing universal concerns within narrow confines of time and space; for example, *Implementation,* a study of a single problem in the city in which he lived, immediately attracted worldwide attention because implementation is a universal problem of governance (see Pressman and Wildavsky 1973; Rose 1995). However, a survey about a single country at a single point in time has something in common with descriptive reports: there are no logical grounds for generalizing findings across time and space.

Robust conclusions about political behavior can only be arrived at if they are tested in different temporal contexts and across national boundaries in order to determine *under what circumstances and to what extent* the findings from a single-country study are generalizable. Even if a national survey is designed to test a general theory, the results are country specific; any claim to be general or universal is speculative rather than substantiated. To reject the influence of time and institutions is to commit the individualist fallacy of "deriving conclusions about a higher level of aggregation from data on individuals" (Reisinger 1995, 339; for a full discussion of the term, see Scheuch 1966).

In reflecting on the chapters in this section, I will argue that political behavior does not exist among isolated individuals; it occurs within a three-dimensional space. It is a function of when and where it occurs as well as who is involved. To understand under what circumstances and to what extent differences in national institutions and history are significant, time and space must be incorporated as variables in the analysis.

Individual behavior = (f) country, historical time, individual attributes + error term

Each of these terms can be expanded greatly, just as individuals differ in many attributes so countries differ in their political institutions and in the timing of modernization. However, one type of influence cannot substitute for another. Whereas national institutions and temporal influences are given at the time of a single national survey, candidates and parties vary from one election to the next, and even more between democratic and undemocratic political systems. Moreover, the political institutions and state boundaries of most European countries have varied at least once and often more than that in the past century. Ignoring the influence of time and space misleadingly assigns to the error term influences that have been left out by a researcher on practical grounds (lack of multinational data) or through lack of awareness of historical context. Bringing society back in turns time and space from constants to variables.

1 WHEN: TIME MATTERS

When research is done affects results, because historical time is a context, not a constant (Pierson 2004). The events of one year are not like another; the conjunction of circumstances can vary from one election to the next; and the sequence of events can either make behavior path dependent or alter what individuals do before and after a given point in time. To conduct a time-series analysis as if it did not make any difference whether time was 1900, 1950, or 2000 is to show a blithe disregard for the way in which individuals, institutions, and societies change their behavior when the historical context changes (cf. Robinson 1979).

1.1 Timeless Behavior?

Political behavior research tends to be conducted in the historical present: results from one year are interchanged with another as if they are timeless in their relevance. For example, the classic and still cited study of *The American Voter* drew its empirical evidence from the relatively placid election of Dwight D. Eisenhower as president in 1952 and 1956 (Campbell et al. 1960). Yet a lot has happened in American politics in the half-century since.

Theories of political socialization support a timeless approach insofar as they emphasize the stability of individual attitudes and behavior. Individuals begin developing attitudes and political awareness in childhood, and what is learned in youth can influence adult behavior and how new experiences are evaluated, reinforcing what was learned earlier. Thus, an individual's political behavior is expected to be relatively stable through his or her lifetime. In addition, attitudes and behavior can persist from one generation to the next insofar as youths acquire a party identification from their parents (Butler and Stokes 1970). Theories of path dependence postulate that attitudes and behavior persist because the costs in time, money, or emotions are greater than the immediately perceived benefits of changing behavior and beliefs (Sewell 1996). Such theories can be invoked to explain the "freezing" of party allegiances (Lipset and Rokkan 1967). The stability of individual behavior can also characterize political institutions. David Easton's (1965) seminal study postulated a regime in a steady-state equilibrium due to a feedback process relating the inputs of citizens, the outputs of governors, and the response that citizens made to government's outputs. In this way, democracies are expected to be "stable" or "consolidated."

Insofar as intergenerational political socialization and path dependence create a steady-state political equilibrium, then the timing of a piece of research may make little difference. However, a steady-state equilibrium is an ideal-type tendency, the mean around which fluctuations occur. In the words of Peyton Young:

Equilibrium can be understood only within a dynamic framework that explains how it comes about (if in fact it does). Neoclassical economics describes the way the world looks once the dust has settled; we are interested in how it goes about settling. This is not an idle issue, since the business of settling may have considerable bearing on how things look afterwards. More important, we need to recognize the dust never really does settle—it keeps moving about buffeted by random currents of air. (1988, 133)

The relatively small fluctuations of a steady-state equilibrium will sooner or later be punctuated by political events that challenge individuals and political elites to alter their behavior (Baumgartner and Jones 1993). The result can be a dynamic reform, in which the political system is intact but a major element is altered. For example, New Zealand's shift from a first-past-the-post to a mixed-member proportional representation system compelled individuals to vote differently because the ballot itself was changed. When elite initiatives cause parties to be launched, break up, or merge, this creates a "floating" party system that offers the opportunity or even forces voters to change their behavior. Similarly, no sooner had Butler and Stokes published their tribute to the British two-party system than political events disrupted the Conservative–Labour duopoly. When the dust settled, there was a three-party system. However, the punctuation of an equilibrium may be followed by a return to the status quo ante. In the United States, third-party candidates for the presidency intermittently challenge the duopoly of Democrats and Republicans, only to be followed by a return to competition between the same two parties as before.

A change in political regime does not challenge institutions but disrupts them. Whether the change is from a democratic to an authoritarian regime or in the other direction, this forces individuals to relearn norms of political behavior. Since the disruption of regimes in Germany and in Spain occurred after the introduction of survey research, there are survey-based studies showing how individuals have adapted to a new regime (Linz 1959; Baker, Dalton, and Hildebrandt 1981; Noelle-Neumann 1995; for Spain, Gunther, Sani, and Shabad 1988, McDonough, Barnes, and Lopez-Pina 1988). The study of modernization in the chapters in this part presume that behavior is not timeless or unchanging.

1.2 Changes over Time

There are limited conditions in which political behavior is free of temporal (that is, historical) influences. Tests of the persistence of attitudes among generations have found that all cohorts tend to respond similarly and substantially to short-term political stimuli (Mishler and Rose 2006; Inglehart in this volume). Theories of modernization imply social changes gradually alter individual behavior, for example, through the spread of industrialization and rising standards of education (cf. Dalton 2006). While it is illogical to extrapolate a trend from a single survey, the temptation to do so is always there.

To ignore influences on political behavior prior to the point at which a survey is conducted is to act as if the past had no empirical existence! Yet the chief variables that constitute a causal model are not fixed once and for all: they are subject to variation across time. A pioneering scholar of modernization, Joseph Schumpeter, saw it as a process of "creative destruction," in which one type of economy succeeded another, a process that occurred with the passage of time. As Schumpeter emphasized (1946: 1), "No decade in the history of politics, religion, technology, painting, poetry and what not ever contains its own explanation." He then added that, in order to understand the impact of modernization and what has since become described as post-modernization, "You must survey a period of much wider span. Not to do so is the hallmark of dilettantism."

In long-established democracies it is necessary to understand the pre-survey-data past in order to understand the evolution of political behavior. Through careful reliance on ecological analysis of aggregate data and records showing how individuals voted before the ballot became secret, Wald (1983) analyzed the impact of religion on English voting from the late nineteenth century onwards. An alternative is to define a long-term research issue in a manner that can appropriately be tested with aggregate data, for example, Bartolini and Mair's (1990) study of the stabilization of European electorates through a century of upheavals from 1885 onwards. It is also the only way to come to grips with important twentieth-century issues such as "Who Voted for Hitler?" (see e.g. Falter 1991).

The passage of time can itself be an influence on political behavior. While an apparently stable regime can disappear almost over night, the consolidation of a regime takes time. When a regime is new, individual decisions about whether to support it can only be based on hopes of the future or rejection or commitment to the old regime. With the passage of time, people gain experience of the new regime. After a decade, people can decide whether to support a new regime (assuming it has survived that long), on the basis of its performance rather than prospective or retrospective judgments.

The Soviet Union was transformed into the Russian Federation at the end of 1991. A decade and one-half afterwards is long enough for a new regime to develop positive support—if its performance and values are evaluated positively by its subjects. With the passage of time the force of political inertia could wear down opposition and cultivate resigned acceptance of the new regime on the grounds that it is a lesser evil or simply that there is no alternative, thus making it "the only regime in town" (cf. Linz 1990). Empirical data to test the impact of the passage of time are available by pooling fourteen New Russia Barometer sample surveys from 1992 to 2005 (see **www.abdn.ac.uk/cspp**). Figure 15.1 shows the extent to which the month-by-month passage of time influences support for the current regime (Steenbergen and Jones 2002; Raudenbush and Bryk 2002; Luke 2004).

The principal influence on the development of support for the current Russian regime is the passage of time. Cumulatively, fourteen years adds 40 points to regime support on a 201-point scale running from plus 100 to minus 100 (see Rose, Mishler, and Munro 2007, ch. 9). The way in which individuals evaluate the Russian economy also has a big impact on regime support, however. Evaluations of the economy go up and down so the direction of its influence fluctuates. By contrast, the impact of the monthly passage of time is consistently in one direction. Even though one might expect that with time Russians would take freedom for granted and its influence on support for the

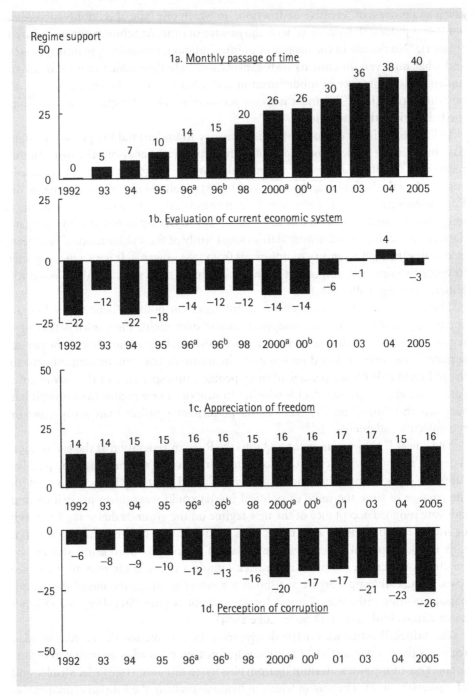

Fig. 15.1 Changing influences on regime support in Russia, 1992–2005

Source: Rose, Mishler and Munro, 2006: Table 9.2, Figure 9.4. Regime support measured on a scale with a range from plus 100 to minus 100.

current regime would wane, this has not happened. An appreciation of gains in freedom under the new regime has remained steady and its impact has remained substantial. Consistently, a big majority of Russians view their regime as corrupt. With the passage of time, this perception of corruption exercises a steadily increasing influence on the evaluation of the Russian regime—and that influence is negative.

2 WHERE: CHANGING PLACES CHALLENGES ASSUMPTIONS

Because national histories and institutions differ, *where* individuals live affects what people think and what people can do. Comparison turns structural attributes of a society from a constant into a variable. For example, elections in both Europe and the United States offer voters a choice, but the form differs between a one-round presidential ballot and a proportional representation list ballot to elect a parliament. Such contextual differences create a logical obstacle to generalizing from a single national study. Even as profoundly individualistic a subject as medical science recognizes this: epidemiologists study variations in the incidence of health and diseases from country to country. Even though quantitative political behavior studies appear different from "thick" prose analyses of area studies, they often share something in common: each can deal with a single country. A more scientific basis for generalization requires testing findings in more than one context and country as demonstrated by most of the chapters in this part.

2.1 Comparing Aggregates without Individuals

The study of comparative politics need not study individual political behavior; it can focus on political institutions. Nor need it be comparative: most studies catalogued under this heading are case studies of a single country different than the author's country of residence. An American SSRC committee chaired by Gabriel Almond and James S. Coleman (1960) pioneered conceptually oriented case studies in seven volumes of research that concentrated on holistic comparisons of national institutions, such as bureaucracies. The SSRC volume on political culture (Pye and Verba 1965) emphasized homogeneity within national cultures as well as comparisons across cultures.[1] Case studies continue to flourish, but they no longer tend to be

---

[1] Characteristic of Gabriel Almond's intellectual breadth, concurrently he produced a five-nation comparative study of *The Civic Culture* that was survey-based (Almond and Verba 1963). However, a major finding—the importance of a mixture of civic, subject, and even traditional outlooks—was ambiguous, leaving open the extent to which this occurred within individuals or at the societal level. Subsequently, Almond and Verba (1980) re-examined changes in their research paradigm and the countries studied over time.

ethnographic descriptions of alien ways. Instead, a case is placed within a conceptual framework that identifies what more general points it relates to.

Comparative research in public policy focuses on the policy outputs of government rather than on individual recipients. This is true whether hypotheses are tested through an institutionally detailed comparison of social policies or by a rigorous quantitative analysis of public expenditure across a dozen or more countries. Huntington's (1996) study of the clash of cultures postulates the existence of transnational civilizations based on religion. He then proceeds to impute behavioral differences to states and individuals belonging to different civilizations (cf. Inoguchi in this volume). However, no individual-level data are offered to support his thesis (for a challenge, see Rose 2002*a*).

Global comparisons can be undertaken with data assembled for as many as 180 countries by the United Nations, the World Bank, and non-governmental producers of data on freedom (**www.freedomhouse.org**) and perceptions of corruption (**www.transparency.org**). There are a multiplicity of global democracy indices produced by university-based political scientists from Bollen (1990) to Vanhanen (2003: for a review, see Munck and Verhuilen 2002). While the number and the variety of countries covered are impressive, none of these databases provides information about individual behavior. Data derived from individuals about such things as literacy or political participation are aggregated and reported as a percentage of the national population. There is no possibility of comparing how individuals within a country vary around the national mean—or whether there are common cross-national influences on within-nation differences in individual behavior.

2.2 Comparing Individuals in Context

Paradoxically, comparative analysis is invariably present in studies of political behavior—but it is a comparison of individuals within a country, for example, accounting for differences in individual behavior due to differences in education, age, gender, or other variables. However, a single-nation study cannot show to what extent social and demographic differences common in many countries have the same or a different influence elsewhere.

The geographical scope for comparison is today very wide and many different reasons can justify the choice of a country or countries (Dogan and Pelassy 1990). The study of political behavior in a single country becomes comparative if it is intended to replicate conclusions established in previous fieldwork in another country. Given the leading role of American political scientists in developing research in political behavior, this most often involves applying American theories in another national setting. However, such research is not comparative in the strict sense, for a generic model was not the starting point and it can be constricted to points common between the first and second country while omitting what is different. For example, a survey study applying the Michigan model of party identification to Russia reported a substantial level of party identification there but overlooked the ephemeral nature of party organizations there. Thus, most of the parties with which respondents were said to identify had disappeared before the research was published.

Comparison of political behavior in countries deemed most similar in their contextual characteristics—for example, Norway and Sweden—holds constant many historical characteristics, for the two countries were formerly under one king and shared the same religion. There is cultural proximity (language is mutually comprehensible between Norwegians and Swedes); the countries have a similar level of socioeconomic development; and their political systems—democratic, unitary, multi-party proportional representation, and welfare state—are also similar.

As the chapters in this section show, the number of countries available for comparison is much enlarged by making comparisons within a universe of countries that have one major characteristic in common. The characteristic can be geographical (Asia: see Inoguchi in this volume); political (democratic); social (high education); or economic (high mean national income). Expanding comparison to two dozen or more countries increases the likelihood of patterns emerging that are statistically reliable. While there may be half a dozen ways in which contextual differences can affect individual behavior, few would go so far as to argue that the configuration of contextual attributes in each of two dozen countries is so distinctive that it constitutes a unique and dominant determinant of individual political behavior.

The European Union provides a politically meaningful context for comparing individual behavior. Its twenty-seven member states are committed to common standards and policies in a variety of fields; government officials are constantly interacting in pan-European meetings; citizens of any country have freedom to travel and study in other countries; and all can vote in elections of the European Parliament. Moreover, the EU's own Eurobarometer survey conducts at least two surveys a year in which the same questions are asked of individuals in all twenty-seven member states of the EU (see **www.europa.eu/public_opinion**). Within the EU context, there are variations in national institutions and even more in national histories. The political socialization of individual citizens of long-established democracies has occurred in a different setting than that of individuals in the eight central and east European countries admitted to the European Union in 2004, who were socialized as subjects of a communist regime.

Modernization theories emphasize the achievement of a high level of socioeconomic development regardless of geography and history. In turn, a high level of economic well-being, education, and urbanization is expected to produce greater cross-national similarities in the behavior of individual citizens, because they are most exposed to "globalizing" (that is, homogenizing) influences (Lipset 1994). Arguably, modern citizens may also be more democratic, for example, because of their higher average level of education. The homogenizing effect of modernization on the political behavior of individuals independent of national context can be tested across four or more continents. If membership in the Organization for Economic Cooperation and Development (OECD) is treated as an indicator of being modern, then the behavior of citizens of Australia, Canada, Japan, Korea, and the United States should be similar to citizens of European countries.[2]

A single-country study can be conceived as a deviant case, examined in order to identify the causes of exceptions from a rule. Singapore can be considered a deviant case, because it is modern but not democratic; it offers a context for testing whether and how this regime is "buying" support from its subjects. My Northern Ireland survey of *Governing without Consensus* was conceived as a deviant case analysis not only within the context of the United Kingdom, but within that of established democracies (Rose 1971). India is the outstanding example of hundreds of millions of illiterate, impoverished, and rural residents participating in elections in a democratic political system.

Deviant case analysis raises a question: What is the norm used to establish deviation? This question is addressed in the literature of American exceptionalism. For Lipset (1996), the norm was a European society in which class politics is prominent, a reflection of his own upbringing in New York City as the offspring of east European immigrants. A further weakness of the American exceptionalism approach is that it assumes homogeneity between the great majority of European or OECD countries (Rose 1991). For Hartz (1955), America's exceptionalism arose from the absence of Europe's feudal history. For students of the American South, exceptionalism arose from the legacy of slavery and incomplete democratization until the federal Voting Rights Act of 1965 (Woodward 1955; Gonzalez and King 2004).

3 What to Study: Inputs, Outputs, and/or Values?

The study of political behavior is not confined to behavioral acts; it also includes examining predispositions, preferences, and values. Each element can be linked in a model that postulates political behavior is a consequence of preferences and predispositions and links both to values. However, each of these statements is probabilistic or contingent. For example, in a repressive regime behavior will reflect what the government wants rather than what individuals prefer and in a totalitarian regime opinions that subjects voice in public can be the opposite of what they think or say in private.

---

[2] The OECD's admission of two developing countries, Turkey and Mexico, is based on the presence there of a significant modern sector as well as developing and more traditional sectors, thus implying grounds for within-country comparisons. The membership of these countries not only reflects their aspirations for national development but also the OECD's desire to expand its scope and influence.

3.1 Political Behavior as Both Inputs and Outputs

The literature of political behavior is unbalanced. Research devotes the great bulk of attention to the inputs of citizens to government through voting and expressing opinions. The demands that government makes on its citizens to pay taxes and to conform with laws and the benefits that public policy provides to individuals and households tend to be neglected. Yet citizens spend more time receiving benefits of public policy and earning money to pay taxes than in voting or going to political meetings. To ignore this fact is to dissociate the study of political (*sic*) behavior from the study of government.

As the chapters in the section on participation document, most citizens have only a limited engagement in politics. While studies of voting are justifiable because of the importance of elections to government, it does not follow that voting is equally important to citizens. Consistently, empirical research shows that the majority of citizens are only voters. Broadening the definition of political behavior to include participation in all types of voluntary organizations increases the proportion who may be deemed to be engaged in politics. However, voluntary organizations such as sports clubs, hobby groups, and choirs do not recruit members on political grounds and the primary benefits they provide are for individual members (Olson 1965).

Politics is not an important part of the lives of most people. In the 2003 European Quality of Life Survey, family comes first: 98 percent say that it is important in their lives and more than nine-tenths of Europeans also regard work, friends, and leisure as important. By contrast, less than half consider politics as at least fairly important and only 11 percent regard it as very important (Rose 2006). Not only do most citizens of democratic systems give political activities a low priority but also many would prefer to leave the big decisions of government to elected representatives. The New Europe Barometer asked citizens in the eight central and east European countries admitted to the European Union in 2004 whether people like themselves or elected politicians should make the big decisions of government. Even though politicians are widely distrusted in the region, 68 percent wanted to leave the business of making major decisions to their representatives as against 32 percent wanting people like themselves to be involved (Rose 2005, 67; see also, Hibbing and Theiss-Morse 2001).

Ordinary people spend more time thinking about their health, their job, their pension, or their children's education than about how to vote. All of these concerns are directly affected by public policies both in European welfare states and in Anglo-American polities in which public, private, and not-for-profit provision of social services are interdependent. However, they are not thought of as "politics" in conventional studies of political behavior (for an exception, see Rose 1989; Kumlin in this volume).

The distinction between politics and policy is artificial, and exacerbated by English-language usage; in continental languages there is not the same contrast between "political" science and "policy" science (Heidenheimer 1986). Consistent with David Easton's (1965) model of a feedback between governors and governed, policy outputs of government that are inputs to the daily lives of ordinary people are also a form of political behavior. These outputs include health care, education, pension income, cash-transfer payments to the unemployed, mothers and the disabled, and housing subsidies. In economic terms, these benefits constitute private goods and services, since recipients could be excluded from them and they could be sold in the market. However, in political terms they are public benefits, because they are authorized by legislation, financed by taxes, and often delivered by public employees.

When behavioral analysis is extended to the outputs of government, then 83 percent of European households are annually involved in policy behavior, that is, the consumption of benefits authorized by legislation and funded by taxation (Figure 15.2). The percentage engaged in policy outputs is thus higher than those who have voted in the last national election. Moreover, policy engagement is much more immediately relevant and has a bigger impact on the life of an ordinary individual than does the indirect and notional effects of voting or attending the meeting of a political organization.

At any given point in time, the median European is the recipient of at least two major public policy benefits, for example, working in the public sector and having children in school, or being a pensioner and receiving health care. One-fifth receive three or more benefits (Figure 15.2). Only one in seven are momentarily in receipt of no benefits, being healthy, earning a good income in the private sector, and without children. If collective goods provided by public policies such as clean air and water are included as individual benefits, then everyone would be involved in politics with every breath of fresh air and every glass of water that they drink.

At some stage in the life cycle, virtually every individual will benefit from major policy outputs. Adult Europeans have already benefited from about a dozen years of

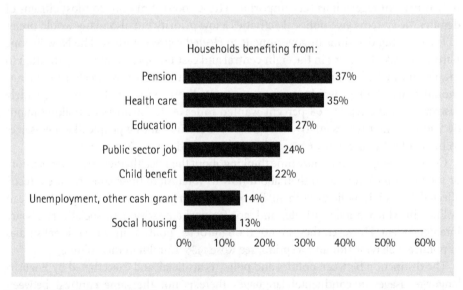

Fig. 15.2 Participation in policy outputs

Source: Percentages based on replies to 2003 European Quality of Life Survey (Dublin: European Foundation for Living and Working Conditions; number of respondents 27,008) with national results weighted to each country's share of the total population of 28 countries. Health care calculated as those with poor or not very good health or having a disability.

education. While most adults do not go to hospital each year and many do not see a doctor, about one-third do have a major need for health care during the year and in the course of a few years, the overwhelming majority of adults use their country's national health service. Government is a major source of income in three different ways: it provides cash benefits for pensioners, the unemployed, and the disabled because they are outside the labour force; it employs a significant fraction of the labour force to deliver public services; and it also provides supplementary cash benefits for child care and for social housing.

3.2 Do World Values Exist?

Whereas behavior is an overt act, values are mental constructs. Values constitute belief systems that are relevant to understanding how individuals view their world, including government. However, many values, for example, about family and child-rearing, relate to contexts remote from politics. Even if people hold values that are politically relevant, most people do not engage in political activities that could advance these values. Even if they did, the connection between individual values and public policy is contingent and remote, since individual values are aggregated in a great variety of intermediary organizations and then input to a policy-making process in which decisions are usually arrived at by bargaining or even by a garbage-can process.

The comparative study of values in Europe was initiated in 1978 by a group of Catholic-oriented sociologists forming the European Value Systems Study Group. Its first survey covered two dozen countries; results were reported in French by Jean Stoetzel (1983) and in English (Harding et al. 1986). The study examined values in the broadest sense, ranging from politics to family life, morality, and religion. A second wave was carried out in 1990, and included the United States and Canada (Ester, Halman, and de Moor 1993; de Moor 1995); a third wave occurred in 1999–2000 (Halman 2001). Ronald Inglehart then initiated a World Values Survey (WVS), which first fielded in 1981, and in 2005 commenced its fifth round of surveys extending to more than seventy-five countries (**www.worldvaluessurvey.com**).

The World Values Survey is a major source of cross-national comparative and trend data. As its name emphasizes, its questionnaire covers a broad range of politically relevant values. Ironically, much of Inglehart's publications have aggregated individual responses into national means, and then aggregated national means into cross-national clusters of cultures (see Inglehart 1997; chapter in this volume). This has produced an Inglehart Values Map of the world (**www.worldvaluessurvey. com/library/index.html**) with eight different clusters characterized principally by religion or geography, such as Protestant Europe and Confucian countries. Seligson (2002) has questioned whether the result is "The Renaissance of Political Culture or the Renaissance of the Ecological Fallacy?" (for a reply, see Inglehart and Welzel 2003; see also Inglehart and Welzel chapters in this volume).

The WVS questionnaire has favored consistency in questions across diverse societies so that cross-national comparisons can be made within each survey. This assumes that there is substantial cross-continental commonality in what constitutes national values to make it meaningful to field a common questionnaire. However, this may produce "an illusory appearance of comparability" (Heath et al. 2005, 321). Assuming that questions suitable in the United States and Europe will be equally suitable for interviewing respondents in many different continents and national contexts risks conceptual overstretch. As Canache, Mondak, and Seligson (2001) have shown, the meaning of a question about satisfaction with democracy can be confusing or problematic between and even within countries. This is consistent with Philip Converse's (1964) caution that asking questions that respondents do not understand or have no interest in can create "non-attitudes."

While social indicators such as education or income may be conceptually uniform, their application in cross-national research becomes problematic. National education systems differ in the minimum number of years of compulsory education; in the types of schools attended and in the certificates that pupils receive. American categories are atypical of educational qualifications in most of the world. Thus, any standardized cross-national indicator of education can only be approximate. Incomes may be compared according to a standard unit of currency (e.g. a US dollar subject to foreign exchange fluctuations); by adjusting currencies for purchasing power parity; or by calculating an individual's position within a national income distribution to assign individuals to high-, medium- and low-income-groups within a society.

The logical implication of expanding research into national contexts that vary as greatly as Asian, African, and Middle East countries is to increase the need to contextualize research by altering or adding questions to take into account the greater differences in context. For example, the meaning of a left–right scale can become problematic (see Mair's contribution to this volume). Not to adapt questionnaires to context risks omitting information that is contextually critical, For example, the fact that regime change cannot be studied in long-established democracies is not a reason for ignoring its impact on political behavior when conducting surveys in post-communist countries, where regime change does occur (Rose, Mishler, and Haerpfer 1998). To ignore such phenomena replaces the minor problem of missing data with the major problem of missing concepts.[3]

If the attitudes of individuals are to influence macropolitical institutions, they must be aggregated into a macro-construct such as political culture. Otherwise, there is no connection between individual values and what governments do. However, as Dieter Fuchs shows in his contribution to this section, there are fundamental problems in aggregating values of individuals into a macropolitical culture. The aggregation of individual opinions, whether on the basis of a dominant tendency (e.g. democratic) or showing a distribution between postmaterialists and others,

---

[3] The same problem faces national income economists in developing countries when they attempt to account for economic behavior by focusing exclusively on economic activities that are officially recorded by national governments in accord with international procedures for measuring gross domestic product. However, the less modern an economy, the greater the volume of economic activity that is omitted, because it takes place as unrecorded cash-in-hand transactions and within the household without any money changing hands (see e.g. Rose 2002a; Thomas 2003).

creates an analytic construct, but such an abstract concept is not, *ipso facto*, a positive causal force. To treat democratic values of individuals as a reified political culture and make it tantamount to a democratic political regime goes further: it leaves out political institutions and the state.

4 Bringing Societies back in

Given the intensity with which political behavior is being analyzed in a single time and place, greater gains in the foreseeable future are more likely to come from broadening research by bringing societies back in. Doing so is the only way to test the universalist assumption that individual behavior is unaffected by national context. Cross-national analysis turns a context that is a constant for respondents of a single survey into a variable. Thus, it becomes possible to test under what circumstances and to what extent findings about individual behavior are or are not affected by differences in space and time. Just as the subjects of behavioral research are expected to calculate according to bounded rationality (Simon 1979), so those who study them should think in terms of bounded generalizability.

Data are no longer a limitation for testing the generalizability of propositions about political behavior. Surveys of political behavior are now available for half the countries in the world with a population of a million or more (Heath, Fisher, and Smith 2005). Moreover, the global expansion of survey research has produced data from many different types of countries, whether differences are defined in political terms (the People's Republic of China and Sweden) or economic terms (India and the United States); or socialization (East and West Germany). Moreover, surveys now cover a span of up to half a century. It is no longer necessary to treat any one national election as typical: such an assumption can be tested empirically and the cumulative influence of the passage of time can be tested over generations. Nor is it necessary to speculate about the development of attitudes in new democracies. Whereas the first wave of democratization occurred more than a century before survey research, the third wave of democratization came after the institutionalization of survey research.

Comparable questions can be found in many national surveys, reflecting a predisposition of researchers to replicate what their peers have already published. In mature social science communities, path dependence can explain the persistence of standard questions across time as a necessary condition of maintaining a time series. In smaller countries and in countries entering survey research later, there is also a readiness to seek integration in "big" political science research. It is also safe to do so, for the professional weight given cross-national replication is much stronger than the encouragement to innovate by asking questions about unfamiliar topics such as participation in policy outputs.

High-speed computers make it easy to analyze multinational data sets with tens of thousands of respondents and statistical methods of multi-level modelling provide the means to apportion variance in individual behavior between differences in individual attributes and contextual attributes, whether context is defined in terms of space or time. This is a boon for contemporary comparative research. Aristotle did not have a computer when he wrote the analysis of politics that inspired Marty Lipset (1960, 7), and Lipset wrote *Political Man* with only a counter-sorter and Juan Linz.

The ideal research project would analyze national surveys of individuals in multiple countries and different temporal contexts. However, the greater the diversity of countries in the data set, the greater the demands for contextual knowledge and the greater the risk that nominally identical questions do not have the same significance in different places. Just as Robert Merton (1957) invoked theories of the middle way, so a span of space and time need not be maximalist—as long as it contains enough variations to provide a robust test of generic hypotheses. In any event, it is self-defeating to stipulate that a maximalist ideal should also be the minimum that is acceptable.

All research involves inclusion *and* exclusion: some things are the focus of research and lots must be left out. The contemporary tendency of social scientists to publish journal articles rather than books greatly reduces the space to include important dimensions of a problem. However, such a limitation is not an adequate justification for totally ignoring time and space. A journal article that is expected to include detailed discussions of samples and of statistical methods should make space for succinct statements about the temporal and spatial context of the research and how this may affect the generalizability of its findings to other times and places. To omit such a consideration buries the influence of time and space on political behavior within the error term.

Cumulative advances in knowledge across space and time require reintegrating political behavior in the social sciences in order to create a political science field that is both psychological *and* sociological. Doing so will return the subject to the interdisciplinary discourse from which it emerged, for the progenitors of political behavior research were not only political scientists but also sociologists (Paul Lazarsfeld, S. M. Lipset, and Stein Rokkan), social psychologists (Philip Converse), and institutionalists (V. O. Key). Many had an excellent grounding in comparative history too (e.g. Gabriel Almond and Rokkan). If cumulative progress is to be made, it will be made by standing on the shoulders of such giants. This is best done by standing on two legs, one reflecting specialist knowledge of individual behavior, and the second reflecting the influences of space and time.

REFERENCES

ALMOND, G., and COLEMAN, J. 1960. *The Politics of Developing Areas*. Princeton: Princeton University Press.
—— and VERBA, S. 1963. *The Civic Culture*. Princeton: Princeton University Press.
—— —— eds. 1980. *The Civic Culture Revisited: An Analytical Study*. Boston: Little, Brown.
BAKER, K., DALTON, R., and HILDEBRANDT, K. 1981. *Germany Transformed: Political Culture and the New Politics*. Cambridge, Mass.: Harvard University Press.

BARTOLINI, S., and MAIR, P. 1990. *Identity, Competition and Electoral Availability: The Stabilisation of European Democracy, 1885–1985*. Cambridge: Cambridge University Press.

BAUMGARTNER, F., and JONES, B. 1993. *Agendas and Instability in American Politics*. Chicago: University of Chicago Press.

BELL, D. 1974. *The Coming of Post-Industrial Society*. New York: Basic Books.

BOLLEN, K. 1990. Political democracy: conceptual and measurement traps. *Studies in Comparative International Development*, 25: 7–24.

BUTLER, D., and STOKES, D. 1970. *Political Change in Britain*, 2nd edn. London: Macmillan.

CAMPBELL, A., CONVERSE, P., MILLER, W., and STOKES, D. 1960. *The American Voter*. New York: John Wiley.

CANACHE, D., MONDAK, J., and SELIGSON, M. 2001. Meaning and measurement in cross-national research on satisfaction with democracy. *Public Opinion Quarterly*, 65: 506–28.

CONVERSE, P. 1964. The nature of belief systems in mass publics. Pp. 206–61 in *Ideology and Discontent*, ed. D. Apter New York: Free Press.

DALTON, R. 2006. *Citizen Politics: Public Opinion and Parties in Advanced Industrial Democracies*. Washington, DC: CQ Press.

DOGAN, M., and PELASSY, D. 1990. *How to Compare Nations*, 2nd edn. Chatham, NJ: Chatham House.

EASTON, D. 1965. *A Framework for Political Analysis*. Englewood Cliffs, NJ: Prentice-Hall.

ESTER, P., HALMAN, L., and MOOR, R. 1993. *The Individualizing Society: Value Change in Europe and Northern America*. Tilburg: Tilburg University Press.

FALTER, J. 1991. *Hitlers Wähler*. Munich: C. H. Beck.

FINER, S. 1997. *The History of Government*, 3 vols. Oxford: Oxford University Press.

GONZALEZ, F., and KING, D. 2004. The state and democratization: the United States in comparative perspective. *British Journal of Political Science*, 34: 193–210.

GUNTHER, R., SANI, G., and SHABAD, G. 1988. *Spain after Franco: The Making of a Competitive Party System*. Berkeley: University of California Press, revised edition.

HALMAN, L. 2001. *The European Values Study: A Third Wave Source Book of the 1999/2000 European Values Study Surveys*. Tilburg: Tilburg University Press.

HARDING, S., PHILIPS, D., and FOGARTY, M. 1986. *Contrasting Values in Western Europe*. London: Macmillan.

HARTZ, L. 1955. *The Liberal Tradition in America*. New York: Harcourt, Brace.

HEATH, A., FISHER, S., and SMITH, S. 2005. The Globalization of Public Opinion Research. *Annual Review of Political Science*, 8: 297–333.

HEIDENHEIMER, A. 1986. Politics policy and policy as concepts in English and continental languages. *Review of Politics*, 48: 3–30.

HIBBING, J., and THEISS-MORSE, E. eds. 2001. *What is it about Government that Americans Dislike?* New York: Cambridge University Press.

HUNTINGTON, S. 1996. *The Clash of Civilizations and the Remaking of World Order*. New York: Simon & Schuster.

INGLEHART, R. 1997. *Modernization and Postmodernization*. Princeton: Princeton University Press.

—— and WELZEL, C. 2003. Democratic institutions and political culture: misconceptions in addressing the ecological fallacy. *Comparative Politics*, 36: 61–80.

INKELES, A. 1983. *Becoming Modern*. New York: Columbia University Press.

LERNER, D. 1958. *The Passing of Traditional Society*. Glencoe, Ill: Free Press.

LINZ, J. 1959. The social bases of West German politics. New York: Columbia University Ph.D. dissertation in sociology.

—— 1990. Transitions to democracy. *Washington Quarterly* (Summer), 143–64.

LIPSET, S. M. 1960. *Political Man*. New York: Doubleday.

—— 1994. The social requisites of democracy revisited. *American Sociological Review*, 59 (1): 1–22.

—— 1996. *American Exceptionalism: A Double-Edged Sword*. New York: W.W. Norton.

—— and ROKKAN, S. eds. 1967. *Party Systems and Voter Alignments*. New York: Free Press.

LUKE, D. 2004. *Multi-Level Modelling*. London: Sage Publications Quantitative Applications in the Social Sciences 07–143.

McDONOUGH, P., BARNES, S., and LOPEZ PINA, A. 1988. *The Cultural Dynamics of Democratization in Spain*. Ithaca, NY: Cornell University Press.

MERTON, R. 1957. *Social Structure and Social Theory*. Glencoe, Ill.: The Free Press, revised and enlarged edition.

MISHLER, W., and ROSE, R. 2006. Generation, age and time: the dynamics of political learning during Russia's transformation. Aberdeen: CSPP Studies in Public Policy No. 412.

MOOR, R. DE ed. 1995. *Values in Western Societies*. Tilburg: Tilburg University Press.

MUNCK, G., and VERHUILEN, J. 2002. Conceptualizing and measuring democracy: evaluating alternative indices. *Comparative Political Studies*, 35: 5–34.

NOELLE-NEUMANN, E. 1995. Juan Linz's doctoral dissertation forty years later. In *Politics, Society and Democracy*, vol. ii, ed. H. E. Chehabi and A. Stepan Boulder, Colo.: Westview Press.

OLSON, M. 1965. *The Logic of Collective Action: Public Goods and the Theory of Groups*. Cambridge, Mass.: Harvard University Press.

PIERSON, P. 2004. *Politics in Time: History, Institutions and Social Analysis*. Princeton: Princeton University Press.

PRESSMAN, J., and WILDAVSKY, A. 1973. *Implementation*. Berkeley: University of California Press.

PYE, L. 1962. *Politics, Personality and Nation Building*. New Haven: Yale University Press.

—— and VERBA, S. eds., 1965. *Political Culture and Political Development*. Princeton: Princeton University Press.

RAUDENBUSH, S., and BRYK, A. 2002. *Hierarchical Linear Modelling: Applications and Data Analysis Methods*, 2nd edn. Thousand Oaks, Calif.: Sage Publications Advanced Quantitative Techniques in the Social Sciences.

REISINGER, W. 1995. The renaissance of a rubric: political culture as concept and theory. *International Journal of Public Opinion Research*, 7: 285–96.

ROBINSON, J. 1979. History versus equilibrium. *Collected Economic Papers of Joan Robinson*, vol. v. Oxford: Oxford University Press.

ROBINSON, W. 1950. Ecological correlations and the behavior of individuals. *American Sociological Review*, 15: 350–7.

ROSE, R. 1971. *Governing without Consensus: An Irish Perspective*. London: Faber & Faber.

—— 1989. *Ordinary People In Public Policy*. London: Sage Publications.

—— 1991. Is American public policy exceptional? Pp. 187–229 in *Is America Different?*, ed. B. Shafer. New York: Oxford University Press.

—— 1995. Aaron Wildavsky: Ein Mensch für die Ganze Welt. In *Budgeting, Policy, Politics: An Appreciation of Aaron Wildavsky*, ed. N. Caiden and J. White. New Brunswick, NJ: Transaction Publishers.

—— 2002*a*. How Muslims view democracy: a Central Asian perspective. *Journal of Democracy*, 13: 102–11.

—— 2002*b*. Economies in transformation: a multidimensional approach to a cross-cultural problem. *East European Constitutional Review*, 11: 62–70.

—— 2005. *Insiders and Outsiders: New Europe Barometer 2004*. Glasgow: Centre for the Study of Public Policy Studies in Public Policy No. 404.

—— 2006. *Participation in Civil Society: A European Society Approach.* Dublin: European Foundation for Living and Working Conditions.

—— MISHLER, W., and HAERPFER, C. 1998. *Democracy and its Alternatives: Understanding Post-Communist Societies.* Oxford: Polity Press and Baltimore: Johns Hopkins University Press.

—— —— and MUNRO, N. 2006. *Russia Transformed: Developing Popular Support for a New Regime.* Cambridge: Cambridge University Press.

SCHEUCH, E. 1966. Cross-national comparisons using aggregate data: some substantive and methodological problems. Pp. 131–67 in *Comparing Nations,* ed. R. Merritt and S. Rokken. New Haven: Yale University Press.

SCHUMPETER, J. 1946. The American economy in the interwar years. *American Economic Review,* 36: 1–10.

SCOTT, J. 1985. *Weapons of the Weak: Everyday Forms of Peasant Resistance.* New Haven: Yale University Press.

SELIGSON, M. 2002. The renaissance of political culture or the renaissance of the ecological fallacy? *Comparative Politics,* 34: 273–92.

SEWELL, W. 1996. Three temporalities: toward an eventful sociology. Pp. 245–80 in *The Historic Turn in the Human Sciences,* ed. T. McDonald. Ann Arbor: University of Michigan Press.

SHLAPENTOKH, V. 2001. *A Normal Totalitarian Society: How the Soviet Union Functioned and How It Collapsed.* Armonk, NY: M. E. Sharpe.

SIMON, H. 1979. Rational decision making in business organizations. *American Economic Review,* 69: 493–513.

STEENBERGEN, M., and JONES, B. 2002. Modelling multilevel data structures. *American Journal of Political Science,* 46: 218–37.

STOETZEL, J. 1983. *Les Valeurs du temps présent.* Paris: Presses Universitaires de France.

THOMAS, J. 2003. Quantifying the black economy: "measurement with theory" Yet Again? *Economic Journal,* 109 (456): 381–9.

VANHANEN, T. 2003. *Democratization: A Comparative Review of 170 Countries.* London: Routledge.

WALD, K. 1983. *Crosses on the Ballot: Patterns of British Voter Alignment since 1885.* Princeton: Princeton University Press.

WEIL, F. 1987. Cohorts, regimes, and the legitimation of democracy: West Germany since 1945. *American Sociological Review,* 52: 308–24.

WOODWARD, C. 1955. *The Strange Career of Jim Crow.* New York: Oxford University Press.

YOUNG, P. 1998. *Individual Strategy and Social Structure: An Evolutionary Theory of Institutions.* Princeton: Princeton University Press.

PART IV

POLITICAL VALUES

PART IX

POLITICAL VALUES

CHAPTER 16

....

POLITICAL VALUES

....

LOEK HALMAN

THE empirical study of political values has gained momentum since Almond and Verba's (1963) seminal study on the *Civic Culture*. They introduced the concept of political culture to understand various political systems. They argued that in addition to the institutional and constitutional features of political systems, the political orientations of the individuals who constitute the political system are also relevant. Up to then, students of politics were mainly concerned "with the structure and function of political systems, institutions, and agencies, and their effects on public policy" (Almond and Verba 1963, 31).

Almond and Verba's pioneering work redirected empirical enquiry from an exclusive preoccupation with institutions and structure and their concept of political culture bridged the gap between macro-level politics and micro-politics. "We would like to suggest that this relationship between attitudes and motivations of the discrete individuals who make up the political systems and the character and performance of political systems may be discovered systematically through concepts of political culture" (Almond and Verba 1963, 32). The concept of political culture refers to "a particular pattern of orientations to political actions" (Pye 1973, 65–6), and these orientations have major implications for the "way the political system operates—to its stability, effectiveness and so forth" (Almond and Verba 1963, 74). Carol Pateman (1980) criticized this assumed relationship between people's orientations and political outcomes, arguing that it remained unclear how the values of people should affect the political system. Indeed, as Barry (1978) pointed out, political culture may better be viewed as the effect and not as the cause of political processes. A correlation between civic culture attitudes and democracy does not say anything about the causal chain. The presumption that a civic culture is conducive to democracy can also be interpreted the other way around, but such a conclusion would be less exiting, namely that "'democracy' produces the 'civic culture'" (Barry 1978, 51–2).

However, Almond and Verba did not consider political culture as determining political structure, but they regarded them as interconnected, mutually dependent, and dynamically interacting. "Political culture is treated as both an independent and a dependent variable, as causing and as being caused by it" (Almond 1980, 29). Beliefs, feelings, and values are the product as well as the cause of a political system.

The *Civic Culture* was one of the first empirical studies using the recently developed research technology "of sample surveys, which led to a much sharper specification and elaboration of the subjective dimensions of stable democratic politics" (Almond 1980, 22). For the first time in history it was possible to "establish whether there were indeed distinctive nation 'marks' and national characters; whether and in what respects and degrees nations were divided into distinctive subcultures; whether social class, functional groups, and specific elites had distinctive orientations towards politics and public policy, and what role was played by what socialization agents in the development of these orientations" (Almond 1980, 15).

The rise of the political culture concept during the 1950s and 1960s was part of the more general ascension of the idea that culture is a prominent explanatory power in the social sciences and history. "Culture was given causal efficacy as well as being caused and political culture...acquired the same traits" (Formisano 2001, 397 quoting Berkhofer). As such, the recent emphasis on the importance of the cultural factor, and the growing awareness that culture in general and values in particular play an important role in human life is far from new. The idea that culture matters was prominent in Weber's intriguing work on the *Protestant Ethic and the Spirit of Capitalism* more than a century ago and earlier, de Tocqueville wrote about the importance of culture in his *Democracy in America*. During the 1940–50s, a rich literature was developed by scholars like Mead, Benedict, McCelland, Banfield, Inkeles, and Lipset, who regarded culture as "a crucial element in understanding societies, analyzing differences among them, and explaining their economic and political development" (Huntington 2000, xiv).

However, during the 1960s and 1970s, interest in culture as a determining factor declined and rational choice theories became dominant. Following the logic of economics, social phenomena were explained as the result of rational calculations made by self-interested individuals who aim at maximizing their own individual utility. Such theories claim that people anticipate the outcomes of alternative courses of action and then decide which of these alternatives will yield the best outcome for them. People choose the alternative that is likely to produce the greatest satisfaction.

In more recent years, interest in the cultural factor rose again, not in the last place because rational choice models appeared to have limited explanatory power, for example, to understand collective action (why do individuals join many groups and associations?), or to understand the survival of social norms such as altruism, reciprocity, and trust. Apparently people are not driven by a narrowly conceived self-interest and thus are not purely rationally calculating and maximizing their own interests. The renaissance of culture as an important factor and the rediscovery of the cultural approach to politics can be seen as a way of counterbalancing the rational choice approach that dominated the sixties and seventies (Lane and Ersson 2005, 2).

The cultural factor was also rediscovered because of the failure of economic factors to explain cross-cultural differences and the differential trajectories of cultural changes over time. As Inglehart (1988, 1203) noted, "there is no question that economic factors are politically important, but they are only part of the story." He referred to the importance of political attitudes, beliefs, orientations, preferences, and priorities that "have major political consequences, being closely linked to the viability of democratic institutions". Culture was again regarded as an important source in human life and treated as a powerful active agent. As a proponent of this view, Wildavsky argued that people's basic orientations, their preferences, beliefs, and interests in particular should be taken into account. He stated, "I wish to make *what people want* [his italics]—their desires, preferences, values, ideals—into the central subject of our inquiry" because preferences "in regard to political objects are not external to political life; on the contrary, they constitute the very internal essence, the quintessence of politics: the construction and reconstruction of our lives together" (Wildavsky 1987, 5).

The unexpected and rapid collapse of communist or socialist authoritarian regimes in central and eastern European countries and the rash unification of both Germanies have further triggered the idea that culture really matters. These events marked the end of the "Cold War" and evoked new or renewed contacts and relationships between East and West. Above all they "have drawn attention to the way regimes legitimate themselves and the way citizens identify themselves, both processes which suggest an important mediating role for culture" (Street 1994, 96). Salient examples in this respect are of course the dramatic events that took place in Yugoslavia and many of the former Soviet countries. Such events are a sad illustration of what can happen when hidden forces and large differences in values within the collective consciousness of people explode into hatred and violence.

The importance of the cultural factor has also been demonstrated more recently in the European process of unification. The integration of nation-states into one Europe has mainly been confined to the political and economic dimensions and this process is not welcomed with great enthusiasm by all Europeans. As soon as the cultural dimension is included, citizens become more reluctant regarding their support for Europe and the European ideal. Many people fear that a further European integration beyond economic and political cooperation undermines the role of the nation-state and that "national" identities, habits, and cultures will slowly disappear. Recent analyses of data collected within the framework of the European Values Study suggest, however, that Europe is far from a cultural unity. European unity appears to be a unity of diversity. There remain significant differences in the basic value orientations of the Europeans (Arts, Hagenaars, and Halman 2003; Arts and Halman 2004; Halman, Luijkx, and Van Zundert 2005). So it will be a demanding task of European leaders to ensure that the European project is in harmony with and reflection of the values of European citizens. That the European project is endangered from this cultural diversity is recognized. Recently, the President of the European Commission installed a reflection group on the Spiritual and Cultural Dimension of Europe. In their concluding remarks this group writes that "because an economic order never evolves in a value-free environment . . . an effective and just economic order must also be embedded in the morals, customs, and expectations of human beings, as well as in their social institutions. So the manner in which the larger European economic area—the common market—is in harmony with the values of European citizens, as varied as these may be, is no mere academic problem; it is a fundamental and political one" (Biedenkopf, Geremek, and Michalski 2004, 7).

The discussion on values is also triggered by the recent influx of migrant minorities and the multicultural society that is developing in many advanced industrial societies. These provoked in many European countries an open debate on the consequences of value diversity and what exactly comprises the cultural entity and identity of nation-states. Also, the disappearance of internal borders between European Union member states, the demise of communism in the east, and the enlargement and further integration of the European Union in the center and the west have put the issues of identity and the survival of national cultures high on the European agenda. The European project seems to have awakened nationalistic sentiments and movements from their slumber and massive migration waves into Europe seem to have triggered exclusionist reactions toward new cultural and ethnic minorities and increased intercultural and interethnic conflict.

Apart from this, globalization of society makes sometimes painfully clear that people around the globe are not the same and adhere to very distinct values. Cultural conflicts over basic human values are frequently in the news and seem to confirm what Huntington predicted in his *Clash of Civilizations.* Major dividing lines in the contemporary world are defined by culture and no longer by ideological, economic, and political features. "In the post-Cold War world, the most important distinctions among peoples are not ideological, political, or economic. They are cultural... The most important groupings of states are no longer the three blocs of the Cold War but rather the world's seven or eight major civilizations" (Huntington 1996, 21).

The discussion of values is often fuelled by a growing preoccupation with the decline of values, in particular those values that make us good citizens and make society and human life good. "Widespread feelings of social mistrust, citizens turning away from prime institutions and political authorities, and engaging less in informal interactions are seen as indicators of the decline of the traditional civic ethic" (Ester, Mohler, and Vinken 2006: 17; Bellah et al. 1992; Etzioni 1996; 2001; Fukuyama 2000; Putnam 2000; 2002). In the current, sometimes heated, debate, the discussion is not so much on the decline of values as such, but more on the decline of decent, (pro-) social behavior. Many politicians and society watchers claim that a growing number of citizens is indifferent and skeptical about politics, and too narrowly focused on pure self-interest. They consider this a severe threat for respect for human rights and human dignity, liberty, equality, and solidarity. In their view, the "good" values have declined or have even vanished and the wrong, "bad" values triumph in today's highly individualized society.

Major causes for this decline are found in modernization processes of individualization, secularization, and globalization that are assumed to have had severe consequences for the values, preferences, beliefs, and ideas that people adhere to. It is also in this vein that we look at political values and will decide on what old and new political values are. But before we enter into that discussion, it seems necessary to shed some light on the concept of values, for it remains unclear what values are. Therefore we start our discussion on old and new values with a short introduction of the concept of values in general and political values in particular.

1 WHAT ARE VALUES AND WHAT ARE POLITICAL VALUES?

Since little theory has developed on values (Dietz and Stern 1995, 264), the concept is not very clear. It is more or less a commonplace to state that values are hard to define properly. The sociological and psychological literature on the subject reveals a terminological jungle. To a large extent, this conceptual confusion is grounded in the nature of values. One obvious problem in (social) research is that values can only be postulated or inferred, because values, as such, are not visible or measurable directly. As a consequence, a value is a more or less open concept. There is no empirically grounded theory of values, which stimulated efforts to distinguish values from closely-related concepts like attitudes, beliefs, opinions and and other orientations. The common notion, however, is that values are somehow more basic or more existential than these related concepts. Attitudes, for example, are considered to refer to a more restricted complex of objects and/or behaviors than values (Reich and Adcock 1976, 20). This type of theoretical argument assumes a more or less hierarchical structure in which values are more basic than attitudes. "A value is seen to be a disposition of a person just like an attitude, but more basic than an attitude, often underlying it" (Rokeach 1968, 124). The same applies to the relations between values and theoretical concepts such as norms, beliefs, opinions, and so on. Most social scientists agree that values are deeply rooted motivations or orientations guiding or explaining certain attitudes, norms, and opinions which, in turn, direct human action or at least part of it. Adhering to a specific value constitutes a disposition, or a propensity to act in a certain way (Halman 1991, 27; Ester, Mohler, and Vinken 2006, 7; van Deth and Scarbrough 1995). Such a definition of values is a functional one and although it is more a description of what values *do* rather than what they actually *are*, it enables us to measure values as latent constructs, that can be observed indirectly, that is, in the way in which people evaluate states, activities, or outcomes.

Having made clear what values are, we need to define political values. Rokeach (1973, 25) argued that values can be classified in domains or institutional spheres. Accordingly, political values can be defined as the category of values that pertain to the political sphere. In line with our values concept, political values can be seen as the foundations of people's political behaviors such as voting and/or protesting or as Almond and Verba (1963) indicated, political values are people's orientations towards political objects. Hence, the individual's concrete political behavior can (at least partly) be explained from his or her political values or orientations. Thus, political values can be seen as perceptions of a desirable order (van Deth 1984), and determining "whether a political situation or a political event is experienced as favorable or unfavorable, good or bad" (Inglehart and Klingemann 1979, 207). Political values enable us to make political judgments.

2 OLD AND NEW?

It is not easy to decide what is old and new when it comes to values. If "old" means that certain values have been emphasized in the past, while "new" refers to the values that have more recently gained prominence, it remains a question if such a qualification makes sense. Old in the sense that in the past certain values were investigated does not mean that other values or orientations did not exist at that moment in time. It may simply mean that these other orientations were not an object of study because no one was interested in these orientations while in more contemporary settings such values have drawn attention and have become fashionable to focus on. For instance, a popular theme nowadays is sustainable development and many studies focus on issues of pollution, saving energy, climate changes, or water management. In times that the environment becomes an important issue, for whatever reason, environmental values come to the fore.

The distinction between old and new may be seen in terms of former versus contemporary, or in terms of traditional versus modern. Former values are those that have been recognized and focused on in the past, while "new" refers to orientations that have been identified recently and that dominate the current discourse. In that sense, "old" does not necessarily imply old and forgotten, but "old" would mean that these values have lost attention or have become less attractive to focus on, while "new" would apply to those values that match the emerging new issues and phenomena in contemporary society.

However, "old" and "new" in the sense of traditional versus modern may be understood in terms of changing values and shifting value adherences among populations. These value changes are linked to significant transformations of economic and social structures and the idea is that the values that prevailed during feudalism are not the same as those associated with industrialism or post-industrialism. In such a view, the distinction between old and new is connected with the themes of modernization and post-modernization. The traditional orientations stressing security, order, respect for authority, and conformity are considered to slowly shifting away whereas values stressing personal autonomy, individual freedom, self-fulfillment, independence, and emancipation are assumed to be on the the rise (Inglehart 1977, 1990, 1997; van Deth 1995).

Certain political values may turn out to be more resistant than others and have not vanished. Thus, in the *Civic Culture*, Almond and Verba identified a number of democratic attitudes that were already identified as important by de Tocqueville, and that are considered (again or still) highly relevant today. Such attitudes of trust, political partisanship, and societal involvement are key concepts of what is recognized as social capital, a notion that regained prominence since the recent works of Putnam, Fukuyama, and others.

3 OLD POLITICAL VALUES?

Since the Enlightenment, liberalism was one of the dominant political forces. Social-ism and social democracy are the two other classical ideological schools of thought which have dominated social and political behaviors of people and politics (see also Rush 1992, 190). Classic themes in politics are of course freedom versus authoritar-ianism, equality versus inequality, the cleavage of labor and capital in society in general, and the class conflict in particular. It has become more or less common practice to classify political opinions on these issues in terms of left and right. The concepts of left and right are "generally seen as instruments that citizens can use to orient themselves in a complex political world" (Fuchs and Klingemann 1989, 203); they "summarize one's stands on the important political issues of the day. It serves the function of organizing and simplifying a complex political reality, providing an overall orientation toward a potentially limitless number of issues, political parties, and social groups. The pervasive use of the Left–Right concept throughout the years in Western political discourse testifies to its usefulness" (Inglehart 1990, 292–3).

In the beginning left and right referred to the distinction between "the clergy (right) and the nobility (left)" (Nevitte and Gibbins 1990, 29). With industrialization, the left–right continuum became associated with the cleavage of labor and capital in general and the class conflict in particular and the core issue in the left–right distinction became equality (Bobbio 1996, 60). Left represents the part of society that stresses greater equality, whereas right is supportive of a "more or less hierarchical social order, and opposing change toward greater equality" (Lipset et al. 1954, 1135). Both notions became increasingly associated with issues like the (re-) distribution of income and wealth and the role of the government in the economy and society. "Left" favors a more just distribution of income and wealth and welcomes state intervention to achieve this, while "right" stresses the principles of a free market economy and independent individuals, and thus strongly favors a reduction of state control. Such cleavages between left and right are still highly relevant in today's society.

The polarization between left and right not only applies to political conflicts; the different outlooks also appear in all kinds of social, moral, and ethical issues, like abortion, euthanasia, nuclear energy, etc. Particularly the development of modern welfare states resulted in a growing number of social issues that are interpreted in terms of the left and right polarity, despite the fact that these issues are not associated with the traditional class conflicts. Issues like the quality of life, environment, nuclear energy, disarmament, foreigners, asylum seekers, and various moral issues have become important topics where left and right express fundamentally different views. Left is regarded to take the sides of the poor, the disadvantaged, the deprived, and minority groups; they are most concerned about the environment and opposed to nuclear energy and arms, and in moral issues left represents the liberal stances. Right is commonly seen as more restrictive and in favor of traditional standpoints. They are the strongest proponents of authority, order, maintaining the status quo, and a strong moral society.

Knutsen argues that the basic conflicts embedded in what he called old left–right were economic in nature, "referring in particular to the role of government in the economy" (Knutsen 1995, 161; 2006, 115). These emerged particularly in industrial society. The main conflict centered around state control and improving equality versus freedom of enterprise and individual achievement. New dividing lines circle around conflicts emerging from advanced industrial and post-industrial society and relate to conflicts between conservative moral and social beliefs versus individual and social freedom (King 1987; Levitas 1986; Knutsen 1995; 2006).

Thus, also with regard to contemporary controversial issues, the left–right schema appears a useful tool to classify people's opinions. However, the left–right distinction is increasingly understood in terms of progressive versus conservative. For example, political parties, their adherents are often described in terms of left–right distinctions. It seems that an "old" concept has survived and can still be applied in contemporary society. In fact, the terms left and right remained popular in political discourse and in the mass media, but in political studies the interest in this left–right dimension appears to have declined.

4 NEW POLITICAL VALUES?

The main reason for the decreased interest in the left–right schema is the claim that a large number of new phenomena cannot be fitted into the ideological struggle between left and right. New issues have emerged on the political agenda and "the simple concepts 'left' and 'right' are too general for analyzing change in value orientations as between industrial and advanced industrial society" (van Deth 1995, 10). Energy, the Cold War, the collapse of communism, the environment, sustainable development, welfare state, the European unification, globalization and internationalization, gay rights, equality for women, international migration, flows of refugees, became topics that increasingly needed serious attention, often resulting in new cleavages: the struggle between the sexes (men against women), active versus inactive people, the division of rich and poor countries, natives versus (im)migrants. These new topics that attracted widespread attention were not the core of the "old" traditional political ideologies that emerged from the French Revolution—that is, conservatism, liberalism and socialism. The old ideologies and traditional values lost their attractiveness and much of the political values inquiries focused on the value orientations that were connected with what is commonly denoted new politics. "New politics, various scholars argued, could only be understood as the reflection of new values" (Lane and Ersson 2005, 258), which center around conflicts emerging from post-industrial society and issues about the meaning of life in such a society (Knutsen 2006). What values classify as new? An even more important question is why these new values have emerged?

The central values of old politics largely relate to economic growth, public order, national security, and traditional lifestyles, conformity, and authority, while the values of new politics emphasize individual freedom, social equality and in particular quality of life (Inglehart 1977, 1990, 1999; and chapter in this volume). For Knutsen (2006), both the materialist–postmaterialist value orientation and libertarian/authoritarian values can be regarded as value orientations associated with new politics. The materialist–postmaterialist dimension reflects the "shift from a preoccupation with physical sustenance and safety values towards a greater emphasis on belonging, self-expression and quality of life issues" (Knutsen 2006, 116; Inglehart 1977, 1990, 1997). Similarly, the libertarian-authoritarian dimension distinguishes between an emphasis on "autonomy, openness, and self betterment" (Knutsen 2006, 116) on the libertarian side and "concerns for security and order,... respect for authority, discipline and dutifulness, patriotism, and intolerance for minorities, conformity to customs, and support for traditional religious and moral values" (Flanagan 1987, 1305) on the authoritarian side. The latter dimension reflects the shift of values from authoritarian to libertarian. More and more people turn away from traditions, the traditional authoritarian institutions, and the prescribed values and norms and increasingly they want to decide for themselves and determine on their own how to live their own lives.

Why have these modern orientations gained prominence? The answer can be found in the major social and political changes that gradually transformed society into postmodern society. There is widespread acceptance of the idea that modernization processes such as individualization, secularization, and globalization have had profound impact on people's (political) values.

5 MODERNIZATION AND POLITICAL VALUE CHANGES

Most perspectives on value changes begin with the observation that there are fundamental qualitative differences between modern industrialized society and late modern, advanced industrial, postmodern society. Further, most perspectives link structural transformations to fundamental shifts in basic value orientations. As for the structural features, most advanced societies have recently experienced unprecedented increases in levels of affluence, growth of the tertiary economic sector at the cost of the first and secondary sectors, improving educational opportunities and rising levels of education, growing use of communication-related technologies, and all have experienced what is known as the "information revolution". Further, these changes resulted in expanding social welfare networks and increasing geographic, economic, and social mobility, specialization of job-related knowledge, and professionalization.

These fundamental structural changes are related with or accompanied by a process in which individuals are increasingly able and willing to develop their own values and norms that do not necessarily correspond to the traditional, institutional (religious) ones. This process seems to be a universal (western) process that brings about not only more modern views, but also more diversity, and it is triggered and strongly pushed by rising levels of education of the population. More education increases people's "breadth of perspective" (Gabennesch 1972, 183), their abilities and cognitive and political skills, which makes them more independent from the traditional suppliers of values, norms, and beliefs, and more open to new ideas and arguments, other providers of meanings, values, and norms. People's actions and behaviors are increasingly rooted in and legitimized by their own personal preferences, convictions, and goals. There is an unrestrained endeavor to pursue private needs and aspirations, resulting in assigning top priority to personal need fulfillment. Self-development and personal happiness have become the ultimate criteria for individual actions and attitudes. Individualization thus entails a process in which opinions, beliefs, attitudes, and values grow to be matters of personal choice. As such, it denotes increasing levels of personal autonomy, self-reliance, and an emphasis on individual freedom and the Self (Giddens 1991). Individualized persons no longer take for granted the rules and prescriptions imposed by traditional institutions which means that the traditional options are less likely to be selected by an increasing number of people. This process of de-traditionalization is characterized by a decline of traditional views in a variety of life domains. The "disciplined, self-denying, and achievement-oriented norms... are giving way to an increasingly broad latitude for individual choice of lifestyles and individual self-expression" (Inglehart 1997, 28).

People's values, beliefs, attitudes, and behavior are based increasingly on personal choice and are less dependent on tradition and social institutions. In other words, a process of privatization causes individual choices to be based increasingly on personal convictions and preferences. Waters (1994, 206) portrayed this as follows: "We may no longer be living under the aegis of an industrial or capitalist culture which can tell us what is true, right and beautiful, and also what our place is in the grand scheme, but under a chaotic, mass-mediated, individual-preference-based culture of post-modernity." Voting, for instance "is no longer the confirmation of 'belonging' to a specific social group but becomes an individual choice..., an affirmation of a personal value system: the 'issue voter' tends to replace the traditional 'party identification voter'" (Ignazi 1992, 4). Since the saliency of ideology has diminished, the once strong ties between party and voter have weakened significantly. The modern voter has become an "issue voter" and politics has become "issue politics" which appears from the gradual shift that has occurred from membership of older style or traditional social movements, such as churches, ethnic groups, unions, or political parties towards membership of issue movements to protect or fight for certain causes, such as sexual liberties, feminism, environment, or even stopping the expansion of an airport or the building of a railroad or road (Barnes 1998, 122). In modern or postmodern societies, old cleavages have disappeared, but increasingly new arenas of conflict have emerged, quite often related to concrete causes (Barnes 1998, 122). Economic development increases this interest in new issues. Inglehart (1997) similarly maintains that economic development and the development of the modern welfare state has led to increasing interest in new issues dealing with the quality of life. People are less concerned with material wealth, and more and more concerned with the environment, emancipation, and personal interests. New groups and organizations will develop to protect these new interests.

The individual in advanced postmodern society also faces a multitude of alternatives as a consequence of internationalization, transnationalization, and globalization. Today's world is a "global village," denoting that the world is a compressed one, and that the consciousness of the world as a whole has intensified tremendously (Robertson 1992, 8). The globalization of social reality is a main effect of the rapid evolution of modern communication technology. Technological developments and innovations in telecommunications, the spread and popularity of computers, and also the increased mobility of major companies and people, as well as the growing exposure to television, radio, video and movies have intensified worldwide social relations and flows of information. In the modern world people encounter a great variety of alternative cultural habits and a broad range of lifestyles and modes of conduct. As such, globalization, "exhausted the old ideas, the traditional ideas, which had therefore lost their truth on the power to persuade" (Rush 1992, 187). Globalization makes people aware of an expanding range of beliefs and moral convictions and thus with a plurality of choices. Because it has been argued that individualized and secularized people are liberated from the constraints imposed by traditional institutions (e.g. religion), globalization implies that people can pick and choose what they want from a global cultural marketplace. Globalization, thus, may be favorable to pluralism because people's choices are increasingly dependent upon personal convictions and preferences.

The emancipation of the individual, the growing emphasis on personal autonomy and individual freedom, the de-unification of collective standards and the fragmentation of private pursuits seem advantageous to "a declining acceptance of the authority of hierarchical institutions, both political and non-political" (Inglehart 1997, 15). Thus, citizens are increasingly questioning the traditional sources of authority and no longer bound by common moral principles. From this, a society emerged where people are mainly concerned in their private matters and they feel no longer committed to the public case. As Fukuyama (2000, 14) says, "a culture of intense individualism . . . ends up being bereft of community." The calculating citizen chooses to "bowl alone" and is increasingly disconnected from the once strong social ties. Because social responsibilities have declined and individual citizens are less embedded in associative relations, a process of deinstitutionalization has occurred appearing as weaker social bonds, people being detached from society, non-affiliated, and without any loyalty to the wider community. Such a society is threatened by disintegration and the individual is threatened by anomie. Durkheim recognized this problem a long time ago, and, more recently, among others Fukuyama warned about the dangers of an individualized society. "A society dedicated to the constant upending of norms and rules in the name of increasing individual freedom of choice will find itself increasingly disorganized, atomized, isolated, and incapable of carrying out common goals and tasks" (Fukuyama 2000, 15).

This unbridled pursuit of private goals and the erosion of collective community life concerns not only many politicians, but also many social scientists. The current debate on the future of citizenship and civil society is directed strongly towards the negative effects of these developments. Individual freedom is "held responsible for rising criminality, political apathy, lack of responsibility, hedonism and moral obtrusion" (Arts, Muffels, and ter Meulen 2001, 467). Communitarians also have expressed their concern for the ultimate consequences of this development towards hedonism, privatism, consumerism, and the "I" culture. They fear a trend towards radical individualism and ethical relativism and the withdrawal of the individual from community life. The only way to solve the problem of individualistic, modern society is, according to proponents of the communitarian theories, the re-establishment of a firm moral order in society by (re-)creating a strong "we" feeling and the (re-)establishment of a "spirit of community" (Etzioni 1996; 2001). What present society needs, they argue, is "a strong moral voice speaking for and from a set of shared core values, that guides community members to pro-social behavior" (Ester, Mohler, and Vinken 2006, 18).

6 CRITICAL AND DISCONTENTED CITIZENS

Apart from pursuing their own interests, being disengaged, and disconnected, contemporary publics are said to be more critical (e.g. Norris 1999). In advanced modern welfare state, people's basic needs are satisfied, which according to some resulted in rising levels of postmaterialism (cf. Inglehart 1997), but which also resulted in increasing demands from citizens towards government. The unprecedented high levels of subjective well-being and wide range of welfare state provisions for unemployment, income maintenance, health, housing, and old age allowed people to take survival and security for granted. Because they can take survival and security for granted, postmaterialist value priorities are rising. These values emphasize individual self-expression and quality of life issues and these bring "new, more demanding standards to the evaluation of political life and confront political leaders with more active, articulate citizens" (Inglehart 1997, 297–8).

The expanded role of the state to protect the individual's interest undermined private initiative and individual responsibility while welfare provisions are increasingly regarded as self-evident and considered a right and entitlement. Unrestrained self-interest makes people not only more demanding but also makes the demands more diverse. It becomes more and more difficult for the government to satisfy all these competing, conflicting, and incompatible demands and needs. The economic crisis has reduced the capacity of the state to guarantee social provisions for all people in society and satisfy their needs. In fact, most welfare states have turned into overloaded political economies, meaning that governments cannot meet both public and private claims. Increasingly there is what Dalton calls a representation gap: the differences between citizens preferences and government policy outputs (Dalton 2004, 66). Such a gap between what people expect from their government and what the government can provide easily results in growing dissatisfaction, public doubts about government, widespread disillusionment with political representatives and political parties, and declining public support. The rise of support for extremist leaders and extremist political parties is often regarded to reflect these feelings of discomfort with government, the current policy, and governing parties.

The economic crisis, the reduction of social security, and the declining levels of public support not only threaten democracy, they also threaten humanitarian solidarity. Fuelled by the process of individualization which induces egocentric, hedonistic, individualistic, and consumeristic behavioral patterns, it is often assumed that cleavages emerge between the employed and unemployed, the older and young people, the sick and disabled versus the healthy people, and between natives and foreigners. Historical processes such as ongoing globalization, the collapse of communism, increasing rates of immigration, and the enlargement of the European Union have been the occasions of a revival of nationalist sentiments, the rise of racial discrimination and ethnic prejudice (Arts and Halman 2005). These have become of great concern to national as well as European Community politicians. The ethnic conflicts in Russia and the Balkans, the increased support for extreme right-wing political parties, the growing popularity among the young of racist and fascist movements in many European countries, and hostilities and assaults towards immigrants delineate major problems contemporary Europe has to cope with and seem to have rapidly fostered feelings of intolerance, racial discrimination, xenophobia, and nationalistic sentiments. Issues of ethnicity, identity, and nationalism have come to dominate European politics because they are considered to be the most explosive and divisive cleavages for the future of European integration (Berglund, Aarebrot, and Koralewicz 1995, 375). Such diversities are regarded as important sources of miscommunication, misunderstandings, intolerance, polarization, intergroup conflict, and violence. The immigration flows are assumed to have triggered ethnocentric and xenophobic counteractions of not only extreme nationalists but also of established populations. If the latter would be the case, bitter cultural (and hence social and political) conflicts could come into being.

7 CONCLUSIONS

The aim of this article was to write about old and new political values put in context. It appeared difficult, not only to decide what values and thus what political values are, but also to define what is old and what is new in this regard. I argued that "old" should not be understood in terms of forgotten and vanished, but more in terms of traditional, while "new" should no be seen as values that are replacing the old ones, but denote values that prevail in contemporary society. Defined in such a way, old and new reflect the changes in values and value priorities. These changes are embedded in broader fundamental societal transformations that often are referred to as modernization of society.

The central claim of modernization theory is that contemporary, modern, post-industrial society differs in many respects from traditional and industrial society, and political values are no longer grounded in political cleavages based on social class conflict but on cleavages based on cultural issues and quality of life concerns. Economic conflicts are likely to remain important, but they are increasingly sharing the stage with new issues that were almost invisible a generation ago: environmental protection, abortion, ethnic conflicts, women's issues, and gay and lesbian emancipation are heated issues today.

As a result, a new dimension of political conflict has become increasingly salient. It reflects a polarization between modern and postmodern issue preferences. This new dimension is distinct from the traditional left–right conflict over ownership of the means of production and distribution of income. A new political cleavage pits culturally conservative against change-oriented progressive individuals, groups, and political parties.

The trajectories of modernization in general and processes of individualization, secularization, and globalization in particular, have transformed the value orientations and priorities in the political realm. In contemporary, highly individualized, secular and globalized order, the "grand world views" have become irrelevant for political orientation. The significance of traditional structures and ties, such as religion, family, class, has receded, enlarging the individual's freedom and autonomy in shaping personal life. People have gradually become self-decisive and self-reliant, no longer forced to accept the traditional authorities as taken for granted. The absoluteness of any kind of external authority, be it religious or secular, has eroded. Authority becomes internalized and deference to authority pervasively declined (Inglehart 1999).

The unrestrained striving to realize personal desires and aspirations, giving priority to individual freedom and autonomy and the emphasis on personal need fulfillment are assumed to have made contemporary individualized people mainly interested in their own lucrative careers and devoting their lives to conspicuous consumption, immediate gratification, personal happiness, success, and achievement. Such people neglect the public interests and civic commitment to the common good is eroding. Evidence of this development is found in increasing crime rates, marital breakdowns, drug abuse, suicide, tax evasion, and other deviant behaviors and practices and the increasing disconnection from family, friends, neighbors, and social structures, such as the church, recreation clubs, political parties, and even bowling leagues (Putnam 2000). Because civic virtues, such as trust, social engagement, and solidarity are on the decline, and since these virtues are considered basic requirement for democracy to survive or to work properly (Putnam 1993), contemporary society suffers a democratic deficit. Democracy is endangered because people are less and less inclined to engage in civic actions.

In Europe, the further integration and intended enlargement of the European Union have fuelled nationalistic sentiments and movements. The recent migration waves into Europe have advanced exclusionist reactions toward new cultural and ethnic minorities and fostered intercultural and interethnic conflicts. These gave rise to new and acute cultural cleavages; and it is precisely because the nations of Europe have failed to become genuine melting pots that so much of European politics now revolves around issues of multiculturalism. Not perpetual peace but nationalist, ethnic, and religious conflicts will occur. So, the ghosts of the past, such as nationalism and racial or religious struggle, still haunt Europe's darker corners, reappear everywhere. In this respect one could speak about the "return of history" (Joffe 1992; Rothschild 1999) for European history is a story of conflicts. Such issues generated interest in and studies on multicultural society (European and multiple) identity, tolerance, and patriotic, nationalistic, ethnocentric, and xenophobic attitudes.

Such orientations are far from new and have been studied before extensively. For example, Stouffer's (1955) classic study of tolerance in America dates back to the fifties, while Sumner (1906/1959) introduced the term ethnocentrism already early in the twentieth century (also see chapter in this volume by Gibson). The question therefore is whether such orientations classify as "new" or "old." It seems better to conclude that there is a renewed interest in such orientations. The same counts for attitudes of trust, civic actions, and societal involvement. Such orientations were already identified as important for democracy in the *Civic Culture* by Almond and Verba (1963). Again, there is nothing really new under the sun. The types of issues that are most salient in the politics of the societies define the values at that moment.

Thus, it seems that it does not make much sense to define and distinguish old and new political values. Old orientations are not replaced by new ones, but value orientations are changing as a result of the transformations of society and modernization processes like individualization, secularization, and globalization. People in modern post-industrial society are no longer constrained in their choices and they favor personal autonomy, individual freedom, and self-direction, quality of life, and the pursuit of subjective well-being. This centrality of the individual generated the rise of values such as emancipation, self-expression, postmaterialism, gender equality, environmentalism, feminism, and ecologism etc. As van Deth (1995, 8) concluded, these new orientations have risen in addition to traditional value orientations.

REFERENCES

ALMOND, G. A. 1980. The intellectual history of the civic culture concept. Pp. 1–26 in *The Civic Culture Revisited*, ed. G. A. Almond and S. Verba. Boston: Little, Brown & Company.

—— and VERBA, S. 1963. *The Civic Culture*. Princeton: Princeton University Press.

ARTS, W., HAGENAARS, J., and HALMAN, L. eds. 2003. *The Cultural Diversity of European Unity*. Leiden: Brill.

—— and HALMAN, L. eds. 2004. *European Values at the Turn of the Millennium*. Leiden: Brill.

—— —— 2005. National identity in Europe today. *International Journal of Sociology*, 35: 69–93.

—— MUFFELS, R., and TER MEULEN, R. 2001. Epilogue: the Future of solidaristic health and social care in Europe. Pp. 473–7 in *Solidarity in Health and Social Care in Europe*, ed. R. ter Meulen, W. Arts, and R. Muffels. Dordrecht: Kluwer Academic Publishers.

BARNES, S. H. 1998. The mobilization of political identity in new democracies. Pp. 117–38 in, *The Postcommunist Citizen*, ed. S. H. Barnes and J. Simon Budapest: Erasmus Foundation and IPAS of HAS.

BARRY, B. 1978. *Sociologists, Economists, and Democracy*. Chicago: University of Chicago Press.

BELLAH, R. N., MADSEN, R., SULLIVAN, W. M., SWIDLER, A., and TIPTON, S. M. 1992. *The Good Society*. New York: Vintage Books.

BERGLUND, S., AAREBROT, F., and KORALEWICZ, J. 1995. The view from EFTA. Pp. 368–401 in *Public Opinion and Internationalized Governance*, ed. O. Niedermayer and R. Sinnott. Oxford: Oxford University Press.

BIEDENKOPF, K., GEREMEK, B., and MICHALSKI, K. 2004. *The Spiritual and Cultural Dimension of Europe*. Vienna/Brussels: Institute for Human Sciences and European Commission.

BOBBIO, N. 1996. *Left & Right: The Significance of a Political Distinction*. Chicago: The University of Chicago Press.

DALTON, R. J. 2004. *Democratic Challenges: Democratic Choices*. Oxford: Oxford University Press.

DIETZ, T., and STERN, P. C. 1995. Toward a theory of choice: socially embedded preference construction. *Journal of Socio-Economics*, 24: 261–79.

ESTER, P., MOHLER, P., and VINKEN, H. 2006. Values and the social sciences: a global world of global values? Pp. 3–29 in *Globalization, Value Change, and Generations*, ed. P. Ester, M. Braun, and P. Mohler. Leiden: Brill.

ETZIONI, A. 1996. *The New Golden Rule: Community and Morality in a Democratic Society*. New York: Basic Books.

—— 2001. *The Monochrome Society*. Princeton: Princeton University Press.

FLANAGAN, S. C. 1982. Changing values in advanced industrial societies: Inglehart's silent revolution from the perspective of Japanese findings. *Comparative Political Studies*, 14: 403–44.

—— 1987. Value changes in industrial societies. *American Political Science Review*, 81: 1303–19.

FORMISANO, R. P. 2001. The concept of political culture. *Journal of Interdisciplinary History*, 31: 393–426.

FUCHS, D., and KLINGEMANN, H. D. 1989. The left–right schema. Pp. 203–34 in *Continuities in Political Action*, ed. J. W. van Deth and M. K. Jennings. Berlin: Walter de Gruyter.

FUKUYAMA, F. 2000. *The Great Disruption*. New York: Touchstone.

GABENNESCH, H. 1972. Authoritarianism as world view. *American Journal of Sociology*, 77: 857–75.

GIDDENS, A. 1991. *Modernity and Self-Identity*. Stanford, Calif.: Stanford University Press.

HALMAN, L. 1991. *Waarden in de Westerse wereld*. Tilburg: Tilburg University Press.

——— LUIJKX, R. and VAN ZUNDERT, M. 2005. *Atlas of European Values*. Leiden: Brill.

HUNTINGTON, S. P. 1996. *The Clash of Civilizations and the Remaking of World Order*. New York: Simon & Schuster.

——— 2000. Cultures Count. Pp. xiii–xvi in *Culture Matters: How Values Shape Human Progress*, ed. L. E. Harrison and S. P. Huntington. New York: Basic Books.

IGNAZI, P. 1992. The silent counter-revolution: hypotheses on the emergence of extreme right-wing parties in Europe. Pp. 3–34 in, *European Journal of Political Research, Special Issue: Extreme Right Wing Parties in Europe*, ed. P. Ignazi & C. Ysmal. Dordrecht: Kluwer Academic Publishers.

INGLEHART, R. 1977. *The Silent Revolution*. Princeton: Princeton University Press.

——— 1988. The renaissance of political culture. *American Political Science Review*, 82: 1203–30.

——— 1990. *Culture Shift in Advanced Industrial Society*. Princeton: Princeton University Press.

——— 1997. *Modernization and Postmodernization*. Princeton: Princeton Universy Press.

——— 1999. Postmodernization erodes respect for authority, but increases support for democracy. Pp. 236–56 in *Critical Citizens*, ed. P. Norris. Oxford: Oxford University Press.

——— and KLINGEMANN, H. D. 1979. Ideological conceptualization and value priorities. Pp. 203–14 in *Political Action: Mass Participation in Five Western Democracies*, ed. S. M. Barnes, M. Kaase, et al. Beverly Hills, Calif.: Sage.

JOFFE, J. 1992. The new Europe: yesterday's ghosts. *Foreign Affairs*, 72: 29–43.

KING, D. S. 1987. *The New Right: Politics, Markets and Citizenship*. Basingstoke: Macmillan Education Ltd.

KNUTSEN, O. 1995. Left-right materialist value orientations. Pp. 160–96 in, *The Impact of Values*, ed. J. W. van Deth and E. Scarbrough. Oxford: Oxford University Press.

——— 2006. The end of traditional political values?. Pp. 115–50 in *Globalization, Value Change, and Generations*, ed. P. Ester, M. Braun and P. Mohler. Leiden: Brill.

LANE, J.-E., and ERSSON, S. 2005. *Culture and Politics*. Aldershot: Ashgate.

LEVITAS, R. ed. 1986. *The Ideology of the New Right*. Oxford: Polity Press.

LIPSET, S. M., LAZARSFELD, P. F. BARTON, A. H., and LINZ, J. 1954. The psychology of voting: an analysis of political behavior. Pp. 1124–76 in *The Handbook of Social Psychology, Vol. II*, ed. G. Lindzey and A. H. Barton. Reading, Mass.: Addison-Wesley.

NEVITTE, N., and GIBBINS, R. 1990. *New Elites in Old States: Ideologies in the Anglo-American Democracies*. Toronto: Oxford University Press.

NORRIS, P. ed. 1999. *Critical Citizens*. Oxford: Oxford University Press.

PATEMAN, C. 1980. The civic culture: a philosophic critique. Pp. 57–102 in *The Civic Culture Revisited*, ed. G. A. Almond and S. Verba. Boston: Little, Brown & Company.

PUTNAM, R. 1993. *Making Democracy Work*. Princeton: Princeton University Press.

——— 2000. *Bowling Alone*. New York: Simon & Schuster.

——— ed. 2002. *Democracies in Flux*. Oxford: Oxford University Press.

PYE, L. W. 1973. Culture and political science: problems in the evaluation of the concept of political culture. Pp. 65–76 in *The Idea of Culture in the Social Sciences*, ed. L. Schneider and C. M. Bonjean. Cambridge: Cambridge University Press.

REICH, B., and ADCOCK, C. 1976. *Values, Attitudes and Behaviour Change*. London: Methuen.

ROBERTSON, R. 1992. *Globalization: Social Theory and Global Culture*. London: Sage.

ROKEACH, M. 1968. *Beliefs, Attitudes and Values*. San Francisco: Jossey-Bass Inc. Publishers.

——— 1973. *The Nature of Human Values*. New York: Free Press.

ROTHSCHILD, E. 1999. Who is Europe? Globalization and the return of history. *Foreign Policy*, 115: 106–17.

RUSH, M. 1992. *Politics and Society. An Introduction to Political Sociology*. New York: Prentice Hall.

STOUFFER, S. 1955. *Communism, Conformity and Civil Liberties*. New York: Doubleday.

STREET, J. 1994. Political Culture: From Civic Culture to Mass Culture. *British Journal of Political Science*, 24: 95–113.

SUMNER, W. G. 1906/1959. *Folkways*. New York: Dover Publications.

VAN DETH, J. W. 1984. *Politieke waarden*. Amsterdam: CT Press.

—— 1995. Introduction: the impact of values. Pp. 1–18 in *The Impact of Values*, ed. J. W. van Deth and E. Scarbrough. Oxford: Oxford University Press.

—— and SCARBROUGH, E. 1995. The concept of values. Pp. 21–47 in *The Impact of Values*, ed. J. W. van Deth and E. Scarbrough. Oxford: Oxford University Press.

VERBA, S., and NIE, N. 1972. *Participation in America: Political Democracy and Social Equality*. New York: Harper & Ro.

WATERS, M. 1994. *Modern Sociological Theory*. London: Sage.

WILDAVSKY, A. 1987. Choosing preferences by constructing instititions: a cultural theory of preference formation. *American Political Science Review*, 81: 3–22.

CHAPTER 17

....

POLITICAL INTOLERANCE IN THE CONTEXT OF DEMOCRATIC THEORY

....

JAMES L. GIBSON

In 1954, in the midst of the infamous McCarthy-led Red Scare in the United States, Samuel Stouffer initiated the modern study of political intolerance with a major survey of both the American mass public and local community leaders. Stouffer, like many others, observed the widespread political repression being undertaken in the name of protecting America and its values from the godless communists, and wondered whether such repression was supported by ordinary people. The results were unequivocal when it comes to the mass public: Of 4,933 respondents interviewed, only 113 people—a paltry 2.3 percent—would not restrict the activities and rights of an admitted communist in some way.[1] Local community leaders, on the other hand, expressed considerably less appetite for intolerance. Out of Stouffer's

* I acknowledge the helpful comments of Jessica Flanigan on an earlier version of this chapter.

[1] Stouffer asked his respondents nine questions about placing restrictions on the activities of an admitted communist. The responses ranged from the 89.6 percent who would fire the communist from a job working in a defense plant (and the 89.4% who would fire the communist from a job teaching in a university) to a "low" of 35.5 percent who would stop buying a brand of soap that was plugged by a communist on a radio show.

research emerged highly influential "elitist" theories of democracy (e.g. Bachrach 1967), as well as an intellectual concern that has persisted for fifty years about the causes and consequences of the intolerance of ordinary citizens (e.g. for a study of British elites and masses see Barnum and Sullivan 1989; on Canadian elites and masses see Sniderman et al. 1996; on Nicaragua see Stein 1999; for contrary findings on elite–mass differences see Rohrschneider 1996).

Intolerance—the unwillingness to put up with disagreeable ideas and groups— has thus become a staple of research on the democratic orientations of citizens throughout the world. The topic is today no less important than it was in the days of Joseph McCarthy (the Republican Senator from Wisconsin who led the Red Scare of the 1950s), since intolerance in one form or another fuels the conflicts in Northern Ireland, the Middle East, Rwanda, and many other areas of the world. And even where intolerance does not directly produce political violence, the failure of democratizing regimes to embrace political freedom for all, even those in the opposition, has become one of the most important impediments to the consolidation of democratic reform throughout the world (as in the so-called illiberal democracies—see Zakaria 2003). Thus, it is important to assess what fifty years of social scientific research have taught us about the causes and consequences of political intolerance. That is the purpose of this chapter.[2]

This chapter begins with an overview of democratic theory, since the meaning of political tolerance (like all concepts) can best be understood within the context of theory. Because tolerance is often confused with other fellow travelers such as permissiveness, it is useful to carefully explicate the concept. The definition of concepts is of course arbitrary, but all concepts acquire their meaning from theory. In the case of political tolerance, the relevant body of thought is democratic theory, and perhaps even more precisely, theories of liberal democracy.[3]

1 THE ROLE OF TOLERANCE IN DEMOCRATIC THEORY

Democracy is of course a system of procedures by which majorities tend to have their way: the majority rules. Liberal democracies require mechanisms of aggregating citizen preferences within majoritarian institutions and this is perhaps the essence of the concept of democracy (e.g. Dahl 1989). But democracy is also a system in which

[2] For an earlier useful review of the tolerance literature see Sullivan and Transue (1999).

[3] This is not to imply that the only legitimate conceptualization of tolerance is that connected to liberal democratic theory (for various theories of tolerance, see Sullivan, Piereson, and Marcus 1982). Indeed, Gibson (2004a) conceptualizes tolerance as an element of "reconciliation" (as in the South African truth and reconciliation process). That conceptualization is not incompatible with liberal democratic theory, even if it places emphasis on a slightly different theoretical approach.

institutionalized respect for the rights of political minorities to try to become a majority must exist. In particular, political minorities in a liberal democracy must be given the means of contestation—the right to try to convince others of the rightness of their positions. Setting up institutions of majority rule turns out to be a comparatively simple task; ensuring the right of unpopular political minorities to compete for political power turns out to be far more difficult.

Without guarantees of the right of all to participate in politics, the "marketplace of ideas" cannot function effectively. The idea of a marketplace is that anyone can put forth a product—an idea—for political "consumers" to consider. The success of the idea is determined by the level of support freely given in the market. The market encourages deliberation, through which superior ideas are found to be superior, and through which the flaws of bad ideas are exposed for all to see (almost as if guided by an invisible hand).[4] Liberal political philosophers (like J. S. Mill) have long been attracted to this marketplace notion, and many consider it an essential element of democratic governance.

Many instances exist in which lack of confidence in the effectiveness of the marketplace of ideas has stimulated governments to place restrictions on the potential entrants to the arena. Some political systems prohibit, for instance, political parties based on religion, others ban all political parties not based on a particular religion. "Extremist" ideas are banned in some systems (as in laws prohibiting Holocaust denials), just as "radical" political parties are prohibited from participating in other systems (e.g. fascist parties in Germany). American policy makers in 1954 (and policy makers throughout much of the world as well) apparently had so little confidence in the ability of ordinary people to consider and reject communism that they banned communists from putting their ideas forward for consideration.[5] Perhaps most common throughout the world today, governments that have become accustomed to political power often seek to prohibit opposition groups from participating in the marketplace of ideas.[6] Without a willingness to put up with all ideologies seeking to compete for the hearts and minds of the citizenry the market is likely to fail. Thus, a fairly simple theory is that democracies require the free and open debate of political differences, and such debate can only take place where political tolerance prevails.

Political tolerance in a democracy requires that all political ideas (and the groups holding them) get the same access to the marketplace of ideas as the access legally extended to the ideas dominating the system. This definition obviously precludes any form of violence and therefore I make no claim that political tolerance extends

---

[4] I do not discount the value of simply allowing all ideas—right and wrong—to have their say, to have what procedural justice scholars refer to as "voice" (e.g. Tyler and Mitchell 1994; Tyler et al. 1997). Procedural justice theories posit that allowing groups voice enhances the legitimacy of the democratic process, especially among those unable to win within majoritarian arenas.

[5] See Gibson (1988) for examples of the types of restrictions put on Communists in the US during the 1940s and 1950s. See also Goldstein (1978).

[6] In the early party of the twenty-first century, examples of this phenomenon are too numerous to catalog. The efforts of Robert Mugabe to maintain his power in Zimbabwe provide an excellent exemplar.

to the right of terrorists to engage in terror. It may, however, protect the speech rights of terrorists, or, more precisely, those who advocate terrorism (e.g. defenders or advocates of suicide bombing).[7] The liberal democratic theory of political tolerance does not protect many forms of non-political expression, such as pornography (except as enlisted in the service of politics) and most types of commercial speech. It does however extend the right of contestation to deeply unpopular ideas, such as the need for a violent revolution or racism or Communism or radical Islam.

Whenever the definition of tolerance is considered, critics question whether certain types of "extreme" speech must be protected. These discussions are useful in principle, but not in practice. From the point-of-view of empirical research on tolerance, the controversies that emerge do not have to do with the most extreme and unusual forms of speech, but rather with the contestation rights of relatively innocuous ideas. In the case of the United States, for instance, even in the twenty-first century, 48 percent of the American people prefer that atheists (someone who is against all religion and churches) be denied the right to hold a public demonstration (see Gibson 2005c). Similar findings have been reported from a Polish survey in 1993 (Karpov 1999, 1536). Only after ordinary people come to tolerate a range of even slightly unorthodox ideas should research then focus on tolerance of the views of the most extreme members of society.

Liberal democratic theory also provides some guidance as to what sorts of activities must be guaranteed to political minorities: Actions and behaviors related to efforts to persuade people and to compete for political power must be put up with. This might include giving public speeches, running candidates for public office, or even publicizing a group by removing trash from the freeways (and claiming credit for doing with so with a publicly erected sign). Obviously, illegal activity need not be countenanced, even if I acknowledge that the line between legal and illegal is often thin, given the power and propensity of majorities to criminalize political activities by the minority.[8]

This theory of the marketplace of ideas anticipates two important (and interconnected) restraints on freedom. First, as I have already mentioned, many fear that the government, typically under the guise of regulation, will usurp power and deny the expression of ideas threatening to the status quo (i.e. the power of the government of the day). Examples of such abuses of minority rights to participation are too widespread to even begin to catalog.

A second constraint on freedom is more subtle: It originates in the political culture of a polity—the beliefs, values, attitudes, and behaviors of ordinary citizens. Restraints on freedom can certainly emanate from public policy; but they can also

---

[7] As I write this, the British are considering new proposals to ban pure speech in support of such activities as suicide bombing. It remains to be seen whether such legislation will be acceptable to British judges and the British people.

[8] This issue is actually a bit more complicated given that political minorities typically need access to specific tactics (e.g. public demonstrations) that the majority does not require or find useful. Thus, regimes sometimes invoke political equality when they ban all demonstrations, even if the effect of such bans falls quite disproportionately on different segments of the political community.

be found in subtle demands for conformity within a society's culture. To the extent that ordinary citizens are intolerant of views challenging mainstream thought, the expression of such viewpoints is likely to generate sanctions and costs. This can in turn create what Noelle-Neumann (1984) has referred to as a "spiral of silence:" A dynamic process in which those holding minority viewpoints increasingly learn about how rare their views are, thereby leading to silence, which in turn makes the ideas seem to be even less widely held, and therefore more dangerous or costly to express. Perhaps the most significant legacy of McCarthyism in the United States was not the limitations imposed on communists and their fellow travelers—legal limitations that were often severe and included imprisonment—but instead was the creation of a "Silent Generation," a cohort unwilling to express views that might be considered controversial or unpopular. And, to complete the circle, mass political intolerance can be a useful form of political capital for those who would in turn enact repressive legislation. To the extent that a political culture emphasizes conformity and penalizes those with contrarian ideas, little tolerance exists, and the likelihood of political repression is high.

1.1 Measuring Political Intolerance

Tolerance thus requires that citizens and governments put up with ideas that are thought to be objectionable. Two components of this definition require further consideration: Which ideas must be put up with, and which activities must be allowed? The answers to both of these questions are intimately related not just to the conceptualization of tolerance, but to its operationalization as well. From the viewpoint of empirical studies of political tolerance, measurement issues of whom and what have become concerns of great importance.[9]

In Stouffer's era, the nature of the perceived threat to the dominant ideology of the time was clear: It came from communists, and their "fellow travelers."[10] Consequently, tolerance questions were framed around the right of communists to compete for political power. To the extent that it is obvious which groups are objects of intolerance in a society, then at least part of the job of measuring mass political intolerance is easy.

For instance, the largest amount of data on political tolerance has been collected by the General Social Survey (GSS) in the United States. This survey, begun in the early 1970s and continuing through today, routinely asks about five groups: someone who is against all churches and religion (atheists), a man who admits he is a communist, a man who admits he is a homosexual, a person who advocates doing away with elections and letting the military run the country, and a person who believes that blacks are genetically inferior. These particular groups are derived from Stouffer's

---

[9] On the measurement of tolerance and other democratic values see Finkel, Sigelman, and Humphries (1999).

[10] Sullivan et al. (1985) make the same argument about Israel.

research and are assumed to be representative today of the fringes of the American ideological continua.

The obvious limitation of these questions is that the replies of those who are themselves atheists, homosexuals, communists, racists, and militarists cannot be treated as valid measures of political tolerance.[11] The flaw with the Stouffer approach to measuring political intolerance was discovered by John Sullivan and his colleagues. Tolerance is putting up with that with which one disagrees. Consequently, it makes no sense to ask one who is a communist whether communists should be allowed to make speeches, etc.[12] Sullivan, Piereson, and Marcus (1982) argued that a valid measure of intolerance requires an "objection precondition," by which they meant that the stimulus presented to every respondent (the ideology or group representing the ideology) must be objectionable. To achieve this, the respondents must be allowed to name a highly disliked group; the researcher does not specify which groups are asked about; rather the respondent must be allowed to designate the group. So as to introduce some degree of comparability across respondents, each is asked to identify the group he or she *dislikes the most*; tolerance questions are then asked about this group. The technique has been named the "least-liked" measurement approach, even though this is a slight misnomer in that the group asked about is actually the most disliked, not, strictly speaking, the least liked.[13]

Some controversies continue to plague the measurement literature, however. Not everyone is convinced of the value of the least-liked approach, at least as it was initially developed by Sullivan, Piereson, and Marcus (see, for examples, McClosky and Brill 1983; Gibson 1986; Sniderman et al. 1989; Chong 1993; and Hurwitz and Mondak 2002). Perhaps the most potent critique of the approach is that it fails to tell us much about the "breadth" of intolerance, by which I mean the range of differences in ideas that is not tolerated. Perhaps many people can name a particular group/idea that they find uniquely offensive (in the twentieth century context, the Ku Klux Klan or Nazis, for instance), and owing to the extraordinary nature of the group/idea, they would not tolerate it. At the same time, however, the category of not-tolerated-ideas/groups is limited to this most extreme instance. Other citizens express intolerance for their most disliked group, but are also willing not to tolerate many other groups that are disliked less than the most disliked. This gives these citizens a broad range of groups, perhaps covering a considerable expanse of ideological territory, that they will not put up with. Most Americans in the 1950s would not tolerate political activity by communists; but most also would not tolerate political activity by socialists, atheists, and even "integrationists."[14] The "breadth" of intolerance signifies

[11] Note that Kuklinski and Cobb (1997) argue on the basis of a "list experiment" that roughly one-half of white males in the American South are racist.

[12] Scholars have tried innovative methods for correcting for such bias (e.g. Wilson 1994; Mondak and Sanders 2003), but it seems likely that the utility of asking questions about these groups will continue to diminish over time.

[13] One important drawback of the least-liked technology is that it is quite costly in terms of questions and interview time and is difficult to administer via telephone interviews.

[14] See Stouffer (1955). For an engaging and insightful analysis of how race and anti-communism got conflated in Texas in the 1950s (and in Houston in particular) see Carleton (1985).

the minimum amount of antipathy that must exist before a respondent is willing not to tolerate. Unfortunately, we know little about the breadth of intolerance of individuals or countries throughout the world.[15]

Another measurement issue has recently been raised by Mondak and Sanders (2003), who have argued that it is useful under some circumstances to conceptualize tolerance as a dichotomy: people are either tolerant (perfectly so, allowing everything by everyone), or they are intolerant (although Mondak and Sanders recognize that the degree of *intolerance* may vary). Their argument is part of an effort to rescue the tolerance measures employed in the General Social Survey (GSS) and elsewhere (e.g. the Polish General Social Survey—see Karpov 1999). Gibson (2005*a*, 2005*b*) has shown that this argument is neither conceptually nor empirically useful, primarily because nearly all people can imagine a group or an activity that they would prefer not be allowed. The number of perfectly tolerant people (allow all groups all activities) is too small to be of any empirical consequence. Moreover, extant cross-national research has shown that most countries are in no danger whatsoever of approaching extreme levels of tolerance! For example, Peffley and Rohrschneider (2003) refer to levels of tolerance in the seventeen countries they study as "a scarce commodity" (248) and "abysmally low" (254), and generally conclude that "intolerance is the norm, tolerance the exception" (248). Most scholars seem to believe that tolerance is a continuum that varies from those who would place fewer restrictions of objectionable ideas and actions to those who would place greater restrictions.

The least-liked approach to measuring intolerance serves well those who are primarily interested in investigating individual differences among people. The technique is less well suited for studying the politics of civil liberties in a society. It one wants to know, for instance, whether there is widespread support for banning a particular idea from the marketplace of ideas, then establishing an objection precondition for each respondent may not be necessary (e.g. Barnum and Sullivan 1989). And, as I have noted, in some societies (e.g. Israel) there is little ambiguity about who the enemy of the status quo is; in such cases, the least-liked technology may not be necessary.[16]

1.2 Pluralistic Intolerance

The least-liked measurement approach is closely connected to one of the most important ideas to emerge from the tolerance literature: the theory of pluralistic intolerance. Sullivan, Piereson, and Marcus (1982) have argued that lack of consensus

[15] To address this issue, one must ask questions about not just the most disliked group, but many different groups. So, for instance, the World Values Survey asked about only a single group, thus providing no information on breadth (Peffley and Rohrschneider 2003). Gibson and Gouws (2003), on the other hand, asked about several groups, giving the authors at least some purchase on the breadth question. Providing a spatial analysis of the breadth of ideological difference deemed legitimate in a society (the breadth of the "loyal opposition") seems to be an important but difficult research question for the field.

[16] Perhaps the only systematic comparison of the least-liked measures of intolerance with the fixed-group approach is the analysis of Gibson 1992*b*. The general conclusion of that research is that, at least under the circumstances of the United States in 1987, the two approaches generate similarly valid and reliable measures.

on who the enemy is—pluralistic intolerance—can neutralize even widespread intolerance. When everyone picks a different "least-liked" group, it may mean that there is insufficient agreement for intolerance to be mobilized into political repression. When intolerance is pluralistic, it is dispersed and may be benign. Indeed, their theory strongly emphasizes the need to identify the factors contributing to the *focusing* of intolerance, for it is focused intolerance that is dangerous and pernicious (see Sullivan et al. 1985).

Unfortunately, little rigorous research at the system level (either over time or cross-nationally) has investigated the theory of pluralistic intolerance. In their research on South Africa, Gibson and Gouws (2003) discovered that intolerance can be both focused and pluralistic, in the sense that many groups, of various ideological affinities, may not be tolerated by people. Gibson (1998a), on the other hand, asserts that intolerance is focused on the far right wing in Russia (see also Gibson and Duch 1993). More research needs to be conducted to determine the "breadth" of tolerance in different societies—the range of ideas that people believe can be legitimately expressed in a society.

1.3 What Tolerance is Not: Intolerance and Intergroup Prejudice

One might naturally expect that intolerance and prejudice are simply different sides of the same coin, and that the literatures on political tolerance and intergroup conflict and prejudice are closely integrated.[17] In fact, that is not so. To an amazing degree, these two bodies of research rarely intersect. That this is so is one of the major enigmas in the tolerance literature (see Gibson 2006).

Stenner has strongly argued that intolerance and prejudice are cut from the same cloth. She asserts: "This work began with the conviction that racial, political and moral intolerance, normally studied in isolation, are really kindred spirits: primarily driven by the same fundamental predispositions, fueled by the same motives, exacerbated by the same fears" (2005, 325). Yet, to date, only partial and inconclusive data have been produced specifically documenting that political intolerance (especially as measured by the least-liked technology) and intergroup prejudice are intercorrelated to any significant degree. For instance, Gibson (2006a) has shown that the two concepts are entirely unrelated in both Russia and South Africa. Gibson's argument is that expressing prejudice toward one's political enemies is simply not a precondition for political intolerance. What groups stand for is a sociotropic factor, which differs greatly from the perceived characteristics of the individual members of the group. For many, it is not necessary to ascribe a series of negative stereotypes to those with whom political disagreements are severe.[18] It is therefore important not

---

[17] For a useful study of interethnic intolerance see Massey, Hodson, and Sekulić? 1999. See also Gibson 2004a.

[18] Conversely, Sullivan, Pierson, and Marcus (1982, 4) argue that: "Tolerance...is not merely the absence of prejudice...The prejudiced person may in fact be tolerant, if he understands his prejudices and proceeds to permit the expression of those things toward which he is prejudiced." They conclude: "Thus, the prejudiced person may be either tolerant or intolerant, depending on what action he or she is prepared to take politically" (1982, 5).

to *assume* that intolerance and prejudice are necessarily cut from the same cloth, and to investigate the relationship carefully in future empirical research.

As I have noted, perhaps one reason why intolerance and prejudice are not always interconnected has to do with the highly influential role of threat perceptions in shaping political intolerance. The strongest predictor of intolerance is the feeling that a group is threatening. Perceptions of threat may be based upon prejudice, but they need not be, and one can well imagine that many perceptions of group threat are based on objective and realistic perceptions that have nothing to do with prejudice. One might find some strains of Islam threatening, for instance, not out of mistaken generalizations about Muslims but rather out of opposition to those who would not put a wall of separation between religion and politics (e.g. Sniderman and Hagendoorn 2007). Secularists and atheists may view a variety of religious groups as threatening, without any degree of prejudice. And conversely, one can easily hold prejudiced views toward groups seen as impotent, and hence not threatening. For instance, it would not be surprising to find that many hold prejudiced views of members of the neo-Nazis today, while believing that the group poses little threat directly owing to the ascribed characteristics (e.g. "neo-Nazis are too stupid to be threatening").

Finally, political tolerance has to do with what one expects of the state, not of oneself. It is easy to imagine the citizen who would fight strongly to protect the rights of a despised political minority, while at the same time being unwilling to share a meal with a member of the group or have her daughter marry a group member. In a democratic society, keeping a great deal of social distance from a group is not incompatible with tolerating its political activities.

Thus, extant theory provides many insights into how political tolerance can be conceptualized and operationalized. Tolerance requires putting up with political activity by groups whose ideas are repugnant. It does so under the liberal democratic theory that all ideas must be free to compete within the marketplace. The intolerance of ordinary people is important not just because it can fuel repressive legislation, but also because it can contribute to a climate of conformity that sanctions the expression of minority viewpoints. As a consequence, social scientists have devoted considerable resources to measuring mass political intolerance, and then to investigating its origins. It is to this last point of emphasis that I turn next.

2 What Causes Some Citizens to be Tolerant but Others Not?

Perhaps one of the most widely investigated questions in the tolerance literature has to do with the etiology of intolerance at the individual level. Many have contributed to identifying predictors of intolerance, ranging from Sniderman's work (1975) on self-esteem and social learning, to Sullivan, Pierson, and Marcus (1982) on threat perceptions, democratic values, and psychological insecurity, to Stenner's book

(2005) on the personality trait authoritarianism. Nearly all agree that some sort of closed-mindedness or psychological rigidity contributes to intolerance, even if the precise label attached to the concept varies across researchers.

In virtually all studies, threat perceptions are one of the strongest predictors of intolerance. Not surprisingly, those who are more threatened by their political enemies are less likely to tolerate them. However, a number of surprises are associated with the threat–tolerance relationship. The strongest predictor of intolerance is the feeling that a group is threatening, but, ironically perhaps, it is not the direct threat to one's own personal well-being (egocentric threat perceptions) that is crucial, but instead perceived threat to the group and/or society (sociotropic threat perceptions) that is so likely to generate intolerance (e.g. Gibson and Gouws 2003; Davis and Silver 2004). Moreover, several studies have now reported that the perceived efficacy of a group (its power or potential for power) has few implications for the other aspects of threat perceptions or for political intolerance (e.g. Marcus et al. 1995; Gibson and Gouws 2003). It seems natural to suggest that intolerance flourishes where the threat of groups and ideas is highest, yet the various processes involved have been found to be fairly complex and the simple relationship does not typically exist.[19]

It is also paradoxical that, even though one might expect perceptions of threat to be shaped by personality characteristics, in fact little convincing evidence has been adduced on this point. The most concentrated effort to identify the personality precursors to threat is the work of Marcus et al. (1995), although many scholars have worked on this problem. If in fact threat perceptions are based on realistic factors (e.g. realistic group conflict) then there is no necessary requirement for psychological variables to be implicated. On the other hand, to the extent that groups represent sociotropic threats, one might well hypothesize that individual personality characteristics (e.g. authoritarianism and chauvinistic nationalism) are activated. Unraveling these relationships—or lack of relationships—is a research problem of considerable importance for the field.

Some of the most interesting work on this score posits an interactive effect of psychological attributes and external environmental factors. No research better demonstrates this effect than that of Feldman (e.g. Feldman and Stenner 1997; Feldman 2003), who has shown that authoritarianism and perceptions of environmental stress interact in creating intolerance. Similarly, Gibson (2002) has shown that Russian intolerance reacts to their perceptions of political and economic stress, and crime in particular. Gibson and Gouws (2003) have also documented that perceptions of an out-of-control crime rate among South Africans can fuel the anxiety that gives rise to enhanced perceptions of threat (see also Huddy et al. 2005). On the other hand, this process is far from automatic—Gibson and Howard (2007) have demonstrated that despite all of the factors being in alignment for Jews to be scapegoated in

---

[19] That sociotropic threat perceptions are the most influential type of threat implies that social identity concerns may play an important role in this process. That hypothesis has been investigated, but the results are too complicated to consider in this essay. For research on the role of group attachments in shaping identities see Gibson and Gouws (2000), and Gibson (2006b).

Russia during the 1990s, in fact anti-Semitic attacks on Jews (formal or informal) failed to materialize. Learning who the enemy is requires a theory of blame, and under many social and political circumstances it is not at all clear who is to blame. The whole process of attributing blame and calculating threat from groups is at present poorly understood.

In the original model of the origins of intolerance, Sullivan, Piereson, and Marcus (1982) demonstrate that tolerance is connected to a more general set of beliefs about democracy (even though the slippage between general commitments to democracy and specific applications to the rights of disliked groups is considerable). Gibson, Duch, and Tedin (1992, see also Gibson 1995) have expanded this research to consider more specifically the connection between tolerance and support for democratic institutions and processes (see also Finkel and Ernst 2005). At least in Russia, such interrelationships are not strong, largely owing to the difficulty of embracing tolerance of hated groups and ideas. In formerly dictatorial systems, people were denied majority rule; consequently, the majoritarian aspects of democracy are readily embraced since they lead to the empowerment of the people. Extending these rights to unpopular minorities requires more intellectual effort than many can muster. Tolerance may be the most difficult democratic value of all; only among those with a fully articulated democratic belief system—which is especially uncommon among people not repeatedly exposed to democratic institutions and processes—do we see close connections between tolerance and the other democratic values.

2.1 Can Intolerance Be Changed?

Little research has directly investigated change in political tolerance over time. A couple of studies have shown intolerance to be sensitive to exogenous environmental stress such as crime and social unrest (e.g. Gibson and Gouws 2003; Gibson 2002; Feldman and Stenner 1997), but micro-level analysis of change is as rare as it is important. One of the most interesting findings to emerge from this limited literature is that, while it is clear that threat perceptions cause intolerance, it may also be the case that intolerance causes threat perceptions (Gibson forthcoming). That is, because tolerant people are in some sense more secure, they are not predisposed to see their political competitors as particularly threatening. It may be that a "spiral of tolerance" can be created in the sense that tolerance breeds lower perceptions of group threat, which breeds more tolerance, etc.

A sizeable body of literature exists on "civic education" (e.g. Nie, Junn, and Stehlik-Barry 1996), and tolerance is one value that researchers seek to foster through education and training programs. Successes (based on rigorous data analysis) have been few and far beyond (e.g. Avery et al. 1993). Recently, efforts have been made to evaluate the programs of the United States government to enhance support for democratic institutions and processes, including political tolerance, but the early results have not been very promising, especially as concerns tolerance (e.g. Finkel 2002, 2003; Finkel and Ernest 2005). It may well be that basic orientations toward foreign and threatening ideas are shaped at an early age, and, although environmental conditions can ameliorate or exacerbate such propensities, core attitudes and values are fairly resistant to change.

One other way in which scholars have studied change in intolerance is through the so-called sober second thought experiment (e.g. Gibson 1998b). Stouffer (1955) long ago theorized that tolerance is a difficult and cognitively demanding position to adopt (see also McClosky and Brill 1983). Indeed, the conventional view among scholars is that tolerance requires deliberation and that in the absence of such deliberation, intolerance likely results, owing to the emotional basis of the response to threatening stimuli (but see Kuklinski et al. 1991). When people take the time and energy to deliberate, they often can discern the costs of intolerance, in addition to the benefits of intolerance that are usually so readily calculable. Thus, one knows immediately that "bad ideas must be repressed," but determining that such repression may actually backfire (e.g. by making the bad ideas more attractive simply because they are forbidden) is a more arduous task. Thus, the conventional hypothesis is that deliberation enhances tolerance. Much of the contemporary literature on deliberative democracy makes this assumption, either implicitly or explicitly.

Empirical research has not been especially kind to this expectation. Perhaps most interesting is the finding that tolerance is considerably more pliable than intolerance. For instance, Gibson (1998b) and others (e.g. Peffley, Knigge, and Hurwitz 2001; Sniderman et al. 1996; Marcus et al. 1995; and Kuklinski et al. 1991) have shown that tolerance and intolerance differ in their pliability—the tolerant can be more readily persuaded to abandon their tolerance than can the intolerant be convinced to become tolerant. For instance, based on the Sober Second Thought Experiment, Gibson reports (1998b, 828) that, while 74.1 percent of intolerant Russians did not budge from their intolerance when presented with three reasons to tolerate, only 44.8 percent of the tolerant remained tolerant when exposed to three pro-intolerance counter-arguments. Other research reports similar asymmetries. This finding has been replicated in both South Africa (Gibson and Gouws 2003) and the United States (Gibson 1996). The susceptibility of tolerance to being trumped by other values is apparently high since democratic belief systems (within which tolerance is embedded) often contain values that conflict. For instance, the desire to protect innocent and weak groups from slander may override a commitment to free speech for all political ideas.[20] Unfortunately, research to date has not been very successful in identifying ideas and arguments that might convert the intolerant into embracing political tolerance. In any event, this asymmetry in the potency of tolerance and intolerance is a finding so important that it warrants considerable additional investigation.[21]

[20] An obvious example of free speech concerns being trumped is legislation and policy against so-called hate speech. For a very interesting study of the impact of hate speech legislation on the intolerance of college students, see Chong (2006).

[21] This asymmetry may also extend to the connection between attitudes and actual behavior, with intolerance more likely than tolerance to produce action. See Gibson and Bingham (1985); Barnum and Sullivan (1990); Marcus et al. (1995); and Gibson (2006a). Since studies of actual behavior are relatively rare, however, less confidence should be vested in this finding, as compared to the findings on persuadability.

As in so many areas of the social sciences, static research dominates. Scholars use cross-sectional analysis to make inferences about change, and macro-level analysis (e.g. cohort analysis and pooled cross-sections) provide additional inferential leverage. However, such analyses can also be highly misleading in that micro-level change is often obscured by macro-level appearance of stasis. The tolerance subfield is almost entirely dominated by cross-sectional research. Until more dynamic theories and data sets are produced, a full understanding of the origins of intolerance will remain elusive and incomplete.

3 WHAT ARE THE CONSEQUENCES OF MASS POLITICAL INTOLERANCE?

Does intolerance matter? This question is difficult to address since it is bound up in complex theories about the role of public opinion in shaping public policy. Moreover, intolerance probably matters most within the context of specific disputes, as in the dispute in Skokie, Illinois, over the rights of American Nazis to hold a demonstration (e.g. Gibson and Bingham 1985). Indeed, one tradition in research on the consequences of intolerance is to pursue what Sniderman (1993) calls "firehouse studies:" studies that respond to specific civil liberties controversies (e.g. Gibson 1987, Gibson and Tedin 1988). Such research is difficult to mount, however, since disputes over civil liberties rarely develop with the periodicity or predictability of other political events, such as elections. As a consequence, some research relies upon hypothetical scenarios to investigate the behavioral implications of intolerance (e.g. Marcus et al. 1995) and to consider the role of contextual factors in shaping intolerance (e.g. Gibson and Gouws 2001).

Another line of research involves determining whether intolerant opinion has the sort of characteristics likely to make it pernicious. Gibson's (1998a) study of Russian opinion adopts this perspective, focusing on whether intolerance is principled (bound up within an ideology), focused, "empowered" in the sense that the intolerant believe their views are in the majority, and common among the more politically relevant subsection of the mass public ("opinion leaders"). In the Russian case, Gibson concludes that mass political intolerance is in fact potentially consequential for the rights of unpopular political minorities.

Connecting mass political intolerance to specific public policies has proven difficult. Gibson, for instance, has shown (1988; see also Page and Shapiro 1983) that repressive state policies against Communists adopted in the 1950s were not a direct consequence of mass public opinion (even if policy was related to elite opinion). On the other hand, there was a connection between mass intolerance and repressive policies during the era of Vietnam War dissent, but the relationship is not as expected. States with opinion that was more tolerant were *more likely* to adopt repressive legislation (Gibson 1989). Gibson shows that tolerance was related to the prevalence of protest, and that protest generated a repressive response. Thus, these relationships are complicated.

As I suggested, a key process by which intolerance affects political freedom in a polity may have to do with cultural norms that encourage or discourage political disagreement. Gibson (1992a) has shown that intolerance within a family does indeed constrain political discussion and affect the extent to which people feel free to express their political views. And a growing body of literature suggests that political homogeneity in social networks reinforces political intolerance (Mutz 2002). Indeed, because networks tend so commonly to be homogeneous, many of the key assumptions of theories of deliberative democracy turn out to be challenged by the empirical evidence available (but see Huckfeldt, Johnson, and Sprague 2005).

3.1 Political Intolerance in Times of Crisis

The attack on the United States on 9/11/2001 by Muslim fanatics ushered in a new, but not entirely unfamiliar, era in American politics. Throughout American history, during times of crisis, civil liberties have been either suspended or limited in important ways (e.g. Epstein et al. 2005). No better chronicling of these episodes has been reported than the encyclopedic work of Goldstein (1978).

The policy response to the 9/11 attack is therefore not unprecedented. What is new, however, is the ability of scholars to launch systematic research efforts to understand how citizens come to balance expectations of personal and societal security with the demands of tolerance and individual liberty. Davis and Silver (2004), for instance, show that people make tradeoffs between liberty and order in arriving at positions on civil liberties policies, and that these tradeoffs are sensitive to several moderating influences (e.g. the degree of trust in government). Undoubtedly, the nature of the tradeoffs varies over time, as external threats wax and wane. Unfortunately, little is understood about the details of this dynamic process.

A familiar complaint against all subfields in public opinion is that attitudes are not important because they do not influence actual behavior (e.g. Weissberg 1998). In general, meta-analyses routinely show this charge to be false (Kraus 1995). The limited research addressing this issue in the tolerance literature also suggests that civil liberties attitudes do indeed influence citizens' political behavior in actual civil liberties conflicts (e.g. Gibson and Bingham 1985). Nonetheless, the political tolerance subfield would undoubtedly profit from greater attention to the consequences of mass political intolerance. In doing so, we ought to cast our nets broadly, remembering that the failure of citizens to put up with views with which they do not agree can influence feelings of political freedom and willingness to discuss and debate (Gibson 1992a), as well as public policy at both the local and national levels.

4 CONCLUDING COMMENTS

The study of political intolerance is a vast enterprise at both the micro- and macro-levels, and research on political tolerance constitutes a subfield much too large to be able to be comprehensively surveyed in a short chapter such as this. I have barely mentioned philosophical or normative studies of intolerance (e.g. Bollinger 1986), detailed studies of how individuals select their targets have not been considered (e.g. stereotype threat, Golebiowska 1996), many case studies of outbreaks of intolerance have not been addressed here (e.g. Strum 1999); and studies of intolerance in nations outside the United States have been slighted (e.g. Sullivan et al. 1985). Nor have I reviewed important issues such as how and why members of the mass public and elites differ on issues of tolerance (see Sullivan et al. 1993), or issues such as whether religion and religiosity and intolerance are inextricably interconnected (e.g. see Karpov 1999). Furthermore, new issues are constantly emerging: It appears inevitable that the neurology of threat perceptions and intolerance will be a hot topic for future research (e.g. Marcus, Wood, and Theiss-Morse 1998). Those interested in pursuing research on the myriad dimensions of political tolerance will find a fresh and vibrant literature on nearly all specific research questions, even if many such questions are beyond the scope of this chapter.

Instead, in this chapter, I have attempted three things. First, I have tried to show that, as a concept, political tolerance derives its rigor and specificity from liberal democratic theory. Political tolerance does not require that everything be put up with under all circumstances; instead, it only requires free and unfettered entry for all views to the marketplace of ideas. Second, I have demonstrated that the origins of intolerance at the micro-level are reasonably well understood, even if some very important enigmas still exist. Intolerance flows most regularly from perceptions of group threat, even if we understand little about how some groups become threatening while others are not. Finally, intolerance has important political consequences. The simplistic view that intolerance directly fuels repressive public policy does not warrant much support, even if intolerance, when having characteristics rendering it pernicious, can on occasion be mobilized by political entrepreneurs. The intolerance of citizens can also affect the nature of deliberation and disagreement in society, and therefore constrain the market even without direct government intervention.

Even if we understand something of the etiology of intolerance and something of the consequence it has for democratic development, a host of important unanswered questions exist. My hope is that some might be stimulated by this chapter to pursue these questions further, and thereby contribute to creating a more tolerant world.

REFERENCES

AVERY, P. et al. 1993. *Tolerance For Diversity of Beliefs: A Secondary Curriculum Unit.* Boulder, Colo.: Social Science Education Consortium.
BACHRACH, P. 1967. *The Theory of Democratic Elitism: A Critique.* Boston: Little, Brown.

BARNUM, D., and SULLIVAN, J. 1989. Attitudinal tolerance and political freedom in Britain. *British Journal of Political Science*, 19 (1): 136–46.

—— —— 1990. The elusive foundations of political freedom in Britain and the United States. *Journal of Politics*, 52 (3): 719–39.

BOLLINGER, L. 1986. *The Tolerant Society: Freedom of Speech and Extremist Speech in America.* New York: Oxford University Press.

CARLETON, D. 1985. *Read Scare!: Right-Wing Hysteria, Fifties Fanaticism, and their Legacy in Texas.* Austin, Tex.: Texas Monthly Press.

CHONG, D. 1993. How people think, reason and feel about rights and liberties. *American Journal of Political Science*, 37 (3): 867–99.

—— 2006. Free speech and multiculturalism in and out of the academy. *Political Psychology*, 27 (1): 29–54.

DAHL, ROBERT A. 1989. *Democracy and Its Critics.* New Haven: Yale University Press.

DAVIS, D., and SILVER, B. 2004. Civil liberties vs. security: public opinion in the context of the terrorist attacks on America. *American Journal of Political Science*, 48 (1): 28–46.

EPSTEIN, L., HO, D., KING, G., and SEGAL, J. 2005. The Supreme Court during times of crisis: how war affects only non-war cases. *New York University Law Review*, 80 (1): 1–116.

FELDMAN, S. 2003. Enforcing social conformity: a theory of authoritarianism. *Political Psychology*, 24 (1): 41–74.

—— and STENNER, K. 1997. Perceived threat and authoritarianism. *Political Psychology*, 18 (4): 741–70.

FINKEL, S. 2002. Civic education and the mobilization of political participation in developing democracies. *Journal of Politics*, 64 (4): 994–1020.

—— 2003. Can democracy be taught? *Journal of Democracy*, 14 (4): 137–51.

—— and ERNST, H. 2005. Civic education in post-Apartheid South Africa: alternative paths to the development of knowledge and democratic values. *Political Psychology*, 26 (3): 333–64.

—— SIGELMAN, L., and HUMPHRIES, S. 1999. Democratic values and political tolerance. Pp. 203–96 in *Measures of Political Attitudes*, ed. J. Robinson et al. New York: Academic Press.

GIBSON, J. 1986. Pluralistic intolerance in America: a reconsideration. *American Politics Quarterly*, 14: 267–93.

—— 1987. Homosexuals and the Ku Klux Klan: a contextual analysis of political intolerance. *Western Political Quarterly*, 40 (3): 427–48.

—— 1988. Political intolerance and political repression during the McCarthy Red Scare. *American Political Science Review*, 82 (2): 511–29.

—— 1989. The policy consequences of political intolerance: political repression during the Vietnam War era. *Journal of Politics*, 51 (1): 13–35.

—— 1992a. The political consequences of intolerance: cultural conformity and political freedom. *American Political Science Review*, 86 (2): 338–56.

—— 1992b. Alternative measures of political tolerance: must tolerance be 'least-liked'? *American Journal of Political Science*, 36: 560–77.

—— 1995. The resilience of mass support for democratic institutions and processes in the nascent Russian and Ukrainian democracies. Pp. 53–111 in *Political Culture and Civil Society in Russia and the New States of Eurasia*, ed. V. Tismaneanu. Armonk, NY: M. E. Sharp.

—— 1996. The paradoxes of political tolerance in processes of democratisation. *Politikon: South African Journal of Political Studies* 23 (2): 5–21.

—— 1998a. Putting up with fellow Russians: an analysis of political tolerance in the fledgling Russian democracy. *Political Research Quarterly*, 51 (1): 37–68.

—— 1998b. A sober second thought: an experiment in persuading Russians to tolerate. *American Journal of Political Science*, 42: 819–50.

—— 2002. Becoming tolerant? Short-term changes in Russian political culture. *British Journal of Political Science*, 32: 309–34.

—— 2004. *Overcoming Apartheid: Can Truth Reconcile a Divided Nation?* New York: Russell Sage Foundation.

—— 2005a. On the nature of tolerance: dichotomous or continuous? *Political Behavior*, 27 (4): 313–23.

—— 2005b. Parsimony in the study of tolerance and intolerance. *Political Behavior*, 27 (4): 339–45.

—— 2005c. Political intolerance in the United States, 2005. Unpublished paper, Washington University in St Louis.

—— 2006a. Enigmas of intolerance: fifty years after Stouffer's *Communism, Conformity, and Civil Liberties. Perspectives on Politics*, 4 (1): 21–34.

—— Forthcoming. Is intolerance incorrigible? An analysis of change among Russians. In *Toleration on Trial*, ed. I. Creppell, R. Hardin, and S. Macedo. Lanham, Md.: Lexington Books.

—— 2006b. Do strong group identities fuel intolerance? Evidence from the South African Case. *Political Psychology*, 27 (5): 665–705.

—— and BINGHAM, R. 1985. *Civil Liberties and Nazis: The Skokie Free Speech Controversy.* New York: Praeger.

—— and DUCH, R. 1993. Political intolerance in the USSR: the distribution and etiology of mass opinion. *Comparative Political Studies*, 26: 286–329.

—— —— and TEDIN, K. 1992. Democratic values and the transformation of the Soviet Union. *Journal of Politics*, 54 (2): 329–71.

—— and GOUWS, A. 2000. Social identities and political intolerance: linkages within the South African mass public. *American Journal of Political Science*, 44 (2): 278–92.

—— —— 2001. Making tolerance judgments: the effects of context, local and national. *Journal of Politics*, 63 (4): 1067–90.

—— —— 2003. *Overcoming Intolerance in South Africa: Experiments in Democratic Persuasion.* New York: Cambridge University Press.

—— and HOWARD, M. M. 2007. Russian anti-Semitism and the scapegoating of Jews: The Dog That Didn't Bark? *British Journal of Political Science*, 37 (2, April): 193–224.

—— and TEDIN, K. 1988. The etiology of intolerance of homosexual politics. *Social Science Quarterly*, 69 (3): 587–604.

GOLEBIOWSKA, E. 1996. The "pictures in our heads" and individual-targeted tolerance. *Journal of Politics*, 58 (4): 1010–34.

GOLDSTEIN, R. 1978. *Political Repression in Modern America.* Cambridge, Mass.: Schenkman.

HUCKFELDT, R., JOHNSON, P., and SPRAGUE, J. 2005. *Political Disagreement: The Survival of Diverse Opinions within Communications Networks.* New York: Cambridge University Press

HUDDY, L., FELDMAN, S., TABER, C., and LAHAV, G. 2005. Threat, anxiety, and support of antiterrorism policies. *American Journal of Political Science*, 49 (3): 593–608.

HURWITZ, J., and MONDAK, J. 2002. Democratic principles, discrimination and political intolerance. *British Journal of Political Science*, 32 (1): 93–118.

KARPOV, V. 1999. Religiosity and political tolerance in Poland. *Sociology of Religion*, 60 (4): 387–402.

KRAUS, S. 1995. Attitudes and the prediction of behavior: a meta-analysis of the empirical literature. *Personality and Social Psychology Bulletin*, 21: 58–75.

KUKLINSKI, J., and COBB, M. 1997. Racial attitudes and the "New South". *American Journal of Political Science*, 59 (2): 323–49.

KUKLINSKI, J., RIGGLE, E., OTTATI, V., SCHWARZ, N., and WYER, R. Jr. 1991. The cognitive and affective bases of political tolerance judgments. *American Journal of Political Science*, 35 (1): 1–27.

MCCLOSKY, H., and BRILL, A. 1983. *Dimensions of Tolerance: What Americans Think about Civil Liberties*. New York: Russell Sage Foundation.

MARCUS, G., WOOD, S., and THEISS-MORSE, E. 1998. Linking neuroscience to political intolerance and political judgment. *Politics and the Life Sciences* 17 (2): 165–78.

—— SULLIVAN, J., THEISS-MORSE, E., and WOOD, S. 1995. *With Malice Toward Some: How People Make Civil Liberties Judgments*. New York: Cambridge University Press.

MASSEY, G., HODSON, R., and SEKULIĆ, D. 1999. Ethnic enclaves and intolerance: the case of Yugoslavia. *Social Forces*, 78 (2): 669–91.

MONDAK, J., and SANDERS, M. 2003. Tolerance and intolerance, 1976–1998. *American Journal of Political Science*, 47 (3): 492–502.

MUTZ, D. 2002. Cross-cutting social networks: testing democratic theory in practice. *American Political Science Review*, 96 (1): 111–26.

NIE, N., JUNN, J., and STEHLIK-BARRY, K. 1996. *Education and Democratic Citizenship in America*. Chicago: University of Chicago Press.

NOELLE-NEUMANN, E. 1984. *The Spiral of Silence: Public Opinion, our Social Skin*. Chicago: University of Chicago Press.

PAGE, B., and SHAPIRO, R. 1983. Effects of public opinion on public policy. *American Political Science Review*, 77: 175–90.

PEFFLEY, M., KNIGGE, P., and HURWITZ, J. 2001. A multiple values model of political tolerance. *Political Research Quarterly*, 54 (2): 379–406.

—— and ROHRSCHNEIDER, R. 2003. Democratization and political tolerance in seventeen countries: a multi-level model of democratic learning. *Political Research Quarterly* 56 (3): 243–57.

ROHRSCHNEIDER, R. 1996. Institutional learning versus value diffusion: the evolution of democratic values among parliamentarians in Eastern and Western Germany. *Journal of Politics*, 68: 442–66.

SNIDERMAN, P. 1975. *Personality and Democratic Politics*. Berkeley: University of California Press.

—— 1993. The new look in public opinion research. Pp. 219–45 in *Political Science: The State of the Discipline II*, ed. A. Finifter. Washington, DC: The American Political Science Association.

—— and HAGENDOORN, L. 2007. *When Ways of Life Collide: Multiculturalism and Its Discontents in the Netherlands*. Princeton: Princeton University Press.

—— TETLOCK, P., GLASER, J., GREEN, D., and HOUT, M. 1989. Principled tolerance and the American mass public. *British Journal of Political Science*, 19 (1): 25–45.

—— FLETCHER, J., RUSSELL, P., and TETLOCK, P. 1996. *The Clash of Rights: Liberty, Equality, and Legitimacy in Pluralist Democracy*. New Haven: Yale University Press.

STEIN, A. 1999. The consequences of the Nicaraguan revolution for political tolerance: explaining differences among the mass public, Catholic priests, and secular elites. *Comparative Politics*, 30 (3): 335–53.

STENNER, K. 2005. *The Authoritarian Dynamic*. New York: Cambridge University Press.

STOUFFER, S. 1955. *Communism, Conformity and Civil Liberties*. New York: Doubleday.

STRUM, P. 1999. *When the Nazis Came to Skokie: Freedom for Speech We Hate*. Lawrence, Kan.: University Press of Kansas.

SULLIVAN, J., PIERESON, J., and MARCUS, G. 1982. *Political Tolerance and American Democracy*. Chicago: University of Chicago Press.

—— and TRANSUE, J. 1999. The psychological underpinnings of democracy: a selective review of research on political tolerance, interpersonal trust, and social capital. *Annual Review of Psychology*, 50: 625–50.

—— SHAMIR, M., WALSH, P., and ROBERTS, N. 1985. *Political Tolerance in Context: Support for Unpopular Minorities in Israel, New Zealand, and the United States*. Boulder, Colo.: Westview Press, Inc.

—— WALSH, P., SHAMIR, M., BARNUM, D., and GIBSON, J. 1993. Why politicians are more tolerant: selective recruitment and socialization among political elites in Britain, Israel, New Zealand and the United States. *British Journal of Political Science*, 23: 51–76.

TYLER, T., and MITCHELL, G. 1994. Legitimacy and the empowerment of discretionary legal authority: The United States Supreme Court and abortion rights. *Duke Law Journal*, 43: 703–815.

—— BOECKMANN, R., SMITH, H., and HUO, Y. 1997. *Social Justice in a Diverse Society*. Boulder, Colo.: Westview Press.

WEISSBERG, R. 1998. *Political Tolerance: Balancing Community and Diversity*. Thousand Oaks, Calif.: Sage Publications.

WILSON, T. 1994. Trends in tolerance toward rightist and leftist groups, 1976–1988: effects of attitude change and cohort succession. *Public Opinion Quarterly*, 58 (4): 539–56.

ZAKARIA, F. 2003. *The Future of Freedom: Illiberal Democracy at Home and Abroad*. New York. W. W. Norton & Company.

CHAPTER 18

SOCIAL AND POLITICAL TRUST

KENNETH NEWTON

THE idea that trust is essential for social, economic, and political life is a very old one going back at least to Confucius who suggested that trust, weapons, and food are the essentials of government: food, because well-fed citizens are less likely to make trouble, trust because in the absence of food, citizens are likely to believe that their leaders are working on the problem, and weapons in case neither of the other two work. In more recent times, Hobbes and Locke also wrote[1] about the importance of trust, and Adam Smith pointed out that, without it, efficient economic transactions are impossible. Tocqueville placed trust, and voluntary association as the mechanism for creating it, at the centre of his understanding of stable democracy, an idea passed on by John Stuart Mill, Georg Simmel, Ferdinand Toennies, Emile Durkheim, and Max Weber into the twentieth century. In the last decade, there has been an explosion of interest in the concept, partly because of evidence of its decline in western societies, and partly because of the intense interest in theories of social capital. Social capital supposedly has important implications for a large number of diverse phenomena—from economic efficiency, educational attainment, and crime to longevity, good health, stable democracy, and life satisfaction—and trust is a central core of social capital, and the best single empirical indicator of it.[2]

---

[1] For a useful account of the development of theoretical work on trust in western social and political thought see Misztal (1996).

[2] This is not to say that trust is the only component of social capital, or that all components will have the same causes and consequences for social, economic, and political life (Knack 2002, 783; and Stolle chapter in this volume).

This chapter considers the nature and importance of the relationship between social and political trust. It starts with an account of the problems of defining trust and identifies its main types. It then outlines how trust is measured in empirical research, and discusses the reliability and validity of these measures, and we consider some of the main theories of trust. It then examines the empirical evidence for these theories, before drawing some rather cautious conclusions. Since trust is a highly contested concept, and since the theories start from different assumptions and reach different conclusions, the purpose of the chapter is less to provide final answers to questions about trust than to outline different approaches to studying trust and different ways of understanding its significance for contemporary society and political life.

1 DEFINING AND MEASURING TRUST AND TYPES OF TRUST

There is much controversy about what social trust is, how it should be defined, and how it is distinguished from similar terms, such as mutuality, empathy, reciprocity, civility, respect, solidarity, and fraternity (see Barber 1983; Baier 1986; Gambetta 1988; Hardin 1996; Misztal 1996; Seligman 1997; Warren 1999). Some claim that there are so many problems with the concept that we should drop the term and replace it with a better one. This seems like throwing out the baby with the bath water. We cannot assumed that any other term would be a better analytical tool until it is subjected to the same close and critical scrutiny as trust, when it would probably prove just as unsatisfactory. Trust is so closely associated with its synonyms that to substitute one of them is to simply pass on all the old problems. It is better to take the pragmatic view that there is no point in defining the essence of trust, because it has none. As Levi (1998, 79) writes, "Trust is not one thing and it does not have one source; it has a variety of forms and causes." Therefore, we use the pragmatic approach of offering a working definition, identifying good measures of it, and seeing where they get us. It turns out that for all the abstract theory about the deficiencies of the concept and its measurement, trust seems to be understood well enough by those who answer survey questions about it, and the attitudes of trust or distrust they express are quite closely aligned with the way they behave.

1.1 A Working Definition of Trust

We define trust as the belief that others will not deliberately or knowingly do us harm, if they can avoid it, and will look after our interests, if this is possible. This is consistent with a common sense idea of what trust is—that we trust others when we feel we can walk the streets without being mugged, will not be treated unjustly by officials, exploited at work, deceived by politicians, treated badly by friends, acquaintances, or strangers, or cheated in everyday life. It is also close to the academic definition of trust. Hardin (1998, 12–15) defines trust as "encapsulated interest", and Gambetta (1988, 217) argues that it is built on the belief that others will act beneficially rather than maliciously towards us. Warren (1999, 311) writes that trust involves shared interests and a lack of malice.

One preliminary point is that we do not either trust or distrust, but do so to varying degrees. In other words, trust is a variable that ranges along a continuum. Thus we use the shorthand terms trust and distrust, rather than the more accurate but clumsy terms such as "tending towards trust rather more than distrust."

1.2 Types of Trust

It is essential to distinguish between social and political trust, or what is sometimes known as horizontal or interpersonal trust and vertical trust. People may trust those around them and not their political leaders, and although there may be a general association between social and political trust, as social capital theory suggests, this is an empirical question. If we are to explore the social foundations of politics, a major task of political sociology, we must maintain a clear conceptual distinction between the social and the political.

In addition, it is now conventional to distinguish between trust in people and confidence in institutions (Seligman 1997; Giddens 1990, 83–8). Citizens may trust in friends, neighbours, colleagues, and countrymen, about whom they have personal knowledge, but have confidence in institutions such as parliament, the state bureaucracy, and the courts, based upon their sense of how these institutions work. Institutions are based on systems, rules, and formal procedures that operate independently of the face-to-face relations of personal trust. Following this distinction, most survey questions ask about trust in people and confidence in institutions. Institutional confidence comes close to the concept of legitimation, which has a more profound importance for the system of government than trust in particular political leaders or the government of the day (Evans 1996; Warren 1999). In Easton's terms (1965, 1975) institutional confidence is a measure of support for the political regime that is more important for our understanding of political stability than more volatile measures of support for authorities.

A third important distinction is between specific, thick, or particularized social trust, on the one hand, and generalized, thin, or abstract trust on the other. The former is based on personal, first-hand knowledge of individuals (trust in a friend), the latter on more general information about social groups and situations. I trust (or distrust) the people I know because I know them, and I trust (or distrust) my fellow countrymen not because I know them personally, but because I have first-hand knowledge of how society generally works: it is safe to walk this street, not that one: it is safe to walk through the park during the day, but not at night: it is safe to trust registered taxi drivers but not the pirate cabs. In modern, large-scale, geographically mobile, mixed and multicultural societies, trust in strangers is particularly important, especially in strangers who are not like us. In Granovetter's (1973) famous phrase, the "strength of weak ties" becomes more important as the scale and impersonality of society grows. This makes theories of generalized trust all the more crucial for understanding the social integration and stability of modern society.

1.3 Measuring Trust

Trust is contingent upon people and circumstance: I trust a friend to recommend a good book but not to drive my car safely; I trust the professionalism of airline pilots but this does not necessarily extend beyond their occupational capacities; I trust a colleague to turn up to lectures on time but not to meet a writing deadline.[3] For this reason, some argue that there is no meaningful survey question about trust in general. Only questions specifying exactly the object and circumstances of trust make sense, but then the question ceases to have general interest or validity.[4] Anything more general is likely to produce unreliable, meaningless, and random responses of the "door-step opinion" kind. Besides, if social scientists themselves cannot arrive at a common understanding of trust, why should survey respondents do so?

Survey research evidence does not support these doubts. First, cross-national surveys hold few surprises. The World Values surveys, for example, ask the standard question about generalized social trust, and finds that Denmark, Norway, Sweden, the Netherlands, and Finland are at the top of the international league table, separated by 50 or more percentage points from Brazil, Tanzania, Uganda, the Philippines, and Romania at the bottom (see Table 18.1). The standard question about confidence in parliament is probably a less reliable indicator, since Vietnam, China, Bangladesh, and Tanzania are at the top of the global league table. Nevertheless, Norway, Luxembourg, the Netherlands, Sweden, and Denmark have scores between 70 and 49 percent, while Macedonia, Peru, Lithuania, South Korea, and Argentina have 11 percent or less (Table 18.2). With some significant exceptions, the confidence in parliament scores are what one might expect. Confidence in parliament correlates significantly with Freedom House scores for democracy (Inglehart 1997; Newton 2001*a*), which suggests that attitudes correspond quite closely with objective measures. Far from being a set of unreliable, random, and meaningless results, these figures are in danger of being yawningly obvious.

Moreover, surveys suggest that the classic set of trust questions—the much tried and tested Rosenberg scale—works well as a reliable and valid measure of social

---

[3] Or as one commentators puts it, "I would trust Clinton with the economy but not my daughter. I would trust George W. Bush with my daughter but not the economy."

[4] Similarly, Fine (2001, 93) argues that social capital is too flexible a concept to have explanatory meaning.

Table 18.1 Generalized social trust in 83 nations, 2000 (%)

Denmark	67	USA	36	Czech Rep.	24	Slovakia	16
Sweden	66	Germany	35	Greece	24	Turkey	16
Iran	65	Ireland	35	Morocco	24	Venezuela	16
Norway	65	Austria	34	Russia	24	Argentina	15
Netherlands	60	Mont'gro	34	Chile	23	El Salvador	15
Finland	58	Italy	33	Estonia	23	Moldova	15
China	56	Belgium	31	Puerto Rico	23	Macedonia	14
Indonesia	52	Pakistan	31	France	22	S. Africa	12
New Zealand	49	UK	30	Hungary	22	Zimbabwe	12
Japan	43	Jordan	28	Slovenia	22	Algeria	11
Belarus	41	Bulgaria	27	Uruguay	22	Colombia	11
Iceland	41	S. Korea	27	Azerbaijan	21	Peru	11
India	41	Ukraine	27	Malta	21	Portugal	10
Vietnam	41	Dom. Rep.	26	Mexico	21	Romania	10
Switzerland	41	Luxembourg	26	Croatia	19	Philippines	8
Australia	40	Nigeria	26	Georgia	19	Uganda	8
N. Ireland	40	Armenia	25	Poland	19	Tanzania	8
Canada	39	Lithuania	25	Serbia	19	Brazil	3
Taiwan	38	Albania	24	Latvia	17		
Egypt	38	Israel	24	Singapore	17		
Spain	36	Bangla.	24	Bosnia	16		

Source: World Values Survey Wave IV, 1999–2000.

Note: Entries are the percentage of the adult population saying "most people can be trusted" when asked the standard generalized social trust question "Generally speaking, would you say that most people can be trusted or that you can't be too careful in dealing with people?"

trust.[5] These questions scale well, showing that the great majority of respondents, whatever they may understand by the questions, answer them in a consistent and non-random way.[6] The measure of generalized trust also seems to do what it claims. Analyzing a survey that asked more than a dozen different kinds of questions about whom and what people trust, Uslaner (2002, 54) finds that the measure of generalized

---

[5] It consists of three questions:

"Generally speaking, would you say that most people can be trusted or that you can't be too careful in dealing with others?" (Generalized trust)

Would you say that most of the time people try to be helpful or are they mostly looking out for themselves? (Helpfulness)

Do you think that most people would try to take advantage of you if they got a chance or would they try to be fair? (Fairness)

[6] A principle component analysis of individual responses to the Rosenberg trust reveals one main component, with KMO measures of between 62 and 74, that explains between 66% and 87% of the variance in thirteen countries (Zmerli, Newton, and Montero 2007).

Table 18.2 Confidence in parliament in 77 nations, 2000 (%)

Vietnam	98	Zimbabwe	50	USA	38	Ukraine	27
China	95	Denmark	49	Belgium	36	Colombia	25
Bangladesh	89	Portugal	49	Germany	36	Slovenia	25
Tanzania	79	Spain	48	UK	36	Greece	24
Uganda	77	Taiwan	46	Chile	35	Croatia	23
Pakistan	76	Albania	45	Moldova	35	Mexico	23
Azerbaijan	74	Nigeria	45	Brazil	34	Serbia	23
Iceland	72	Finland	44	Hungary	34	Japan	22
Iran	70	Switzerland	44	Italy	34	Morocco	22
Norway	70	Indonesia	43	Algeria	33	Bosnia	20
Egypt	68	Turkey	43	Poland	33	Romania	19
Jordan	65	Slovakia	42	Montenegro	33	Russia	19
Luxembourg	63	Uruguay	42	Australia	31	New Zealand	15
Philippines	62	Austria	41	El Salvador	31	Czech Rep.	12
S. Africa	60	Canada	41	Ireland	31	Dom. Rep.	12
India	55	France	41	Armenia	30	Argentina	11
Netherlands	55	Georgia	41	Latvia	28	S. Korea	11
Malta	52	N. Ireland	40	Bulgaria	27	Lithuania	11
Sweden	51	Belarus	38	Estonia	27	Peru	10
				Ukraine	27	Macedonia	7

Note: The figures are the percentages who respond "a great deal/quite a lot" to the question "for each item listed, how much confidence do you have in them, is it a great deal, quite a lot, not very much, or none at all? Parliament."

trust loads heavily on trust in strangers.[7] He concludes that the question really does measure generalized trust. Finally Yamagishi and colleagues (Yamagishi, Hayashi, and Jin 1994; Yamagishi and Yamagishi 1994) provide some experimental evidence to show that those who express trusting attitudes also tend to behave in a trusting way.

Surveys of trust and confidence do not find the large and random fluctuations in responses that one would expect of questions of doubtful reliability, validity, and meaning. On the contrary, they show a good deal of stability over time. For example, Delhey and Newton (2005) find a correlation of 0.88 (Pearson's r,) between trust scores for thirty-two countries in 1990 and 1995.[8] Uslaner (2002, 66–7) finds that individual responses to the standard trust question in a three-wave panel study (1972–4–6) show remarkable consistency over time, and concludes that trust is an

---

[7] Factor analysis shows three independent dimensions that correspond to trust in strangers (generalized social trust), trust in friends and family (particularized social trust), and trust in government (political trust). This validates empirically the distinctions between social and political trust, and particularized and specific social trust.

[8] On the stability of national trust scores over time see also Knack and Keefer (1997, 1262).

enduring value. Similarly, case studies of large changes in confidence in parliament in four developed democracies find that they correspond to real political and economic events, as we will see later in this chapter. None of this suggests that respondents are not able to answer the trust and confidence questions sensibly or consistently, or that there is no such thing as generalized trust as against trust in particular people and institutions in particular circumstances.

2 THEORIES OF SOCIAL TRUST

Trust is not a natural or innate characteristic (Ridley 1997). It is a form of learned behavior, and because it involves taking risks—a willingness to bank on the trust-worthiness of others—individuals update their sense of trust according to daily experiences (Dasgupta 1988; Hardin 1993; also Uslaner 2002). The question naturally arises of why and under what circumstances we decide to take the risk and trust others or invest institutions with a degree of confidence? There are different approaches to this apparently simple question, depending on the type of trust, but also on fundamentally different approaches to social science explanation.

2.1 Particularized Trust in Small Communities

The simplest kind of trust of the thick or specific type is the easiest to explain. It is typically found in comparatively small, clearly bounded and strongly bonded communities consisting of similar kinds of people who are dependent upon each other, and who interact closely together (Williams 1988). The members of such communities are socialized into a relatively homogeneous culture. Social sanctions are powerful and difficult to escape because the community is clearly bounded. The great merit of specific trust is that it binds the community strongly. Its problem, of course, is that out-groups and strangers are likely to be distrusted (Gambetta 1988). This raises the important point that trust, like social capital, has its good and bad aspects. Trust within a closed circle of mafia members is good for the mafia, but not necessarily for anybody else. Trust within the Protestants and Catholic communities of Northern Ireland is one thing, trust that spans religious, ethnic, or class groups in society is another. It may even be that distrust of the wider society forces people back to intense particular trust in the family—the amoral familism on which Edward Banfield (1958) writes—just as authoritarian and totalitarian political systems seem to undermine generalized trust and oblige citizens to rely in daily life on particularized trust (Mischler and Rose 1997; Sztompka 2000). At any rate, modern large-scale and heterogeneous society cannot be based upon particularized or thick trust, which is why attention has concentrated heavily on generalized social trust.

2.2 Generalized Trust in Large-scale Society

Modern, large-scale societies do not necessarily lack thick or specific trust, but generalized trust in strangers is also important because in these societies much social interaction is between people who neither know one another nor share a common social background. At the same time, urban societies have a double problem. First, small and intense communities of the kind capable of teaching and sustaining thick trust, are increasingly rare in modern, large-scale societies. They have to rely on more diffuse and amorphous mechanisms to sustain generalized trust. Yet, at the same time, generalized social trust is more difficult to explain and assimilate than particularized trust. I understand why I should trust or distrust the people I know, but why should I trust comparative strangers, some of whom may not be of my religion, ethnic background, or culture? Where does such trust come from? There are three main theories: rational-choice, social-psychological, and societal ones.

2.2.1 Rational-choice Trust

Rational-choice theorists see generalized social trust as a rational, tit-for-tat calculation, in which we recognize that we have to treat others in a trustworthy manner to have any hope of them doing the same for us. Rational trust of this kind is self-interest rightly understood.[9] The problem is the difficulty of falsifying the proposition. To do so we need a way of distinguishing between actions that are self-interested and other-interested, and in the same way that we can construe everything and everything we do as the pursuit of pleasure, so we can define all our actions as self-interested. If man serves himself by serving others then even the most altruistic and selfless action can be interpreted as the clever and far sighted pursuit of self-interest. On the other hand, a less restricted approach suggests that there seem to be many examples of people acting in a trustworthy manner even though it seems not to be in their own interests, or at least in their own immediate interests. If it is rationally self-interested to betray trust, defect from agreements, and free-ride on the occasions where we can get away with it, then many people are not rational a lot of the time. Most people do not see the world this way because other calculations and values enter into their social relations. Finally, trust is a "bootstraps" concept; we need a minimum of trust before we can even enter into normal trusting relationships. In the same way that purely economic relations need trust as a precondition for their existence, a degree of trust is a precondition for establishing the kind of social relations on which social trust can develop.[10] To this extent, the rational explanation of trust seems to assume away the puzzle of its existence (cf. Blackburn 1998; Warren 1999).

2.2.2 Social-psychological Theories

One way of avoiding this problem is to argue, as social-psychologists do, that trust is learned in early childhood and becomes part of a core personality syndrome.

---

[9] The phrase "self interest rightly understood" is Tocqueville's (1945, 129–32) where he argues, as does Adam Smith, that "man serves himself in serving his fellow creatures."

[10] This is Durkheim's critique of rational, self-interested utilitarianism (see Misztal 1996: 42–9).

According to this theory, people acquire a trusting or distrusting disposition as a result of relations with adults in early childhood, particularly with a mother or mother figure. Once established, trusting dispositions tend to persist as a central feature of the individual's psychological make-up, unless challenged by trauma (Uslaner 2002, 89). Consequently, people carry their sense of trust with them through their lives and in different sorts of circumstances. Trust is an intrinsic part of a larger syndrome of personality characteristics, including a sense of optimism, a sense of control over ones own life, and a belief in the possibility of cooperation with others. (Erikson 1950; Allport 1961; Cattell 1965; Rosenberg 1956, 1957; Uslaner 1999, 2000, 2002). In short, this approach maintains that trust is learned at an early age, when it becomes a core feature of a personality syndrome that includes having a confident, optimistic, and cooperative disposition.

A variation of the social-psychology approach places less importance on early childhood socialization than on everyday experiences in later life. According to this view, trust is not a core personality trait so much as a product of an individual's life experience. This approach looks for correlations between trust and objective individual characteristics often associated with patterns of life experience (class and income, education, age, gender, religion, ethnicity, and personal experiences such as unemployment, divorce, and having a close circle of friends), and with subjective attitudes such as job satisfaction, life satisfaction, happiness, and perhaps a sense of anxiety, insecurity, and lack of control in life.

Both social-psychological approaches see trust as a bottom-up phenomenon based on individual psychology and experience. Both expect to find a connection between trust and the personal psychological or social characteristics of individuals. According to Portes (1998, 21) "the greatest theoretical promise of social capital lies at the individual level," as Bourdieu (1986) and Coleman (1988, 1990) conceived it.

2.2.3 Societal Theories

A different view of generalized social trust sees it not so much as the property of individuals, but as a collective feature of society. When answering the survey questions about trust, respondents tell us less about themselves and their personal inclinations, and more about how they evaluate the trustworthiness of the people in the world around them. Those who believe that others generally behave in a trustworthy manner are likely to say that they trust; those who believe that others are not trustworthy are likely to express distrust. In this sense, social trust is based on daily experience of social relations, and responses to the generalized trust question can be taken as a measure—a litmus paper test—of how people actually treat each other in the respondent's society. Trust is not a mindset that people have inside themselves, but a collective property of social systems. It forms the context of social relations and it is based on experience of social relations; therefore it influences how individuals relate to others, and it influences how individuals respond to survey questions about generalized trust (Levi 1996; Putnam 2000; Newton 2001b; Maloney, Smith, and Stoker 2001).

Individuals can both consume and produce trust, but they do so in the sense of consuming and producing an indivisible social good. Acting in a trustworthy manner reinforces the climate of trust, and helps to preserve a virtuous circle in which others do the same. The more trustworthy others are, the more it makes sense to take the risks implicit in trust, the more trustworthy my own behavior and that of others is likely to be, and the more trust is likely to be expressed by society in general.[11]

The individual and the societal views of trust are clearly not incompatible. Individuals in a given society may vary in their willingness to trust according to their personality types formed by early socialization or by later life experiences. Some societies may have higher levels of trust than others according to their social, economic, and political circumstances, irrespective of their distribution of personality and social types. This view is consistent with the argument that generalized social trust in modern, large-scale society is associated with a wide range of institutional mechanisms of social control that are designed, among other things, to reinforce trustworthy behavior.

A mental experiment illustrates this view of trust. Imagine taking a taxi in Copenhagen in the middle of the night and trusting the taxi driver not to cheat you. After all, Copenhagen is a law abiding place, the taxi has a meter and a number, the city and the country has an elaborate set of local rules governing the taxi business, and a reliable system of implementing and monitoring them. Then imagine taking another taxi ride in the middle of the night with, as it happens, exactly the same driver, but this time in Rio de Janeiro, one of the world's more lawless and low-trust cities, where the taxi has no meter, no number, and no back-up system of control. Now I am a trusting sort of chap, but should I be as trusting in Rio as in Copenhagen? It would not be wise.

This account of trust and trustworthiness may throw light on the nature of trust but it does not explain where it comes from. One answer is the classical theory that we learn to trust by interacting with others in voluntary associations. These are the "free schools of democracy" that teach us "the habits of the heart" on which democracy and social harmony rest—reciprocity, empathy, understanding, trust, cooperation, compromise, and a capacity to rub along in an adequately peaceful way with others so that we all benefit in the end. Voluntary associations represent our interests in the conflicts over public policies but they also draw us into civic engagement and get us involved in our communities in a satisfying and productive manner.

A different account of trust in modern society brings institutions back in, that is institutions with a bearing on trustworthy behavior. These include public bureaucracies, especially the police, courts, the law, and state bureaucracies, and their universal code of operation, as well as a wide range of professional and commercial organizations and their codes of practice. Every time we visit the dentist, the doctor,

---

[11] It does not follow that trust or social capital is equally distributed across all sections of the population in a society. It is not (Hall 1999; Edwards and Foley 2001; Maloney, Smith, and Stoker 2004; Li, Savage, and Pickles 2003).

the bank, a restaurant, a shop, or a cinema, and every time we use a lift, travel on a bus, train, or plane, even cross a bridge or walk in the street, we trust the individuals, equipment, infrastructure, and public regulation of these things. We do this not because we know much, if anything, about the particular people or equipment or rules of conduct involved, but because we place trust in a system that trains people for their jobs, monitors their performance and health, regulates their working hours, checks the safety of brakes, engines, machinery, the public health provisions of public places, and the brick and metalwork of buildings, bridges, and railways. Even the teaching and research of university professors are increasingly regulated, monitored, and evaluated.

It does not follow that the institutionalized monitoring and regulation of behavior is the only source of social trust in the modern world, for it surely is not. Nor does it follow that monitoring and regulation always have their desired effect, for they surely do not. In fact, their increasing use by public and private agencies may undermine trust because their very use signals an unwillingness to trust people in the first place. As O'Neill (2002, 19) puts it, "Plants don't flourish when we pull them up too often to check how their roots are growing: political, institutional and professional life too may not flourish if we constantly uproot it to demonstrate that everything is transparent and trustworthy". One of the paradoxes of trust is that it involves risk, but modern society often goes to extreme lengths to minimize risk, so it imposes elaborates rules to enforce trustworthiness, which undermines trust.

2.3 Individual-level Empirical Research

Empirical research at the individual level has not been conspicuously successful in establishing the origins and the consequences of social trust or its connection with political trust. There is some evidence that the socially trusting are the winners in society, as measured by money, status, education, job and life satisfaction, and subjective happiness (Newton 1999a; Whiteley 1999; Putnam 2000; Patterson 1999; Delhey and Newton 2003; Stolle 2001). It is not difficult to imagine why the relatively affluent, well-educated, and high-status members of society tend to express trust, whereas those in the slums do not.

Political trust and confidence do not seem to overlap much, if at all, with social trust (Kaase 1999; Newton 2001b). Most research finds that the social trust is independent of political confidence, and the politically trusting are, if anything, even more randomly distributed among social groups than the socially trusting (Abramson 1983; Lawrence 1997).[12] Political trust is better explained by political rather than social variables—support for the governing party or coalition, national pride, interest in politics, and belief in open government (Newton 1999b; Newton and Norris 2000; Anderson and LoTempio 2002). Once again, it is not surprising that

---

[12] However, low and insignificant correlations between generalized social trust and political confidence may be the result of poor and blunt measures of these variables—see Zmerli, Newton, and Montero (forthcoming).

social trust at the individual level is best explained by social variables, whereas political trust is best explained by political factors.

At the same time, the most notable thing about attempts to explain individual variations in social trust is the poor results. Statistically, the associations between generalized social trust and individual characteristics are rather weak and patchy, and even the strongest combination of variables usually explains a rather small proportion of the variance. In this sense individual variables, social or psychological, have not explained social trust at all well, although they should not be completely dismissed.

One notable absentee from the list of variables associated with social and political trust is membership of voluntary associations. Although group membership is heavily emphasized by many major social theorists of the nineteenth and twentieth centuries, as well as the recent civil society and social capital literatures, there is little evidence to support the claim. By and large, research shows that involvement with voluntary associations (membership of, multiple membership of, and activity in) has a weak bearing on trust, and on many other forms of social attitudes and behavior (Stolle 2001; Delhey and Newton 2003; Wollebaek and Selle 2003; Uslaner 2006). The association with political attitudes and behavior is even weaker (Van Deth 2000; Dekker, Koopmans, and van den Broak 1997; Knack and Keefer 1997; Torcal and Montero 1999; Newton 1999a, 1999b; Stolle and Rochon 2001; Whiteley 1999; Booth and Richard 2001; Vazquez and Olmos 2003). Two recent reviews of the literature bluntly reject the claim that we learn to trust by interacting with others in voluntary associations (Uslaner 1999,145–6; Hooghe 2003a, 2003c). Nor is there a strong link between social trust and civic engagement (Uslaner 2002, ch. 5).

On reflection it is difficult to see why voluntary associations might be important in this particular respect. Most people do not devote a great deal of time or emotional energy to them, compared with their jobs, family, neighborhood, and school (Newton 1997, 579). It is as likely that the trusting join associations, as that associations generate trust (Stolle and Hooghe 2004; Stolle 2001; Jennings and Stoker 2004). Besides, it is difficult to know how contact with people we know can teach us trust in people we do not know, especially when voluntary associations are usually composed of like-minded people with a similar social background (Rosenblum 1998; Uslaner 2006).

In sum, social and political trust when viewed from the individual level is a puzzle. As a dependent variable it is difficult to explain; and as an independent variable it does not seem to explain much. Indeed, from the individual perspective, it is difficult to know what all the fuss is about.

2.4 Cross-national Empirical Research

Fortunately, cross-national research shows a much stronger connection between social and political trust, and between social trust and a variety of social, economic, and political circumstances. Most studies find significant correlations between generalized social trust and a string of political measures such as satisfaction with democracy, satisfaction with government, confidence in public institutions (police, courts, parliament, civil service, cabinets, and government) and objective measures of democracy and the workings of democratic government (Newton 1999*b*, 2001*b*; Newton and Norris 2000; Inglehart 1997, 1999). Political systems and institutions that perform with fairness and impartiality encourage individuals to behave the same way, pay their taxes, respect the public interest, play their part as citizens, support the institutions of government, not free-ride, and trust their fellow citizens (Dunn 1990; Foley and Edwards 2001; Levi 1998; Brehm and Rahn 1997; Scholz 1998; Pagden 1988; Offe 1999; Rothstein 2000; Rothstein and Stolle 2003; Huysseune 2003). The implications are that not only can social trust between citizens help to create social conditions that underpin stable democratic government, but systems of government can make it possible for citizens to behave in a trustworthy manner by virtue of institutions that regulate social relations (police and the courts) and that set frameworks for all sorts of social activities (education, civil service, local government).[13]

Putnam, Pharr, and Dalton (2000, 26; see also Newton and Norris, 2000; Van der Meer 2003) extend this line of reasoning to the "rainmaker hypothesis." This argues that in the same way that rain from the skies falls on the just and the unjust alike, so also the operation of government institutions affect all citizens in a country to a greater or lesser extent, irrespective of whether they are trusting or distrusting individuals. Trusting attitudes and trustworthy behavior is more likely in countries with an honest and corruption-free police force, legal system, and public bureaucracy to enforce the social order. These institutions create a framework that makes it possible to behave in a trustworthy manner and not suffer for it.[14] Citizens are less likely to pay their taxes in a climate of distrust where bureaucrats are corrupt (Scholz 1998). Social distrust goes hand in hand with institutionalized corruption (Delhey and Newton 2005). Trust is higher in welfare systems based on universal principles than in those using means testing, which are more likely to create distrust and suspicion among the public and between citizen and welfare officials (Rothstein 1998; Rothstein and Stolle 2003). Elections can create social trust (Rahn, Brehm, and Carlson 1999), just as authoritarian or totalitarian governments can help to destroy it (Mischler and Rose 1997).

Although any country has its particular distribution of trusting personality types, the differences between countries like Denmark and Sweden, where 67 and 66 percent of the population expresses trust, and Brazil and Tanzania, where 3 and 8 percent do, is likely to be attributable to social and political institutions as much as to social-psychological factors. The Norwegians and Danes trust each other because their daily experience suggests that this is sensible, and it is sensible because they live in societies whose institutions facilitate trustworthy behavior. In other words, Danes and Norwegians say they trust their fellow citizens because their fellow citizens are

---

[13] Solt (2004) is one of the few aggregate studies that finds nothing to support social capital.

[14] There is a stronger correlation between generalized social trust and confidence in the police and legal system, than confidence in other public institutions, because, it might be argued, the police and the courts are particulary important for relations of social trust between ordinary citizens (Newton 2001*a*, 1134).

trustworthy. And Danish and Norwegian society is trustworthy because (at least in part) their institutions of democracy, administration, law enforcement, civil society, and welfare are relatively fair, just, impartial and corruption-free in their operations. These make it easier and normal to behave in a trustworthy manner, while not being unduly disadvantaged by a minority who might be prepared to exploit the trusting.

2.5 Systems of Social and Political Trust

Cross-national comparative research shows that social and political trust are generally embedded in a larger complex of social, economic, and political features of society (Putnam 1993; Knack and Keefer 1997; Tyler 1998; Booth and Richard 2001; Newton 2001b; Inglehart and Welzel 2005; Weingast 1998; Levi and Stoker 2000; Knack 2002; Begum 2003; Warner 2003). Four sets of influences seem to be particularly closely associated with generalized social trust (Delhey and Newton 2005). The first, good government, is a composite index of national measures of the rule of law, government effectiveness, political stability, years of democracy, and a law and order index (Delhey and Newton 2005). These variables themselves form a tight part and parcel of a single syndrome of national characteristics. Second, national wealth (a simple measure of GDP per capita) and income equality are associated with high trust. It seems that for poor countries it is wealth that matters, but for rich countries it is income equality that matters so far as social trust is concerned. Third, and further back in the causal chain, trust is associated with ethnic homogeneity. The more ethnically, religiously, or linguistically fragmented a society, the lower its social trust is likely to be. And last, of all the world's religions, a Protestant majority (or large minority) is the only one that seems to make a difference to trust levels.

These factors are often so closely associated with one another that they are difficult to disentangle. Protestantism is closely aligned historically with capitalism, economic growth, and income equality. Wealthy nations are often democratically developed with effective and efficient public institutions that command the confidence of their citizens. Ethnic homogeneity makes it easier to govern, and may facilitate the redistribution of wealth. There is a connection between the individualism and self-government of the Protestant ethic and democracy. In short, generalized social trust is often part of a tight syndrome of social, economic, and political features of nations.

3 CONCLUSIONS

Research on social and political trust is a difficult project. Trust is a complicated concept, difficult to define and closely tied, conceptually and empirically, to many social and political attitudes and forms of behavior. It is claimed to be a major factor in a long and varied list of social goods: trusting individuals are said to live longer, happier, and more healthy lives; high-trust societies are said to be wealthier and more democratic; trusting communities are supposed to have better schools and lower crime rates. The fact that trust can be simultaneously cast as (1) both an individual and collective property; (2) a private and a collective good; (3) something that individuals and society people can produce and consume; (4) both a possible cause and consequence of a wide range of important social and political attitudes and behaviors; and (5) both a foundation and product of democratic institutions and politics, further complicates matters.

The importance of trust is that it might lie at the heart of a powerful explanatory social nexus, but this only produces the difficulty that it is also part of a close family of social, economic, and political phenomena that are difficult to study empirically, and virtually impossible to disentangle one variable from another. If trust is linked in so many ways to so many things, how can we be sure that it is trust that matters, and not some combination of its close correlates? And even if we can isolate trust as an important variable, how are we to decide whether it is cause or effect? There is good evidence that income equality is linked to trust, but does trust make it easier to redistribute income, or is it that greater equality encourages trust? Does the fact that social trust and democracy go together tell us that it is easier to build democracy in a society where individuals trust each other, or that democracy creates trust? At the same time, it is easy to fall into circular arguments: trust helps to generate a social outcome; and we can judge the existence and importance of trust from the presence of this outcome (Portes 1998).

Given all these difficulties it is not unexpected that theoretical and empirical research is controversial and often inconclusive. But in an attempt to cut through some of the difficulties it might be helpful to offer three tentative conclusions based on the theory and evidence covered in this chapter. First, voluntary associations do not seem to matter. It may well be that voluntary associations count in all sorts of other ways, but where social capital and civil society theories are concerned, it is notable that most individual and aggregate studies find little support for the idea that membership of, or activity in, voluntary associations generates social trust. It may be that current work on bonding and bridging associations will find the evidence, but meanwhile there is little to encourage the classical theory that links voluntary involvement with the habits of the heart that sustain social integration and democratic stability.

Second, individual-level studies of social and political trust have not generally produced particularly strong or robust results that help us understand the origins of trust or its consequences. Social trust is generally rather weakly associated with individual characteristics of an objective and subjective nature. It is true that social trust seems to be a privilege of the rich, successful, and educated, and it is true that the trusting people are often happy and satisfied with their life, but the pattern is not a notably strong one. In regression analysis terms, these sorts of variables explain only a small proportion of the variance. Political trust is usually even more randomly distributed between social groups. It is more closely associated with political variables such as national pride, support for the governing party or coalition, and interest in politics. Most studies find slight connection between social and political trust, and between social trust and forms of social participation, democratic behavior, and civic engagement. In this sense trust is a puzzling concept: its individual origins are largely unexplained; and its individual effects are hard to find.

Third, the good and positive news is that there is stronger and more consistent evidence that social and political institutions and the way they work have profound implications for social trust, as well as political trust and confidence. For example, generalized social trust is higher the better a nation's Freedom House score for democracy, the longer the nation has been a democracy, the more it is run according to the rule of law, the more effective its government institutions, and the less corruption there is. Generalized social trust is higher in countries that express more confidence in parliament and greater satisfaction with democracy. Social trust is higher in wealthier societies, and among wealthier societies it is higher in more equal ones. It is higher in states with universalistic rather than selective welfare systems. This suggests that trust may well be a top-down phenomenon that is influenced by the nature and operation of social and political institutions, as much as a bottom-up phenomenon built upon patterns of childhood socialization and the life experiences of individual citizens. If this is so, then research on social and political trust of a cross-national research or aggregate nature is likely to yield better returns than studies that take individuals as their unit of analysis.

REFERENCES

ABRAMSON, P. 1983. *Political Attitudes in America: Formation and Change*. San Francisco: W. H. Freeman.

ALLPORT, G. W. 1961. *Pattern and Growth in Personality*. New York: Holt, Rinehart & Winston.

ANDERSON, C. J., and LoTEMPIO, A. J. 2002. Winning, losing, and political trust in America. *British Journal of Political Science*, 32: 335–51.

BAIER, A. 1986. Trust and anti-trust'. *Ethics*, 96: 231–60.

BANFIELD, E. C. 1958. *The Moral Basis of Backward Society*, Glencoe, Ill.: Free Press.

BARBER, B. 1983. *The Logic and Limits of Trust*. New Brunswick, NJ: Rutgers University Press.

BEGUM, H. 2003. *Social Capital in Action: Adding up Local Connections and Networks*. London: National Council for Voluntary Associations.

BLACKBURN, S. 1998. Trust, co-operation and human psychology. Pp. 28–45 in *Trust and Governance*, ed. V. Braithwaite and M. Levi New York: Russell Sage Foundation.

BOOTH, J. A., and RICHARD, P. B. 2001. Civil society and political context in central America. Pp. 43–55 in *Beyond Tocqueville: Civil Society and the Social Capital Debate in Comparative Perspective*, ed. R. Edwards, M. W. Foley, and M. Diani. Hanover, NH: Tufts University Press.

BOURDIEU, P. 1986. The Forms of Capital. Pp. 241–58 in *Handbook of Theory and Research for the Sociology of Education*, ed. J. G. Richardson. New York: Greenwood Press.

BREHM, J., and RAHN, W. 1997. Individual-level evidence for the causes and consequences of social capital. *American Journal of Political Science*, 41: 999–1023.

CATTELL, R. B. 1965. *The Scientific Analysis of Personality*. Baltimore: Penguin Books.

COLEMAN, J. S. 1988. Social capital in the creation of human capital. *American Journal of Sociology*, 94: 95–120.

—— 1990. *Foundations of Social Theory*, Cambridge: Belknap.

DASGUPTA, P. 1988. Trust as a commodity. Pp. 49–71 in *Trust: Making and Breaking Cooperative Relations*, ed. D. Gambetta. Oxford: Blackwell.

DELHEY, J., and NEWTON, K. 2003. Who trusts? The origins of social trust in seven countries. *European Societies*, 5: 93–137.

—— —— 2005. Predicting cross-national levels of social trust: Global pattern or Nordic exceptionalism?, *European Sociological Review*, DOI:10.1093/esr/jci022.

DEKKER, P. KOOMANS, R., and VAN DEN BROAK A. 1997. Voluntary associations, social movements and individual political behavior in western Europe. Pp. 220–40 *Private Groups and Public Life*, ed. J. van Deth. London: Routedge.

DUNN, J. 1990. Trust and political agency. Pp. 45–61 in *Interpreting Political Responsibility*, ed. J. Dunn. Cambridge: Polity Press.

EASTON, D. 1965. *A Systems Analysis of Political Life*. New York: Wiley.

—— 1975. A re-assessment of the concept of political support. *British Journal of Political Science*, 5: 435–57.

EDWARDS R., and FOLEY, M. W. 2001. Civil society and social capital: a primer. Pp. 1–16 in *Beyond Tocqueville: Civil Society and the Social Capital Debate in Comparative Perspective*, ed. R. Edwards, M. W. Foley, and M. Diani. Hanover, NH: University of New England Press.

ERIKSON, E. H. 1950. *Childhood and Society*. New York: Norton.

EVANS, P. 1996. Government action, social capital and development: reviewing the evidence on synergy. *World Development*, 24: 1119–32.

FINE, B. 2001. *Social Capital Versus Social Theory*. London: Routledge.

FOLEY M., and EDWARDS, R. 1996. The paradox of civil society. *Journal of Democracy*, 7: 38–52.

—— —— 1997. Escape from politics?: social theory and the social capital debate. *American Behavioral Scientist*, 40: 550–61.

GAMBETTA, D. 1988. Mafia: the price of distrust. Pp. 158–75 in *Trust: Making and Breaking Cooperative Relations*, ed. D. Gambetta. Oxford: Blackwell.

GIDDENS, A. 1990. *The Consequences of Modernity*. Stanford, Calif.: Stanford University Press.

GRANOVETTER, M. S. 1973. The strength of weak ties. *American Journal of Sociology*, 78: 1360–80.

HALL, P. 1999. Social capital in Britain. *British Journal of Political Science*, 29: 417–61.

HARDIN, R. 1991. Trusting persons, trusting institutions. Pp. 185–209 in *The Strategy of Choice*, ed. R. J. Zeckhauser. Cambridge, Mass.: MIT Press.

—— 1993. The street-level epistemology of trust. *Politics and Society*, 21: 505–29.

—— 1996. Trustworthiness. *Ethics*, 107: 26–42.

—— 1998. Trust in government. Pp. 9–27 in *Trust and Governance*, ed. V. Braithwaite and M. Levi. New York: Russell Sage.

HOOGHE, M. 2003a. Value congruence and convergence within voluntary associations: ethnocentricism in Belgian organisations. *Political Behavior*, 25: 151–75.

—— 2003b. Participation in voluntary associations and value indicators: the effects of current and previous participation experiences. *Nonprofit and Voluntary Sector Quarterly*, 32: 47–69.

—— 2003c. Voluntary associations and democratic attitudes: value congruence as a causal mechanism. Pp. 89–112 in *Social Capital: Civil Society and Institutions in Comparative Perspective*, ed. M. Hooghe and D. Stolle. Basingtoke: Palgrave.

HUYSSEUNE, M. 2003. Institutions and their impact on social capital and civic culture: the case of Italy. Pp. 211–30 in *Social Capital: Civil Society and Institutions in Comparative Perspective*, ed. M. Hooghe and D. Stolle. Basingtoke: Palgrave.

INGLEHART, R. 1997. *Modernization and Post-Modernization: Cultural, Economic and Political Change in 43 Societies.* Princeton: Princeton University Press.

—— 1999. Trust, well-being and democracy. Pp. 88–120 in *Democracy and Trust,* ed. M. E. Warren. Cambridge: Cambridge University Press.

—— and WELZEL, C. 2005. *Modernization, Cultural Change and Democracy.* New York: Cambridge University Press.

JENNINGS, M. K., and STOKER, L. 2004. Social trust and civic engagement across time and generations. *Acta Politica,* 39: 342–79.

KAASE, M. 1999. Interpersonal trust, political trust and non-institutionalised political participation in Western Europe. *West European Politics,* 22: 1–23.

KNACK, S. 2002. Social capital and the quality of government: evidence from the states. *American Journal of Political Science,* 46: 772–85.

—— and KEEFER, P. 1997. Does social capital have an economic payoff? A cross-country investigation. *Quarterly Journal of Economics,* 112: 1251–88.

LAWRENCE, R. Z. 1997. Is it really the economy stupid? Pp. 111–32 in *Why Americans Mistrust Government,* ed. J. S. Nye, P. D. Zelikow, and D. C. King. Cambridge, Mass.: Harvard University Press.

LEVI, M. 1996. Social and unsocial capital: a review essay of Robert Putnam's *Making Democracy Work. Politics and Society,* 24: 45–55.

—— 1998. A state of trust. Pp. 77–101 in *Trust and Governance,* ed. V. Braithwaite and M. Levi. New York: Russell Sage Foundation.

—— and STOKER, L. 2000. Political trust and trustworthiness. Pp. 475–508 in *Annual Review of Political Science,* Vol. 30, ed. N. W. Polsby. Palo Alto, Calif. Annual reviews.

LI, Y., SAVAGE, M., and PICKLES, A. 2003. Social capital and social exclusion in England and Wales. *British Journal of Sociology,* 54: 497–526.

LUHMANN, N. 1979. *Trust and Power,* New York: Wiley.

MALONEY, W., SMITH, G., and STOKER, G. 2001. Social capital and the city. Pp. 83–96 in *Beyond Tocqueville: Civil Society and the Social Capital Debate in Comparative Perspective,* ed. B. Edwards, M. W. Foley, and M. Diani. Hanover, NH: Tufts University/University of New England Press.

MALONEY, W., SMITH, G., and STOKER, G. 2004. Building social capital in city politics: scope and limitations at the inter-organisational level. *Political Studies,* 52: 508–30.

MISCHLER, W., and ROSE, R. 1997. Trust, distrust, and skepticism: popular evaluations of civil and political institutions in post-communist societies. *Journal of Politics,* 59: 418–51.

MISZTAL, B. A. 1996. *Trust in Modern Societies.* Oxford: Blackwell.

NEWTON, K. 1997. Social capital and democracy. *American Behavioral Scientist,* 40: 575–86.

—— 1999*a*. Social capital and democracy in modern Europe. Pp. 3–24 in *Social Capital and European Democracy,* ed. J van Deth et al. London: Routledge.

—— 1999*b*. Social and political trust in established democracies. Pp. 169–87 in *Critical Citizens,* ed. P. Norris. Oxford, Oxford University Press.

—— 2001*a*. Social capital and democracy. Pp. 225–34 in *Beyond Tocqueville: Civil Society and the Social Capital Debate in Comparative Perspective,* ed. B. Edwards, M. J. Foley, and M. Diani. Hanover, NH: Tufts University Press.

—— 2001*b*. Trust, social capital, civil society, and democracy. *International Political Science Review,* 22: 201–14.

—— and NORRIS, P. 2000. Confidence in public institutions: faith, culture, or performance? Pp. 52–73 in *Disaffected Democracies: What's Ailing the Trilateral Democracies?,* ed. S. Pharr and R. Putnam. Princeton: Princeton University Press.

OFFE, C. 1999. How can we trust our fellow citizens? Pp. 42–87 in *Democracy and Trust*, ed. M. Warren Cambridge: Cambridge University Press.

O'NEIL, O. 2002. *A Question of Trust: The BBC Reith Lectures 2002*. Cambridge: Cambridge University Press.

ORREN, G. 1997. Fall from grace: the public's loss of faith in government. Pp. 77–107 in *Why Americans Mistrust Government*, ed. J. S. Nye, P. D. Zelikow, and D. C. King. Cambridge, Mass.: Harvard University Press.

PAGDEN, A. 1988. The destruction of trust and its economic consequences in the case of eighteenth-century Naples. Pp. 127–41 in *Trust: Making and Breaking Cooperative Relations*, ed. D. Gambetta. Oxford: Blackwell.

PATTERSON, O. 1999. Liberty against the democratic state: on the historical and contemporary sources of American distrust. Pp. 151–207 in *Democracy and Trust*, ed. M. E. Warren. Cambridge: Cambridge University Press.

PORTES, A. 1998. Social capital: its origins and applications in modern sociology. *Annual Review of Sociology*, 24, Annual reviews: 1–24.

PUTNAM, R. D. 1993. *Making Democracy Work: Civic Traditions in Modern Italy*. Princeton: Princeton University Press.

—— 2000. *Bowling Alone: The Collapse and Revival of American Community*. New York: Simon & Schuster.

—— PHARR, S., and DALTON, R. J. 2000. Introduction: what's troubling the trilateral democracies? Pp. 3–27 in *Disaffected Democracies: Whats Troubling theTrilateral Countries?*, ed. S. J. Pharr and R. D. Putnam. Princeton: Princeton University Press.

RAHN, W. M., BREHM, J., and CARLSON, N. 1999. National elections as institutions for generating social capital. Pp. 110–60 in *Civil Engagement in American Democracy*, ed. T. Skocpol and M. Fiorina. Washington, DC: Brookings Institution.

RIDLEY, M. 1997. *The Origins of Virtues: Human Instincts and the Evolution of Cooperation*. New York: Viking.

ROSENBERG, M. 1956. Misanthropy and political ideology. *American Sociological Review*, 21: 690–5.

—— 1957. Misanthropy and attitudes towards international affairs. *Journal of Conflict Resolution*, 1: 340–5.

ROSENBLUM, N. L. 1998. *Membership and Morals*. Princeton: Princeton University Press.

ROTHSTEIN, B. 1998. *Just Institutions Matter: The Moral and Political Logic of the Universal Welfare State*. Cambridge: Cambridge University Press.

—— 2000. Trust, social dilemmas, and collective memories. *Journal of Theoretical Politics*, 12: 476–501.

—— and STOLLE, D. 2003. Social capital, impartiality and the welfare state: an institutional approach. Pp. 191–209 in *Social Capital: Civil Society and Institutions in Comparative Perspective*, ed. M. Hooghe and D. Stolle. Basingstoke: Palgrave.

SCHOLZ, J. T. 1998. Trust, taxes and compliance. Pp. 135–66 in *Trust and Governance*, ed. V. Braithwaite and M. Levi. New York: Russell Sage.

SELIGMAN, A. B. 1997. *The Problem of Trust*. Princeton: Princeton University Press.

SOLT, F. 2004. Civics or structure? Revisiting the origins of democratic quality in the Italian regions. *British Journal of Political Science*, 34: 123–35.

STOLLE, D. 2001. Getting to trust: an analysis of the importance of institutions, families, personal experiences and group membership. Pp. 118–33 in *Social Capital and Participation in Everyday Life*, ed. P. Dekker and E. Uslaner. London: Routledge.

—— and HOOGHE, M. 2004. The roots of social capital: attitudinal and network mechanisms in relation between youth and adult factors of social capital. *Acta Politica*, 39: 422–41.

—— and ROCHON, T. R. 2001. Are all associations alike: member diversity, associational type, and the creation of social capital. Pp. 83–96 in *Beyond Tocqueville: Civil Society and the Social Capital Debate in Comparative Perspective*, ed. B. Edwards, M. W. Foley, and M. Diani. Hanover, NH: Tufts University/University of New England Press.

SZTOMPKA, P. 2000. *Trust: A Sociological Theory.* Cambridge: Cambridge University Press.

TOCQUEVILLE, A. DE 1945. *Democracy in America,* vol. ii. New York: Vintage Books.

TORCAL, M., and MONTERO, J. R. 1999. Facets of social capital in new democracies, Pp. 213–39 in *Social Capital and European Democracy,* ed. J. van Deth et al. London: Routledge.

TYLER, T. 1998. Trust and democratic governance. Pp. 269–94 in *Trust and Governance*, ed. V. Braithwaite and M. Levi. New York: Russell Sage Foundation.

USLANER E. M. 1999. Democracy and social capital. Pp. 121–50 in *Democracy and Trust*, ed. M. Warren. Cambridge: Cambridge University Press.

USLANER, E. M. 2000. Producing and consuming trust. *Political Science Quarterly*, 115: 569–90.

—— 2002. *The Moral Foundations of Trust.* New York: Cambridge University Press.

—— 2006. Trust as a moral value. In *Handbook of Social Capital*, ed. D. Castiglione, J. W. van Deth, and G. Wolleb. Oxford: Oxford University Press.

VAN DER MEER, J. 2003. Rain or fog? An empirical examination of social capital's rainmaker effects. Pp. 133–51 in *Social Capital: Civil Society and Institutions in Comparative Perspective,* ed. M. Hooghe and D. Stolle. Basingtoke: Palgrave.

VAN DETH, J. W. 2000. Interesting but irrelevant: social capital and the saliency of politics in Western Europe. *European Journal of Political Research*, 37: 115–47.

VAZQUEZ, F. H., and OLMOS, H. C. 2003. In whom we trust? The development of particularised trust inside associations. *European Political Science*, Summer: 56–60.

WARNER, A. 2003. Social capital as a societal resource for building political support in new democracies. *European Political Science*, Summer: 61–7.

WARREN, M. E. 1999. Democratic theory and trust. Pp. 310–45 in *Democracy and Trust*, ed. M. Warren. Cambridge: Cambridge University Press.

WEINGAST, B. 1998. Constructing trust: the political and economic roots of ethnic and regional violence. Pp. 163–200 in *Where is the New Institutionalism Now?*, ed. V. Haufler, K. Soltan, and E. Uslaner, Ann Arbor: University of Michigan Press.

WHITELEY, P. F. 1999. The origins of social capital. Pp. 25–44 in *Social Capital and European Democracy*, ed. J. van Deth et al. London: Routledge.

WILLIAMS, B. 1988. Formal structures and social reality. Pp. 3–15 in *Trust: Making and Breaking Cooperative Relations*, ed. D. Gambetta. Oxford: Blackwell.

WOLLEBAEK, D., and SELLE, P. 2003. Participation and social capital formation: Norway in a comparative perspective. *Scandinavian Political Studies*, 26 (1): 67–91.

YAMAGISHI, T., HAYASHI, N., and JIN, N. 1994. Prisoner's dilemma networks: selection strategy versus action strategy. Pp. 233–50 in *Social Dilemmas and Cooperation*, ed. U. Schulz, W. Albers, and U. Mueller. New York: Springer-Verlag.

—— and YAMAGISHI, M. 1994. Trust and commitment in the United States and Japan. *Motivation and Emotion*, 18: 129–166.

ZMERLI, S., NEWTON, K., and MONTERO, J. R. 2007. Trust in people, confidence in political institutions, and satisfaction with democracy. Pp. 21–37 in *Citizenship and Involvement in European Democracies*, ed. J. W. van Deth, J. R. Montero, and A. Westholm. London: Routledge.

CHAPTER 19

THE WELFARE STATE: VALUES, POLICY PREFERENCES, AND PERFORMANCE EVALUATIONS

STAFFAN KUMLIN

CITIZENS' attitudes towards welfare state policies merit attention for at least two reasons.[1] First, such policies comprise a sizeable share of total public spending in rich industrialized countries. Thus, welfare state attitudes concern a cornerstone of public policy. Second, such attitudes not only reveal substantive political preferences, but also hint at which type of democracy citizens favor. As discussed at length in the chapter by Thomassen, a long-standing tension in democratic thought concerns the values of equality and freedom. Both are intrinsic to democracy, but their precise nature and balance are contested. The welfare state is relevant here as it is arguably the main policy instrument for altering the balance and nature of equality and freedom.

[1] This research has received financial support from The Bank of Sweden Tercentenary Foundation, The Swedish Collegium for Advanced Study in the Social Sciences, and the Swedish Council for Working Life and Social Research. The author would like to thank Linda Berg, Jonas Edlund, Mikael Hjerm, Sören Holmberg, Henrik Oscarsson, Maria Oskarson, Maria Pettersson, and Stefan Svallfors, for useful comments.

Empirical research on welfare state attitudes has grown exponentially over the last thirty years. Initially, a slow development took place within countries, building on national data sources such as election studies. In a later phase, national data were painstakingly assembled and analyzed by comparative pioneers such as Coughlin (1980). In recent years, the availability of genuinely comparable and repeatedly collected data has fueled an impressive development. Also, the spread of democracy has generated scientific attention to countries outside the older and richer western democracies, not least the post-communist countries of central and eastern Europe (Wegener 2000; Örkény and Székely 2000). Still, as this review will inevitably reveal, a disproportionate amount of research efforts have been carried out in roughly the OECD area.

Many researchers have found it worthwhile to think about welfare state attitudes in terms of a hierarchy of abstraction levels. For instance, Coughlin (1980) concluded that mass publics in western countries differed from each other with respect to generalized, ideological welfare state support, with citizens in low-spending countries being more generally suspicious towards the welfare state. At the same time, attitudes towards specific programs and services tended to be largely positive in most countries. Similarly, Goodsell (1983) reported that whereas a majority of Americans were ideologically suspicious of public welfare and government spending, only a minority tended to be dissatisfied with how public schemes perform in practice.

Based on findings such as these, I distinguish between three levels of welfare state attitudes. At each level one can further separate between different dimensions, objects, and aspects. First, at the most abstract level we find symbolic, generalized, and value-laden orientations towards overarching concepts such as "equality," "redistribution," "the public sector," "taxation," and "privatization." As shorthand, one may refer to this level as "general welfare state support." Second, at a middle level we have specific policy prefer-ences about various aspects or parts of the welfare state. Third, at the bottom of the hierarchy one finds even more specific evaluations of welfare state-related "performance."

I consider each of these levels in turn, after which I proceed to a number of explanatory themes and topics around which empirical findings have accumulated. These themes include (1) macro-contextual factors and development over time; (2) the role of social class in structuring attitudes; (3) the impact of narrow self-interest; (4) distributive and procedural justice concerns; and (5) policy feedback effects on attitudes and behavior. I finish by hinting at three promising emerging areas that will hopefully receive more attention in the future.

1 WELFARE STATE ATTITUDES AS GENERAL POLITICAL VALUES

At their most general level, welfare state attitudes are conceptually and empirically related to the left–right conflict. While the meaning of left and right varies across space and time, one of the more universal components of this conflict is the question of how much the state should intervene in the market economy and its outcomes (see chapter by Mair in this volume). Because welfare state policies comprise a large portion of total state intervention, general attitudes towards the welfare state tell us something about people's stands in the more general state intervention conflict. Indeed, researchers sometimes even measure positions in the state intervention conflict (or "economic left–right" as it is often called) using survey items concerning the preferred general size and redistributive impact of welfare state arrangements. Generally speaking, those who favor a high level of social equality, a large public sector, and a highly redistributive tax system, are more likely to label themselves as leftists and to vote for parties of the left. However, the strength of such correlations varies tremendously across countries.

One should also note that not all measures of state intervention orientations are related to general welfare state support. For instance, based on data from nine western European countries, Borre and Viegas (1995) found that attitudes towards how much the government should intervene in the macroeconomy rarely correlate strongly with welfare-related state intervention responses such as "cut government spending." It is unsafe, then, to assume that attitudes towards all types of state intervention form one single dimension, or to assume that general welfare state support spawns all types of state intervention.

Finally, it is worthwhile to distinguish between attitudes towards the output and input side of the welfare state. Output attitudes are about the normative appeal and functioning of policy products such as transfers and services, whereas input attitudes concern the financing of those products, in particular taxation. Downs (1960) initially suggested that there are important differences between citizens' relations to inputs and outputs respectively. He argued that whereas there is usually a direct link between costs and benefits in the market, the two are often divorced in the public sphere. This may reduce support for public spending among the ordinary citizen: "since his payments to the government are not related to the benefits he receives from it, he finds himself contributing to things that do not benefit him" (Downs 1960, 548).

This prediction has not gone unchallenged. According to a very different hypothesis citizens tend to underestimate costs of public service provision, and their support for public spending on various services tends to go down if they are informed about the real burden for taxpayers (Winter and Mouritzen 2001). More than this, citizens are sometimes said to want "something for nothing." According to this view, the fact that in most countries citizens are relatively friendly toward the welfare state is explained by citizens expressing expansionist preferences without thinking about tax burdens. Still, analyses of "priced" survey questions—where respondents are explicitly reminded of the link between additional spending and additional taxation—nevertheless reveal preferences that largely resemble unpriced priorities (Confalonieri and Newton 1995).

2 WELFARE STATE ATTITUDES AS SPECIFIC POLICY PREFERENCES

Specific policy preferences, although typically correlated with higher-level ideological dimensions (Kaase and Newton 1995), are more complex than can be neatly captured by general measures of state intervention orientations and left–right ideology (Ullrich 2000). Moreover, although research commonly finds that both general and specific support for the welfare state are high, studies of specific preferences also show a more complex picture where support varies substantially across different parts of the welfare state. For example, in *The Scope of Government* (Borre and Scarbrough 1995), Roller (1995) and Pettersen (1995) examined west Europeans' attitudes towards the parts of the welfare state that are mainly aimed at the creation of "equality" (including policies aiming at redistribution or equal life chances) and "security" (including for example basic pensions and unemployment benefits). The results showed that "although equality policies receive relatively high support, they are, none the less, the less popular part of the welfare state" (Roller 1995, 196). The interpretation was twofold. First, "Because of the ambiguous character of 'equality' in Western societies ... we suggest that policies designed to achieve socio-economic security win more support than policies designed to achieve socio-economic equality." Second, it was argued that more people have an interest invested in security policies (Pettersen 1995, 188).

Inspired by Roller (1992), these authors also distinguished between the *range* and *degree* aspects of welfare state policy preferences. The former refers to the range of areas within which citizens think the government bears a responsibility for solving problems. Scholars often argue that this is the most fundamental indicator of welfare state acceptance (Roller 1999*a*, 1999*b*). In contrast, degree refers to "how much" the government should intervene, and whether spending cuts and increases are advocated. There are empirical arguments for making this distinction. For instance, while the two aspects (unsurprisingly) tend to correlate, the correlation is far from perfect. Moreover, Roller (1999*a*) notes that even citizens advocating cutbacks in an area simultaneously display strong support for basic government responsibility. Finally, the range of support tends to be more stable at a higher level of support, compared to the degree of support (Borre 1995; Huseby 1995).

Finally, at an even more concrete level, public support varies tremendously across particular policies (Coughlin 1980). Van Oorschot (2006, 24–5) aptly explained that "All over modern, Western welfare states, in various decades, the public was found to be most in favor of social protection for old people, closely followed by protection for sick and disabled people, while the support schemes for families with needy children less, schemes for unemployed people less still, and supports social assistance schemes least of all." These differences in support seem to be a common element in the popular welfare culture of present western welfare states.

Why such differences? Ullrich (2000) argued that we are largely lacking studies that explicitly test competing explanations for differences in support across policies. Nevertheless, below we discuss a series of indirect findings that imply that the pattern is due to a combination of self-interest, social justice perceptions, and feedback effects of policy design.

3 WELFARE STATE ATTITUDES AS PERFORMANCE EVALUATIONS

While general welfare state support and specific policy preferences are repeatedly measured in comparative public opinion surveys, perceptions and evaluations of welfare state performance are not as thoroughly researched. One explanation could be that the popularity of the economic voting program (see Lewis-Beck and Stegamaier chapter in this volume) has crowded out non-economic forms of government performance from the mainstream of political behavior research.

This may be about to change, not least as performance dissatisfaction is becoming increasingly salient in real-world politics. Policy researchers argue that many countries are entering an era of "permanent austerity," in which it is becoming difficult to finance previous welfare state commitments (Pierson 2001). Moreover, there are indications that welfare state performance matters for political orientations and behavior. Performance dissatisfaction is associated with both higher support for increased spending on the target of dissatisfaction (Edlund 2004), as well as higher probability of program-specific political participation (Goul Andersen and Hoff 2001).

In addition, more general orientations and behavior may be affected. Using data from eight countries, Huseby (2000) examined the impact of macro-performance, as well as individual performance evaluations, in three policy areas—the economy, basic social welfare, and the environment. She found that all three affected trust in the functioning of the current political system (though not support for more abstract democratic principles). There are similar results for East Germany, where citizens' comparisons between the communist and post-communist welfare state tend to be unflattering for the latter, which has negative consequences for political trust (Roller 1999b). Moreover, drawing on data from fifteen western European countries, Kumlin (2007) finds that dissatisfaction with public health services and education is negatively associated with political trust in all countries, but typically unrelated to general welfare state support. Interestingly, in most countries there is a significant impact on Euro-scepticism; many dissatisfied Europeans direct their dissatisfaction also to the European Union (Kumlin 2004a). Finally, in several countries dissatisfaction has a significant negative impact on the probability of voting for a government party, controlling for social class, ideology, and retrospective economic evaluations.

Other findings suggest that citizens' personal experiences with welfare state institutions affect political attitudes and behavior. This appears to hold true for contexts as different as the US (Soss 1999; Mettler 2002; Campbell 2005) and Sweden (Kumlin 2004b; Kumlin and Rothstein 2005). Such effects may come as a surprise as much previous research—especially the "economic voting" literature—suggests that even when people do have relevant personal experiences from which they could draw political conclusions, they nevertheless typically fail to do so (see Lewis-Beck and Stegamaier chapter in this volume). Instead, perceptions of aggregated economic experiences have stronger effects. Such "sociotropic" perceptions are seen as the results of information provided by political elites, experts, and the mass media. In contrast, personal experiences may play a more important role in performance evaluations of the welfare state.[2]

4 EXPLANATORY THEMES: TIME AND CONTEXT

The rest of the chapter discusses a number of explanatory themes around which empirical results have accumulated. For example, several influential theories predict that social change has systematically affected welfare state attitudes over time. According to some accounts, continuous modernization processes produce social differentiation and individualism, as well as increasing difficulties for welfare states to maintain the quality of transfers and services. This is thought to undermine support for equality, redistribution, and taxation (Offe 1987). In stark contrast, theories of "government overload" predict that as welfare states expand, citizens come to expect that it is the state's responsibility to solve any new social problems appearing on the agenda by means of public schemes (Crozier, Huntington, and Watanuki 1975).

Most empirical studies, however, do not reveal a spiral of generally rising demands on governments, nor systematically declining levels of welfare state support. Likewise, endorsement of the principles of progressive taxation is reportedly widespread and stable (Confalonieri and Newton 1995; Edlund 1999). In the few countries where a long-term decline in welfare state support can be observed, such as in Germany, the drop is nevertheless modest, with large majorities still supporting state responsibility in core welfare state areas (Roller 2000).

---

[2] I have suggested two explanations for this apparent difference across policy domains Kumlin (2004b). First, the nature of available political information differs, with a better supply of general, sociotropic information about collective experiences in the economic realm compared to welfare state territory; this makes personal economic experiences less crucial from an informational point of view. Second, the nature of political responsibility varies across the two policy domains, with a clearer and closer link between responsible politicians and personal welfare state experiences, than between politicians and ups and downs in the personal pocketbook.

Instead, most opinion changes appear to be cyclical. In particular, many advanced industrial countries experienced a dip in welfare state support at some point during the late 1970s and 1980s. In most cases, however, support recovered or even strengthened relatively quickly, often in response to cuts in spending and benefits, and to increasing inequality levels (Shapiro and Young 1989; Aalberg 2003). Further, these short-term dips have typically concerned general welfare state support whereas preferences concerning specific policies have proven to be highly stable over time (Taylor-Gooby 1985; Svallfors 1996).

Furthermore, in contrast to overload theory, demands for state expansion tend to be higher in countries with less developed welfare states and a higher level of socioeconomic inequality (Roller 1995; Borre and Viegas 1995). These discoveries suggest that "public opinion is not irreversible," but rather that "demands for government spending on some services seem to level off in wealthier nations compared with poorer ones" (Kaase and Newton 1995, 73).

These difficulties in finding linear developments over time point toward the influence of short-term contextual factors. For example, welfare state attitudes become more expansionist in times of recession and unemployment. Such hardship could fuel welfare demands because it increases the felt risk of becoming unemployed, because it brings social needs to the forefront of political debate, and because unemployment is less easily explained in terms of individual causes. In support of these arguments, Blekesaune and Quadagno (2003) analyzed survey data from twenty-four countries, including both old and post-communist democracies. They found that current unemployment levels accounted for roughly one-third of national-level variation in support for welfare policies directed at the old, sick, and unemployed.

Organized interests and elite opinion formation are also key contextual factors. For example, adherents of "the power mobilization hypothesis" have emphasized that the strength of trade unions has affected support for welfare state policies, especially among the working class (Korpi 1983). Similarly, recent accounts of welfare state politics emphasize that the policies that tend to escape cutbacks are policies where interest organizations are able to mobilize popular support (Pierson 1994). Also, opinion shifts in the rightist, anti-welfare direction are often preceded by changes or active opinion formation attempts by parties and prolific politicians. The usual examples include Mogens Glistrup and his anti-tax party in Denmark in the 1970s, Ronald Reagan in the US, and Margaret Thatcher in the UK, during the 1980s.

5 SOCIAL CLASS

Researchers have devoted considerable effort to explaining variation between individuals. The most common approach considers socioeconomic status and class. For example, the working class usually displays higher general welfare state support than the middle class. The same can be said for certain specific policies aimed at class-correlated social risks. Such patterns exist in older mature western democracies (Borre and Scarbrough 1995), as well as in post-communist societies (Örkény and Székely 2000).

When class effects occur, there is typically almost as much class-related variation within the middle class and the working class, as there is variation between them. Unskilled workers are significantly more supportive than skilled workers, and middle-class citizens with "routine non-manual" jobs are significantly more supportive than the more educated and well-off "service class" and the self-employed (Svallfors 2006). Moreover, while the extent of class-based voting decreased in western countries during much of the second half of the twentieth century (see Knutsen chapter), the link between class and welfare state support remains intact (Roller 2000). Drawing on data spanning three decades and several west European countries, Pettersen (1995, 230) concluded that "theories of class formation provide a superior explanation for people's public spending preferences over the entire time period analyzed." I hasten to add, however, that there is much variation across studies in the actual magnitude of class effects (Ullrich 2000). Additionally, there seems to be systematic variation across countries. For example, in a four-country comparison Svallfors (2006) found that class effects on general welfare state support were strongest in Sweden, weakest in the US, with Britain and Germany falling somewhere in between.

The variation across countries and studies begs the question of how links between class and welfare state support can be explained. One possibility is that they are due to individual differences in risks, interests, resources, and education levels. Empirically however, it has proven hard to account for class differences with more proximate individual-level variables, such as education, income, self-interest, economic resources, risk exposure on the labour market, or work conditions (Svallfors 2006). Although such variables are often important for welfare state support in their own right, they can rarely explain class-support links. Similarly, it is difficult to account for class effects in terms of individual differences in adherence to distributive ideals and values. Lewin-Epstein, Kaplan, and Levanon (2003, 20) found that when status variables "simply indicate one's position in the social hierarchy, such as education and income, the entire effect is mediated through the image of society and preferred principles of distributive justice. In contrast, social characteristics which serve as focal points for collective identification in addition to hierarchical position, such as class and ethnicity, have a strong unmediated effect on support redistribution policies."

These findings, then, suggest that class patterns in support are forged at the group level, and are driven by group interests and solidarity rather than by individual-level differences in interests and values. A long tradition in political science tells us that a relationship between social stratification and political alignments does not normally arise without the assistance of organized group mobilization at the intermediate level provided by parties and interest organizations. Such factors may help explain the variation across studies and countries in the actual magnitude of class effects. Svallfors (2006) suggested that it is not the actual stratification in individuals' life chances, resources, and interests that determine the strength of the class-attitude nexus. Rather, it seems more dependent on elite-level class articulation and politicization, as well as on the extent to which the existing institutional character of the welfare state itself makes political actors and citizens think about redistributional topics. Testing such predictions for a larger group of countries should be a worthwhile task for future efforts.

A related causal motor of group-oriented thinking may be driven by "social communication" of the kind discussed in the chapter by Huckfeldt. Because members of different classes live in different informational environments it is usually easier for, say, upper middle-class citizens to adopt anti-welfare and rightist preferences for the simple reason that so many people in their vicinity communicate information that foster such preferences. Moreover, such interests may be articulated and disseminated by politically attentive "opinion leaders" within social groups, rather than being calculated separately by each individual, based on independently gathered information. Because political preferences within a group are socially contagious, a strong correlation between class interests and political preferences can emerge, even if nobody but a few sophisticated opinion leaders has clear perceptions of the stakes involved. An associated possibility is that the link between class and welfare state attitudes partly operates through early socialization mechanisms, where parents' political orientations are adopted by their children. Using a panel design and a sample of parents and children, Westholm (1991) discovered that general attitudes towards "social welfare" were reproduced by such family socialization. Such findings, taken together with the fact that class affiliations are partly inherited, help explain correlations between class and welfare state support.

6 SELF-INTEREST

The fact that individual-level interest-variables are not good at explaining social class differences in welfare attitudes does not exclude the possibility that self-interest is important in its own right. The self-interest hypothesis holds that welfare state attitudes are not reflections of affectively charged and stable values. Rather, people are instrumental and narrowly egoistic in a material sense, choosing on the basis of personal benefits and risk-reducing consequences of policies. Interestingly, such assumptions lie at the heart of most influential theories of welfare state development (Mau 2003). Empirically, self-interest explanations are regularly used to understand differences in support across policies, as such variation seems to correspond broadly to the proportion of the population who currently benefit, or who can reasonably expect benefits in the future.

When it comes to specific policy preferences, self-interest indeed seems to matter. This becomes especially clear whenever researchers have access to sharp measures of interests—rather than distant "socioeconomic" proxies—either in terms of future risk or in terms of current benefit or service reception. For instance, Iversen and Soskice (2001) looked for attitude differences between those with "specific" and "general" professional skills respectively. The premise was that specific skills—that is, those that are not easily transferable from one firm or one part of the labor market to another—generate higher personal risks of needing support from income replacement schemes. In an analysis of ten countries, they found that general skills diminish support for public spending on unemployment benefits, health care, pensions, and job protection in declining industries.[3] Moreover, drawing on data from several European countries, Pettersen (1995, 2001) found that various indicators of self-interest structure acceptance for increased spending on particular policies. Additionally, current personal benefit reception strengthens performance evaluations of, and support for, those particular programs and services (Johansson, Nilsson, and Strömberg 2001). Taken together, these findings imply that differences in aggregate levels of support across policies are partly due to self-interest.

However, most research tells us self-interest is considerably less important at higher levels of attitude abstraction. Dunleavy (1979) identified a trend where more middle-class citizens became dependent on public services. He argued that this produced a political cleavage between those who consume public services and those who do not, and between those who are employed in the public sector and those who are not. This logic predicts that heavy public service consumers and public employees are more likely to express general welfare state support, for instance by voting for leftist parties.

The public–private employment part of these predictions has fared quite well in empirical research (see Bean and Papadakis 1998). However, signals are mixed when it comes to the prediction that public welfare and service *consumers* are more inclined than others to generally support the welfare state. Studies in Britain in the 1970s and 1980s primarily analyzed party choice (cf. Dunleavy 1979). There was indeed some support for the predictions, but the findings were criticized by Franklin and Page (1984), who interpreted the explanatory power as unimpressive compared to those of other relevant independent variables.

A similar skepticism has emerged on the other side of the Atlantic. In an extensive empirical study of the Californian "tax revolt" in the 1970s, Sears and Citrin (1982, 212–13) concluded that self-interest effects "could only be seen on attitudes most directly and tangibly related to the welfare of the interested person. For example, self-interest did foster preferences for increased spending on services of direct personal benefit, but not the desire for a larger public sector in general." Similarly, comparative studies from the 1990s point to equally weak effects of current welfare state usage on general welfare state support (Bean and Papadakis 1998; Goul Andersen 1993; Svallfors 1996).

There is one theoretical and one methodological explanation for why self-interest appears to matter greatly for specific policy preferences, but only moderately for general support. The theoretical explanation is that the impact of self-interest increases when choices are concrete because the personal stakes associated with different alternatives become larger and more visible (Sears and Funk 1991; Huseby 1995). Other things equal, concrete policy choices raise the likelihood that citizens recognize,

---

[3] Unfortunately, the analysis of Iversen and Soskice (2001) did not include very detailed class controls. Therefore, it will be an interesting question for future research to determine (1) the extent to which relationships between skill profiles and attitudes are spurious or hold up controlling for class and (2) the extent to which skill profiles in fact channel class effects on attitudes.

calculate, and choose on the basis of consequences for personal, short-term, material interest. Thus, whereas it is relatively easy to know whether one benefits from spending on, say, "unemployment benefits" or "public child care," it is difficult for many to know whether one benefits from spending on welfare state policies generally. And it may be ever harder to make this calculus when asked for one's attitude towards "redistribution," "equality," or some other value-laden concept.

While there is empirical merit to this argument (see Sears and Funk 1991), there is also a methodological reason for the apparently weak impact of self-interest on general welfare state support. Much previous research has used data lacking extensive information about personal welfare state usage and interests. Such data constraints have forced scholars to rely on rough measures of welfare state self-interest. For instance, Hadenius (1986) used a small number of rough dummy variables as indicators of welfare state self-interest (whether people were pensioners, had received sickness benefits, had children at home, or whether they had received unemployment benefits). These dummies proved to have weak effects on attitudes towards public expenditure and taxation. Similarly, based only on information about whether Danish respondents were unemployed, disabled, early retired, or old-age pensioners, Goul Andersen (1993, 37–8) "found virtually no evidence confirming that people's personal relationship to the welfare state . . . has any impact upon their welfare state attitudes." He concluded that "interests are almost irrelevant as determinants of welfare state support in Denmark" (Goul Andersen 1993, 43).

Studies drawing on more wide-ranging information have suggested that self-interest may be a more potent explanation of general welfare state support than most studies have been able to show. Kumlin (2004b) used data on whether respondents received service from about twenty-five different policies. Some of the information was pulled from public records rather than from respondents themselves. These data revealed self-interest effects on general welfare state support of a magnitude that approached that of social class, one that was stronger than the joint impact of education and income. Similarly, drawing on Danish data, Goul Andersen (1999) has somewhat modified his previous conclusion that welfare state self-interests are "almost irrelevant." He analyzed a more elaborate self-interest measure than the one he had previously used and found that both public employees as well as the publicly supported display higher general welfare state support and are more likely to vote for socialist parties than other categories. Again, self-interest effects on general welfare state support approached those of social class.

7 SOCIAL JUSTICE

Researchers often suggest that people evaluate the welfare state in terms of *social justice* just as much as they are trying to maximize their personal gain. To capture the idea, theorists have used terms like "dual utility function" (Rothstein 1998), "contingent consent" (Levi 1997), or "moral economy" (Svallfors 1996; Mau 2003).

Citizens are thought to compare the actual functioning of welfare state policies with some sort of normative expectations. If the actual state of affairs matches normative social justice expectations, support for the welfare state, and even political and social trust, may be boosted. Moreover, evaluations of social justice are presumably independent of one's self-interest. The latter is a vital prediction as a social justice perspective loses its appeal if such evaluations are nothing but "self-interest in disguise," that is, if they are reflections of the extent to which one's personal and material self-interest is served by the welfare state (cf. Lind and Tyler 1988).

While there is less research on social justice aspects of welfare state performance than on the self-interest aspect, there is by now an emerging accumulation of findings. Some research focuses on "distributive justice," where support for social and political institutions is contingent on whether such institutions are perceived to distribute outcomes fairly. Other studies investigate the role of "procedural justice," where support is contingent on whether the processes in which citizens and the state interact match normative expectations.

As for distributive justice, analysts often suggest that citizens distinguish between the "deserving" and "undeserving" poor. Van Oorschot (2006) analyzed twenty-three countries in western and central/eastern Europe. He found that Europeans share a common deservingness culture, one that largely corresponds with the variations of support across policies described previously: the old are perceived as the most deserving of public welfare, followed by the sick and disabled, and then the unemployed. Immigrants are seen as the least deserving of all.

Citizens use heterogeneous criteria in forming deservingness perceptions. Tyler and his colleagues summarized social psychological research on distributive justice by noting that "principles of distributive justice are situationally based. People do not simply apply general principles of justice to all settings. Instead, they have situational frameworks that indicate that different principles of justice matter in different settings" (Tyler et al. 1997, 56). Thus, van Oorschot (2000) distilled five criteria of "deservingness" from a large number of previous studies. First, people are thought to assess "control over neediness," where those who cannot help their predicament are more deserving. Control was the most important criteria for cutback preferences. Second, the greater the "level of need" the greater the perceived deservingness. Third, "identity" is thought to matter, i.e. mainly needy people who "belong to us" are deserving. A fourth criterion taps the attitudes of beneficiaries, while a fifth criterion concerns the "reciprocal relationship" between benefactors and beneficiaries. The solidarity of the former is thought to be contingent on whether the latter adhere to certain behavioral norms (cf. Mau 2003).

A somewhat different conceptualization of distributive justice separates between distribution principles, rather than between groups. Scholars distinguish between at least three broad categories of distributive ideals: "equality," which means everyone in a particular situation receives the same outcomes, "equity," where personal outcomes should match personal contributions, and "need," where outcomes vary according to personal need (Deutsch 1985).

Distributive justice evaluations of welfare state performance seem to influence support. For instance, there is evidence that perceptions of group deservingness have a genuine causal impact on how generous welfare benefits people would like (Appelbaum 2001). Moreover, Biel, Eek, and Gärling (1997) analyzed the impact of distributive justice perceptions on willingness to pay for public childcare. They found that a perceived discrepancy between personal distributive justice ideals and the actual perceived distribution of childcare services reduced willingness to support public childcare. Moreover, Mau (2003) presents cross-sectional survey evidence showing that support for poverty policies in Britain and Germany is associated with judgments of the extent to which beneficiaries are seen as truly deserving and whether they "fiddle the system." Likewise, thinking that less generous benefits enhance welfare clients' motivation to provide for themselves is associated with less support for unemployment policies. Taken together, these findings suggest that the differences in public support across policy areas are not only due to self-interest, but also to whether redistribution to groups is seen as fair and just.

Other studies have used broader political orientations as dependent variables. Tyler, Rasinski, and McGraw (1985, 716) found that evaluations of the incumbent US president were positively associated with perceptions of distributive justice. Those approving of the way benefits were distributed also tended to endorse their president, controlling for a series of potentially confounding factors such as self-interest. Moreover, drawing on American and Norwegian evidence, Miller and Listhaug (1999) concluded that distributive justice perceptions affect political trust. This was true both for "sociotropic" judgments of distributive justice as well as for personally experienced distributive justice.

Similar to research on distributive justice, procedural justice studies emphasize a rather broad spectrum of variables (see Lind and Tyler 1988; Tyler et al. 1997). These include the efficiency and speed with which people get service outcomes, whether people are treated with dignity and respect, whether there is consistency and predictability in procedures across time and people, and whether citizens experience "voice opportunities" in their dealings with street-level bureaucrats.

Studies from social psychology conclude that perceived procedural justice is an ingredient in individuals' evaluations of a wide range of social situations (for an overview, see Tyler et al. 1997: chapter 4). These situations range from court experiences to work-life settings to interpersonal relations. People who perceive procedural aspects of allocation processes as fair are more inclined to express satisfaction, accept decisions, and comply with rules and restrictions. These effects are often relatively independent of personal material gain and perceptions of distributive justice. Procedural justice perceptions thus influence attitudes even among people who receive comparable outcomes from a process, and who make similar distributive justice judgments of those outcomes.

Unfortunately, only a few studies have extended these ideas to the welfare state setting. *The Bureaucratic Encounter* (Katz et al. 1975) discovered that positive perceptions of procedures tended to generate positive generalized attitudes towards government and the political system. Similarly, other studies conclude that procedures have stronger positive effects than either personal self-interest or distributive justice perceptions (Tyler, Rasinski, and McGraw 1985; Miller and Listhaug 1999). Kumlin (2004b) found that perceptions of both distributive justice and procedural justice in experiences with welfare state institutions tend to diminish political trust—but not general welfare state support—net of what would be suggested by respondents' self-interest.

8 POLICY FEEDBACK

In recent years, researchers have increasingly drawn inspiration from "the new institutionalism" in political science. A key question is how various features of welfare state policies—once established—exercise *feedback effects* on welfare state attitudes. Scholars argue that the design of welfare state institutions may affect both self-interest and social justice-related performance evaluations, which may shape both concrete preferences and general welfare state support (Rothstein 1998). In addition, the nature of welfare state policies may have the capacity to both increase and suppress political participation and trust (Schneider and Ingram 1997; Mettler and Soss 2004; Campbell 2006).

The empirical evidence can be divided into two categories. In one of them, researchers look at the country level for evidence of policy feedback. Most efforts draw on Esping-Andersen's (1990) welfare state regime typology. It has been investigated whether citizens in "liberal" welfare states display more resistance to public welfare, and whether people in "social democratic" regimes endorse such policies. A second hypothesis holds that the effect of social class on welfare state support is stronger in liberal welfare regimes and weaker in social democratic regimes. One causal mechanism is that in social democratic regimes public services are also heavily used by the middle classes. Where differences in the degree of public service usage are less correlated with traditional social structure, the impact of social structure on welfare state support might be diluted. In addition, researchers predict that gender conflicts are particularly pronounced in social democratic regimes, whereas "insider-outsider" conflicts are thought to be more important in conservative regimes.

The jury is still out on these issues. On the one hand, effects of socioeconomic characteristics do not seem to vary across countries in ways suggested by a regime approach (Svallfors 1997, 2006), although such findings have been criticized on theoretical and methodological grounds (Linos and West 2003). Other studies, on the other hand, have discerned regime-consistent country differences in welfare state support (Coughlin 1980; Svallfors 1997; Svallfors 2003; Jæger 2006), and Mau (2003) reports that citizens' distribution ideals seem highly dependent on principles that have long been enshrined in institutional welfare legacies. For example, the British tend to favor flat-rate benefits, whereas Germans more often endorse income related solutions. Confusingly however, a series of studies have failed to uncover regime-consistent country variations in welfare state-related attitudes (Bean and Papadakis 1998; Lapinski et al. 1998; Aalberg 2003). For instance, van Oorschot and Halman (2000, 20) found "no direct relation between how a country's population tends to perceive the causes of poverty ... and ways in which welfare states are designed." In stark contrast, Larsen (2008 forthcoming) reports macro evidence in favor of the hypothesis, with Scandinavians being the least prone to agree poverty is caused by "laziness and lack of will power."

The two latter studies agree, however, that Americans are more prone to individual, rather than structural, explanations of poverty than Europeans. Moreover, they also found that citizens in post-communist countries in 1990 were more prone to individual explanations than western Europeans. This difference, however, seems to have shrunk since then. Kreidl (2000, 173) concludes, "During socialism, as well as after its collapse, the elite was interested in supporting negative individualistic explanations of poverty, and it's only gradually that populations in these countries come to see either structural or positive individualistic causes... structural explanations gained in generality in the postcommunist societies since 1991" (cf. Wegener 2000; Örkény and Székely 2000).

The second group of studies has conceptualized policy feedback in terms of differences across policies within countries (for overviews, see Mettler and Soss 2004; Campbell 2006). This research highlights the effects of personal experiences, rather than the general impact of living in a welfare state with a particular design. In addition, it does not only employ welfare state support as the dependent variable, but rather analyzes a broad spectrum of dependent variables, including trust and political participation. Feedback is also usually conceived both in terms of how policies distribute material and political resources between and within different recipient groups (Mettler 2002; Campbell 2005), as well as in terms of broader "interpretive" lessons about politics and the welfare state that policies may convey (Pierson 1993).

As for the latter, one group of studies conceptualizes policy design in terms of the power relation between the citizen and the bureaucrat. Power relations can be affected by a multitude of institutional and policy features. For example, Soss (1999) compared Americans with experiences of the AFDC (Aid to Families with Dependent Children) and the SSDI (Social Security Disability Insurance) respectively. He found that AFDC experiences had negative effects on electoral participation and beliefs about the responsiveness of government whereas SSDI experiences did not. This difference could not be attributed to socioeconomic differences that existed prior to welfare interaction. Rather, it seemed to be due to AFDC having more power over its clients than the SSDI, and to the AFDC being worse at considering clients' views and preferences. By giving citizens the feeling of being underdogs in relation to the state, AFDC experiences generated negative attitudes towards public institutions and the political system. Similarly, Kumlin (2004b) studied the political impact of personal welfare state experiences in Sweden, and concluded that the direction of experience effects vary depending on the design of experienced policies. Experiences of "customer institutions"—where bureaucratic discretion and means-testing are rare, but exit-options frequent—tend to generate positive perceptions of social justice, and in turn positive effects on general welfare state support and political trust. Exactly the opposite appears true of experiences with "client institutions," where discretion and means-testing is frequent and exit-options rare (cf. Hoff 1993; Möller 1996). These results suggest that the large differences in support across policies are not just due to self-interest or perceptions of group deservingness, but also to differences in how the interaction between citizens and state is institutionalized.

As discussed by Goodsell (1981) and Campbell (2006), there are numerous other ways in which differences between welfare state policies can be conceptualized and put to empirical use. Hence, continued theoretical and empirical work on the topic of policy feedback seems to be a promising area for future efforts.

9 Outlook: Three Suggestions for Future Research

Let me finish by pointing to three avenues for future research. While none of them is untouched, there is less research to draw on compared to the areas reviewed above. First, on a methodological note, we need to pay more attention to issues related to *direction of causality*. The relationships between values, policy preferences, and performance evaluations are arguably sometimes, to some extent, reciprocal. But most research has drawn on cross-sectional data, and so we know far too little about how they affect each other over time. Research on policy feedback effects at the regime level suffers from a similar problem: To the extent that attitude constellations do vary across regimes, one wonders whether there has really been a truly causal impact of policy on opinion. Both these examples illustrate a need for research designs that can better accommodate reciprocal causation, including panel data, time-series data, or—for research questions where it is feasible—experiments.

A second area has to do with the relationship between *identity, ethnicity, race, and welfare state support*. On the macro-level, it is well known that redistribution and egalitarian policies are more developed in ethnically and racially homogeneous societies (Alesina and Glaeser 2004). Further, as noted above, citizens invariably see "immigrants" as the most undeserving group all across Europe (van Oorschot 2006). In the US, Gilens (1999) and others have shown that the unpopularity of welfare is partly due to the fact that "the American public thinks that most people who receive welfare are black, and second, the public thinks that blacks are less committed to the work ethic than are other Americans." In a similar vein, Luttmer (2001, 501) found that Americans "increase their support for welfare spending as the share of local recipients from their own racial group increases."

As our societies grow increasingly diverse in ethnic and racial terms, it becomes increasingly important to understand these patterns. Do we simply have at hand the self-interested preferences of ethnic and racial majorities? Or can the pattern be explained in terms of more deeply entrenched territorial attachments, ethnic identities, or perhaps even racism, where some citizens are genuinely unwilling to redistribute to those who are not perceived to belong to, or who do not look like, "us." Alternatively, can the patterns be understood in terms of less intrinsic problems related to perceived deficiencies in the attitudes and behavior of recipient groups, as well as in the perceived effects of particular policy designs on recipients? Interestingly, Gilens (1999, 7) came down strongly in favor of the latter possibilities in his US study: "whites' belief that blacks are lazy and the opposition to welfare that grows out of this belief do not primarily reflect either a general animus toward African Americans or racial conflict over tangible resources. As a consequence, antipoverty programs that are not seen as rewards for the lazy can gain widespread approval among white Americans, even if these programs are strongly identified with blacks."

Moreover, Gilens's results indicated that both the media and citizens tend to significantly overestimate the proportion of welfare recipients that are black, and that support for welfare spending tends to increase among the few citizens whose perceptions are correct. This observation suggests a third potentially fruitful research area. The question is how generally *informed, deliberated, and considered* people's values, policy preferences, and performance evaluations are. While similar questions have inspired political behavior research for some time, they have yet to find their way into the mainstream of the field reviewed here.

A number of studies do indicate that misperceptions and low knowledge levels among Americans are biased in the anti-welfare direction, which attenuates public support for welfare state policies (cf. Bartels 2005). Of course, low knowledge levels may theoretically just as well be skewed *in favor* of the welfare state. In particular, one can imagine this to be the case in countries where the culturally dominant ideology is less concerned with individual, but more with collective rationality. Indeed, Aalberg (2003) found that perceptions of poverty rates and income inequality were clearly associated with actual poverty and inequality levels. However, she also found evidence of underestimation in some countries, but overestimation in others. Similarly, Taylor-Gooby and Hastie (2002) found a broad resemblance between public perceptions and the actual spending on various areas, but also some striking misperceptions. On the one hand, spending on unemployment benefits is exaggerated: this may hold back support for welfare spending because a group that is typically seen as relatively undeserving is also seen as consuming a disproportionably large share of the welfare budget. On the other hand, the authors reported a sizeable overestimation of defense spending and a slight overestimation of child poverty. Perceptions such as these are arguably biased in favor of welfare state spending versus other types of outlays. Interestingly, a bivariate analysis also revealed that (mis)perceptions may affect welfare state support, where overestimation of actual spending is associated with lower support for increased taxation and spending in particular areas.

Scattered findings such as these suggest a need to know more about the levels and consequences of knowledge about relevant social and policy-related facts. Would highly and equally informed citizens perceive other groups to be deserving and undeserving respectively? Would informed citizens be less—or perhaps more—responsive to narrow personal interests? Would informed citizens favor other institutional solutions and welfare mixes than the ones currently at work in their societies?

References

AALBERG, T. 2003. *Achieving Justice: Comparative Public Opinion on Income Distribution.* Leiden: Brill.

ALESINA, A., and GLAESER, E. L. 2004. *Fighting Poverty in the US and Europe: A World of Difference.* New York: Oxford University Press.

APPELBAUM, L. D. 2001. The influence of perceived deservingness on policy decisions regarding aid to the poor. *Political Psychology,* 22: 419–42.

BARTELS, L. M. 2005. Homer gets a tax cut: inequality and public policy in the American mind. *Perspectives on Politics*, 3: 15–31.

BEAN, C., and PAPADAKIS, E. 1998. A comparison of mass attitudes towards the welfare state in different institutional regimes, 1985–1990. *International Journal of Public Opinion Research*, 10: 211–36.

BIEL, A., EEK, D., and GÄRLING, T. 1997. Distributive justice and willingness to pay for municipality child care. *Social Justice Research*, 10: 63–80.

BLEKESAUNE, M., and QUADAGNO, J. 2003. Public attitudes toward welfare state policies: a comparison of 24 nations. *European Sociological Review*, 19: 415–27.

BORRE, O. 1995. Beliefs and the scope of government. Pp. 367–87 in *The Scope of Government*, ed. O. Borre and E. Scarbrough. Oxford: Oxford University Press.

—— and SCARBROUGH, E. eds. 1995. *The Scope of Government*. Oxford: Oxford University Press.

—— and VIEGAS, J. M. 1995. Government intervention in the economy. Pp. 234–80 in *The Scope of Government*, ed. O. Borre and E. Scarbrough. Oxford: Oxford University Press.

CAMPBELL, A. 2005. *How Policies Make Citizens: Senior Political Activism and the American Welfare State*. Princeton: Princeton University Press.

—— 2006. Policy feedbacks and the political mobilization of mass publics. Unpublished paper, Department of Political Science, Massachusetts Institute of Technology.

CONFALONIERI, M. A., and NEWTON, K. 1995. Taxing and spending: tax revolt or tax protest. Pp. 121–48 in *The Scope of Government*, ed. O. Borre and E. Scarbrough. Oxford: Oxford University Press.

COUGHLIN, R. M. 1980. *Ideology, Public Opinion, and Welfare policy: Attitudes toward Taxes and Spending in Industrialized Societies*. Berkeley: Institute of International Studies University of California.

CROZIER, M., HUNTINGTON, S. P., and WATANUKI, J. 1975. *The Crisis of Democracy*. New York: New York University Press.

DEUTSCH, M. 1985. *Distributive Justice: A Social-Psychological Perspective*. New Haven: Yale University Press.

DOWNS, A. 1960. Why the government budget is too small in a democracy. *World Politics*, 12: 541–63.

DUNLEAVY, P. 1979. The urban basis of political alignment: social class, domestic property ownership and state intervention in consumption processes. *British Journal of Political Science*, 9: 409–43.

EDLUND, J. 1999. Progressive taxation farewell? Attitudes to income redistribution and taxation in Sweden, Great Britain, and the United States. Pp. 106–34 in *The End of the Welfare State?*, ed. S. Svallfors and P. Taylor-Gooby. London: Routledge.

—— 2004. Trust in the capability of the welfare state and general welfare state support 1997–2002. *Acta Sociologica*, 49: 395–417.

ESPING-ANDERSEN, G. 1990. *The Three Worlds of Welfare Capitalism*. Cambridge: Polity Press.

FRANKLIN, M. N., and PAGE, E. C. 1984. A critique of the consumption cleavage approach in British voting studies. *Political Studies* 32: 521–36.

GILENS, M. 1999. *Why Americans Hate Welfare: Race, Media, and the Politics of Antipoverty Policy*. Chicago: Chicago University Press.

GOODSELL, C. T. ed. 1981. *The Public Encounter. Where State and Citizen Meet*. Bloomington: Indiana University Press.

—— 1983. *The Case for Bureaucracy. A Public Administration Polemic*. Chatham, NJ: Chatham House Publishers.

GOUL ANDERSEN, J. 1993. Sources of welfare state support in Denmark: self-interest or way of life? Pp. 25–48 in *Welfare Trends in the Scandinavian Countries*, ed. E. J. Hansen, S. Ringen, H. Uusitalo and R. Erikson. London: M. E. Sharpe.

—— 1999. Changing labour markets, new social divisions, and welfare state support. Pp. 13–33 in *The End of the Welfare State?*, ed. S. Svallfors and P. Taylor-Gooby. London: Routledge.

—— and HOFF, J. 2001. *Democracy and Citizenship in Scandinavia.* New York: Palgrave.

HADENIUS, A. 1986. *A Crisis of the Welfare State?* Uppsala: Almquist & Wiksell.

HOFF, J. 1993. Medborgerskab, brukerrolle og magt. Pp. 53–85 in *Medborgerskab: Demokrati och politisk deltagelse*, ed. J. Andersen, A.-D. Christensen, K. Langberg, B. Siim, and L. Torpe. Viborg: Systeme.

HUSEBY, B. M. 1995. Attitudes towards the size of government. Pp. 87–118 in *The Scope of Government*, ed. O. Borre and E. Scarbrough. Oxford: Oxford University Press.

—— 2000. *Government Performance and Political Support: A Study of How Evaluations of Economic Performance, Social Policy and Environmental Protection Influence the Popular Assessments of the Political System.* Trondheim: Department of Sociology and Political Science, Norwegian University of Technology (NTNU).

IVERSEN, T., and SOCKICE, D. 2001. An asset theory of social policy preferences. *American Political Science Review*, 95: 875–93.

JÆGER, M. M. 2006. Welfare Regimes and Attitudes towards Redistribution: The Regime Hypothesis Revisted. *European Sociological Review*, 22.

JOHANSSON, F., NILSSON, L., and STRÖMBERG, L. 2001. *Kommunal demokrati under fyra decennier.* Malmö: Liber.

KAASE, M., and NEWTON, K. 1995. *Beliefs in Government.* Oxford: Oxford University Press.

KATZ, D., GUTEK, B. A., KAHN, R. L., and BARTON, E. 1975. *Bureaucratic Encounters: A Pilot Study in the Evaluation of Government Services.* Ann Arbor: Survey Research Center, Institute for Social Research, The University of Michigan.

KORPI, W. 1983. *The Democratic Class Struggle.* London: Routledge.

KREIDL, M. 2000. Perceptions of poverty and wealth in western and post-communist countries. *Social Justice Research*, 13: 151–76.

KUMLIN, S. 2004a. Blaming Europe: why welfare state dissatisfaction breeds Euroscepticism. Paper presented at Annual Meeting of the American Political Science Association, Chicago.

—— 2004b. *The Personal and the Political: How Personal Welfare State Experiences Affect Political Trust and Ideology.* New York: Palgrave-Macmillan.

—— 2007. Overloaded or undermined? European welfare states in the face of performance dissatisfaction. In *The Political Sociology of the Welfare State*, ed. S. Svallfors. Stanford, Calif.: Stanford University Press.

—— and ROTHSTEIN, B. 2005. Making and breaking social capital: the impact of welfare state institutions. *Comparative Political Studies*, 38: 339–65.

LAPINSKI, J. S., RIEMANN, C. R., SHAPIRO, R. Y., STEVENS, M. F., and JACOBS, L. R. 1998. Welfare state regimes and subjective well-being: a cross-national study. *International Journal of Public Opinion Research*, 10: 2–24.

LARSEN, C. A. 2008. Forthcoming. The institutional logic of welfare attitudes: How welfare regimes influence public support. *Comparative Political Studies*, 41.

LEVI, M. 1997. *Consent, Dissent, and Patriotism.* New York: Cambridge University Press.

LEWIN-EPSTEIN, N., KAPLAN, A., and LEVANON, A. 2003. Distributive justice and attitudes toward the welfare state. *Social Justice Research*, 16: 1–27.

LIND, A. E., and TYLER, T. R. 1988. *The Social Psychology of Procedural Justice.* New York: Plenum Press.

LINOS, K., and WEST, M. 2003. Self-interest, social beliefs, and attitudes to redistribution. *European Sociological Review*, 19: 393–409.

LUTTMER, E. F. P. 2001. Group loyalty and the taste for redistribution. *Journal of Political Economy,* 109: 500–28.

MAU, S. 2003. *The Moral Economy of Welfare States: Britain and Germany Compared.* London: Routledge.

METTLER, S. 2002. Bringing the state back into civic engagement: policy feedback effects of the G.I. bill for World War II veterans. *American Political Science Review,* 96: 351–65.

—— and SOSS, J. 2004. The consequences of public policy for democratic citizenship: bridging policy studies and mass politics. *Perspectives on Politics,* 2: 55–73.

MILLER, A., and LISTHAUG, O. 1999. Political performance and institutional trust. Pp. 204–16 in *Critical Citizens: Global Support for Democratic Governance,* ed. P. Norris. Oxford: Oxford University Press.

MÖLLER, T. 1996. *Brukare och klienter i välfärdsstaten: Om missnöje och påverkansmöjligheter inom barn- och äldreomsorg.* Stockholm: Publica.

OFFE, C. 1987. Democracy against the welfare state? Structural foundations of neoconservative political opportunities. *Political Theory,* 15: 501–37.

ÖRKÉNY, A., and SZÉKELY, M. 2000. Views on social equality and the role of the state: posttransformation trends in eastern and central Europe. *Social Justice Research,* 13: 199–218.

PETTERSEN, P. A. 1995. The welfare state: the security dimension. Pp. 198–233 in *The Scope of Government,* ed. O. Borre and E. Scarbrough. Oxford: Oxford University Press.

PIERSON, P. 1993. When effect becomes cause: policy feedback and political change. *World Politics,* 45: 595–628.

—— 1994. *Dismantling the Welfare State?* Cambridge: Cambridge University Press.

—— ed. 2001. *The New Politics of the Welfare State.* Oxford: Oxford University Press.

ROLLER, E. 1992. *Einstellungen der Bürger zum Wohlfartsstaat der Bundesrepublik Deutschland.* Opladen: Westdeutscher Verlag.

—— 1995. The welfare state: the equality dimension. Pp. 165–97 in *The Scope of Government,* ed. O. Borre and E. Scarbrough. Oxford: Oxford University Press.

—— 1999*a.* Shrinking the welfare state: citizens' attitudes towards cuts in social spending in Germany in the 1990s. *German Politics,* 8: 21–39.

—— 1999*b.* Sozialpolitik und demokratische Konsolidierung: Eine empirische analyse für die Neuen Bundesländer. Pp. 313–46 in *Wahlen und politische Einstellungen in Deutschland und Österreich,* ed. F. Plasser, O. W. Gabriel, J. W. Falter, and P. A. Ulram. Frankfurt: Peter Lang.

—— 2000. Ende des sozialstaatlichen Konsenses? Zum Aufbrechen traditioneller und zur Entstehung neuer Konfliktstrukturen in Deutschland. Pp. 88–114 in *Demokratie und Partizipation: Festschrift für Max Kaase,* ed. O. Niedermayer and B. Westle. Wiesbaden: Westdeutscher Verlag.

ROTHSTEIN, B. 1998. *Just Institutions Matter: The Moral and Political Logic of the Universal Welfare State.* Cambridge: Cambridge University Press.

SCHNEIDER, A. L., and INGRAM, H. 1997. *Policy Design for Democracy.* Lawrence: University Press of Kansas.

SEARS, D. O., and CITRIN, J. 1982. *Tax Revolt. Something for Nothing in California.* Cambridge, Mass.: Harvard University Press.

—— and FUNK, C. L. 1991. The role of self-interest in social and political attitudes. *Advances in Experimental Social Psychology,* 24: 1–91.

SHAPIRO, R. Y., and YOUNG, J. T. 1989. Public opinion and the welfare state: the United States in comparative pespective. *Political Science Quarterly,* 104: 59–89.

SOSS, J. 1999. Lessons of welfare: policy design, political learning, and political action. *American Political Science Review,* 93: 363–80.

SVALLFORS, S. 1996. *Välfärdsstatens moraliska ekonomi: Välfärdsopinionen i 90-talets Sverige.* Umeå: Boréa.

SVALLFORS, S. 1997. Worlds of welfare and attitudes to redistribution: a comparison of eight western nations. *European Sociological Review*, 13: 283–304.

—— 2003. Welfare regimes and welfare opinions: a comparison of eight western countries. *Social Indicators Research*, 64: 495–520.

—— 2006. *The Moral Economy of Class: Class and Attitudes in Comparative Perspective.* Stanford, Calif.: Stanford University Press.

TAYLOR-GOOBY, P. 1985. *Public Opinion, Ideology, and State Welfare.* London: Routledge & Kegan Paul.

—— and HASTIE, C. 2002. Support for goverment spending: has New Labour got it right? Pp. 75–96 in *British Social Attitudes: The 19th Report*, ed. A. Park, K. Thomson, L. Jarvis, C. Bromley, and J. Curtice. London: Sage.

TYLER, T. R., RASINSKI, K. A., and McGRAW, K. M. 1985. The influence of perceived injustice on the endorsement of political leaders. *Journal of Applied Social Psychology*, 15: 700–25.

—— BOECKMANN, R. J., SMITH, H. J., and HUO, Y. J. 1997. *Social Justice in a Diverse Society.* Boulder, Colo.: Westview Press.

ULLRICH, C. G. 2000. Die Soziale Akzeptans des Wohlfartsstaates: Ergebnisse, Kritik und Perspektiven einer Forschungsrichtung. *Soziale Welt*, 51: 131–52.

VAN OORSCHOT, W. 2000. Who should get what, and why? On deservingness criteria and the conditionality of solidarity among the public. *Policy and Politics*, 28: 33–48.

—— 2006. Making the difference in social Europe: deservingness perceptions among citizens of European welfare states. *Journal of European Social Policy*, 16: 23–44.

—— and HALMAN, L. 2000. Blame or fate, individual or social? An international comparison of popular explanations of poverty. *European Societies*, 2: 1–28.

WEGENER, B. 2000. Political culture and post-communist transition-a social justice approach: introduction. *Social Justice Research*, 13: 75–82.

WESTHOLM, A. 1991. *The Political Heritage: Testing Theories of Family Socialization and Generational Change.* Uppsala Universitet: Statsvetenskapliga institutionen.

WINTER, S., and MOURITZEN, P. E. 2001. Why people want something for nothing: the role of assymetrical illusions. *European Journal of Political Research*, 39: 109–43.

CHAPTER 20

....

CITIZEN OPINION ON FOREIGN POLICY AND WORLD POLITICS

....

RICHARD C. EICHENBERG

Because of citizen protests during the Vietnam War, the European antinuclear protests of the 1980s, and the global demonstrations against the Iraq War in 2003, scholars have argued that the study of foreign and national security policy can no longer be based solely on the military aspects of deterrence, coercion, and war. Rather, as Michael Howard put it, governments and scholars must pay attention to *reassurance*, the requirement of governments to "persuade one's own people, and those of one's allies, that the benefits of military action, or preparation for it, will outweigh the costs" (1983, 317).

This chapter proceeds from the assumption that public opinion will be an important concern in debates about international issues, especially concerning issues of war and peace. It is therefore all the more important to clarify exactly what "public opinion" means, how it can be measured, and how it behaves. There is fertile ground for such an inquiry. Over the last thirty years, public opinion polling has spread to most corners of the globe, making cross-national comparisons much easier than was the case previously (Pew Research Center 2005). Moreover, scholarship on public opinion and foreign policy has yielded something of a revolution in the way scholars understand the process of opinion formation. In particular, research has brought new answers to three sets of important questions:

(1) *What do public opinion polls measure?* How do citizens, who are generally uninformed about foreign policy and world affairs, form opinions on these matters? Quite simply, how can we measure "public opinion?"

(2) *How "rational" is public opinion?* Is it stable or volatile? Are opinions coherent? Do opinions plausibly reflect the flow of world events? Does public opinion respond to what governments do? Precisely what is the form of that response?

(3) *How universal are the determinants of citizen opinion, especially on crucial issues of war and peace?* Are the findings in broad, cross-national comparisons the same as those in the US or European contexts?

In this chapter, I review the scholarly literature on these questions and present data from public opinion surveys to illustrate the discussion. In the immediately following section, I describe in more detail why the answers to an individual survey question can be close to meaningless, but I also present two examples to show that analysis of many questions on policy issues can be combined to measure the public's "mood" on policy choices. Subsequent sections examine the questions of how "rational" these opinions are; precisely how opinion moods fluctuate in response to government policies; and the extent to which citizen opinions across the globe reveal both universal logics and the logic of specific national characteristics.

1 MEASURES: FROM SINGLE QUESTIONS TO POLICY MOOD

1.1 Ambivalence and "Mood"

Scholars of public opinion are aware of a paradox: the very grist of their studies—the single survey question at a single point in time—is close to meaningless in gauging "public opinion." Responses to a single survey question are highly sensitive to the wording of that question (Eichenberg 1989, 2005; Mueller 1973, 1994; Asher 2004).

Why are citizen responses to survey questions so sensitive to the wording of the question? One reason is that some policies may involve technical issues or questions that are distant from citizens' daily lives; unless events conspire to make them salient to citizens, opinion surveys are likely to yield a fair percentage of disinterested or uninformed opinions. A second reason is that citizens lack information about world affairs and therefore look for cues to help resolve uncertainty about complex policy issues. We know, for example, that different questions about the possibility of war with Iraq evinced highly different percentages within many countries. The mention of Saddam Hussein, casualties, or ground troops in questions about the Iraq War provided cues that conditioned the percentage who favored the war (Eichenberg

2005, 2006; Everts and Isernia 2005). Each word in a survey question framed a different aspect of a possible war with Iraq. When survey questions mentioned the United Nations or the support of allies for the war, this produced different percentages, for these are quite distinct cues. Lacking detailed information about a range of foreign policy issues, citizens do not engage in an expensive search for that information, but often use inexpensive cues that are contained in the question itself. Similar cues might come from the morning headlines or a conversation over the water cooler, a fact that helps explain why even an identical question might yield different percentages over the course of a week or even several days.

A second explanation for the instability of individual responses is contained in a simple yet elegant theory of survey responses developed by John Zaller and Stanley Feldman (Zaller 1992; Zaller and Feldman 1992). Zaller and Feldman argue not only that citizens are relatively uninformed about issues, but more importantly that they are also *ambivalent and conflicted*. On controversial issues such as social equality or war and peace, citizens are likely to possess competing or even contradictory opinions. One may, for example, strongly prefer the peaceful resolution of a particular international conflict while at the same time acknowledging that military force might become necessary or approve it after it is employed. For any particular issue or policy choice, individuals possess a range of ambivalent sentiments (Zaller and Feldman 1992, 583–5).

How is this ambivalence resolved when an individual is presented with a survey question that requests a relatively simple response? According to Zaller and Feldman, individuals consult a number of "considerations" that are most salient in memory at the moment of the survey, that is, information that is most accessible in the thinking of respondents. For those who have thought little about the specific issue, this might reduce to the considerations that are communicated by the question itself—mentioning the UN might resolve the ambivalence for some in the direction of "peace." Other considerations might be communicated by additional questions in the same survey. For example, if the survey questionnaire includes a long series of items about the casualties that could occur in war, this will likely affect the responses to subsequent questions about using military force (Zaller and Feldman 1992, 586–7; see also Mueller 1994, 1–11).

Of course, even ambivalent citizens are not empty vessels. They bring their values and policy preferences to any political question, and these longer-term considerations also condition their responses to survey questions. We know, for example, that women are more sensitive to casualties in war (Sapiro and Conover 1993; Eichenberg 2003); that US conservatives and the European right are generally more supportive of militant policy options (Wittkopf 1990; Holsti 2004; Asmus, Everts, and Isernia 2003, 2004); and that citizens with higher levels of education respond faster to the cues contained in major events and policy debates (Zaller 1992). Thus, the response to a survey question by any particular citizen will result from a combination of the information that is communicated by the question itself, by short-term events, and by the resonance of personal values and characteristics such as ideology, partisanship, gender, race, or education (Holsti 2004, 163–239 reviews the effect of each of these variables in detail).

These observations make clear why the responses to a single survey question are of limited value. Single questions are rooted in one specific wording at a single moment in historical context, and they evoke a particular set of considerations for respondents. Individuals may formulate their answers differently in response to another question that evokes different considerations at a different moment in time. The implications for students of public opinion are clear. One can only gain a summary assessment of "public opinion" on a particular issue or policy choice by studying as many variations in question wording as possible. Further, to fully understand how events external to the survey influence the considerations of respondents, one has to study how opinions unfold over time. The examples in the following two sections illustrate these points.

1.2 The US Mood on Defense Spending

In his study of the attitudes of US citizens toward the role of government, Stimson (1999) describes his concept of a public "mood." He observes that there are many hundreds of survey questions on the issue of increasing or decreasing the role of the US government in the domains of social security, health care, education, and many other policy areas, with each question revealing a different level of support for increasing or decreasing the US governmental role. Nonetheless, Stimson demonstrates that the movement over time of these survey items has much in common—they tend to move up or down together. There is, he argues, a "common disposition" to favor (or oppose) an increase in the role of government in citizens' lives. The utility of Stimson's insight is heightened by the fact that his index of policy mood based on this myriad of questions is a very good predictor of election outcomes in both US presidential and congressional elections. Citizens know what they want, and they vote accordingly (Stimson 1999, 97–120).

We can extend Stimson's logic to the field of international affairs and illustrate the use of multiple opinion measures by studying citizen support for defense spending in the United States. The defense budget represents the core of national security policy making, and considerable evidence discussed below shows that the public's influence on budgeting outcomes is significant. Yet ascertaining the public's support for defense spending is no easy task. Table 20.1 summarizes the results of eight survey questions in 1976 that employed typical question formats for ascertaining US citizen support for spending ("is spending too little/increase spending?"). In the Table, I measure *support* as the percent favoring increased spending divided by the total percentage that favor either an increase or decrease. Not surprisingly given what I have said about individual survey responses, there are large disparities among these polls, ranging from 66 percent support in one question that happens also to mention "strengthening our military" to 38 percent in the standard Gallup poll on defense spending.

Nonetheless, Figure 20.1 shows that the US public's defense spending "mood" was fairly consistent over time. The figure shows four separate series of questions that measure support for defense spending. The first two, by the Gallup organization and the General Social Survey (GSS), ask slightly different versions of the question

Table 20.1 Nine questions on support for defense spending in the US in 1976

	Increase defense	Decrease defense	Net support (%)
There's a lot of talk these days about cutting back on government spend-ing. How do you feel–would you like to see the government spend more money, less money, or just about what they are spending now on: Defense (Jan 21–8, 1976, Time/ Yankelovich)	27	27	50
There is much discussion as to the amount of money the government in Washington should spend for national defense and military purposes. How do you feel about this: Do you think we are spending too little, too much, or about the right amount? (Jan 30– Feb 2, 1976, Gallup Poll)	22	36	38
We are faced with many problems in this country, none of which can be solved easily or inexpensively. I'm going to name some of these prob-lems, and for each one I'd like you to tell me whether you think we're spending too much money on it, too little money, or about the right amount. Are we spending too much, too little, or about the right amount on … the military, armaments and defense? (Feb/Apr 1976, General Social Survey)	24	27	47
Now again remembering that gov-ernment spending has to be paid for out of our taxes, let me mention some other types of programs. Considering the situation today at home and abroad do you think the total amount the United States is now spending for defense and military purposes should be increased, kept at the present level, reduced, or ended altogether? (June 1976, The Gallup Poll/Potomac Associates)	27	21	56
Which of these statements is closest to your opinion? 1. We need to ex-pand our national defense and strengthen our military; 2. Our defense is just right now and should	39	20	66

(Continued)

Table 20.1 (*Continued*)

neither be increased nor decreased; 3. Too much is spent on **defense**, we would be safe **spending** less. (Oct 1976, Cambridge Reports).			
In general do you favor increasing or decreasing the **defense** budget of the United States, or keeping it the same as it is now? (Dec 17–23, 1976, Louis Harris)	25	27	48

Note: Net support is "increase" divided by the sum of "increase" and "decrease."

Source: IPOLL database, Roper Center for Public Opinion Research, University of Connecticut (also available through Lexis-Nexis).

of whether defense spending is "too much...too little...or just right?" (the exact question wording is shown in Table 20.1). The third is actually the average of many different surveys on defense spending collected by Hartley and Russett, including many in addition to the Gallup and GSS series (Hartley and Russett 1992). The fourth series is constructed from a defense spending scale that is presented to respondents in

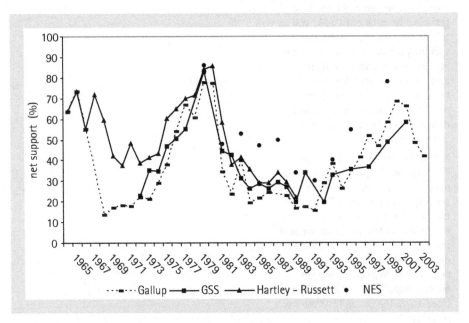

Fig. 20.1 Four measures of net support for defense spending in the US

Note: "Net Support" is defined as "increase" divided by the sum of "increase" and "decrease" in surveys on defense spending.

Source: Gallup and GSS surveys are available through the IPOLL database of the Roper Center for Public Opinion Research at the University of Connecticut. See Hartley and Russett (1992) for the source of their series, which is an average of six survey questions for each year. The NES responses are available from the NES website: http://www.umich.edu/~nes/nesguide/toptable/tab4d_3b.htm, accessed August 31, 2005.

the US National Election Study (NES).[1] For each of the four series, I calculate support for defense spending as follows: the percentage that favors an increase divided by the total favoring either an increase or a decrease in spending. Put briefly, the measure represents support for defense as a percentage of the total who express an opinion on increasing or decreasing the defense budget.

Not surprisingly, different question formats do yield different levels of support. Nonetheless, the four series clearly move together, suggesting that each is reflective of a collective disposition on the question of increasing the defense budget. These survey questions on defense spending therefore confirm that something coherent can be measured from what at first blush appears to be a cacophony of separate items. Later in this chapter, we see that these same opinions respond in a systematic fashion to the government's actual defense spending decisions and that the US government subsequently responds systematically to the public's mood. Thus, from the raw materials of individual survey questions, we can begin to construct a picture of the democratic politics of defense policy.

1.3 The Mood in Europe

Can the analysis of policy mood be generalized to public opinion elsewhere? One might argue along with Stimson (1999, xxii) that "Public opinion is about as institution-free as anything in politics can be. And it is the specifics of political institutions that so restrict our ability to create theories of general interest. The happy message, then, is that a model of public opinion that works for the American case ought to transfer across national boundaries with a minimum of difficulty." According to this logic, the cognitive processes of citizens everywhere are likely to be the same: the same lack of specific information about foreign policy; the same ambivalence on difficult political issues; and the same tendency to resolve uncertainty and ambivalence by using the cues that are contained in the wording of survey questions, the considerations that are evoked by major political events, and by referencing their values, partisanship, gender, and other personal characteristics. If correct, we should find general dispositions in public opinion outside the American political system.

Consider the process of European integration, which began modestly in 1957 with the establishment of a common market. During the 1980s and 1990s, the process accelerated rapidly with an expansion from six to fifteen members, the further liberalization of the European market, and the announcement of a transition to a single European currency in the Maastricht Treaty of 1992. By 2004, the European Union (EU) had expanded to twenty-five members and had dramatically increased the number of policy domains that are covered by the union's legislative authority. It had also established the euro as the common currency for all of Europe. At the same time, public support for the process of integration grew in importance. The public reacted very negatively to the Maastricht Treaty, which caused the union's governing body—the European Council—to aver in 1996 that "citizens are at the core of the European construction: the Union has the imperative to respond concretely to

[1] The scale ranges from 1 (greatly decrease spending) to 7 (greatly increase spending). In the graphic, I use all values representing increases (5,6,7) and decreases (1,2,3), ignoring the scale value in the precise middle (4).

their needs and concerns" (Presidency Conclusions, European Council, Turin, March 29, 1996, 1).

Not surprisingly, the EU conducts a great deal of polling to monitor the "needs and concerns" of its citizens. Yet measuring support for "integration" is hardly easy. To be sure, the technical meaning of the word is fairly clear; integration is a process of gradually merging the authority of what were formerly separate sovereign states. But in practice "European integration" has had at least three purposes in both official and scholarly discourse. First, the establishment of the original common market was accomplished quite explicitly in the pursuit of *peace*, following the cosmopolitan argument that the causes of war are rooted in the competitive anarchy of a system of separate sovereign states. Second, the common market and European Union were designed to increase European *prosperity*. Finally, framed as it was by the Cold War, the common market obviously had implications for European *power*. Power would flow to Europe by combining the resources and influence of the individual member states and by eliminating their separate and even competing voices on the world scene.

All three of these purposes have been reflected in survey questions about European integration, many of them sponsored by the EU commission. Figure 20.2 displays the European average in response to three survey questions (for comprehensive analyses of surveys on European integration, see the contributions to Niedermayer and Sinnot 1995). The first, labeled *unify* evokes the cosmopolitan notion of eliminating sovereignty by asking: "In general, are you for or against efforts being made to *unify* Western Europe?" A second question—*benefit*—addresses the more utilitarian concern of prosperity by asking starkly if respondents feel that "(*your country*) has on balance *benefited or not* from being a member of the EC (common market)?" The benefit question also subtly excludes cosmopolitan sentiment by presenting the issue in terms of national benefits rather than a unified community. Finally, a question on community *membership* offers elements of both utilitarian and cosmopolitan sentiment by asking simply if "you think that (*your country's*) *membership* of the European Community [common market] is a *good* thing, neither good nor bad, or a *bad* thing?" On the one hand, the reference to "your country" and the "good versus bad thing" juxtaposition probably weights the question in a nationalist, instrumental direction, while the reference to membership in the European Community has mild cosmopolitan overtones.

Figure 20.2 reveals that until the mid-1990s, the three questions did reveal a clear hierarchy of support. The cosmopolitan overtones of the "unify" question evoked the most favorable responses, followed by the mixed message of membership and the starkly utilitarian question on "benefit." However, beginning with the collapse of support on all three measures that followed the Maastricht Treaty in 1992, benefit and membership appear to have become close to identical. Anticipating the theme of the next section of this chapter, I would argue that this is a perfectly rational evolution, for it was after the Maastricht Treaty that the EU expanded its powers into more and more policy areas that affected the material interests of European citizens—there was a lot more cost and benefit to be concerned about (Eichenberg and Dalton 2003). The fact that Europeans would increasingly interpret the membership question in a

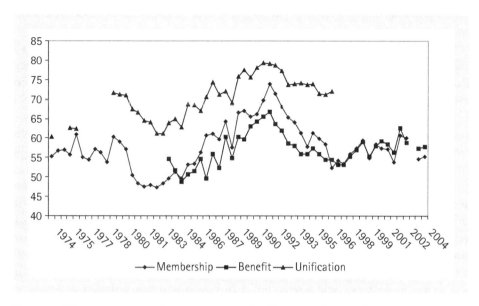

Fig. 20.2 Three survey questions on support for European integration

Note: The graphic shows the average responses from surveys in all EU states that have members since 1985.

Source: Commission of the European Union, *Standard Eurobarometer* (bi-annual), available from: http://europa. eu.int/comm/public_opinion/standard_en.htm, accessed August 31, 2005.

fashion similar to the benefit question therefore suggests that citizens had correctly identified the shifting nature of the integration process.

In any case, the differences in the average level of support for integration evinced in the three questions demonstrates once again that citizens resolved any uncertainty or ambivalence by responding to the cosmopolitan or utilitarian considerations evoked by the question and by changing policy circumstances. Nonetheless, Figure 20.2 also suggests that a common disposition—what we might call a "European integration mood"—also permeates these sentiments. Although the membership question did peak somewhat higher at about the time of the Maastricht Treaty in 1992, clearly there is a great deal of common movement in the measures.

2 Is Public Opinion on Global Issues "Rational?"

We have seen that there are common dispositions ("moods") in the collective opinions of US and European citizens and that these moods are sensitive to particular considerations operating at any moment in time. The combined impact of short-term considerations and the personal predilections of survey respondents produces opinion moods that ebb and flow in ways that make a good deal of sense given what we know about the policy issues.

This pattern of stable, sensible movement in citizen opinion contradicts a long-standing consensus concerning public opinion on national security and foreign policy. Prior to the 1980s, the prevailing view of scholars was that an uninformed, disinterested public was almost by definition incapable of producing a "rational" public opinion on foreign policy matters (the substantial literature surrounding this view is reviewed in detail in Holsti 2004, 25–98). In particular, public opinion was characterized as irrational in several specific senses of the word. First, it was argued that public opinion was highly changeable, indeed *unstable*, in the sense of revealing large swings from one opinion to another for no apparent reason. Second, public opinion was *incoherent*: an opinion on one foreign policy issue was unlikely to be related to views on other, even similar issues. Finally, public opinion could therefore not reveal any real relation to world events or policy actions, for the information level needed to form such opinions was low; public opinion was too changeable and incoherent to produce any *plausible* relationship between the real world and public opinion. And if opinion was so irrational, how could foreign policy be governed democratically?

All of this changed after Shapiro and Page's landmark study of American public opinion and foreign policy between 1935 and 1985 (1988). They argued that a description of public opinion in its collectivity must be based on as many individual questions as possible. They therefore amassed an extensive database of survey questions on foreign policy in the US between 1935 and 1985 and calculated the magnitude of change between any two identical, adjacent items (1988, 215). Their analysis is telling: public opinion turned out to be very stable indeed. In fact, in half of more than 1,000 surveys, there was no opinion change between adjacent time points. Among those questions that did reveal change, the largest share was rather modest. Moreover, Page and Shapiro examined reversals in the direction of opinion that might suggest a fickle or capricious public. Such fluctuations were very rare: they occurred in only 18 percent of the relevant survey questions, leading Shapiro and Page to conclude that "This would not seem to support the notion that the public has fickle and vacillating moods toward either foreign or domestic affairs" (1988, 219).

Stability also characterizes a variety of opinions on foreign policy and national security in the west European countries for which historical survey materials are available. In 1989, after studying a large number of west European public opinion surveys on the East–West military balance, nuclear weapons and arms control, defense spending, and the NATO alliance, I concluded that "continuity in public opinion was far more prevalent than change" (Eichenberg 1989, 198). Similarly, employing data from over 1,000 survey questions in France, Germany, and Italy, Isernia, Juhász, and Rattinger (2002) found results that were strikingly close to those of Page and Shapiro for the United States. Overall, opinion was characterized by moderate change, and reversals in the direction of opinion change were rare.

In summary, research demonstrates that public opinion in the United States and western Europe is neither highly changeable nor fickle and vacillating. A separate question is whether individual opinions are coherent, that is, whether views on one issue or set of issues are correlated with views on similar issues. For example, if one has a generally favorable view of the United Nations, should one not also favor securing the approval of that organization before using military force to resolve conflicts? Similarly, if one is positively disposed to defense spending and generally supportive of using national military forces for purposes of deterrence or resolving conflicts, should one not also downplay the role of the United Nations?

These sorts of question have animated a substantial body of scholarly research over the last twenty years, and the results prevailing in these studies is that individual opinions are in fact coherent. The most historically comprehensive research on this issue has been conducted by Eugene Wittkopf in the US context. Wittkopf studied the questions administered in the quadrennial surveys of the Chicago Council on Foreign Relations on *American Public Opinion and US Foreign Policy* (Wittkopf 1990, 1996). The Chicago Council surveys are particularly valuable because they include a very large number of questions on a variety of political, military, and economic issues. Analysts are therefore not dependent on single questions, and more importantly, one can investigate the degree to which citizens' views on one set of issues (such as international institutions) are correlated with their views on other issues (such as the use of military force).

Wittkopf's most important finding is that Americans have long been divided on a crucial question: the role of *military force in international relations*. Americans divide into three groups on this question: a "hardliner" group that largely endorses the threat or use of military force and consider issues of power balance and competition to be primary in international relations; an "accommodationist" group that is critical of military force and therefore favors the use of multilateral international institutions to resolve global conflicts; and a mixed "internationalist" group who favor elements of both militant and cooperative engagement in world affairs. There is also a small isolationist group that opposes all types of international engagement (1990, 26).

Equally important, Wittkopf finds that citizen opinions on a range of international issues tend to cluster together within these groups—indeed the strong correlation among many survey items is what defines the groups. Thus, a citizen who favors a strong role for the UN is also likely to be critical of military power; to favor trade as a tool for building international cooperation; and to disdain unilateralism while endorsing multilateralism (Wittkopf 1990, 1996). A militant internationalist would have largely opposite opinions. The key point is that citizen responses to many different questions are correlated in this way. Their opinions are, in a word, coherent.

Studies of public opinion in western Europe reveal the same coherence. What is interesting about these studies is the similarity to Wittkopf's finding for US public opinion: a citizen's opinion about the role of military force in international relations seems to be the factor that most strongly conditions the world-view. For example, Ziegler (1987) studied European public opinion toward transatlantic relations during the 1980s, including survey items on NATO, defense spending, and support for missile deployment in France, Germany, Italy, and the United Kingdom. Like Wittkopf, he found that opinions tend to cluster into a relatively militant group (generally favoring military solutions) and a more dovish group, with a "mixed group" also existing. Everts (1995) found a similar structure in Europe, and Jenkins-Smith, Herron, and

Mitchell (2004) found that American and British attitudes on a variety of nuclear issues formed a similar pattern. Asmus, Everts, and Isernia (2003, 2004) studied responses in the United States and seven European countries using the comprehensive yearly surveys of US and European attitudes conducted by the German Marshall Fund of the United States (GMFUS 2005; see also Isernia and Everts 2004). They found opinion clusters much like those in the US. Like individual opinions, moreover, these clusters of attitudes are relatively stable; they have existed in all GMF surveys from 2002 through 2005 (GMFUS 2005).

We thus have evidence that public opinion is "rational" in the dual sense of exhibiting *stability* and *coherence*. But what of *plausibility*? Does public opinion change in ways that reflect events occurring in the global environment or in reaction to government policies? And what is the form of that response? The examples described earlier in this chapter have already provided substantial evidence that public opinion moves plausibly in reaction to events and policy. Other studies provide additional evidence. For example, I have noted that Shapiro and Page found that public opinion rarely reverses direction. Based on extensive analysis of a number of foreign policy opinions, they further concluded that "These changes have seldom, if ever, occurred . . . without reasonable causes, such as the actions of foreign friends or enemies or changes in the United States' position in the world" (1988, 220–1).

Can we generalize about the *form* taken by the reactions of the public? Some opinion change is clearly instrumental; it reacts to the success or failure of government policy. For example, the evaluations of European integration that I described earlier are strongly correlated with the EU's economic policy performance. Europeans react negatively to bad economic news, for example, but positively to the gains made from expanding trade (Eichenberg and Dalton 1993, 2003; Gabel 1998). Aside from this instrumentality, there is also evidence in several contexts that the reaction of the public reflects a desire for moderation in policy. For example, Nincic (1988) studied American evaluations of foreign policy toward the Soviet Union under Presidents Carter and Reagan. Nincic's principal question was whether public opinion considered presidential policies too "hard" or too "soft." The results were clear: under Carter, respondents tended to argue that policy was too "soft," and under Reagan too "hard." Nincic (1988) labels this pattern the "policy of opposites" and suggests that the public essentially reacts by expressing a desire to "reign in" presidents who move too far in either direction. The pattern of "opposites" in public reactions to defense and foreign policy also suggests the more general relevance of Stimson's notion of a moderate zone of acceptability in citizen issue opinions. When government policy moves outside the zone of what the public will accept (or tolerate), public opinion will react by demanding a return to acceptable policies (Stimson 1999, 122–3).

There is substantial evidence of this pattern of "opposites" in public reactions to changes in the level of defense spending in both the US and in western Europe. Wlezien conceptualizes the pattern in terms of a "thermostat" metaphor: if policy (in this case defense spending) moves below or above the public's desired level, opinion will react in the opposite direction by demanding an increase or decrease for subsequent years. Following this metaphor, we would expect to see a negative correlation between changes in the defense budget and public opinion, and this is precisely what Wlezien finds in several studies (1995, 1996, 2004). Indeed, the "thermostat" phenomenon characterizes citizens' reaction to budgetary change in both the defense and domestic policy domains in the US, the United Kingdom, and elsewhere (Eichenberg and Stoll 2003; Wlezien 2004; Soroka and Wlezien 2004, 2005). Moreover, the evidence suggests that governments subsequently adjust budgets to reflect public preferences, a finding that holds in the US and several European countries (Hartley and Russett 1992; Wlezien 1995; Eichenberg and Stoll 2003). In both domestic and foreign policy, then, the thermostat reaction suggests that for the public, moderation is a virtue—and governments do take notice.

This is something that we might have inferred from the studies of opinion clusters discussed immediately above. Citizens with very hawkish or dovish views are not the majority in either the US or Europe. Rather, the plurality or even majority of citizens are "pragmatists" (Asmus, Everts, and Isernia 2003, 2004) or "internationalists" (Wittkopf 1990) who prefer a mixture of forceful and conciliatory policies. Not surprisingly, therefore, if policy moves too far in either direction, there is a substantial number of citizens who will signal the opinion that the thermostat should be turned back in a more moderate direction.

3 ARE THERE UNIVERSAL PATTERNS IN GLOBAL PUBLIC OPINION?

Because most scholarship is based on US and European public opinion, a question arises: how universal are patterns in public opinion on world politics, especially on the crucial issues of war and peace that have preoccupied global audiences over the last fifteen years?

The attitudes of US citizens on war and peace issues—the use of military force— are now well understood. Two early studies by Jentleson and Britton showed that the support of US citizens for using military force is heavily influenced by the objective for which force is used, what Jentleson calls the "principal policy objective" (Jentleson 1992; Jentleson and Britton 1998). Support for restraining or defending against foreign adversaries (foreign policy restraint) is very high, as is support for humanitarian relief operations, presumably because these actions enjoy normative and legal legitimacy and because the military requirements of success are fairly clear. In contrast, support for involvement in civil wars—internal political conflicts in Jentleson's terminology—is low, because such actions enjoy less legal legitimacy and perhaps also because they are risky and potentially costly operations. In a study of all US military interventions since 1981, Eichenberg (2005) confirms the importance of the principal policy objective and also finds that US citizen support for peacekeeping missions is low, perhaps because they engender involvement in civil strife situations.

These findings have been replicated in a number of studies with similar results, although each new study also offers a theoretical improvement (for comprehensive reviews of this literature, see Klarevas 2002; Holsti 2004; and Eichenberg 2005). Most important is the work of Larson, who argues that US public support for military operations is a *cost benefit calculation*: citizens evaluate the potential benefits of the action in terms of the stakes involved and the probability of success, and the costs of the action in terms of the human and financial costs. In three studies of a number of military conflicts involving the US, Larson finds robust support for his argument (Larson 1996, Larson and Sarych 2005). The importance of rational calculation is also confirmed in additional studies that find that the stakes, human cost, and relative success of the mission are key determinants of citizen support, although the principal policy objective remains a key influence on base levels of support (Feaver and Gelpi 2004; Gelpi, Feaver, and Reifler 2004; Eichenberg 2005).

How universal are these patterns? Do the considerations that influence the opinions of US citizens also operate elsewhere around the globe, or do opinions elsewhere differ from findings in the US setting? Until recently, it was difficult to answer these questions. Although there have been studies of citizen opinion in individual European societies (Mendel 1961; Everts 2000; Everts and Isernia 2001; Bobrow and Boyer 2001) or concerning individual historical conflicts (Sobel and Schiraev 2003; Everts and Isernia 2005), there have been no truly comparative, historical studies of the sort that characterize scholarship on US public opinion. Moreover, public opinion outside of Europe and the US has received limited attention. True, there has been a tremendous growth in truly comparative, global polling, especially concerning American foreign policy, the war in Afghanistan, and the war in Iraq (Pew Research Center 2005; GMFUS 2005). Nonetheless, scholars have only begun to tap these global sources in basic research on the sources of attitudes (Goldsmith, Horiuchi, and Inoguchi 2005).

Certainly there are clues to the determinants of support for using military force in global public opinion. For example, both in Europe and elsewhere, there is substantial evidence that the legitimacy surrounding the action is a key influence, as evidenced by the endorsement of international institutions, coalitions, or alliances (Everts 1995; Everts and Sinnot 1995; Sobel and Schiraev 2003; Everts and Isernia 2005). Public opinion in Europe also shows a sensitivity to risk and casualties (Everts 2000), and one cross-national study of opinion in sixty-three countries showed that support for the US war against Afghanistan in 2001 varied with such national characteristics as alliance memberships, trade with the US, past experience with terrorism, and the percentage of Muslims in the population (Goldsmith, Horiuchi, and Inoguchi 2005; see also Pew Research Center 2005). There is, in short, some limited evidence that support for using military force demonstrates both universal aspects that condition support in all countries (international legitimacy), and national variations in which the characteristics and international position of a country influences the level of support for military actions.

I examined these two sets of variables, which I labeled *universal logics* and *national characteristics*, in a study of public support for using military force in eighty-one countries. The study included public opinion surveys before and during the Persian Gulf War, the wars in Bosnia and Kosovo, and the US-led wars against Afghanistan and Iraq (Eichenberg 2006). The data in this study provide a rare cross-national insight into the determinants of support for military action.

An important result of the study is that there is indeed a universal logic to support for using military force. That is, even controlling for such national characteristics as relative wealth, military power, trade relationships, and religious composition of the population, variables relating to the principal policy objective of the action, the degree of international legitimacy attached to the action, the participation of international forces, and the risk and costliness of the action remain very strong correlates of support for using military force. One example illustrates the importance of these universal logics. Generally, societies with large Muslim populations have been skeptical of using military force. However, during the Gulf War in 1991, nineteen survey questions about coalition military action against Iraq were asked in Bahrain, Oman, Saudi Arabia, Turkey, and the United Arab Emirates, all countries with majority Muslim populations. Support for military action against Iraq averaged 50 percent in these countries and approached 60 percent in Saudi Arabia and Turkey. In the other conflicts, support for using force averages 25 percent in predominantly Muslim societies.

This finding reinforces the universal importance of policy objectives and international legitimacy to support for using force. The restraint of a demonstrably aggressive neighbor in the Persian Gulf overrode whatever doubts that Muslims in the region might have had about the use of force against Iraq in 1991. The fact that the coalition military effort had been endorsed by the United Nations was also no doubt a factor (Eichenberg 2006, 60). Some considerations, it appears, are indeed universal.

Yet national characteristics are also important. In particular, even when controlling for universal logics, the effect of important national characteristics, such as relative wealth, relative military power, alliance commitments, and religious composition of the population, remain strong correlates of support for using force. Put briefly, poor, weak societies that are not allied with the US are far less supportive of using military force than are wealthy, powerful allies of the US. My conclusion concerning these relationships is this:

The experience and interests that are captured by national characteristics form something of a structural baseline in national perspectives. Citizens of a country that is poor, militarily weak, and outside the alliance orbit of the international system's dominant powers are unlikely to look positively on the use of military force to resolve conflicts, especially when it is the military of the system's most powerful actors that form the core of the forces involved. Nonetheless, this structural baseline is not immutable. There are also political and normative logics that move support above and below the baseline of support. (Eichenberg 2006, 51–2).

The different levels of support of Muslim citizens during the Gulf War of 1991 and the Iraq War of 2003 is a perfect illustration. Support was low in the latter case because its objective was regime change; it was carried out by just a few international actors led by the US; and it was not endorsed by the international community. In the former case, the action aimed to reverse a clear case of aggression; it was sanctioned by the international community; and it was carried out by a broad coalition of actors.

4 Conclusions

In the past, research on citizen opinions of world affairs was something of a hard case for those who hope for democratic control of policy. Citizens in most countries are not well informed on global issues, and on many issues they are understandably ambivalent. As a result, when the pollsters ask complicated questions about truly difficult decisions—such as the decision to go to war—citizens are likely to sway one way or the other, depending on the exact words that are put before them.

Yet a review of scholarship on public opinion concerning issues of foreign policy, national security, and war and peace reveals that citizens in most countries have quite sensible reactions to these complexities. Although survey organizations are prone to place quite different questions before respondents, we have seen that their responses reveal identifiable "moods." Citizens notice the nuances of policies that are queried in public opinion surveys, and the "mood" of citizens reveals itself. These moods are in turn quite reasonable given the policy choices surrounding them, and the evidence suggests that governments represent this sentiment in subsequent policy. Equally important, citizen opinions are "rational," in the sense that they are relatively stable, coherent, and plausibly related to world events.

Finally, there is some evidence that citizen opinions on world affairs, especially on issues of war and peace, share some universal judgments. Citizens in all countries value the international legitimacy that flows from the endorsement of international institutions. Citizens in all countries shy away from risky actions and from the possible loss of life in war. But it is also true that attitudes are formed from a national perspective. Citizens of rich and powerful states are more comfortable with the use of force in international relations. Citizens of poorer and weaker states are far less enthusiastic. The conversation between the citizens of these two groups represents an important challenge for the future.

References

Asher, H. 2004. *Polling and the Public.* Washington, DC: Congressional Quarterly Press.

Asmus, R., Everts, P., and Isernia, P. 2003. Power, war and public opinion: thoughts on the nature and structure of the Transatlantic divide. Washington, DC: German Marshall Fund of the United States, www.transatlantictrends.org/doc/2003_english_essay.pdf

———— ———— ———— 2004. Across the Atlantic and the political aisle: the double divide in U.S.-European relations. Washington, DC: German Marshall Fund of the United States, www.transatlantictrends.org/doc/2004_english_analytical.pdf

BOBROW, D., and BOYER, M. 2001. Public opinion and international policy choices: global commitments for Japan and its peers? *Japanese Journal of Political Science*, 2 (1): 67–95.

EICHENBERG, R. 1989. *Public Opinion and National Security in Western Europe: Consensus Lost?* Ithaca, NY: Cornell University Press.

———— 2003. Gender differences in public attitudes toward the use of force by the United States, 1990–2003. *International Security*, 28: 134–5.

———— 2005. Victory has many friends: US public opinion and the use of military force, 1981–2005. *International Security*, 30: 140–77.

———— 2006. Global public opinion from the first Gulf War to the invasion and occupation of Iraq. Paper delivered to the Convention of the International Studies Association, San Diego, March 22–5.

———— and DALTON, R. 1993. Europeans and the European Union: the dynamics of public support for European integration. *International Organization*, 47: 507–34.

———— ———— 2003. Post-Maastricht blues: the welfare state and the transformation of public opinion on European integration, 1973–2002. Department of Political Science, Tufts University.

———— and STOLL, R. 2003. Representing defense: democratic control of the defense budget in the United States and Western Europe. *Journal of Conflict Resolution*, 47: 399–422.

EVERTS, P. 1995. NATO, the European Community, and the United Nations. Pp. 402–29 in *Public Opinion and Internationalized Governance*, ed. O. Niedermayer and R. Sinnott. London: Oxford University Press.

———— 2000. Public opinion after the Cold War: a paradigm shift. Pp. 177–94 in *Decision-Making in a Glass House: Mass Media, Public Opinion, and American and Foreign Policy in the 21st Century*, ed. B. Nacos, R. Shapiro, and P. Isernia. Lanham, Md.: Rowman & Littlefield.

———— and ISERNIA, P. eds. 2001. *Public Opinion and the International Use of Force*. London: Routledge.

———— ———— 2005. The polls: the war in Iraq. *Public Opinion Quarterly*, 69: 264–323.

———— and SINNOT, R. 1995. European publics and the legitimacy of internationalized governance. Pp. 431–57 in *Public Opinion and Internationalized Governance*, ed. O. Niedermayer and R. Sinnott. London: Oxford University Press.

FEAVER, P., and GELPI, C. 2004. *Choosing Your Battles: American Civil-Military Relations and the Use of Force*. Princeton: Princeton University Press.

GABEL, M. 1998. *Interests and Integration*. Ann Arbor: University of Michigan Press.

GELPI, C., FEAVER, P., and REIFLER, J. 2004. Casualty sensitivity and the war in Iraq. Department of Political Science, Duke University.

GMFUS (German Marshall Fund of the United States). 2005. *Transatlantic Trends 2005*. www.tranatlantictrends.org

GOLDSMITH, B., HORIUCHI, Y., and INOGUCHI, T. 2005. American foreign policy and global public opinion. *Journal of Conflict Resolution*, 49: 408–29.

HARTLEY, T., and RUSSETT, B. 1992. Public opinion and the common defense: who governs military spending in the United States? *American Political Science Review*, 86: 905–15.

HOLSTI, O. 2004. *Public Opinion and American Foreign Policy*. Ann Arbor: University of Michigan Press.

HOWARD, M. 1983. Reassurance and deterrence. *Foreign Affairs*, 61: 309–20.

ISERNIA, P., and EVERTS, P. 2004. Partners apart? The foreign policy attitudes of the American and European publics. *Japanese Journal of Political Science*, 5: 229–58.

ISERNIA, P., EVERTS, P., JUHÁSZ, Z., and RATTINGER, H. 2002. Foreign policy and the rational public in comparative perspective. *Journal of Conflict Resolution*, 46: 201–24.

JENKINS-SMITH, H., MITCHELL, N., and HERRON, K. 2004. Foreign and domestic policy belief structures in the U.S. and British publics. *Journal of Conflict Resolution*, 48: 287–309.

JENTLESON, B. 1992. The pretty prudent public: post-Vietnam American opinion on the use of military force. *International Studies Quarterly*, 36: 49–74.

—— and BRITTON, R. 1998. Still pretty prudent: post-Cold War American public opinion on the use of military force. *Journal of Conflict Resolution*, 42: 395–417.

KLAREVAS, L. 2002. The "essential domino" of military operations: American public opinion and the use of force. *International Studies Perspectives*, 3: 417–37.

LARSON, E. 1996. *Casualties and Consensus: The Historical Role of Casualties in Domestic Support for U.S. Military Operations*. Santa Monica, Calif.: Rand.

—— 2000. Putting theory to work: diagnosing public opinion on the U.S. intervention in Bosnia. In *Being Useful: Policy Relevance and International Relations Theory*, ed. M. Nincic and J. Lepgold. Ann Arbor: University of Michigan Press.

—— and SAVYCH, B. 2005. *American Public Support for U.S. Military Operations from Mogadishu to Baghdad*. Santa Monica, Calif.: Rand.

MENDEL, D., JR. 1961. *The Japanese People and Foreign Policy: A Study of Public Opinion in Post-Treaty Japan*. Berkeley: University of California Press.

MUELLER, J. 1973. *War, Presidents and Public Opinion*. New York: John Wiley.

—— 1994. *Policy and Opinion in the Gulf War*. Chicago: University of Chicago Press.

NACOS, B., SHAPIRO, R., and ISERNIA, P. eds. 2000. *Decision-making in a Glass House: Mass Media, Public Opinion, and American and Foreign Policy in the 21st Century*. Lanham, Md.: Rowman & Littlefield.

NIEDERMAYER, O., and SINNOTT, R. eds. 1995. *Public Opinion and Internationalized Governance*. London: Oxford University Press.

NINCIC, M. 1988. The United States, the Soviet Union, and the politics of opposites. *World Politics* 40: 452–75.

Pew Research Center for the People and the Press. 2005. *The Pew Global Attitudes Project*. http://people-press.org

SAPIRO, V., and CONOVER, P. 1993. Gender, feminist consciousness, and war. *American Journal of Political Science*, 37: 1079–99.

SHAPIRO, R., and PAGE, B. 1988. Foreign policy and the rational public. *Journal of Conflict Resolution*, 32: 211–47.

SOBEL, R., and SHIRAEV, E. eds. 2003. *International Public Opinion and the Bosnia Crisis*. New York: Lexington Books.

SOROKA, S., and WLEZIEN, C. 2004. Degrees of democracy: public opinion and policy in comparative perspective. *Center for Advanced Study in the Social Sciences, Working Paper Series*. Madrid: Juan March Institute.

—— —— 2005. Opinion-policy dynamics: public preferences and public expenditure in the UK. *British Journal of Political Science*, 35 (04): 665–89.

STIMSON, J. 1999. *Public Opinion in America: Mood, Cycles, and Swings*. Boulder, Colo.: Westview Press.

WITTKOPF, E. 1990. *The Faces of Internationalism: Public Opinion and American Foreign Policy*. Durham, NC: Duke University Press.

—— 1996. What Americans really think about foreign policy. *Washington Quarterly*, 19: 91–106.

WLEZIEN, C. 1995. The public as thermostat: dynamics of preferences for spending. *American Journal of Political Science*, 39: 981–1000.

—— 1996. Dynamics of representation: the case of US spending on defense. *British Journal of Political Science*, 26: 81–103.

—— 2004. Patterns of representation: dynamics of public preferences and policy. *Journal of Politics*, 66: 1–24.

ZALLER, J. 1992. *The Nature and Origins of Mass Opinion*. Cambridge: Cambridge University Press.

—— and FELDMAN, S. 1992. A simple theory of the survey response: answering questions versus revealing preferences. *American Journal of Political Science*, 36 (August): 579–616.

ZIEGLER, A. 1987. The structure of European attitudes toward Atlantic cooperation. *British Journal of Political Science*, 17: 457–77.

CHAPTER 21

....

NORMS OF
CITIZENSHIP

....

JAN W. VAN DETH

In the last few years the concept of citizenship has endured a remarkable revival in both academic and political debates. This fashion is closely related to several major problems that supposedly trouble contemporary democracies. Particularly prominent is a lament about the increase of social egoism, declining feelings of solidarity and community, a public withdrawal from the "dirty" realm of politics, and the decrease of social and political engagement. There seems to be a widespread consensus that a revival of citizenship can compensate and make up for the assumed deficiencies of modern democracies and especially offer a cure for welfare states confronted with severe budgetary constraints. If governments increasingly lose confidence in their own capabilities and withdraw from the public space, a renewed focus on the roles of citizens is obvious.

Citizenship—broadly understood as a relationship between an individual and a state in which the individual owes loyalty to the state and is entitled to its protection—has behavioral, attitudinal, and normative aspects. In that way, the concept covers the whole area of political behavior ranging from casting a vote in national elections to combating the ideals of a local interest group.[1] This chapter highlights the normative aspects of citizenship; that is, support for "norms of citizenship." These norms refer to the *image of a "good citizen"* which is characterized by the acceptance of such norms as being active in politics and public life, showing solidarity with other people, paying taxes and fees, and obeying laws and regulations. The main question, then, is not whether people indeed are politically active

---

[1] Citizenship is also used to refer to all aspects of individual political behavior. See for a broad conceptualization of citizenship as virtually identical with political behavior in democratic systems: Carmines and Huckfeldt (1996) or Nie et al. (1996).

or actually obey the laws. Instead, I examine the normative considerations about the position of citizens in democratic systems. Which norms characterize a "good citizen?" Are these norms of citizenship widely spread among the citizenries of mass democracies?

Studying norms of citizenship in addition to behavioral and attitudinal aspects of democratic politics is important for two purposes. First, although norms, attitudes, and behavior are not simply identical, people will engage in politics and public affairs in ways consistent with their norms of citizenship. For example, those who support the idea that citizens have a duty to cast a vote will be much more likely to participate in elections than other people do. Second, norms of citizenship provide *reasons* why citizens behave in specific ways. Those who strongly support the duty to vote will give different reasons for their participation in an election than those who consider politics and elections from a more instrumental view (cf. Theiss-Morse 1993; Verba et al. 1995).

1 Citizenship

A "good citizen" can be defined in many ways. Political philosophers from Aristotle and Plato to Michael Walzer and Benjamin Barber have dealt with the relationships between the requirements of the community on the one hand, and the rights and obligations of people living in that community on the other. Probably no community can exist on the basis of power and control only—without some minimum level of acceptance of its basic principles by its members, the persistence of any community is endangered. Discussions about citizenship concentrate on the exact definition of the rights and duties of people living in particular communities, usually states. The interdependence between the needs of a community and the features of a "good" member of that community typically is taken for granted. Following this argument, people living in democratic communities have to meet the requirements of democratic social life. These requirements are summarized under the label citizenship and include such things as engagement in public and political affairs, responsibility, solidarity, equal opportunities, and individual rights.[2] In fact, the very recognition of these requirements transforms people living in some community or state into citizens living in a democratic polity. For that reason, applying the concept

---

[2] In public debates "citizenship" is also used as a synonym for nationality as an official status and a legal concept ("obtaining British citizenship"). Although rights and duties of people also define this use of the concept of citizenship, the formal and legal aspects related to nationality are not relevant for our discussion about the much more general concept of norms of citizenship. See for a discussion of the "Problem of Inclusion" from a theoretical point of view: Dahl (1989, 119–32). The character of citizenship as a right is illustrated by Dahl's first characterization of a polyarchy: "Citizenship is extended to a relatively high proportion of adults" (1989, 220). A detailed analysis of the historical development of citizenship in the United States is presented by Schudson (1998). See Heater (2004) for a general overview of the history of the concept.

citizenship only makes sense if people are citizens and not simply subjects. Understood in this way, advanced and widely ensured citizenship, by definition, is democratic citizenship. This specification does not imply, of course, that citizenship only makes sense when applied to liberal democracies in Europe or North America. For democratic political systems in Africa or Latin America, the notion of citizenship is as important as it is for any other democratic system. And although one could think of people living under non-democratic regimes as citizens-without-rights, the concepts democracy and citizenship cannot be disconnected without fundamentally changing the meaning of each of them.

Even if we restrict citizenship to democratic citizenship, many types of rights and obligations can be distinguished: legal rights and obligations, political rights and obligations, social rights and obligations, and participation rights and obligations (cf. Janoski 1998). Starting with Pericles' speech more than 2,400 years ago politicians and political theorists have defended the notion that a well-developed democracy relies on the *combination* of private engagement and political involvement among its citizens.[3] In the winter of 431–430 BC the citizens of Athens gathered to bury their casualties of the first year of the Peloponnesian War. Pericles delivered the funeral oration and he used the opportunity to emphasize the extraordinary high culture and love of freedom of his native city with pride. Besides, he stressed the obligations of a "good citizen":

An Athenian citizen does not neglect the state because he takes care of his own household; and even those of us who are engaged in business have a fair idea of politics. We alone regard a man who takes no interest in public affairs, not as a harmless, but as a useless character; and if few of us are originators, we are all sound judges of policy. (Sabine and Thorson 1973, 28)

This dual responsibility still defines the obligations of a "good citizen" fairly accurate and it can be seen as a core requirement for the establishment and endurance of democratic political systems (cf. Portis 1985, 458).

Since comprehensive citizenship presumes a democratic community the concept obtained significant political relevance with the American and French Revolutions. In the "Declaration of the Rights of Man and of the Citizen" the French National Assembly in August 1789 proclaimed that "Men are born and remain free and equal in rights" and the final end of every political institution being "the natural and inalienable rights of man." The Virginia "Bill of Rights"—published thirteen years earlier than the French text—also stressed the universal nature of these rights and the correspondence between individual political rights and the "common interest" (cf. Schudson 1998, 28). According to these documents, the power of a state should be based on the consent of its citizens and the protection of individual rights. Every (independent) person has basic and equal rights, but only in a democracy is the state the property of its own citizenry. And only in a democracy have people particular rights as citizens. This double recognition of individual rights and "ownership" of the

---

[3] See Weintraub (1997) for an excellent overview of the "public/private distinction" and its relevance for political theory. Especially feminist approaches focus on this distinction (cf. Lister 2003) or Hobson (2000) for a more general approach.

state indicates a radical break with previous thinking and the accentuation of citizenship as an important aspect of democratic governance.

Ever since the late eighteenth century the protection of individual rights and its counterpart—the limitations of state power—determine our understanding of citizenship and democracy. Thomas Marshall (1950) summarized the idea of citizenship and its relevance for contemporary discussions of democracy and political behavior is his seminal contribution on the history of citizenship. He distinguished between three types of rights: civil, political, and social rights. According to Marshall, citizenship is a status granted to individuals who meet specific requirements; it transforms people from subjects of political processes to participants and doers. It defines both rights and duties of citizens; that is, it defines both the entitlements of each person against the community or the state as well as its obligations towards these institutions (Marshall 1950, 41–3, 45–6).

A citizen concentrating on his or her own household and business is—as Pericles remarked—a "useless character" and clearly not somebody entitled to citizenship. This sense of duty towards "public affairs" is characteristic for most conceptualizations of citizenship. According to Marshall citizenship requires "a direct sense of community membership based on loyalty to a civilisation which is a common possession. It is a loyalty of free men endowed with rights and protected by a common law" (1950, 24). Divergent approaches of citizenship all accept the notion of "loyalties" on the one hand, and "rights" of "free men" on the other. What distinguishes different approaches, however, is the way they deal with conflicts of interests between these notions: what should happen in cases of clear conflicts of interest between "the good of the community" and individual citizens using their rights? What is to be done when Marshall's "free men" decide to use their rights in such a way that they abstain from being loyal? Are rights only available to those persons that are loyal? Is a "sense of community" based on, say, purely egoistic motives instead of "loyalty to a civilisation" acceptable as a hallmark of citizenship? As Dahl noticed: "If a society could exist in which there were no conflicts of interest, no one would have much need for personal rights: What any citizen wanted, everyone would want" (1989, 220). Since conflicts and incompatibilities are normal in every community and state, guidelines are required how to deal with them. Different approaches to citizenship define various ways to handle these conflicts and incompatibilities.[4]

Broadly speaking, contemporary authors on citizenship present liberal, social democratic, communitarian, and republican ways to handle conflicts of interests or incompatibilities between various principles (cf. Janoski 1998, 17–23; Hemerijck 2001, 138–40). In *liberal approaches* freedom from undesired intervention by the state or other citizens ("negative freedom") and equality of opportunities are stressed. *Social*

---

[4] Several authors have argued that these conflicts and incompatibilities are unavoidable because the state has a monopoly on the use of force, which is mutually exclusive with legitimacy understood as the deliberate acceptance of rules. See Hoffman (2004) for an extensive discussion of this line of reasoning, or Crouch et al. (2001) for discussions about the limitations of citizenship and the decline of the nation state.

democratic approaches usually have a lot in common with liberal approaches, but rely on the idea that people should have sufficient resources to utilize opportunities ("positive freedom"). The two other approaches stress the importance of the community. *Communitarian approaches* reject the focus within liberal and social democratic traditions on rights at the expense of obligations. They stress the interdependency between the individual and the community rather than individual rights. *Republican approaches* accentuate the political community as opposed to some "natural" community emphasized by communitarians, and the rights, obligations, and loyalties of citizens are directly linked to the political system.

The close connection between concepts of citizenship and democracy can be illustrated easily by fashionable communitarian proposals as presented by Benjamin Barber. Basically relying on similar arguments as Pericles, Barber (1984; 1995) makes a strong case for a much more "participatory democracy" as an alternative for liberal "thin democracy" and "politics as zookeeping." A "good citizen" can only exist in a "strong democracy," which "requires unmediated self-government by an engaged citizenry" (Barber 1984, 261). The main characteristic of such a healthy democracy is that it is "the politics of amateurs, where every man is compelled to encounter every other man without the intermediary of expertise" (Barber 1984, 152). Barber repeatedly stresses that participation can be learned by active citizens in order to develop citizenship. Hence, engagement in politics is not to be considered as a specific type of activity—it is an integral part of social life and essential for citizenship. A "good citizen" is someone who does not accept the distinction between political and non-political activities and orientations.

This concise overview of various approaches to the concept citizenship yields two conclusions. First, advanced citizenship is concerned with duties (obligations, loyalties) and rights (privileges) of citizens as "free men" in democratic societies; that is, it is based on the relationship between private and public affairs. This conceptualization underlines the direct relationships between democracy and citizenship, and excludes the use of citizenship for non-democratic political systems. Second, it cannot be presumed that the rights and duties of citizens are simply compatible with the rights and duties of fellow citizens or with the needs of the community or the state.

2 NORMS OF CITIZENSHIP

Empirical research on citizenship has been mainly concerned with citizenship as a synonym for political behavior. The early voting studies, but especially Almond and Verba's *Civic Culture* (1963), seem to rely on the presumption that anything a citizen does or thinks about politics is an aspect of citizenship. As indicated, the focus here is more limited and directed toward the normative aspects of citizenship. With respect to the extensive conceptualizations and century-old discussions among political philosophers about the various meanings of citizenship and the norms of citizenship, it is remarkable that empirical research on the normative aspects is rare. What image do citizens have of norms of citizenship; that is, what image do they have about a "good citizen?" How are norms of citizenship distributed in democracies? Do people recognize a distinction between private and public affairs? Astonishing as it might be, not much empirical information is available to answer these questions. Besides, the available evidence is almost completely restricted to liberal democracies in Europe and North America.

2.1 Images of a "Good Citizen"

A first way to get information about the images of a "good citizen" among citizens is simply to ask citizens what they consider important aspects of "good citizens." This can be done by using open-ended questions in surveys, by in-depth interviews, or by organizing discussions among focus groups. Lane (1962) interviewed fifteen Eastport men about their views on citizenship. Focus groups have been selected by Pamela Johnston Conover and her collaborators (1990, 1991, 1993, 2004) in their extensive comparisons of the ideas about citizenship among British and American citizens.

In order to obtain empirical information about the way citizens think about their rights and duties, Conover and her colleagues initially organized focus group discussions. Contrary to standardized surveys, in-depth interviews and focus groups encourage participants to rely on their own vocabulary and ways of arguing. Researchers confronted the groups with a number of hypothetical dilemmas as well as more abstract questions about citizenship. More recently, they expanded the research design to cover local contexts and the function of citizenship ideas in different communities. The results of these studies provide very interesting information about what citizens think about citizenship and the language they use to articulate these ideas. Besides, especially opinions about privileges and rights among focus groups appeared to be much more coherent than expected:

many citizens share common understandings of the content, nature, and origins of rights. But American and British citizens operate with different schemas. When American citizens think about rights, they most naturally think about civil rights. Underlying this shared focus is a legalistic, basically negative understanding of the nature of rights, an understanding that fits easily with the existence of civil rights but that in their minds is incongruent with the existence of positive social rights. When British citizens think about their rights they most naturally think about social rights. Underlying this common perspective is a contractual conception of rights, accompanied by a sense that these rights have gradually accumulated over the centuries in the course of popular campaigns and struggles. (Conover et al. 1990, 11; cf. Conover et al. 1991, 812; Conover et al. 1993, 158)

These two different understandings of citizens' rights imply a very uneven representation of the three conventionally distinguished civil, political, and social rights. Although American participants do recognize political and social rights, the emphasis undoubtedly lies on civil rights (freedom of speech, freedom of religion, etc.) and "liberal" approaches. This is especially remarkable since many political theorists have argued for a much broader understanding of citizenship stressing emancipatory aspects and guarantees that basic needs are met by the community. In Britain, the emphasis is on social rights and "communitarian" approaches are dominant, and less importance is attached to political and civic rights. For explanations of the origin of rights, citizens in both countries refer to "communitarian" ideas. Political rights do not seem to be very relevant for the meaning of citizenship in both countries.

A widely shared "liberal" understanding also characterizes the way people think of responsibilities and duties of citizens. Central to the "liberal" understanding of core responsibilities of citizens in both countries

are fundamental duties necessary for the preservation of civil life (e.g., obedience to the law, respect for the rights of others) and the political system (e.g., paying taxes, serving on juries, and, occasionally, voting). But people differ sharply over other forms of citizen behavior. Most argue that other types of citizen behavior (e.g., public services, aid to the needy, political participation beyond voting) are not so much responsibilities of citizenship as they are virtuous behaviors that individuals might or might not choose to do. (Conover et al. 1993, 163; cf. Conover et al. 1990, 18; Conover et al. 1991, 818)

The differences observed in the arguments about these last kinds of "virtuous behaviors" are based on different ideas about the relationship between individuals and the community. Focus group members discern liberal, communitarian, and mixed approaches, varying from duties as merely legal requirements to duties as moral imperatives based on a sense of solidarity and concern. Yet, virtually all participants place a high value on these "virtuous behaviors"—what distinguishes them is the arguments they use to legitimate these activities. Both American and British participants rely on "liberal" approaches, although especially in Britain citizens express significant "communitarian" ideas (Conover et al. 1990, 18). More recent and more extensive research on local communities in both countries corroborates and enhances these findings (Conover et al. 2004). Responding to the question what they "might do to be better citizens" British and American respondents "are more likely to think about civic engagement than about electoral participation or democratic deliberation." Frequently used concepts and images are: "taking care of the environment, helping the elderly and the ill, participating in community organizations, taking a general interest in the community, giving to charity, and (in Britain) caring for animals" (Conover et al. 2004, 1060).

From these focus group discussions and local interviews the outline of a "good citizen" is fairly clear. A "good citizen" understands his or her rights mainly as civil rights (US) or social rights (Britain) and does not consider political rights to be equally important or relevant. Second, a "good citizen" understands his or her duties mainly as duties and responsibilities that are required to preserve civil life. A "good citizen" certainly values social engagement and active involvement in community matters, but no consensus exist about the reasons for these activities. This outline of citizenship is both remarkably limited and surprisingly sophisticated. The limitations are indicated by the dominance of the "liberal" approach to citizenship and interpretations of rights and duties as individual rights and duties. However, this dominance certainly does not exclude more sophisticated arguments about the need for social concern and collective action in the United States or in Britain.

Although Conover and her colleagues collected and analyzed their material with extraordinary care and presented very original and unusual views on the ideas of citizens about citizenship, the problematic aspects of their studies are obvious. The strong emphasis on "liberal" approaches to citizenship and the "mixture" of "liberal" and "communitarian" arguments are hardly surprising for British and American participants. Furthermore, for conclusions about the distributions of norms of citizenship among citizens representative samples of these populations are required. In other words: we need to go beyond results of focus groups and local interviews and should try to avoid a possible Anglo-Saxon bias by using comparative studies.

2.2 Support for Norms of Citizenship

Listening to discussions in focus groups and using open-ended questions are excellent ways to trace images of citizenship. However, these research strategies do not allow for inferences about the distribution of various aspects of norms of citizenship among the populations of mass democracies. In order to deal with that last question, representative surveys and structured interviews are required. Here, too, the amount of available empirical evidence is rather disappointing. Attempting to combine explorative methods and large-scale research Theiss-Morse (1993) used Q-factoring to develop an instrument distinguishing four main types of citizenship in two American cities—only one of these types include political activities beyond voting. Tyler (1990) presented strong evidence that people rely on images of procedural justice instead of outcomes when they decide to obey the law, but did not focus on citizenship.

Major examples of international studies which permit reliable comparisons of at least some aspects of norms of citizenship among the populations of democratic polities are the Citizenship, Involvement, Democracy project (CID) and the first wave of the European Social Survey (ESS).[5] The questions on the personal image of a "good citizen" used in the CID and ESS are based on a extensive battery developed as part of a Swedish citizenship study, which focuses on four dimensions: solidarity, participation, law obeying, and autonomy (Petersson et al. 1998, 129–30). Although the exact number of items has been reduced considerably, both the CID and the ESS can trace support for these four aspects of citizenship in many countries empirically. The questions direct the respondents' attention to the contested meaning of the concept as well as to his or her personal opinions about the "good citizen:"

---

[5] The network "Citizenship, Involvement, Democracy" (CID) was funded by the European Science Foundation; see: www.mzes.uni-mannheim.de/projekte/CID for further information. For the European Social Survey see: ess.nsd.uib.no/2003

As you know, there are different opinions as to what it takes to be a good citizen. I would therefore like to ask you to examine the characteristics listed on the card. Looking at what *you personally* think, how important is it:

    A. To show solidarity with people who are worse off than yourself
    B. To vote in public elections
    C. Never to try to evade taxes
    D. To form your own opinion, independently of others
    E. Always to obey laws and regulations
    F. To be active in organizations
    G. To think of others more than yourself
    H. To subject your own opinions to critical examination.

Respondents express their opinion for each item on an eleven-point scale ranging from "very unimportant" to "very important." A shorter instrument is used by the ESS including the items A, B, D, E, and F as well as an additional item "Be active in politics."

Analyzing the ESS data Rossteutscher (2005) reports high levels of support for law obeying, solidarity, and autonomy in European democracies. About 70–90 percent of the populations consider these three aspects as "very important" features of a "good citizen." This high level of support can also be revealed for the norm to vote in public elections. Much lower, however, is the support for the norm to be active in organizations (Rossteutscher 2005, 183–9). Denters, Gabriel, and Torcal analyzed the more extensive version cited above and could confirm the expected dimensionality as well as the remarkable high level of support for the first three aspects of being a "good citizen":

We have found that in the hearts and minds of citizens the support for various citizenship norms is closely linked and that in all countries analysed here widespread support for the norms of law-abidingness, critical and deliberative values, and solidarity exists. Moreover, we also found that in each of our countries a majority of citizens has internalized a fully integrated concept of citizenship, based on simultaneous strong support for each of the three basic components of citizenship. (Denters, Gabriel, and Torcal 2007)

The results of both the CID and ESS findings are summarized in Figure 21.1. In spite of the use of different items and different sets of countries the results are remarkably similar for the two studies. Support for norms of citizenship is high for each of the four major aspects. Autonomy and law obeying are unreservedly supported by about 70 percent of the respondents, whereas voting and solidarity are considered to be important by about 60 percent.[6] On the other hand we see that the Tocquevillian idea that engagement in voluntary associations is an important aspect of being a "good citizen," is supported by about one out of every four respondents only. Even more remarkable is the clear lack of support for the idea that a "good citizen" should be active in politics: only 10 percent of the respondents support the norm that a "good citizen" is—generally speaking—a political active citizen. In a similar way, Dekker and de Hart (2002) show that politics is an astonishingly unimportant aspect of the image of a "good citizen" in The Netherlands. As Figure

---

    [6] The World Values Survey contains an extended measure for the acceptance of pro-social norms. The results obtained with this measure underline the conclusion that pro-social norms are widely accepted in democratic states (cf. Gabriel et al. 2002, 73–9).

21.1 makes clear, for the majority of respondents being a "good citizen" includes casting a vote in elections, but no further political activities are required to obtain this qualification. In other words, a "good citizen" is someone who visits the ballot box—not someone who is engaged in public and political affairs beyond voting.[7] Moreover, these findings do not support the idea that engagement in voluntary associations can be seen as a substitute for political engagement. People are consistently reluctant to place much value on both social and on political participation as core aspects of being a "good citizen" (cf. Theiss-Morse and Hibbing 2005, 242–5). Obviously, the "ideal citizen is not the enlightened political participant cognizant of the common good but the effective one" (Gross 1997, 233). This is a remarkably restricted conception of the participatory aspects of citizenship, which is far away from ideas presented by political theorists from Pericles to Benjamin Barber.

Figure 21.1 presents the average levels of support for various aspects of being a "good citizen." A closer look at the results for each country suggests substantive differences between the support for each aspect. One might expect that support for norms of citizenship is well established in the older democracies of north-western Europe and that citizens with less experience with democratic decision making still hesitate to show that support. This expectation is only confirmed for Spain, which shows a consistently

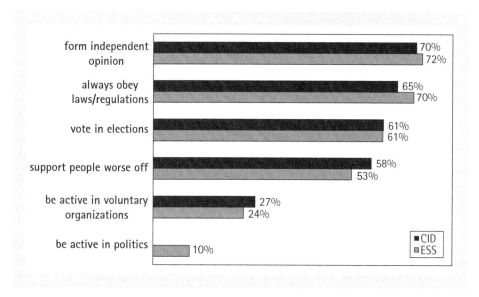

Fig. 21.1 Aspects of being a "good citizen" (percentages of respondents scoring 8, 9, or 10)

Source: ESS: Austria, Belgium, Switzerland, Czech Republic, Germany, Denmark, Spain, Finland, France, United Kingdom, Greece, Hungary, Ireland, Israel, Italy, Luxembourg, the Netherlands, Norway, Poland, Portugal, Sweden, Slovenia.
CID: Denmark, Germany, Moldova, the Netherlands, Norway, Portugal, Romania, Russia, Slovenia, Spain, Sweden, Switzerland.

---

[7] Surveys relying on similar measures as the CID-project arrive at similar conclusions. See Patty, Seyd, and Whiteley (2004, 48–50) for British results about the high levels of support for "civic duties and obligations" and a corresponding limited "sense of duty to become politically engaged" beyond voting.

lower level of support for almost each aspect mentioned. Especially citizens of the newer democracies in eastern and central Europe (Slovenia, Moldova, Romania) are much more willing to support aspects of "good" citizenship than the average figures indicate. In fact, people living in well-established democracies like Switzerland, Belgium, or the Netherlands show consistently lower levels of support for many of the aspects of citizenship mentioned. Apparently, stressing norms of citizenship is more important for people having limited experiences with democracy only—in well-established democracies these norms are taken for granted. This conclusion, however, should not be taken too literally since deviations from this rule can be easily documented.

Recognizing the importance of rights and obligation of a "good citizen" from a personal point of view obviously is the most important, but not the only way to conceptualize citizenship. In addition, one could use a societal point of view; that is, consider which society people prefer to live in. The CID study includes the following question dealing with this view:

I will now read some statements about how society could look. Could you tell me for each of these statements whether or not you would like to live in a society which emphasizes that . . .
  A. people are industrious and diligent
  B. people take responsibility for each other
  C. people stick to the rules
  D. people are self-confident and critical
  E. people can do whatever they want
  F. people live in economic security and wealth
  G. people are politically active
  H. people can realize themselves.

Although this question is not developed to observe support for norms of citizenship a confrontation of the four main aspects of being a "good citizen" with the aspects of the society people prefer to live in, can provide information about the individual or societal nature of citizenship. Table 21.1 presents the levels of support for norms of citizenship from both the individual and the societal points of view. These results confirm the conclusion that norms of citizenship are widely shared and supported. Furthermore, people clearly attach more importance to solidarity as a societal than as an individual feature. Since even more respondents would like to live in a society that enable "people to live in economic security and wealth," the additional accentuation of societal solidarity as compared to individual solidarity is probable due to fears for economic insecurity. Instead to rely on help and assistance from individual fellow citizens who behave as "good citizens" many people simply want to live in a society were economic security is provided. In a similar way, support for law- and rule-obeying norms is also somewhat higher from a societal than from an individual point of view. The results for the autonomy items indicate that especially forming independent opinions is supported from the individual perspective. And once again, the items referring to participation present the most remarkable findings. The majority of respondents consider casting a vote as an aspect of being a "good citizen." Yet only one in three believes that political participation in general is important from a societal point of view. Obviously, casting a vote is seen very clearly as a private duty and not as a public virtue. The relatively low

Table 21.1 Norms of citizenship from individual and societal perspectives (percentages of respondents scoring 8, 9, or 10)

Individual perspective	Support (%)	Support (%)	Societal perspective
As you know, there are different opinions as to what it takes to be a good citizen. I would therefore like to ask you to examine the characteristics listed on the card. Looking at what *you personally* think, how important is it ...			I will now read some statements about how society could look. Could you tell me for each of these statements whether or not you would like to live in a society which emphasizes that ...
A. to show solidarity with people who are worse off than yourself	56	71	B. people take responsibility for each other
G. to think of others more than yourself	32	–	–
B. to vote in public elections	63	–	–
F. to be active in organizations	29	–	–
	–	33	G. people are politically active
E. always to obey laws and regulations	62	69	C. people stick to the rules
C. never to try to evade taxes	57	–	
	–	28	E. people can do whatever they want
	–	67	H. people can realize themselves
D. to form your own opinion, independently of others	73	58	D. people are self-confident and critical
H. to subject your own opinions to critical examination	51	–	–
		58	A. people are industrious and diligent
		72	F. people live in economic security and wealth

Source: CID: Denmark, Germany, Moldova, the Netherlands, Norway, Portugal, Romania, Slovenia, Sweden, Switzerland.

level of support for political activities from a societal point of view is in line with the very low level of importance for such actions as reported for the "good citizens" in Figure 21.1 above and underlines the marginal position of political participation beyond voting as a norm of citizenship.

The country-specific differences noted in our discussion of Figure 21.1 are not confirmed for the results presented in Table 21.1. Very large differences can be found in the support for norms of citizenship from the two perspectives in many countries. Citizens of newer democracies such as Moldova and Slovenia overwhelmingly support rule-obeying, autonomy, and participatory aspects, whereas these aspects are less important for people from Switzerland or the Netherlands. Especially in Switzerland, the levels of support are relatively low for both perspectives. Here, too, we observe a tendency for citizens of established democracies to take these norms for granted—but the pattern is not consistent and several deviations can be observed.

Country-specific information is also available in other studies. In spite of the fact that this balancing of rights and duties of citizens is crucial to distinguish liberal, sociodemocratic, communitarian, or republican approaches to citizenship, not much empirical information is available on this topic. The British *Citizenship Survey 2003* includes the statement "You can't demand rights as someone living in the UK without also accepting responsibilities." A very large majority (66 percent) agreed with this assertion, while only 1 percent "definitely disagreed." That individual accomplishments cannot replace social provisions is clearly indicated by the fact that in the same survey only 36 percent agreed with the statement "If people would mind their own business, our society would be a better place" (Home Office Research 2004, 23).

The peculiar position of political activities as an aspect of citizenship is also reflected in the study of social activists in the United States. Focusing on the reasons these activists give for political inactivity the neutral response "I don't have enough time" is followed immediately by "I should take care of myself and my family before I worry about the community or nation" and "The important things in my life have nothing to do with politics" (Verba et al. 1995, 129).[8] Yet those who are politically active refer to "the desire to do their duty as a member of the community, to make the community or nation a better place to live, or to do their share" as the most important reasons for their engagement (Verba et al. 1995, 117). Apparently, social activists justify political activities with norms of citizenship whereas political inactivity is defended by pointing to the unimportance of politics as compared to other areas of life. Here, too, people do not consider political activities as being an obvious part of their involvement in public and social affairs.

The scarce amount of empirical information on the distribution of support for norms of citizenship provides a consistent picture. Representative surveys show that large majorities of citizens in each democratic polity support norms and obligations related to solidarity, obeying laws, and autonomy both from an individual and a societal perspective. Much less support is available for the participatory aspects of citizenship. Although many respondents underline the need to cast a vote in elections, not much emphasis is placed on engagement in voluntary associations or being politically active beyond voting. In current democracies the image of a "good citizen" is widely shared and supported. With the exception of social and political

---

[8] See van Deth (2000) for a more extensive discussion of the relative importance of politics as compared to other areas of life.

involvement beyond voting, this image assembles all aspects of the concept of citizenship as discussed by political theorists consistently.

3 CONCLUSION

Norms of citizenship rely on the notion that citizens should be engaged in both private and public affairs. No empirical evidence is available to assess the optimal balance between these areas that citizens might have in mind. What we do have, however, is information on the images of a "good citizen" and on the support for various norms of citizenship both at the individual and the societal level. These findings do not confirm popular images about the erosion of social virtues.

For example, Mitchell (2005) observed a significant change in the ways US courts and lawmakers define citizenship. This new concept is "marked by a radical individualism and extreme libertarianism" and is labeled "The S.U.V. model of citizenship: floating bubbles, buffer zones, and the rise of the 'purely atomic' individual" (Mitchell 2005, 77). The average citizen does not seem to think of citizenship in these terms. On the contrary. The empirical evidence available—although imperfect—clearly rejects fashionable impressions about an ongoing erosion of citizenship norms among mass publics. In all democracies normative considerations about solidarity, obeying laws, autonomy, and electoral participation are widely shared and supported. Much less convinced are citizens that participating in voluntary associations or being politically active are features of a "good citizen."

Empirical information on norms of citizenship, then, are neither in line with negative pictures of a rapid decline of public virtues, nor with overenthusiastic expectations about citizens eagerly looking for opportunities to participate in "thick democracy." Whether such participation, in turn, would have positive consequences for the development of citizenship norms still is a controversial topic. Some authors strongly argue that participation does not seem to be necessary for the development of norms such as solidarity (cf. Segall 2005). Others draw a more complicated picture (cf. Theiss-Morse 1993; Mansbridge 1999; Verba et al. 1995, 500) or underline the benevolent impacts of "deliberation" (Fishkin and Luskin 2005).

Reviewing the empirical accomplishments of a number of approaches Carmines and Huckfeldt conclude that "a revised model of citizenship has emerged—a model of the citizen as a cost-conscious consumer and processor of political information who, while taking her duties seriously, has successfully reduced the impulse to be consumed by politics and political affairs" (1996, 250). Based on completely different sources Schudson (1998) describes the rise of "monitorial citizens" in modern democracies in a similar way: they are "perhaps better informed" and "have no more virtue than citizens of the past—but not less, either." The crucial point is that they "tend to be defensive rather than proactive" (Schudson 1998, 311). This idea of a "monitorial citizen" seems to be generally supported by the empirical evidence available.

The scarce empirical evidence available does not show a trace of the rise of a "S.U.V. model of citizenship" or the arrival of "thick democracy" in the near future. Contrary to these fashionable interpretations, people have a much more realistic view of their role in democracies. They do take their rights and duties as citizens seriously, but they are reluctant to get involved in public and political affairs beyond voting. This should not be used to condemn citizens as "useless characters" or current political systems as "thin democracies" only. These finding underline the fact that many citizens have a much more down-to-earth orientation towards politics than many professional observers trust them to have.

References

ALMOND, G., and VERBA, S. 1963. *The Civic Culture: Political Attitudes and Democracy in Five Nations.* Boston: Little, Brown.

BARBER, B. 1984. *Strong Democracy: Participatory Politics for a New Age.* Berkeley: University of California Press.

—— 1995. *Jihad vs McWorld.* New York: Times Books.

CARMINES, E. G., and HUCKFELDT, R. 1996. Political behavior: An overview. Pp. 223–54 in *A New Handbook of Political Science*, ed. R. E. Goodin and H.-D. Klingemann. Oxford: Oxford University Press.

CONOVER, P. J., CREWE, I. M., and SEARING, D. D. 1990. *Conceptions of Citizenship among British and American Publics: An Exploratory Analysis.* Colchester: University of Essex. Essex Papers in Politics and Government, 73.

—— —— —— 1991. The nature of citizenship in the United States and Great Britain: empirical comments on theoretical themes. *Journal of Politics*, 53/3: 800–32.

—— —— —— 2004. Elusive ideal of equal citizenship: political theory and political psychology in the United States and Great Britain. *Journal of Politics*, 66/4: 1036–68.

—— LEONARD, S. T., and SEARING, D. D. 1993. Duty is a four-letter word: democratic citizenship in the liberal polity. Pp. 147–71 in *Reconsidering the Democratic Public.* ed. G. E. Marcus and R. L. Hanson. Pennsylvania: Pennsylvania State University Press.

CROUCH, C., EDER, K., and TAMBINI, D., ed. 2001. *Citizenship, Markets, and the State*, Oxford: Oxford University Press.

DAHL, R. A. 1989. *Democracy and Its Critics*, New Haven: Yale University Press.

DEKKER, P., and HART, J. DE 2002. Burgers over burgerschap. Pp. 21–35 in *Modern Burgerschap: Het Sociaal Debat Deel 6.* ed. R. P. Hortulanus and J. E. M. Machielse. The Hague: Elsevier.

DENTERS, B., GABRIEL, O., and TORCAL, M. 2007. Norms of good citizenship. Ch. 4 in *Citizenship and Involvement in Europe.* ed. J. W. van Deth, J. R. Montero, and A. Westholm.

FISHKIN, J. S., and LUSKIN, R. C. 2005. Deliberation and "better citizens". http://cdd.stanford.edu/research/papers/2002/bettercitizens.pdf (May, 12 2005).

GABRIEL, O. W., KUNZ, V., ROSSTEUTSCHER, S., and VAN DETH, J. W. 2002. *Sozialkapital und Demokratie: Zivilgesellschaftliche Ressourcen im Vergleich.* Vienna: WUV-Universitätsverlag.

GROSS, M. L. 1997. *Ethics and Activism: The Theory and Practice of Political Morality.* Cambridge: Cambridge University Press.

HEATER, D. 2004. *A Brief History of Citizenship.* Edinburgh: Edinburgh University Press.

HEMERIJCK, A. 2001. Prospects for effective social citizenship in an age of structural inactivity. Pp. 134–70 in Crouch, Eder, and Tambini 2001.

HOBSON, B. ed. 2000. *Gender and Citizenship in Transition.* Houndmills: MacMillan.

HOFFMAN, J. 2004. *Citizenship beyond the State.* London: Sage.

HOME OFFICE RESEARCH. 2004. *2003 Home Office Citizenship Survey: People, Families and Communities.* London: Home Office Research Study 289.

JANOSKI, T. 1998. *Citizenship and Civil Society: A Framework of Rights and Obligations in Liberal, Traditional, and Social Democratic Regimes.* Cambridge: Cambridge University Press.

LANE, R. E. 1965. *Political Ideology: Why the American Common Man Believes What He Does.* New York: Free Press.

LISTER, R. 2003. *Feminist Theory & Practice of Citizenship.* Paper presented at the meeting of the German Political Science Association (DVPW), Mainz, September 2003.

MANSBRIDGE, J. 1999. On the idea that participation makes better citizens. Pp. 291–325 in *Citizen Competence and Democratic Institutions.* ed. S. L. Stephen and S. K. Edward. Pennsylvania: Pennsylvania State University Press.

MARSHALL, T. H. 1950. *Citizenship and Social Class,* ed. T. Bottomore. London: Pluto Press (1992 edn.)

MITCHELL, D. 2005. The S.U.V. model of citizenship: floating bubbles, buffer zones, and the rise of the "purely atomic" individual. *Political Geography,* 24: 77–100.

NIE, N. H., JUN, J., and STEHLIK-BARRY, K. 1996. *Education and Democratic Citizenship in America.* Chicago: University of Chicago Press.

PATTY, C., SEYD, P., and WHITELEY, P. 2004. *Citizenship in Britain: Values, Participation and Democracy.* Cambridge: Cambridge University Press.

PETERSSON, O., HERMANSSON, J., MICHELETTI, M., TEORELL, J., and WESTHOLM, A. 1998. *Demokrati och Medborgarskap: Demokratiradets Rapport 1998.* Stockholm: SNS Förlag.

PORTIS, E. B. 1985. Citizenship & personal identity. *Polity,* 18: 457–72.

ROSSTEUTSCHER, S. 2005. Die Rückkehr der Tugend? Pp. 175–200 in *Deutschland in Europa.* ed. J. W. van Deth. Wiesbaden: VS-Verlag.

SABINE, G. H., and THORSON, T. L. 1973. *A History of Political Theory,* 4th edn. Hinsdale, Ill.: Dryden Press.

SCHUDSON, M. 1998. *The Good Citizen: A History of American Civic Life.* Cambridge, Mass.: Harvard University Press.

SEGALL, S. 2005. Political participation as an engine of social solidarity: a skeptical view. *Political Studies,* 53: 362–78.

THEISS-MORSE, E. 1993. Conceptualizations of good citizenship and political participation. *Political Behavior,* 15/4: 355–80.

—— and HIBBING, J. R. 2005. Citizenship and civic engagement. *American Review of Political Science,* 8: 227–49.

TYLER, T. R. 1990. *Why People Obey the Law.* New Haven: Yale University Press.

VAN DETH, J. W. 2000. Interesting but irrelevant: social capital and the saliency of politics in Western Europe. *European Journal of Political Research,* 37: 115–47.

VERBA, S., SCHLOZMAN, K. L., and BRADY, H. E. 1995. *Voice and Equality: Civic Voluntarism in American Politics.* Cambridge, Mass.: Harvard University Press.

WEINTRAUB, J. 1997. The theory and politics of the public/private distinction. Pp. 1–42 in *Public and Private in Thought and Practice: Perspectives on a Grand Dichotomy.* ed. J. Weintraub and K. Kumar. Chicago: University of Chicago Press.

C H A P T E R 2 2

DEMOCRATIC VALUES

JACQUES THOMASSEN

DEMOCRATIC values refer to the basic principles of democratic governance. The extent to which people in a particular polity share these basic principles is essential for the democratic quality of a political regime. First, a democratic regime almost by definition is a *legitimate* regime as it is supposed to be based on the consent of the people. Legitimacy in turn is usually defined in terms of basic democratic values or principles. According to Rawls's *liberal principle of legitimacy* "our exercise of political power is proper and hence justifiable only when it is exercised in accordance with a constitution the essentials of which all citizens may reasonably be expected to endorse in the light of principles and ideas acceptable to them as reasonable and rational" (Rawls 1996). Or in shorthand: "Groups regard a political system as legitimate or illegitimate according to the way in which its values fit with theirs." (Lipset 1966, 77). Second, the legitimacy of a democratic political system is generally considered as one of the most important conditions for its feasibility and stability.

In Easton's conceptual framework basic political principles or values are an important, if not *the* single most important source of the legitimacy of the regime. A sense of legitimacy derives from "the conviction on the part of the member that it is right and proper for him to accept and obey the authorities and to abide by the requirements of the regime." It is a strong kind of support because "it is not contingent on specific inducements or rewards of any kind, except in the very long run.... [I]f there is a strong inner conviction of the moral validity of the authorities or regime, support may persist even in the face of repeated deprivations attributed to the outputs of the authorities or their failure to do so" (Easton 1965, 278).

Parts of this chapter are based on Thomassen 1995.

The dependence of the stability of a democratic system of government on its legitimacy and therefore on the extent to which people subscribe to the democratic values behind it, is a persistent issue in the literature on democratic government and political culture. In a seminal essay Lipset (1966) explained why in the 1930s countries like Germany, Austria, and Spain fell for fascism whereas other countries did not. In his view this was because the democratic regimes in these countries were not legitimate. Therefore, when the effectiveness of these governments broke down in the 1930s these regimes missed the "reservoir of good will" that helped equally ineffective other democratic regimes in Europe to survive the economic crisis.

The collapse of the communist regimes in central and eastern Europe since 1989 and their transition towards democracy gave a new boost to studies exploring the feasibility of the new democratic regimes given their effectiveness and legitimacy. Once more the question is to what extent the democratic values of the citizens of these new regimes are well enough developed to sustain the new democratic regimes even if their immediate performance is disappointing.

The exploration of the relationship between legitimacy and the stability of democracy is beyond the purpose of this chapter. We only refer to it in order to indicate how important people's support for democratic values is for our understanding of the fate of democracy.

In this chapter we first assess the extent to which people across the world support democracy as a form of government. We then argue that such an assessment is not very informative as long as we are uncertain what people mean by democracy. We then confront the main connotations people associate with democracy with the main democratic values discerned in normative democratic theory. We then try to assess to what extent people uphold these more specific values of democracy if they are asked to apply them in specific circumstances.

1 SUPPORT FOR DEMOCRACY

In 1989 Francis Fukuyama declared the end of history. In his view a remarkable consensus concerning the legitimacy of liberal democracy as a system of government had emerged throughout the world. Although there still are many parts of the world in which liberal democracy has not yet triumphed, there is an increasing acceptance of the idea that liberal democracy in reality constitutes the best possible solution to the human problem (Fukuyama 1989, 1992).

This, of course, is a fascinating and provocative statement. But what is the empirical evidence for it? Fukuyama's major argument is that liberal democracy has no serious ideological rivals left after having defeated its major ideological rivals, fascism and communism. This might be true, but at least two questions remain. First, it might be true that liberal democracy has defeated fascism and communism as serious rival ideologies. But does this really imply that a large majority of the people around the world now embrace the values underlying liberal democracy? Second, one might wonder whether the "end of history" did not end on September 11, 2001 (Owens 2003). Should we seriously believe that liberal democracy finds much support in the Muslim world or are recent developments more in line with Huntington's equally challenging thesis of a clash of civilizations (Huntington 1996)?

These are the two empirical questions we will address in this section. In order to avoid the use of an eclectic collection of data from all kinds of sources, we will mainly rely on the cumulative results of the two most recent waves of the World Values Survey (WVS), conducted in 1995–6 and 2000–2. Based on questionnaires that explore values and beliefs in more than seventy countries, the WVS is an investigation of sociocultural and political change that encompasses over 80 percent of the world's population (Inglehart and Norris 2003; Inglehart and Welzel 2005). These studies asked two general questions that are supposed to measure general support for democracy as a form of government. The first one asks people whether they think having a democracy is a good way of governing their country. The second question asks them to what extent they agree with the statement "Democracy may have many problems but it's better than any other form of government."

The answers to these questions seem to prove Fukuyama right. An overwhelming majority of the people from every corner of the world agree that democracy is an ideal form of government. No matter how one subdivides the countries in the world, according to their geographic location, the age of their democracy and even according to the distinction between western and Islamic societies, the results are the same: in each category more than 80 percent of the people value democracy positively (Bratton, Mattes, and Gyimah-Boadi 2004; Dalton and Shin 2006; Inglehart and Norris 2003; Klingemann 1999; Rose 2002; Rose, Mishler, and Haerpfer 1998; Shin 2005; Tessler 2002).[1]

How deeply embedded these convictions are, is a different matter. According to Inglehart and Welzel (2005, 268–70) "The contemporary world is no longer divided between those who favor and those who oppose democracy; the vast majority favors democracy, and the main distinction now is whether people support democracy for instrumental or intrinsic reasons." They show that in post-industrial democracies intrinsic supporters constitute the great majority of those who support democracy. In eastern ex-communist countries and low-income societies high proportions of the public express overt support for democracy, but intrinsic supporters form only a minority of them. A majority supports democracy for instrumental reasons. These instrumental motives do not reflect a high valuation of democracy per se; they reflect support for democracy insofar as it is thought to be linked with prosperity and order. This type of support can quickly vanish if a society's experience under democracy is disappointing.

[1] See also chapter by Doh Shin in this volume and the information on the websites in the next note. For a report on support for democracy in Latin America, see http://democracia.undp.org/Default.Asp. Also, see the Pew global attitudes project and the Gallup VOP surveys, both of which have also examined support for democracy with a broad international framework: http://pewglobal.org/

Therefore, knowing that people around the world tend to support democracy as an ideal form of government is merely a starting point if we want to unveil people's support for democratic values. Is it more than lip service, more than a thin layer of civilization that will easily evaporate when people are tested on more specific values of democracy and their implications? If it is not, these figures are as convincing as representatives of totalitarian regimes serving on the human rights commission of the United Nations. Therefore, in the next section we first try to assess what people mean with democracy. Then we see to what extent these views match normative theories of democracies. From this confrontation we develop what we consider as the most important values of democracy. Next, we see to what extent people support these more specific aspects of democracy and—even more important—to what extent they uphold these values when they are asked to apply them in specific circumstances.

2 DEMOCRACY: WHAT DOES IT MEAN?

The best way to find out what people mean by democracy is by asking them. The most appropriate way to do this is by an open-ended question in a survey. Such a question was asked in Regional Barometer surveys conducted around the turn of the millennium.[2] The findings from these studies are unequivocal. People across the globe associate democracy primarily with liberty, followed at a far distance by more procedural aspects of democracy like "government by the people," "electoral choice," and this other basic value, "equality (before the law)" (Afrobarometer 2002; Albritton and Bureekul 2004; Bratton, Mattes, and Gyimah-Boadi 2004; Ikeda, Yamada, and Kohno 2004; Simon 1976). The answers to this question make perfect sense from the perspective of generally accepted conceptions of democracy. Liberty is the first value the immortal battle cry of the French Revolution, *Liberté, Egalité, et Fraternité*, refers to. Liberty, equality, and solidarity stand for the basic values of democracy, but they clearly have a different weight in people's mind. Liberty obviously is by far the most important value people associate with democracy. Equality and solidarity are much less frequently mentioned.

In particular the concepts of *freedom* and *equality* are essential in any conception of democracy. Significantly, both the American Declaration of Independence and the French Déclaration des Droits de l'Homme et du Citoyen, the magnificent

---

[2] The regional barometers consist of the (East) Asian Barometer, the New Europe Barometer, the Latinobarometro and the Afrobarometer. In 2001 these regionally organized surveys formed a global consortium of comparative surveys across emerging democracies and transitional societies, the Global Barometer Survey (GBS). For a comprehensive overview, and links to the websites of these regional surveys, see **www.idea.int/democracy/global-barometers.cfm**. Each of these sites offers extensive documentation, including working papers etc.

documents forming the intellectual justification for the two great democratic revolutions at the end of the eighteenth century, start with an outspoken commitment to these basic values. Also, the preamble to the United Nations' Universal Declaration of Human Rights starts with the statement "All human beings are born free and equal in dignity and rights."

3 Two Conceptions of Democracy

Throughout history both liberty and equality have been considered as fundamental values of democracy. But this is not to say that they easily travel together. A classic dilemma in democratic theory is: the more liberty the less equality, and the more equality the less liberty. Although liberty and equality are usually seen as twin concepts, they stand for two different strands of thought that can be distinguished in democratic theory. In the literature different labels are used to indicate essentially the same distinction: the Individualist versus the Collectivist theory (Pennock 1979), or the Anglo-American or Liberal versus the French or Continental tradition (Sabine 1952), or Madisonian versus Populist democracy (Dahl 1956).[3] The difference between the two perspectives can also be indicated by the distinction between the concept of the Rule of Law or the "*Rechtsstaat*" and democracy in the limited sense of "popular sovereignty."

These two democratic traditions had their points of origin respectively in the two great European revolutions which mark the beginnings of modern European politics: the English revolution of 1688 and the French Revolution a century later. Partly because of the different historical context in which these revolutions originated they developed a different view on the relationship between state and society and between state and citizens. "What the English revolution contributed to the democratic tradition was the principle of freedom for minorities, together with a constitutional system both to protect and to regulate that freedom.... It assumes that the area within which a government ought to act is limited, is defined by law, and cannot extend over all the interests and activities of its citizens (Sabine 1952, 457).

The French revolution introduced the concept of equal national citizenship into modern politics and as its counterpart the concept of the sovereign national state, supreme over every other form of social organization. A democratic society should be one in which absolutely nothing stands between man and the state (Sabine 1952, 462–4).

It might be clear that the distinction between the two democratic traditions is an *analytical* one and hardly one of political practice. Democracy and the Rule of Law have different intellectual roots but have been integrated in western democratic institutions. Therefore, democracy can be considered as a historical compromise

---

[3] Also, Lijphart's distinction between a majoritarian and a consensus model of democracy can be considered as an institutional translation of the same distinction (Lijphart 1999).

between two different principles. The first one is the principle of *popular sovereignty*: the sovereign power is exercised by or in the name of the people. The second and at least as important principle is that the liberty of individual citizens must be protected against the power of the state, whether or not this is legitimized by the (majority of the) people. Although these two principles clearly exist as different views on democratic values and institutions, it might be better to consider them as ideal types in the Weberian sense: it is possible to indicate the theoretical pure extremes on a continuum, but in reality we will seldom find these pure types but rather mixed types. This compromise is expressed in the concept of liberal democracy, or the *demokratische Rechtsstaat* as it is called in Germanic languages.

As far as the one principle could be institutionalized without the other, we would no longer speak of a liberal democracy. In the prototypical Prussian *Rechtsstaat* the rule of law was maintained to some extent but because neither the principle of popular sovereignty nor political equality were recognized as principles of government nobody in its right mind would call Friedrich the Great's Prussia a democracy. Likewise, Dahl argued that "Madisonian democracy" as originally developed by the American founding fathers was at best a one-sided conception of democracy. The founding fathers tried to find a compromise between two principles, majority rule or "the republican principle" and the protection of the liberties of minorities. But they were so obsessed by the second principle that they pushed it "as far as it is possible to go while still remaining within the rubric of democracy" (Dahl 1956, 31–2). But Dahl also opposes any definition of democracy in terms of the "absolute sovereignty of the majority:" "so far as I am aware, no one has ever advocated, and no one except its enemies has ever defined democracy to mean, that a majority would or should do anything it felt an impulse to do. Every advocate of democracy of whom I am aware, and every friendly definition of it, includes the idea of restraints on majorities" (Dahl 1956, 36).

But as much as these two principles together constitute the modern conception of democracy, there is no fixed balance between them. The relative weight of the two principles can be different in different states, it can be different within one state at different periods of time, and different people can give different weights to these two principles. Typologies of democratic systems often distinguish types of democracy according to their position on the continuum between these two principles, between individualism and collectivism. Fuchs and Klingemann for instance distinguish the libertarian, the liberal, and socialist types of democracy.[4] The libertarian and socialist types form the end poles of the continuum in the real world of democracies, with the liberal model in between. In the libertarian model the individual and not the state bears the principal responsibility for shaping and determining a person's life (Nozick 1974). Also, the relationship between individual citizens is characterized by competition and little solidarity. In the socialist type the state is primarily responsible

---

[4] In addition they distinguish a fourth type, the republican or communitarian model. However, the difference between this and the other three types is not defined by the relationship between state and citizen but by the mutual relationship between citizens.

and solidarity is high. In contrast to the libertarian model the liberal model (Rawls 1996) accepts a role of the state in order to further the equality of opportunity, but the role of the government is more restricted than in the socialist model. In the event of a conflict, individual freedom always has unrestricted priority over the equal distribution of the other primary goods (Fuchs and Klingemann 2002). Elsewhere I have argued that the extent to which people value the one over the other principle can be assessed by measuring their attitudes towards a number of pairs of concepts: liberty versus equality, small versus big government, pluralism versus the common good, and an instrumental versus a developmental view of participation (Thomassen 1995). For reasons of space and the availability of data we will limit ourselves in this chapter to an assessment of the extent to which people across the world support the basic principles of liberty and equality and how they view the role of the state.

4 LIBERTY

It would be too simple to say that the difference between the two conceptions of democracy reflects the classic tension between liberty and equality. Liberty plays a prominent role in both theories, but the interpretation of liberty associated with these two theories is different. In both theories, liberty refers to the relationship between the citizen and the state, but in a different way.

According to the collectivist theory, a free citizen is a citizen who takes part in the process of decision making, who actively participates in politics. Rousseau represents this idea of democracy in its most extreme form. In his view, freedom and participation in the legislative process are the same thing. Participation in law-making means that the citizen still has to obey the laws but, because these laws are of his own making, he remains his own master. According to this "positive" concept of liberty (Berlin 1969), there is a logical relationship between liberty and self-government, participation, and democracy. It is anything but inconsistent with equality.

The individualist view on liberty is totally different, and is usually referred to as the "negative" or protective concept of freedom (Berlin 1969; Rose 1995). Freedom is interpreted as freedom from constraints by other human beings, in particular by the state or the government. This view supports the desirability of civil liberties such as freedom of speech and press, of association, assembly, and religion, the rights of privacy and lifestyle, the right of due process, the protection and tolerance of minorities, and cultural and political diversity (McClosky and Brill 1983). The protection of these basic rights is a central component of the "democratic creed" (Dahl 1961). Therefore, the extent to which citizens support their protection is a significant test of people's democratic value orientations.

A long range of studies yields a very clear picture on people's endorsement of these basic principles of democracy. As long as people are asked in the abstract whether they endorse these principles an overwhelming majority of people responds according to the democratic textbook. But as a range of studies on political tolerance show, for a disquieting number of people this endorsement is not more than lip service (Klosko 2000). Political tolerance implies the willingness to respect the civil rights of individuals who espouse ideas or points of view to which one is opposed. But as early as the 1950s studies in the United States showed that a large number of people failed this test (Prothro and Grigg 1960; Stouffer 1955). Only a minority of the people was willing to extend civil liberties like the freedom of speech to communists. Although a replication of the same study in the 1970s suggested that Americans had become more tolerable (Nunn, Crockett, and Williams 1978), these findings were later criticized as being biased by political developments. Many questions referred to people's tolerance of communists, socialists, and atheists. As the general hostility towards these groups had decreased in the decades since the McCarthy area it was no wonder that tolerance towards these groups had increased.

In order to overcome this bias Sullivan et al. developed a "content-controlled" measure of political tolerance (Klosko 2000; Sullivan, Piereson, and Markus 1982). Respondents were no longer asked to express their feelings towards a number of groups selected by the researchers. Instead they were first asked to identify groups to which they were opposed and then were asked about extending civil liberties to them. Quite predictably, respondents with liberal views identified right-wing groups, while right-wing respondents did the reverse. When this research strategy was applied an increase of the level of tolerance could no longer be observed. Moreover, the research of Sullivan and his associates confirmed once more that the tolerance towards less liked groups was remarkably low. Only 19 percent for instance would allow members of less liked groups to teach in public schools. Similarly, only 16 percent believed that members of their least liked group should not be banned from being president of the United States. Accordingly, Sullivan and his colleagues argued: "though tolerance of communists and atheists has increased over the years, tolerance as a more universal attitude may not have changed much at all" (Klosko 2000, 51–2).

There are several interpretations of why the level of tolerance is so much lower when applied to specific situations and specific groups than when people are asked for their support for general principles. The first one attributes them to cognitive skills. In order to apply abstract principles to specific cases people must see the logical relationship between the abstract principles and the specific situation at hand. This is an important reason that education increases tolerance. It fosters "greater acquaintance with the logical implications of the broad democratic principles" (Klosko 2000: 57; see also Gibson 1992).

A second interpretation is what Klosko (2000, 57) refers to as the "tacit qualification" view. Although most people have no hesitation to subscribe to general principles of democracy, in particular civil liberties, most people will tend to qualify this general position when they face uncomfortable situations. Should Neo-Nazis be allowed to organize anti-Semitic demonstrations in Germany? Should Orangists be allowed to march provocatively through Catholic neighbourhoods in Belfast? Different people will answer these questions differently but it would be hard to find people who will make no exceptions to the application of civil rights when really pushed (Gibson 1998; Gibson 2002; Hurwitz and Mondak 2002; Rohrschneider 1999; Sniderman et al. 2000).

These two interpretations are not independent from each other. Better educated people tend to respond more tolerantly to specific cases and must be harder pushed to qualify their general principles. But democratic values are not just a matter of education. The political institutions and the political culture of a country are equally important. Democracy breeds democratic attitudes. This is clearly shown by findings from comparative research. In the most recent waves of the World Values Study political tolerance was measured according to the method developed by Sullivan et al. Respondents were first asked which of a number of groups they disliked most. Next they were asked whether they were willing to extend to a disliked group the right to (1) hold public office and (2) hold demonstrations. Using data from the 1995–7 study Peffley and Rohrschneider show that citizens in mature democracies are both more politically tolerant and more consistent in their application of general democratic norms to disliked minorities than people in newly established democracies (see also Gibson 2002).

However, this finding is overshadowed by the fact that even in mature democracies political tolerance is a scarce commodity; the highest percentage allowing members of a disliked group to hold office is found in the USA (14%). The vast majority of respondents thus appear to deny disliked groups the right to hold public office. Publics are a bit more willing to permit a disliked group to demonstrate, but again this is only a minority of 28 percent (in Australia) at the most. Therefore, with respect to both rights intolerance appears to be the norm, tolerance the exception (Peffley and Rohrschneider 2003).

5 EQUALITY

The principle of equality can be interpreted either as *political* or *social equality*. There is no inherent tension between political equality and liberty. Quite the contrary: the individualist interpretation of democracy demands that, once it is recognized that the people should make political decisions, then all the constituent individuals should have an equal say (Holden 1988). There is a possible tension between liberty and social equality however. The individualist theory of democracy emphasizes that any policy to enforce social equality is a threat to liberty. But the extent to which this is the case depends on the form of equality referred to. One form refers to *equality of opportunity*. In its most basic form, this means no more than that individuals should have equal chances. This can hardly be seen as a threat to liberty. However, the matter becomes more complicated when it is maintained that opportunities for certain groups are, in fact, not equal because they do not have an equal start. From this perspective, it can be argued that government policy should improve the opportunities of disadvantaged groups, for instance by affirmative government action to compensate women, blacks, and other minorities. Such policies can be enforced only by limiting the freedom of people to a certain extent.

The welfare state can be seen as the embodiment of this broader concept of democracy, in which not only civil rights and political equality, but also social rights and social equality are considered fundamental rights. In this context the ideal of social equality tends to imply not only the equality of opportunity but also *equality of condition*. If social equality is literally supposed to mean that all people have available the same resources, this is obviously inconsistent with the principle of liberty. It could only be attained and maintained by suppression. Thus, no society which adheres to both liberty and equality can define equality as equality of condition (Pennock 1979, 36), at least not in an absolute sense. At the same time, for reasons of legitimacy, no political system can afford to be insensitive to the fact that an unlimited liberty will lead to an inequality of condition which will not be acceptable to its citizens (Dahl 1982). The most obvious case is the responsibility of the government to reduce the income gap between rich and poor. Therefore, all countries will need to find a compromise between the two extremes of unlimited liberty at the risk of extreme differences in the social condition of its people, and complete social equality which can—and even then in theory only—be achieved by an oppressive political system. But even in a mild form the reduction of social inequality will not come into being spontaneously. It will have to be enforced by government intervention.

Equality of condition as compared to equality of opportunity finds little support across the world. The choice between these two interpretations of equality was measured in successive waves of the European and World Values Studies in a somewhat peculiar way. Respondents were asked to respond to the following question:

Imagine two secretaries, of the same age, doing practically the same job. One finds out that the other earns considerably more than she does. The better paid secretary, however, is quicker, more efficient and more reliable at her job. In your opinion, is it fair or not fair that one secretary is paid more than the other.

A great majority of people across the world agrees that this is fair indeed. This might be interpreted as support for the equality of opportunity. People who disagree with this statement apparently think that the two secretaries are entitled to the same salary despite the difference in quality between them. This betrays support for the equality of condition. Although a substantial majority of the people in all countries represented in either of these studies agrees that one secretary should be paid better, this majority varies from 54 percent in Norway to over 96 percent in Egypt and the Czech Republic. A rough comparison of different parts of the world (see Table 22.1) reveals that the highest support for the idea of equality of condition is

Table 22.1 Attitudes on liberty, equality, and the role of the state

Region	Agreement "fair that a faster secretary is paid more."[a]	Government responsible that everyone is provided for (average).[a] [b]	Liberty above equality [c]
Africa	77.6 % (8)	6.7	
Asia	84.3 % (14)	6.1	
Europe ("old")	71.9 % (20)	4.7	53.0 %
Former communist countries [d]	87.7 % (23)	6.2	53.6 %
Latin America	74.9 % (10)	5.7	
North America	87.5 % (2)	4.6	
Australia and New Zealand	86.6% (2)	5.1	

[a] *Source*: World Values Study 1999–2001.
[b] Average score on ten-point scale. The lower the score, the higher the support for government responsibility.
[c] *Source*: European Values Study.
[d] Former communist countries in central and eastern Europe and the former Soviet Union.

found in the "old" Europe with its advanced welfare states.[5] In the advanced industrial democracies in the new worlds of North America and Oceania it is much less. Perhaps more surprising is the strong support for competitiveness in former communist countries. As people in these countries have been socialized into the doctrine of an egalitarian society one might have expected to find the remnants of this socialization process in people's reaction to this dilemma (Fuchs 1999; Rohrschneider 1999).

Different views on social equality imply different views on the role of the state. The advancement of social equality almost by definition implies a strong role of the state. A strong role of the state fits in the collectivist theory of democracy. The state is the embodiment of popular sovereignty. Therefore, it is the role of the state to direct societal development and to take care of the welfare of the people. Government intervention and regulation are not inimical to democracy but accepted democratic instruments to steer society according to the view of the elected government. According to the individualist view, government intervention should be limited to a minimum. The identification of the power of the state with the will of the people, and hence the argument that the power of the state needs no constraints, is considered as the very definition of a totalitarian state, because it makes no distinction between the will of the people as a whole and the right of individual citizens to be protected against that will. Even though this extreme version of the collectivist

[5] In my contribution to *Citizens and the State* I predicted and actually found that the support for the equality of condition would have decreased in western Europe during the more recent decades. This finding was based on data until 1990. In most countries this trend has not continued between 1990 and 2000.

view has few adherents in western democracies, from the individualist perspective increasing government intervention and regulation are seen as a fundamental threat to the essential value of democracy—individual freedom (Hayek 1994).

The development of the welfare state, in particular in Europe, seems to leave no doubt about which view has won the argument. It is widely recognized—even in the constitution of some countries—that the government is responsible for public welfare; for example, for minimum wages, public health, public transport, education, full employment, public housing, incomes and prices, in addition to individual rights to liberty. However, in most countries increasing state intervention and regulation has become a political issue. For several reasons, the idea that the government should direct and regulate societal developments has become less popular and the governments of most advanced industrial democracies have tried to reduce the role of government. The extent to which these attempts have been successful differs from country to country and is related to the degree to which citizens and their representatives are willing to accept these changes.

To what extent do people across the world support the view that the state is responsible for public welfare? In the World Values Study of 1995–6 and 1999–2002 respondents were asked to position themselves on a ten-point scale with the following end poles: "The government should take more responsibility to ensure that everyone is provided for" and "People should take more responsibility to provide for themselves." In the second column of Table 22.1 the average scores on this scale for different parts of the world are presented. There are obvious differences between them. The support for a caring state is nowhere as high as in North America, i.e. Canada and the USA. If we would single out the US, the support would be even higher (4.29). Support for a strong role of the state is also relatively high in western Europe and in Australia and New Zealand. Therefore, in general we find the highest support for a strong responsibility of the state in advanced industrial democracies (see also Verba et al. 1987).

6 Two Conceptions of Democracy?

Above we suggested that the relative weight of the conceptions of democracy can be different in different states, that it can be different within one state at different periods of time, and that different people can give different weights to these two conceptions.

In the two previous sections we presented evidence on the extent to which people across the world support the values of liberty and equality and how much responsibility they want to allocate to the state. Liberty and equality represent two distinct and coherent political-philosophical conceptions of democracy. In addition to a different emphasis on liberty and equality these different conceptions are reflected in a different view on the role of the state, to a different appreciation of pluralism vs. the general interest and a different interpretation of the meaning of political participation in a democracy. We will only be able to find systematic differences in the weight different people assign to the two conceptions of democracy if these distinct conceptions of democracy are reflected in people's value orientations. This implies that these value orientations should form a clear pattern or belief system, reflecting these. In other words, if somebody is inclined to value liberty above equality, (s)he should also be inclined to value pluralism positively and to support an instrumental view on political participation.

Elsewhere (Thomassen 1995) I have shown that people's attitudes on these different aspects of democracy do indeed form a coherent pattern, consistent with the two conceptions of democracy. I also showed that in western Europe people's attitudes gradually shifted towards the individualist pole of the continuum between an individualist and a collective view on democracy. Fuchs and Klingemann (2002) show that people in different parts of the world tend to prefer consistently different types of democracy on the continuum libertarian-liberal-socialist. The libertarian type of democracy is most strongly supported in the United States. In Europe people tend to assign more responsibility to the state. In the former communist countries of central and eastern Europe people still tend to support a socialist type of democracy. The value orientations in western Europe can be characterized as supportive of the liberal model, but tending towards the socialist model. Australia and New Zealand take a position between the US and western Europe.

Here we will take a different approach. Since we have presented people's attitudes on liberty, equality, and the role of the state the question is whether we can explain the differences in support for these basic principles between the people of various countries.

Referring to differences in political culture between countries is not very helpful since attitudes towards democracy are part of that culture. A promising theoretical approach is *institutional learning* (Rohrschneider 1999). It predicts that when citizens are exposed to the values and norms underlying a nation's institutional configuration they will be influenced by it. In general, a nation's institutional configuration will form a coherent pattern and mainly be based either on the individualist (the consensus model of democracy) or on the collectivist conception of democracy (the majoritarian model of democracy) (Lijphart 1999). However, it is difficult to assess the pure effects of differences in institutional configurations by comparative research because it is hard to meet the *ceteris paribus* clause: other things are rarely equal.

But the recent transition of a number of countries from communism to liberal democracy offers new research opportunities. In particular comparing the two parts of Germany after reunification is as close as one can get to a controlled experiment if one wants to study the effect of being socialized under different institutions and different ideologies. Using this unique opportunity Rohrschneider tested two alternative hypotheses on how people learn democratic values. In addition to the institutional learning hypothesis he also tested the diffusion hypothesis according to which the development of democratic attitudes in socialist-authoritarian systems is to be attributed to the exposure to western-style values, even during the old regime.

Just as the institutional learning hypothesis predicts, people in East Germany in the middle of the 1990s were more inclined to support socialist values than people in West Germany. In contrast to their fellow citizens from West Germany a majority of them emphasized social equality over political liberty. They also valued direct democracy more but were less convinced that pluralism contributes positively to democracy.[6] These findings not only support the institutional learning hypothesis but also provide evidence for the hypothesis that attitudes on liberty vs equality, on political participation, and pluralism vs. the general interest form a consistent pattern, even among the mass public.

Still, as nice as the German case is from a methodological point of view it is only one country and it is not immediately clear whether these findings can be generalized. The data in Table 22.1 offer the opportunity for a rough test of the institutional learning hypothesis for a large number of countries. According to this hypothesis we should expect that people from countries that until recently were under communist rule would value the equality of outcome and a strong role for the state more than people in the established liberal democracies of western Europe, America, and Oceania. Also, we would expect them to value equality over liberty. However, this is not the case at all. As far as there is a difference it is in the opposite direction. People in the former communist countries value the equality of outcome less than people in western Europe. Their support for a strong role of the state on average is lower than in established democracies, whereas the average percentage valuing liberty above equality is exactly the same as in western Europe. Why these findings are so different from Rohrschneider's is not immediately clear. Therefore, as much as it is a cliché, further and more detailed research is needed to assess and explain differences between countries with regard to the support of various democratic values.

7 IN CONCLUSION

Do people across the world support democratic values? The answer to this question depends on how we define democracy. There is hardly any doubt about people's support for democracy as a form of government. Democracy is seen as a superior form of government by a firm majority of the people in countries across the world. This finding is reassuring both for the world of established and developing democracies.

There has been an ongoing debate on the alleged crisis of democracy in established democracies. Because of a decline of political involvement, at least in conventional

---

[6] This latter attitude was found among political elites but was not measured in the survey among the mass public.

politics, of trust in politicians and even in political institutions we seem to be witnessing a gradual decline of the legitimacy of democracy. But as we argued throughout this chapter the legitimacy of a political regime refers to the consistency of its political institutions with the value orientations of its citizens. And in this respect Fukuyama seems to be right: there is no serious ideological rival to democracy in the world of established democracies. People are dedicated to democracy as a system of government. Therefore, as far as there is a crisis of democracy it is not because people want something else than democracy. People who are dissatisfied with the functioning of democracy want more rather than less democracy (Dalton 2004; Klingemann and Fuchs 1995; Norris 1999).

In developing democracies the situation is not very different. In contrast to the 1930s there is no indication that people will be easily seduced by a totalitarian ideology, although it is still to be seen how robust their support for democracy will be after a longer period of poor performance of the new democratic regimes.

However, this sunny picture has a shadow side. Democracy is more than a system of government. It also implies that government, even if it is legitimized by a majority of the people, will respect the civil rights of each and every individual citizen. There is ample empirical evidence to show that the respect for these rights is not deeply embedded in most people's mind. Therefore, there might be not much of a buffer against a political movement or government denying certain civil rights to particular groups of people. In that sense democracy is not necessarily a perfect guardian of democracy.

References

Afrobarometer. 2002. What do Africans Think about Democracy and Development? In *Afrobarometer Briefing Paper.*

Albritton, R. B., and Bureekul, T. 2004. Developing democracy under a new constitution in Thailand. In *Asian Barometer Working Paper Series*, ed. A. B. P. Office. Taipei: National Taiwan University and Academia Sinica.

Berlin, I. 1969. *Four Essays on Liberty.* Oxford: Oxford University Press.

Bratton, M., Mattes, R., and Gyimah-Boadi, E. 2004. *Public Opinion, Democracy, and Market Reform in Africa.* Cambridge: Cambridge University Press.

Dahl, R. A. 1956. *A Preface to Democratic Theory.* Chicago: University of Chicago Press.

—— 1961. *Who Governs?* New Haven: Yale University Press.

—— 1982. *Dilemmas of Pluralist Democracy: Autonomy vs. Control.* New Haven: Yale University Press.

Dalton, R. J. 2004. *Democratic Challenges, Democratic Choices: The Erosion of Political Support in Advanced Industrial Democracies.* Oxford: Oxford University Press.

—— and Shin, D. C. eds. 2006. *Citizens, Democracy and Markets around the Pacific Rim: Congruence Theory and Political Culture.* Oxford: Oxford University Press.

Easton, D. 1965. *A Systems Analysis of Political Life.* New York: John Wiley.

Fuchs, D. 1999. The democratic culture of unified Germany. Pp. 123–45 in *Critical Citizens: Global Support for Democratic Governance*, ed. P. Norris. Oxford: Oxford University Press.

—— and KLINGEMANN, H.-D. 2002. Eastward enlargement of the European Union and the identiy of Europe. *West European Politics*, 25 (2): 19–53.

FUKUYAMA, F. 1989. The end of history. *The National Interest*, 16: 3–18.

—— 1992. *The End of History and the Last Man*. New York: Avon Books.

GIBSON, J. L. 1992. Alternative measures of political intolerance: must tolerance be "least-liked"? *American Journal of Political Science*, 36: 560–77.

—— 1998. Putting up with fellow Russians: an analysis of political intolerance in the fledging Russian democracy. *Political Research Quarterly*, 51 (1): 37–68.

—— 2002. Becoming tolerant? Short-term changes in Russian political culture. *British Journal of Political Science*, 32: 309–34.

HAYEK, F. 1994. *The Road to Serfdom*. Chicago: University of Chicago Press.

HOLDEN, B. 1988. *Understanding Liberal Democracy*. Deddington: Philip Allan.

HUNTINGTON, S. P. 1996. *The Clash of Civilizations and the Remaking of the World Order*. New York: Simon & Schuster.

HURWITZ, J., and MONDAK, J. 2002. Democratic principles, discrimination and political intolerance. *British Journal of Political Science*, 32 (1): 93–118.

IKEDA, K., YAMADA, Y., and KOHNO, M. 2004. Japanese attitudes and values toward democracy. In *Asian Barometer Working Paper Series*, ed. A. B. P. Office. Taipei: National Taiwan University and Academia Sinica.

INGLEHART, R., and NORRIS, P. 2003. The true clash of civilizations. *Foreign Policy* (March/April): 67–74.

—— and WELZEL, C. 2005. *Modernization, Cultural Change, and Democracy: The Human Development Sequence*. Cambridge: Cambridge University Press.

KLINGEMANN, H.-D. 1999. Mapping political support in the 1990s: a global analysis. Pp. 31–56 in *Critical Citizens: Global Support for Democratic Governance*, ed. P. Norris. Oxford: Oxford University Press.

—— and FUCHS, D. eds. 1995. *Citizens and the State*. Oxford: Oxford University Press.

KLOSKO, G. 2000. *Democratic Procedures and Liberal Consensus*. Oxford: Oxford University Press.

LIJPHART, A. 1999. *Patterns of Democracy: Government Forms and Performance in Thirty-Six Countries*. New Haven: Yale University Press.

LIPSET, S. M. 1966. *Political Man*. London: Mercury Books.

McCLOSKY, H., and BRILL, A. 1983. *Dimensions of Tolerance: What Americans Believe about Civil Liberties*. New York: Russell Sage Foundation.

NORRIS, P. ed. 1999. *Critical Citizens: Global Support for Democratic Governance*. Oxford: Oxford University Press.

NOZICK, R. 1974. *Anarchy, State, and Utopia*. New York: Basic Books.

NUNN, C. Z., CROCKETT, H. J., and WILLIAMS, J. A. 1978. *Tolerance for Nonconformity*. San Francisco: Jossey-Bass Publishers.

OWENS, M. T. 2003. The end of the "end of history". **www.ashbrook.org/publicat/oped/owens/03/9-11.html**

PEFFLEY, M., and ROHRSCHNEIDER, R. 2003. Democratization and political tolerance in seventeen countries: a multi-level model of democratic learning. *Political Research Quarterly*, 56 (3): 243–57.

PENNOCK, J. R. 1979. *Democratic Political Theory*. Princeton: Princeton University Press.

PROTHRO, J., and GRIGG, C. 1960. Fundamental principles of democracy: bases of agreement and disagreement. *Journal of Politics*, 22: 276–94.

RAWLS, J. 1996. *Political Liberalism*. New York: Columbia University Press.

ROHRSCHNEIDER, R. 1999. *Learning Democracy: Democratic and Economic Values in Unified Germany*. Oxford: Oxford University Press.

ROSE, R. 1995. Freedom as a Fundamental Value. *International Social Science Journal* 47: 457–71.

—— 2002. Does Islam make people anti-democratic? A central Asian perspective. *Journal of Democracy*, 13 (4).

—— MISHLER, W., and HAERPFER, C. 1998. *Democracy and Its Alternatives: Understanding Postcommunist Societies*. Baltimore: Johns Hopkins Press.

SABINE, G. H. 1952. The Two Democratic Traditions. *The Philosophical Review* 61 (4): 451–474.

SHIN, D. C. 2005. Is democracy the only game in town? *Journal of Democracy*, 16: 89–101.

SIMON, J. 1976. Popular conceptions of democracy in post-communist Europe. In *Studies in Public Policy*, ed. U. o. G. Centre for the Study of Public Policy. Glasgow.

SNIDERMAN, P. M., PERI, P., DE FIGUERIDO, R., and PIAZZA, T. 2000. *The Outsider: Prejudice and Politics in Italy*. Princeton: Princeton University Press.

STOUFFER, S. A. 1955. *Communism, Conformity, and Civil Liberties*. Garden City, NY: Doubleday.

SULLIVAN, J. J, PIERESON, J., and MARKUS, G. E. 1982. *Political Tolerance and American Democracy*. Chicago: University of Chicago Press.

TESSLER, M. 2002. Islam and democracy in the Middle East: the impact of religious orientations on attitudes toward democracy in four Arab countries. *Comparative Politics* 34 (3).

THOMASSEN, J. J. A. 1995. Support for democratic values. Pp. 383–416 in *Citizens and the State*, ed. H.-D. Klingemann and D. Fuchs. Oxford: Oxford University Press.

VERBA, S., KELMAN, S., ORREN, G., MIYAKE, I., WATANUKI, J., KABASHIMA, I., and FERREE, D. Jr. 1987. *Elites and the Idea of Equality: A Comparison of Japan, Sweden and the United States*. Cambridge, Mass.: Harvard University Press.

NEW DEBATES IN POLITICAL BEHAVIOR

PART V

NEW DEBATES
IN POLITICAL
BEHAVIOR

CHAPTER 23

....

AN INSTITUTIONAL THEORY OF POLITICAL CHOICE

....

PAUL M. SNIDERMAN
MATTHEW S. LEVENDUSKY

WHY do voters choose one candidate over another? Why do citizens choose one policy alternative over another? Two types of answers predominate—rational choice and psychological. The two have been treated as rivals. This chapter focuses on the emergence of a perspective that takes them to be allies—an institutional theory of political choice (see, for relevant extant work, Adams, Merrill, and Grofman 2005; Bendor, Diermeier, and Ting 2003; Bendor, Kumar, and Siegel 2005; Sniderman 2000; Jackman and Sniderman 2002; Sniderman and Bullock 2004). The purpose of the chapter is to serve as a billboard advertisement for innovative research developing this theory. This research comes in different flavors, some more formal, some more psychological.[1] But

* We have many to thank but none more than Stephen Haber, James H. Kuklinski, and Arthur Lupia. It is a pleasure to acknowledge our debt to them.

[1] Terminology is treacherous. The study of political behavior is standardly styled as a behavioral approach. Focusing on what is doing the work of explanation, rather than what is being explained, psychological is more apt. The behavioral approach we lay out here is a combination of formal and psychological perspectives.

there is a shared explanatory taste. Each points to the role of political institutions in structuring political choices.

The key intuition is this. In politics, citizens do not get their choice of choices. They must select from an organized menu of choices. It follows that a theory of political choice requires two types of explanatory mechanisms—an internal one to account for choice between alternatives plus an external one to account for the alternatives on offer. Political behavior research has traditionally concentrated on the former (e.g. see Mutz chapter and chapters on electoral choice in this volume); formal theoretic accounts, on the second. This chapter lays out a theoretical framework for integrating the internal and external explanatory mechanisms.

The broad strategy of turning attention to the role of external factors in structuring choice is being pursued on a number of fronts—for example, the work of Kuklinski and his colleagues on information environments (Kuklinski et al. 2001; Jerit, Barabas, and Bolsen 2006); Druckman on framing (2004, 2001a, 2000b; Druckman and Nelson 2003); and Saris (2004) on the structure of the task. All bring out conditions of choice that shape the actual choices made. We shall nonetheless formulate the problem differently. What is needed, we believe, is a formulation that does double duty. For one, it accounts for the way that choices citizens make are organized—why, for example, are political choices framed as they are and not some other way? For another, it accounts for the fit between the external organization of choice sets and internal processes of choice—why exactly do patterns of consistency imposed by external factors mesh with patterns of consistency generated by internal ones? We accordingly lay out an institutional theory of political choice.

Institutions are a notoriously big tent construct. We are concerned with only one small corner of political institutions—the logic of electoral competition mediated by political parties. An institutional theory of political choice still has its training wheels on. But we believe it brings—and not merely promises—advances on two fronts. First, it picks out a common mechanism, political parties, regulating the organization of alternatives on offer and conditioning choices between them. Second, it points to an explanation of (Herbert) Simon's puzzle: how can citizens make approximately coherent political choices given the limits on their informational fund and computational capacities?

1 BEHAVIORAL ECONOMICS AS A MODEL

A leg-in-both-camps approach can be awkward. It can even appear self-contradictory. Rational choice is an effort to explain choices assuming full rationality under the circumstances. A behavioral approach is an effort to account for choices where a full rationality approach falls short (Camerer, Loewenstein, and Rabin 2004). The appearance of awkwardness is real. The appearance of self-contradiction is not.

Behavioral economics offers a model of how to tie rational and psychological perspectives together.

Three premises underpin behavioral economics. The first is that actors aim to maximize their welfare. The second assumption is that they have limited computational capacities and attention. The third is that their expectations about the actions of others and desires are fixed (Kreps 2004). These three premises—utility maximization, bounded rationality, and the endogeneity of beliefs and tastes—generate the signature research program of behavioral economics: the discovery and analysis of systematic departures from axiomatic choice (Camerer 2003). To the degree that observed choice diverges from strictly rational choice, and a principled explanation of the difference can be developed, a behavioral approach is value-added.

So, too, with political choice, though with a difference in starting point. In economics, the presumption is that people must (on the whole) be making rational choices: otherwise, they would have gone under. In the study of political behavior, the presumption is just the other way around. It is easier to see how they get things wrong than how they can get them right. Under ordinary circumstances, after all, ordinary citizens pay minimal attention to, and are minimally knowledgeable about, politics (e.g. Delli Carpini and Keeter 1996). It is far from obvious how they nonetheless can make coherent choices[2]—which, of course, begs the question of whether they indeed can make any reasonable choices at all (Bartels 2003).

In the judgment of many, a solution to the problem of coherent choice compatible with any heavy breathing representation of democratic citizenship is a chimera. From our vantage point, the problem of coherent choice has seemed intractable because of the one-legged stance of traditional studies in political behavior. They have proceeded on the assumption that citizens organize their preferences relying on their own resources. A two-legged stance is necessary. Choices among distinct alternatives depend not only on the attributes of the chooser, but also on the properties of choice sets (McFadden 1974). Citizens are capable of making coherent choices to the degree that political institutions, and particularly political parties, do the heavy lifting of organizing coherent choice sets.

2 PROPERTIES OF POLITICAL CHOICE SETS

Students of Comparative Politics not infrequently acknowledge they are taking their lead from advances in American politics. It gives us pleasure to reciprocate. Students of comparative politics have brought out the foundational role of electoral systems, and in

---

[2] By a coherent choice we mean selection of the available policy alternative most consonant with a citizen's general view of the matter. Note that this is a narrower version of Hurwitz and Peffley's (1987) concept of vertical linkage.

so doing they have called attention to the institutional structuring of political alterna-tives (e.g. Cox 1997). Our focus, though, is proximal, not distal—not the underlying structure of political systems, but political choice sets produced by party systems.[3]

The policy location of the parties (candidates) in spatial voting models has been the most thoroughly examined property of choice sets in politics (Downs 1957). Over the last four decades modelers have productively explored the logical implications of varying Downs's postulates, bringing into play among other factors, the entry of third parties (Palfrey 1984), the participation decisions of potential party activists (Aldrich 1983), uncertainty of voters' about the policy locations of candidates and of candidates about the policy locations of voters (e.g. Wittman 1983; Palfrey 1984; Calvert 1985; Roemer 2001; for an excellent overview see Grofman 2004). It is noteworthy, however, that a basic identification problem has just been identified. Fiorina (2005) shows how candidates moving in a policy space over time can make it appear as if voters are changing over time. Assume that candidates become polarized. Moderate voters then can choose only between two extreme candidates. In turn, they appear to be extreme themselves—even though they have remained moderate. It is necessary, it follows, to take account of the spatial locations of candidates over time to identify the factors that lead voters to favor one candidate over the other at each point in time (see also van Houweling and Sniderman 2004).

We shall examine spatial reasoning in the context of political institutions, but we begin by considering non-spatial properties of choice sets in politics, among them, the number, polarity, and labeling of alternatives.

3 NUMBER OF ALTERNATIVES

A restriction on the number of alternatives on offer is a strategic property of political choice sets. In a break-the-mold study, Glaser (2002) assessed the impact of separable versus bundled choices. The issue was support for or opposition to a new school bond. In one experimental condition, respondents were presented with the total package of improvements to vote up or down; in the other condition, the three major components of the package—improvements in heating system, in computers, and in the gymna-sium—were put to voters as three independent choices. When the alternatives were bundled together as one package, the bond issue failed to get the necessary 60 percent support. When the alternatives were independently presented, each component of the bond issue got the necessary 60 percent. Glaser's study points to the broad variety of ways in which the structure of choices can affect a political outcome.

---

[3] We came across Kriesi's (2005) study of the politics of referenda in Switzerland too late in the process of preparing this chapter to take full advantage of it. It is the most developed account to date of what it means analytically to take the view that party elites structure choice sets in politics, and thereby condition both the processes by which choices are made and the choices that in fact are made.

As a general proposition, the coherence of choice should vary inversely with the number of alternatives: as the number increases, the probability of choosing the policy alternative closest to one's general view of the matter decreases. We have no evidentiary cards to pull out of the deck to document directly the cost of larger numbers of alternatives; but a fair amount of side information suggests this is a reasonable hypothesis.

A research literature on choice overload has emerged.[4] Decreasing the variety of product types at an online grocery store increases sales (Boatwright and Nunes 2001). Presenting people with either a large number of alternatives or a small one affects the likelihood that they will take satisfaction in the choice they have made (Iyengar and Lepper 2000; see also Iyengar, Huberman, and Jiang 2004). Increasing the number of alternatives decreases the likelihood that a choice will be made (Dhar 1997). As for explicitly political choices, Niemi and Westholm (1984) have shown that temporal stability of policy positions is higher in multi-party Sweden than in two-party America; while Gordon and Segura (1997) make the intriguing suggestion that levels of political sophistication are lower in multi-party systems due to their institutional configuration.

The classic literature on belief system consistency also bears on the connection between number of alternatives and consistency of choice, although again indirectly. Constraint is the ground floor measure of coherence in mass belief systems. Some years ago, Nie, Verba, and Petrocik (1976) announced that constraint had shot up in the mid-1960s from the minimal levels of the 1950s reported by Converse (1964). Their explanation: the politics of the sixties was more engaging than that of the fifties. In an elegant experiment, Sullivan, Piereson, and Marcus (1978) demonstrated that the change in levels of constraint was instead a function of the introduction of a different question format—one in which respondents are asked to choose between two policies rather than whether they support or oppose one policy (see also Bishop, Tuchfarber, and Oldendick 1978).

This methodological dust-up throws some light on the properties of choice sets in politics—in particular, on the optimal number of alternatives to maximize the translation of general political orientations into consistent policy preferences. It may be thought the optimal number is one. Then voters cannot be distracted by a second. But the studies of Sullivan et al. and Bishop et al. show that voters can connect their positions on different issues more consistently when they are con-fronted with a choice between two competing alternatives rather than simply voting a policy up or down. It is as though the contrast between alternatives makes clearer what is at stake. A deeper point about validity has not been noticed in the shadows. To get a fix on the abilities of citizens to think coherently about political questions, it is necessary to put questions in the way they actually are presented to them in politics. This may sound a truism. It is anything but. The post-1964 format more nearly approximates the shape of choices in a competitive party system than the pre-1964 one; and it is in response to the post-1964 format that citizens show more

---

[4] We are indebted to Scott Nicholson for directing us to this research literature.

constraint. Curiously, the conclusion that has been drawn is that constraint has remained low. It is a curious conclusion because the post-1964 format has more external validity than the pre-1964 format; which suggests that the more likely interpretation is that constraint was as high before 1964 as after, not that constraint was as low after the mid-sixties as before.

Ideological coherence is the most demanding standard of consistency for mass belief systems. A path-breaking set of studies in the Political Action Project (see Barnes et al. 1979) explored levels of ideological consistency in mass belief systems across several nations. Fuchs and Klingemann (1989) made a meticulous comparison of West Germany, the Netherlands, and the United States. West Germans and the Dutch are more readily able to define what the terms left and right mean in the political parlance of their respective countries than are Americans in theirs. "On the basis of these data," they argue, "we have to conclude that the left–right schema is not currently institutionalized in the United States to the same extent and in the same way as it is in the two European countries" (Fuchs and Klingemann 1989, 209).

This observation may be taken as a property of public opinion that conditions the political strategies of party elites. It is our suggestion, however, to reason the other way around—to endogenize public opinion. Whether or not citizens think in ideological terms depends on whether elites stimulate citizens to think in those terms or not. In the 1970s and 1980s, when the Political Action Project studies were conducted, party politics was less ideologically coherent in the United States than in western Europe. With less ideologically distinct parties, citizens in the US needed to make a larger inferential leap to see politics as a left–right game. Now, American elites are more ideologically distinct (Poole and Rosenthal 1997). In response, the belief systems of Americans should have become more ideologically congruent, as indeed they have (Layman and Carsey 2002; Levendusky 2006). In equilibrium, levels of ideological understanding are conditional on levels of ideological polarization among partisan elites, not the other way around.

4 POLARIZATION OF ALTERNATIVES

The first generation of framing studies of political choice (e.g. Zaller 1992) demonstrated that large numbers of ordinary citizens could be moved from one side of an issue to the opposite, depending on whether the policy was framed in a way to elicit support *or* to evoke opposition. Understandably, this "flip-flop" result has been interpreted as evidence of inconsistency of political choice; indeed, of the absence of genuine attitudes even on major issues of public policy. Sniderman and Theriault (2004) hypothesized, however, that under the pressure of electoral competitions, choice sets in politics become bipolar: if citizens oppose one course of action, they act as though it follows that they should support the other, and the other way about.

Their experiment reproduced the design of previous framing experiments where only one frame was presented to respondents, but it added an alternative version where both frames are presented. Presented with one frame at a time, their results replicate the earlier studies: respondents swing first to one side of an issue, then to the other. But when they are presented with "competing" frames, rather than being confused by contradictory perspectives, their thinking is clarified; and they become more, not less, likely to choose the policy alternative closest to their general view of the matter. It is worth noting that this stabilizing effect is as least as pronounced for the less educated as for the more.

Druckman's ensuing research program on framing effects has been hat-doffing. He has investigated the role of credible sources (Druckman 2001a); deliberation (Druckman and Nelson 2003); elite competition (Druckman 2004); and framing—strictly construed as preference reversals over logically equivalent alternatives (Druckman 2004). One of many pertinent findings concerns the effect of political argument. The consequence of simultaneous exposure to competing frames, he demonstrates, is to extinguish framing effects, or very nearly so.

The results of Druckman and of Sniderman and Theriault point to the potential value of rethinking the ingrained image of public opinion as superficial and incoherent. The first generation of framing experiments put respondents in an artificial situation. They were allowed to hear only one side of the argument. But in real politics, no party can control public debate. They compete both about what position should be adopted and how an issue should be framed—it is hard, after all, to do one without the other. Studying reactions in an artificial situation, in which only one way to think about an issue is presented, public opinion analysts have concluded that confused citizens can easily be swayed to one side or the other of issues. Studying reactions in a situation more akin to politics suggests a different conclusion. The clash of competing considerations, so far from confusing citizens, helps clarify the choices before them.

The polarization of alternatives, conditional on the party system in place, also throws light on the meaning of consistency in political choice. It is a natural tendency, and often an appropriate one, to take maximizing self-interest as a condition of consistency. On this view, inconsistency consists in selection of the alternative on offer at odds with economic self-interest. It seems so obvious that when some take a choice at odds with self-interest, this is in and of itself a proof of ignorance. So Bartels (2005) has concluded that the strong plurality support for Bush's tax cut is entirely attributable to simple ignorance. This interpretation is understandable, particularly in a discipline with a tradition of concern about false consciousness. Lupia et al. (2005), however, observe that this judgment of mass ignorance presupposes that there is just one perspective a reasonable person can take on the tax cut—an economic one. A reasonable presupposition often. But frequently in politics, and perhaps distinctively in politics, there is a clash of points of view—different conceptions of what is just; of how to achieve it; even of how economies and societies work. Then there is no one right answer that all reasonable people should reach. The "right" answer hinges on the perspective they adopt; and reasonable people can adopt different perspectives. Thus Lupia and his colleagues show that well-informed liberals opposed the Bush tax cut; and conservatives—whether well-informed or not—favored it. It is not excessive to count as rational the choice of the policy alternative most appropriate to one's overall outlook on politics. It is all the more ironic, then, that the presumption that there is only one rational answer has obscured the rationality of citizens' political choices.

5 LABELING OF ALTERNATIVES AND POLITICAL SIGNALING

The classic hypothesis of ideology by proxy (Campbell et al. 1960) posited that signals of salient social groups enable voters to take coherent ideological positions, even in the absence of their understanding an ideology. They could, for example, take consistent positions on racial policies without an understanding of the policies themselves. They need to know only how they felt about black Americans and whether the policies help or hinder them—hardly an arcane level of knowledge. Analysis of endorsement effects advanced the study of political signaling another step. In a classic study, Lupia (1994) showed that voters used information providers' reputations as reliable signals (see also Lupia and McCubbins 1998).

Signaling has thus been in the analytical cupboard for some time. Yet, curiously studies of political signaling have focused on implicitly political groups, not explicitly political ones. Interest groups like labor or blacks have been studied; political parties neglected. No doubt it sounds odd to say so. There is a warehouse of studies of party identification, including the role of parties, as an inner gyroscope signaling choice (e.g. Jacoby 1988). But party identification is one side of the coin, and not the obviously most relevant side for analysis of parties as strategic actors. Party loyalties endure, indeed strengthen, over a lifetime. Moreover, they tend to be passed from father and mother to son and daughter. So party loyalties run across as well as within political generations; which is to say that the responses they evoke are sunk in the politics of a generation or more ago, not those of today or even those of yesterday. The persisting influence of party identification is thus one more illustration of the truth of William Faulkner's epigram: The past is never dead. It's not even past.

All the more reason, then, to complement analysis of the enduring loyalties of party supporters with analysis of political parties as strategic actors in the here and now. They marshal resources; they direct attention; they signal positions. More broadly, on our view, it is the logic of electoral competition operating through the medium of political parties that organizes psychological processes, not the other way around. In an ingenious study, Druckman (2001b) examined a paradigmatic experiment of Kahneman and Tversky—the classic Asian disease problem. In one arm of the experiment, the K-T procedure was replicated; in the second arm, the risk-averse and risk-seeking alternatives were labeled the Democrat's and the Republican's programs, respectively; in the third arm, the party labels on the risk-averse and risk-seeking alternatives were reversed. Without party labels, Druckman's results mirror the irrational preference reversals of Kahneman and Tversky. With party labels, preference reversals disappear for partisans of one party, and are greatly reduced for partisans of the other—an example of the anchoring role of attachments to political parties worth reflection.

Druckman's results are consistent with an interpretation of party labels as affective tags, evoking responses at the present moment because of loyalties acquired in the past. As partisan elites have polarized, however, they have sent an increasingly clear institutional signal about what it means to be a Democrat or a Republican: Democrats stand for X, Republicans stand for Y, and X and Y are distinct policy programs (Poole and Rosenthal 1997; Ansolabehere, Snyder, and Stewart 2001). Party labels are now brand names.

Party brand names are, of course, not the only political brand names. Nearly as important are ideological labels. It is a cardinal feature of (many) party systems that the party and ideology brand names now go hand in hand. Of course, in the nature of things the two sometimes diverge: liberal parties put up a conservative candidate; conservative parties a liberal one. Huckfeldt and his colleagues (2004, 2005) have exploited the imperfect correlation between the two major brand names in American politics to pry apart two possible interpretations of party as a brand name—psychological and ideological. They zero in on reactions when party and ideology signals conflict—the off-diagonals as they style them; and show that ideology dominates partisanship in the off-diagonals—a result that ingeniously suggests the importance of political ideas in politics.

The polarization of elite politics has of course had the effect of depopulating the off-diagonals, but not in the way commonly supposed. It is a cliché of contemporary American politics that their supporters have polarized as party activists have polarized. America, it is incessantly said, is now divided between blue states and red. In a tour de force, Fiorina (2005) has shown that most Americans remain moderate; indeed as moderate now as three decades ago, and what is more, moderate also on hot button issues like abortion and homosexuality. Levendusky (2006), however, has discovered an underlying shift. As party elites have gone through a process of polarization, their supporters in response have gone through a process of sorting: they have increasingly brought their politics into line with party attachments. They are not more likely to be at the extremes than they were, but they are markedly more likely to be on the same side politically as their party leaders. Party leaders and party supporters have thus traveled parallel paths but unequal distances.

Or more exactly, party leaders have been traveling on one path, and their supporters on separate but parallel paths. In what sense separate paths? In what sense parallel? The theoretical perspective we are developing posits that party leaders structure political choices. But what does it mean for them to impose a structure? If their supporters must conform, must they conform across the board? If not, why not? Carmines and Layman (1997) and Layman and Carsey (2002) have transformed our understanding of the structure of public opinion, showing that the basic organization units of mass belief systems are policy agendas. The role that government should play on providing a safety net and health care are examples of issues on the social welfare agenda; abortion and homosexuality, of issues on the social values agenda; government job training programs and business loans for blacks, of issues on the race agenda. Party supporters tend to take consistently liberal (or conservative) positions on each pair of issues, consistent with their party's overall stance on the issues. They also are more consistent, the more strongly they identify with their party and know how its position differs from the competing party's position. The question thus is not whether mass publics are capable of constraint; substantial numbers are. It is, when are their beliefs constrained and why?

This research demonstrates that citizens take consistent positions for issues on the same agenda; but the positions they take for issues on one agenda have little to do with the positions they take on another. With reflection, it is obvious why. Believe that governmental job training programs promote government bureaucracy and undercut individual initiative and responsibility—and you have a relevant reason to believe that governmental public housing programs will do the same. But what is the relevant reasoning connecting support for a job-training program and support for gay rights? In short, the question is not why people often fail to make connections across policy agendas. The question is rather why should they?

The linkage across agendas is weak, but links in a chain can be tightened. Under what conditions can the linkage in mass belief systems be strengthened?

To bring out the importance of party brand names in generating issue constraint, Tomz and Sniderman (2005) presented party-labeled policy alternatives (as they are in real life) to a medley of policies in one experimental condition, and non-labeled (as they are in standard public opinion surveys) policy alternatives in another. Their experimental results show that party branding policy alternatives does not increase constraint for party supporters for issues on the same policy agenda (corroborating Carmines, Layman, and Carsey's results by a different method). On the other hand, party labels *do* increase constraint for issues on different agendas.

The interpretation of this finding may appear obvious. It has become an epistemological reflex to view more consistency in the political thinking of ordinary citizens as normatively more desirable than less; understandably so against the background of decades of research reporting their patchy knowledge of public affairs and miscellaneous combinations of ideas. How can one not cheer in the face of evidence that ordinary citizens are not so hopelessly muddle-headed as they sometimes appear to be? Party signals are a heuristic enabling them to take consistent stands across a number of fronts, in a word, to engage politics in more nearly the same overarching terms as elites engage it.

Tomz and Sniderman point to a less happy interpretation of the signaling finding. It makes sense that ordinary citizens should treat policy agendas as separate matters since, in fact, they are separate matters. Protection for the environment and government assistance for the disadvantaged do not logically fit together. It is otherwise for party elites. They are tied together organizationally, if not logically. Consider Stimson's (2004) theory of career incentives and low dimensionality politics. From time to time, party activists and leaders find themselves in the minority on an issue that comes to the fore (e.g. pro-life Democrats). Since recruitment tends to operate on the basis of the majority position, the size of the majority steadily increases. And since retirement cycles inexorably roll on, the size of the minority steadily decreases. Voice quickly becomes ineffective and exit always is costly; indeed, usually career-ending. Parties are coordination devices: they bring together activists with different agendas. They accordingly have strong incentives to achieve consensus, or at any rate to avoid dissensus.[5] Hence the paradoxical simplicity of political thought of the cognitively complex and politically engaged.

Party activists, then, have a good reason to keep to a common line. Party supporters do not: they pay no price for either voice or exit. Two quite different interpretations of Tomz and Sniderman's link-tightening finding now suggest themselves. The first is the familiar one. Party is a heuristic that enables people to take politically coherent stands, and thus come a little bit closer to the democratic ideal of a citizen. The second interpretation, however, has a bitter rather than a sweet normative taste. Rather than political signals acting as an epistemological crutch, they render party adherents susceptible to manipulation by their party's elites, who can and do induce them to take positions they would not on their own.

Another study has brought out a companion quandary, focusing on the process of spatial reasoning (van Houweling and Sniderman 2004). So far as voters follow Downs's rule, choosing the candidate whose issue position is closer to theirs, the logic of electoral competition puts pressure on candidates to take positions similar to the voters' positions. Of course other considerations—for example, uncertainty of voter positions—can intervene (see Grofman 2004). But spatial reasoning in all its variations, neo-Downsian as well as Downsian, assumes that voters respond identically—and accurately—to candidate positions. But what reason is there to believe that the positions candidates take are the positions that voters perceive them to take? Candidates wave party banners for a reason: because it encourages party supporters to see the candidate as one of them. We like those who are like us not least because they are like us. In turn, we think that they think what we think. So the more strongly voters identify with their party, the more likely they are to judge that the candidate of their party represents their views.

Notice that the hypothesis, then, is *not* that the power of party identification moves party adherents to support the candidate of their party for reasons of sentiment, although it most certainly does. The hypothesis instead is that party loyalty biases spatial reasoning itself. To investigate this biasing hypothesis, van Houweling and Sniderman (2004) carried out a large-scale experiment ($N=7,000$). In one experimental condition, respondents were presented with the (randomly assigned) positions of party branded candidates. In the other condition, they were presented with competing candidates who were not party labeled. Respondents then were asked which candidate, if either, represents their position. It was not a surprise to observe partisan bias. It was staggering

---

[5] The idea that issues from different agendas—say, gay rights and support for the disadvantaged—are tied together at a deep level should by no means be dismissed. The deep connections between temperament and ideology remain to be plumbed.

to observe the magnitude of the bias. An absolute majority of strong party identifiers judge the position of the candidate of their party to correspond to theirs, even when the position of the candidate of the other party *unambiguously* is closer to theirs. This finding of partisan bias underlines the centrality of a political dynamic that formal models of representation have put on the sidelines. If a party candidate can unambiguously disagree with his supporters, yet his supporters perceive him to agree with them, party elites have more freedom of maneuver than has been acknowledged.

Candidates do not have unbounded freedom of maneuver, ironically for the same reason that they have a good deal of freedom. As Cox and McCubbins (1993) established in their pioneering analysis of party brand names, parties want to have an effective brand name. A clear and consistent brand is an asset for Congressional candidates. If a voter knows a candidate's party, then they know (more or less) where he stands on a host of issues; no less important, where he *should* stand on them. In turn, if he violates his party's reputation, he loses the reputational advantage and possibly worse. Even so, so far as van Houweling and Sniderman's results generalize, party elites have more freedom of maneuver than has been recognized.

6 Institutions and Rational Expectations

When voters make choices in an election, they need to form expectations about what will happen down-stream. "If [a voter] is rational," as Downs (1957) observed, "he knows that no party will be able to do everything it says it will do. Hence he cannot merely compare platforms; instead he must estimate in his own mind what the parties would actually do were they in power" (39). In the spirit of Downs, we borrow the phrase rational expectations. In what ways can citizens, looking down the game tree, make current choices in the light of accurate expectations about future conditions?

A number of neo-Downsian theories have explored the dynamics of rational expectations so understood. Grofman's (1985), for example, has focused attention between the status quo and rational discounting of candidate positions and the status quo. The status quo is sticky and is known to be so. Extreme candidates are therefore unlikely to be able to carry out policies as advertised. A rational person will accordingly discount their extreme positions, imputing to them the more moderate policies they actually will pursue when they are in office. Grofman's status quo hypothesis is interesting politically, and not merely psychologically, since the effect of discounting is to strengthen the hand of non-centrist candidates.

Fiorina's (2003) policy balancing model offers an institutionally differentiated model of rational expectations. Some citizens, he hypothesizes, split their vote, supporting one party for the executive, its opponent for the legislature, to promote a more moderate policy than either party would put into law if they had control of both executive and legislature (see also Alesina and Rosenthal 1995). Citizens, Fiorina cautions, might not consciously pursue this strategy of offsetting votes. They nevertheless can, and some evidence suggests do, act as if they were pursuing it.

Lacy and Paolino (2003, 1998) have mounted a two-front research program on separation of powers and vote choice. On the formal front, they have developed the first balancing model unencumbered by standard—and implausible—assumptions of homogeneous parties or nationwide districts. On the empirical front, they have developed a direct measure of expected policy positions of successful presidential candidates, providing for the first time a bridge to move from hypothetical as if reasoning to empirical hypothesis testing.

Multi-party systems invite theories of rational expectations. The field of comparative politics has generated an abundant literature on strategic voting (see Cox 1997 for a review). As a concrete example of the role of political institutions in structuring choice sets, consider coalition bargaining in a PR system. In such a system, citizens understand that (except in atypical cases) no single party will be able to form the government on its own. A coalition government will be formed, and the voter must calculate what combination of parties will best realize his policy aims. Kedar (2005) provides an exemplary study, developing and empirically testing a decision-theoretic model of policy balancing in parliamentary elections. She shows that moderate voters do better by voting for extreme parties to balance out forces on the other side of the ideological spectrum than by voting for the party whose platform matches their own preferences.

Rational expectations is thus another illustration of our most fundamental theoretical premise: to understand choice in politics, *it is necessary to take account not only of the attributes of choosers but also the properties of choice sets.*[6]

7 Political Parties and Political Reasoning

The role of political parties as focal points brings out another aspect of the institutional structuring of choice. Political parties have incentives to focus attention selectively, to bring some issues to the fore and relegate others to the background. In turn, voters will see one party better representing them than another, depending on whether their attention is directed to one set of concerns rather than another. Political parties are not the only institutional mechanism for focusing attention. They are, however, the prime one for competing elites to focus attention as an electoral strategy.

---

[6] Many studies using the Comparative Study of Electoral Systems (CSES) data are relevant to this point, although we cannot review them here due to space constraints. We refer the interested reader to **www.cses.org/resources/results/results.htm** for a comprehensive listing of the relevant work.

Johnston et al. (1992) present a dramatic example of the role of parties in focusing attention. In the 1988 federal election in Canada, two issues dominated the agenda. One was the Meech Lake Accord, redefining federalism to give the province of Quebec a greater measure of autonomy; the other, ratification of the North American Free Trade Agreement (NAFTA). At the start of the campaign, both issues were front and center. The Meech Lake Accord, however, threatened to split the eastern and western wings of the Conservative party. So the Conservative party focused on NAFTA. The Accord also threatened the Liberal party, plus NAFTA opened the door to demagogic appeals to national identity. So it, too, focused on NAFTA. The result was to retire one of the two issues at the forefront of public attention at the start of the campaign, and through the strategic calculation of party elites, restrict the menu of choice to a single issue.

Under the pressure of electoral competition, politicians cannot avoid strategic choices of focal points: what concern, which goal, to spotlight? Stimson (2004) has drawn the main lines of the strategic logic of parties in focusing attention; while Dickson and Scheve (2006) offer a display window example of formal theory exploiting psychological assumptions, to specify conditions under which incentives bring considerations of identity to the fore. A fully articulated theory of attention is the next step.

Attention is one thing; the intake of information another. To what extent—and, more fundamentally, in what way—are citizens capable of updating their beliefs? The study of motivated reasoning has documented citizens' strain to consistency in their political thinking (Lodge and Taber 2000). The strength of a strain to consistency is not invariant. Motivated skepticism, for example, depends strongly on the strength of people's attitude toward the object and their knowledge about the object (Taber and Lodge 2006). All the same, as a first approximation, it is reasonable to say that people have a pronounced tendency to resist updating. Instructively, people does not just mean the ordinary citizen. It includes the political expert. In a landmark study of expert political predictions, Tetlock offers a striking example of cognitive conservation. When experts make errors in prediction, even unambiguous ones, they often fail to acknowledge that the prediction itself was erroneous. The claim is not that individuals are unaware of new information, which is true enough. It goes farther and posits that they commonly do what it takes cognitively to interpret new information as consistent with their priors. As Tetlock (2005) observes, "There are good reasons for expecting smart people to be bad Bayesians ... people tend to be balky belief updaters who admit mistakes grudgingly and defend their prior positions tenaciously" (125–6). Of course, we would emphasize, the correct conclusion is *not* that people—even experts—fail to value rationality. They do, more than is commonly appreciated. "They draw the desired conclusion only if they [believe they] can muster up the evidence necessary to support it"—to support, that is, a conclusion that would convince an impartial observer (Kunda 1990, 483). Their reasoning is biased without their being aware it is biased; indeed, biased in the face of their desire that it be unbiased.

Formal models of learning characteristically presume that belief updating is unproblematic. As Keynes would have it, when the facts change, the people change their minds. Formal models of credibility are still more strongly committed to strong versions of updating; so much so that, in some versions, one act of deception strips a source of trustworthiness (e.g. Sobel 1985). Consider, then, Bullock's (2005) gun-at-your head demonstration of cognitive conservatism. Bullock gave subjects information about a Republican candidate before they evaluated him. Then he informed a subset that the information was false. Finally, he asked all subjects to evaluate the candidate again. Democrats who learned the information was false revised their opinion of the Republican candidate—but only by a half of the amount they should on Bayesian premises. Republicans did not revise their opinion of the Republican candidate at all. Bullock's experiment thus suggests that belief updating in the face of deception is anything but unproblematic: false information seems to have power even after it is known to be false.

Voters are not blind to the world they live in, even if much of the traditional public opinion literature represents them as deaf and dumb. They are, however, resistant to revising their priors about how problems in the world should be dealt with. But policy preferences nonetheless are updated. How does this happen?

As a rule parties as well as voters are resistant to updating their priors. The tendency of every rational party, Downs (1957) argued, is to maintain continuity in its policies. But parties are also the primary organizational medium through which candidates compete for electoral office. Periodically, they have incentives, because of changes in circumstances or on account of compositional changes in their base, to modify the policy alternatives on their menus. In the early 1970s, for example, the parties took muted stances on the issue of legal abortion, and in fact, many Republican elites were more liberal than their Democratic counterparts. By the 1990s, there had been a turnabout at the elite level. Democrats were clearly the pro-choice party and Republicans were the pro-life party (see Adams 1997).

Here, we believe, is the largest part of the answer to the question of how party adherents update. When parties update their policy menus, their supporters favor their party's new offering for much the same reason they favored its previous one—namely, their attachment to their party and the broad outlooks on politics associated with it. Of course, some cast away their partisan attachments when new policies conflict with their political convictions. More commonly, though, party identification is their anchor, and it is their views on issues—even on hot button issues such as abortion—that swing around to be consistent with their party loyalties, not the other way around (Miller 2000).[7] The process may give the impression of blind loyalty. But in responding to changes in circumstances, it is in the interest of political parties to give the best response in their repertoire. So far as parties update their alternatives on offer in response to incentives from changed circumstances, party supporters need not update

---

[7] This is typically, although not always, the case. In an exemplary study, Carsey and Layman (2006) discuss the conditions under which citizens who hold views out of step with their party will change either their partisanship or their issue positions. They show that changing partisanship to accommodate your issue position is most likely when citizens are aware of party differences and find the issue to be salient. These conditions (salience and awareness of party differences) are the exception rather than the rule. For most citizens faced with conflicting issue positions and party ID, they change their issue position if they change at all.

on their own to locate the response they would rationally judge best—best, that is to say, conditional on their priors. Realignments aside, the primary mechanism of change in policy preferences, paradoxically, is continuity of party attachments.

8 ENVOI

There is an emerging consensus on the value of combining formal and behavioral approaches; on specifying relationships between political institutions and strategic choice; on exploring further the centrality of party loyalty to political choice. Or perhaps better, an emerging synthesis of the three. Combined, they make plain that a theory of choice in politics must take account not only of attributes of the chooser, as has research in the past, but also of properties of the choice set.

Not the least reason that this new direction seems to us progressive is that it is continuous with the established one. It may appear otherwise. Our primary focus has been the role of properties of choice sets in facilitating consistency of belief and choice. To some in public opinion research and to most outside it, the focal theme appears just the opposite—inconsistency. This impression is understandable. The exceptional virtues of Converse and Zaller's contributions have overshadowed the main current of research, what has run in just the opposite direction, concentrating on the analysis of consistency. Online processing, core values, affect, judgmental heuristics, motivated reasoning, even Bayesian updating, all have been brought into play as consistency generators. It would be odd indeed to mount so large and persistent an effort to specify mechanisms of consistency, if there was not a presumption of some substantial measure of consistency in mass belief systems. This presumption is by no means universally shared, of course. The growing body of research on ambivalence is exhibit number one of a persisting interest in inconsistency (see, for example, Alvarez and Brehm 2002; Basinger and Lavine 2005). It has all the same been a side current to this point, not the main one. So far from being at odds with previous work, the research we have reviewed is an extension of it. It is an effort to understand how consistency is imposed by the conditions of choice as well as by the tastes and aptitudes of the chooser.

It is all the more important, then, to flag a major weakness of the new institutional research program. The test of a theory is not just that it is capable of giving an account of newly observed regularities. It must also be capable of giving an account of previous ones. It may give a different interpretation of them. But it must account, as it were, for all the cards on the table. The research we have laid out cannot do so. It cannot account in a satisfying way for the instability and lack of consistency (variously defined) that are the hallmark of Converse and Zaller's landmark works. Some measure of inconsistency is better understood as measurement error as Achen (1975) demonstrated some time ago, and consistency in any case is a matter of degree. But a good deal of muddle remains, and while the view we have laid out does not deny there is lability in political preference, it cannot give a satisfying in principle explanation of it. Somewhere down the road a more encompassing synthesis will have to be developed.

We are aware that the account that we have set out is not a theory dressed in its Sunday best. We nonetheless think it has some virtues. It calls attention to a new component of a theory of choice, namely, properties of the choice set. It ties properties of political choice sets to political institutions, above all, political parties. And it has the virtue of telling a political story about political choice. Parties are the common focal point of candidates and voters, and the cumulative morale of this body of research is the power of party elites. They manifestly are under pressure to respond to popular preferences. But they can exercise an important measure of autonomy, not merely by their power to persuade their adherents to follow their line, but more deeply, by their power to structure the alternatives on offer and so the choices citizens make. No doubt there is more to the story.

REFERENCES

ACHEN, C. 1975. Mass political attitudes and the survey response. *American Political Science Review*, 69: 1218–31.

ADAMS, G. 1997. Abortion: evidence of issue evolution. *American Journal of Political Science*, 41: 718–37.

ADAMS, J., MERRILL, S., and GROFMAN, B. 2005. *A Unified Theory of Party Competition*. New York: Cambridge University Press.

ALDRICH, J. 1983. A Downsian spatial model with party activism. *American Political Science Review*, 77: 974–90.

ALESINA, A., and ROSENTHAL, H. 1995. *Partisan Politics, Divided Government, and the Economy*. New York: Cambridge University Press.

ALVAREZ, R. M., and BREHM, J. 2002. *Hard Choices, Easy Answers: Values, Information and American Public Opinion*. Princeton: Princeton University Press.

ANSOLABEHERE, S., SNYDER, J., and STEWART, C. 2001. Candidate positioning in U.S. House elections. *American Journal of Political Science*, 45: 136–59.

BARNES, S., KAASE, M., ALLERBECK, K., FARAH, B., HEUNKS, F., INGLEHART, R., JENNINGS, M. K., KLINGEMANN, H., MARSH, A., and ROSENMAYR, L. 1979. *Political Action: Mass Participation in Five Western Democracies*. Beverly Hills, Calif.: Sage.

BARTELS, L. 2003. Democracy with attitudes. Pp. 48–82 in *Electoral Democracy*, ed. M. MacKuen and G. Rabinowitz. Ann Arbor: University of Michigan Press.

—— 2005. Homer gets a tax cut: inequality and public policy in the American mind. *Perspectives on Politics*, 3: 15–31.

BASINGER, S., and LAVINE, H. 2005. Ambivalence, information and electoral choice. *American Political Science Review*, 99: 169–84.

BENDOR, J., DIERMEIER, D., and TING, M. 2003. A behavioral model of turnout, *American Political Science Review*, 97: 261–80.

—— KUMAR, S., and SIEGEL, D. 2005. V.O. key formalized: retrospective voting as adaptive behavior. Paper presented at the Annual Meeting of the Midwest Political Science Association, Chicago.

BISHOP, G., TUCHFARBER, A., and OLDENDICK, R. 1978. Change in the structure of American political attitudes: the nagging question of question wording. *American Journal of Political Science*, 22: 250–69.

BOATWRIGHT, P., and NUNES, J. 2001. Reducing assortment: an attribute-based approach. *Journal of Marketing*, 65: 50–63.

BULLOCK, J. 2005. The enduring power of false information. Manuscript: Stanford University.

CALVERT, R. 1985. Robustness of the multidimensional voting model: candidate motivations, uncertainty and convergence. *American Journal of Political Science*, 29: 69–95.

CAMERER, C., 2003. *Behavioral Game Theory*. Princeton: Princeton University Press.

—— LOEWENSTEIN, G., and RABIN, M. eds. 2004. *Advances in Behavioral Economics*. Princeton: Princeton University Press.

CARMINES, E., and LAYMAN, G. 1997. Issue evolution in postwar American politics: old certainties and fresh tensions. In *Present Discontents*, ed. B. Shafer. Chatham, NJ: Chatham House.

CAMPBELL, A., MILLER, W., CONVERSE, P., and STOKES, D. 1960. *The American Voter*. New York: Wiley.

CARSEY, T., and LAYMAN, G. 2006. Changing sides or changing minds? Party identification and policy preferences in the American electorate. *American Journal of Political Science*, 50: 464–77.

CONVERSE, P. 1964. The nature of belief systems in mass publics. Pp. 206–61 in *Ideology and Discontent*, ed. D. Apter. New York: Free Press.

COX, G. 1997. *Making Votes Count*. New York: Cambridge University Press.

—— and MCCUBBINS, M. 1993. *Legislative Leviathan: party government in the House.* Berkeley: University of California Press.

DELLI CARPINI, M., and KEETER, S. 1996. What Americans know about politics and why it matters. New Haven: Yale University Press.

DHAR, R. 1997. Consumer preference for a no choice option. *Journal of Consumer Research*, 24: 215–31.

DICKSON, E., and SCHEVE, K. 2006. Social identity, political speech and electoral competition. *Journal of Theoretical Politics*, 18: 5–39.

DOWNS, A. 1957. *An Economic Theory of Democracy*. New York: Harper & Row.

DRUCKMAN, J. 2001a. On the limits of framing effects: who can frame? *Journal of Politics*, 63: 1041–66.

—— 2001b. Using credible advice to overcome framing effects. *Journal of Law, Economics, and Organization*, 17: 62–82.

—— 2004. Political preference formation: competition, deliberation and the (ir)relevance of framing effects. *American Political Science Review*, 98: 671–86.

—— and NELSON, K. 2003. Framing and deliberation: how citizens' conversations limit elite influence. *American Journal of Political Science*, 47: 729–45.

FIORINA, M. 2003. *Divided Government*, 2nd edn. New York: Longman.

—— with ABRAMS, S., and POPE, J. C. 2005. *Culture War*. New York: Pearson Longman.

FUCHS, D., and KLINGEMANN, H. 1989. The left–right schema. Pp. 203–34 in *Continuities in Political Action*, ed. M. K. Jennings, J. van Deth, et al. Berlin: Walter de Gruyter.

GLASER, J. 2002. White voters, black schools: structuring racial choices with a checklist ballot. *American Journal of Political Science*, 46: 35–46.

GORDON, S., and SEGURA, G. 1997. Cross-national variation in the political sophistication of individuals: capability or choice? *Journal of Politics*, 59: 126–47.

GROFMAN, B. 1985. The neglected role of the status quo in models of issue voting. *Journal of Politics*, 47: 230–37.

—— 2004. Downs and two-party convergence. *Annual Review of Political Science*, 7: 25–46.

HUCKFELDT, R., MONDAK, J., CRAW, M., and MOREHOUSE MENDEZ, J. 2004. Terms and conditions of candidate choice: partisan versus ideological heuristics. In *Interdisziplinare Sozialforschung: Theorie und Emprische Anwedugen. Festschrift zum 65. Geburtstag von Franz Urban Pappi*, ed. C Henning and C. Melbeck. Frankfurt: Campus Verlag.

—— —— —— —— 2005. Making sense of candidates: partisanship, ideology, and issues as guides to judgment. *Cognitive Brain Research*, 23: 11–23.

HURWITZ, J., and PEFFLEY, M. 1987. How are foreign policy attitudes structured? A hierarchical model. *American Political Science Review*, 81: 1009–120.

IYENGAR, S., and LEPPER, M. 2000. When choice is demotivating: can one desire too much of a good thing? *Journal of Personality and Social Psychology*, 79: 995–1006.

—— HUBERMAN, G., and JIANG, W. 2004. How much choice is too much: determinants of individual contributions in 401K retirement plans. Pp. 83–95 in *Pension Design and Structure: New Lessons from Behavioral Finance*, ed. O. Mitchell and S. Utkus. Oxford: Oxford University Press.

JACKMAN, S., and SNIDERMAN, P. 2002. The institutional organization of choice spaces: a political conception of political psychology. In *Political Psychology*, ed. K. Monroe. Mahway, NJ: Lawrence Erlbaum.

JACOBY, W. 1988. The impact of party identification on issue attitudes. *American Journal of Political Science*, 32: 643–61.

JERIT, J., BARABAS, J., and BOLSEN, T. 2006. Citizens, knowledge and the information environment. *American Journal of Political Science*, 50: 266–82.

JOHNSTON, R., BLAIS, A., BRADY, H., and CRETE, J. 1992. *Letting The People Decide: Dynamics of a Canadian Election*. Stanford, Calif.: Stanford University Press.

KEDAR, O. 2005. When moderate voters prefer extreme parties: policy balancing in parliamentary elections. *American Political Science Review*, 99: 185–99.

KREPS, D. 2004. Beliefs and tastes: confessions of an economist. Pp. 113–42 in *Models of a Man: Essays in Memory of Herbert A. Simon*, ed. M. Augier and J. March. Cambridge, Mass.: MIT Press.

KRIESI, H. 2005. *Direct Democratic Choice: The Swiss Experience*. Lanham, Md.: Lexington Books.

KUKLINSKI, J., QUIRK, P., JERIT, J., and RICH, R. 2001. The political environment and citizen competence. *American Journal of Political Science*, 45: 410–24.

KUNDA, Z. 1990. The case for motivated reasoning. *Psychological Bulletin*, 108: 480–98.

LACY, D., and PAOLINO, P. 1998. Downsian voting and the separation of powers. *American Journal of Political Science*, 42: 1180–99.

—— —— 2003. Policy expectations voting in executive elections: the role of institutions. Paper presented at the Annual Meeting of the American Political Science Association, Philadelphia.

LAYMAN, G., and CARSEY, T. 2002. Party polarization and conflict extension in the American electorate. *American Journal of Political Science*, 46: 786–80.

LEVENDUSKY, M. 2006. Sorting: explaining change in the U.S. electorate. Ph.D. Dissertation: Stanford University.

LODGE, M., and TABER, C. 2000. Three steps toward a theory of motivated reasoning. Pp. 182–213 in *Elements of Reason*, ed. A. Lupia, M. McCubbins, and S. Popkin. New York: Cambridge University Press.

LUPIA, A. 1994. Shortcuts versus encyclopedias: information and voting behavior in California Insurance reform elections. *American Political Science Review*, 88: 63–76.

—— and McCUBBINS, M. 1998. *The Democratic Dilemma*. New York: Cambridge University Press.

LUPIA, A., LEVINE, A., MENNING, J., and SIN, G. 2005. Were Bush tax cut supporters "simply ignorant?" A second look at conservatives and liberals in "Homer gets a tax cut". Manuscript: University of Michigan.

McFADDEN, D. 1974. The measurement of urban travel demand. *Journal of Public Economics*, 3: 303–28.

MILLER, W. 2000. Temporal order and causal inference. *Political Analysis*, 8: 119–40.

NIE, N., VERBA, S., and PETROCIK, J. 1976. *The Changing American Voter*. Cambridge, Mass.: Harvard University Press.

NIEMI, R., and WESTHOLM, A. 1984. Issues, parties and attitudinal stability: a comparative study of Sweden and the United States. *Electoral Studies*, 3: 65–83.

PALFREY, T. 1984. Spatial equilibrium with entry. *Review of Economic Studies*, 51: 139–56.

POOLE, K., and ROSENTHAL, H. 1997. *Congress: A Political-Economic History of Roll Call Voting*. New York: Oxford University Press.

ROEMER, J. 2001. *Political Competition: Theory and Applications*. Cambridge, Mass.: Harvard University Press.

SARIS, W. 2004. Different judgment models for policy questions: competing or complementary? In *Studies in Public Opinion*, ed. W. Saris and P. Sniderman. Princeton: Princeton University Press.

—— and SNIDERMAN, P. eds. 2004. *Studies in Public Opinion*, Princeton: Princeton University Press.

SNIDERMAN, P. 2000. Taking Sides: A Fixed Choice Theory of Political Reasoning. Pp. 67–84 in *Elements of Reason*, ed. A. Lupia, M. McCubbins, and S. Popkin. New York: Cambridge University Press.

—— and BULLOCK, J. 2004. A consistency theory of public opinion and political choice: the hypothesis of menu dependence. Pp. 337–58 in Saris and Sniderman 2004.

—— and THERIAULT, S. 2004. The structure of political argument and the logic of issue framing. Pp. 133–65 in Saris and Sniderman 2004.

SOBEL, J. 1985. A theory of credibility. *Review of Economic Studies*, 52: 557–73.

STIMSON, J. 2004. *Tides of Consent*. New York: Cambridge University Press.

SULLIVAN, J., PIERSON, J., and MARCUS, G. 1978. Ideological constraint in the mass public: a methodological critique and some new findings. *American Journal of Political Science*, 22: 233–49.

TABER, C., and LODGE, M. 2006. Motivated skepticism in the evaluation of political beliefs. *American Journal of Political Science*, 50: 755–69.

TETLOCK, P. 2005. *Expert Political Judgment: How Good Is It? How Can We Know?* Princeton: Princeton University Press.

TOMZ, M., and SNIDERMAN, P. 2005. The organization of mass belief systems. Paper presented at the Annual Meeting of the Midwest Political Science Association, Chicago.

VAN HOUWELING, R., and SNIDERMAN, P. 2004. The political logic of a Downsian space. Paper presented at the Annual Meeting of the Midwest Political Science Association, Chicago.

WITTMAN, D. 1983. Candidate motivation: a synthesis of alternative theories. *American Political Science Review*, 77: 142–57.

ZALLER, J. 1992. *The Nature and Origins of Mass Opinion*. New York: Cambridge University Press.

CHAPTER 24

THE DECLINE
OF SOCIAL CLASS?

ODDBJØRN KNUTSEN

SOCIAL class represents a classic structural cleavage in industrial society. Social class became a major determinant for political attitudes and voting behavior when the political systems of western nations democratized in the late nineteenth century and early twentieth century. Today the main issue regarding the class cleavage is whether it is persisting, declining, or is undergoing a transformation.

This chapter focuses on various aspects of the class cleavage. I first outline Marx's and Weber's conceptions of social class and place the class cleavage within the context of political behavior in the famous Lipset and Rokkan model for political cleavages in industrial societies. I then discuss the various phases in the study of class voting, and outline a possible new trend in class-voting analyses. I outline class schemas and statistical measurements to tap social class and class voting in the various stages of class-voting studies. The chapter next reviews important debates in the studies of class voting, such as the political orientation of the service class and the persistence of class voting. I review findings about trends in class voting. Finally, I outline explanations of cross-national differences in class voting and systematic empirical tests of such explanations.

1 CLASS ANALYSES, THE CLASS CLEAVAGE, AND POLITICAL BEHAVIOR

Class analyses can be traced back to the study of conflict within the social sciences. Karl Marx and Max Weber are the central theorists in this tradition. Although their concepts of social class differed, both considered social class as vitally important for shaping the material interests and important experiences of individuals.

Marx defined social classes in terms of the relationship of groups of individuals to the means of production. Marx's class model emphasizes two fundamental classes based on their relation to property. A minority of "non-producers", who control the means of production, can use this position of control to extract from the majority of "producers" the surplus product that is the source of their livelihood. Control of the means of production yields political control, and a dominant class seeks to stabilize its position by advancing a legitimating ideology.

In capitalist society property rights in the means of production generate three classes: capitalists who own the means of production and hire workers, workers who sell their labor power to capitalist and petty bourgeois who own and use the means of production without hiring others. Although Marx differentiated classes on objective terms, he was primarily interested in the emergence of class consciousness among the depressed strata to create a sense of shared class interests that would provide a basis for conflict with the dominant class. A group that held a number of objective characteristics in common, but lacked class consciousness, meant that it could not play the role of a historically significant class.

Weber's notion of social classes emphasized the market. Class refers to any group of people who share the same class situation, and the chances in the market that presents a common condition for the individual's fate. Classes are founded on different economic interests in market relationships. Weber strongly emphasized a pluralistic conception of classes and distinguished between "ownership" classes and "acquisition" classes. While the former classes were based on property ownership, the other acquisition classes were based on the "marketable skills" that they possess, in particular educational qualifications. This was the basis for various middle classes between the privileged classes and the "negative privileged" classes (those who possess neither property nor marketable skills).

A basic difference between these concepts of class is that whereas the Marxist approach focuses on the realm of production and does not recognize that some line of cleavages other than capital/labor could constitute the *primary* source of political antagonism, the Weberian approach considers the class cleavages as only one among many primary sources of cleavage.

In Lipset and Rokkan's (1967) seminal work on the formation of social cleavages in western democracies, the class cleavage was essentially a cleavage between owners and employers on the one side, and tenants, laborers, and workers on the other. It sprang out of the Industrial Revolution and proved much more uniformly divisive than the other major cleavages. The rising masses of workers resented their working conditions and the insecurity of their contracts. This resulted in the formation of labor unions and the development of nationwide socialist parties. The uniformity of the labor market cleavage across nations implied that it produced similar structures of party systems. Conflicts along the other social cleavages tended to generate diverse national patterns, but the owner-worker cleavages moved the party system in a common direction. The Russian Revolution also brought about a more divisive party structure among parties articulating working-class interests. Significant communist parties emerged in some countries, which sometimes created a split with the socialist parties.

The labor market cleavage is the central class cleavage, but another class cleavage is the conflict between peasants and others employed in the primary sector and those who wanted to buy the products from the primary sector, particularly the urban population. This cleavage also sprang out of the Industrial Revolution. Such conflicts did not invariably prove party forming. In many countries, the religious interests of the rural population were more influential than the strictly economic ones, and the economic interest articulation took place within Christian parties. Distinct agrarian parties emerged only in some countries where strong cultural opposition had deepened and embittered the strictly economic conflicts (Lipset and Rokkan 1967). Rokkan developed an elaborate model based on the two economic cleavages in an important work on the Norwegian cleavage structure (Rokkan 1966).

2 THE THREE GENERATIONS OF CLASS VOTING

Early attempts to study the class-vote link used ecological techniques to infer the vote preference of different occupation and income groups. The advent of election surveys around 1960 made possible more direct testing of the relationship between social class and voting behavior. The accumulation of national election surveys since then has produced detailed examination of the association between social class and party choice over time. Most of these studies analyzed data from a single country, although there are some comparative longitudinal analyses.

Nieuwbeerta (1995, ch. 1) groups studies of class voting into three "generations". The three generations are distinguished by the research problems that were formulated in the studies, the content of the major hypotheses, measurement procedures, data collection, and methods of data analysis.[1]

The first generation of class voting studies was during the 1950s and 1960s. This research focused attention on a broad range of research problems concerning the relationship between social class and voting. The basic question was whether an individual's social and economic position was related to voting behavior. Researchers addressed this question by examining a limited number of data sets and using simple measures of social class (see for example Alford 1964; Korpi 1983; Lipset 1981).

The second generation started in the late 1960s. The aim was to increase the amount of variance in voting behavior explained by adding variables to the equation, rather than focusing upon the relationship between social class and party choice in

---

[1] See Nieuwbeerta's (1995, ch. 1) more extensive presentation of the three generations of class voting.

detail. The empirical analyses were more sophisticated than those of the first generation (see for example Franklin et al. 1992; Inglehart 1990).

The first two generations of class voting found that the manual working class tended to support the left-wing political parties, while the non-manual classes generally supported the right-wing parties. Researchers discovered substantial cross-national differences, although studies from different countries were restricted in their comparability. Class voting was largest in the Nordic countries, then in Britain and Australia, and then the Continental countries, and considerably smaller in USA and Canada. On the basis of available published cross-tabulations from the early studies of class voting from the first two generations, Nieuwbeerta (1995: 53, table 3.5) compiled the level of class voting in about fifteen countries. On average, the level of class voting in the Nordic countries was 48 percentage points in the 1945–60 period according to the Alford index (see below), followed by Britain (37), Australia (33), Continental counties (25), and finally Canada and USA (12). Similar differences existed for the 1960s.

The third generation emerged around the mid-1980s. These studies used a detailed cross-nationally comparable class scheme, and applied log odds-ratios and non-linear statistical techniques. The researchers of the third generation argued more specifically that measures based on percentage differences (so-called absolute class voting) were sensitive to the general popularity of the political parties, and that measures of so-called relative class voting based on log-odds ratios should be used instead.

All three generations of class voting relied on a dichotomous party choice variable that grouped parties of the left into one category and all other parties (non-socialist or rightist parties) into the other category.

3 A New Forth Generation of Class Voting Research?

Hout, Brooks, and Manza (1995) introduced the idea of distinguishing between "traditional" and "total" class voting. Traditional class voting meant the portion of the statistical association between class and voting behavior that arises from blue-collar classes supporting left-leaning parties and white-collar classes voting for right-leaning parties. Total class voting includes, by contrast, all sources of the relationship between social classes and party choice where classes and parties are treated as separate categories on both variables (including non-voting). Here I will advance this distinction a bit further by differentiating between:

(1) "Total class voting," which considers class differences (based on a detailed class schema) in voting between all the parties in the party system.

(2) "Overall or total left–right class voting," which examines the left–right voting of all social classes.
(3) "Traditional (left–right) class voting," which examines the left–right division of parties and only two social classes (the manual/non-manual division).

The party choice variable has (nearly) always been dichotomized into left–right in class-voting research. This division can be questioned in advanced industrial societies. There is some evidence that social cleavages, and the class cleavage in particular, cut across the left–right division of parties. The New Left parties gain stronger support from the higher educated strata and the new middle class, while the New Right parties gain strongest support from the less educated and the workers. Therefore, newer research on class voting should consider all parties as separate categories (see Knutsen 2004a, 2006).

4 CLASS SCHEMA

The first two generations of class voting used a traditional two-class schema between manual workers and all other classes (Nieuwbeerta 1995). More recent class-voting studies use more detailed class schemas. Prominent among these schemas are the so-called Erikson/Goldthorpe (hereafter EG) class schema originally developed in connection with social mobility studies (Goldthorpe 1980; Erikson and Goldthorpe 1992).[2] This is the most influential conceptualization and operationalization of social class in European sociology (Savage 1991). The third generation of class-voting studies typically used this class schema.

The EG schema is derived mainly from classic sources, in particular from Marx and especially Weber. The schema differentiates positions within *labor markets* and *production units*—more specifically, to separate such positions in terms of the employment relations that they entail (Erikson and Goldthorpe 1992, 37). The basic distinction in the schema is within the category of employees.

The schema distinguishes between employees involved in a service relationship with their employers and those whose employment is essentially regulated by a labor contract. A "service relationship," rather than one formulated in terms of a labor contract, exists where the employees are required to exercise *delegated authority* or *specialized knowledge and expertise* in the interest of their employing organization (Goldthorpe 1982; Erikson and Goldthorpe 1992, 42).

A main division exists between the predominantly salaried professional—higher technical, administrative, and managerial—positions, and the predominantly

---

[2] It is also called the EGP class schema, owing to the contribution of Portocarero (Erikson, Goldthorpe, and Portocarero 1979).

wage-earning manual occupations. The former are positions with a service relationship, and thus constitute the basis of the "service class" or the "salariat"[3] of modern
industrial society. The latter, where the labor contract usually prevails, constitute the
basis of the working class. The service class comprises administrators and managers,
employed professionals, higher-grade technicians, and supervisors of non-manual
workers. It is divided into a higher and a lower level according to administrative
responsibility and educational training.

Routine non-manual employees in the EG schema do not belong to the new
middle class or the service class. This includes routine non-manual positions, usually
involving clerical, sales, or personal-service tasks, which exist on the fringes of
professional, administrative, and managerial bureaucracies (Goldthorpe 1980, 40).

The working-class group comprises skilled and unskilled manual wage-earners in
all branches of industry, as well as supervisors of manual workers (foremen) and
lower-grade technicians.

5 MEASUREMENTS OF CLASS VOTING

Most analyses of class voting use a dichotomous party choice variable (socialist/non-
socialist parties) and a dichotomous class variable (manual versus non-manual social
classes). The traditional measure of class voting calculates the percentage difference.
The so-called Alford index is simply the percentage difference in support for the left
or socialist parties between the manual and the non-manual social classes (Alford
1964, 79–80).

Newer research on class voting emphasizes the difference between absolute and
relative class voting, and suggests that log-odds ratios are a better measure of
(relative) class voting. This measure, in contrast to the Alford index, is insensitive
to changes in the overall support for parties or party groups (Heath, Jowell, and
Curtice 1985; Hout, Brooks, and Manza 1993; Nieuwbeerta 1995). This measure—still
based on a dichotomous class variable—is called the Thomsen index.[4]

When the assumption of only two social classes is replaced by more classes, as in
the EG class schema, the analyses become more complicated. Hout, Brooks, and
Manza (1995) suggest using the *kappa index*.[5] The higher the value of the kappa
index, the higher is the level of class voting. The kappa index has several desirable

---

[3] "Salariat" was introduced as a synonym of service class in order to avoid confusion between the
service class and "service workers" and the service sector of employment (Goldthorpe 1995).

[4] Named after Søren Risbjerg Thomsen, who was one of the first to apply the log-odds ratio in
research on politics and political cleavages.

[5] The kappa index calculates several log-odds ratios between a reference category on the class variable
and each of the other classes and uses the standard deviation of these log-odds ratios as a measure of class
voting.

statistical properties. The most desirable property is that the index is based on log-odds ratios and therefore not dependent on the marginal distributions of the independent or dependent variables.

Kappa values can be calculated for each political party. For example, it can analyze total class voting where the research question examines the class profile of individual parties and compare parties and party families in a comparative analysis (see Knutsen 2006, ch. 4) "It provides a uniform metric for comparative and historical analyses based on suitable class and voting typologies" (Hout, Brooks, and Manza 1995: 814).[6] Several newer studies of class voting use the kappa index (Nieuwbeerta 1995; Weakliem and Heath 1999b).

6 THE DEBATE ABOUT THE POLITICAL ORIENTATIONS OF THE SERVICE CLASS

The class structure in western democracies has changed largely from a typical industrial society to advanced industrial or post-industrial society. The most important change is the decline of the working class and the increase in those who belong to the service class. These important changes in the class structure have triggered a debate about the political orientations of the service class.

The literature on the service class (the new middle class) disagrees about the political orientations and party choice of this class. This is important since the service class has grown in size and may shift left–right class voting since it is considered as a non-manual class. If it is essentially a conservative class, its increasing size might strengthened or at least stabilize class voting. If it is a left-wing class, it might decrease left–right class voting.

John Goldthorpe formulated an influential theory of the political orientations of the service class: the service class "will constitute an essentially *conservative* element within modern society" (Goldthorpe 1982, 180). The service class is employees who are subordinate to some form of higher agency, but the main characteristic of the service-class occupations is that they exercise authority and/or specialized knowledge and expertise. They perform their work tasks and roles with some significant degree of authority and discretion, and enjoy conditions of employment that are decidedly advantaged relative to other grades of employees. This represents a unifying structural location that determines their basic social and political outlook, which will be conservative and status quo-oriented (Goldthorpe 1982, 168–70).

---

[6] The kappa index assumes a dichotomous party choice variable, and cannot be calculated when the party choice variable is a nominal-level variable based on all parties. Therefore it cannot be used as a measure of the overall correlation between social class and party choice in a multi-party system.

In the British debate, Lash and Urry (1987) argued that the service class will be an innovative and disruptive force in capitalism. They couple the service class with the rise of new social movements and the weakening of the old patterns of political alignments. Savage (1991) found considerable internal divisions within the service class. He showed that party divisions within the service class are considerably greater than in other social classes. Heath and Savage (1995) showed considerably variations within the service class's party identification. However, structural characteristics like sector employment and employment status have only limited power for explaining these differences.

Similar findings about divisions within the service class with regard to participation in new social movements and party choice are found for several continental European countries (Müller 1999; Kriesi 1998, 168–72). In Scandinavia, sector employment has a large impact of voting, and the division within the service class in particular is substantial. The service class in the public sector is more likely to support left-wing parties than the service class in the private sector (Knutsen 2001). The same applies to most west European countries although not to the same degree (Knutsen 2005).

7 The Debate about the Persistence or Decline of Class Voting

It once was considered conventional wisdom that class voting was declining in all advanced democracies, but recent research has seriously challenged this wisdom. Leading scholars like Seymour Martin Lipset (1981) and Ronald Inglehart (1984) initially documented a decline in class voting in several countries mainly by using a simple measure of social class (the Alford index). In Britain, a variety of electoral researchers expressed this conventional view (Franklin 1984; Rose and McAllister 1986; Särlvik and Crewe 1983).

In the United States, Clem Brooks, Michael Hout, and Jeff Manza challenged this conventional view. By using a more detailed class schema, as well as more sophisticated statistical techniques that measure relative class voting instead of absolute class voting, they argued that social class has a quite permanent overall impact on American party choice (Brooks and Manza 1997; Manza and Brooks 1999; Hout, Brooks, and Manza 1995).

In Britain, the British Election Study teams of the 1980s and 1990s—the so-called Nuffield team—also disputed the claims about class dealignment. Using newer statistical techniques and a more elaborate class schema (the EG class schema), they differentiated between absolute and relative class voting and found more trendless fluctuation than decline in class voting (Heath, Jowell, and Curtice 1985; Heath et al. 1991; Evans, Heath, and Payne 1991). Anthony Heath has recently shown—and admitted—that class voting is declining in both Britain and the USA, as well as in France, somewhat contrary to his previous position (Weakliem and Heath 1999*a*; 1999*b*). Others within the Nuffield group, however, have defended the view that class voting in Britain is constant (Goldthorpe 1999) and argued that the comparative studies of the decline in class voting are disputable (Evans 1999).[7]

Those who support the persistence of class voting belong to the third generation of class-voting researchers. They argue that newer and more sophisticated statistical techniques and a more elaborate class schema (the EG class schema), are major reasons why their findings differ from the conventional dealignment argument. However, other researchers in the third generation find clear evidence of decline in class voting (see below).

8 TRENDS IN CLASS VOTING

8.1 Comparative Studies from Advanced Democracies

Nieuwbeerta's (1995) pioneering work is the most extensive analysis of class voting in a comparative perspective. He uses the new class schemas and the new statistical techniques, but his findings conformed to the conventional wisdom: Class voting had declined in most western democracies, according to both the Thomsen and the kappa indices.

Nieuwbeerta studied class voting in twenty countries over time, and found that—based on 324 class-voting tables in the time span 1945–90—the correlation between the Alford index and the log-odds ratios (Thomsen index) was 0.97. Nieuwbeerta also found that the measures did not yield substantively different results (1995, 52–5).

Nieuwbeerta analyzed class voting trends based on the EG-classes by using the kappa index. He again found clear trends towards a decline in class voting in nearly all countries, and the trends are fairly similar to those found based on a dichotomous class variable. Nieuwbeerta's (1995) general results were that various measurements of the level of class voting and the amount of decline were highly correlated despite the fact that different measurement and very different class schemas were used.

In a more recent analysis, Nieuwbeerta and Manza (2002) expanded the database to include additional data from the 1990s. In a comparative analysis of six countries (Australia, Austria, Britain, Germany, the Netherlands, and USA) there were significant long-term decline in total left–right class voting in all countries.

Knutsen (2006) has studied absolute and relative class voting in eight west European countries from the mid-1970s to the late 1990s. He found a decline in

---

[7] The debate about class voting is also reflected in discussion between the main contributors within the field. Many of these contributions are included in Clark and Lipset (2001).

class voting; the average decline was 47 percent of the original strength in the late 1970s (based on the Alford and Thomsen indices), and 36 percent for kappa index for four social classes. The decline in class voting was largest in Denmark and the Netherlands, then Britain, France, and Italy and smallest in Belgium, Germany, and Ireland. Knutsen also found strong correlations between the various measures of class voting.

Both studies found the decline in class voting is greatest in the countries where class voting has been largest, in particular the Nordic countries. Thus, class voting is converging to a fairly low level across western democracies.

Knutsen (2006) found that total class voting was declining by examining the correlations between party choice treated as a nominal-level variable and the EG-classes. However, the decline in class voting is smaller when several social classes were examined (as the findings based on the kappa index referred to above indicated) and when all parties are included in the analyses. Nevertheless, there is a significant decline. Class voting was largest for support for the communist, social-democrat (who got strongest support from workers), and liberal parties (who got strongest support from employers and service class), and smallest for the greens, Christian democrats, and the nationalist parties (Knutsen 2006).

8.2 Class Voting in Some West European Countries

8.2.1 *France*

Studies of French electoral sociology have come to different conclusions regarding the strength of class voting over time. Lewis-Beck (1984) analyzed data from 1958 to 1981 and concluded that "social class continued to shape party choice with undiminished force" (Lewis-Beck 1984). Weakliem and Heath (1999a) analyzed total class voting and traditional class voting from the mid-1940s to 1992. They found considerable fluctuation in total class voting over time but no long-term trend, but they showed a considerable decline for traditional left–right class voting. The Alford index declined from around 30 to 10 percentage points during the period. Another study showed that the Alford index declined from around 20 percentage points in the 1970–80s to less than 5 in the 2002 elections (Cautès 2004).

Boy and Mayer (2000, 157–61) found a clear decline in class voting between manual and non-manual employee groups regarding support for the socialist parties from 1978 to 1997. The workers had increasingly declined from supporting the leftist parties and increasingly supported the National Front. The self-employed class was, however, still strongly supporting the established right-wing parties. They concluded by stating that "the principle differences exist no longer between manual workers and clerical workers, but between the self-employed and wage earners, with a resurgence of the left among salaried upper and middle classes compensations for its decline among the working class" (Boy and Mayer 2000, 161). Given that the non-manual employees comprise five times as large a portion of the workforce in France, class voting has nevertheless declined largely.

8.2.2 *Germany*

In Germany Dalton (2003) found a clear decline in class voting based on the German Election Studies from 1953 to 2002. The decline in class voting was primarily caused by changes in the new middle-class vote. This stratum moved from the CDU/CSU camp in the 1950s to the SPD in the 1970–80s. Schnell and Kohler (1995) similarly found a strong decline in the explanatory power of social class on party choice in Germany based on data from 1953 to 1992 and statistical methods from the "third generation." Most of the decline takes place from 1953 to around 1970.[8] Other studies also find a clear decline in class voting (Pappi 1990; Pappi and Mnich 1992).

Walter Müller's (1999) examined surveys from 1976–94 and used the EGP class schema and divided the service class into three groups according to the relationship to organizational power and the tasks performed. Müller found "a quite astonishing constancy in the differences in party orientation among the antagonists of the classical class cleavage" (Müller 1999, 178).

8.2.3 *Scandinavia*

Class voting has been comparatively very high in Scandinavia. Class voting was 44 and 51 percentage points according to the Alford index in the first election studies in Norway and Sweden. In Denmark the Alford index of class voting was about 50 points in the mid-1960s. Class voting has gradually declined in these countries to about 30 percentage points around 1990. In Denmark and Norway there was a dramatic further decline to only 6 percentage points in 2001/2002, while the level of class voting in Sweden was stable at 25–9 percentage points (Knutsen 2004*b*).

More specifically, class voting declined because workers supported the socialist parties to a smaller extent than previously, while the new middle class increased their support for the socialist parties. Differences in class voting between the wage-earner classes decreased for social democrats and the rightist (conservative and radical right combined) parties. However, "class voting" increased for the left socialist parties,

---

[8] Schnell and Kohler coupled their findings to Ulrich Beck's individualization hypothesis. See the debate about the decline in the influence of social class and religion and the coupling of these findings to Beck's hypothesis which followed the publication of Schnell's and Kohler's article (Müller 1997; Jagodzinski and Quandt 1997) and the reply of Schnell and Kohler (1997). Nieuwbeerta and Manza (2002) show a clear linear decline in total class in Germany from 1969 to 1998. In their six-nation study the decline is largest in Australia, Britain, and Germany.

which have concentrated their support among the new middle class. These findings strongly support the perspective of the "two lefts" which are rooted in different social classes (Knutsen 2001).

8.3 Eastern Europe

The general shape of the cleavage structure underpinning the post-communist party systems in eastern and central Europe has been studied from different angles. By some observers post-communist societies were unorganized in intermediate civic groups, and these societies lacked social differentiation and ideological commitments that might structure attitudes and party choice. The political parties that emerged were not programmatic parties, but were charismatic and clientelistic parties that lacked societal and political anchors. Other researchers countered this *tabula rasa* hypothesis and argued that it left little room for variations within and across post-communist polities (see Evans and Whitefield 1993; Whitefield 2002). For example, Whitefield (2002) identified the social and political factors that might shape cleavages in post-communist systems in a causal chain from pre-communist historical and cultural factors, in the form of communist rule or transition from it, in the institutional choices and party strategies and in the character of economic and social post-communist experiences itself.

Evans and Whitefield (2000) conducted the broadest empirical investigation of political divisions in eastern Europe based on twelve countries in the mid-1990s. They found a variety of social and ideological bases of party competition. Social class (apart form the urban-rural division regarding farmers versus other classes) was only among the significant predictors of party choice in a few countries.

The literature on social cleavages emphasized the impact of social class on party choice when eastern European voters in several countries voted post-communist, left-wing successor parties into parliamentary power beginning in 1993. Several authors argued that the values and cultural issues that had dominated the first years of post-communist politics were partly replaced by an economic left–right axis and class politics (Kitschelt 1992; Szelényi, Fodor and Hanley 1997). The supposed increase in class was linked to the conflicts related to the pace and extent of market reforms (Pettai and Kreuzer 1999). These reforms transformed the class structure and created larger income and wealth inequality (Slomczynski and Shabad 1997).

Restitution and privatization led to the emergence of a class of proprietors and entrepreneurs, and the growth of this new class contributed to the formation of traditional class cleavages. Due to delayed modernization of industrial structures, the size of the working class had not declined, which meant that is still represented a significant social force (Mateju and Reháková 1997).

However, only in Russia and the Czech Republic do such perspectives receive considerable empirical support. Evans and Whitefield (1999) found that class political alignments in Russia became more left–right/working-middle class by the mid-1990s, increased in magnitude accordingly, and have remained relatively stable since. They argued that as voters learned about the class implications of markets and about the party system in the new democracy, they exhibited a growing capacity to link their class position to their partisan choices. These differences remain stable even as "catch-all" or "surge" parties increase their level of popular support. This perspective is supported by evidence that economic left–right orientations and economic experiences strongly—and increasingly over time—reduce the direct impact of social class on voting when these variables are included as intermediate variables in a causal analysis.

Similar results appeared in other post-communist nations. According to Mateju and Reháková (1997; Mateju, Reháková, and Evans 1999), the increase in the vote for the Czech Social Democrats during the 1990s was accompanied by a class-party realignment caused by the crystallization of political interests and attitudes in the electorate. Szelényi, Fodor, and Hanley (1997) find similar trends towards increased class voting in Hungary and Poland although the pattern for Poland is "weaker and more contradictory."

However, these patterns do not apply to all eastern European countries. In a comparative analysis of five east European countries (Bulgaria, Czech Republic, East Germany, Hungary, and Poland) and nine west European countries based on data from the 1990s, Gijsberts and Nieuwbeerta (2000, 411–15) found that total class voting was much weaker in the eastern European countries. In these countries, hardly any class differences in voting behavior existed, except for the Czech Republic. Moreover, in Bulgaria and Hungary, patterns of class voting were opposite to those found in the west. The non-manual classes voted more left-wing than members of the manual classes. The authors also examined class differences in economic left–right attitudes and found similar class contrasts in the east and west. These economic values did not explain differences in class voting in the eastern countries apart from in the Czech Republic, as they did in the west (Gijsberts and Nieuwbeerta 2000, 414–20). In brief, the cleavage structure had not crystallized according to the economic left–right class cleavage.

8.4 Asia

In Japan, class voting has been consistently low. In the 1950s, the main difference between the conservatives and the socialists arose from a conflict between traditional and modern values; age and education were the major determinants of the vote, not social class. Watanuki (1967, 456–60) labeled this pattern of conflict "culture politics."

During the 1960s, these cultural issues declined in importance, and social class became more important. Farmers and employers have been the strongholds for the Liberal Democratic Party (LDP), while white-collar and blue-collar workers have voted similarly from the 1960 to the late 1980s. Among employees, unionized employees were much more likely to support the left, while the non-unionized supported the LDP or the new parties in the center. The impact of union member-ship was similar for the wage-earners (Flanagan 1984; Watanuki 1991). These patterns seem to have continued into the 1990s (Watanuki 2001).

In India, social class is only weakly related to party support. A major explanation is that the dominant Congress Party was a heterogeneous, catch-all, centrist party, which developed its support in the independence movement, thereby allowing it to mobilize voters who were first mobilized into mass politics during the independence movement (Chhibber and Petrocik 1989). Supporters of the Congress Party represent a variety of social classes and occupation groups, religions, and languages. For example, in the 1971 election the Congress vote was 15 percentage points higher among the lower classes than among the higher classes in urban areas, while there was no class effect in the rural areas (Chhibber and Petrocik 1989). However, the Congress Party and other parties mobilized different social groups in different states in the federal structure, and intergroup party conflicts are more geographically specific. This implies that within the various states the class cleavage has been substantial.

During the 1990s, the Indian party system changed largely and the dominance of the Congress party came to an end. The right-wing Bharatiya Janata Party (BJP) emerged as the largest party in parliament. This party mobilized Hindu, middle-class, and forward caste voters. Class voting and other types of cleavage voting increased considerably at the national level (Chhibber 1999).

8.5 Latin America

Dix (1989, 26–9) argued that the coming of universal suffrage and political mobilization in Latin America did not produce the kind of class-mass parties familiar in the West. Instead, catch-all parties are the predominant type of party in Latin America in the 1980s and later. Single-class parties have tended to be relatively peripheral to party systems that have revolved around an axis of one or more multi-class parties. Additional structural explanations for the low level of class voting are the small size of the industrial working class compared to employees in agriculture and the service sector and the weaker union movement (Dix 1989).

Torcal and Mainwaring (2003) found that class had a modest influence on party choice in Chile in the 1990s. Unskilled workers, skilled workers, and marginalized self-employed were most likely to supported the centre-left, while the service class, the petty bourgeoisie and the routine non-manual were more likely to support the parties of the right. They also compared the impact of social class in 1973 (before the military coup) and in the 1990s. The impact of social class before the period of military dictatorship was larger than in the 1990s. Class voting declined because the political elites were aware of how disastrous the extreme polarization of class issues had been in earlier periods. Therefore, the party leaders played down class and redistributive themes and underscored the desirability to restore democracy.

In an extensive comparative analysis of seven Latin American and seven west European countries in the mid-1990s, Mainwaring and Torcal (2003) found that class voting was much weaker in Latin America than in the West. The authors did not find any consistent trends among the Latin American countries for some classes to vote for specific party families. For example, the service class was not significantly more likely to support the parties of the right and skilled workers only engaged in class voting in a few of these comparisons. Arguments that conservative parties have an upper-class core constituency and that left parties have a pronounced working-class base are not accurate for Latin America.[9]

9 THEORETICAL EXPLANATIONS FOR VARIATION IN CLASS VOTING

A new set of studies by Nieuwbeerta (Nieuwbeerta 1995; Nieuwbeerta and Ultee 1999) and Knutsen (2006) try to explain the changes in class voting over time or to explain the differences between advanced industrial countries.[10]

The decline in class voting has occurred in a period of post-industrial transformation. The transformation of labor markets produced a dramatic shift in the employment structure, often referred to as "deindustrialization" whereby employment in service industries increased, and employment in manufacturing decreased considerably. The size of the working class also decreased, while the number of white-collar workers, and service workers in particular, increased. These transformations were accompanied by considerable economic growth and rising prosperity (post-Second World War until the early 1970s), although growth rates have since declined. Analysts often argue that these transformations generated growing economic and social insecurity, despite the economic growth, for large sections of the populations. This insecurity is frequently associated with an increase in unemployment, and unstable labor markets. Social inequality had also risen in many advanced industrial

---

[9] Torcal and Mainwaring control for religious activity (church attendance) and urban/rural residence in their analysis of the class cleavage.

[10] Some studies discuss the causes of cross-national variations for a limited number of countries at a specific time (Alford 1964), while other studies use only a few explanatory variables (Korpi 1983; Weakliem and Heath 1999a).

societies, and tighter fiscal constraints reduced the capacity of governments to cope with new problems through expansion of the public sector (Iversen and Wren 1998). Some of these factors might increase class voting, but class voting has been declining (independent of the way it is measured). However, some of these factors might explain the cross-national variation in class voting.

Deindustrialization and the transformation of the class structure are often coupled with the rise of other social cleavages and value-based conflicts that replace or supplement the class cleavage, and the increasing influence of these other cleavages could therefore cause a decline in class voting (Dalton, Beck, and Flanagan 1984; Inglehart 1984, 1990).

Several variables may explain the levels of class voting in advanced industrial societies. Some of the variables primarily explain the comparative differences in class voting, whole others explain changes in class voting over time within countries.

Economic Prosperity. Several analyses of declining class voting assume that economic prosperity decreases class voting. Rising incomes, improved standards of consumption, the spread of home ownership, and greater leisure in the working class lead affluent workers to identify with the middle classes and embrace its attitudes and lifestyles (Goldthorpe et al. 1968). Feelings of class solidarity and the attachment to labor unions also weaken in advanced industrial society (Dalton, Beck, and Flanagan 1984). This produces a decline in support for socialist parties among the working class.[11] Class-voting levels are lower in the more prosperous countries, and decrease over time when the standard of living increases.

Unemployment. Lipset's extensive discussion of electoral political sociology maintains that leftist voting is associated with insecurity, and groups with high unemployment rates should strongly vote for the left. Lipset finds support for this thesis from studies of different countries (Lipset 1981). Since the working class have less secure employment and are more likely to be unemployed than others, a high level of unemployment could cause a high level of class voting.

The relationship between unemployment and class voting has not been discussed theoretically and is seldom examined empirically. The literature on support for the New Radical Right parties emphasizes that these parties get strong support from marginalized and underprivileged social groups like unskilled workers, and unemployed and jobless persons (Betz 1994). With higher unemployment, these groups might vote for the radical right, thereby contributing to a decrease in left–right class voting. However, Weakliem and Heath (1999*a*, 116) do not find a significant impact of unemployment on class voting in analyses of class voting in Britain, France, and the United States.

Employment in Industry. The decline in industrial employment and the increased employment in the service sector is a major trait of a post-industrial society. Class voting is declining over time partly for the same reasons as those formulated in connection with the decline of the working class (discussed below), and partly because

---

[11] An extensive test of the thesis for social democratic parties in Scandinavia did not support the thesis (Sainsbury 1985).

deindustrialization implies that new conflicts over material and non-economic issues supplants the class cleavage in advanced welfare states.

The Size of the Working Class. Parties no longer appeal to class issues related to the economic left–right dimension to the same degree as previously. The main leftist parties cannot successfully appeal to all groups and they face an electoral tradeoff in appealing to different groups of voters. Przeworski (1980; Przeworski and Sprague 1986) formulated the best-known discussion of this perspective. Left parties whose core constituencies are manual workers face an electoral dilemma: Since the working class is an electoral minority, these parties must also appeal to middle-class voters if they are to win elections. However, such strategic maneuvers have class-demobilizing effects because these parties presumably lose workers' support when they appeal to the middle classes. When social democrats extend their class appeal to other social classes, they cannot appeal to interests and issues specific to workers as a collectivity—those that constitute the public good for workers as a class—but only those that workers share with other social classes (Przeworski 1980). In brief, class voting decreases when the size of the working class diminishes.

Union Density. Previous research found that the higher the level of union density, the higher the level of left–right class voting. This relationship is, however, ambiguous for two reasons: (1) a higher level of unionization among the non-manual strata increases the probability that these groups will vote for the left, thereby decreasing the level of traditional left–right class voting, and (2) not all unions have been socialist or linked to the left parties.

Despite the ambiguity of unionization among the non-manual classes, union density among employees is strongly linked to class voting. Researchers have found a strong correlation between union density and class voting based on eighteen OECD countries in the 1970s and a larger set of west European countries over a longer time span (Korpi 1983).

Income Inequality. Income differences are closely related to standard of living between social classes and social strata. When income inequality is large between social classes, this may foster class voting since classes will win or lose more in an economic sense by voting for a leftist or a rightist party (Nieuwbeerta and Ultee 1999).

Religious Fragmentation and the Size of the Secular Group. The religious cleavage tends to cut across the class cleavage because religious voters tend to vote for the Christian parties, regardless of their social class. Therefore, class voting should be lower in countries with a high level of religious fragmentation.[12] One might also argue that the size of the secular or religiously unaffiliated segment of the population is important. Class voting is most evident among the secular segment because the cross-cutting character of the religious cleavage occurs among the religious segment.[13]

---

[12] Religious and ethno-linguistic heterogeneity (fragmentation) is also strongly associated with the electoral strength of the leftist parties. Religious and ethno-linguistic fragmentation decreases the strength of the left in a comparative setting (Bartolini 2000). This might be associated with the lower level of left–right class voting in highly religious and ethno-linguistic systems because workers in these settings vote for non-socialist parties.

[13] The fragmentation measurement accounts for the number and respective sizes of religious denominations, in addition to the size of the non-religious group. It is questionable whether the size of the various religious denominations in religiously mixed countries affects the level of class voting. In addition, the fragmentation measurement is problematic regarding the size of the unaffiliated group.

Left–Right Polarization. Left–right polarization in the party system is also connected to class voting. A large polarization implies that there are clear differences between the parties regarding the dominant class issues, while smaller differences imply that choices are less clear regarding class issues (Evans, Heath, and Payne 1999). If there is a convergence of the two main left and right parties, segments of the working class become alienated from the left, and may be tempted to vote for the right, even the radical right. According to many observations and empirical studies, such convergence between the major left-wing and right-wing parties has occurred in many advanced industrial countries (Kitschelt 1995; Knutsen 1998).

The Impact of New Politics Values. Some theories argue that New Politics issues, such as environmental quality and cultural issues, will gradually replace Old Politics issues and the core of Old Politics cleavage—social class (Inglehart 1984; Kitschelt 1994, 1995). As New Politics issues begin to cause significant party conflict, and transform the political space in advanced democracies, the class cleavage may become weaker. The old class cleavage is partly turned upside down since higher educated service-class voters support the New Left parties, and a portion of the working class supports the New Right parties.

10 COMPARATIVE ANALYSES OF EXPLANATIONS OF CHANGES IN CLASS VOTING

Nieuwbeerta (1995; Nieuwbeerta and Ultee 1999) analyzed some of these explanations of the comparative differences in class voting over time in twenty countries. He found that four variables were significantly correlated with the level of class voting across nations: union density, the percentage of manual workers, religious-ethnical diversity, and income differences. The three first correlations were in the expected direction. However, class voting was largest in countries with the smallest income differences. In the longitudinal analysis, the standard of living and the percentage of manual workers correlated significantly with class voting in many countries.[14]

Knutsen (2006, ch. 7) analyzed a larger set of explanatory variables but with fewer countries (eight) and a shorter time span (from the mid-1970s to the late 1990s). He analyzed all three types of class voting mentioned above. He found that the level of class voting was significantly correlated with level of unemployment, union density, the size of the working class, the portion of the workforce working in industry,

---

[14] In addition the percentage of mobile persons decreased the level of class voting over time. Class mobility is an additional factor to the list of explanatory factors in this chapter.

economic prosperity, and the size of the secular group in the expected directions. Income inequality and the impact of New Politics values on the party system were also correlated with the two measures of class voting based on the EG-class variable. The analysis showed that three variables correlated with the decline in class voting in all eight countries: GNP per capita, the size of the working class, and the portion of the workforce employed in industry. Union density, the impact of New Politics, the overall polarization in the party system, and the left–right distance between the major leftist and rightist parties were correlated with changes in class voting in 4–5 of the eight countries.

The analysis of explanation of trends in class voting focused in particular on the changes in the party systems and the political strategies of political parties. *A detailed empirical investigation of changing location of the major parties and political strategies of the major leftist parties showed a consistent pattern where a decisive move towards the centre was accompanied with a decline in class voting* (Knutsen 2006).

Finally in a pooled cross-sectional time-series analysis, union density, the size of the working class, the portion of the workforce employed in industry and (with a strong negative correlation) GDP per capita had the strongest correlations with class voting. Income inequality and the size of the secular group were negatively correlated with class voting, but these correlations were less robust. The ideological distance between the largest left-wing and right-wing parties was positively correlated with class voting. Regression analyses show that union density, the size of the working class and the size of the workforce employed in industry had significant effect on total class voting. The impact of union density was generally the largest and most consistent predictor.

11 Conclusions

Class voting was generally largest in western democracies during the industrial phase, although there was considerable cross-national variation in the strength of the class cleavage. Class voting is much lower in Asia, Latin America, and in the emergent democracies in eastern and central Europe. In these latter regions, there is no trend towards class dealignment. There are some trends towards an increasing impact of social class on the vote. All evidence indicates however, that class voting in these countries will remain lower than in the western countries during the industrial phase.

Class voting is definitely declining in advanced western democracies. Traditional indicators for the post-industrial transition can explain the decline in class voting from an industrial to an advanced industrial society: Growing prosperity, the decline of the workforce that is workers and work in industry. The decline in class voting is also strongly associated with the centrist strategies of the main political parties of the left and right.

How would class voting develop in the future and what would the study of class voting focus upon? Given the importance of structural variables connected with the post-industrial transformation for explaining the decline in class voting, it is natural to predict that class voting will remain low. The convergence between the political parties also appears to persist. However, if larger left–right polarization between the political parties emerges, for example regarding welfare state retrenchment, class voting might increase.

Class-voting studies should increasingly focus more on total class voting and overall left–right class voting, instead of traditional class voting. In particular, total class voting should focus on party families as the basis for comparative studies of class voting instead of the left–right division of parties.

Studies of social class effects on voting behavior will increasingly use interaction models where other variables are analyzed in connection with social class. Such interaction variables will include, for example, organizational tasks at work, sectoral employment, and political-economic marked locations like whether one works in the sectors exposed to international competition or sectors oriented towards domestic and local markets.

Whether such interaction models are significant, or whether these latter variables would explain voting behavior much better than social class remains to be seen. If these interaction models do not yield significant results, class-voting studies will be seen as increasingly irrelevant, and alternative structural variables will supplant studies of social class and voting behavior, not only supplement it.

REFERENCES

ALFORD, R. 1964. *Party and Society. The Anglo-American Democracies.* London: Rand McNally.

BARTOLINI, S. 2000. *The Political Mobilization of the European Left, 1860–1980: The Class Cleavage.* Cambridge: Cambridge University Press.

BETZ, H. 1994. *Radical Right-Wing Populism in Western Europe.* Basingstoke: Macmillan.

BOY, D., and MAYER, N. 2000. Cleavage voting and issue voting in France. In *How France Votes*, ed. M. New York: Chatham.

BROOKS, C., and MANZA, J. 1997. Class politics and political change in the United States, 1952–1992. *Social Forces*, 76: 379–408.

CAUTÈS, B. 2004. Old wine in new bottles? New wine in old bottles? Class, religious and the vote in the French electorate. In *The French Voter: Before and after the 2002 Elections*, ed. M. Lewis-Beck. Basingstoke: Palgrave Macmillan.

CHHIBBER, P. 1999. *Democracy without Associations: Transformation of the Party System and Social Cleavages in India.* Ann Arbor: University of Michigan Press.

—— and PETROCIK, J. 1989. The puzzle of Indian politics: Social cleavages and the Indian party system, *British Journal of Political Science*, 19: 191–210.

CLARK, T., and LIPSET, S. eds. 2001. *The Breakdown of Class Politics: A Debate on Post-industrial Stratification.* Baltimore: Johns Hopkins University Press.

DALTON, R. 2003. Voter choice and electoral politics. In G. Smith, et al., *Developments in German Politics.* London: Macmillan.

DALTON, R., BECK, P., and FLANAGAN, S. 1984. Electoral change in advanced industrial democracies. In *Electoral Change in Advanced Industrial Democracies*, ed. R. Dalton, S. Flanagan, and P. Beck. Princeton: Princeton University Press.

DIX, R. 1989. Cleavage structures and party systems in Latin America. *Comparative Politics*, 22: 23–37.

ERIKSON, R., and GOLDTHORPE, J. 1992. *The Constant Flux: A Study of Class Mobility in Industrial Societies*. Oxford: Clarendon Press.

—— —— and PORTOCARERO, L. 1979. Intergenerational class mobility in three Western European societies: England, France and Sweden. *British Journal of Sociology*, 30: 415–41.

EVANS, G. 1999. Class and vote: disputing the orthodoxy. In *The End of Class Politics? Class Voting in Comparative Context*, ed. G. Evans. Oxford: Oxford University Press.

—— HEATH, A. and PAYNE, C. 1991. Modeling trends in class/party relationship 1964–87. *Electoral Studies*, 10: 99–117.

—— —— —— 1999. Class: Labour as a catch-all party? In *Critical Elections: British Parties and Voters in Long-Termed Perspective*, ed. G. Evans and P. Norris. London: Sage.

—— and WHITEFIELD, S. 1993. Identifying the Bases of Party Competition in Eastern Europe, *British Journal of Political Science*, 23: 521–48.

—— —— 1999. The emergence of class politics and class voting in post-communist Russia. In *The End of Class Politics? Class Voting in Comparative Context*, ed. G. Evans. Oxford: Oxford University Press.

—— —— 2000. Explaining the formation of electoral cleavages in post-communist societies. In *Elections in Central and Eastern Europe: The First Wave*, ed. H. Klingemann, E. Mochmann, and K. Newton. Berlin: Sigma.

FLANAGAN, S. 1984. Electoral change in Japan: a study of secular realignment. In *Electoral Change in Advanced Industrial Societies*, ed. R. Dalton, S. Flanagan, and P. Beck. Princeton: Princeton University Press.

FRANKLIN, M. 1984. How the decline in class voting opened the way to radical change in British politics. *British Journal of Political Science*, 14: 483–508.

—— MACKIE, T., VALEN, H., et al. 1992. *Electoral Change: Responses to Evolving Social and Attitudinal Structures in Western Countries*. Cambridge: Cambridge University Press.

GIJSBERTS, M., and NIEUWBEERTA, P. 2000. Class cleavages in party preferences in the new democracies in Eastern Europe: a comparison with Western nations. *European Societies*, 2: 397–430.

GOLDTHORPE, J. 1980. *Social Mobility and Class Structure in Modern Britain*. Oxford: Clarendon Press.

—— 1982. On the service class, its formation and future. In *Social Class and the Division of Labour*, ed. A. Giddens and G. Mackenzie. Cambridge: Cambridge University Press.

—— 1995. The service class revisited. In *Social Change and the Middle Classes*, ed. T. Butler and M. Savage. London: UCL Press.

—— 1999. Modeling the pattern of class voting in British elections, 1964–1992. In *The End of Class Politics? Class Voting in Comparative Context*, ed. G. Evans. Oxford: Oxford University Press.

—— et al. 1968. *The Affluent Worker: Political Attitudes and Behavior*. Cambridge: Cambridge University Press.

HEATH, A., JOWELL, R., and CURTICE, J. 1985. *How Britain Votes*. Oxford: Pergamon Press.

HEATH, A. et al. 1991. *Understanding Political Change: The British Voter 1964–87*. Oxford: Pergamon Press.

—— and SAVAGE, M. 1995. Political alignments within the middle classes, 1972–89. In *Social Change and the Middle Classes*, ed. T. Butler and M. Savage. London: UCL Press.

HOUT, M., BROOKS, C., and MANZA, J. 1993. The persistence of classes in post-industrial societies, *International Sociology*, 8: 259–77.

—— —— —— 1995. The democratic class struggle in the United States, 1948–1992. *American Sociological Review*, 60: 805–28.

INGLEHART, R. 1984. The changing structure of political cleavages in Western societies. In *Electoral Change in Advanced Industrial Societies*, ed. R. Dalton, S. Flanagan, and P. Beck. Princeton: Princeton University Press.

—— 1990. *Cultural Shift in Advanced Industrial Society*. Princeton: Princeton University Press.

IVERSEN, T., and WREN, A. 1998. Equality, employment, and budgetary restraint: the trilemma of the service economy. *World Politics*, 50: 507–46.

JAGODZINSKI, W., and QUANDT, M. 1997. Wahlverhalten und Religion im lichte der Individualisierungsthese: Anmerkungen zu dem Beitrag von Schnell und Kohler. *Kölner Zeitschrift für Soziologie und Sozialpsychologie*, 49: 761–82.

KITSCHELT, H. 1992. The formation of party systems in East Central Europe. *Politics and Society*, 20: 7–50.

—— 1994. *The Transformation of European Social Democracy*. Cambridge: Cambridge University Press.

—— 1995. *The Radical Right in Western Europe: A Comparative Analysis*. Ann Arbor: The University of Michigan Press.

KNUTSEN, O. 1998. Expert judgments of the left–right location of political parties: a comparative longitudinal study. *West European Politics*, 21 (2): 63–94.

—— Social class, sector employment, and gender as party cleavages in the Scandinavian countries: a comparative longitudinal study, 1970–95. *Scandinavian Political Studies*, 24: 311–50.

—— 2004a. *Social Structure and Party Choice in Western Europe: A Comparative Longitudinal Study*. Houndmills: Palgrave Macmillan.

—— 2004b. Voters and social cleavages. In *Nordic politics*, ed. K. Heidar. Oslo: Universitetsforlaget.

—— 2005. The impact of sector employment on party choice: a comparative study of eight West European countries. *European Journal of Political Research*, 44: 593–621.

—— 2006. *Class Voting in Western Europe. a comparative longitudinal study*. Lanham, Md.: Lexington.

KORPI, W. 1983. *The Democratic Class Struggle*. London: Routledge & Kegan Paul.

KRIESI, H. 1998. The transformation of cleavage politics: the 1997 Stein Rokkan lecture. *European Journal of Political Science*, 33: 165–85.

LASH, S., and URRY, J. 1987. *The End of Organized Capitalism*. Cambridge: Polity Press.

LEWIS-BECK, M. 1984. France: the stalled electorate. In *Electoral Change in Advanced Industrial Societies*, ed. R. Dalton, S. Flanagan, and P. Beck. Princeton: Princeton University Press.

LIPSET, S. 1981. *Political Man: The Social Basis of Politics*. London: Heinemann.

—— and ROKKAN, S. 1967. Cleavage structure, party systems, and voter alignments: an introduction. In *Party Systems and Voter Alignments*, ed. S. Lipset and S. Rokkan. New York: The Free Press.

LOCKWOOD, D. 1995. Introduction: Marking out the middle class(es). In *Social Change and the Middle Classes*, ed. T. Butter and M. Savage. London: UCL Press.

MAINWARING, S., and TORCAL, M. 2003. The political mobilization of class voting: Latin America and Western Europe in the 1990s. Paper presented at the American Political Science Association's annual meeting. Philadelphia, August 27–31.

MANZA, J., and BROOKS, C. 1999. *Social Cleavages and Political Change: Voter Alignments and U.S. Party Coalitions.* Oxford: Oxford University Press.

—— HOUT, M. and BROOKS, C. 1995. Class voting in capitalist democracies since World War II: dealignment, realignment, or trendless fluctuation? *Annual Review of Sociology,* 21: 137–62.

MATEJU, P., and REHÁKOVÁ, B. 1997. Turning left or class realignment? Analysis of the changing relationship between class and party in the Czech Republic, 1992–96. *East European Politics and Societies,* 11: 501–42.

MATEJU, P., REHÁKOVÁ, B., and EVANS, G. 1999. The politics of interests and class realignment in the Czech Republic, 1992–1996. In *The End of Class Politics? Class Voting in Comparative Context,* ed. G. Evans. Oxford: Oxford University Press.

MÜLLER, W. 1997. Sozialstruktur und Wahlverhalten: Eine Widerrede gegen die Individualisierungsthese. *Kölner Zeitschrift für Soziologie und Sozialpsychologie,* 49: 447–60.

—— 1999. Class cleavages in party preferences in Germany—old and new. In *The End of Class Politics? Class Voting in Comparative Context,* ed. G. Evans. Oxford: Oxford University Press.

NIEUWBEERTA, P. 1995. *The Democratic Class Struggle in Twenty Countries 1945–1990.* Amsterdam: Thesis Publishers.

—— and MANZA, J. 2002. Klassen-, Religions- und Geschlechterspaltungen: Parteien und Gesellschaften in vergleichender Perspektiv. In *Das Ende der politisierten Sozialstruktur?,* F. Brettschneider, J. van Deth, and E. Roller. ed. Opladen: Leske & Budrich.

—— and ULTEE, W. 1999. Class voting in Western industrialised countries, 1945–1990: systematizing and testing explanations. *European Journal of Political Research,* 35: 123–60.

PAPPI, F. 1990. Klassenstruktur and Wahlverhalten im sozialen Wandel. In *Wahlen und Wähler: Analysen aus Anlass der Bundestagswahl 1987,* ed. M. Kaase and H. Klingemann. Opladen: Westdeutscher Verlag.

—— and MNICH, P. 1992. Germany, in *Electoral Change: Responses to Evolving Social and Attitudinal Structures in Western Countries,* ed. M. Franklin, T. Mackie, and H. Valen. Cambridge: Cambridge University Press.

PETTAI, V., and KREUZER, M. 1999. Party politics in the Baltic states: social bases and institutional context, *East European Politics and Societies* 13: 148–89.

PRZEWORSKI, A. 1980. Social democracy as a historical phenomenon. *New Left Review,* 20: 27–58.

—— and SPRAGUE, J. 1986. *Paper Stones: A History of Electoral Socialism.* Chicago: Chicago University Press.

ROKKAN, S. 1966. Norway: numerical democracy and corporate pluralism. In *Political Oppositions in Western Democracies,* ed. R. Dahl. New Haven: Yale University Press.

ROSE, R., and MCALLISTER, I. 1986. *Voters Begin to Choose: From Closed-Class to Open Elections in Britain.* London: Sage.

SAINSBURY, D. 1985. The electoral difficulties of the Scandinavian social democrats in the 1970s: the social bases of the parties and structural explanations of party decline. *Comparative Politics,* 18: 1–19.

SÄRLVIK, B., and CREWE, I. 1983. *Decade of Dealignment: The Conservative Victory of 1979 and Electoral Trends in the 1970s.* Cambridge: Cambridge University Press.

SAVAGE, M. 1991. Making sense of middle-class politics: a secondary analysis of the 1987 British election survey. *Sociological Review,* 39: 26–54.

SCHNELL, R. and KOHLER, U. 1995. Empirische Untersuchung einer Individualisierungshypothese am Beispiel der Parteipräferenz von 1953–1992. *Kölner Zeitschrift für Soziologie und Sozialpsychologie* 47: 634–657.

—— —— 1997. Zur Erklärungskraft Sozio-Demographischer variablen im Zeitverlauf. *Kölner Zeitschrift für Soziologie und Sozialpsychologie*, 49: 783–95.

SLOMCZYNSKI, K., and SHABAD, G. 1997. Systemic transformation and the salience of class structure in East Central Europe. *East European Politics and Society*, 11: 155–89.

SZELÉNYI, I., FODOR, É., and HANLEY, E. 1997. Left turn in postcommunist politics: bringing class back in? *East European Politics and Societies*, 11: 190–224.

TORCAL, M., and MAINWARING, S. 2003. The political re-crafting of social bases of party competition: Chile, 1973–95. *British Journal of Political Science*, 33: 55–84.

WATANUKI, J. 1967. Patterns of politics in present-day Japan. In *Party Systems and Voter Alignments*, ed. S. M. Lipset and S. Rokkan. New York: The Free Press.

—— 1991. Social structure and voting behavior. In *The Japanese Voter*, ed. S. C. Flanagan. New Haven: Yale University Press.

—— 2001. Japan: from emerging to stable party system? In *Party Systems and Vloter Alignments Revisited*, ed. L. Karvonen and S. Kuhnle. London: Routledge.

WEAKLIEM, D., and HEATH, A. 1999a. The secret life of class voting: Britain. France, and the United States since the 1930s. In *The End of Class Politics? Class Voting in Comparative Context*, ed. G. Evans. Oxford: Oxford University Press.

—— 1999b. Resolving disputes about class voting in Britain and the United States: definitions, models, and data. In *The End of Class Politics? Class Voting in Comparative Context*, ed. G. Evans. Oxford: Oxford University Press.

WHITEFIELD, S. 2002. Political cleavages and post-communist politics. *Annual Review of Political Science*, 5: 181–200.

....

CHAPTER 25

THE EFFECTS OF RELIGION AND RELIGIOSITY ON VOTING BEHAVIOR

....

YILMAZ ESMER

THORLEIF PETTERSSON

THE significant role played by religion on shaping election outcomes is as old as the ballot box itself. From its day of inception, electoral politics has been significantly influenced by the "divine." The degree of this impact has varied in time and space, but it would not be an exaggeration to state that "worldly concerns" have yet to enjoy a complete reign over voting decisions anywhere on the globe. This chapter tries to show that this statement is valid in all types of societies including the post-industrial and highly developed ones.

Although the accuracy of the figures is debated, it is estimated that there are roughly 2.1 billion Christians, 1.3 billion Muslims, 900 million Hindus, 376 million Budhists, and 14 million Jews in the world. Of the 6.5 billion (**www.prb.org**) inhabitants of the globe, almost 85% belong to a religion, while those classified as "secular/nonreligious/agnostic/atheist" number about 1.1 billion (**www.adherents. com**). For the majority of people in the world, religion is much more important in their lives than politics. The World Values/European Values Surveys, for example, asked almost

100,000 people around the world how important politics and how important religion was in their lives. According to these surveys, for about 16 percent of the world's population, politics is more important than religion; for about 29 percent they are equally important; and for the remaining 55 percent religion is more important than politics. Religion is a very important factor in people's lives and its relation to politics and particularly electoral behavior is the focus of this chapter.

Religion's enviable status as *the* source of political legitimacy for so many centuries was seriously challenged, at least in the Occident, by the ideas of the Enlightenment. It may come as a surprise to many that neither the "positivist revolution" nor the processes of rapid industrialization and modernization spelled an end to religious influences on politics in general and voting preferences in particular as predicted by the secularization theory. Yet for others, religion in some form or another is *the* answer to a basic human need; part of the *condition humaine*, so to speak. Thus, it follows that religion always has and will continue to exert considerable influence on human behavior, political or otherwise. This is obvious even if one limits oneself to the first few years of the twenty-first century and to the most affluent societies of the world. From the heated discussions on the now defunct constitution of the European Union to laws on stem cell research and to the American presidential elections, the pervasive role of religion in politics is all too evident to ignore even in those societies where the Enlightenment has had its greatest impact.

This chapter delineates the extent to which religion influences political and, in particular, voting behavior in the contemporary world and, data permitting, attempts to identify the major factors behind this influence.

A meaningful starting point for the analysis of the interaction of religion and politics is the intellectual movement that is broadly referred to as the Enlightenment which, above all, was a concerted effort to dethrone religion (no doubt, some Enlightenment thinkers would have liked to banish it altogether) and replace it with human rationality and the scientific method. "The Enlightenment was eager to deny religious transcendence and to affirm that everything was to be found within a single, orderly System of Nature" wrote Gellner (1992, 82) who pointed out that one of the basic tenets "of scientific method, of the cognitive procedure discovered in the course of the Scientific Revolution and codified by the Enlightenment" is the refusal to allow any "privileged or a priori *substantive* truths" and to grant equal status to "all facts and truths." This, he argued "at one fell swoop, eliminates the sacred from the world" (Gellner 1992, 80). Indeed, at its very core, the Enlightenment was a direct challenge to the basic teachings and doctrines of the church. From that viewpoint, secularization in the modern sense of the term is the offspring of the Enlightenment (Girvin 2000).

If rationality is to govern all human action and if science and the scientific method rather than revelation and divine authority are to guide the course of human development, it follows that governments should also be organized according to these same principles. Put differently, politics needs no guidance from religion.

Legal-rational authority, to use Weber's terminology, is a natural outcome of the philosophy of the Enlightenment.

Indeed, the Enlightenment thinking found its way into the political sphere without delay and served as a source of inspiration for both the American Constitution and the French Revolution, although the two nations took very different paths with respect to the role of religion in government and in society at large. These two very dissimilar interpretations of secularism have existed to date and are very much alive in the United States and France, respectively. From a historical perspective, the American Declaration of Independence and the Constitution sought to protect religion and religious freedoms of citizens. Experience had taught the Founding Fathers that governments could and would seriously curtail religious freedoms and attempt to suppress "unofficial" religions and denominations. This threat against individual religious freedoms was very much in the minds of the authors of the American Constitution who took great pains to prevent such an undesirable outcome. In de Tocqueville's eloquent words, it is one of the fundamental principles of the "Republic" that "every man is allowed freely to take that road which he thinks will lead him to heaven" (de Tocqueville 1945, 436). Therefore, Article 1 of the Bill of Rights of the Constitution of the United States stipulates that "Congress shall make no law respecting an establishment of religion, or prohibiting the exercise thereof." It is entirely consistent with this tradition that the United States Department of State regularly publishes reports on religious freedom in the World, focusing on the regulation and restriction of religious faith and practices by governments. From this perspective, how religions may restrict the state and the political sphere is not an issue that deserves much attention. Hence, the wide use of religion and religious symbols in government is viewed as compatible with this brand of secularism. American secularism, it seems, can coexist with assigning religion—Christian religion, to be specific—a highly visible standing in the political arena. Religion is an important ingredient of the political debate in that country. In contrast, the United States Supreme Court has upheld secular principles on several occasions handing down decisions which, to some, appeared as outright anti-religious. Thus, in this particular brand of secularism, even brief morning prayers are not allowed in public schools but government buildings can openly display religious symbols and the Bible is permitted, even required, to be an indispensable paraphernalia of the court system.

In contrast, French secularism, or *laicité*, placed paramount importance on keeping religion at a comfortable distance from government. The French Revolution was not very sympathetic to religion, to say the least. The so-called Jacobins took an openly hostile view of religion and aspired to abolish the Catholic Church. Jacobin rule was brief but the understanding that the state needs to be protected from religion just as much as the citizens' religious freedoms have to be protected from state interference has prevailed. The French Constitution declares the secular characteristic of the Republic and France most strongly opposed the proposal to include a reference to God in the proposed (and subsequently rejected) European Union Constitution. It is noteworthy that the rise of Islamic fundamentalism in Europe prompted certain western European governments led by France to resort to this notion of secularism in banning all religious symbols from public schools.

More than two centuries after the American and the French Revolutions, the question of how much religion is to be allowed in governmental affairs is still not resolved even in secular countries. Both ideologically and in practice, Europe can be said to be the most secular region in the world. Nevertheless, at the beginning of the twenty-first century, France and Turkey are the only two among the EU member or candidate countries that include an explicit reference to secularism in their constitutions and make it a defining characteristic of the state.

By and large, Europeans have freedom *from* religion if they so choose. Yet, the separation of state and church is hardly an undisputed fact even in Europe. Although it has no practical significance, the monarch of the United Kingdom is still the head of the Anglican Church. The influence of the Catholic Church in the political life and laws of such countries as Poland, Ireland, and Malta is apparent. The Orthodox Church is extremely visible in the public and the political sphere in Greece. As noted above, whether the draft constitution of the European Union would make a reference to the "Christian heritage of Europe" was a matter for serious debate. As a compromise, the draft did not include a reference to the Christian heritage but did mention the "religious heritage." Can a secular constitution refer to religion, any religion, in any context? The strictly secularist answer to this question is an emphatic no. Nevertheless, Ireland stands at the other extreme. The Preamble of the Constitution of Ireland starts like a hardcore religious text with references to the Holy Trinity and Jesus Christ.[1] Greece is another case "where more traditional church-state norms are maintained" (Girvin 2000, 21), as well as other examples.[2] Thus, even in "secular" and "secularizing" Europe, states can have official religions and constitutions can read like Vatican edicts.

We are all aware that religion has some impact on political and voting behavior in all societies and we know that the magnitude of the effect is highly variable. One existing framework for explaining this variability is secularization theory. We now briefly consider the basic claims and predictions of the secularization theory with a view to their relevance for the relationship between religion and voting.

1 Secularization Theory

"Secular" is a rather ambiguous term referring to more than one concept.[3] Secularization can refer to a characteristic of the government. One can also talk about a

---

[1] "In the Name of the Most Holy Trinity, from Whom is all authority and to Whom, as our final end, all actions both of men and States must be referred, We, the People of Eire, humbly acknowledging our divine obligations to our Divine Lord, Jesus Christ...." Preamble of the Constitution of the Republic of Ireland.

[2] The Constitution of Poland, to cite but one example, mentions "our culture rooted in the Christian heritage of the Nation." However, it is noteworthy that the Polish Constitution refers explicitly to those who believe in God and those "not sharing such faith" and guarantees equal rights to both.

[3] For a brief excursion into the origins of the term, see Berger 1969, 106 ff.

"secular society" where the role of religious institutions on non-religious spheres (e.g. economic and social matters, international relations, etc.) has been minimized. Adopting this viewpoint, Berger defines secularization as "the process by which sectors of society and culture are removed from the domination of religious institutions and symbols" (Berger 1973, 113). In agreement, Chaves (1994) argues that it is more productive to define secularization not in terms of a religious decline, but rather "as the declining scope of religious authority."

In addition to "secular governments" and "secular societies," there are "secular individuals." At the micro-level, too, the term has a range of meanings extending from the person for whom religion is a private matter of faith that does not interfere with his/her behavior pertaining to non-religious matters[4] all the way to the person who has no place for religion in any sphere, that is, the agnostic or the atheist. Therefore, it is necessary to avoid using secular and non-secular as mutually exclusive categories with no overlap but rather to view *secularization as an ongoing process*.

Secularization theory asserts that modernization, a process that is inseparable from rational thinking, will decrease the need for and the significance of religion both at the macro- and the micro-levels. The passage from the traditional to modern society (which the early modernists saw as inevitable) is not good news for organized religion or any faith looking for an authority beyond the physical world. The move from "traditional" to "modern" involves related changes in various spheres. Most significant is the transition from an agrarian to an industrial (and later on post-industrial) mode of production; increasing levels of economic welfare for all citizens; high levels of specialization; greater mass participation particularly in political life; drastically lower fertility rates; and, perhaps most importantly for our concerns here, the ever-increasing emphasis on secular mass education. Mandatory education with curricula based on human rationality and the scientific method directly challenges the teachings of traditional religion. Secularization theorists have argued that all of these developments would minimize the role of religion in modern society where, to the extent that it existed at all, it would be a private affair of the individual, providing certain rules of moral conduct. The effect of religion on social and political spheres would be minimal.

Many of the founding scholars of sociology were advocates of secularization theory in one form or another. "The seminal social thinkers of the nineteenth century—August Comte, Herbert Spencer, Emile Durkheim, Max Weber, Karl Marx, and Sigmund Freud—all believed that religion would fade in importance and cease to be significant with the advent of industrial society" (Norris and Inglehart 2004, 3). From Marx's well-known definition of religion "as the opium of the masses," that is, as an instrument the ruling classes use to pacify the oppressed, to Durkheim's more favorable approach,[5] the common thread of thought is that

---

[4] This is referred to as the compartmentalization of the mind similar to structural differentiation at the societal level. See, for example, Dobbelaere (2002).

[5] While joining others in rejecting the supernatural character of religion and agreeing that it was a product of society, Durkheim nevertheless assigned a positive function to this "man-made institution." Religion, in Durkheim's view, enhances solidarity and is essential for the proper functioning of the social system.

religion and religious explanations are basically non-scientific and that religion is a human construct. In a society where the young are socialized in secular schools for long years and where the traditional culture is no longer supported by the new structures, there would be little need for superstitions and metaphysical explanations. Whether it was going to be Comte's positivistic stage, or Marx's classless society, or Weber's legal-rational authority that would characterize the future of advanced societies, the role of religion would necessarily be much more limited and confined.

Variants of secularization theory have been popular in mainstream modern sociology as well until very recently. Gorski (2003, 111) notes that except for Parsons "postwar sociologists of religion all agreed that the public influence of religion was shrinking, and many thought that private belief itself was bound to decline or even disappear." This basic understanding of secularization at the macro-level is shared even by those who have declared that "it is high time to bury most of the commonly shared assumptions of a steadily declining religion at the graveyard of failed theories" (Stark and Finke 2000).

However, secularization theories have recently been the object of bitter criticism. Some went so far as to suggest that "secularization should be erased from the sociological dictionary" in an article aptly entitled "Towards Elimination of the Concept of Secularization" (Martin 1969). Secularization theories have even been accused of being used "to legitimate myths about the decline in moral standards in contemporary life. By doing so they tend to become divorced from their original coordinates of space and time, and hence appear to justify notions for which they had little or no relevance at the outset." Thus, the concept has "attained a mythological significance in the study of society similar to that of scientific myths in the natural sciences" (Glasner 1977, 9).

Although most secularization theorists agree on the differentiation at the macro-level between religion and secular society, there is much disagreement on the extent and the consequences of this differentiation.

One line of argument assumes that popular religious involvement has decreased over time. A common measure of this decline in religiosity is the decrease in church attendance rates particularly manifest in western Europe, where there is strong evidence of a continued trend toward less religion (see, for example, Casanova 1994; Dogan 1996). To quote Gorski (2003, 110) "The trends are quite clear: In most parts of the West, Christian belief and practice have declined significantly, at least since Word War II, and probably for much longer." Broughton and ten Napel (2000b, 2) concur: "The overwhelming evidence [in Europe] of the last thirty years is that fewer and fewer are attending church, that respect for Church traditions and norms has declined rapidly and that even amongst the remaining 'faithful', the motivations for and justifications of 'religious behavior' are often mixed and blurred." A conspicuous exception to secularization theories that is still awaiting a plausible explanation is the United States, where church attendance levels are not only much higher than most of Europe but also have somewhat increased over time (Stark and Finke 2000).

Another line of argumentation is that the differentiation between religion and the secular society leads to the privatization of the former. It is assumed that as religious and secular institutions become differentiated, religion remains significant to personal and private matters (Turner 1991). Thus, religion is assigned basically to the home—family life, love, intimacy—and becomes a matter of individual and private taste. Secularization, thus understood, does not call for a decline in individual religiosity and will not concern itself with public and political matters.

Researchers have recently questioned the privatization of religion thesis. Critics argue that examples such as the obvious political significance of North American Protestant fundamentalism, the popularity enjoyed by Evangelical Christianity particularly in the United States, the strong impact of Catholicism on the Sandinista revolution in Latin America, or the strong Catholic basis of the Solidarity movement in Poland demonstrate that contemporary religion refuses to accept the marginal role given to it by secularization theories. The recent rise of political Islamism, the new or the renewed interest in Eastern as well as unconventional religions, the immense prestige and recognition recently enjoyed by the Vatican, are all assumed to further demonstrate that, in fact, contemporary religion has *de*-privatized and has become increasingly relevant for the political sphere. These and similar developments have shaken the conviction in the validity of secularization theories. The assumption that macro-level differentiation of the religious and the political spheres must necessarily lead to the privatization of religion is no longer tenable (Casanova 1994).

In addition, there is no denying that, apart from directly influencing policy decisions and laws, religion is a major force in determining election outcomes as well. The American and the Iranian presidential elections of 2004 and 2005, respectively, are only two most recent and well-known examples.

Thus, today, the main prediction of the secularization theory faces serious challenge. Berger, once a forceful defender of secularization theory, previously wrote that "the same secularizing forces have now become worldwide in the course of westernization and modernization. Most of the available data, to be sure, pertain to the social-structural manifestations of secularization rather than to the secularization of consciousness, but we have enough data to indicate the massive presence of the latter in the contemporary West" (Berger 1969, 108). What happened to the "universal process" and the "massive evidence?" Berger (1999) now believes that the basic prediction of secularization theory has simply proven to be false.[6] He is seemingly overwhelmed by a "resurgence of religion" and now argues that secularization is certainly not the rule but rather the exception. He further states that "religious movements and institutions that have made great efforts to conform to a perceived modernity are almost everywhere on the decline" (Berger 1999, 6) and relates modernity to what he sees as an unmistakable rise in orthodox and fundamentalist movements with reference to the human intolerance for uncertainty. Since modernity "undermines all the old certainties" people eagerly accept anything that promises to

---

[6] For arguments challenging the predictions of secularization theories, see: Casanova 1994; Haynes 1998.

remove this uncomfortable state and restore certainty. Now, this turns secularization theory upside down: modernization brings about uncertainty which in turn creates a demand for orthodox religions since these leave no room for doubt or uncertainty. In other words, modernization increases fundamentalism, conservatism, and ortho- doxy! A rather paradoxical and ironic outcome indeed.

Whether the contemporary world is secularizing or desecularizing is a hotly debated issue. Published in the same year as *The Desecularization of the World* (Berger 1999), Halman and Riis's (1999) study is entitled *Religion in Secularizing Society* as if to emphasize the scholarly disagreement on the matter. Norris and Inglehart (2004) also take issue with the desecularization thesis and find evidence that confirms at least a modified version of secularization theory. They analyze the European/World Values Survey and conclude that the outlook for secularization theory is not as bleak as some argue. They show that with respect to both practice and faith, religiosity has been declining in advanced industrial societies over the last half-century. These societies have moved towards secularism. The United States is the major and well-known exception to this otherwise predictable trend. However, Norris and Inglehart add that the move towards more secular societies and more secular individuals in the most advanced industrial societies does not mean that religiosity is decreasing globally. Quite to the contrary, the number of traditionally religious people is increasing in absolute terms. The explanation is simply related to differential fertility rates in the first and third worlds. At the core of Norris and Inglehart's revised theory is the empirical observation that secularism is strongly correlated with economic security and affluence. They "believe that the importance of religiosity persists more strongly among vulnerable populations, especially those living in poorer nations, facing personal survival-threatening risks" (Norris and Inglehart 2004, 4).

Norris and Inglehart present ample evidence to demonstrate their point. However, as a simple test, we look here at the correlations between the importance of God in one's life[7] and the UNDP's 2002 Human Development Index as well as the individual components of this composite index (UNDP 2004). If modernization leads to secularization, then we should observe negative correlations between the importance of God in one's life and Human Development indicators that are commonly used as measures of modernization. Indeed, data from sixty-five countries ranging from the wealthiest and most developed to the poorest do yield significant negative correl- ations with the Human Development Index and with every one of its three com- ponents. The Pearson r coefficients between the importance of God scale and the Human Development Index, as well as its components, are:

Human Development Index	−.648
Life Expectancy 2002	−.501
Education Index 2002	−.669
GDP 2002	−.581

[7] This variable is taken from the World Values and European Values Surveys. It is a ten-point scale about the importance of God in respondent's life. Surveys were conducted roughly around the year 2000.

Interestingly, the correlations between the importance of God and the Human Development Index as well as the Education Index are greater than the correlation between two components (i.e. between education index and life expectancy index) of the HDI. At least at the macro-level, it is difficult to refute the prediction of the secularization theory. In addition, the negative correlation is strongest between importance of God and the Education Index component of the Human Development Index. Transmitting rational thinking and scientific method, which is the basic function of the modern school system, does have the effect the Enlightenment thinkers wished for and predicted, at least when aggregated data are analyzed.

A number of studies using different indicators of religiosity have confirmed these findings. Norris and Inglehart (2004, 59) note that "religious participation, values and beliefs remain widespread in poorer developing nations, but today they engage less than the majority of the publics in the most affluent postindustrial societies." The authors emphasize that both Pew Global Attitudes Survey and the Gallup International Millennium Survey validate these patterns. According to the former, in the forty-four countries surveyed, "all wealthier nations except the United States place less importance on religion than in poorer developing countries" (Norris and Inglehart 2004, 62).

2 "SUPPLY-SIDE" THEORIES

A relatively recent critique of secularization theories is referred to as "the supply side theories of religion" which challenge the claim that modernization necessarily leads to secularization.[8] Supply-side theories argue that the degree of religiosity in a society is determined by the nature of the "religious market" in that society. In places where a given religion or denomination enjoys a monopoly, lack of competition leads to complacency, resulting in lower church attendance and generally lower levels of religiosity. In direct analogy to the market, competition should stimulate higher productivity and better performance which translate into more and better "customers" for the competing "products." Thus, facing the threat of losing their congregations to the competition, churches work harder to spread their gospel and this results in increased levels of religiosity. To complete the free market analogy, state regulation of religion is presumed to be negatively correlated with religiosity. Religious involvement is assumed to increase as religious markets offer more choice *and* are free of government intervention.

---

[8] As we pointed out above, the United States stands out as the most blatant exception to the contentions of secularization theories See, for example, Finke and Stark (1992; 2003).

Explaining levels of religiosity by the degree of competition may have some validity for the United States and may also help to explain some of the variance at the community level. Aggregated society-level data may mask the diversity effects that are observable when the unit of analysis is the community (Hamberg and Pettersson 2002). Nevertheless, supply-side explanations fail the test in a number of places. For example, in many Islamic societies where this religion enjoys as perfect a monopoly as one can find, religiosity—both belief and practice—are among the highest in the world. According to the World Values Surveys, four of the five nations with the highest proportions of persons defining themselves as religious are pre-dominantly Muslim (and *predominantly the same denomination within Islam*) and the sixth nation is overwhelmingly Catholic.[9] Furthermore, there is considerable variation in the levels of religiosity among societies where one can meaningfully speak of a competitive religious market. For such societies, Jelen and Wilcox (2002, 318) "hypothesize that the market metaphor which underlies 'supply side' theories of religious adherence and participation is simply irrelevant when the possibility of religious switching seems remote."

3 RELIGION IN POLITICS

Scholars cannot agree on what determines the levels of religiosity in a given society or whether religious practice and belief are rising or declining in the contemporary world. However, there is agreement that the divorce between religion and politics—if there ever was one—has never been complete. Ronald Reagan once said that "religion and politics are necessarily related" (quoted in Wald 1987, 1). This is the case despite the Enlightenment, massive industrialization and post-industrialization, the phenomenal spread of mass education, scientific advances, and unprecedented economic welfare and security in the West. Indeed, "one of the central points of tension since the Enlightenment has been between religion and politics" (Girvin 2000, 7). Therefore, the appropriate question in analyzing the association between religion and politics is not whether or not the relationship exists. It does. Instead, one should ask:

a. To what extent is religion still effective in shaping political institutions and processes at the macro-level?
b. To what extent is individual political behavior affected by religion?

[9] Inglehart et. al. (2004, table F 034). These six countries are: Egypt (99% religious, 94% Muslim); Bangladesh (97% religious, 83% Muslim); Nigeria (97% religious, 50% Muslim, 40% Christian); Iran (95% religious, 99% Muslim); Morocco (95% religious, 99% Muslim); Poland (94% religious, 95% Catholic).

c. Does the variance in the strength of the relationship at both macro- and micro-levels conform to the predictions of the major theories that claim to explain this variance?

In these questions, religion and religiosity are the independent variables. More specifically, one should look at the effects of belonging to a certain religion or denomination; the effects of the level of religiosity within a given religion or denomination; and the effects of the degree of religious homogeneity within a given society.

A full treatment of all of these questions is beyond the scope of this chapter. Thus, we limit ourselves to one specific but important aspect of political behavior, voting, and offer some insights into the relationship between religion, religiosity, and electoral choice.

Studies of voting behavior and religion fit into two broad categories. The first category includes studies that compare the electoral choices of voters belonging to different religions or denominations. Second, there are attempts to correlate levels of religiosity—both belief and practice—with voting behavior. Studies that belong to the first category outnumber those in the second group mostly due to the literature that emanates from the United States. Although the more common tendency is to assign socioeconomic and demographic factors the primary role in explaining electoral behavior, hardly any study of American voters has failed to observe the impact of religion on the choice of parties and candidates.

One of the relatively earlier studies[10] of American voting behavior found that "No matter what demographic variable is controlled, the relationship between Catholic affiliation and party preference significantly remains. Not only that, but the religious affiliation (and the ethnic differences it represents) appears to be a stronger influence upon vote than any other single factor" (Berelson, Lazarsfeld, and McPhee 1954, 65). Many studies in widely differing locations have confirmed this finding. American Catholics, Jews, and Protestants of differing churches have been analyzed repeatedly with respect to their voting behavior.[11] It is now almost common knowledge that religion is important in American politics. In the elections of the last few decades, Catholics and Jews have been more likely to vote Democratic while certain Protestant denominations and particularly Evangelicals have been much more supportive of Republican candidates. The latter have played a major role in determining the outcome of the 2000 and 2004 presidential elections in the United States.[12]

The importance of religion as a determinant of voting is confirmed in comparative studies as well. In 1969, Rose and Unwin's (1969) study of sixteen Western nations concluded that religion was a more important factor than social class in explaining voting behavior. Ten years later, Lijphart (1979, 442) reached the same conclusion in a

[10] Stuart A. Rice, who published in the 1920s is generally credited with the first voting study of an academic nature.

[11] For earlier works, see, for example, Berelson, Lazarsfeld and McPhee (1954); Campbell, et al. (1960); Lenski (1963); Lipset and Rokkan (1967). Some examples of the more recent works are: Nie, Verba, and Petrocik (1976); Hertzke (1988); Miller and Shanks (1996); Layman (2001); Leege, et al. (2002).

[12] Extensive and very useful data on religion and religiosity in the United States are available at www.thearda.com

different set of western democracies noting that "Among the determinants of party choice, religion emerges as the victor, language as a strong runner up, and class a distant third." Recently, in a longitudinal study of eight western European countries covering the period 1970 to 1997, Knutsen (2004, 99) concluded that "Despite the paucity of explicitly religious issues and the lack of religious themes in most campaigns, religious beliefs have proven to be a strong predictor of party choice in many western European democracies."

These and many other similar studies that conclude that religion is an important predictor of vote have two things in common. First, their conclusions concern western democracies. This is understandable given that competitive free elections are a prerequisite for the subject matter of these studies. Furthermore, surveys on voting behavior are a relatively new phenomenon outside the western world. Second, the independent variable in these studies is religion (belonging or not belonging to particular faiths) and not religiosity.

However, in analyzing the relationship between religion and politics, a second question is the level of an individual's commitment to a particular faith. There is a fundamental difference between being a devout and deeply committed member of a faith and belonging to it nominally. Therefore, in the context of voting studies, the term religious cleavage should also consider the potential differences between the devoted and the secular.

There is evidence that the degree of religiosity may explain even more of the variance in electoral choice than religious denomination. Deeply dedicated Protestants and Catholics in a given society may make similar electoral choices which are different from the choices of the uncommitted members of their own church. As a case in point "In Germany, for example, the main religious divide appears to be between those who are better integrated into their church and those who are not, rather than on the basis of a purely denominational division between Protestants and Catholics" (Broughton and ten Napel 2000c, 203). Manza and Wright (2003, 306) point out that "A number of analysts have argued that a religiously rooted set of cultural conflicts have emerged, with religious conservatives of all denominations lined up on one side and liberals and seculars on the other." In contrast, there are at least two aspects of religious commitment: practice, very often operationalized as attendance, and faith. In one of the earliest empirical studies on the topic, Lenski (1963) distinguishes between religion (denomination), doctrinal orthodoxy, and devotionalism and separately explores the effects of these dimensions on political, social, and economic life.

Most studies that analyze the religiosity dimension use church attendance as the independent variable (Knutsen 2004, 99). Jagodzinski and Dobbelaere (1995) use the term "church religiosity" to refer to this aspect of religiosity. Clearly, church attendance is not the ideal indicator of religious commitment and practice. While some religions, for example Catholicism, emphasize and require regular attendance at church services, this is not the case for others. Furthermore, going to church can, in many places, be interpreted as a social rather than a religious commitment. We need better measures of religiosity.

The "Importance of God" scale is a good indicator of faith for the adherents of the three monotheistic religions, although it has debatable value outside the Christian, Islamic, and Jewish communities. Luckily, several international survey programs, such as the WVS, the ISSP, and the CSES, include multiple indicators of religious practice and faith as well as electoral choice (see chapter by Kittilson in this volume). With the availability of longitudinal and comparative data from these surveys, we are now in a much better position to tackle some important questions for a good number of societies. Among them:

a. Is the process of secularization moving along as predicted or have we entered an era of desecularization?
b. Is modernization or the structure of religious markets a better predictor of religiosity? Or could it be that both have validity under certain conditions?
c. How is religion related to voting behavior and party choice? Is denomination or degree of religiosity a better predictor of electoral behavior?

4 SECULARIZATION OR DESECULARIZATION?

Of the various meanings of the term we mentioned above, we are here referring to secularization at the level of the individual. Thus, the establishment of a theocratic government in a given country does not mean that the individuals in that society as a whole become less or more secularized. Similarly, citizens of a highly secularized country can become progressively more religious. A case in point is the United States where court decisions consistently change political institutions in a secularist direction but the larger population, by and large, moves in the opposite direction.

It is hard to disagree with Berger (1999) that we cannot, by any stretch of the imagination, assume that we live in a seculariz*ed* world. That is not the question, however. The question is whether or not we live in a seculariz*ing* world. Berger (1999, 12) predicts "with some assurance" that "There is no reason to think that the world of the twenty-first century will be any less religious than the world today." From this viewpoint, the world is not secularizing and will not secularize in the twenty-first century; if anything, the trend is in the opposite direction.

We believe a more balanced answer to the secularization-desecularization question calls for a conditional answer: it depends on where you are looking. For instance, one would be hard put to deny the secularization process that has been occurring in Europe (particularly western Europe). The disagreement is whether, from a global perspective, this is an exception or part of a wider trend. According to Eurobarometer data, church attendance has declined in nine out of ten western countries during the two decades between 1978 and 1998 (Norris and Inglehart 2004, 72). The only seeming exception is Italy where the decline had started earlier and stabilized in the 1980–90s.

Europe, by and large, has been secularizing and there is no reason to think that this trend will reverse in the decades to come. An equally well-known fact is that in the United States, religion is as important as ever. That being the case, as a rule, religiosity (both practice and belief) in affluent societies is either decreasing or already low. Unfortunately, we do not have systematic data for the developing world. We know that religion is much more important in these societies, but it is difficult to speak about general trends due to the lack of long-term data. Globally, however, available evidence is largely in favor of theories that predict a negative correlation between religiosity on the one hand and economic and human development on the other.

5 MODERNIZATION OR DIVERSITY?

With societies as the unit of analysis, Norris and Inglehart conclude that the evidence is not supportive of supply-side explanations. They find no significant relationships between religious diversity and religiosity. They write:

Contrary to the predictions of supply-side theory, the correlations between religious pluralism and religious behavior all prove insignificant in post-industrial societies... The results *lend no support to the claim of a significant link between religious pluralism and participation,* and this is true irrespective of whether the comparison focuses on the frequency of attendance at services of worship or the frequency of prayer... the theory does indeed fit the American case, but the problem is that it fails to work elsewhere. (Norris and Inglehart 2004, 100, emphasis original)

While Norris and Inglehart's global analyses fail to find any diversity effects, it is plausible to think that different religious traditions provide different contexts which might affect the relationship between the structure of religious markets and levels of religious involvement. Even a casual observation, for instance, suggests that Christian and Muslim traditions might differ in this respect. As we have mentioned, predominantly Islamic societies, where there is hardly any diversity on the supply side and where "market" regulation by the political authority is at its highest, display extremely high levels of religious involvement as well.

An analysis of thirty-seven predominantly Christian societies[13] suggests that modernization and cultural diversity may *both* be correlated with religiosity, the former negatively and the latter positively, as the respective theories would expect. The analysis, using European and World Values Survey data, is summarized in

[13] Argentina, Austria, Belarus, Belgium, Bulgaria, Canada, Chile, Croatia, Czech Republic, Denmark, Estonia, Finland, France, Germany, Greece, Hungary, Iceland, Ireland, Italy, Latvia, Lithuania, Luxembourg, Malta, Mexico, the Netherlands, Philippines, Poland, Portugal, Romania, Russia, Slovakia, Slovenia, South Africa, Spain, Sweden, Ukraine, and United States.

Table 25.1 Effects of micro- and macro-level factors on church involvement and on views concerning the role of religious leaders in politics

	Religious Involvement	Influence of Religion on Politics
Micro-level factors		
Age	.01*	.00
Gender	.32*	.07*
Education	−.02*.	−.01
Having children	.04*	.02
Life satisfaction	.04*	.00
Macro-level factors		
Human well-being	−.03*	−.01
Cultural diversity	.26	.16*
Catholic tradition	1.20*	−.17.
Orthodox tradition	.83	−.24

Note: Unstandardized regression coefficients from two multi-level hierarchical linear regressions. Coefficients significant at .001 level are marked by an asterisk.

Source: 1999–2000 EVS/WVS data for 39,200 respondents from 37 countries.

Table 25.1, which reports the effects (regression coefficients)[14] of individual-level variables, human well-being, cultural diversity, and denomination. Cultural diversity does seem to have a positive impact on religiosity or on attitudes toward the role of religion in politics. Important though it is, modernization may not be the sole universal cause for religious decline.

If it is true that modernization (security, affluence, education, etc.) decreases the importance of religion, and if cultural/religious diversity effects are in the opposite direction as Table 25.1 suggests, we find ourselves in a rather paradoxical situation. Modernization means lower levels of religiosity. Modernization also means more diversity. But diversity has a positive impact on religiosity. Therefore, in a rather roundabout way, modernization can mean more and not less religion. Berger's reasoning about modernity being a factor that supports fundamentalism was mentioned above. Taking both arguments into consideration, can modernization indeed increase religiosity and fundamentalism? Clearly, more analyses, preferably with

[14] For readers who are not statistically oriented, regression coefficient denotes the unit of change in the dependent variable when the independent variable changes by one unit. For instance, reading from Table 25.1, one unit increase in "cultural diversity scale" is expected to produce 0.26 units of increase in "religious involvement scale" while other independent variables are held constant. By the same token, one unit of increase in the level of education is expected to decrease religious involvement by 0.02 units. Multi-level analysis estimates regression coefficients for different units of analysis simultaneously. Thus, it allows us to consider, for instance, individual, community and society level variables in the same equation.

longitudinal data and in different institutional and structural contexts, are needed to solve this puzzle.

6 RELIGION AT THE BALLOT BOX

Manza and Wright (2003, 299–300) distinguish four religious cleavages that can affect voting behavior.[15] We have noted the need to differentiate between at least two different meanings of religious voting: (*a*) voting according to one's religion or religious denomination; and (*b*) voting according to one's level of religious commitment. Most studies of religion and voting behavior concentrate on the effects of the former on electoral choice. If secularization theory is accurate in its predictions, "religion voting" as well as "religiosity voting" should become less and less pronounced with modernization. The content matter of the doctrine as well as global/local political and social environments will no doubt affect the speed of this process. Short-term fluctuations are also quite possible. Nevertheless, the long-term general trend should be in the predicted direction. As an example for the first effect, Catholic, Protestant, and Islamic societies, not to mention Hindu or Buddhist ones, are not expected to exhibit equal levels of secularization *ceteris paribus*. Gellner (1992, 6) is not alone in asking "Why should one particular religion [Islam] be so secularization resistant?" and thinking that "in Islam, we see a pre-industrial faith, a founded, doctrinal, world religion in the proper sense, which, at any rate for the time being, *totally and effectively defies the secularization thesis*" (Gellner 1992, 19, emphasis ours).

Islamic populations resist secularization and some of them move in the opposite direction for lengthy periods of time. But to argue that this is a "defiance of the secularization thesis" would not do justice to the theory which does not claim that great amounts of extremely ill-distributed wealth will lead to secularization. Affluence and material security of *the masses* is only one aspect of modernization. It is the whole modernization syndrome, not just one slightly observable symptom that should lead to secularization. Thus, Islam's problem is more likely to lie elsewhere, that is, its resistance to modernization (Huntington 1996). A few figures from the *2002 Arab Human Development Report*[16] should lend enough support for this viewpoint. For instance, total factor productivity in the Arab world decreased between 1960 and 1990 while it increased rapidly in most other parts of the world. The per capita output in twenty-two Arab countries is half of what it is in Korea. In 1999, the total GDP in all Arab countries combined was less than that of Spain alone. At the present rate, decades will elapse before illiteracy is eradicated or education enrollments reach the level attained by developed countries in the mid-1990s. Around

---

[15] The four cleavages that Manza and Wright (2003) identify are: "(a) church attendance; (b) doctrinal beliefs; (c) denominational groups; and (d) local/contextual aspects of congregational membership."

[16] 2002 is the first year that the UNDP released a Human Development Report for the Arab Region.

15 percent of the labor force is unemployed. Women hold 3.5 percent of parliamentary seats in Arab countries; and in a number of Arab countries women do not even have the legal right to vote or to run for office. One in every two Arab women is illiterate. The Arab region has the lowest ICT (Information and Communication Technologies, e.g. internet connectivity) access rate compared to any other region in the world. The number of books translated in Spain each year is about the same as the number of books translated into Arabic in the last one thousand years.

Under these conditions, secularization theory would not predict a decline in the importance of religion. Indeed, survey data indicate very high levels of religiosity in the Islamic world. In fact, comparison of Muslim and non-Muslim populations in multi-religion countries shows that the former attaches much more importance to faith than the latter (Esmer 2002*a*). It is no surprise, therefore, that when relatively free elections are held in the Islamic world—which itself is a rare phenomenon—Islamist groups make a very strong showing. Islam, and even radical Islam, is very much present at the election polls. The election of Mahmoud Ahmadinejad as the President of Iran in August 2005 and the electoral victory of Hamas in Palestine a few months later are two most recent cases in point. Even in Turkey, a country with a long tradition of secularism, religiosity plays an important role in determining the outcome at the ballot box (Esmer 2002*b*). Religiosity is a major factor influencing voting behavior throughout the Islamic world.

Such a sweeping conclusion would not be appropriate for the western world where there is much more variation with respect to the impact of religion and religiosity on electoral behavior. However, a look at the changes in various indicators of religiosity between 1981 and 2000 in fourteen highly developed western societies shows that the overall trend is towards secularization, that is, a decline in the importance of religion in the lives of individuals (Table 25.2). For instance, in 1981 the proportion of those not belonging to any religious denomination in Belgium was 16.2 percent. The corresponding figure around the year 2000 was 36.5 percent, representing an increase of 125 percent. Indeed, the fourteen-country means (unweighted) for every one of the seven indicators given in Table 25.2 have changed in the expected direction. The proportion of those who do not belong to any religious denomination increases around 118 percent during these two decades. The importance of God (country means on a ten-point scale) has decreased in eleven out of fourteen countries. It remained about the same in the United States (where it was and is still the highest in the developed world) and Sweden (where it was and still is very low) while increasing only in Italy. Of the fourteen societies included in Table 25.2, Ireland is of particular interest from the secularization theory point of view. Ireland ouperformed all other societies in the table in terms of change in the Human Development Index of Ireland between 1975 and 2000 (UNDP 2005). Religiosity indicators for Ireland have also changed significantly in the direction of a more secular world-view.

The general trend in the developed world, with notable exceptions such as the United States, is towards a more secular society and more secular individuals. This should decrease the overall effect of religiosity on voting behavior. Extensive analyses of European survey data lead Jagodzinski and Dobbelaere (1995, 115) to the same

Table 25.2 Change in religiosity indicators in 14 high human development Western societies, 1981–2000

Nation	Belong to no religious denomination (%)		Attend religious service once a week (%)		Is a religious person (%)		Believe in God (%)		Shared rel. belief very important for marriage (%)		Confidence in church (%)		Importance of God -mean, 10-pt scale.	
	1981	1999	1981	1999	1981	1999	1981	1999	1981	1999	1981	1999	1981	1999
BELGIUM	16.2	36.5	30.3	17.5	81.5	67.4	86.7	70.9	28.1	18.3	65.1	40.1	5.94	5.19
CANADA	10.6	31.4	32.3	25.1	76.6	73.5	93.5	89.2	33.5	12.7	70.2	58.8	7.37	7.18
DENMARK	5.6	10.0	3.3	2.7	73.9	76.5	68.3	68.9	18.8	12.7	49.8	59.2	4.47	4.02
FRANCE	26.3	42.5	12.0	7.6	55.6	46.6	68.0	61.5	19.3	13.0	56.2	45.7	4.72	4.40
G.BRITAIN	9.3	16.6	13.8	14.4	59.2	41.6	82.6	71.8	21.2	13.7	48.6	34.4	5.69	4.92
GERMANY[a]	8.9	23.4	21.8	13.6	69.5	55.8	81.9	67.8	19.9	14.9	47.4	39.5	5.68	5.04
ICELAND	1.3	4.3	2.4	3.2	68.5	73.9	81.3	84.4	18.6	10.1	74.5	64.5	6.45	6.24
IRELAND	1.3	9.3	82.4	56.9	66.1	74.0	97.1	95.5	39.9	26.3	78.2	52.2	8.03	7.41
ITALY	6.5	17.8	36.0	40.5	85.7	85.8	89.5	93.5	25.9	23.4	60.7	67.1	6.96	7.43
N. IRELAND	3.3	13.9	52.2	48.5	62.8	62.3	96.6	93.2	41.3	32.8	71.4	43.6	7.49	7.07
THE NETHERLANDS	36.5	55.2	26.9	13.9	70.4	61.8	72.2	59.6	25.1	11.3	41.1	28.6	5.35	4.93
SPAIN	8.9	17.0	41.3	25.2	65.4	61.4	91.9	84.8	30.7	20.6	50.8	42.0	6.39	5.88
SWEDEN	6.9	24.2	5.7	3.8	34.2	38.9	60.4	53.4	17.9	12.8	39.1	45.4	4.08	4.10
USA	6.1	21.5	43.7	45.2	83.6	82.5	97.9	95.7	43.9		77.0	74.6	8.43	8.47
mean, Europe + N. America	10.6	23.1	28.9	22.8	68.1	64.4	83.4	77.9	27.4	17.5	59.3	49.7	6.22	5.88
mean, Europe	10.9	22.6	27.3	20.7	66.1	62.2	81.4	75.4	25.6	17.5	56.9	46.9	5.94	5.55

[a]In 1981, West Germany.

Source: European Values Studies, www.europeanvalues.nl

conclusion. "Politics and religion will become even more differentiated; church guidelines on political questions will no longer be accepted; they may even provoke a negative reaction. The crumbling of church integration may, in the long run, change voting patterns and the appeal of Christian parties." Some years later, Halman and Pettersson's (2004, 336) analysis of European survey data similarly concludes that there is no "widespread preference for religion to be a potent actor in the political and public realm."

Nevertheless, it would be a mistake to exaggerate the trend. Very sizeable proportions of devout individuals exist in even the most developed societies. Therefore, if any religiosity effects on voting behavior exist, they should still be observable in survey data in spite of the general trend in the opposite direction. Indeed, evidence shows that even in western Europe, religion and religiosity still have considerable impact on voting behavior. A review of politics and religion in twelve European countries confirms this conclusion. Even in the Netherlands, a highly secularized country by any measure, 40 percent of the population is of the opinion that "religion is a good guide in politics" (Broughton and ten Napel 2000a).

We do not have the space here to comment on individual countries. Recent data for seventeen European countries[17] indicate that religiosity still significantly shapes electoral choice in most European countries. We examined the relationship between party preference and three religiosity measures: religiosity scale, frequency of church attendance, and frequency of prayer. By and large, the devout and the pious are more likely to vote for the political right and the Christian Democratic parties. In thirty of the thirty-five comparisons, there is a statistically significant relationship between the religiosity measure and partisanship. In five out of seventeen countries, there is no significant relationship between any of the three indicators of religiosity and political party preferences. All of these countries are Northern European: three Scandinavian countries (Denmark, Norway, and Sweden), Estonia, and the United Kingdom.

One would have to introduce a number of control variables before reaching any definitive conclusions, but it is very doubtful that many of those statistically significant relationships will disappear altogether when one controls for socioeconomic status and demographic variables. Rather, it is reasonable to conclude that religiosity still has an effect on voting preferences in most of Europe—the most secularized region within the monotheistic world. There is also some evidence that religiosity increases the probability of electoral participation and that the higher the religiosity the more stable the individual's party preference.

The strong impact of Judaism on politics and voting behavior is also evident in Israel where "the state was originally a nationalist state for the Jewish people, but there are growing demands for it to be a religious state as well. There are also demands ... even to amend the Law of Return so as to give Orthodox rabbis the authority to determine whom the state of Israel recognizes as a Jew" (Stepan 2005, 20).

Outside of the monotheistic tradition, Japan with its lack of the concept of a life to come but with over half a century of free and competitive elections deserves some

---

[17] Data are available from http://ess.nsd.uib.no

attention. Toyoda and Tanaka (2002, 280) write that "one cross-national study ... shows that the Japanese, compared with five other nations, had the most negative reaction to religious parties." However, even in Japan, it is hard to deny the existence of some relationship between religion, religiosity, and electoral choice. For example, according to most recent World Values Survey data, the following proportions of the supporters of major parties say they "draw comfort and strength from religion:"

Liberal Democratic Party (Jiminto): 47%
Democratic Party of Japan (Minshuto): 34.7%
Clean Government Party (Komeito): 87.2%
Communist Party (Kyosanto): 27.1%

These figures show that Komeito, the major explicitly religious party (Toyoda and Tanaka 2002), draws a disproportionate amount of support from pious voters. Furthermore, as expected, the constituency of the Communist Party is the least religious of all.

India, the land of not one but many Gods, also has had its share of conflicts between the secular and the religious segments of the population. Very much like Kemalist Turkey, India initially was erected on secular-nationalist foundations. Nevertheless, today the supporters of the secular Congress Party and the traditionalist Bharatiya Janata Party have differing views on religion.

7 CONCLUSIONS

We have tried to review the available evidence as well as the theoretical wisdom concerning the relationship between religion and voting behavior. We concentrated on this one aspect of political behavior without in any way implying that other forms of political participation were of less significance. Our basic conclusions can be summarized as follows.

Evidence does not suggest that the predictions of prominent Enlightenment thinkers about the decreasing importance of religion were completely wrong. To be sure, this is not a linear process without setbacks. Nevertheless, the negative correlation between modernization (a process which, above all, emphasizes the scientific method and rational thinking) and religiosity is hard to ignore.

It follows that it would not be appropriate to send either the concept of secularization or the secularization theory to the "graveyard."

Secularization theory, however, should be amended to take into account additional factors that affect the process. Among these, the belief system and organizational structure of a religious tradition and the diversity at the religious marketplace are particularly worthy of mention. For instance, predictions of secularization theory vis-à-vis Islam can be of special interest in view of the arguments that Islam is unique in showing strong resistance to change and modernization.

Religious diversity seems to have a positive effect on religiosity especially in the United States, and perhaps in the Christian world as a whole, but it may not have much predictive use if the probability of or the opportunities for freely switching are remote.

A full explanation should also account for the social and the political context. It is possible to observe a process of desecularization when religion is used to mobilize masses for political or ideological reasons such as when religion becomes a symbol for resistance against perceived oppression, exploitation, and the like.

Religious cleavages still have a significant impact on voter behavior in many parts of the globe. This observation is valid even in many European societies which have undergone a noticeable process of secularization. Neither "religion voting" nor "religious voting" has disappeared yet but, with the possible exception of East Asia, the region where the impact of religion on voting is minimal is Scandinavia. As a general rule, the more religious a person is, the more likely he/she is to vote for a conservative or a right-of-center party. This observation, however, is not without exceptions.

With respect to the availability of data, thanks to a number of international survey programs that collect data from many societies at regular intervals, we are in a much better position to answer certain questions than we have ever been before. However, there is still a serious deficiency of longitudinal data for the non-Christian world. From a methodological perspective, multi-level analyses which can simultaneously analyze individual-, community-, and society-level data hold greater promise to widen and deepen our understanding of the complex relationship between politics and religion.

REFERENCES

Article 1 of the Bill of Rights declared on December 15, 1791.

BERELSON, B., LAZARSFELD, P., and McPHEE, W. 1954. *Voting: A Study of Opinion Formation in a Presidential Campaign*. Chicago: The University of Chicago Press.

BERGER, P. 1969. *The Sacred Canopy: Elements of a Sociological Theory of Religion*. New York: Doubleday.

—— 1973. *The Social Reality of Religion*. Harmondsworth: Penguin.

—— 1999. The desecularization of the world: a global overview. Pp. 1–18 in *The Desecularization of the World: Resurgent Religion and World Politics*, ed. P. Berger. Grand Rapids, Mich. Eeerdmans.

BROUGHTON, D., and TEN NAPEL, H. eds. 2000a. *Religion and Mass Electoral Behaviour in Europe*. London: Routledge.

—— —— 2000b. Introduction. Pp. 1–6 in Broughton and ten Napel 2000a.

—— —— 2000c. Conclusion: European exceptionalism. Pp. 198–209 in Broughton and ten Napel 2000.

CAMPBELL, A. et al. 1960. *The American Voter*. New York: John Wiley.

—— 1966. *Elections and the Political Order*. New York: John Wiley.

CASANOVA, J. 1994. *Public Religions in the Modern World*. Chicago: University of Chicago Press.

CHAVES, M. 1994. Secularization as declining religious authority. *Social Forces*, 72: 749–74.

DE TOCQUEVILLE, A. 1945 edn. *Democracy in America*. vol. i, ed. P. Bradley. New York: Vintage Books; originally published 1835.

DOBBELAERE, K. 2002. *Secularization: An Analysis of Three Levels*, Oxford: P.I.E. Peter Lang.

DOGAN, M. 1996. Erosion of class voting and of the religious vote in Western Europe. *International Social Science Journal*, 47: 525–38.

ESMER, Y. 2002a. At the ballot box: determinants of voting behavior. Pp. 91–114 in *Politics, Parties and Elections in Turkey*, ed. S. Sayari and Y. Esmer. Boulder, Colo.: Lynne Rienner.

—— 2002b. Is there an Islamic civilization? *Comparative Sociology*, 1: 265–98.

FINKE, R. and STARK, R. 1992. *The Churching of America, 1776–1990*. New Brunswick: Rutgers University Press.

—— —— 2003. The dynamics of religious economies. Pp. 96–109 in *Handbook of the Sociology of Religion*, ed. M. Dillon. Cambridge: Cambridge University Press.

GELLNER, E. 1992. *Postmodernism, Reason and Religion*. New York: Routledge.

GIRVIN, B. 2000. The political culture of secularisation: European trends and comparative perspectives. Pp. 7–27 in *Religion and Mass Electoral Behaviour in Europe*, ed. D. Broughton and H. ten Napel. London: Routledge.

GLASNER, P. E. 1977. *The Sociology of Secularisation: A Critique of a Concept*. London: Routledge & Kegan Paul.

GORSKI, P. S. 2003. Historicizing the secularization debate: an agenda for research. Pp. 110–22 in Dillon 2003.

HALMAN, L., and RIIS, O. eds. 1999. *Religion in Secularizing Society: The European's Religion at the End of the 20th Century*. Tilburg: Tilburg University Press.

—— and PETTERSSON, T. 2004. Normative orientations towards the differentiation between religion and politics. Pp. 317–39 in *European Values at the Turn of the Millennium*, eds. W. Arts and L. Halman. Leiden: Brill.

HAMBERG, E. M., and PETTERSSON, T. 2002. Religious markets: supply, demand, and rational choices. Pp. 91–114 in *Sacred Markets, Sacred Canopies: Essays on Religious Markets and Religious Pluralism*, ed. T. Jelen. Lanham, Md.: Rowman-Littlefield.

HAYNES, J. 1998. *Religion in Global Politics*. New York: Longman.

HERTZKE, A. 1988. *Representing God in Washington*. Knoxville: University of Tennessee Press.

HUNTINGTON, S. 1996. *The Clash of Civilizations and the Remaking of the World Order*. London: Touchstone.

INGLEHART, R. et. al. 2004. *Human Beliefs and Values*. Mexico: Siglio XX1 Editores.

JAGODZINSKI, W., and DOBBELAERE, K. 1995. Secularization and church religiosity. Pp. 76–119 in *The Impact of Values*, ed. J. W. van Deth and E. Scarbrough. Oxford: Oxford University Press.

JELEN, T., and WILCOX, C. 2002. The political roles of religion. Pp. 314–24 in *Religion and Politics in Comparative Perspective: The One, The Few and the Many*, ed. T. Jelen and C. Wilcox. Cambridge: Cambridge University Press.

KNUTSEN, O. 2004. Religious denomination and party choice in western europe: a comparative longitudinal study from eight countries, 1970–97. *International Political Science Review*, 1: 97–128.

LAYMAN, G. 2001. *The Great Divide: religious and cultural conflict in American party politics*. New York: Columbia University Press.

LEEGE, D. et al. 2002. *The Politics of Cultural Differences: social change and voter mobilization strategies in the post-New Deal period*. Princeton: Princeton University Press.

LENIN, V. 1967. Imperialism, the highest stage of capitalism. In *Lenin, 1897 to January 1917, Selected Works*, vol i. New York: International Publishers; originally published 1917.

LENSKI, G. 1963. *The Religious Factor: A Sociologist's Inquiry*. New York: Anchor Books.

LIJPHART, A. 1979. Religious vs. linguistic vs. class voting: the "crucial experiment" of comparing Belgium, Canada, South Africa and Switzerland. *American Political Science Review*, 2: 442–58.

LIPSET, S. M., and ROKKAN, S. eds. 1967. *Party Systems and Voter Alignments*. New York: Free Press.

MANZA, J., and WRIGHT, N. 2003. Religion and political behavior. Pp. 297–314 in *Handbook of the Sociology of Religion*, ed. M. Dillon. Cambridge: Cambridge University Press.

MARTIN, D. 1969. *The Religious and the Secular*, London: Routledge.

MILLER, W., and SHANKS, J. M. 1996. *The New American Voter*. Cambridge, Mass.: Harvard University Press.

NIE, N., VERBA, S. and PETROCIK, J. 1976. *The Changing American Voter*. Cambridge, Mass.: Harvard University Press.

NORRIS, P., and INGLEHART, R. 2004. *Sacred and Secular: Religion and Politics Worldwide*. Cambridge: Cambridge University Press.

ROSE, R., and UNWIN, D. 1969. Social cohesion, political parties and strains in regimes. *Comparative Political Studies*, 2: 7–67.

STARK, R., and FINKE, R. 2000. *Acts of Faith: Exploring the Human Side of Religion*. Berkeley: University of California Press.

STEPAN, A. 2005. Religion, democracy and the "twin tolerations." Pp. 3–23 in *World Religions and Democracy*, ed. L. Diamond, M. F. Plattner, and P. J. Costopoulos. Baltimore: Johns Hopkins University Press.

TOYODA, M. A. and TANAKA, A. 2002. Religion and politics in Japan. Pp. 269–86 in Jelen and Wilcox 2002.

TURNER, B. S. 1991. *Religion and Social Theory*. London: Sage.

UNDP. 2004. *Human Development Report 2004*. New York: UNDP.

—— 2005. *Human Development Report 2005*. New York: UNDP.

WALD, K. D. 1987. *Religion and Politics in the United States*. New York: St Martin's Press.

CHAPTER 26

RACE AND POLITICAL BEHAVIOR

SHAMIT SAGGAR

DuBois wrote that "the problem of the twentieth century is the problem of the colour line." However, it is a considerable leap from his sagacious observation to the concerns of students of political behavior. In fact research priorities of political science have been shaped as much by academic trends and reactive pursuits as any underlying claims about the centrality of race and colour in political representation and organization.

Political behavior has recently taken political inquiry in the direction of examining, empirically where possible, the underlying sources of political difference. A powerful conditioner of such difference is the idea that social identity is linked to, and largely driven by, racial or ethnic categories of political community or political collective interest. For example, a number of voting studies have demonstrated the impact of racial or ethnic background on both party choice and issue preferences. This has been clouded by the need to isolate interaction effects between race and ethnicity on one hand, and the role of social class, income, education, geography, age, gender, and additional factors on the other. Political behaviorialists have, in addition, had the responsibility to explain and quantify the significance of racial or ethnic prisms for thinking about and shaping the policy agenda. In tackling aspects of social exclusion, therefore, public policy specialists are frequently concerned with understanding why forms of disadvanatge and deprivation that are linked to factors such as poverty or education are thought of as being racial in nature by the policy, press, and electoral communities.

This insight is potentially very significant since it can underpin large, generalized assertions about the process of racialization of political identity, sentiment, and behavior. This chapter considers this insight although, to be fair, it notes that political scientists and social theorists often see far too much into associated generalizations about the role played by race in political behavior. Nevertheless, our discussion begins with the need to unpick a variety of claims about the nature of behavior that is both politically and racially related at one and the same time.

This chapter is necessarily selective in its approach and coverage. As a survey it cannot hope to be comprehensive and certain themes and debates are therefore given greater attention than others. The purpose is to draw together several central themes found in the literature, and to evaluate the broad trends in the volume of research. The interests of researchers, however, have tended to be patchy and clustered around several major topics and approaches.

1 POLITICAL BEHAVIOR AND ELECTORAL ENGAGEMENT

Basic questions of electoral engagement cannot be overlooked in studying modern politics and the involvement of ethnic minorities in elective politics requires close attention for two reasons. First, taking part in the electoral process, and exerting political leverage through the democratic decision-making process is a useful marker for involvement in mainstream society. Consequently, different levels of mainstream electoral participation among different ethnic groups may be proxy indicators of wider integration patterns. If particular racial or ethnic groups shun participation in mainstream schooling, housing, and other areas, we can surmise that electoral involvement likely follows a similar pattern, according to this argument.

The evidence, interestingly, often follows this general path but there are a number of exceptional cases. One, obvious example is the relative high levels of participation in mainstream electoral politics among urban Hispanic and African-Americans in the US, while patterns of engagement in employment and housing markets have trailed behind (Tate 1993; De La Garza and DeSipio 2004; Verba, Schlozman, and Brady 1995; Dawson 1994). This is most often linked to particular opportunity structures that are open (or sometimes pried apart) in party political institutions and local electoral law and its application via courts that are increasingly sensitized to claims of latent racial bias.

Second, the underlying reputation of liberal democracies—and increasingly among emerging democracies—can be at stake in assessing the breadth of involvement of all groups within society. Democratic processes and institutions can be harmed in the longer run, it is feared, if large pockets of the would-be electorate remain aloof from participative norms. This argument, to be sure, developed into something of a received wisdom on the question of threatened black abstention in the 2004 US presidential race. It was echoed in a number of local electoral contests in the US where concerns about racial disenfrancisement were publicly aired.

Empirical research on electoral regustration and turnout in a number of western democracies indicates a lower level of involvement and engagement among immigrant-descended ethnic minorities in comparison with whites. This implies that fairly serious mobilization problems exist and it is important to assess whether these are circumstantial and linked to social background, or not. In the meantime, these data confirm many existing suspicions that some serious problems for democratic participation exist in western democracies.

In the British case, concerns often focus on simple South Asian-black distinctions. Participation deficits are found, to varying degrees, *among* most minority groups, whilst for Indians talk of deficits is entirely misplaced. Ultimately, the real significance of these figures lies in their cumulative effect upon participation once registration (and legal eligibility) is taken into account. Electoral registration in Britain varies from one ethnic group to another, with Indians standing closest to the rate found among whites. Studies of ethnic minority voting in the UK suggest that minority registration rates are lower than that found among whites ranging from 3 to 24 points. Among South Asian groups there is scant evidence of any ethnic group falling appreciably below the 9 in 10 prevailing level. South Asian Indians lead the minority cohort with registration rates that match those of whites. Similar figures have been found in earlier local-level studies suggesting that these rates are credible. Black Africans are dramatically lower than most ethnic minorities, while black Caribbean registration rivals the very high rates seen among whites and Asian Indians. It would appear that earlier, pre-election claims about significant levels of black Caribbean under-registration were *very* wide of the mark.

Elsewhere in European countries of mass immigration, gathering realible data on electoral inclusion has been difficult. Research data that does exist generally points to lower level of engagement, arguably driven by circumstantial and socioeconomic factors as much as anything. Minority or immigrant group interest in and commitment to civic participation and culture can sometimes point to higher levels of engagement relative to the indigenous population group but systematic evidence on this front has been scant (Fennema and Tillie 2001).

The paltry turnout figures found among black Caribbeans in Britain are not reflected in their registration rate, which ranks extremely close to the "highly registered" Indians and whites. The conclusion appears to be that black Caribbean participation patterns exhibit deficiency at some point *after* registration. Electoral mobilization thus centers on why this group has such large numbers of abstainers from among those who hold registered valid votes. In the case of their black African counterparts, genuine deficits are apparent in both realms, suggesting that mobilization problems are rather more general and enduring as opposed to focused and specific. Finally, among Pakistanis and Bangladeshis it appears that mobilization problems do exist and are similarly two-pronged in character (see Table 26.1).

Table 26.1 Turnout by ethnic group, 1997 (%)

	White	Indian	Pakist	Bang	Bl-Af	Bl-Car	Misc	
Did you manage to vote in the *General Election*								
Yes	78.7	82.4	75.6	73.9	64.4	68.7	65.1	
No	21.2	17.6	24.4	26.1	35.6	30.6	34.9	
Don't know	0.0	0.0	0.0	0.0	0.0	0.7	0.0	
Total *N*	2,601	227	123	46	101	147	83	[3,328]
Total %	100.0	100.0	100.0	100.0	100.0	100.0	100.0	

Source: BES 1997, merged file.

The image of high-involvement Asian Indians in Britain is reflected in their turnout rate that exceeds whites by a far from negligible margin. The remainder of the picture is equally familiar. First, there is little to distinguish between the Pakistani and Bangladeshi turnout rates: both were reasonably high and not significantly out of line with that of whites. Second, a rather different story is told among both black Africans and black Caribbeans. In both cases, turnout rates dipped far below those of all other ethnic groups suggesting, at the minimum, the existence of a serious mobilization problem.

These low rates certainly resemble some earlier studies, and it is worth recalling that this sense of looming black political alienation in Britain and America under-pinned a number of debates about minority politics. Such debates expressed concern about black abstention on the basis of polling data that showed an even lower possible black turnout. It is hard to deny that a serious issue for democratic participation is bound up in these figures. If the factors driving significantly lower black turnout rates are other than circumstantial—that is because of geography (lower turnout associated with inner urban constituencies) or social class (generally higher among middle-class than working-class groups)—then it is likely that some fairly specific racial considerations are at play. Such considerations might reasonably include black political alienation that is based on racial exclusion and distancing from mainstream society.

Systematic patterns of discrimination, bound up with repetitive tendencies towards repressive or oppositional self-identity, cannot be ruled out as powerful processes linked with such racially defined indicators of political involvement. This is an important issue of democratic participation facing not just these communities but also democratic institutions such as political parties and elected government more generally.

In British politics, this argument on exclusion is regularly rehearsed by small yet astute black and minority pressure groups, with tacit backing from liberal commen-tators, public figures, and think-tanks. Press reports of the 1997, 2001, and 2005 general elections all gave widespread coverage to this allegation, partly articulated by reformist-minded politicians within mainstream parties and also by external pressure groups. The concern has undoubtedly been further underlined in a period with significant declines in propensity to register to vote and turn out, particularly among younger, urban based would-be electors.

France's suburban riots and disorder in autumn 2005 drew fresh attention to the argument that second- and third-generation groups from North African decent are isolated and feel unbound by larger French republican norms about civil society and mainstream political mobilization. Moreover, if non-participation cannot be accounted for in social class or circumstantial terms, one obvious worry is that democratic institutions such as political parties are at fault. At the very least, parties and politicians cannot make unfettered claims about the quality of the democratic system.

It is necessary to introduce some basic qualifications first. The most pressing need is to isolate the degree to which legal citizenship defines other rights, including voting rights. In the wake of large-scale post-war immigration, the United Kingdom tended to recognize voting rights on more generous terms than in many countries across continental Europe and indeed elsewhere. Immigration from New Commonwealth sources to the UK was usually associated with the enjoyment of full political rights by the immigrant newcomers at or shortly after the point of entry. This legacy has meant that examinations of the electoral participation of ethnic minority groups does not involve any prior assumptions as to whether these groups are likely to enjoy political rights or not. This is something of a vexed question in countries such as Germany and Italy but largely irrelevant in Britain.

There is a further variant in France where political rights exist and are assured among most ethnic minorities, and yet the nature of their political involvement and how it is described by the political parties is colorblind. The granting of voting rights to the children of children of earlier immigrants may not be at issue, but the treatment of such voting-based opportunities in electoral race is clearly the subject of great dispute. The anxiety over this mismatch is further intensified in the policy arena where uncertainty prevails in judging the degree to which racial or ethnic sensitization of public policy can follow from colorblind assessments about political behavior.

Poor registration rates amongst minorities are linked to voter disinterest and disillusionment across western democracies. Little can be done in the short run to tackle the root causes of such alienation, though pressure groups and other campaigners will encourage abstainers onto the register. The work of Operation Black Vote (OBV), jointly established by Charter 88 and the 1990 Trust a year before the UK 1997 election, is one campaign that stands out. Its central message was to encourage minority voters to place themselves on the register, equipping literally new voters with the basic tools for democratic involvement. Furthermore, OBV's cutting edge was sharpened by its genuinely non-partisan stance. The US Democratic Party's drive to recruit black and other minority groups to the point of electoral registration in 1992 is another illustration (Highton and Wolfinger 1998).

It is unlikely that parties will overlook such efforts if they can be shown to raise registration levels. The difficulty lies in assessing the relevance of this initially powerful argument beyond the participation-voter interest effects of single elections.

Understanding turnout data needs to be added to the picture, to help us distinguish between casual abstainers (citing ad hoc circumstantial factors disrupting an intention to vote), hardcore abstainers (showing no real interest in an election or its outcome) and serial abstainers (those who rarely, if ever, vote). Parties tend to focus on trying to engage those who are somewhat doubtful about going out to vote. Minority voters can pose very serious challenges in terms of large groups of abstainers thought to be highly unlikely to engage in the democratic process. Language difficulties can create further obstacles on top of this.

Taken together, various studies indicate that some identifiable variations exist in the degree to which different ethnic groups are engaged in the democratic process (see for example Lien 1994, comparing Asian-Americans with Mexican Americans as one typical study that has highlighted such variation). However, the magnitude of some of the intergroup differences is perhaps less than might be thought or predicted. Most minorities share a lot in common with most other minorities in their electoral involvement, contrasting only at the margin with their white counterparts. A few groups falls dramatically short of the underlying minority rate of engagement, though some occasionally remain above. Arguments emphasizing substantial underparticipation among minorities must take care to evaluate these variations accordingly.

2 RACE, CONFLICT, AND POLITICAL BEHAVIOR

Racial conflict and related policy issues have not occupied a major strand within academic writing on political behavior. However, the existing research has focused on major—and more familiar—questions of political science and political philosophy such as democracy, representation, and power. An illustration of this conditional interest can be seen in Myrdal's 1944 study of race relations in the United States, *An American Dilemma*, which clearly sought to address itself to the application of democracy in the first democratic nation (Myrdal 1944). Indeed, the more one examines the literature in this field, the more one is struck by the extent of scholars' interest in the subject matter for broader purposes (Saggar 1992a).

Notwithstanding the latent motives underscoring academic research in this field, it is important to note that *specifically* political analyses of race and racism remain relatively sparse and underdeveloped compared with other disciplines of social enquiry. Chief amongst this larger and longer developed literature has been the contribution of sociology and, to a lesser degree, social psychology and social anthropology (see for example Park 1950; Cox 1948; Barth 1969; Hechter, Friedman, and Appelbaum 1982; Weinreich 1986).

A cursory glance at writing in this field reveals a preponderance of research on, *inter alia*, the electoral participation of racial and ethnic minorities, state immigration policy, public policy governing minority–majority relations, race and class, and autonomous black political thought and activity. Political behavior themes are spread across these areas of academic inquiry. Empirical political scientists have concentrated on the former two areas, while the recent theoretical debates centers around the latter areas.

Many of the substantive studies of the race–politics nexus have concentrated on a number of important questions about political behavior. These include, for example, the relationship between racial groups and levels and forms of political participation, single-issue interest group activity, and group mobilization towards areas of political protest and/or violence. Starting from this perspective, one can see the different ways in which race shapes not merely formal political processes but also a wide range of underlying social tensions including differential public service delivery and competition for scarce resources in urban political environments. Of course, much of this research asks to what extent race plays either a determining or conditioning role. Or put another way, do black or other minority groups—and indeed other less or non-racialized ethnic minority groups—in a society such as the United States differ from their white counterparts in terms of the level and type of public service consumption or political participation as a result of their racial background or because of other factors such as economic or educational status?

Of course, the most immediate rejoinder to this kind of question is to acknowledge that it is the degree to which race-specific or related characteristics condition behavior that really matters. Indeed, precisely because of very strong patterns of conditioning—as seen in the US Democratic Party's domination of the black vote—it is easy to miss the vital influence of other factors. Multivariate analysis has been particularly useful in casting light on these kinds of influence. Race, as many US electoral observers have commented, undoubtedly trumps social class in the voting patterns of the black electorate, but this does not deny the impact and significance of class-based political outlooks and behavior. Previous research on this broad question finds that while a correlation between race and political behaviour exists in many western democracies, the task of demonstrating causal explanation has proved more difficult.

The significance of race as a concept frequently stems from its potential as an exclusionary variable. Thus, its capacity to focus shared values and backgrounds cannot be underestimated, since, unlike other similar variables, it usually operates in an unambiguous, dichotomous manner. Social class, ethnic group, regional origin, generational cohort and other familiar variables of political analysis differ from race in that they exhibit various degrees of internal overlap and conceptual imprecision. In contrast, the political impact of race, while regularly burdened by theoretical and empirical confusion linked to collective ethnic group action, has been analysed in rather clearer and more tangible terms. To take the well-documented example of residential segregation between black and white communities in the United States, researchers have encountered *relatively* few methodological difficulties in assigning individual behaviour to forms of group cohesion (see Borjas 1998, in relation to segregation, housing choice and group dynamics for instance). The difficulty arises in accounting for political action based on such cohesion, particularly in the absence of external constraints fuelling racially specific shared interests such as legally sanctioned force (as in South Africa since the early 1960s) or technical obstacles to electoral participation (as in parts of the United States until the mid-1960s).

It is not sufficient to suppose that discrimination alone will result in collective political action on the basis of race, although there is plenty of scope for it do so. The processes behind such action, if it is to occur, are commonly more complex and involve a wide range of social interaction between, and political integration of, different racial groups (Verba and Nie 1972, 149–73; Saggar 2000).

The voting behaviour of ethnic minority groups in advanced industrial states appears to confirm this point. Studlar (1983), Williams (1982), St Angelo and Puryear (1982) and Saggar (2000) all pointed to variance in black and others ethnic minority voting patterns in Britain and the United States. They show that black voters do *not* respond uniformly to their shared experiences as subjects of discrimination or exclusion. Equally important is the generally high level of similar voting patterns among ethnic minority groups. Using survey data from 1997 and 2001, Saggar (2003) described the "iron law" of black and South Asian voting in the UK whereby, for almost thirty years, four in five of all black and Asian votes that were cast went to the Labour Party. The importance of this is not to be understated since it showed the loyalty or stickiness of the party's support from one section of the electorate regardless of Labour's wider standing with the electorate at large.

Of course, racial differences are not only significant in terms of their impact on formal political participation, but are also closely intertwined with the distribution of power. Indeed, in several polities that have been characterized by overt legal discrimination on racial grounds—such as South Africa during the Apartheid era and indeed the southern United States during the Jim Crow era—underlying power relations excluded certain groups from key social and economic resources. In doing so, the skewed picture of control and influence below the level of formal participation served to reflect what was already apparent at the level of mass party politics. Moreover, as Wilson reminds us, the power relationship between racial groups is invariably uneven: "Differential power is a marked feature of racial-group interaction in complex societies; the greater the power discrepancy between subordinate and dominant racial groups, the greater the extent and scope of racial domination" (Wilson 1978, 18).

Why should domination necessarily extend beyond the political realm? The response to this question must point to sociological and historical understanding of power as a multifaceted concept which goes further than the use of coercive force in the face of interest confrontation. Economic and cultural dependency, for example, are both key forms through which domination has occurred "and facilitated the emergence of still another, more sophisticated form of control: psychosocial dominance" (Baker 1983, 80). This historical process was exemplified by the former white-dominated South African and Southern Rhodesian cases, but it is important to note that, despite great emphasis placed on coercive and structural dominance, it has perhaps been the psychosocial that has had the most enduring consequences (Baker 1983, 81).

The counter-forces of black African nationalism have been conspicuous by their diluted impact in both these societies compared with numerous other post-colonial African states. Moreover, as many writers have commented, white hegemony in terms of cultural awareness and discussion of inter-race power relations has transcended the nominal southern African divide, and is manifest in several diverse multi-racial societies (Wilson 2001; Finkel 2002). For example, the adoption of European-based parliamentary systems by a number of black African states following the struggles for independence has inevitably shaped political development in ways that have sometimes conflicted with local circumstances. The relative inability of these states to reform their political infrastructures—beyond that associated with large-scale political violence—is perhaps further testimony to the persisting dominance of European, Enlightenment-based philosophical assumptions concerning repres-entation, individual rights, and the reach of the state. Moreover, as Smith (1986, 223–5) notes, considerable problems of political instability have occurred in many black African states owing to their diverse plural compositions and structures; in a number of cases such as Nigeria, Sierra Leone, Uganda, Ethiopia, and Chad this mismatch has been closely linked to the colonial legacies of past European-imposed constitutional-legal settlements (Davidson 1983).

Elsewhere, a succession of civil rights leaders in the United States have observed, and constructed quasi-political issues over, the lexicon of race in political debate. In the 1960s radical black leaders in the United States fashioned a new rejectionist philosophy of anger leading to positive mobilization of black communities. Their analysis centered on opposition to perceived white-dominated cultural categories that had historically viewed black thought and contributions as marginal to main-stream society. In this context, they launched a campaign for black self-awareness in which it was declared, "I am a man—I am somebody", a cry echoed during the 1980s by the Reverend Jesse Jackson's call for the hyphenated term "African-Ameri-can" to displace "black" as the collective reference for the black minority he (then) sought to lead.

3 Behaviorial Frameworks of Enquiry and Understanding

In common with the major trends in political science since the 1950s, specialist studies of race and politics have mainly followed institutional and behavioral frame-works of enquiry. That is to say, the rise of racially and ethnically plural societies—most notably in European and North American countries—have had several important consequences for the operation of different political systems. These consequences, commonly impacting on areas such as party competition, labor migration and civil rights policies, have captured the attention of researchers and have been at the forefront of research in this field (see for example Welch and Secret 1981; Layton-Henry and Rich 1986; Welch and Studlar 1985; Pinderhughes 1987; Ali and O'Cinneide 2002). Institutional and behavioral approaches have dominated investigations of the race–politics nexus, and thus the literature does not present any new or particularly novel questions for the understanding of this topic.

This guiding framework includes several specific studies of the political impact of race. One such area is state immigration policy, which has resulted in a veritable trove of research on the western European experience in particular (Rogers 1985; Freeman 1979; Castles, Booth, and Wallace 1984; Brubaker 1992; Hollifield 1999; Hansen 2000). Various national governments sought to fill domestic labour shortages through foreign recruitment in the 1950s and 1960s, but this became an increasingly politicized dimension by the 1970s and 1980s. The popular-cum-electoral politicization of these policies came about not least because of the non-European origin of much of the labour force involved in this process, and the negative anti-immigrant backlash it provoked in many receiving countries. A more recent aspect of this public concern is the claim that the public consensus underlying large welfare state programs can and has been undermined by growing ethnic heterogeneity (Goodhart 2004).

Several writers emphasize the economically related aspects of such immigration policies and their eventual reversal during the 1970s and 1980s. Writing on the former West German case, Katzenstein argued that the appearance of the immigration issue in domestic politics compelled "policy-makers to confront the social consequences of decisions made largely for economic reasons" (Katzenstein 1987, 213). Elsewhere the electoral spoils of explicit anti-immigrant platforms appeared most vividly in Britain (during the 1970s) France (beginning in the 1980s and peaking in the 2002 presidential run-off), Denmark (where a far right, anti-immigration party made up part of the governing coalition after 2001), the Netherlands (where anti-immigrant political sentiment reached a peak in 2002), and Austria (whose national political landscape has been scarred by such sentiment since the late 1990s). The National Front's run-off against Chirac in the French presidential contest, the inclusion of a far right parties in the Austrian and Danish center–right coalitions, and the anti-immigrant zeal of the Berlusconi first and second administration in Italy, are all cases in point.

Researchers have extended their interest to the processes underlying and resulting from the politicization of immigration. There is growing interest, for example, in areas such as the political rights of immigrant workers (Layton-Henry 1989), the experience of racism and racially exclusionary public policies (Castles, Booth, and Wallace 1984), and the anti-immigrant backlash of the right (Husbands 1989). However, this literature has emerged from within the conventional lines that have shaped the discipline and, in general, has not attempted to challenge or reach beyond them. Thus, political scientists and commentators dispensed with the politics of race with comparative ease. Underlying conflicts and issues of power relations involving race have been largely neglected for the same reason that such broader critical approaches to political analysis were themselves overlooked and relegated to the fringes of the discipline for so long. For example, almost two decades ago, writers on British politics such as Dearlove and Saunders (1984) convincingly argued that preoccupations with narrow views of politics will preclude fuller understanding not only of British politics as a whole but also of key interlocking aspects of the broader picture (such as divisions of race, gender, and so on). The political analysis of race has usually taken as its frame of reference an unsatisfactorily narrow view of politics, and thus has merely replicated the dominant scholastic frameworks of the discipline on a smaller scale.

4 COMPARATIVE POLITICS, RACE, AND POLITICAL BEHAVIOR

The bulk of research activity and insights discussed in this chapter have centered on political behavior in a western industrial setting. Certainly the long-running legacy of the racial scar on the US political landscape has driven the ongoing importance of and interest in racially and ethnically related theories of political engagement and mobilization. The arrival and settlement of significant numbers of immigrants and ethnic minorities in European post-war societies has similarly fuelled academic pursuit of such theories.

The non-western context contains a number of significant national cases as well as a rich research literature examining the impact and influence of race and ethnic categories on political engagement. The great interest in the South African case is not surprising. Gibson and Gouws (2000) have noted the continuing importance of social identity in shaping citizen attitudes towards tolerance and intolerance in South African society. The solidarity of strong group identity, chiefly a legacy of the past, has emerged as a major obstacle to building a more inclusive national identity and political culture. The democratic setting for this challenge arguably makes it an even greater task.

The democratic setting of Indian politics makes for an even richer study of the role of racial and ethnic categories in political behavior. The most striking example is the successive attempts to deliver political and economic emancipation for the country's disadvantaged caste communities as well as some of its religious minorities. But again, in common with western examples, the recurring test is one of identifying the underlying causes of political behavior that are distinguishable from the poor social and economic conditions of these groups (see Pande 2003, for example, Varshey 2001). The dynamic of ethnic and religious conflict in Indian politics and society has added a further twist in attempting to specify how far racial or ethnic identity can be described as a causal driver of political behavior rather than as a symptom of long-standing divisions (Singh 2000).

The multi-ethnic and multi-racial setting of Brazilian politics provides another major example for political research. In the recent era, the patterns of political mobilization that have interwoven social class and race in Brazil have been central to understanding political change. Fry (2000), Marx (1998), and Hanchard (1994) all dwelt on this aspects of racial politics in Brazil and emphasized political struggles based around blackness and constructed black political identity. Incorporating political rights, citizenship, and civic rights into the realm of political participation remains the core challenge of modern Brazilian politics. In this regard, the political engagement of discrete racial groups gives rise to patterns of political identity and socialization within this wider backdrop. The centenary of the abolition of slavery in 1998 created a mixed response in Brazilian society (Winnant 1992). This included for example a major set of protests by those who complained about the "myth" of abolition. Substantive racial emancipation remains elusive according to this critique. Underpinning this kind of political grievance lay the reality of settled racial disadvantage, a pattern that has tended to recreate over generations. The politics of settled racial grievance is a familar aspect of Brazilian society and politics. It is also familiar to observers of other societies that have sought to address deep binary divisions based around racial codes.

Non-western frames of reference therefore add another dimension to the understanding of race and political behavior. The insight that arguably matters most is the need to account for the interplay between race and ethnicity and a number of other forces of identity. National self-identify is one such example, particularly in countries that have attained modern, stable nationhood in the post-war period. Racial politics is often been easier to identify than to account for as a result. Meanwhile, the politics of race and mass political behavior in countries such as France or Australia is awkward and generally marked by a reluctance to acknowledge the depth or permanence of racial categories. Reactions to mass, non-white immigration tends to be the dominant explanatory framework. The racialized aspects of political behaviour are been difficult to deflect, but are equally hard to incorporate successfully into theories of political participation.

REFERENCES

ALI, R., and O'CINNEIDE, C. 2002. *Our House? Race and Representation in British Politics.* London: Institute for Public Policy Research.

BAKER, D. 1983. *Race, Ethnicity and Power: A Comparative Study,* London: Routledge & Kegan Paul.

BARTH, F. ed. 1969. *Ethnic Groups and Boundaries.* Bergen: Universitetsforlaget.

BORJAS, G. 1998. To ghetto or not to ghetto: ethnicity residential segregation. *Journal of Urban Economics,* 44: 228–53.

British Election Study. 1997. www.data-archive.ac.uk/findingData/snDescription.asp?sn=3891

BRUBAKER, R. 1992. *Citizenship and Nationhood in France and Germany.* Cambridge, Mass.: Harvard University Press.

CASTLES, S., BOOTH, H., and WALLACE, T. 1984. *Here for Good: Western Europe's New Ethnic Minorities*, London: Pluto Press.

COX, O. 1948. *Caste, Class and Race*. New York: Monthly Review Press.

DAWSON, M. 1994. *Behind The Mule: Race And Class in African-American Politics*, Princeton: Princeton University Press.

DAVIDSON, B. ed. 1983. *Africa South of the Sahara*. London: Europa Publications.

DEARLOVE, J., and SAUNDERS, P. 1984. *Introduction to British Politics*. Oxford: Polity Press.

DE LA GARZA, R., and DESIPIO, L. eds. 2004. *Muted Voices: Latinos and the 2000 Elections*, Lanham, Md.: Rowman & Littlefield.

FENNEMA, M., and TILLIE, J. 2001. Civic community, political participation and political trust of ethnic groups. *Connections*, 24 (1): 26–41.

FINKEL, S. 2002. Civic education and the mobilization of political participation in developing democracies. Paper prepared for the conference on Political Participation: Building a Research Agenda, Princeton University, October 12–14, 2000.

FREEMAN, G. 1979. *Immigrant Labour and Racial Conflict in Industrial Societies: The French and British Experience, 1945–75*, Princeton: Princeton University Press.

FRY, P. 2000. Politics, nationality, and the meanings of "race" in Brazil. *Daedalus*, 129 (2): 83–118.

GIBSON, J., and GOUWS, A. 2000. Social identities and political intolerance: linkages within the South African mass public. *American Journal of Political Science*, 44 (2): 278–92.

—— and MOYNIHAN, D. 1963. *Beyond the Melting Pot*. Cambridge, Mass.: MIT Press.

—— and YOUNG, K. eds. 1983. *Ethnic Pluralism and Public Policy: Achieving Equality in the United States and Britain*. London: Heinemann.

GOODHART, D. 2004. "Too diverse?", *Prospect* (Feb.), 30–7.

HANCHARD, M. 1994. *Orpheus and Power: The "Movimento Negro" of Rio de Janeiro and Sao Paulo, Brazil 1945–1988*. Princeton: Princeton University Press.

HANSEN, R. 2000. *Citizenship and Immigration in Post-war Britain*. Oxford: Oxford University Press.

HECHTER, M., FRIEDMAN, D., and APPELBAUM, M. 1982. A theory of ethnic collective action. *International Migration Review*, 16: 412–34.

HIGHTON, B., and WOLFINGER, R. 1998. Estimating the effects of the National Voter Registration Act of 1993. *Political Behavior*, 20: 79–104.

HOLLIFIELD, J. 1999. Ideas, institutions and civil society: on the limits of immigration control in liberal democracies. *IMIS-Beitraege*, 10: 57–90.

HUSBANDS, C. 1989. *Race and the Right in Contemporary Politics*. London: Pinter.

KATZENSTEIN, P. 1987. *Policy and Politics in West Germany: The Growth of a Semi-Sovereign State*, Philadelphia: Temple University Press.

LAYTON-HENRY, Z. ed. 1989. *The Political Rights of Migrant Workers in Western Europe*. London: Sage Publications.

—— and RICH, P. eds. 1986. *Race, Government and Politics in Britain*. London: Macmillan.

LIEN, P. 1994. Ethnicity and political participation: a comparison between Asian and Mexican Americans. *Political Behavior*, 16: 237–64.

MARX, A. 1998. *Making Race and Nation: A Comparison of South Africa, the United States, and Brazil*. Cambridge: Cambridge University Press.

MYRDAL, G. 1944. *An American Dilemma*. New York: Harper Brothers.

PANDE, R. 2003. Can mandated political representation increase policy influence for disadvantaged minorities? Theory and evidence from India. *American Economic Review*, 93: 1132–51.

PARK, R. ed. 1950. *Race and Culture*. New York: Free Press.

PINDERHUGHES, D. 1987. *Race and Ethnicity in Chicago Politics*. Chicago: University of Illinois Press.

PRESTON, M., HENDERSON, L. J., JR., and PURYEAR, P. eds. 1982. *The New Black Politics: The Search for Political Power*, New York: Longman.

REX, J., and MASON, D. eds. 1986. *Theories of Race and Ethnic Relations*, Cambridge: Cambridge University Press.

ROGERS, R. ed. 1985. *Guests Coming to Stay: The Effects of European Migration on Sending and Receiving Countries*, Boulder, Colo.: Westview Press.

SAGGAR, S. 1991. *Race and Public Policy: A Study of Local Politics and Government*, Aldershot: Avebury.

—— 1992*a*. Race and politics. In ed. M. Hawkesworth and M. Kogan, *The Routledge Encyclopedia of Government and Politics*, London: Routledge, 1992, 534–54.

—— 1992*b*. The politics of racial pluralism and problems of evaluation. In ed. R. Barot and K. Flanagan, *Social Order in Post-Classical Sociology*, London: The Edwin Mellen Press, 1995,166–92

—— 2000. *Race and Representation*. Manchester: Manchester University Press.

—— 2003. Immigration and the politics of public opinion. *Political Quarterly*, special issue on migration by invitation, 178–94.

ST ANGELO, D., and PURYEAR, P. 1982. Fear, apathy and other dimensions of black voting. Pp. 109–30 in *The New Black Politics: The Search for Political Power*, ed. M. Preston, L. J. Henderson Jr., and P. Puryear. New York: Longman.

SINGH, G. 2000. *Ethnic Conflict in India*. New York: St Martin's Press.

SMITH, M. G. 1986. Pluralism, race and ethnicity in selected African countries. In *Theories of Race and Ethnic Relations*, ed. J. Rex and D. Mason. Cambridge: Cambridge University Press.

STUDLAR, D. 1983. The ethnic vote, 1983: problems of analysis and interpretation. *New Community*, 11: 92–100.

TATE, K. 1993. *From Protest to Politics: The New Black Voters in American Elections*. New York: Russell Sage Foundation; Cambridge: Harvard University Press.

VARSHEY, A. 2001. *Ethnic Conflict and Civil Society: India and Beyond*. New Haven: Yale University Press.

VERBA, S., and NIE, N. 1972. *Participation in America: Political Democracy and Social Equality*. New York: Harper & Row.

—— SCHLOZMAN, K., and BRADY, H. 1995 *Voice and Equality: Civic Voluntarism in American Politics*. Cambridge: Harvard University Press.

WEINREICH, P. 1986. The operationalisation of identity theory in racial and ethnic relations. In *Theories of Race and Ethnic Relations*, ed. J. Rex and D. Mason. Cambridge: Cambridge University Press.

WELCH, S., and SECRET, P. 1981. Sex, race and political participation. *Western Political Quarterly*, 34: 5–16.

—— and STUDLAR, D. 1985. The impact of race on political behaviour in Britain. *British Journal of Political Science*, 15: 528–40.

WILLIAMS, E. 1982. Black political progress in the 1970s: the electoral arena. in *The New Black Politics: The Search for Political Power*, ed. M. Preston, L. J. Henderson Jr., and P. Puryear. New York: Longman.

WILSON, R. 2001. *The Politics of Truth and Reconciliation in South Africa: Legitimizing the Post-Apartheid State*. Cambridge: Cambridge University Press.

WINNANT, H. 1992. Rethinking race in Brazil. *Journal of Latin American Studies*, 24: 173–92.

CHAPTER 27

ECONOMIC
MODELS
OF VOTING

MICHAEL S. LEWIS-BECK

MARY STEGMAIER

DURING the 1980 US presidential election campaign that pitted incumbent President Jimmy Carter against challenger Ronald Reagan, Reagan asked American voters a peremptory question:

Next Tuesday all of you will go to the polls, will stand there in the polling place and make a decision. I think when you make that decision, it might be well if you would ask yourself, are you better off than you were four years ago? (US Presidential Debate, Oct. 28, 1980)

President Reagan's quote provides an ideal starting point to introduce the fundamentals of economic voting. The basic idea behind economic voting is referred to as the reward–punishment hypothesis. This hypothesis holds that when the economy is good, voters will reward the incumbent with their vote. Conversely, when the economy is bad, voters will punish the incumbent by casting their vote for the challenger. Given the poor condition of the US economy in the fall of 1980, Reagan wagered that voters would punish the Carter administration on Election Day.

While Reagan certainly wasn't the first to believe that voters might consider economics when casting their vote, he asked the question at a pivotal point in the study of economic voting. At the time, scholars such as V. O. Key and Anthony Downs had laid the foundations for the contemporary study of economic voting, but very few studies testing these theories had been published. Thus, political scientists had only tentative answers to many fundamental questions as to the precise nature of economic voting.

One of these questions concerns the direction of voters' gaze. Do voters assess the past economic performance of the government or do they look to the future? The idea that voters review the performance of the incumbent government is referred to as retrospective voting. President Reagan's quote above provides us with a neat example of a retrospective question, since the time reference is over the past four years. Retrospective economic voting theory has its origins in V. O. Key (1966, 61) and his argument about the electorate's crucial "role of appraiser of past events, past performance, and past actions. It judges retrospectively." Morris Fiorina (1981, 26) later applied Key's view, seeing "an electorate that treats elections . . . as referenda on the incumbent administration's handling of the economy."

But, do voters only consider the past? Anthony Downs (1957, 39) suggested that voters look to the future: "When a man votes, he is helping to select the government which will govern him during the coming election period. . . . He makes his decision by comparing future performances he expects from the competing parties." The theory that voters look to the future and vote according to economic expectations is called prospective economic voting. Questions surrounding the importance of retrospective versus prospective voting weave their way through many of our reviewed studies of economic voting.

A second question in the economic voting literature deals with the types of economic conditions voters consider. The conventional wisdom among politicians and the public is that voters vote according to their pocketbook. We see this in Reagan's quote, as he asks "are you" rather than "is the nation" better off now than four years ago.[1] The theory of pocketbook voting says that when personal or household financial conditions have deteriorated, voters will punish the incumbent. If personal financial conditions have improved, voters will reward the incumbent. In the overwhelming majority of studies, researchers have found that instead of emphasizing personal finances, voters are much more likely to be considering the national economic situation when casting their vote. The theory that national economic conditions matter to individual vote choice is called sociotropic voting.

To measure sociotropic retrospective and prospective evaluations, survey items of the following general form are standard:

Retrospective question: "Looking back over the past year, would you say the national economic situation has gotten worse, better, or stayed the same?"
Prospective question: "Looking ahead to the next year, do you think the national economic situation will be worse, better, or stay the same?"

By substituting the words "national economic situation" with the words "personal financial situation" the questions will then tap into pocketbook voting. Surveys in democratic countries include these and other political questions that enable researchers to determine the impact that the economy has on vote choice relative to other factors.

---

[1] In expanding on this question, Reagan mentions not only personal economic conditions, but also the national unemployment rate (a sociotropic consideration) as well as non-economic issues. The Commission on Presidential Debates website contains the full text of the debate: www.debates.org/

1 SELECTION OF STUDIES

The fundamental questions concerning economic voting have been studied and addressed in democracies around the globe. Today, the study of economic voting is in full flower with approximately 400 books and articles published on the subject. Obviously, not all of these works can be discussed, or even mentioned, here. However, for readers interested in economic voting in specific countries not reviewed here, we provide a list of recent studies in footnote two.[2] And, as a further library aid, we refer readers to additional earlier reviews (Anderson 1995, ch. 3; Lewis-Beck 1988, chs. 2 and 3; Lewis-Beck and Paldam 2000; Lewis-Beck and Stegmaier 2000; Monroe 1984; Nannestad and Paldam 1994; Norpoth 1996).

Because these investigations have become so numerous, an organizing theme is doubly necessary. Our first step is to emphasize micro-level, survey research, at the expense of the macro-level, aggregate, time-series research. Besides reducing the workload, the strategy has an academic logic. The initial studies were macro-, examining economic growth, unemployment, inflation, and the like (Frey and Garbers 1972; Goodhart and Bhansali 1970; Kramer 1971; Rosa and Amson 1976). These pioneering efforts suggested that voters strongly responded to the economy. But these results forced the ecological inference question: do voters really think and act this way, or is the aggregate finding simply spurious? The answer appeared to lie with investigation of individuals in election surveys.

Survey research of this sort has focused more on the US case than any other. Hence we start with it, moving to the next most-studied cases, Britain and France. Next, multinational studies from different regions of the democratic world are explicated. After this review, conclusions are drawn about the workings of economics on democratic vote choice, and suggestions are made for future research.

In selecting studies to discuss, we stress first-order elections, that is presidential or parliamentary elections, deeming them more important than second-order contests. With respect to theory, the ordering principle is the reward–punishment model of the economic vote. Accordingly, voters are held to vote for the incumbent in economic good times, and vote against the incumbent in economic bad times. There are minor variants on this notion of economic voting, but it is the classic reward–punishment scheme, and the likelihood of its existence, that gives the theory its interest and power. While our country studies focus on the much-studied established democracies, the power of the economic voting theory is further buttressed by studies of post-socialist

---

[2] Survey research has examined economic voting in many democracies other than those covered in this chapter. Here we offer one recent study for a sampling of countries not reviewed in this article: Argentina (Canton and Jorrat 2002); Australia (Mughan, Benn, and McAllister 2003); Canada (Blais et al. 2002); Costa Rica (Seligson and Gomez 1989); Denmark (Borre 1997); Germany (Fröchling 1998); Ghana (Youde 2005); Hungary (Anderson, Lewis-Beck, and Stegmaier 2003); Israel (Nannestad, Paldam, and Rosholm 2003); Italy (Bellucci 2002); Mexico (Domínguez and McCann 1995); the Netherlands (Irwin and van Holsteyn 1997); New Zealand (Allen 2000); Nicaragua (Anderson, Lewis-Beck, and Stegmaier 2003); Poland (Bielasiak and Blunck 2002); Russia (Colton 1996); Spain (Fraile 2002); Taiwan (Hsien, Lacy, and Niou 1998); and Zambia (Posner and Simon 2002).

democracies (Anderson, Lewis-Beck, and Stegmaier 2003; Colton 1996, 2000; Duch 2001; Hesli and Bashkirova 2001; Mishler and Willerton 2003) and developing countries around the globe (Bratton et al. 2005; Canton and Jorrat 2002; Pacek and Radcliff 1995; Posner and Simon 2002; Remmer 1991; Youde 2005). Indeed, the economic voting paradigm has come to rival other political behavior models—party identification, social cleavages, and issue voting. As we shall see below, it appears a worthy adversary.

2 THE MOST STUDIED CASES: THE UNITED STATES, GREAT BRITAIN, AND FRANCE

2.1 The United States

The retrospective economic voter hypothesis in the US was thoroughly pursued in Kiewiet's (1983) seminal analyses of the 1960–1980 American National Election Studies (ANES). In these, and subsequent ANES studies, two items have received special attention. The first, a pocketbook item, concerns the individual's financial well-being. The second, a sociotropic item, concerns the economic conditions of the entire nation. Kiewiet's (1983, 35) finding, that pocketbook voting is weak in presidential elections, whereas sociotropic voting is strong, has continued to characterize survey research from subsequent elections (Alvarez and Nagler 1995, 1998; Kinder, Adams, and Gronke 1989; Lanoue 1994).

Results from the 2004 US presidential election suggest that sociotropic voting is alive and well. Bivariate analysis of the 2004 ANES shows that among those who thought the national economy was "better," about 87 percent said they voted for Bush. In contrast, among those who thought it was "worse," only 20 percent voted for Bush. This 67-percentage point difference implies that the economic effect can be quite large. Of course, this is only a preliminary, bivariate result. What do recent multivariate studies show? It is helpful to consider the model generally estimated. Here is a stylized version of the standard specification, across many studies.

Vote = economics + other issues + party identification + socioeconomic status

The investigations by Alvarez and Nagler (1995, 1998) on the 1992 and 1996 elections, respectively, conform to this general specification. They found powerful sociotropic effects, while finding no pocketbook effects. For example, in 1996, voters who saw the national economy as "better" were 38 percent more likely to vote for Clinton, when compared to those who saw it as "worse." Morover, this economic effect was greater than that of any issue studied (Alvarez and Nagler 1998, 1360–2). In his examination of the 2000 election, Norpoth (2004, 54) reports that the parameter estimate for the national economy "is strong." He further observes that, in that election, the economy ranked about the same in importance for voters as it had in 1992 and 1996 (Norpoth 2004, 53).

An important argument is that these reported strong economic effects exaggerate the true impact of the economy, because they are based on perceptions, which contain random and systematic error (Kramer 1983). To test this possibility, Markus (1988, 1992) measured the national economy objectively with election year Real Disposable Income (RDI). By grafting that measure to each respondent in a pooled analysis of the 1956–88 ANES surveys, he found significant and strong RDI effects, with a one-percentage point increase expected to raise incumbent support 2.5 percent. Nadeau and Lewis-Beck (2001, 164) replicated this finding on an extended pool, 1956–96. Further, they showed that a subjective measure of the national economy, a national business index (NBI), exercised a still stronger effect. For each election year, NBI equals the percent who said the economy was "better" minus the percent who said it was "worse." To illustrate, for 1996, "better" = 54.5 percent, "worse" = 26.5 percent, so NBI = 54.5 − 26.5 = 28. When NBI changes one standard deviation, the expected incumbent support changes 5.5 percent. (Nadeau and Lewis-Beck 2001, 165). They also explored other aspects of economic voting that we have not yet touched on: the time dimension and the institutional context.

Thus far, the assumption has been that economic voting is entirely retrospective. However, there are some scholars who have argued that voting is equally prospective, perhaps more so (Clarke and Stewart 1994; MacKuen, Erikson, and Stimson 1992). Scattered evidence from different presidential election surveys suggests a prospective component exists. Fiorina (1981, 139) found that expectations about which party would better handle economic problems helped account for the 1976 presidential vote. Studying the 1984 election, Lewis-Beck (1988, 121) uncovered significant prospective effects, as did Lanoue (1994) for 1988. Lockerbie (1992), looking at 1956–88 ANES surveys, decided that prospective effects exceed retrospective ones. Nadeau and Lewis-Beck (2001, 172–5), in their pooled analysis above, examined the impact of an Economic Future Index (EFI), equal to the percentage who think business conditions over the next twelve months will be "good" minus the percentage who think they will be "bad." Comparing coefficients, it has about the same impact as NBI.

In American presidential elections, then, it appears that economic voting can be prospective as well as retrospective. Moreover, these two components appear weighted, depending on whether or not the sitting president is running for re-election. When he runs, the economic vote is mostly retrospective. This makes good sense. Voters know that he has been president, and tend to hold him responsible for his economic record. However, when the party candidate is not the president himself, they tend not to hold him responsible, since he was obviously not in the driver's seat (Nadeau and Lewis-Beck 2001, 175). This was the case in 2000, when Al Gore, not Bill Clinton, was the candidate. Gore could not make much of the economic boom going into that contest, because he was not the incumbent president. (Norpoth 2004 makes this point quite well.)

What we see is that the strength of economic voting can vary with the institutional and political context. This is not surprising, once we consider that the classic reward-punishment model rests psychologically on the attribution of responsibility. Whom do I praise or blame for economic performance? In US presidential elections, it is more likely to be the sitting president, contrasted to a mere candidate from the president's party. Rudolph and Grant (2002) do show, in a special 2000 election survey, that respondents who specifically attributed economic responsibility to the president were much more likely to vote for Al Gore. However, in this contest, only 24.6 percent of the respondents were in that attribution group (Rudolph and Grant 2002, 811). The other groups attributed economic responsibility to business leaders, Congress, or the Federal Reserve. As the authors note, "The failure of Al Gore to garner more support was not due to the status of the economy, but to his inability to make the case that it was the Clinton-Gore administration that was responsible for the economy. Failure to do so meant that others received credit and Gore lost votes" (Rudolph and Grant 2002, 818).

As the above example reminds us, economic perceptions may be interactive, or heterogeneous. That is, while the typical elector has an average response to the economy, indicated by an additive regression coefficient, subgroups of electors may have a response different from the average, as indicated by a non-additive regression coefficient. The attribution group may not only affect the impact of sociotropic perceptions; it can also affect the relative importance of pocketbook versus socio-tropic effects.[3] Nevertheless, the main point should not be lost: in study after study, presidential election after presidential election, strong sociotropic economic effects have manifested themselves in the general voting population. Further, of all issues facing the American electorate, economic ones are generally at the top of the list in terms of their impact on voter choice.

2.2 Great Britain

In Britain, scholars have the well-executed national British Election Study (BES) to investigate economic voting questions. The BES has been ongoing for over forty years, and its early investigators were attuned to the economic voting hypo-thesis. In the classic words of pioneers Butler and Stokes (1969, 392), "the electorate's response to the economy is one under which voters reward the Government for the conditions they welcome and punish the Government for the conditions they dislike." Their focus was especially on personal economic expectations for the future. They found that Conservative Government support "changed between the elections of 1959 and 1964 according to whether the individual sees his economic well-being as having improved or not ... [in] a strong trend" (Butler and Stokes 1969, 403–4).

---

[3] For examples of heterogeneity in US economic voting see: Weatherford (1978); Feldman (1982); Welch and Hibbing (1992); Gomez and Wilson (2001).

Of the subsequent investigations of the BES, the most comprehensive for our purposes is that of Sanders (2003), who examines the effects of party identification and economic perceptions in five separate general elections between 1974 and 1997. (But see also Alt 1979; Studlar, McAllister, and Ascui 1990.) Because of data availability, he limits himself to assessing the sociotropic retrospective variable, based on an item asking if national economic conditions have worsened or not over the last year. He finds, as expected, that "the governing party loses support among those voters who believe that economic conditions have worsened" (Sanders 2003, 261). For example, according to the 1974 logistic analysis, believing the economy has worsened doubled the odds of a vote for the Conservatives. Even restricting the samples to strong party identifiers, the sociotropic impact remains clear, and shows no relative deterioration over time. Specifically, examining the Conservative vote, the ratio of the party identification effect to the economic perception effect varies from about 3:1 to 4:1 across the series, beginning at 3.85 (in 1974) and ending at 3.85 (in 1997).

A vigorous tradition in British voting studies explores the impact of regional differences (McAllister and Studlar 1992). In terms of economic voting, a telling example comes from Johnston et al. (2000). They examine the role of local context on national retrospective economic voting in the 1997 general election. They find that, when the voter's neighborhood is perceived as less well off, or has relatively high unemployment, any positive sociotropic evaluation of the national economy is much reduced. On the basis of their logistic regressions, they conclude that there is "strong evidence of spatial variations in economic voting in England and Wales at the 1997 general election" (Johnston et al. 2000, 141).

Currently, the British Election Study (2001, 2005) seems especially vital. Clarke et al. (2004) recently published a thorough volume on the 2001 general election, *Political Choice in Britain*. This text, along with the venerable *Political Change in Britain* (Butler and Stokes 1969), nicely book-end thirty-five years of election survey research in Britain. Clarke et al. (2004, 83) note, as did their predecessors, that economics matters for British elections. The controversy rests with how, and how much.

Labour, as the ruling party, went into the 2001 election under economic blue skies. Unemployment and inflation rates were low, at just over 3 percent, and interest rates were falling. The perceptual data from the 2001 BES reflect these positive economic indicators: 70 percent saw the economic past as the "same or better," and 68 percent saw the economic future as the "same or better" (Clarke et al. 2004, 84–5). Further, as an issue priority, economics ranked second after the National Health Service (Clarke et al. 2004, 90). In attempting to explain vote choice for or against Labour, the authors posit the following competing models: sociodemographic, party identification, issue-proximity, economic voting, issue performance, and feelings about party leaders. In terms of fit, the economic voting model does better than all but the party identification and party leader models (Clarke et al. 2004, 104).

The authors blend these rival models into a composite model. The estimation, of Labour vs. opposition vote, correctly classifies 87.6 percent of the choices (Clarke et al.

2004, table 4.10). Interestingly, the pocketbook variables, both retrospective and prospective, cease to be significant. The national economy variables, both retrospective and prospective, remain significant, and carry coefficients of almost equal magnitude. Given the rigorous controls, this much strengthens the case that British economic voters are prospective as well as retrospective. Further, the potency of the general judgments about the national economy supports an old notion from Butler and Stokes (1969, 391), who seemed to see such judgments as catch-all expressions of economic particulars: "the dominant mode of popular response to economic goals seems to be one that approves at the same time of full employment, larger pay packets, stable prices, and . . . a strong currency and balanced international payments." In other words, the standard sociotropic items are well phrased, capturing the many rivulets of the complex modern economy.

In terms of vote probabilities, the effect of a perceptual shift in national economic conditions, prospective or retrospective, is almost as great as a shift to a Labour party identification (Clarke et al. 2004, 113). In addition, investigation of the influences on party leader images reveals indirect effects of economic perceptions. Overall, the Clarke et al. (2004, 123) conclusion seems incontestable: "reactions to the economy had substantial effects on electoral choice in 2001." Further, their careful work caps the more general point: economic issues figured prominently in shaping the British voter's decision.

2.3 France

The French example would seem to offer an especially good test of the economic voting idea, because of the uniqueness and complexity of its political system. It has many parties, a dual executive, and two rounds of balloting. One might easily imagine that, under such rules, the economic signal would be lost before reaching the ballot box. But such is not the case, as numerous studies have shown.

Election surveys have a long tradition in France, and explanations of declared voter preference are vigorously pursued. (On recent elections, see Boy and Mayer 1993, 1997; Cautrès and Mayer 2004.) Alas, a full battery of economic perception questions has not been regularly posed. However, when they have been, the results merit attention. Further, these results can be supplemented by judicious use of the Euro-barometer data, as seen below.

The first micro-study of economics and the French voter examined economic perception items in the Eurobarometer, 1970–8 (Lewis-Beck 1983). When these disparate 55 items are correlated with left–right vote intention, average $r = .20$ (Lewis-Beck 1983, 350). In regression models predicting left–right legislative vote in 1973 and 1978, personal and collective economic items reach statistical significance, in the face of strong controls on ideology, class, religion, and region (Lewis-Beck 1983, 356).

A follow-up study fielded a full battery of economic items in certain of the 1983 and 1984 Eurobarometers, France included. An idealized model of legislative vote intention (incumbent vs. opposition), with only economic perceptions as predictor variables, was initially postulated, yielding a respectable percentage of variance explained (Lewis-Beck 1988, 56). A fully specified single-equation model, including class, religion, and ideology as controls, demonstrated statistically significant effects from national retrospective and prospective items (not to mention an item on economic anger). Interestingly, no retrospective pocketbook effects were revealed (Lewis-Beck 1988, 56, 82). A general finding—significant retrospective sociotropic effects, but no retrospective pocketbook effects, has persisted across subsequent studies, to which we now turn.

The first serious battery of economic questions was administered in the 1995 French National Election Studies (FNES). At the bivariate level, the economic voting hypothesis appeared promising in these 1995 data. For example, among those who saw a brighter economic future, 72 percent expressed a second-round presidential preference for Chirac, in contrast to only 18 percent among those who saw a dark economic future. Analyzing economic effects on the first presidential ballot via a logistic regression, Lewis-Beck (1997) established there was an economic vote, more sociotropic than personal, and prospective as well as retrospective. He further showed that French economic voters were more sophisticated than naive. First, economic perceptions tended to influence only votes for major party candidates. The French voter, rightly, did not attribute economic responsibility to lesser parties, such as the Ecologists, and so did not vote for them on those grounds. Second, voters did not vote against Jospin if they perceived a deteriorating economy, even though he was the candidate of Socialist president Mitterrand. Instead, they voted against the incumbent Prime Minister Balladur, whom they rightly perceived as in charge of the economy, under conditions of cohabitation (prime minister and president of different parties).

Lewis-Beck and Nadeau (2000) generally pursue French economic voting in the face of systematically changing institutional conditions such as cohabitation, election type, and ballot order. The following is a widely agreed upon, baseline specification of the vote choice in French national elections:

$$\text{Vote} = \text{class} + \text{religion} + \text{left–right ideology} + \text{economics}$$

In their regression estimations, Lewis-Beck and Nadeau modify this specification to incorporate cohabitation effects in conjunction with economic effects. Thus, focus is on coefficients for these independent variables: retrospective sociotropic evaluation, retrospective sociotropic evaluation times ($\times$) cohabitation. The dependent variable is incumbent vote (prime minister party vs. not), and the data are a pool of eight Euro-barometer surveys 1984–94. According to the results, under cohabitation, the impact of the economic vote is cut in half. French voters see the prime minister as primarily responsible for running the economy, and reward or punish him (or her) accordingly. However, they also recognize that, failing unity with the president, economic power is inevitably diluted, so they punish less.

Analysis of surveys from the 1988 and 1995 presidential elections, both occurring under cohabitation, exposes more economic voting dynamics (Lewis-Beck and Nadeau 2000, 177–80). First, economic voting is stronger in presidential elections than in legislative contests. Second, in presidential contests, perceived economic gains enhanced the vote for candidates from the prime minister's party coalition (not the president's), as voters held it economically responsible. Finally, economic voting in presidential contests is greater when, on the second ballot, one of the candidates is the prime minister. In that case, that candidate has an actual economic track record in office, and voters are more willing and able to attribute blame or praise.

Repeated survey analyses of national elections in Fifth Republic France manifest strong and complex patterns of economic voting. It is largely sociotropic and more or less equally retrospective or prospective, depending in part on the institutional context. The French voter is sophisticated, knowing whom and how much to blame. When government is unified, the president is the lightning rod for economic discontent. However, under cohabitation, the burden shifts to the prime minister. Smaller parties are blamed less than large parties, legislative candidates are blamed less than presidential candidates, and presidential candidates who are prime minister are blamed more than presidential candidates who are not prime minister. These dynamics illustrate how powerful the economic pulse can be in guiding the elector across complex political waters.

3 Comparing Democracies: Cross-National Studies

Thus far, we have considered single-country studies in established democracies. There are, however, a growing number of studies that examine multiple countries. The following aggregate-level pooled analyses, on nation-samples from different parts of the world, have all found important economic voting effects: Lewis-Beck and Mitchell (1990), on the five major western European countries; Chappell and Veiga (2000), on thirteen western European nations; Pacek (1994) and Tucker (2001) on central European samples; Remmer (1991) on twelve Latin American countries; Pacek and Radcliff (1995) on eight low-income nations; Wilkin, Haller, and Norporth (1997) on a worldwide sample of countries. While generally positive, the findings were not always so (Paldam 1991).

Further, the results are not always consistent across countries. Lewis-Beck (1988) found that economic voting strength descended in this order: Britain, Spain, Germany, France, and Italy. He argued the main reason was "coalitional complexity" (Lewis-Beck 1988, 105). For example, for Britain the incumbent was one party, for

Italy it was five. The more parties in the incumbent coalition, the more "diffusion of government responsibility" (Lewis-Beck 1986, 341). In other words, when responsibility for managing the economy is less clear, it is harder for the voter to attach blame, and the economic vote is diluted.

The clarity of responsibility hypothesis has received fullest attention in the work of Powell and Whitten (1993), in their investigation of nineteen industrial democracies, 1969–88. They argue that if "the legislative rules, the political control of different institutions, and the lack of cohesion of the government all encourage more influence for the political opposition, voters will be less likely to punish the government for poor performance of the economy. Responsibility for that performance will simply be less clear" (Powell and Whitten 1993, 393). To assess the political context, they look at five indicators: voting cohesion of governing parties, formation of the committee system, opposition from the upper chamber, minority government, and coalition government. They find that, in countries where the assignment of government responsibility is made unclear, there are no significant economic effects on the vote, in contrast to strongly significant economic effects where responsibility is clear.

Other pooled analyses on nations have demonstrated that the electoral impact of economics depends on political or institutional context. First is the replication of the above result, with forty new cases and clarity of responsibility measures refined (Whitten and Palmer 1999). Second, these works have begun to extend beyond western Europe. Roberts and Wibbels (1999) investigate sixteen Latin American nations across the 1980s and 1990s, reporting that the impact of economics depends on election type. Samuels (2004) looking at a mostly Latin American sample, finds the institutions of presidentialism affect the strength of the economic vote. Benton (2005), in a comparative analysis of thirteen Latin American countries, discovers that when electoral laws are more restrictive, economic voting is heightened.

The foregoing studies suggest strongly that political institutions and context condition the economic vote. Nevertheless, since all these studies are aggregate, they can be no more than suggestive. To confirm these conditional effects, we need to explore comparative analyses of individual-level electoral surveys. The first comparative survey examination of the economic vote was done by Lewis-Beck (1986, 1988). He analyzed economic voting in Britain, France, Germany, Italy, and Spain, examining simple hypotheses on the differing findings from survey to survey; however, he never pooled them into one data set (Lewis-Beck 1988, ch. 7). There are some relevant fully pooled survey studies, and they are reviewed below.

Anderson (2000) examines the impact of political context on economic voting, in a pool of thirteen European country surveys, from the 1994 Eurobarometer. The dependent variable of principal interest is incumbent vote (for any of the parties in the coalition) versus otherwise. The independent economic variables are retrospective pocketbook and retrospective sociotropic, with controls on ideology, religiosity, and social class. Political context variables include Powell and Whitten's (1993) clarity of responsibility index, strength of the governing party, and number of available alternatives. He shows that sociotropic voting is consistently enhanced by political context, such as clarity of responsibility, governing party strength, and a small number of parties. He concludes that, "Taken together, these findings suggest that voters' ability to express discontent with economic performance is enhanced when accountability is simple. Voters' economic assessments have stronger effects on government support when it is clear who the target is, when the target is sizable, and when voters have only a limited number of viable alternatives to throw their support to" (Anderson 2000, 168).

Nadeau, Niemi, and Yoshinaka (2002) extend Anderson's analysis in space and time, looking at a pooled cross-sectional time series of eight countries surveyed in the 1976–92 Eurobarometers. They elaborate the clarity of responsibility measure, including the long-term cross-national institutional components of Powell and Whitten (1993), as well as short-term components that can vary within a country, such as number of parties in the ruling coalition and longevity of government. The dependent variable, in logistic regression analyses, is the dichotomy of vote for (or against) a party in government. Control variables are left–right self-placement, and a socioeconomic status battery. The economic measure comes from the standard retrospective sociotropic item, aggregated into an index assigned to each respondent, in a manner similar to that followed by Nadeau and Lewis-Beck (2001) in their pooled analysis of the ANES.

They find here that economic voting is stronger where there is more clarity of responsibility, which can vary within a country as well as across countries. In the high clarity countries—Britain, France, Ireland, Germany—"economic evaluations are a moderately strong force on intended vote.... In the remaining countries [Denmark, the Netherlands, Belgium, Italy], economic evaluations...make a much smaller contribution" (Nadeau, Niemi, and Yoshinaka 2002, 414–15). However, "[e]ven in those countries where clarity of responsibility for governmental action tends, on average, to be low, voters will, under propitious conditions, credit or blame the government for the economic situation" (Nadeau, Niemi, and Yoshinaka 2002, 418–19). In other words, economic voting as a government sanction is always possible.

The above investigations have looked at political context. Hellwig (2001) looks at economic context, tying the political economy literature on globalization to the economic voting question. Because of globalization, that is, international economic integration, governments are less able to manage their national economics. There-fore, as electorates perceive this, we should expect to see less economic voting. He looks at a pool of nine national surveys, from the Comparative Study of Electoral Systems data (1999). The dependent variable is vote intention for the incumbent (versus otherwise). The economic perception item is the standard sociotropic retro-spective one, and there are controls on ideology and socioeconomic status. Global-ization of a nation is operationalized with export and import dollars as a proportion of GDP. When this variable is assigned to each respondent and interacted with the sociotropic variable, one observes the expected result, i.e. there is a significant decrease in economic voting in the face of more open trade.

4 SUMMARY AND CONCLUSIONS

According to Lewis-Beck (1988, 162), "the generalization of the economic voting model across nations" was "ripe for challenge." The review at hand roundly refutes that challenge, showing the robustness of economic voting theory, regardless of national democratic setting. It is not important whether the democracy is much studied or little studied, resilient or fragile, the economy reliably moves voters to hold their government accountable in national elections. When they see prosperity, they give support. When they see business conditions in decline, they withdraw support. This reward–punishment pattern can be counted on, election after election, country after country.

How strong are these effects on individual voters? There are different ways to answer. When sociotropic assessments change from "better" to "worse," reported vote probability shifts are never trivial and are sometimes quite strong. Even when the probability shift is small, cumulatively it can generate a critical increase or decrease in the aggregate electoral share for the incumbent. Economic opinion can be decisive, for it is short-term and can seriously change, unlike more inertial forces. Compared to other issues, it regularly produces a stronger structural impact, as measured by its regression coefficients. Further, it is the rare election where economic matters are not at the top of the public's political agenda. This is not surprising given it is a valence issue (Stokes 1992). No one opposes prosperity. Its valence strength allows it to rival, even occasionally surpass, in importance other factors, such as party identification or social cleavages.

How does economic voting work? The outline is simple enough. First, voters attribute to the incumbent responsibility for managing the economy. Second, they judge economic conditions. Third, they blame or praise accordingly with their vote. Slight variation in the process can occur at any of these decision points. Voters may define the political economic incumbent differently, for example, prime minister, president, or legislature. They may have differing assessments of economic conditions, for example, some may see things as better, others worse. They may vary in the intensity of their blame; for example, workers might react more strongly to recession (Weatherford 1978). Such variations in the reasoning chain, when systematically linked to identifiable psychological or sociological groups, expose heterogeneity in economic voting. Trust, individualism, sophistication, education, and gender have all been found, at least at certain times, to condition the economic vote.

Just as group membership can condition the economic vote, so can political context. It has enduring aspects, mostly from institutions, and malleable aspects, mostly from the game of politics. The essentially fixed, institutional features of a polity, often written in the constitution or standing legislation—term definitions, power divisions, electoral laws, ballot rules, election type—can alter the direction and weight of the economic vote. The fluctuating, short-run concerns of politics—composition of the ruling coalition, opposition strength, multi-party dynamics, government time in office—also impact the economic vote. Besides the political context, there is the economic context, of which globalization is but one example. These contextual variables vary across nations and within nations, ever-shaping the economic vote coefficient. In democracies, economic currents sway electors, forging new streams as context dictates, arriving at the ballot box as the river arrives at the sea.

When voters look at the economy, what aspects are relevant? They may look directly or indirectly at a host of formal indices, such as the GDP growth rate, and informal indicators, such as their own pocketbook. In general, voters observe several indices, weigh them, and make a summary economic judgment. In these evaluations, the nation consistently appears as a more important object of evaluation than lower political units, e.g. states and counties, or lower social units, e.g. the neighborhood and the individual. These summary judgments are not totally unrelated to objective measures of the economy. On the contrary, when this question has been studied, subjective assessments are found predictive of objective assessments. Take our leading examples, of the US, Britain, and France. Subjective national economic assessments, when aggregated, correlate very highly with standard macroeconomic indicators of growth, inflation, and unemployment (see respectively, Nadeau and Lewis-Beck 2001; Sanders 2000; Bélanger and Lewis-Beck 2004, 232–4).

While economic voters give emphasis to the well-being of the nation, their gaze may be retrospective, prospective, or a mix of the two, depending in part on the political context. When the incumbent party candidate has a clear track record, presumably from having served a term or two, past considerations weigh more heavily. In contrast, when the incumbent party candidate has an ambiguous track record, economic voting is more likely to be prospective.

In terms of future survey research on economic voting, we believe three general areas deserve special attention: the composition of sociotropic perceptions, the modeling of economic effects, and the stability of the economic vote. We consider each of these, in turn, beginning with the first. What information on the economy do voters have? There is work here, which serves as a beginning (Blendon et al. 1997; Holbrook and Garand 1996; Sanders 2000). And, we need to know more about how they weigh the information in arriving at their summary judgment of the national economy. We know little at the individual level about the particular subjective and objective economic assessments that feed into the voter's overall evaluation of the economy.

We would expect these components to change over time, in part because of how the media "frames" economic news (Behr and Iyengar 1985; Goidel and Langley 1995; Haller and Norpoth 1997; Hetherington 1996; Mutz 1994). As job insecurity and income inequality continue to rise, in fact and in media reports, national economic performance could change from a consensus issue to a conflict issue. That is, economic voters might become focused on growth in their particular share of the pie, rather than growth of the whole pie, as now. (There is some indirect evidence for this, in the effects of the "jobs" variable in the forecast of current US elections; see Lewis-Beck and Tien 2004). In such a circumstance, the impact of the standard sociotropic measures would decline, and distributional measures would have to take their place.

With respect to modeling, economic perceptions routinely manage statistical significance, even in the face of controlling, or over-controlling. The single-equation format, followed by almost all practitioners in this field, poses collinearity risks that need to be recognized. One possible solution moves to a multi-equation format. Another, perhaps preferable, solution gives more attention to verifying the exogenous status of the independent variables. Worry has been expressed that the economic perception variables are endogenous, in part determined by partisanship (Anderson, Mendes, and Tverdora 2004; Evans 1999; Evans and Andersen 2006; Wlezien, Franklin, and Twiggs 1997). A first step, of course, is to include partisan variables as controls, but that is only a first step. It may be necessary to exogenize the economic perception variables by some sort of instrumental variables procedure. More importantly, the partisan variables may need to be made exogenous, on the grounds that they are absorbing too much variance explained and suppressing the economic effects (Lewis-Beck 2006). This seems to be the logic Fiorina (1981, 170) employed, when he lagged party identification and converted it into an instrument, before estimating economic effects. His more or less forgotten exercise suggests that panel data, rather than cross-sectional data, are the way out of this endogeneity-exogeneity dilemma.

Once the exogeneity of the independent variables has been assured, the analyst can better focus on the key question of the impact of the economic issue, relative to other issues. In his analysis of the major western European democracies, Lewis-Beck (1988, 160) concluded that economics provided the "premier issue set." Alvarez and Nagler (1995, 1998) and Alvarez, Nagler, and Bowler (2000) make much the same argument for the US and Britain. In terms of "issue voting" models, the expectation is that economics can be demonstrated generally to be the top issue for the electorate, both in terms of rank and structural effect. Already, in the studies at hand, it has been shown a respectable rival to partisan identification, in terms of impact. As the exogeneity issues come to be resolved, it may appear in even closer competition.

Some have questioned the value, not to say the reality, of the economic voting hypothesis, because of the instability of coefficients across studies. First, recall that even the parameter estimates from the anchoring variables of social cleavage and party identification have varied from election to election without diminishing their acknowledged importance in models of democratic vote choice. Second, the findings reviewed here suggest the instability of the economic vote is more apparent, a product of neglecting contextual effects. Once the long-term institutional or the short-term political framework is modeled, the economic coefficients settle down in understandable ways. For example, effects are predictably larger in presidential elections, compared to legislative contests, predictably smaller when the ruling government is multi-party rather than single party. Third, among issue variables, economics must inherently produce more stable coefficients than most, because it is the central valence issue of domestic democratic politics. Just as everyone wants peace abroad, they want prosperity at home. When governments fail to deliver on that economic promise, citizens hold them accountable.

REFERENCES

ALLEN, M. W. 2000. Self-interest, economic beliefs, and political party preference in New Zealand. *Political Psychology*, 21 (2): 323–45.

ALT, J. 1979. *The Politics of Economic Decline*. Cambridge: Cambridge University Press.

ALVAREZ, R. M., and NAGLER, J. 1995. Economics, issues and the Perot candidacy: voter choice in the 1992 presidential elections. *American Journal of Political Science*, 39: 714–44.

—— 1998. Economics, entitlements, and social issues: voter choice in the 1996 presidential election. *American Journal of Political Science*, 42: 1349–63.

—— NAGLER, J., and BOWLER, S. 2000. Issues, economics, and the dynamics of multiparty elections: the British 1987 general election. *American Political Science Review*, 94 (1): 131–49.

ANDERSON, C. J. 1995. *Blaming the Government: Citizens and the Economy in Five European Democracies*. Armonk, NY: M. E. Sharpe

—— 2000. Economic voting and political context: a comparative perspective. *Electoral Studies*, 19: 151–70.

—— MENDES, S. M., and TVERDOVA, Y. 2004. Endogenous economic voting: evidence from the 1997 British election. *Electoral Studies*, 23: 683–708.

ANDERSON, L., LEWIS-BECK, M. S., and STEGMAIER, M. 2003. Post-socialist democratization: a comparative political economy model of the vote for Hungary and Nicaragua. *Electoral Studies*, 22: 469–84.

BEHR, R., and IYENGAR, S. 1985. Television news, real-world cues, and changes in the public agenda. *Public Opinion Quarterly*, 49: 38–57.

BÉLANGER, E., and LEWIS-BECK, M. S. 2004. National economic voting in France: objective versus subjective measures. Pp. 231–42 in *The French Voter: Before and After the 2002 Elections*, ed. M. S. Lewis-Beck. New York: Palgrave Macmillan.

BELLUCCI, P. 2002. From class voting to economic voting: patterns of individualization of electoral behavior in Italy, 1972–1996. Pp. 261–83 in *Economic Voting*, ed. H. Dorussen and M. Taylor. New York: Routledge.

BENTON, A. L. 2005. Dissatisfied democrats or retrospective voters? Economic hardship, political institutions, and voting behavior in Latin America. *Comparative Political Studies*, 38 (4): 417–42.

BIELASIAK, J., and BLUNCK, D. 2002. Past and present in transitional voting: electoral choices in post-communist Poland. *Party Politics*, 8: 563–85.

BLAIS, A., NADEAU, R., GIDENGIL, E., and NEVITTE, N. 2002. The impact of issues and the economy in the 1997 Canadian federal election. *Canadian Journal of Political Science*, 35: 409–21.

BLENDON, R. J., BENSON, J. M., BRODIE, M., MORIN, R., ALTMAN, D. E., GITTERMAN, D., BROSSARD, M., and JAMES, M. 1997. Bridging the gap between the public's and economists' views of the economy. *Journal of Economic Perspectives*, 11 (3): 105–18.

BORRE, O. 1997. Economic voting in Danish electoral surveys 1987–1994. *Scandinavian Political Studies*, 20 (4): 347–65.

BOY, D. 1997. *L'Électeur a ses raisons*. Paris: Presses de Sciences Politiques.

—— and MAYER, N. 1993. *The French Voter Decides*. Ann Arbor: University of Michigan Press.

BRATTON, M., MATTES, R., and GYIMAH-BOADI, E. 2005. *Public Opinion, Democracy and Market Reform in Africa*. New York: Cambridge University Press.

BUTLER, D., and STOKES, D. 1969. *Political Change in Britain: Forces Shaping Electoral Choice*. New York: St Martin's Press.

CANTON, D., and JORRAT, J. R. 2002. Economic evaluations, partisanship, and social bases of presidential voting in Argentina, 1995 and 1999. *International Journal of Public Opinion Research,* 14 (4): 413–27.

CAUTRÉS, B., and MAYER, N. 2004. *Le Nouveau Désordre électoral, les leçons du 21 avril 2002.* Paris: Presses de Sciences Politiques.

CHAPPELL, H. W., JR., and VEIGA, L. G. 2000. Economics and elections in Western Europe: 1960–1997. *Electoral Studies,* 19: 183–97.

CLARKE, H., and STEWART, M. 1994. Prospections, retrospections, and rationality: the "bankers" model of presidential approval reconsidered. *American Journal of Political Science,* 38: 1104–23.

—— SANDERS, D., STEWART, M. C., and WHITELEY, P. 2004. *Political Choice in Britain.* Oxford: Oxford University Press.

COLTON, T. J. 1996. Economics and voting in Russia. *Post-Soviet Affairs,* 12 (4): 289–317.

—— 2000. *Transitional Citizens: Voters and What Influences Them in the New Russia.* Cambridge, Mass.: Harvard University Press.

DOMÍNGUEZ, J. I., and McCANN, J. A. 1995. Shaping Mexico's electoral arena: the construction of partisan cleavages in the 1988 and 1991 national elections. *American Political Science Review.* 89: 34–48.

DOWNS, A. 1957. *An Economic Theory of Democracy.* New York: Harper & Row.

DUCH, R. M. 2001. A developmental model of heterogeneous economic voting in new democracies. *American Political Science Review,* 95 (4): 895–910.

EVANS, G. 1999. Economics and politics revisited: exploring the decline in Conservative support, 1992–1995. *Political Studies,* 47: 139–51.

—— and ANDERSEN, R. 2006. The political conditioning of economic perceptions. *Journal of Politics,* 68: 194–207.

FELDMAN, S. 1982. Economic self-interest and political behavior. *American Journal of Political Science,* 26: 446–66.

FIORINA, M. 1981. *Retrospective Voting in American National Elections.* New Haven: Yale University Press.

FRAILE, M. 2002. The retrospective voter in Spain during the 1990s. Pp. 284–302 in *Economic Voting,* ed. H. Dorussen and M. Taylor. New York: Routledge.

FREY, B. S., and GARBERS, H. 1972. Der Einfluss wirtschaftlicher variabler auf die popularität der regierung—eine empirische analyse. *Jahrbücher für Nationalökonomie und Statistik,* 186: 281–95.

FRÖCHLING, H. 1998. *Ökonomie und Wahlen in Westlichen Demokratien: Ein Vergleichende Rational-Choice-Analyse.* Weisbaden: Westdeutscher Verlag.

GOIDEL, R. K., and LANGLEY, R. E. 1995. Media coverage of the economy and aggregate economic evaluations: uncovering evidence of indirect media effects. *Political Research Quarterly,* 48: 313–28.

GOMEZ, B. T., and WILSON, J. M. 2001. Political sophistication and economic voting in the American electorate: a theory of heterogeneous attribution. *American Journal of Political Science,* 45 (4): 899–914.

GOODHART, C. A. E., and BHANSALI, R. J. 1970. Political economy. *Political Studies,* 18: 43–106.

HALLER, H. B., and NORPOTH, H. 1997. Reality bites: news exposure and economic opinion. *Public Opinion Quarterly,* 61: 555–75.

HELLWIG, T. T. 2001. Interdependence, government constraints, and economic voting. *Journal of Politics,* 63 (4): 1141–62.

HESLI, V. L., and BASHKIROVA, E. 2001. The impact of time and economic circumstances on popular evaluations of Russia's president. *International Political Science Review,* 22: 379–98.

HETHERINGTON, M. 1996. The media's role in forming voters national economic evaluations in 1992. *American Journal of Political Science*, 40: 372–95.

HOLBROOK, T., and GARAND, J. 1996. Homo economus? Economic information and economic voting. *Political Research Quarterly*, 49: 351–75.

HSIEN, J. F., LACY, D., and NIOU, E. M. S. 1998. Retrospective and prospective voting in a one-party-dominant democracy: Taiwan's 1996 presidential election. *Public Choice*, 97: 383–99.

IRWIN, G., and VAN HOLSTEYN, J. 1997. Where to go from here? Revamping electoral politics in the Netherlands. *West European Politics*, 20 (2): 93–118.

JOHNSTON, R., PATTIE, C., DORLING, D., McALLISTER, I., TUNSTALL, H., and ROSSITER, D. 2000. Local context, retrospective economic evaluations, and voting: the 1997 general election in England and Wales. *Political Behavior*, 22 (2): 121–43.

KEY, V. O. 1966. *The Responsible Electorate*. New York: Vintage.

KIEWIET, D. R. 1983. *Macroeconomics and Micropolitics: The Electoral Effects of Economic Issues*. Chicago: University of Chicago Press.

KINDER, D., ADAMS, G., and GRONKE, P. W. 1989. Economics and politics in the 1984 American presidential election. *American Journal of Political Science*, 33: 491–515.

KRAMER, G. 1971. Short-term fluctuations in U.S. voting behavior, 1896–1964. *American Political Science Review*, 65: 131–43.

—— 1983. The ecological fallacy revisited: aggregate- versus individual-level findings on economics and elections, and sociotropic voting. *American Political Science Review*, 77: 92–111.

LANOUE, D. J. 1994. Retrospective and prospective voting in presidential-year elections. *Political Research Quarterly*, 47: 193–205.

LEWIS-BECK, M. S. 1983. Economics and the French voter: a microanalysis. *Public Opinion Quarterly*, 47: 347–60.

—— 1986. Comparative economic voting: Britain, France, Germany, Italy. *American Journal of Political Science*, 30: 315–46.

—— 1988. *Economics and Elections: The Major Western Democracies*. Ann Arbor: University of Michigan Press.

—— 1997. Le porte-monnie en question. Pp. 239–61 in *L'Électeur a ses raisons*, ed. D. Boy and N. Mayer. Paris: Presses de la Foundation Nationale des Sciences Politiques.

—— 2006. Does economics still matter? Econometrics and the vote. *Journal of Politics*, 68: 208–12.

—— and MITCHELL, G. 1990. Modelos transnacionales de voto economico: estudio de un conjunto de paises europeos. *Revista del Instituto de Estudios Economicos*, 4: 65–81.

—— and NADEAU, R. 2000. French electoral institutions and the economic vote. *Electoral Studies*, 19: 171–182.

—— and PALDAM, M. 2000. Economic voting: an introduction. *Electoral Studies*, 19: 113–21.

—— and STEGMAIER, M. 2000. Economic determinants of electoral outcomes. *Annual Review of Political Science*, 3: 183–219.

—— and TIEN, C. 2004. Jobs and the job of president: a forecast for 2004. *PS: Political Science and Politics*, 37: 753–58.

LOCKERBIE, B. 1992. Prospective voting in presidential elections, 1956–1988. *American Politics Quarterly*, 20: 308–25.

McALLISTER, I., and STUDLAR, D. T. 1992. Region and voting in Britain, 1979–87: territorial polarization or artefact? *American Journal of Political Science*, 36 (1): 168–99.

MACKUEN, M., ERIKSON, R., and STIMSON, J. 1992. Peasants or bankers? The American electorate and the U.S. economy. *American Political Science Review*, 86: 597–611.

MARKUS, G. 1988. The impact of personal and national economic conditions on the presidential vote: a pooled cross-sectional analysis. *American Journal of Political Science*, 32: 137–54.

—— 1992. The impact of personal and national economic conditions on presidential voting, 1956–1988. *American Journal of Political Science*, 36: 829–34.

MISHLER, W., and WILLERTON, J. P. 2003. The dynamics of presidential popularity in post-communist Russia: cultural imperative versus neo-institutional choice? *Journal of Politics*, 65: 111–41.

MONROE, K. R. 1984. *Presidential Popularity and the Economy*. New York: Praeger.

MUGHAN, A., BEAN, C., and MCALLISTER, I. 2003. Economic globalization, job insecurity and the populist reaction. *Electoral Studies*, 22: 617–33.

MUTZ, D. 1994. Contextualizing personal experience: the role of the mass media. *Journal of Politics*, 56: 689–715.

NADEAU, R., and LEWIS-BECK, M. S. 2001. National economic voting in U.S. presidential elections. *Journal of Politics*, 63: 159–81.

—— NIEMI, R. G., and YOSHINAKA, A. 2002. A cross-national analysis of economic voting: taking account of the political context across time and nations. *Electoral Studies*, 21: 403–23.

NANNESTAD, P., and PALDAM, M. 1994. The VP function: a survey of the literature on vote and popularity functions after 25 years. *Public Choice*, 79: 213–45.

—— PALDAM, M., and ROSHOLM, M. 2003. System change and economic evaluations: a study of immigrants and natives in Israel. *Electoral Studies*, 22: 485–501.

NORPOTH, H. 1996. The economy. Pp. 299–318 in *Comparing Democracies: Elections and Voting in Global Perspective*. ed. L. LeDuc, R. G. Niemi, and P. Norris. Thousand Oaks, Calif.: Sage.

—— 2004. Bush v. Gore: the recount of economic voting. Pp. 49–64 in *Models of Voting in Presidential Elections*, ed. H. F. Weisberg and C. Wilcox. Stanford, Calif.: Stanford University Press.

PACEK, A. C. 1994. Macroeconomic conditions and electoral politics in East Central Europe. *American Journal of Political Science*, 38: 723–44.

—— and RADCLIFF, B. 1995. Political economy of competitive elections in the developing world. *American Journal of Political Science*, 39: 745–59.

PALDAM, M. 1991. How robust is the vote function? A study of seventeen nations over four decades. Pp. 9–31 in *Economics and Politics: The Calculus of Support*, ed. H. Norpoth, M. S. Lewis-Beck, and J. D. Lafay. Ann Arbor: University of Michigan Press.

POSNER, D. N., and SIMON, D. J. 2002. Economic conditions and incumbent support in Africa's new democracies: evidence from Zambia. *Comparative Political Studies*, 35 (3): 313–36.

POWELL, G. B., and WHITTEN, G. D. 1993. A cross-national analysis of economic voting: taking account of the political context. *American Journal of Political Science*, 37: 391–414.

REMMER, K. L. 1991. The political impact of economic crisis in Latin America in the 1980s. *American Political Science Review*, 85: 777–800.

ROBERTS, K. M., and WIBBELS, E. 1999. Party systems and electoral volatility in Latin America: a test of economic institutional, and structural explanations. *American Political Science Review*, 93 (3): 575–90.

ROSA, J. J., and AMSON, D. 1976. Conditions économiques et elections: une analyse politico-économetrique (1920–1973). *Revue Française de Science Politique*, 26: 1101–24.

RUDOLPH, T. J. and GRANT, J. T. 2002. An attributional model of economic voting: evidence from the 2000 presidential election. *Political Research Quarterly*, 55(4): 805–23.

SAMUELS, D. 2004. Presidentialism and accountability for the economy in comparative perspective. *American Political Science Review*, 98: 425–36.

SANDERS, D. 2000. The real economy and the perceived economy in popularity functions: how much do the voters need to know? A study of British data, 1974–97. *Electoral Studies*, 19: 275–94.

——— 2003. Party identification, economic perceptions, and voting in British general elections, 1974–97. *Electoral Studies*, 22: 239–63.

SELIGSON, M. A., and GOMEZ, M. 1989. Ordinary elections in extraordinary times: the political economy of voting in Costa Rica. Pp. 158–84 in *Elections and Democracy in Central America*, ed. J. A. Booth and M. A. Seligson. Chapel Hill: University of North Carolina Press.

STOKES, D. E. 1992. Valence politics. Pp. 141–62 in *Electoral Politics*, ed. D. Kavanagh. Oxford: Clarendon Press.

STUDLAR, D. T., McALLISTER, I., and ASCUI, A. 1990. Privatization and the British electorate: microeconomic policies, macroeconomic evaluations, and party support. *American Journal of Political Science*, 34: 1077–101.

TUCKER, J. A. 2001. Economic conditions and the vote for incumbent parties in Russia, Poland, Hungary, Slovakia, and the Czech Republic from 1990 to 1996. *Post-Soviet Affairs*, 17 (4): 309–31.

WEATHERFORD, M. S. 1978. Economic conditions and electoral outcomes: class differences in the political response to recession. *American Journal of Political Science*, 22: 917–38.

WELCH, S., and HIBBING, J. 1992. Financial conditions, gender, and voting in American national elections. *Journal of Politics*, 54: 197–213.

WHITELEY, P. F. 2005. Forecasting seats from votes in British general elections. *British Journal of Political Science and International Relations*, 7 (2): 165–73.

WHITTEN, G. D., and PALMER, H. D. 1999. Cross-national analyses of economic voting. *Electoral Studies*, 18: 49–67.

WILKIN, S., HALLER, B., and NORPORTH, H. 1997. From Argentina to Zambia: a world-wide test of economic voting. *Electoral Studies*, 16: 301–16.

WLEZIEN, C., FRANKLIN, M., and TWIGGS, D. 1997. Economic perceptions and vote choice: disentangling the endogeneity. *Political Behavior*, 19 (1): 7–17.

YOUDE, J. 2005. Economics and government popularity in Ghana. *Electoral Studies*, 24: 1–16.

CHAPTER 28

NEW DIMENSIONS OF POLITICAL CLEAVAGE

KEVIN DEEGAN-KRAUSE

A NEWCOMER to studies of political cleavage may be forgiven for thinking that the only common denominator of contemporary scholarship is an obligatory reference to Seymour Martin Lipset and Stein Rokkan's 1967 "Cleavage Structures, Party Systems, and Voter Alignments." As in many fields of study related to democratic politics, research on cleavage faces a recent surplus of novelty:

- new cases in Latin America, Central and Eastern Europe, Africa and Asia;
- new data and new methods;
- new conceptual understandings of the term "cleavage."

With this explosion of possibilities, a general theory of cleavage seems even less likely today than in 1967, but a survey of scholarship on new cleavages—and new thinking on old cleavages—can outline broad patterns and point to areas for further research. Such a survey must ask what scholars now mean when they talk about cleavages and what recent studies reveal about the contours of new cleavages, their origins, and their consequences.

1 NEW WORDS FOR CLEAVAGE?

A baffling array of inconsistently used terms plagues contemporary scholarship on cleavage. Precise definition was not Lipset and Rokkan's main goal and their article's provocative ambiguity may explain its endurance. Subsequent researchers have attempted to introduce more precision, most prominently Bartolini and Mair who specify that cleavage entails

an empirical element, which identifies the empirical referent of the concept, and which we can define in social-structural terms; a normative element, that is the set of values and beliefs which provides a sense of identity and role to the empirical element, and which reflect the self-consciousness of the social group(s) involved; and an organizational/behavioral element, that is the set of individual interactions, institutions, and organizations, such as political parties, which develop as part of the cleavage. (1990, 215)

For Bartolini and Mair a cleavage involves *all* of these differences at the same time. They emphasize that "cleavages cannot be reduced simply to the outgrowths of social stratification; rather, social distinctions become cleavages when they are organized as such.... A cleavage has therefore to be considered primarily as *a form of closure of social relationships*" (216). While many authors take issue with particular aspects of this definition, it is remarkable the degree to which the major works in the field accept the three elements. Research on cleavage most often entails the search for: (*a*) self-conscious demographic groups; (*b*) sharing a common mindset; and (*c*) a distinct political organization.

The scholarly quest to identify cleavages with all three elements yields fruitful results for some cases in some eras but not for others. Analysis of those cases that lack one or more of the three elements has been hampered by the lack of common vocabulary for "something less" than Bartolini and Mair's cleavage definition. It is helpful, therefore, to first establish a common basis for "something less" than cleavage. The conceptual model presented in Figure 28.1 offers a suggestion for simplifying the current conceptual discussion down to seven key relationships across three levels, accepting or adapting current usage wherever possible.

One Cleavage Element: A Difference. "Difference" nicely captures the notion of a lone cleavage element. This chapter uses the general term "structure" to include the "empirical," "ascriptive," or "demographic" categories found in cleavage research. The heading "attitude" here refers to "normative" or "value" categories. The heading "institution" refers to activity elsewhere labeled as "political," "organizational," or "behavioral."

Two Cleavage Elements: A Divide. The term "divide" which is already in relatively common use effectively captures the notion of distinct sides but without the sheer quality of a cleavage. Three such pairs are possible:

(1) *Structure plus Attitudes.* The term "position divide" offers an alternative to various teleological notions such as "non-politicized cleavage" used to describe the alignment of structural and attitudinal difference without an accompanying political alignment. "Position" carries connotations both of structural location and of individual attitude.

(2) *Structure plus Institutions.* Knutsen and Scarborough's "pure structural voting" (1995) accurately captures the notion, but does not lend itself to easy use. The phrase "census divide," echoing Horowitz's "census elections" (1985), captures the alignment of group identity and political choice without attitudinal trappings.

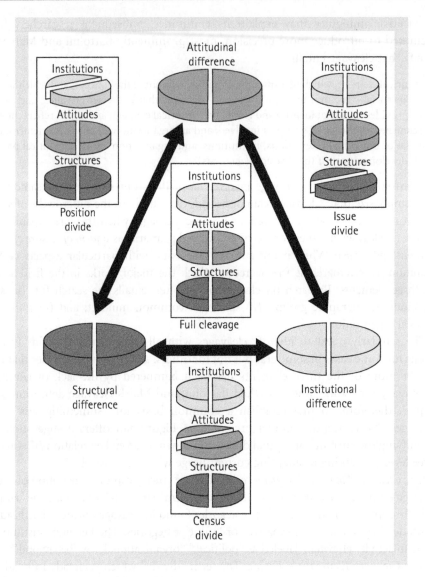

Fig. 28.1 Model of difference, divide, and cleavage

(3) *Attitudes plus Institutions.* This relationship has spawned the greatest variety of alternatives and stands in greatest need of clarity. The word "issues" emerges regularly in scholarship in this area and refers to the interplay between attitude and partisanship.

Three Cleavage Elements: Full Cleavage. The word "cleavage" has been used in so many ways that it can serve here only as a generic term for division. The phrase "full cleavage" is necessary to specify Bartolini and Mair's threefold concept.

2 NEW TYPOLOGIES OF CLEAVAGE?

In a handbook on political behavior it is appropriate to begin with *political* differences and assess the degree to which these overlap with attitudinal differences to form issue divides or with structural differences to form census divides or with both to form full cleavages.

Much scholarship on "cleavage" focuses on how institutional and attitudinal differences interact to form issue divides. A profusion of new surveys has made such studies easier, but there are other reasons for starting with issue divides. Issue divides apparently have increased in importance, accompanying or perhaps supplanting structurally based divides. A sign of the importance of issue divides is the number of attempts to create comprehensive schemas of issue divides. Sartori (1976) begins with the primacy of programmatic left and right emphasizing questions of market and state distribution of economic resources. His preliminary four-dimensional schema also recognizes other potentially programmatic conflicts including secularism against denominations, ethnicity against integration, and democracy against authoritarianism. Others have proposed additional categories including material vs postmaterial values (Inglehart 1977), foreign policy questions (Lijphart 1984), and domestic protectionism against processes such as international integration, immigration and globalization (Stubager 2003; Cole 2005; Kriesi 1998).

Of course structure retains an important role. Lipset and Rokkan's definition of key structural elements has survived the test of time not only because its labels elegantly captured key structural differences but also because they have proven highly adaptable:

- "urban–rural" cleavage now represents geographic difference;
- "owner–worker" cleavage represents socioeconomic status;
- "center–periphery" cleavage represents cultural difference, particularly ethnicity;
- "church–state" cleavage represents differences in cultural values and religiosity.

Thus adapted, Lipset and Rokkan's list leaves little room for additional categories. Tóka notes that "The requirement of social closure implies that only a few quasi-demographic differences (class, ethno-religious or regional identity, urban-rural residence) can serve as the bases of cleavages" (Tóka 1998, 596). The few serious rival claimants include generational difference and education level (Inglehart 1977), economic sector (Kriesi 1998), and gender (Brooks, Nieuwbeerta, and Manza 2006).

3 NEW CONTOURS OF CLEAVAGE?

On the basis of these lists we can explore the contours of cleavages. This involves several fairly obvious questions built around the above-mentioned conceptual framework: (1) the importance of various issue divides; (2) the interaction among various issue divides; and (3) the structural roots of issue divides and of those institutional differences without attitudinal components. Many accepted categories remain useful, even though they were derived from a limited number of mid-twentieth-century democracies. In other respects, however, early twenty-first-century politics challenges the boundaries and pushes the old metaphors to the breaking point, even in long-standing democracies.

3.1 Advanced Industrial Democracies

The divides and cleavages of western Europe have received constant attention from scholars for the past half-century. Their efforts document considerable areas of stability coupled with certain specific changes. Attitudes on economic questions have continued to shape partisan choice as have, to a lesser extent, questions about religion and related cultural values. Furthermore, both social class and religiosity still exhibit a significant relationship to partisanship and in some countries (see chapters by Knutsen and Esmer and Pettersson), as have regional, ethnic, or linguistic differences. Yet much has changed. New institutional differences have emerged with the rise of Green and extreme right parties (and in some countries the collapse of major parties). Established democracies have also experienced the rise of issue divides based on political participation, environmental protection, sex- and repro-duction-related issues, and immigration.

Scholars continue to debate the independence of these "new" attitudinal differences from differences on more established socioeconomic and religious issue questions. Moreno (1999) finds a wide variation in the degree to which respondents' positions on "new" questions reflected their positions on socioeconomic questions, but in most countries exhibited a relatively high degree of independence between the two issue dimensions. Moreno also finds considerable diversity in the degree to which these attitudinal differences align with party preference. In some countries party systems are arrayed across two dimensions, while in other countries parties lay close to a single line on a redistribution vs market dimension or a postmodern vs fundamentalist dimension or a combined postmodern/redistribution vs. fundamentalist/market dimension. Kitschelt and Rehm (2004) find considerably less variation. Although they array parties in a two-dimensional space defined by support for redistribution of income and support for "superior goods" (environment, culture, and education), average party supporters in each of their nine cases line up close to a diagonal line defined by extremes that the authors label as left-libertarian and right-authoritarian, though the clustering and the steepness of the slope differ from case to case.

It is noteworthy that these disagreements tend to fall within fairly narrow bounds. These authors agree about the basic issue dimensions on which parties compete, and they find that postmodern attitudes sometimes align with anti-market attitudes but almost never with *pro*-market attitudes. Researchers disagree more strongly about the degree to which institutional differences and issue divides depend on structural elements. Three decades of research has demonstrated the weakening of party loyalty and the weakening of working-class support for left-wing parties (Nieuwbeerta and Ultee 1999). Brooks, Nieuwbeerta, and Manza (2006) also report a decline in the relationship between religiosity and voting in the Netherlands, a country noted for its strong church vs state cleavage. Many who emphasizes the progress of structural dealignment also note "an increased effect of issues on the vote" which "compensated more or less precisely for the decline in cleavage politics" (Dalton 1996, 335). Much of the increase in issue effects came precisely from the emergence of independent postmaterialist or libertarian issues that exhibited weak relationships to class, religion, or other social structures. In 1988 Knutsen argued that even economic-related attitudes had lost their structural roots: "the Left–Right dimension has altered from a structural class or status cleavage to an independent ideological cleavage" (349). In 1995 Knutsen and Scarbrough found a major rise in the significance of issue dimensions: between 1973 and 1990 attitudes alone came to explain partisan choice better than either structures alone or structures plus attitudes.

Other research, however, suggests merely a shift in the type of structures that underpin issue divides. According to Kriesi (1998) and Kitschelt and Rehm (2004) the redistributionist-libertarian vs market-authoritarian issue divide rests upon strong, cleavage-like roots in non-class structures such as age and gender and of newly disaggregated class categories such as "sociocultural professional" and "routine office worker." A growing number of studies based on diverse data sources and analytical methods suggest a degree of consensus on the emergence of such cleavage patterns in much of western Europe. It appears, however, that quite different patterns exist in cases such as Belgium, Spain, Canada, the United States, and Ireland in which geography and ethnicity play a larger role. Other emerging issue divides may also have the potential to disrupt existing patterns, but despite the enormous economic and cultural role of the European Union, a distinct "integration-independence" issue divide has yet to emerge (Hix 2002).

3.2 Post-communist Europe

Post-communist Europe offers a remarkable laboratory for political development. Although its cleavages bear some similarity to those of industrial democracies, they differ in ways that have important theoretical implications. The first challenge is to establish whether any form of cleavage exists in the region. Innes (2002) challenges the notion that post-communist attitudes and party voting coincide by pointing to large "instant catch-all" parties. She argues that "When party labels become this meaningless, it raises the question of how stable partisanship and consequently system stabilization can be established" (2002, 100). In spite of this programmatic "flexibility," studies demonstrate a measurable degree of regularity and consistency among most eastern European parties' electorates. Gijsberts and Nieuwbeerta (2000) show a narrower distribution of partisan attitudes in post-communist Europe than in Western Europe but similar overall patterns. Economic issues, furthermore, are not necessarily the best way to compare the strength of issue divides in East and West.

Although economy-related divides emerged throughout post-communist Europe, non-economic issue also aligned closely with party preference. Evans and Whitefield's (2000) cross-national analysis from the mid-1990s identifies a large set of countries in which issues other than economic liberalism formed the primary ideological basis of party competition.

Defining the specific contours of these other issue dimensions requires some departure from frameworks created for western Europe. Issue divides on cultural questions vaguely resembled western counterparts, but with significant differences. In western Europe, Moreno contrasts cultural "fundamentalism" with "postmodernism," but in post-communist Europe he finds few characteristically postmodern elements such as "environmental politics" or "sexual preference" (1999, 22) and instead contrasts fundamentalism with cultural "liberalism." Post-communist cultural issue divides primarily involve such questions as the role of the church, abortion, pornography, and consumerism, all filtered through a lens of decades of communist restrictions.

Even more unusual (from a western European perspective) are post-communism's nation-related issue divides. Questions of minority rights form one subset of this category, and these resemble questions about ethnic rights in Spain, Belgium, and Northern Ireland. What differentiates national-related issue divides in the east, however, is the degree to which conflicts over minority rights occur *within* as well as across ethnic lines. These intra-national debates over minorities often form part of a larger issue divide related to national sovereignty and the magnitude of threats to national security (Deegan-Krause 2006). This nationalism issue divide, present in many of the region's new states, has few direct parallels in contemporary industrial democracies except perhaps mid-twentieth-century Ireland, whose divides may be less "exceptional" than scholars have assumed.

A significant share of the post-communist European cases also experienced deep divides over democracy itself. Klingemann (2005) finds that that competition over past authoritarianism continues to shape party competition long after the demise of the authoritarian government. Todosijević, furthermore, finds evidence in Serbia of a contemporary divide "between parties of authoritarian and democratic orientation" (Todosijević 2003, 79, and other surveys). Surveys suggest that this authoritarianism-democracy divide emerged in Slovakia, Croatia, Belarus, Ukraine, and some other former Soviet republics as well. These divides differed from western Europe's authoritarian-libertarian divides to the extent that post-communist authoritarianism had less to do with the democracy's quality than with its very existence.

Post-communist Europe demonstrated not only a wider range of active issue divides than western Europe, but also a far greater diversity of combinations. In some countries, for example, national and economic divides ran parallel while in others the two divides were perpendicular. In the parallel cases, furthermore, some countries' nationalists tended to support market reforms while nationalists elsewhere opposed reforms. The relationship between economic and cultural divides also varied, though cultural and market divides usually formed two independent dimensions. The most consistent combination involved the tendency of authoritarianism to line up with nationalism (Kitschelt 1992), but even here it would be premature to see an inherent link. Since fewer than half of the region's national divides were accompanied by authoritarianism-democracy issue divides it would appear that authoritarians need nationalism more than nationalists need unaccountable authority.

Much of this diversity in issue divides apparently results from a variety of historical circumstances in the region, but another source is the weakness of structural roots for many divides. The nearly perfect correlation between minority ethnicity and voting for minority ethnic parties offers a rare example of a full cleavage. However, such cleavages often had few direct political consequences because of the small size of minority populations. More important divides exhibited weaker roots. Gijsberts and Nieuw-beerta (2000) find that the relationship between social class and economic *attitudes* to be almost as strong in post-communist Europe as in western Europe, but economic attitudes related to party choice only in the Czech Republic. In other countries voters recognized their class interests, but rarely voted according to those interests.

Other structural differences did not even produce significant position divides. The vast majority of ethnic majority voters did not choose nationalist parties, and nationalist attitudes among majority-group voters have proven hard to explain. Since the specific details of nation-related issue divides differed from country to country, broad comparative calculations are difficult, but single-country analyses find that within ethnic populations there were few ascriptive markers for nationalist attitudes (Todosijević 2003; Deegan-Krause 2006). The same absence of a clear demographic profile also characterized authoritarian parties especially during the first half of the 1990s before the younger, educated, urban voters realized the consequences of authoritarian leadership for international integration.

3.3 Latin America

As another regional laboratory, Latin America raises questions about the relevance of cleavage analysis. Scholarship on the region often focuses on the absence of clear attitudinal or structural bases for party support. Conaghan sees "floating politicians and floating voters" (1995, 450). Roberts notes "a shift from fixed and durable bonds to more fluid and contingent forms of support" and a "severe erosion of both encapsulating and programmatic linkages" (2000, 14–15).

A small number of quantitatively based pieces suggest the weakness of cleavages in Latin America relative to other regions and their further weakening over time. Main-waring and Torcal find a considerably smaller relationship between voters' left–right orientation and their party choice in Latin America than in western Europe (2003a). Luna and Zechmeister (2005), note "tremendous heterogeneity." They find western-strength issue divides in some countries (Chile and Uruguay) but in many other countries they find little meaningful relationship. For those countries where patterns were visible, researchers have attempted to identify broader regional patterns. Moreno finds economic issue divides throughout the region but he argues that in most countries these are less important than regime- and culture-related issue divides. He parti-cularly emphasizes the importance of "democracy-authoritarianism" divides in many countries, an observation confirmed by case studies such as Mainwaring and Torcal's analysis of Chile (2003*b*, 83). In the second half of the 1990s, however, Moreno shows that most democracy-related divides had weakened in favor of emerging divides related to cultural questions such as "abortion, religiosity, and nationalist sentiments" (1999, 22).

Notably missing from these assessments is a divide between materialists and post-materialists along western European lines. Moreno (1999) finds only small pockets of post-materialism in Latin America, and as with post-communist Europe, he contrasts fundamentalism with liberalism rather than postmodernism. As in post-communist Europe, furthermore, he shows that authority questions tend to stand on their own and concern the rejection of recent authoritarian regimes rather than political participation. Also missing from the list of major Latin America issue divides are ethnic or linguistic questions. Yashar (1998) notes a growing politicization of indigenous populations and issues specific to those populations, but with relatively minor and indirect effects on national-level party competition.

Even to the extent that Latin American politics is "about something," the attitudes and party choice have little basis in structural elements. Roberts notes that:

Few Latin America party systems have ever lived up to [Bartolini and Mair's] exacting three-dimensional cleavage standards. In particular, the cleavage structures of most Latin American party systems have had shallower roots in sociological distinctions of class and ethnicity. As pointed out by Dix, most political parties in Latin America draw support from a heteroge-neous cross-section of society. (2002, 8)

Using survey evidence from the mid-1990s, Mainwaring and Torcal concluded that:

On average, Latin American voters have weaker individual level attachments to political parties than Western European voters. They are not strongly anchored to parties through the traditional social cleavages that Lipset and Rokkan (1967) emphasized.... Even after decades of some apparent erosion of such cleavages in Western Europe, they remain far more important in anchoring the vote than in most of Latin America. (2003*a*, 17)

The results are not uniform, however, and some countries demonstrate considerably higher class voting. Roberts (2002) uncovers stronger structural roots for "labor-mobilizing party systems" in Argentina, Bolivia, Brazil, Chile, Mexico, Nicaragua, Peru, and Venezuela than in the region's many "elitist party systems." He also notes that neoliberalism and globalization have further undermined these already weak cleavages. Mainwaring and Torcal find class voting to be statistically significant only in Brazil, Argentina, and Peru (2003*a*). Molina and Perez (2004) find unexpectedly weak class voting even for Venezuela under Hugo Chavez.

3.4 Middle East

In the Middle East only a few countries have produced competitive political systems and comparative research on cleavages focuses on Turkey and Israel. While the specific issues and groups differ, the two countries exhibit some similarities, particularly the emergence of "full cleavages" through the emergence of issue divides that parallel structural differences. According to Shamir and Arian "issues involving identity dilemmas...have become increasingly important in structuring the vote. Such dilemmas amalgamate policy issues and social allegiances, while reinforcing existing cleavage structures" (1999, 265). In Turkey, relationships between structural, attitudinal, and institutional elements have also strengthened over time and Hazama argues that "social cleavages and the party system in Turkey seem to be heading for convergence" (2003, 379). This process diverges from the western European patterns not only in the direction of movement—toward full cleavages rather than away—but in the nature of the issues and structures. In Israel as in Turkey, the full cleavages emerge around questions of identity related to ethnicity religious sects, and degree of religiosity. In the process, socioeconomic issue divides and socioeconomic structures have lost importance in political conflict except to the extent that economic position depends on religious or ethnic identity.

3.5 Asia

As in the Middle East, few Asian countries followed western European cleavage patterns. Although Japan comes closest to the western European model, its relatively prominent left–right divide "had more to do with foreign policy and defense" than with class issues, and upheavals in Japanese party politics in the mid-1990s led "the demise of left–right ideological politics in Japan" (Weisberg and Tanaka 2001, 90). In Korea and Taiwan politics experienced even weaker socioeconomic divides and tended instead toward democracy-related and nation-related issue divides, though Wong argues that Taiwan's political parties remained largely "nonprogrammatic" on socioeconomic questions whereas anti-authoritarian parties in Korea were more deeply "anchored in a vision of socioeconomic transformation" (2004, 1221–2). Korean parties, however, depended heavily on non-attitudinal elements including structural "regionalism" and "personality dominated, clientelistic parties, built on the basis of vast networks of patron-client relations and informally institutionalized intra-party factions" (Croissant 2002a, 250).

In Southeast Asia, a combination of ethnic structures and clientelist networks (sometimes overlapping and sometimes not) tended to dominate politics with little role for issues that were not immediately reducible to group or clan claims. Croissant argues that "party systems in Asia exhibit a much lower ideological or programmatic orientation than party systems in the Western world" (2002b, 347). In some countries, however, group differences also overlapped broader attitudinal differences, particularly in Indonesia where some party voters exhibited attitudinal and structural characteristics that might be defined as "Islamist" and "secular" (Qodari 2005) and in Thailand where the emergence of a significant new party helped to produce a higher degree of overlap between party choice, attitudes toward redistribution, and socioeconomic position (at the individual and regional levels) (Croissant and Pojar 2005).

In South Asia, observers note a shift from clientelist networks to ethnic structures. Chhibber argues that the past two decades have witnessed "an erosion of traditional clientelist politics [and] a marked increase in the political saliency of essentialized identities of caste, religious community, and ethnicity (subnationalism)" (Chhibber 1999, 493–4). These increasingly salient structures, furthermore, have become alternative mechanisms for extracting state resources and the focus on "state resources . . . as streams that can be channeled toward those who have the power to control them" has prevented competition over "the basic framework of the economy" (Mehta 1997, 64). At the same time the sheer diversity of groups in India has exerted a restraining influence on the emergence of nationwide structural divides, and caste differences within the Hindu population have weakened the structural basis of a Hinduism-related cleavage" (Ganguly 2003, 22).

3.6 Africa

In Africa, unlike the regions above, most party systems do not give even a supporting role to attitudinal differences and issue divides. Research in the region begins (and often ends) with the role of structural elements. Young's research on Africa in the mid-1990s identified "few cases . . . where political alignments are not significantly affected by communal solidarities," because candidates rely on "vague slogans expressing desire for change and opposition to incumbents" rather than "defining alternative visions of society" (1996, 61–2). Nearly a decade later, van de Walle argued that "the low salience of ideology for the majority of [African] parties is unmistakable" (2003, 304). African voting thus depends on a combination of the highly individual and the highly structural and "election campaigns have been conducted almost entirely on the basis of personal and ethno-regional appeals for support. In most countries, . . . ethnic identity provides a remarkably precise prediction of voting behavior" (305). Posner cautions against an oversimplified view of structural elements, however, noting that "in-group/out-group distinctions" and other "axes of social differentiation" are complex and may emerge on the basis of language, religion, as well as "tribal affiliation, clan membership, geographic region of origin, or race" (2001, 2). He further notes that since no single group is likely to produce an electoral majority, ambitious politicians must engage in coalition building that transcends structural differences. Mozaffar concurs, arguing that the "formation of multiethnic electoral coalitions" may offer some degree of choice and may lead to "variations in the configuration of resulting ethnopolitical cleavages" (Mozaffar, Scarritt, and Galaich 2003, 389–90).

3.7 Patterns and Trends

Despite what seems an irreducible degree of diversity in the world's cleavage patterns, some regularities do emerge and some developments prove widespread enough to bear comment. Except in many African states, attitudes play an almost uniformly important role in political choice. The character of the most salient attitudes differs, however, not only from region to region but from country to country. Only among western democracies do issue divides show signs of an emerging pattern. Even in those countries, the claim to regularity is weak: most western countries exhibit a socioeconomic issue divide between state and market distribution that partially overlaps an issue divide between postmaterialism and materialism (or libertarianism and authoritarianism). Other regions exhibit more change and richer variety. An issue divide between pro-market and pro-redistribution parties emerged in nearly all countries, but it frequently played a secondary or tertiary role to issue divides that involved policy on national or religion questions or questions about democracy itself. The variety extends, furthermore, to include patterns of interaction among issue divides, supporting Stimson's speculation that "what seems to go together" depends less on "logical connections" than on "psychology (what symbols are shared) and social learning (what kinds of ideas are learned together in one's social background). If nothing is naturally connected, the corollary is that anything can come to seem connected" (2002, 7).

Despite western research that shows the declining role of class voting, structures have also remained robust, particularly those defined by linguistic and other ethnic boundaries. Rare is the party whose support cuts across such ethnic lines or the ethnicity that does not have at least one party that claims to represent ethnic interests. Party support rarely transcends ethnic lines except in cases where two or more groups band together in response to a competing group. The link between ethnicity and politics is extremely strong in Africa and nearly so in parts of Asia and the Middle East, but it is hardly less significant in post-communist Europe. Nor are such cleavages absent in ethnically heterogeneous western democracies. Structures related to religion have proven nearly as robust, particularly fundamentalist Christianity in parts of North America, Roman Catholicism in parts of post-communist Europe and certain sects of Islam in the Middle East and parts of Africa and Asia. Even the shrinking role of class in western countries may reflect less the decline of structure than a shift in salient structural markers away from class hierarchy and toward occupational and sectoral categories.

The relationship between attitudes and structure has also developed new complexities. The growing importance of attitudes may contribute to a further disappearance of many census divides—the non-attitudinal relationship between structure and voting—as structural groups develop attitudinal frames around their collective demands. Issue divides, by contrast, appear capable of surviving without extensive structure, but for some this apparent independence may simply reflect the shift to new and little-studied structural categories. Furthermore, new research suggests that structures can play a different *kind* of role than standard models predict. Examples of the new configuration can be found in many societies with significant ethnic cleavages. Majority and minority ethnic groups may hold very different attitudes about minority rights, but attitudes often differ within those groups as well (especially within majority groups) and in many countries the attitude toward minority rights shapes the central issue divide *within* the majority groups. A similar phenomenon often occurs over religion in the form of sharp disagreements among adherents of a dominant religious sect regarding the role of religion in politics. The central debates of many newer democracies are actually debates within structural segments about whether that structural segment should become the defining element of politics. In a sense, these are *issue divides* about the acceptance or rejection of a particular *full cleavage*. When ethno-nationalists or fundamentalists win convincing victories, full cleavages become more likely. When they fail, issue divides may shift to some other question (perhaps about whether to politicize yet another structural difference). Where the forces are relatively evenly matched, the issue divides concerning the acceptability of nationalism or religious fundamentalism may remain significant for an indefinite period.

Finally, it is necessary to extend the search for structural and attitudinal components of voting into realms that currently receive insufficient attention in cleavage research. The alternatives to structural and attitudinal voting tend to fall under one of three headings: personalism, by which individuals vote on the basis of a candidate's personality or credentials regardless of policy proposals or group affiliations; clientelism, by which individuals exchange their ballot for direct, tangible reward; and pocketbook voting—a combination of clientelist and personalist elements—by which individuals seek tangible reward on the basis of expectations about general economic performance rather than policy proposals. On the map of cleavage politics, these alternatives represent blank spaces, but it is not necessary to cede all of this territory. Cleavage analysis should not ignore the structural nature of clientelism, which often involves large and close-knit social networks. Such networks may be difficult to quantify (especially for outsiders) but to the extent that they perform many of the same functions as ethnic or religious groups and offer a high degree of social closure, they can be understood in structural terms as census-divides or cleavages. Furthermore, pocketbook voting may depend to an unexpected degree on economic program rather than economic performance. Recent findings by Tucker suggest that economic slowdowns in post-communist Europe hurt parties which oppose redistribution more than those "responsible" for the slowdown (Tucker 2006). Finally, much voting that looks random or purely "personal" may simply reflect the absence of appropriate survey questions. Ostiguy (1998), for example, posits a "high-low" divide in Argentina between "stiff and respectable" and "folksy and coarse" that cuts across standard attitudinal and even structural categories. The multi-country surveys necessary to shed light on the broader cleavage patterns are particularly likely to miss such idiosyncratic divides, particularly those connected with national identity or character. Small-scale, thick description thus remains necessary to prevent big, thin surveys from looking at an unusual cleavage and seeing nothing.

4 NEW EXPLANATIONS FOR CLEAVAGE

Current work in cleavage studies extends beyond the discernment of patterns to the understanding of causal mechanisms. Much research in the field presents itself as a "classic dichotomy" between those who emphasize the top-down role of political elites against those who emphasize the bottom-up role of society (Hagopian 2004, 5). The best work in the field seeks not to anoint a winner—it is unlikely that one side is right and the other wrong—but to identify the interaction between elites and society and circumstances that may favor one side or the other.

Although nearly all recent scholarship acknowledges a role for individual choice, many scholars still focus on the constraints that make some choices more likely than others. In their study of post-communist Europe, Evans and Whitefield (2000) argue that voters with little experience and little information will "respond best to the party appeals which most closely relate to their own significant social experiences, identities and values." Parties, in turn, will emphasize "historic social and ideological divisions within the country," and the "most pressing contemporary challenges" rather than tempting fate by "impos[ing] divisions on society." Even those who emphasize structural constraints do not agree on their relative influence. Kitschelt, for example, stresses the legacies of economic development in twentieth-century Europe whereas Evans and Whitefield emphasize significant ethnic and religious differences. Structural accounts have their limits, furthermore. They provide a solid basis for understanding which cleavages are *least* likely to emerge, but in countries with more than one kind of structural fracture, they have difficulty predicting which cleavages will emerge as dominant or how they will align with others. Nor can they easily account for the emergence of issue divides without underlying structural preconditions.

Even Kriesi's work on "social divisions" acknowledges that such divisions "are not translated into politics as a matter of course, but that they are decisively shaped by their political articulation" (1998). Recent cleavage studies empirically demonstrate the effects of political agency both on the attitudinal and structural elements of cleavage. In their most limited form, claims about the relationship between agency and structure emphasize the potential of political actors to "mitigate social divisions" or "politicize them" through "strategic policy choices" (Chhibber and Torcal 1997). Neto and Cox (1997, 167) refer to "exploitable cleavages" and Mozaffar, Scarritt, and Galaich (2003, 390) view ethnicity as "a strategic resource that is contingently politicized." Research provides numerous examples of the reverse principle by which parties *de*-emphasize structural differences when they "identify the common ideological denominator and establish an organizational structure that allows for the aggregation of interests" (Enyedi 2005, 701). Posner further demonstrates that in the right circumstances the amalgamation may even unite groups that otherwise display a high degree of antagonism (Posner 2001). More expansive claims suggest that parties not only increase the political salience of *existing* structural differences but actually create *new* structural differences. Sartori (1969), Zuckerman (1975), and Przeworski and Sprague (1986) emphasizes the capacity for parties to create identities and form communities. Kriesi documents the role of party-organized "collective actions" (1998, 172) to reinforce the "structural and cultural distinctiveness" of left-libertarian sociocultural professionals and of rival segments of the "new middle class" in managerial positions.

Other research focuses on the relationship between political elites and attitudes. Mainwaring argues that "political elites emphasize some issues and muffle others.

Especially before the institutionalization of a party system, their choices affect the issues that emerge as salient in different political systems" (1999, 59). Other recent research emphasizes the ability of parties to shape issue divides not only by influencing the political salience of attitudes but also by the shaping the attitudes themselves, particularly toward issues of low salience. Layman and Carsey use panel surveys to demonstrate that parties can link previously unrelated attitudes. They find that United States voters "change their issue positions in response to changes in the stands of political elites who share their political predispositions" (2002, 202). Party elites can therefore shape alignments among issue divides: "When party elites polarize on multiple issue agendas, rather than just one, the parties in the electorate may well follow suit" (201). A further strong consequence of "party-driven attitudinal conversion" is that parties with relatively stable electorates may actually be able to restructure the fundamental relationship between structure and attitudes. Enyedi (2005), for example, finds that Hungary's Young Democrat party succeeded not only in attracting more authoritarian voters while maintaining a younger-than-average base, but also, perhaps, in increasing levels of authoritarianism among young Hungarians.

Not all elite-led efforts face equal odds for success, however, and recent research tests the conditions favoring politicization or depoliticizaiton of attitudes and structures. It appears, for example, that a larger number of raw structural differences increase the role of elites simply by allowing for more choices about *which* difference to politicize (Deegan-Krause 2006). Institutional factors also matter. Mainwaring's work on Brazil demonstrates how states influence cleavages by shaping party systems (1999). Neto and Cox (1997), Posner (2001), van de Walle (2003), and Burgess and Levitsky (2003) emphasize the role of electoral systems design and party organization. Hagopian (2004) and van de Walle (2003) note that clientelist institutions undermine efforts to politicize particular issues while Chhibber suggests that the weakness of civil society magnifies leaders' influence over cleavages (1999). Most of these works are individual-country case studies, however, and there is a significant need for comparative research that can specify the type of elite influence on cleavage formation and test the conditions under which it may occur.

5 New Consequences of Cleavage?

Extensive comparative research is easier to justify when the phenomenon under study has a significant impact. New research about how cleavages affect democracy points both to new levels of complexity and to new and significant dangers. By far the most frequent justification for the importance of cleavages is its role in creating conditions for stable democratic competition. According to Whitefield's brief summary of conventional wisdom, "the presence of cleavages...can contribute to democratic stability by solidifying party-public ties and increasing the predictability of political outcomes"

(2002, 181–2). Yet research suggests that predictability may not necessarily require full cleavages with structural elements. Tóka's (1998) survey of post-communist Europe shows that structure played little role in stabilizing voting patterns while attitudes played a significant stabilizing role. The question is further complicated by disputes over the dangers of electoral volatility. Some scholars suggest that structurally based cleavages may actually threaten democracy since volatility that is too low may produce "winner-take-all exercises between polarized communities" (van de Walle 2003, 305), and Tóka argues that high volatility may on occasion be "an instrument of electoral control" and calls for "some scepticism . . . regarding its alleged regime-destabilizing potential" (592). The most significant dangers of volatility are more subtle. Tóka acknowledges that "constant and predictable weakness of party loyalties may undermine the accountability and responsiveness of elected office-holders" (1998, 592), and Dalton worries that without "fixed systems of cleavage systems and alignments, . . . modern governments may face increasing difficulty in generating a political consensus in favor of any policy" (Dalton 1996, 341). While not instantaneously fatal, persistent volatility resulting from the absence of cleavages could reduce a democracy's ability to survive over time.

A more concrete, but often neglected reason for caring about divides and cleavages is that these have a decisive impact on outcomes. Cleavages have sides, and the side that wins will—in theory, at least—get more of what it wants than the side that loses. Oscillation between rival positions is well understood in the realm of socioeconomic policy and in industrial democracies the relatively narrow swings between market- and state-oriented policies usually evoke little concern. Many newer democracies face more difficult challenges. Not only are their oscillations wider, but they occur along more dangerous lines. In most cases, even sharp swings between more or less redistributive policies pose little threat to civil and political liberties. The same cannot always be said for swings across national, religious, or especially democratic divides. The good news is that the victory of democratic and inclusive politicians may produce policies that are even more democratic and inclusive than the society as a whole. The bad news, as many countries have discovered to their peril, is that the imbalance sometimes favors authoritarianism and ethnic or religious exclusion. The questions that divide a country thus shape its destiny.

References

BARTOLINI, S., and MAIR, P. 1990. *Identity, Competition, and Electoral Availability: The Stability of European Electorates, 1885–1985*. Cambridge: Cambridge University Press.

BROOKS, C., NIEUWBEERTA, P., and MANZA, J. 2006. Cleavage-based voting behavior in cross-national perspective: evidence from six postwar democracies. *Social Science Research*, 35: 88–128.

BURGESS, K., and LEVITSKY, S. 2003. Explaining populist party adaptation in Latin America: environmental and organizational determinants of party change in Argentina, Mexico, Peru, and Venezuela. *Comparative Political Studies*, 36: 881–911.

CHHIBBER, P. 1999. *Democracy without Associations: Transformation of the Party System and Social Cleavages in India*. Ann Arbor: University of Michigan Press.

CHHIBBER, P., and TORCAL, M. 1997. Elite strategy, social cleavages, and party systems in a new democracy: Spain. *Comparative Political Studies*, 30: 27–54.

COLE, A. 2005. Old Right or New Right? The ideological positioning of parties of the far Right. *European Journal of Political Research*, 44: 203–30.

CONAGHAN, C. 1995. Politicians against parties: discord and disconnection in Ecuador's party system. Pp. 434–58 in *Building Democratic Institutions in Latin America*, ed. S. Mainwaring and T. R. Scully. Palo Alto, Calif.: Stanford University Press.

CROISSANT, A. 2002a. Electoral politics in South Korea. Pp. 233–76 in *Electoral Politics in Southeast and East Asia*, ed. A. Croissant. Singapore: Friedrich-Ebert-Stiftung.

—— 2002b. Electoral politics in Southeast and East Asia: a comparative perspective. Pp. 231–68 in *Electoral Politics in Southeast and East Asia*, ed. A. Croissant. Singapore: Friedrich-Ebert-Stiftung.

—— and POJAR, D. 2005. Quo vadis Thailand? Thai politics after the 2005 parliamentary election. *Strategic Insights*, 4: 6, **www.ciaonet.org/olj/si/si_4_6/si_4_6_005.pdf**.

DALTON, R. J. 1996. Cleavage politics, issues and electoral change. Pp. 319–42 in *Comparing Democracies: Elections and Voting in Comparative Perspective*, ed. L. LeDuc, R. G. Niemi, and P. Norris. London: Sage.

DEEGAN-KRAUSE, K. 2006. *Elected Affinities: Democracy and Party Competition in Slovakia and the Czech Republic*. Palo Alto, Calif.: Stanford University Press.

ENYEDI, Z. 2005. The role of agency in cleavage formation. *European Journal of Political Research*, 44: 697–720.

EVANS, G., and WHITEFIELD, S. 2000. Explaining the formation of electoral cleavages in post-communist democracies. Pp. 36–70 in *Elections in Central and Eastern Europe: The First Wave*, ed. H.-D. Klingemann, E. Mochmann, and K. Newton. Berlin: Sigma.

GANGULY, S. 2003. The crisis of Indian secularism. *Journal of Democracy*. 14: 11–25.

GIJSBERTS, M., and NIEUWBEERTA, P. 2000. Class cleavages in party preferences in the new democracies in Eastern Europe: a comparison with western democracies. *European Societies*, 2: 397–430.

HAGOPIAN, F. 2004. Economic liberalization, party competition, and elite partisan cleavages: Brazil in comparative (Latin American) perspective. Paper presented at the Workshop on the Analysis of Political Cleavages and Party Competition, Duke University, **http://cas.uchicago.edu/workshops/cpolit/papers/uchicago_1201.doc**

HAZAMA, Y. 2003. Social cleavages and electoral support in Turkey: toward convergence? *The Developing Economies*, 61: 362–87.

HOROWITZ, D. 1985. *Ethnic Groups in Conflict*. Berkeley: University of California Press.

HIX, S. 2002. Parliamentary behavio with two principals: preferences, parties, and voting in the European parliament. *American Journal of Political Science*, 46: 688–98.

INGLEHART, R. 1977. *The Silent Revolution: Changing Values and Political Styles among Western Publics*. Princeton: Princeton University Press.

INNES, A. 2002. Party competition in postcommunist Europe: the Great Electoral Lottery. *Comparative Politics*, 35: 85–105.

KITSCHELT, H. 1992. The formation of party systems in East Central Europe. *Politics and Society*, 20: 7–50.

—— and REHM, R. 2004. Socio-economic group preferences and partisan alignments. Paper presented at the 14th International Conference of Europeanists, Chicago, **http://cas.uchicago. edu/workshops/cpolit/papers/kitschelt.pdf**

KLINGEMANN, H.-D. 2005. Post-autocratic party systems and the regime cleavage in new democracies. Pp. 95–135 in *Democracy under construction: Patterns from Four Continents*, ed. U. van Beek. Bloomfield Hills: Barbara Budrich Publishers.

KNUTSEN, O. 1988. The impact of structural and ideological party cleavages in West European democracies: a comparative empirical analysis. *British Journal of Political Science*, 18: 323–52.

—— and SCARBROUGH, E. 1995. Cleavage politics. Pp. 493–523 in *The Impact of Values*, ed. J. W. van Deth. Oxford: Oxford University Press.

KRIESI, H. 1998. The transformation of cleavage politics. *European Journal of Political Research*, 33: 165–85.

LAYMAN, G. C., and CARSEY, T. M. 2002. Party polarization and party structuring of policy attitudes: a comparison of three NES panel studies. *Political Behavior* 24: 199–236.

LIJPHART, A. 1984. *Democracies*. New Haven: Yale University Press.

LIPSET, S. M., and ROKKAN, S. 1967. Cleavage structures, party systems, and voter alignments: an introduction. Pp. 1–64 in *Party Systems and Voter Alignments: Cross-National Perspectives*, ed. S. M. Lipset and S. Rokkan. New York: Free Press.

LUNA, J., and ZECHMEISTER, E. 2005. Political representation in Latin America: a study of elite-mass congruence in nine countries. *Comparative Political Studies*, 38: 388–416.

MAINWARING, S. 1999. *Rethinking Party Systems in the Third Wave of Democratization: The Case of Brazil*. Palo Alto, Calif.: Stanford University Press.

—— and TORCAL, M. 2003a. Individual level anchoring of the vote and party system stability: Latin America and Western Europe. Paper presented at the European Consortium of Political Research, Edinburgh, **www.essex.ac.uk/ecpr/events/jointsessions/paperarchive/edinburgh/ws19/TorcalMainwaring.pdf**

—— —— 2003b. The political recrafting of social bases of party competition: Chile, 1973–95. *British Journal of Political Science*, 33: 55–84.

MEHTA, P. 1997. India: fragmentation amid consensus. *Journal of Democracy*, 8: 56–69.

MOLINA, J., and PÉREZ, C. 2004. Radical change at the ballot box: causes and consequences of electoral behavior in Venezuela's 2000 elections. *Latin American Politics and Society*, 46: 103–34.

MORENO, A. 1999. *Political Cleavages: Issues, Parties and the Consolidation of Democracy*. Boulder Colo.: Westview Press.

MOZAFFAR, S., SCARRITT, J., and GALAICH, G. 2003. Electoral institutions, ethnopolitical cleavages, and party systems in Africa's emerging democracies. *American Political Science Review*, 97: 379–90.

NETO, O., and COX, G. 1997. Electoral institutions, cleavage structures, and the number of parties. *American Journal of Political Science*, 41: 149–74.

NIEUWBEERTA, P., and ULTEE, W. 1999. Class voting in Western industrialized countries, 1945–1990: systematizing and testing explanations. *European Journal of Political Research*, 35: 123–60.

OSTIGUY, P. 1998. Peronism and Anti-Peronism: class-cultural cleavages and political identity in Argentina. Doctoral dissertation, University of California, Berkeley.

POSNER, D. 2001. Regime change and ethnic cleavages in Africa. Paper presented at the Workshop on Democracy in Africa in Comparative Perspective, Stanford University, **http://democracy.stanford. edu/Seminar/Posner.htm**

PRZEWORSKI, A., and SPRAGUE, J. 1986. *Paper Stones: A History of Electoral Socialism*. Chicago: University of Chicago Press.

QODARI, M. 2005. Indonesia's quest for accountable governance. *Journal of Democracy*, 16: 73–87.

ROBERTS, K. 2000. Party-society linkages and democratic representation in Latin America. Paper presented at the Conference on Threats to Democracy in Latin America, University of British Columbia.

—— 2002. Social inequalities without class cleavages: party systems and labor movements in Latin America's neoliberal era. *Studies in Comparative International Development*, 36: 3–33.

SARTORI, G. 1969. From the sociology of politics to political sociology. Pp. 65–100 in *Politics and the Social Sciences*, ed. S. M. Lipset. New York: Oxford University Press.

SARTORI, G. 1976. *Parties and Party Systems.* New York: Cambridge University Press.

SHAMIR, M., and ARIAN, A. 1999. Collective identity and electoral competition in Israel. *American Political Science Review,* 93: 265–77.

STIMSON, J. 2002. The dimensionality of issues in two party politics. Paper presented at the Conference on Elections, Columbia University, **www.unc.edu/~jstimson/ColPaper.pdf**

STUBAGER, R. 2003. Cleavages re-formulated: the development of a sociostructurally anchored definition. Paper presented at the European Consortium of Political Research, Edinburgh, **www.ps.au.dk/stubager/Project1/ Cleavages%20Reformulated% 20ECPR%2003.pdf**

TODOSIJEVIĆ, B. 2003. Serbia. Pp. 493–548 in *The Handbook of Political Change in Eastern Europe,* 2nd edn. ed. S. Berglund, J. Eckman, and F. Aarebrot. Cheltenham: Edward Elgar.

TÓKA, G. 1998. Party appeals and voter loyalty in New Democracies. *Political Studies,* 46: 589–610.

TUCKER, J. 2006. *Regional Economic Voting: Russia, Poland, Hungary, Slovakia and the Czech Republic from 1990–99.* Cambridge: Cambridge University Press.

VAN DE WALLE, N. 2003. Presidentialism and clientelism in Africa's emerging party systems. *Journal of Modern African Studies,* 41: 297–321.

WEISBERG, H., and TANAKA, A. 2001. Change in the spatial dimensions of party conflict: the case of Japan in the 1990s. *Political Behavior,* 23: 75–101.

WHITEFIELD, S. 2002. Political cleavages and post-communist politics. *Annual Review of Political Science,* 5: 181–200.

WONG, J. 2004. Democratization and the left: comparing East Asia and Latin America. *Comparative Political Studies,* 37: 1213–37.

YASHAR, D. 1998. Contesting citizenship: indigenous movements and democracy in Latin America. *Comparative Politics,* 31: 23–42.

YOUNG, C. 1996. Africa: an interim balance sheet. *Journal of Democracy,* 7: 53–68.

ZUCKERMAN, A. 1975. Political cleavage: a conceptual and theoretical analysis. *British Journal of Political Science,* 5: 231–48.

CHAPTER 29

PARTISANSHIP RECONSIDERED

SÖREN HOLMBERG

WHEN the authors of the *The American Voter* introduced the concept of party identification they knew they had struck scientific gold. As all good scientific breakthroughs their idea was simple. Party identification was invented to "characterize the individual's affective orientation to an important group-object in his environment" (Campbell et al. 1960, 121). Since modesty was not a dominate trait among the Michigan Four, they themselves provided a frame of reference for their discovery. The language they used and the conclusions they drew were practically carved in stone: "Evidently no single datum can tell us more about the attitude and behavior of the individual as presidential elector than his location on a dimension of psychological identification extending between the two great parties" (Campbell et al. 1960, 142–3).

The political science community of the day agreed. The concept of party identification was seen as "the glory variable of the 1950s and early 1960s" that "brought fame to the Michigan group, provided the basic structure for most studies of voting over a decade or two, and provided a key element in the revision of democratic theory..." (Shively 1980, 219). The success was not limited to United States. The concept of party identification was exported abroad and applied to other democratic multi-party systems.

No tree reaches the stars, however. Inevitably, dissenting voices began to be heard, especially after partisanship started to decline in America in the late 1960s. Between the presidential elections of 1964 and 1972, the proportion of party identified Americans dropped from 77 percent to 64 (Wattenberg 1998). What was happening? Was not party identification supposed to be stable? Was this the beginning of dealignment or yet another example of realignment in the American two-party system? A great debate commenced, and it still continues to this day.

Three topics are at the center of the discussion. (1) What is party identification? How can it be defined theoretically and measured empirically? Is it meaningful to talk about the direction and strength of party identification on one and the same dimension? (2) The unmoved mover—is party identification stable or does it move? If it moves, what about short-term versus long-term change, and aggregate-versus individual-level mobility? (3) What moves the mover? How do we explain party identification? Is it created by childhood socialization and by non-political affective forces, or do political and economic factors play a role as well. And where is party identification located in the funnel of causality—way back as an almost exogenous variable, or closer to the mouth of the funnel as an endogenous factor? This chapter will examine each of these three points.

1 What is Party Identification?

The original delineation of the party identification concept by the Michigan School was based on social psychology (Belknap and Campbell 1952; Campbell et al. 1960). Reference group theory pointed to the fact that humans identify with collectivities such as parties just like they identify with religious and ethnical groups as well as with social classes. In *The American Voter* they wrote: "Both reference group theory and small-group studies of influence have converged upon the attracting or repelling quality of the group as the generalized dimension most critical in defining the individual-group relationship, and it is this dimension that we will call identification" (1960, 121).

Reference group theory has today evolved into social identity theory. But proponents of the new identity theory still embrace the original conception of party identification as "a precursor of social identity theory years ahead of its time" (Greene 2004, 36). Social identity is a basic aspect of partisanship, they claim. The founding father of identity theory defined social identity as "that part of an individual's self concept which derives from his knowledge of his membership of a group (or groups) together with the value and emotional significance attached to the membership" (Tajfel 1978). Clearly, affect and group-belonging is emphasized, not cognitive factors and rational considerations.

This emotional and non-rational, non-political definition of party identification was and still is the main target of the critique leveled at the Michigan School of voting behavior, whether it be the old version or the new social identity variety. Most of the critique emanates from rational choice theory (Downs 1957). Party identification as an information-economizing device was an idea inspired by Downs (Goldberg 1969; Robertson 1976; Shively 1979). Morris Fiorina, however, is the leading scholar among these critics. Fiorina's (1981) emphasis on the importance of cognitive factors and retrospective political evaluations as formative factors behind party identification has become the most prominent alternative definition of party identification.

Whereas the Michigan Four spoke of a stable, affective, and identity-based party identification of almost exogenous status, Fiorina saw a potentially volatile, rational, policy-based party identification with a clear endogenous position in the funnel of causality. To Fiorina party identification was not primarily identity. Instead it was a weighted average of past evaluations of the parties—a "running tally" of reactions to past political and economical happenings. Today, Fiorina is joined by many scholars who find a growing consistency between ideology and partisanship, and a sizeable rational component to party identification in the US (Abramowitz and Saunders 2004).

In Europe, the concept of party identification was received with mixed feelings—more positively in Scandinavia, while scholars on the Continent were more skeptical. However, rendering the directional component of the concept useful in multi-party systems was a major concern all across Europe. In Norway, Denmark, and Sweden, a modified and more politicized version of the Michigan model was accepted (Campbell and Valen 1961; Särlvik 1970; Listhaug 1989; Holmberg 1994; Borre and Goul Andersen 1997; Berglund 2004). But, of course, in practice most analyses dealt with the strength component of party identification. The directional component was too close to actual party choice, with correlations well above .90.

If critique was modest in Scandinavia, it has been much more fundamental in Great Britain and in the Netherlands, questioning altogether the usefulness of the concept. Budge, Crewe, and Farlie practically judged party identification a non-entity. Talking about "past regularities" and "present intentions" they sarcastically asked, "how theoretically interesting is the statement that electors vote for the party to which they feel closest?" (1976, 11). Thomassen is equally critical but more specific. He sums up his critique in three points: (1)"Party identification is less stable than the vote. (2) What little evidence exists to the effect that party identification and vote preference can be distinguished can also be explained as unreliability of measurement. (3) There is strong evidence that party identification is not causally prior to the vote" (1976, 77).

Later studies confirmed that party identification tends to be less stable than the vote in the Netherlands (Visser 1992), but also that the Netherlands is a deviant case. In panel studies in countries like Britain, Canada, USA, and Sweden, party identification is more stable across elections than the vote (LeDuc 1981; Holmberg 1994). For example, in the four latest inter-election panels in Sweden, covering the years 1988 to 2002, the proportion of voters who have changed their party vote but not party identification has been around 10–11 percent while the corresponding percent for voters who have switched party identification but not the vote has varied between 5 and 7 percent. Thus, party identification is still more stable than the vote in Sweden. What has changed, however, is the proportion of people who switch both party identification and the vote. This double volatility group has increased from 11 percent in the 1973–6 Swedish panel to 20 percent in the 1998–2002 panel.

Double volatility as such is not irreconcilable with the Michigan model of party identification. However, there cannot be too much volatility and not too often. Party identification should be a stable, possibly lifelong attachment that is expected to change only under extraordinary circumstances, such as those of a critical election or a realignment period (Key 1955; Rosenof 2003). Obviously, the prevalence of double volatility in Europe does not reconcile well with such a model. The original model has to be revised in order to accommodate systems where party identification is more volatile; maybe into a version that conceptualizes party identification less as a fixture and more as an endogenous variable amenable to some short-term change. In America scholars like Jackson (1975), Page and Jones (1979), and Markus and Converse (1979) have suggested useful revisionist models along these lines.

The debate over how to empirically measure party identification in the United States has been less heated. The American National Election Studies (ANES) has maintained the same standard set of three survey questions all the time since 1952. The result is a unidimensional seven-point classification from strong Democrats, over pure Independents, to strong Republicans, with weak identifiers and leaners in between. Measurement concerns have mainly focused on two problems—the status of leaners and whether the seven-point scale is truly unidimensional. The first concern has arisen because American leaners sometimes behave more partisan than weak identifiers (Petrocik 1974) and sometimes behave more like independents (Miller 1991). What are they, partisans or independents?

The dimensionality issue is more esoteric and American. Should independence be a separate dimension from the partisan divide between Democrats and Republicans, and consequently be measured separately? (Weisberg 1980). In multi-party systems it has always been natural to define and measure the strength and directional components of the party identification concept on two different dimensions. However, today most American scholars agree "that the seven-point scale does reasonably well in measuring partisanship in the current era" (Niemi and Weisberg 2001: 323). Thus, the old ANES workhorse is still acceptable.

2 UNMOVED MOVER

When people started to question the concept of party identification in the 1970s, the first and most obvious point to attack was the notion that party identification was supposed to be unmovable except during infrequent periods of party realignment. Very early on, however, it was quite obvious that party identification was not nearly as stable as the stereotype Michigan model predicted, neither on the aggregate level nor on the individual level (Dreyer 1973). Even as early as in the presidential election of 1964, aggregate party identification changed more dramatically than any time before or after. Democrats spiked to 61 percent and Republicans dropped to 31 percent (see Figure 29.1). Subsequent elections proved that it was not the start of a realignment strengthening the Democrats. Lyndon Johnson was only a one-election wonder. What we saw in 1964 was only dramatic short-term change. Beginning with

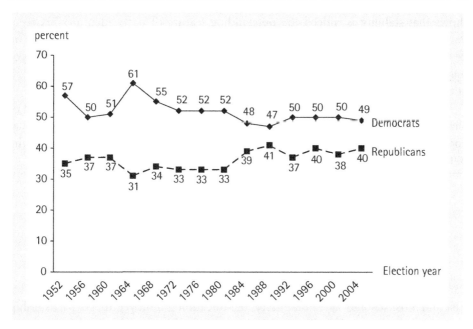

Fig. 29.1 Party identification in the United States, 1952–2004

Comment: The percentages do not add up to 100 because a politicals and independents are not included in the figure. Leaners, however, are included.

Source: American National Elections Studies (ANES).

the Reagan elections of 1980 and 1984, however, it is more plausible to talk of an evolving Republican realignment, increasing the Republican voter share from 33 percent in 1980 to 40 percent in 2004 (Meffert, Norporth, and Ruhil 2001). Nevertheless, in ANES data, Democrats are still the largest party with the support of 49 percent of Americans in 2004.

Aggregate party identification in America has exhibited even more movement if we look at other sets of time-series data than is provided by ANES, for example, the Gallup survey or the *CBS News* and *New York Times* survey. In 1989 MacKuen, Erikson, and Stimson pioneered the use of surveys like that in measuring what they called macropartisanship—a proxy for aggregated party identification—measured monthly, not every other year as is the case for the Michigan studies.

Michael Meffert and his collegues comment thus on the new volatile findings: "The study of party identification has entered the twilight zone... Gone seems the days when partisanship was regarded as an immovable object... There is no question that macropartisanship... has exhibited substantial movement over the last half century" (Meffert, Norpoth, and Ruhil 2001, 953). And they go on and ask the central questions—how serious can we take the movements and where do they originate from?

Meffert et al. take the movements seriously, as do Erikson et al., but others are more skeptical and prove that parts of the movements are due to measurement errors. Error correction models make shifts in macropartisanship more sluggish. And the conclusion bolsters the original Michigan idea. "In the end, the accumulated scholarship shows that stability is indeed the outstanding feature of party identities" (Green, Palmquist, and Schickler 2001, 363). Robert Erikson and colleagues do not agree: "The key to understand the macropartisanship series is its long memory. The response of macropartisanship to new economic and political inputs may be imperceptibly small at the time of occurrence, but it will be long-lasting" (Erikson et al. 2001, 370).

As Niemi and Weisberg conclude: "The question becomes whether the amount of change that occurs is better characterized as large enough to be meaningful or small enough to be ignored" (2001, 334). We are reminded of the classic problem—is the bottle half empty or half full?

3 WHAT DOES THE MOVER MOVE?

Party identification as a mover is not under contention. The Michigan Four said it first and most scholars agree that party identification is a mover, that is partisanship to a degree affects political attitudes like issue positions, policy evaluations, and leader popularity. Party identification creates a sort of perceptual screen and helps organizing voters' political world-view (Sniderman, Brody, and Tetlock 1991; Rahn 1993; Brader and Tucker 2001b). Party sympathies structure peoples' perceptions of and attitudes toward, the body politic.

And, of course, party identification has a strong effect on behavior as well, most prominently on party or candidate choice, but also more generally on electoral participation. However, the effect on voting and campaign activity is more pronounced than the effects on other forms of political activity (Finkel and Opp 1991; Bäck and Teorell 2005). The decline in the strength of party identification in most west European countries has been accompanied by a fall in turnout levels at the polls. If you do not find a party to identify with why bother to vote?

Reciprocal causation, however, is a potential problem in this context. Party identification is shaping behaviors, attitudes, and perceptions at the same time as it is shaped by attitudes and perceptions as well as by behaviors. Consequently, our estimates of the effects of party identification tend to be on the high side, exaggerating the impact. We need clever experiments and more panel studies to be able to better sort out this reciprocal causation problem.

4 WHAT MOVES THE MOVER?

That party identification is a mover is not an issue, and has never been. What is contentious, however, is what moves the mover. The original claim in *The American Voter* is that party identification in essence is a non-political attitude formed mainly by socialization during childhood and adolescence. Thereafter party identification is supposed to be immune to politics and economic change, except under really rare circumstances when a realignment can occur. Party identification was conceived as an exogenous variable affecting politics but not being affected by politics.

Critics of this notion of taking politics out of party identification have been around since the beginning but more noticeably since the 1970s. The counter-theory among the revisionists is that party identification is a political variable influenced in the short term as well as the long term by political factors like ideological inclinations, economic fluctuations, issue positions, and evaluations of government and candidate performance. In short, in studies of voting behavior, party identification should be treated as an endogenous variable, not be sanctified as an unmoved mover.

It is probably most fair to say that most empirical studies tend to support the revisionist school. As Niemi and Weisberg (2001) say: "party identification does vary with some other factors . . . regardless of whether one believes party identification to be sticky, no one would argue that it does not change at all, either at the individual or the aggregate level" (334). And the other factors have to do with politics as well as with economic circumstances, and not only childhood socialization.

Defenders of the immune non-political version of party identification, including Warren Miller (1992; Miller and Shanks 1996), do not dispute that there is some movement in party identification and that there is some impact of politics. But their argument is that political effects and all changes are minor when we consider measurement errors and factors like generational replacement. We are back to the problem of the half-full or half-empty bottle, although most scholars would probably opt for the half-full interpretation. Politics do have an impact on party identification, even in the short term.

In western Europe, the debate is less heated, but in a way very similar to the American discussion. The European focus, however, is on the strength component of party identification, not on the directional part. The issue is to what extent political considerations are driving the strength of partisanship among voters. One view is that political competition factors play a prominent role (Schmitt and Holmberg 1995), another that modernization and cognitive mobilization has rendered party identification less functional for voters, hence the decline in partisanship in western democracies (Shively 1979; Dalton 1984; Dalton and Wattenberg 2000). The first view—like the revisionists in America—sees party identification as clearly affected by politics, while the second view tends to place politics in the back seat and instead emphasizes the importance of more sociological factors and the general development of society.

A recent European study involving six countries tests both these views and comes up with an ambivalent verdict for the modernization hypothesis as well as for the political hypothesis (Berglund et al. 2005). Party identifiers have become less numerous over time, as the modernization theory predicts. Partisanship is slowly eroding. But the development is far from monotonous and the same across countries. An interesting note is that strength of party identification is increasing somewhat, not decreasing, in recent elections in three of the European countries—Germany in 2002,

Denmark in 2005, and the Netherlands in 2002. The same small upward shift in partisanship is also noticeable in the American presidential elections in 2004. Clearly, nation-specific factors play a role. There is no uniform, secular trend downwards for partisanship in western democracies. The pattern differs rather dramatically by country. Furthermore, the micro-theory underpinning the modernization theory is not supported. Contrary to expectations, cognitive mobilization operationalized as high education does not uniformly lead to less strength in partisanships. The political competition theory did fare a bit better. As expected, on the aggregated national level there is some effect of left–right polarization on strength of partisanship. Individual-level analysis confirms the results. Berglund and associates (2005) conclude: "The more polarized a party system is, the more partisans we find. But again, these political correlates of the development of party identification are modest at best, and cannot fully explain what goes on in the six West European countries . . . Political polarization is one factor in the evolution of partisanship, but certainly not the only one and perhaps not even a very powerful one" (124). A rather somber conclusion, which once again proves that empirical tests seldom lead to clear-cut results.

However, the polarization idea gets some support, when applied to the US situation. In America, strong identifiers have been on the increase since the low-point elections in the 1970s—from 24 percent in 1976 to 34 percent in 2004. At the same time, the American party system has become more polarized. Studies show that people perceive more differences between Democrats and Republicans today than in the 1970s (Wattenberg 1998; Hetherington 2001). The American parties have become more different and distinct in the eyes of the voters, making it easier and more meaningful to identify strongly with one of them.

As a contrast—and in support of the notion that polarization is important for partisanship—data from Sweden, where strength of party identification is falling, show that people over the last twenty years perceive fewer and fewer ideological differences between the parties, especially between the Social Democrats and the largest non-socialist party, the Conservatives (Holmberg and Oscarsson 2004).

The results in Figure 29.2 show the development of strong party identifiers in America in comparison with Sweden. The two curves highlight two very different, and for some people maybe surprising, developments. Strong identifiers are on the increase in America while they are becoming fewer in Sweden. It is worth repeating the American result since many political pundits in the US seem unaware of the fact that strength of party identification has *not* been going down for the last thirty years, and when it comes to strong identification, it has actually been on the increase.

Thus, parties are strengthening their position among voters in America and weakening their hold in Sweden. According to the political theory of party identification, one important reason for these developments is increased party polarization in the US and decreased polarization in Sweden. And observe that modernization theory cannot explain the difference between the USA and Sweden unless we entertain the notion that America has become less modernized during the last couple of decades.

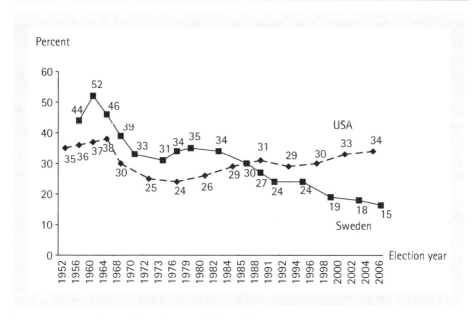

Fig. 29.2 Strong Party Identifiers in USA and in Sweden since the 1950s

Comment: The measurement of party identification is not exactly identical but very similar between USA and Sweden. In the Swedish case, the measurement was somewhat different in the elections 1956–64 compared to in the later elections. For details on how party identification is measured in Sweden, see Holmberg (1994).

5 EVIDENCE FROM EMERGING DEMOCRACIES

Most research on party identification has been done in established democracies, especially in the United States. However, emerging democracies with newformed party systems give us a golden opportunity to study the origins and development of partisanship in new ways. Data from new democracies are useful to supplement knowledge from established democracies. In the latter case—in the older democracies— "the origins of partisanship are obscured by the fog of history. At best, scholars can study the processes of socialization and conversation" (Greenstein 1965; Jennings and Niemi 1981; Shively 1979, cited from Brader and Tucker 2001a, 1). In new democracies the Big Bang of party birth can be studied when it happens, not decades afterward.

So far, results are scattered and rather ambiguous, especially concerning the Russian case. Studies using self-identification measures tend to find few party identifiers and more people with multiple attachments in Russia and Eastern Europe (White, Rose, and McAllister 1997; Schmitt forthcoming). Other studies relying on indirect measures of party attachment find more evidence of the emergence of enduring partisanship in Russia. When it comes to the processes behind the crystallization of party attachments most studies point at the importance of rational, deliberative, and political factors (Miller and Klobucar 2000; Brader and Tucker

2001*b*; Dalton and Weldon 2005). Social identity theory gets weak support in Russia. Peoples' social place in society have only modest and indirect effects on the strength and origin of partisanship (Brader and Tucker 2001*b*).

Results from research on partisanship in emerging democracies in Latin America point in the same direction as the studies from eastern Europe. Party identification is mainly shaped by political factors, not social variables. And it is not an especially stable phenomenon. For example, dealignment trends are already visible in new democracies in Latin Amreica (Sanchez 2003; Hagogian 1998; Dalton and Weldon 2005).

6 What to do?

The answer is not to wring our hands and conclude that party identification is a fuzzy concept with foggy empirical foundations. Instead, the answer must be the usual and rather cheerful one—keep on working. Party identification deals with a much too important phenomenon to be abandoned. As long as party-based democracies are around, people's different relationships with the major actors—the parties—must be conceptualized and measured. Maybe the Michigan invention from the 1950s is not the best solution or the only possible solution.

Fifty years of research using the *American Voter's* version of handling party attachments has proved party identification to be an extremely useful, yet a profoundly unclear concept. However, the problems that have appeared have less to do with the original version of the concept of party identification. After all the Michigan Four created a fairly concise variable with the intent of measuring a primarily affective relationship between people and their preferred party. Cognitions and politics were not supposed to play a large role. But when researchers—including to a degree the Michigan Four themselves—began to use the concept and interpret results, problems surfaced. Scholars started to broaden the concept and read in more phenomena than were originally intended.

This critique strikes the revisionists in particular. They try to change a non-political and affective concept into a cognitive and political concept. Party identification according to the Michigan Four is a different idea than party identification according to Fiorina and the revisionist school. We are talking about two different theoretical notions that ideally should be measured and tested separately. A concept and a theory which try to lump everything together is not very useful. Lean and mean concepts are more scientifically useful.

Consequently, we should not try to bridge the two or more sides of the discussion. Compromise or looking for middle ground is not the way to go. On the contrary, we should specify different concepts and create different operationalized measures. For example, one concept focused on affective relationships between voters and parties and another for more cognitive and evaluative relationships. The former concept could preferably retain the name party identification, while the latter concept could be called partisanship. Ideas like this are not new. They have been discussed by, among others, Mikael Gilljam (2003).

A consequence might be that the old Michigan concept with the accompanying seven-point measuring scale has to go. There are already ideas and suggestions for different measuring techniques in the social identity literature (Brewer and Silver 2000; Greene 2004). How to conceptionalize and measure the new partisanship variable is a challenge for the revisionists. There is no lack of possibilities already in use in election studies around the world. Like-dislike scales, party sympathy or closeness questions, and questions evaluating party policies come immediately to mind.

A solution along these lines is tempting but maybe unviable given all theoretical and measurement problems in keeping the two concepts separate. For example, will not affective party identification and evaluative partisanship be too closely correlated, making them difficult to use separately in practical studies? Well, that is an empirical question that can be answered when we have defined and started to systematically measure the new concepts of party identification and partisanship.

The gauntlet is thrown down.

REFERENCES

ABRAMOWITZ, A., and SAUNDERS, K. 2004. Rational hearts and minds: social identity, ideology, and party identification in the American electorate. Paper delivered at the Annual Meeting of the American Political Science Association, Chicago, 2004.

BÄCK, H., and TEORELL, J. 2005. Party attachemnt and political participation: a panel study of citizen attitudes and behavior in Russia. Paper presented at a Studying Political Action meeting at Karlstad University, June 2005.

BELKNAP, G., and CAMPBELL, A. 1952. Political party identification and attitudes toward foreign policy. *Public Opinion Quarterly*, 15: 601–23.

BERGLUND, F. 2004. *Partiidentifikasjon og politisk endring: En studie av langsiktige tillknytninger blant norske velgere 1965–1997*. Oslo: Thesis/Unipax.

—— HOLMBERG, S., SCHMITT, H., and THOMASSEN, J. 2005. Party identification and party choice. Pp. 106–24 in *The European Voter*, ed. J. Thomassen. Oxford: Oxford University Press.

BORRE, O., and GOUL ANDERSEN, J. 1997. *Voting and Political Attitudes in Denmark*. Aarhus University Press.

BRADER, T., and TUCKER, J. 2001a. Pathways to partisanship in new democracies: evidence from Russia. Paper presented at an AAASS meeting in Washington, DC, November 2001.

—— —— 2001b. The Emergence of Mass Partisanship in Russia, 1993–1996. *American Journal of Political Science*, 45 (1): 69–83.

BREWER, M., and SILVER, M. 2000. Group distinctiveness, social identity and collective mobilization. Pp. 153–71 in *Self, Identity and Social Movement*, ed. S. Stryker, T. Owens, and R. White. Minneapolis: University of Minnesota.

BUDGE, I., CREWE, I., and FARLIE, D. 1976. *Party Identification and Beyond*. London: John Wiley & Sons.

CAMPBELL, A., and VALEN, H. 1961. Party identification in Norway and the United States. *Public Opinion Quarterly*, 25: 245–68.

—— CONVERSE, P., MILLER, W., and STOKES, D. 1960. *The American Voter.* New York: John Wiley & Sons.

DALTON, R. 1984. Cognitive mobilization and partisan dealignment in advanced industrial societies. *Journal of Politics*, 46: 264–84.

—— and WATTENBERG, M. 2000. *Parties without Partisans: Political Change in Advanced Industrial Democracies.* Oxford: Oxford University Press.

—— and WELDON, S. 2005. Partisanship and party system institutionalization. Paper presented at National Democratic Institute, Washington, DC, August 2005.

DOWNS, A. 1957. *An Economic Theory of Democracy.* New York: Harper & Row.

DREYER, E. 1973. Change and stability in party identification. *American Journal of Political Science*, 35: 712–22.

ERIKSON, R., MACUEN, M., and STIMSON, J. 2001. Macropartisanship: the permanent memory of partisanship evaluation. Pp. 364–70 in *Controversies in Voting Behavior*, ed. R. Niemi and H. Weisberg. Washington DC: CQ Press.

FINKEL, S., and OPP, K-D. 1991. Party identification and participation in collective political action. *Journal of Politics*, 53: 339–71.

FIORINA, M. 1981. *Retrospective Voting in American Presidential Elections.* New Haven: Yale University Press.

GILLJAM, M. 2003. *Kommentarer till Frode Berglunds avhandling.* Göteborg: Department of Political Science.

GOLDBERG, A. 1969. Social determination and rationality as a basis of party identification. *American Political Science Review*, 63: 5–25.

GREEN, D., PALMQUIST, B., and SCHICKLER, E. 2001. Partisan stability: evidence from aggregate data. Pp. 356–63 in *Controversies in Voting Behavior*, ed. R. Niemi and H. Weisberg. Washington DC: CQ Press.

—— —— —— 2002. *Partisan Hearts and Minds: Political Parties and the Social Identities of Voters.* New Haven, Conn.: Yale University Press.

GREENE, S. 2004. Social Identity Theory and Party Identification. *Social Science Quarterly*, 85: 136–53.

GREENSTEIN, F. 1965. *Children and Politics.* New Haven: Yale University Press.

HAGOPIAN, F. 1998. Democracy and political representation in Latin America in the 1990s: pause, reorganization, or decline? In *Fault Lines of Democracy in Post-Transition Latin America*, ed. F. Agüero and J. Stark. Coral Gabels: North/South Center Press, University of Miami.

HETHERINGTON, MARK. 2001. Resurgent mass partisanship: the role of elite polarization. *American Political Science Review*, 95 (3): 619–32.

HOLMBERG, S. 1994. Party identification compared across the Atlantic. Pp. 93–121 in *Elections at Home and Abroad: Essays in Honor of Warren E. Miller*, ed. K. Jennings and T. Mann. Ann Arbor: University of Michigan Press.

—— and OSCARSSON, H. 2004. *Väljare: Svenskt väljarbeteende under 50 år.* Stockholm: Norstedts Juridik.

JACKSON, J. 1975. Issues, party choice, and presidential votes. *American Journal of Political Science*, 19: 161–85.

JENNINGS, K., and NIEMI, R. 1981. *Generations and Politics: A Panel Study of Young Adults and their Parents.* Princeton: Princeton University Press.

KEY, V. O. 1955. A Theory of Critical Elections. *Journal of Politics*, 17: 3–18.

LeDuc, L. 1981. The dynamic properties of party identification: a four-nation comparison. *European Journal of Political Research*, 9: 257–68.

Listhaug, O. 1989. *Citizens, Parties and Norwegian Electoral Politics 1957–1986: An Empirical Study.* Trondheim: Tapir.

MacKuen, M., Erikson, R., and Stimson, J. 1989. Macropartisanship. *American Political Science Review*, 83: 1125–42.

Markus, G., and Converse, P. 1979. A dynamic simultaneous equation model of electoral choice. *American Political Science Review*, 73: 1055–70.

Meffert, M., Norpoth, H., and Ruhil, A. 2001. Realignment and macropartisanship. *American Political Science Review*, 95: 953–62.

Miller, A., and Klobucar, T. 2000. The development of party identification in post-Soviet societies. *American Journal of Political Science*, 44: 667–86.

Miller, W. 1991. Party identification, realignment, and party voting: back to the basics. *American Political Science Review*, 85: 557–68.

—— 1992. Generational change and party identification. *Political Behavior*, 14: 333–53.

—— and Shanks, M. 1996. *The New American Voter.* Cambridge, Mass.: Harvard University Press.

Niemi, R., and Weisberg, H. eds. 2001. *Controversies in Voting Behavior.* Washington DC: CQ Press.

Page, B., and Jones, C. 1979. Reciprocal effects of policy preferences, party loyalties and the vote. *American Political Science Review*, 83: 1071–89.

Petrocik, J. R. 1974. An analysis of intransitivities in the index of party identification. *Political Methodology*, 1: 38–48.

Rahn, W. 1993. The role of partisan stereotypes in information processing about political candidates. *American Journal of Political Science*, 37: 472–96.

Robertson, D. 1976. Surrogates for party identification in the rational choice framework. Pp. 365–81 in *Party Identification and Beyond*, ed. I. Budge, I. Crewe, and B. Farlie. London: John Wiley & Sons.

Rosenhof, T. 2003. *Realignment: The Theory that Changed the Way We Think about American Politics.* Lanham, Md: Rowman & Littlefield.

Sanchez, F. 2003. Dealignment in Costa Rica: a case study of electoral change. St Anthony's College, University of Oxford.

Särlvik, B. 1970. *Electoral Behavior in the Swedish Multiparty System.* Göteborg: Department of Political Science.

Schmitt, H. forthcoming. Multiple party identifications. In *The Comparative Study of Electoral Systems*, ed. H. Klingemann.

—— and Holmberg, S. 1995. Political parties in decline? Pp. 95–134 in *Citizens and the State*, ed. H.-D. Klingemann and D. Fuchs. Oxford: Oxford University Press.

Shively, P. 1979. The development of party identification among adults: explanation of functional model. *American Political Science Review*, 73: 1039–54.

—— 1980. The nature of party identification: a review of recent developments. In *The Electorate Reconsidered*, ed. J. Pierce and J. Sullivan. Beverly Hills, Calif.: Sage.

Sniderman, P., Brody, R., and Tetlock, P. 1991. *Reasoning and Choice.* Cambridge: Cambridge University Press.

Tajfel, H. 1978. Social categorization, social identity, and social comparisons. Pp. 61–76 in *Differentiation between Social Groups*, ed. H. Tajfel. London: Academic Press.

Thomassen, J. 1976. Party identification as a cross-national concept: its meaning in the Netherlands. Pp. 63–79 in *Party Identification and Beyond*, ed. I., Budge, I. Crewe, and D. Farlie. London: John Wiley & Sons.

VISSER, M. 1992. The role of group indentifications in dutch politics. Paper presented at the ECPR Workshop in Limerick 1992.

WATTENBERG, M. 1998. *The Decline of American Political Parties 1952–1988*. Cambridge, Mass.: Harvard University Press.

WEISBERG, H. 1980. A multidimensional conceptualization of party identification. *Political Behavior*, 2: 33–60.

WHITE, S., ROSE, R., and MCALLISTER, I. 1997. *How Russia Votes*. Chatham, NJ: Chatham House.

CHAPTER 30

THE PERSONALIZATION OF POLITICS

IAN MCALLISTER

In a trend that has been shared by all of the liberal democracies, politics has become increasingly personalized. It is now commonplace for governments to be named after their leader, rather than after the party that holds office, particularly if the party and its leader have won successive elections. This phenomenon is often traced to the election of Margaret Thatcher in Britain in 1979 and Ronald Reagan in the United States in 1980, two strong, charismatic leaders whose profile within the electorate easily eclipsed that of their respective parties. However, it is often forgotten that the earliest post-war manifestation of a leader surpassing the popularity of his party was Pierre Trudeau's election as Canadian prime minister in 1968, when newly enfranchised younger voters responded to the new prime minister's "swinger" image by giving birth to "Trudeaumania".

Nor is the trend towards the personalization of politics restricted to presidential systems, its traditional institutional home. The popular focus on leaders now appears commonplace across almost all of the major parliamentary systems, where parties once occupied center stage. The focus on leaders within parliamentary systems has been so marked over the past two decades that it has spawned a large literature that variously labels it the "presidentialization of politics" (Mughan 1993; Poguntke and Webb 2005), "institutional presidentialization" (Maddens and Fiers 2004), and "presidential parliamentarism" (Hazan 1996). Despite the diverse labels, the common underlying theme of these works is that the operation of democratic systems is experiencing fundamental change, without any concomitant change in their formal institutional structures.

Explanations for the personalization of politics vary, but one that is often advanced is the growth of the electronic media and its consequences for politics, particularly in the conduct of national elections (Bowler and Farrell 1992; Glaser and Salmon 1991). The electronic media are seen as crucial in shaping the way that governments communicate with voters and in how they seek to convert them. At the same time, party leaders exploit their exposure in the electronic media in order to attract votes. Whatever the importance of the media in this process, no single explanation accounts for the increasing personalization of politics in democratic societies, and it is clear that a complex and multi-causal process is at work. This chapter examines the evidence for leaders becoming more important, and reviews the explanations that are advanced to explain it. The final section examines the potential consequences of this change.[1]

1 LEADERS AND DEMOCRACY: THE EVIDENCE

Considerable impressionistic evidence supports the idea that leaders have become more important in democratic societies. Studies of election campaigns routinely find major party leaders gain consistently stronger recognition as polling day draws closer, while the visibility of minor party leaders exhibits little change (Bartels 1988; Miller et al. 1990; Page and Shapiro 1992). However, rigorous tests of the proposition are rare, for three reasons. First, collecting consistent overtime data is difficult, and making such estimations across a range of countries even more so. Second, since the personalities (and the popularity) of leaders changes continuously, observing any consistent trend becomes fraught with methodological problems as leaders fade in and out of the public's view. Third, the types of qualities that voters see as most important in their leaders has changed, and at least part of that change may well be a consequence of increases in voters' levels of education, as much as other changes (Miller, Wattenberg, and Malanchuk 1986).

Substantial evidence supports the view that leaders are increasingly visible to the mass public during elections.[2] Particularly important is the mass media's propensity to mention candidates rather than the parties to which they belong during elections campaigns. Table 30.1 shows the ratio of candidate to party mentions for five advanced democracies for periods ranging from 1952 onwards. The results show that in four of the six countries there is a marked and consistent trend towards more candidate than party mentions in news stories. For example, in the 1952 US presidential election there were 1.7 candidate mentions for every one party mention;

---

[1] For longer discussions of these issues, see McAllister (1996, 2006).

[2] Wattenberg (1991; updated in McAllister 1996, 291) shows an increasing likelihood that voters will refer to economic evaluations in their mention of US presidential candidates.

Table 30.1 The ratio of candidate to party mentions during elections in five democracies

	United States	United Kingdom	Austria	France	Canada
1952	1.7				
1956	2				
1957					1.2
1958		0.7			
1959					1.3
1960	3				
1964	3				
1965				4.3	
1966		0.8	0.4		
1968	3.6				1.7
1972	3.6				
1974		0.9		4.4	2
1975			0.4		
1976	4.5				
1980	5.2				
1981				3.7	
1983		1.3			
1984					1.1
1986			1		
1987		1.1			
1988	5.2			5.4	
1992		1.1			
1995			1.3	5.6	
1996	5.6				
1997		1.3			1.6

Source: Dalton, McAllister, and Wattenberg (2000, table 3.6).

by the 1996 election this ratio had increased to 5.6 candidate mentions for each party mention, more than a threefold increase. There was also a threefold increase in Austria between 1966 and 1995, and an almost twofold increase in the United Kingdom. The only exception to the upward trend is Canada.

Other research comes to similar conclusions. Evidence from parliamentary systems directly relating the popularity of leaders to the probability of voting for a party show consistently strong effects, although of a much lesser degree than is often supposed once other factors are taken into account (for a discussion, see Holmberg and Oscarsson 2006). Graetz and McAllister (1987) used summary (thermometer) scores of the party leaders in the 1974, 1979, and 1983 British general elections to show that while leader evaluations had a major impact on defection and conversion between the parties, the net effect on the three election outcomes was comparatively small. The largest effect was in 1983, when the relative standing of the two major party leaders—Margaret Thatcher and Michael Foot, both of whom were from the radical wings of their respective parties—influenced the vote by about 4 percent. In a comparative study of Australia and Britain, Bean and Mughan (1989, 1174) reach similar conclusions.[3]

Interest in the electoral appeal of political leaders comes at a time when scholarly research has concluded that the way in which a voter accumulates information about a candidate—personal as well as political—is an essential tool that enables her to make judgments about the suitability of the competing candidates for elective office. Miller, Wattenberg, and Malanchuk's (1986) study of how US voters viewed presidential candidates between 1952 and 1984 found that "the overall basic structure employed in candidate appraisals" remained stable over the period of the surveys. However, there was a trend towards such attributes as competence, integrity, and reliability becoming more important over the period. There was also some evidence that non-political, personal mentions had decreased overtime, although the authors concluded that much of that change could be attributed to the diverse personalities of the candidates being evaluated rather than to any underlying structural change in how voters evaluate candidate traits.

Similar findings have come from research by Wattenberg (1991; see also Huang and Price 2001; Keeter 1987; McAllister 1996, 291) who examined the proportion of US voters who mentioned economic, partisan, and sociological factors for voting either for or against a presidential candidate over a forty-year period. In line with the decline in partisanship, the proportion of the American electorate who spontaneously evaluated the candidates along partisan lines declined from around one-third in 1952, to just 14 percent in 1992. Sociological factors, such as group-related mentions, remained relatively constant over the period. The major change was the proportion of respondents who mentioned economic factors in their evaluations of presidential candidates, rising from 13 percent of all voter evaluations in 1968 to 57 percent in 1992. This supports the contention that political leaders have become electorally important in their own right, by personifying the policy platforms of their respective parties.

These findings derive, of course, from a presidential system. Do they also hold for parliamentary systems as well? Bean (1993, 129) suggested that they do, and provided evidence from Australia and New Zealand to support his assertion. His caveat is that in presidential systems, candidates act as surrogates for their parties and as a consequence absorb the programmatic traits that would otherwise be the responsibility of their party. In parliamentary systems, by contrast, since parties are stronger and more disciplined, leaders are more likely to be evaluated on their non-political, personal qualities. In their study of Australia, Britain, and the United States, Bean

---

[3] See also the country chapters in Poguntke and Webb (2005).

and Mughan (1989) found evidence to support this proposition, although the differences they detect were not large. As a result, Bean (1993, 129) concluded that the weight of performance evaluations on the vote is similar "across both national and temporal boundaries, for parliamentary as well as presidential political systems and for many different individual political leaders, whether they have stronger or weaker images and whether they are incumbents or non-incumbents."

In shaping electoral outcomes, leaders clearly matter, though by a much lesser margin than is often supposed, once a wide range of other factors are taken into account. There is also substantial evidence that voters judge candidates against certain traits that enable them to make a summary evaluation about the likely performance of the candidate if he or she is elected to office. However, much of the evidence is country-specific, and firm conclusions are complicated by the changing personalities involved and by the specific events and circumstances surrounding particular elections. While the evidence is therefore tentative, it does suggest that voters in parliamentary systems are becoming more candidate-centered in their voting, compared to voters in presidential systems. At the same time, it would appear that voters in presidential systems are evaluating candidates in a more instrumental and less partisan way. In the sections that follow, some explanations for these trends are advanced.

2 Institutions and Political Leadership

Variations in institutional arrangements have clear and important effects on the nature and style of political leadership, with the major distinction being between presidential and parliamentary systems (McAllister 1996).[4] Almost all presidents are popularly elected, usually by means of direct election, or occasionally through some form of electoral college.[5] Regardless of the electoral system, presidential systems conform to Verney's (1959, 75) defining characteristic of the type, namely, that "the executive is responsible to the electorate." Presidentialism generally encourages individual responsibility, since executive authority resides with an individual who is elected to the position for a fixed period of time. In addition, party discipline is often weak in presidential systems, since the president's political survival does not depend on the unity of the governing party.

---

[4] Within the established and newly emerging democracies, the major distinction in executive leadership is between presidentialism and parliamentarism. Countries that have had interrupted periods of democratic government often display the characteristics of both systems, at different points in time, such as Bangladesh. Other countries have adopted hybrid constitutional systems. Among the established democracies, Switzerland is perhaps the most difficult country of all to classify; France is also a difficult case.

[5] An exception is Taiwan, where the president is elected for a six-year term by the National Assembly; the sole purposes of this body are to select the president and to amend the constitution, although it also has the power to recall the president in certain circumstances.

Among parliamentary systems, there is a distinction between systems that have coalition arrangements, a pattern that is found throughout Europe (Laver and Schofield 1990), and those (mainly democracies in the Westminster tradition) that have majoritarian arrangements. Parliamentary arrangements encourage collective responsibility, so that the executive is both dependent upon the confidence of the members of legislature and accountable to them. The operation of parliamentarism also encourages party government, so that in contrast to presidential systems, party discipline is a primary factor in maintaining executive authority (Katz 1986). In parliamentary systems, parties frequently go to considerable lengths to retain the loyalty of their elected members, and to ensure party discipline, since these are the attributes on which their political survival rests (Bowler, Farrell, and Katz 1999).

Presidential systems have fixed terms for their leaders, so retaining office is not normally dependent upon the day-to-day confidence of the legislature. This permits presidents greater flexibility in formulating and implementing policy without the risk of an unexpected election to upset their plans. In parliamentary systems, by contrast, the survival of the executive depends upon the confidence of the legislature. The executive can therefore be removed at any time by the legislature, usually following the passing of a vote of no confidence. In practice, this means that a prime minister must make it a priority to retain the confidence of his or her party colleagues and to more carefully refine his or her performance in office, since the date when the government will be judged by the electorate at the polls is less certain.

It follows that presidents have much greater executive authority than their prime ministerial counterparts, and they also have more autonomy in their ability to shape policy—though not necessarily in their power to implement it. While we need to distinguish effects which can be attributed to specific personalities, there is clear evidence that the post-war operation of parliamentary systems has moved closer to this presidential model. Like presidents, many post-war British prime ministers have accumulated considerably greater power and authority when compared to their pre-war counterparts (King 1994; Rhodes 1995). In many Westminster systems, it is often argued that government based on collective cabinet responsibility has been undermined by these changes, in part by the increased complexity of modern decision making, but also by the centralization of prime ministerial authority. Moreover, in majoritarian parliamentary systems, the prime minister now exercises unprecedented power in shaping ministerial careers, a crucial tool in ensuring compliance and centralizing authority.

The type of electoral system also can influence the nature and direction of political leadership, although it is difficult to measure and highly variable across countries. Electoral systems are easily manipulated by politicians and parties since they are rarely constitutionally embedded, unlike presidentialism or parliamentarism.[6] There is increasing debate about electoral reform in the established democracies, such as Italy, Japan, New Zealand, Israel, the UK, and Canada; this is in addition to debates

---

[6] Sartori has characterized the electoral system as "the most specific manipulative instrument of politics" (1976, 273).

about the electoral systems most suited to the wide range of newly democratizing countries (see Taagepera 2002). Among the list of items that feature in these deliberations is the nature and degree of linkage between politicians and voters. This is viewed as a major factor behind the recent fashion for mixed systems, whose principal virtue is supposedly that they represent a balance between the proportionality found in multi-member systems, while preserving the personal link between the politician and the voter (Shugart and Wattenberg 2001).[7]

Traditionally, electoral systems are evaluated for their ability to "represent" social and ethnic groups. More recently, attention has shifted to the choice that is offered to voters, the consequences of such choice for democratic stability, and in the way that voters exercise their choices to evaluate candidates (Farrell and McAllister 2006). Electoral systems that permit voters to discriminate between candidates have more potential for leaders to influence the vote than, for example, party list systems where parties determine the order of candidates. The main distinction is between ordinal systems (such as preferential systems like STV) where voters have more choice, either by selecting multiple candidates or by rank ordering them, and categorical ballots (such as closed list) where voters have few choices in determining the fate of individual candidates (Bowler and Farrell 1993; Shugart 2001).

The new democracies of central and eastern Europe represent a special case in the role of political institutions in shaping political leadership. The autocratic nature of the old communist regimes has been a legacy that many have found difficult to leave behind, and political instability and economic stress have combined to influence many voters to seek a "strong leader" to overcome their problems. This has been most notable in Russia, where Vladimir Putin has exploited this widespread popular desire in order to centralize political authority (Rose and Munro 2002). Across most of the post-communist societies, institutional arrangements (whether presidential or parliamentary) often matter less than particular individuals and the constellation of issues that shape political conflict (Baylis 1996). However, research by Beliaev (2006) in twenty-two post-communist societies has concluded that presidential systems with stronger executive powers have fared worse in democratic performance compared to either parliamentary systems or presidential systems with weak executive powers.

The nature of legislative, executive, and electoral institutions moulds the style and substance of political leadership within a country. However, many of the changes in political leadership that are taking place, particularly in parliamentary systems, occur in the absence of any significant institutional change. This holds in countries such as Britain, that have unwritten, evolving constitutions, as well as in countries with formally defined constitutional rules. There has been a changing interpretation of the formal and informal rules that govern how politics operates with respect to political leaders. While there are instances of institutional reforms that promote the

---

[7] In Italy, the 1994 move from PR to a mixed system appears to have greatly enhanced the role of the main leaders, since the winner almost invariably becomes the prime minister. In Germany, Klingemann and Weßels (2001) show that in the single-member district ballot, there is a sizeable personal vote for candidates.

personalization of politics—electoral reform, for example, or the direct election of the prime minister in Israel—such examples are few. In the next three sections non-institutional explanations for the personalization of politics are evaluated.

3 THE ELECTRONIC MEDIA AND PERSONALIZATION

Many of the observed changes in the role of political leaders in the established democracies is traced back to the growth of the electronic media, and especially television during the 1950s and 1960s. In the early years of television's development, relatively few resources were devoted to the coverage of politics, which was seen as not well suited to the new medium (Patterson 1993). That view changed rapidly as the potential of television to market politics to voters became apparent (Schudson 2002). In the 1952 US presidential election campaign, Dwight D. Eisenhower, the successful candidate, made extensive use of television advertising for the first time. His expos-ure on television is credited with portraying him to voters as a warm and friendly personality, in contrast to his opponent, Adlai Stevenson, who refused to follow suit and appeared aloof and detached (Barkin 1986; West 2001).

While television had an early role in US politics, it was slower to demonstrate its potential in the major parliamentary systems. Nevertheless, by the 1960s the television coverage of politics—and especially political leaders—was established, and television began to influence the way in which voters viewed their leaders. In Britain, the 1964 general election was the first to be systematically covered by television;[8] perhaps coincidentally, it was the first election in Britain where analysts used the term "presidential" to describe the character of the campaign (Mughan 2000, 27). Similar findings showing the link between television and personalization have been observed in other parts of Europe, although the effects are uneven, and often contingent on the types of personalities involved, the electoral context, and the issues that dominate during the campaign (Kaase 1994; Kleinnijenhuis et al. 2001). By the late 1960s, television was an indispensable tool for modern election campaigning in virtually all of the established democracies (Bowler and Farrell 1992; Norris et al. 1999).

One indication of the profound nature of the impact of television on political leaders is the increasing importance of televised leaders' debates during national election campaigns (Hellweg, Pfau, and Brydon 1992). The first debate was held in the United States between John F. Kennedy and Richard Nixon during the 1960 presidential election campaign and is credited with winning Kennedy the presidency.

[8] The two major parties were allocated seventy-five minutes each of free television broadcasting (McAllister 1985).

In the words of one television executive at the time, "Kennedy was bronzed beautifully...Nixon looked like death" (quoted in Druckman 2003, 563). The next televised leaders' debate was not until the 1976 election, when Gerald Ford debated with Jimmy Carter. The two 1976 debates were seen as significantly increasing not just the personal profiles of the two major candidates, but in improving voters' knowledge of the issues (for a review, see Holbrook 1999).

Largely as a consequence of the US experience with televised debates, by the 1980s the idea of a leaders' debate had spread to the established parliamentary democracies. Of forty-five democracies that were examined in the mid-1990s, all but four had held a leaders' debate at the immediate past election (LeDuc, Niemi, and Norris 1996, 45–8). Perhaps the only established parliamentary democracy where a leaders' debate is consistently resisted is Britain.[9] In most other countries, the debate is now an established and formal part of the election campaign, the only point of disagreement between the parties being the number of debates and their closeness to polling day, with the incumbent wishing to minimize the risks of a live television debate by having fewer and earlier debates, the challenger wishing to maximize it by later and more frequent debates (Schroeder 2000).

The new democracies of central and eastern Europe have been quick to utilize television for political purposes. With many of these countries still in the early stages of democratic consolidation and with fragmented, unstable party systems and voters who exhibit few partisan loyalties, the media has exercised an undue influence in shaping election outcomes. In Russia, the pro-Putin state television network had a major influence on the outcomes of the 1999 parliamentary and 2000 presidential elections (White and McAllister 2006; White, Oates, and McAllister 2005). It is hardly surprising, then, that across many of the new democracies, media laws and the accompanying financial arrangements are a major source of dispute among politicians (Voltmer 2006).

Television's concentration on the personalities of the political leaders and the way in which it uses those personalities to frame political issues and events has several explanations. The most obvious is how television presents information to its viewers. Because of the way in which it communicates information through visual images, it is easier for television to disseminate information through a familiar personality rather than through an abstract document or an institution (Glaser and Salmon 1991; see also Ranney 1983). In turn, these visual images make it easier for viewers to develop a rapport with the politicians they see on television, and to empathize with their goals. Viewers may place themselves in the role of the candidates they see on television, or in the role of the interviewers who interrogate them, and as a consequence gain a better understanding of the politician's views. For television, political leaders represent a convenient visual shortcut to capture and retain the viewer's attention, particularly if the information overlaps with the leader's personality.

---

[9] In defense of not having a formal debate, it is usually argued that scrutiny of party policies and the competence of the leaders is best left to professional media interviewers. Schudson (2002, 264) observes that British television interviewing style, "once formal and deferential" has changed to being "aggressive and critical."

While it is tempting to see television as the prime mover behind the personaliza tion of politics, political parties also play a key role in the process. Parties find it easier to market political choices to voters through a familiar personality, who can promote the party's policies much more effectively to voters when compared to the simple dissemination of a press release or through the publication of a policy document. When framed within the visual context of television, the leader can promote the policy and then be questioned by an interviewer, who vicariously represents the interests of voters, further heightening popular interest in the policy. When the party is in government, the reinforcement of policy and personality that television can deliver—emphasizing such values as authority and competence—can enhance the already substantial advantages that accrue to incumbency, benefiting the government's popularity (McAllister 1996).

The desire of voters to hold governments accountable for their actions provides a further explanation for the emphasis on the personalities of the leaders. Voters prefer to hold an individual accountable for government performance (or, occa-sionally, for the performance of the opposition), rather than an abstract institution or a political ideal (Bean and Mughan 1989). This tendency is more important in a parliamentary system, where collective cabinet responsibility and the fortunes of the government as a whole may blur accountability in the eyes of the public. Personalization can be especially problematic in a coalition arrangement where accountability is more difficult to assign. By focusing attention on the prime minister as the individual who is accountable for the government's collective performance, the public finds it easier to deliver reward or punishment, when compared to an abstract collectivity. As a result, there is a general trend towards a stronger correlation overtime between prime ministerial popularity and the pub-lic's rating of government in both Australia and Britain (Lanoue and Headrick 1994; McAllister 2003).

4 TELEVISION AND "POLITICAL PRIMING"

A further refinement on the way in which television projects the personalities of political leaders is the phenomenon of "political priming." Political priming is the process by which leaders are evaluated by voters, based on a leader's performance on the issues that are considered to be of importance to voters. Since voters cannot make an exhaustive evaluation of all aspects of a leader's performance, "their evaluations depend on a modest sample of what they know, and a sample of convenience at that" (Kinder 1998, 181). Typically, voters focus on a small number of issues, which are systematically linked to the leader and their performance on those issues continuously evaluated (Iyengar and Kinder 1987). As new information emerges about political leaders and their performance, this modifies how voters view the leader's key personality traits. Ultimately, such popular evaluations of political leaders, aggregated over a period of time, come to influence electoral outcomes (for a review, see Krosnick and Kinder 1990).

Political priming is consistently important in presidential systems, since the exclusive focus on the president provides the electronic media with the greatest opportunity to evaluate presidential performance across a wide range of issues, domestic and international. Not surprisingly, most research on priming in presidential systems comes from the United States (for a review, see Kinder 1998).[10] Priming also takes place in parliamentary systems, by focusing on the prime minister, but the evaluation of prime ministerial performance is more difficult if there is one or more opposition leaders whose performance must also be taken into account by the public. The extreme case is a multi-party system where there are several political leaders, and in these instances the media must provide a distinct message about the performance of each (Gunther and Mughan 2000).

Television has a central role to play in determining how and in what way this priming takes place, by shaping how the issue is framed and presented to the public. Television news executives decide whether or not to focus on a particular issue or event. Since the range of potential issues is vast, from moral issues like abortion or euthanasia, to economic issues involving inflation or general economic management, television must make a choice on which ones to concentrate on. What the media decides, and how often they choose to cover a topic in their news stories, plays a key role in making an issue politically salient, by priming voters on it (Mutz 1992). The decisions that the electronic media take can even determine whether or not voters are likely to have a view on the issue in the first place. Television can imply that a leader is responsible for creating a problem in the first place. Even if the leader is not responsible for creating the problem, as in the case of a natural disaster, then the leader can be held responsible if it is not solved (Iyengar 1991; Iyengar and Kinder 1987; Kinder 1998).

Political priming by the media occurs most frequently on issues of war or peace, or foreign policy, where the options are clear and where the performance of the leader in handling the issue is easily understood within the electorate. Several studies show the importance of the electronic media in shaping the performance of the United States president on such issues as the 1991 Gulf War and the bombing of Iraq (Edwards and Swenson 1997; Krosnick and Brannon 1993), and European studies have show the importance of priming on such issues as European integration, where there is also a clear choice (de Vreese 2004). Priming is obviously more difficult if the issues are complex, particularly where they involve economic management, and if it is an issue on which party cues are weak. In contrast, the growth in education in the second half of the twentieth century provides voters with more cognitive skills with which to process the necessary information, thus diminishing uncertainty and risk in the process of priming (Alvarez 1997).

[10] An exception is de Vreese's (2004) study of Norway, and Gidengil et al. (2002) in Canada.

Does the way in which television portrays leaders and their personal characteristics influence the vote? There is little doubt that the presence of the visual images and non-verbal cues conveyed by television has significant effects on how voters evaluate candidates. Druckman (2003; see also Graber 2001) conducted an experiment to show that those who saw a visual replay of the 1960 Kennedy–Nixon debate reacted differently to those who listened to the audio version. Those who saw the visual version placed greater reliance on their personal perceptions of the candidates than those who listened to the audio version. Nevertheless, generalized conclusions are problematic, because of the complexities involved in evaluating the direct electoral influence of television (Miller and Krosnick 2000). We can say with certainty that while television exposure is a necessary condition to ensure a leader's electoral competitiveness, it is not a sufficient condition for his or her electoral success.

5 THE DECLINE OF PARTIES AND ELECTORAL PARTICIPATION

Popular perceptions of political leaders are usually traced back to political socialization, and to the experiences of adolescents in the years before they join the active electorate (Conover and Searing 2000; Jennings and Niemi 1974). This process of socialization is also linked to the emergence of partisanship, and across most of the established democracies for which reliable data are available how people view their leaders is strongly associated with feelings of partisan attachment (Miller, Wattenberg, and Malanchuk 1986). The link between partisan attachment and leader image is particularly strong in parliamentary systems. Some of the earliest voting studies in Britain found that citizens' views of the party leaders were associated with the popular images of the parties themselves, to the extent that they were almost indistinguishable (Milne and Mackenzie 1954; see also Butler and Stokes 1974). Similar findings emerge from other parliamentary systems (Bean 1993; Graetz and McAllister 1987).

If partisanship is declining, then it follows that how voters view their leaders will also change significantly as a result. The widespread partisan dealignment in most advanced democracies in the past several decades is the most profound change that has taken place in voting behaviour since the 1920s (Clarke and Stewart 1998; Dalton and Wattenberg 2000; Webb, Farrell, and Holliday 2002). With weaker partisan loyalties, and in the absence of strong social links to specific parties, such as class or religion, voters are more likely to switch their vote between elections, or to abstain. In these circumstances, weaker voter attachments to parties should enhance the role of the leader in both the mobilization and conversion of the vote. In the absence of party cues, voters will rely more heavily on the appeal of the candidates' personalities in order to decide their vote.

In line with many other social and technological changes in the advanced democracies, the traditional concept of the mass party has been in decline for more than half a century, most notably in the Westminster systems where they first originated (Scarrow 2000). The decline of parties as mass organizations and the increasing difficulty that parties encounter in mobilizing the vote has often shifted citizens' attentions away from local election campaigns and towards the national political stage, a trend that has been hastened by the growth of the electronic media. At the same time, the major parties have shifted their emphasis during election campaigns from local candidates to national political leaders, in turn elevating to high office those who they believe will exercise the maximum geographical and social appeal to voters (McAllister 1996). As a result, there is now less emphasis on a party's policies than in the past, and more emphasis on the personalities of the leaders who will have to implement those policies if they win election (Wattenberg 1991, 13–30).

A further change in the political context that influences the role of leaders in electoral choice is the decline of electoral participation. Turnout has declined across the established democracies (Blais 2000 and chapter in this volume; Wattenberg 2002), and after an initially high level, among the newly democratized post-communist states as well (Kostadinova 2003). The assumption is that declining turnout will enhance the role of the president or the prime minister, by focusing greater attention on the leader's role in mobilizing the vote, above and beyond party considerations. In addition, the decline in electoral participation should produce voters who may be more motivated by economic self-interest in reaching their voting decision, since their more apathetic counterparts would abstain. This conclusion is in line with findings which show that the greater propensity of late deciding voters in Australian, British, and US elections are more likely to be rational and calculating, rather than capricious or disinterested. In such a context, the role of the leader in framing and promoting policies to attract these voters may well become more important over the course of time (McAllister 2002).

This change in the partisan and electoral context has several important consequences for the personalization of politics. First, political leaders are now important not just for voter conversion, but for mobilization as well, traditionally the major function of the political parties. To the extent that voters respond to the personalities of the leaders (either positively or negatively) their probability of voting will increase. Second, leaders now hold their positions by virtue of a personalized mandate, rather than because of a support base within the party (Poguntke and Webb 2005, 9). This means that leaders can appeal to voters over the heads of the party, bypassing party factions and activists.[11] Third, once a leader is popularly elected, the personalized mandate that he or she possesses will convey considerable policy autonomy, with little or no recourse to the party machinery (see Poguntke and Webb 2005 for longer discussion).

---

[11] As Poguntke and Webb (2005, 22) note, this is both an advantage and a disadvantage: "as long as they can ride the tiger of an increasingly fickle public opinion, they can 'go it alone'; once public support begins to dwindle, however, they are left with few allies."

6 THE CONSEQUENCES

There is little doubt that politics has become more personalized over the past half-century. The trend is especially pronounced within the established parliamentary democracies, where the character and style of election campaigning, the presentation and promotion of policies, and the executive authority of the prime minister have all changed markedly from what was observed a generation earlier. The phenomenon of personalization has also emerged in the former post-communist states, although here its origins lie in the lack of confidence in political institutions engendered by the communist legacy, which has given greater prominence to political personalities (Rose and Mishler 1994). While the causes of the personalization of politics are numerous and complex, it does appear that international trends in political communications have become so uniform and pervasive that they dwarf all other explanations (Negrine 1996; Schudson 1995).

What are the consequences of the personalization of politics for electoral politics? The trend towards the emphasis on leaders is likely to further exacerbate the decline in political parties, since their programmatic function is being steadily absorbed by the major party leaders who, in any event, hold a personalized rather than a party mandate. There may be greater electoral volatility, which is already occurring as a result of partisan dealignment and the declining political influence of social structure (Dalton and Wattenberg 2000). As leaders come and go, and electoral mobilization and conversion comes increasingly to depend on political personality rather than party program, there is scope for even more electoral volatility. At the same time, election campaigns will become more important in determining outcomes, featuring personal images as much (or more than) parties and policies; this is already a trend which is one of the more visible consequences of personalization (Bowler and Farrell 1992; Mancini and Swanson 1996).

What are the consequences of the personalization of politics for democratic governance? First, leaders will enjoy much greater autonomy in policy making because of their personalized mandate; a dramatic recent example was the commitment of troops to Iraq by Australia and Britain, largely as a consequence of their respective prime ministers' personal commitment to the US president, George W. Bush. Second, the increasing presidentialization of parliamentary systems will lead to demands for institutional reform to accommodate these new practices. One example has been calls for the direct election of the prime minister (Maddens and Fiers 2004). To date, this was implemented only in Israel, between 1992 and 2001 (Hazan 1996), but it has been considered in countries as diverse as Japan, the Netherlands, and Italy.[12] The motivation behind the proposal is to prevent the parliamentary system from being undermined by an undue emphasis on the

---

[12] The major consequence in Israel appears to be a weakening of the parties, and what Arian and Shamir (2001, 706) call "the privatization of the electoral system."

personalities of the major party leaders, and a consequent weakening in the legitimacy of the parliamentary system itself.

The personalization of politics has also progressed significantly in the parliamentary democracies. With the profound political changes that will result from internet communication technology, the next decades may see at least as much change in political leadership as the past few decades. Since the main changes in political leadership that have occurred are in style and informal convention rather than in legal rules, we can expect greater pressure to reform institutional structures in order to curb personal political authority and personalized mandates; some embryonic attempts have already been made in that direction. But in the absence of any radical changes, the personalization of politics will remain a—and perhaps *the*—central feature of democratic politics in the twenty-first century.

REFERENCES

ALVAREZ. R. 1997. *Information and Elections*. Ann Arbor: University of Michigan Press.

ARIAN, A., and SHAMIR, M. 2001. Candidates, parties and blocs: Israel in the 1990s. *Party Politics*, 7: 689–710.

BARKIN, S. 1986. Eisenhower's secret strategy: television planning in the 1952 campaign. *European Journal of Marketing*, 20: 18–28.

BARTELS, L. 1988. *Presidential Primaries and the Dynamics of Public Choice*. Princeton: Princeton University Press.

BAYLIS, T. A. 1996. President versus prime ministers: shaping executive authority in Eastern Europe. *World Politics*, 48: 297–323.

BEAN, C. 1993. The electoral influence of party leader images in Australia and New Zealand. *Comparative Political Studies*, 26: 111–32.

—— and MUGHAN, A. 1989. Leadership effects in parliamentary elections in Australia and Britain. *American Political Science Review*, 83: 1165–79.

BELIAEV, M. V. 2006. Presidential powers and consolidation of new postcommunist democracies. *Comparative Political Studies*, 39: 375–98.

BLAIS, A. 2000. *To Vote or Not to Vote: The Merits and Limits of Rational Choice Theory*. Pittsburgh: University of Pittsburgh Press.

BOWLER, S., and FARRELL, D. eds. 1992. *Electoral Strategies and Political Marketing*. London: Macmillan.

—— —— 1993. Legislator shirking and voter monitoring: impacts of European parliament electoral systems upon legislator-voter relationships. *Journal of Common Market Studies* 31: 45–69.

—— —— and KATZ, R. eds. 1999. *Party Discipline and Parliamentary Government*. Columbus, Oh.: Ohio State University Press.

BUTLER, D., and STOKES, D. 1974. *Political Change in Britain*. London: Macmillan.

CLARKE, H., and STEWART, M. 1998. The decline of parties in the minds of citizens. *Annual Review of Political Science*, 1: 357–78.

CONOVER, P., and SEARING, D. 2000. A political socialization approach. Pp. 91–124 in *Rediscovering the Democratic Purposes of Education*, ed. L. M., McDonnell, P. M. Timpane, and R. Benjamin. Lawrence, Kan.: University of Kansas Press.

DALTON, R., MCALLISTER, I., and WATTENBERG, M. 2000. The consequences of partisan dealignment. Pp. 37–63 in Dalton and Wattenberg 2000.

—— and WATTENBERG, M. eds. 2000. *Parties without Partisans: Political Change in Advanced Industrial Democracies*. Oxford: Oxford University Press.

DE VREESE, C. 2004. Primed by the Euro: the impact of a referendum campaign on public opinion and evaluations of government and political leaders. *Scandinavian Political Studies*, 27: 45–64.

DRUCKMAN, J. 2003. The power of television images: the first Kennedy Nixon debate revisited. *Journal of Politics*, 65: 559–71.

EDWARDS, G., and SWENSON, T. 1997. Who rallies? The anatomy of a rally event. *Journal of Politics*, 59: 200–12.

FARRELL, D. M., and MCALLISTER, I. 2005. *The Australian Electoral System: Origins, Variations and Consequences*. Sydney: University of NSW Press.

FRANKLIN, M., MACKIE, T., and VALEN, H. 1992. *Electoral Change: Responses to Evolving Social and Attitudinal Structures in Western Countries*. Cambridge: Cambridge University Press.

GIDENGIL, E. et al. 2002. Priming and campaign context: evidence from recent Canadian elections. Pp. 76–91 in *Do Political Campaigns Matter? Campaign Effects in Elections and Referendums*, ed. D. M. Farrell and R. Schmitt-Beck. London: Routledge.

GLASER, T., and SALMON, C. 1991. *Public Opinion and the Communication of Consent*. New York: Guilford.

GRABER, D. A. 2001. *Processing Politics*. Chicago: University of Chicago Press.

GRAETZ, B., and MCALLISTER, I. 1987. Political leadership and electoral outcomes in Britain, 1974–1983. *Comparative Political Studies*, 19: 484–507.

GUNTHER, R., and MUGHAN, A. eds. 2000. *Democracy and the Media: A Comparative Perspective*. Cambridge: Cambridge University Press.

HAZAN, R. 1996. Presidential parliamentarism: direct popular election of the prime minister. *Electoral Studies*, 15: 21–38.

HELLWEG, S., PFAU, M., and BRYDON, S. 1992. *Televised Presidential Debates*. New York: Praeger.

HOLBROOK, T. 1999. Political learning from presidential debates. *Political Behavior*, 21: 67–89.

HOLMBERG, S., and OSCARSSON, H. 2006. Party leader effects on the vote. In *Political Leaders and Democratic Elections*, ed K. Aarts, A. Blais, and H. Schmitt. Oxford: Oxford University Press.

HUANG, L.-N., and PRICE, V. 2001. Motivations, goals, information search and memory about political candidates. *Political Psychology*, 22: 665–92.

IYENGAR, S. 1991. *Is Anyone Responsible? How Television Frames Political Issues*. Chicago: University of Chicago Press.

—— and KINDER, D. 1987. *News that Matters: Television and American Opinion*. Chicago: University of Chicago Press.

JENNINGS, M., and NIEMI, R. 1974. *The Political Character of Adolescence: The Influence of Families and Schools*. Princeton: Princeton University Press.

KAASE, M. 1994. Is there personalization in politics? Candidates and voting behavior in Germany. *International Political Science Review*, 15: 211–30.

KATZ, R. 1986. Party government: a rationalistic conception. Pp. 124–39 in *The Future of Party Government*, ed. F.G. Castles and R. Wildemanns. Berlin: de Gruyter.

KEETER, S. 1987. The illusion of intimacy: television and the role of candidate personal qualities in voter choice. *Public Opinion Quarterly*, 51: 344–58.

KINDER, D. 1998. Communication and opinion. *Annual Review of Political Science*, 1: 167–97.

KING, A. 1994. Chief executives in Western Europe. Pp. 150–63 in *Developing Democracy*, ed. I. Budge and D. McKay. London: Sage.

KLEINNIJENHUIS J., MAURER, M., KEPPLINGER, H., et al. 2001. Issues and personalities in German and Dutch television news: patterns and effects. *European Journal of Communication*, 16: 337–59.

KLINGEMANN, H.-D., and WEßELS, B. 2001. Political consequences of Germany's mixed member system: personalization at the grass-roots.' Pp. 279–97 in *Mixed-Member Electoral Systems: The Best of Both Worlds?*, ed. M. Shugart, and M. Wattenberg Oxford: Oxford University Press.

KOSTADINOVA, T. 2003. Voter turnout dynamics in post-Communist Europe. *European Journal of Political Research*, 42: 741–59.

KROSNICK, J., and BRANNON, L. 1993. The impact of the Gulf War on the ingredients of presidential evaluation: multidimensional effects of political involvement. *American Political Science Review*, 87: 763–75.

—— and KINDER, D. 1990. Altering the foundations of support for the president through priming. *American Political Science Review*, 84: 497–512.

LANOUE, D., and HEADRICK, B. 1994. Prime ministers, parties and the public. *Public Opinion Quarterly*, 58: 191–209.

LAVER, M., and SCHOFIELD, N. 1990. *Multiparty Government: The Politics of Coalition in Europe*. Oxford: Oxford University Press.

LEDUC, L, NIEMI, R., and NORRIS, P. eds. 1996. Introduction: the present and future of democratic elections. Pp. 4–17 in *Comparing Democracies: Elections and Voting in Global Perspective*, ed. L. LeDuc, R. Niemi, and P. Norris. Thousand Oaks, Calif.: Sage.

MCALLISTER, I. 1985. Campaign activity and electoral outcomes in Britain, 1979 and 1983. *Public Opinion Quarterly*, 49: 300–15.

—— 1996. Leaders. Pp. 278–96 in *Comparing Democracies: Elections and Voting in Global Perspective*, ed. L. LeDuc, R. Niemi, and P. Norris. Thousand Oaks, Calif.: Sage.

—— 2002. Calculating or capricious? The new politics of late deciding voters. Pp. 22–40 in *Do Political Campaigns Matter? Campaign Effects in Elections and Referendums*, ed. D. M. Farrell and R. Schmitt-Beck. London: Routledge.

—— 2003. Prime ministers, opposition leaders and government popularity in Australia. *Australian Journal of Political Science*, 38: 259–77.

—— 2006. Political leaders in Westminster systems. In *Political Leaders and Democratic Elections*, ed. K. Aarts, A. Blais, and H. Schmitt. Oxford: Oxford University Press.

MADDENS, B., and FIERS, S. 2004. The direct PM election and the institutional presidentialisation of parliamentary systems. *Electoral Studies*, 23: 769–93.

MANCINI, P., and SWANSON, D. L. 1996. Politics, media, and modern democracy: introduction. Pp. 3–11 in *Politics, Media, and Modern Democracy: An International Study of Innovations in Electoral Campaigning and their Consequences*, ed. P. Mancini and D. L. Swanson. Westport, Conn.: Praeger.

MILLER, A., WATTENBERG, M., and MALANCHUK, O. 1986. Schematic assessments of presidential candidates. *American Political Science Review*, 80: 521–40.

MILLER, J., and KROSNICK, J. 2000. News media impact on the ingredients of presidential evaluations. *American Journal of Political Science*, 44: 295–309.

MILLER, W. et al. 1990. *How Voters Change*. Oxford: Oxford University Press.

MILNE, R., and MACKENZIE, H. C. 1954. *Straight Fight*. London: Hansard Society.

MUGHAN, A. 1993. Party leaders and presidentialism in the 1992 British election: a postwar perspective. In *British Elections and Parties Yearbook, 1993*, ed. D. Denver et al. London: Harvester Wheatsheaf.

MUGHAN, A. 2000. *Media and the Presidentialization of Parliamentary Elections.* London: Palgrave.

MUTZ, D. 1992. Mass media and the depoliticization of personal experience. *American Journal of Political Science,* 36: 483–508.

NEGRINE, R. 1996. *The Communication of Politics.* London: Sage.

NORRIS, P., CURTICE, J., SANDERS, D., SCAMMELL, M., and SEMETKO, H. 1999. *On Message: Communicating the Campaign.* London: Sage.

PAGE, B. I., and SHAPIRO, M. 1992. *The Rational Public.* Chicago: University of Chicago Press.

PATTERSON, T. 1993. *Out of Order.* New York: Knopf.

POGUNTKE, T., and WEBB, P. eds. 2005. *The Presidentialization of Politics in Democratic Societies.* Oxford: Oxford University Press.

RANNEY, A. 1983. *Channels of Power: The Impact of Television on American Politics.* New York: Basic Books.

RHODES, R. 1995. Introducing the Core Executive. Pp. 1–8 in *Prime Minister, Cabinet and Core Executive,* ed. R. A. W. Rhodes and P. Dunleavy. London: Macmillan.

ROSE, R., and MISHLER. W. 1994. Mass reaction to regime change in Eastern Europe: polarization or leaders and laggards? *British Journal of Political Science,* 24: 159–82.

—— and MUNRO, N. 2002. *Elections without Order: Russia's Challenge to Vladimir Putin.* Cambridge: Cambridge University Press.

SARTORI, G. 1976. *Parties and Party Systems.* Cambridge: Cambridge University Press.

SCARROW, S. 2000. Parties without members? Party organization in a changing electoral environment. Pp. 79–101 in *Parties without Partisans: Political Change in Advanced Industrial Democracies,* ed. R. J. Dalton and M. P. Wattenberg. Oxford: Oxford University Press.

SCHROEDER, A. 2000. *Presidential Debates: Forty Years of High Risk TV.* New York: Columbia University Press.

SCHUDSON, M. 1995. *The Power of News.* Cambridge, Mass.: Harvard University Press.

—— 2002. The news media as political institutions. *Annual Review of Political Science* 5: 249–69.

SHUGART, M. 2001. Electoral "efficiency" and the move to mixed-member systems. *Electoral Studies,* 20: 173–93.

—— and WATTENBERG, M., eds. 2001. *Mixed-Member Electoral Systems: The Best of Both Worlds?* Oxford: Oxford University Press.

TAAGEPERA, R. 2002. Designing electoral rules and waiting for an electoral system to evolve. Pp. 248–65 in *The Architecture of Democracy: Constitutional Design, Conflict Management, and Democracy,* ed. A. Reynolds. Oxford: Oxford University Press.

VERNEY, D. 1959. *The Analysis of Political Systems.* London: Routledge & Kegan Paul.

VOLTMER, K. ed. 2006. *Mass Media and Political Communication in New Democracies.* London: Routledge.

WATTENBERG, M. 1991. *The Rise of Candidate-Centered Politics.* Cambridge, Mass.: Harvard University Press.

—— 2002. *Where Have all the Voters Gone?* Cambridge, Mass.: Harvard University Press.

WEBB, P., FARRELL, D., and HOLLIDAY, I. eds. 2002. *Political Parties at the Millennium: Adaptation and Decline in Democratic Societies.* Oxford: Oxford University Press.

WEST, D. 2001. *Air Wars: Television Advertising in Election Campaigns, 1952–2000.* Washington, DC: Congressional Quarterly Press.

WHITE, S., and MCALLISTER, I. 2006. Politics and the media in post-communist Russia. Pp. 210–27 in *Mass Media and Political Communication in New Democracies,* ed. K. Voltmer. London: Routledge.

—— OATES, S., and MCALLISTER, I. 2005. Media effects and Russian elections, 1999–2000. *British Journal of Political Science,* 35: 191–208.

CHAPTER 31

THE INTERACTION OF STRUCTURES AND VOTER BEHAVIOR

CHRISTOPHER J. ANDERSON

DOES institutional performance affect people's sense of whether their political system is legitimate? Does the economy influence voter support for incumbent governments? Do citizens' policy preferences shape their vote choice? Do domestic institutions affect whether citizens are willing to transfer authority to supranational and international institutions? These are all questions social scientists have asked for some time. As it turns out, more often than not the answer is a resounding "it depends." Specifically, political scientists have come to realize that the answers to these questions depend on understanding the interaction of countries' macro-characteristics and individual differences among citizens.

Relying on so-called multi-level models, which combine information about individuals and the contexts to which they are exposed, scholars of behavioral politics have started to comprehend more systematically than ever before the conditions under which the relations mentioned above exist or are strengthened and weakened (Kedar and Shively 2005). As I describe below, such models are a growth industry in the comparative study of behavioral politics because of advances in scholarly understandings of institutions and context as well as significant advances in statistical

* I am grateful to André Blais, Shaun Bowler, Ray Duch, Matt Gabel, John Huber, Orit Kedar, Michael McDonald, and Phil Shively for their many helpful suggestions.

techniques that allow the analysis of exciting new survey data that cover much of the globe. Returning to the questions posed above, we know, for example, that the impact of corruption on system support is conditional on whether citizens are supporters of the incumbent government (Anderson and Tverdova 2003; Seligson 2002), that the economy has a stronger impact on voters when institutions produce clear responsibility for policy making (Powell and Whitten 1993), and that citizens will be more likely to support transfers of authority away from national institutions if inferior performance of national institutions is coupled with high opinions of supranational ones (Rohrschneider 2002). In this chapter, I review the growing literature on the nexus of macro-level structures and individual behavior that these studies are part of with an eye toward the effects that macro-level institutions and contexts have on citizen behavior as well as how political institutions and the environment in which citizens form opinions and act moderate the effects of individual-level factors on citizen behavior.

1 The Comparative Study of Structures and Political Behavior: Citizens in Context

People do not live in a vacuum. They form attitudes and make choices in variable environments, which come in the form of formal institutional rules that govern people's behavior or in the form of differential economic, social, and political conditions that shape people's interpretations and actions. In a very basic way, then, context and behavior are intimately connected, and this connection is at the heart of political life in at least two fundamental ways: first, formal and informal rules affect people's political behavior, and people's preferences, attitudes, and behavior affect the establishment and functioning of such rules. Second, citizens are exposed to variable social, political, and economic environments that they are called upon to understand and interpret and that they may seek to shape based on these understandings and interpretations.

While the influences of context on individuals should be obvious, students of comparative politics traditionally have paid less attention to contextual than to individual-level factors in explanations of citizen attitudes and behavior (but see, for example, Verba, Nie, and Kim 1978). The reasons for this are varied, but they are likely to include the historical leadership role and the intellectual underpinnings of the behavioral revolution in survey research, in which the American National Election Studies (ANES) at the University of Michigan have played an important role for shaping scholarly debates about politics and citizen behavior for many years.

The Michigan researchers relied upon psychological concepts as primary explanatory factors. This approach focused attention on the actions of citizens as autonomous individuals, without much regard for the political context of their neighborhoods, communities, or work environments. In the ensuing decades, the Michigan approach to understanding citizen politics dominated scholarly debates. Moreover, because of the dominance of American political science and the institutionalization of the ANES, this approach was exported to various corners of American and international universities (see the chapter by Kittilson in this volume). These efforts played a critical role in establishing an international infrastructure of research institutes, data archives, and researchers versed in the science of survey research and following the Michigan paradigm. Yet, despite this internationalization of survey research, explicitly cross-national surveys that included comparable measures and that were collected at similar points in time for many years were quite rare.[1]

Starting in the 1980s, however, much of this changed, and several collaborative cross-national survey projects were initiated (see the chapter by Kittilson in this volume). The expansion and proliferation of cross-national survey projects coincided with several particularly auspicious trends in the real world and in the world of ideas. In the real world, the rapid expansion of electoral democracies around the world in the 1980s and 1990s provided a significantly enlarged universe of country cases that could be studied with an eye toward democratic institutions, processes, behaviors, and attitudes, and where surveys could be conducted reliably and repeatedly. Moreover, this period saw significant advances in desktop computing technologies and, more recently, statistical techniques appropriate for conducting cross-national and multi-level research (Steenbergen and Jones 2002).

In the world of ideas, the 1980s and 1990s saw a renewed focus on institutional questions across political science, with new theories that could be tested with better data. In addition, there was a renewed interest in developing a more sophisticated understanding of contextual theories of political behavior (Huckfeldt and Sprague 1995; Zuckerman 2005). As a result of this confluence of factors, the comparative study of behavioral politics has been significantly shaped in recent years by the emphasis on institutions in comparative politics and on context in behavioral research, a greater number of democracies around the world in which to test arguments cross-nationally, better and more varied cross-national comparable data, and finally advances in statistical techniques (multi-level or hierarchical modeling) along with increased computational ease. Most significantly, this has led to an upsurge in scholarship that combines the (cross-national) study of institutions and other macro-political features with individual-level data and concerns about individual behavior.

That is, there is now a renewed and systematic attempt to connect the experiences people have as participants in the political process and how they interact with the constraints any particular political system or situation provides. And this has had implications for the role of institutions and structures in studies of political behavior and, in turn, for our understanding of institutions.

---

[1] Notable exceptions include Almond and Verba's *Civic Culture* study or Barnes, Kaase, et al.'s *Political Action* study, for example.

2 MODELING STRUCTURES AND BEHAVIOR

People form opinions and make decisions in specific and frequently dissimilar political, economic, and social contexts (Huckfeldt and Sprague 1995; Zuckerman 2005). These contexts vary from the immediate social environment to macro-level structures at the level of countries or even beyond (Anderson and Paskeviciute 2005; Beck et al. 2002). And following what has now become a common definition of an institution as any socially imposed constraint upon human behavior, institutions are the "rules of the game" for human interaction (North 1981) that do not have to be formal or written rules but can also include informal constraints, such as widely accepted norms of behavior that have long been the focus of cultural theories of politics.

At the meso-level, recent years have seen a revival of scholarship into the connection between individuals' social environments and political behavior with a focus on how people obtain information from social others and how people's discussion networks shape their understanding of and participation in the political world around them (Huckfeldt and Sprague 1995; Huckfeldt, Johnson, and Sprague 2004). While this research has been based predominantly on data collected in the United States, scholars have applied the basic insights from this research to understanding behavior in other countries as well (Huckfeldt, Ikeda, and Pappi 2005).

Predominantly, however, the comparative study of behavioral politics has seen investigations of macro-level contexts or structures. These usually come in one of two forms: *institutions* and *structural conditions*.[2] Aside from being variable across space and time, these contexts are commonly the product of social choices human societies make. Moreover, they typically produce differential costs and incentives for differently situated individuals. For instance, in one national context it may be more difficult to vote or to participate in politics in other ways. Moreover, these environments have variable and non-neutral consequences for different kinds of people and so provide individuals with incentives and conditions for viewing the world and behaving in particular and distinct ways. Put simply, then, even in the same national context, the environment may affect different people differently.

Such a picture of the interaction between structures and behavior presumes several things. First, that politics is about the interaction of people's values and the rules and conditions that govern the implementation of those values; second, that the rules and realities in which citizens make choices are themselves a function of people's values (Riker 1980). Put another way: contexts are critical for understanding the decisions people make because they affect different people differently, and people's decisions, in turn, shape the nature, shape, and stability of these contexts.

---

[2] For example, electoral rules or the rules governing executive-legislative relations are frequently investigated features of the institutional environment, while countries' levels of corruption or ethnic heterogeneity are examples of the macro-contexts in which citizens find themselves.

Over the years, much has been written about how formal institutions affect mass political behavior—be it turnout, vote choice, or participation generally—by shaping the incentives of citizens to act in certain ways, and similar amounts of attention have been paid to the question of how macro-level contexts affect the resources and incentives of citizens to act in the political arena. Examples of this kind of approach are now common in the comparative study of political behavior.

Perhaps the most extensively researched area has dealt with the question of how electoral systems shape voter behavior. To mention some of the most prominent examples, students of electoral systems have long maintained that voters' choices are conditioned by the political context and electoral rules (Duverger 1954; Cox 1997). A plethora of studies have found that different electoral rules produce systematic differences in election outcomes (number of parties, success of certain kinds of candidates, electoral volatility, etc.) (e.g. Lijphart 1990; Rae 1967).

And there is ample evidence in other, related areas to suggest that individuals are constrained actors within particular, and variable, political environments. For example, turnout is said to be low in the United States because registration requirements are cumbersome (Powell 1986), more proportional electoral systems are said to generate incentives that favor multi-party systems and strategic voting (Cox 1997), political participation in some countries is said to be low because corruption undermines citizens' beliefs that their participation matters (Bravo and Hojman 2003), and informal understandings of the relationships between, say, legislators and constituencies are said to shape voters' choices (Cox, Rosenbluth, and Thies 1998).

The analytical strategies underlying the examples given above presume that macro-contexts are exogenous; that is, external to individual political behavior. Moreover, such a view takes the political environment—be it institutional or broadly contextual—as static. Another way to think about this is to say that the relationship between citizen behavior and context is assumed to run from context to behavior.[3] Thus, the most common approach takes some aspect of behavior as the dependent variable and a structural feature of a polity as the independent variable, and assumes that the latter is exogenous and stable. What is more, the effect of contextual factors is typically examined as if it were direct. Perhaps unsurprisingly, there are reasons to question the assumptions that underlie this approach. Here I will focus on the notion that institutions have direct effects on behavior since it is likely that any effect we find for contexts is only an average for the population as a whole that hides significant heterogeneity in people's behavior. The next section discusses these issues in more detail.

---

[3] While I will mostly follow these assumptions of exogeneity and stability here, I also wish to note that some students of politics and behavior have sought to proceed from alternative premises, namely that institutions may perhaps be neither exogenous nor in equilibrium. A number of studies have investigated the institutional choices societies make—for example, with the help of referendums or founding elections—and a rich research tradition has examined what shapes changes in the macro-context citizens live in.

3 EFFECTS OF STRUCTURES ON VOTER BEHAVIOR: CONCEPTUAL AND METHODOLOGICAL ISSUES

Structures can affect voters in three basic ways: directly, indirectly, and interactively (or contingently).[4] By *direct effects*, I mean that citizens' decisions are affected by the incentives the rules or context provide. For example, rational choice models of voter turnout presume that voters consider the costs and benefits of going to the polls and that turnout is expected to be lower when the costs are greater. Among the most frequently studied institutional constraints that impose costs on voters are registration requirements and the timing of elections. Part of the costs imposed by such rules comes in the form of time—when voting takes more time, voters will participate less. Thus, in a study of data from the United States, Gimpel and Schuknecht (2003) found, for example, that citizens who have to travel longer distances to reach their polling station are less likely to vote, with a five-mile increase in distance from the polling station leading to a more than 2 percent decrease in voter turnout. And through simulations based on Canadian data, Blais found that increasing the time involved in voting from 15–30 minutes to 45 minutes reduced turnout by about 2 percent among regular voters (Blais 2000, 89). In this set-up, structural features directly affect the costs of participation—in this example, the time-costs of going to the polls. One way to consider this relationship is displayed with the help of fictitious data in Figure 31.1. As the cost of voting increases, the probability of turnout decreases.

At first glance, many comparative studies of political behavior seem to resemble such a simple "direct effects" model, at least empirically. Yet, upon closer inspection, even if they investigate the impact of institutional features on behavior as if it were direct, many studies of the effects of structures on behavior turn out to be either models of indirect or contingent effects when considered up close.

Theoretically speaking, *indirect effects* imply that structures affect some intervening variable, which, in turn, is the immediate cause of the dependent variable. For example, we could hypothesize that electoral rules—say, a high electoral threshold—affect the formation of particular parties by producing differential incentives for political entrepreneurs, whose behavior via the resulting formation of particular parties and thus the supply of choices, in turn, affects voter choices. Or, to use another example, the degree or kind of ethnic heterogeneity in a country may affect citizens' identification with their ethnic group or their views of other groups, which, in turn, affect whether they engage in peaceful or violent political action.

In the former example, institutions will be correlated with vote choice as if they had direct effects on behavior. In truth, however, electoral rules affect the calculations

---

[4] For an excellent introduction to the politics of context, see Huckfeldt (1986).

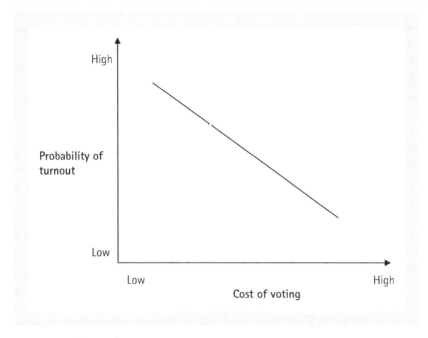

High

Probability of
turnout

Low

Low   High
Cost of voting

Fig. 31.1 Direct effects of institutions on turnout

and behaviors of political elites, which, in turn, affect citizen choices. And in the latter example, social structures will be correlated with behavior as well, and the mechanism by which this occurs is that social structures affect the attitudes of citizens about their ethnic group, which in turn affect their behavior. The main point here is that, theoretically and empirically speaking, we view structure as having consequences, but that these consequences have secondary, or indirect effects on behavior rather than direct ones.

In addition to such indirect effects, structures can have *contingent effects*. This means that the effect of some structural feature on voter behavior is strengthened or weakened, depending on the presence of some third variable. Alternatively, structure can be the intervening variable that helps determine the relative impact an independent variable may have on the dependent variable, where the independent variable can be an individual-level factor.

These contingent effects can be presented visually with fictitious data as shown in Figure 31.2. Panel (*a*) shows both an individual as well as a contextual effect. At the individual level, voters with many resources are always more likely to vote than voters with few resources, regardless of institutional context, as shown by the gap between the dashed and solid lines. At the macro-level, people in countries where the cost of voting is high are less likely to vote than people in countries where the cost of voting is low. Finally, the graph also shows that each variable's effect depends on the other. People with few resources are much less likely to vote if they live in a country where the cost of voting is high than if they live in a country where the cost of voting

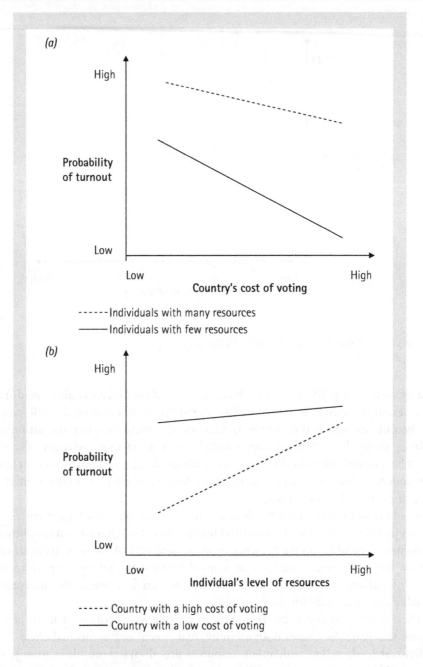

Fig. 31.2 Interactive effects of institutions and individual characteristics on turnout

is low. Conversely, individuals with many resources are only slightly less likely to vote in countries where the cost of voting is high. Put another way: the turnout gap between individuals with many and few resources is particularly pronounced in countries where the cost of voting is high.

Alternatively, as the fictitious data in panel (b) show, at the individual level, an individual's resources enhance the probability of turnout across the board. Similarly, at the level of countries, turnout is higher in countries where the cost of voting is low, as evidenced by the gap between the dashed and solid lines. At the same time, however, the extent to which a country's cost of voting affects the individual voter's probability of turning out is contingent on an individual's level of resources: the institutional context (cost of voting) has a much more powerful effect among individuals with few resources than individuals rich in resources.

In multivariate analyses, these designs are typically analyzed with interaction terms (or analogous analytic strategies, such as split sample estimations or so-called two-step estimations). Typically, such models involve a relatively small number of macro-units (typically countries) and a large number of micro-observations (typically individual respondents) per macro-unit.[5] Analyses of such micro-macro interactions constitute an area of comparative behavioral scholarship where researchers have made significant progress over the past few years and more work is being done every day.

Such interactions are ubiquitous not only in work on behavioral politics, but in comparative politics more generally. Usually, this has to do with important theoretical considerations: "Even where variables are not explicitly nested, they will be implicitly so in theory, as in questions about the relationship between democracy and economic development; though these are both macro-level variables, all arguments about their relationship involve assumptions about how various subsystem players (labor, capital, the military, etc.) interact under varying system-level conditions. Comparative politics, dealing as it does with how politics operates in varying political systems, appears by its very nature to be multi-level. Indeed, one could reasonably claim that all Comparative Politics is multi-level" (Kedar and Shively 2005).

This would imply that behavioral politics, especially when conducted from a comparative perspective, is inherently contingent.[6] A few examples may help explain the logic of this approach and the kinds of powerful insights it can generate. Perhaps the area where analyses of interactions between structures and voting have been most widespread is in scholarship on economic voting, but other areas (on voting behavior more generally and political legitimacy) have seen their fair share of multi-level analyses as well. In the following sections I will provide an overview of some of the research in these areas to demonstrate how scholars have productively analyzed the interaction of structures and behavior.

---

[5] For good introductions regarding the methodological issues involved, see Brambor, Clark, and Golder (2005); Steenbergen and Jones (2002), and Western (1998) as well as the papers in the special issue of *Political Analysis*, 13 (4), 2005.

[6] Not all of this work is or has to be cross-national in nature. It is equally possible to examine cross-regional differences as contextual influences. While there are fewer studies that exploit cross-regional variation, these generally follow the same logic. An example is Jesuit (2003).

4 INTERACTIONS OF STRUCTURES
AND BEHAVIOR IN RESEARCH
ON ECONOMIC VOTING

In recent years, a number of studies have focused on how the nature of a country's representative structures interacts with the willingness of voters to punish governments for bad economic performance. Most of this literature argues that the impact of a bad economy hinges on the ability of voters to assign responsibility to governments for economic performance. This ability has come to be thought of as being affected by structural features of polities, which act as institutional barriers that make it difficult for voters to obtain the necessary information about the representative's activities.

Institutions thus either facilitate or hamper citizens' ability to reward or punish governments. Institutions allow representatives to shift blame—an example is the frequent practice of coalition government in the continental European countries— and the complexity of political institutions makes it difficult for voters to figure out which one among the possibly honest officeholders or parties is to blame for a bad economy. As a result, the impact of the economy—in the form of evaluations of the economy, for example—on voting behavior for or against the government is expected to vary in strength and perhaps even direction, depending on the institutional context that varies across countries.[7]

Exactly how this may work has been the subject of much research (Anderson 2000; Dorussen and Taylor 2001; Norpoth 2001; Paldam 1991; Powell and Whitten 1993; Rudolph 2003; Samuels 2004). In revising the traditional model of economic voting, attempts to incorporate politics more explicitly in these models were pushed along by the publication of a paper by G. Bingham Powell and Guy Whitten (1993). Powell and Whitten classified political systems into those where government policy responsibility is clear and those where it is not, based on factors such as one-party versus multi-party rule, decision-making powers for opposition parties in parliament, or party cohesion. They found that economic voting effects were stronger in those countries that had clearer levels of responsibility (see also Royed, Leyden, and Borrelli 2000 for a dissenting view).[8]

Another view of how political context may mediate the relationship between economy and government support suggests that clarity of responsibility also varies over time within (and across) countries because of election outcomes that change the

---

[7] An additional factor has been added by Pacek and Radcliff (1995b) who find that more extensive welfare states cushion impact of a bad economy on the vote. In addition, scholars recently have begun to examine the impact of the international economic environment on economic voting (cf. Hellwig 2002).

[8] Recently, Samuels (2004) has pushed the Powell and Whitten classification to include the distinction between presidentialism vs parliamentarism (as well as the existence of concurrent or non-concurrent presidential and legislative elections). He finds that the impact of clarity of responsibility on presidential election outcomes is conditional upon whether legislative elections are held concurrently.

balance of power and elite bargaining, both of which periodically reshape the political context in which voters seek to affix credit and blame (Anderson 1995a; Bengtsson 2004; Nadeau, Niemi, and Yoshinaka 2002).[9] For example, democracies shift the power to govern and enact policy at more or less regular intervals by way of the electoral process. And every election offers different choices to changing electorates (Bengtsson 2004). Elections and inter-election events also shuffle the cards of government and depending on the political system—they install new actors, change the partisan composition of governing coalitions, or confirm political parties and executives in office with an expanded (reduced) or large (small) mandate. Thus, even when formal institutions do not change or vary, the extent to which voters are able to assign responsibility to political actors changes because of the political dynamics created by electoral systems, party systems, process of government formation, and the like (Anderson 1995a, 2000).

Finally, this new contextual branch of economic voting research has documented that the ability of voters to retain or throw incumbents out of office is also contingent on the presence of credible alternatives. Thus, clarity of responsibility really matters only when voters perceive that there are viable alternatives to the current incumbents (Sanders 1991). Yet, unsurprisingly, perhaps, the extent to which voters have such or perceive such choices varies considerably, and this, as we well know, is the result of a country's structural features and political dynamics (Anderson 1995b).

Fragmented party systems, volatile party systems, or party systems dominated by one dominant party should make it more difficult for voters to identify a clear alternative to the incumbent government (Anderson 2000; Paldam 1991). In such countries there tends to be greater uncertainty about the likely shape of an alternative future government that will form after the election has been held, and this results in a diminished likelihood that voters will turn out the incumbent government even when economic conditions are bad (Anderson 2000).

The contextual model of economic voting has been expanded in theoretical complexity as well as in geographic reach. Samuels (2004), for example, considers economic voting in presidential regimes, which are quite common in Latin America and eastern Europe, and the role of concurrently held presidential and parliamentary elections. And contextual factors have been used to understand what some have considered "anomalies" in economic voting outside of the advanced industrialized societies, including Africa, Asia, and Latin America as well as the transition states of eastern Europe (Pacek and Radcliff 1995a; Posner and Simon 2002; Remmer 1993; Stokes 1996; Tucker 2005; Weyland 1998).

---

[9] For a different version of how context affects the economy-support relationship, see Duch and Stevenson (2005) who differentiate among systems depending on whether they tend to experience exogenous shocks or competence shocks. The theory implies that the economy will matter more to the voter's expected utility calculations when the variance in administrative competence across politicians is large relative to the variance in exogenous economic shocks. Under these conditions, movement in the economy (which is observed by the voter) is a good signal of the competence of incumbents (which is not directly observed).

While the different approaches to understanding contingent effects from an institutional or contextual perspective differ—some focus on formal features of a political system while others focus on the political context of the day, some focus on incumbents while others consider the alternatives voters have—they all view voters as willing to reward and punish, but being thwarted by contextual conditions that prevent the truthful translation of policy evaluations into a vote because of difficulty to assign responsibility to the right actor or the lack of alternative choices. Following the discussion in the previous section, then, the relations among the key variables are viewed as both *indirect* and *contingent*. The effects of a bad economy on vote choice are *indirect* in that they work through voters' willingness to reward and punish the government. The impact of voters' motivations to reward and punish, in turn, is *contingent* on political structures. Cumulatively, this body of research demonstrates that the relationship between the state of the economy and voter behavior is highly conditional at the cross-national (or cross-institutional) level or cross-temporally. Thus, democratic institutions and political contexts frequently serve to weaken the impact of economic conditions on voting behavior and election outcomes in systematic ways.

While I have framed this discussion in terms of research on economic voting, the general argument should apply to issue-based voting more generally. Depending on the issue voters happen to care most about—be it the environment, health, education, or foreign policy—the general logic should work here as well: Macro-level conditions should affect voters' choices via voters' understandings and motivations to reward and punish, and these, in turn, can be expected to affect voters' choices differently, depending on the political structures that exist in a country.

4.1 Extensions and Other Ways of Incorporating Institutions

The basic insight of this work—that differences in representational structure matter for how voters behave and that they matter in contingent ways—has been pursued in other domains as well. For example, Huber, Kernell, and Leoni (2005) examine the relationship between institutional features and partisan attachment across twenty-five new and established democracies around the globe. They find that institutions that encourage retrospective clarity of responsibility foster the formation of party attachments. Moreover, institutional context has differential effects: features of political systems that make it more difficult to form party attachments have their biggest impact on individuals who have the fewest cognitive resources.

Addressing different questions in a similar way, Kedar (2005) examines how institutional context conditions the relationship between voter goals and voter behavior. Based on evidence from two highly majoritarian democracies and two very consensual ones, she finds that voters incorporate the way institutions convert votes to policy into their choices. Since policy is often the result of institutionalized multi-party bargaining and since votes are thus watered down by power sharing, voters often compensate for this by supporting parties whose positions differ from (and are often more extreme than) their own.

In related studies, Klingemann and Weßels (2000) and Gschwend (2003) examine the likelihood that individuals will vote sincerely or strategically. They find that voters' tendency to vote sincerely or strategically is dependent on district magnitude, proportionality, allocation rules, and party system (supply). In particular, they argue that sincere voting is more likely among individuals living in countries with electoral systems characterized by large district magnitude and a high degree of proportionality.

To give yet another example of the kinds of insights multi-level approaches can generate, electoral institutions and the outcomes they produce can lead to reinterpretations of what we know about the effect of institutions on voter behavior. For example, Brockington (2004) and Jusko and Shively (2005) examine the effect of party systems and coalition government on voter turnout—a question that has received significant attention in the behavioral literature—to see if the impact of party systems differ for different kinds of voters. Consistent with much previous research on the effects of proportional representation on turnout, they find that, for high-information voters, participation in elections rises as the number of parties in the system increases. Thus, among these voters, more choice improves participation rates. However, for citizens with more limited political information, increases in the number of parties in party systems depresses voting turnout. This leads to the ironic conclusion that PR, which is intended to lead to a more fair representation system, increases the information gap by complicating political choices and thus disenfranchises the less informed relative to the better informed.

These examples demonstrate that the systematic incorporation of well-known institutional features into models of political behavior can produce novel insights and help resolve well-known theoretical puzzles or empirical debates—Why does a bad economy sometimes lead voters to throw governments out of office but sometimes does not? Why is turnout higher in some proportional representation systems than others? Why do scholars find support both for proximity and directional models of voting?—and add a richness that models based on direct and unconditional effects do not possess.

5 INTERACTIONS OF VOTE CHOICE AND STRUCTURES IN RESEARCH ON LEGITIMACY: REVERSING THE CAUSAL ARROW

While most work in behavioral politics seeks to explain behavior with the help of attitudinal constructs (or attitudes with other attitudes), recent research focuses on vote choice as the independent variable. This research examines the consequences of voters' decisions, how these affect voters, and how these effects are mediated by political institutions; or, alternatively, how contextual factors affect people's attitudes differently, depending on how they voted.

This approach has been most fully developed in the area of political legitimacy. Here, scholars have examined how election outcomes—whether voters cast their ballot for the party or parties in office after the election or those in the opposition—and the nature of representative institutions affect voters' subsequent attitudes and behavior. This stream of scholarship investigates the role institutions play in moderating the sense of loss or victory citizens feel. Findings to date indicate that losers' incentives to develop low levels of support for the political system are significantly affected by a country's political context. This means that institutions have a role in blunting or exacerbating the rougher edge of losing or the thrill of success.

This research starts with the assumption that losing produces negative attitudes towards politics while winning does the opposite (Anderson et al. 2005). And winning and losing, once experienced, are expected to affect subsequent attitudes.[10] Political institutions, in turn, are important because they shape the responses of winners and losers. This means that the extent to which citizen attitudes toward democratic institutions, and by implication the potential for protest or unrest among the losers, for example, are channeled by a country's particular political context (Anderson and Guillory 1997). Individuals who belong to the political minority have more negative attitudes toward government than those in the majority if institutions are designed such that losses have particularly weighty consequences (Anderson et al. 2005).

For example, different democratic systems determine the extent to which the winners may do what they want and what rights the losers have to prevent unfettered majority rule (Colomer 2001). Institutions thus determine the rules of the game and how much of a say citizens have in selecting the new government—that is, the specify the process by which losers are created—but second, and as importantly, they also determine how power is exercised. The basic theoretical model implies that the impact of the election outcome on winners' and losers' attitudes and behaviors is constrained by attitudes and institutional arrangements. Thus, again, the relations among the basic set of variables are viewed as contingent: the impact of an individual-level factor (the attitudes associated with winning and losing) on beliefs about the legitimacy of the political system is conditional upon the context in which winning and losing are given meaning.[11]

---

[10] Support for the empirical leverage of this individual-level distinction has been found with data from around the globe, ranging from western Europe, to the post-communist states, Latin America, Asia, and Africa (Anderson et al. 2005; Cho 2004; Karp and Bowler 2001; Stebe 2003).

[11] A related and growing literature examines how being among the winners or losers of elections affect other attitudes, as well as how winner-loser status affects the impact of macro-factors on behavior. Thus, Anderson and Tverdova (2003) find, for example, that the negative impact of corruption on support for democratic institutions is stronger among losers and muted among winners, and Anderson, Mendes, and Tverdova (2004) find that perceptions of the economy improve systematically as a result of being on the winning side in elections.

6 MULTI-LEVEL MODELS AND MULTI-LEVEL GOVERNANCE: CITIZENS AND THE EUROPEAN UNION

Finally, an area of scholarship that seems almost ideally suited to the exploration of multi-level models is the emerging EU polity. Not only do political scientists have an increasingly sophisticated understanding of the EU as a political system and citizens' attitudes and behavior regarding the EU, but there also are extensive sources of data to analyze the differences in contexts and voter behavior across the member states of the Union. What is more, there is considerable variation in institutional and other structures across the current twenty-seven member states that facilitate cross-national analyses.

Perhaps the most extensively developed aspect of multi-level scholarship on EU politics deals with understanding citizen support for various aspects of EU integration, including membership in the Union, support for further integration (widening and deepening), or various policy-specific aspects of integration. While early studies of support for integration examined mostly macro-level characteristics as predictors (Eichenberg and Dalton 1993), recent research examines the individual-level determinants of integration with a focus on domestic politics (Anderson 1998; Hooghe and Marks 2005). Yet, exactly how domestic politics in EU member states affect individuals' willingness to support further integration is still uncertain. While some research stresses the importance of some variables over others—say, identity vs instrumental motivations (cf. Hooghe and Marks 2005)—others model the interactions among individual-level factors and member states' structural features to explain variations in public opinion.

Variously, this scholarship focuses on how domestic (and hence cross-nationally variable) political or economic structures affect different people's propensity to exhibit supportive attitudes and behaviors toward the EU. On the political side of things, Rohrschneider (2002) finds that, when citizens perceive that they are unrepresented in the EU, their support for the EU is reduced. More importantly, this reduction is especially strong in nations with well-functioning domestic institutions. In this formulation, the impact of attitudes about the quality of representation on support for Europe is contingent upon the quality of domestic institutions.

Along parallel lines, Christin (2005) examines attitudes about the EU in central and east European countries and finds an interaction between individual-level attitudes about domestic reforms and macro-level variables. When domestic macro-political and economic performance is weak, citizens' views on domestic reforms are not particularly powerful predictors of opinions about the EU. However, if the performance of the country is good, those who have favorable attitudes towards the free market or democracy exhibit significantly more positive attitudes towards the EU than those who have negative attitudes. This understanding is based on contingent relations as well: attitudes about markets and democracy are stronger or weaker determinants of support for the EU, depending on whether macroeconomic and political performance is good.

On the political economy front, researchers have also identified important cross-level interactions within the EU. Specifically, recent studies demonstrate the inter-active effects between individuals' skill endowments and the nature of the (macro-) political economy on attitudes about the EU. At the individual level, skill endowments are a particularly potent predictor of support for European integration, with lower-skilled citizens particularly likely to have more negative evaluations of the EU (Gabel 1998). Going one step further and embedding individuals with different skills in different political economies, Brinegar and Jolly (2005) find that low-skilled workers in countries with high-skill economies exhibit significantly less support for European integration, and respondents with higher education in low-skill-endowment countries support European integration less than low-skilled workers. This suggests that cross-national differences in economic institutions and economic structures condition the importance of human capital in shaping attitudes towards European integration.

Finally, some work is investigating the interdependence among national differences, differences across political parties, and individual citizens (cf. Steenbergen and Jones 2002). This research models the process of opinion formation within and across member states by focusing on the frequency or nature of the messages sent by party elites to citizens about the EU. Examining the relative impact of instrumental motivations vs identity on support for the EU, Hooghe and Marks (2005), for example, investigate how the political consequences of identity are contested and shaped in national contexts. They find that the more national elites are divided, the more citizens are likely to be cued to oppose European integration, and this effect is particularly pronounced among citizens who see themselves as exclusively national.

7 DISCUSSION

Institutions have long figured prominently in the study of politics, and the idea that (cross-national) differences in political contexts are powerful forces in shaping citizen behavior is nothing new. Almost thirty years ago, Verba, Nie, and Kim's (1978) study of citizen participation in seven developed and developing countries examined the extent to which institutional constraints amplified and attenuated individuals' propensities to be politically engaged. Despite their pathbreaking effort, however, contextual explanations of political behavior have only recently grown in importance in the comparative study of how citizens think and act.

In part, this trend toward constructing explanations that connect macro- and micro-levels of analysis is undoubtedly due to the increasing availability of large cross-national survey data sets that allow for the integration of individual behavior and institutional or contextual features as well as the improved statistical and computing tools to analyze such data efficiently. In addition, the movement toward multi-level theories of behavioral politics is in no small measure due to the renewed emphasis on and sophisticated understanding of political institutions and their consequences, as well as a more advanced understanding of contextual theories of political behavior.

Scholars' growing ease of connecting micro- and macro-levels of analysis holds significant promise for integrating the study of behavioral politics with other areas of political science scholarship by linking institutions and behavior or by developing and testing more complex models of the interaction of elite behavior and party behavior with the study of citizen politics. In addition, this area of inquiry holds much promise for integrating the all-too frequent study of established democracies with research on emerging and transitioning democracies, as well as the institution-alization of multi-level polities such as the European Union or interactions among international politics, subnational politics, and citizen behavior.

In this chapter, I focus on two particular kinds of interactions of structures and behavior that I label *contingent*: first, cases where individual-level factors have differential effects, depending on the institutional environment; second, cases where the structural features of a polity have differential effects, depending on individual or other structural factors. Viewing individual voters as embedded in and interacting with the institutional and structural contexts in which they live and act is relatively new in the comparative study of behavioral politics. But significant research streams aimed at both the methodology of investigating such multi-level relationships as well as the substance of particular sets of questions have been developed over the past decade. These are particularly extensive in the areas of economic voting and political legitimacy, and there are related but currently less extensive efforts underway in the areas of electoral turnout and vote choice as well as political behavior in the European Union as an emerging supranational polity.

These endeavors carry with them distinct and frequently unstated assumptions about the political world that are worth keeping in mind. Importantly, they assume that the structural contexts are exogenous and stable. While these assumptions may be safe under many conditions, on occasion they are liable to be controversial. In fact, one of the perhaps more interesting yet undeveloped research areas in this subfield of political science could be the rigorous analysis of the conditions under which these assumptions are safe or should be challenged.

Moreover, an important assumption concerns the stability of contextual features over time. While political science is mostly a quasi-experimental science, there are, on occasion, situations that allow scholars of institutions to take advantage of "natural experiments" to investigate their claims. One fruitful area, for example, concerns the role of electoral systems in shaping or being shaped by political behavior. Some scholars have traveled down this path—some studies, for example, have sought to understand how New Zealand's voters reacted to the changes in electoral rules in that country (Banducci, Donovan, and Karp 1999; Karp and Bowler

2001), and in particular how different kinds of voters were affected differently by alternative electoral system designs. Others have examined the impact of voter behavior on institutional change in an experimental setting (Bowler and Donovan 2004), and there are liable to be many instances where institutional change affects voters and voters themselves seek to effect such change. The fluidity or stability of structures—and concomitantly the exogeneity and endogeneity of institutions—is particularly likely to differ systematically in old versus new democracies, with the presumption of greater endogeneity or at least potential for it in newer democracies.

This area of scholarship holds much untapped promise, but several questions remain: The first question, naturally, is *whether* and *how* institutions and structural features of polities matter for citizen behavior. Given that research to date has focused mainly on voters' electoral choices and decisions to participate in elections, this first generation of scholarship needs to establish which institutions matter, and what kinds of behavior they matter for. One can easily imagine a proliferation of studies that examine the interactive effects of institutional features and individual-level factors, but absent some more general theories about the interactions of structures and voting, such efforts are unlikely to yield cumulative understandings of either institutions or behavior. A second, but also critical, question is how much institutions matter in which domains and how much they matter relative to individual-level factors. To establish that institutions matter and how is one thing—to establish that they make a significant difference and by how much they do so is quite another but also essential matter.

At the end of the day, what is particularly noteworthy about cross-level investigations of behavioral politics is that they hold the promise of producing a more nuanced and contextualized understanding of political life by connecting hitherto unconnected streams of scholarship in the areas of institutions, political economy, policy, and behavior and allowing us a better and more complex empirical and theoretical handle on the hows and whys of citizen politics.

References

ANDERSON, C. 1995a. *Blaming the Government: Citizens and the Economy in Five European Democracies*. Armonk, NY: M. E. Sharpe.

—— 1995b. Party systems and the dynamics of government support: Britain and Germany, 1960–1990. *European Journal of Political Research*, 27 (1): 93–118.

—— 1998. When in doubt, use proxies: attitudes toward domestic politics and support for European integration. *Comparative Political Studies*, 31 (5): 569–601.

—— 2000. Economic voting and political context: a comparative perspective. *Electoral Studies*, 19 (2–3): 151–70.

—— and GUILLORY, C. 1997. Political institutions and satisfaction with democracy: a cross-national analysis of consensus and majoritarian systems. *American Political Science Review*, 91 (1): 66–81.

—— MENDES, S., and TVERDOVA, Y. 2004. Endogenous economic voting: evidence from the 1997 British election. *Electoral Studies*, 23 (4): 683–708.

—— and PASKEVICIUTE, A. 2005. Macro politics and micro behavior: mainstream politics and the frequency of political discussion in contemporary democracies. Pp. 228–48 in *The Social Logic of Politics*, ed. A. S. Zuckerman. Philadelphia: Temple University Press.

—— and TVERDOVA, Y. 2003. Corruption, political allegiances, and attitudes toward government in contemporary democracies. *American Journal of Political Science*, 47 (1): 91–109.

BLAIS, A., BOWLER, S., DONOVAN, T., and LISTHAUG, O. 2005. *Losers' Consent: Elections and Democratic Legitimacy*. New York: Oxford University Press.

BANDUCCI, S., DONOVAN, T., and KARP, J. 1999. Proportional representation and attitudes about politics: results from New Zealand. *Electoral Studies*, 18 (4): 533–55.

BECK, P., DALTON, R., GREENE, S., and HUCKFELDT, R. 2002. The social calculus of voting: interpersonal, media, and organizational influences on presidential choices. *American Political Science Review*, 96 (1): 57–73.

BENGTSSON, Å. 2004. Economic voting: the effect of political context, volatility and turnout on voters' assignment of responsibility. *European Journal of Political Research*, 43 (5): 749–67.

BLAIS, A. 2000. *To Vote or not to Vote: The Merits and Limits of Rational Choice Theory*. Pittsburgh: University of Pittsburgh Press.

BOWLER, S., and DONOVAN, T. 2004. Reasoning about institutional change: losers' support for electoral reforms. Paper presented at the 2004 Midwest Political Science Association Meeting, Chicago.

BRAMBOR, T., CLARK, W., and GOLDER, M. 2006. Understanding interaction models: improving empirical analyses, *Political Analysis* 14 (1): 63–82.

BRAVO, C., and HOJMAN, D. 2003. Political animals and civic participation. Unpublished ms., Department of Economics, Harvard University.

BRINEGAR, A., and JOLLY, S. 2005. Location, location, location: national contextual factors and public support for European Integration. *European Union Politics*, 6 (2): 155–80.

BROCKINGTON, D. 2004. The paradox of proportional representation: the effect of party systems and coalitions on individuals' electoral participation. *Political Studies*, 52 (3): 469–90.

CHO, W. 2004. Political institutions and satisfaction with democracy in Sub-Saharan Africa. Michigan State University, Afrobarometer Working Paper No. 39.

CHRISTIN, T. 2005. Economic and political basis of attitudes towards the EU in Central and East European Countries in the 1990s. *European Union Politics*, 6 (1): 29–57.

COLOMER, J. 2001. *Political Institutions: Democracy and Social Choice*. New York: Oxford University Press.

COX, G. 1997. *Making Votes Count: Strategic Coordination in the World's Electoral Systems*. New York: Cambridge University Press.

—— ROSENBLUTH, F., and THIES, M. 1998. Mobilization, social networks, and turnout: evidence from Japan. *World Politics*, 50 (3): 447–74.

DORUSSEN, H., and TAYLOR, M. 2001. The political context of issue-priority voting: coalitions and economic voting in the Netherlands, 1970–1999. *Electoral Studies*, 20 (3): 399–426.

DUCH, R., and STEVENSON, R. 2005. Context and the economic vote: a multi-level analysis. *Political Analysis*, 13 (4): 387–409.

DUVERGER, M. 1954. *Political Parties: Their Organization and Activity in the Modern State*. London, Methuen.

EICHENBERG, R., and DALTON, R. 1993. Europeans and the European Community: The dynamics of public support for European integration. *International Organization*, 47 (4): 507–34.

GABEL, M. 1998. *Interests and Integration: Market Liberalization, Public Opinion, and European Union.* Ann Arbor: University of Michigan Press.

GIMPEL, J., and SCHUKNECHT, J. 2003. Political participation and the accessibility of the ballot box. *Political Geography,* 22: 471–88.

GSCHWEND, T. 2003. Comparative politics of strategic voting: a hierarchy of electoral systems. Paper presented at the Annual Meeting of the American Political Science Association. August, Philadelphia.

HELLWIG, T. 2002. Interdependence, government constraints and economic voting. *Journal of Politics,* 63 (4): 1141–62.

HOOGHE, L., and MARKS, G. 2005. Calculation, community, and cues: public opinion on European integration. *European Union Politics,* 6 (4): (forthcoming).

HUBER, J., KERNELL, G., and LEONI, E. 2005. The institutional origins of party identification. *Political Analysis,* 13 (4): 365–86.

HUCKFELDT, R. 1986. *Politics in Context.* New York: Agathon.

—— and SPRAGUE, J. 1995. *Citizens, Politics, and Social Communication: Information and Influence in an Election Campaign.* New York: Cambridge University Press.

—— IKEDA, K., and PAPPI, F. 2005. Patterns of disagreement in democratic politics: comparing Germany, Japan, and the United States. *American Journal of Political Science,* 49 (3): 497–514.

—— JOHNSON, P., and SPRAGUE, J. 2004. *Political Disagreement: The Survival of Diverse Opinions within Communication Networks.* New York: Cambridge University Press.

JESUIT, D. 2003. The regional dynamics of European electoral politics: participation in national and European contests in the 1990s. *European Union Politics,* 4 (2): 139–64.

JUSKO, K., and SHIVELY, W. P. 2005. Applying a two-step strategy to the analysis of cross-national public opinion data. *Political Analysis,* 13 (4): 327–44.

KARP, J., and BOWLER, S. 2001. Coalition politics and satisfaction with democracy: explaining new Zealand's reaction to proportional representation. *European Journal of Political Research,* 40 (1): 57–79.

KEDAR, O. 2005. When moderate voters prefer extreme parties: policy balancing in parliamentary elections. *American Political Science Review,* 99(2): 185–99.

—— and SHIVELY, W. P. 2005. Introduction: Special issue on multilevel modeling for large clusters. *Political Analysis,* 13 (4): 297–300.

KLINGEMANN, H.-D., and WEßELS, B. 2000. Voter rationalities in different electoral systems. Paper prepared for delivery at the XVIIIth World Congress of the International Political Science Association. August 1–5, 2000, Québec City, Canada.

LIJPHART, A. 1990. The political consequences of electoral laws, 1945–85. *American Political Science Review,* 84 (2): 481–96.

—— 1999. *Patterns of Democracy.* New Haven: Yale University Press.

NADEAU, R., NIEMI, R., and YOSHINAKA, A. 2002. A cross-national analysis of economic voting: taking account of the political context across time and nations. *Electoral Studies,* 21 (3): 403–23.

NORPOTH, H. 2001. Divided government and economic voting. *Journal of Politics,* 63 (2): 414–35.

NORTH, D. 1981. *Structure and Change in Economic History.* New York: W. W. Norton.

PACEK, A., and RADCLIFF, B. 1995a. The political economy of competitive elections in the developing world. *American Journal of Political Science,* 39 (3): 745–59.

—— —— 1995b. Economic voting and the welfare state: a cross-national analysis. *Journal of Politics,* 57 (1): 44–61

PALDAM, M. 1991. How robust is the vote function? Pp. 9–32 in *Economics and Politics: The Calculus of Support,* ed. H. Norpoth, M. Lewis-Beck, and J. Lafay. Ann Arbor: University of Michigan Press.

POSNER, D., and SIMON, D. 2002. Economic conditions and incumbent support in Africa's new democracies: evidence from Zambia. *Comparative Political Studies*, 35 (3): 313–36.

POWELL, G. B. 1986. American voter turnout in comparative perspective. *American Political Science Review*, 80 (1): 17–43.

—— and WHITTEN, G. 1993. A cross-national analysis of economic voting: taking account of the political context. *American Journal of Political Science*, 37 (2): 391–414.

RAE, D. 1967. *The Political Consequences of Electoral Laws*. New Haven: Yale University Press.

REMMER, K. 1993. The political economy of elections in Latin America, 1980–1991. *American Political Science Review*, 87 (2): 393–407.

RIKER, W. 1980. Implications from the disequilibrium of majority rule for the study of institutions. *American Political Science Review*, 74 (2): 432–46.

ROHRSCHNEIDER, R. 2002. The democracy deficit and mass support for an EU-wide government. *American Journal of Political Science*, 46 (2): 463–75.

ROYED T., LEYDEN, K., and BORRELLI, S. 2000. Is "clarity of responsibility" important for economic voting? Revisiting Powell and Whitten's hypothesis. *British Journal of Political Science*, 30 (4): 669–85.

RUDOLPH, T. 2003. Institutional context and the assignment of political responsibility. *Journal of Politics*, 65 (1): 190–215.

SAMUELS, D. 2004. Presidentialism and accountability for the economy in comparative perspective. *American Political Science Review*, 98 (3): 425–36.

SANDERS, D. 1991. Government popularity and the outcome of the next general election. *Political Quarterly*, 62 (2): 235–61.

SELIGSON, M. 2002. The impact of corruption on regime legitimacy: a comparative study of four Latin American countries. *Journal of Politics*, 64 (2): 408–33.

ŠTEBE, J. 2003. Consequences of voting on changes in satisfaction with democracy in post-socialist countries. Paper presented at the CSES Plenary Session. October, Stockholm, Sweden.

STEENBERGEN M., and JONES, B. 2002. Modeling multilevel data structures. *American Journal of Political Science*, 46 (1): 218–37.

STOKES, S. 1996. Public opinion and market reforms: the limits of economic voting. *Comparative Political Studies*, 29 (5): 499–519.

TUCKER, J. 2005. *Regional Economic Voting: Russia, Poland, Hungary, Slovakia, and the Czech Republic, 1990–1999*. New York: Cambridge University Press.

VERBA, S., NIE, N., and KIM, J. 1978. *Participation and Political Equality: A Cross-National Comparison*. New York: Cambridge University Press.

WESTERN, B. 1998. Causal heterogeneity in comparative research: a bayesian hierarchical modelling approach. *American Journal of Political Science*, 42 (4): 1233–59.

WEYLAND, K. 1998. Swallowing the bitter pill: sources of popular support for neoliberal reform in Latin America. *Comparative Political Studies*, 31 (5): 539–68.

ZUCKERMAN, A. ed. 2005. *The Social Logic of Politics*. Philadelphia: Temple University Press.

CHAPTER 32

PERSPECTIVES ON ELECTORAL BEHAVIOR

ANTHONY HEATH

THE chapters in this volume demonstrate the tremendous intellectual vitality of political science research on electoral behavior, with an explosion of scientific papers over recent decades, a great increase in the range and variety of data, new theoretical developments and even some degree of cumulation (normally rare in the social sciences) with new findings building on older ones and integrating them into a more comprehensive framework.

From its inception the study of electoral behavior has been heavily influenced by American research, especially by the three traditions of the more sociological Columbia school, with its emphasis on processes of social influence, the socio-psychological Michigan model with its emphasis on party identification and the "funnel of causality," and the economics-inspired rational choice models of Anthony Downs and his successors. The Michigan model has been particularly influential with the export of election studies from the United States, first to other developed countries and more recently to a much wider range of developing countries.[1]

Historically these three intellectual traditions largely focused on the more micro issues of how voters decide, but one of the more exciting developments in recent decades, documented very clearly by these chapters, is the growing interest in comparative research and more macro questions. The study of electoral behavior is

---

[1] One early export of the Michigan model to a non-western country was that to India in 1967, leading to a series of remarkable election studies. See Eldersveld and Ahmed (1978).

also now international in scope, not only in the countries studied but also in the range of scholars who contribute.

As a first approximation, we can integrate these different foci (and the present chapters) within the original Downsian framework of electors with their distributions of attitudes and preferences (treated as exogenous in the original framework although in practice largely shaped by sociological factors such as class, religion, ethnicity, or generation), of parties with their records and policy stances together with the institutional rules such as proportional representation or single member plurality systems, and the decision rules whereby electors decide which party if any to support or which other courses of political action to take in the light of their preferences and political opportunity structure. Thus some scholarship has focused on the changing social bases of political interests and action, some on deeper understanding of the decision rules, and some on the impact of the institutional framework.

In the classic Downsian framework, voters' preferences were seen to be largely exogenous, voters' decision rules were assumed to be psychological universals, invariant with respect to either preferences or political opportunity structures, and only the party positions were seen to be endogenous, parties shifting their positions in response to the distribution of voter preferences. Comparative research (comparative both across time and space) is clearly essential for understanding the impact of the institutional framework and of the ways in which parties change their policy positions. But comparative research is now also exploring how far the decision rules and related micro-processes are generalizable from the American context in which they were first formulated or whether they vary across different social and institutional contexts. And comparative research also has the potential to explore whether the distribution of voters' preferences is truly exogenous. More generally, we are now coming to see that all three elements of the classic Downsian framework are in fact interrelated.

This is clearly evident in the work on micro-processes. As Sniderman and Levendusky emphasize in their chapter "Institutions organize psychological processes, we are suggesting, not the other way around." This is perhaps most evident in the case of the Michigan model and the role of party identification cross-nationally. From the very first export of the Michigan model to Europe, Europeans wondered if the concept of party identification was as useful and worked in the same way as it did in the United States (see, for example, Butler and Stokes 1969). And Holmberg's review raises the question of whether party identification is as useful a concept in the new democracies of eastern Europe or of Latin America as it has been in the longer-established democracies. A related point was made long ago by Klingemann (1972) in a classic paper; he suggested that in some European countries voters' conceptions of themselves as left or right functioned in a way similar to party identification in the United States, an argument which was reiterated, extended, and subjected to empirical study in later publications (Inglehart and Klingemann 1978; Fuchs and Klingemann 1990).

While much of the European critique of party identification has focused on the descriptive question of whether it has the stability across the life course originally postulated or whether it largely moves in tandem with vote (and thus has little explanatory power), the literature reviewed also suggests that the nature of the parties and the political options facing voters will themselves influence the psychological development of attachments to parties. As Berglund and his colleagues suggest "The more polarized a party system is, the more partisans we find" (quoted in Holmberg in this volume).

At all events, the applicability of the Michigan model, and specifically the role of party identification in the decision-making process, is now clearly seen as variable across democracies. Indeed, it may well be that the United States is actually unusual for the large role that party identification historically has played. Furthermore, but less definitely, the role of party identification should now be seen as endogenous and should be seen as potentially a response, as Holmberg suggests, both to properties of the political structure and also to properties of the social structure, with modernization tending to reduce the role of party identification (and perhaps reducing the role of affective attachments more generally). Of course, this does not mean that there are no psychological universals in the decision-making process: where party identification does operate, the mechanisms involved (such as the perceptual screen that it provides) may be universal but the crucial point is that how we model the decision-making process—the equation that we fit to the data—should not be assumed to be constant across democracies.

The same point is made even more clearly and persuasively in the literature on economic voting which follows the Downsian tradition. To be sure, Lewis-Beck and Stegmaier suggest that in one sense the economic voting model is a universal: "It is not important whether the democracy is much-studied or little-studied, resilient or fragile, the economy reliably moves voters to hold their government accountable in national elections." However, Lewis-Beck's own work and that of a growing body of other scholars suggests that the extent to which the economy moves voters is markedly variable across democracies, varying in particular according to the diffusion of government responsibility (Lewis-Beck 1986). This body of work (e.g. Powell and Whitten 1993; Anderson 2000) has been a particularly impressive achievement of comparative research on electoral behaviour and suggests a model that could for example also be applied to the cross-national study of the way in which the role of party identification varies across democracies.

Much less work has been done on the earliest of the three models of how voters decide, that is the tradition of the Columbia school with its emphasis on the role of personal influence, although one might perhaps argue that the social cleavage literature is indirectly following on from the more sociological concerns of the Columbia school. Huckfeldt and his colleagues (Huckfeldt, Johnson, and Sprague 2004; Huckfeldt and Sprague 1995) have kept this tradition alive with important work on the role of social context. While social network analysis has been one of the more vigorous intellectual developments in other social sciences, it has been curiously absent from political science. Nor has there been much systematic cross-national comparison of the role of the social influence comparable to the cross-national studies or party identification or of economic voting (for exceptions see Huckfeldt, Ikeda, and Pappi 2005; Ikeda and Huckfeldt 2001). This is partly because of the difficulty and expense of obtaining the detailed network data that is required, but we should be careful to remember that "absence of evidence does not imply evidence of absence." Lack of data on the role of social networks, either nationally or internationally, does not imply that such social processes do not operate.

Sociological aspects of societies and their influence on vote have, of course, been much studied with the vigorous debates on whether the influence of social class, and of other social cleavages such as ethnicity and religion, vary across democracies and over time (see for example the chapters by Knutsen, Saggar, and Esmer and Pettersson). Much of this work has been largely descriptive but the most recent work in this area again shows how the operation of these cleavages may be contingent upon the changing political structure, analogous perhaps to the way in which economic voting is contingent on the organization of politics. As Knutsen shows in his chapter, much of the earlier work has tried to document whether and by how much class voting had declined. Explanation, however, has to focus on the interaction between the changing preferences of voters and changing party positions. As Knutsen explains in his recent book, "A detailed empirical investigation of changing location of the major parties and political strategies of the major leftist parties showed a consistent pattern where a decisive move towards the centre was accompanied with a decline in class voting" (2006, 22).

1 LOOKING TOWARD THE FUTURE

What of the future? I think we can expect this trend towards comparative research, towards understanding the generalizability of our models to non-Western contexts, and towards understanding the interplay between macro- and micro-processes to continue and to be consolidated. The growth of comparative research reflects a number of different factors which are likely to continue. First of all, as Anderson points out in his chapter, there has been the spread of democracy around the world so that there are now a great many more countries in which patterns of electoral behaviour can be studied.[2] A second factor is the increasing availability of (more or less) good quality data (see chapter by Kitilson). High-quality survey data was for many years the preserve of a few wealthy western countries most notably the USA but also (and rather later) Britain, Germany, or Denmark. More recently

---

[2] Of course, this is not the whole story since there have been quite a number of non-western democracies (most notably India, which must surely be regarded as the world's most remarkable democracy) which have been in existence throughout the post-war period when modern political science emerged and yet have been singularly neglected by western political scientists. Costa Rica, Venezuela, and Sri Lanka have also had continuous histories of contested elections for around fifty years, but it surely has to be said that our understanding of what determines election outcomes in these countries falls some way short of the depth of sophistication evident in analyses of, say, the US or UK.

the Comparative Study of Electoral Systems (CSES) project has included modules of questions from over forty countries around the world—still heavily concentrated to be sure on western Europe and North America but now including countries such as Brazil, Mexico, Peru, Taiwan, and Thailand.

A third factor is the emergence of real-world phenomena (and quite worrying phenomena too), most notably the Far Right, in some countries but not others. In this way the real world has intruded on our scientific studies and demanded some explanation of why the Far Right has surfaced in some contexts but not in others. This has given a powerful impetus towards the development of models that focus on the role of the political context. Kitschelt's work has been notable here in focusing both on what he terms the "political opportunity structure" as well as on the distribution of preferences among the electorate (Kitschelt 1995).

While it is foolhardy to predict real-world developments, it is probably a safe working assumption that in the foreseeable future we will continue to have a wide range of democracies to study and growing data sources for their study. Comparative research is thus likely to continue as a growth area within the discipline.

One pressing issue that needs to be studied, however, is the quality and comparability of the data becoming available for cross-national study. Surveys tend to differ in their populations covered, their sampling methods (quota, random route, or probability samples), their modes (face to face, self-completion, or telephone), their response rates, and their extent of supervision in the field and interviewer training. These differences will surely have some consequences for data quality, particularly for bias and reliability. If we find a weaker association between, say, class or party identification and vote in one country than another, can we be sure that this reflects the "real world" or is it simply that there is more noise in one data set than other? This difficulty is compounded by the fact that the information one needs about survey methods and data quality are rarely reported in sufficient detail. (See, for example, the references cited in Heath, Fisher, and Smith 2005; Saris and Kaase 1997.)

There may also be good reasons why survey methods might vary around the world, reflecting for example the nature of the market research infrastructure. It should not be assumed however that western data sets are necessarily more reliable than non-western ones. Given the evidence of falling response rates in the West with the concomitant risk of increased response biases, it may well be that the net balance works in the opposite direction with non-western data sets being of higher quality on average than western ones. At any rate, treating data as unproblematic and of equal scientific value around the world could potentially lead to quite misleading conclusions. A priority for future cross-national research is therefore to investigate how far results might be artefacts of methodological differences, response biases, and the like. (See Heath, Fisher, and Smith 2005 for further discussion of these issues.)

It may not only be the conduct of surveys that varies around the world, but also the responses of respondents to those surveys. A particular issue when questions on citizens' attitudes and preferences are the focus of the investigation is that "yea saying" may be a particular problem when there are big gaps between the social standing of the interviewer and of the respondent. There may also be cross-national variation in the extent of social desirability bias. Increased use of cross-national data ought therefore to go hand in hand with increased methodological sophistication on the part of the data analyst and a recognition that methodological assumptions that work quite well in western contexts may not hold nearly as well elsewhere.

Turning to more substantive issues, we need to continue to explore the general-izability of our western models of electoral choice to the newer democracies in the way that has already begun to be done for party identification and economic voting. For example, one factor that might repay investigation is what electorates hold their governments responsible for. It is probably true that all electorates hold their governments responsible for the performance of the economy (as Lewis-Beck suggests). It would be surprising if they did not also hold them responsible for war and peace. The importance of Margaret Thatcher's success in the Falklands War for her subsequent electoral successes was one of the most lively recent debates in the British study of electoral behaviour. (See, for example, Sanders, Ward, and Marsh 1987; Norpoth 1987; Clarke, Mishler, and Whiteley 1990.) As Clarke and his colleagues conclude "non-economic variables are also relevant...and popularity functions that model them correctly will enhance our understanding of both the economics and the politics of party support" (Clarke, Mishler, and Whiteley 1990, 63).

It may also be worth considering whether the range of responsibilities that electorates attribute to governments varies systematically around the world. There may be both cultural and structural factors at work. Historically, the former com-munist regimes provided a much wider array of services for their citizens than did the liberal market economies, most notably the US with its tradition of small govern-ment. Health care, pensions, education are also differently organized in different countries and, where they are organized centrally, governments may be held respon-sible for their performance. At the other extreme, less developed countries have much smaller welfare states, and rather different challenges, of which corruption and internal security are perhaps the most pressing. It is quite possible that models of economic voting that do not include such variables will be mis-specified.

The dominant models of electoral choice also continue to be largely individualistic and it is not clear that such models will be as appropriate in non-western contexts. Individualistic models may well be appropriate in much of the developed world, and if the arguments of Ulrich Beck (Beck 1992; Beck and Beck-Gernsheim 2002) and others about the processes of individualization that tend to occur in post-industrial societies are correct, the reality of established western democracies may slowly be coming closer to the assumptions of our models. However, it is not clear that individualistic models are so appropriate in societies where processes of individual-ization may have not progressed as far as they have in the West. Processes of social influence may well have a much greater role in Africa or South Asia than they do in the developed world. The more sociological aspects of a newer democracy, in particular the nature and strength of its social groups and the extent (and depth) of its modernization, may well determine the way social influences impact on vote. We should also remember that newer democracies may be much less homogeneous than we are used to in the West, with large modernized sectors coexisting with extensive rural populations with limited education and literacy. We should therefore be prepared for much greater voter heterogeneity within the country than we are used to in the West: individualistic models may fit highly educated respondents in urban settings quite well but fit rather badly in remoter rural areas.

It is not just the nature of the social structure that may be relevant. The nature of the political rules of the game may also affect whether social relations are important (analogously to the way in which party polarization may affect partisanship). For example, where politics is organized around patron–client relations, or perhaps where corruption is more tolerated and the spoils of office can be distributed to the winner's supporters, social relations are likely to be more significant factors in electoral choice.

Comparative research, then, will give us further opportunities to see how far western models of electoral choice can be applied elsewhere and to explore the ways in which these models are contingent upon particular features of the social structure and the political institutions and context. These are fairly straightforward extensions of the work already impressively carried out in the areas of economic voting and party identification.

A more ambitious program might be to explore the interdependence of the political and social structures. In an important but perhaps neglected work Przeworski and Sprague (1986) have shown how the logic of social change impacts on the strategies chosen by socialist parties. But the reverse process may also happen. Sociologists have long suggested that socialist governments may have important consequences for levels of social inequality and the degree of social fluidity in a country (although these claims tend to be based on the rather weak evidence of cross-sectional correlations between parties in office and levels of inequality). To be sure, there are powerful arguments that, in a globalized world, political parties can have little medium-term influence even on simple economic factors such as the level of unemployment, but in an interesting recent paper Alderson and Nielsen (2002) have shown that the increasing inequality that appears to have accompanied globalization in recent decades was specific to a rather limited number of countries that also happened to have introduced Reaganite tax-cutting policies. Globalization may not have reduced the scope for government intervention quite as much as had been supposed, and in any event the impact of globalization (as measured by economic measures such as openness of the economy) varies very considerably from country to country.

A quite different kind of example comes from India where policies of reservation for scheduled castes appear to be having important repercussions on the nature of caste in contemporary India and on the formation of castes as political actors. Gandhi had opposed such measures before independence on the grounds that, by politicizing the divisions, they might serve to exacerbate rather than diminish caste differences in India, but the measures were introduced nonetheless. And more recently they were extended to the "other backward classes" by a Janata Dal government looking for a vote maximizing strategy in classic Downsian fashion.

Subsequently, parties such as the Bahujan Samaj Party (BSP) catering to specific caste communities have emerged, but the crucial point is that, as Gandhi had feared, the consequence has been to politicize caste and to transform the operation of castes as social formations. The reverse process might be happening in the West where the tendency of formerly socialist parties to move to the centre might have the effect of depoliticizing class and in turn reducing citizens' awareness of class interests and divisions. Rather than being exogenous, citizens' preferences might be importantly shaped by party programs.

It is important to recognize that any investigation of these kinds of interdependencies needs to include both a dynamic as well as a comparative dimension. Purely cross-sectional analyses will not be persuasive if we want to understand the nature of the reciprocal relations between social and political institutions. We need pooled time-series and comparative data sets. We also need the appropriate statistical techniques for such analyses. It is very easy to obtain spurious results if inappropriate methods are used. For example, if we have ten countries and ten sets of election results for each, we apparently have 100 country-level observations, which considerably improves our chances of obtaining "significant" results. But we actually need to model the data as a three-level multi-level structure with individuals nested within years nested within countries. This is, of course, well known but it serves to emphasize that comparative research will tend to become quantitatively more sophisticated as a result, perhaps with the danger of reducing the ability of colleagues to communicate.

There is also a danger that statistical sophistication will not always go hand in hand with the methodological sophistication about data quality mentioned earlier. And there is a danger too that it may not always be accompanied by an adequate understanding of the historical and institutional contexts of each country. For example, was the 2004 victory of Congress over the Bharatiya Janata Party (BJP) in India a classic example of economic voting, as many commentators assumed, or was it rather a consequence of the changing pattern of alliances that the two main parties made with their regional partners? Without detailed knowledge of the way that Indian politics works on the ground, it would be easy to arrive at erroneous conclusions that fit our western theories about what decides election. (For a brief introduction to how Indian politics works see Heath, Glouharova, and Heath 2005.) It may prove wise for comparativists to team up with country experts rather than to think that they can do it all on their own.

REFERENCES

ALDERSON, A. S., and NIELSEN, F. 2002. Globalization and the great U-turn: income inequality trends in 16 OECD countries. *American Journal of Sociology,* 107 (5): 1244–99.

ANDERSON, C. J. 2000. Economic voting and political context: a comparative perspective. *Electoral Studies,* 19: 151–70.

BECK, U. 1992. *Risk Society: Towards a New Modernity*. London: Sage.

—— and BECK-GERNSHEIM, E. 2002. *Individualization: institutionalized individualism and its social and political consequences*. London: Sage.

BUTLER, D., and STOKES, D. 1969. *Political Change in Britain*, 1st edn. London: Macmillan.

CLARKE, H. D., MISHLER, W., and WHITELEY, P. 1990. Recapturing the Falklands: models of Conservative popularity, 1979–83. *British Journal of Political Science*, 20: 63–81.

ELDERSVELD, S. J., and AHMED, B. 1978. *Citizens and Politics: Mass Political Behaviour in India*. Chicago: University of Chicago Press.

FUCHS, D., and KLINGEMANN, H.-D. 1990. The left–right schema. Pp. 203–38 in *Continuities in Political Action: A Longitudinal Study of Political Orientations in Three Western Democracies*, ed. M. K. Jennings and J. Van Deth. Berlin: de Gruyter.

HEATH, A. F., FISHER, S., and SMITH, S. 2005. The globalization of public opinion research. *Annual Review of Political Science*, 8: 297–333.

—— GLOUHAROVA, S., and HEATH, O. 2005. India: two-party contests within a multiparty system. Pp. 137–156 in *The Politics of Electoral Systems*, ed. M. Gallagher and P. Mitchell. Oxford: OUP.

HUCKFELDT, R., IKEDA, K., and PAPPI, F. 2005. Patterns of disagreement in democratic politics: comparing Germany, Japan, and the United States. *American Journal of Political Science*, 49: 497–514.

—— JOHNSON, P., and SPRAGUE, J. 2004. *Political Disagreement: The Survival of Diverse Opinions within Communication Networks*. New York: Cambridge University Press.

—— and SPRAGUE, J. 1995. *Citizens, Politics, and Social Communication*. New York: Cambridge University Press.

IKEDA, K., and HUCKFELDT, R. 2001. Political communication and disagreement among citizens in Japan and the United States. *Political Behavior*, 23: 23–52.

INGLEHART, R., and KLINGEMANN, H.-D. 1978. Party identification, ideological preference, and the left–right dimension among western mass publics. Pp. 243–73 in *Party Identification and Beyond*, ed. I. Budge, I. Crewe, and D. Farlie. London: Wiley.

KITSCHELT, H. 1995. *The Radical Right in Western Europe: A Comparative Analysis*. Ann Arbor: University of Michigan Press.

KLINGEMANN, H. D. 1972. Testing the left–right continuum on a sample of German voters. *Comparative Political Studies*, 5: 93–106.

KNUTSEN, O. 2006. *Class Voting in Western Europe: A Comparative Longitudinal Study*. Lanham, Md.: Lexington.

LEWIS-BECK, M. S. 1988. *Economics and Elections: The Major Western Democracies*. Ann Arbor: University of Michigan Press.

NORPOTH, H. 1987. The Falklands war and government popularity in Britain: rally without consequences or surge without decline. *Electoral Studies*, 6: 3–16.

POWELL, G. B., and WHITTEN, G. D. 1993. A cross-national analysis of economic voting: taking account of the political context. *American Journal of Political Science*, 37: 391–414.

PRZEWORSKI, A., and SPRAGUE, J. 1986. *Paper Stones: A History of Electoral Socialism*. Chicago: University of Chicago Press.

SANDERS, D., WARD, H. and MARSH, D. 1987. Government popularity and the Falklands war. *British Journal of Political Science*, 17: 281–313.

SARIS, W. E., and KAASE, M. eds. 1997. *Eurobarometer—Measurement Instruments for Opinions in Europe*. ZUMA Nachrichten Spezial, Bd. 2. Mannheim: ZUMA.

PART VI

POLITICAL
PARTICIPATION

CHAPTER 33

TURNOUT IN ELECTIONS

ANDRÉ BLAIS

THERE are more and more democratic elections throughout the world. In each of these elections, citizens must decide not only which party or candidate they wish to support but also, and perhaps more fundamentally, whether they wish to support anyone, that is, whether they will vote or not.

Voting is, besides filling an income tax return, the most frequent and basic form of political activity (Blais 2000). It is very simple yet its meaning is complex. Because it is so basic, a substantial amount of research has been devoted to the question of who votes and why. This research has produced many interesting findings, which I will try to summarize here. But the more we study it, the more we realize that voting may not be as simple as we may think, or at least the reasons for which people do or do not vote are more complex than we initially thought.

Turnout can be analyzed from two perspectives, the aggregate and the individual. At the aggregate level, we can look at overall turnout, compare it over time and/or across space. The questions are then whether turnout is higher in some countries than in others, in some types of elections (presidential versus legislative, for instance), and whether it increases or decreases over time. At the individual level, we are interested in the decision to vote or not to vote, and then the questions are who votes and why.

I first address turnout from an aggregate perspective and I compare the level of turnout across space and over time. I deal with "simple" descriptive questions. How many people vote in a typical democratic election? Does turnout vary a lot or just a little from one country to another? Is turnout relatively constant over time (in a given country)? Has it declined recently?

Once the basic patterns have been established, I move to the more difficult and important "why" questions. Why is turnout higher in some countries than in others? Why does it increase or decrease over time?

Finally, I move to the individual level. I first consider "who" votes. One concern is that electoral participation be concentrated among the better off in society and that the voice of the poor is not heard in the process (Verba, Schlozman, and Brady 1995). How much of a socioeconomic divide is there in turnout? I finally examine the factors that shape individuals' decision to vote or not to vote. In that vein, I review the most influential models that have been proposed to explain electoral participation.

1 Patterns and Trends

In most nations there are many types of elections. In Norway, for instance, citizens typically have only two elections every five years; Americans vote in a seemingly endless stream of city, county, state, and federal elections (Crewe 1981). This chapter focuses on democratic legislative elections, the elections for which the data are most widely available and comparable.

Our first step is to describe the number of people who turnout to vote in legislative elections. The data presented in Tables 33.1 and 33.2 include all democratic legislative elections since 1972 in all democratic nations (democracy is defined as having a score of 1 or 2 on the Freedom House ratings of political rights in the year the election was held). A total of 533 elections and 106 countries are included. Turnout is measured as the percentage of those registered who cast a vote. Some studies use "voting age population" as the denominator but that denominator includes people who do not have the right to vote and it is measured at the time of the last census, which can be out of date (see Blais and Dobrzynska 1998, and Franklin 2004). The United States, which have a peculiar registration procedure, are excluded from these two tables.[1]

In a typical legislative election, three-quarters of eligible citizens turn out to vote (the mean is 75.5 percent and the median 76.5 percent). As is well known, electoral participation tends to be the most common form of political activity in most nations. Turnout varies immensely across countries, however. It is beyond 90 percent in nine countries and is it below 50 percent in nine others. There is no concentration around the mean (or median). There are as many countries with mean turnout in the 80 percent range ($n=31$) or in the 60 percent range ($n=25$) as in the 70 percent range ($n=29$).

Turnout tends to be relatively stable from one election to the next within a given country (Franklin 2004). The mean change in turnout between a given election and the previous one is five percentage points, which is far from negligible. Over time variations are more limited in established democracies, where mean change is "only" three points. Across-country variations in turnout are greater than over time changes but the latter should not be underestimated.

---

[1] Turnout in the United States is usually expressed as a percentage of the voting age population. McDonald and Popkin (2001) have shown that this underestimates "true" turnout because the denominator includes non-citizens and prisoners.

Table 33.1 Mean turnout by country (1972–2004)

Country	Mean	Country	Mean	Country	Mean
Malta	95.7	Norway	80.1	Croatia	69.1
Australia	95.0	Philippines	80.1	Cape Verde	68.6
Belgium	93.3	Kiribati	80.0	Ecuador	68.0
Cyprus	93.3	Malawi	80.0	Japan	67.9
Nauru	92.4	Belize	78.4	St. Kitts & Nevis	67.0
Fiji	91.6	Costa Rica	77.9	Lesotho	66.7
Czechoslovakia	90.5	Israel	77.6	Barbados	66.6
Uruguay	90.4	Honduras	77.3	Botswana	66.5
Bahamas	90.2	Slovakia ,	76.6	Papua New Guinea	66.5
Luxembourg	88.8	San Marino	76.5	Hungary	66.1
Iceland	88.5	Panama	75.3	South Korea	65.7
Italy	88.3	Namibia	74.4	Sao Tome & Principe	65.0
Nepal	88.1	Bolivia	74.3	Taiwan	64.5
Liechtenstein	88.0	Jamaica	74.1	Solomon Islands	63.8
Guyana	87.7	Portugal	74.1	Benin	63.4
Sweden	87.7	Surinam	73.8	St. Lucia	63.1
Austria	87.0	Spain	73.7	Dominican Republic	62.7
Sri Lanka	86.7	United Kingdom	73.1	Grenada	61.9
Chile	86.5	Vanuatu	73.1	Trinidad & Tobago	61.6
Denmark	86.2	Slovenia	72.7	Bangladesh	61.5
New Zealand	85.8	Gambia	72.4	Estonia	61.5
Mauritius	85.1	Finland	72.2	Madagascar	60.1
Germany	84.6	France	72.2	India	59.5
Mongolia	84.3	Ghana	72.2	Lithuania	58.1
South Africa	84.3	Latvia	71.7	El Salvador	53.7
Turkey	82.4	Ireland	71.2	Mexico	49.4
Samoa	82.3	St. Vincent & Gren.	71.2	Poland	47.4
Tuvalu	81.9	Bulgaria	71.1	Switzerland	46.5
Argentina	81.7	Antigua & Barbuda	71.0	Zambia	45.4
Netherlands	81.6	Thailand	70.9	Columbia	41.3
Andorra	81.4	Romania	70.7	Burkina Faso	40.2
Venezuela	81.2	Monaco	70.6	Lebanon	39.0
Peru	80.7	Canada	70.3	Nigeria	38.9
Palau	80.3	Moldova	69.6	Mali	21.1
Brazil	80.2	Czech Republic	69.4		
Greece	80.1	Dominica	69.4		
Total mean	75.5				

Turnout is measured as the percent of those registered who cast a vote. Data compiled by the author.

Table 33.2 Mean turnout by period

	Period				No. Elections
	1970–9	1980–9	1990–9	2000–4	
All cases (106 countries)	78.9	78.5	74.2	70.7	533
Established democracies (29 countries)	83.1	81.5	78.4	73.9	246

Researchers have debated whether there is a general trend upwards or downwards in turnout levels (Blais 2000; Dalton and Wattenberg 2000; Wattenberg 2002). Table 33.2 shows that mean turnout across all these nations has declined over time. Election turnout was close to 80 percent in the 1970s and 1980s, and it is now just slightly over 70 percent. Average turnout has declined by about 8 points, and that decline started only in the 1990s. The decline could be more apparent than real and could stem from the recent inclusion of new democracies. The second row of Table 33.2 compares turnout among a stable group of countries that have had a constant score of 1 or 2 on the Freedom House ratings since the 1970s, and a similar decline of 9 points since the 1980s emerges in that group as well. Thus, there has been a rather substantial turnout decline and that decline is recent.

The data reported above deal with national legislative elections. Is turnout substantially higher or lower in presidential versus legislative elections, or in local versus national elections? The available information is limited. Blais (2000) indicates that turnout is slightly higher in presidential elections (the median difference is two points) and more substantially lower in local elections (with a median difference of 13 points). The slightly higher turnout observed in presidential elections may indicate that more personalized campaigns have greater appeal. The lower turnout in local elections may reflect the lesser importance given to local government but it may also result from weaker media coverage.

The following section discusses the factors that explain differences in election turnout across nations, producing the aggregate patterns in Table 33.1. Then, the following section considers the factors that might explain the longitudinal trends in Table 33.2.

2 Explaining Turnout Variations across Countries

Table 33.1 shows the existence of substantial variations in turnout across countries. Why is turnout so high in Malta and so low in Mali? Do high turnout countries share common characteristics? Researchers have been examining the factors that could account for these differences. Three sets of factors have been identified: the socioeconomic environment, the institutional set-up, and the party system (Powell 1982; Blais and Dobrzynska 1998).

Many studies confirm the hypothesis that turnout tends to be higher in economically advanced societies (Powell 1982; Blais and Dobrzynska 1998; Norris 2002; Fornos, Power, and Garand 2004). The hypothesis is confirmed, however, only in those studies that have examined a wide array of countries or that have not been confined to the developed world. Within older democracies, there is no income effect, and so the real difference is between poor and other countries, be they very or only somewhat rich (Blais and Dobrzynska 1998).

Research has mainly focused on the impact of institutions. Among institutional variables, four have been examined particularly closely: compulsory voting, the nature of the electoral system, the salience of the election, and voting (or registration) facilities.

Every piece of research supports the view that compulsory voting laws "work," that is, they foster turnout.[2] Compulsory voting is typically estimated to increase turnout by approximately 10 to 15 points. For instance, Australia has a rigorous system of compulsory voting, and turnout rates have averaged 95 percent for the past thirty years.[3]

We do not know, however, what it takes to "convince" voters that they should vote even if they are not predisposed to, more precisely we do not know whether sanctions are required, how stiff sanctions need to be, and how strictly they must be enforced. Blais, Dobrzynska, and Massicotte (2002) report that compulsory voting without sanctions has no impact but they do not indicate which sanctions do and do not work nor whether sanctions need to be (firmly) enforced. Fornos, Power, and Garand (2004) find that the stronger the sanctions the greater the impact of compulsory voting legislation but they do not ascertain the effect of enforcement as such. More research is needed to specify how and why compulsory voting does or does not work.

It is usually believed that PR should stimulate turnout. On the one hand, PR produces more parties, which means that voters have more choice. On the other hand, there are not the wasted votes that are typically discussed in single-member plurality systems. The proposition that a more proportional system with large district magnitude[4] fosters turnout has been supported by about every study pertaining to advanced democracies (Powell 1986; Jackman 1987; Blais and Carty 1990; Franklin 1996; for a review see Blais and Aarts 2006). The pattern does not seem to hold in Latin America, however (Pérez-Liñán 2001; Fornos, Power, and Garand 2001) and when the analysis includes a wide array of countries, the impact of PR appears quite limited (Blais and Dobrzynska 1998).

---

[2] Norris (2002) qualifies the verdict; she finds that the effect is confined to older democracies.

[3] Compulsory voting prevails in twenty-six countries around the world. In eight countries (Australia, Belgium, Cyprus, Fiji, Luxembourg, Nauru, Singapore, and Uruguay) there are sanctions for abstention and these sanctions appear to be enforced (see **www.idea.int/vt/ compulsory_voting.cfm** and Bilodeau and Blais 2005).

[4] District magnitude refers to the number of seats in a given district. Typically, in a first past the post system one member is elected in each district. In a PR system, districts can be relatively small (let us say five members to be elected) or large (let us say twenty). The larger the districts, the easier it is for small parties to obtain seats.

It is not clear, in fact, why PR would contribute to a higher turnout. The most direct impact of PR is to increase the number of parties (Taagepera and Shugart 1989; Blais and Carty 1991; Lijphart 1994; Cox 1997) yet the available evidence suggests that turnout *decreases* when there are many parties (see below). Some researchers argue that the presence of safe seats in single-member districts reduces turnout (Franklin 2004) but there are also safe seats in PR systems, and the probability of casting a decisive vote remains extremely small.[5] In short, the common sense view that turnout is higher under PR needs to be questioned (for an exhaustive review of this question, see Blais and Aarts 2006).

It makes sense to assume that the more important the election, the higher the turnout. The importance of an election is directly related to the relative power of the body that is being elected. From that perspective, one would expect turnout to be highest for the election to the most powerful institution in a given country. This means that where there are two elective chambers in a country, turnout should be higher for the most powerful chamber, usually the lower house.[6] In the same vein, where there is a directly elected president, turnout should be higher at the presidential election (than at the legislative election) if (and only if) the president has more power than the legislature.

The United States, with its varied systems and levels of elections seems to underscore the significance of electoral importance; turnout is generally highest in presidential elections, lower in congressional off-year elections, lower still in most state elections, and even lower in city and county elections. As far as I can tell, however, these propositions have not been systematically tested across nations. Blais (2000, 40) notes that in three countries where the directly elected president has little power (Austria, Iceland, and Ireland), mean turnout for the presidential election is almost as high as mean turnout in the legislative election (a tiny difference of two points), which suggests that the "importance" of the election may not be as crucial as we are prone to believe.

The literature has examined whether turnout in lower house national elections is systematically lower in those countries where the lower house has to share power with an upper house or a president or because the national government has to share power with subnational entities. The hypothesis that turnout is reduced with bicameralism has been confirmed in some studies (Jackman 1987; Jackman and Miller 1995; Fornos, Power, and Garand 2004) but disconfirmed in others (Blais and Carty 1990; Pérez-Liñán 2001; Radcliff and Davis 2000). The idea that turnout in legislative elections is lower where there is a "relevant" elected president or strong regional governments (Siaroff and Merer 2002) or where parliamentary responsibility is weakened (Franklin 2004) seems to be supported. But the evidence does not corroborate the assertion that turnout in national elections is lower in federal states (Blais and Carty 1990).

---

[5] More specifically, it may be quite obvious that my preferred party will win one seat (neither more nor less) in my PR district and whether I vote or not will make no difference. It could still be, however, that people are less likely to think that their vote is wasted in a proportional representation system.

[6] Obviously, all these propositions hold only when and where elections for the different offices are held at different points in time.

Finally, Blais and Dobrzynska (1998) create a summary measure of the national lower house's overall leverage (which they call "decisiveness") and they find that measure to be correlated with a higher turnout.

The findings are inconsistent, perhaps a reflection of the fact that the indicators of the relative power of legislatures may not be accurate enough. Despite these inconsistencies, I am inclined to conclude that turnout is higher when the body to be elected has greater political leverage. The relationship may not be as strong as we tend to assume, however. It is useful to keep in mind that turnout for the election of "powerless" presidents has been over 80 percent in Austria and Iceland.

The last type of institution that should matter concerns the adoption of rules that facilitate voting. The assumption is that people are more likely to vote if it is easy than if it is difficult. So everything else being equal, turnout should be higher when and where voting takes place during weekends or holidays, over a longer time period, if employers are forced to provide time off for their employees to vote, and if special procedures like advance or postal voting are available.

Unfortunately, we know relatively little about the actual impact of such measures on turnout. Franklin (1996) initially reported that postal (absentee) voting and Sunday voting increase turnout but his subsequent analyses of turnout changes (Franklin 2004) indicate no independent impact. Norris (2004) examines the effect of a variety of rules (number of polling days, polling on rest day, postal voting, proxy voting, special polling booths, transfer voting, and advance voting) and finds no effect. Blais, Massicotte, and Dobrzynska (2003) create a scale indicating the presence or absence of advance, postal, or proxy voting and they indicate that the scale is associated with higher turnout. Again the findings do not appear to be very robust, possibly because information about these rules is not always very accurate. It makes sense to assume that people are more willing to vote when it is easy than when it is difficult. But we still do not know which measures are the most efficient or how much difference they make. If "marginal increases in cost [of voting] ... matter only marginally" (Blais 2000, 89), then decreasing these costs through voting facilities measures should produce only a small boost in turnout.

Cross-national variations in turnout can partially be explained by institutional variables that affect the importance of elections or the simplicity of voting (registration). That being said, the literature has not produced consistent findings on the impact of such institutions, perhaps because the indicators that have been used have not been as precise as they should be.

The last set of factors that is thought to affect turnout is the party system. Research has focused on two dimensions: the number of parties and party competitiveness. Intuitively we might expect turnout to increase when there are more parties. Voters have more options to choose from and they are more likely to find a party that is relatively close to their own points of view. Yet the empirical evidence suggests that turnout is depressed when the number of parties increases (Jackman 1987; Blais and Carty 1990; Blais and Dobrzynska 1998; Radcliff and Davis 2000; Kostadinova 2003; Fornos, Power, and Garand 2004).

Two interpretations have been advanced to "explain" this intriguing finding. First, the presence of a multi-party system usually leads to the formation of coalition governments; thus elections are less *decisive* in these cases because the final composition of the government depends on the deals that the parties are willing to make, deals about which voters have no say (Downs 1957; Jackman 1987). That interpretation is contradicted, however, by the finding that turnout is not higher in elections that produce single-party majority governments, elections which are, according to that perspective, decisive (Blais and Carty 1990; Blais and Dobrzynska 1998).

Second, the number of parties increases information costs for voters who must compare the positions of many parties on the main issues of the day (Blais and Dobrzynska 1998). Long Jusko and Shively (2005) present data that support such an interpretation; they show that it is only among the less informed that the number of parties depresses turnout. Yet this may not be a very robust finding because the information measures utilized in this study are not easily comparable. Furthermore, voters do not have to assemble information about each and every party, they can decide to confine their search to two or three options. All in all, then, the literature does not offer a compelling explanation for why turnout appears to be higher when there are fewer parties.

Findings are more robust concerning the second party system variable, competitiveness. There is consistent evidence that the closer the electoral contest the higher the turnout (Blais and Dobrzynska 1998; Blais 2000; Franklin 2004). And there is a simple and rather compelling explanation. People are more likely to feel that their vote "counts" when an election is close and that feeling fosters turnout (Blais 2000). Yet it is also striking that closeness matters but only at the margin. As Blais (2000, 78) puts it, "a close election is likely to increase turnout by a few percentage points, but the fact remains that people vote in a national election even if the outcome of the election is a foregone conclusion."

The impact of party system variables on turnout is not entirely clear. On the one hand, there is a puzzling negative correlation between the number of parties and turnout. On the other hand, people are more likely to vote in a close election but the link is not very strong.

3 EXPLAINING THE RECENT TURNOUT DECLINE

As can be seen in Table 33.2, turnout has declined by 7 or 8 points since the 1990s. That decline has spurred concerns about the legitimacy of political institutions and it has nourished demands for institutional reform (Dalton 2004). Three main interpretations have been offered to explain the recent turnout decline.

The first interpretation focuses on the effect of generational replacement. Miller and Shanks (1996; see also Lyons and Alexander 2000) argued that the main source of turnout decline in the United States was the replacement of the pre-New Deal generation (born before 1932) with the post-New Deal generation (born after 1964). The most recent generation is simply much less likely to vote than the previous two generations (New Deal and pre-New Deal), even taking into account life-cycle effects. This raises the question of why the most recent generation is less prone to vote. Miller and Shanks note that members of the post-New Deal generation have weaker party attachments and community integration and lower interest in politics but they candidly admit that "we have not . . . been able to identify or account for the essential causal elements" (Miller and Shanks 1996, 112).

Blais et al. (2004), for their part, look at the socio-demographic sources of turnout decline in Canada and conclude that the main reason lies in the lower turnout of the post baby boomers, a verdict similar to that of Miller and Shanks. They note that the most recent generation pays less attention to politics and has a weaker sense of duty and they suggest that this reflects a larger cultural change. These studies show clear evidence of generational effects but they offer no compelling explanation of what triggers these generational differences.

An alternative explanation is proposed by Franklin (2004). Franklin is interested in explaining the ups and downs of turnout within countries between 1945 and 1999, and not specifically in the recent turnout decline. His basic proposition is that turnout increases or decreases from one election to another depending on the "character" of the election, mostly the degree of electoral competition. His theory is completely at odds with the previous accounts. According to him, turnout varies because the character of elections changes over time, not because the character of voters changes (as the "generational" accounts suggest).

Franklin points out two main sources of turnout decline. The first is what he calls "young initiation," which is the lowering of the voting age from 21 to 18 in most democracies. According to Franklin, people face their first election at a very bad moment, when they are attending college or they are just starting to establish themselves in a community. He adds that voting is very much a habit and that those who do not vote in their first election are prone to abstain in the following ones. The second factor is the decline of what he calls "majority status" elections. Because of the fractionalization of party systems, leading parties are "falling further and further below the 50 percent support threshold that would deliver total control of the legislature into their hands" (Franklin 2004, 192), thus making elections less decisive.

There is little doubt that the lowering of the voting age had a detrimental effect on turnout (Blais and Dobrzynska 1998). But most established democracies lowered the voting age in the 1970s yet turnout started to decline only in the 1990s. Likewise, Japan, which has not changed its voting age (20), shows the same decline in turnout. This suggests that voting age legislation is not the main culprit, contrary to Franklin's claim.

The second reason for the turnout decline according to Franklin is the increased fractionalization in party systems and its detrimental effects on election decisiveness. This line of reasoning assumes that decisiveness (or the lack of it) is a major determinant of turnout. Unfortunately, studies that have used more direct measures of decisiveness (whether the government that is formed after the election is a single-party majority one) have found no relationship with turnout (Blais and Carty 1990; Blais and Dobrzynska 1998), and so the interpretation is not very compelling.

The third interpretation is that turnout has declined because of declining group mobilization. This is the thesis defended by Gray and Caul (2000), who examine turnout decline between 1950 and 1997.[7] They show in particular that turnout has declined more substantially in countries where union density and labor party vote share have been going down. And so they point to the decline of unions and labor parties as responsible for the turnout decline. This is an interesting argument but it is not entirely compelling. On the one hand, these two variables show up as less powerful predictors of turnout decline than changes in population size, number of parties, and percent of population between 30 and 69. On the other hand, the median decline in union density and labor party vote share in those countries was only 4 and 5 percentage points, and so these two factors combined would "explain" only about one point of the 10-point decline.

Our understanding of the factors responsible for the recent turnout decline is limited. There is strong evidence that recent cohorts are less inclined to vote but we lack a compelling account of why it is so. It is plausible that the lowering of the voting age contributed to turnout decline but we lack a compelling account of why turnout did not decline in the 1980s.

4 THE DECISION TO VOTE OR NOT TO VOTE

The last question to be examined is why some individuals vote (most of the time) and others do not. Before directly addressing that question, it is useful to specify the socio-demographic characteristics of voters and abstainers.

Wolfinger and Rosenstone (1980) provided a systematic analysis of who votes (and who abstains) in the United States, an analysis based on a huge survey of more than 88,000 individuals. They show that the two crucial variables are first education and second age. They also found that government employees, the less mobile, and married people were substantially more likely to vote.

Blais (2000) performed the same kind of analysis, pooling together surveys conducted in nine democratic countries. He reports that age and education are the two most significant factors, followed by religiosity, income, and marital status.

These two studies converge on the basic conclusion that age and education are the two most important socio-demographic characteristics that distinguish voters and abstainers. Age reflects the influence of both generational differences and life-cycle effects. As we have seen in the previous section, turnout is lower among the most recent cohorts. Moreover, the probability of voting increases as one gets older.

---

[7] Rosenstone and Hansen (1993) also impute much of the turnout decline in the United States to declining party mobilization. The problem with this interpretation is that it is not clear that turnout actually declined in the United States (see McDonald and Popkin 2001).

Turnout is also substantially higher among the better educated. The presence of an educational cleavage indicates that class differences emerge even with respect to such a simple act as voting. At the same time, it must be pointed out that it is the amount of education that one has that seems to count not how rich or poor that person is. The obvious follow-up question is then: Why are the better educated and the older more prone to vote than the less educated and the youth? To answer this question we need to review general theories of electoral participation.

Brady, Verba, and Schlozman (1995, 271) argue that if one asks why people do not participate, three answers suggest themselves: "because they can't, because they don't want to, or because nobody asked." I would add at least another possible answer: because it does not matter.

Each of these responses can be related to a model of electoral participation. "They can't" suggests that what distinguishes voters and abstainers is resources. One important model of electoral participation, indeed of general political participation, most elegantly articulated by Verba, Schlozman, and Brady (1995), is the *resource* model. A second model, the *psychological engagement* model, argues that what really matters is whether people care about politics, whether they have developed an interest in politics. The third approach, the *mobilization* model, most forcefully developed by Rosenstone and Hansen (1993), proposes that the decision to vote or not to vote depends on the individual's environment. An individual is likely to vote if she is invited, asked, or pressured to, and she is likely to abstain otherwise. The fourth and last model suggests that people may decide not to vote because they realize that their vote does not make a difference. This is the kind of interpretation advanced by the rational choice approach (see Downs 1957).

The first model argues that the most crucial determinant of political activity is resources, more specifically money, time, and civic skills (Verba, Schlozman, and Brady 1995; Brady, Verba, and Schlozman 1995). The model was developed to explain political participation in general but it is less relevant in the case of voting, which is quite an easy activity, requiring little time and skills. The authors acknowledge this, concluding that "political interest is much more important than resources if our main project is to explain voting turnout" (Brady, Verba, and Schlozman 1995, 283), and "what matters most for going to the polls is not the resources at voters' disposal but, rather, their civic orientations, especially their interest in politics" (Verba, Schlozman, and Brady 1995, 361).

The psychological engagement model is both appealing and disappointing. There is indeed strong evidence that political interest is closely associated with turnout. The more interested one is, the more likely one is to vote. Those who have developed a taste for politics are likely to vote and those who have no taste are inclined to abstain. There are two related problems with this interpretation. On the one hand, the explanation looks trivial. It would be very surprising to find that those who are less interested in politics are more willing to engage in political activities. On the other hand, the challenge becomes to explain why some people are more interested than others in politics.

Verba, Schlozman, and Brady (1995) examine the factors responsible for the development of political interest. They focus on two factors: education and parental influence. Education has a strong direct link with political interest but it has also indirect connections because it fosters involvement in non-political organizations, which in turns fosters political interest. Parental influence is also crucial, as exposure to politics at home is one of the strongest predictor of political interest.[8] We need more in-depth analyses of what makes people tune in or out of politics but the available evidence suggests that the possession of such basic resources as vocabulary skills is important for the development of political interest. In that sense, voting may be easy but politics is not an easy topic and the resource model alerts us to crucial antecedents of the motivations that nourish the willingness to go to the polls.

The third model that has been proposed to explain why some people vote and others do not focuses on the role of mobilization. Rosenstone and Hansen (1993) note that from a strictly individualistic perspective it does not make much sense to vote because one's vote will not make a difference (see below) and so the explanation "must move beyond the worlds of individuals to include family, friends, neighbors, and co-workers, plus politicians, parties, activists, and interest groups" (23).

Rosenstone and Hansen (1993) show that voters who are contacted by parties are much more likely to vote, even controlling for a host of other factors. Their finding has been replicated in many other studies (Rallings and Trasher 1990; Wielhouwer and Lockerbie 1994; Clarke et al. 2004; Karp, Banducci, and Bowler forthcoming), and so there is little doubt that, everything else being equal, a person is more likely to vote if she has been directly contacted by the parties or candidates. At the same time, it is hard to believe that mobilization or the lack of it is the most powerful factor that drives the decision to vote or abstain.

According to a fourth line of interpretation, many people do not vote because they consider that their vote is very unlikely to make a difference, that is, to decide who wins the election. This is the kind of interpretation that is advanced by the rational choice model. According to that model, people estimate the benefits and costs of voting and they decide to vote if the benefits are greater than the costs and to abstain otherwise. The costs of voting (the time it takes to go to the polls and to inform oneself in order to decide how to vote) are small but not nil. The benefits are even smaller because the probability that one individual vote will decide who wins is tiny. As a consequence, the "rational" citizen abstains because the costs outweigh the benefits (Downs 1957; see also Aldrich 1993).

The rational choice model would seem to explain why some people do not vote, but it cannot account for the fact that a clear majority still votes in national elections. And indeed the most thorough evaluation of the model (Blais 2000) concludes that this perspective has "considerable limitations" (139). Because voting is a low-stake decision, citizens do not pay a high price for making the "wrong" choice. The consequence is that the rational choice model should perform less well for this kind of behavior.

The rational choice model has the advantage of forcing us to think about what induces citizens to vote when, from a purely individualistic point of view, the most reasonable

---

[8] The other strongest predictor, according to Verba, Schlozman, and Brady (1995), is involvement in school activities. One wonders, however, whether those who participate in school activities are not those who have already developed some interest in public affairs.

option is abstention. Riker and Ordeshook (1968) point out that people may well derive an intrinsic benefit from the mere fact of voting, possibly a feeling of satisfaction derived from accomplishing one's civic duty. Indeed many people think that it is the duty of every citizen to vote in a democracy and that feeling is strongly correlated with the decision to vote (Blais 2000). This raises still another question about the nature and sources of such feelings. How do people get socialized to the view that voting is a "moral obligation" and why do some people feel more strongly so than others?

The extant literature has shown that people vote because some are interested in politics, many believe it is their duty to do so, and a few are directly contacted (and they prefer to say "yes" to "no"). Others do not vote because they are not really interested, they sort of know that their own vote will not make a difference, and they have not been asked. Among all these factors, psychological engagement and sense of duty appear to be the most important but the challenge is to understand how these values are developed.

5 CONCLUSION

Turnout has been declining recently but typically close to three-quarters of those who have the right do vote in national legislative elections. Turnout is lower in poorer countries and it is higher when the election is perceived to be important and close or when voting is compulsory. At the individual level, the propensity to vote increases with age and education. The correlation with age is particularly strong and reflects the combination of life-cycle and generational effects. The latter are particularly important when it comes to explaining the recent turnout decline. That decline is concentrated among the younger cohorts. The presence of an educational gap reminds us that even if voting is easy, following politics and nourishing an interest for public affairs are not.

The decision to vote or not to vote hinges on many considerations but the two most important ones appear to be whether one is interested in politics or not and whether one feels that voting is a civic duty. And so the challenge is to come up with compelling explanations for why people tune in or off politics and for why they come to believe that voting is a moral obligation or simply an individual choice option.

REFERENCES

ALDRICH, J. 1993. Rational choice and turnout. *American Journal of Political Science*, 37: 246–78.
BILODEAU, A., and BLAIS, A. 2005. Le vote obligatoire a-t-il un effet de socialisation politique? Paper presented to the Colloque international sur le vote obligatoire, Institut d'études politiques de Lille, October 20–1.

BLAIS, A. 2000. *To Vote or not to Vote? The Merits and Limits of Rational Choice*. Pittsburgh: University of Pittsburgh Press.

—— and CARTY, K. 1990. Does proportional representation foster voter turnout? *European Journal of Political Research*, 18: 167–81.

—— —— 1991. The psychological impact of electoral laws: measuring Duverger's elusive factor. *British Journal of Political Science*, 21: 79–93.

—— and DOBRZYNSKA, A. 1998. Turnout in electoral democracies. *European Journal of Political Research*, 33: 239–61.

—— MASSICOTTE, L., and DOBRZYNSKA, A. 2003. Why is turnout higher in some countries than in others? Research paper published by Elections Canada.

—— GIDENGIL, E., NEVITTE, N., and NADEAU, R. 2004. Where does turnout decline come from? *European Journal of Political Science*, 43: 221–36.

—— and AARTS, K. 2006. Electoral system and turnout. *Acta Politica*, 41, 180–96.

BRADY, H., VERBA, S., and SCHLOZMAN, K. 1995. Beyond SES: a resource model of political participation. *American Political Science Review*, 89: 271–94.

CLARKE, H., SANDERS, D., STEWART, M., and WHITELEY, P. 2004. *Political Choice in Britain*. Oxford: Oxford University Press.

COX, G. W. 1997. *Making Votes Count*. New York: Cambridge University Press.

—— and MUNGER, M. 1989. Closeness, expenditures, and turnout in U.S. House elections. *American Political Science Review*, 83: 217–31.

CREWE, I. 1981. Electoral participation. Pp. 216–63 in *Democracy at the Polls*, ed. D. Butler et al. Washington, DC: American Enterprise Institute.

DALTON, R. 2004. *Democratic Challenges, Democratic Choices: The Erosion of Political Support in Advanced Industrial Democracies*. Oxford: Oxford University Press.

—— and WATTENBERG, M. 2000. *Parties without Partisans: Political Change in Advanced Industrial Democracies*. Oxford: Oxford University Press.

DOWNS, A. 1957. *An Economic Theory of Democracy*. New York: Harper.

FORNOS, C. A., POWER, T. J., and GARAND, J. C. 2004. Explaining voter turnout in Latin America, 1980 to 2000. *Comparative Political Studies*, 37 (8): 909–40.

FRANKLIN, M. 1996. Electoral participation. Pp. 216–35 in *Comparing Democracies: Elections and Voting in Global Perspective*, ed. L. LeDuc, R. Niemi, and P. Norris. Thousand Oaks, Calif.: Sage Publication.

—— 2004. *Voter Turnout and the Dynamics of Electoral Competition in Established Democracies since 1945*. Cambridge: Cambridge University Press.

GRAY, M., and CAUL M. 2000. Declining voter turnout in advanced industrial democracies, 1950 to 1997: the effects of declining group mobilization. *Comparative Political Studies*, 33: 1091–122.

JACKMAN, R. W. 1987. Political institutions and voter turnout in industrial democracies. *American Political Science Review*, 81: 405–24.

—— and MILLER R. A. 1995. Voter turnout in the industrial democracies during the 1980s. *Comparative Political Studies*, 27 (4): 467–92.

KARP, J., BANDUCCI, S., and BOWLER, S. forthcoming. Getting out the vote: party mobilization in a comparative perspective. *British Journal of Political Science*.

KOSTADINOVA, T. 2003. Voter turnout dynamics in post communist Europe. *European Journal of Political Research*, 42 (6): 741–59.

LIJPHART, A. 1994. *Electoral Systems and Party Systems*. Oxford: Oxford University Press.

LONG JUSKO, K., and PHILIPS SHIVELY, W. 2005. Applying a two-step strategy to the analysis of cross-national public opinion data. *Political Analysis*, 13: 327–44.

LYONS, W., and ALEXANDER, R. 2000. A tale of two electorates. *Journal of Politics*, 62: 1014–34.

McDONALD, M. P., and POPKIN, S. 2001. The myth of the vanishing voter. *American Political Science Review*, 95: 963–74.

MILLER, W. E., and MERRILL SHANKS, J. 1996. *The New American Voter*. Cambridge, Mass.: Harvard University Press.

NORRIS, P. 2002. *Democratic Phoenix: Reinventing Political Activism*. Cambridge: Cambridge University Press.

—— 2004. *Electoral Engineering: Voting Rules and Political Behavior*. New York: Cambridge University Press.

PÈREZ-LIÑÁN, A. 2001. Neoinstitutional accounts of voter turnout: moving beyond industrial democracies. *Electoral Studies*, 20 (2): 281–97.

POWELL, G. B. 1982. *Comparative Democracies: Participation, Stability and Violence*. Cambridge, Mass.: Harvard University Press.

—— 1986. American voter turnout in comparative perspective. *American Political Science Review*, 80 (1): 17–43.

RADCLIFF, B., and DAVIS, P. 2000. Labor organization and electoral participation in industrial democracies. *American Journal of Political Science*, 44 (1): 132–41.

RALLINGS, C., and TRASHER, M. 1990. Turnout in English local elections: an aggregate analysis with electoral and contextual data. *Electoral Studies*, 9: 79–90.

RIKER, W. H., and ORDESHOOK, P. C. 1968. A theory of the calculus of voting. *American Political Science Review*, 62: 25–43.

ROSENSTONE, S., and HANSEN, J. M. 1993. *Mobilization, Participation, and Democracy in America*. New York: Macmillan.

SIAROFF, A., and MERER, J. W. A. 2002. Parliamentary election turnout in Europe since 1990. *Political Studies*, 50: 916–27.

TAAGEPERA, R., and SHUGART, M. S. 1989. *Seats and Votes: The Effects and Determinants of Electoral Systems*. New Haven: Yale University Press.

VERBA, S., SCHLOZMAN, K., and BRADY, H. 1995. *Voice and Equality: Civic Voluntarism in American Politics*. Cambridge, Mass.: Harvard University Press.

WATTENBERG, M. 2002. *Where Have All the Voters Gone?* Cambridge, Mass.: Harvard University Press.

WIELHOUWER, P., and LOCKERBIE, B. 1994. Party contacting and political participation 1952–90. *American Journal of Political Science*, 38: 211–29.

WOLFINGER, R., and ROSENSTONE, S. 1980. *Who Votes?* New Haven: Yale University Press.

CHAPTER 34

POLITICAL ACTIVISM AND PARTY MEMBERS

SUSAN E. SCARROW

POLITICAL parties are at the heart of democratic political institutions, and party members are at the heart of some of these parties. And in many parties, members have been gaining increasing responsibility for decisions such as candidate selection, decisions that ultimately have a great impact on their country's politics. Because party members are so close to the center of politics, political scientists have long been concerned to understand their motivations and priorities. In recent years this interest has stimulated a wealth of research on the attitudes and activities of party members. Perhaps paradoxically, this enthusiasm for studying party members has come at a time of rapidly waning enrollments in parties in established democracies. This chapter will discuss what members have meant to parties in the past, what we have learned from recent research about those who join parties, and what this research may suggest about the likely future of membership-based political organizing.

1 PARTIES AS MEMBERSHIP ASSOCIATIONS

The advent of membership-based parties roughly coincided with the extension of the franchise in Europe and in former British colonies. The European Socialist parties of the late nineteenth and early twentieth centuries were the first parties to pursue a strategy of mass enrollment, a strategy which initially focused on newly enfranchised voters and on those who hoped to win voting rights. The largest of these parties boosted enrollment figures by corporate membership schemes, whereby members of trade unions or other organizations were automatically registered as party members (for instance, the British Labour party in its first decades). Such arrangements increased membership and generally strengthened party finances, but they did not necessarily represent an increase in individual-level political participation. However, some of these original "mass" parties did strive to make individual party membership a meaningful experience that both included and went beyond politics, offering their members opportunities for education, recreation, and economic benefits such as access to insurance schemes.

Other parties took note of the electoral success of the socialist parties, and sought to emulate their organizational strategies by building up their own popular organizations. But these efforts were limited, and prior to the Second World War parties with large memberships remained more common on the left than the right. Even on the left, large memberships were not universal (Scarrow 2000). It was only in the 1950s and 1960s that party membership soared on both the left and the right across the western democracies. These decades were the hey-day of the membership party, the years when Maurice Duverger was predicting that mass-based parties were the future norm (Duverger 1963). In these years, parties in many established democracies boasted enrollments of well over 10 percent of the electorate (for instance, Austria, Denmark, Finland, New Zealand, Norway, Sweden, and Switzerland). Yet by the 1980s these figures had begun to drop, and the membership highs of the 1950s and 1960s began to look more like an anomaly than the norm (Katz, Mair, et al. 1992; Scarrow 2000; Mair and van Biezen 2001).

At first, this decline was not uniform across countries, or unidirectional within them. Moreover, some of the drop was easily discounted, reflecting as it did an improvement in party record keeping, as national parties began to keep databases of individual members, and as they adopted changing rules about who counted as a current member. In some cases, these new definitions made it much easier for individuals to obtain membership, and should have boosted membership by lowering the costs of joining, turning membership into an easy credit-card transaction rather than a personal act, one which in some cases required a prospective member to be vetted by local party leaders and even vouched for by member sponsors. But in other cases, the new rules clearly reduced the size of the paper membership, for instance by introducing national databases with individual records, something that stopped local parties from reporting inflated membership figures. And some of the drop was relative: because electorates were growing, the proportion of the electorate enrolled in political parties dropped more rapidly than the absolute numbers of members. Still, by the beginning of the twenty-first century all methods of measuring membership indicated a widespread and long-term enrollment decline in party membership in established democracies, with little to suggest that this was anything other than a permanent change. Even in the Scandinavian countries, where membership parties had deep roots, and where party enrollments had been well in excess of 10 percent of the electorate, all of the established parties experienced sharp drops in their memberships. Nor was this decline in party memberships completely offset by interest in newer parties. In the 1980s new parties like the Greens gained solid electoral footholds in many countries, but their membership organizations remained relatively small compared to the mass parties of the past. By the beginning of the twenty-first century, there were few established democracies in which parties claimed to enroll more than 8 percent of the electorate, and self-reported membership in opinion surveys showed a similar decline from the 1980s to the 1990s, though there was perhaps some leveling off of that trend in the 1990s (Scarrow 2000; Mair and van Biezen 2001). Table 34.1 shows self-reported membership in a variety of established and new democracies. Although self-reports may be prone to over-representation in the same way as

Table 34.1 Participation in political parties[a] (**party members as % of population**)

Established Democracies		Newer Democracies	
Country	% Members	Country	% Members
Iceland	19.0	S. Africa	9.2
Austria	11.8	Slovakia	6.9
India	11.4	Croatia	5.0
Sweden	10.3	Bulgaria	4.7
The Netherlands	9.3	Peru	4.7
Greece	7.9	Argentina	4.5
Belgium	7.0	Mexico	4.5
Denmark	6.6	Philippines	4.3
Malta	6.2	Czech Republic	4.1
Canada	6.1	Slovenia	3.0
Finland	6.1	S. Korea	2.7
Luxembourg	5.1	Chile	2.5
Ireland	4.3	Romania	2.3
Italy	4.1	Lithuania	2.0
Japan	3.5	Latvia	1.9
Germany	2.9	Estonia	1.7
United Kingdom	2.6	Hungary	1.7
France	1.9	Poland	0.9
Spain	1.7		
Portugal	1.6		

[a] Membership in Political Party or Groups.

Sources: World Values Survey 1999–2001.

self-reported turnout, they do give a sense of the proportion of the electorate who were engaging in politics through political party membership.[1]

Yet even amid signs of waning membership in these countries there were other signs in the 1990s that membership-based party organization was not altogether obsolete. Outside of the established democracies new parties in at least some of the third-wave democracies were creating and building up new membership associations. For instance, in the Czech Republic, Hungary, and Slovakia, the enlistment of members in new and newly democratized parties brought membership rates close to the levels of those in some of their western European counterparts. This was achieved despite the membership losses of the former communist parties in the years immediately after the establishment of democratic electoral competition (Mair and van Biezen 2001 and Table 34.1). In Latin American and Asian democracies some parties have also used membership organization to mobilize their supporters. For instance, in some populist-oriented parties local leaders have cultivated grass roots support and enhanced their own political positions by building local party organizations (e.g. the PRI in Mexico, or the Peronists in Argentina), and in these countries patronage benefits have increased the incentives for individuals to join the parties which control national or regional governments (Serrano 1998; Calvo and Murillo 2004). Although firm membership figures are hard to come by in these countries, surveys show self-reported membership levels that are at least as high as in established European democracies.

Even in parties that have been run as patronage organizations, and that have attracted members with individual economic incentives more than with political benefits, membership has not necessarily been meaningless when considered as a form of political participation. For instance, in the two Latin American parties named above, party members have recently gained rights to participate in party primaries. Indeed, parties throughout Latin America recently have been experimenting with new rules for candidate selection that include party members (as have some Asian parties) (Martz 2000; Langston 2001; Wu 2001; de Luca, Jones, and Tula 2002). As this suggest, in many of the newer democracies there seems to be a strong commitment to organizational ideas that are built around membership bases. In most contemporary democracies, new or established, the parties enroll only a small minority of citizens. But these individuals may wield disproportionate, and apparently increasing, political influence.

1.1 Explaining Membership Decline (and Growth)

What factors account for the declining popularity of party membership in the established democracies? Those who have studied this phenomenon disagree as to whether it should be ascribed more to parties' loss of interest in enrolling members

---

[1] The 1999–2001 World Values Survey question asked about membership in "political parties and groups" rather than just "political parties", but to the extent that can be judged from other surveys, these figures do not seem to have been inflated by the changed question wording.

(demand-side factors), or to changing lifestyles which make citizens less interested in enrolling (supply-side factors) (Scarrow 1996).

On the one hand, parties may be less interested in recruiting because some tasks once performed by party members now can be more easily handled in other ways. In many countries, parties which once relied on member donations now receive a large portion of their revenues from state subsidies, and at least in national elections, labor-intensive campaign methods have been displaced by mass media campaigns. For all these reasons, some suspect that party leaders are not as eager to recruit as formerly, not least because maintaining a large membership is not cost free. Parties which want to attract and maintain members generally offer services and benefits to members in addition to the opportunity to attend local party meetings. These benefits may include "insider" information (via newsletters or password protected websites), participation opportunities (for instance, party primaries, party congresses), and often, non-political advantages, whether this be selective access to jobs and other resources controlled by the state, or benefits of the types that non-party organizations may also offer (consumer discounts, credit cards, vacation clubs, etc.). Parties may be reluctant to pay the costs of providing these benefits unless they view party members as an electoral asset.

On the other hand, many would ascribe declining party memberships to changing lifestyles and values among parties' core supporters, changes that have reduced the supply of potential members. Citizens have access to a much greater range of leisure activities than they did a half-century ago, and they also have much greater opportunities to participate in politics in other ways, whether in single-issue movements or via the internet (Dalton 2006). Against this background, participation in political parties is not as attractive as it once was.

These supply-side and demand-side explanations for declining memberships are compatible, but the relative emphasis given to each has implications for expectations about where this trend is headed. Those who emphasize demand-side explanations cast doubt on whether parties will really want to enroll members, but all agree that if they do they are more likely to boost enrollments by offering incentives for participation that evolve along with citizens' priorities and lifestyles (for instance, Seyd and Whiteley 1992). In either case, even if there are some changes that may enable parties to combat their waning appeal, it seems unlikely that we will soon see a major growth in party memberships in established democracies. What is less clear is whether parties in newer democracies can hold onto, and perhaps boost, their memberships, or whether these, too, will decline in the face of changing lifestyles, and changing campaign styles.

Yet even if memberships are in decline in many countries, we need to put this development into perspective. As has been made clear above, in most democracies party members are, and always have been, a small subset of the wider electorate. But the importance of membership parties may not be indicated by their size alone. Parties with well-developed memberships may contribute to political integration through their local networks, and they may thereby foster political stability. This was a claim of some mid-twentieth century analysts (for instance, Neumann 1965;

Rokkan 1966; Weiner and LaPalombara 1966), and it is one that continues to resonate. Some contemporary advocates of democratic development argue that parties *must* have active and internally empowered members if they are to compete successfully, and if they are to contribute to democratic stability. For instance, one well-funded democracy-promotion institution has proclaimed that "the strength and stability of a national political party and the success of its candidates for elective office at every level are closely related to the number of active, enthusiastic party members and supporters at the local level" (National Democratic Institute 2003, 10). Few academic students of party development would go quite this far in proclaiming party members to be either the *sine qua non* of democracy, or of a party's electoral success. Nevertheless, many would agree that they can be very influential. Even if memberships are neither as broad-reaching nor as large as they once were, in most democracies party membership and party activism remain important outlets for political participation, and the extent and structures of party's membership organizations can have important consequences that affect national political life. This makes it important to ask what types of people join parties, what motivates them, and the extent to which they help to shape political outcomes. Recent scholarship has greatly improved our ability to answer these questions.

2 THE STUDY OF PARTY MEMBERS

Until the 1980s, most of what we knew about party members came from studies of single towns or regions. These snap shots still provide good portraits of party life in an earlier era, but they gave little basis for generalization, and they provided little information about the attitudes and motives of individual party members. This changed with the advent of more systematic surveys of party members. These surveys were made possible to a large extent by organizational changes within the parties themselves, as national parties developed better membership databases, and as national party organizations became more professionalized, and therefore more sympathetic to social science methods. Some parties initially entrusted such studies to party-affiliated researchers (for instance, in Germany Falke 1982; Becker and Hombach 1983; Reif and Schmitt eds. 1987), but by the 1990s party leaders in several countries proved surprisingly willing to let independent political scientists survey their members and publish the results. In the UK Patrick Seyd and Paul Whiteley led the way with surveys of Labour and then Conservative party members (Seyd and Whiteley 1992; Whiteley, Seyd, and Richardson 1994). These were complemented by surveys of Liberal Democrat members and even a survey of the members of the tiny British Green party (Rüdig, Bennie, and Franklin 1991). Their findings helped to spur similar efforts in other countries, including Canada, Denmark, Germany, Ireland, the Netherlands, and Norway. Similar studies were also conducted in the United States, where research focused on parties' active supporters, in the absence of formal membership provisions (Stone, Rapoport, and Schneider 2004). Although the survey frameworks for these studies were only loosely coordinated, all were linked by a common interest in several overlapping themes, something which makes it relatively easy to compare their findings. In addition, researchers profited from the cooperation of national political parties in conducting more systematic studies of those who were most active within parties, the party convention delegates (for instance, Reif et al. 1980; Kirkpatrick 1976).

About the same time as these surveys were being conducted, and sometimes in conjunction with them, researchers began to more systematically investigate the electoral impact of party members and other party volunteers. In addition to this research on campaign effects, an increased number of national election studies began to use questions and research designs that made it possible to compare the actions and attitudes of party members with those of other party supporters. Together these studies have helped to flesh out our picture of the motives of party members, and their impact on policies. So perhaps ironically, even as party memberships have been declining in established democracies, we have gained a much greater understanding of the relations between parties and their members in these countries. This research, summarized below, can also help us to understand how the loss of members may affect the ways that parties carry out their traditional activities.

3 Party Members and Linkage: How Representative are Members?

3.1 The Demography of Membership

Ever since the first systematic studies of political participation, it has been clear that those who join parties, like those whose participate in most types of political activities, are not a demographically representative sample of the electorate (Verba, Nie, and Kim 1978; Parry, Moyser, and Day 1992). Party members tend to have above-average levels of education and income. They are more likely to be male than female. They tend to be older than the population average (see especially Widfeldt 1995). While the age structure is not unexpected for this kind of political activity, it is notable that in many parties the average age of membership seems to be increasing.

There are a few exceptions to these general demographic patterns. For instance, Green parties tend to have comparatively younger memberships, something which probably reflects their relative newness (they have fewer long-term members who have aged within the party), not just the youthfulness of their political appeal. The British Conservative party is notable for the gender parity in its membership

(Whiteley, Seyd, and Richardson 1994). Historically, parties of the left have tended to be more inclusive than other parties in terms of the education and income levels of their members. However, in recent years the difference between left and right parties on this score has been declining in many countries, reflecting the broadened appeal of left parties as well as the increasing educational levels in society. Because of this shift, parties of the left do not stand out as they once did as organizations that help to counteract the social disparities that are evident in almost all other forms of political participation. Since participatory skills acquired in one arena can empower individuals to be active in other areas (Verba, Schlozman, and Brady 1995), this change within the parties may exacerbate the inequality in the ranks of those who participate in politics more generally.

The demographic disconnect between party members and the broader society could have several types of political consequences. At the least, if a party's membership does not reflect the electorate it hopes to represent, the party's credibility may suffer. For instance, it will be more difficult for a party to campaign on a platform of improved rights for women if it has few female members within its ranks, and particularly if the lower ratio of female members translates into a lower proportion of female candidates. More generally, a party's membership can help it to sustain informal contacts in its communities. Conversely, if the party lacks members from particular groups, its links with those groups are weakened. An even worse consequence of this demographic disconnect could arise if a party's decisions reflected the interests of its most engaged supporters rather than those of its target constituencies. For instance, if retirees and those close to retirement make up a majority of party members, parties may be more inclined to shield retiree benefits in economic crises, even at the cost of social services for younger (and probably more numerous) voters. This disparity of interests might be most evident, and most likely to matter, in parties that give members a large role in selecting candidates and in determining party policies.

In fact, it remains an open question whether demographic differences really lead to a huge disconnect between the policy preferences and attitudes of party members and other potential party voters. Thus, one study found little difference in the left–right self-placement of party members and party supporters despite their different backgrounds, suggesting that demographic disparities did not have significant political consequences (Widfeldt 1995). More detailed studies of members' views have found a bit more evidence that these differences might affect policy outcomes. For instance, a study of nine Danish parties found that female members were significantly more interested in social issues than their male counterparts—a potentially significant difference given that women were under-represented in all the parties (Pedersen 2004). If there are similar systematic preference differences on other issues and in other parties, the demographic composition of party memberships could affect political outcomes, possibly making parties less electable, or, even if they win, making them less effective in representing the interests of those who vote for them. However, there is little hard evidence that these differences are big enough to pose a major challenge for most parties.

3.2 Are Party Members Radicals?

The potential disconnect between the priorities of members and other party supporters could be exacerbated by non-demographic differences. It is widely suspected
that party members may have more intensely held, and therefore more radical or
ideological, political views than other party supporters. This suspicion, which is
almost as old as organized parties themselves, was formalized and extended by the
Australian political scientist John May, who dubbed it the "Special Law of Curvilinear Disparity" (1973). According to May, both ordinary party members and those
who hold public office may be more interested in politics than those who merely vote
for the party. But because party office-seekers and higher officeholders have personal
reasons to care about winning elections, they are likely to be concerned about
attracting moderate voters as well as about pursuing ideological agendas. In contrast,
the chief reason for supporters to join a party is to help advance their favored causes
and beliefs. As a result, "mere" party members are likely to be more ideologically
motivated than either the mass of the party's voters, or the pragmatists who hold
public office. If this assumption is true, it suggests that party members will often be
dissatisfied with party leaders, whom they are likely to view as too willing to
compromise. The exception to this may occur where party members have a large
say in nomination and leadership selection procedures. But candidates selected this
way might be less appealing to a party's target electorate than candidates selected by
party bosses who had kept an eye on opinion polls. In other words, if May was right
about this disparity of views, the expansion of democracy within parties would be
likely to detract from the quality of democracy within a polity by creating parties that
are less representative of the broader constituencies they are seeking to serve. But *was*
May right about this?

Although there is a great deal of anecdotal evidence to support the idea that party
activists hold more radical views than other party supporters, systematic investigations have provided only slim evidence for the validity of May's "Special Law." In fact,
most studies show that the views of party activists largely resemble those of less active
party members, and that to the extent there are differences among those with
different levels of involvement, it is the party officeholders and party candidates,
not the mid-level activists, who hold the most radical views (Norris 1995; Narud and
Skare 1999; Gallagher and Marsh 2004). In the United States, studies from the 1970s
onward have found that party convention delegates do seem to be less centrist than
most party supporters, but they have found little curvilinearity in this phenomenon—office-seekers at the top of the party did not seem to moderate their views
(Kirkpatrick 1976; Miller 1988; Herrera and Taylor 1994). In Europe, a few studies
have indeed found limited evidence of the predicted curvilinearity between the
attitudes of representatives, mid-level elites, and other party members or supporters,
but these differences have mostly been confined to ideologically charged issues, and
to certain types of parties (Kitschelt 1989; Narud and Skare 1999).

Thus, research suggests that the attitudes and priorities of party members are not
all that different from those of other voters, despite the differences in members'

backgrounds, and the differences in the intensity of their political engagement. This should be reassuring to those who advocate getting party members more involved in party decision making. Furthermore, even if members might be more ideological on some subjects, we still do not have much evidence about how party members' views affect their actions. Counterbalancing the anecdotal evidence of radical—and un-electable—candidates chosen by members in party primaries are stories of party members being more pragmatic than some leaders about putting electability ahead of ideological purity when choosing party programs and candidates (for example, the German Greens in the early 1990s, or the British Labour party in the 1980s). When confronted with the evidence of opinion polls, and the specter of electoral defeat, party activists and elites might prove to be equally motivated by electoral consider-ations (Abramowitz et al. 1983). Finally, even if active members are ideological purists, in some situations articulating distinctive positions may be a better strategy than courting the median voter. In other words, while the demography of party membership suggests that parties tend to do badly in forming grassroots connections with all parts of society, or even with all parts of their target electorate, studies of members' attitudes suggest that the political implications of this incongruence are less than might be feared. And studies of parties' policy outputs—their party programs—suggest that their positions are largely in line with those of their sup-porters, but where they diverge they are if anything less, not more, radical than those of their supporters. This congruence occurs despite the fact that most party programs need to win the approval of the supposedly most radical group of party activists, the party convention delegates (Klingemann 1995).

4 Participation within Parties and the Democratic Process

To what extent do party members actively participate in politics? Of course, merely joining counts as a form of participation, and enrolling and maintaining membership status represents a greater amount of political engagement than most citizens are willing to undertake. And "merely" enrolling is not an insignificant act, because parties may benefit from the endorsement provided by those who are willing to join, and because the act of joining may reinforce an individual's loyalty to a political cause. But, as noted above, in many cases today the act of party affiliation has become an impersonal credit card transaction that can be completed on the internet, without any personal contact with party organizers, and with no require-ments of further activity. Given this, it is not surprising that the amount of activity associated with membership varies widely. So it is worth asking to what extent members engage in political activities within their parties? And to what extent do their parties seem to gain electoral advantages from these activities? The answer to this latter question can help us to understand possible implications of the rise or decline in party memberships.

In fact, most studies have shown that many party members are largely inactive within their parties, while others are engaged primarily at times of high mobilization, such as national election campaigns. These numbers do vary across parties, however. It is not clear what determines the level of activity within any particular party, or whether the ratio of active to passive members is fixed or changeable within them. If the ratio is generally fixed, activity levels in parties would rise and fall along with enrollment figures. However, if the number of people involved is determined more by the size of the job to be done—the number of local government candidacies to fill, the number of leaflets to deliver—the number of members active within a local party could remain fairly constant even as membership fluctuates. In the latter case, declining membership numbers would have less of an immediate impact on the parties' outreach activities.

Surveys of party members and national election surveys give inconsistent evidence on these points. In some countries, self-reported activity within parties did increase even as membership declined in the 1980s, suggesting that parties were left with smaller memberships but more active members (Scarrow 2000). But surveys focused on party members give a different picture. For instance, in Norwegian parties in the 1990s self-reported rates of participation by individual members did not increase as membership fell, nor did most members shift their activity patterns in response to parties' creation of new internet-based communications channels (Heidar and Saglie 2003). In these parties, the loss of party members seemed to translate directly into diminished party activity. Surveys of the British Labour party in the 1990s suggested an even worse picture for the party, with absolute membership levels declining, and with the remaining members reporting that they were less active than they had been (Seyd and Whiteley 2004; 358). Although Fine Gael membership did not decline in the 1990s, its members also were more likely to describe themselves as less rather than more active than they used to be (Gallagher and Marsh 2004; 91).

So there is good reason to think that a variety of changes may be adding up to diminished activity at the parties' grassroots. Still, this does not mean that the remaining membership activity is altogether unimportant. Party members may continue to help their party's electoral efforts in concrete and active ways, including fundraising, helping with campaigns, helping with year-round activities, filling candidacies, and reaching out to other supporters in less formal ways. What do we know about how well party members perform these tasks, and about how, if at all, their activities have changed in recent decades?

4.1 Party Members and Party Finances

In most parties, membership involves a financial commitment, and members are often approached to make additional contributions to support the party cause. Indeed, Duverger described members' financial contributions as one of their crucial functions, something that was key to the success of mass membership parties of the left. In his words, the invention of the dues-paying mass membership was equivalent to the invention of savings bonds to finance wars: in both cases, large sums were raised from small amounts (Duverger 1963, 63). But how important are members' contributions today, when parties of the left can attract the large-scale support of businesses as well as of trade unions, and when parties of all political stripes are increasingly reliant on public subsidies?

In many parties, donating money is one of the activities which sees the highest levels of member participation. In the countries for which we have such information, members who listed providing financial support as among the activities in which they were most likely to engage were over 80 percent of British Labour and Conservative party members, and of Canadian party members; almost 70 percent of German party members, over 50 percent of Dutch party members, almost 50 percent of Norwegian party members. In most cases, these donations were in addition to regular dues payments (Seyd and Whiteley 1992, 95; Whiteley, Seyd and Richardson 1994, 74; Cross and Young 2004, 27; Heinrich, Lübker, and Biehl 2002, 30; Van Holsteyn 2001, 13 Heidar and Saglie 2003, 770).

How much difference such contributions make is another matter. Although good figures on party finance are notoriously hard to obtain, it seems unlikely that members' contributions are a main source of revenue for major parties in any of the established democracies. Moreover, the relative importance of such contributions has almost certainly declined in many (though not all) countries as parties have obtained access to other funds, particularly to public subsidies (Katz and Mair 1994). On the other hand, the importance of these donated sums may exceed their monetary value. In Germany, for instance, parties rely heavily on public subsidies, but they are required to raise at least half of their funds from non-public sources. Members' contributions help them to meet this requirement. Even where parties do not operate under the same legal constraints, the marginal value of members' contributions may be high, particularly when these support parties' local organizations and activities (Pedersen et al. 2004, 377).

4.2 Party Members and Campaigning

In recent decades much has been written about the professionalization of election campaigns (sometimes described as "Americanization"). This is usually equated with the increasing centralization and homogenization of national-level contests, as parties strive to present a single unified message. Many have assumed that nationalized, professionalized campaigns would have little room for local efforts, which is one reason for anticipating a declining demand for party members. Despite these predictions, in most countries parties do still attempt some forms of grassroots campaigning, and these campaigns are an important part of local party life: to the extent that party members ever participate in partisan activities, it is most likely to be in campaign efforts. Rates of reported participation in campaign activities ranged from one-quarter and one-third of party members in Denmark, Norway, and in the British Conservative Party, up to well over 50 percent of members in Germany, Canada, the Netherlands, in the Irish Fine Gael, and in the British Labour party (Pedersen et al. 2004, 377; Heidar and Saglie 2003, 770; Whiteley, Seyd, and Richardson 1994, 74; Heinrich, Lübker, and Biehl 2002, 30; Cross and Young 2004, 27; Van Holsteyn 2001, 13; Gallagher and Marsh 2004, 232; Seyd and Whiteley 1992, 95).

So, many members are mobilized at election times, but do their efforts matter? Recent research suggests that such activities are more than a mere vestige of past campaign eras. Studies from Ireland, Canada, the United States, and the United Kingdom have found that the efforts of active local parties and/or of active party members can have a positive and politically significant impact on their parties' election results (Huckfeldt and Sprague 1992; Denver and Hands 1992; Seyd, and Whiteley 1992; Whiteley, Seyd, and Richardson 1994; Carty and Eagles 1999; Gallagher and Marsh 2004). If local activity seems to have an impact in countries like the United States and the United Kingdom, where campaigns are highly professionalized and highly nationalized, there is every reason to believe that local party activists elsewhere could have a similar impact by mobilizing and motivating voters. Their efforts may be even more important in local and regional elections, where media campaigns generally play a smaller role. In sum, grassroots campaigning by party members may not be the most visible aspect of contemporary election contests, but it is by no means an obsolete or irrelevant form of political participation.

4.3 Party Members and Year-Round Activities

One of the distinctive features of many membership parties has been their active existence between national elections. They have engaged supporters in year-round activities, giving them opportunities to participate in politics, and providing social opportunities that reinforce political identities. Yet while some local *parties* may be active year round, many of their *members* are not. In most parties only a minority of party members regularly attend local party meetings or other events. This picture of passive members should not be overdrawn. In three countries where members have been surveyed on the question, and in the British Labour party, a majority reported attending at least one local party event per year (though figures from Norway and from the British Conservatives were lower) (see Table 34.2). This suggests that at least in some places, membership was more than a mere paper transaction, even if it did not lead to intensive involvement. However, far fewer were highly active, attending meetings regularly throughout the year, or giving large amounts of time each month. German party members seem to be the exception. Though they did not report on their meeting attendance in quite the same way, 47 percent listed themselves as giving five hours or more to party work per month (Heinrich, Lübker, and Biehl 2002, 29). With this one exception, it seems clear that it is only a small fraction of party members who treat party activities as a focal point of their leisure activities; the rest are probably linked to their party more by impersonal communications (news-

Table 34.2 Attendance at local party meetings (%)

	Never	1–2 times/year	Frequently
Canada	39	27	21
Denmark	43	27	30
Ireland (Fine Gael)	18	44	14
Norway	52	29	19
United Kingdom	68 (C) 36 (L)	14 (C) 14 (L)	11 (C) 30 (L)

Canada Frequently = 6 or more times per year
Denmark Frequently = more than twice a year
Ireland Frequently = 6 or more times per year
Norway Frequently = 5 or more times per year
United Kingdom Frequently = 6 or more times per year (Conservatives); Frequently = "Frequently"
(Labour party); 1–2 times/year = "Rarely" (Labour party)

Sources: Seyd and Whiteley 1992; Whiteley, Seyd, Richardson 1994; Heidar and Saglie 2003; Cross and Young 2004; Gallagher and Marsh 2004; Pedersen et al. 2004.

letters, e-mails) than by face-to-face contacts. This is perhaps one reason some parties which practice intra-party democracy have favored postal ballots rather than holding local caucuses to decide issues—because mailed ballots are likely to engage a much broader, and possibly more representative, segment of the membership.

4.4 Party Members and Candidate Recruitment

In most parties with formal memberships, party members have traditionally been the chief source of parties' candidates for local and national offices. Some members may join a party in hopes of gaining a nomination, but it is just as likely that parties actively recruit from among the membership to obtain a sufficient number of nominees, particularly for local government elections and for non-winnable national seats. The amount of candidate recruiting to be done depends on the number of layers of elected government, as well as on the size and partisanship of local councils. However, whatever the electoral structures, it is to be expected that members of small parties are more likely than others to be called upon to serve as party candidates, because there is greater need for their services relative to the number of seats to be contested. This was especially obvious in Germany in the 1990s, where members of small parties stood as candidates at much higher rates than their counterparts in larger parties: 46 percent of Green party members, 49 percent of FDP members, compared with 31 percent of SPD and 33 percent of CDU members. The same phenomenon could also be observed cross-regionally, with those in the membership-weak eastern German branches much more likely to have been called upon to be candidates than their western counterparts: 57 percent of SPD members, and 48 percent of

CDU members, well above their parties' national averages (Heinrich, Lübker, and Biehl 2002, 31). In other countries where members have been surveyed, rates of candidacies have been lower, but still impressive considering the proportion of members who are completely inactive: over 5 percent of members in the Irish Fine Gael and in the British Conservative party, and at least 15 percent of members in Danish parties and the British Labour party (Seyd and Whiteley 1992; Whiteley, Seyd, and Richardson 1994; Gallagher and March 2004; Pedersen et al. 2004). Even in the larger parties it seems likely that many who are politically engaged enough to join a party will stand for office at some point, though far fewer of them will wind up securing a public office.

4.5 Party Members and Informal Outreach

In addition to participating in party activities, members can support their parties by the ways they relate to their communities in informal settings, sharing party messages with friends and co-workers, and mobilizing others by their own example. This may be especially likely to happen in a country like Germany, where 80 percent of party members report that they are also active members of non-party organizations, including social clubs, sports clubs, trade unions, and professional societies (Heinrich, Lübker, and Biehl 2002, 24). But even where party members hold fewer formal memberships in other groups, they may still have an influence on their immediate milieu. For instance, over 80 percent of British party members reported that they had discussed politics with non-party members, while over 40 percent of Danish party members and over 50 percent of Dutch party members reported that they had tried to persuade others to vote for their party (Seyd and Whiteley 2004, 362; Pedersen et al. 2004, 378; van Holsteyn 2001). Lacking similar information from other parties, it is hard to know whether such personal endorsements are typical, and it is hard to measure the impact of such informal contacts, but these figures do reinforce the assumption that members are likely to benefit their parties by their "ambassadorial" engagement outside the party realm.

4.6 Party Members and Internal Decision making

In many countries, party members are playing an increasingly important role in party decision making. In countries where democratic and transparent procedures are held in high regard, including members in party decisions can enhance the legitimacy of the results. Party leaders may agree to such changes in part because of the perceived popularity of inclusive procedures. In other cases, they may do so in hopes of diffusing conflicts between intra-party factions by giving clear rules for resolving leadership disputes. Whatever the reasons, in recent years party members in many countries have assumed more responsibility for selecting candidates, whether in party primaries or in local party caucuses (Martz 2000; Scarrow et al. 2000; Bille 2001; Wu 2001). In addition, party members are increasingly asked to weigh in on the selection of national party leaders. In some instances, they are also asked to vote in party-internal "referendums" to help set party policies on controversial issues that might otherwise split their parties. Even if the new rules do not necessarily resolve the internal conflicts, the procedural changes have increased the political content of membership for those who chose to be active within their parties. Voting rights can be a meaningful membership privilege, one that encourages supporters to join, and encourages would-be candidates to enlist their supporters. The introduction of these voting rights can change the meaning of party membership in other ways as well. When parties use postal ballots to make their decisions, members are able to be active participants whether or not they have any other contact with their local parties. As a result, party membership may become simultaneously a less active commitment, but also a potentially more influential form of political participation.

5 PARTY MEMBERS AND POLITICAL PARTICIPATION: DECLINE, NOT OBSOLESCENCE?

The preceding discussion makes clear that the decline of party membership is not necessarily the same as the obsolescence of this form of political participation. In today's membership parties few members are extremely active, but many do occasionally participate in campaign events, in meetings, or at the very least through their extra donations. Because of this, political parties remain organizations that help their members to develop their individual political resources, and, in doing so, they indirectly benefit the wider societies by encouraging citizens to be active and engaged. Increasingly, those who enroll gain an enhanced role in national and local politics because they gain opportunities to affect the selection of party candidates and policies. These benefits of membership are not one sided, because members also remain a resource for their parties. Even in an age of highly developed mass communications strategies in campaigns, and of generous state subsidies for party activities, parties which can enroll and mobilize large memberships apparently still gain advantages, if only marginal ones, from the various kinds of support that their members provide. Members help in party fund-raising and as election foot-soldiers, and they also aid their parties by their informal contacts, spreading party messages in ways that mass communication cannot achieve. In short, party membership is not obsolete either for the individuals who enroll, or for the parties which seek to establish and maintain broad popular organizations.

But even if party membership is not obsolete as an individual activity, or as an organizational strategy, many parties clearly are finding it difficult to attract and retain members. Despite the big increase in knowledge about the motivations of members, it is still hard to predict whether recent drops in membership in established parties are a sign of the imminent disappearance of this form of political organization, or whether parties which want to stabilize their membership enrollments may be able to do so by changing the benefits offered to members. If they attempt this, it is likely that the mix of incentives that attract members may vary among different societies, and may be specific to particular political climates. So it is difficult to judge the extent to which locally based membership organizations are likely to be an important part of future parties' organizational strategies. But to the extent that party members gain or maintain privileged positions as gatekeepers for party nominations, and as arbiters of party policies, engagement within political parties will remain an important form of political participation.

References

ABRAMOWITZ, A. et al. 1983. The party isn't over: incentives for activism in the 1980 presidential nominating campaign. *Journal of Politics*, 45: 1006–15.

BECKER, H., and HOMBACH, B. 1983. *Die SPD von Innen*. Bonn: Verlag Neue Gesellschaft.

BILLE, L. 2001. Democratizing a democratic procedure: Myth or reality? *Party Politics*, 7: 363–80.

CALVO, E., and MURILLO, M. V. 2004. Who delivers? Partisan clients in the Argentine electoral market. *American Journal of Political Science*, 48 (4): 742–57.

CARTY, K., and EAGLES, M. 1999. Do local campaigns matter? Campaign spending, the local canvass and party support in Canada. *Electoral Studies*, 18: 69–87.

CROSS, W., and YOUNG, L. 2004. The contours of political party membership in Canada. *Party Politics*, 10: 427–44.

DALTON, R. 2006. *Citizen Politics*, 4th edn. Washington, DC: CQ Press.

DE LUCA, M., JONES, M. P., and TULA, M. 2002. Back rooms or ballot boxes? Candidate nomination in Argentina, *Comparative Political Studies*, 35: 413–36.

DENVER, D., and HANDS, G. 1992. Constituency campaigning. *Parliamentary Affairs*, 45: 528–44.

DUVERGER, M. 1963. *Political Parties*. New York: Wiley. First French edition 1954.

FALKE, W. 1982. *Die Mitglieder der CDU*. Berlin: Duncker & Humblot.

GALLAGHER, M., and MARSH, M. 2004. Party membership in Ireland: the members of Fine Gael. *Party Politics*, 10: 407–25.

HEIDAR, K., and SAGLIE, J. 2003. A decline of linkage? Intra-party participation in Norway, 1991–2000, *European Journal of Political Research*, 42: 761–86.

HEINRICH, R., LÜBKER, M., and BIEHL, H. 2002. *Parteimitglieder in Vergleich*. Working Paper: Potsdam University.

HERRERA, R., and TAYLOR, M. 1994. The structure of opinion in American political parties. *Political Studies*, 42: 676–89.

HUCKFELDT, R., and SPRAGUE, J. 1992. Political parties and electoral mobilization: political structure, social structure, and the party canvas. *American Political Science Review*, 86: 70–86.

KATZ, R. and MAIR, P. eds. 1994. *How Parties Organize*. London: Sage Publications.

—— —— et al. 1992. The membership of political parties in European democracies, 1960–1990. *European Journal of Political Research*, 22: 329–45.

KIRKPATRICK, J. 1976. *The New Presidential Elite.* New York. Russell Sage Foundation.

KITSCHELT, H. 1989. The internal politics of parties: the law of curvilinear disparity revisited. *Political Studies*, 38: 400–21.

KLINGEMANN, H.-D. 1995. Party positions and voter orientations. Pp. 183–205 in *Citizens and the State*, ed. H.-D. Klingemann and D. Fuchs. Oxford: Oxford University Press.

LANGSTON, J. 2001. Why rules matter: changes in candidate selection in Mexico's PRI, 1988–2000. *Journal of Latin American Studies*, 33: 485–511.

MAIR, P., and VAN BIEZEN, I. 2001. Party membership in twenty European democracies, 1980–2000. *Party Politics*, 7: 5–21.

MARTZ, J. 2000. Political parties and candidate selection in Venezuela and Colombia. *Political Science Quarterly*, 114: 639–59.

MAY, J. 1973. Opinion structure of political parties: the special law of curvilinear disparity. *Political Studies*, 21: 135–51.

MILLER, W. E. 1988. *Without Consent.* Lexington: University of Kentucky Press.

NARUD, H., and SKARE, A. 1999. Are party activists the party extremists? The structure of opinion in political parties. *Scandinavian Political Studies*, 22: 45–65.

National Democratic Institute. 2003. *A Guide to Political Party Development.* Washington, DC: National Democratic Institute.

NEUMANN, S. 1965. *Die Parteien der Weimarer Republik.* Stuttgart: W. Kohlhammer Verlag. First published 1932.

NORRIS, P. 1995. May's law of curvilinear disparity revisited. *Party Politics*, 1: 29–47.

PARRY, G., MOYSER, G., and DAY, N. 1992. *Political Participation and Democracy in Britain.* Cambridge: Cambridge University Press.

PEDERSEN, K. et al. 2004. Sleeping or active partners? Danish party members at the turn of the millenium. *Party Politics*, 10: 367–83.

REIF, K., and SCHMITT, H. eds. 1987. *Neumitglieder in der SPD.* Neustadt: Verlag Neue Pfälzer Post.

—— et al. 1980. National political parties' middle-level elites and European integration. *European Journal of Political Research*, 8: 91–112.

ROHRSCHNEIDER, R. 1994. How iron is the iron law of oligarchy? *European Journal of Political Research*, 25: 207–38.

ROKKAN, S. 1966. Electoral mobilization, party competition, and national integration. Pp. 241–65 in *Political Parties and Political Development*, ed. J. LaPalombra and M. Weiner Princeton: Princeton University Press.

RÜDIG, W., BENNIE, L., and FRANKLIN, M. 1991. *Green Party Members: A Profile.* Glasgow: Delta Publications.

SAGLIE, J., and HEIDAR, K. 2004. Democracy within Norwegian political parties: complacency or pressure for change? *Party Politics* 10: 385–405.

SCARROW, S. 1996. *Parties and their Members.* Oxford: Oxford University Press.

—— 2000. Parties without members? Party organization in a changing electoral environment. Pp. 79–101 in *Parties without Partisans*, ed. R. Dalton and M. Wattenberg. Oxford: Oxford University Press.

—— et al. 2000. From social integration to electoral contestation: the changing distribution of power within political parties. Pp. 129–53 in *Parties without Partisans*, ed. R. Dalton and M. Wattenberg. Oxford: Oxford University Press.

SERRANO, M. 1998. *Governing Mexico: Political Parties and Elections.* London: Institute of Latin American Studies.

SEYD, P., and WHITELEY, P. 1992. *Labour's Grass Roots.* Oxford: Oxford University Press.

—— —— 2004. British party members: an overview. *Party Politics*, 10: 355–66.

STONE, W., RAPOPORT, R., and SCHNEIDER, M. 2004. Party members in a three-party election. *Party Politics*, 10: 445–69.

VAN HOLSTEYN, J. 2001. Neither threat nor challenge. Paper presented at the ECPR Joint Sessions of Workshops, April 6–11. Grenoble, France.

VERBA, S., NIE, N., and KIM, J. 1978. *Participation and Political Equality*. Cambridge: Cambridge University Press.

—— SCHLOZMAN, K. L., and BRADY, H. E. 1995. *Voice And Equality: Civic Voluntarism in American Politics*. Cambridge, Mass.: Harvard University Press.

WEINER, M., and LAPALOMBARA, J. 1966. The impact of parties on political development. Pp. 399–435 in *Political Parties and Political Development*, ed. J. LaPalombara and M. Weiner. Princeton: Princeton University Press.

WHITELEY, P., SEYD, P., and RICHARDSON, J. 1994. *True Blues: The Politics of Conservative Party Membership*. Oxford: Oxford University Press.

WIDFELDT, A. 1995. Party members and party representativeness. Pp. 134–82 in *Citizens and the State*, ed. H.-D. Klingemann and D. Fuchs. Oxford: Oxford University Press.

WU, C. 2001. The transformation of the Kuomintang's candidate selection system. *Party Politics*, 7: 103–18.

CHAPTER 35

SOCIAL CAPITAL

DIETLIND STOLLE

ANALYSES of institutional performance, the quality of democracy, and economic development have recently focused on resources derived from the society itself, namely social capital. While many dimensions of the concept of social capital are far from new, major social science contributions have provoked new research and much debate over the last decades (Coleman 1988, 1990; Putnam 1993, 2000). Scholars are increasingly concerned with this key social resource that seems to oil the wheels of the market economy and democratic politics.

The importance of social capital seems to be intuitive and captures the imagination of many people—academics and politicians included—but there is considerable disagreement about the conceptualization and measurement of social capital and its sources. Analysts also disagree about how and why it is important and whether social capital is declining in western democracies. This chapter assesses the current state of research within these debates.[1] The chapter starts with a discussion of the various roots, conceptions, and measurements of social capital. The following section discusses the various consequences and benefits of social capital. Since social capital is viewed as such a precious resource, it is particularly alarming that some aspects may be declining in western democracies; yet not all scholars agree with this assessment. The next section considers the main theoretical frameworks, competing ideas, and evidence on the sources of social capital. The chapter asks why some countries, regions, villages, or individuals possess more of this important resource than others. Finally, the chapter provides an overview of future issues in social capital research.

---

[1] Earlier accounts are linked to the work of Tocqueville [1835], even though he does not use the term social capital.

1 ROOTS AND CONCEPTIONS
OF SOCIAL CAPITAL

The concept of social capital has several interdisciplinary roots, each of which has a distinct emphasis in its conceptions. The most important recent conceptualizations of social capital are found in the work by Coleman, Lin, and Putnam (see the main distinctions in their conceptions summarized in Table 35.1).

James Coleman introduced the concept of social capital in his research of educational attainment and performance. For him, social capital inheres "in the structure of relations between persons and among persons, and is lodged neither in individuals nor in physical implements of production" (Coleman 1990, 302 ff.). Coleman discusses several aspects of social relations that constitute useful resources, such as obligations and expectations, information channels (such as networks or friends), norms and effective sanctions (for example norms of high achievement, sanctions against crime in a neighborhood), authority relations (social capital is concentrated in one person), and social organizations and their side products (for example, a parent–teacher association). In sum, social capital exists in social relations of all sorts, especially within the family or community social organizations, and takes on a variety of forms. Coleman's examples range from the neighborhood norm of watching out for neighbors' children to parental involvement in school matters.

Table 35.1 Similarities and differences between various approaches to social capital

	Coleman	Lin et al.	Putnam
Definition	Aspects of social structure that provide resources to actors to fulfill their interests	Investment in social relations with a return in the marketplace	Networks, norms of reciprocity, and trust for mutual collective benefit
Which aspects of social interactions are important	Closure, norms, values	Several aspects of social interactions, e.g. density of networks, resources in networks	Selected dimensions: horizontal versus vertical structures, selected networks, *generalized* trust and reciprocity
Benefits	Various individual and collective benefits (often focuses on human capital benefits), also externalities	Individual nature: jobs, promotions, economic resources, etc.	Solves collective action problems (collective pay-offs; effectiveness of democratic institutions; economic development)
Awareness of benefits	Somewhat	Purposeful	Not necessary

Depending on the context, social capital may have different pay-offs to the individuals involved in the social relationship, or to the collective as an externality of the social interaction. In the latter sense, social capital is a public good and a by-product of social interaction.

Nan Lin and associates offer a different sociological conceptualization of social capital (Lin 2001; Lin, Cook, and Burt 2001; Portes 1998). Social capital is seen as an investment in social relations with an expected return in the marketplace (Lin 2001, 19 ff.). Social capital is also characterized as the resources that are embedded in social networks. The view that social relationships have value or offer resources stems from the fact that they enhance the flow of information, allow for the possibility of influence, offer social credentials or reputation and emotional reinforcement (Lin 2001, 20 ff.). Most importantly, actors are cognitively aware of these resources and consciously choose to access them. Social capital thus becomes a conscious investment in one's social networks. An example here is the occupational diversity of one's acquaintances (Erickson 2001).

Putnam's (1993, 2000) view of social capital builds on Coleman's work, but has a narrower focus on specific aspects of social interactions that matter for well-performing governments and ultimately for democracy. By social capital, Putnam refers to norms of generalized reciprocity, trust, and networks of civic engagement that are organized horizontally (also see chapter by Newton in this volume). These ingredients of social capital reduce the information costs about the trustworthiness of other citizens and foster cooperation. Associations, voluntary organizations, and mass-based political parties represent such networks and they inculcate such norms and trust. In conditions where public life is organized hierarchically, engagement in horizontal social and cultural associations does not exist, and thus norms of trust and cooperation cannot prevail. In this view, social capital has mostly positive civic attributes as a societal resource that links citizens to each other and enables them to pursue their common objectives more effectively. It taps the potential willingness of citizens to cooperate with each other and to engage in civic endeavors collectively. In later formulations of his work, Putnam (2000) broadens the concept of social capital to include a variety of other types of social interactions such as the writing of greeting cards, families eating together, or entertaining friends at home. This later formulation emphasizes the overall importance of social interactions, and retreats from the view of social capital as civicness.

Whereas Putnam builds his argument on the work by Almond and Verba (1963), who were mostly interested in the frequency and overall means of participation, awareness of political issues, and political efficacy, Putnam goes beyond the pure quantity of social and political participation and stresses context and quality. For example, not all associations and types of trust are alike; it matters whether we look at associations that are based on horizontal ties or at associations based on hierarchy. These are not the same to Putnam! Similarly, Putnam makes a distinction between conventional voting, which can be based on patron–client relationships, and voluntary referenda voting, where the pure interest in public affairs matters. He also distinguishes generalized trust, which includes a wide radius of people, and generalized reciprocity, which spans over a wide time horizon, from all other attitudes such as knowledge-based trust or immediate reciprocity ("tit for tat") that seem oriented only towards close others, family, or people personally known.

There is a strong contrast between the various conceptions of social capital and their use in the social sciences. Coleman's wide definition, which includes a variety of aspects of social interactions and values such as trust and obligations, must be understood in their context and specific situation.[2] There is no theory or explicit causal claim behind Coleman's formulation, and social capital consists of whatever informal mechanisms facilitate productive social interactions. Putnam's narrower view in his earlier work, which equates social capital with civicness, practically represents an attitudinal approach of social capital theory, as networks of civic engagement come causally prior to civic attitudes such as trust and reciprocity. These civic attitudes are so vital because they facilitate collective action. Several researchers have followed Putnam's original lead and focused on civic attitudes as the ultimate indicators of social capital. Lin's is probably the narrowest conception of social capital, with a clear focus on social networks as instrumental resources that individuals can access—this sociological view is often called the network approach to social capital theory. What the various approaches of social capital theory have in common is their common focus on the value of networks, and they therefore share conceptual roots.

Besides the scope of the conceptualization, the approaches also differ in their emphasis on social capital as a collective or individual good. Coleman stresses it as a resource that is available both to individuals and collectives, while Lin emphasizes the individual aspects and Putnam points to social capital as a collective resource. Yet this divergence does not capture fundamental conceptual differences; instead what differentiates the approaches here is the choice of dependent variables, which differ according to the social science discipline in which the concept is used. These varying consequences of social capital are the subject of the next section. In sum, the major distinctions between the approaches lie in their central focus on what exactly captures social capital, its conceptual scope, and the choice of the types of phenomena that are explained.

2 THE CONSEQUENCES OF SOCIAL CAPITAL

Why is there so much interest in social capital? Certainly, social capital is so attractive because of its promising effects in various areas of political, economic, and personal life. Sociologists focus on the effects of social networks on personal benefits, whereas political scientists are mostly concerned with the consequences of the density of

---

[2] Critics of Putnam's use of social capital have noted this point. They suggest that generalized attitudes and norms that inhere in individuals are context dependent and cannot be captured adequately with survey questions (Foley and Edwards 1999; Hardin 2004).

voluntary associations and networks and the spread of generalized trust on a variety of societal outcomes, while economists analyze its potential economic impacts.

So, for example, sociologists stress the importance of parental social networks for the performance of schoolchildren (Coleman 1988); they write about the importance of diverse personal networks for one's success in the job market and job promotions (Burt 1998; Granovetter 1973), or how informal social resources are utilized to accomplish occupational mobility (Lin, Cook, and Burt 2001). Participation in social networks and voluntary associations is also linked to political mobilization and participation although not without doubts (Galston 2004; Seligson 1999). Associations purportedly foster the training of civic skills (Verba et al. 1995), a civic spirit and volunteerism (Putnam 2000, 121 ff.), and a sense of political efficacy (Berry et al. 1993). Through an enhanced information flow based on the expansion of social relationships, association members might experience a higher probability of being solicited for political action (Teorell 2003). All of these authors share a focus on the *individual* advantages that result from direct or indirect participation in certain types of social networks.[3]

Political science places more stress on social capital as a collective concept, which influences outcomes such as democracy, institutional performance, and social cohesion. From this perspective, what constitutes social capital to a set of parents, for example, is not so much their relationship with *one* specific neighbor in their town who watches out for their children at the playground. Instead, the focus is on the wide distribution of cooperative values, norms, and attitudes that constitute the social capital of a town, city, region, or larger unit. These resources benefit the collective and the wider society.

The most prominent research finding here results, of course, from Putnam's earlier work on Italy, which shows that networks of civic engagement and resulting generalized trust and norms of reciprocity foster the better performance of regional democratic governments (1993). Putnam's work builds on Almond and Verba (1963) who argued that a culture of trust is one of the important prerequisites to democratic stability. Similarly, Inglehart (1999) claims that economic development leads to certain cultural changes, particularly in trust, which help to stabilize democracy. In his view, a culture of trust serves as an essential underpinning to the acceptance of democratic rules, for example, allowing the opposition taking over after an election. Social capital is also evoked in debates about ethnic conflict. In determining the roots and factors of Hindi and Muslim riots in India, Varshney (2002) shows that in cities where both communities have little informal social interaction, communal conflict periodically descends into violence, whereas social interactions that bridge between these groups transcend community boundaries and often channel conflict into peaceful avenues.

Generalized trust and other attitudinal aspects of social capital are also associated with economic development and growth. Fukuyama (1995) claims that a lack of

---

[3] The effects of associations and social networks for the development of civic attitudes and trust are discussed in the section on "sources of social capital."

generalized trust prevents the building of large-scale professionally managed modern economic organizations. Knack and Keefer (1997) demonstrate how trust (and not voluntary associations) is an important predictor of economic growth. Zak and Knack (2001) show that even controlling for various institutional aspects that facilitate investment and growth, such as the protection of property rights, contract enforceability, and the lack of corruption, generalized trust is still an important additional predictor of economic growth.

Although in political science social capital is mostly viewed as a collective resource, several studies show its beneficial effects at the individual level as well. For example, not only do trusters engage in mutually beneficial relations more frequently (Yamagishi 2001), but they are generally more socially active, engaged, tolerant, and more inclined to support liberal rights such as minority rights and free speech (Uslaner 2002). Such individuals are also more likely to serve jury duty in the United States (ibid.), an important behavioral indicator of cooperation. Experimental evidence shows fairly conclusively that generalized trust matters for cooperation, especially in one-shot situations and in multiple n-person games, and trusters are more likely to give people a second chance (Yamagishi 2001). Clearly, generalized trust is an advantage to people and societies that possess it, as trusters are more likely to initiate cooperative relations that might be beneficial for themselves as well as for their social environment, which benefits from cooperation.

3 THE DECLINE DEBATE

Since social capital is widely seen as a useful resource to individuals or societies, Robert Putnam (1995, 2000) struck a sensitive nerve when he argued that in America this resource has steadily declined over the last decades. His description of falling membership in voluntary associations, declining volunteerism, political apathy, and rising political and social distrust seemed to confirm the civic disarray that America had experienced in recent decades. Scholars have debated and re-examined Putnam's alarming interpretations, and their applicability to other western democracies (Stolle and Hooghe 2005; Putnam 2002; Uslaner 2002).

Concerns about the erosion of social ties and social interactions are not new in the social sciences. Authors like Tönnies, Durkheim, and Weber wondered how social order and cohesion could be maintained given the political and economic modernization of western societies. Almost two decades ago, Robert Bellah and his team warned that more individualistic motivations are threatening the traditional social bonds in American society (1985). Recently, Stephen Macedo and his colleagues expressed their concern with regard to the status of political and social engagement in American society (Macedo et al. 2005).

What is the decline argument all about? According to Putnam, the loss of confidence and degradation of social ties pervades all aspects of American society. Drawing on commercial lifestyle surveys, Putnam finds a negative trend for various forms of social interactions involving face-to-face contact beyond formally organized engagements. Not only do Americans socialize less with each other, join fewer associations, and come together around the dinner table less often than some decades ago, they also refrain from conventional political involvement. For example, he shows that since the 1960s Americans have been losing trust in their government and in government institutions (see also Nye, Zelikow, and King 1997; Pharr and Putnam 2000). In addition, voter turnout and membership in traditional political groups such as parties has followed a downward spiral (Teixeira 1992; Putnam 2000, 2002; for the entire decline argument see also Macedo et al. 2005).

The underlying message is quite clear: the trend warns that the loss of community in American society may eventually destabilize democratic civic culture, which may have negative consequences for the performance of political institutions and the viability of democracy itself.

These arguments have encountered fierce academic opposition. The *Bowling Alone* thesis has been variously characterized as overly pessimistic, too traditional, or plainly wrong. A number of authors claim that the decline thesis idolizes the vanished world of the 1950s (Talbot 2000; Lowndes 2000), depicting it as pure nostalgia, a manifestation of the longing for a civic and engaged era that has clearly ended (Pollitt 1996; Lappé and Du Bois 1997). Putnam's sweeping statements have stirred reinterpretations of the available evidence on civic participation and social cohesion (Ladd 1996; Paxton 1999), in addition to a multiplicity of new comparative research efforts (Hall 1999; Putnam 2002; Torpe 2003). Three criticisms are highlighted here in particular: (1) the change from a conceptually narrow to a "kitchen sink" approach to social capital; (2) the argument about American exceptionalism; and (3) the rise of new modes of citizen involvement and social interaction.

First, the ground covered in this debate is both extremely broad and vaguely bounded. It runs the gamut of participatory and behavioral indicators. For example, measurements of social interaction, networks, trust between citizens, civic engagement and often even political participation are thrown into the debate together. Such a kitchen-sink approach to the social capital concept are criticized by adherents of the more stringent network perspective as well as by others who had hoped that Putnam's original contribution would highlight important aspects of political culture instead of expanding the notion of political culture altogether (Lin 2001; Laitin 1995).

A second critique invoked against the *Bowling Alone* thesis is that the erosion of civic life might be uniquely American. Is it true that similar trends cannot be detected in other western societies? We should distinguish between the political indicators of participation and more classic measures of social capital that are lumped together in the *Bowling Alone* account. Clearly, in Europe too, political parties and trade unions have lost members in recent decades (Ebbinghaus and Visser 1999; Mair and van

Biezen 2001). With the notable exception of the Scandinavian countries, voter turnout also shows a downward trend in most industrialized countries (Gray and Caul 2000; Jackman and Miller 1998). Scholars have recorded a systematic decline of political trust in most European countries, with notable exceptions in Germany and the Netherlands (Norris 1999; Dalton 2004). Overall, European societies are plagued, as is the United States, by political disenchantment, increasing cynicism, and political alienation.

With regard to classic social capital indicators such as generalized trust, there is no evidence of a general downward trend across European societies (Dekker and van den Broek 1998; Putnam 2002), with the exception of some Anglo-Saxon democracies (Putnam 2002, 393 ff.). Nor do the various countries assembled in *Democracies in Flux* offer any support for a clear pattern of decline in non-political associational membership in European countries (Putnam 2002). For example, associational membership is stable in Britain, and has risen in countries such as Sweden, Japan, or West Germany (ibid.). Faced with this evidence, even Putnam has acknowledged: "At the most general level, our investigation has found no general and simultaneous decline in social capital throughout the industrial/postindustrial world over the last generation" (2002, 410). So whereas most democratic countries struggle with a decline in conventional political participation, such as voting, party membership, and even political trust, social relations are not threatened to the same extent. This finding limits the generalization of the *Bowling Alone* thesis beyond the United States and at the same time offers new insights about the sources of the downward slope. If not all western democracies exhibit such similar trends, universal western experiences such as economic prosperity cannot solve the puzzle of this decline.

Finally, there is obvious disagreement about the interpretation of a downward trend. Some scholars argue that diminishing social and civic involvement indicates that citizens are quite happy and satisfied with their lives (Schudson 1998), while others believe that citizens are moving away from and are fed up with mainstream political institutions and politics and are increasingly becoming apathetic, self-oriented, and disinterested in collective issues (Bellah et al. 1985; Putnam 2000). Yet other scholars emphasize that citizens are developing a multitude of new and more suitable ways to engage in social and civic arenas, which they find more meaningful, more efficient, and more direct. For this last group of scholars, the decline in conventional social interaction and political action is not worrisome. Rather, we should expect citizens to turn away from mass political organizations, associations, and traditional social engagements (Inglehart 1997). What can be concluded about this claim so far?

Empirical research about the transformations in civic engagement and social interactions is still scarce. First analyses find a steady increase in the number of people involved in newly emerging ways of civic engagements such as internet campaigns, anti-globalization protest movements, political consumerism, and alternative lifestyle communities (Bennett 1998; Dalton 2004; Stolle, Hooghe, and Micheletti 2005). Moreover, citizens in western democracies do not just engage in the political process differently, but the changing patterns also affect the style of socializing: citizens use fewer face-to-face and traditional organizational structures in favor of horizontal and more flexible ones (Castells 1998; Wuthnow 1998). This transformation can be seen in that citizens engage more in virtual communication with each other, with effects on social contacts more generally (Shklovski, Kiesler, and Kraut forthcoming). Also, citizens rely more on informal ways of volunteering or they support organizations financially to sponsor a cause. This latter phenomenon is called the rise of checkbook memberships (Skocpol 1996).

Currently, researchers debate whether the counter-trend of new modes of citizen political engagement and social interaction might substitute for the loss in traditional and conventional engagement and interaction. In the Putnamian conceptualization of social capital and citizen engagement, face-to-face social interaction and conventional political involvement, such as in voluntary organizations, serve as a standard litmus test for the health of a given society. They are valued over the newer or emerging forms for several reasons. First, the socialization function of face-to-face interaction implies that they train citizens or members of associations into a more civically oriented mindset, which in turn leaves them better disposed toward cooperation, trust, and reciprocity. The available evidence on this effect, however, is at best rather mixed (see more on this below). Second, doubters of emerging forms of participation and interaction point out that they are usually performed alone, and tend to be much more individualized and less collective in nature (hence the title "*Bowling Alone*") than face-to-face interactions or conventional participation. To use the image of bowling, if people bowl alone or simply with friends instead of in leagues, the danger is that they are exposed only to a narrow range of the population—which again limits socialization effects. Similarly, for emerging forms of participation, most participants simply perform such acts alone or outside the framework of traditional political organizations. They can access a political website at home before their computer screen, forward a political email from their office, sign a petition on the street, or purchase or boycott products for political reasons in the supermarket alone. The question is whether individualized actions might still address collective issues and concerns (Micheletti 2003). Third, face-to-face interactions in voluntary associations in particular are seen as important because of the external link they provide between citizens and the state. They offer vital (if, for the most part, indirect) access for citizens wanting to influence state and governmental affairs. Intermediary organizations aggregate individual interests, and thus contribute to processes of complexity reduction and gatekeeping that are necessary for a political system to function effectively.

Finally, critics claim that newly emerging action repertoires establish even stronger patterns of persistent inequalities than conventional forms of participation (Verba, Schlozman, and Brady 1995; Skocpol 2003), as they may exclude a large group of the population from broad-based participation. However, before we can draw any conclusions about the potential of these emerging forms of political engagement and social interactions for substituting the functions of the conventional forms, more systematic analyses of their character, style, and consequences are needed. This is no easy undertaking: Given that these forms of participation and engagement are more fluid, sporadic, less organized, and consequently much harder to detect accurately, particularly through the means of survey research, their empirical study is a particular challenge compared to the study of institutionalized, conventional forms of action.

4 THE SOURCES OF SOCIAL CAPITAL

If social capital possesses all the advantages evinced by the theory and empirical research to date, the question of how it can be produced, maintained, or even destroyed logically follows. Why do some people have more resourceful networks or can more easily engage in trusting relationships than others? Why can citizens in some regions or villages join together and solve their collective action problems easily while others cannot? These questions are prompted by the growing conviction that the answers are crucial to personal well-being, political stability, and to economic development.

Two discussions shape the debate here. One concerns the extent to which local, regional, or national patterns of social capital are formed by historical factors or by contemporary forces. Another disagreement exists between those who view the origins of social capital from a bottom-up perspective versus those who prefer a top-down approach. The former scholars view social capital as residing mainly in the realm of civil society, centered chiefly in groups of voluntary associations, and largely disconnected from the state and political institutions (Putnam 1993; Fukuyama 1995). The latter group argues that social capital flourishes when it is embedded in and linked to formal political institutions (Levi 1998; Rothstein 2005; Rothstein and Stolle in press; Tarrow 1996). In this latter account, the capacity of citizens to develop cooperative ties is also determined by the effects of state policy so that institutional engineering might foster social capital. The following section reviews the most important debates and empirical findings about the causes and origins of social capital.

4.1 The Institutional Sources of Social Capital

Institutionalists highlight the role and independent impact of the state and *contemporary* political institutions in shaping societal patterns of and individual access to social capital vis-à-vis other factors. In addition, there is a debate about which institutional aspects and characteristics matter most for the successful development of social capital. These two debates will be discussed in the remainder of this section.

Putnam (1995), Fukuyama (1995), and Banfield (1958) draw a bottom-up model of social capital creation. Putnam (1993), for example, traces social capital in medieval

Italy, explaining how, in the south, Norman mercenaries built a powerful feudal monarchy with hierarchical structures, whereas in the north, communal republics based on horizontal relationships fostered mutual assistance and economic cooperation. Putnam seeks to demonstrate that the "civicness" of the north survived natural catastrophes and political changes. In addition, he points out that the civic regions were not wealthier in the first place. The implications of this view have left many social scientists and policy makers dissatisfied: societies that are low on social capital are simply stuck in a path-dependent quagmire of distrust, and there seems to be little that can be done about it. However, in his later work Putnam (2000) makes clear that we need to make a distinction between short-term and long-term influences on social capital although they are left unspecified.

Sidney Tarrow has thoroughly criticized the bottom-up model that Putnam presents; he argues that the "state plays a fundamental role in shaping civic capacity" (Tarrow 1996, 395). Similarly, Margaret Levi (1998) disapproves of Putnam's exclusive concentration on historical patterns and societal origins of social capital and suggests that policy performance can be just as much a source of trust as a result.[4] Skocpol, Ganz, and Munson (2000) also argue that historically the development of voluntary associations as large umbrella organizations depended much on state support.

To what extent do states have an independent effect on social capital? At the most aggregate level, political systems have been identified as being related to social capital (Almond and Verba 1963; Paxton 2002). Generally, authoritarianism, or what Booth and Bayer Richard (1998) label "repression level" in their analysis of selected Central American countries, is found to have a strong, negative influence on social capital. Repressive governments disturb civic developments in two other major ways: first, they discourage spontaneous group activity, and second, they discourage trust (Booth and Bayes Richard 1998, 43). Even though totalitarian governments, such as communist regimes, mobilize civil society through party and other governmental organizations, associations are always state controlled and often not voluntary (Howard 2003). Generally, authoritarian and totalitarian governments seem partially to build their strength on the foundation of distrust among their citizens (however, see Letki and Evans 2005 for an alternative view). A good example of this is found in the activities of the (East) German Democratic Republic's state secret police, which pitted citizens against each other and provoked tight social control among friends, neighbors, and colleagues, and even within the family (Sztompka 1995). From this perspective, the Norman Kingdom in Southern Italy should be primarily viewed as an oppressive regime that damaged and destroyed social capital, yet the difference from Putnam's interpretation here is that these long-term effects could be overcome with the implementation of different types of institutions.

These insights about the role of political systems have also been widely documented empirically. For example, the density of associational memberships and other

---

[4] This insight has also been pointed out by Brehm and Rahn (1997). Although they did not use an institutional structural approach, at the individual level they found that within a US sample using the GSS confidence in institutions has a larger effect on interpersonal trust than the other way around, even though they see both types of trust as influencing each other (Brehm and Rahn 1997, 1014 ff.).

formal networks, as well as generalized trust levels, are significantly lower in countries that have experienced periods of non-democratic governments (Howard 2003; Inglehart 1997). Although authoritarian and democratic regimes seem related to substantial differences in social capital at the country level, various types of democratic systems also differ in the patterns and levels of social capital.

So, what aspects of democratic government shape social capital? Although empirical research is still scarce, there are many arguments about how types of welfare states and regimes affect the availability and access to social capital. For example, researchers claim that universal welfare states are better able to constrain the socioeconomic inequalities within their population, and there is no doubt that such inequalities influence patterns of social cohesion and interaction. Citizens who see their fellow citizens as equals and as "one of their own" might more easily make a leap of faith, engaging with and giving a "trust credit" to people they do not necessarily know. Evidence shows that such correlations exist, and, in addition, temporal variations in trust levels strongly correlate with temporal variations in income equality in the United States (see Uslaner 2002).

Second, welfare state institutions also influence the values, attitudes, and civic spirit in a given country. Some welfare states might emphasize values of impartiality, fairness, and procedural justice more than others; this in turn affects the fabric of how people relate to one another. The most plausible distinction can be made between selective and *universal* forms of public service (Kumlin and Rothstein 2005; Rothstein and Stolle in press). Selective programs have a divisive character. In their essence, welfare states that are predominantly based on such programs are designed to pit groups of the population against each other. Alternatively, the principle of universality means that access to many social programs (such as old-age pensions, health care, childcare, child allowances, and health insurance) is not targeted to "the poor," but instead covers the entire population (or easily defined segments) without consideration of their ability to pay (Kumlin and Rothstein 2005; Rothstein and Stolle in press; Esping-Andersen 1999; Rothstein 2005).

This last discussion points to important overall characteristics of state institutions that seem related to patterns of social capital: the implementation of the principles of impartiality and fairness. If institutions of law and order, which detect and punish people who break contracts, offer or take bribes or engage in corrupt and biased practices themselves, citizens make inferences from such practices to other citizens. They will conclude that corruption causes their fellow citizens to act in a corrupt manner, and they will feel obliged themselves to engage in corrupt practices. So, if citizens cannot trust the institutional effectiveness and fairness of the judicial system and the police because of corruption, then their view of others is compromised; conversely, fair and impartial practices facilitate trust and social interactions (Levi 1998; Rothstein and Stolle forthcoming).

In sum, social-democratic type welfare states as well as countries with non-corrupt state institutions have features that enable broad high levels of social capital within the population. The empirical evidence confirms that people in these countries exhibit the highest levels of social capital in the western world. As far as we know, generalized trust levels are the highest in Scandinavia and have been maintained there, as opposed to the United States or other Anglo-Saxon democracies, where they gradually declined over the last decades (Putnam 2000). Similarly, there is a strong correlation between corruption indices and institutional impartiality measures and social capital (Delhey and Newton 2005; Rothstein and Stolle forthcoming; You 2005).

Although the institutional approach delivers an important addition to the debate about the sources of social capital, which implies that this societal resource is embedded in its institutional context, there are still problems with this approach. Whereas the correlations between selected institutional characteristics and social capital are very strong and the causal mechanisms well thought out, there are still several accounts that deliver the exact opposite interpretation of the causal arrow. Inglehart (1997) insists on a causal logic from political culture to the stability of democracy. Similarly, Newton and Norris (2000) interpret a positive correlation between political and social trust at the aggregate national level as evidence that social capital "can help build effective social and political institutions, and this in turn encourages confidence in civic institutions." As in the logic presented in Putnam's work, social relationships shape the experience of governmental institutions and ultimately their performance. These contradictory interpretations of the strong relationship between social capital and institutions imply that much more work needs to be done to disentangle the causal arrows and mechanisms. Better analyses of institutional change over time and its effects on social capital could strengthen the institutionalist accounts, whereas societal interpretations would benefit from a better discussion of the causal mechanisms involved.[5] These issues are part of the social capital research agenda.

4.2 The Role of Voluntary Associations and Social Interactions

Most accounts of social capital rely predominantly on the importance of social interactions and voluntary associations and thus pay less attention to the institutional accounts presented above. In this section we distinguish between the network-oriented and the attitudinal approaches to social capital. In the former, more sociological tradition, the structure of networks (such as differences between weak and strong ties) determines the access to social capital and related resources provided in these social relationships (Granovetter 1973; see also section 2 above). The latter follows the Tocquevillian tradition, and associations or social groups are seen as creators of social capital because of their socialization effects on democratic and cooperative values and norms. Associations and social interactions function as

---

[5] For example, if social capital influences institutional performance, little is known *how* trusting people create better service performance and more democratically responsive local politicians, although see a discussion in by Boix and Posner (1998).

"learning schools for democracy." We focus here more on network characteristics and their expected socialization effects in the political science tradition.

The attitudinal approach that focuses on the primacy of networks and associations as sources of civic values starts from a collective logic. It claims that in areas with stronger, dense, horizontal, and more cross-cutting networks, there is a spillover from the membership in organizations to the development of cooperative values and norms that citizens develop (Putnam refers to this effect as the "rainmaker" effect, see Pharr and Putnam 2000). The problem with this approach is the lack of an apparent theory on how social interactions at the individual level generate civic values, as well as empirical findings that support such a theory.

There is some evidence that countries with dense social networks also exhibit more generalized trust and other civic values at the individual level (Putnam 1995; Inglehart 1997). However, evidence for a causal flow from joining to trusting has not been confirmed so far (Uslaner 2002; Stolle 2001; Delhey and Newton 2005; Claiborn and Martin 2000). Uslaner (2002, ch. 5) generally uncovers minimal effects of group membership, calling civic engagement "moral dead ends." Moreover, while associational members are often found to be more trusting in western democracies, Stolle (2001) shows that this is due mostly to processes of self-selection.

The importance of groups and social interactions for the development of civic values and attitudes has not been dismissed entirely. Instead the research agenda has changed in three different ways. First, research is determining which aspects of social interactions and group membership are supportive and facilitative of civic values. Second, the notion of group membership has expanded to include not just formal memberships in voluntary associations, but also informal social interactions. And third, whereas adult socialization effects in groups are rarely found, there is a renewed interest in how adolescents are shaped by various group experiences. We will examine these issues briefly in turn.

Several hypotheses guide the research on which types of groups are more important for the development of civic attitudes and values. First and most important, face-to-face interactions should be more productive of civic attitudes than so-called "checkbook" organizations in which members do not interact directly. However, Wollebaek and Selle (2003) have shown that there is not necessarily a significant difference between active or passive association members. Second, memberships in hierarchical associations, such as the Catholic Church in southern Italy, which do not create mutuality and equality of participation, do not have the same effect as memberships of social capital-rich groups (Putnam 1993). This distinction turns out difficult to test. Third, the group experiences might be even more pronounced in their impact when the members of the group are diverse and from different backgrounds. This type of group interaction, which is called bridging (Putnam 1993, 90), brings members into contact with people from a cross-section of society. As a result, the formative experience is likely to be more pronounced than if the association is a narrowly constituted segment of society (Putnam 2000; Rogers et al. 1975).

So far, none of these hypotheses has been successfully confirmed by empirical research. The research agenda has shifted to include more informal social relationships that are perhaps more frequent and allow potentially for more diverse interactions. Scholars who work on gender relations have echoed this move, as women in particular tend to prefer more informal social networks (Lowndes 2000).

The debate about the importance of bridging ties in formal and informal settings has opened a whole new agenda in social capital research. This discussion is embedded in the larger debate about rising diversity in western democracies. Changing patterns of immigration, perceptions of the increase in the numbers of refugees and asylum seekers in Europe, tighter battles about distributional policies in the wake of crumbling welfare states, the overdue rising visibility of ethnic and racial minorities in public institutions, as well as increasing socioeconomic inequalities in North America, have certainly contributed to an expanding debate about the consequences of diversity for social cohesion or social capital.

Contrary to original beliefs, studies on how the composition of neighborhoods influences civic attitudes found that increasing levels of diversity pose a challenge to generalized trust and redistributive values in our modern democratic societies (Soroka, Helliwell, and Johnston 2006; Costa and Kahn 2003; Alesina and La Ferrara 2000). However, other studies have not confirmed such negative effects or show that social interactions in heterogeneous places were more beneficial than those in places where people were more racially similar (Marschall and Stolle 2004). And looking at a very different kind of diversity, Mutz found that political discussions in diverse networks with others who hold opposing viewpoints also have been found to positively influence political tolerance (Mutz 2002). These seemingly contradictory results about the effects of diversity on social cohesion or attitudinal social capital call for further investigation into how racial, ethnic, or political compositions across various units influence the societal fabric and the ability to cooperate.

Finally, if there is an effect of membership in associations and other types of social interactions on civic attitudes, it seems plausible that it will be more pronounced during the early period of one's life. The available research on political socialization strongly suggests that experiences during childhood, youth, and adolescence— whether in the family, at school, or within peer groups—shape enduring patterns of social and political attitudes (see Jennings chapter in this volume; Allerbeck, Jennings, and Rosenmayr 1979; Hess and Torney 1968; Youniss, McLellan, and Yates 1997). The most recent research opens the social capital agenda to the insights of socialization, family, and youth research.

In sum, the study of associations, networks and groups as sources of social capital has made many advances despite its inherent theoretical and empirical problems. The widespread accusations that social capital research ignores the fact that certain associations or groups are detrimental for the provision of resources, norms, and trust is now utterly outdated. The research agenda has advanced far beyond the pure insight that networks have value.

5 CONCLUSION

Social capital is an important societal resource. In social science, the concept of social capital is currently receiving considerable academic attention, and rightly so, because it has been shown to play a considerable role in our political and social lives. Furthermore, the concept of social capital allows us to operationalize important aspects of political culture and to use political culture as an explanatory variable in cross-national settings. Several cross-national data collections are currently being constructed in order to address the various patterns and levels of social capital across a variety of political systems, institutions, and societal traditions (see the discussion of the World Values Survey, European Social Survey, and other projects in the chapter by Kittilson in this volume).

Perhaps the most interesting aspect of social capital is that this concept has a variety of interdisciplinary roots, which lead to some fundamentally different approaches to studying and measuring social capital. Managing these different approaches under the umbrella of the social capital concept is a challenge. Although the differences in the political science and sociological approaches to social capital can mostly be captured in the varying emphasis on which component of social capital matters (attitudes versus networks) and which type of outcome variables are studied, this has often led to sharp mutual criticisms and misunderstandings. For example, one paradox elucidated in this chapter is that in network approaches, the effects of social ties and group memberships are treated as consequences of social capital, whereas in attitudinal approaches membership in networks and groups might be viewed as sources of social capital.

Besides these interdisciplinary challenges, the social capital research agenda should help to disentangle issues of cause and effect. Since this is not yet resolved, researchers run into the paradox that the relationship between social capital and political institutions, for example, is interpreted both as a consequence and as a cause of social capital. Although the discovery of larger patterns is interesting, this does not resolve policy issues of how social capital can be maintained and nurtured, for example. It is therefore essential that research on social capital predominantly adopts research designs that go beyond pure correlations. Longitudinal and cross-national data collections as well as field experiments in this area should be encouraged. The attention to childhood experiences and youth socialization are also welcome innovations that further advance this rich research agenda.

REFERENCES

ALESINA, A., and LA FERRARA, E. 2000. The determinants of trust. NBER working paper series, No. 7621.

ALLERBECK, K., JENNINGS, M. K., and ROSENMAYR, L. 1979. Generations and families. Pp. 487–521 in Political Action, ed. S. Barnes, M. Kaase, et al. Beverly Hills: Sage.

ALMOND, G. A., and VERBA, S. 1963. *The Civic Culture*. Princeton: Princeton University Press.

BANFIELD, E. C. 1958. *The Moral Basis of a Backward Society*. New York: The Free Press.

BELLAH, R. et al. 1985. *Habits of the Heart*. Berkeley: University of California Press.

BENNETT, W. L. 1998. The uncivic culture: communication, identity, and the rise of lifestyle politics. *Political Science and Politics*, 31 (4): 741–61.

BERRY, J., PORTNEY, K., and THOMSON, K. 1993. *The Rebirth of Urban Democracy*. Washington, DC: Brookings.

BOIX, C., and POSNER, D. 1998. Social capital: explaining its origins and effects on government performance. *British Journal of Political Science*, 28 (4): 686–95.

BOOTH, J., and BAYER RICHARD, P. 1998. Civil society and political context in Central America. *American Behavioral Scientist*, 42: 33–46.

BREHM, J., and RAHN, W. 1997. Individual level evidence for the causes and consequences of social capital. *American Journal of Political Science*, 41: 999–1023.

BURT, R. 1998. The gender of social capital. *Rationality and Society*, 10: 5–46.

CASTELLS, M. 1997. *The Rise of the Network Society*. Oxford: Blackwell.

CLAIBORN, M. P., and MARTIN, P. S. 2000. Trusting and joining? An empirical test of the reciprocal nature of social capital. *Political Behavior*, 22: 267–91.

COLEMAN, J. S. 1988. Social capital in the creation of human capital. *American Journal of Sociology*, 94: S95–S120.

—— 1990. *Foundations of Social Theory*. Cambridge, Mass.: Belknap.

COSTA, D., and KAHN, M. 2003. Civic engagement and community heterogeneity: an economist's perspective. *Perspectives in Politics* 1 (1): 103–11.

DALTON, R. 2004. *Democratic Challenges, Democratic Choices: The Erosion of Political Support in Advanced Industrial Democracies*. Oxford: Oxford University Press.

DEKKER, P., and VAN DEN BROEK, A. 1998. Civil society in comparative perspective: involvement in voluntary associations in North America and Western Europe. *Voluntas*, 9 (1): 11–38.

DELHEY, J., and NEWTON, K. 2005. Predicting cross-national levels of social trust: global pattern or nordic exceptionalism? *European Sociological Review*, 21 (4): 311–27.

EBBINGHAUS, B., and VISSER, J. 1999. When institutions matter: union growth and decline in Western Europe, 1950–1995. *European Sociological Review*, 15 (2): 135–58.

ERICKSON, B. 2001. Good networks and good jobs: the value of social capital to employers and employees. Pp. 127–58 in *Social capital: Theory and Research*, ed. N. Lin, K. Cook, and R. Burt. New York: Aldine de Gryuter.

ESPING-ANDERSEN, G. 1999. *Social Foundations of Postindustrial Economies*. Oxford: Oxford University Press.

FOLEY, M., and EDWARDS, B. 1999. Is It Time to Disinvest in Social Capital? *Journal of Public Policy* 19 (2): 141–73.

FUKUYAMA, F. 1995. *Trust: The Social Virtues and Creation of Prosperity*. London: Hamish Hamilton.

GALSTON, M. 2004. Civic renewal and the regulation of nonprofits. *Cornell Journal of Law and Public Policy*, 13 (289): 401 ff.

GRANOVETTER, M. S. 1973. The Strength of Weak Ties. *American Journal of Sociology*, 78: 1360–80.

GRAY, M., and CAUL, M. 2000. Declining voter turnout in advanced democracies. *Comparative Political Studies*, 33 (9): 1091–121.

HALL, P. A. 1999. Social capital in Britain. *British Journal of Political Science*, 29 (3): 417–61.

HARDIN, R. 2004. *Trust and Trustworthiness*. New York: Russell Sage Foundation Pubs.

HERREROS, F. 2004. *The Problem of Forming Social Capital: Why Trust?* New York: Palgrave/ Macmillan.

HESS, R., and TORNEY, J. (1968). *The Development of Political Attitudes in Children*. Garden City, NY: Doubleday.

HOWARD, M. 2003. *The Weakness of Civil Society in Post-Communist Europe*. Cambridge: Cambridge University Press.

INGLEHART, R. 1997. *Modernization and Postmodernization: Cultural, Economic, and Political Change in 43 societies*. Princeton: Princeton University Press.

—— 1999. Trust, well-being and democracy. Pp. 88–120 in *Democracy and Trust*, ed. M. E. Warren. Cambridge: Cambridge University Press.

JACKMAN, R. W., and MILLER, R. A. 1998. Social capital and politics. *Annual Review of Political Science*, 1: 47–73.

KNACK, S., and KEEFER, P. 1997. Does social capital have an economic payoff? A cross-country investigation. *Quarterly Journal of Economics*, 112: 1251–88.

KUMLIN, S., and ROTHSTEIN, B. 2005. Making and breaking social capital: the impact of welfare state institutions. *Comparative Political Studies*, 38: 339–65.

LADD, E. C. 1996. The data just do not show the erosion of America's social capital. *Public Perspective*, 7: 1, 5–6.

LAPPÉ, F. M., and DU BOIS, P. M. 1997. Building social capital without looking backward. *National Civic Review*, February 14.

LAITIN, D. D. 1995. The civic culture at 30. *American Political Science Review*, 89: 168–73.

LETKI, N., and EVANS, G. 2005. Endogenizing social trust: democratization in East-Central Europe. *British Journal of Political Science*, 35: 515–29.

LEVI, M. 1998. A state of trust. Pp. 77–101 in *Trust and Governance*, ed. V. Braithwaite and M. Levi. New York: Russell Sage Foundation.

LIN, N. 2001. *Social Capital: A Theory of Social Structure and Action*. Cambridge: Cambridge University Press.

—— COOK, K., and BURT, R. 2001. *Social Capital: Theory and Research*. New York: Aldine de Gruyter.

LISTHAUG, O. 1995. The dynamics of trust in politicians. Pp. 261–97 in *Citizens and the State*, ed. H.-D. Klingemann and D. Fuchs. Oxford: Oxford University Press.

LOWNDES, V. 2000. Women and social capital. *British Journal of Political Science*, 30 (3): 533–7.

MACEDO, S. et al. 2005. *Democracy at Risk*. Washington, DC: Brookings Institution.

MAIR, P., and VAN BIEZEN, I. 2001. Party membership in twenty European democracies, 1980–2000. *Party Politics*, 7 (1): 5–22.

MARSCHALL, M., and STOLLE D. 2004. Race and the city: neighborhood context and the development of generalized trust. *Political Behavior*, 26 (2): 126–53.

MICHELETTI, M. 2003. *Political Virtue and Shopping: Individuals, Consumerism, and Collective Action*. New York: Palgrave.

MUTZ, D. C. 2002. Cross-cutting social networks: testing democratic theory in practice. *American Political Science Review*, 96 (1): 111–26.

NEWTON, K., and NORRIS, P. 2000. Confidence in public institutions. Pp. 52–73 in *Disaffected Democracies: What's Troubling the Trilateral Countries*, ed. S. J. Pharr and R. D. Putnam. Princeton: Princeton University Press.

NORRIS, P. ed. 1999. *Critical Citizens: Global Support for Democratic Government*. Oxford: Oxford University Press.

NYE, J., ZELIKOW, P., and KING, D. eds. 1997. *Why People don't Trust Government*. Cambridge, Mass.: Harvard University Press.

PAXTON, P. 1999. Is social capital declining in the United States? A mutiple indicator assessment. *American Journal of Sociology*, 105 (1): 88–127.

—— 2002. Social capital and democracy: an interdependent relationship. *American Sociological Review*, 67: 254–77.

PHARR, S., and PUTNAM, R. eds. 2000. *Disaffected Democracies*. Princeton: Princeton University Press.

POLLITT, K. 1996. For whom the ball rolls. *The Nation*, 262 (April 15): 9.

PORTES, A. 1998. Social capital: its origins and applications in modern sociology. *Annual Review of Sociology*, 24: 1–24.

PUTNAM, R. D. 1993. *Making Democracy Work*. Princeton: Princeton University Press.

—— 1995. Bowling alone: America's declining social capital. *Journal of Democracy*, 6 (1): 65–78.

—— 2000. *Bowling Alone: The Collapse and Revival of American Community*. Simon & Schuster.

—— 2002. *Democracies in Flux: The Evolution of Social Capital in Contemporary Society*. Oxford: Oxford University Press.

ROGERS, D., BULTENA, G., and BARB, K. 1975. Voluntary associations membership and political participation: an exploration of the mobilization hypothesis. *Sociological Quarterly*, 16: 305–18.

ROTHSTEIN, B. 2005. *Social Traps and the Problem of Trust*. Cambridge: Cambridge University Press.

—— and STOLLE, D. In press. Political institutions and generalized trust. In *The Handbook of Social Capital*, ed. D. Castiglione, J. W. van Deth, and G. Wolleb. Oxford: Oxford University Press.

—— —— Forthcoming. The State and Social Capital: An Institutional Theory of Generalized Trust. *Comparative Politics*.

SCHUDSON, M. 1998. *The Good Citizen*. New York: Free Press.

SELIGSON, A. 1999. Civic Association and democratic participation in Central America: a test of the Putnam thesis. *Comparative Political Studies*, 32 (3): 342–62.

SHKLOVSKI, I., KIESLER, S. and KRAUT, R. E. Forthcoming. The internet and social interaction: a meta-analysis and critique of studies, 1995–2003. In *Domesticating Information Technology*, ed. R. Kraut, M. Brynin, and S. Kiesler. Oxford: Oxford University Press.

SKOCPOL, T. 1996. Unravelling from above. *American Prospect*, 25: 20–5.

—— 2003. *Diminished Democracy: From Membership to Management in American Civic Life*. Norman: University of Oklahoma Press.

—— GANZ, M., and MUNSON, Z. 2000. A nation of organizers: the institutional origins of civic voluntarism in the United States. *American Political Science Review*, 94: 527–46.

SOROKA, S., HELLIWELL, J., and JOHNSTON, R. 2006. Measuring and Modelling Trust. Pp. 95–132 in *Social Capital, Diversity and the Welfare State*, ed. Fiona Kay and Richard Johnston. Vancouver: UBC Press.

STOLLE, D. 2001. Clubs and congregations: the benefits of joining an association. Pp. 202–44 in *Trust in Society*, ed. K. Cook. New York: Russell Sage Foundation.

—— and HOOGHE, M. 2005. Inaccurate, exceptional, one-sided or irrelevant? The debate about the alleged decline of social capital and civic engagement in western societies. *British Journal of Political Science*, 34 (4): 703–21.

—— —— and MICHELETTI, M. 2005. Politics in the super-market—political consumerism as a form of political participation. *International Review of Political Science*, 26 (3): 245–69.

SZTOMPKA, P. 1995. Vetrauen: Die fehlende Ressource in der Postkommunistischen Gesellschaft. Pp. 254–76 in *Politische Institutionen im Wandel*, ed. B. Nedelmann. Special Issue of *Kölner Zeitschrift fur Sozialwissenschaft* 35.

TALBOT, M. 2000. Who wants to be a legionnaire? A book review of Robert D. Putnam's Bowling Alone: The Collapse and Revival of American Community. *New York Times*, June 25.

TARROW, S. 1996. Making social science work across space and time: a critical reflection on Robert Putnam's Making Democracy Work. *American Political Science Review*, 90: 389–97.

TEIXEIRA, R. 1992. *The Disappearing American Voter*. Washington, DC.: Brookings Institution.

TEORELL, J. 2003. Linking social capital to political participation: voluntary associations and networks of recruitment in Sweden. *Scandinavian Political Studies*, 26 (1): 49.

TOCQUEVILLE, A. DE 1961. *Democracy in America*. New York: Schocken Books; originally published 1835.

TORPE, L. 2003. Social capital in Denmark: a deviant case? *Scandinavian Political Studies*, 26 (1): 27.

USLANER, E. M. 2002. *The Moral Value of Trust*. Cambridge: Cambridge University Press.

VARSHNEY, A. 2002. *Ethnic Conflict and Civic Life: Hindus and Muslims in India*, New Haven: Yale University Press.

VERBA S., SCHLOZMAN K., and BRADY, H. 1995. *Voice and Equality: Civic Volunteerism in American Politics*. Cambridge, Mass.: Harvard University Press.

WOLLEBAEK, D., and SELLE, P. 2003. The importance of passive membership for social capital formation. Pp. 67–88 in *Generating Social Capital*, ed. M. Hooghe and D. Stolle. New York: Palgrave.

WUTHNOW, R. 1998. *Loose Connections: Joining Together in America's Fragmented Communities*. Cambridge, Mass.: Harvard University Press.

YAMAGISHI, T. 2001. Trust as a form of social intelligence. Pp. 121–47 in *Trust in Society*, ed. K. Cook. Thousand Oaks, Calif.: Sage Publication.

YOU, J.-S. 2005. Corruption and inequality as correlates of social trust: fairness matters more than similarity. Unpublished Working Paper.

YOUNISS, J., McLELLAN, J., and YATES, M. 1997. What we know about engendering civic identity. *American Behavioral Scientist*, 40: 620–35.

ZAK, P. J., and KNACK, S. 2001. Trust and Growth. *Economic Journal*, 111 (470): 295–321.

CHAPTER 36

CIVIL SOCIETY AND DEMOCRATIZATION

EDMUND WNUK-LIPIŃSKI

For much of the twentieth century the concept of civil society was hardly at the center of attention of sociological and political thought. Researchers somewhat neglected the concept, or at least less frequently mentioned it as one of the primary analytical categories of social science. They believed that civil society was but an epiphenomenon of a democratic state. Only the democratic state, it was thought, was capable of facilitating the freedom of association, that *sine qua non* of civil society. Furthermore, researchers felt that civic virtues evolved and were learned within the voluntary associations of free people; civic skills and virtues were not inherited but were gained from the democratic environment, above all through the participation in voluntary associations. These skills and values are then internalized and adopted as one's own, as individualized forms of participation in the life of a community organized and protected by a democratic state. This way of thinking continues to function to this very day (e.g. Walzer 1992; Kotzé and du Toit 2005*a*).

If the existence of civic society is derived from a democratic state, then it is only natural to focus on the state and on the democratic system of government rather than on civil society itself. However, this begs the question of how democratic systems emerge in the first place; they must have been created by those who, though functioning in a non-democratic environment, felt that democratic procedures and values were better than what they had previously experienced. History teaches us that although the democratic system of government provides "continuing education" on civic values, of equal importance, and epistemologically more interesting, is a

* I would like to thank Hans-Dieter Klingemann and Russell Dalton for helpful comments on the draft version of this chapter.

situation in which the attachment to civic values is shared only by some individuals or groups, despite the undemocratic environment in which they live.

Developments in central and eastern Europe as well as in South Korea, the Philippines, and a number of Latin American countries over the final decades of the twentieth century turned analysts' attention to grassroots social movements that build civic attitudes against a backdrop of non-democratic regimes and whose actions eventually lead to the erosion and collapse of non-democratic systems. In particular, the emergence of the Solidarity movement in Poland in 1980 created a strong impulse for students of democracy to pay closer attention to the role of civil society as such, and particularly its role in the process of the democratization of autocratic states.

This is not to say that the idea of civil society was invented concurrently with the collapse of communism. Its variants have accompanied systematic reflection upon the organization of human societies at least since Aristotle. Aristotle's "political community" may be regarded as the beginning of a long chain of ideas established to account for that special category of human communities whose members are not only able to transcend the requirements of individual survival but who also posses the ability and the will to influence the ways in which the community functions. This category of communities, known to ancient Romans as *societas civilis*, was defined as a community of citizens who are free and equal before the law and who are governed according to explicit rules embedded in shared norms and values. *Societas civilis* captures the essence of the kind of community which is today often referred as civil society. This type of community is the main interest of this chapter. Our secondary interest is democratization, the process of transition from a non-democratic to a democratic system of government, especially in what Huntington (1991) called "the third wave of democratization" in the late twentieth century.

I begin with an elucidation of the concept of civil society, as there is a considerable, and one might say rather usual within the social sciences, confusion about its meaning, particularly when the relationship between civil society and the state is considered.

I must also clarify the notion of democratization, understood here as the transition from an autocratic to a democratic system of government. Democratization in South America, Southeast Asia, and notably the collapse of the global communist system and the resulting changes in eastern and central Europe challenged not only the extant theories of civil societies, but also the theories of transition from autocratic to democratic systems of government.

The changes in eastern and central Europe are epistemologically interesting for yet another reason. The liberation of nation-states from external domination when combined with democratization leads to a reintegration of society around new collective objectives, values, and norms. Two separate dimensions of the formation of a community are simultaneously set in motion by democratization of this type: the national and civic. Both of these dimensions are governed by separate operational principles, both define the status of an individual differently; both set separate criteria for community membership.

The relationship between these two aspects, the *ethnos* and the *demos* of a community position the individual within the key dimensions of social reality. Analysis of this relationship enables us to elaborate upon the nature of the system emerging from the process of democratization. Finally, this chapter addresses the question of the quality of a civil society arising from the transition to democracy from a previously undemocratic system. I focus on that facet of civil society which is primarily determined by the political culture.

1 CIVIL SOCIETY: A CONCEPTUALIZATION

A variety of conceptualizations of civil society can be found in literature (also see chapter by Stolle in this volume). For the most part, theoretical differences in this area result not so much from diverse assumptions, or even from diverse research objectives, but from substantive considerations of deeper theoretical significance, namely a conception of the relationship between the individual and society. Additionally, such differences result from the conception of citizens' rights and the role of citizens in public life. Finally, and most importantly, these variations result from explicit or implicit assumptions regarding the role of the state and its relation to various social groupings, organized and functioning within the public sphere.

Under the simplest of definitions, civil society *is the totality of non-state institutions, organizations and civic associations functioning in the public domain. These are grassroots organizations which are relatively autonomous from the state and based on voluntary membership.*

Even this rather general definition does not yield a common denomination of various approaches to the concept of civil society. A number of approaches incorporate markets (Pérez-Díaz 1996), while others view civil society as a social space (Colás 2002), filled with "non-coerced human association and also a set of relational networks" (Walzer 1992, 89). There are also more elaborate treatments of civil society as a normative model, separate from the economy and the state and which possess the following components: (1) *Plurality*: families, informal groups, and voluntary associations whose plurality and autonomy allow for variety of forms of life; (2) *Publicity*: institutions of culture and communication; (3) *Legality*: structures of general laws and basic rights needed to demarcate plurality, privacy, and publicity from, at least, the state and (...) the economy. Together, these structures secure the institutional existence of a modern differentiated civil society" (Cohen and Arato 1992, 346).

Given this multiplicity of approaches, it is not feasible to develop a single framework to contain them all, especially if they are considered in the context of democratization. Therefore, for the purpose of the present argument, I shall conceptualize "civil society" from a somewhat different angle.

As Charles Taylor (1994) noted, we can think of civil society in three different forms. In the most general sense, civil society exists everywhere where there is room for the existence of free associations that are not controlled by the state. In a narrower sense, we would restrict the term "civil society" only to a situation in which society as a whole is able to organize and coordinate its activities without state supervision. Finally, we may understand civil society as a network of associations which are able to significantly influence current state policies or may even produce a change to state policy in a certain area. In the first meaning, some elements of civil society may even exist in a non-democratic environment (dissident groups of citizens in authoritarian states whose existence is tolerated by the state, for example). The second meaning refers to civil society in democratic states and is the standard understanding of the concept in the literature. The third meaning indicates the possible effects of autonomous civic activities in relation to the state (democratic and autocratic alike). Charles Taylor's distinction is particularly helpful in tracing the ways in which the democratization of autocratic regimes is brought about through the pressure of internal social forces which are self-organized against the oppressive, non-democratic state.

I begin with the specification of the key prerequisites that must be met for a civil society to emerge. These prerequisites determine whether the social space for a civil society is available and what shape the civil society will eventually take. I shall then consider the factors facilitating the willingness of citizens to participate in civil society. Moreover, I locate civil society in a social space and present the various types of relations between the diverse organizational structures of civil society and how they relate to society at large. Finally, I describe the functions that can be attributed to the various forms of social activity undertaken within civil society.

The conceptualization presented here relates to a civil society that is formed and then operates within the ramifications of a democratic nation-state. Indeed, it is difficult to imagine the existence of civil society without its indispensable point of reference, namely the nation-state. Linz and Stepan go even further as they treat the prior existence of statehood as the necessary prerequisite of a democratic system of government. "Democracy," they argue, "is a form of governance of a state. Thus, no modern polity can become democratically consolidated unless it is first a state" (Linz and Stepan 1996, 7). This begs the question of utmost theoretical importance: What comes first—the democratic state followed by a civil society or, conversely, a grass-roots social movement that is harbinger of civil society appears first in order for the authoritarian state to evolve into its democratic version?

Under the former scenario, the democratization of the state is an undertaking of social elites: the dissenting elites forming within the *ancien régime* and the dissident counter-elites emerging as a result of a crisis of the previous system. Under the latter perspective, the democratization process results from the mobilization of the masses, capable of self-organizing into a social movement and aiming at regaining the social space appropriated and controlled by the authoritarian state. A successful repossession of that social space is, in turn, the precondition for the unrestrained self-organization of various social forces. This mode of self-organization presages the emergence of a plural civil society.

It is analytically possible to distinguish three types of relations between the state and civil society: (1) Civil society is the opposite of the state. (2) Civil society supplements the state. (3) The state supplements civil society. The first type of relationship is likely to unfold particularly during the "bottom-up" type of democratization and relates to the democratization process of eastern and central Europe. I discuss this type of the process later in this chapter. For now, let us briefly note that this type of relationship is rather short-lived, as it is characteristic of the declining phase of autocratic states and the primary stage of the creation of a democratic state. However, some authors claim that the antagonistic relationship between society and the state endures because the state constitutes the realm of power, within which legal coercion is used, while the realm of civil society is governed by the principle of voluntary participation (Bobbio 1997).

The second type of relationship features especially prominently in republican and occasionally in communitarian theoretical, if not ideological, perspectives. Within these perspectives the emphasis is on the benefits of civil society which stem from its concentration on the areas in which the state lacks competency or is less effective than is civil society. The third type of relationship, following in the footsteps of the liberal perspective, is formulated on the basis of the principle of the minimalism of the state on the one hand, and on the basis of the principle of subsidiarity on the other. The principle of subsidiarity conveys the notion that the state is needed only where civil society is ineffective or lacks requisite competency. In summary, the first type of relationship features antagonistic relations between the state and civil society, while the remaining two feature non-antagonistic relationships based on cooperation, mutual supplementation, and relatively harmonious coexistence.

One may expect civil society to emerge in the event of the following three prerequisites being met: (1) The existence of the public space allowing for the unrestrained self-organization of nascent social forces; (2) the existence of channels of social communication which are not controlled by the state; (3) the existence of free markets, wherein the exchange of goods and services occurs, along with the protection of private property. If the public sphere is unavailable to the unrestrained self-organization of social forces, as is the case when it is controlled by a non-democratic state, then it is impossible for organizations and associations autonomous from the state and which comprise the institutional expression of civil society to emerge. Under such circumstances, quasi-civil organizations and associations appear; they are often controlled by the state and it is the state which brings them into existence (as was often the case of autocratic states before transition and, presently, is typical for state-led civil society in China). However, history shows that under such circumstances various informal counter-culture and dissident groupings form which, though functioning outside of the state-controlled public sphere, outgrow the level of social micro-structures (primary groups) and locate themselves in social niches which possess only diffused boundaries. In a non-democratic environment such dissident groups may form *proto-civil society*, which puts some pressure on state policies and may eventually bring about the liberalization of the system,

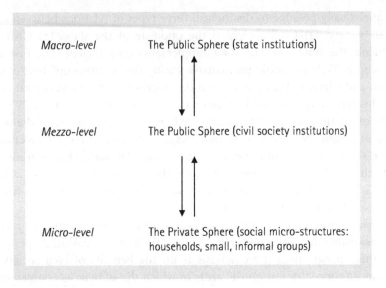

Fig. 36.1 Civil society in social space

and, finally, its democratization. "This destabilizing combination of concession from above and liberalizing pressure from below can produce harsh crack-downs as well as a further broadening of civil and political liberties" (Kaufmann 1988, 93).

Social communication serves to define and negotiate group interests, allows for agreement upon the shared values and purposes of various social groups, which allows for their institutionalization.

Finally, the markets, autonomous from the state, along with mechanisms allowing for the protection of private property ensure the state-independent economic foundations of civil society. When looking at command economies (of the type that existed in the former Eastern Bloc and which still operates in North Korea and Cuba), in place of civic attitudes, the public sphere features clientelist attitudes towards the sponsor. In other words, the central state controls all economic resources and their redistribution.

Civil societies fill the whole of the public sphere extending between the level of the state and the elemental level of households. The entire social space consists of three levels, which are presented graphically in Figure 36.1.

2 Functions of Civil Society

According to various traditions of political philosophy, we may distinguish four basic functions of civil society: (1) Protection from state arbitrariness; (2) observation and control of state power; (3) democratic socialization of citizens; and (4) creation of the public sphere and the provision of the actors who operate in this sphere (Merkel 1999). The first function Merkel (1999) labels as "Lockeian," for it stems from the liberal tradition dating back to John Locke. This function includes both the protection of the autonomy of the individual, private property, and room for a community life without the arbitrary interference of the state. The second function refers to the Montesquieu theoretical tradition and the concept of checks and balances. On the one hand, a network of intermediary organizations controls the state, while on the other hand these organizations bridge state and society. "High organizational density in society among all classes but especially among the subordinate classes is an important counterweight to the power of the state apparatus" (Rueschemeyer, Stephens, and Stephens 1992, 66). The third function—called "the Tocquevillean" by Merkel—implies that civil society acts as an incubator of citizens and civic virtues such as trust, tolerance, reciprocity (Putnam 1993). Finally, the fourth function of civil society—"Habermasian," as Merkel puts it—is the formation of effective channels of civic discourse, representation, and mobilization around values and interests.

Since a civil society is situated at the intermediate level, a fundamental role played by the plurality of civic settings is the *mediation* between the level of the state and the elemental level of the household.[1] Within the mediating role, civil society actually fulfils a whole array of more specific functions and tasks related to the above-mentioned four basic functions. The following tasks merit a mention: (1) Control; (2) Articulative; (3) Integrative; and (4) Educational. To be more precise, these tasks are fulfilled to varying degrees by specific, organized structures which operate within the boundaries of civil society. Since a civil society is, to use Walzer's (1992, 98) phrase, "a setting of settings: all are included, none is preferred," the specific settings of citizens, and not civil society at large, are the collective actors which fulfill all the functions and tasks of civil society.

The *Control* function refers to the activity of the various watchdog NGOs which monitor whether state power is kept within legal limits and that the commonly shared rules of the game are observed in public life.

The *Articulative* function of these settings consists of transforming dispersed "personal troubles" into more coherent "public issues." It aggregates aspirations, objectives, needs, and values, which at the level of micro-structure are quite diffused, into broader agendas. It also includes the representation of those agendas vis-à-vis both the state and public opinion.

---

[1] Norberto Bobbio (1997) views the relationship between the state and civil society differently. In his opinion it is the state that assumes the mediating role with regard to pluralist civil society, due to the fact that within the latter, economic, social, ideological, and religious conflicts occur, while the role of the state is to maintain law and order through conflict mediation, prevention, or suppression. This is unlikely to be accurate. Nations undergoing democratization, along with mature democracies, both witness conflicts between the state and various institutions of civil society while conflicts between various organizations of civil society which would lend themselves to state mediation are less frequent. Bobbio's stance runs into difficulty when one considers that if the relationship between the state and civil society is permanently antagonistic, then the mediating function ought to be contested through antagonistically predisposed social agencies of civil society.

The *Integrative* function of civic settings consists of coalescing their membership around aggregated objectives that are transformed into public endeavors. For example, the mobilization of participation in organized forms of collective action in the public sphere, or, at a minimum, the mobilization of support for the aims of a given organization or association.

The *Educational* function of civic settings has dual nature. First, it propagates civic attitudes and virtues among their respective members. It stimulates the internalization of democratic ground rules (procedures) which regulate activities undertaken within the public sphere. It habituates participation in public life and thereby of exercising the prerogatives stemming from the status of citizenship. This is the uniquely important process of learning democracy through action. It improves the quality of political culture and in young democracies helps active members to change clientelist attitudes (widespread under non-democratic regimes) into the civic ones. Second, through elevating their aims to the status of public objectives and their inclusion into social discourse, civic settings sensitize public opinion to issues that would otherwise be absent from social dialogue and would remain unnoticed by public opinion and political actors.

3 DEMOCRATIZATION

Democratization is a social process, or, more precisely, a spectrum of complex and interweaving processes that can be separated from each other only analytically. This observation leads to a number of theoretical approaches (Heine 2005) that emphaze a certain aspect of the process. Since democratization is not an instant act but, rather, a cluster of complex processes, it has its primary, climax, and final outcome. Moreover, such a cluster of processes has a morphogenetic (Archer 2000) character, by which I mean that certain phases of democratization are conditioned by the changes produced by earlier phases of the same process. Simplifying the matter, one can differentiate the following phases of transition to democracy. (1) The "Initial" phase, in which "transformative" social processes are set in motion; a "transformative strength"[2] of a given process is characterized by its ability to change the *ancien régime* into a new social system. (2) The "Trans-Systemic" phase, in which the old system no longer functions but the new is only beginning to emerge. (3) The "Consolidation" phase, during which the democratic system of government is stabilized and, in practice, becomes the only place in public life available for the

---

[2] "Transformative strength" is understood as being either a process set in motion by rebellious masses that generates an ad hoc counter-elite (open revolution) or as a pact between an old elite and a counter-elite backed by the masses which, in practice, concludes the old system and paves the way to a new system.

interplay of interests and values.[3] However, the question of what it is that sets the transformative processes in motion remains open. Both Linz and Stepan (1996) and Charles Tilly (2000) emphasize the role of the power elite of the *ancien régime* in producing major change in public life. If the authoritarian power elite for whatever reasons (economic crisis, pressure from the international environment, social unrest, military defeat, radical social change in neighboring countries or the internal struggle for power after the death of a charismatic leader) introduces incremental alterations to public life leading to liberalization then we have, as a result, at least two important effects: (1) A split of the elite into "hardliners" and "reformers", and (2) growing expectations of the society for further liberalization and, eventually, democratization. The split of the elite lessens the oppressiveness of the system, places the question of power legitimacy on the agenda and—in turn—reinforces the pressure from the society for further liberalization whilst generating an alternative counter-elite which expresses popular expectations. The institutional conditions for "negotiated revolution" (Bruszt 1991) are, thereby, established and the transition to democracy may unfold. This way of reasoning, inspired by de Tocqueville (1994) along with his observations concerning the causes of the French Revolution, is now a fairly common approach to the process of democratization and transition to democracy.

4 TRANSITION TO DEMOCRACY AND THE EMERGENCE OF CIVIL SOCIETY

Since the 1970s or, more precisely, since the democratic revolution in Portugal in 1974, the transition to democracy from authoritarian rule has been observed in a growing number of countries. Samuel Huntington (1991) coined this global tendency, "a third wave of democratization." Democratization and, eventually, the transition to democracy reached southern Europe, Latin America, and several Asian countries, but the third wave of democratization received an enormous boost after the collapse of the Soviet Bloc. In most of these countries, democratization opened the public space for the emergence of civil society. In a few countries, it was civil society that pushed an autocratic system on democratic trajectory.

---

[3] Pérez-Diaz (1996) introduces different analytical categories. In his approach each systemic change consists of three different, though overlapping, processes: transition, consolidation, and institutionalization. Transition is the period of negotiating between the actors of public life some basic rules of the game; consolidation is the widely spread conviction that the new system will survive and its basic rules of the game are equally widely respected; institutionalization means that the new system is recognized as legitimate by a majority of the society and the new rules of the game are internalized by politicians and by society. This categorization, however, can hardly be used for an analysis of civil society development under the process of radical systemic change.

4.1 Civil Society and Democratization in Southern Europe and Latin America

The beginning of the third wave of democratization is associated with the military *coup d'état* that abolished the authoritarian regime of Antonio Salazar in Portugal in 1974. However, the Spanish transition to democracy is considered to be paradigmatic for much of Latin America. Spain was a country in which elements of civil society emerged and operated in a basically non-democratic institutional environment. The initial phase of transition, launched by the elite, but under pressure from below, began immediately upon the death of Franco in 1975. The *trans-systemic* phase was relatively short because "democratic crafters and supporters inherited a civil society already robust and reasonably differentiated, an economic society that needed restructuring but was already institutionalized, a state apparatus tainted with authoritarianism but usable (...) and a reasonably strong recent tradition of the rule of law" (Linz and Stepan 1996, 113). The consolidation of the new democracy was achieved as early as 1982, with the socialist opposition victory in the general election.

In many Latin American countries as well, some elements of civil society were present in public life before the transitions to democracy in the 1980s and 1990s, due to the fact that the "military-bureaucratic authoritarian regimes" (O'Donnell 1973) did not execute total control over the public space. In Chile, for example, the repressive authoritarian regime disbanded civil organizations and weakened civil society. Democratic opposition found shelter under the umbrella of the Catholic Church and this social capital enabled the launch of an initial stage of transition (known as "participatory revolution") and the rejection of Pinochet and his authoritarian system in the 1988 referendum (Kotzé and du Toit 2005*b*). In Brazil, civil society was weaker and a significant proportion of the population (around 40 percent in 1988) wanted the return of military rule (Linz and Stepan 1996). Across several Latin American nations, however, the liberation theology of Catholic reformers and the activities of labor union activists were seen as creating at least the beginnings of a civil society. And when the democratization process began, these groups and their members were often active participants in democratization.

4.2 Civil Society in Eastern and Central Europe

Numerous authors correlate the collapse of communism in eastern and central Europe and the reinvigoration of interest in civil society in western social thought. Indeed, this is an actual correlation not a coincidence, because the defeat of communism occurred in a spectacular and, for the most part, bloodless fashion, although—contrary to the authoritarian regimes of Latin America and southern Europe—communism in Soviet Bloc countries was reinforced by the so-called "Brezhnev Doctrine."[4] In some countries

---

[4] The Brezhnev Doctrine assumed that each country of the Soviet Bloc could count on the military support of Warsaw Pact troops in the event of an internal or external threat to the communist regime. The doctrine was intended to legitimize the invasion of Czechoslovakia in 1968.

(e.g. Poland) civil society was decisive in defeating communism (Linz and Stepan 1996), whereas in most of the other ex-communist countries, civil society emerged only after the transition to democracy (Gyarfasova 1995; Palous 1995; Horvát and Szakolczai 1992). Civil society in Poland evolved in opposition to the communist state and was, particularly during the initial phase of its development, charged with moral objectives that were shared by a range of generally weak dissident groups in Hungary, East Germany, and Czechoslovakia (Havel 1988). The evolution of civil society in opposition to the communist state impacted on its shape and its relation to the state, as characterized by mutual distrust rather than by a harmonious cooperation. This reverberates to the present day. The second ingredient, the spectacular success of the non-violent social movements which emerged in 1989 (and in 1980 in Poland) created renewed interest in western thought with regard to the question of civil society.

The formative phases of civil society in Poland merit closer attention because they became the model for other countries in the region, especially Hungary, the Czech Republic, and Slovakia. To a large extent this model determined both how the functions of civil society came to be defined (i.e. largely in opposition to the state) and how the process of democratization and the awakening of civil society unfolded.

During the trans-system phase of the shift to democracy, three processes took place in almost every country emerging from the ruins of communism. First was the pluralization of proto-civil society, initially united in the effort to challenge the old system, the common enemy. Second was the partial demobilization of the original movement (a phenomenon observed earlier in Latin America). Third was the process of developing institutional forms of various social forces and civic initiatives at the intermediate level.

The partial withdrawal of the demobilized fraction of the masses into the private sphere underlined the level of social disillusionment at the trajectory of the radical changes that were occurring. It also indicated the fear of the emergent ground rules that were not internalized. The other group of mobilized masses remained in the public sphere and was instrumental in creating the foundations of civil society. The proportion of one group to another is, of course, relevant from the view point of the emerging civil society. Put simply, the greater the level of social demobilization during this phase, the weaker civil society becomes, while the metamorphosis of clientist attitudes typical for the old system into civic attitudes becomes more limited. These factors are decisive with respect to the quality of the nascent democratic system.

During the consolidation phase, the democratic system of government and its procedures became—to use Linz and Stepan's metaphor (1996, 5)—"the only game in town." The formal ground rules, now constitutionally codified, are becoming the normative basis of the entire system while regulating the workings of the state, of civil society, and the foundations of the participation of citizens in the social arena. Provided that these conditions are met, a democratic system of government can be viewed as consolidated while the transition process to that system as successful.

4.3 Civil Society in Asia

Basically, Asiatic societies (first of all China) belong to the cultural zone which can roughly be called "Confucian" (Inglehart and Baker 2000), although Korea is a mix of Buddhist and Christian, and the dominant system in Japan is related to Shintoism. These different philosophical and religious systems create a cultural frame of reference which makes a significant difference in the substantial aspect of the emergence of civil society and transition to democracy, although the formal aspect of these processes may look familiar to a western student of democracy. A number of authors (de Bary 1994; Wei-Ming 1994; Frolic 1997; Gawlikowski 2002a, 2002b) indicate that within this civilization, the place of the individual in society as well as his/her relations with others is different from western societies. The character of the communities also differs from western models. The western concept of citizenship has a predominantly individualistic character, whereas the Asiatic (and particularly—Chinese) variety is rather communitarian, and not so much anti-state but rather in harmony with state policy. This conforms with the Confucian emphasis on the duties and obligations of citizens towards community and state rather than their rights. From this perspective, western public life is based on an adversarial system of relations, whereas the Asiatic system, in contrast, is an interplay of fiduciary communities (Gawlikowski 2002b, 28). However, such a cultural background should be fertile ground for the emergence of the vibrant local communities and organizations which normally operate within civil society. From this point of view, Asiatic countries vary enormously. In Korea, civil society was instrumental in the transition to democracy (Kotzé and du Toit 2005a; Kim 2000) and, after successful transition, membership in organizations of civil society doubled between 1981 and 1990 (Dalton 2006). In China, organizations of this type are controlled by the state, and truly autonomous organizations are limited to the bare minimum, especially since 1989. Nevertheless, even in China, the number of these organizations is growing and is forming a peculiar "state-led civil society" (Frolic 1997; Gawlikowski 2002a).

4.4 The Post-Autocratic Citizen

Each autocratic system, even if it is highly oppressive, enjoys genuine support in part of the population. This is usually a minority (predominantly privileged functionaries of the system and their families) but sufficient for the system to function and to reproduce. Transitions to democracy have left the problem of those who served the autocratic system but who—due to the transition—have lost their privileged position. However, nostalgia towards former, autocratic regimes is felt not only by those who have lost privileges, but also by those who were the clients of the autocratic regime and who have difficulty adjusting to the new rules of the game. The category of those who, for whatever reason, represent "positive attitudes and beliefs associated with the autocratic regime" was coined by Hans-Dieter Klingemann (2005, 121) as "post-autocratic citizens." Whatever the nature of the autocratic regime (military dictatorship, apartheid, communist rule), after its collapse it leaves a group of "post-autocratic citizens" who are able to convert their beliefs from post-autocratic to democratic only by means of a relatively long process of re-education. According to surveys, the size of this category in the mid-1990s (i.e. a couple of years after transition) varied from 12 percent in South Korea, through 22 percent in South Africa, 25 percent in Poland, 36 percent in East Germany, to up to 38 percent in Chile (Klingemann 2005, 123).

4.5 Membership of Voluntary Associations

Membership of voluntary associations is one of the standard indicators of civic engagement. Data from the World Values Survey shows that membership varies substantially among democratic nations: from around 70 percent in Scandinavian countries and the USA to less than 30 percent in Japan and southern European nations. Moreover, citizens of the USA and Scandinavian countries engage, on average, in a greater number of associations (Schofer and Fourcade-Gourinchas 2001, 807).

Membership of voluntary organizations for a selected set of countries is shown in Table 36.1. As we see from the table, civil society in the US is far more active in joining various voluntary associations than other nations. In contrast, Japanese and Polish societies seem rather passive in this area. The differences in civic engagement may be interpreted according to four different models of explanation: economic and cultural, with the remaining two referring to political determinants (Curtis, Baer, and Grabb 2001). One explanation links the level of civic engagement to the level of economic development of a given society: the higher the standard of living, the more

Table 36.1 Membership of voluntary organizations in selected countries (%)

Organizations	USA	South Africa	South Korea	Japan	Poland
Religious	57.1	52.4	42.1	10.6	5.7
Educational or cultural	37.3	20.0	19.1	11.0	2.2
Sports or recreational	36.0	22.9	24.7	14.1	3.1
Labour unions	13.6	9.3	5.6	6.5	10.3
Political groups	19.2	11.5	2.7	3.5	0.7
Conservation and environmental	15.6	3.9	6.2	3.2	1.2
Professional associations	28.0	5.3	8.8	4.8	4.3

Note: Table entries are the percentage of respondents indicating that they "belong to" selected organizations in 1999–2002.

Sources: Dalton (2006); Kotzé and du Toit (2005b).

likely citizens are to engage in voluntary associations. A second explanation links the level of civic engagement to the dominant religious tradition: Protestantism—in contrast to Orthodox Christianity, Islam, Confucianism, and even Catholicism—"is seen as promoting an ethic in which, rather than relying on the state or the church establishment to provide for the needs of community, people are encouraged to join together voluntarily as free individuals to fulfil various societal functions" (Curtis, Baer, and Grabb 2001, 785). A third explanation concentrates on the nature of the democratic system: both liberal and social welfare models of democracy encourage citizens to public engagement, whereas a more corporate model of democracy is less favourable to civic engagement. Fourthly, the stability and continuity of democracy positively correlates with civic engagement: the older and more stable a democracy is, the more likely citizens are to join voluntary associations (Curtis, Baer, and Grabb 2001, 787). In fact, all four explanations supplement each other and help us to understand variations in civic engagement in different democratic societies.

5 CIVIL SOCIETY AND NATIONHOOD

With the downfall of communism, many observers feared that nationalism rather than civic communities would appear from its ruins. These concerns were not without foundation. Ethnic conflicts in the former Yugoslavia, the Caucasian republics of the former USSR, and the ethnicity-based tensions between Hungary and Romania all testified vividly to the rebirth of nationalism in the region. However, civil societies were also reborn.

According to Szacki (1997, 39), "civil society and nationhood are two different and frequently competing types of 'imagined communities' that Europe had to deal with in the course of the last several centuries. The former brings to mind that which is common to all civilized societies, while the latter that which establishes the unique identity of every society."

However, as I mentioned earlier, civil society functions within the confines of the nation-state and, in creating its normative foundations, draws from the resources of shared understandings and values shaped by specific national heritage. Hence within modern democratic systems of government, which allow for the development of modern concepts of citizenship and of the rules of its operation in the public sphere, these two dimensions are interwoven and are difficult to separate, even through analytical means. As a consequence, civil society, operating in the context of a specific nation-state is the realm within which the supranational liberal-democratic principles are realized. However, the nation-state also breathes life into these principles by providing them with localized meaning.

6 POLITICAL CULTURE AND THE QUALITY
OF CIVIL SOCIETY

The quality of democracy and of civil society is determined by citizens' political culture and social capital (also see chapter by Newton in this volume). This issue, undoubtedly also relevant to mature democracies, is particularly important in the case of young democracies, in which new procedures and ground rules must compete with memories of practices established under the previous system, particularly if these informal rules are also effective. As Putnam (1993, 180) correctly points out, "informal norms and culture change more slowly than formal rules, and tend to remould those formal rules, so that the external imposition of a common set of formal rules will lead to widely divergent outcomes." As mentioned earlier, civic culture may be defined within categories of prevailing attitudes towards other participants in public life (trust, tolerance of different points of view), by the level of competence in public affairs, by the awareness of collective purposes, for example, interests transcending one's own particularities (Śpiewak 1998), and by the adherence to the formal rules of conduct governing the public sphere.

Low civic culture occurs when the level of trust towards others is low, tolerance of different viewpoints is fragile, when the desire to realize particular interests, irrespective of their consequences for the wider community, prevails, and when the knowledge of the basic mechanisms of public life is negligible, while formal rules are routinely violated.

According to Putnam (1993, 177–8), the principles of reciprocity and trust, on the one hand, and the principles of dependency and exploitation, on the other, are both effective as social bonds. However, the level of institutional and civic effectiveness is different depending on which principles prevail. High civic culture, comprising social resources of trust, norms, and ties, are accumulated and "amplify" each other. As a result, a positive social equilibrium arises. This equilibrium is characterized by a high level of social cooperation, high levels of trust, mutual support, significant levels of civic engagement, and, generally, increased welfare of the community.

Low civic culture behaves in a mirror fashion: particularity, the absence of trust, exploitation, and the escape into the private sphere and, as a result of these factors, social and economic stagnation. All of these factors tend to amplify each other and to accumulate. This negative equilibrium, once created, tends to be stable over time, while the process of reversing it is problematic even should a section of society so desire. This is so due to the fact that the social attitudes of those influenced by the negative equilibrium view the behavior of those wishing to break from it as being highly peculiar and naive, and are exploited mercilessly.

Low civic culture leads to the phenomenon known as "amoral familism" (Banfield 1958), that is, to the maximalization of any benefits that accrue to individuals and their families at the expense of society at large. The prevailing assumption is that others do the same. Strategies for obtaining these particularist benefits are either outside the formal ground rules or stand in contradiction to those rules. If these strategies are effective, they become quite resilient and find many followers. It is in this context that permissiveness towards corruption, illegal lobbying, the identification of legal loopholes, or tax fraud reigns. The relative effectiveness of such informal norms of behavior leads to a gradual deterioration of the formal rules; the latter are downgraded to the status of vacuous rituals; democratic institutions, including institutions of civil society, become a mere veneer behind which "the real life" takes place. O'Donnell (1997, 46) argues that, "Many new polyarchies do not lack institutionalization, but a fixation on highly formalized and complex organization prevents us from seeing extremely influential, informal, and sometimes concealed institutions: clientelism and, more generally, particularism."

In the countries that emerged from communism and that have successfully concluded the transition to democracy, the consolidation of the democratic system is undermined in two ways. On the one hand, the dubious heritage of habitual, informal ties forged during the previous system continues to operate (Staniszkis 1999). On the other hand, there are strategies created with the purpose of ensuring the successful functioning of the new system. A good example of such a strategy is the conversion of political capital into economic capital during the transition from command economy to market economy (Wasilewski and Wnuk-Lipinski 1995; Lane 2000). Similar strategies were formed during the trans-systemic phase, when new ground rules were evolving, and while their enforcement was weak. These strategies, effective as a means of securing the particularist interests of various interest groups during the trans-systemic phase and often applied on the border between the polity and the economy, remain present in the consolidation phase. They consist of finding ways around the formal rules, while the ties to the power elites guarantee immunity from prosecution. This results, at the level of state institutions, in the spread of corruption; at the intermediate level, to the deceleration of the evolution from clientelism to citizenship; at the level of micro-structures, such strategies broaden the appeal of the notion that formal rules are a mere façade, behind which people of power and money realize their particularist interests at the expense of public welfare.

Only a vibrant civil society can tame this insidious process which undermines the consolidation, or perhaps even the legitimization, of the democratic regime. Civil society presents itself to the individual as the place of continuing civic education and, through democratic procedures and free media, as a controlling device helping to prevent the degeneration of the sphere of power.

REFERENCES

ARCHER, M. S. 2000. *Being Human: The Problem of Agency.* Cambridge: Cambridge University Press.

BANFIELD, E. C. 1958. *The Moral Basis of a Backward Society.* Chicago: The Free Press.

BOBBIO, N. 1997. Społeczeństwo obywatelskie. In *Ani książę ani kupiec: Obywatel* [Civil Society, from: Neither Prince Nor Merchant: A Citizen], ed. J. Szacki. Kraków: Znak.

BRUSZT, L. 1991. The negotiated revolution of Hungary. Pp. 213–25 in *Democracy and Political Transformation,* ed. G. Szoboszlai. Budapest: Hungarian Political Science Association.

COHEN, J. L., and ARATO, A. 1992. *Civil Society and Political Theory.* Cambridge, Mass.: MIT Press.

COLÁS, A. 2002. *International Civil Society.* Cambridge: Polity.

CURTIS, J. E., BAER, D. E., GRABB, E. G. 2001. Nations of joiners: explaining voluntary association membership in democratic societies. *American Sociological Review,* 66 (6): 783–805.

DALTON, R. J. 2006. Civil society, social capital and democracy. In *Citizens, Democracy and Markets around the Pacific Rim,* ed. R. Dalton and D. Shin, Oxford: Oxford University Press.

DE BARY, T. W. 1994. Konfucjanizm i społeczeństwo obywatelskie. In *Europa i społeczeństwo obywatelskie. Rozmowy w Castel Gandolfo,* [Confucianism and civil society. Pp. 179–200 in *Europe and Civil Society. Talks in Castel Gandolfo*] ed. K. Michalski. Kraków: Znak.

DE TOCQUEVILLE, A. 1994. *Dawny ustrój i rewolucja* [Old system and the Revolution]. Kraków: Znak.

DOORENSPLEET, R. 2000. Reassessing three waves of democratization. *World Politics,* 52: 384–406.

FROLIC, B. M. 1997. State-led civil society. In *Civil Society in China,* ed. T. Brook and M. B. Frolic. Armonk, NY: M. E. Sharpe.

GASIOROWSKI, M. J., and POWER, T. 1998. The structural determinants of democratic consolidation: evidence from the third world. *Comparative Political Studies,* 31 (6).

GAWLIKOWSKI, K. 2002*a.* Formowanie się społeczenstwa obywatelskiego w Chinach w XX w. in: Chiny: Rozwój społeczenstwa i panstwa na przelomie XX i XXI wieku [Emergence of civil society in 20th century China. Pp. 9–34 in *China: Development of Society and State on the Threshold of the 20th and 21st Centuries*], ed. K. Gawlikowski and K. Tomala. Warszawa: ISP PAN—TRIO.

—— 2002*b.* Jednostka i władza w cywilizacji wschodnioazjatyckiej. In *Korea: Doświadczenia i perspektywy,* [The individual and power in East-Asiatic civilization. Pp. 15–71 in *Korea: Experiences and Prospects*], ed. K. Gawlikowski and E. Potocka. Torun: A. Marszalek.

GYARFASOVA, O. 1995. Slovakia after split: dilemmas of the new citizenship. Pp. 165–80 in *Citizenship East and West,* ed. A. Liebich and D. Warner. London: Kegan Paul International.

HAVEL, V. 1988. Anti-political politics. In *Civil Society and the State. New European Perspectives,* ed. John Keane. New York: Verso.

HEINE, J. 2005. Institutional engineering in new democracies. Pp. 65–94 in *Democracy under Construction: Patterns from Four Continents,* ed. U. van Beek. Opladen: Barbara Budrich Publishers.

HORVÁT, A., and SZAKOLCZAI, A. 1992. The discourse of civil society and the self-elimination of the party. In *Democracy and Civil Society in Eastern Europe,* ed. P. Lewis. New York: St Martin's Press.

HUNTINGTON, S. P. 1991. *The Third Wave: Democratization in the Late Twentieth Century,* Norman: University of Oklahoma Press.

INGLEHART, R., and BAKER, W. 2000. Modernization, cultural change, and persistence of traditional values, in *American Sociological Review,* 65 (1): 19–51.

KAUFMAN, R. R. 1988. Liberalization and democratization in South America: perspectives from the 1970s. Pp. 85–107 in *Transition from Authoritarian Rule: Comparative Perspectives,* ed. G. O'Donnell, P. Schmitter, and L. Whitehead. Baltimore: Johns Hopkins University Press.

KIM, S. 2000. *The Politics of Democratization in Korea: The Role of Civil Society.* Pittsburgh: University of Pittsburgh Press.

KLINGEMANN, H. D. 2005. Post-autocratic party systems and the regime cleavage in new democracies. in *Democracy under Construction: Patterns from Four Continents,* ed. U. van Beek. Opladen: Barbara Budrich Publishers.

KOTZÉ, H., and DU TOIT, P. 2005a. Civil society and democracy. Pp. 243–58 in *Democracy under Construction: Patterns from Four Continents*, ed. U. van Beek. Opladen: Barbara Budrich Publishers.

—— —— 2005b. Data analyses, comparisons and synthesis. Pp. 305–36 in *Democracy under Construction: Patterns from Four Continents*, ed. U. van Beek. Opladen: Barbara Budrich Publishers.

LANE, D. 2000. Russia: the old elite's evolution, divisions, and outlooks. Pp. 179–98 in *Elites after State Socialism: Theories and Analysis*, ed. J. Higley and G. Lengyel. New York: Rowman & Littlefield.

LINZ, J. J., and STEPAN, A. 1996. *Problems of Democratic Transition and Consolidation: Southern Europe, South America, and Post-Communist Europe*. Baltimore: Johns Hopkins University Press.

MERKEL, W. 1999. Civil society and democratic consolidation in Eastern Europe. *Society and Economy in Central and Eastern Europe*, 21 (3).

O'DONNELL, G. 1973. *Modernization and Bureaucratic Authoritarianism: Studies in South American Politics*. Berkeley: Institute of International Studies.

—— 1997. Illusions about consolidation. In *Consolidating the Third Wave Democracies*, ed. L. Diamond, M. F. Plattner, Y. Chu, and H. Tien. Baltimore: Johns Hopkins University Press.

PALOUS, M. 1995. Questions of Czech citizenship. Pp. 141–59 in *Citizenship East and West*, ed. A. Liebich and D. Warner. New York: Kegan Paul International.

PÉREZ-DIAZ, V. 1996. *Powrót społeczeństwa obywatelskiego w Hiszpanii* [*Return of Civil Society in Spain*]. Kraków: Znak.

PUTNAM, R. D. 1993. *Making Democracy Work: Civic Traditions in Modern Italy*. Princeton: Princeton University Press.

RUESCHEMEYER, D., STEPHENS, E., and STEPHENS, J. 1992. *Capitalist Development and Democracy*. Cambridge: Polity Press.

SCHOFER, E., and FOURCADE-GOURINCHAS, M. 2001. The structural contexts of civic engagement: voluntary association membership in comparative perspective. *American Sociological Review*, 66 (6): 806–28.

STANISZKIS, J. 1999. *Post-communism: The Emerging Enigma*. Warsaw: Institute of Political Studies, Polish Academy of Sciences.

ŚPIEWAK, P. 1998. *W stronę wspólnego dobra*, [*Towards the Common Good*]. Warszawa: Fundacja ALETHEIA.

SZACKI, J. 1997. Powrót idei społeczeństwa obywatelskiego. In *Ani książę ani kupiec: Obywatel*, [Return of the idea of civil society, in *Neither Prince nor Merchant: A Citizen*], ed. J. Szacki. Kraków: Znak.

TAYLOR, C. 1994. Kiedy mówimy: społeczeństwo obywatelskie. in *Europa i społeczeństwo obywatelskie: Rozmowy w Castel Gandolfo*, [When we speak: civil society. Pp. 54–80 in *Europe and Civil Society: Talks in Castel Gandolfo*], ed. K. Michalski. Kraków: Znak.

TILLY, C. 2000. Processes and mechanisms of democratization. *Sociological Theory* 18 (1): 1–16.

WALZER, M. 1992. The civil society argument. in *Dimensions of Radical Democracy: Pluralism, Citizenship, Community*, ed. C. Mouffe. London: Verso.

WASILEWSKI, J., and WNUK-LIPINSKI, E. 1995. Poland: the winding road from communist to post-solidarity elite. *Theory and Society*, 24.

WEI-MING, T. 1994. Humanizm konfucjański i demokracja. in *Europa i społeczeństwo obywatelskie: Rozmowy w Castel Gandolfo*, [Confucian humanism and democracy. Pp. 201–21 in *Europe and Civil Society: Talks in Castel Gandolfo*], ed. K. Michalski. Kraków: Znak.

WNUK-LIPIŃSKI, E. 1987. Social dimorphism. Pp. 159–76 in *Society in Transition*, ed. I. Białecki, J. Koralewicz, and M. Watson. London: Berg Publishers.

CHAPTER 37

SOCIAL MOVEMENTS

RUUD KOOPMANS

MUCH of political science focuses on the daily business of democracy: elections, institutions, legislation, policies, lobbying, and so forth. Voters, governments, legislatures, courts, political parties, and established interest groups are the actors that figure centrally in such analyses. There are good reasons for such an emphasis because these are most of the time the central processes and actors in democratic politics. Policy making tends to take place within narrow margins and political change in democracies is usually a gradual and orderly affair. In spite of a political rhetoric full of references to change, upheaval, and renewal, even "landslide" elections rarely cause more than a ripple of change in the lives of ordinary citizens. There is much groping in politics and in political science about why most citizens in democracies show so little—and declining—interest in political affairs, but the banal heart of the matter is that such lack of interest often springs from a realistic assessment of the impact of elections and of who governs on people's daily lives.

Because democracies ultimately draw legitimacy from popular involvement, politicians have good reason to worry about the lack of enthusiasm among the citizenry, to undertake efforts to increase accountability and transparency, and to contemplate new avenues to promote citizens' participation. However, from a somewhat broader perspective, the unobtrusive nature of democratic politics is a virtue rather than a vice. Democracy has liberated people from overly obtrusive, non-democratic political systems and has allowed citizens the liberty to construct their lives without worrying too much about politics. Even in democracies, not every citizen can enjoy this freedom to the same extent, and such inequalities remain important issues of contestation, even if the degree to which they are amenable by policies is often limited. By and large, however, the momentous political changes that touch people's lives do not emerge from the ordinary democratic political process, but from those more rare occasions when the boundaries of democratic politics itself are at stake.

The most obvious case in point is the process of democratization. Democratization has most of the time not been orderly and gradual, but has progressed by way of revolutionary upheavals and mass social movements. The earliest thrusts towards modern forms of democracy—e.g. in England, the United Dutch Provinces, the United States of America, or France—were the result of national independence struggles and political revolutions, rather than of gradual reform and an orderly expansion of political rights. This pattern has held up to the present day, as exemplified by the sudden and unexpected mass mobilizations that led to the fall of communism, the disintegration of multinational states, and the establishment of a multitude of new democracies in eastern Europe.

When originally established, democracies are seldom inclusive in the sense that they extend political rights to all citizens. The early democracies were all elite affairs that excluded much of the population on the basis of wealth, gender, and where relevant also race. Further expansion of democracy has rarely happened without intense political struggle by social movements on behalf of these excluded groups. The eradication of wealth and class as criteria for voting rights required a long battle by labor movements; the women's movement played a similar role in the expansion of political rights to women, and long years of courageous extra-institutional mobilization were necessary to do away with racial apartheid in the USA and in South Africa. In the establishment of the latest wave of new democracies, exclusion along the lines of class, gender, or race has usually not been a contested issue, but this has been all the more the case for the demarcation of political boundaries along the lines of ethnicity and religion. Once again, such struggles over the boundaries of democratic politics have not been contained within the arenas of parliaments, government, or the courts, but have spilled over into, or more often been taken over by extra-institutional and not seldom bloody struggles among various ethnic and religious groups. Even in the "old" western European and North American democracies, the struggle over the boundaries of democracy continues, as indicated by fierce struggles over the civic and cultural rights of new immigrant groups, which are again only very partially contained within parliamentary and party politics.

The expansion of democracy is not only a question of including clearly demarcated social groups such as workers or women, but also concerns the substantive agenda of politics; the issues around which politicians and parties compete with each other for the support of the citizenry. The routine political process is able to deal reasonably well—and certainly better than any conceivable alternative—with issues that have an established place on the political agenda. Politicians can monitor the public's opinion on these issues through polls and other survey instruments; in their campaigns they can inform voters about their parties' standpoint on them; and citizens can hold politicians accountable for their performance on these issues when they cast their votes. However, parliaments, governments, and parties are much less well-placed for—and often not interested in—bringing new themes and issues to the public's attention and onto the political agenda. One example of such a new issue, which by now has become well established, is that of the protection of the environment and the conservation of energy sources. This issue was launched from outside the regular channels of institutional democracy by worried experts, local citizens' initiatives, and emergent environmental organizations, and was often only with great reluctance taken up by established political actors, which in turn opened up opportunities for the establishment of new, "green" political parties. Other examples from the same epoch of the 1960s and 1970s are the issues that were launched by the new women's movement and other identity movements, who under the banner "the personal is political" advanced the claim that issues such as reproductive rights, homosexuality, or the distribution of tasks in the family were legitimate issues of public concern that required political action.

We should, however, beware of sketching a too benign picture of social movements as if their historical role has been only to contribute to ever more inclusive versions of democracy. Extra-institutional challenges to the boundaries of democracy just as often go in the other direction, towards more exclusive political rights, or even towards abolishing democracy altogether. The two great totalitarian challenges of the last century, communism and fascism, are obvious examples, but so are most movements for ethnic emancipation, national independence, or religious revival, whose demands for inclusion often go hand in hand with the exclusion or even physical elimination of the members of rival ethnicities and religions. The same is true for current struggles over the rights of immigrants, in which extreme-right groups oppose claims for inclusion and seek to retain or return to a notion of citizenship that privileges the dominant ethnic group.

1 THEORETICAL PERSPECTIVES ON SOCIAL MOVEMENTS

1.1 Classic Theoretical Approaches

What do theories of social movements tell us about the causes and conditions of the mass mobilizations that have redefined the boundaries of democratic politics? Until the 1960s, a decidedly negative view on the role of social movements prevailed. Various strands of theory in this early work all agreed that "collective behavior"—a summary term that included not only social movements but also mobs, panics, and crazes—was an irrational and destructive phenomenon. The earliest of these theoretical traditions posits that when people coalesce in groups, they lose their individuality and become susceptible to irrational behavior, which may include great bravery and sacrifice for the group, but also uncontrolled violence towards outsiders. Originally formulated by Gustave Le Bon (1960 [1895]), such crowd-psychological ideas can also be traced in the thinking of Max Weber on charismatic leadership and of Émile Durkheim on the collective conscience.

Post-war theories of "mass society" introduced a more social-structural variation on the same theme (e.g. Kornhauser 1959). Based on Durkheim's conception of "anomie," rapid social change was seen as breaking down traditional social ties and norms. In search for new social anchors, the uprooted and isolated individuals of mass society were seen as easy targets for totalitarian mass movements of the left and right. Such movements were moreover seen as attracting particular types of "authoritarian" personalities (Adorno et al. 1950). Within the Parsonian tradition with its emphasis on functionally integrative normative systems, "deviant" social movements could not appear in a very positive light, either. Neil Smelser (1962) provided the most elaborated version of the structural-functionalist view that associated social movements with "structural strain," which paved the way for the spread of irrational and disintegrative "generalized beliefs."

Theories of relative deprivation are a final strand of scholarship in this classical tradition. In the most influential version of this argument, Ted Gurr (1970) built on social-psychological frustration-aggression theory. Relative deprivation is a gap between what people get and what they expect and aspire to get on the basis of past trends and comparisons with other groups. Deprived individuals experience psychological frustration and this leads them to strike out violently at the perceived sources of their anger, without, in essence, much further reflection. As Gurr, James Davies (1962), and others argued, relative deprivation does not need to be associated with economic downturns but can, as in the case of the movements of the 1960s, also occur in times of affluence, as long as the rise of aspirations exceeds the capacities of the economic and political systems to satisfy them.

The predominance of theories emphasizing the irrational and violent aspects of social movements and describing their participants as easily susceptible, socially uprooted, and frustrated, can in large part be explained by the ideological and social distance between the predominant social movements and the scholars that studied them. Most academics of those days had little sympathy for the labor movement, and the rise of fascism and Stalinism only strengthened the aversion within academia for popular politics. Not coincidentally, the only areas of study where classical explanations are still prevalent nowadays are those that deal with social movements for which social scientists have little sympathy, for instance extreme right and xenophobic protests, which are often ascribed to the frustration and lack of social integration of the "losers of modernity" (e.g. Heitmeyer et al. 1992).

1.2 Resource Mobilization

Apart from these holdouts in the study of "unsympathetic" movements, the protest waves of the 1960s and 1970s, in which students and academics were centrally involved, led to a radical shift in the predominant view on social movements. Inspired by Mancur Olson's (1965) economic theory of collective action, a new "resource mobilization" school (e.g. Oberschall 1973; McCarthy and Zald 1977) emerged, which contradicted the classical theories in almost every conceivable way. In the spirit of Olson, social movements were interpreted as rational, utility-maximizing actors, and a whole new vocabulary was invented that spoke no longer of charismatic leaders but of "movement entrepreneurs" who set up "social movement organizations" and larger "social movement industries," which offered their products to a clientele not of frustrated and irrational individuals, but of "conscience con-stituents" who considered the profitability of investing their "discretionary re-sources" in social movement activities. Regarding the social-structural conditions for mobilization, resource mobilization theorists emphasized group solidarity and the integration of individuals into social networks rather than the breakdown of norms and the social uprooting of the classical perspectives.

Numerous studies confronted the predictions of the classical approaches with those of the resource mobilization perspective, and generally found strong support for the latter. In particular, the participants in social movements tended to be well integrated into their communities, and were mobilized by way of tight social networks, rather than as isolated individuals (e.g. Useem 1980; Jenkins and Perrow 1977). Moreover, Charles Tilly and his colleagues (1978; Shorter and Tilly 1974; Tilly, Tilly, and Tilly 1975) amassed evidence that demonstrated that there was no direct link between rapid social change and surges in social movement mobilization. As Piven and Cloward (1977, 1992)—two of the very few dissident voices at the time—pointed out, these supportive results were partly due to the fact that resource mobilization theorists often focused on movements or sections of movements that were relatively well organized, reformist, and middle class, and tended to downplay the more eruptive and disruptive aspects of social movements.

The core theoretical problem with such a rationalist, economic view of social movements—namely Mancur Olson's free rider problem of collective action—has never been quite resolved. The solution proposed by Olson, the provision of selective incentives, is not only problematic on theoretical grounds—because it leads to a second-order problem of collective action, see Oliver 1980—but is also empirically improbable for the case of resource-poor, weakly organized, and emergent social movements, which have little to offer their members in return for their often costly and risky participation. In the absence of a solution, many social movement scholars have simply shifted Olson's dilemma aside as irrelevant in view of the empirical ubiquity of collective action (e.g. Fireman and Gamson 1979; Melucci 1980). Others have tried to salvage the notions of rationality and selective incentives by introducing various "solidary," "purposive," and "psychic" incentives (e.g. Muller and Opp 1986; Marwell and Oliver 1993), which Olson had already decidedly rejected as tautological in his original statement of the collective action problem (1965, 160).

Another problem of resource mobilization theory is its limited appreciation of the external context in shaping the strategies, organizational forms, and mobilization opportunities of social movements. Social-structural changes appear in resource mobilization theory mainly in the form of economic growth, which increases the availability of "discretionary resources" such as spare time and disposable income among middle-class "conscience constituents," which can be tapped by social move-ment organizations (McCarthy and Zald 1977). Resource mobilization theory's attention for political actors in the environment of social movements such as political parties and governments is likewise restricted to a view of them as potential sources of resource support for movement organizations.

1.3 Political Opportunity Structure

Criticism of this lack of attention for the political environment of social movements in resource mobilization theory led to the elaboration of the concept of "political opportunity structures", which was introduced by Peter Eisinger (1973) and further developed by, among others, Charles Tilly (1978) and Doug McAdam (1982). Contrary to the strong focus on movement-internal factors in resource mobilization theory, proponents of the "political process" approach argue that variations in the amount and types of social movement activity can be explained by variations in the political context that they confront. Eisinger, for instance, showed that urban movements fluctuated with the structures and openness of local politics, and McAdam linked the rise of the civil rights movement in the USA to shifts in the electoral constituencies of Democrats and Republicans as a result of migration of blacks to the northern states, and the erosion of the Democrats' hold on southern whites. In Europe, the political opportunity structure concept was especially fruitful in stimulating cross-national research, e.g. Herbert Kitschelt's (1986) comparison of anti-nuclear energy movements in various countries, Donatella della Porta's (1995) comparison of the New Left in Germany and Italy, or the comparison of new social movements in Germany, France, the Netherlands, and Switzerland by Hanspeter Kriesi and his collaborators (1995).

These comparative studies connected social movement studies to the concerns of mainstream political science, by showing how the timing, strategies, and volume of social movement mobilization were related to factors such as electoral volatility, the composition of the party system, institutional centralization, separation of powers, and conflict-resolution strategies of political elites. Kriesi et al.'s study in particular revealed a strong tendency for social movements to adapt to, and reflect the character-istics of the very political systems that they challenged. For instance, the availability of multiple channels of access and consensus-oriented elite strategies in Switzerland are mirrored by relatively moderate, continuous, and decentralized social movements. The centralization of French politics and the insulation of its political elites from popular pressure, by contrast, lead to more radical, intermittent, and centralized challenges.

Figure 37.1 shows that going from the open and decentralized Swiss political system to the closed, centralized French polity, the overall level of mobilization of social movements decreases markedly. This tendency is however entirely due to the high level of conventional mobilization in Switzerland in the form of petitions, referendum signature drives, and organizational membership. Participation in unconventional protest, by contrast, follows the exact reverse pattern, with France having the highest level, and Switzerland the lowest. Within the category of unconventional protest, France, moreover, has the highest rate of violent protest followed by Germany, the Netherlands, and finally Switzerland (not shown in the figure, see Kriesi et al.

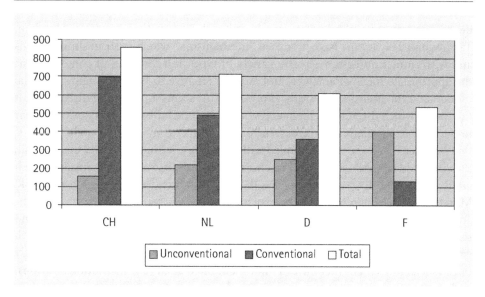

Fig. 37.1 Levels of mobilization of social movements in four European countries, 1975–1989, in thousands of participants per million inhabitants

Note: Calculated on the basis of Kriesi et al. 1995, 45. Unconventional protest includes demonstrations, strikes, civil disobedience, and political violence. Conventional mobilization includes petitions, signature drives for referendum campaigns, as well as membership in new social movement organizations and labor unions.

1995, 50). Thus, in line with the political opportunity structure perspective, more disruptive and radical forms of mobilization flourish in countries such as France that offer relatively few channels of access to social movements, whereas open, inclusive political systems invite moderate forms of movement mobilization.

While particularly in cross-national comparative work, the political process approach offers a powerful set of explanatory tools, there has been more criticism of its application to the dynamics of contention. Although it carries the word "process" in its name, the political process perspective is, as McAdam, Tarrow, and Tilly (2001) have convincingly argued, not really a dynamic theory. According to these authors, the search for stable regularities in the relations between structural variables and movement action that characterizes much work in the political process perspective is largely futile. Examples are the many—and indeed quite inconclusive—studies that look for "the" effects of repression on mobilization (for a recent overview, see Davenport et al. 2005), as if there were some universal law of repression to be discovered that is independent of the insertion of concrete interactions between movements and authorities in time and space (Koopmans 2004a). The same can be said for studies of the effects of political opportunity structures more generally, which have sometimes revealed strongly divergent effects (including no effect at all) of the same variables across studies (Meyer 2004; Meyer and Minkoff 2004).

An alternative is needed for the fruitless search for universal causal laws of political contention, which simultaneously avoids the equally unattractive alternative of ad hoc descriptive accounts, thinly disguised in cultural-constructivist rhetoric. McAdam, Tarrow, and Tilly (2001) have proposed "mechanisms," which recur in similar forms and with similar outcomes across a variety of types and instances of contention, as the appropriate focus of analyses, and as an alternative to both invariant, universal models and the holistic case-study approach. This seems a promising direction, but the way in which the authors themselves have developed the idea does not yet appear to be a viable alternative to the current political process model. The main reason is that McAdam et al. are so preoccupied with avoiding any kind of general theory at all, that they end up with a long and open-ended list of dozens of mechanisms, which are not meaningfully related to one another within a broader theoretical framework. Moreover, each phenomenon to be explained seems to require its own set of mechanisms, and if the same mechanisms are used to explain several cases, they often tend to have divergent effects, which leads one to doubt whether we are dealing here with genuine mechanisms at all. Finally, some of the mechanisms that figure prominently in the social movement literature are not mentioned at all (e.g. institutionalization), and in the absence of a coherent theoretical framework one is left to wonder why (Koopmans 2003).

2 CURRENT CHALLENGES

2.1 Culture and Discourse

The dominant position of political process theory in the field has recently been challenged from a number of directions. A first line of criticism grants that there is much that political process theory has illuminated, but also much that it has neglected. In particular, the political process perspective is faulted for having an over-politicized view of social movements, which neglects their cultural dimensions and their dependence not just on political institutions but increasingly also on the nature of public discourse, especially as it takes place in the mass media. While the demands and strategies of some social movements—e.g. the peace and anti-nuclear energy movements—primarily address political authorities, other movements—such as the women's and gay movements or religious movements—have a much wider range of demands and addressees, among which political authorities do not necessarily figure very centrally. The women's movement, for instance, is in spite of its obvious importance conspicuously absent from the analyses of political process scholars, simply because many of its actions and demands are not addressed at policy makers, but are submerged within social institutions and the "private" sphere.

Social movement scholars have become increasingly aware of the centrality of discursive struggles in a variety of arenas for setting the public agenda, framing issues in particular ways, and defining collective identities. This discursive side of social movements has received attention in several variants. David Snow and his collaborators (Snow et al. 1986; Snow and Benford 1992) have emphasized the strategic employment of framing techniques by social movement organizations in order to mobilize adherents and convince the public. From a more structural perspective, others have emphasized how public discourse can, next to institutional politics, be seen as a parallel "discursive opportunity structure," in which media discourse plays a central role and which ascribes credibility, relevance, and legitimacy to certain issues and points of view, but not to others (Koopmans and Statham 1999; Ferree et al. 2004; Koopmans and Olzak 2004). Using this perspective, Ferree et al. (2004) have shown how the discourse on abortion in the United States differs radically from public debates on the same issue in Germany. As Ferree shows, this has important consequences for the mobilization opportunities of feminist movements in the two countries: "The destigmatizing claims that are most ridiculed and excluded in German feminism are among the most acceptable in the United States, and the unattainable 'moral high ground' of state support for reproductive rights in the United States is part of the protectionist mainstream in Germany" (Ferree 2003, 338–9).

A recent study uses a similar theoretical approach to study immigrant mobilization in several European countries and shows that even the collective identities around which social movements mobilize can be strongly affected by the discursive opportunity structure (Koopmans et al. 2005). As Figure 37.2 shows, there are striking cross-national differences in the degree to which immigrants make public claims around racial, religious, or ethnic identities, or on the basis of their common status as immigrants. In Germany, more than two-thirds of all immigrant claims are made in the name of national ethnic categories such as Turks or Bosnians, while in France and Britain such national and ethnic identities are emphasized in less than 20 percent of all claims. By contrast, French immigrants tend to mobilize on the basis

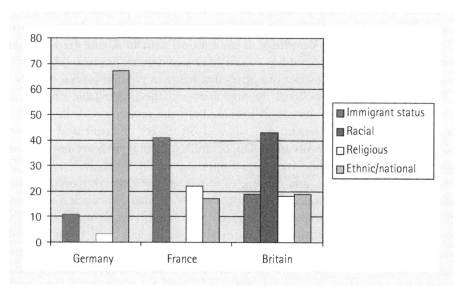

Fig. 37.2 Main types of collective identities in public claims making of immigrant organizations in three European countries (% of claims)

Note: Calculated on the basis of Koopmans et al. (2005, 118–19).

of their common immigrant status, whereas their British counterparts formulate demands that target racially defined categories such as blacks. The authors show that these differences are largely independent of the composition of the immigrant populations, and relate them instead to the dominant discourses on citizenship and immigrant integration, which emphasize national origin in Germany, race in Britain, and which delegitimize differentialist identities in France.

2.2 Agency and Emotions

A second element of what some have labeled—somewhat wishfully—as the "cultural turn" in social movement studies is the criticism of the conception of agency in the political process model (e.g. Goodwin and Jasper 1999; Whittier 2002; Kurzman 2004). In sharp contrast to the self-image of movement activists as innovative and boundary-transgressing actors, the political opportunity perspective often leaves little room for agency and sees movement actors as being shaped and channeled by anonymous political structures and power configurations. How exactly these structural variables affect movement activists' choices usually remains vague, but implicitly most political process theorists have, like resource mobilization theory, relied on rational choice as the micro-foundation of their theories.

In addition to the still unresolved free rider problem, the use of rational choice as the connection between political opportunity structures and movement action leads to a number of additional problems. The first is that only political opportunities that are perceived as such can affect movement actions (Gamson and Meyer 1996). Given the complexity of the interactions among multiple actors in political processes, and the distance between concrete movement action and abstract political structures, this is a qualification with major ramifications. It is highly improbable that movement activists have the detailed knowledge of institutional structures, elite divisions, and electoral alignments that would be necessary to base an even approximately reliable strategic calculus on the abstract categories that figure in political process models.

The indeterminacy of political opportunities and the unavoidable uncertainty of complex contentious interactions provide both the necessity and the leverage, the critics argue, for movement activists and organizers to define and attribute meaning to their strategic situation. Opportunities, in this view, are not external and objective variables, but are to an important extent made and revealed by the creativity, imagination, and courage of movement activists. Moreover, because rational calculation is inconclusive in situations of limited information and high uncertainty, emotions such as anger, indignation, and pride have an important role to play in empowering people to engage in the kind of risky and costly behaviors with uncertain outcomes that social movement activity almost invariably entails (Jasper 1997; Gould 2004). In a way, then, these criticisms constitute a re-appreciation of some of the social-psychological mechanisms that were central to the classical approaches, albeit with the important difference that these emotions are seen as products of social construction, and as enabling agency, rather than as forces that overwhelm actors in such a way that they lose their capacity for reflexive action.

While there is certainly merit in these arguments against the structuralism and rationalism of the political process approach, a major problem with the social constructionist alternative is that it has not itself given us much in the way of testable propositions or causal explanations. The social constructionist perspective risks leading the field towards descriptive accounts of movement histories or activist careers, without giving much theoretical leverage on how to systematize these findings. For instance, its advocates have thus far failed to make clear how the constructionist perspective could be usefully employed to answer the kind of questions that the political process perspective has rightly focused its attention on. Why do movements arise at the particular points in history that they do? What accounts for the important differences that we find between similar movements in different political and cultural contexts? What explains the shifts in strategies, aims, and organizational forms that we regularly observe over the course of protest waves?

2.3 Evolutionary Approaches

An alternative that avoids the voluntarism of constructivism without regressing into the structural determinism of the political process perspective is to employ an evolutionary mode of explanation to connect structure and action. Evolutionary models consist of the well-known mechanisms of variation, selection, and retention/diffusion (Campbell 1973), and focus on the interplay of movement-external (environmental selection) and internal (variation/innovation and retention/diffusion) elements. In the evolutionary approach, structures do not enter the explanation as abstract forces that somehow compel actors, but in the concrete form of the reactions by other political contenders (positive or negative selection, e.g. by way of concessions, media attention, stigmatization, or repression) that a particular movement action provokes (or fails to provoke).

An advantage of evolutionary explanations is that they do not require strong assumptions about the cognitive or psychological mechanisms that generate the strategic decisions of movement activists and their opponents, which makes them compatible with several micro-theories, reaching from expected utility versions of rational choice, via bounded rationality and emotions, to even a completely random input of strategies. In evolutionary models, it is to some extent arbitrary how variety is generated in the inputs, as long as there is some degree of variety with which environmental selection can work. The persistence and proliferation of patterns of action are not explained by their prior rationality or emotional salience, but by the outcomes that they generate (see Thorndike's [1898] famous "law of effect"). For example, whether a movement will radicalize towards violence will neither be fully explained by prior, forward-looking strategic analyses of activists, nor by their emotional states of anger or despair, but by the fact that in order to diffuse, violence must generate the kind of outcomes (e.g. media attention or concessions) that lead those who experiment with violence to retain it, and that convince other activists to adopt it into their strategic repertoires.

At present, this evolutionary alternative is still in its infant stages. Apart from first theoretical statements (Koopmans 2004a, 2005), Oliver and Myers (2003a, 2003b) have begun to explore evolutionary dynamics in formal mathematical models and numeric simulations. In addition, there are first examples of empirical analyses that use event data to analyze the evolution of political contention (Koopmans and Olzak 2004; Koopmans 2004b). Whether the evolutionary approach can fulfill its promise, both theoretically and empirically, still remains to be seen, but the approach does seem to have the potential to act as a bridge between agency-oriented and structural perspectives within social movement research.

3 THE PLACE OF SOCIAL MOVEMENTS IN POLITICAL SCIENCE

As challengers to the boundaries of democratic politics, social movements have been central players in the expansion of democracy, but also figure prominently among democracy's greatest past and current threats. In view of their crucial role in virtually every major instance of political change, it is surprising that the study of social movements occupies a rather marginal place within political science. In the United States, the main political science journals rarely contain work on social movements, and the topic is largely left in that country to sociology, where it constitutes one of the most vibrant and prominent subfields in that discipline. In Europe, the study of social movements is generally considered as belonging to the domain of political science, but it tends to be fragmented into subtopics—e.g. currently lively fields dealing with political extremism or with immigrant participation—and to wax and wane with the ups and downs of particular types of social movements.

A striking example of the latter phenomenon concerns the so-called "new social movements" (ecology, peace, women's emancipation, and so forth), which emerged during the 1970s and 1980s in western Europe, and which spurred a large number of influential studies on both sides of the Atlantic (e.g. Brand 1985; Tarrow 1989; Dalton and Kuechler 1990; Rucht 1994; Kriesi et al. 1995). However, with the institutionalization of these movements and their incorporation into established politics, the formerly thriving field of social movement studies has largely disappeared again from the mainstream of European political science.

During times of routine politics, such lack of attention for social movements may seem justified because they appear mostly as actors without much influence, operating at the marginal fringes of politics. But when it comes to understanding the major waves of democratization, the rise of new political values and issues, as well as the current threats to democracy, there are hardly any political actors that are more relevant to study than social movements. A more institutionalized place within political science for the study of social movements therefore still remains an important desideratum.

REFERENCES

ADORNO, T. W., FRANKEL-BRUNSWICK, E., LEVINSON, D. J., and SANFORD, R. N. 1950. *The Authoritarian Personality*. New York: Harper & Row.

BRAND, K.-W. ed. 1985. *Neue soziale Bewegungen in Westeuropa und den USA: Ein internationaler Vergleich*. Frankfurt: Campus.

CAMPBELL, D. T. 1965. Variation and selective retention in socio-cultural evolution. Pp. 19–49 in *Social Change in Developing Areas. A Reinterpretation of Evolutionary Theory*, ed. H. R. Barringer, G. I. Blanksten, and R. W. Mack. Cambridge, Mass.: Schenkman.

DALTON, R. J., and KUECHLER, M. 1990. *Challenging the Political Order. New Social and Political Movements in Western Democracies*. Cambridge: Polity Press.

DAVENPORT, C., JOHNSTON, H., and MUELLER, C. eds. 2005. *Repression and Mobilization*. Minneapolis: University of Minnesota Press.

DAVIES, J. C. 1962. Towards a theory of revolution. *American Sociological Review*, 27: 5–18.

DELLA PORTA, D. 1995. *Social Movements, Political Violence and the State*. Cambridge: Cambridge University Press.

EISINGER, P. K. 1973. The conditions of protest behavior in American cities. *American Political Science Review*, 67: 11–28.

FERREE, M. M. 2003. Resonance and radicalism: feminist framing in the abortion debates of the United States and Germany. *American Journal of Sociology*, 109: 304–44.

—— GAMSON, W. A., GERHARDS, J., and RUCHT, D. 2002. *Shaping Abortion Discourse: Democracy and the Public Sphere in Germany and the United States*. Cambridge: Cambridge University Press.

FIREMAN, B., and GAMSON, W. A. 1979. Utilitarian logic in the resource mobilization perspective. Pp. 8–44 in *The Dynamics of Social Movements*, ed. M. N. Zald and J. D. McCarthy. Cambridge, Mass.: Winthrop.

GAMSON, W. A., and MEYER, D. S. 1996. Framing political opportunity. Pp. 275–90 in *Comparative Perspectives on Social Movements: Political Opportunities, Mobilizing Structures, and Cultural Framings*, ed. D. McAdam, J. D. McCarthy, and M. N. Zald. Cambridge: Cambridge University Press.

GOODWIN, J., and JASPER, J. M. 1999. Caught in a winding, snarling vine: the structural bias of political process theory. *Sociological Forum*, 14: 27–54.

GOULD, D. B. 2004. Passionate political processes: bringing emotions back into the study of social movements. Pp. 155–76 in *Rethinking Social Movements: Structure, Meaning, and Emotion*, ed. J. Goodwin and J. M. Jasper. Lanham, Md.: Rowman & Littlefield.

GURR, T. R. 1970: *Why Men Rebel*. Princeton: Princeton University Press.

HEITMEYER, W. et al. 1992. *Die Bielefelder Rechtsextremismus-Studie*. Munich: Juventa.

JASPER, J. M. 1997. *The Art of Moral Protest: Culture, Biography, and Creativity in Social Movements*. Chicago: University of Chicago Press.

JENKINS, C., and PERROW, C. 1977. Insurgency of the powerless: farm workers movements (1946–1972). *American Sociological Review*, 42: 249–68.

Langzeituntersuchung zur politischen Sozialization männlicher Jugendlicher. Munich: Juventa.

KITSCHELT, H. 1986. Political opportunity structures and political protest. *British Journal of Political Science*, 16: 57–86.

KOOPMANS, R. 2003. A failed revolution—But a worthy cause. *Mobilization*, 8: 116–19.

—— 2004a. Protest in time and space: the evolution of waves of contention, Pp. 19–46 in *The Blackwell Companion to Social Movements*, ed. D. A. Snow, S. A. Soule, and H. Kriesi. Oxford: Blackwell.

—— 2004b. Movements and media: selection processes and evolutionary dynamics in the public sphere. *Theory and Society*, 33: 367–91.

—— 2005. The missing link between structure and agency: outline of an evolutionary approach to social movements. *Mobilization*, 10: 19–36.

—— and OLZAK, S. 2004. Discursive opportunities and the evolution of right-wing violence in Germany. *American Journal of Sociology*, 110: 198–230.

—— and STATHAM, P. 1999. Ethnic and civic conceptions of nationhood and the differential success of the extreme right in Germany and Italy. Pp. 225–51 in *How Social Movements Matter*, ed. M. Giugni, D. McAdam, and C. Tilly. Minneapolis: University of Minnesota Press.

—— —— GIUGNI, M., and PASSY, F. 2005. *Contested Citizenship. Immigration and Cultural Diversity in Europe.* Minneapolis: University of Minnesota Press.

KORNHAUSER, W. 1959. *The Politics of Mass Society.* Glencoe, Ill.: Free Press.

KRIESI, H., KOOPMANS, R., DUYVENDAK, J. W., and GIUGNI, M. G. 1995. *New Social Movements in Western Europe: A Comparative Analysis.* Minneapolis: University of Minnesota Press.

KURZMAN, C. 2004. The poststructuralist consensus in social movement theory. Pp. 111–20 in *Rethinking Social Movements. Structure, Meaning, and Emotion*, ed. J. Goodwin and J. M. Jasper. Lanham, Md.: Rowman & Littlefield.

LE BON, G. 1960 [1895]. *The Crowd. A Study of the Popular Mind.* New York: Viking Press.

McADAM, D. 1982. *Political Process and the Development of Black Insurgency, 1930–1970.* Chicago: University of Chicago Press.

—— TARROW, S. and TILLY, C. 2001. *Dynamics of contention.* Cambridge: Cambridge University Press.

McCARTHY, J. D., and ZALD, M. N. 1977. Resource mobilization and social movements. *American Journal of Sociology*, 82: 1212–41.

MARWELL, G., and OLIVER, P. 1993. *The Critical Mass in Collective Action: A Micro-Social Theory.* Cambridge: Cambridge University Press.

MELUCCI, A. 1980. The new social movements: a theoretical approach. *Social Science Information*, 19: 199–226.

MEYER, D. S. 2004. Protest and political opportunities. *Annual Review of Sociology*, 30: 125–45.

—— and MINKOFF, D. C. 2004. Conceptualizing political opportunity. *Social Forces*, 82: 1457–92.

MULLER, E. N., and OPP, K.-D. 1986. Rational choice and rebellious collective action. *American Political Science Review*, 80: 473–87.

OBERSCHALL, A. 1973. *Social Movements and Social Conflicts.* Englewood Cliffs, NJ: Prentice Hall.

OLIVER, P. E. 1980. Rewards and punishments as selective incentives for collective action: theoretical investigations. *American Journal of Sociology*, 85: 1356–75.

—— and MYERS, D. J. 2003a. The coevolution of social movements. *Mobilization*, 8: 1–24.

—— —— 2003b. Networks, diffusion, and cycles of collective action. Pp. 173–204 in *Social Movement Analysis: The Network Perspective*, ed. M. Diani and D. McAdam. Oxford: Oxford University Press.

OLSON, M. 1965. *The Logic of Collective Action.* Cambridge, Mass.: Harvard University Press.

PIVEN, F. F., and CLOWARD, R. A. 1977. *Poor People's Movements. Why They Succeed, How They Fail.* New York: Vintage Books.

—— —— 1992. Normalizing collective protest. Pp. 301–25 in *Frontiers in Social Movement Theory,* ed. A. D. Morris and C. Mueller. New Haven: Yale University Press.

RUCHT, D. 1994. *Modernisierung und Neue Soziale Bewegungen. Deutschland, Frankreich und USA im Vergleich.* Frankfurt: Campus.

SHORTER, E., and TILLY, C. 1974. *Strikes in France, 1830–1968.* Cambridge: Cambridge University Press.

SNOW, D. A., and BENFORD, R. D. 1992 Master frames and cycles of protest. Pp. 133–55 in *Frontiers in Social Movement Theory,* eds. A. D. Morris and C. Mueller. New Haven: Yale University Press.

—— ROCHFORD, E. B. Jr., WORDEN, S. K. and BENFORD, R. D. 1986. Frame alignment processes, micromobilization, and movement participation. *American Sociological Review,* 51: 464–81.

SMELSER, N. J. 1962. *Theory of Collective Behavior.* New York: Free Press.

TARROW, S. 1989. *Democracy and Disorder: Protest and Politics in Italy 1965–1975.* Oxford: Clarendon Press.

THORNDIKE, R. 1898. Animal intelligence: an experimental study of the associative processes in animals. *Psychological Review* (Monograph Supplement) 2(8).

TILLY, C. 1978. *From Mobilization to Revolution.* Reading, Mass.: Addison-Wesley.

—— TILLY, L., and TILLY, R. 1975. *The Rebellious Century. 1830–1930.* Cambridge, Mass.: Harvard University Press.

USEEM, B. 1980. Solidarity model, breakdown model, and the Boston anti-busing movement. *American Sociological Review,* 45: 357–69.

WHITTIER, N. 2002. Meaning and structure in social movements. Pp. 289–308 in *Social Movements, Identity, Culture, and the State,* ed. D. S. Meyer, N. Whittier, and B. Robnett. Oxford: Oxford University Press.

CHAPTER 38

THE SPREAD OF PROTEST POLITICS

DIETER RUCHT

In daily language, protest means the "symbolic and/or physical expression of dissent to something or somebody."[1] In this broad sense, protest occurs in many forms and many places. A child protests against finishing his or her soup. A football player protests against a dubious decision of the referee. These protests are articulated individually and outside a political context. By contrast, the term "protest politics" (Dalton 2002, ch. 4) usually denotes the deliberate and public use of protest by groups or organizations (but rarely individuals) that seek to influence a political decision or process, which they perceive as having negative consequences for themselves, another group or society as a whole.

In political life, some groups exist for the very purpose of protesting, or they at least use protest as a key mechanism to get their voices heard. This, for example, applies to Greenpeace, which is, according to various surveys, one of the best-known and most trusted associations in contemporary societies. Other groups, for example an association of fishermen or an automobile club, typically rely on other means to pursue their interests. Yet they may use protest occasionally or as a last resort. Accordingly, the kinds of groups that protest vary greatly, ranging from an informal citizen initiative to a big, hierarchical association to a radical political party. Even a government may resort to protest, for example by sending a written critical note to another government. As a rule, however, political protest is carried out by intermediary bodies that link citizens on the one hand and political power-holders on the other. Thus, the classical protest actors are loosely structured groups, campaigns, and social movements, and—to a lesser extent—interest groups and political parties.

---

[1] The original meaning of the Latin term *protestare* was "to bear witness" and therefore did not necessarily imply the act of rejecting something or somebody.

In addition to the kinds of actors, the content, aims, levels, and forms of political protest also vary extremely. Protest can refer to any political and social issue that is debated and contested, whether it is an utterance of a political leader, an administrative directive, or a political regime as a whole. The aim of protest can be narrow or broad, reformist or revolutionary, realistic or utopian. Some protests last only a few minutes, others, e.g. site occupations, may last over months or years. Some protests are spontaneous activities, others are carefully crafted and planned over a year or even longer. Still others take place on a regular basis. One example would be the annual worker protests on the First of May (existing since 1890). Another example is the weekly protest of the *Madres de Plaza de Mayo* who, since April 1977, have urged the prosecution of those who tortured or killed their children during the authoritarian regime in Argentina.

Regarding the spatial dimension, the issue may range from the concern of a small neighborhood to one of the world population. Political protests, if collective at all, can therefore be carried out by a handful of people in front of the town hall, but may also be an activity of the masses, as was the case with the millions who protested in many countries against the imminent war in Iraq on February 15, 2003, arguably the largest protest event in history. The forms of protest, too, include a broad range of activities, for example writing a petition, participating in a collection of signatures, attending a march or a gathering, blocking traffic, destroying property, injuring or even killing people.

As long as protest occurs in public, it should be conceptualized as a triangular communication process rather than a bipolar struggle. Besides the actors who protest and those who are targeted, third parties come into play, be they mediators or control agencies, be they physically present bystanders or the general public, which learns about the protest activity only via mass media. The role of the audience of protest should not be underestimated. Quite often, protest groups invest more energy in attracting the attention and probably even support of the audience than in trying to have a direct impact on their opponent. In some cases, the very act of protest would not occur without the assumed presence of media.

In the following, different perspectives and theories on protest politics will be described briefly. The main section of this chapter presents empirical findings on the patterns of protest, its determinants, and effects. The main results will be summarized in a few concluding remarks.

1 PERSPECTIVES AND THEORIES ON PROTEST POLITICS

Until the twentieth century, protest politics was widely seen as an irrational outburst of the "dangerous classes," which threatened the public order. This view of the "madding crowd" (McPhail 1991) included the peasant revolts in the sixteenth and seventeenth centuries as well as the workers' protests in the nineteenth and early twentieth centuries. The activities of machine breakers in Britain (Luddites) appeared to be an especially clear-cut example of the "blind fury" of the mob. Power-holders and their supporters were not interested in understanding the motives of their challengers, but rather in ways of discrediting and oppressing these groups. The scholarly world echoed this prejudice of emotionalized protesters, even in some historical analyses of protest (Mousnier 1968; Beloff 1938). It was probably most pronounced in the mass psychology that flourished in the late nineteenth and early twentieth centuries, as represented in the writings of Gustave Le Bon, Gabriel Tarde, and others. In this view, "crowd behaviour" was the result of uncontrolled emotions that spread like a disease, resulting from or in the breakdown of "normal" situations. This breakdown perspective was applied in some versions of collective behaviour theory that were especially prevalent in the USA until the mid-1960s. However, other theoretical currents, ranging from Marxism to symbolic interactionism to structural functionalism to rational choice perspectives, took a more serious and better grounded view of protest politics.

During the 1960s, the naive and distorted view of protest politics as irrational behaviour was replaced by perspectives that considered protest politics as a fairly rational and instrumental means to promote a political or social cause. Protest was seen as a "political resource" (Lipsky 1968) that, under certain conditions, proved to be quite effective (Gamson 1990). This interpretation became dominant even in analyses of the ghetto riots in the USA (Solznick 1969). Theories of relative deprivation were especially helpful in understanding the reasons for protest (Davies 1969; Gurr 1970). Relative deprivation convincingly explained why the objectively most deprived people were not necessarily those who protested the most.[2]

The strongest attack against the older view of irrational protest came from two strands, the resource mobilization approach and the rational choice theories. The former approach (McCarthy and Zald 1977), generally focusing on groups rather than on individuals, emerged within the broader framework of social movement studies (see Koopmans's chapter in this volume). It underlined the organized nature of protest and used analogies to economic behaviour, as indicated by the use of terms such as "social movement industry." Researchers extended this approach by considering the cognitive aspects of protest mobilization and the political processes and context in which protest groups and social movements are embedded (Tilly 1978; McAdam 1982; Tarrow 1998). In contrast, rational choice theories focus on the individual who, in light of perceived costs and benefits, chooses to take part in or abstain from protest activities (Finkel et al. 1989; Muller 1986; Opp 1989; Chong 1991). In this context, values and attitudes held by individuals are seen as the most important predictors of protest participation. This rationalist turn in the interpretation of protest politics in the USA

[2] This is also an important finding from survey analyses on protest. "In short, protest in advanced industrial democracies is not simply an outlet for the alienated and deprived; just the opposite often appears" (Dalton 2002, 67). While Dalton explains this finding basically by use of the resource model (which indeed has an explanatory power), one should also acknowledge the fact that people first must feel some sort of deprivation before they seek to find ways of overcoming it.

was partly a result of the experiences of a new generation of scholars, who had been involved in, or at least sympathized with, "progressive" movement activities.

In Europe, the early mass psychology did not fall on fertile ground. In light of the emblematic case of the labour movement, the organized and instrumental nature of protest politics was all too obvious. At a later stage, the resource mobilization and political process theories coming from the USA could easily be adopted and combined with the new social movement theories (Klandermans 1991) that, unlike the US approaches and social psychology theories also represented in Europe (Klandermans 1984), focused on the "why" rather than on the "how" of participation in protest.

The dominance of rationalist and structuralist perspectives in the 1980s and 1990s was challenged by new approaches that were inspired by constructionist theories and culturalist approaches. While these approaches emphasized the role of identity building, protest culture, morality, and emotions in protest activity (Johnston and Klandermans 1995; Jasper 1997; Goodwin and Jasper 1999), they did so without falling back on the prejudices of early mass psychology.

Today, the study of protest is no longer dominated by one single, encompassing theoretical perspective. Rather, we find an array of specific approaches that highlight and explore different aspects, such as: organizing and networking, motivating participants, identity building, framing of issues, strategy and tactics, agenda setting, and influencing policies. These approaches are anchored in different theoretical traditions and disciplines. In addition, there are attempts to integrate various perspectives into a broader conceptual framework (Neidhardt and Rucht 1993). All in all, the study of the causes, patterns, and consequences of political protest has become more complex, more context oriented, and more sophisticated; that is, it has become a matter for specialists rather than for grand theorists working with universal schemes and seeking parsimonious explanations.

2 THE SPREAD OF PROTEST POLITICS: EMPIRICAL FINDINGS

2.1 Methodologies

Along with the elaboration of theoretical and conceptual instruments, researchers have developed methodological tools for the empirical study of protest politics. On the one hand, methods inspired by ethnographic fieldwork have concentrated on analyses of the course and the details of a single act of collective protest. To this purpose, participant observers were trained and posted to register the behavior and physical constellation of protesters, describing their clothes, slogans, banners, speeches, interactions, etc. In such a case, much energy is invested in getting an in-depth view of just one or a few single protest incidents (McPhail and Miller 1973; McPhail and Wohlstein 1983).

On the other end of the methodological spectrum, protest event analysis covers a large number of protests in a potentially big territory over a considerable time span. Because researchers cannot be physically present in all these places, let alone witness protests that have occurred far back in history, they rely on existing sources such as police archives or newspaper reports to code certain features of protest such as location, size, theme, form, etc. (Rucht and Ohlemacher 1992; Kriesi et al. 1995; Fillieule 1996; Rucht, Koopmans, and Neidhardt 1999; Koopmans and Rucht 2002). Of course, the selectivity and biases of these sources has to be taken into account. As a recent extension to this method, claims analysis encompasses not only acts of protest but all demands and claims made by actors who publicly engage in a conflictive matter or in a broader policy domain (Koopmans and Statham 1999).

These methods allow researchers to identify the patterns of different aggregates of protest, for example regarding numbers of participants, claims and forms of protest across time, themes, and territory. Based on protest event analysis, for example, researchers have studied the protest activities of the so-called "new social movements" in four European countries (Kriesi et al. 1995) and environmental movements in seven European countries (Rootes 2003). Although these event analyses are instructive in many respects, they include only little and often superficial information about each single event.

A frequently used method for analysing protest is the case study that focuses on a single campaign, issue, or policy field. A case study can include a set of more specific methods such as content analysis of written documents, interviews, and participant observation. It goes beyond a single protest incident and allows for a better understanding of processes and interactions in a particular context. Yet this method has the disadvantage of not being representative for a larger number of cases, let alone the universe of protests in a given period and territory.

Another conventional and frequently applied method is to concentrate on individuals or groups rather than protests or campaigns as units of observation. Representative surveys can study the population's attitude toward protest groups and causes as well as the respondents' potential or actual participation in protest activities. This kind of research usually relates protest activity to socio-demographic, attitudinal, and other characteristics of the respondents to investigate the predictors for participation in different forms of protest (Barnes, Kaase, et al. 1979; Inglehart 1990; Jennings, van Deth, et al. 1990; Norris 2002; Dalton 2002).

Occasionally, researchers also have interviewed protesters on the spot or in other settings as members of a particular organization, thereby getting a more detailed and contextualized picture of who protests why and when. This method, for example, has been applied to study peace protesters in Britain in the 1960s (Parkin 1968) and more recently in other contexts (van Aelst and Walgrave 2001; Andretta et al. 2003; Agrikoliansky and Sommier 2005; Walgrave and Rucht forthcoming). In addition, individuals can be tapped as valuable sources of information on groups, organizations, and broader networks and alliances. Materials produced by these groups also serve as important sources of information. Unlike in other research areas, however, experimental methods and focus groups rarely have been used in the context of protest politics and social movements (some of the prominent exceptions are Touraine 1978; Melucci 1984).

In summary, a broad range of sources and methods are available to study different dimensions and aspects of protest. Although these methods can be, and in fact have been, adapted to the specific subject under study, none is exclusively reserved to protest politics. The increasingly systematic use of these methods during the last few decades has generated a large body of empirical knowledge about protest politics, of which some of the results are presented below with regard to the specific spread of protest politics.

2.2 The Multidimensional Spread of Protest Politics

2.2.1 *Frequency and mobilization capacity*

Protest politics is by no means a relic of pre-democratic or semi-democratic societies. Advanced western democracies, despite their broad set of institutionalized mechanisms to feed the interests of the citizenry into the decision-making process, experience the frequent use of protest.

Although few longitudinal and reliable data on the aggregate of political protest are available, there are indications that the frequency of political protest is increasing rather than decreasing. In Germany, for example, the number of political protests has grown considerably from the 1950s to the 1990s (Rucht 2003b). In France, the number of demonstrations has dramatically increased in the last few decades (Fillieule 1997; Tartakowsky 2004). Researchers have coined terms such as "demonstration democracy" (Etzioni 1970), "participatory revolution" (Kaase 1984), "movement society" (Neidhardt and Rucht 1993; Meyer and Tarrow 1998), and "protest society" (Pross 1992) to designate this development. Etzioni noticed that "demonstrations are becoming a part of the daily routine of our democracy and its most distinctive mark" (1970, 1).

The likelihood of an increasing use of political protest is supported by a series of population surveys in several countries (Barnes et al. 1979; Jennings et al. 1990; Norris 2002; Dalton 2002, 2004). According to these surveys, the citizenry exhibits a growing readiness for, and actual participation in, various forms of protest. Protest, in other words, has become a "normal" part of politics (Fuchs 1991). Even its frequent use is not necessarily perceived as a sign of destabilization or crisis of the political order. Rather, the opposite seems to be true. According to the World Values Survey undertaken from 1999 to 2002, participation in different forms of protest tends to be significantly higher in the well-established western and non-western democracies than in the more recent democracies in both eastern/central Europe and in a number of less "developed" countries from the southern part of the globe (see Table 38.1). Only when it comes to participation in the most disruptive form of protest under investigation (occupying buildings or factories) do the least developed countries exceed the advanced non-European countries (though not the western European ones).

The gap in protest participation between western Europe (including southern and northern Europe) and eastern/central Europe is also confirmed by data from the European Social Surveys conducted in 2002 and 2004. Moreover, participation in four

Table 38.1 Participation in various forms of protest according to world regions (%)[a]

Region	Signing a petition	Attending lawful demonstrations	Joining in boycotts	Joining unofficial strikes	Occupying buildings or factories
West European countries[b]	56.0	27.3	13.4	6.9	4.5
Advanced non-European countries[c]	61.8	20.2	14.5	6.5	2.1
East/central European countries[d]	29.3	15.0	4.9	3.4	1.1
Less developed "southern" countries[e]	16.3	12.7	8.0	5.2	3.5

[a] Source: World Values Survey 1999–2002. Respondents who, regarding the items listed, answered "have done."
[b] Austria, Belgium, Denmark, Finland, France, Germany, Great Britain, Greece, Iceland, Ireland, Italy, Luxembourg, the Netherlands, Portugal, Spain, Sweden.
[c] Canada, Israel, Japan, Republic of Korea, USA.
[d] Czech Republic, Estonia, Hungary, Poland, Slovakia, Slovenia, Russian Federation, Ukraine.
[e] Argentina, India, Indonesia, Mexico, Pakistan, Philippines, South Africa, Uganda.

activities during the last twelve months ("signing a petition," "boycotting products," "wearing or displaying campaign badges/stickers," "taking part in a lawful public demonstration") has increased in western Europe and, with the exception of boycotts, has also increased in eastern Europe from 2002 to 2004.

2.2.2 Issues and Claims

While social groups and ideological camps were broad but relatively few in number in the eighteenth and nineteenth centuries, today's advanced democracies rest on a highly differentiated social structure with a plethora of diverse groups, each living in specific conditions and therefore pursuing specific interests and political claims. Accordingly, the themes and issues around which protest is organized have grown enormously. Traditional cleavages (such as left vs. right, local vs. central, secular vs. religious) still exist, yet they have lost their significance relative to the multitude of other and new cleavages. Many problems and issues, such as genetic engineering, the depletion of the ozone layers, or the risks of nuclear power production, cannot be interpreted by means of the traditional cleavages. In addition, many problems affect only distinct social or professional groups whose demands can no longer be adopted and represented by broader generic groups (e.g. farmers, workers, shop owners). Rather, specific groups, such as retirees, nurses, cleaners, single mothers, lesbians, or lorry drivers, enter the stage as relatively homogeneous protest actors.

2.2.3 *Social categories*

Related to the growth of issues is the spread of protest into almost all social strata in established democracies. While protest was previously a domain primarily of under-privileged groups (though hardly the most deprived), today it is accessible to almost all kinds of social groups. We not only witness protests of workers in precarious jobs but also of dentists, policemen, and university professors. Because protest has diffused into many pockets of the populace and is increasingly seen as part of "normal politics," even high-ranking political leaders may participate in protest activities. This was the case in Germany, when several ministers of the Bavarian government headed a street demonstration against the jurisdiction of the Supreme Court in November 1995 or when leading representatives of the German federal government participated in marches against right-wing extremism and xenophobia in 1992 and 2000. By the same token, the kinds of organizations calling for protest are becoming more variegated. Not only the usual suspects, such as leftist radicals, trade unions, or student associations but also more "traditional" associations, for example nature conservation groups or Christian groups, become infected by the protest virus, although protest may not be part of their regular action repertoire. Across the board, representative surveys show a consistent link between the level of education and the propensity to engage in various protest activities. Regarding all four groups of countries included in Table 38.1, a clear-cut pattern is visible: the higher the level of education, the higher the percentage of people who engage in protest. This "iron law" applies to all five items under scrutiny in the World Social Survey of 1999 to 2002 as well as to all four items of the European Social Survey in 2004.

2.2.4 *Forms of Action*

During the course of the twentieth century, the forms and channels of protest have also become more numerous and diversified. In pre-modern societies, protest tended to be limited to either humble and modest claims of the subjects, usually expressed in petitions, letters to the king, etc., or, if these channels were blocked, the claimants resorted to rebellion. By contrast, modern democracies are marked by a steep increase of protests that range between the extremes of humble claims and violent outbursts.[3] The great bulk of protest politics is restricted to moderate and legal forms of expressing dissent. In most countries, police have developed a routine to regulate these kinds of protests (della Porta and Reiter 1998). In Berlin, for example, 2,000 to 2,500 protests have taken place annually in the last few years. Most frequently, we find collections of signatures, tabling, picketing, marches, gatherings, press releases, etc. With the increased availability of procedural complaints and litigation, these chan-nels are also becoming more widely used. In some cases, tens of thousands or even

---

[3] See the conceptual scheme representing different spectres of "unconventional behaviour" as pre-sented by Marsh (1997, 42) and refined by Dalton (2002, 61). Dalton distinguishes between partially overlapping zones of "orthodox" and "unorthodox" political behavior. The latter category includes direct action, illegal action and violence, again partially overlapping each other. At the end opposite to violence, the authors locate conventional politics, such as voting, lobbying, formal interest groups, etc.

hundreds of thousands of people have formally objected to techno-industrial projects such as nuclear reactors, airports, dams, channels, pipelines, etc. In addition to these strictly legal protests, more disruptive though still non-violent forms of protest have also increased in significance. Blockades, squatting, occupation of construction sites, and the politically motivated refusal to participate in a census or to pay certain taxes belong to this category. While some protest groups practise "direct action" for purely instrumental reasons, others do so strictly in the spirit of civil disobedience that is bound to a number of non-trivial conditions. Whatever the specific form and spirit of such activities, they are less frequent when compared to the legal protests, and they attract far fewer participants. Representative surveys show that the younger generation exhibits a greater propensity to engage in more disruptive forms of protests when compared to older age cohorts. According to the data of the World Values Survey in 1999 to 2002, this pattern is especially pronounced in western European countries. Whereas 6.9 percent of the respondents in the age group up to 25 years reported having participated in occupations of buildings or factories, 4.7 percent in the age group from 26 to 50 and only 3.0 percent of those aged more than 50 years reported doing so. Disruptive action is also predominantly a male activity. In all four world regions listed in Table 38.1, the proportion of women engaged in occupying buildings or factories (ranging from 1.8 percent in eastern/central Europe to 3.8 percent in western Europe) was lower than the proportion of men. By contrast, nearly as many women as men signed a petition in western Europe and eastern/central Europe. In the group of advanced non-European countries, a significantly greater number of women compared to men reported having signed a petition.

2.2.5 *Territory*

Finally, and probably most remarkably during the last decades, protest politics has also spread in a territorial sense, i.e. across countries and continents. With modern means of communication, in particular television and video technology, protest activities occurring in a given place can literally be watched worldwide (Gitlin 1980). This applies, to mention just a few outstanding examples, to the demonstrations around the Democratic Convention in Chicago in 1968, the student protests during the Olympic Games in Mexico City in 1968, the Tiananmen square protests in Beijing in 1998, and the Orange Revolution in Ukraine in 2005. It comes as no surprise that certain ideas, claims, and protest tactics are rapidly diffused to other places (McAdam and Rucht 1993). Relatively cheap and fast means of travelling, together with the use of the internet, facilitate such diffusion. These means are are also instrumental in building networks of activists and organizing joint campaigns.

Immigration across countries and continents contributes to the territorial spread of protest. Immigrant groups in western democracies often raise problems (hunger, economic exploitation, political repression, etc.) in their home countries, thereby broadening the range of issues and social carriers in their host society. For example, Algerian immigrants protested in Paris in 1961 against the French colonial regime in their home country (a protest event during which more than a hundred largely peaceful participants were killed by police); political refugees coming from Chile to Europe blamed the Pinochet government for torture and massacres after the *coup d'état* in 1973; Kurds in Germany blocked a highway to draw attention to repression in eastern Turkey throughout the 1990s. In many of these cases, the immigrant groups were supported by domestic advocacy groups. More generally, prominent groups such as Amnesty International and Human Rights Watch help to raise awareness about usually geographically distant but severe violations of human and civil rights.

During the last few years, cross-border networking and protesting has been boosted in the context of what the media have labelled "anti-globalization groups" and which the activists refer to as "global justice movements." While the origins of these movements can be traced at least as far back as the third world groups of the 1960s, they have been perceived as a new phenomenon, especially since the Zapatista uprising in 1996 and the protest campaign against the meeting of the World Trade Organization in Seattle in 1999 (Lichbach and Almeida 2001). Since then, a number of "counter summits" and other mass protests (Pianta 2001) have contributed to the image of a stunning worldwide protest movement—a "movement of movements" whose smallest common denominator is the struggle against the globalizing neoliberalism and its proponents, be they multinational corporations or international governmental institutions like the WTO, the World Bank, and the International Monetary Fund (Rucht 2003*a*; della Porta and Tarrow 2005; Tarrow 2005). The Global Justice Movements not only reactively mobilize against these targets on the occasion of official summits, they have also begun to establish a more permanent infrastructure by forming broad alliances (e.g. Attac, Peoples' Global Action), creating multi-issue communication networks (such as Indymedia), and engaging in the Social Forum process. The latter gained momentum with the first World Social Forum in Brazil in 2001 as a direct response to the well-established and elitist World Economic Forum which takes place in the Swiss mountain resort of Davos on an annual basis. Within only a few years, the World Social Forum has become an activity in its own right, with masses of participants from all continents. The forum idea has also spread to the continental level (for example, with four European Social Forums to date in Florence, Paris, London, and Athens, respectively). Finally, national and local forums were set up in a considerable number of countries. In Europe, the forum idea is probably strongest in Italy, with some 150 loosely coordinated local groups and a capacity to mobilize, in cooperation with a plethora of many other leftist groups, hundreds of thousands of people in street protest. With their generic aim to abolish neoliberalism or, from the perspective of left-radical groups, capitalism and neo-imperialism, these groups have set a goal that is extremely difficult to reach. However, when it comes to raising consciousness regarding the negative side effects of economic globalization, they have made considerable progress in the last few years. Moreover, partly with the support of some national governments, they were able to reach more limited goals such as thwarting the Multilateral Agreement on Investment in 1997, banning anti-personnel landmines by the late 1990s, and reaching a partial debt relief for the poorest countries of the globe in the early 2000s.

2.3 Determinants and Effects of Protest

Numerous empirical studies have disproved the common assumption that the greater the grievances, the more likely people will engage in social or political protest. Only when additional factors come into play do grievances result in actual protest. Different theoretical schools have emphasized different sets of factors such as: the perception and interpretation of grievances and their causes, the expected impact of protest, the resource base, the structural commonalities of the protesters and their organizational embeddedness and the context structure including political, economic, cultural, and discursive opportunities and restrictions on protest. The relevance of these sets of factors has been demonstrated by the use of different data, most using representative population surveys, surveys of participants in actual protest events, and protest event and claims-making data derived from newspaper reports or police archives. The latter were particularly useful in demonstrating the role of context factors, such as access to the decision-making system, the availability of allies, and state capacity (Kriesi et al. 1995). The role of different context structures is particularly striking when comparing the Spanish Basque country with other regions in Spain. Based on police data, Casquete has calculated that the "demonstration density rate," measured as the number of demonstrations per thousand inhabitants, is "roughly 18.3 times higher in the Basque country" than in the rest of Spain in the five-year period from 1996 to 2000 (Casquete 2003, 17). This difference, to a large extent, has to be explained by political and cultural structures.

Survey research, on the other hand, was useful in highlighting the role of socio-demographic characteristics, attitudes, values, and cost-benefit calculus. More recently, surveys have also been used to test the relevance of different factors on participation in protest, including not only socio-demographics but also economic, political, and cultural factors. Using the World Values Survey in 1990/1991, Roller and Weßels (1996) showed that the organizational context, measured as an individual's embeddedness in organizations, contributes more to the explanation of legal protest than to that of illegal protest. Regarding the wider context of political protest, their analysis suggests that the more modern a society (measured by a set of socioeconomic factors and political factors), the higher the extent of protest participation. Dalton and van Sickle, drawing on the World Values Survey undertaken from 1999 to 2002, tested the relative impact of resource, structural, and cultural bases of protest (for their dependent variable, see the items listed in Table 38.1). The authors come to a straightforward conclusion: "In summary, protest is facilitated by a syndrome of factors found in advanced industrial democracies: affluence, open and effective political institutions, and post-materialist (self-expressive) values. Each of these variables shows a strong bivariate relationship to protest, and they continue to display independent influence on our multivariate models" (Dalton and van Sickle 2005, 16).

Though being of tremendous scholarly and political interest, the study of the impact of protest still suffers from a lack of systematic comparative data (Giugni 1998; Kolb 2006). Relative to the abundance of literature dealing in some way with the effects of protest, few robust findings are available. In part, this is due to conceptual difficulties in identifying and measuring the multitude of independent, intervening, and dependent factors that come into play. Some effects of protest may materialize only after a considerable time span or in interaction with factors other than protest. Even the complete failure of a given protest may contribute to the success of another protest, provided that the actors have learned their lesson—a fact that may escape scholarly attention. Another problem stems from the fact that protesters sometimes modify their goals during the course of a campaign, making the reference point for success and failure arbitrary.

It is safe to say that the size and forms of protest are at best indirectly linked to the outcomes. On the one hand, some protests, even including large and intense ones, do not seem to produce concrete results. On the other hand, even small protests may occasionally result in a substantial political change. Disruptive protest can trigger considerable concessions by the authorities or strengthen the moderate protesters by a so-called "radical flank effect" (Haines 1988). Yet in other circumstances, it may also create a deep split among the protesters' ranks, turn away people who otherwise would sympathize with the cause of protest, or legitimize severe repression by the authorities.

While protest often fails to achieve a complete or substantial policy success, quite often it at least has a limited impact in one of several dimensions of outcomes, such as influencing public opinion, strengthening or weakening protest organizations, (de-) legitimating the opponents, modifying voting behaviour, affecting the rules of the game, etc. Whether or not protest matters depends much on the circumstances, among them the media resonance of the protest, the credibility of the protesters, the strength of the opponents, the cultural resonance of the protesters' frames, and precipitating incidents. In a few exceptional moments, protest is able to "make history," as the peaceful revolutions in eastern Europe in the late 1980s demonstrated. In other situations, protest unintentionally provokes strong counter-protest and therefore fails. In a historical perspective, it is evident that many achievements that we tend to take for granted are the outcome of numerous and sustained protest activities. This is true, for example, for the constitutional guarantee of elementary human, civic, and social rights. But it is also worth noting that such achievements are attacked by anti-democratic and xenophobic groups, who use various forms of protest to promote their views.

3 CONCLUSION

During the last two centuries, and probably most clearly during the course of the last three decades, protest politics underwent significant changes. Broadly speaking, polit-ical protest appears to have increased in terms of the frequency of events and number of participants, broadened and diversified regarding the range of issues, forms, and social carriers, diffused spatially across countries and continents, and shifted to the trans-national level. In all these respects, a remarkable spread of protest politics can be observed. During these processes, protest has lost much of its former image as an "unconventional" and "disturbing" phenomenon. At least the moderate forms of procedural, appellative, and demonstrative protest are accepted, and occasionally practised, by large segments of the population, though predominantly by the better-educated social strata. To a much smaller extent, confrontational forms of protest (direct action, civil disobedience) have also increased. As for violent protest, no reliable cross-national and longitudinal data are available. The trends seem to vary considerably from country to country.

With the exception of violent activities, protest politics has not just normalized in the sense that we have become used to it, it has also gained legitimacy. Advocates of a participatory democracy consider protest as a necessary and healthy element of a "strong" democracy (Barber 1984). To the extent that conflict is acknowledged as a constitutive element of the democratic game and the role of the citizen as the "democratic phoenix" (Norris 2002) is not limited to periodic voting, the citizens' pursuit of interest will continue to include protest activities, both those that respect human rights and embrace democracy, but also those which disregard or even conflict with democratic values.

REFERENCES

AGRIKOLIANSKY, E., and SOMMIER, I., eds. 2005. *Radiographie du mouvement altermondialiste.* Paris: La Dispute.

ANDRETTA, M., DELLA PORTA, D., MOSCA, L., and REITER, H. 2003. *No global—new global: Identität und Strategien der Antiglobalisierungsbewegung.* Frankfurt/M.: Campus.

BARBER, B. 1984. *Strong Democracy: Participatory Politics for a New Age.* Berkeley: University of California Press.

BARNES, S. H., KAASE, M., et al. 1979. *Political Action: Mass Participation in Five Nations.* Beverly Hills, Calif.: Sage.

BELOFF, M. 1938. *Public Order and Popular Disturbances, 1660–1714.* Oxford: Oxford University Press.

CASQUETE, J. 2003. From imagination to visualization: protest rituals in the Basque country. Wissenschaftszentrum Berlin für Sozialforschung. Discussion Paper SP IV 2003–401.

CHONG, D. 1991. *Collective Action and the Civil Rights Movement.* Chicago: University of Chicago Press.

DALTON, R. J. 2002. *Citizen Politics: Public Opinion and Political Parties in Advanced Industrial Democracies,* 3rd edn. New York: Chatham House.

—— 2004. *Democratic Challenges, Democratic Choices: The Erosion of Political Support in Advanced Industrial Democracies.* Oxford: Oxford University Press.

—— 2006. *Citizen Politics: Public Opinion and Political Parties in Advanced Industrial Democracies* 4th edn. Washington, DC: CQ Press.

—— and VAN SICKLE, A. 2005. The resource, structural, and cultural bases of protest. Center for the Study of Democracy (University of California, Irvine). Paper 05'11 (http://repositories.cdlib.ord/csd/05–11).

DAVIES, J. C. 1969. The J-curve of rising and declining satisfactions as a cause of revolution and rebellion. Pp. 415–36 in *The History of Violence in America,* ed. H. D. Graham and T. Gurr. New York: Bantam Books.

DELLA PORTA, D., and REITER, H. eds. 1998. *Policing Protest: The Control of Mass Demonstrations in Western Democracies.* Minneapolis: University of Minnesota Press.

—— and TARROW, S. eds. 2005. *Transnational Protest and Global Activism.* Lanham, Md.: Rowman & Littlefield.

ETZIONI, A. 1970. *Demonstration Democracy.* New York: Gordon & Breach.

FILLIEULE, O. 1996. Police records and national press in France: issues in the methodology of data-collections from newspapers. Working Paper of the Robert Schuman Centre, No. 96/25. Florence: European University Institute.

—— 1997. *Stratégies de la rue.* Paris: Presses de Sciences Po.

FINKEL, S. E., MULLER, E. N., and OPP, K.-D. 1989. Personal influence, collective rationality, and mass political action. *American Political Science Review,* 83: 885–903.

FUCHS, D. 1991. The normalization of the unconventional: forms of political action and new social movements. Pp. 148–65 in *Political Participation and Democracy in Poland and West Germany,* ed. G. Meyer and F. Ryszka. Warsaw: Wydawca.

GAMSON, W. 1990. *The Strategy of Social Protest,* 2nd edn. Belmont, Calif.: Wadsworth.

GITLIN, T. 1980. *The Whole World is Watching: Mass Media and the Making and Unmaking of the New Left.* Berkeley: University of California Press.

GIUGNI, M. 1998. Was it worth the effort? The outcomes and consequences of social movements. *Annual Review of Sociology,* 98: 371–93.

GOODWIN, J., and JASPER, J. M. 1999. Caught in a winding, snarling vine: the structural bias of political process theory. *Sociological Forum,* 14: 27–54.

GURR, T. R. 1970. *Why Men Rebel.* Princeton: Princeton University Press.

HAINES, H. H. 1988. *Black Radicals and the Civil Rights Mainstream, 1954–1970.* Knoxville: University of Tennessee Press.

INGLEHART, R. 1990. *Culture Shift in Advanced Industrial Society.* Princeton: Princeton University Press.

JASPER, J. M. 1997. *The Art of Moral Protest: Culture, Biography, and Creativity in Social Movements.* Chicago: University of Chicago Press.

JENNINGS, M. K., VAN DETH, J., et al. 1990. *Continuities in Political Action: A Longitudinal Study of Political Orientations in Three Western Democracies.* Berlin: de Gruyter.

JOHNSTON, H., and KLANDERMANS, B. eds. 1995. *Social Movements and Culture.* Minneapolis: University of Minnesota Press.

KAASE, M., 1984. The challenge of the "participatory revolution" in pluralist democracies. *International Political Science Review,* 5: 299–318.

KLANDERMANS, B. 1984. Mobilization and participation: social psychological expansions of the resource mobilization theory. *American Sociological Review,* 49: 583–600.

—— 1991. New social movements and resource mobilization: the European and the American approach. Pp. 17–44 in *Research on Social Movements: The State of the Art in Western Europe and the USA,* ed. D. Rucht. Frankfurt/M: Campus.

KOLB, F. 2006. Protest, opportunities, and mechanisms: a theory of social movements and political change. Free University of Berlin. Unpublished Ph.D. dissertation.

KOOPMANS, R., and RUCHT, D. 2002. Protest event analysis. Pp. 231–59 in *Methods in Social Movement Research,* ed. B. Klandermans and S. Staggenborg. Minneapolis: University of Minnesota Press.

—— and STATHAM, P. 1999. Political claims analysis: integrating protest event and public discourse approaches. Pp. 203–22 in *Mobilization 4. Special Issue: Protest Event Analysis,* ed. D. Rucht and R. Koopmans.

KRIESI, H., KOOPMANS, R., DUYVENDAK, J. W., and GUIGNI, M. G. 1995. *New Social Movements in Western Europe. A Comparative Analysis.* Minneapolis: University of Minnesota Press.

LICHBACH, M. I. and ALMEIDA, P. 2001. Global order and local resistance: the neoliberal institutional trilemma and the battle of Seattle. University of California, Riverside. Unpublished Paper.

LIPSKY, M. 1968. Protest as a political resource. *American Political Science Review*, 62: 1144–58.

McADAM, D. 1982. *Political Process and the Development of Black Insurgency, 1930–1970*. Chicago: University of Chicago Press.

—— and RUCHT, D. 1993. Cross-national diffusion of social movement ideas and tactics. *The Annals of the American Academy of Political and Social Sciences, Special Issue on Citizens, Protest, and Democratic Politics*, ed. R. Dalton. Vol. 528: 56–74.

McCARTHY, J. D., and ZALD, M. N. 1977. Resource mobilization and social movements: a partial theory. *American Journal of Sociology*, 82: 1212–41.

McPHAIL, C. 1991. *The Myth of the Madding Crowd*. New York: Aldine de Gruyter.

—— and MILLER, D. L. 1973. The assembling process: a theoretical and empirical investigation. *American Sociological Review*, 38: 721–35.

—— and WOHLSTEIN, R. 1983. Individual and collective behaviors within gatherings, demonstrations, and riots. *Annual Review of Sociology*, 9: 579–600.

MARSH, A. 1977. *Protest and Political Consciousness*. Beverly Hills, Calif.: Sage.

MELUCCI, A. ed. 1984. *Altri Codici: Aree di movimento nella metropoli*. Bologna: Il mulino.

MEYER, D., and TARROW, S. eds. 1998. *The Social Movement Society: Contentious Politics for a New Century*. Lanham, Md.: Rowman & Littlefield.

MOUSNIER, R. 1968. *Fureurs paysannes: les paysans dans les révoltes du XVIIe siècle (France, Russie, Chine)*. Paris: Calman-Lévy.

MULLER, E. N. 1986. Rational choice and rebellious collective action. *American Political Science Review*, 80: 471–87.

NEIDHARDT, F. and RUCHT, D. 1993. Auf dem Weg in die "Bewegungsgesellschaft"? Über die Stabilisierbarkeit sozialer Bewegungen. *Soziale Welt*, 44: 305–26.

NORRIS, P. 1999. *Critical Citizens: Global Support for Democratic Governance*. Oxford: Oxford University Press.

—— 2002. *Democratic Phoenix: Reinventing Political Activism*. Cambridge, Cambridge University Press.

OPP, K.-D. 1989. *The Rationality of Political Protest: A Comparative Analysis of Rational Choice Theory*. Boulder, Colo.: Westview Press.

PARKIN, F. 1968. *Middle Class Radicalism: The Social Bases of the British Campaign for Nuclear Disarmament*. Cambridge: Cambridge University Press.

PIANTA, M. 2001. Parallel summits of global civil society. Pp. 169–94 in *Global Civil Society 2001*, ed. H. Anheier, M. Glasius, and M. Kaldor. Oxford: Oxford University Press.

PROSS, H. 1992. *Protestgesellschaft: Von der Wirksamkeit des Widerspruchs*. Munich: Artemis & Winkler.

ROLLER, E., and WEßELS, B. 1996. Contexts of political protest in western democracies: political organization and modernity. Pp. 91–134 in *Extremism, Protest, Social Movements, and Democracy and Society*, vol. iii, ed. F. Weil et al. Greenwich: JAI Press.

ROOTES, C. ed. 2003. *Environmental Protest in Western Europe*. Oxford: Oxford University Press.

RUCHT, D. 2003a. Social movements challenging neo-liberal globalization. Pp. 211–28 in *Social Movements and Democracy*, ed. P. Ibarra. New York: Palgrave Macmillan.

—— 2003b. Bürgerschaftliches Engagement in sozialen Bewegungen und politischen Kampagnen. Pp. 17–155 in *Bürgerschaftliches Engagement in Parteien und Bewegungen*, ed. Enquete-Kommission "Zukunft des Bürgerschaftlichen Engagements." Deutscher Bundestag. Opladen: Leske & Budrich.

—— and OHLEMACHER, T. 1992. Protest event data: collection, uses and perspectives. Pp. 76–10 in *Studying Collective Action*, ed. R. Eyerman and M. Diani. Beverly Hills, Calif.: Sage.

—— KOOPMANS, R., and NEIDHARDT, F. eds. 1999. *Acts of Dissent: New Developments in the Study of Protest*. Lanham, Md.: Rowman & Littlefield.

SOLZNICK, J. H. 1969. *The Politics of Protest*. (Task Force on Violent Aspects of Protest and Confrontation of the National Commission on the Causes and Prevention of Violence). New York: Simon & Schuster.

TARROW, S 1998. *Power in Movement. Social Movements and Contentious Politics*, 2nd edn. Cambridge: University of Cambridge Press.

—— 2005. *The New Transnational Activism*. Cambridge: University of Cambridge Press.

TARTAKOWSKY, D. 2004. *La Manif en éclat*. Paris: La Dispute.

TOURAINE, A. 1978. *Le Voix et le regard*. Paris: Seuil.

TILLY, C. 1978. *From Mobilization to Revolution*. Reading, Mass.: Addison-Wesley.

VAN AELST, P., and WALGRAVE, S. 2001. Who is that man in the street? From the normalisation of protest to the normalisation of the protester. *European Journal of Political Research*, 39: 461–86.

WALGRAVE, S., and RUCHT, D. eds. Forthcoming. *Protest Politics: Anti-war Mobilization in Western Democracies*. Minneapolis: University of Minnesota Press.

CHAPTER 39

NEW FEMINIST CHALLENGES TO THE STUDY OF POLITICAL ENGAGEMENT

PIPPA NORRIS

As we enter the twenty-first century, why are so few women leaders found in the corridors of power in legislative, executive, and judicial office, even in many long-standing democracies? And why are women usually under-represented as activists within party organization, unions, interest groups, and community associations? The phenomenon of the "activism gap" among women and men has been well documented at mass and elite levels in numerous studies, both within the United States and in many other countries. Given the immense changes in men and women's lifestyles during recent decades—in education, the workforce, and the family—the continuance of the familiar activism gap is an important and intriguing puzzle. This chapter considers some of the key research questions and the recent theoretical advances seeking to explain the activism gap, focusing upon feminist challenges to the conventional study of political behavior.

To explore these issues, section 1 of this chapter considers some of the reasons—political, intellectual, and organizational—for the growth of scholarship on gender studies in recent decades. Section 2 documents the extent of the contemporary "activism gap" among women and men as citizens and politicians reported in numerous studies. Section 3 discusses the distinguishing features and theoretical assumptions of the rival frameworks seeking to explain the activism gap. Section 4 highlights selected studies concerning the role of cultural attitudes and resources to illustrate supply-side explanations. Section 5 summarizes alternative demand-side perspectives on the root causes of women and men's political activism, emphasizing the role of mobilizing organizations and gendered institutions. The conclusion reflects on the implications of these contrasting perspectives for our knowledge of gender politics and the broader challenges of feminist theories for political behavior in general.

1 THE GROWTH OF THE SUBFIELD

Earlier reviews of the literature have traced the emergence of the study of women and politics and mapped out the main contours of the burgeoning literature. Scholars have reflected upon the growing body of work on feminism and political theory, gender gaps in partisanship and public opinion, gender and international conflict, women in comparative politics, and the impact of public policy on issues of sex and gender (see, for example, Sapiro 1991; Carroll and Zerilli 1993; Sigel 1996; Staudt and Weaver 1997; Lovenduski 1998; Ritter and Mellow 2000; Burns 2002; Carroll 2003). This chapter builds upon these insights and focuses on what is known about the activism gap between women and men in the field of political behavior.

To clarify the core concepts in the literature, following the now conventional distinction, "*sex*" is understood here as the biological or physical differences that distinguish male and female, for example in muscle strength, reproductive capacities, or levels of testosterone. Sex is conceptualized as an individual attribute or demographic characteristic. "*Gender*" refers to the socially constructed meanings associated with being a woman or a man. Both sex and gender can be regarded as continuums (for example, some women are physically strong, some men are relatively weak) but sex is almost always measured at the most basic and simplest level as a dichotomy. Sex and gender may have direct effects on political behavior, or they may have an indirect impact by interacting with cross-cutting cleavages, for example where women and men differ in their lifestyles and experiences through their care of dependants, dependence on state benefits, or patterns of occupational segregation, as well as by interacting with cleavages of ethnicity and class.

Research draws attention to the way that sex and gender may influence many dimensions of political behavior, including through: (i) shaping political attitudes, beliefs, opinions, and policy preferences; (ii) influencing political activism through electoral-oriented channels typified by voting, parties, and campaigns, as well as through civic arenas such as interest groups, the mass media, voluntary associations, and community organizations; (iii) determining patterns of voting choices and partisan attachments; (iv) affecting group identification and mobilization through new social movements and organizations concerned with feminism, masculinity, and sexual choice; (v) influencing the public policy agenda on issues such as gay and lesbian rights, abortion, childcare, same-sex marriage, welfare reform, gender quotas in politics, pay equity, sex discrimination, sexual harassment, and equal opportunities in the workplace; and lastly, at elite levels, (vi) shaping women and men's routes into elected office, political representation in legislatures, and the role of women as leaders and heads of state.

Questions about the significance of sex and gender in politics hardly raise "new" debates; indeed these are some of central issues that have long motivated the study of political behavior ever since sex was monitored as a standard face-sheet variable in surveys. Herbert Tingsten's pioneering book on *Political Behavior* (1937) provided the earliest empirical work, documenting systematic differences in men and women's political preferences and voting turnout. This was followed by Maurice Duverger's seminal *The Political Role of Women* (1955), comparing women as voters and in elected office in western Europe. Just as studies have long focused upon the classic cleavages of class, religion, and race/ethnicity, so also for the last half-century, at least *sotto voce*, sex and gender have provided one of the enduring foundations for political sociology and political psychology. But when survey research started in the post-war decade other social cleavages such as class, religion, and race/ethnicity were widely regarded as primary.

Berelson, Lazarsfeld, and McPhee's path-breaking *Voting* (1954) illustrates some of the earliest survey analysis in political sociology. They examined the role of social groups in determining party support in the 1948 presidential election in Elmira, New York. Social class, age/generation, and Protestant or Catholic religious identities were regarded as the main social influences on Democratic and Republican support. The role of sex was acknowledged, as women were less politicized than men. Women also derived weaker voting cues from class identities, as well as being more Republican-leaning in voting intentions. But sex differences were never treated systematically as a major part of their puzzle of electoral behavior. Similar treatments can be found among other seminal studies which established the field of political sociology during the 1950s and 1960s (e.g. Lipset 1960; Almond and Verba 1963). Subsequent feminist critiques have often noted that where sex was discussed in this early literature, the importance of any differences between women and men were sometimes exaggerated and stereotyped, based on the limited evidence and the modest size of any gender gaps, and differences between women and men were assumed to be relatively unproblematic (Bourque and Grossholtz 1974; Carroll 1979; Goot and Reid 1984).

In subsequent decades, the issue of the impact of sex and gender on political behavior arose with renewed vigor on the contemporary research agenda. This was fueled by intellectual developments in feminist scholarship, rethinking predominant frameworks, methods, and concepts, sweeping through the social sciences and humanities. Political sociology lagged behind developments in disciplines such as history, philosophy, and anthropology, but beginning in the early-1970s the study of women and political behavior became established as a distinctive subfield within the American profession of political science. This development was fuelled by ground-breaking work on women's behavior as voters, activists, and elected representatives published by a handful of scholars (Amundsen 1971; Kirkpatrick 1974; Diamond 1977;

Githens and Prestage 1977; Baxter and Lansing 1983). The study of gender politics gradually emerged as a distinct subfield in political science in many other countries as well, as demonstrated by strong international networks and popular research sections in the main national and regional political science organizations, such as IPSA and the ECPR. The Women and Politics research section of APSA was founded in 1986; almost two decades later it has more than 600 political scientists as members, ranking 11th out of 34 sections. Participation by women scholars as paper-givers at APSA's annual meeting has surged; the proportion of women quadrupled from only 43 (8%) in 1971 to a peak of 1053 (36%) in 2003 (Gruberg 2005). The major shift occurred from 1971 to 1991, followed by a slower and more modest rise.

This expansion is also demonstrated by the burgeoning range of books, monographs, and conference papers on women and politics, as well as on men, masculinity, and the politics of sexual choice. University courses on women and politics now exist in about three-quarters of all US political science departments (Brandes et al. 2001). The rapid increase in the number of women students and academics in political science has transformed the profession; in the US, women are now almost one-half of all undergraduates in political science, one-quarter of all faculty, and almost one-third (29% or 3,491) of APSA's official membership (Brandes et al. 2001). Not all women in the profession study gender politics, by any means; nevertheless patterns of recruitment have indirectly encouraged the intellectual expansion of the subfield. A comparable surge has occurred among female graduates in political science, suggesting that this trend will continue as doctoral students gradually percolate through the profession (Brandes et al. 2001). In other countries, women are often a smaller proportion of political scientists, but evidence suggests that their numbers have grown over the years. In Britain, for example, the proportion of women faculty in political science rose from 10 percent in 1978 to 24 percent in 2002 (Bennie 2002). At the same time, the study of women and politics continues to face some important hurdles in achieving full recognition; for example, the major scholarly journals in political science, such as the APSR, continue to include few papers reflecting feminist epistemology and theory (Kelly and Fisher 1993; Kelly, Williams, and Fisher 1994; Mathews and Andersen 2001), and some scholars have detected recent signs of a possible backlash against women within the profession. The subfield of women and politics, and gender studies, has therefore made important strides over the years, expanding in scope and sophistication, but some of the core issues which first stimulated work continue to remain on the research agenda.

2 The Puzzle of the Activism Gap

The core puzzle in the literature focuses on the "activism gap" among women and men, a phenomenon found at mass and elite level. The key question is why this gap persists despite the transformation of women's lives in post-industrial societies during the late twentieth century. Women have now flooded into universities and the paid workforce in record numbers, they have made striking advances in the professions and management, and there is substantial evidence that social attitudes favoring gender equality have become widespread in affluent societies (Inglehart and Norris 2003). Yet developments in politics, particularly at the apex of power, seem to lag behind these trends.

The earliest studies of political behavior in western Europe and North America, conducted during the 1920s and 1930s shortly after the female franchise was granted in many countries, commonly observed that men were more likely to vote than women (Merriam 1924; Gosnell 1930; Tingsten 1937; Durant 1949). For Lipset (1960), sex was one of the standard variables to explain mass levels of electoral turnout and conventional forms of political participation, alongside the most powerful predictors of age, class, and education. During the 1960s and early 1970s, Verba, Nie, and Kim (1978) compared voting turnout, party membership, contact activity, and community organizing, all "conventional" forms of political participation, in seven nations. The study concluded: "*In all societies for which we have data, sex is related to political activity; men are more active than women.*" The activism gap persisted, even after controlling for differences between women and men in their education, trade union membership, and psychological involvement in politics. During the early 1970s, Barnes, Kaase et al. (1979) expanded the scope of activity in their study of "protest politics", comparing eight post-industrial nations. They established that women were usually less engaged in demonstrations, occupations, and illegal strikes.

In post-industrial societies, given the substantial changes in men and women's lifestyles, educational opportunities, and workplace participation, there are many reasons why the gender gap in activism may have diminished, or possibly even reversed. This pattern seems to have occurred in countries where women now regularly cast ballots in significantly higher proportions than men (Christy 1987; Norris 2001). In the United States, in every presidential election since 1980, the proportion of eligible female adults who voted has exceeded the proportion of eligible male adults who voted (Conway, Steuernagel, and Ahern 1997). Burns, Schlozman, and Verba (2001) found that the gender gap in voting turnout had closed by the mid-1990s, but American women are still less engaged than men in election-oriented arenas, such as in attending public meetings, campaign contributions, affiliation with political organizations, and contacting public officials, as well as involvement in other dimensions of civic life, including attending meetings or organizing to solve community problems. Nor was this pattern confined to the United States. For comparison, in Britain, Pattie, Seyd, and Whiteley (2004) reported that gender was not significantly related to the total number of political actions. Women, however, were slightly *more* engaged than men in individual acts (such as boycotting a product) although at the same time they were marginally *less* involved in collective acts (such as party membership). Gender differences were also evident in cultural attitudes, with women proving less politically knowledgeable, interested, and engaged in political discussions.

In a broader comparison based on eighty nations contained in the World Values Survey, Inglehart and Norris (2003) established that women remain less engaged than men in many common modes of political life. The gender gap in participation is usually modest in size, but also consistent; men continue to predominate in traditional forms of activism, as members in voluntary organizations, community associations, and new social movements, and in the common forms of protest politics. Nevertheless the size of gender differences was greater in poorer developing societies rather than in post-industrial nations so that in the longer term, due to processes of societal development, the activism gap may gradually diminish. Moreover, in post-industrial societies, the activism gap was smallest among the youngest cohort, which is another important indicator of long-term generational change (Inglehart and Norris 2003). There have also been studies of the role of women as actors in democratic transitions in Latin America and post-communist Europe, where pre-existing networks are found to play an important role in whether women are mobilized (Baldez 2003). In these regions, there has also been considerable research on the use of quotas for elected office, which were commonplace but subsequently reduced or abandoned in post-communist Europe, whilst simultaneously experiencing a substantial revival of usage in Latin America (Dahlerup 2005).

Some have theorized that women may be under-represented in the conventional electoral arenas but they may, instead, predominate elsewhere as the grassroots volunteer workers engaged in community and social organizations. Yet, organizational membership also remains segmented by gender in the United States, as well as in most nations (Inglehart and Norris 2003; Norris and Inglehart 2005). The greatest contrast is less in the total number of clubs, groups, and organizations that men and women join, but rather in the horizontal divisions within associational life. Today in many countries certain types of organizations remain disproportionately male, including political parties, sports clubs, the peace movement, professional groups, labor unions, and community associations. By contrast, women still predominate in associations related to traditional female roles, including education and the arts, religious and church organizations, providing social welfare services for the elderly or handicapped, as well as women's groups. This matters if horizontal segmentation into same sex-related bonding groups has positive functions for members, and yet may generate negative externalities (reinforcing gender divisions) for society as a whole. In a perfectly sex-segmented society, the problem is not that women are not bowling, but rather that they are bowling in women's leagues.

At elite level, at the apex of power, there is an even larger gap in the proportion of women who become candidates, elected officials, and leaders, with women constituting about 15 percent of parliamentarians worldwide (Inter-Parliamentary Union 1997, 2000). Despite the lack of substantial progress worldwide, women politicians have moved ahead far further and faster in some places more than in others. It is well known that women parliamentarians do best in the Nordic nations, where they are on average 39 percent of MPs in the lower house. The proportion of women members of parliament elsewhere is lower, including in the Americas (16%), Asia (14%), Europe excluding the Nordic states (14%), sub-Saharan Africa (12%), and the Pacific

(12%). The worst record for women's representation is the Arab region, where women are less than 5 percent of elected representatives, and they continue to be barred by law from standing for parliament in Kuwait, Quatar, Saudi Arabia, Oman, and the United Arab Emirates. Therefore despite many official declarations of intent made by governments, NGOs, and international agencies pledged to establish conditions of gender equality in the public sphere, in practice major barriers continue to restrict women's advancement in public life.

To summarize what is known, the general consensus in the literature suggests that many decades after achieving full citizenship, women in post-industrial societies now participate equally at the ballot box, or even cast slightly more votes than men. Yet women still lag behind men slightly as activists in other types of campaign and party politics, as well as in voluntary associations and community organizations. Gender gaps remain most marked at the apex of power, in legislatures, cabinets, and as heads of state (Reynolds 1999).

3 RIVAL INTELLECTUAL THEMES AND EXPLANATORY FRAMEWORKS

What best explains this continuing activism gap? The main explanations in the literature can be categorized into the supply-side and demand-side approaches, namely:

Supply-side factors:

- *Resource-based explanations* emphasizing the social characteristics that facilitate political engagement, notably education, work status, occupation, time, and income, with education, in particular, closely associated with the acquisition of political information and civic skills;
- *Cultural accounts* focusing upon the motivational attitudes that bring people into public affairs, exemplified by a sense of political efficacy, interest, ambition, social trust, institutional confidence, knowledge, group identities, partisan affiliation, and civic duty;

Demand-side factors:

- *Agency explanations* prioritizing the role of mobilizing organizations which draw people into public life, such as churches, parties, community groups, and unions, as well as the impact of the news media and informal social networks; and lastly,
- *Institutional explanations* suggesting that political institutions matter, including the formal and informal rules, legal regulations, social conventions, standard procedures, and political processes which structure opportunities for activism.

Earlier decades were dominated by social psychological theories stressing the role of sex-role socialization. This process presumably shaped both the acquisition of cultural attitudes, such as a sense of political efficacy and interest, and the possession of certain resources, such as educational qualifications and professional occupations. The democratic norm was the active citizen and the key research question became why many women (and indeed many men) failed to live up to this ideal. In recent decades, this approach has come under increasing challenge from theories emphasizing that citizens become active when mobilized by political agencies and within a context of opportunities regulated by institutional rules, practices, and conventions. As Rosenstone and Hansen (1993) theorize, understanding patterns of political activism requires us to pay attention both to the characteristics of individual citizens (the supply-side "push") but also the particular social and political context within which they operate (the demand-side "pull"). Supply-side accounts suggest that, in a democracy, there is something about women which makes them decide not to undertake political acts. By contrast, demand-side arguments suggest that there is something about political organizations and institutional practices which are gendered, thereby reinforcing the predominant status quo and limiting opportunities for women's activism.

Of course we should not assume that any single monocausal explanation lies at the heart of this phenomenon; instead research needs to carefully disentangle the relative importance of each of these factors for comprehensive accounts of the gender gap in political activism. Researchers presently face the problem that it is far easier to study the individual through the standard approaches of survey methodology, and hence to focus attention upon individual resources and attitudes, than it is to study the individual-within-context, and hence how gendered practices within organizations and institutions may systematically mobilize men and silence women. The challenge lies in understanding the complex interaction between supply and demand, without assuming that one or the other can necessarily be regarded as "primary" in causal models. This sounds obvious, in many regards, yet this simple observation is often overlooked. The feminist challenge to the conventional intellectual framework remains a work in process and it is far from complete, with the older interpretation remaining the most pervasive in the literature. Nevertheless this shift in theoretical emphasis provides new insights valuable for interpreting both the underlying processes that drive gendered political participation at mass and elite levels, and the ways in which these could be altered.

Other reviews of the literature, notably Carroll and Zerilli (1993), identified two broad perspectives, mainstream and transformationalist, which they suggested divided the literature. Mainstream scholars, they suggested, have focused upon comparing women and men as political actors, adopting the discipline's conventional epistemology (positivism, with scientific explanation and prediction as the goal), concepts (such as voting, parties, political attitudes, recruitment, and participation), and methods (quantitative, survey research). In contrast, more radical feminist approaches commonly challenge some of these assumptions by employing a postpositivist epistemology (empirical, with interpretation as the goal), new concepts (largely drawn from the feminist movement and from untraditional theoretical frameworks and vocabularies), and innovative methodologies (often qualitative, in-depth interviews, participant observation, post-structural, and ethnographic). The transformational perspective emphasizes that women's politics have appeared in many so-called non-conventional political arenas outside of the electoral arena, exemplified by voluntary associations, mutual aid societies, churches, battered women's shelters, and around policy areas such as sexual harassment and reproductive rights, as well as in more mainstream political institutions such as in legislatures and the courts (see also Staudt and Weaver 1997; Ritter and Mellow 2000).

The distinction between "mainstream" and "transformational" research on political behavior remains evident but these approaches have gradually shaded into each other during the last decade. Far from focusing exclusively on the core institutions of government or participation via electoral arenas, for example, "mainstream" behavioral studies have revived their interest in alternative forms and channels of activism, including the social networks and voluntary associations linked to theories of social capital. This was stimulated by Robert Putnam's (2000) work and the study of new social movements, protests, demonstrations, and "contentious politics" (Tarrow 1994; Tilly 2004). This development generated a substantial outpouring of new research on interest groups, voluntary associations, community organizations, social movements, and transnational policy networks, as well as forms of protest politics, demonstrations, petitioning, consumer politics, internet mobilizing, and collective action occurring outside of conventional electoral and party channels. The literature has widely recognized the important role of gender in these forms of activism; for example, Putnam's work on the causes of an erosion of social capital in the United States considers the gradual entry of more women into the workplace, and the impact of dual responsibilities at home and work on time pressures, which may restrict their organizational and networking roles in traditional community associations. Burns, Schlozman, and Verba's (2001) analysis of women and men's political participation, while based on standard survey methods, expanded the research well beyond the electoral arena, to consider participation in a diverse range of voluntary organizations which can be regarded as the "private roots of public action", including churches, community groups, charities, unions, fraternal groups, hobby clubs, neighborhood associations, and so on. Comparative work has developed similar themes elsewhere (Norris 2002; Inglehart and Norris 2003; Norris and Inglehart 2005). The extensive literature on the growth of new social movements and transnational advocacy networks also recognizes the modern women's movement as central to these developments (Zald and McCarthy 1987).

Contemporary "mainstream" studies of political behavior have also gradually expanded the range of methodological tools used for studying behavior, venturing beyond the standard cross-sectional national sample survey exemplified by the American National Election Study. Political science now more commonly develops and blends multi-method and multi-level models drawing upon many alternative data sources, including cross-national and panel surveys, qualitative focus groups and structured personal interviews, historical narratives, intensive case studies, quasi-experimental studies, participant observation, aggregate data, content analysis, and event analysis. On balance, therefore, although differences continue between "mainstream" and "transformational" studies of political behavior, these approaches have experienced some merger in recent years. This does not imply that a consensus exists, even within the more quantitative behavioral tradition, about the most appropriate theoretical framework, methodology, or research designs used to explain patterns of gendered political behavior at mass and elite levels. The contrasts between these rival frameworks can be illustrated by comparing some of the literature in more depth.

4 SUPPLY-SIDE FACTORS: CULTURAL ATTITUDES AND CIVIC RESOURCES

The predominant framework in the early literature of the 1960s and 1970s was based upon social psychological theories of socialization emphasizing the role of cultural attitudes and social resources as "supply-side" factors when mobilizing men and women into political life. The emphasis on the social and cultural construction of gender served a useful function in this literature by debunking previous biologically determinist accounts of sex differences, although its assumptions ultimately proved equally conservative. Political socialization is understood as the process whereby people learn what is expected of them in a political system. Formative experiences early in childhood and adolescence presumably generate fixed and enduring attitudes towards appropriate social norms and behaviors associated with roles which persist into adult life. Socialization theory was developed in a series of publications, notably by Easton and Dennis (1969), Hess and Torney (1968), and Greenstein (1961). The central puzzle in this approach concerns how women and men come to acquire distinctive political attitudes, values, opinions, and resources during their formative years in childhood and adolescence.

The cultural attitudes and psychological orientations most closely associated with political participation are typically expressions of interest in public affairs, a sense of confidence in the ability to influence government and the policy process (internal political efficacy), levels of information, feelings of civic duty, and a sense of partisan identification. At elite level, political ambition is regarded as important for how far women and men seek to become candidates for elected office. In turn, gender differences in attitudes, values, beliefs, and orientations are thought to lead in later life towards the activism gap at mass and elite levels (Clark and Clark 1986; Sapiro 1983).

Through shaping social norms about sex roles in the family, workplace, and public sphere, the socialization process also indirectly influences women and men's experiences, resources, and lifestyles. This process leads to inequalities in civic assets such as skills, knowledge, experience, time, and money. Possession of these assets makes some better placed than others to take advantage of the opportunities for participation

(Verba, Schlozman, and Brady 1995). Resources are perhaps most obviously useful in fostering more demanding forms of activism, such as the value of social networks in campaign fund-raising, the need for leisure time to volunteer in a community association, the assets of flexible careers for the pursuit of elected office, the advantages of communication skills to produce the local party newsletter, and the organizational abilities that help mobilize social movements.

The socialization paradigm became pervasive in the voting behavior studies of the 1960s and 1970s, and its core theoretical assumptions continue to resonate today (see, for example, Conway, Steuernagel, and Ahern 1997, 17–31). One implication concerns processes of cultural change. If the socialization process stamps enduring orientations towards the most appropriate division of sex roles in early childhood and adolescence, then these patterns of behavior should persist throughout a person's lifetime. Socialization theory is thus most appropriate for explaining patterns of cultural stability—as parental attitudes and values are passed on to their offspring—but it has problems in accounting for the dynamics of change. Working within this tradition, however, Ronald Inglehart developed an influential theory of how cultural attitudes and values change; he suggests that substantial generational shifts in cultural values can and do occur, including important shifts in traditional attitudes towards gender equality in post-industrial societies (Inglehart 1977, 1990, 1997, chapter in this volume; Inglehart and Welzel 2005). For Inglehart, these value shifts reflect decisive events and the distinctive experiences of each cohort, including the gradual emergence in affluent societies of self-expression values which emphasize gender equality. This theory emphasizes that value change occurs primarily at societal level, rather than among individuals during their lifetimes. The erosion of traditional attitudes towards a strict division of sex roles in the home, schools, and workplace is evident in the predominant cultural attitudes found in agrarian, industrial, and post-industrial societies, among successive generational cohorts within each society, and among sectors such as the rich and poor, rather than between women and men within each society.

Therefore the primary explanatory framework for gender gaps in political activism focuses on socialization processes and how this influences cultural attitudes towards appropriate sex roles in the public and private spheres, the acquisition of civic resources, and therefore common forms of participation. As Burns, Schlozman, and Verba (2001) summarize this pattern, women and men differ in their "stockpile of participatory factors," exemplified by their levels of educational attainment, experience in the workforce, income, and psychological predispositions, with women found to be less politically informed, less interested in politics, and less efficacious than men. Social psychological explanations are also advanced at elite level to explain why there are fewer women as candidates for elected office, focusing upon the core concept of political "ambition." Lawless and Fox (2005), for example, work within socialization theory to suggest that even among the pool of eligibles with considerable educational and occupational resources, women remain less interested in running for elected office, due to the continuing impact of traditional sex roles within the home and family.

In short, supply-side explanations remain the predominant approach in the contemporary literature today, particularly within the United States. In Europe, by contrast, a more structural comparative perspective often highlights and emphasizes the importance of formal institutions for generating significant variations in political behavior, including the activism gap (compare, for example, Lawless and Fox with Lovenduski 2005).

5 DEMAND-SIDE FACTORS: MOBILIZING AGENCIES AND GENDERED INSTITUTIONS

In recent years, core assumptions made in the supply-side approach have come under increasing challenge. Approaches emphasizing the broader context provide important additional insights into the ways that citizens are pulled into political activism through social networks, organizational efforts, community events, and the structure of opportunities that are available for political expression and communications. Conventions and practices within parties, the media, or legislative bodies may appear gender neutral, but in practice they may reinforce certain ways of doing things and certain patterns of behavior that reflect the dominant group and which thereby unintentionally deter women.

"Demand"-side approaches emphasize the role of mobilizing agencies that draw people into politics (Rosenstone and Hanson 1993). The simplest claim is that civic organizations such as parties, churches, unions, and advocacy groups are not passive; instead they actively drum up potential members and ask supporters to become engaged through joining local branches, attending meetings, donating funds, or holding leadership positions (Cassell 1999). Associational membership represents a direct form of political activism, and also an important indirect influence upon other forms of participation. Get-out-the-vote drives, canvassing, advertising, and membership mail-in campaigns are the most obvious examples of such mobilizing processes. Civic associations provide opportunities for supporters to become active through organizing demonstrations, write-in campaigns to elected officials, election campaigns, and recruiting people for elected office. The process of political communications, through the news media and through informal personal discussions with friends, neighbors, and colleagues, is also capable of activating and mobilizing citizens (Norris 2000). As Rosenstone and Hanson (1993) argue: "Citizens participate in elections and government both because they go to politics and because politics goes to them." Piven and Cloward (2000) suggest that Democrats and Republicans have failed to mobilize the poorer and less educated sectors of the American electorate, as well as women and African-American citizens. Voter turnout has also been depressed by restrictive practices in ballot access, exemplified by limits on the voting rights of ex-felons.

If campaign mobilization drives are important, the key question becomes who is targeted and recruited into politics, and whether women constitute an important part of the mobilization efforts. Studies of participation face the challenge of how to examine this form of organizational activity with systematic evidence. Standard surveys allow us to monitor individual-level behaviour, including self-reported attempts by organizations to contact potential supporters (for example, surveys ask whether citizens were contacted by a party or candidate during the campaign). But it is far more difficult to gain reliable insights into the strategic decisions that organizations make on who they target and how they try to persuade supporters to become active members. Case studies of the activities of specific associations, local election campaigns, groups, or parties provide some evidence, for example gathering information from membership surveys, officer surveys, and/or participant observation, but it is often difficult to generalize from such evidence across a wide range of different types of organizations.

Mobilizing activities are widely recognized as important, even if difficult to study using the standard approaches in political behavior. But feminists have gone further than this conventional approach. In a related demand side, institutional theories also emphasize the importance of the broader structural context on political participation, particularly the influence of agencies, formal rules, and informal practices. An institutional focus also helps to account more satisfactorily for some of the striking contrasts in women's participation in politics found in different nations worldwide, even among countries within broadly similar cultural regions, such as the proportion of women elected to parliaments in western Europe. The key insight of this perspective suggests that the formal and informal rules and practices of political life are rarely gender neutral; instead, they reflect and reinforce gendered patterns of power and hierarchical authority, which need to be explicitly recognized and, for feminists, challenged and reformed (Acker 1989, 1992; Lovenduski 1998, 2005). In this regard, research on race and ethnicity has long used the concept of "institutionalized racism" to explain how certain systematic practices, rules, and routines function to reinforce the disadvantage, exclusion, or marginalization of ethnic minorities, even though these practices are not directly related to racist attitudes or intentions to discriminate (Carmichael and Hamilton 1967; Miles 1989). A simple illustration concerns job specifications that require a certain minimal height to join the security forces, a practice which may disproportionately exclude members of certain minority groups who commonly fall below this physical stature. Standard requirements for certain tests of physical strength or endurance which are gender-blind may also penalize women who wish to enter the military.

A more radical approach along similar lines has been developed by feminists who propose the idea of "gendered political institutions" to identify certain standard practices, operating procedures, and formal rules that are often taken for granted within organizations but with consequences that unintentionally prevent women and men from playing an equally active role in public affairs (Acker 1989, 1992; Kenney 1996; Lovenduski 1998; Duerst-Lahti 2002; Hawkesworth 2003). Such rules and practices do not refer to gender per se, indeed there is no explicit intention to discriminate. Nevertheless the outcomes of these practices differ systematically for women and men. Feminist theorists emphasize that divisions in power and disadvantage associated with gender are generated and reinforced by state institutions through laws, policies, rules, and conventional practices, as well as by granting women and men different rights, for example in education, occupation, immigration, the welfare state, citizenship, and office-holding. As such, it is not sufficient to ask how gender influences institutions, where gender is regarded as preceding institutions; instead one key question becomes how political and social institutions generate and reinforce social constructions of gender. Simple illustrations include holding party, union, or community group meetings in the evening, or failing to provide childcare facilities at meetings, which might make participation more difficult for anyone with primary care of dependants at home. Such practices may appear gender neutral, but in practice, given the usual patterns of family responsibilities, they affect women more than men. Along similar lines in recruitment practices, selectors may favor candidates with sufficient financial resources to fund their own campaigns, or those drawn from occupations such as lawyers or business, and again in practice these sorts of requirements may disadvantage women more than men (Norris and Lovenduski 1993, 1995). Certain standard conventions common in legislatures that appear gender neutral may also discourage women—such as evening or all-night hours of sitting, the aggressive style of adversarial parliamentary debates, the allocation of committee assignments based on seniority, or low rates of incumbency turnover (Schwindt-Bayer 2005).

Institutional practices may also shape attitudes as well as behavior. For example, studies usually show, in many surveys in many countries, that women continue to express less interest in politics, even in established democracies (Inglehart and Norris 2003). One explanation may concern the gendered characteristics, practices, and rules of political institutions. For example, Burns, Schlozman, and Verba (2001) found that women seeking or holding elected office in American politics have an impact upon the political engagement of women at the mass level, boosting women's political interest, knowledge of the candidates, and sense of political efficacy. They reason that more visible women in politics may act as role models sending signals to women citizens that politics is an arena open to them. Alternatively the presence of women in public office might suggest to women citizens that their interests will be reflected in the policy-making process. Along similar lines, Norris, Lovenduski, and Campbell (2004) found that in districts with a female MP, women voters were more likely to turn out, to be interested in politics, to express willingness to work in the campaign, and to have a stronger sense of external efficacy about the benefits of government. There could well be reciprocal effects at work, but the evidence in the US and Britain suggests that the election of women may well encourage participation by women as citizens.

In principle, of course, certain gendered institutional practices may also favor women, in female-dominated institutions (such as the nursing profession). In practice, however, this is less common in politics since most implicit routines and practices usually preserve and reinforce the existing status quo within governing institutions. As Kenney (1996) notes, the size of the predominant group matters for the conventions and practices within each institution. Attitudes regarded as individualistic in the socialization approach, for example if women appear to lack ambition for elected office, may instead reflect gendered relations and practices built into institutional structures, notably the paucity of women in leadership roles. Hawkesworth (2003) illustrates this process in a detailed study combining in-depth qualitative interviews with a case study of legislative practices in Congress to illustrate the marginalization of Congresswomen of color.

The understanding that institutional practices are rarely gender neutral also reflects growing recognition of the role of positive action strategies and institutional political reforms as policy options designed to achieve greater equality for women's participation in appointed and elected office. The most common initiatives include the use of gender quotas within party candidate selection processes, a growing practice in many nations, whether implemented by constitutional convention, by law, or by party rules (Bonder and Nari 1995; Jones 1996, 1998; Caul 2001; Htun and Jones 2002; Tinker 2004). Administrative electoral reforms may also mobilize mass-level voting behavior, for example the use of all-postal ballots may be particularly important for encouraging voting participation among the home-bound, including women who are responsible for care of dependants or who are elderly. Parliamentary reforms to create more women-friendly procedures, rules, and facilities are another part of this effort. The importance of the electoral system for women's representation is well established, notably the way that on average almost twice as many women are usually elected under proportional representation electoral systems than under majoritarian rules (Rule 1981, 1987; Rule and Zimmerman 1994; Norris 2004).

Rather than regarding political attitudes as enduring individual-level psychological predispositions, the feminist challenge suggests that these should be understood as relatively malleable characteristics which are open to being altered, even relatively rapidly, through the process of structural reforms. In this view, for example, gender differences in political ambition for elected office, commonly reported in a series of studies, should be understood as reflecting female responses to a male-dominated environment and gendered relations embodied in party, electoral, and legislative institutions. Understood in this way, a lack of ambition is less an individual quality acquired via sex-role socialization than a rational assessment of the opportunities available to women, given the institutional environment and practices.

6 CONCLUSIONS

The research agenda on gendered political behavior has focused on the activism gap usually found in many countries in the most common types of political participation, including patterns of voting turnout, membership of political parties, and mobilization through interest groups and social movements. Although debate continues, a gender gap also exists in social capital, including activism within a range of voluntary associations, and in alternative types of protest politics. The most visible activism gap is in positions of political leadership, through elected and appointed office at local, state or national levels.

The supply and demand perspectives present alternative views about the most appropriate analytical and theoretical framework that can explain gender gaps in political participation at mass and elite levels. The supply-side perspective remains predominant in the conventional literature, reflecting the individualistic tradition of survey-based political behavioral methods. But there is growing evidence that the institutional practices which stimulate individuals to become active may well matter. In short, these accounts suggest that women participate less than men in political life either because they can not (they lack resources), because they will not (they are not interested), because nobody asked them (they lack political networks), or because gendered institutional practices limit their opportunities. These approaches differ in their emphasis on the primary motors driving human behavior, their expectations about the pace of change, and also their assumptions about the ability of formal institutional rules to alter, rather than adapt to, deeply embedded and habitual social norms and cultural habits.

The tension between these approaches is far from unique to the study of women and politics, instead it runs as a pervasive dividing line throughout political behavior. But feminist perspectives are particularly important for challenging the conventional interpretation of behavior and for demanding more innovative methodological approaches to understand how gendered institutional practices systematically discourage, silence, and mobilize some groups over others. New interpretive frameworks are developing which help to explain patterns of political participation associated with gender, as well as related disparities by ethnicity and class. The importance of these feminist challenges is to challenge the conventional methods and theories of political behavior, and indeed to suggest that richer and more compelling explanations are produced when the individualistic approaches common in survey research are replaced by more comprehensive understandings of the complex patterns of individual-behavior-within-context.

References

ACKER, J. 1989. Hierarchies, job bodies: a theory of gendered institutions. *Gender and Society*, 4: 139–58.

—— 1992. From sex role to gendered institutions. *Contemporary Sociology*, 21 (5): 565–9.

ALMOND, G., and VERBA, S. 1963. *The Civic Culture: Political Attitudes and Democracy in Five Nations*. Princeton: Princeton University Press.

AMUNDSEN, K. 1971. *The Silenced Majority: Women and American Democracy*. Englewood Cliffs, NJ: Prentice Hall.

BALDEZ, L. 2003. Women's movements and democratic transition in Chile, Brazil, East Germany, and Poland. *Comparative Politics*, 35 (3): 253.

BARNES, S., KAASE, M., et al. 1979. *Political Action: Mass Participation in Five Western Democracies*. Beverly Hills, Calif.: Sage.

BAXTER, S., and LANSING, M. 1983. *Women and Politics*. Ann Arbor: University of Michigan Press.

BENNIE, L. 2002. Survey of the profession. *Political Studies Association News*, October.

BERELSON, B., LAZARSFELD, P., and MCPHEE, W. 1954. *Voting*. Chicago: University of Chicago Press.

BONDER, G., and NARI, M. 1995. The 30 percent quota law: a turning point for women's political participation in Argentina. Pp. 183–93 in *A Rising Public Voice: Women in Politics Worldwide*, ed. A. Brill. New York: The Feminist Press of the City University of New York.

BOURQUE, S., and GROSSHOLTZ, J. 1974. Politics an unnatural practice: political science looks at female participation. *Politics and Society*, 4: 225–66.

BRANDES, L. et al. 2001. The status of women in political science: female participation in the professoriate and the study of women and politics in the discipline. *PS: Political Science & Politics*, 34 (2): 319–26.

BURNS, N. 2002. Gender: public opinion and political action. Pp. 462–87 in *Political Science: The State of the Discipline*, ed. I. Katznelson and H. V. Milner. New York: W. W. Norton/ APSA.

—— SCHLOZMAN, K., and VERBA, S. 2001. *The Private Roots of Public Action*. Cambridge, Mass.: Harvard University Press.

CARMICHAEL, S., and HAMILTON, C. 1967. *Black Power: The Politics of Liberation in America*. New York: Vintage Books.

CARROLL, B. 1979. Political science Part I: American politics and political behavior. *Signs*, 5: 289–306.

CARROLL, S. ed. 2003. *Women and American Politics: New Questions, New Directions*. New York: Oxford University Press.

—— and ZERILLI, L. 1993. Feminist challenges to political science. Pp. 55–77 in *The State of the Discipline II*, ed. A. Finifter. Washington, DC: American Political Science Association.

CASSEL, C. 1999. Voluntary associations, churches and social participation theories of turnout. *Social Science Quarterly*, 80 (3): 504–17.

CAUL, M. 2001. Political parties and the adoption of candidate gender quotas: a cross-national analysis. *Journal of Politics*, 63 (4): 1214–29.

CHRISTY, C. 1987. *Sex Differences in Political Participation: Processes of Change in Fourteen Nations*. New York: Praeger.

CLARK, C., and CLARK, J. 1986. Models of gender and political participation in the United States. *Women and Politics*, 6 (1): 5–25.

CONWAY, M., STEUERNAGEL, G., and AHERN, D. 1997. *Women and Political Participation: Cultural Change in the Political Arena*. Washington, DC: CQ Press.

DAHLERUP, D. ed. 2005. *Women, Quotas and Politics*. New York: Routledge.

DELLA PORTA, D., and DIANI, M. 1999. *Social Movements: An Introduction*. Oxford: Blackwell.

DIAMOND, I. 1977. *Sex Roles in the State House*. New Haven: Yale University Press.

DUERST-LAHTI, G. 2002. Governing institutions, ideologies, and gender: toward the possibility of equal political representation. *Sex Roles*, 47 (7–8): 371–88.

DURANT, H. 1949. *Political Opinion*. London.

DUVERGER, M. 1955. *The Political Role of Women*. Paris: UNESCO.

EASTON, D., and DENNIS, J. 1969. *Children in the Political System*. New York: McGraw Hill.

GITHENS, M., and PRESTAGE, J. 1977. *A Portrait of Marginality*. New York: David McKay.

GOOT, M., and REID, E. 1984. Women: if not apolitical, then conservative. In *Women and the Public Sphere*, ed. Janet Siltanen and Michelle Stanworth. London: Hutchinson.

GOSNELL, H. 1930. *Why Europe Votes*. Chicago: The University of Chicago Press.

GREENSTEIN, F. 1961. Sex-related political differences in childhood. *Journal of Politics*, 23 (2): 353–71.

GRUBERG, M. 2005. Participation by women in the 2004 APSA annual meeting. *PS: Political Science & Politics*, 1: 113–14.

HAWKE3WORTH, M. 2003. Congressional enactments of race-gender: toward a theory of race-gendered institutions. *American Political Science Review*, 97 (4): 529–50.

HESS, R., and TORNEY, J. 1968. *The Development of Political Attitudes in Children*. Chicago: Aldine.

HTUN, M., and JONES, M. 2002. Engendering the right to participate in decision-making: electoral quotas and women's leadership in Latin America. Pp. 32–56 in *Gender and the Politics of Rights and Democracy in Latin America*, ed. N. Craske and M. Molyneux. New York: Palgrave.

INGLEHART, R. 1977. *The Silent Revolution: Changing Values and Political Styles among Western Publics*. Princeton: Princeton University Press.

—— 1990. *Culture Shift in Advanced Industrial Society*. Princeton: Princeton University Press.

—— 1997. *Modernization and Postmodernization: Cultural, Economic and Political Change in 43 Societies*. Princeton: Princeton University Press.

—— and NORRIS, P. 2003. *Rising Tide: Gender Equality and Cultural Change around the World*. New York: Cambridge University Press.

—— and WELZEL, C. 2005. *Modernization, Cultural Change, and Democracy: The Human Development Sequence*. Cambridge: Cambridge University Press.

INTER-PARLIAMENTARY UNION. 1997. *Men and Women in Politics*. Reports and Documents Series 28. Geneva: IPU.

—— 2000. *Participation of Women in Public Life*. Geneva: IPU.

JONES, M. 1996. Increasing women's representation via gender quotas: the Argentine Ley de Cupos. *Women and Politics*, 16 (4): 75–98.

—— 1998. Gender quotas, electoral laws, and the election of women: lessons from the Argentine provinces. *Comparative Political Studies*, 31 (1): 3–21.

KECK, M., and SIKKINK, K. 1998. *Activists beyond Borders: Advocacy Networks in International Politics*. Ithaca, NY: Cornell University Press.

KELLY, R., and FISHER, K. 1993. An assessment of articles about women in the "top 15" political science journals. *PS: Political Science and Politics*, 26: 544–58.

—— WILLIAMS, L., and FISHER, K. 1994. Women & politics: an assessment of its role within the discipline of political science. *Women & Politics*, 14 (4): 3–18.

KENNEY, S. 1996. New research on gendered political institutions. *Political Research Quarterly*, 49 (2): 445–66.

KIRKPATRICK, J. 1974. *Political Women*. New York: Basic Books.

LARANA, E., JOHNSTON, H., and GUSFIELD, J. eds. 1994. *New Social Movements: From Ideology to Identity*. Philadelphia: Temple University Press.

LAWLESS, J., and FOX, R. 2005. *It Takes a Candidate: Why Women Don't Run for Office*. Cambridge: Cambridge University Press.

LIPSET, S. 1960. *Political Man: The Social Basis of Politics*. New York: Doubleday.

LOVENDUSKI, J. 1998. Gendering research in political science. *Annual Review of Political Science*, 1: 333–56.

—— 2005. *Feminizing Politics*. Cambridge: Polity.

MATHEWS, L., and ANDERSEN, K. 2001. A gender gap in publishing? Women's representation in edited political science books. *PS: Political Science and Politics*, 34: 143–7.

McADAM, D., McCARTHY, J., and ZALD, M. 1996. *Comparative Perspectives on Social Movements*. New York: Cambridge University Press.

MERRIAM, C. 1924. *Non-Voting: Causes and Methods of Control*. Chicago: The University of Chicago Press.

MILES, R. 1989. *Racism*. London: Routledge.

NORRIS, P. 2000. *A Virtuous Circle? Political Communications in Post-industrial Democracies*. Cambridge: Cambridge University Press.

—— 2001. Women's power at the ballot box. In IDEA *Voter Turnout from 1945 to 2000: A Global Report on Political Participation*. 3rd edn. Stockholm: International IDEA.

—— 2002. *Democratic Phoenix: Reinventing Political Activism*. Cambridge: Cambridge University Press.

—— 2004. *Electoral Engineering*. Cambridge: Cambridge University Press.

—— and INGLEHART, R. 2005. Gendering Social Capital: Bowling in Women's Leagues?' Pp. 73–98 in *Unequal Returns: Gender, Social Capital and Political Engagement* ed. B. O'Neill and E. Gidengil. New York: Routledge.

—— and LOVENDUSKI, J. 1993. If only more candidates came forward . . . Supply-side explanations of candidate selection in Britain. *British Journal of Political Science*, 23: 373–408.

—— —— 1995. *Political Recruitment: Gender, Race and Class in the British Parliament*. Cambridge: Cambridge University Press.

—— —— and CAMPBELL, R. 2004. *Closing the Activism Gap: Gender Perspectives and Political Participation*. London: UK Electoral Commission.

OBERSCHALL, A. 1993. *Social Movements: Ideologies, Interests and Identities*. New Brunswick: Transaction.

PARRY, G., MOYSER, G., and DAY, N. 1992. *Political Participation and Democracy in Britain*. Cambridge: Cambridge University Press.

PATTIE, C., SEYD, P., and WHITELEY, P. 2004. *Citizens and Politics: Democracy and Participation in Twenty-First Century Britain*. Cambridge: Cambridge University Press.

PIVEN, F., and CLOWARD, R. 2000. *Why Americans Still Don't Vote: And Why Politicians Want It that Way*. Boston: Beacon Press.

PUTNAM, R. 2000. *Bowling Alone: The Collapse and Revival of American Community*. New York: Simon & Schuster.

REYNOLDS A. 1999. Women in the legislatures and executives of the world: knocking at the highest glass ceiling. *World Politics*, 51 (4): 547.

RITTER, G., and MELLOW, N. 2000. The state of gender studies in political science. *Annals of the American Academy of Political and Social Science*, 571: 121–34.

ROSENSTONE, S., and HANSEN, J. 1993. *Mobilization, Participation and Democracy in America*. New York: Macmillan.

RULE, W. 1981. The critical contextual factors in women's legislative recruitment. *Western Political Quarterly*, 34: 60–77.

—— 1987. Electoral systems, contextual factors and women's opportunity for election to parliament in twenty-three democracies. *Western Political Quarterly*, 40 (3): 477–98.

—— and ZIMMERMAN, J. eds. 1994. *Electoral Systems in Comparative Perspective: Their Impact on Women and Minorities*. Westport, Conn.: Greenwood Press.

SAPIRO, V. 1983. *The Political Integration of Women: Roles, Socialization, and Politics*. Urbana: University of Illinois Press.

—— 1991. Gender politics, gendering politics: the state of the field. In *Political Science: Looking Towards the Future*, ed. W. Crotty. Evanston, Ill.: Northwestern University Press.

SCHWINDT-BAYER, L. 2005. The incumbency disadvantage and women's election to legislative office. *Electoral Studies*, 24 (2): 227–44.

SIGEL, R. 1996. *Ambition and Accommodation: How Women View Gender Relations*. Chicago: University of Chicago Press.

STAUDT, K., and WEAVER, W. 1997. *Political Science and Feminisms: Integration or Transformation?* New York: Twayne.

SWERS, M. 2001. Research on women in legislatures: what have we learned, where are we going? *Women & Politics*, 23 (1–2): 167–85.

TARROW, S. 1994. *Power in Movement*. Cambridge: Cambridge University Press.

TILLY, C. 2004. *Social Movements, 1768–2004*. New York: Paradigm Publishers.

TINGSTEN, H. 1937. *Political Behavior: Studies in Election Statistics*. Reprinted Totowa, NJ: Bedminster Press (1963).

TINKER, I. 2004. Quotas for women in elected legislatures: do they really empower women? *Womens Studies International Forum*, 27 (5–6): 531–46.

TRUE, J., and MINTROM, M. 2001. Transnational networks and policy diffusion: the case of gender mainstreaming. *International Studies Quarterly*, 45 (1): 27–57.

VERBA, S., NIE, N., and KIM, J. 1978. *Participation and Political Equality: A Seven-Nation Comparison* New York: Cambridge University Press.

—— SCHLOZMAN, K., and BRADY, H. 1995. *Voice and Equality: Civic Voluntarism in American Politics*. Cambridge, Mass.: Harvard University Press.

ZALD, M., and McCARTHY, J. eds. 1987. *Social Movements in an Organizational Society*. New Brunswick, NJ: Transaction Books.

CHAPTER 40

NEW MODES OF CAMPAIGNING

RÜDIGER SCHMITT-BECK

In democracies, actors like politicians, parties, governments, interest groups, or social movements must be concerned about public opinion. Without its support, they cannot attain most of their goals. Campaigning can be seen as a rational reaction to this, a means of political actors to take their fate in their own hands. Instead of subjecting themselves passively to the ebb and flow of public sentiment, they seek to increase their own freedom of action and prospects of success by waging political campaigns—planned, coordinated communication efforts that aim to shape public opinion in a favorable way. In recent decades political actors of all sorts have increasingly come to view political campaigning as no less crucial than policy-making itself. Ever more efforts and resources are invested into public communication activities, so that campaigning is now seen by some observers as a core feature of the political process in contemporary democracies, having transformed them into "Public Relations Democracies" (Davis 2002).

Political campaigns are attempts by political actors to influence how citizens see the political world. Target audiences are provided with carefully selected, and usually biased, information. Pictures of political reality are designed and communicated that campaigners wish to be adopted by citizens, and to become part of their "subjective political reality" (Swanson 1991). Campaigns may seek to initiate processes of learning on the part of citizens, to mobilize them into political action, to activate their latent political predispositions, to stimulate them to use certain pieces of information and not others when taking their decisions, and to persuade them to change

* This chapter profited from stimulating exchanges with David Farrell, Ralph Negrine, and Katrin Voltmer.

their political attitudes and preferences. Which of these goals are prominent depends on a particular campaign's type and situational setting.

Election campaigns see parties and their candidates waging battles for votes and public office. Referendum campaigns, more numerous today as democracies open up new channels for direct citizen participation in political decision making, see proponents and opponents of the relevant issues attempting to steer votes in their preferred direction. Issue-based campaigns see government agencies, interest groups, or social movements attempting to have an issue or policy proposal placed high on the political agenda, and to have it favorably framed in public debate, while image campaigns are launched to paint the public perception of political actors, including even nation states' images in other countries, in a more favourable light. Public or private agencies' information campaigns seek to enhance citizens' understanding of certain problems or policies.

This chapter focuses mostly on election campaigns, as these—due to their core role in the political process of representative democracies—have been much more thoroughly studied than any other type of campaigns. First, recent trends in electioneering are discussed, with particular emphasis on how old and new democracies across the world are adopting new modes of campaigning and are thus becoming "Americanized." Subsequently, the available evidence is reviewed on whether and under what conditions campaigns, and particularly the new modes of electioneering, actually "matter" for public opinion and citizens' political choices.

1 THE "AMERICAN" STYLE OF ELECTIONEERING

Campaigning has not only moved from the sidelines to centerstage of contemporary politics; but campaigns are also conducted very differently from what they used to be. To describe these changes, analysts have suggested a developmental logic, construing the current style of electioneering as the most recent of three stages (Farrell 1996). According to an influential conceptual framework suggested by Norris (2000), campaigning in many countries has, through an evolutionary process of gradual modernization, moved from a "pre-modern" style over a "modern" style to a mode for which the term "postmodern" has gained wide acceptance (although this allusion to French social philosophy must be seen more as a metaphor than as an analytical concept). Originating in the nineteenth century with the extension of the franchise, "pre-modern" campaigns were essentially decentralized local affairs, run at the grass roots by party activists on a short-term and ad hoc basis, with personal contacts and partisan newspapers being the main channels of campaign communcations. Their main purpose was to mobilize faithful supporters by activating their partisan pre-dispositions. "Modern" campaigning gradually emerged since the 1950s. It was characterized by a growing importance of strategic thinking and central coordination by national party organizations, the emergence of national television news as the predominant channel of campaign communications, and the beginning influx of technical expertise from outside the parties. Persuasion, rather than just mobilization and activation became increasingly important during this phase.

While all this continues to be relevant, the essence of contemporary "postmodern" campaigning is a general trend towards more fragmented, but also more extended, if not permanent campaigns, that are to an even larger extent centrally controlled and professionally conducted. Especially in America, pundits claim we are moving toward an era of the perpetual campaign (Blumenthal 1982). Complementing this recent development, is a strategic move from "selling" ideologically predefined policies to "political marketing" that puts "customers" first, and seeks to offer them political "products" that fit their needs and wants. Concomitantly, the parties are shifting their principal orientation from an emphasis on ideological identity to "vote-seeking" (Harmel and Janda 1994) and "chasing" instead of merely mobilizing voters (Rohrschneider 2002).

At the same time campaign practices seem to become more similar in democratic countries worldwide. Different hypotheses have been put forward about the nature of this process of convergence. The notion of "*Americanization*" (Butler and Ranney 1992; Mancini and Swanson 1996; Negrine and Papathanassopoulos 1996) suggests that it is to be seen as a transnational unidirectional diffusion of modes of campaigning that were first developed in the United States, but are becoming—through export and wholesale adoption—the staple of electioneering more or less everywhere where democratic elections are held (Plasser and Plasser 2002, 15–20; Sussman and Galizio 2003). To evaluate this claim it is helpful to examine more carefully how electioneering for higher political offices, especially the presidency, nowadays works in the United States.

American campaigns are entirely *centered on candidates*. Like ideal-typical political entrepreneurs, ambitious individuals decide whether, when, and how they want to run for public office. Successive waves of reform have turned the general public, as opposed to parties and their leaders, into the relevant selectorate to which aspiring candidates need to appeal for nomination. Because of the primary process and the nature of campaign funding, each candidate needs to create a personal campaign organization, often years before the election. At presidential races such organizations are very large and enormously complex. They include hundreds of citizen volunteers and party regulars, but the key positions are given to hired experts from the private sector. This *professionalization* of electioneering started in the 1960s. Since then, campaign consultancy has turned into big business, with hundreds of firms offering dozens of highly specialized services to campaign organizations at all levels of the political system. The key role of hired professionals in contemporary American campaigns, in particular the part played by pollsters, is seen by some as an indication of a "*scientification*" of campaigning (Swanson and Mancini 1996), although in-depth studies show that it is not so much academic expertise on which campaigns consultants draw, but rather some sort of political folk wisdom that emerges out of campaign practice itself and proves its worth through electoral success (Scammell 1998).

In any case, this can be interpreted as a determined attempt to *rationalize* the conduct of campaigns, leaving as little as possible to chance, and seeking the most efficient means for achieving the ultimate goal of gaining votes. The rational approach to electioneering also incites "*targeting*" as the key strategy for approaching voters. Just like business operations, campaigns have become very conscious about the fact that resources are scarce and must be allocated wisely. Therefore, "shotgun" approaches to contact a large undifferentiated set of voters do not recommend themselves. Each campaign first "segments" the electorate with the help of social science research tools, and then defines for itself a sufficiently large "winning coalition" of voters whose members it then attempts to attract. Carefully tailored messages are conveyed through media with a high likelihood to reach exactly these voters. In addition, geographic targeting is considered essential, zeroing in on "battleground states" that may deliver the pivotal votes to win a race. Research also plays an important role in developing the *messages* that a campaign seeks to convey. Guided by the logic of *political marketing*, campaigns explore what prospective voters want, design their themes accordingly, and monitor constantly how their messages resonate with voters (Newman 1999). The candidate is the central theme of a campaign communications that is highly *personalized*. How to design the candidate's public image is one of the key decisions in campaign strategy. Through "deliberate priming" (Medvic 2000), concentrating on a small number of carefully selected topics and repeating these over and over again, campaigns aim to influence which considerations voters bring to bear when reasoning about whom to elect.

Naturally, evaluative messages are a core component of campaign communications. In that respect, recent American campaigns have displayed a marked tendency to "*go negative*," especially in television advertising (Ansolabehere and Iyengar 1997). More and more, candidates have come to resort on attacking their political opponents rather than on emphasizing their own positive sides, thereby creating the impression that contemporary campaigns are battles of determined mudslingers rather than debates about political issues and the best solutions for society's most pressing problems. Since the late 1980s the incidence of negativism in political advertising increased enormously. At the 2000 presidential election, more than two-thirds of all television ads were classified as negative, with a clear increase from the primaries to the final phase of the campaign (Kaid and Johnston 2000; West 2005).

US campaigns are mainly conducted through the *mass media*. Paid *television advertising* is the dominant channel for campaign communications, amounting to several times the quantity of news and current affairs programming in election periods. But campaign organizations also consider the media's regular editorial content as extremely important. The campaigns seek to instrumentalize the news media for their own purposes by means of conventional press relations and sophisticated "*news management*." This emphasis on "earned media" forces campaign organizations to adapt to the logic of politically autonomous, commercial media, that are guided by audience-centered criteria of newsworthiness. Due to an increasingly critical stance, if not outright hostility of American media towards politics and political elites, and decreasing attention that they pay to elections, campaigners increasingly have a hard time exploiting the "free media," such as feature stories that the media produce or other free media coverage (Patterson 2000). In their dealings with the mainstream media, candidates are thus operating in unfriendly territory, and find themselves often deprived of opportunities to "go public" through the news. Another challenge is the proliferation of special-interest television channels brought about by the spread of cable, and the ensuing fragmentation of the audience. As a consequence, candidates are always eager to find means to circumvent the journalistic filters. One of them is *talkshow campaigning* which became fashionable in the 1990s. Recent years have also seen a proliferation of new channels for campaign communications, that combine the two advantages of being fully controlled by the campaigns, like advertising, and at the same time particularly well suited for targeting specific subgroups. Foremost among these is direct mail, but telephone campaigning, cable television, and the internet are also convenient *"narrowcasting"* media. The twofold tendency towards more fragmented audiences, but also increased targeting is the core feature distinguishing "postmodern" campaigns from the previous stage (Norris 2000).

One of the last functioning resorts of "broadcast campaigning" are the *televised debates* between challengers and incumbents—highly stylized, ritualized media events that still attract considerable audiences. Since the famous debate of 1960 that was widely believed to have helped John F. Kennedy to gain the presidency because of the un-telegenic appearance of his opponent, Vice-President Richard Nixon, televised candidate "duels" have become a staple of electioneering not only in the United States but in all OECD countries (remarkably, with the single exception of Britain) as well as in many countries of the less developed regions of the world (Norris 2000, 153; Plasser and Plasser 2002, 188–91; Coleman 2000). The importance of these ultimate pseudo-events is seen not only in the events themselves, and the impressions of the candidates that they give to their audiences, but similarly strongly in the resonance they find in other media's reporting. Who emerges from electors' direct and mediated impressions as the "winner" and the "loser" of the debate is seen as one of the decisive factors with regard to the candidates' success at the ballots (Lanoue and Schrott 1991).

Obviously, American campaigns are enormously complex endeavors. Campaigning therefore requires skilled professionals, and this contributes to the escalating costs of contemporary *"capital-intensive"* campaigns (Farrell 1996). From 1952 to 1996 total campaign spending in the US is estimated to have grown more than thirty-fold (Maisel 2002, 381). Financial activity of 2004 presidential candidates and national conventions totaled more than $1 billion, an increase of 56 percent compared to the previous campaign. In addition, individuals, parties, and interest groups spent another $192.4 million independently, supporting or attacking one of the presidential candidates (www.fec.gov). Above all it is the "air war" (West 2005) of television advertising that eats up large chunks of candidates' campaign coffers. Since—with the exception of a limited option at presidential elections—public funding is unavailable for American campaigns, they must operate in a business-like manner, refunding their expenditures themselves and permanently raising money to keep going. Hence, fund-raising experts are among the key advisers in any typical American campaign organization.

Yet, while all this is the more spectacular face of current electioneering in the United States, it must not be overlooked that "pre-modern" *grass roots* components continue to play a far from negligible role. The "ground war" of a large "volunteer infantry" of local activists, coordinated by local and county party organizations as well as local branches of the candidates' own campaign organizations, swarming out in their neighborhoods to recruit voters through personal contact, is still alive and well, although an apparent fascination with centralized hi-tech campaigning seems to keep scholarly interest in these rather mundane, though vibrant activities unduly low (but see Beck et al. 1997).

2 "SHOPPING" ON THE AMERICAN MARKET

US style campaigning is a complex package of specific agents, strategic philosophies, messages, and communication channels. If "Americanization" is supposed to indicate a process of imitation, whereby this entire bundle is exported to other regions of the world and adopted wholesale, then this simply does not take place. The changing modes of campaigning in other democracies are much better described by the "*shopping model*" (Farrell 2002; Plasser and Plasser 2002). By "*modernizing*" their campaign practices (Swanson and Mancini 1996), political elites in established democracies all over the world are trying to adapt to similarly changing technical, institutional, and social circumstances. Most notably, these include the advent of television and the more current revolution of new information technologies, the growing institutional autonomy of the audiovisual media, brought about by a worldwide trend of deregulation and commercialization, and the dealignment trend (Dalton 2000) that in established democracies renders growing portions of electorates unavailable for mere activation, forcing campaign organizations to rely increasingly on the more demanding task of persuasion. Similar problems pose themselves in many new democracies, with often weak and "floating" party systems that lack anchors in these countries' "prealigned" electorates.

The United States is unique in having experienced these changes earlier than most other democracies. In addition, in many respects the environment of electioneering in the United States has been particularly conducive to the emergence of the specific features of "modern" and "postmodern" campaigning. As a consequence, political actors from other countries can find an abundance of practices in the American campaigners' toolbox that can be considered as potential improvements for campaigning in their own domestic settings. Yet, whether and how American modes of campaigning are adopted by parties in other countries depends on a whole range of contextual conditions, each of them relevant for specific facets of the complex package of American style electioneering (Farrell 2002; Swanson and Mancini 1996; Norris 2000; Plasser and Plasser 2002). Hence, campaigners from many countries more or less selectively "shop" on the American—but to some degree also the west European—market of modes of electioneering, and try to fuse the newly acquired tools into their traditional styles of campaigning.

Clearly, institutional aspects of *systems of government* are important mediators. For instance, presidential systems lend themselves more easily to candidate-centered and personalized electioneering than parliamentary democracies (Poguntke and Webb 2005; Aarts, Blais, and Schmitt forthcoming). *Electoral systems* are highly significant, with majority systems inviting a focus on individual candidates, whereas systems of proportional representation tend to strengthen the role of parties. There are also huge variations between democracies with regard to the extent to which *campaigning practices are regulated by law*. The legal environment of American campaigns is uniquely liberal, while other countries, especially in Asia, have strict rules for even specific details of campaign communications. Television advertising is subject to restrictions in most countries (Kaid and Holtz-Bacha 1995). But campaign laws in countries like, for instance, Japan regulate even how often, where and at what times candidates can hold meetings, usage of microphones, and the number of leaflets they are allowed to distribute at these occasions. While calling voters on the phone is allowed, contacting them through direct mail and email is prohibited to candidates, and even the number of loudspeaker cars they can send out in cities and villages is restricted. Also, there are strict rules for the size, number, and even design of campaign posters and newspaper ads (Plasser and Plasser 2002).

Also critical are characteristics of *party systems*. Two-party systems with zero-sum competition encourage different strategic calculations than multi-party systems where parties may need to form coalitions after elections. Parties' material resources are another important feature, and for these, in turn, it makes a difference whether or not parties have access to public funding. In addition, features of the *parties* them-selves, for instance their ideological heritage, are crucial (Gibson and Römmele 2001). Similarly important are structures of *media systems*. Across the world, countries differ enormously with regard to the number of media, the types of media that are dominant, the media's reach in society, the available technical standards, and so on. The extent to which media operate according to commercial instead of political imperatives is also essential.

Another group of factors concerns the *electorate*. Incentives to apply techniques of persuasive communication are certainly strongest in societies where ties to political parties are weak and electoral volatility is high, since the reservoir of voters that are available for influence is larger than elsewhere. *Political cultures* make a difference, too, as they circumscribe boundaries for acceptable political practices. For instance, consensus-oriented cultures that place high value on accommodation and balancing interests can be expected to be less open than cultures characterized by a more competitive, confrontational style of conducting politics (Lijphart 1999) to adapt the new techniques of attack electioneering that have recently become common in the US. In fact, despite movements in a similar direction in countries like Britain or Israel, no other country has so far adopted an equally negativistic mode of campaigning (Plasser and Plasser 2002, 90–7).

Taken together, these conditions constitute characteristic patterns of constraint and opportunity within each country that channel which of the many facets of American electioneering may be adopted and which cannot easily be wedded to an existing setting. Sometimes, there is simply not much leeway for the adoption of American techniques. However, as long as winning votes in competitive elections is the dominant motive of campaign organizations they will always seek ways to improve their campaigns. It does not really matter whether the effectiveness of a mode of campaigning is proven or not—the stakes are simply too high for campaigners to neglect any activity that *might* be helpful in gaining votes. They tend to operate under the assumption that their competitors will at all times seek to maximize their effectiveness by taking advantage of any innovative tool available to them, in order to prevail in the contest. The competitive pressures inherent in elections thus creates a momentum towards expanding campaign arsenals, ever more sophisticated campaigns, and correspondingly rising costs. Looking at the US (or, for that matter, other countries with more advanced styles of electioneering) for modes of campaigning that can—within the limits imposed by the formal and informal features of one's own political setting—augment one's toolbox is, then, certainly something that suggests itself.

The consequence of this is a *hybridization* of campaign development, producing distinct national patterns of electioneering, each of them being a unique blend of "modern" or even "postmodern" practices and more traditional modes. Accordingly, there are countries that mirror the American model relatively closely in many respects, whereas others remain distinctly different. While ultimately each country has its own unique style and trajectory of campaigning, considerable similarities exist nonetheless within families of countries that share important contextual features (Plasser and Plasser 2002).

Due to especially favorable opportunity structures, *Latin American* countries have adapted particularly strongly to the US paradigm (Waisbord 1996; Espindola 2002; Plasser and Plasser 2002, 271–3). Presidential political systems and weak party systems as well as relatively liberal legal regimes governing campaigns have encouraged a style of electioneering that is centered around television, with paid advertising playing a key role. The electoral process is highly personalized, and outside consultancy is widely used, largely replacing party officials in the conduct of campaigns. While the Southern cone is an important market for US-based consultants, a significant indigenous industry has emerged in recent years. To varying degrees the contextual conditions are similar in Russia and other *post-communist new democracies*. In these countries, campaigns are a hybrid combination of "modern" television operations with a clear focus on political leaders, reliance on contracted consultants, and more or less intense usage of administrative resources of governments, especially state-dependent electronic media, in order to control campaign communications (Mickiewicz and Richter 1996; Nivat 2000; Plasser and Plasser 2002, 273–5). Many new democracies display signs of "leapfrogging"—bypassing the "pre-modern" era of mass politics, to enter the era of electoral politics immediately the "modern", if not the "postmodern" way (Pasquino 2001).

The marketing logic has also gained ground in *west European* campaigning, with an increased role for research, targeting, media management, careful planning of messages, and centralized coordination of campaign activities. A tendency towards more professionalized campaigning is also not to be overlooked. Yet, in stark contrast to the US or Latin America, it is mainly taking place inside, rather than outside of parties. West European parties nowadays regularly include contracted specialists into their campaigns, but have also increased the professionalism of their own staff. Local campaigns have been rationalized through extensive usage of modern information and communication technologies, although they otherwise remain a stronghold of the "pre-modern" style of campaigning. Paid television advertising plays only a marginal role. On the whole, in western Europe parties stay firmly in control of the electoral process, but the selective adoption of American modes of campaigning tends to strengthen the power of their leaders at the expense of members and traditional functionaries (Farrell 2002; Plasser and Plasser 2002, 269–71).

The latter phenomenon can be seen as part and parcel of a broader trend of a "presidentialization" of politics in parliamentary democracies, revealing itself not only in the growing power and autonomy of political leaders within political parties and political executives, but also in the emergence of increasingly leadership-centered electoral processes (Mughan 2000; Poguntke and Webb 2005). There is a tendency for campaigns to be run by temporary special units with some organizational autonomy within parties and a high degree of personal loyalty to party leaders, as exemplified by New Labour's Milbank Tower and the German SPD's "Kampa". In addition, the content of campaign communications seems to be becoming more personalized, although less dramatically than often assumed. Manifesting itself in parties' advertising strategies as well as in the increasing reliance on candidate-centered media formats like televised debates and talkshows, the growing emphasis on leaders does not mean that political competition mutates into some sort of apolitical beauty contest where entertainment values prevail. Politicians' private lives still play only a marginal role. Rather, candidates increasingly serve as vehicles for simplifying complex issue debates, and as far as personality traits are concerned, emphasis is placed mostly on managerial qualities like determination and assertiveness, rather than on whether they are nice fellows (Holtz-Bacha 2000; Keil 2003).

In *East Asian* democracies like Japan or Taiwan traditional modes of campaigning that draw heavily on local networks and support groups continue to coexist with "modern" television campaigning, including extensive use of "paid media," and "postmodern" hi-tech campaigning through the internet (Curtis 1992; Plasser and Plasser 2002, 275–7). On the whole, these campaigns are candidate rather than party-centered. In many countries of the *Third World* campaign organizations' ability to adopt American techniques of electioneering is seriously hampered. Although professional advice, the marketing logic, and to a limited degree also modern "video style" campaigning through paid advertising do play a role, campaigns need to be at their core rather "low-tech." As television has not yet fully penetrated these societies, personal appearances of candidates at rallies and interpersonal communication remain the central channels of campaign communications (Plasser and Plasser 2002, 277–81).

3 Do Campaigns Matter?

Active participants in the political game like politicians, consultants, or journalists tend to see campaigning as one of the biggest movers in the political process. In stark contrast to those directly involved, political scientists have long tended towards pronounced skepticism. In the 1940s the Columbia school's "minimal effects" model (Lazarsfeld et al. 1944) became the generally accepted view of how campaigns might affect voters. It held that election campaigns primarily activate voters' latent predispositions and bring about voting preferences that correspond to their social-structural and ideological characteristics. Once having come to the fore, they were believed to be reinforced by campaigns until election day, so that voters did not stray from their fold. Conversion, that is, voting against one's predispositions, was an uncommon, and, if it occured, an unpredictable event. This view effectively stalled research into campaign effects for decades.

However, during the 1990s, following the general revival of interest in campaigns and campaigning, the question of whether and how campaigns might "matter" slowly re-engaged the attention of political scientists, especially in the US (Miller 1990; Holbrook 1996; Farrell and Schmitt-Beck 2002; Johnston and Brady 2006). Although still fragmentary, the general impression emerging from recent analyses in this emerging field is that the Columbia scholars were not all that wrong. Even in the age of television and "modern," if not "postmodern," campaigning, activation and reinforcement appear as the dominant processes during campaign periods. Predispositions like partisanship or ideology, and pre-campaign assessments of governments' performance, candidates' quality, as well as the economy are better predictors of electors' choices than campaign-induced changes in these variables (Finkel 1993). Correspondingly, at least at American presidential elections, forecasting models have proven fairly accurate in predicting candidates' vote shares from pre-campaign aggregate values of similar "fundamental variables" (e.g. Campbell and Garand 1999). However, this must not indicate that campaigns are meaningless. Rather, they could in fact be the very reason for the forecasting models' success—if it were not for parties and politicians waging highly visible election campaigns these models might actually fail. As Campbell notes, "[t]he reason that elections are predictable is not that campaigns have no effect, but that campaign effects themselves are largely predictable" (Campbell 2000, 187). In essence, from this perspective campaigns can be understood as periods of high intensity information flows that make voters aware of the "true values" of the basic variables, thus helping them to cast "enlightened" votes (Gelman and King 1993; Holbrook 1996).

Obviously, this is a highly abstract perspective on campaigns that ignores all the details of campaign practices with which both practicioners and students of the new modes of campaigning are preoccupied. It may be tempting to conclude from these studies that it is irrelevant how political actors campaign, if only they do it with sufficient intensity. Yet, some studies suggest that at least at the margins there may well be some space left for effects not of *campaigning* as such, regardless of how it is done, but rather of specific *campaigns*, waged in particular ways. For instance, conversion, although rare, does appear to occur to some extent during campaign periods (Finkel 1993). Analyses of US presidential elections found that campaign effects were largely systematic and thus predictable, but small shifts of election results were also attributable to "unsystematic" effects that could not be predicted from long-term variables. Rather, they seem to have been connected to the specific circumstances of particular elections. While "national conditions" define a charac-teristic baseline for the division of votes at each election (Holbrook 1996), in very close races such unpredictable campaign effects may even become pivotal, as seems to have been the case on several occassions during the last century (Campbell 2000). In addition, as the cases of the two previous US presidential elections show, forecasting models may even go wrong. Arguably, that Al Gore lost in 2000 despite economic conditions that should have made him the safe winner, can be attributed to the fact that he abstained from emphasizing the economy in his campaign, and thus to a wrong strategic decision on his part. Hence, campaigns may not automatically transform "fundamental variables" into electoral outcomes, but only when candi-dates decide to campaign on these issues (Johnston, Hagen, and Jamieson 2004). All this suggests that "campaign effects are more than the unfolding of the historically inevitable" (Johnston et al. 1992, 6).

It is thus necessary to take a closer look at how campaigns are waged in order to disentangle the contribution of specific campaign features to narrowing the explana-tory gap that remains after the systematic effects of campaigning are taken into account. One line of study inspects the dynamics of campaigns as chains of *key events*. It seems clear that occurences like nomination conventions or candidates' televised debates can have substantial effects on voters' sympathies (Holbrook 1996; Johnston et al. 1992). But important related questions have not yet been decisively resolved. For instance, it is debated whether the effects of such events are attributable to direct exposure, or moderated by how the mass media deal with these events. Also at issue is whether how such events are staged is important for their influence on public opinion. Several studies indicate that event-induced "bumps" in candidates' voter support have only small net effects on vote divisions, due to a mutual cancellation of the gross effects of competing events, thus suggesting no particular role for differing modes of staging them. Furthermore, the controversy is unsolved whether the effects of events are lasting, as predicted by the "online" model of political information processing, or rather short-lived, and thus potentially decaying until polling day, as expected by memory-based models of decision making (Johnston, Hagen, and Jamieson 2004).

Another stream of research goes inside the black box of the campaign organization and its activities, usually zeroing in on one component of campaigning and measuring the influence this might have on voters. These studies are primarily interested in the relevance of differences in the *resources* political actors invest for campaign purposes as well as in the *channels and modes* they use for communicating their messages. In countries like Britain, Canada, and the US, territorial district single-member electoral systems have stimulated numerous inquiries into the role of local campaign expenditures for electoral success. While local campaigns are no key components of the notion of "Americanized" campaigns, such studies of constituency campaigning provide evidence that with regard to votes, at least one component of modern campaigning does seem to work: spending. Apparently, "capital-intensive" campaigns are more effective campaigns (Jacobson 1980, 1990; Pattie, Johnston, and Fieldhouse 1995; Gerber 2004).

Other studies demonstrate more directly that local party activists' manpower and the intensity of their canvassing efforts make a difference for the success of campaigns (e.g. Huckfeldt and Sprague 1992; Denver and Hands 1997). Clearly, the seemingly old-fashioned local campaign with its emphasis on unmediated contacts between campaigners and electors still has an important role to play in contemporary campaigns—one that, if anything, in recent years has become more rather than less important. Yet, campaign modernization did not bypass local campaigning. British party organizations increasingly channel their material resources to selected con-stituencies. To the degree that well-resourced local campaigns are more effective in gaining seats, this testifies to the important role of geographical targeting for electoral success. One study of the British general election of 1997 compares the effectiveness of "modern" and "postmodern" practices in local campaigns. While "modern" tools unequivocally helped getting votes, no similarly clear evidence emerges with regard to "postmodern" practices like advance preparation, computer use, direct mail, and telephone canvassing (Denver and Hands 2002). Several other studies also suggest that the impersonal mode of contacting voters by telephone, direct mail, or email is not as effective as genuine face-to-face canvassing (Green and Gerber 2004). Hence, the "Americanization" of campaigning with regard to constituency campaigns appears as a mixed blessing. It makes sense to pool resources strategically in key constituencies, but whether the newest communications tools also work better in these campaigns is highly doubtful.

There is also some evidence that the professionalization of campaigning yields results. A study of US congressional elections indicates that the more campaign functions candidates assign to hired consultants, the more votes they get (Medvic 2000). Due to its central importance in US campaigns, research into the effects of television advertising has flourished, and is one of the most productive areas of campaign effects research (Goldstein and Ridout 2004). TV ads can affect voters' opinions on issues and candidate images. Yet, only few studies provide evidence that candidates can actually win votes by running ads (Shaw 1999; Johnston, Hagen, and Jamieson 2004). Remarkably, despite the fact that press advertisements have by no means disappeared from contemporary campaigns but rather, at least in west

European contests, still eat up large chunks of parties' campaign budgets and gain wide attention among electors, they have attracted much less scholarly interest. There is only fragmentary evidence about such ads' content (Keil 2003), and virtually nothing is known about their effects on voters.

Our knowledge is even more fragmentary, when it comes to the role played by the *communication strategies* and the specific *appeals, themes, and messages* that campaigns convey. Some studies suggest that campaigns may indeed bring about opinion change, especially with regard to perceptions of parties' ability to deal with certain issues (Bowler et al. 1992; Schmitt-Beck 2001). Others indicate that campaign communications may effectively reshape the ways leaders are perceived by the public (Johnston et al. 1992; Johnston, Hagen, and Jamieson 2004). However, on the whole it appears that the prospects of a "rhetoric" strategy of direct persuasion (Riker 1983), that is, the strategy of trying to gain votes by convincing voters to re-evaluate certain objects that are relevant for their decisions, are rather limited (Zaller 1992). Thus, it often cannot be the high road to gaining votes.

More promising is a "heresthetic" strategy (Riker 1983) of indirect persuasion that does not attempt to alter citizens' assessments of candidates, parties, or issues, but rather tries to manipulate the salience of the considerations that electors take into account when deciding how to vote. The battle of effective campaign communications is, then, not about whether things ought to be seen positively or negatively, but rather about which factors voters will think of when constructing their overall evaluations of the competitors on election day. Campaigns that work seek resonance with favorable opinions on parties or candidates that voters already hold, stimulating them to think of these aspects, while at the same time trying to de-emphasize less favorable topics. Successful campaigns "prime" issues that parties already "own" instead of trying to "appropriate" new themes or "riding the wave" of the current news agenda (Budge and Farlie 1983; Ansolabehere and Iyengar 1994; Iyengar and Simon 2000; Simon 2002; Druckman 2004). Available evidence thus suggests that campaigners are well advised to let their communications strategies be guided by the strengths they already possess in the eyes of the electorate instead of trying to "reposition" themselves by moving around in political space, as suggested by political marketers, or of attempting to "re-educate" citizens about how things should be evaluated. Whether or not at a given election pre-campaign "basic variables" like the economy actually play the role ascribed to them by forecasting models, also seems to hinge to a considerable degree on whether or not campaigns choose to thematize these issues (Johnston, Hagen, and Jamieson 2004).

Since campaigns change citizens' communications environments in many ways, they may—in addition to their effects on voting—also have consequences that were not intended, or anticipated, by the campaign organizations. Such *unintended effects* may be positive, for instance, if, from being exposed to campaigns, voters become motivated to follow politics more closely (Lazarsfeld, Berelson, and Gaudet 1944), and thereby become better informed about politics more generally (Norris and Sanders 2003). Starting with Patterson and McClure (1976), research has repeatedly demonstrated how television spots have clear cognitive effects, contributing to a general increase in levels of awareness of the candidates and their policies (cf. e.g. Freedman, Franz, and Goldstein 2004). Other studies suggest that campaigns can even induce positive short-term changes in citizens' political trust and system support (Banducci and Karp 2003). However, some analysts are concerned that campaigns may also have a detrimental effect on citizens' attitudes towards the political process and its actors (Norris 2000).

In particular, the rising tide of negativism in campaign advertising in the US has nourished worries that this may lead to increased political cynicism among citizens and consequentially be responsible for depressing voter turnout (Ansolabehere and Iyengar 1997). A huge body of research has been accumulated around this hotly debated topic, but evidence so far is mixed (Lau et al. 1999; Lau and Sigelman 2000). Some studies seem to confirm the null hypothesis that the tone of ads is unrelated to turnout (Garramone et al. 1990; Clinton and Lapinski 2004). But other research suggests that attack ads alienate voters and thus indeed have a demobilizing effect at elections (e.g. Ansolabehere and Iyengar 1997; Ansolabehere, Iyengar, and Simon 1999). Yet, according to a third group of studies negative ads can also have the opposite effect: to stimulate citizens' involvement in the electoral process, thereby creating a more interested, engaged, and thus more, rather than less participatory electorate (Finkel and Geer 1998; Wattenberg and Brians 1999; Freedman and Goldstein 1999; Vavreck 2000; Freedman, Franz, and Goldstein 2004). Thus, the debate is yet undecided whether attack advertising indeed has detrimental consequences for the health of civic life. Yet, one thing at least does seem to be clear—it is no more effective in attracting votes than other advertising (Lau and Sigelman 2000).

4 Preconditions of Effective Campaigns

How campaigns may be effective, is highly conditional. They matter in ways that are dependent on a multitude of factors, often interacting with each other in complex patterns. Hence, "efforts to study campaigns as 'main effects' [...] are doomed to fail" (Iyengar and Simon 2000, 163; Schmitt-Beck and Farrell 2002; Kriesi 2002). Some of these factors concern the campaigns themselves, others the campaign's recipients—the electorates and the individuals of which they are composed. For instance, campaigns may matter very differently depending on the *type of decision event*. On the whole, referendum campaigns can be expected to be more effective than election campaigns, especially if they concern unfamiliar and complex issues that are unrelated to the sociopolitical cleavage structures of organized party conflict (LeDuc 2002; De Vreese and Semetko 2004). In the cases of campaigns for elections or for referendums over established issues with clear partisan connotations, the story is mostly one of activation and reinforcement. However, if referenda concern *new, unclear and complex issues* opinions cannot be activated but must be formed, and there is considerable scope for conversion through campaign information, leading to unpredictable outcomes.

Both the intensity or *"loudness"* of campaigns and their degree of directional *balance or one-sidedness* are also important for their outcomes. The predictability of campaign effects at American presidential election campaigns may occur because these campaigns are both highly intense, and balanced (Campbell 2000). In contrast to this, in more one-sided contests more intensely campaigning parties are advantaged (Zaller 1992), and even partisans may be deflected from their predispositions (Lachat and Sciarini 2002). On the other hand, the systematic effects of more balanced campaigns presuppose a certain minimum *length* of the campaign period (Stevenson and Vavreck 2000).

The scope for campaign influence can also vary dramatically depending on the types of *voters* involved. One obvious conditioning factor is whether voters are at all *available* to be influenced by campaigns. This is not the case if they have taken their decisions long before a campaign started. Yet, the number of late-deciders on whom campaigns can only be expected to have effects (Campbell 2000; Lachat and Sciarini 2002; Fournier et al. 2004), has grown in recent decades, as a consequence of partisan dealignment (Dalton, McAllister, and Wattenberg 2000). In general, *political predispositions* like ideology, and, above all, partisanship feature as important moderating factors for campaign influence, at least if campaigns bear a relationship to existing cleavage structures and organized party conflict. Zaller (1992) also attaches importance to the mediating role of the extent to which voters pay attention and understand campaigners' messages and their implications, that is, their *political awareness*. More sophisticated voters are more inclined to receive campaign messages, and therefore more likely to be "primed" about issues and candidate images. However, when it comes to direct persuasion, political awareness increases the likelihood of activation while inhibiting the likelihood of conversion.

5 CONCLUSION

In recent decades campaigning has undergone a worldwide process of modernization, that has also led to some degree of cross-cultural convergence, especially with regard to the role of the audiovisual media as central conveyors of campaign messages and the personalization of politics. Yet, what we see is not a wholesale adoption of the "American" model of electioneering, but a rather selective "shopping" on the US market, where the new modes of campaigning have developed earliest and to the highest level. Rather than being imitated wholesale, "Americanized" campaign techniques are fused with existing practices in other countries, leading to hybrid styles of electioneering.

It is the guiding spirit with regard to campaign principles and strategies rather than the techniques per se that characterizes the current processes of transnational diffusion of campaign practices best. Contemporary modes of electioneering can be understood as an increasingly *rationalized* way of seeking votes and winning elections, attempting to always make the best conceivable, most efficient use of available means of mobilization and persuasion, within the boundaries of given contextual circumstances. This, in turn, seems to be connected to a marked tendency on the part of political elites to act more and more like *Schumpeterian* political entrepreneurs who are primarily moved by the desire to attain public office (Schumpeter 1994). Concomitantly, campaigning has become increasingly centered around leaders, either outside of parties that function as mere service institutions for candidates, like in the United States, or inside of parties, like in western Europe, where the new way of campaigning seems to strengthen the party organizations' top strata.

Yet, whether "modern" or "postmodern" campaigns are actually more effective than old-fashioned "pre-modern" campaigns is, on the whole, not proven. While some aspects seem to "work", others have not yet substantiated their effectiveness. At the same time, there are clear indications that traditional modes of campaigning, especially those relying on personal contacts with voters, help candidates and parties to gain votes.

In any case, it is doubtful that successful campaigns by necessity produce "enlightened" preferences that are in the voters' best interest. Clever campaigners may be able to shift the terms of debate to those areas where they can prevail more easily. Perhaps even more worrisome is the heavy advantage that well-funded campaign organizations enjoy at the polls. An important implication of this well-documented pattern is that by way of campaigning, economic inequality can translate into political inequality, thereby undermining one of the key prerequisites of democratic politics. Some findings also suggest that the increasing negativism of contemporary election campaigns may have consequences for citizens' political involvement that may be, although unintended, nonetheless detrimental for democracy. Citizens' direct involvement in campaign activities is on the decline in many established democracies (Dalton et al. 2000), although it is not clear whether this is largely the effect or the cause of the global trend of campaign modernization. In any case, when being asked themselves, voters do not seem to approve of the new modes of electioneering (Medvic et al. 2000; Lipsitz et al. 2005).

On the other hand, in today's dealigned societies where many citizens tend to tune out of electoral politics, modern electioneering may also have an important positive role to play as a stimulant for engaging otherwise detached citizens with politics, mobilizing them to take part in selecting political leaders through elections, informing them on the issues that are at stake in these contests, and helping them to form opinions on the candidates that compete for their votes. In particular this concerns the rather uninvolved segments of the citizenry which lack the necessary competence to form autonomous judgments on complicated political matters. For them, the simple, yet appealing emotional messages of modern campaigns—lamented by proponents of a more deliberative politics as a deterioration of the quality of political debate—may serve as valuable cues that make otherwise incomprehensible politics more accessible. By increasing its inclusiveness it thus contributes to the quality of the democratic political process. Arguably, the scope for manipulation and a merely virtual politics is limited, since no campaign organization is able to control the entire campaign discourse. Other actors' communications, including those from competing parties and candidates, but also interest groups and above all the media, as well as citizens' everyday experiences may serve as checks against such tendencies that otherwise would have a potential to seriously hamper the mechanisms of elite responsiveness and "vertical accountability" through elections that are at the very heart of representative democratic politics (Diamond and Morlino 2004).

REFERENCES

AARTS, K., BLAIS, A., and SCHMITT, H. eds. Forthcoming. *Political Leaders and Democratic Elections*, Oxford: Oxford University Press.

ANSOLABEHERE, S., and IYENGAR, S. 1994. Riding the wave and claiming ownership over issues: the joint effects of advertising and news coverage in campaigns. *Public Opinion Quarterly*, 58: 335–57.

—— —— 1997. *Going Negative: How Political Advertisements Shrink and Polarize the Electorate*. New York: Free Press.

—— —— and SIMON, A. 1999. Replicating experiments using aggregate and survey data: the case of negative advertising and turnout. *American Political Science Review*, 93: 901–9.

BANDUCCI, S. A., and KARP, J. A. 2003. How elections change the way citizens view the political system: campaigns, media effects and electoral outcomes in comparative perspective. *British Journal of Political Science*, 33: 443–67.

BECK, P. A., DALTON, R. J., HAYNES, A., and HUCKFELDT R. 1997. Presidential campaigning at the grass roots. *Journal of Politics*, 59: 1264–75.

BLUMENTHAL, S. 1982. *The Permanent Campaign*. New York: Simon & Schuster.

BOWLER, S., BROUGHTON, D., TODD, D., and SNIPP, J. 1992. The informed electorate? Voter responsiveness to campaigns in Britain and Germany. Pp. 204–22 in *Electoral Strategies and Political Marketing*, ed. S. Bowler and D. M. Farrell. New York: St. Martin's Press.

BUDGE, I., and FARLIE, D. 1983. Party competition—selective emphasis or direct confrontation? An alternative view with data. Pp. 267–305 in *Western European Party Systems: Continuity and Change*, ed. H. Daalder and P. Mair. Beverly Hills, Calif.: Sage.

BUTLER, D., and RANNEY, A. eds. 1992: *Electioneering: A Comparative Study of Continuity and Change*. Oxford: Clarendon.

CAMPBELL, J. E. 2000. *The American Campaign. U.S. Presidential Campaigns and the National Vote*. College Station: Texas A & M University Press.

—— and GARAND, J. C. ed. 1999. *Before the Vote: Forecasting American National Elections*. Thousand Oaks, Calif.: Sage Publications.

CLINTON, J. D., and LAPINSKI, J. S. 2004. "Targeted" advertising and voter turnout: an experimental study of the 2000 presidential election. *Journal of Politics*, 66: 69–96.

COLEMAN, S. ed. 2000. *Televised Election Debates: International Perspectives*. New York: St Martin's Press.

CURTIS, G. L. 1992. Pp. 222–43 in *Electioneering: A Comparative Study of Continuity and Change*, ed. D. Butler and A. Ranney. Oxford: Clarendon.

DALTON, R. J. 2000. The decline of party identifications. Pp. 19–36 in *Parties without Partisans: Political Change in Advanced Industrial Democracies*, ed. R. J. Dalton and M. P. Wattenberg. Oxford: Oxford University Press.

—— MCALLISTER, I., and WATTENBERG, M. P. 2000. The consequences of partisan dealignment. Pp. 37–63 in *Parties without Partisans: Political Change in Advanced Industrial Democracies*, ed. R. J. Dalton and M. P. Wattenberg. Oxford: Oxford University Press.

DAVIS, A. 2002. *Public Relations Democracy. Public Relations, Politics and the Mass Media in Britain*. Manchester: Manchester University Press.

DE VREESE, C. H., and SEMETKO, H. 2004. *Political Campaigning in Referendums: Framing the Referendum Issue*. London/New York: Routledge.

DENVER, D., and HANDS, G. 1997. *Modern Constituency Electioneering*. London: Frank Cass.

—— —— 2002. Post-Fordism in the constituencies? The continuing development of constituency campaigning in Britain. In Farrell and Schmitt-Beck 2002: 108–26.

DRUCKMAN, J. N. 2004. Priming the vote: campaign effects in a U.S. Senate election. *Political Psychology*, 25: 577–94.

DIAMOND, L., and MORLINO, L. 2004. The quality of democracy: an overview. *Journal of Democracy*, 15: 20–31.

ESPINDOLA, R. 2002. Professionalised campaigning in Latin America. *Journal of Political Marketing*, 1 (4): 65–81.

FARRELL, D. M. 1996. Campaign strategies and tactics. Pp. 160–83 in *Comparing Democracies: Elections and Voting in Global Perspective*, ed. L. LeDuc, R. G. Niemi, and P. Norris. Thousand Oaks, Calif.: Sage.

—— 2002. Campaign modernization and the West European party. Pp. 63–83 in *Political Parties and Democracy in Western Europe*, ed. K. R. Luther and F. Müller-Rommel. Oxford: Oxford University Press.

—— and SCHMITT-BECK, R. ed. 2002. *Do Political Campaigns Matter? Campaign Effects in Elections and Referendums*. London: Routledge.

FINKEL, S. E. 1993. Reexamining the "minimal effects" model in recent presidential campaigns. *Journal of Politics*, 55: 1–21.

—— and GEER, G. G. 1998. A spot check: casting doubt on the demobilizing effect of attack advertising. *American Journal of Political Science*, 42: 573–95.

FOURNIER, P., NADEAU, R., BLAIS, A., GIDENGIL, E. and NEVITTE, N. 2004. Time-of-voting decision and susceptibility to campaign effects. *Electoral Studies*, 23: 661–81.

FREEDMAN, P., FRANZ, M., and GOLDSTEIN, K. 2004. Campaign advertising and democratic citizenship. *American Journal of Political Science*, 48: 723–741.

—— and GOLDSTEIN, K. 1999. Measuring media exposure and the effects of negative campaign ads. *American Journal of Political Science*, 43: 1189–208.

GARRAMONE, G. M., ATKIN, C. K., PINKLETON, B. E., and COLE, R. T. 1990. Effects of negative political advertising on the political process. *Journal of Broadcasting & Electronic Media*, 34: 299–311.

GELMAN, A., and KING, G. 1993. Why are American presidential election campaign polls so variable when voters are so predictable? *British Journal of Political Science*, 23: 409–51.

GERBER, A. S. 2004: Does campaign spending work? *American Behavioral Scientist*, 47: 541–74.

GIBSON, R., and RÖMMELE, A. 2001. Changing campaign communications: a party-centered theory of professionalized campaigning. *Harvard International Journal of Press/Politics*, 6: 31–43.

GOLDSTEIN, K., and RIDOUT, T. N. 2004. Measuring the effects of televised political advertising in the United States. *Annual Review of Political Science*, 7: 205–26.

GREEN, D. O. and GERBER, A. S. 2004. *Get Out the Vote! How to Increase Voter Turnout.* Washington, DC: Brookings Institution Press.

HARMEL, R., and JANDA, K. 1994. An integrated theory of party goals and party change. *Journal of Theoretical Politics,* 6: 259–87.

HOLBROOK, T. M. 1996. *Do Campaigns Matter?* Thousand Oaks, Calif.: Sage.

HOLTZ-BACHA, C. 2000. *Wahlwerbung als politische Kultur.* Wiesbaden: Westdeutscher Verlag.

HUCKFELDT, R., and SPRAGUE, J. 1992. Political Parties and Electoral Mobilization: Political Structure, Social Structure, and the Party Canvass. *American Political Science Review,* 86: 70–86.

IYENGAR, S., and SIMON, A. 2000. New Perspectives and Evidence on Political Communication and Campaign Effects. *Annual Review of Psychology,* 51: 149–69.

JACOBSON, G. 1980. *Money in Congressional Elections.* New Haven: Yale University Press.

—— 1990. The effects of campaign spending in house elections: new evidence for old arguments. *American Journal of Political Science,* 34: 334–62.

JOHNSTON, R., and BRADY, H. E. eds. 2006. *Capturing Campaign Effects.* Ann Arbor: University of Michigan Press.

—— HAGEN, M. G., and JAMIESON, K. H. 2004. *The 2000 Presidential Election and the Foundations of Party Politics.* Cambridge, Mass.: Cambridge University Press.

—— BLAIS, A., BRADY, H. E., and CRÊTE, J. 1992. *Letting the People Decide: Dynamics of a Canadian Election.* Montreal: McGill-Queen's University Press.

KAID, L. L., and HOLTZ-BACHA, C. eds. 1995. *Political Advertising in Western Democracies: Parties and Candidates on Television.* Thousand Oaks, Calif.: Sage.

—— and JOHNSTON, A. 2000. *Videostyle in Presidential Campaigns: Style and Content of Televised Political Advertising.* Westport, Conn.: Praeger.

KEIL, S. I. 2003. *Wahlkampfkommunikation in Wahlanzeigen und Wahlprogrammen.* Frankfurt: Lang.

KRIESI, H. 2002. Individual opinion formation in a direct democratic campaign. *British Journal of Political Science,* 32: 171–91.

LACHAT, R., and SCIARINI, P. 2002. When do election campaigns matter, and to whom? Results from the 1999 Swiss election panel study. Pp. 41–57 in Farrell and Schmitt-Beck 2002.

LANOUE, D. J., and SCHROTT, P. 1991: *The Joint Press Conference: The History, Impact, and Prospects of American Presidential Debates.* Westport, Conn.: Greenwood.

LAU, R. R., and SIGELMAN, L. 2000. Effectiveness of negative political advertising. Pp. 10–43 in *Crowded Airwaves: Campaign Advertising in Elections,* ed. J. A. Thurber, C. J. Nelson, and D. Dulio. Washington, DC: Brookings Institution.

—— —— L., HELDMANN, C., and BABBITT, P. 1999: The effects of negative political advertisements: a meta-analytic assessment. *American Political Science Review,* 93: 851–76.

LAZARSFELD, P. F., BERELSON, B., and GAUDET, H. 1944. *The People's Choice: How the Voter Makes up his Mind in a Presidential Campaign.* New York: Columbia University Press.

LEDUC, L. 2002: Referendums and elections: how do campaigns differ? Pp. 145–62 in Farrell and Schmitt-Beck 2002.

LIJPHART, A. 1999. *Patterns of Democracy.* New Haven: Yale University Press.

LIPSITZ, K., TROST, C., GROSSMANN, M., and SIDES, J. 2005. What voters want from political campaign communication. *Political Communication,* 22: 337–54.

MAISEL, L. S. 2002. *Parties and Elections in America: The Electoral Process,* 3rd edn. Lanham, Md.: Rowman & Littlefield.

MANCINI, P., and SWANSON, D. L. 1996. Politics, media, and modern democracy: introduction. Pp. 1–26 in *Politics, media and Modern Democracy,* ed. D. Swanson and P. Mancini. New York: Praeger.

MEDVIC, S. K. 2000. Professionalization in congressional elections. Pp. 91–109 in *Campaign Warriors: Political Consultants in Elections*, ed. J. A. Thurber and C. J. Nelson. Washington, DC: Brookings Institution Press.

—— DULIO, D. A., THURBER, J. A. and NELSON, C. J. 2000. Citizens' attitudes toward campaigns and campaigners. *Votes and Opinions*, 3: 18–19.

MICKIEWICZ, E., and RICHTER, A. 1996. Television, Campaigning, and Elections in the Soviet Union and Post-Soviet Russia. Pp. 107–27 in *Politics, Media, and Modern Democracy: An International Study of Innovations in Electoral Campaigning and their Consequences*, ed. D. L. Swanson and P. Mancini. Westport, Conn.: Praeger.

MILLER, W. 1990. *How Voters Change: The 1987 British Election Campaign in Perspective*. Oxford: Clarendon.

MUGHAN, A. 2000. *Media and the Presidentialization of Parliamentary Elections*. Houndmills: Palgrave.

NEGRINE, R., and PAPATHANASSOPOULOS, S. 1996. The "Americanization" of political communication: a critique. *Harvard International Journal of Press/Politics*, 1: 45–62.

NEWMAN, B. I. ed. 1999. *Handbook of Political Marketing*. Thousand Oaks, Calif.: Sage.

NIVAT, A. 2000. Russian presidential campaign coverage. *Harvard International Journal of Press/Politics*, 5: 92–97.

NORRIS, P. 2000. *A Virtuous Circle: Political Communications in Postindustrial Societies*. Cambridge: Cambridge University Press.

—— and SANDERS, D. 2003. Message or medium? Campaign learning during the 2001 British general election. *Political Communication*, 20: 233–62.

PASQUINO, G. 2001. The new campaign politics in Southern Europe. Pp. 183–223 in *Parties, Politics, and Democracy in the New Southern Europe*, ed. N. Diamandouros and R. Gunther. Baltimore: Johns Hopkins University Press.

PATTERSON, T. E. 2000. The United States: news in a free-market society. Pp. 241–65 in *Democracy and the Media: A Comparative Perspective*, ed. R. Gunther and A. Mughan. Cambridge: Cambridge University Press.

—— and McCLURE, R. D. 1976. *The Unseeing Eye: The Myth of Television Power in National Politics*. New York: Paragon.

PATTIE, C. J., JOHNSTON, R. J., and FIELDHOUSE, E. A. 1995. Winning the local vote: the effectiveness of constituency campaign spending in Great Britain, 1983–1992. *American Political Science Review*, 89: 969–83.

PLASSER, F., and PLASSER, G. 2002. *Global Political Campaigning: A Worldwide Analysis of Campaign Professionals and Their Practices*. Westport, Conn.: Praeger.

POGUNTKE, T., and WEBB, P., eds. 2005. *The Presidentialization of Politics: A Comparative Study of Modern Democracies*. Oxford: Oxford University Press.

RIKER, W. H. 1983. Political theory and the art of heresthetics. Pp. 47–67 in *Political Science: The State of the Discipline*, ed. A. Finifter, Washington, DC: APSA.

ROHRSCHNEIDER, R. 2002. Mobilizing versus chasing: How do parties target voters in election campaigns? *Electoral Studies*, 21: 367–82.

SCAMMELL, M. 1998. The wisdom of the war room: U.S. campaigning and Americanization. *Media, Culture and Society*, 20: 251–75.

SCHMITT-BECK, R. 2001. Ein Sieg der "Kampa"? Politische Symbolik im Wahlkampf der SPD und ihre Resonanz in der Wählerschaft. Pp. 133–61 in *Wahlen und Wähler*, ed. H. Klingemann and M. Kaase. Wiesbaden: Westdeutscher Verlag.

—— and FARRELL, D. M. 2002. Do political campaigns matter? Yes, but it depends. Pp. 183–93 in Farrell and Schmitt-Beck 2002.

SCHUMPETER, J. A. 1994. *Capitalism, Socialism, and Democracy*. London: Routledge; originally published 1942.

SHAW, D. R. 1999. A study of presidential campaign event effects from 1952 to 1992. *Journal of Politics*, 61: 387–422.

SIMON, A. F. 2002. *The Winning Message: Candidate Behavior, Campaign Discourse, and Democracy.* Cambridge: Cambridge University Press.

STEVENSON, R. T., and VAVRECK, L. 2000. Does campaign length matter? Testing for cross-national effects. *British Journal of Political Science*, 30: 217–35.

SUSSMAN, G., and GALIZIO, L. 2003. The global reproduction of American politics. *Political Communication*, 20: 309–28.

SWANSON, D. L. 1991. Theoretical dimensions of the U.S.-French presidential campaign studies. Pp. 9–23 in *Mediated Politics in Two Cultures: Presidential Campaigning in the United States and France,* ed. L. L. Kaid, J. Gerstlé, and K. R. Sanders. New York: Praeger.

—— and MANCINI, P., ed. 1996. *Politics, Media and Modern Democracy.* New York: Praeger.

VAVRECK, L. 2000. How does it all "turnout"? Exposure to attack advertising, campaign interest, and participation in American presidential campaigns. Pp. 79–105 in *Campaign Reform: Insights and Evidence,* ed. L. M. Bartels and L. Vavreck. Ann Arbor: University of Michigan Press.

WAISBORD, S. 1996. Secular politics: the modernization of Argentine electioneering. Pp. 207–26 in *Politics, Media, and Modern Democracy: An International Study of Innovations in Electoral Campaigning and their Consequences,* ed. D. L. Swanson and P. Mancini. Westport, Conn.: Praeger.

WATTENBERG, M. P., and BRIANS, C. L. 1999. Negative campaign advertising: demobilizer or mobilizer? *American Political Science Review*, 93: 891–900.

WEST, D. 2005. *Air Wars: Television Advertising in Political Campaigns, 1952–2004,* 4th edn. Washington, DC: CQ Press.

ZALLER, J. R. 1992. *The Nature and Origins of Mass Opinion.* New York: Cambridge University Press.

CHAPTER 41

E-GOVERNMENT
AND DEMOCRACY

MICHAEL MARGOLIS

WHEN graphical browsers and the World Wide Web popularized the internet in the mid-1990s, political visionaries joined their business counterparts in predicting radical changes for governance in addition to those for commerce. Just as the internet would restructure accepted business models, so it would renew western democracy. Interaction among citizens in cyberspace would enrich public opinion and increase participation in democratic politics. In contrast to the established mass media, computer mediated communication would afford ordinary citizens opportunities to become their own publishers. Political activists—"netizens," so to speak—would employ email, newsgroups, and websites to form new political groups and build new coalitions. Cyber-democrats like Howard Rheingold, Rhonda and Michael Hauben, Andrew Shapiro, and John Perry Barlow heralded the internet's promise for realizing formerly impossible dreams of informed engagement in political and civic affairs (Rheingold 1993; Hauben and Hauben 1997; Shapiro 1999; Barlow 1996). They anticipated that once citizens discovered this potential, the internet would foster greater individual freedom as well as viable new parties and interest groups that would challenge the dominant political groups.

It hasn't happened. Established parties, together with their candidates and office-holders, dominate political activity not only offline, but also on the internet (Margolis, Resnick, and Levy 2003; Margolis, Resnick, and Wolfe 1999). Moreover, cyberspace is replete with heavily advertised websites of familiar commercial and political interests, websites that reflect their overwhelming dominance of economic, political, and civic affairs. In short, contrary to cyber-democrats' predictions that the internet would broaden democracy through citizens' increased involvement in and influence over public affairs, we have witnessed a normalization of the politics of cyberspace, the emergence of a political order that largely replicates that found in the physical world (Gibson, Nixon, and Ward 2003).

When democratically inclined social scientists began studying the political impact of the internet in the early 1990s, they hoped to discover many popular new political groups online whose members exercised intelligent civic and political participation that affected public policy in the real world. Their research showed that they had been overly optimistic, however, particularly with regard to policy inputs, the process of translating citizens' preferences into laws and regulations. Instead of revolutionizing policy formulation in the real world, netizens' political activities tended to reflect and reinforce the familiar patterns of behavior they had brought from that world (Fisher, Margolis, and Resnick 1996a, 1996b; Margolis and Resnick 2000, ch. 1). Nevertheless, the internet did present new possibilities for enlightened democratic participation, especially with regard to the policy outputs of government.

Taxpaying citizens are not merely the government's financiers; they are also its customers. As such they expect—even demand—that government implement public policies efficiently and effectively, particularly when those policies affect them personally. Indeed, the burgeoning numbers of governmental agencies online can be seen as efforts to realize the efficiency and good will that stem from doing business via the internet. And whether or not governments intend it, providing services online increases the opportunities for democratic political participation.

Scholars have argued that nations that aspire to modernity must deploy information technology (IT) via the internet in order to benefit from the global economy. If the argument holds, it follows that regardless of their ability to control (or avoid) elections, modern governments must allow citizens to access millions of networked databases. It seems likely, therefore, that if authoritarian governments seek prominence in world affairs, they must loosen restrictions on externally generated information and must allow citizens to use such information for purposes that inevitably develop new economic and political resources, which lie beyond the governments' customary spheres of control. This hypothesis seems plausible. Even though institutional change lags behind technological innovation, governments with advanced technological sectors but few democratic traditions, such as Singapore, China, Malaysia, and several eastern European nations of the former Soviet bloc, seem to be tolerating more openness in domestic affairs as they seek more significant roles in the global economy (West 2005, ch. 10 and Appendix II).

The next section contains a discussion of the proximate intellectual roots of cyber-democracy: the "New Left" and the "counter-culture" movements of the 1960s and early 1970s. I suggest that cyber-democrats saw the internet as the means to break away from the cycle of soaring promise and failed fulfillment that each new mass medium had engendered since the Industrial Revolution. The following section examines the difficulties of implementing direct democracy despite the increased powers the internet affords each citizen. It also questions the advantages of citizens' direct participation in policy making in comparison to citizens' judging the results of those policies. The final section discusses the advantages and dangers of democratic participation that emphasizes the output side of politics. The discussion reviews how institutional arrangements, internet access, and citizens' habitual behaviors affect various desiderata, such as privacy, individual liberty, civic values, national security, and domestic and global economic progress. It argues that political uses of the internet must take these arrangements and behaviors into account, and it concludes that encouraging citizens to react to how governmental policies affect them seems more promising for achieving positive democratic outcomes than does encouraging them to participate directly in formulating those policies. In the end, however, the evidence and the argument hark back to a familiar theory of democracy. Neither IT nor any particular institutional arrangement can substitute for a democratically inclined citizenry that holds its freely chosen governmental officials to account.

1 THE ROOTS OF CYBER-DEMOCRACY

The 1960s in the USA saw the growth of two distinct but interrelated radical movements, the New Left and the Counterculture. They shared a number of fundamental values, but had separate political agendas. Both were anti-elitist and egalitarian; they valued openness, sharing, community, and cooperation rather than competition. They opposed the manipulation of wants and desires that characterizes a commercial economy. Many who participated in them shared similar musical tastes, clothing styles, and recreational drugs, but the two movements differed in political strategy.

The New Left viewed participatory democracy as a means for citizens to re-establish control of their lives. Citizens would realize that their private problems had public causes and political solutions, and they would transform the bureaucratic, impersonal society that had pacified them. Participatory democracy would wrest power and control from the corporate and governmental elite (Thayer 1973; Hauben n.d.). Adherents of the counter-culture also rejected corporate America, but unlike the political activists of the New Left, they did so by dropping out rather than engaging in political struggle. They created alternative communities in which they could live as they pleased, unconstrained by the values, assumptions, material possessions, and laws that governed the rest of society. They aimed to establish a new way of life based on joy and liberation, and a new politics worked out directly by the people themselves without interference from the repressive structures of traditional American society. While the New Left saw itself as struggling to transform American society through organized political activity, the counter-culture saw itself as subverting that society by creating freer and more attractive alternatives.

The radicalism of the 1960s had roots in previous radical movements. Many of the early leaders of the New Left were so called "red diaper" babies, children of radicals who had been members of left-wing parties and active in the trade union movement. The Students for a Democratic Society (SDS), for instance, was born in 1959 when the

Student League for Industrial Democracy (SLID), the campus wing of the League for Industrial Democracy, a socialist group that went back to 1905, changed its name to the SDS (Davis 1996, ch. 8).[1]

The Counterculture was also connected with earlier forms of protest. Its rejection of established cultural values owed much to the revolt against the moral, sexual, and artistic conventions of bourgeois society exemplified by a variety of nineteenth- and early twentieth-century European avant-garde movements. To the extent that it tried to establish alternative societies, the counter-culture also borrowed ideas from the anarchists and the Utopian Socialists. While utopianism was an anathema to the Old Left, a deviation to be avoided, the counter-culture gave it a positive spin. To be utopian was to be realistic: one could reject corrupt society, drop out, and join a commune (Reich 1971; Roszak 1969).

Both movements fell short of their goals. The New Left's leaders were mainly campus intellectuals who aimed to organize students and poor people to struggle for self-determination and participatory democracy. Unfortunately, they picked difficult target groups. Students and poor people had been among the least likely groups to engage in sustained political activity during the post-Second World War period (Campbell et al. 1960; Verba and Nie 1972). The New Left's efforts failed to bring about fundamental changes in the American economic and the political system, and the counter-culture failed to popularize their alternative ways of living. The masses weren't ready to engage in widespread political activism, nor were they ready to abandon the capitalist norms of hard work and conformity.

Yet both movements helped to democratize the American polity and by dint of the American mass media to inspire political and cultural protests abroad (Tunstall 1977). Even though we cannot ascertain how much credit the New Left and the counter-culture deserve in comparison to other social, political, and demographic pressures, the United States has become more open and inclusive *de jure* than it was in the early 1960s as have Japan, Australia, New Zealand, Mexico, and most eastern and western European nations where the political and cultural unrest of the late 1960s also took place (Wiki 1960s).

Elsewhere David Resnick and I distinguished three categories of internet politics: politics *within the net* (intra-net politics), political *uses of the net*, and *politics that affect the net*. Politics within the net encompasses the political life of virtual communities and other identifiable online groups that regulate their own affairs, settle their own disputes, and develop their own online lifestyles. Political uses of the net refers to the ways in which the net can be used by ordinary citizens, political activists, organized interests, political parties, and governments to achieve their real world political goals, which often have little to do with the internet per se. Politics that affect the net refers to policies and actions that governments and other powerful

---

[1] Even though they opposed McCarthyism and other excesses of the Cold War, the New Left's leaders also rejected Soviet style communism. They embraced the critiques of post-war radicals like C. Wright Mills and Herbert Marcuse. The former had intellectual ties to American Progressivism; the latter had ties to the Frankfurt School.

institutions take to regulate the internet as a new form of mass communication and as a vehicle for commercial activity. The first two types of internet politics are relevant for sorting out the cyber-democrats' claims for the democratizing potential of political activity on the internet. The last type is most relevant for explaining why so much of that potential remains unrealized.

Online communities in the early days of cyberspace, each with their own intra-net politics, looked like a reincarnation of the counter-culture. Freedom could be achieved in this new type of space, a virtual state of nature in which people freely formed their own communities independent of the values, traditions, and legal constraints of the ordinary world. Communities could exercise authority over their own domains, based on a set of implicitly derived rules or "netiquette," without interference from outsiders. Enthusiasts proclaimed that terrestrial governments should not attempt to extend their jurisdiction into cyberspace. Indeed, some argued that the very structure of the internet itself made the attempt to impose outside regulation futile:

Governments derive their just powers from the consent of the governed. You have neither solicited nor received ours. . . . Cyberspace does not lie within your borders. Do not think that you can build it, as though it were a construction project. You cannot. It is an act of nature and it grows itself through our collective action. (Barlow 1996)

What the counter-culture promised, cyberspace could deliver. Intra-net politics was humanistic, egalitarian, and voluntary in contrast to the corrupt politics of organized special interests of the real world. Enthusiasts claimed that cyberspace created possibilities for liberation that even the most radical counter-cultural theorists had not imagined. In cyberspace people no longer were restricted to their own bodies and the cultural baggage that they contained. Anyone could create a new identity, indeed, a multiplicity of identities. The familiar trio of race, class, and gender could be transcended in cyberspace—recall the famous *New Yorker* cartoon of a canine at a monitor proclaiming, "On the Internet, no one knows you're a dog" (Steiner 1993). Others saw the possibility of cyberspace deepening and strengthening identities that were denigrated in the real world.

Hopes for change did not rely solely on the expectation that powerful identities could be forged in cyberspace. Activists saw political uses of the internet as dynamic means for consciousness raising and political organizing in the real world. By generating a public space for a true deliberative democracy the internet would enable citizens to fulfill their democratic potentials. Citizens no longer needed to accept the corporate dominated mass media's interpretations of reality. The internet could furnish alternative sources of information. Because they could access information on their own, citizens could make up their own minds without so-called experts to guide them. An informed citizenry could engage in political debate armed with all the information and opinions they could possibly use. Governmental officials could not hide their mistakes nor could they claim that issues were too complex for ordinary citizens to grasp. Information, full and free, would empower an invigorated democratic citizenry (Margolis 1979; Barber 1984, 1998; Davis 2005).

Political uses of the net were just beginning. Grassroots politics would flourish. Citizens would access information with speed and ease, and they would use electronic networks to communicate and exchange ideas with each other or with their elected representatives and governmental officials. Open sources of information would deepen democratic discussions and debates. The internet presented the possibility of virtual communities actualizing the dreams of participatory democracy and political liberation. The independence of the internet communities, coupled with the internet's egalitarian architecture, would render politics that affect the net impotent.

2 THE REAL WORLD EXPERIENCE

Cyber-democrats tend to give short shrift to how real world politics affect the internet. They concentrate instead on how politics within the net can bring about political liberation and how political uses of the net can influence public opinion and the conduct of real world politics. They point to virtual communities whose members carry on active civic lives even though they may never meet one another in the flesh. For populists of both the left and the right, political participation in cyberspace can approximate an ideal type of communitarian democracy emphasizing mutuality. If democratic policy making consists of resolving differences among competing interests, building coalitions for cooperative action, or some combination of the two, the internet's capacity to share equal access to vast stores of information and equal power to send and receive that information provides the means for realizing it.

Civic life, however, extends beyond formal issues of public policy. People interact over a variety of matters, and a sense of community often grows among those who share mutual interests. Thousands of virtual interest groups run Usenet newsgroups, listserv mailing lists, web-based chat rooms, blogs, and the like. Some virtual communities, such as The WELL, act as cooperative societies in which dues-paying members participate in conferences without the expectation of a quid pro quo for any particular information or service they provide (WELL). Others like Wikipedia have fostered a freely accessible international encyclopedia "written collaboratively by people from all around the world."[2] Moreover, real communities throughout the world have established their own Freenets or Community networks designed to enrich their civic life.[3]

Nevertheless, nothing compels virtual communities to function as mutual benefit societies. Traditional democratic politics attempts to work out acceptable solutions

---

[2] As of December 2005 the collaboration involved over "13,000 active contributors working on over 1,800,000 articles in more than 100 languages" (Wiki About).

[3] For lists, see Organization for Community Networks or Freenets & Community Networks.

through complex exchanges that involve pressuring and bargaining. In cyberspace, however, like-minded netizens can form online communities that insulate members from exchanges with those who may hold different opinions. While hate groups like Stormfront and Aryan Nations are notorious for countenancing only those who espouse their groups' particular views, researchers have uncovered many other virtual communities that exist largely to promote their own interests, whether political or non-political, and to reinforce their own like-mindedness. These communities also make those who disagree unwelcome to join and uncomfortable if they choose to participate (Aryan; Bimber 1998; Hill and Hughes 1998, 71–5; Galston 2002; Putnam 2000, ch. 22; Stormfront; Wiki Aryan; Wiki Stormfront).

Like today's cyber-democrats, political philosophers and pundits who favored active citizen participation in policy making in the past viewed each new mass medium that emerged as the means to create an active, informed, enlightened, and sophisticated body politic. They predicted that the development of cheap newsprint, film, sound recording, radio, and television in turn would not only provide the populace with information on public affairs but also expose them to foreign cultures and the great artistic achievements of humanity. From the popular press to community access cable television, each medium has had some impact on political and civic life, but none has fostered the enlightened democratic participation that its boosters prophesied. For better or for worse, most people generally have neither the time nor the desire to scrutinize the day-to-day affairs of governmental policy making. Most become politically involved only when a particular public policy output impinges upon their personal interests or upon the interests of friends, relatives, or associates whom they hold dear.

A mass medium's high production costs favor content that attracts a mass audience to whom investors, advertisers, or sponsors can be sold access. Producers assemble this audience chiefly by responding to popular tastes, not by attempting to raise civic, cultural, and educational standards. Popular tastes tend to reflect the prevalent norms, which include mostly the unenlightened selfish interests and the vulgar intellectual and artistic preferences that the philosophers and pundits proclaimed the new medium would elevate. By the time most people begin to use each medium regularly, therefore, lofty goals largely have been cast aside.

News media on the web have not escaped this fate. Unorthodox web news providers may have arrived first, but the established news media now predominate. Major newspapers, magazines, radio and television networks have the expertise and resources to gather, organize, and display more information more expeditiously than their upstart rivals. They also can pay more to advertise online and offline to direct traffic to their sites. Finally, they have better name recognition and more good will to draw upon than do their challengers. Most people, who are largely indifferent to public affairs to begin with, will turn to familiar names for the headline news they occasionally desire.

So far, our discussion has ignored the proverbial "elephant in the room," the ever-present digital divide. If the internet—or any advancement of digitally based IT—is to democratize politics, it must be easily accessible to the vast majority of adult citizens. Notwithstanding the increasing numbers of users for whom new technologies have provided internet access, two major dimensions of the divide persist: divisions between nations and divisions within. Simply put, citizens of wealthy nations comprise disproportionately large numbers of internet users. And within nations, the wealthier citizens similarly comprise disproportionately large numbers of users.

Even though rapidly expanding numbers of users combined with new technologies for access make it difficult to measure individuals' specific use of the internet for political purposes, our imperfect measures can still reveal relationships that persist over time. Tables 41.1 and 41.2 provide a snapshot of the two major dimensions of the digital divide as of November 2005.

Table 41.1 indicates that those living in wealthy regions comprise disproportionately large numbers of internet users. Denizens of Europe, North America, and Australia number less than 20 percent of the world's population, but they comprise a majority of the world's internet users. In contrast, those of Asia and Africa, who number more than 70 percent of the world's population, comprise less than one-third of internet users. The populations of African and Middle Eastern nations are most egregiously under-represented. The contrasts regarding proportions with internet access are even sharper: fewer than one in ten residents of Asia, Africa, and the Middle East have access in comparison to over one-third of Europeans, a majority of Australians, and two-thirds of North Americans. Moreover, the distribution of access within regions is hardly uniform. In low access regions, countries with relatively higher median incomes, such as Israel, Kuwait, United Arab Emirates (Middle East),

Table 41.1 Internet access and usage by region, November 2005

Region	Population est. 2005 (millions)	% world population	Internet users (millions)	Usage growth 2000–5%	% internet penetration	% world users
Africa	896.7	14.0	23.9	429	2.7	2.5
Asia	3,622.9	56.4	327.1	186	9.0	33.9
Europe	804.6	12.5	283.5	170	35.2	29.4
Middle East	187.3	2.9	15.5	370	8.3	1.6
N. America	328.4	5.1	223.9	107	68.2	23.2
C. & S. America (incl. Mexico)	546.7	8.5	72.8	303	13.3	7.5
Australia/Oceania	33.4	0.5	17.7	131	52.8	1.8
World Total	6,420.1	100.0	964.3	167	15.0	100.0

Sources: Demographic (Population) numbers are based on data contained in the world-gazetteer website; internet usage information comes from data published by Nielsen//NetRatings, by the International Telecommunications Union, by local NICs, and by other other reliable sources. For definitions, disclaimer, and navigation help, see the Site Surfing Guide. www.internetworldstats.com/stats.htm (updated 11/9/05).

Table 41.2 Digital divide indicators within selected OECD nations

Nation	Internet Penetration 2000		Internet Penetration 2000	
	lowest income (%)	% increase 1998–2000	highest income (%)	% increase 1998–2000
Australia	20	217	50	85
Canada	8	55	45	20
France	3	70	50	60
Japan	5	na	45	na
Netherlands	7	48	67	67
United Kingdom	3	200	50	53
United States	11	80	77	32

1. Australia: Lowest income: less than AUD 50,000; highest income: more than AUD 50,000.
2. Canada: Lowest: second decile; highest: tenth decile. 1999 level. 1998–9 growth.
3. France: Lowest: less than FRF 80,000; highest: more than FRF 450,000. 1999–2000 growth for internet.
4. Japan: Lowest: less than JPY 3 million; highest: more than JPY 12 million. For internet 2000 only; no growth available.
5. Netherlands: Lowest: first quartile of income; highest: fourth income quartile. 1998–9 growth.
6. United Kingdom: Lowest: second decile; highest: tenth decile. 1998–9 and 1999–2000 respectively instead of 1998 and 2000.
7. United States. Lowest: less than USD 15,000; highest: more than USD 75,000.

Source: OECD 2001, 17.

Egypt, South Africa (Africa), Japan, South Korea, Taiwan and Singapore (Asia), denizens have access rates that are from two to eight times as great as the regional average.[4] Similarly, nations of the European Union have an internet access rate of 49 percent–nearly treble that of non-member nations. Even if the five-year trend of higher growth rates of internet usage among poorer nations were to continue, it would take more than a decade for their levels of access to approach those of their wealthier counterparts.

Using internet access rates to measure the digital divide across nations, however, does not tell the whole story. Greater proportions of the populations of wealthier nations can afford access to high-quality broadband capacity than can the populations of poorer nations. Moreover, the internet itself has a decidedly Anglo-American tilt. Nearly 90 percent of links to secure commercial servers went to pages in English in 2000, and over one-third of all types of websites were written in English in 2005. While these percentages will decrease as global (especially American-based) corporations go multilingual, the dominant languages are likely to remain those of the wealthier nations: i.e. English, French, German, Spanish, Italian, Portuguese, Dutch, Chinese, Japanese, Korean, and Russian (Nationmaster.com; OECD 2001,

---

[4] As of this writing (Nov. 2005) the access rate for Iraq is one-tenth of one percent (0.1%). See links on Internet World Stats for details.

23).[5] New schemes are underway to manufacture and distribute durable handheld and laptop computers that cost less $100 (US) and can access the internet. But it remains to be seen if wealthy nations will in fact support the massive subsidies necessary not only to pay for these computers, but to assure that those who receive them have sufficient broadband access. As long as the internet remains primarily a commercially oriented vehicle, it will be tilted toward providing people more access as customers than as citizens (Media Lab 2005; BBC News 2005; Coleman 2005; Redling 2005).

Table 41.2 displays parallel aspects of the digital divide within economically advanced nations of the Organization for Economic Cooperation and Development (OECD). For every country listed greater proportions of those with high incomes have access to the internet than do those with low incomes. Once again, the lower-income groups generally show faster acceleration in expanding their access, but they still lag years behind. The data for PC ownership (not shown) for these countries reflect the same relationships. Along with income, OECD finds that other indicators of affluence, such as higher education (especially among adults under 50), urban residence, owning a PC and having children in the household, belonging to economically advantaged ethnic groups, and being able to afford higher access charges, are also positively associated with more time spent online. Rafts of academic research and popular reports have uncovered similar patterns.[6] Once again we must remember that access is a necessary but not a sufficient condition for making political uses of the internet. Many people use the internet, but most of them use it for activities other than politics. And among those who do use it for politics E. E. Schattschneider's well-known observation still applies: "The flaw in the pluralist heaven is that the heavenly choir sings with a strong upper-class [male] accent" (Schattschneider 1960, 35; OECD 2001, 21; Davis 2005, 71–2; West 2005, 173).

To be sure, notable new political and civic groups have organized via the internet, but these groups generally hold narrower views and deliberately attempt to activate narrower groups than do mass political parties, daily newspapers, news magazines, or broadcast news. Cyberculture tends to reinforce pro-business/free market initiatives and to fragment rather than build the "social capital" of the communities where people actually live (Norris 2001, chs. 9–10; Schier 2000, chs. 1, 2, and 6; Putnam 2000, ch. 22).

Meetup.com is a major exception: an online organization devoted to fostering Putnam's idea of social capital throughout the developed world. Meetup.com helps "people [to] find others who share their interest or cause, and form lasting, influential, local community groups that regularly meet face-to-face" regardless of their particular views (Meetup; Putnam 2000, ch. 24). Established in 2002, its civic

---

[5] This predominance of English and developed nations' languages holds for articles written for Wikipedia and for the directors of and the websites associated with ICANN, the International Corporation for the Assignment of Names and Numbers (see ICANN).

[6] See Norris 2001, chs. 3–6; West 2005, chs. 7–10 and numerous reports released by the Pew Internet and American Life Project (**www.pewinternet.org/reports.asp**).

and political groups enjoyed phenomenal growth in the run-up to the November 2004 American presidential election, and the organization prospered from fees paid by commercial venues where "Meetups" took place, as well as from "unobtrusive text ads" on affiliated groups' websites and from optional group members' fees for "Meetup Plus" services. After the election, however, when political interest waned (as usual) and memberships declined, Meetup.com announced that beginning May 2005 affiliated groups would have to pay fees for its services (Wiki Meetup). On May 9, 2005, Townhall, a politically conservative–and largely Republican–group, severed its relationship with Meetup.com substituting a "custom solution [called 'TownSquare' that will] better cater to the needs of our local groups." In September 2005 Democracy for America, the legacy group of Howard Dean's presidential organization, also set up its own customized tool, "DFA-Link," to organize its local group meetings independently of Meetup (Townhall; DFA-Link).[7]

In July 2005 Meetup.com had approximately 1.6 million registered members and over 58,000 groups worldwide, and it claimed that individual memberships had increased slightly since fees were imposed. The number of groups had declined 50 percent, however, partially due to purging those with fewer than five members. The loss of Townhall and DFA (27,500 and 137,500 members in 423 and 707 groups respectively) undoubtedly hurt its bottom line, even though most Meetup groups are not devoted to political activism. Indeed, notwithstanding its prestigious board of directors, Meetup.com may need to compromise its idealistic goals severely in order to survive.[8]

That political uses of the Net have not produced a significant restructuring of democratic politics should not surprise us. Political scientists have found time and again that most voters don't know very much about the particular policy issues and that except when cataclysmic events like war, social upheaval, or economic depression impinge on their daily lives, most people's participation in policy making is limited to casting ballots in elections. Researchers have noted the difficulty of mobilizing citizens to challenge the domination of the major parties and the interest groups that support them, especially when they perceive social and economic conditions as relatively benign. Why should we expect access to the internet to change these habits? (Gibson, Römmele, and Ward 2004, ch. 10.)

We should not confuse the flowering of email lists, websites, and blogs touting all sorts of worthy causes, movements, and interests with a shift in social power in the

---

[7] While the new fees obviously motivated these changes, Townhall nonetheless boasted that the added "improvements" would include: "Conservatives only! No Deaniacs, no liberals."

[8] The five-member board includes (former) US Senator Bill Bradley and Esther Dyson, past Chairman of the ICANN Board. The nine-member Advisory Council includes Chuck De Feo, eCampaign Manager, Bush-Cheney '04; Jane Fountain, Director of the National Center for Digital Government, and Phil Noble, Founder of PoliticsOnline. Despite its initial success, Meetup.com could go the way of "Third Voice," a browser companion program that permitted users to post comments on websites visible only to other Third Voice users. Introduced with some fanfare in the late 1990s, it initially stirred controversy, but it failed to sustain interest and went out of business early in 2001. See Margolis and Resnick 1999.

real world. This is not to deny that the internet can facilitate fund-raising, petition and letter-writing campaigns, organizing political demonstrations, or creating flash mobs with political agendas. Such uses of the net are impressive, but we should remember that the high water mark of post-Second World War democratic activism in Europe and America occurred in the late 1960s and early 1970s, years before the internet took root.

Using the internet as an alternative or supplement to traditional methods of political participation seems more appropriate than using it to move toward direct–or even deliberative–democracy. Electronic voting, for instance, seems like a live option, provided problems of the security and privacy of ballots and the inequalities of the digital divide can be overcome (Alvarez and Hall 2004, ch. 8). Those who extol citizens' using the internet to participate more fully in formulating public policy seem to forget that representative institutions are not second-best solutions to the problem of self-rule created in the technological dark ages before simultaneous communication among citizens became feasible. Do we have any reason to believe that direct democracy would actually work the way its advocates hope? Where is the sign that citizens of large, pluralistic, advanced industrial or post-industrial societies care to take on the burdens of crafting public policy? While we have placed a greater reliance on public opinion polls of late, do we really believe that government by public opinion polls would be good for democracy? Legislatures, executives, and judiciaries, chosen according to constitutionally agreed upon rules, may not produce the wisest policies, but do we really think that it would be preferable to rely upon millions of cyber-citizens to formulate such policies over the internet? (Mill 1962; Lippmann 1993; Alvarez and Hall 2004, ch. 4.)

As suggested above, using the internet to make the output side of government more responsive to citizens looks like a better strategy for encouraging responsible democratic participation. Citizens can judge from personal experience how well governmental officials have implemented the internet's capabilities to ease access to information, to arrange delivery of services, and to conduct routine transactions, such as obtaining licenses or permits, bidding on contracts, paying taxes, and so forth. They know the extent to which they can transact business with government at convenient times and places as opposed to visiting particular offices during restricted hours. How easily can they contact officials via e-mail or telephone? Can forms be processed reliably online, or must citizens submit hard copies? How easily can citizens use the internet to register or to vote, to obtain relevant information about candidates, issues, or policies, or to provide feedback—both praise and complaint—to relevant public officials about how governmental policies affect them or the people, values, and interests they hold dear? (Curtin, Sommer and Vis-Sommer 2003; Lam 2004.)[9]

---

[9] Curtin became editor of the newly established *Journal of E-Government*, which completed its second year of publication in Fall 2006.

3 ADVANTAGES AND DANGERS
OF E-GOVERNMENT

Throughout history many politicians, political philosophers, and scholars have argued that direct democracy tended toward tyranny of the majority, mobocracy, or worse. They have contended that evidence—systematic or anecdotal—demonstrates that citizens are better at judging the effects of governmental policies retrospectively than they are at predicting them. From the Enlightenment forward democratic theorists have advocated representative institutions that take account of diverse interests in society, elected representatives who accommodate the wishes of the majority to those of various minorities, and a citizenry that uses its reason to judge their representatives' (or their parties') performance more upon the results of their recent policies than upon their promises for the future (Chapman and Pennock 1968; Pitkin 1967; Budge et al. 1972, ch. 3; Fiorina 1981). In line with these arguments, this chapter has suggested that we look to the internet's potential for improving citizens' retrospective judgments of the consequences of governmental policies rather than stress its potential for encouraging citizens' direct participation in formulating those policies. Let us examine how political uses of the internet can be structured to accomplish this.

Modern technology has outdistanced the capabilities of eighteenth-century-based democratic political institutions, especially elected legislatures, to deal with it. As a result, bureaucratic elites, both public and private, play increasingly influential roles in formulating and implementing governmental policies that deal with technologically complex problems that affect the distribution of wealth, the natural environment, the military, public health, public safety, medical care, the movement of capital, and the like. Moreover, legislatures have been notoriously slow in adopting IT necessary for them to engage effectively with the executive in formulating these policies, while executive-controlled bureaucracies have been far quicker to adopt these technologies and to use them to shield information about policy outputs from legislative oversight. Paradoxically, the internet has contributed to the trend toward the weakening of legislatures and the strengthening of executive centered government (West 2005, ch. 1; Margolis and Resnick 2000, ch. 4; Davis 1999, chs. 1 and 7).

This shift toward executive government—buttressed by IT—raises new threats to democracy. Just as the internet can provide citizens with information about public policy, it can provide governments and other powerful interests with information about citizens' private lives. Just as it can provide citizens with the means to communicate their reactions to public policies, so too it can provide the means for governmental officials and other established groups to distort, manipulate, or otherwise control accessible information. Realizing this dark potential could produce a totalitarian nightmare like Orwell's *1984* where citizens fear or revere an all-seeing Big Brother, or a seemingly benign hedonistic society like Huxley's *Brave New World,* where a conditioned citizenry happily accepts the existing social order. In short, the institutional arrangements for managing the net greatly affect the extent to which citizens can use it to exercise democratic control (Gibson, Römmele, and Ward 2004, ch. 1; Fountain 2001, ch. 11).

Until the early 1990s governments—especially agencies of the United States—and non-profit organizations, such as educational institutions and foundations, largely underwrote the internet. Users were disproportionately young, male, affluent, college educated, politically active, and libertarian. Self-selected groups made and enforced rules of intra-net politics (sometimes capriciously) in accordance with their inter-pretations of netiquette. Commercial usage and spam were largely excluded. By the late 1990s, however, cyberspace began to resemble ordinary space. Governments sold off or otherwise turned over most of the internet to private hands. As simplified protocols associated with the World Wide Web drew millions of novices to cyber-space, commercial enterprises, governmental agencies, and other established social and political organizations jumped online, lest they lose touch with customers and clientele or lose out on new markets for goods and services. The "dot.coms," which multiplied most quickly, sought to safeguard their investments by developing rules and regulations that resembled those with which their customers were already familiar. Together with real world allies–governmental and non-governmental–they soon rendered netiquette as obsolete as Emily Post for controlling transactions via the internet (Fisher, Margolis, and Resnick 1996b; Margolis and Resnick 2000, ch. 2).

Consumer oriented business models became the norm. Websites offered visitors—customers, if you will—information, goods, or services for a price. That price might involve a direct monetary exchange like an ordinary purchase in the real world or an exposure to a particular set of messages analogous to a series of commercials on radio or television. But the internet's powers allow advertisers to extract more information about potential customers than was possible with any previous mass medium. Websites can record the pages each visitor views, the visitor's IP address, the advertisements shown, and the length of time spent on each page, and whether or not the visitor clicked on any particular advertisement. "Cookies" can be implanted on visitors' computers so that subsequent visits will trigger advertisements or suggestions that cater to the interests inferred from their behavior during previous visits. (Users often will be denied service if they do not set their browsers to accept all cookies.) Moreover, if visitors can be enticed to leave their e-mail (or postal) addresses and demographics, advertisers and other interested parties can be sold access to pre-screened potential customers or supporters without the seller revealing specific information about any individual on the list.[10]

Executive agencies control nearly all the most frequently visited governmental websites. As these sites emulate the customer service features of commercial websites, citizens can conduct personal transactions interactively, frequently on a "24/7" basis. And just as commercial sites can extract information about their visitors, so too can

---

[10] For instance, an informational website might invite users to register for chances to win a big ticket item in exchange for permission to allow the website to forward them information from sellers who would offer products about which they had inquired during recent visits. Alternatively, an e-mail service like Yahoo's might sell political parties, candidates, or interest groups access to users who live in particular locales or have expressed interest in particular social or political issues of causes.

governments use the internet's monitoring capacities to extract information about theirs. The service is convenient, but the danger here is obvious: it is no trick for executive agencies to assemble and to "mine" data on how each citizen uses the internet. Jane Fountain, director of the National Center for Digital Government, observed, "using information technology to network government [is] relatively simple. The more complex and difficulty challenges are to address issues of accountability, equity, and democratic process" (Fountain 2005). Unless the people's representatives—elected legislators, ombudsmen, or their designates—demand unfettered access to nearly all the executive branch's digitized information, there is little to stop the executive from deploying the data its agencies gather to exploit the internet's dark potential. Formal legislation or regulations that require accountability are not self-enforcing. Unless the burden of demonstrating the necessity of restricting information accords with criteria laid down by general legislation or through exclusions granted by special legislation, the executive can deny citizens and their representatives the means to fairly assess policy outcomes.

To rectify this imbalance legislators need to exert more control and better oversight over governments' use of the internet and to reinforce that control through assuring citizens' easy access to digitized information about how public policies are implemented. They must also provide effective means for citizens to communicate to their representatives and other governmental officials regarding how those policies are affecting them.

No solution is perfect, however. Even though these reforms would increase the power of the people's elected representatives relative to the largely unelected executive branch and its technologically adept bureaucracy, they would also increase the danger of demagogic legislators—and their financial backers—acquiring new powers to exploit for selfish or nefarious purposes. Some unscrupulous legislators would undoubtedly exploit their privileged access to information for private advantage, as they have done in the past. But consider the alternatives. Should unelected bureaucrats and technological elites control the information? What assurances do we have that they will act in the public interest more often than will the legislators? Periodically legislators must answer directly to the citizenry; the others need not. Nonetheless, to argue that strengthening the legislature's control over government's information will promote democracy requires two leaps of faith. First, that the great majority of the people's representatives will use their unfettered access to the government's digitized information to expose to public scrutiny the false claims and deleterious consequences of their colleagues' actions as well as those of the executive. And second, that citizens will judge the information against their own experience and will vote to oust the unscrupulous and return responsible representatives in their place.

That citizens or their representatives use the internet to acquire the information required to make intelligent judgments about the consequences of public policies is necessary—but not sufficient—for actualizing the retrospective type of cyber-democracy this chapter has discussed. Information must be organized and presented in a manner that people can understand, citizens and representatives must be encouraged to pay attention to one another's communications, and institutional arrangements must prevent powerful moneyed interests (national and international) from controlling information necessary for legislators to determine the likely consequences of their laws and policies or—worse yet—from buying those laws and policies outright. Many such arrangements, albeit more with regard to policy inputs than to retrospective judgments of policy outputs, have been discussed elsewhere at length. These include education vouchers as awards for community service volunteers, protection for knowledgeable whistleblowers, facilitators or moderators for online discussion groups, methods of accounting that include environmental costs and other externalities, public interest representatives appointed to serve on corporate boards, and various reforms of campaign finance and of methods for casting and counting ballots. (See Margolis 1979, ch. 7; Budge 1996, chs. 1 and 7; Barber 1998, ch. 2; Davis 2005, ch. 6; Schier 2000, ch. 6.)

In the last analysis, however, no set of institutional arrangements can guarantee that citizens make effective political uses of the net. As in the real world, a viable democracy requires that its citizens pay at least a modicum of attention to the quality of governmental services and the consequences of public policies for the polity, not merely to how well they receive governmental services and how public policies affect their personal interests. John Stuart Mill said it very well in 1861, when western nations contemplated massive expansions of their electorates:

Thus, a people may prefer a free government, but if, from indolence, or carelessness, or cowardice, or want of public spirit, they are unequal to the exertions necessary to preserve it; if they will not fight for it when it is directly attacked; if they can be deluded by the artifices used to cheat them out of it; if by momentary discouragement, or temporary panic, or a fit of enthusiasm for an individual, they can be induced to lay their liberties at the feet even of a great man or trust him with powers that enable him to subvert their institutions; in all these cases they are more or less unfit for liberty; and though it may be for their good to have had it, even for a short time, they are unlikely long to enjoy it. (Mill 1962, ch. 1)

In this regard, the internet changes nothing.

References

ALVAREZ, R. M., and HALL, T. E. 2004. *Point, Click & Vote: The Future of Internet Voting*. Washington, DC: Brookings.

Aryan Nations. www.aryan-nations.org/ (accessed 9/1/05).

BARBER, B. R. 1984. *Strong Democracy: Participatory Politics for a New Age*. Berkeley: University of California Press.

—— 1998. *A Place for Us: How to Make Society Civil and Democracy Strong*. New York: Hill & Wang.

BARLOW, J.P. 1996. A declaration of independence of cyberspace. http://homes.eff.org/~barlow/Declaration-Final.html (accessed 9/1/05).

BBC NEWS. 2005. Sub-$100 laptop design unveiled. September 29. http://news.bbc.co.uk/1/hi/technology/4292854.stm (accessed 11/19/05).

BIMBER, B. 1998. The internet and political transformation: populism, community, and accelerated pluralism. *Polity*, 31(1): 133–60.

BUDGE, I. 1996. *The New Challenge of Direct Democracy.* Cambridge, Mass.: Polity Press.
—— et al. 1972. *Political Stratification and Democracy.* London: Macmillan.
BURKE, E. 1774. Speech to the electors of Bristol (November 3).
CAMPBELL, A. et al. 1960. *The American Voter.* New York: Wiley.
CHAPMAN, J. W., and PENNOCK, J. R. eds. 1968. *Representation.* New York: Atherton Press.
COLEMAN, N. 2005. Beware a "digital Munich." *Wall Street Journal,* November 7.
CURTIN G. G., SOMMER, M., and VIS SOMMER, V. eds. 2003. *The World of E-Government.* New York: Haworth Press.
DAVIS, R. 1999. *The Web of Politics: The Internet's Impact on the American Political System.* New York: Oxford University Press.
—— 2005. *Politics Online: Blogs, Chatrooms, and Discussion Groups in American Democracy.* New York: Routledge.
DFA-LINK. http://tools. democracyforamerica.com/link/ (accessed 9/8/05).
EULAU, H. et al. 1958. The role of the representative. *American Political Science Review,* 53: 742–56.
FIORINA, M. P. *Retrospective Voting in American National Elections.* New Haven: Yale University Press, 1981.
FISHER, B., MARGOLIS, M., and RESNICK D. 1996a. A study of civic life on the internet. Vol. ii, pp. 986–91 in *1995 Proceedings of the Section on Survey Research Methods of the American Statistical Association.* Alexandria, Va.: American Statistical Association.
—— —— —— 1996b. Surveying the internet: democratic theory and civic life in cyberspace. *Southeastern Political Review,* 24: 399–429.
FOUNTAIN, J. E. 2001. *Building the Virtual State: Informational Technology and Institutional Change.* Washington, DC: Brookings Institution Press.
—— 2005. The virtual state is not a virtual corporation. P. 27 in *Taubman Center Annual Report.* Cambridge, Mass.: Kennedy School of Government. www.ksg.harvard.edu/digitalcenter/ (accessed 9/9/05).
FREENETS & COMMUNITY NETWORKS. www.lights.com/freenet/ (accessed 9/1/05).
GALSTON, W. 2002. The impact of the internet on civic life: an early assessment. Pp. 40–58 in *Governance.com: Democracy in the Information Age,* ed. E. C. Kamarek and J. S. Nye. Washington, DC: Brookings Institution Press.
GIBSON, R., NIXON, P., and WARD S. eds. 2003. *Net Gain? Political Parties and the Impact of New Information Communication Technologies.* London: Routledge.
—— RÖMMELE, A., and WARD, S. J., eds. 2004. *Electronic Democracy: Mobilisation, Organisation and Participation via new ICTs.* London: Routledge.
HAMILTON, A., JAY, J., and MADISON J. 1787–8. *The Federalist Papers.*
HAUBEN, M. (n.d.). Participatory democracy from the 1960s and SDS into the future on-line. www.columbia.edu/~hauben/CS/netdemocracy-60s.txt (accessed 12/9/05).
—— and HAUBEN, R. 1997. *Netizens: On the History and Impact of Usenet and the Internet.* Los Alamitos, Calif.: IEEE Computer Society Press.
HILL, K. A., and HUGHES, J. E. 1998. *Cyberpolitics: Citizen Activism in the Age of the Internet* (Lanham, Md.: Rowman & Littlefield).
ICANN (Internet Corporation for Assigned Names and Numbers). www.icann.org/ index.html (accessed 12/8/07).
Internet World Stats. www.internetworldstats.com/stats.htm (accessed 11/18/05).
LAM, W. 2004. Integration challenges toward increasing e-government maturity. *Journal of E-Government,* 1 (2): 45–58.
LIPPMANN, W. 1993. *The Phantom Public.* New Brunswick, NJ: Transaction Publishers.
MARGOLIS, M. 1979. *Viable Democracy.* New York: St Martin's Press.

MARGOLIS, M., and RESNICK, D. 1999. Third voice: vox populi vox dei? *First Monday,* 4 (10) www.firstmonday.dk/issues/issue4_10/margolis/index.html

—— —— 2000. *Politics as Usual: The Cyberspace "Revolution."* Thousand Oaks, Calif.: Sage Publications, Inc.

—— —— and LEVY, J. 2003. Major parties dominate, minor parties struggle: US elections and the internet. pp. 53–69 in Gibson, Nixon and Ward 2003.

—— —— and WOLFE, J. 1999. Party competition on the internet: minor versus major parties in the UK and the USA. *Harvard International Journal of Press/Politics,* 4(3): 24–47.

MEDIA LAB. 2005. http://laptop.media.mit.edu/ (accessed 11/19/05).

MEETUP. www.meetup.com/about (accessed 9/1/05).

MILL, J. S. 1962 [1861]. *Considerations on Representative Government.* Chicago: Regnery.

NationMaster. www.nationmaster.com (accessed 11/18/05).

NORRIS, P. 2001. *Digital Divide: Civic Engagement, Information Poverty, and the Internet Worldwide.* Cambridge: Cambridge University Press.

OECD. 2001. *Understanding the Digital Divide.* Paris: OECD Publications.

ORGANIZATION FOR COMMUNITY NETWORKS. www.ofcn.org/ (accessed 9/1/05).

PEW INTERNET AND AMERICAN LIFE PROJECT. *Reports.* www.pewinternet.org/reports.asp (accessed 11/19/05).

PITKIN, H. 1967. *The Concept of Representation.* Berkeley: University of California Press.

PUTNAM, R. D. 2000. *Bowling Alone: The Collapse and Revival of American Community.* New York: Simon & Schuster.

REDLING, V. 2005. Icann? We all can. *Wall Street Journal,* November 11.

REICH, C. A. 1971. *The Greening of America.* New York: Bantam.

RHEINOLD, H. 1993 *The Virtual Community: Homesteading on the Electronic Frontier.* Reading, Mass.: Addison-Wesley.

ROSZAK, T. 1969. *The Making of a Counter Culture: Reflections on the Technocratic Society and Its Youthful Opposition.* New York: Doubleday.

SCHATTSCHNEIDER, E. E. 1960. *The Semisovereign People: A Realist's View of Democracy in America.* New York: Holt, Rinehart & Winston.

SCHIER, S. E. 2000. *By Invitation Only: The Rise of Exclusive Politics in the United States.* Pittsburgh: University of Pittsburgh Press.

SHAPIRO, A. L. 1999. T*he Control Revolution: How the Internet is Putting Individuals in Charge and Changing the World We Know.* NY: PublicAffairs.

STEINER. P. 1993. *New Yorker,* July 5, p. 61.

STORMFRONT. www.stormfront.org/forum (accessed 1/29/07).

THAYER, F. C. 1973. *An End to Hierarchy! An End to Competition! Organizing the Politics and Economics of Survival.* New York: New Viewpoints.

TOWNHALL. www.townhall.com/meetup/ (accessed 8/22/05).

TUNSTALL, J. 1977. *The Media are American.* New York: Columbia University Press.

VERBA, S., and NIE, N. H. 1972. *Participation in America: Political Democracy and Social Inequality.* New York: Harper & Row.

WELL, The. www.well.com/ (accessed 9/1/05).

WEST, D. 2005. *Digital Government: Technology and the Public Sector.* Princeton: Princeton University Press.

WIKI 1960s. http://en. wikipedia.org/wiki/1960s (accessed 11/1/05).

WIKI ABOUT. http://en.wikipedia.org/wiki/Wikipedia:About (accessed 12/7/05).

WIKI ARYAN. http://en.wikipedia.org/wiki/Aryan_Nations (accessed 9/1/05).

WIKI MEETUP. http://en.wikipedia.org/wiki/Meetup (accessed 9/8/05).

WIKI STORMFRONT. http://en.wikipedia.org/wiki/Stormfront (accessed 9/1/05).

CHAPTER 42

PERSPECTIVES ON POLITICAL PARTICIPATION

MAX KAASE

In six yearly issues, *Political Science Abstracts*, which operates under the auspices of the International Political Science Association (IPSA), covers about 1,000 political science journals worldwide and the articles therein. These abstracts are published electronically or in a print version in English despite the fact that many articles are not written in English in the original. If one furthermore considers that an estimated 40,000 political scientists around the world regularly work on political science subjects, then one gets an idea about the wealth of scholarly information that is continuously produced on politics and the political science process. But how relevant is this wealth of information for research and teaching, and can and is it digested systematically by the scholarly community considering the fact that only a small, even if ever increasing part of these materials is written in today's lingua franca, English? This is a complex issue which is aggravated by the fact that most of the international canon of political science theory, epistemology and methodology is dominated by approaches in the field which have been developed and institutionalized in North America and Europe.

This is, of course, not by accident because political science is intimately linked with democratic governance of the liberal pluralist kind and could only thrive under the freedom of thought which is an essential element of this type of political order. As it has recently spread and continues to spread, in whatever adaptation, to other parts of the world, the multiplicity and complexity of findings from research grows and has to be accommodated, at least in the medium to long run, by Handbooks like the one for which this chapter has been written.

Looking at the science system at large, its internationalization—not the least through the internet—has created a worldwide community of scholars who are in constant immediate interaction and competition. This is now the general practice especially in the sciences, and direct or indirect cooperation between scholars enhances the understanding of physical and biological processes dramatically. What makes the sciences special is that they are not bound to nation-state borderlines because they build on a canon of theories, findings and research methodologies that are united through a common understanding and acceptance of criteria that determine what the scientific status quo, scientific quality and progress are and how they can be further developed. In the social sciences, some scholars have not given up on coming closer to this unified approach of theory building and research practices. But there is also reason for skepticism, given the enormous variability of the human nature and the institutions and organizations which have emerged through historical time. However, as a look through the nine chapters of this part of the Handbook shows, in almost all fields of political participation one finds at least some crystallized knowledge of a more general nature which reflects an improved scholarly understanding of the structures and processes regarding the various elements of political participation.

What are some of the conditions that have favored this development? One is the continued existence of the nation state which despite its processes of internationalization and integration still defines most of the institutional frames in which processes of political participation occur, like electoral laws for national and subnational elections. The chapter by Blais on "Turnout in Elections" is an excellent example of how research can and must draw on such institutional variability when trying to explain turnout and its changes as well as to analyze them comparatively.

A second point is that through the internationalization of the science system diffusion of theoretical approaches for the analysis of political phenomena has, at least in principle, facilitated the cumulation of knowledge through common frames of reference. This is not withstanding the fact that the under-canonization of approaches to the study of social and political phenomena makes the integration of findings from different sources often difficult, if not impossible. However, as political science has become more institutionalized in universities and transnational organizations like the European Consortium for Political Research (ECPR) and IPSA, which are fostering collaborative research networks beyond national boundaries, important incentives for systematic comparative research have materialized. The impact of these developments is also clearly visible in the chapters of this part of the Handbook.

Finally, there is a remarkable trend from the early days of segmented national cross-sectional studies to longitudinal studies both within and across countries as indicated in the survey field e.g. by the various Barometer studies in four continents (Euro, Latino, Africa, Asia), the World Values Surveys, or the European Social Survey which, through their unified databases covering a large number of nation states, now permit comparative micro-macro analyses across countries and time. These studies vary in methodological rigor and complexity, and they almost exclusively address representative samples of national populations. As became visible in some of the previous chapters, they are well suited to contribute to fields like turnout in elections, social capital, political protest, and female political engagement. For other fields, similar comparative longitudinal databases are not so easily available or available at all, for example, with respect to party membership, social movements, or new modes of campaigning. But even where the databases are more satisfactory, they do not always suffice to answer all questions posed, like why we have observed a rather sizeable decline in turnout in national elections between 1970 and 2004.

1 What Have We Learned?

1.1 Civil Society and Social Capital

Political Science, as many other fields in the social sciences and the humanities, is not free of scholarly fads. At this point in time, it is not clear whether the concept of civil society will, twenty years from now, also fall into the fad category. One can easily agree with Wnuk-Lipinski that civil society belongs to the intermediate level of society, that is (mostly) private organizations which operate between the individual and the macro-institutions of society, most noteworthy the state, but not only the state. De Tocqueville's *Democracy in America*, Kornhauser (1959), or the early Putnam (1993) have all pointed to the important function of voluntary associations for a stable and effective democracy. It is therefore telling that the concept of civil society only re-emerged, under this name, as a dominant concept in the social sciences in the context of democratization and transition research with a particular focus on central and eastern Europe, as those countries moved—more or less successfully—from totalitarian to democratic political rule, a point that is forcefully made in the chapter by Wnuk-Lipinski. In those countries, civil society was the intermediate crystallization of private citizens that had emerged in opposition to the monolithic totalitarian state. But this chapter does little to conceptualize civil society in a way that would make it an analytically useful tool to systematically guide research in a way not thought about and used before.

There is, however, an obvious, though implicit link to a related concept that took on in the 1990s theoretically in sociology from Coleman and in political science from Putnam: social capital. The theoretical and empirical ambiguities of this concept have been laid out perfectly in the chapter by Dietlind Stolle. The main reason why the concept has triggered so much response from political scientists is the claim that social capital, that is networks of civic engagement which build cohesion and trust between citizens, is an essential resource for the well-functioning and stability of democratic governments and governance.

Here, again, the connecting thread to civil society is the role intermediary organizations play in the functioning of pluralist democracies—and nothing new at that.

What made the topic so attractive for contemporary political scientists (most of the publications Stolle cites in her chapter date after 1995) was Putnam's claim (e.g. 2000) of the decline in social capital, first in the US and then beyond, and its implications for an eventual destabilization of western democracy. It cannot come as a surprise that this claim as well as the overall concept of social capital were soon challenged both on theoretical, methodological, and empirical grounds. Nevertheless, as Stolle convincingly shows, social capital can connect to a broad variety of topics in political science, and while there are many questions which remain to be tackled by empirical research, social capital turns out to be one of the most important innovations on the research agenda for the conditions under which democratic governance can flourish.

1.2 Turnout and Campaigning

The simple act of voting, as it was once called, has remained the essential source of legitimation for democratic governments. Constitutional and institutional factors influence the way in which a vote cast by an individual citizen is transformed into positions of collective political power. Little wonder, then, that from the early days of democratic governance, elections have constituted a core research interest for the social sciences at large well beyond the narrow realm of political science.

Traditionally, there have been different ways of looking at turnout: high turnout as an indication of citizen democratic engagement versus high turnout as an indication of systemic unrest, protest, and disaffection; low turnout as an indication of democratic satisfaction or of democratic alienation. While research has shown that any of those interpretations at certain points in time and under special contextual circumstances may be valid, high turnout for a long time in a large number of stable democracies is associated with civicness and system identification. In fact, this perspective has normatively prevailed in some democracies to the point where voting became compulsory (very worthwhile reading on an imagined situation of evaporating turnout makes a 2004 novel by 1998 Literature Nobel Prize Laureate José Saramago). Research into voting participation dates back to the early twentieth century. Since vote counting is a public task and responsibility, it is little wonder that excellent public records are available for scrutiny. In Blais's well-composed chapter, he distinguishes between aggregate data, usually from public sources and complete for all members of the population entitled to vote, and individual data from (mostly) representative sample surveys. In an aggregate analysis of national elections in ninety-nine democratic countries since 1972—altogether 537 elections— he shows that, with a great deal of country-specific variance, on average about three-quarters of those eligible to vote do so. Blais naturally is particularly interested in those institutional factors influencing turnout, and he finds such factors, partly expected ones and partly unexpected ones. Since these findings are derived from a wealth of different studies with different variable constellations, though, the statistical impact of these various factors cannot be precisely quantified and, even worse, generalized. Unfortunately, the same is also true for the observed average ten-percentage point decline in turnout in the thirty-year period under scrutiny. Thus, it appears that despite the wealth of available empirical data on voting it is not possible to really understand the individual and collective meaning behind the observed overall decline in turnout.

Blais's analysis concentrates on systematic and individual properties that may influence the individual and collective decision to go or not to go to the polls. However, individual predispositions and institutional properties naturally are also influenced by the input side of the structures and processes which provide political information and motivation. Both at elections usually come from electoral campaigns and the related strategies and efforts by the political actors. In the early voting studies, it seemed common wisdom that campaigns activate and reinforce, but do not change, political preferences. But this is no longer to be assumed because of three major recent developments. The first is the evaporation of traditional cleavage structures firmly attaching citizens to particular parties. The second is changes in party systems, internal party structures, and party membership. The third and probably most important is changes in the structure of media systems and the resulting changes in campaign strategies.

It is this latter point which Schmitt-Beck has taken up in his excellent chapter on "New Modes of Campaigning." The key issue here is whether the "Americanization" of electoral campaigns has become a general feature for democracies around the world. Personalization, the creation of pseudo-events including candidate TV debates, negative campaigning, and the underpinning of campaign strategies by social research are indeed features which have spread almost worldwide. Needless to say that all this happens against the backdrop of nation- and culture-specific conditions and is thus ameliorated in its effects on the popular vote. Schmitt-Beck, in his conclusion, discusses the potential positive and negative effects of modern campaigning, and this field for obvious reasons is one of the best researched in political science. However, elections in pluralist democracies are extremely complex processes. For instance, modern campaign strategies cannot be easily used for manipulation because information on these strategies among political actors and citizens diffuses so easily in knowledge societies. One important question, namely whether modern campaign styles have had an impact on the shrinking trust in and satisfaction with democratic political institutions and governments, has not been asked in this chapter and therefore awaits future clarification.

1.3 Political Participation through Parties

The observed decline in party membership has begun to challenge the notion that without political parties the democratic process cannot function, an assumption which had even found its way into the German Constitution in 1949. Thus, it is not by chance that in Scarrow's entry on "Political Activism and Party Members" the existence and role of political parties for the functioning of the democratic process is taken for granted and therefore not addressed.

Given this premise, the question is even more in need of systematic scrutiny how political parties as membership organizations have fared in the last decades. Research on party membership has demonstrated that it is not easy to measure it, and this is especially true as modern computer-based book-keeping techniques can now give a much more reliable and up-to-date account of the status of party membership than before. Whatever measurement procedure is applied, though, the general outcome at least in the European multi-party systems is that since the 1980s there has been an across the board decline in membership. Looking at the three factors of dealignment, growth of direct action politics and the medialization of politics through centralized campaigns alone should make it plausible why such a decline occurred which, incidentally, has not been compensated in the aggregate by the emergence of new parties like the Greens.

Scarrow in her chapter emphasizes that over the last two decades scholars have conducted a lot of research into party members, their demography, issue preferences, beliefs, and level of internal party activity. However, these studies have been loosely integrated across national boundaries and lack, most importantly, a systematic longitudinal dimension—both in the aggregate and on the individual level. Thus, it is difficult to assess the long-term implications of the observed membership decline for the internal functioning of parties. Needless to say, these findings will also lead to the questions about the effects of changes in the structure, membership composition, and level of internal membership engagement on the legitimacy of the institution of party in democratic politics and on the functioning of interest aggregation in the democratic process.

1.4 The Gender Gap in Political Participation

For a long time in political sociology, it fared as certified truth that men were more politically active than women. That this is no longer true, at least not in established democracies, is documented in an encompassing way by Norris's excellent chapter on "New Feminist Challenges to the Study of Political Engagement." To assess the structure and dynamics of female political engagement is, incidentally, not the least due to the fact that through the development of the survey methodology and comparative and longitudinal studies in the twentieth century, the data necessary for this kind of analysis was collected on a regular basis. We will not discuss the details of the many results which Norris presents. It may suffice to say that by now the previous gender gap in political involvement in modern democratic societies has disappeared in voting, is hardly visible—if not even reversed—for unconventional forms of political action, remains visible in horizontal divisions of associational life, and is most marked for representation in legislatures and cabinets. Although Norris does not address this point, it must be added that an even larger gap exists when it comes to high-ranking positions in the business world.

To explain such differences, Norris points to cultural attitudes and civic resources that according to the literature operate as important explanatory approaches for the engagement gender gap. But also structural factors must come into consideration, since developed societies differ in the extent to which societal resources are made available which enable women in family-like structures or individually to balance the roles of both mother and professional.

Beyond this, the introduction of demand-side aspects systematically enriches theoretical perspectives in the gender gap research. For one, this refers to the influence of organizations, formal rules, and informal practices that help to maintain gender gaps in political and social life. On the other hand, Norris refers to the feminist concept of gendered institutions in the sense that the functioning of institutions can implicitly or explicitly reinforce divisions in resource allocation which influence gendered career patterns.

In sum, then, the analysis of gender differences in political involvement and participation is an excellent example of how existing databases can be scrutinized under innovative theoretical perspectives which in turn can stimulate new research and new research methodologies.

1.5 Social Movements and Protest Politics

It is not by chance that about the same time—in the late 1960s and early 1970s—both social movements and protest politics became new objects of political science scrutiny. The established, election-centered politics had become commonplace—for many people even boring and unsatisfactory. The post-war economies in Europe and North America blossomed, and educational reforms began to create more resourceful segments of the population. These developments jointly became harbingers of emerging value changes that also entailed quests for participatory rights beyond the vote. Student protest around the western world, but also race riots in the US and large-scale opposition against the Vietnam War engagement of that country challenged institutionalized means of political participation. In the beginning, it was not at all clear whether such protests implied a challenge to established structures and modes of democratic governance to a point where transformations to some kind of a socialist/ communist system were imminent. But it did not take long before it became clear that the challenge was not a basic one to the pluralist democratic system but to what was perceived by some as the vote not being a sufficient way to utter and implement political preferences (Barnes, Kaase, et al. 1979).

Rucht, in his handbook entry, rightly points out that research in this field has neither resulted in a convergent theoretical perspective nor in integrated research strategies. This is not the least due to the fact that protest—that is activities outside the realm of the institutionalized political process—has become manifold in form and ubiquitous in occurrence. They now belong to the normal political repertory of practically all groups of society. (Rucht mentions that in the German capital of Berlin between 2,000 and 2,500 protest rallies take place every year.) Thus, it would not be wrong to speak of protest as a non-institutionalized normal mode of political engagement (the concept of normality does, of course, no longer apply in case protest actions become violent).

If used as a political strategy to achieve political goals, protest has to define target actors in institutionalized politics. One of the topics where research has been largely missing is the question of the impact of protest activities on political outcomes. Next to the observation that effects will most likely become visible when local problems and actors are targeted, certainly the rise and organization of the protest groups as well as the societal reach of the issue at stake come into view. And this is the link to the related topic of social movements, that is, organizations with an internal structure of some permanence and a concentration on a reasonably well-defined segment of the overall political issue agenda.

In political sociology, the concept of social movements was initially used for developments at a time when in the process of democratization mediating structures like parties and associations were established; the workers movement is a case in point. The reinvention of the concept then occurred in the 1970s under the label of new social movements because of similarities in structure and organization to the old ones, but with different issue agendas. Here, the most prominent examples are the environmental, the peace, and the women's movements, although this list is not exhaustive.

The chapter by Koopmans is almost exclusively concerned with the theoretical underpinnings of movement research. Probably most interesting, beyond the various theoretical approaches he discusses, is his concern that social movement research must find a way between the futile search for universal laws reigning this phenomenon and unsatisfactory ad hoc descriptive accounts. Given that the chapter finds it difficult to systematize empirical findings from movement research, one must conclude that, whatever theoretical approach is chosen at the end, it requires more comparative and longitudinal research not the least to demarcate the line between social movements and NGOs and to determine whether social movements are a passing fancy or not.

1.6 The World Wide Web and Electronic Government

One of the issues challenging political thinkers and scientists alike is the promises and frailties of direct democracy. This topic is mentioned here not for detailed scrutiny. Rather, it is addressed because in the chapter by Margolis he looks at the promises and problematiques for the democratic political process originating from the increasing availability of the internet.

One of the topics that has intrigued social researchers from the beginning is the notion of the digital divide within and between countries: this refers to the observation that access to the internet and to the necessary hardware depends nationally on economic development and individually on resources like education and income. But for those political scientists working in and on advanced established democracies, the digital divide is at best a passing fancy and does not impinge in principle on the positive options foreseen for participatory advancement. However, Margolis, in his encompassing review of the literature, pours a lot of water into this wine in pointing out that almost all of the promises associated with the internet promoting political participation have not come true or have shown a double face. Nevertheless, given the wide use that governments, parties, and social groups make of the internet, the problematique remains a viable one for political research.

2 POLITICAL PARTICIPATION: PAST ACHIEVEMENTS AND FUTURE VISIONS

2.1 Will Democracy Prevail?

It is a trivium these days that political participation is inextricably related to the democratic process. There cannot be any democracy without the inclusion of the populus and its institutionalized right to determine by whom it is governed through regular elections in order to ascertain that a change in those who hold democratic offices is possible. Also, there can be no question that the overarching one-person-one-vote principle and the inclusiveness of the right to vote are the essence of democratic politics, encompassing principles which it took a century to install in liberal pluralist democracies operating under legal rule in a Rechtsstaat.

It is another trivium that liberal pluralist democracy is not an "easy" political system. Huntington (1991) has shown that the "velvet revolution" in central and eastern Europe is another step in a difficult process of the establishment, breakdown, and then re-establishment of democratic rule in the twentieth century. Thus, while there are now more democracies in the world than in any other historical period before, their consolidation can never be taken for granted.

This consideration at first view may be least pertinent for the established democracies of North America and western Europe. However, increasing streams of migrants into those regions from economically disadvantaged parts of the world create new challenges for democratic governance. A major problem which is related to the concept of inclusiveness arises from different value systems of the inhabitant and immigrating population. Citizenship and civicness are at stake, and this has recently become most visible in western Europe in the clash of religious beliefs which has led to conflicts between particularistic and universalistic values and results, in its extreme, in terrorist attacks like the ones in the US, the United Kingdom, and Spain.

The issue of multiculturalism and its integration in the context of the nation-state is aggravated by the decreasing role of the nation-state in framing the political involvement of its citizens in its capability to provide binding legal rules for action in all areas of life. The internationalization of business, capital movements, communication, and travel already is a challenge in its own right. On top of this comes the emergence of multifaceted international quasi-state and intermediary organizations like the European Union and the NGOs which all impinge on the nation-state's capacity to act on its own account, not to speak of the legitimation problems which arise from these processes of internationalization.

Given the apparent exhaustion of viable alternatives of political organization to democratic rule, one may speculate that it will be only a matter of time until this type of political system will prevail around the world given its institutionalized emphasis on the rule of law, equality, freedom, individual rights, and rejection of violence as a political means. Research has amply demonstrated, though, that the institutions of democracy can take many shapes, and this is already true for the western world. As liberal pluralist democracy spreads around the world, then, the question arises whether western values of individualism square well with other, deeply embedded value systems like familialism in Asia, a question which is answered in the negative, for example by Jang (2006). One systematic consideration from the above observations is that the spread of democratic rule is also a major challenge for comparative political science research to extend its reach beyond Europe and North America to properly understand the conditions under which democratic governance continues to thrive both in the established and in the less established democracies.

In methodological terms, these developments open new avenues for the better understanding of how institutional (macro), intermediary (meso), and individual (micro) factors interact in creating particular social and political outcomes which help democracies to thrive. As was mentioned in the beginning, political scientists have gone a long way already to establish longitudinal databases for the study of individual political, social, and cultural beliefs. And as these databases are becoming increasingly harmonized, the future challenge will be to find valid and reliable indicators which can succinctly characterize the institutional and organizational make-up of nation states in order to permit the micro-macro analyses of democratic processes and governance so badly needed.

2.2 The Future Scope of Political Participation

Given the essential role of elections in the allocation of temporary power to reigning elites in democracies, it cannot surprise anybody that voting studies have been the core topic for research on participation for a long time. With the institutionalization of survey-based voting studies in many countries, some of them having become increasingly complex as panels and through the inclusion of media studies, there is now an enormous body of empirical evidence helping to understand why citizens go to the polls and why they vote for one of the party choices offered in the particular polity. It has to be added that the options for the empirical study of elections has been enhanced by the fact that, starting almost fifty years ago, the primary researchers on elections have helped to engage in the building of data archives around the world which have made access to election study data easy and cost-effective for secondary research. Still, given the institutional diversity of democratic systems, it cannot come as a surprise that the comparative study of elections has lagged behind for a long time and continues to lag despite the existence of the Comparative Study of Electoral

Systems (CSES). Nevertheless, election studies have been and will remain a core pillar of participation research around the democratic world.

If one looks back at the first empirical study of political participation (Milbrath 1965), then one can easily see that it concentrated on acts related to the vote. With the protest movements of the 1960s previously alluded to, participation research extended in the realm of uninstitutionalized political participation, like signing petitions, joining boycotts, going to demonstrations and—a little later—joining a citizen action group. The first major piece of comparative research into this field was the eight-nation Political Action Study (Barnes, Kaase, et al. 1979). One of its major findings was that these participatory acts, at least the non-violent ones, indicated an extension of the citizen's political action repertory within the realm of democratic engagement, but did not signal a turn away from liberal pluralist democracies, as some of the crisis theories emerging at the time had suspected. Ongoing research in this field has corroborated, as Rucht points out in his chapter in this volume, that one can almost speak of a normalization of non-violent uninstitutionalized forms of political participation.

This is an important finding because it speaks to the adaptability of democracies to processes of social and political change, thereby making democratic systems stronger and not weaker. The most recent corroboration of this conclusion is an analysis by Norris (2006) on the basis of the about eighty countries around the world included in the year 2000 wave of the World Values Study. Not only does her analysis confirm findings from Political Action and beyond; by introducing a macro-distinction between fragile and stable democracies and autocracies she can show the different impact of direct action politics on both types of political systems in that it encourages strong democracies and tends to destabilize autocratic regimes. This is a telling example of what deeper insights can be gained by combining micro- and macro-data from a broad variety of countries.

Since these are findings on the democratic process that can be generalized across democracies, one would expect that the extension of the participatory repertory would also raise or keep at least at a high level the legitimacy of democratic polities. However, as Dalton (2004) has shown in a comparative longitudinal analysis of survey data, such a conclusion is premature, or rather outright wrong. The fact of the matter is rather that since the early 1990s western democracies have experienced a considerable decline in political trust and satisfaction. This decline has not yet reached the dimension of acceptance of democracy as such, but not only targets the political authorities, but also reaches out into the realm of democratic political institutions. Along similar lines goes the analysis by Putnam (e.g. 2000) about a decline in social capital which he views as a challenge and danger for the established democracies (for details of the social capital discussion see the chapter by Stolle in this volume).

These are surprising findings indeed not only because the eclipse of totalitarian communism at the time of the beginning of the downturn has eliminated the only viable competitor to democracy, but also because Roller (2005) has shown that, different from what the crisis of democracy theories have implied, there was no loss in effectiveness in democratic performance in that period.

Dalton (2004) has tried to explain the observed decline in support and satisfaction with macro-variables like changing values, media effects, and lack of economic performance, but concludes that the effects of these and other macro-variables on the decline are small indeed and may point to a convergence of causes, without, though, being able to put this conclusion on safe quantitative grounds. Another explanation of a more basic kind, although not testable empirically with the data at hand is that the loss of the communist counterpart has people made more aware of the weaknesses of the democratic process, weaknesses which surely have existed also before 1990, but may, of course, then have become more visible and therefore issues of public debate.

Benjamin Barber's strong democracy concept (1984) emphasizes the need for more democratic participation by the citizenry, and this squares well with the ongoing debate on direct democracy (e.g. Budge 1996), electronic and deliberative democracy (Kaase 2002), the planning cell (Dienel 1991), and representative citizen parliaments (e.g. Dahl 1989; Fishkin 1995). These approaches share the notion that the time has come to install new modes of democratic involvement beyond the vote in order to increase democratic legitimacy. Interestingly enough, the empirical evidence is ignored that even in democracies political affairs continue to rank rather low in the list of priorities citizens give to a variety of life domains and that referenda are open for manipulation by powerful interests.

Already for quite some time research has shown in particular for the Swiss example that direct democracy works well—and best—on the local level. Cain, Dalton, and Scarrow (2003) have thoroughly scrutinized the available evidence on institutional changes that have been implemented in various polities in the dimensions of representative, direct, and advocacy democracy where citizens become directly involved in the policy formation process. This analysis shows that there have been, indeed, over the last two or three decades substantial advances in opening up avenues beyond the vote in order to permit citizens more influence in political decision-making. Neither can these analyses document, though, that such efforts have enhanced democratic legitimacy nor do they adequately address the problem of democratic equality which had been so elegantly solved by the one-person-one-vote logic a century ago. This consideration directly leads to the essential democratic challenge of accountability: which political decisions for the polity are taken legitimately by whom, how can the responsible actors be held accountable for decisions they have taken, and what are the defined channels to revoke such decisions if the need arises?

The farthest political scientists have gone in their reaction to the observed crisis of democratic support and satisfaction can be found in a report by Schmitter and Trechsel (2005) for the Council of Europe under the title "The Future of Democracy in Europe." In this document, they present a "wish list" of twenty-eight democratic reforms pertaining to greatly enhanced participatory rights embedded in large institutional reforms of the democratic political process. We cannot discuss these proposals here at any length. We reference this work only to show that many ideas along these lines vagabond in scholarly discourse although they avoid any detailed discussion on implementation and its consequences for the operation of the political process.

3 In Lieu of a Conclusion

Part VI of this volume gives a very good overview of the state of participation research in political science. It documents what has been achieved, the extent to which knowledge and understanding of participatory phenomena has been enhanced over the years, and the lacunae of missing knowledge that still exist. In order to improve the understanding of what has been shown to be a moving target, surely three weaknesses need to be confronted: better theoretical underpinnings are needed, an extension of the polities to be included in empirical research is to be aimed for, and more sophisticated multi-level-dynamic research designs must be developed to cope with the growing complexity of the participatory space.

References

Barber, B. 1984. *Strong Democracy: Politics for a New Age.* Berkeley: University of California Press.

Barnes, S. H., Kaase, M., et al. 1979. *Political Action: Mass Participation in Five Western Democracies.* Beverly Hills, Calif.: Sage.

Budge, I. 1996. *The New Challenge of Direct Democracy.* Cambridge: Polity Press.

Cain, B. E., Dalton, R. J., Scarrow, S. E. 2003. *Democracy Transformed?* New York. Oxford University Press.

Dahl, R. A. 1989. *Democracy and its Critics.* New Haven: Yale University Press.

Dalton, R. J. 2004. *Democratic Challenges, Democratic Choices: The Erosion of Political Support in Advanced Industrial Democracies.* Oxford: Oxford University Press.

Dienel, P. C. 1991. *Die Planungszelle: Der Bürger plant seine Umwelt. Eine Alternative zur Establishment-Demokratie.* Opladen: Westdeutscher Verlag.

Fishkin, J. S. 1995. *The Voice of the People: Public Opinion and Democracy.* New Haven: Yale University Press.

Huntington, S. P. 1991. *The Third Wave: Democratization in the Late Twentieth Century.* Norman: The University of Oklahoma Press.

Jang, D.-J. 2006. East Asian perspectives on liberal democracy: a critical evaluation. Pp. 37–56 in *Democracy in Asia, Europe and the World: Toward a Universal Definition?*, ed. C.-S. Ahn and B. Fort. Singapore: Marshall Cavendish Academic.

Kaase, M. 2002. Elektronische Demokratie: Wird ein Traum wahr? Pp. 260–83 in *Bürger und Demokratie in Ost und West*, ed. D. Fuchs, E. Roller, B. Wessels. Wiesbaden: Westdeutscher Verlag.

Kornhauser, W. 1959. *The Politics of Mass Society.* New York: The Free Press.

Milbrath, L. W. 1965. *Political Participation.* Chicago: Rand McNally.

Norris, P. 2006. Political protest in fragile states. Paper presented at the 20th World Congress of the International Political Science Foundation (IPSA). Fukuoka, Japan.

Putnam, R. D. 1993. *Making Democracy Work: Civic Traditions in Modern Italy.* Princeton: Princeton University Press.

—— 2000. *Bowling Alone: The Collapse and Revival of American Community.* New York: Simon & Schuster.

ROLLER, E. 2005. *The Performance of Democracies: Political Institutions and Public Policy.* Oxford: Oxford University Press.

SARAMAGO, J. 2004. *Ensaio sobre e lucidez.* Lisbon: Editorial Caminho.

SCHMITTER, P. C., and TRECHSEL, A. H. 2005. *The Future of Democracy in Europe: Trends, Analyses and Reforms.* Strasbourg: The Council of Europe.

PART VII

DOES PUBLIC OPINION MATTER?

....

CHAPTER 43

THE RELATIONSHIP BETWEEN PUBLIC OPINION AND POLICY

....

CHRISTOPHER WLEZIEN
STUART N. SOROKA

DOES public opinion matter? Many of the preceding chapters presuppose that it does—that belief systems, political values, socialization, and the many determinants of voting behavior are of fundamental importance to the study of politics. Political beliefs and voting behavior are certainly important enough on their own to warrant study. But their significance to political scientists is most often rooted in the sense that—perhaps through changing preferences or through shifts in voting behavior—public opinion can affect policy outcomes. The link between public opinion and public policy is thus fundamental to the study of political behavior. In the words of Erikson, Wright, and McIver (1993, 1), "Ultimately, virtually all public opinion research bears on the question of popular control."

The significance of an opinion-policy link is by no means exclusive to work on public opinion. The vast body of research on electoral representation—on the link

* We thank the editors, Russell Dalton, Hans-Dieter Klingemann, and Robert Shapiro for helpful comments.

between the distribution of votes and seats—is at its heart interested in the extent to which public preferences will be reflected in policy (e.g. Lijphart 1994; Taagepera and Shugart 1989; Cox 1997). This connection is explicit in Powell's (2000) recent work, which shifts the focus of electoral institutional analysis away from votes and seats. A critical test of electoral institutions, Powell suggests, is the link between citizen preferences and government policy positions. While not examining public opinion and policies directly, this work highlights the centrality of the opinion-policy link in the study of representative democracy.

The current chapter reviews the empirical literature testing a general model in which policy is considered to be a function of public preferences. The mechanics by which preferences are converted to policy are considered along with extensions of the basic model—extensions through which the magnitude of opinion representation varies systematically across issues and political institutions. For much of the chapter, then, and in contrast with preceding chapters, public opinion is an *independent* variable—an important driver of public policy change. In a concluding section, we reconsider opinion as a dependent variable, specifically, its responsiveness to policy change. The ongoing existence of both policy representation *and* public responsiveness is critical to the functioning of representative democracy.

1 Opinion Representation in Theory and Practise

A fundamental principle of democratic government is that policy will be a function of opinion (see e.g. Dahl 1971; Weale 1999; Pitkin 1967). We can express this expectation formally, as follows:

$$P = f\{O\}, \tag{1}$$

where P designates policy and O opinion.[1] To be absolutely clear, we expect a positive relationship between opinion and policy—when the public wants a lot of policy, they should get a lot of policy. Whether and the extent to which this is true is a critical indicator of representative governance, and versions of this simple function have generated no small amount of attention from political scientists.

1.1 Dyadic Representation

Early empirical work on the opinion-policy link was sparked in large part by Miller and Stokes's (1963) "Constituency influence in Congress." These authors brought together

---

[1] This is not meant to be a complete model of policy of course, as we know that many other things also matter (Kingdon 1973; Jacobs and Shapiro 2000). The equation is used solely to characterize the relationship between opinion and policy.

data on public preferences by constituency, and both surveys and roll call voting behavior of US members of congress (MCs) on social welfare, foreign affairs, and civil rights. Correlations between constituency preferences and MC's behavior suggested that the latter was guided in part by constituency opinion. The finding was striking at the time, empirically demonstrating a mode of representation quite different from the party-centered work that had preceded it.

This seminal study—alongside other critical early works such as Mayhew's (1974) *Congress: The Electoral Connection,* Clausen's (1973) *How Congressmen Decide,* and Kingdon's (1973) *Congressmen's Voting Decisions*—spawned a vast literature seeking to establish links between the voting behavior of representatives and some combination of constituency opinion, constituency aggregate demographics, and representatives' own demographic traits and party affiliations.[2] The research is largely restricted to the US, where roll call votes are readily available (and party discipline has been weak), though there are important and informative exceptions (e.g. Barnes 1977; Converse and Pierce 1986; Matthews and Valen 1999).[3]

Referred to as studies of *dyadic* representation (Weissberg 1978), the literature on roll call voting asserts that representation is to be found in the relationship between individual constituencies and individual representatives. A good amount of work bears out significant connections in the US House of Representatives and Senate (Erikson and Wright 1997, 2000; Wright and Berkman 1986; Wright 1989a, 1989b). That representation in this work is at the constituency level—focusing on the behavior of legislators—is important, as we shall see below.

1.2 Collective Representation

Another body of work examines relationships between aggregated public preferences and system-level policy outcomes. This research is based on a view of representation ontologically different from that which guides work on dyadic representation. Here, representation is viewed as a systemic property, located not in the behavior of individuals but in the overall functioning of the entire representative policy-making system. The difference is partly a function of outcome variables: for the roll call voting literature, the outcome is clearly MC's votes; for the literature on collective representation, the outcome is policy. And policy is of course not the outcome of a single legislator, but the entire policy-making system. Concordance between individual legislators' actions and constituency preferences is thus a helpful but not sufficient condition for policy representation; most individual representatives could in fact vote against the majority opinion in their district. So long as the various district preferences were reflected in the votes of other districts' representatives, policy outcomes could still be representative of the (national) majority preference (e.g. Hurley 1982). What is critical

[2] For other prominent work on roll call voting, see e.g. Fiorina (1974); Stone (1979); Erikson (1978, 1990); Achen (1978); Kuklinski (1977, 1978); McCrone and Kulinski (1979); Shapiro et al. (1990); Bartels (1991).

[3] See also related cross-national work on party manifestos, e.g. Budge, Robertson, and Hearl (1987); Klingemann, Hoffebert, and Budge (1994).

in this view aren't the individual votes that contribute to the policy outcome, but the outcome itself—and of course the extent to which that outcome is in agreement with aggregated public preferences.

The notion of representation as a function of system-level policy outcomes underlies a vast literature on the "opinion-policy nexus." The literature is wide and varied; we offer a brief review here, distinguishing between three different approaches: (1) consistency; (2) covariation; and (3) congruence.[4] These approaches are differentiated to a large extent by data availability, though as we shall see each has its advantages.

1.2.1 *Policy Consistency: Preferences for Change*

We draw the "policy consistency" designation from Monroe (1979, 1998), whose work on the US provides an archetypal example of this line of analysis. This research asks, *To what extent is policy change consistent with a proximate public preference for policy change?* The approach involves identifying a single survey question asking about policy change, and examining the relationship between the proportion of respondents favoring that change and the existence of proximate changes in policy. "Consistency," then, refers to the match between public preferences for change and actual policy change. Across 556 cases from 1981 to 1993, for instance, Monroe finds a consistency score of 55 percent.

Consistency scores can be estimated for separate policy domains or different time periods. Indeed, this is where consistency scores are most interesting—they can indicate those domains in which opinion representation is particularly good (or bad). What consistency scores cannot do is establish a clear causal connection between public opinion and policy change. As Monroe (1998, 12) himself notes, the best this kind of analysis can do is to establish the coincidence of a public preference for change and actual policy change. A demonstration that preferences *lead* policy requires an analysis of data over time—data that can show, at least, that the public preference for change precedes the policy change.

The principal advantages of the consistency approach relate to the fact that it requires relatively little data—indeed, each case requires just one survey result, and the capacity to assess whether there was a proximate change in policy in that domain. As a consequence, the approach can easily include a wide range of policy issues. Where overall policy responsiveness is concerned, the inclusion of as many policy domains as possible is critical. Polling questions deal with issues of some level of public salience, so estimated overall responsiveness will be based on a rather restricted set of policy domains. Moreover, because policy responsiveness is likely greatest for salient issues—as we shall discuss further below—an estimate of overall policy responsiveness will almost necessarily be biased upwards, relying as it does on only those salient issues about which pollsters ask questions (see Burstein 2003). The consistency approach, by requiring just a single question, can encompass a broader spectrum of policy issues than do the more data-intensive covariation or congruence approaches described below.

[4] These terms have been used in past reviews of this literature. It is typical to distinguish between consistency and congruence, for instance (Monroe 1998). We add the intermediary "covariation" category here, based in part on Weissberg's (1976) early methodological review. For other reviews, see Manza and Cook (2002); Kuklinski and Segura (1995).

Relatively light data requirements also mean that the consistency approach has been quite easily exported outside the US to countries where comparatively less opinion data are available (e.g. Brooks 1985, 1987, 1990; Petry 1999; Petry and Mendelsohn 2004; Brettschneider 1996). These studies compare preferences for policy change at a single point with actual policy change within a subsequent period—usually the next twelve months—and in so doing add much to our understanding of the opinion-policy link across countries. The ongoing interaction between opinion and policy is however more adequately captured by the covariation and congruence approaches, as we shall see.

1.2.2 *Policy Covariation I: Policy and Opinion, Before and After*

Policy covariation studies involve a slightly more data-intensive approach to the link between opinion and policy. While consistency studies measure preference for policy change at a single point in time, covariation studies rely on cases in which the same policy question was asked at two different points in time. Changes in the distribution of responses over that period are compared with proximate policy change. Measures of policy also tend to be more comprehensive in this approach. Policy is typically examined both before and after the period of opinion change, so it is clearer when opinion precedes policy, or vice versa. The central question, then, is: *To what extent do changes in policy follow related changes in public preferences for policy?*

Studies of policy covariation go further than consistency studies in examining both opinion and policy over time, and are thus better equipped to examine the causal order of opinion and policy change. The best-known and most comprehensive study of policy covariation is Page and Shapiro's (1983) study of over 300 federal US policy issues from the mid-1930s to the late 1970s. These authors compare measures of opinion and policy across domains and institutions, similar to Monroe, but with the additional advantage of being able to ascertain whether policy change followed or preceded opinion change. Indeed, a critical insight offered by this approach is that policy change often *precedes* measured opinion change. Page and Shapiro (1983) find that policy may have affected opinion in almost half their cases.

The covariation approach has been used outside the US as well (e.g. Bélanger and Pétry 2005; Isernia, Juhasz, and Rattinger 2002). The approach has much to recommend it: it is not so data intensive as to be difficult outside the US, but at the same time it gathers enough information to get a general sense for the direction of causality between opinion and policy. Still, as with consistency, the limited period over which preferences and policies are measured makes it difficult to ascertain which came first. Preferences can change at a particular point in time because of previous policy changes, for instance. This ongoing interaction over time is missed by the covariation approach, but captured in the congruence approach below.

1.2.3 *Policy Covariation II: Policy and Opinion across Space*

An additional policy covariation model examines the relationship between policy and opinion across space—typically, across US states. Like the Page and Shapiro method, this approach is based on variation in both opinion and policy. Here, however, the variation is not across two points in time, but across contexts. The central question, then, is *To what extent do levels of policy vary across states alongside public preferences for policy?* Erikson, Wright, and McIver's (1993) *Statehouse Democracy* stands out as the best-known example of this kind of research. These authors examine the relationship between estimated state ideology scores and a measure of state policy liberalism; results show quite a strong relationship between the two.

The analysis of opinion and policy relationships across space has been used elsewhere, particularly in work on US state abortion policy (e.g. Goggin and Wlezien 1993; Norrander and Wilcox 1999). The methodological approach is a powerful one, though its use outside the US has been limited, presumably due to a lack of sufficient data at the subnational level. Much the same has been true cross-national research. There was some early work focusing on the convergence between mass and elite views on issues (especially Dalton 1985; also see Thomassen and Schmitt 1997), but only very recently have scholars begun to directly assess the relationships between opinion and policy across countries (e.g. Brooks and Manza 2006).

1.2.4 *Policy Congruence: Dynamic Representation*

The central questions in the study of the opinion-policy nexus are, *To what extent is policy development congruent with changes in public preferences for policy?*, and *To what extent do public preferences for policy react to policy change?* These questions are best addressed using an analysis of time-series data on both public preferences and policy—we refer to this here as the congruence approach. To really tease out the dynamic relationship between opinion and policy, we need dynamic data.

Early work on dynamic representation preceded the development of the time-series econometrics which have come to characterize the field. In *The Attentive Public*, Devine's (1970) analysis includes plots of (survey-based) mean policy support measures for different publics, alongside appropriations in those domains. Similarly, Weissberg (1976) plots opinion measures alongside spending measures for eleven different US policy domains, and Burstein (1979) tracks opinion and antidiscrimination policy. In each case, over-time analysis consists mainly of visual interpretations of graphs. Nevertheless, these authors' broader longitudinal outlook makes their work the clear precursor to more recent research on dynamic representation.

The term "dynamic representation" is drawn from Stimson, MacKuen, and Erikson's (1995) article of the same title, a critical and representative example of what congruence analyses have come to look like. The article posits a model in which policy is a function of public preferences, either directly through politicians' reactions to shifts in opinion, or indirectly through elections that result in shifts in the partisan composition of the legislature. The authors then examine relationships between a survey-based measure of "opinion liberalism" and policy-voting measures for the president, House, Senate, and Supreme Court. There is strong evidence that policy-makers respond to changes in public opinion.

While Stimson and colleagues were developing a dynamic model of the link between public opinion and multiple US political institutions, Wlezien (1995, 1996) was developing a "thermostatic" model of the (dynamic) reciprocal links between preferences and government spending—that is, a model which examined both opinion representation over time and public responsiveness to policy change. Dynamic models such as these are likely best equipped for investigating the causal relationships between opinion and policy. Work along these lines includes analyses of defense spending by Hartley and Russet (1992) and Eichenberg and Stoll (2003), recent work by Erikson, MacKuen, and Stimson (2002) and by Soroka and Wlezien (Soroka 2003; Wlezien 2004; Soroka and Wlezien 2004, 2005) as well as Johnson, Brace, and Arceneaux's (2005) research on environmental policy.

The drawback to dynamic models is they require a good deal of data, and to date this is available across many policy domains in a very limited number of countries: the US, Canada, and the UK. Work on dynamic representation has thus been restricted to polling-rich Anglo-American democracies, and mainly to salient policy domains. What the approach lacks in generalizability, however, it makes up for in the detail with which it can analyze opinion-policy relationships. This, we hope, will become clear in the sections that follow.

2 THE MECHANICS OF REPRESENTATION

Representation can occur in two familiar ways. The first way is indirect, through elections, where the public selects like-minded politicians who then deliver what it wants in policy. This is the traditional pathway to representation and is deeply rooted in the literature on responsible parties (Adams 2001). In effect, the public chooses among alternative policy visions and then the winning parties put their programs into place after the election. The second way to representation is direct, where sitting politicians literally respond to what the public wants. This pathway reflects an active political class, one that endeavors to stay closely attuned to the ebb and flow of public opinion and adjust policy accordingly. The two ways to representation actually are related. That is, the first way implies the second, at least assuming incumbent politicians are interested in remaining in office or clse motivated to represent our preferences for other reasons. This is how we think of representative democracy, how we think it should work, i.e. we expect responsiveness. Responsiveness is dynamic—responsive politicians follow preferences as they change. Policy change is the result.

We can formally express these expectations by revising our equation 1 for policy (P) as follows:

$$P = g\{O, I\}, \tag{2}$$

where O still is opinion and I is introduced to represent partisan control of government. Here policy is conceived to be directly responsive to opinion and indirectly responsive, through changes in partisan composition owing to elections. Of course, the indirect linkage presupposes a connection between public opinion and party control of government, that is:

$$I = h\{O\}. \tag{3}$$

These models apply across both space and time. We can characterize the relationships between opinion and governments and policy across countries or, say, provinces or states within a country. There is relatively little work across countries, as good comparative data are hard to come by, though scholarly explorations are underway. There is more work on the US states, as we have seen, and Erikson, Wright, and McIver's (1993) classic examination reveals both connections: general policy differences across states reflect the partisan composition of government and opinion, and the partisan composition reflects opinion.

We also can characterize relationships over time, as preferences change, following the study of dynamic representation. This sort of analysis allows us to explicitly assess policy "responsiveness." Erikson, MacKuen, and Stimson (2002) do just this, focusing on the number of major pieces of legislation in the US. They show that policy change nicely follows opinion over time independently of party control. Wlezien (1996, 2004) shows the same focusing on budgetary policy. This does not mean that politicians actually respond to changing public preferences, for it may be that they and the public both respond to something else, e.g. the perceived "need" for spending. All we can say for sure is that the research captures policy responsiveness in a statistical sense—whether and the extent to which public preferences directly influence policy change, other things being equal.

Of course, policy responsiveness is an institutional outcome. In parliamentary systems, this is straightforward—the government can change policy fairly directly, assuming that it does not face a realistic threat of a vote of (no) confidence. In presidential systems, agreement across institutions usually is required, as in the US. Presidential responsiveness to public preferences is conceptually quite simple: The president represents a national constituency and is expected to follow national preferences. Congressional responsiveness is more complex, even putting aside bicameralism, as members of the legislature represent districts. Although preferences differ across constituencies (see e.g. Erikson and Wright 1980, 1997, 2000; Erikson, Wright, and McIver 1993), there is reason to suppose that preferences in different constituencies move together over time (see e.g. Bartels 1991), just as movement of opinion across states (Erikson, Wright, and McIver 1993) and various demographic subcategories of the American public (Page and Shapiro 1992) is *largely* parallel. To the extent that they are responsive to public preferences, then, both the president and Congress should move in tandem, and predictable policy change is the logical consequence, even in the presence of divided government. Here we have a good amount of evidence, as we have seen.

How exactly do politicians know what public preferences are? Elections likely provide a good deal of information, but direct representation between elections requires something further. Politicians may learn about preferences through interactions with constituents; they may just have a good intuition for public preferences (Fenno

1978). Polls likely also play a critical role. Particularly given developments in polling technology, policy makers have in principle relatively easy access to public opinion on policy matters (Geer 1996). And while we know that policy makers' use and interpretation of polls can vary (e.g. Kingdon 1995; Herbst 1998), there is considerable evidence of the importance of polls, both public and private, in policy making (e.g. Beal and Hinkley 1984; Jacobs 1993; Jacobs and Shapiro 1995, 1995–6; Heith 1998). This work is critical. It shows one means by which politicians learn about public preferences. As we have noted, politicians have other, more direct sources of information as well.

3 ISSUES AND REPRESENTATION

Representation does not occur in all policy domains in all countries. The characteristics of domains appear to matter, for instance. Representation is likely to reflect the political importance (or "salience") of issue domains, if only due to the possible electoral consequences. Let us briefly trace the logic.

3.1 Issue Salience

In its simplest sense, a salient issue is politically important to the public. People care about the issue and have meaningful opinions that structure party support and candidate evaluation (see e.g. Miller et al. 1976; van der Eijk and Franklin 1996). Candidates are likely to take positions on the issue and it is likely to form the subject of political debate (Graber 1989). People are more likely to pay attention to politicians' behavior on an important issue, as reflected in news media reporting or as communicated in other ways (Ferejohn and Kuklinski 1990). Politicians, meanwhile, are likely to pay attention to public opinion on the issue—it is in their self-interest to do so, after all (Hill and Hurley 1999). There are many different and clear expressions of this conception of importance. In issue domains that are not important, conversely, people are not likely to pay attention to politicians' behavior, and politicians are by implication expected to pay less attention to public opinion in these areas. This reflects a now classic perspective (see e.g. McCrone and Kuklinski 1979; Jones 1994; Geer 1996; Hill and Hurley 1999; also see Jacobs and Shapiro 2000).

This not only implies variation in representation across domains; it implies variation in responsiveness within domains over time, as salience evolves. When an issue is not very salient to the public, politicians are expected to be less responsive. As salience increases, however, the relationship should increase (Jones 1994; Franklin and Wlezien 1997; Soroka 2003). That is, to the extent that salience varies over time, the relationship between opinion and policy itself may vary. Though the expectation is clear, there is little research on the subject. We simply do not know whether representation varies much over time. Indeed, we still do not know much about the variation in issue importance (see Wlezien 2005).[5]

3.2 Specific Versus Global Representation

Public preferences in the different policy domains are not entirely unique—they tend to move together over time. This patterned movement in preferences is well documented in the US (Stimson 1991; Wlezien 1995) but also is true elsewhere, in the US and UK. The pattern has led some scholars to conclude that the public does not have preferences for policy in different areas, but rather a single, very general preference for government activity (e.g. Stimson, MacKuen, and Erikson 1995; Wood and Hinton-Andersson 1998). From this perspective, measured preferences in various domains largely represent (multiple) indicators of a single, underlying preference for government action. When compared with the more traditional perspective, this characterization of public opinion implies a very different, *global* pattern of representation.

Some research shows that, although preferences in different areas do move together over time, the movement is not entirely common (Wlezien 2004). Preferences in some domains share little in common with preferences in others; these preferences often move quite independently over time. In short, this work indicates that preferences are some combination of the *global* and *specific*—moving together to some degree, but exhibiting some independent variation as well. This research also shows that policy makers reflect the specific variation, at least in some policy domains. Not surprisingly, these domains tends to be highly salient to voters, the ones on which they pay close attention to what policy makers do. In other less salient domains, policy only follows the general global signal (also see Druckman and Jacobs 2006). In yet other, very low salience domains, policy seemingly does not follow preferences at all. Recent research (Soroka and Wlezien 2004, 2005) indicates that the patterns differ significantly across countries, which points to possible institutional differences.

4 INSTITUTIONS AND REPRESENTATION

Polities differ in many ways, and some of these differences should have significant implications for the nature and degree of representation. Of fundamental importance are political competition and mass media openness. Without some level of political competition, of course, governments have less incentive to respond to public opinion. At the very least, the incentive would be less reliable. Likewise, some level of mass media competition is essential in modern democracies. Without it, people

---

[5] There is however a related body of literature in policy making that reveals variance in "attentiveness" over time. See Baumgartner and Jones (2005).

cannot easily receive information about what government actors do, and thus cannot effectively hold politicians accountable for their actions.

Even where we have essential levels of media and political competition, as in most modern democracies (including new ones), institutional differences may have important implications for policy representation. Here we have a growing body of empirical work, particularly on electoral systems.

4.1 Electoral Systems

Most of this research focuses on the differences between the majoritarian and proportional visions, using Powell's (2000) language, and mostly on how these differences matter for policy respresentation. Lijphart (1984) provides the first direct statement on the matter. He distinguishes between "consensual" democracies—characterized by, most notably, proportional representation, multi-party systems, and coalition governments—and "majoritarian" systems—characterized by simple plurality election rules, a two-party system, and single-party government (exactly as Duverger (1951) would predict). Most importantly, Lijphart suggests that consensual democracies provide better descriptive representation and general policy congruence than do majoritarian systems.

Powell (2000) provides further empirical support, focusing specifically on the differences between majoritarian and proportional election rules and their implications for representation. Powell finds that proportional representation tends to produce greater congruence between the government and the public; specifically, that the general ideological disposition of government and the ideological bent of the electorate tend to match up better in proportional systems. According to Powell, this reflects the greater, direct participation of constituencies the vision affords (also see Miller et al. 1999).

Powell's results pertain to elections and their immediate consequences. But what about in the periods between elections? Are coalition governments more responsive to ongoing changes in opinion? Although proportional systems may provide more indirect representation, it is not clear that they afford greater direct representation. There is reason to think that governments in majoritarian systems actually are more responsive to opinion *change*. First, it presumably is easier for a single party to respond to changes than a multi-party coalition, as coordination in the latter is more difficult and costly. Second, majoritarian governments may have more of an incentive to respond to opinion change. Since a shift in electoral sentiment has bigger consequences on election day in majoritarian systems, governments there are likely to pay especially close attention to the ebb and flow of opinion.[6] Thus, it may be that the two systems both work to serve representation, but in different ways, where proportional systems provide better *indirect representation* via elections and majoritarian systems better *direct representation* in between elections. There is little empirical work on the subject, however.[7]

---

[6] This generalizes Rogowski and Kayser's (2002) argument relating to the comparatively higher seats-votes elasticities in majoritarian systems.

[7] Very recent work (Hobolt and Klemmensen 2005) suggests that one proportional system (Denmark) is more responsive than one majoritarian one (the UK), at least as regards what governments *say.*

4.2 Government Institutions

Just as electoral systems may matter, so too may government institutions. In particular, research suggests that the horizontal division of powers may structure the relationships between opinion and policy over time.[8] The concentration of powers in parliamentary systems—as opposed to presidential systems—affords voters more direct control over government on election day. This presumably aids indirect representation: To the extent election outcomes reflect public opinion, then policy representation will follow quite naturally, at least to the extent we have responsible parties.

The same seemingly is not true about direct representation, and there is reason to suppose that parliamentary governments are less reliable in their attendance to public opinion over time.[9] Scholars have long noted the dominance of cabinets over parliaments (see e.g. the classic statements by Bagehot 1867 and Jennings 1959; also see Laver and Shepsle 1996; Cox 1987; Tsebelis 2002). These scholars portray a world in which cabinet governments exercise substantial discretion, where the cabinet is the proposer—it puts legislation to the Commons—and the legislature ultimately has only a limited check on what the government does. Strom (2003) concludes that parliamentary government deals much better with "adverse selection" than it does "moral hazard." Once established, the cabinet is difficult to control on a recurring basis.

This has fairly direct implications for government responsiveness. When there are differences between what the cabinet and parliament want, the latter cannot effectively impose its own contrary will. The process of amendment and veto is compromised, at least by comparison with presidential systems. In the latter the executive cannot effectively act without the legislature, at least with respect to statute. The legislature is the proposer—it puts statute to the executive—and while the executive can veto legislation the legislature can typically override. Most changes in policy require agreement between the executive and legislature, or else a supermajority in the latter. This is likely to reduce disjunctures between public opinion and policy change.

Although the separation of powers makes presidential systems much more deliberate in their actions, therefore, it may also make them more reliably responsive to public opinion over time. We still expect representation in parliamentary systems, of course—after all, governments in these systems are more easily held accountable for their actions, as responsibility is far clearer, particularly in a majoritarian context. In between elections, however, there is little to make parliamentary cabinets accountable except for the prospect of a future electoral competition. Though important, the

---

[8] The vertical division of powers also may be important, via public opinion itself: increasing the mix of governments involved in policy making may dampen public information, which may have consequences for representation in turn (Soroka and Wlezien 2004, 2005).

[9] Note that this argument bears some similarities to Risse-Kappen's (1991) work on foreign policy making, in which he argues that the centralization or strength of government institutions determines the extent to which policy makers will follow or lead public preferences.

incentive is imperfect. Research comparing the US, UK, and Canada bears out these expectations (Soroka and Wlezien 2004, 2005).

5 On Political Equality

We make regular reference to "public opinion" and "public preferences." This is what policy makers are expected to represent. But what exactly is the public? Is it the collection of all of us, with each person's preferences given equal weight? Or is it a more narrowly drawn public, including some people's preferences but not others? *Who* gets what they want in policy?

In one conception, the public consists of all citizens, all adults at least. Citizens are all, more or less, equally entitled to vote, and each person has but one vote. Perhaps then we should all have equal weight where policy making is concerned. This is an ideal, the stuff of civics textbooks; in reality, however, there is good reason to think that preferences are not equal, and that some people's preferences are more important than others. In particular, we might expect politicians to pay special attention to the preferences of active voters. These are the people who matter on election day, after all—they are the ones who put (and keep) politicians in office.

The representation of voters rather than citizens would not matter much if voters were a random sample. But we know that there are differences between the voting and non-voting public: voters tend to be better educated, have better jobs, and have higher incomes. Not surprisingly, voters tend to be more conservative than their non-voting counterparts. If politicians are more attentive to this group, and follow the median *voter*, then policy will be more conservative than the median *citizen* would like. This is of obvious importance. We still know relatively little empirically, however, though scholarly interest is on the rise, particularly in the US. Griffin and Newman (2005) reveal that politicians pay more attention to the opinions of voters than those of non-voters. Bartels' (2005) and Gilens' (2005) recent research shows that US politicians are most attuned to the opinions of high-income voters. There may be related socio-demographic manifestations, across race for example.

Political equality also may have explicitly partisan expressions. It may be, for instance, that politicians are more responsive to in-partisans, as Hill and Hurley (2003) have argued. This and the other work on inequality in representation is important. It only scratches the surface, however. We need to know more about the breadth and depth of the inequality, both at particular points in time and over time. To the extent that there is inequality, are politicians more responsive to the opinions of the better-educated, higher-income, more right-wing voting population? Much work remains to be done.

6 THE IMPORTANCE OF PUBLIC RESPONSIVENESS

We have thus far concentrated on policy representation—on the effect of opinion on policy. But policy representation ultimately requires that the public notices and responds to what policy makers do. Without such responsiveness, policy makers would have little incentive to represent what the public wants in policy—there would be no real benefit for doing so, and there would be no real cost for not doing so. Moreover, expressed preferences would be of little use even to those politicians motivated to represent the public for other reasons.

Despite ongoing concerns about the ignorance and irrationality of the average citizen (Converse 1964), a growing body of recent work shows that the average citizen may be more informed than initially thought. This is not to say that the average citizen knows very much about politics; but there is accumulating evidence that individuals may be capable of basic, rational political judgments. Moreover, even in the face of individual ignorance, aggregate preferences often react sensibly to real-world trends (Page and Shapiro 1983, 1992). Wlezien (1995) reveals a public that reacts to both real-world affairs and policy itself, much like a thermostat. That is, the public adjusts its preferences for "more" or "less" policy in response to policy change, favoring less (more) policy in the wake of policy increases (decreases), *ceteris paribus*. This conceptualization fits nicely with the functionalist models proposed by Easton (1965) and Deutsch (1966), where policy outputs feed back on public inputs into the policy-making process.

Empirical analysis shows that public responsiveness, like policy representation, varies across policy domains and political institutions (Wlezien 1995; Soroka and Wlezien 2004, 2005). That representation is likely to be greater in salient domains is largely the product of representatives reacting in domains in which publics themselves are monitoring and reacting to policy change, for instance. Salient domains are characterized by a higher degree of both representation and responsiveness; more precisely, public responsiveness and policy representation co-vary. This is not equally true across contexts, however. Fundamental to public responsiveness is the acquisition of accurate information about what policy makers are doing, and so responsiveness will be lower when the acquisition of information is more difficult. So for instance, federalism, by increasing the number of different governments making policy, and thus making less clear what "government" is doing (see e.g. Downs 1999) may decrease responsiveness and representation.[10] The horizontal division of powers may also be important, though here our expectations are less clear. Regardless, where information is easier to acquire, public responsiveness—and by implication policy representation—should be greater.

Ultimately, we expect variance across domains and institutions in both policy representation and public responsiveness. Yet the existence of each connection between

---

[10] It evidently does not preclude responsiveness. Consider work on the US (Wlezien 1995) and Canada and the UK (Soroka and Wlezien 2004, 2005) and research on opinion about the European Union (Franklin and Wlezien 1997; Dalton and Eichenberg 1998; Gabel 1998).

opinion and policy—indeed, the existence of *both* connections—is critical to the functioning of representative democracy. Insofar as research seeks to understand what public preferences are, and how these are formed, then, it can be viewed as an examination of the potential for, or success of, representative democratic institutions. The work makes a contribution to our understanding of one of the most significant and enduring questions in the study of politics: does democracy work? In some cases, it appears as though it may work better than many of us anticipated.

REFERENCES

ACHEN, C. H. 1978. Measuring representation. *American Journal of Political Science*, 22: 475–510.

ADAMS, J. 2001. *Party Competition and Responsible Party Government: A Theory of Spatial Competition Based upon Insights from Behavioral Voting Research.* Ann Arbor: University of Michigan Press.

BAGEHOT, W. 1867 (1966). *The English Constitution.* Ithaca, NY: Cornell University Press.

BARNES, S. H. 1977. *Representation in Italy: Institutionalized Tradition and Electoral Choice.* Chicago: University of Chicago Press.

BARTELS, L. M. 1991. "Constituency opinion and congressional policy making: the Reagan defense build up. *American Political Science Review*, 85 (2): 457–74.

—— 2005. Economic inequality and political representation. Paper presented at the Annual Meeting of the American Political Science Association, Boston, September 2002. Revised August 2005.

BAUMGARTNER, F. R., and JONES, B. D. 2005. *The Politics of Attention: How Government Prioritizes Problems.* Chicago: University of Chicago Press.

BEAL, R. S., and HINCKLEY, R. 1984. Presidential decision making and opinion polls. *Annals of the American Academy of Political and Social Sciences*, 472: 72–84.

BÉLANGER, E., and PÉTRY, F. 2005. The rational public? A Canadian test of the Page and Shapiro argument. *International Journal of Public Opinion Research*, 17: 190–212.

BRETTSCHNEIDER, F. 1996. Public opinion and parliamentary action: responsiveness in the German Bundestag in comparative perspective. *International Journal of Public Opinion Research*, 8: 292–311.

BROOKS, C., and MANZA, J. 2006. Social policy responsiveness in developed democracies. *American Sociological Review*, 71: 474–94.

BROOKS, J. E. 1985. Democratic frustration in the Anglo-American polities: a quantification of inconsistency between mass public opinion and public policy. *Western Political Quarterly*, 38: 250–61.

—— 1987. "The Opinion-Policy Nexus in France—Do Institutions and Ideology Make a Difference?" *Journal of Politics* 49: 465–80.

—— 1990. The opinion-policy nexus in Germany. *Public Opinion Quarterly*, 54: 508–29.

BUDGE, I., ROBERTSON, D., and HEARL, D. eds. 1987. *Ideology, Strategy and Party Change: Spatial Analyses of Post-War Election Programmes in 19 Democracies.* Cambridge: Cambridge University Press.

BURSTEIN, P. 1979. Public opinion, demonstrations, and the passage of antidiscrimination legislation. *Public Opinion Quarterly*, 43: 157–72.

—— 2003. The impact of public opinion on public policy: a review and an agenda. *Political Research Quarterly*, 56 (1): 29–40.

CLAUSEN, A. R. 1973. *How Congressmen Decide: A Policy Focus.* New York: St Martin's Press.

CONVERSE, P. E. 1964. The nature of belief systems in mass publics. Pp. 201–61 in *Ideology and Discontent,* ed. D. E. Apter. New York: Free Press.

—— and PIERCE, R. 1986. *Political Representation in France.* Cambridge, Mass.: Harvard University Press.

COX, G. W. 1987. *The Efficient Secret: The Cabinet and the Development of Political Parties in Victorian England.* Cambridge: Cambridge University Press.

—— 1997. *Making Votes Count: Strategic Coordination in the World's Electoral Systems.* Cambridge: Cambridge University Press.

DAHL, R. 1971. *Polyarchy: Participation and Opposition.* New Haven: Yale University Press.

DALTON, R. J. 1985. Political parties and political representation: party supporters and party elites in nine nations. *Comparative Political Studies,* 18: 267–99.

—— and EICHENBERG, R. 1998. Citizen support policy integration. Pp. 250–82 *Supranational Governance: The Institutionalization of the European Union,* ed. W. Sandholz and A. Stone. Oxford: Oxford University Press.

DEUTSCH, K. W. 1966. *The Nerves of Government: Models of Political Communication and Control.* New York: Free Press.

DEVINE, D. J. 1970. *The Attentive Public: Polyarchical Democracy.* Chicago: Rand McNally.

DOWNS, W. M. 1999. Accountability payoffs in federal systems? Competing logics and evidence from Europe's newest federation. *Publius: The Journal of Federalism,* 29 (1): 87–110.

DRUCKMAN, J. N., and JACOBS, L. R. 2006. Lumpers and Splitters: The public opinion information that politicians collect and use. *Public Opinion Quarterly,* 70: 453–76.

DUVERGER, M. 1951. *Les Partis politiques.* Paris: Seuil (English trans. *Political Parties: Their Organization and Activity in the Modern State.* New York: Wiley, 1954).

EASTON, D. 1965. *A Framework for Political Analysis.* Englewood Cliffs, NJ: Prentice-Hall.

EICHENBERG, R., and STOLL, R. 2003. Representing defence: democratic control of the defence budget in the United States and Western Europe. *Journal of Conflict Resolution,* 47: 399–423.

ERIKSON, R. S. 1978. Constituency opinion and congressional behavior: a reexamination of the Miller-Stokes representation data. *American Journal of Political Science,* 22: 511–35.

—— 1990. Roll calls, reputations, and representation in the U.S. senate. *Legislative Studies Quarterly,* 15 (4): 623–42.

—— MacKUEN, M. B., and STIMSON, J. A. 2002. *The Macro Polity.* Cambridge: Cambridge University Press.

—— and WRIGHT, G. C. 1980. Policy representation of constituency interests. *Political Behavior,* 2: 91–106.

—— —— 1997. Voters, candidates, and issues in congressional elections. Pp. 67–92 in *Congress Reconsidered,* 6th edn., ed. L. C. Dodd and B. I. Oppenheimer. Washington, DC: CQ Press.

—— —— 2000. Representation of constituency ideology in Congress. Pp. 148–77 in *Continuity and Change in House Elections,* ed. D. W. Brady, J. F. Cogan, and M. P. Fiorina. Stanford, Calif.: Stanford University Press.

—— —— and McIVER, J. P. 1993. *Statehouse Democracy: Public Opinion and Policy in the American States.* Cambridge: Cambridge University Press.

FENNO, RICHARD F. JR. 1978. *Home style: House Members in their Districts.* Boston: Little, Brown.

FEREJOHN, J. A., and KUKLINSKI, J. H. eds. 1990. *Information and Democratic Processes.* Urbana: University of Illinois Press.

FIORINA, M. P. 1974. *Representatives, Roll Calls, and Constituencies.* Lexington, Mass.: Lexington Books.

FRANKLIN, M., and WLEZIEN, C. 1997. The responsive public: issue salience, policy change, and preferences for European Unification. *Journal of Theoretical Politics,* 9: 347–63.

GABEL, M. 1998. Economic integration and mass politics: market liberalization and public attitudes in the European Union. *American Journal of Political Science*, 42: 936–53.

GEER, J. G. 1996. *From Tea Leaves to Opinion Polls: A Theory of Democratic Leadership*. New York: Columbia University Press.

GILENS, M. 2005. Inequality and democratic responsiveness. *Public Opinion Quarterly*, 69: 778–96.

GOGGIN, M., and WLEZIEN, C. 1993. Abortion opinion and policy in the American states. Pp. 190–202 in *Understanding the New Politics of Abortion*, ed. M. Goggin. Newbury Park, Calif.: Sage.

GRABER, D. 1989. *Mass Media and American Politics*, 3rd edn. Washington, DC: CQ Press.

GRIFFIN, J. D., and NEWMAN, B. 2005. Are voters better represented? *Journal of Politics*, forthcoming.

HARTLEY, T. and RUSSETT, B. 1992. Public opinion and the common defence: who governs military spending in the United States? *American Political Science Review*, 86: 905–15.

HEITH, D. J. 1998. Staffing the White House public opinion apparatus: 1969–1988. *Public Opinion Quarterly*, 62 (2): 165–89.

HERBST, S. 1998. *Reading Public Opinion: How Political Actors View the Democratic Process*. Chicago: University of Chicago Press.

HILL, K. Q., and HURLEY, P. A. 1999. Dyadic representation reappraised. *American Journal of Political Science*, 43: 109–37.

—— —— 2003. Beyond the demand-input model: a theory of representational linkages. *Journal of Politics*, 65 (2): 304–26.

HOBOLT, S. B., and KLEMMENSEN, R. 2005. Responsive government? Public opinion and policy preferences in Britain and Denmark. *Political Studies*, 53: 379–402.

HURLEY, P. A. 1982. Collective representation reappraised. *Legislative Studies Quarterly* 7 (1): 119–36.

ISERNIA, P., JUHASZ, Z., and RATTINGER, H. 2002. Foreign policy and the rational public in comparative perspective. *Journal of Conflict Resolution*, 46: 201–24.

JACOBS, L. R. 1993. *The Health of Nations: Public Opinion and the Making of American and British Health Policy*. Ithaca, NY: Cornell University Press.

—— and SHAPIRO, R. Y. 1995. The rise of presidential polling: the Nixon White House in historical perspective. *Public Opinion Quarterly*, 59: 163–95.

—— —— 1995–6. Presidential manipulation of polls and public opinion: the Nixon administration and the pollsters. *Political Science Quarterly*, 110 (4): 519–38.

—— —— 1996. Toward the integrated study of political communication, public opinion, and the policy-making process. *PS: Political Science & Politics* 29: 10–13.

—— —— 2000. *Politicians Don't Pander: Political Manipulation and the Loss of Democratic Responsiveness*. Chicago: University of Chicago Press.

JENNINGS, I. 1959. *Cabinet Government*, 3rd edn. Cambridge: Cambridge University Press.

JOHNSON, M., BRACE, P., and ARCENEAUX, K. 2005. Public opinion and dynamic representation in the American states: the case of environmental attitudes. *Social Science Quarterly*, 86 (1): 87–108.

JONES, B. D. 1994. *Reconceiving Decision-Making in Democratic Politics: Attention, Choice, and Public Policy*. Chicago: University of Chicago Press.

KINGDON, J. W. 1973. *Congressmen's Voting Decisions*. New York: Harper & Row.

—— 1995. *Agendas, Alternatives, and Public Policies*. New York: Harper Collins Publishers.

KLINGEMANN, H.-D., HOFFERBERT, R. I., and BUDGE, I. 1994. *Parties, Policies, and Democracy*. Boulder, Colo.: Westview Press.

KUKLINSKI, J. H. 1977. District competitiveness and legislative roll call behavior: a reassessment of the marginality hypothesis. *American Journal of Political Science*, 20: 627–38.

Kuklinski, J. H. 1978. Representation and elections: a policy analysis. *American Political Science Review,* 72: 165–77.

—— and Segura, G. 1995. Endogeneity, exogeneity, time, and space in political representation: a review article. *Legislative Studies Quarterly,* 20 (1): 3–21.

Laver, M., and Shepsle, K. A. 1996. *Making and Breaking Governments: Cabinets and Legislatures in Parliamentary Democracies.* Cambridge: Cambridge University Press.

Lijphart, A. 1977. *Democracy in Plural Societies.* New Haven: Yale University Press.

—— 1984. *Democracies: Pattern of Majoritarian and Consensus Government in Twenty-One Countries.* New Haven: Yale University Press.

—— 1994. *Electoral Systems and Party Systems: A Study of Twenty-Seven Democracies, 1945–1990.* Oxford: Oxford University Press.

—— 1999. *Government Forms and Performance in Thirty-Six Countries.* New Haven: Yale University Press.

McCrone, D. J., and Kuklinski, J. H. 1979. The delegate theory of representation. *American Journal of Political Science,* 23: 278–300.

Manin, B., Przeworski, A., and Stokes, S. C. 2002. *Democracy, Accountability and Representation.* Cambridge: Cambridge University Press.

Manza, J., and Cook, F. L. 2002. A democratic polity? Three views of policy responsiveness to public opinion in the United States. *American Political Research,* 30: 630–67.

Matthews, D. R., and Valen, H. 1999. *Parliamentary Representation: The Case of the Norwegian Storting.* Columbus, Oh.: Ohia State Press.

Mayhew, D. R. 1974. *Congress: The Electoral Connection.* New Haven: Yale University Press.

Miller, A. H., Miller, W. E., Raine, A. S., and Browne, T. A. 1976. A majority party in disarray: policy polarization in the 1972 election. *American Political Science Review,* 70: 753–78.

Miller, W. E., and Stokes, D. E. 1963. Constituency influence in Congress. *American Political Science Review,* 57 (1): 45–56.

—— Pierce, R., Thomassen, J., Herrera, R., Holmberg, S., Esaisson, P., and Wessels, B., 1999. *Policy Representation in Western Democracies.* Oxford: Oxford University Press.

Monroe, A. 1979. Consistency between constituency preferences and national policy decisions. *American Politics Quarterly,* 12: 3–19.

—— 1998. Public opinion and public policy 1980–1993. *Public Opinion Quarterly,* 62: 6–28.

Norrander, B., and Wilcox, C. 1999. Public opinion and policymaking in the States: the case of post-Roe abortion policy. *Policy Studies Journal,* 27: 707–22.

Page, B. I., and Shapiro, R. Y. 1983. Effects of public opinion on policy. *American Political Science Review,* 77: 175–90.

—— —— 1992. *The Rational Public: Fifty Years of Trends in Americans' Policy Preferences.* Chicago: University of Chicago Press.

Persson, T., Roland, G., and Tabellini, G. 1997. Separation of powers and political accountability. *Quarterly Journal of Economics,* 112 (4): 1163–202.

Petry, F. 1999. The opinion-policy relationship in Canada. *Journal of Politics,* 61: 540–50.

—— and Mendelsohn, M. 2004. Public opinion and policy making in Canada, 1995–2001. *Canadian Journal of Political Science,* 27: 505–29.

Pitkin, H. F. 1967. *The Concept of Representation.* Berkeley: University of California Press.

Powell, G. B. 2000. *Elections as Instruments of Democracy: Majoritarian and Proportional Views.* New Haven: Yale University Press.

Risse-Kappen, T. 1991. Public opinion, domestic structure, and foreign policy in liberal democracies. *World Politics,* 43 (4): 479–512.

Rogowski, R., and Kayser, M. 2002. Majoritarian electoral systems and consumer power: price-level evidence from the OECD countries. *American Journal of Political Science,* 46 (3): 526–39.

SHAPIRO, C. R., BRADY, D. W. BRODY, R. A., and FEREJOHN, J. A. 1990. Linking constituency opinion and senate voting scores: a hybrid explanation. *Legislative Studies Quarterly*, 15 (4): 599–621.

SOROKA, S. N. 2003. Media, public opinion and foreign policy. *Harvard International Journal of Press and Politics*, 8 (1): 27–48.

—— and WLEZIEN, C. 2004. Opinion representation and policy feedback: Canada in comparative perspective. *Canadian Journal of Political Science*, 37 (3): 531–60.

—— —— 2005. Opinion-policy dynamics: public preferences and public expenditure in the United Kingdom. *British Journal of Political Science*, 35: 665–89.

STIMSON, J. A. 1991. *Public Opinion in America: Moods, Cycles, and Swings*. Boulder, Colo.: Westview Press.

—— MacKUEN, M. B., and ERIKSON, R. S. 1995. Dynamic representation. *American Political Science Review*, 89: 543–65.

STONE, W. J. 1979. Measuring constituency-representative linkages: problems and prospects. *Legislative Studies Quarterly*, 4 (4): 623–39.

STRØM, K. 2003. Parliamentary democracy and delegation. Pp. 55–106 in *Delegation and Accountability in Parliamentary Democracies*, ed. K. Strøm, W. Muller, and T. Bergman. Oxford: Oxford University Press.

TAAGEPERA, R., and SHUGART, M. S. 1989. *Seats and Votes: The Effects and Determinants of Electoral Systems*. New Haven: Yale University Press.

THOMASSEN, J., and SCHMITT, H. 1997. Policy representation. *European Journal of Political Research*, 32: 165–84.

TSEBELIS, G. 2002. *Veto Players: How Political Institutions Work*. New York: Russell Sage Foundation.

VAN DER EIJK, C., and FRANKLIN, M. N. 1996. *Choosing Europe? The European Electorate and National Politics in the Face of Union*. Ann Arbor: University of Michigan Press.

WEAKLIEM, D. 2003. Public opinion research and political sociology. *Research in Political Sociology*, 12: 49–80.

WEALE, A. 1999. *Democracy*. New York: St Martin's.

WEISSBERG, R. 1976. *Public Opinion and Popular Government*. Englewood Cliffs, NJ: Prentice-Hall.

—— 1978. Collective vs. dyadic representation in Congress. *American Political Science Review*, 72: 535–47.

WLEZIEN, C. 1995. The public as thermostat: dynamics of preferences for spending. *American Journal of Political Science*, 39: 981–1000.

—— 1996. Dynamics of representation: the case of U.S. spending on defense. *British Journal of Political Science*, 26: 81–103.

—— 2004. Patterns of representation: dynamics of public preferences and policy. *Journal of Politics*, 66: 1–24.

—— 2005. On the salience of political issues: the problem with "most important problem." *Electoral Studies*, 24 (4): 555–79.

WOOD, B. D., and HINTON-ANDERSON, A. 1998. The dynamics of senatorial representation, 1952–1991. *American Journal of Political Science*, 60: 705–36.

WRIGHT, G. C. 1989a. Policy voting in the U.S. senate: who is represented? *Legislative Studies Quarterly*, 14: 465–86.

—— 1989b. Level-of-analysis effects on explanations of voting: the case of U.S. senate elections. *British Journal of Political Science*, 18: 381–98.

—— and BERKMAN, M. B. 1986. Candidates and policy in U.S. senatorial elections. *American Political Science Review*, 80: 576–90.

CHAPTER 44

POLITICAL ELITES

JEAN BLONDEL

FERDINAND MÜLLER-ROMMEL

In what was probably the first comprehensive empirical study of political elites, published in 1976, Robert Putnam claimed that the main defect of the studies undertaken in the field was that "the gap" was "unusually large...between abstract, general theories and masses of unorganised empirical evidence" (1976, ix). The only reservation to be made about this statement might be that the empirical evidence, at the time the book was written, had a "mass" character. Putnam then indicated that the questions of "who rules?" and of "who should rule?" were "central" in empirical and normative political science respectively. He added: "Sage commentators, from Plato and Aristotle to our nightly television newscasters, tell us much about power and leadership, but their profundities, when carefully examined, often turn out to be incomplete and ambiguous" (1976, 2). Thanks to Putnam's own work and to the many studies, sometimes comparative, during the last quarter of the twentieth century, the overall assessment made in 1976 can be modified in part: much is still unknown or only partly known, however. In particular, the geographical scope of the generalizations that can be made on the basis of the collected evidence remains limited.

The key changes, which have occurred since 1976, have gone in three directions. The first change concerns the balance between theoretical and empirical studies. Perhaps the emergence of democracy in the West in the nineteenth century led to widespread dissatisfaction as the contrast between ideal and reality seemed to be vast: the very concept of "elite" thus became a battleground. That concept may have had a positive flavor for those who felt that the people needed guidance, a guidance that was provided by the newly established representative systems. Probably for many more, the adjective "elitist" and the substantive with which it was closely connected, "elitism", indicated dislike, even rejection. That is because writers at the time stressed that rulers tended to use their authority to frustrate democracy. Hence the passionate debates between those who regarded the elite, not only as a necessity, but as a beacon, and those who felt that members of the elite were merely exploiting the positions of privilege in which they found themselves. These views gave rise to the "abstract theories" to which Putnam referred. Since the third quarter of the twentieth century, these heated debates have abated, however. Instead, detailed empirical studies gradually began to show that, at any rate in the West, "extremist" viewpoints about the role of the elite were simply unrealistic.

A second major change is connected to the spread of empirical studies (see the chapter by Hoffmann-Lange in this volume). The political elite came to be seen increasingly as autonomous from other segments of the national elite. Early studies had an essentially global sociological outlook; they apparently took for granted, indeed sometimes plainly stated, that there was *one* elite and that its political component was not merely closely associated to, but indeed undistinguishable from its social and even economic components. On the contrary, empirical studies showed that the political elite were different from other elite groups. At least in the West, this distinction occurred both because of recruitment and career characteristics and because of the nature of the problems which political elites had to address, nationally and internationally.

Third, empirical studies gradually demonstrated that the dichotomous opposition between elite and mass was an unrealistic simplification. In western democracies, groups of various kinds contributed to filling the gap between the two levels. Moreover, among those who could reasonably be regarded as part of the elite, one needs to introduce major distinctions, such as among party activists, parliamentarians, and members of governments. Above all, twentieth century political life was at least ostensibly orchestrated, if not dominated, by leaders, who seemed markedly more powerful than the rest of the political elite.

Despite these three major changes, all of which resulted from the increase in the number and scope of empirical studies, much remains to be done to ensure that we have a true overall picture of the nature and role of political elites in the contemporary world. There are some comparative studies, to be sure, but almost all of these have a limited geographical scope. Putnam's 1976 work was in many ways a heroic attempt at undertaking a worldwide survey, but the author was the first to recognize that what could be said on the basis of empirical data about political elites outside the West was limited in the extreme. The situation has not changed markedly in this respect in the subsequent three decades. Despite the fact that analyses of political elites outside the western world would provide an alternative perspective on the nature of elites, the bulk of the studies on political elites are still devoted to western countries–basically to western and central eastern Europe as well as to Latin and North America (Czudnowski 1982, 1983; Dogan 1989, 2003; Higley and Gunther 1992; Higley and Dogan 1998; Higley et al. 2002; Williams and Lascher 1993; Yesilada 1999). The empirical evidence at our disposal about the composition of political elites outside the West has improved over the past thirty years but can still be described as patchy. Differences in the nature of the political elite are manifestly large, enormous perhaps, between traditional and "developing" political systems, between dictatorships and democratic polities, including among the many types of "emerging" democratic polities, as well as between military and civilian regimes. Yet, one can only provide some insights into the nature of these elites, not give robust evidence of a truly general character.

This chapter thus begins by examining the forms which political elite theory took from the end of the nineteenth century to the 1960s and 1970s. This theory constitutes the background against which empirical studies were subsequently developed. The chapter then concentrates in its second section on career patterns and looks at forms of recruitment as well as at duration and turnover among the political elite. In this respect, the bulk of the findings are drawn mainly from western experience. The third section examines the role of the political elite. Research often suggests that in some countries, despite apparent divisions, the political elite are socially and ideologically united. In the West at least, matters are appreciably more complex. There is a tension, both within the political elite and between that political elite and what can be loosely described as rather inchoate and often unrealistic expectations coming from below. Therefore, it does not seem that the western political elite is fundamentally united; nor is it true either that it is fundamentally disunited. More realistically, its various elements oscillate between efforts at broad compromises and attempts at implementing sharply contested viewpoints.

1 THE THEORETICAL DEBATES ON POLITICAL ELITES

The classical elite theory is associated with Gaetano Mosca (1939), Vilfredo Pareto (1968), and Robert Michels (1962). Their work developed at the end of the nineteenth century when the authority of the old political elite was threatened by the extension of the voting rights to the masses. Even more importantly, this was the time of increasing socialist ideology. During the period, Mosca, Pareto, and Michels questioned the basis of a democratic development in Europe and offered a "realistic" elite theory in contrast to "radical" Marxism. In their view, every society consists of rulers and ruled. Only the former hold the political power and dominate the masses. According to Mosca, the political power of any society must be in the hands of a small ruling elite, because the masses are usually unqualified to exercise power. Pareto refers to different innate personal qualities leading to oligarchic structures. Michels introduces the idea that every organization consists of a division of labour where some skilled persons are the leaders and others are the followers. That is, all three classical elite theorists agreed that there was an "iron law" of oligarchy. Thus, it was argued that in large organizations it appears inevitable that elites will direct the organization even if the goal was to have the members play an active decision-making role. Furthermore, they agreed that the political elite select their successors from the privileged classes that basically share the same value system. Thus, according to the classical elite theorists, the ruling elite are recruited largely in a self-perpetuating manner from the upper class of the society. Finally, all three elite theorists shared the view that the political elite should be autonomous in exercising power. These basic ideas of the classical elite theorists are thus often described as conservative or anti-democratic (Nye 1977).

In the mid-1950s C. Wright Mills (1956) extended these theories. He portrayed a power elite of the post-war USA that consisted of top-position holders in business, in political administration, and in the military. Members of these groups hold overlapping elite positions or have successively held influential positions in various sectors. According to Mills, members of the American power elite are socially homogeneous: they derive from the upper social strata of the society and for this reason they have common interests and similar value systems. The intense communication and cooperation among the top-position holders in the various sectors produces a power elite with an enormous manipulative impact on the majority of the citizens.

Inspired by these theoretical ideas, Robert Dahl (1961) was the first political scientist who linked the debate about the political power of the elite to questions of political legitimacy and participation. Based on empirical findings deducted from a local elite study in the City of New Haven, Dahl concluded that the political elite are divided into leaders and sub-leaders. The latter are highly specialized experts who organize the daily business of politics. Furthermore, their socio-demographic background is closer to the average citizens than that of the leaders. For these reasons the sub-leaders reduce the distance between the political elite and the masses and legitimize the democratic structures of a political system. Dahl also argued that the recruitment into the caste of top leaders was not limited to aristocrats, but open to a wider group of citizens. All persons with specific individual resources such as income, prestige, education, and occupation may in principle belong to the political elite. Thus, the political elite in modern democracies consist of distinct groups of individuals with varying socio-demographic backgrounds and occupational positions. Most of these individuals are highly specialized and politically influential in single policy sectors. Perhaps the key finding of Dahl, however, was that his evidence showed that no elite group had a dominant impact on all political issues. Thus Dahl's "revision" of what could be described as the "classical" elite theories gave impulse to a more detailed examination of the elites and indeed opened the way to the kind of empirical studies which Putnam also advocated.

2 THE NATURE OF THE POLITICAL ELITE IN THE CONTEMPORARY WORLD

Let us now turn to what empirical studies tell us about the characteristics of the political elite in the contemporary world. Although we will concentrate on findings from western countries, we can at least point out to similarities and differences on the basis of broad distinctions among traditional political systems, authoritarian systems of the more "modern" and of the more "traditional" types, and emerging democracies, these categorizations being no more than an indicative nomenclature.

The characteristics of the political elite vary markedly from one of these types of political systems to another. On the one hand, there are *two elements*, which all political elites share. First, the social composition of political elites does not reproduce even in broad terms the social structure of the citizenry. In many cases, that composition bears almost no relationship with the way the nation is structured. Second, leaders are distinct from and more powerful than the bulk of the political elite.

Meanwhile, there are *four ways* in which political elites differ profoundly from each other. These are, first, whether the political elite of a country is distinguishable or not from the social and economic elite of that country, second, the extent to which the elite is internally differentiated into lower and uppermost echelons, third, the nature of mechanisms by which individuals are recruited in the political elite and, fourth, the patterns of duration and turnover of members who belong to the political elite.

The following sections examine the shared characteristics of elites, and then the characteristics that differentiate elites.

2.1 Similarities: The Social Composition of the Political Elite

The social composition of the political elite is always different from the social structure of a country. The political elite are not only much smaller than the citizenry in terms of numbers: in no political system is it a microcosm of the nation. This is true of traditional systems, where members of the political elite are almost exclusively drawn from among the "upper classes" (Eulau and Czudnowski 1976). This is also true of dictatorships, whether "modern" or not, where the political elite is composed of those segments of the society from which supporters, indeed strong supporters, of the regime are typically to be found, for instance from the military or from a party created by the regime. This is even true of democracies, including long-established western democracies. In parliaments, for instance, the working class (even where trade unions are strong) or the peasantry, as well as women, are typically underrepresented, often grossly underrepresented. Putnam (1976, 37) refers in this context to the "law of increasing disproportion:" as the level of elite status increases, the bias in the social characteristics among the elite also increases.

There have been changes, admittedly, in the social composition of western European parliaments in the course of the last two centuries. There has been a marked decline in the number of upper-class parliamentarians, but this has not led to a corresponding increase of the representation of all social groups, as some, especially on the left, wanted to achieve. Instead there developed a preponderance of lawyers, teachers, or civil servants, indeed increasingly professional politicians, and to a lesser extent, businessmen (Best and Cotta 2000, 499–501). As a matter of fact, although moves towards a more accurate "social representation" occurred to an extent with the emergence of socialist parties in the twentieth century, a decline in the working-class composition of parliaments subsequently took place in western European parties of the left. There was no such move in the United States where the traditional two parties continued to prevail. Only the increased representation of women in the last years of the twentieth century can be said to have led to a fairer social composition of western parliaments (Lovenduski and Norris 1993; Norris and Lovenduski 1995; Kittilson 2006).

2.2 Similarities: The Power of the Leaders

The small number of traditional political systems are still dominated by hereditary monarchs, while more "modern" authoritarian systems are typically ruled by dictators. In both cases, the role of leaders is ostensibly overwhelming. Indeed the whole regime, especially in the case of dictatorships, largely depends on the leader—with the corollary that the political elite is ultimately dependent on the leader as well, when it has not been wholly created by the leader (Hermassi 1972; Sadri 1997).

The power of leaders in dictatorships is based on a combination of characteristics, and the combination changes over time in many cases. One element which generally exists is fear: dictatorships typically begin by rounding up opponents or forcing them into exile, while various freedoms, such as the freedom of the press and the freedom of demonstration, are abolished or severely curtailed. Fear is combined, however, in many cases with a variety of forms of support. This support ranges from admiration for what the leader may have previously achieved, for instance in liberating the country from occupying forces or from its colonial status, to the recognition by a segment of the population that the new regime is bringing about social and economic arrangements which that section of the population prefers.

Yet democratic leaders are also typically very powerful in many systems, including western systems, whatever may have been originally thought by those who put forward the concept of representative government. Indeed, the pessimistic views of many early twentieth-century observers, such as Michels, were partly due (or were claimed to be due) to the fact that leadership was regarded as preponderant, including in socialist parties. The nature of the institutions accounts in part for this preponderance. In the case of the presidential systems, researchers have argued that the long history of failures of presidentialism in Latin America could be attributed to the power that constitutions gave to presidents. The same holds true in the case of post-communist Russia, where the communist legacy as well as the presidential power led to the rise of a new powerful political elite (Klingemann, Stoess, Weßels 1991; Sinyavsky 1997; Steen and Gelman 2003).Yet strong leadership is found in parliamentary systems as well. Those regimes with weak leadership, such as that of France up to 1958, and which were unable to meet the challenges that they faced, have tended to be replaced by authoritarian systems or have introduced stronger forms of leadership. As a result, while the political elite in western countries does not entirely depend on the leaders of these countries, as they do in traditional systems or in more "modern" dictatorships, democratic leaders can at least shape in many ways the composition of the political elite. These western elites often induce their members to follow policies which these leaders together with perhaps a small entourage have put forward.

2.3 Differences: The Distinction between the Political Elite and the Rest of the Elite

Many elite theorists did not distinguish the political elite from the socioeconomic elite. In non-democratic systems, the political elite are indeed undistinguishable from the rest of the elite, but in one of two entirely different ways. First, in traditional systems there is no political elite as such because the "pyramidal" social structure inherited from the past constitutes the backbone of political life. This is the case in some of the traditional monarchies which remain in the contemporary world, for instance Saudi Arabia or "emirates" in the Arabian peninsula (Perthes 2004). In these nations, there are no political institutions as such, merely a monarch who rules. Second, where traditional systems become unable to meet demands for change arising in some quarters of the society, these systems tend to be replaced. This often occurs through brutal revolutions, by dictatorships based on the military (not a "political institution" in the strict sense of the word) or on an entirely newly created single party arrangement (or a combination of both). There are many examples of such a development in the contemporary world, Libya being one of the most clear-cut cases. Especially where a single party is created, a new elite attempts to impose, as in the case of communist or of some other "progressive" regimes, not just a different form of politics but a different social and economic structure. The political elite become so preponderant that it seems to encompass the whole of the elite. Thus, in this case, too, political and social and economic elites remain undistinguishable (Taras 1989).

This is not the case in western democracies and indeed to a large extent in "emerging" or "less consolidated" democracies (Best and Becker 1997; Eyal, Szelenyi, and Townsley 1998; Higley and Lengyel 2000; Shlapentokh et al. 1999). A democracy cannot be set up unless political institutions, such as a parliament and a pluralistic system of parties, are set up. Meanwhile, the pre-existing social structure is maintained or at most modified only gradually. Therefore, those who operate the new political institutions have at least to "coexist" with those who are socially or economically powerful, even if numerous clashes occur. Gradually, the political institutions acquire greater strength if the democratic system is successfully maintained: a kind of *modus vivendi* emerges. A political elite, distinct from the social and economic elites, has come to be in existence (Borchert and Zeiss 2003).

2.4 Differences: The Internal Differentiation of the Political Elite

In political systems where the political elite are created *de novo* around a single political party, the political elite are usually united. In communist systems, for instance, both in eastern Europe and in the former Soviet Union as well in those Asian countries where communism continues to prevail, China and Vietnam, for instance, the party is in control and the leadership of that party effectively appoints the members of the parliament, the members of the government and holders of key positions at regional or local level (Steen 1997, 2003; Zang 2003). This is also the case in other types of single-party systems or in "non-party" military regimes, for instance in Africa and the Middle East. The new elite hopes in this way to transform the society (Oyediran 1979; Daloz 2002; Kerstiens 1966).

In the case of democratic systems or even in "emerging democracies" the political elite is institutionally divided both "horizontally" and "vertically." The existence of a pluralistic party system inevitably leads to a "horizontal" development of a number of segments of the political elite, which are autonomous from each other. A "vertical" differentiation also occurs between at least three of these segments, the parties, and especially the party "elites," the members of the legislature (parliament or congress) and the governments. This differentiation occurs even though there are naturally links between parties, legislature, and governments. As a matter of fact, there are subdivisions of these three sets of institutions: the parties between the centre and the regional and local bodies, the legislatures between important committee members and the rank-and-file, and governments between top ministers or secretaries and junior ministers or assistant secretaries (Blondel and Müller-Rommel 1993).

The differentiation in the career background of members of legislatures and members of governments can be particularly sharp, especially in presidential systems. This is not so in most parliamentary systems, and in particular in Europe, as members of the government tend to be drawn from among members of parliament. Yet this is not universally the case even in these systems. In some western European countries, France, Austria, the Netherlands, for instance, about a quarter of members of governments are drawn directly from the civil service or from business (Blondel and Thiebault 1991). The strong distinction between legislature and executive results in the fact that most important public decisions are initiated by that executive. The parliament or the congress tends to be at the receiving end of these proposals, even if the views of members of parliaments or congresses have to be discussed and taken into account. Thus, in institutional terms, a vertical division exists between the lower and upper echelons of the political elite in democratic systems, a distinction which does not really exist in dictatorships where leadership commands and the others are only there to obey.

2.5 Differences: Patterns of Recruitment to the Political Elite

In democratic political systems, there is always some leeway and in some cases even full autonomy in the recruitment of the political elite (Eulau and Czudnowski 1976). It is rare for one to be able to accede to the top without having gone at least for a period through a number of steps in the "cursus honorum:" such a progression is normal in most walks of life. In addition, in democratic systems, including emerging democracies, the power to decide on the selection of members of the political elite may be devolved at levels below, perhaps substantially below, the centre of power, while this is typically not the case in authoritarian systems (Laurentiu 2004).

The first step in the recruitment process in democracies is at the party level. Parties select their "elites" typically by means of elections, admittedly often not strongly contested; parties also select candidates for local governments, regional or state governments and national legislatures, though in a few cases, and above all in the United States, the membership at large is involved in that selection by means of the primaries (Hibbing 1991). Elsewhere, the nomination of party candidates to the legislative elections is appreciably less open. Where the electoral districts are small, the nomination process at least takes place in the local committees of the parties. National party leaders interfere to an extent in these nomination processes. This is, however, sometimes done to stop the nomination of candidates whose views do not coincide with those put forward by the party nationally. There are other reasons for such interference. Yet, from the end of the twentieth century in particular, many western European parties have made efforts to nominate a substantial proportion of women among the candidates (Vianello and Moore 2000; Kittilson 2006). Since there were difficulties in ensuring that a substantial number of women should put themselves forward as candidates, many established democracies have recently introduced a system of "quotas" stipulating that there should be at least a given proportion of women candidates (Carroll 2003; Norris 1997).

Party selection committees can be expected to be somewhat biased in their search for the "best" possible candidates to represent the party at the elections. These biases may well account in part for the middle-class composition of members of legislatures. However, the recruitment of candidates is also dependent on the "supply" of candidates. Where the chances of success at the election are low, generally or in a particular district, the "supply" is likely to be low.

Recruitment to the government is appreciably less open. In some parliamentary systems, an indirect influence of the rank-and-file members of parliament can find its way to the top if, the executive of the opposition parliamentary party is elected by the parliamentarians. When the party subsequently comes to power, some members of that executive may become ministers. In general, however, ministers are chosen by the leader of the party or at most by the leaders of the parties belonging to the government coalition (Pennings 2000; Tavares, Costa Pinto, and Bermeo 2003). In presidential systems, especially in the United States, as this is less the case in many Latin American presidential governments, the president is almost entirely free to select the various secretaries and assistant secretaries who will be in the government. Patterns of recruitment to the political elite become more "elitist" as one moves up towards the national leadership (Blondel 1985).

2.6 Difference: Patterns of Duration and Turnover

Perhaps the most striking features of democratic political elites are the rapidity of the turnover and the shortness of the career. In contrast, there is a much slower turnover of political personnel in traditional regimes and in many dictatorships. In democratic systems, the turnover of elites tends to be low at what might be regarded as the "periphery" of the political elite, for instance in some of the party positions (as Michels had noted with respect to socialist parties in their early development). Meanwhile, members of legislatures, whether parliaments or congresses, remain in their seats, on average, for about a decade and a half. Elites exit from office not just because they are not re-elected, but also because, especially in the United States, they are not re-selected as candidates. Or, sometimes candidates withdraw because the excitement or rewards that the job provides do not match the expectations that the members may have originally had. Thus the parliamentary or congressional elites are renewed entirely, on average, twice in each generation.

Yet this tenure is long when compared to the tenure of members of governments of democratic systems. On average, ministers and secretaries in western Europe are in office for three to four years, with a substantial minority being in office for shorter periods (Blondel and Thiebault 1991). The picture is different in post-communist central eastern Europe: in these countries the duration of ministers in office is only two years on average (Blondel, Müller-Rommel, and Malova 2006). Admittedly, many of these government members will have been junior ministers or assistant secretaries for periods of about the same length. Yet, even if both these periods are added and indeed even if the average duration of tenure in the legislature (in parliamentary systems) is taken into account, one is rarely a member of the political elite for life in democratic systems. Only a few "stars" can be regarded as having made their whole career in politics. The former foreign minister of Germany, Hans Dietrich Genscher, is, for instance, a case in point. This may be regarded as a positive characteristic from the point of view of the "circulation of elites." Thus, this feature of democracies can be regarded as providing further evidence of the superiority of democratic systems over all others. In contrast, a short career at the top implies that many members of democratic governments do not have the time to play a truly significant part in the development and implementation of policies. This may suggest, as has often been claimed, that a rapid turnover of the political elite entails that governments count rather little in comparison with permanent bureaucracies (Dogan 1989).

3 THE ROLE OF THE POLITICAL ELITE

The role of the political elite is particularly difficult to assess outside the West, as the absence of genuine empirical studies makes it very difficult to distinguish between claims and reality. For instance, the political elite cannot be truly separated from the rest of the elite in traditional regimes, such as traditional monarchies, many of which are in the Middle East. This makes it meaningless to assess the role of the political elite. But, even if we consider the role of the elite in general in these political systems, it is difficult to determine precisely how and to what extent the elite does affect the society. Customs are very strong in these regimes and this strength renders change almost impossible to achieve. The members of the elite usually do not want to introduce change on a substantial scale. As a result, only very long and very thorough inquiries could make it possible to conclude whether the elite has a truly significant part to play in the way a particular regime is developing. Such inquiries do not exist, both for these reasons and because access is typically difficult to obtain.

The same conclusion has to be drawn with respect to "modern" dictatorships, whether these are based on a single party, on the military, or on both. Here, too, the distinction between the political elite and the social and economic elite is impossible to draw, given that the members of the new elite are anxious to change society and that they use the political instruments at their disposal to attempt to do so. How far these changes are achieved, however, is more problematic. In most cases, the old elite are eliminated. It is true, as was the case in European communist states, that the institutions are profoundly reshaped and the way politics is conducted becomes consequently different. Whether a change of mentalities is obtained as a result is markedly less clear. In contrast, as seems to be shown by way in which, once the regime has collapsed, political life takes once more a more "normal" turn (Rose and Mishler 1994; Colton and Tucker 1995).

Therefore, we concentrate on democratic political systems and particularly western systems in order to answer to the question of the role of the political elite. Yet, even in the context of these societies, realistic conclusions are difficult to draw, partly because empirical studies devoted to this matter are still rather rare and partly because, as Putnam stated, generalizations have too often been made on the basis of theories only. We first need to examine the empirical validity of the claims made by those theories that assert that the role of the political elite is dominant, even in democratic societies. Second, we need to see to what extent one can delineate the role of the political elite in shaping the characteristics of democratic societies.

3.1 The Political Elite: United and Dominant?

Classical theories assert the dominant character of the political elite is that the divisions within democratic political elite are illusory because, when it comes to "fundamental" problems, the social and ideological unity of that elite re-emerges and frustrates efforts to radically change the character of the society. As was pointed out above, this stand was taken in a variety of different ways and especially under the labels of the "ruling class," of the "power elite," and of the "establishment."

The view that the political elite in western democracies are "fully" united is, however, unrealistic. If the people in western democracies do not support "truly" radical policies, it is not surprising that only few members of the political elite should support these policies. Meanwhile, the members of that elite are divided in many ways, even if they do not constitute a mirror image of the population in terms of their social composition. Their ideological standpoints are far from being as close to each other as the supporters of the "radical" theories suggest, even if the divisions which exist are "merely" between conservatism and reform. Their attitudes to specific policies are also frequently profoundly different and these disagreements are also expressed in very strong terms, whether in parliament or elsewhere. It is therefore simply not true that the political elite is "fundamentally" united in western democracies: what is in question is how "disunited" that elite happens to be and how far it is more disunited in some countries than in others or at some points in time than at others.

3.2 Patterns of Conflict and Consensus within the Political Elite

In some countries or at some occasions, members of the political elite tend to come to agree about adopting a common stance over key policies. More commonly, "consensual politics" has characterized a number of western European countries with respect to social or economic policies; other countries typically practiced "confrontational politics." Moreover, in societies with strongly identifiable "pillars," such as the Netherlands or Belgium, the idea often prevails that the parties representing these pillars should either govern together or at least be permanently associated in some of the key social policies affecting the country (Lijphart 1968, 1999).

Such developments may provide a strong argument in favor of the view that the political elites are "fundamentally united." Yet not only are these developments supported by the populations concerned, but they are also regarded by some scholars, and in particular by Lijphart, as a higher form of democracy than the forms practiced by the countries in which the political elite is sharply divided between government and opposition. Democracy is regarded by many as meaning above all broadly-based participation rather than perpetual conflict. Thus, the kinds of arrangements at the levels of "peak" interest groups, parties, and national executives seem to provide better mechanisms for lower social strata participation than confrontational systems in which only a part of the population supports governmental policies.

The most powerful criticism that can be levelled against the "consensual system" is that it enables the members of the elite to enjoy a more "cosy" life, somewhat sheltered from electoral fluctuations. The key parties may act together in ways that are regarded by some as being of the nature of a "cartel" (Katz and Mair 1995).

Thus the political elite may or may not be ideologically united in western democracies. But the unity or disunity of the political elite reflects the extent to which that elite develops policies that are at least acceptable to the mass of the population. This does not mean that the relationship between the political elite and the mass of the population is always easy or that the people play always or even often a significant part in the policy directions taken by the political elite (see the section on mass–elite representation below). This only means that in western democracies the relationships within the political elite and between the political elite and the population are more complex and more subtle than the theorists had suggested (Strom, Müller, and Bergman 2003). This also means that there is a great need for more empirical studies which would make it possible to determine with precision what are the realistic limits of the divisions within the political elite and to what extent and in what circumstances a united political elite is at unison with the broad mass of the people.

4 CONCLUSION

The concept of the political elite developed gradually out of the broader concept of the elite which sociologists came to use, especially in the later nineteenth century, to attempt to summarize the nature of the link between the rulers and the ruled. The concept of elite was perhaps easily applicable to those countries in which the social structure was relatively stable or where changes brought about by a revolution tended to be imposed from above. Its validity came to be markedly more dubious in the context of the politically complex societies which democracies, and especially western democracies, have become. This is probably why theories about the character and role of the elite have been more numerous up to the middle of the twentieth century than afterwards.

It does not follow that the concept of the political elite should be discarded, for instance in favour of purely institutional definitions. The concept of the political elite has a twofold advantage. On the one hand, it induces scholars to reflect upon the links between the members of the different political institutions which play a part in shaping the nature of political decision making. On the other hand, the concept also forces scholars to consider the relationships between the political elite and the social and economic elite. Yet it does remain the case that the concept of elite is necessarily relatively imprecise and that it minimizes to a substantial extent the levels which exist among those who belong to it and indeed the clashes that occur among elites. The use of the concept of political elite can therefore help markedly our understanding of political life, but on condition that it be treated, not as a rigid notion which is uniformly applicable, but as a flexible tool which takes into account the immense complexities of the power relationships between human beings.

REFERENCES

BEST, H., and BECKER, U. eds. 1997. *Elites in Transition: Elite Research in Central Eastern Europe.* Opladen: Leske & Budrich.
—— and COTTA, M. eds. 2000. *Parliamentary Representatives in Europe 1848–2000.* Oxford: Oxford University Press.

BLONDEL, J. 1973. *Comparative Legislatures.* Englewood Cliffs, NJ: Prentice Hall.

—— 1985. *Government Ministers in the Contemporary World.* London: Sage.

—— and MÜLLER-ROMMEL, F. eds. 1993. *Governing Together.* London: Macmillan.

—— —— and MALOVA, D. 2007. *Governing New European Democracies.* London: Macmillan/Palgrave.

—— and THIEBAULT, J. L. eds. 1991. *The Profession of Government Minister in Western Europe.* London: Macmillan.

BORCHERT, J., and ZEISS, J. eds. 2003, *The Political Class in Advanced Industrial Democracies.* Oxford: Oxford University Press.

CARROLL, S. ed. 2003. *Women in American Politics.* Oxford: Oxford University Press.

CAMP, R. A. 1995. *Political Recruitment across Two Centuries: Mexico 1884–1991.* Austin: University of Texas Press.

COLTON, T., and TUCKER, R. eds. 1995. *Patterns in Post-Soviet Leadership.* Boulder, Colo.: Westview Press.

CZUDNOWSKI, M. ed. 1982. *Does Who Governs Matter? Elite Circulation in Contemporary Societies.* DeKalb: Northern Illinios University Press.

—— ed. 1983. *Political Elites and Social Change.* DeKalb: Northern Illinios University Press.

DAHL, R. 1961. *Who Governs?* New Haven: Yale University Press.

DALOZ, J. P. 2002. *Élites et representations politiques.* Pressac: Presses universitaires de Bourdeaux.

DOGAN, M. ed. 1989. *Pathways to Power.* Boulder, Colo.: Westview Press.

—— ed. 2003. *Elite Configuration at the Apex of Power.* Leiden: Brill Press.

EULAU, H., and CZUDNOWSKI, M. eds. 1976. *Elite Recruitment in Democratic Polities.* London: SAGE.

EYAL, G., SZELENYI, I., and TOWNSLEY, E. 1998. *Making Capitalism without Capitalists: Class Formation and Elite Struggles in Post-Communist Central Europe.* London: Verso Publications.

FERNANDES, J. A. 1970. *The Political Elite in Argentina.* New York: New York University Press.

HERMASSI, E. 1972. *Leadership and National Development in Africa: A Comparative Study.* Berkeley: University of California Press.

HIBBING, J. R. 1991. *Congressional Careers: Conteurs of Life in the U.S. House of Representatives.* Chapel Hill: University of North Carolina Press.

HIGLEY, J., and DOGAN, M. eds. 1998. *Elites, Crisis, and the Origins of Regimes.* Oxford: Oxford University Press.

—— and GUNTHER, R. eds. 1992. *Elites and Democratic Consolidation in Latin America and Southern Europe.* Cambridge: Cambridge University Press.

—— and LENGYEL, G. eds. 2000. *Elites after State Socialism.* Lanham, Md.: Rowman & Littlefield.

—— et al. eds. 2002. *Postcommunist Elites and Democracy in Eastern Europe.* London: Macmillan/Palgrave.

KATZ, R., and MAIR, P. 1995. Changing models of party organization and party democracy: the emergence of the cartel party. *Party Politics* 1: 5–29.

KERSTIENS, T. 1966. *The New Elite in Asia and Africa.* New York: Praeger Press.

KITTILSON, M. 2006. *Challenging Parties, Changing Parliaments: Women and Elected Office in Contemporary Western Europe.* Columbus, Oh.: Ohio State University Press.

KLINGEMANN, H., STOESS, R., and WESSELS, B. eds. 1991. *Politische Klasse und politische Intitutionen.* Opladen: Westdeutscher Verlag.

KLUGMAN, J. 1989. *The New Soviet Elite.* New York: Praeger Press.

LAURENTIU, S. 2004. *Patterns of Elite Recruitment in Post-Socialist Romania.* Bukarest: Editura Ziua.

LIJPHART, A. 1968. *The Politics of Accomodation*. Berkeley: University of California Press.

—— 1999. *Patterns of Democracy*. New Haven, Conn.: Yale University Press.

LOVENDUSKI, J., and NORRIS, P. 1993. *Gender and Party Politics*. London: SAGE.

MICHELS, R. 1962. *Political Parties*. New York: Free Press.

MILLS, C. W. 1956. *The Power Elite*. Oxford: Oxford University Press.

MOSCA, G. 1939. *The Ruling Class*. New York: McGraw-Hill.

NORRIS, P. ed. 1997. *Passages to Power: Legislative Recruitment in Advanced Democracies*. Cambridge: Cambridge University Press.

—— and LOVENDUSKI, J. 1995. *Political Recruitment: Gender, Race and Class in British Parliaments*. Cambridge: Cambridge University Press.

NYE, R. A. 1977. *The Anti-Democratic Sources of Elite Theory: Pareto, Mosca, Michels*. London: Sage.

OYEDIRAN, O. 1979. *Nigerian Government and Politics under Military Rule*. London: Macmillan.

PARETO, V. 1968. *The Rise and the Fall of the Elites*. Totowa: Bedminster.

PENNINGS, P. 2000. Consequences of ministerial recruitment for the functioning of cabinets in western Europe. *Acta Politica*, 1: 86–103.

PERTHES, V. ed. 2004. *Arab Elites*. London: Lynne Riemer.

PUTNAM, R. D. 1976. *The Comparative Study of Political Elites*. Englewood Cliffs, NJ: Prentice Hall.

ROSE, R., and MISHLER, W. 1994. *Representation and Effective Leadership in Post-Communist Political Systems*. Glasgow: University of Strathclyde Press.

SADRI, H. A. 1997. *Revolutionary States, Leaders, and Foreign Relations: A Comparative Study of China, Cuba, and Iran*. New York: Praeger Press.

SHLAPENTOKH, V. et al. eds. 1999. *The New Elite in Post-Communist Eastern Europe*. College Station, Tex.: Texas A&M University Press.

SINYAVSKY, A. 1997. *The Russian Intelligensia*. New York: Columbia University Press.

STEEN, A. 1997. *Between Past and Future: Elites, Democracy and the State in Post-Communist Countries. A Comparison of Estonia, Latvia and Lithuania*. Aldershot; Ashgate Press.

—— 2003. *Elites in the Politics of the New Russia*. London: Routledge.

—— and GELMAN, V. eds. 2003. *Elites and Democratic Development in Russia*. London: Routledge.

STROM, K., MÜLLER, W., and BERGMAN, T. eds. 2003. *Delegation and Accountability in Parliamentary Democracies*. Oxford: Oxford University Press.

TARAS, R. ed. 1989. *Leadership Change in Communist States*. Boston: Unwin Hyman Press.

TAVARES DE ALMEIDA, P., COSTA PINTO, A., and BERMEO, N. eds. 2003. *Who Governs Southern Europe. Regime Change and Ministerial Recruitment 1850–2000*. London: Frank Cass.

VIANELLO, M., and MOORE, G. eds. 2000. *Gendering Elites: Economic and Political Leadership in 27 Industrialised Societies*. London: Macmillan.

WILLIAMS, S., and LASCHER, E. L. eds. 1993. *Ambition and Beyond: Career Paths of American Politicians*. Berkeley: University of California Press.

YESILEDA, B. A. ed. 1999. *Comparative Political Parties and Party Elites*. Ann Arbor: University of Michigan Press.

ZANG, X. 2003. *Elite Dualism and Leadership Selection in China*. London: Routledge.

CHAPTER 45

POLITICAL REPRESENTATION AND DEMOCRACY

BERNHARD WEßELS

POLITICAL representation is at the heart of liberal democracies. Whereas democracy is the idea of popular rule or effective fate control of the people, representation is the mean to realize the democratic idea of giving people a voice in large states. Representation is the "process in which one individual or groups (the representative) act on behalf of other individuals or groups (the represented) in making or influencing authoritative decisions, policies, or laws of a polity" (Thompson 2001, 11696). Representation may occur in many circumstances. Representation in combination with democracy implies parliamentary representation and representation of the people by governments. The crucial question is how representation comes about. How can democracy guarantee that the popular will steers authoritative political action? There is no simple answer to the question how policy preferences of represented have any influence upon policies enacted by representatives. However, from a normative point of view, the relationship between citizens' interests and policy decisions of representatives should be a causal one. Responsiveness is one of the features democracy stands for (Etzioni 1968; Eulau and Karps 1977). Some scholars even regard it as a defining element of democracy. John D. May, for example, states that democracy means responsive rule (May 1978, 1).

In democracies, the major link, which establishes a "causal" relationship between the wishes of the people and acts of governance, are elections. Bingham Powell's book title *Elections as Instruments of Democracy* is programmatic in this regard (Powell 2000). Public opinion as an important driver of public policy change has been emphasized in earlier chapters (Wlezien and Soroka, and McIver in this volume).

Here, the mechanisms that shape the degree and character of political representation will be explored somewhat more in detail. The question is which institutional provisions allow democracy as a process of delegation and accountability to be effective and representatives to act in accordance with the wishes of the people, instead of substituting elites' private desires for promised public policy goals (Laver 1997).

This chapter argues that the quality and character of policy representation varies, depending on the institutional settings of democracies, namely the electoral system and candidate selection, that is, institutions provide incentives or disincentives for representatives to be responsive. The first two sections serve to explore the theoretical backbone of political representation. The remaining sections review the literature with regard to the impact of institutions on representatives, their relation with voters, and policy representation.

1 Norms and Models of Political Representation

The basic idea of representative democracy comprises a more or less simple chain of delegation, or "authorized representation" as Bingham Powell prefers to term it (Powell 2000, 10 ff.). Citizens' preferences translate into voting behavior, the latter into election outcomes, which in turn determine policy making. However, there are obvious differences between parliamentary and presidential systems. In parliamentary democracy, the chain of delegation runs from voters to elected representatives, that is, parliamentarians; from legislators to the executive branch; and from there to the heads of executive departments. Parliamentary democracy is based on the supremacy of parliament. In terms of principal-agent theory, accountability is simple, following the singularity principle, that is, "single or non-competing agents for each principal; a single principal for each agent." Parliament is accountable to voters, government accountable to the parliament. In contrast, in presidential systems, voters are the principal for the legislature and the president. Heads of executive departments may face more than one principal (Strøm 2000, 268–70). As proposed by Dieter Fuchs, political representation is a sequence of action products. Citizens have demands, which parties turn into political issues. Political parties bundle demands into political programs. These programs steer the behavior and the decisions of their representatives in parliament and government. Governments implement decisions via their administrations, policies are accepted by citizens (or not), affect outcomes, which in turn might gear new demands (Fuchs 1993, 23–35). Common to any perspective on political representation is that it is regarded as a multi-level process; as a process, because it has a time sequence, as a multi-level phenomenon, because not any instance is directly accountable to the sovereign, the people. However, whether it is parliamentary or presidential democracy, the principal of possible principals are the people, who delegate or authorize representation to the directly elected.

The way in which this link between representatives, normally members of parliament, and represented is conceptualized, differs. Concepts of representation seem to relate to different visions of democracy, that is, "Majority Control vision" and the "Proportionate Influence vision" (Huber and Powell 1994). The basic distinction between these two visions of democracy is whether government should be responsive to the majority of people or to as many people as possible (Lijphart 1984), thus the distinction between majoritarian Westminster democracy and proportional (consensus) democracy. In general, the majoritarian vision of democracy goes along with an election rule entailing single-member districts, the proportional vision with multi-member districts (Powell 2000). The majoritarian vision produces normally a small party system, and a one-party dominance in parliament and government. The proportional vision produces multi-party systems and coalition governments. From these features result different motivations and patterns of representation, more personalized in the majoritarian, more partisan in the proportional vision, more regionalized in the first, and more collectively oriented in the latter. Furthermore, there is leeway for different types of representation within a vision of democracy (see the contribution of Thomassen in this volume for different values of democracy).

The most influential empirically testable model in comparative research is the famous Miller–Stokes diamond, introduced by the well-known article "Constituency influence in congress," published in 1963 (Miller and Stokes 1963). Applied to a majoritarian system with single-member districts, the diamond model comprises constituency's attitudes, representative's attitudes, their perception of constituency's attitudes, and their roll call behavior. Two ideal types of representation are embedded in this model. The first ideal type is the delegate conception of representation, which means that representatives correctly perceive constituency's attitudes and transform them directly into their roll calls. This is the instructed delegate. The second ideal type demands no imperative relation between constituency's attitudes and roll calls. The representative decides solely on basis of her or his attitudes. By chance (or systematically) these attitudes may be the same or similar to those of the constituency. If congruence between representative and represented results by chance, the ideal type corresponds to what Edmund Burke had in mind in his famous speech to the voters of Bristol—the independent deputy. Thomassen (1991) has criticized these two conceptions for two reasons. First, "pure Burkean role conception of deputies, who think that the will of their constituents should not be decisive for their behavior, can by definition not be an instrument to implement people's will" (Thomassen 1991, 261). Second, the instructed-delegate model seems to assume that representative democracy is only a sorry substitute for real, that is, direct democracy and does not reflect that in modern parliament the task to perform is not to defend local interests against central government but national policy making. Furthermore, both conceptions and thereby the Miller–Stokes model do not take into account the role of political parties which are very important in all democracies and in particular in the European context (Thomassen 1991, 265–6).

However, this is not the only interpretation possible, in particular because Miller and Stokes themselves argue that the congruence between the attitudes of representatives and their constituency may not result from instruction of the deputies by the voters, but from the choice of the voters for a candidate with the respective attitudes (Miller and Stokes 1963, 50). Nevertheless, this conception is dyadic in contrast to models of collective representation like the responsible party model. Accountability rests on the direct relation between constituency's voters and the deputy, who may be punished in the next elections. This view is inspired by the majority control vision of representation, which certainly underlies single member district (SMD) systems such as in Britain and Australia.

Even in some SMD systems, and certainly in proportional systems, accountability is organized differently, and can be best conceptualized in terms of the responsible party model. Thomassen makes this a central point of his critique of the dyadic model of representation (Thomassen 1991) and most empirical representation studies in Europe have applied the approach of collective party representation. This proportional vision of democracy has in fact, though not necessarily constitutionally, implemented a system of accountability in which political parties offer an implicit contract between voters and elected. Voters vote for a program offered by one of the parties, parties commit their MPs to this program, and by this commitment "parties are essential for making the democratic accountability of MPs meaningful" (Müller 2000, 311). In terms of the principal-agent approach: delegation runs from voters to parties, from parties to MPs and government officials, accountability consequently from government officials and MPs to political parties, and from political parties to voters. This is a totally different conception of representation than in the dyadic model, and is more typical of systems such as the Netherlands or Sweden. In addition, Miller and Stokes acknowledge in their classic study of political representation that constituency control is "opposite to the conception of government by responsible *national* parties" (Miller and Stokes 1963, 45). Obviously, these two conceptions of democracy produce different demands for representatives.

The question is what are the driving forces that guarantee responsiveness of representatives to the electorate? Empirical research into political representation has provided empirical and systematic insights to illuminate these mechanisms.

2 INSTITUTIONS AND POLITICAL REPRESENTATION

The way in which responsiveness and accountability work in terms of delegation, namely with regard to the foremost relation between voters and elected stressed in democratic theory, depends on the vision of democracy that is embedded in the political institutions. With regard to the link of voters and representatives, obviously the electoral law is important. Two additional factors influence the link as well: the selection procedures of candidates and the structure of the party system.

Starting from Duverger's law and Rae's seminal work, researchers have studied electoral formula effects on the allocation of seats and the structure of party systems (Duverger 1954; Rae 1967). In recent years, however, researchers have also investigated the effects of the (strategic) behavior of candidates and parties (Cox 1997). Carey and Shugart put the problem in a nutshell: "If a party has more candidates than the number of seats it wins, then the electoral formula must specify a means for determining which candidates take the party's seat" (Carey and Shugart 1995, 417). Electoral formulas distribute the precious commodities, that is, legislative seats among the candidates, and give incentives for candidates, either to rely on their party's reputation or on their personal reputation. If party reputation is all that matters for each politician's electoral prospect, then they will rely on the party. If, however, "electoral prospects depend on winning votes cast for the individual politician instead of, or in addition to, votes cast for the party, then politicians need to evaluate the trade-off between the value of personal and party reputation" (Carey and Shugart 1995, 419). Closed-list PR systems, for example, do not need to trade-off between party's and personal reputation. Single non-transferable vote systems, or SMD plurality systems with open endorsement, on the other hand, provide incentives for candidates to work on their personal reputation as a means for winning elections. Carey and Shugart analyze all the effects of election system variants and show that district magnitude, in combination with the electoral formula, strengthens or loosens the effects: in closed-list systems, the value of personal reputation decreases with magnitude, in all other systems the value increases (Carey and Shugart 1995, 430).

These insights can also be evaluated in terms of delegation and accountability. Electoral laws that provide incentives toward personal voting obviously authorize personal representation and make candidates directly accountable to the voters. The United States is normally considered the archetypical example of this model. In closed-list systems to the contrary, voters authorize party representation and only can make political parties accountable. The intervening variable in this process is candidate selection. This refers to the controls to protect the principal, the voters, *ex ante*. These controls are exercised by the party organization, and (democratic) intra-party selection processes.[1]

Ex-post controls include "police patrol" and "fire alarm" oversight (McCubbins and Schwartz 1984). "Police patrol" refers to direct monitoring and investigation of MPs activities and matters of concern to constituents by the voters themselves. It is costly for the voters and only likely in districts of low magnitude. However, the German case, for example, illustrates that, for the personal vote, this kind of oversight indeed matters (Klingemann and Weßels 2001). "Fire alarm" oversight is exercised by third parties, which could be interest groups and associations, but is normally done by the opposing parties (Mitchell 2000). It includes the monitoring of actions and

---

[1] The contributions in Norris, 1997.

decisions, confrontation with pledges, etc., thus the ordinary means in the interplay between government and opposition.

In general—although not in every case given party regulations for member or even voter primaries—knowing the election law means to know the incentive structure for candidates and elected. The more personal the vote, the less accountable are candidates and elected to their party and the more to their constituencies. This is typically the case in first-pass-the-post electoral systems like in the United States of America, India, Great Britain, and a number of African countries. Closed-list systems, to the contrary, generate full accountability to the party because candidate selection generally depends solely on the selection criteria of the party. Such electoral systems exist in the Scandinavian countries and a number of other democracies in Europe (Czech Republic, Slovakia, the Netherlands, and Spain, for example), but also in Israel, Argentina, and Chile.

The basic hypothesis following from these considerations is that where parties are in full *ex ante* control, it is in the interest of candidates and elected officials to follow the demands of their party. Where this is not the case, and where the fortune of the party depends on the choice possibilities between single candidates, a party is well advised to leave room for individual candidates to gain personal reputation. This includes an incentive for the candidate in case of doubt to defect from or to weaken party reputation by staking out own positions. The first case quite often is an institutionalization of the "Proportionate Influence vision" of representation, the latter of the "Majority Control vision" of democracy. When institutions embedding these different visions of democracy are effective, this should translate into orientations and the behavior of representatives and affect policy representation accordingly.

In representation research, three questions dominate. Whom do legislators want to represent? How do they do it? How representative or responsive are they with regard to voters' views and policy demands? The first two questions relate to the old question of role orientations of MPs and they are strongly inspired by the instructed delegate–independent controversy.

3 WHOM TO REPRESENT: THE FOCUS OF REPRESENTATION

Focus and its counterpart, the style of representation, regard the role orientations of representatives. Role orientations are not merely attitudes, but translations of social expectations into individual norms of behavior. Approaches applying sociological role theory to political representation argue that roles mediate between the deputy as an individual and the deputy as an element of an institution, namely a representative body. "The chief utility of the role-theory model of the legislative actor is that, unlike other models, it pinpoints those aspects of legislators' behavior which make the legislature an institution" (Wahlke et al. 1962, 9).

However, for a long time, research on the sources of legislators' role orientations was fragmented and sometimes contradictory (Jewell 1970, 483). The same was true with regard to the effects of role orientations (Alpert 1979). Kuklinski and Elling even doubted that it would be worthwhile continuing such research (Kuklinski and Elling 1977). Jewell suggested that broadening the comparative scope might help to overcome these shortcomings, because he expected norms of political culture and the structure of the political system to have an impact on legislators' orientations (Jewell 1970). Another reason for the failure of the role orientation approach was seen in the problem that collective party action was inadequately accounted for in research inspired by US traditions (Holmberg 1989; Thomassen 1991). Due to the increasing consideration of the role of political parties in most parliaments, research results clearly show that institutional settings shape the acquisition of legislators' representational roles. Furthermore, roles influence policy representation and thus are an intervening or intermediary element between institutions and individuals.

In many European political systems, the focus of representation is biased towards party. On average across west European countries, party is the dominant focus of representation, followed by nation. Constituency as a focus of representation is on average of minor importance and even more so representation of particular groups (Kielhorn 2001, 86). However, variations across countries are huge and, in some countries, nation dominates over party; in France, constituency dominates other foci. Even in Scandinavia, differences between countries are striking. In Sweden and Norway, for example, around 70 percent of the deputies or more regard party representation as a very important task. In Denmark and Iceland, it is the majority, in Finland a minority.

Differences in the role of parties are presumably related to differences in the political system, either the electoral rule or the nomination procedures. "It appears that the individual-focused electoral system in Finland affects members' view of their party... Danish representatives, who are chosen through an electoral system with a certain individual focus, are only a little bit less party-oriented than their Norwegian and Swedish counterparts, who are strictly chosen by party list... In addition, the comparatively moderate views on party representation held by Icelandic members of parliament can be traced to the nominating system" (Esaiasson 2000, 61–2). Barnes found that in order to secure preference votes candidates in Italy put more emphasis on local political activity than party activist activities (Barnes 1977, 149). In Germany, candidates for districts and regional lists regard different criteria as important for their nomination. For district nomination, the ability to win votes is regarded as most important, for regional list nomination the political position within the party, Porter found, interviewing candidates at both levels (Porter 1995, 84–6; Weßels 1997, 78–81). The same motivations seem to underlie the degree of constituency services of MPs in majoritarian democracies. Findings indicate that in Canada with its first-past-the-post electoral system, constituency service is used to initiate or sustain a political career (Clarke 1978). In Australia, also a majoritarian system, but using an alternative vote (preferential) system, however, marginality has no positive effect on constituency service. The explanation is that partisanship is very strong among voters so that the personal vote does not exceed approximately 3 percent of the total vote.

This gives parties the disciplinary resource of the "threat of 'deselection', the removal as the party candidate in the district" (Studlar and McAllister 1996, 73). Thus, party service plays a more important role in Australia despite the fact that it is a majoritarian system, because there is an incentive for incumbents and possible candidates to show party loyalty if they want to run in the next election.

Even in new democracies where institutions have not had the same time to affect orientations and behavior, the effects of institutional incentives are noticeable. In Hungary, for example, from early after the transformation onwards, we can observe striking effects of the electoral rules. MPs elected by personal vote had a representation focus to represent the electorate or the whole country. MPs elected by list vote, to the contrary, also emphasized party (Ilonszki 1994, 246). Nomination for and placement on party lists in Estonia depends on the quality of party services. In Lithuania, which has a mixed system, to be well known in the district is more important for candidate selection than party service (Ruus 2003, 68, 74).

Incentives to cultivate a personal vote thus are set by nomination procedures, which are strongly affected by electoral laws. On a broader comparative scope, the effects Carey and Shugart attribute to district magnitude are clearly visible (Carey and Shugart 1995, 430–2). Despite their theoretical argument that this is true only in closed-list systems, the general argument of Cox that district magnitude is the most important factor for strategic behavior both for electors and elites because it indicates the degree to which elections are personalized or particized (Cox 1997, 228), holds up across western Europe (Kielhorn 2001, ch. 4.1; Weßels 1999b).

4 How to Represent: The Style of Representation

The "style" dimension of representation, that is, whether a representative's role is defined in terms of a delegate or a trustee, to take the extremes of the continuum, is regarded as relatively useless in representation research. The reason is a simple one: many, though not all constitutions, define members of parliament as independent and responsible only to their own conscience. There are variations, however, but doubtless, the old Burkean controversy does not seem to exist any longer. The German, French, Greek, and Spanish constitutions explicitly demand or guarantee that a representative is not bound by orders and instructions. In addition, some constitutions state that the representative or the parliament represents the nation, the country, or the entire people (in Luxembourg, the Netherlands, and Italy for example). In Sweden, a similar paragraph has been deleted from the Riksdag Act by a revision of the constitution in the early 1970s; but it still remains impossible for parties or voters to recall a mandate (Esaiasson and Holmberg 1996, 50).

Although an imperative mandate is virtually illegal in all representative democracies and thus the independence of members of parliament is guaranteed, in practical terms, in many democracies representatives follow their party. Given the constitutional provisions, most MPs' self-conception is that of an independent representative. However, if confronted with a demand for party discipline or contradicting preferences of different potential principals, MPs often go with the party. Barnes found, that two-thirds of the Italian deputies agreed that a representative should vote as the party asks. In the case of a difference between their own conviction and the party stand, still more than half agreed to vote with the party (Barnes 1977, 129, 132). In Sweden, MPs decide dominantly, that is, 47 percent, in line with the party if their own view or their perception collides with the party's view (Esaiasson and Holmberg 1996, 54). In France, the proportion is roughly 40 percent (Converse and Pierce 1986, 663–71).

Similar patterns can be found in the new democracies in eastern and central Europe, as Linek and Rakunasova have demonstrated for the Czech Republic (Linek and Rakusanova 2004, 113) and Čular for Croatia (Čular 2003). Not only does the party's opinion often count more than the MP's own opinion or voters' opinion, the style of representation is related to the electoral system. In Hungary, for example, a higher proportion of MPs elected by list vote compared to those elected by personal vote think that they are bound by party instructions (Ilonszki 2003).

Even more than their attitudes and reports about their behavior, the actual votes of MPs strikingly point to representation following the responsible party model. Party unity in voting is very high in most established democracies, although it shows some characteristic variations. It is very high in the Nordic countries of Europe, that is Denmark, Iceland, Norway, and Sweden (the Rice-index of party cohesion is in the high nineties). Only Finland is somewhat lower (Jensen 2000, 217–20), which may have the same explanation as the deviation of Finland's MPs with regard to the focus of representation. In Belgium, the UK, and Germany, parties show high unity in voting, too.

The figures seem to be lower in new democracies, for example in the Czech Republic and Russia, where the Rice-index is in the 80s or even 70s. In the case of the Czech Republic, this is attributed to the oversize of the winning majorities which made it cheap for MPs to defect (Linek and Rakusanova 2004, 114–15), in Russia to the weakness of parties (Legutke 2001). Whatsoever, comparing Russia and the United States, both presidential systems, differences vanish. Party unity of the post-communists in Russia in many years of the Duma's legislative term is even higher than for US Democrats and Republicans. This shows that even where party unity is not as strong as in many western countries, institutional effects are noticeable. In Russia, list deputies are significantly more likely to vote with the majority of their faction than SMD deputies (Haspel et al. 1998; Kuklinski and Elling 1977).

These findings give ample evidence for aspects central to political representation. First, institutional structures can be a constraint and facilitator of norms and behavior (Kuklinski and Elling 1977). Obviously, they provide incentives inherent in the career patterns of politicians to make it more likely that politicians think and behave as institutional settings demand. This does not imply an institutional determinism, which would be as poor an explanation as the old sociological determinism. Findings refer to probabilities, not determination. Second, political representation in liberal democracies more often than not is party representation. Accountability works the way researchers of political representation have claimed, namely as responsible party model, and in terms of expected sanctions, as Müller proposed in his principal-agent model of party democracy (Müller 2000). However, where institutional incentives are weaker in this direction, party representation is also weaker. The most interesting point is that the choice between different visions of democracy at the macro-level (a system or an institution like the whole parliament) shows its imprint on attitudes and behavior. This means that, even at the micro-level, where institutional incentives for individual representatives differ within a system, for example with regard to types of mandate, institutional settings have a differentiating impact, steering attitudes and behavior more to the one or the other direction of models of representation.

5 ISSUE CONGRUENCE AND POLICY REPRESENTATION

If institutionalized visions of democracy leave their imprint in role orientations of representatives and representational roles gear behavior, then this should be reflected in policy representation. However, representation is a multi-level process. At the end of the process, legislation and governmental action should be responsive to voters' wishes and demands. To reach this point, however, there is a long way to go and individual acts of representation may fail in the end. To represent and to win a majority in parliament are two different things. This is why studies of issue congruence between representatives and represented claim to study policy representation. Without articulating demands, there would not be a chance to realize policy goals. Articulation of policy goals, however, does not necessarily imply that the proposals will get through (Weßels 1993). The study of issue congruence between elected and electors is at the heart of empirical research into political representation. The starting point was the study "Representation in the United States Congress" by Miller and Stokes in the sixties. Its idea and design quickly spread around the world and similar research programs were started in Europe and South America (Miller 1999).

The original program focused on dyadic correspondence between district opinions and representative's opinions. This perspective, however, did not hold up in Europe, were collective representation by party was supported by research results. Barnes found for Italy a nil relation between district and representative opinion but a considerably strong congruence between a deputy and the supporters of his party (Barnes 1977, 121 f.). Similar patterns have been found in Germany (Farah 1980), Sweden, France (Converse and Pierce 1986, 721–4), and even the US (Esaiasson 1999).

These findings contribute to our research question: Why do institutional structures matter for issue congruence, that is, for policy representation?

Given the limited comparative scope of representation analyses, research into the impact of institutional differences on policy representation almost did not exist at all. Dalton (Dalton 1985) was probably one of the first, if not the first, who comparatively studied issue congruence explicitly dealing with the impact of electoral laws and party organization. He argued both from the perspective of parties as strategic actors, and candidates' dependency on parties. Parties in a plurality system tend to gravitate toward the center of public's opinion distribution, and in proportional systems "more accurately represent voters in numerical and policy terms" in order to avoid vote losses to new parties which may form to fill the gaps left (Dalton 1985, 286 f.). Furthermore, he argued that party structures have an impact on issue congruence: the more centralized the procedures for selecting parliamentary candidates, the higher the congruence between party voters and their representatives. It was not accidental that he investigated these hypotheses with data on the elections to the European Parliament in 1979, this data included mass samples for the nine member countries at that time and a survey of MEP candidates, thus providing a first chance to study policy representation comparatively. Dalton found the party structure hypothesis was supported somewhat more than the electoral system hypothesis (Dalton 1985, 287, 291). Fifteen years later, for the 1994 European elections, the electoral system hypothesis was confirmed again for EP candidates and for elected MEPs (Marsh and Weßels 1997).

Until the mid-1990s, any attempt to study issue congruence at the national level in a comparative perspective had to rely on secondary analysis of existing studies. A group of researchers around Warren Miller started such a project with the explicit goal to find system differences. Relying on ten representation studies from five countries— France (1968), Germany (1988/9), the Netherlands (1971, 1977, 1989), Sweden (1968, 1985, 1988), and the US (1958, 1986/7)—a variety of issues were addressed.[2] Researchers asked: Did the behavior of individuals of mass electorates and the match of preference distributions between electors and elected offer empirical support for the responsible party model; did local representation play a different role in varying systems; and did incentives offered to deputies by majoritarian or proportional systems make a difference for policy representation (Miller et al. 1999)? This research produced mixed or partly contradictory evidence concerning the variation in degree of a responsible party model across systems (Pierce 1999). However, the incentive effects of electoral law came out very clear. Deputies solved the representational trade-off between median and party voter in majoritarian systems by skewing representation in favor of the median, in proportional systems skewing it in favor of the party voters (Weßels 1999a). The rank order of countries with regard to the strength of the trade-off between median voter representation and party voter representation matches the rank-order of countries on the majoritarian-proportional

---

[2] For France see Converse and Pierce (1986); for Germany Herzog, Rebenstorf, and Weßels (1993); for the Netherlands Irwin and Thomassen (1997); for Sweden Esaiasson and Holmberg (1996, 1989); and for the US Herrera, Herrera, and Smith (1992) and Miller and Stokes (1963).

continuum of democracy almost perfectly and is rather stable over time. The two majoritarian systems USA and France rank highest in this trade-off, indicating that issue congruence to the median voter is increased at the expense of lower congruency to party voters. In the Netherlands and Sweden, almost ideal-types of the proportional vision of democracy, distances to party voters are much lower than to the median voter. Germany as mixed system ranks in between (see Figure 45.1). This trade-off in responsiveness to the median and the party voter correlates −0.83 with the disproportionality of the electoral system and 0.91 (Weßels 1999a, 151) with the consensus score of Lijphart and Crepaz (Lijphart and Crepaz 1991). The concept for this score was developed by Lijphart in his book "Democracies" in order to differentiate political systems on the majoritarian-consensual dimension (Lijphart 1984). Other findings for the USA at the district level show that there is no full convergence of district candidates' positions

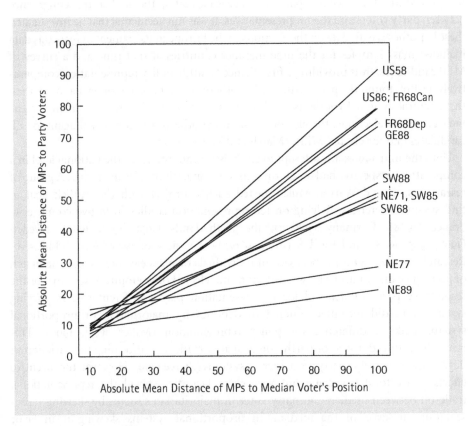

Fig. 45.1 Party- vs. median-voter trade-off in policy representation

Source: Weßels 1999a, 149

The figure represents the regression lines of trade-offs between policy distances of representatives to the median voters and the party voters for a variety of policy issues (mean number of issues around 10; mean number of comparisons 57 per study).

Abbreviations indicate country (FR: France; GE: Germany; NE: The Netherlands; SW: Sweden; US: United States of America), year of the study, and for France whether the sample was candidates or elected representatives.

of the Republican and the Democratic party but that candidates of both parties are the more conservative the more conservative the constituency is (Ansolabehere, Snyder, and Stewart 2001). This finding supports the trade-off hypothesis because it implies that, irrespective of party affiliation, candidate positions move with the median opinion in the constituency. These results indicate that different visions of democracy embedded in the institutional structure had an impact on responsiveness in the expected direction and were very much in line with the findings on representational role orientations.

G. Bingham Powell (Powell 2000) took a different route to investigate representation at the national level comparatively. His aim also was to demonstrate trade-offs in representation induced by different institutional versions of democracy. Using the left–right dimension rather than single issues, he compared citizen orientations from mass surveys with those of legislatures and governments for which positions were independently measured by expert judgments. In analyzing the normative premises of the majority and the proportional model of democracy, Powell found a variety of effects of institutional structures on representative performance (Powell 2000). Of the many relevant findings, two are of particular interest here. The two visions of democracy—majority control and proportionate influence—clearly work distinctively well with regard to left–right congruence, the proportional systems outperforming the majoritarian systems. Nevertheless, measuring the two types of democracy against their own ideals with regard to election process and responsiveness to elections, both perform equally well. Powell's (2000) study shows that elections in majoritarian systems produce easily identifiable (one-party) government majority, provide the opposition with little influence on policy bargaining and government policies, resulting in a clear mandate and accountability. To the contrary, in countries with the proportional constitutional design, coalition governments prevail, the opposition has a proportional influence on policy bargaining and government policies, and representation in the legislature is more proportional. In other words, different types of democracy realize their different goals by different institutions equally well (Powell 2000, 237–46).

Whether the impact of institutions on policy representation also works in new democracies, is still an open question. On the one hand, one might argue that adaptation to the effects of institutions needs time in terms of learning and experience. On the other hand, research on role orientations of representatives shows that the incentives set by institutions are well perceived. Empirical research is rare. However, Kitschelt et al. (Kitschelt et al. 1999) showed that issue congruence between voters and elites in Bulgaria, the Czech Republic, Hungary, and Poland is strongly shaped by the character of party competition. The party competition structure leads to different ways of representation. Polarizing trusteeship—Esaiasson and Holmberg would call it "representation from above" (Esaiasson and Holmberg 1996)—occurs in significant dimensions of party competition, mandate relationships in other areas (Kitschelt et al. 1999, ch. 9). Parties and their representatives react strategically to competition structures with regard to issues or issue dimensions. It is thus quite likely that they also react strategically to institutions, which shape the competition like electoral rules. However, at present no empirical evidence is available, neither in favor nor against this hypothesis.

6 Conclusion

Political representation is a multi-level and multifaceted core element of liberal democracy. Without an acceptable degree of responsiveness, the legitimacy of democratic governance would be questioned. This article has tried to draw attention to the question as to what degree political institutions guarantee democratic representation. This is not a trivial question because representative institutions cannot act without individuals giving life to them. Thus, the more precise question is whether institutions provide incentives for individual actors like legislators or collective actors like parties and their individual representatives to act according to the expectations with regard to representation.

The research in this area implies that institutions indeed increase the chances that representatives are acting as they ought to do. Institutional incentives provide two interrelated aspects relevant for political representation: representational role orientations and issue congruence. Role orientations with regard to the focus, that is, whom to represent, and the style of representation (trustee-delegate /continuum), can be seen as the basis of representatives' action. Both aspects of representational role vary systematically with system characteristics, the electoral system in the first place, and the nomination system in the second place. Furthermore, the degree or character of issue congruence, that is, policy representation, also varies systematically with system differences. Thus, one can conclude that institutions shape action orientations, which results in the respective outcomes, that is, policy representation. The institutional impact points consistently into the expected direction for both aspects, also giving room for variation according to the expectations of different visions of democracy.

It would certainly overstate the results to say institutions make representation work. It would not work without the individual deputies. Nevertheless, as one can say that deputies breathe life into representative institutions, one can conclude from the reported findings that institutions help to make representatives perform as is normatively expected.

References

ALPERT, E. J. 1979. A reconceptualization of representational role theory. *Legislative Studies Quarterly*, 4: 587–603.

ANSOLABEHERE, S., SNYDER, J. M., JR., and STEWART, C., III. 2001. Candidate positioning in U.S. House elections. *American Journal of Political Science*, 45: 136–59.

BARNES, S. H. 1977. *Representation in Italy: Institutionalized Tradition and Electoral Choice*. Chicago: University of Chicago Press.

CAREY, J. M., and SHUGART, M. S. 1995. Incentives to cultivate a personal vote: a rank ordering of electoral formulas. *Electoral Studies*, 14: 417–39.

CLARKE, H. D. 1978. Determinants of provincial constituency service behaviour: a multivariate analysis. *Legislative Studies Quarterly*, 3: 601–28.

CONVERSE, P. E., and PIERCE, R. 1986. *Political Representation in France*. Cambridge, Mass.: Belknap Press.

COX, G. W. 1997. *Making Votes Count. Strategic Coordination in the World's Electoral Systems*. Cambridge: Cambridge University Press.

ČULAR, G. 2003. The Croatian parliament 1990–2002: a site for democratic consolidation? Pp. 68–75 in *Representative Elites in Post-Communist Settings*, ed. H. Best and M. Edinger. Jena: SFB 580, Gesellschaftliche Entwicklungen nach dem Systemumbruch.

DALTON, R. J. 1985. Political parties and political representation: party supporters and party elites in nine nations. *Comparative Political Studies*, 18: 267–99.

DUVERGER, M. 1954. *Political Parties: Their Organization and Activity in the Modern State*. New York: John Wiley & Sons.

ESAIASSON, P. 1999. Not all politics is local: the geographical dimension of policy representation. Pp. 110–36 in *Policy Representation in Western Democracies*, ed. W. E. Miller, R. Pierce, J. Thomassen, R. Herrera, S. Holmberg, P. Esaiasson, and B. Weßels. Oxford: Oxford University Press.

—— 2000. How Members of Parliament define their task. Pp. 51–82 in *Beyond Westminster and Congress: The Nordic Experience*, ed. P. Esaiasson and K. Heidar. Columbus, Oh.: Ohio State University Press.

—— and HOLMBERG, S. 1996. *Representation from Above: Members of Parliament and Representative Democracy in Sweden*. Aldershot: Dartmouth.

ETZIONI, A. 1968. *The Active Society*. London: Collier-MacMillan.

EULAU, H., and KARPS, P. D. 1977. The puzzle of representation: specifying components of responsiveness. *Legislative Studies Quarterly*, 2: 233–54.

FARAH, B. G. 1980. *Political Representation in West Germany: The Institution and Maintenance of Mass Elite Linkages*. University of Michigan, Michigan.

FUCHS, D. 1993. A metatheory of the democratic process. Discussion paper FS III 93–203. Berlin: Wissenschaftszentrum Berlin für Sozialforschung.

HASPEL, M., REMINGTON, T. F., and SMITH, S. S. 1998. Electoral institutions and party cohesion in the Russian Duma. *Journal of Politics*, 60: 417–39.

HERRERA, C. L., HERRERA, R., and SMITH, E. R. A. N. 1992. Public opinion and congressional representation. *Public opinion Quarterly*, 56: 185–205.

HERZOG, D. REBENSTORF, H., and WEßELS, B. ed. 1993. *Parlament und Gesellschaft*. Opladen: Westdeutscher Verlag.

HOLMBERG, S. 1989. Political representation in Sweden. *Scandinavian Political Studies*, 12: 1–36.

HUBER, J. D., and POWELL, G. B., Jr. 1994. Congruence between citizens and policymakers in two visions of liberal democracy. *World Politics*, 46: 291–326.

ILONSZKI, G. 1994. Parliament and parliamentarians in Hungary in comparative perspective. Pp. 237–51 in *The Emergence of East Central European Parliaments: The First Steps*, ed. A. Ágh. Budapest: Hungarian Centre of Democracy Studies.

—— 2003. A moving target? Research experiences and research findings about professionalization of Hungarian representative elites. Pp. 26–32 in *Representative Elites in Post-Communist Settings*, ed. H. Best and M. Edinger. Jena: SFB 580, Gesellschaftliche Entwicklungen nach dem Systemumbruch.

IRWIN, G. A., and THOMASSEN, J. 1997. Issue-consensus in a multi-party system: voters and leaders in the Netherlands. *Acta Politica*, 10: 389–420.

JENSEN, T. K. 2000. Party cohesion. Pp. 210–36 in *Beyond Westminster and Congress: The Nordic Experience*, ed. P. Esaiasson and K. Heidar. Columbus, Oh.: Ohio State University Press.

JEWELL, M. E. 1970. Attitudinal determinants of legislative behaviour: the utility of role analysis. Pp. 460–500 in *Legislators in Developmental Perspective*, ed. A. Kornberg and L. D. Musolf. Kingsport: Kingsport Press.

KIELHORN, A. 2001. *Rollenorientierungen von Abgeordneten in Europa.* Freie Universität Berlin, Berlin.

KITSCHELT, H., MANSFELDOVÁ, Z., MARKOWSKI, R., and TÓKA, G. 1999. *Post-Communist Party Systems: Competition, Representation, and Inter-Party Cooperation.* Cambridge, Mass.: Cambridge University Press.

KLINGEMANN, H.-D., and WEßELS, B. 2001. Political consequences of Germany's mixed-member system: personalization at the grass-roots? Pp. 279–96 in *Mixed Member Electoral Systems: The Best of Both Worlds?*, ed. M. S. Shugart and M. P. Wattenberg. Oxford: Oxford University Press.

KUKLINSKI, J. H., and ELLING, R. C. 1977. Representational role, constituency opinion, and legislative roll-call behavior. *American Journal of Political Science*, 21: 135–47.

LAVER, M. 1997. *Private Desires, Political Action.* London: Sage.

LEGUTKE, A. 2001. *Die Organisation der Parteien in Russland.* Wiesbaden: Westdeutscher Verlag.

LIJPHART, A. 1984. *Democracies: Patterns of Majoritarian and Consensus Government.* New Haven: Yale University Press.

—— and CREPAZ, M. M. L. 1991. Corporatism and consensus democracy in eighteen countries: conceptual and empirical linkages. *British Journal for Political Science*, 21: 235–56.

LINEK, L., and RAKUSANOVA, P. 2004. The more parties vote and the bigger their majority is, the less united they are. Pp. 102–19 in *Central European Parliaments—First Decade of Democratic Experience and Future Prospectives*, ed. Z. Mansfeldová and D. M. Olson. Prague: Academy of Sciences of the Czech Republic.

McCUBBINS, M. D., and SCHWARTZ, T. 1984. Congressional oversight overlooked: police patrols versus fire alarms. *American Journal of Political Science*, 28: 165–79.

MARSH, M., and WEßELS, B. 1997. Territorial representation. *European Journal of Political Research*, 32: 227–41.

MAY, J. D. 1978. Defining democracy. *Political Studies*, 26: 1–14.

MILLER, W. E. 1999. Elite-mass linkages in representative democracies: introduction. Pp. 1–8 in *Policy Representation in Western Democracies*, ed. W. E. Miller, R. Pierce, J. Thomassen, R. Herrera, S. Holmberg, P. Esaiasson, and B. Weßels. Oxford: Oxford University Press.

—— and STOKES, D. E. 1963. Constituency influence in congress. *American Political Science Review*, 57: 45–56.

—— PIERCE, R., THOMASSEN, J., HERRERA, R., HOLMBERG, S., ESAIASSON, P., and WEßELS, B. 1999. *Policy Representation in Western Democracies.* Oxford: Oxford University Press.

MITCHELL, P. 2000. Voters and their representatives: electoral institutions and delegation in parliamentary democracies. *European Journal of Political Research*, 37: 335–51.

MÜLLER, W. C. 2000. Political parties in parliamentary democracies: making delegation and accountability work. *European Journal of Political Research*, 37: 309–33.

NORRIS, P. ed. 1997. *Passages to Power: Legislative Recruitment in Advanced Democracies.* Cambridge: Cambridge University Press.

PIERCE, R. 1999. Conclusion: mixed signals. Pp. 162–5 in *Policy Representation in Western Democracies*, ed. W. E. Miller, R. Pierce, J. Thomassen, R. Herrera, S. Holmberg, P. Esaiasson, and B. Weßels. Oxford: Oxford University Press.

PORTER, S. R. 1995. *Political Representation in Germany: The Effects of Candidate Selection Committees.* University of Rochester, Rochester, New York.

POWELL, G. B. 2000. *Elections as Instruments of Democracy. Majoritarian and Proportional Visions.* New Haven: Yale University Press.

RAE, D. W. 1967. *The Political Consequences of Electoral Laws*. New Haven: Yale University Press.

RUUS, J. 2003. The changing composition of Estonian legislative elites: from de-Sovietification to professionalism. Pp. 68–75 in *Representative Elites in Post-Communist Settings*, ed. H. Best and M. Edinger. Jena: SFB 580, Gesellschaftliche Entwicklungen nach dem Systemumbruch.

STRØM, K. 2000. Delegation and accountability in parliamentary democracies. *European Journal of Political Research*, 37: 261–90.

STUDLAR, D. T., and MCALLISTER, I. 1996. Constituency activity and representational roles among Australian legislators. *Journal of Politics*, 58: 69–90.

THOMASSEN, J. 1991. Empirical research into political representation: a critical reappraisal. Pp. 259–74 in *Politische Klasse und politische Institutionen: Probleme und Perspektiven der Elitenforschung*, ed. H.-D. Klingemann, R. Stöss, and B. Weßels. Opladen: Westdeutscher Verlag.

THOMPSON, D. F. 2001. Political representation. Pp. 11696–8 in *International Encyclopedia of the Social & Behavioral Sciences*, ed. N. J. Smelser and P. B. Baltes. Amsterdam: Elsevier.

WAHLKE, J. C., EULAU, H., BUCHANAN, W., and FERGUSON, L. 1962. *The Legislative System: Explorations in Legislative Behavior*. New York: John Wiley & Sons.

WEßELS, B. 1993. Politische Repräsentation als Prozeß gesellschaftlich-parlamentarischer Kommunikation. Pp. 99–137 in *Parlament und Gesellschaft*, ed. D. Herzog, H. Rebenstorf, and B. Weßels. Opladen: Westdeutscher Verlag.

—— 1997. Germany. Pp. 76–97 in *Passages to Power: Legislative Recruitment in Advanced Democracies*, ed. P. Norris. Cambridge, Mass.: Cambridge University Press.

—— 1999a. System characteristics matter: empirical evidence from ten representation studies. Pp. 137–61 in *Policy Representation in Western Democracies*, ed. W. E. Miller, R. Pierce, J. Thomassen, R. Herrera, S. Holmberg, P. Esaiasson, and B. Weßels. Oxford: Oxford University Press.

—— 1999b. Whom to represent? Role orientations of legislators in Europe. Pp. 209–34 in *Political Representation and Legitimacy in the European Union*, ed. H. Schmitt and J. Thomassen. Oxford: Oxford University Press.

CHAPTER 46

PERSPECTIVES ON REPRESENTATION: ASKING THE RIGHT QUESTIONS AND GETTING THE RIGHT ANSWERS

JAMES STIMSON

REPRESENTATION is an idea that gained prominence in the eighteenth century. It structures much of what we think democracy means. But as scholarship it has been largely fallow ground. We knew just a little bit more about the facts of representation in the late twentieth century than we did 200 years earlier.

And then we started to learn again, asking novel questions and getting answers to them. In this chapter it is my task to make some sense of this pattern, to explain the stop and start character of the scholarship. That I will do. I will have little to say about the previous chapters because I find them very self-contained. A reader who has read and understood them should be spared a repetition of what he or she already knows. Clearly the same themes will emerge.

I will first say a few words about the normative issues that haunt the representation literature. Then I will move on to design issues, focusing on the question of why cross-sectional studies of representation have not been particularly fruitful. Then I move to longitudinal studies, cross-polity analyses (very briefly), and thinking about politics as a system.

1 NORMATIVE AND EMPIRICAL

Much of what we call representation research is actually normative discussions of representation. We have asked, at least since Burke (1889) how should representatives behave and what should representation be. If I just tell the truth here, the design of what is to come in this chapter will make more sense to the reader. I find this discussion tedious. I think we could have it over and over again for a thousand years without gaining a wit of worthwhile understanding.

Contrast Mansbridge's (2003) recent work on the topic. An alleged normative theorist, Mansbridge instead asks what models of process we ought to formulate to square our thinking about representation with the message of empirical studies. How we should think about processes which we have closely observed is indeed a useful discussion, in a word—maybe unintended—science.

Starting with the traditional model, which she labels "promissory"—the member promises to do something during the election campaign and then later does it while in office—Mansbridge develops three other types that square with empirical scholarship. "Anticipatory" representation occurs when the member in office anticipates what will please voters at a later election, rather than being tied to promises made in the previous one. Based on the work of Arnold (1990) and on my own developments with Erikson and MacKuen (Stimson, MacKuen, and Erikson 1995 and Erikson, MacKuen, and Stimson 2002), the anticipatory model is more realistic when one postulates rational members eager to be re-elected. The idea that one would represent only by honoring past promises is less than rational behavior; the politician can benefit also by representing on emerging and changing issues to please future voters. (And if voters change their minds, as for example on the Iraq War in the United States, then it would be neither smart nor responsive to be bound by promises from an earlier time.)

Mansbridge's "gyroscopic" model has members doing their own thing, following an internal compass. Insofar as voters know what direction a member will follow, and take it into account in their voting decisions, then meaningful representation takes place even without the member consciously taking into account constituent preferences or interests. This notion clearly seems applicable to the emerging polarized parties of American politics. One selects a Democrat or a Republican and, with great predictability, gets a string of liberal or conservative votes as a consequence.

The electoral district-member connection is broken in the final model of "surrogate" representation. In this account members choose to represent others, usually like themselves, but beyond the confines of the legally defined electoral district. If, for example, a Hispanic member chooses to look out for the interests of Hispanics everywhere (and not just his or her voters), it would be a case of surrogate representation.

2 THE EVIDENCE

This discussion might imply that I think little of representation, which is not the case. But I think all the fun is in the empirical sphere, in trying to nail down evidence of what, if anything, it is and how it works. That is the sole focus of the rest of this chapter.

2.1 Cross-sectional

Begin with the sort of evidence we acquire from the classic Miller and Stokes (1963) representation study. It shows that for at least some issue domains that average district opinion in the United States is congruent with member voting behavior.[1] That is a straightforward fact, now often replicated and found also in a variety of different sorts of studies. But what does this fact mean? The Miller and Stokes analysis saw it as a psychological process model, the famous diamond diagram, telling us that actual district views became member perceptions of the district, which interacted with member policy attitudes to determine behavior.[2]

I wish to take a different tack here and ask a research design sort of question about causality. Having viewed positive correlations between district public opinion and member votes, I want to ask what models of behavior for both citizens and members would predict the positive evidence that we in fact observe. Asking this question will illustrate the frustrating limits of cross-sectional design.

I want to think about varying voter behavior (as between self-conscious member selection by platforms and expressed views or voting unconsciously), varying member

---

[1] Converse (2006) writes that average district opinion was far from Miller's prior theory or research design, that Miller saw representation as individual congruence—between voter and representative—and turned to aggregate district views later to save a study that would otherwise have ended in total failure. There was nothing there at the individual level. That representatives represent "people" is a charming idea that gives way to the reality and better modern theory that representation is necessarily of aggregates. Empirical failure led Miller to do what modern theories would now propose a priori.

[2] The discussion section of the Miller and Stokes article raises an issue no longer much read or remembered. That is the inconsistency between finding, on the one hand, that candidates for office seem quite well informed about what their potential constituents want and the knowledge, derived from the same set of studies, that citizens are actually communicating almost nothing of their views. Miller and Stokes leave us with a puzzle, that while constituents fail to have views about public policy and fail to express those that they actually hold, candidates for office actually succeed in receiving the messages that are not sent. This is notable for two reasons. One is that it illustrates a remarkable change in journal practices—and not for the better—where modern authors dare not admit any confusion, inconsistency, and puzzling result lest their work end up in the dustbin of rejection. That's a shame, because author admissions of anomaly are vastly more important for stimulating useful research than are the tedious "suggestions for future research" so commonly seen. Substantively, this admission of inconsistency *now* can be taken as evidence that the prevailing theory of the time, that representatives were subject to "pressure" from constituent opinion and responded to it with no more intelligence than does a billiard ball to the pool cue, was deeply wrong. The rational expectations perspective, coming to political science three decades later, resolves the puzzle. Constituents have no need to express their views because rational politicians will be driven by electoral ambition to do an exceedingly good job of anticipating them.

behavior (as between observed district views as a guide to action or just "doing one's own thing") and other processes that might also explain positive correlation.

2.2 Three Models of Process

Consider three quite different processes and states of the world.

Responsive members. Begin with the most obviously "representative" behavior by members, observing district views and adjusting behavior to fit. That would produce positive correlations and none would doubt that the correlations implied representation in its fullest sense. That clearly does not exhaust the possibilities.

Selective voters. Assume in contrast that members pay no heed to district views or changes in them. Could we still produce positive correlations? We could. If voters paid attention to the policy positions of alternative candidates and factored that into their voting decisions, then this also would produce the basic evidence of congruence. Even if no member ever thought about what his or her district wanted, that is, policy conscious selection by voters would still produce the known positive correlations. This is clearly representation, Mansbridge's "gyroscopic" type, if not quite responsiveness.

Distinctive district views. Consider now the prospect that no member ever pays heed to district views and no voter is influenced by policy considerations. Could we still produce the Miller–Stokes evidence—positive correlation between district opinion and member votes? We could. Assume that on at least some issues, some of the time, that district views are distinctive. By that I mean that mean attitudes differ more than randomly between one district and another. Perhaps urban districts typically think handguns should be tightly controlled and rural districts typically think the opposite. Then imagine that voters choose their candidates randomly—or alternatively by some irrelevant criterion, say eye color. Then because election is an act of sampling, the members elected will tend to have whatever views are distinctive in the district (by accidental, not conscious, selection). And again we produce the congruence evidence.

But is it evidence of representation? Clearly, it is not representation in a meaningful sense where neither the representative nor the represented act consciously to achieve congruence. And thus we come face to face with the ugly fact of cross-sectional congruence. It is consistent with actual representative behavior and it is also consistent with the absence of representative behavior. The evidence itself cannot tell us which we are observing, or in what proportions the meaningful and accidental are mixed.

What we need to break out of this trap is experimental variation in "x," change in constituent attitudes. Change requires us to observe relationships over time.

2.3 Cross-temporal

Because "representation" has always been seen in the United States as political geography, a cross-sectional question at its core, we have little evidence of temporal representation, changing public opinion followed by changing behavior of representatives in government. But our intuition of it is as a process—the representative receives a signal of opinion or opinion change and then at some later time chooses whether or not to act on it. So we have observed cross-sectional evidence to infer an unobserved dynamic process. And that has left us in the design trap noted earlier.

In one of the most innovative studies ever, Kuklinski and Stanga (1979) observed public opinion as expressed in a California initiative measure to decriminalize marijuana use. They asked whether (unelected) judges would be sensitive to the initiative outcomes in their own areas. They found that sentencing for marijuana use, while not significantly related to the initiative results before the initiative, became so after. Thus, not only did they have rare control over time order of independent and dependent variables, they also in one stroke demonstrated representation of a sort without any electoral motive.

The earliest approach to observing policy representation dynamics comes in the pioneering work of Page and Shapiro (1983) (updated in Page and Shaprio 1992). Page and Shapiro employ a quasi-experimental approach which locates instances of substantial public opinion changes and then asks whether policy also changed in the interval bracketing opinion change, and if it did, whether the direction of that change was or was not congruent with the direction of opinion change. They found congruence. Opinion changes regularly preceded policy changes in the numerous cases for which measurement of both was possible. This is strong evidence for the inference of a dynamic representation effect (also see Wlezien and Soroka in this volume for a discussion of cross-national evidence).

This style of work allows one to infer process, but does not itself describe it. One knows, that is, that something consistent with representative behavior happened, but the experimental approach does not elucidate that process. Observing the process requires a time-series design in which both opinion and policy can be quantified as time series and then the causal link between them may be modelled.

There are two sub-brands of such a time-series approach. One is a focus on policy domains for measurement of both opinion and policy. Bartels (1991) focuses on defense spending and finds that public attitudes toward the proper level of defense spending vary considerably over time and regularly predict enacted policy in the form of defense budgets. Wlezien (1995, 1996) takes a more general approach, looking at a number of domestic policy areas and finds similar within-domain patterns of representation.

The second sub-brand, seen in my own work with Robert Erikson and Michael MacKuen (1995, 2002), assumes that attitudes are more meaningfully global—on the ubiquitous left–right scale of public rhetoric and party conflict—rather than specific. It measures both opinion (Public Policy Mood) and policy as generalized movements toward left or right over time and finds quite conclusive evidence of connection in the expected—opinion $\rightarrow$ policy—direction. Consistent with the Bartels and Wlezien accounts, the global approach points not only to significant links between opinion and policy change, but also surprisingly strong ones. For elected bodies, House, Senate, and presidency in the US, those links are essentially one to one. Every unit change in opinion produces a unit change in policy, and does so almost immediately. For the US Supreme Court, not expected to be responsive and normatively preferred not to be, the link between opinion and Court decisions is also quite strong.

Beyond establishing the fact of dynamic representation, the theoretical tilt of this work is a focus on mechanism. In particular, it allows causal flow through the means of elections, as enshrined in democratic theory and built into the US constitutional structure. Its more novel mechanism posits that rational politicians pay close heed to signals of public opinion change and adjust to them, while they are going on, to optimally position themselves for future electoral gain. This representation by "rational anticipation" can substantially change outcomes with little—and in principle, no—change of governing personnel. It is also very fast, producing policy change in real time while public opinion is in process of evolving to some new demand.

For the United States at least, the longitudinal evidence confirms what decades of cross-sectional findings suggest, that governing bodies do respond to public opinion—and perhaps more important, to changes in public opinion. The modern understanding alters our understanding of the process from the mechanistic view embedded in the constitution and in traditional theory. That has voters actively communicating their preferences to representatives, who then act on them before those same voters will reward or punish the representative in elections to come. Those voter acts require a level of information and motivation that, though not impossible, are atypical of mass electorates. The revised understanding is that rational and ambitious politicians do an excellent job of anticipating what their constituents want and how they will respond to policy changes (even those they do not now know) in the future. Rational activist politicians, that is, eliminate the need for a rational activist electorate.

But is it only the United States in which such systems of representation exist, or is the US simply the easiest case (with single member districts and plurality elections) and most studied case of a more universal phenomenon? Thinking about representation in other democracies requires a more speculative mood.

2.4 Cross-national

I begin with an admission that I am not fully competent in this literature—and maybe even worse than that. So this will be a very partial treatment, no match for example with the Wessels chapter which precedes it. Although I am engaged in representation research in the UK and in France, I am limited by my mainly American politics focus of a professional lifetime.

I wish to pursue here understandings that are cross-national *and* cross-temporal. The reason for this focus is the same as I noted above, that cross-sectional work can establish a kind of reduced form understanding of representation, that evidence for it does or does not exist, but cannot discriminate between several possible processes which might account for the evidence. My tone is speculative here because this style of work is an intriguing possibility more than a reality.

There is nothing in the theories of Bartels, Wlezien, or Stimson, MacKuen, and Erikson for the American case that is specifically American (also see Miller et al. 1999). Whether for the policy domain ideas or for the global dynamic representation versions, all that is required for the representation dynamics to emerge are ambitious politicians operating with some electoral accountability mechanism. That is present in all real democratic states, so the theory ought to be applicable to all.[3] But while the theory easily extends to other nation-states, the measurement system in the American case may travel considerably less well. In particular, in states featuring coalition government with disciplined parties, it is considerably more challenging to quantify the drift of public policy.

Wlezien and Soroka have pushed forward with a parallel study of the US, UK, and Canada (Soroka and Wlezien 2004a, 2004b, 2005). Focusing on domain-specific opinion and budgetary measures of policy, as in Wlezien's work in the US, they find robust representation of opinion into policy in the US and UK, but less in Canada. Their work illustrates that dynamic representation can be studied outside the US context, but also that the difficulties of measuring both opinion and policy over time are daunting. There is a promising beginning in Sweden.[4] We will not see a flood of such work because data requirements are very great and the effort required to produce time series from raw numbers does not tempt scholars with a short time horizon for completion.

The existence of the Manifesto project (Budge, Robertson, and Hearl 1987; Klingemann, Hofferbert, and Budge 1994) should become a considerable aid to such research programs as in Erikson, MacKuen, and Stimson (2002), but application of these crucial data has been limited to date.

3 SYSTEMS

When we think about representation we usually abstract it out of its context. We ask questions like "Does a change in opinion at time t affect policy at time $t+1$?" But that ignores an important complication: policy change is also likely to feed back to opinion change. This is explicit in Wlezien's (1995) thermostatic conception (see also Durr 1993). And it is explicitly modelled in most of the longitudinal work I have already discussed.

The feedback in all conceptions is negative, the essence of the thermostatic conception. When policy goes too far in one direction, the public calls for correction in the opposite direction. If one conceives of the public as moderate, relative to those

---

[3] It may not work as well in PR and party list electoral systems as in the single-member case, but that is speculation. Where electoral sanction mechanisms exist, it should work to some degree.

[4] See Holmberg (1989) and Essiasson and Holmberg (1996).

who have their hands on the levers of policy, then movements away from the moderate equilibrium in either direction generate public demand for restored equilibrium—that is, movement opposite the most recent acts of government. Thus, a simplified time lagged conception is:

$$\text{Public Opinion}_{t-1} \rightarrow \text{Policy}_t \rightarrow \text{Public Opinion}_{t+1}$$

where the second causal link is understood to be negative.

Now, if we inquire about the ultimate effect of exogenously changing either opinion or policy, our prediction is going to be indeterminant, depending upon the parameters in both causal links. Ultimate effects could explosively amplify representation findings, cancel them out entirely, produce dampened stable behavior, stable oscillation, or even explosive oscillation. All of these possibilities could arise from this simple little model. Where the second linkage is negative and weaker than the first, as it generally is, then only the stable alternatives exist. But this still alerts us that abstracting these relationships out of their system—simple though it is here—creates the potential for seriously misinterpreting the process.

But this two-variable system is itself a considerable simplification of what we believe to be the case in politics. Policy changes might generate satisfaction or dissatisfaction with outcomes. And public opinion changes certainly affect elections in a democratic state. So we see that our little system is itself embedded in a bigger one, one of seventeen variables in the itself-over-simple version of macro-politics developed with my colleagues Erikson and MacKuen (2002, 2003).

And if that isn't complicated enough, things get *really* interesting in politics because some relationships have a knife-edge character. Moving the two-party presidential vote from 49.99 percent to 50.01 percent, for example, changes the winner, and that changes everything.[5] With presidential elections like Kennedy vs. Nixon in 1960 and Bush vs. Gore in 2000, this argument is far from hypothetical.

The import of admitting that politics involves a web of complex relationships, some of which are decidedly non-linear, is that our ability to know the secondary and tertiary effects of any sort of change in one of the key components of the system is seriously overestimated. When feedback is combined with knife-edge outcomes, one quickly loses the ability to predict the medium-term impact of anything—even its direction!

3.1 An Illustration

Consider the system of Figure 46.1 from MacKuen, Stimson, and Erikson (2002). This is the system model of American politics derived from *The Macro Polity*, a grand summary of many—but far from all—of the macro-relationships explored in that volume.[6] One can see that the little opinion-policy model above finds itself embedded in the bottom line of relationships in Figure 46.1.

---

[5] And the same story is true for legislative party control.
[6] I note here that much of this section reports collaborative work.

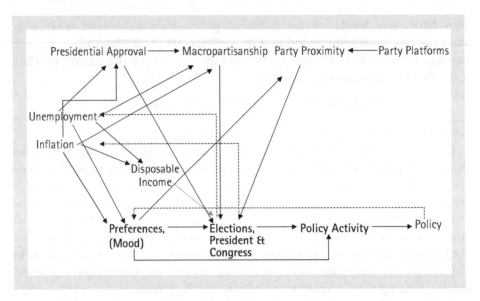

Fig. 46.1 The system model of the macro polity (Erikson, MacKuen, and Stimson 2002)

Now since the model is fully endogenous—every variable in it affects the values of almost every other variable at later times—the modelled connection between opinion and policy now runs through complex and contingent connections that quickly exceed what the mind can grasp. Their connection, that is, is not only the direct arrows that imply simple causality, but also through every possible indirect path, of which there are very many.

As a starting point I note that both dynamic representation and policy to opinion feedback remain in the system form of the model, which is an assumption based upon empirical results more than a "finding." We "find" these processes operative, that is, because the model includes parameters that were estimated recursively in the normal way, and these parameters are statistically significant in those conventional analyses.

What we can do with such a modeling exercise is not to "test" it; assumptions cannot be tested. Its use instead is more exploratory. It allows us to ask "what if?" sorts of questions by tinkering with its pieces and observing the effects of that tinkering over thousands of runs, each with different stochastic errors. The "what if" in this brief illustration is an issue central to the study of political behavior, what if voters were more (or less) responsive to government than they actually are?

We begin by choosing a single actor, the president, and observing a single output, the percent of votes gained or lost by the president's party at the election which follows a policy action. We ask how the president's actions impinge on his (or his party's) electoral fate. Our framework is explicitly Downsian; presidents optimize electoral success by pleasing the median voter, paying at the polls for any deviation to left or right.

Inherent in our model (and in American politics) is that programmatic parties tend always to overshoot, to go further in their policy path than the median voter commands. We understand that parties have principles to which most officeholders and the party's loyal base of workers, contributors, and supporters are deeply committed. Thus presidents (and parties generally) always face a tension between the moderate course of the median voter and the more extreme (and principled) actions that appeal to the party base. Thus real presidents do not optimize electoral success by following the median voter, but instead craft a compromise somewhere between the median and the party base, wanting to be re-elected but also wanting to change policy in the direction of the party's principles.

Thus presidents create a signal of policy excess which highly attentive voters could see. But voters we know are not on average highly attentive. They are mostly tuned out, picking up stray bits and pieces of the policy signal, but not the whole. Our question then is this: How much does it matter that an inattentive electorate does not get the whole picture of presidential policy? Mathematics can tell us what to expect of logical extremes. If attentiveness were zero, then presidents could do whatever they wanted without paying any electoral price. If it were total, then presidents would be sharply constrained, with even small deviations from moderation punished. But these extremes are beyond the range of empirical possibility. We'd like to know how much attentiveness matters within the range where it might reasonably vary.

From the real experience of the late twentieth century we have a parameter estimate which captures the policy-to-opinion feedback process of actual electorates. Now we can ask, what if that parameter were larger or smaller than the actual one, that is, what would happen if the electorate were more (or less) attentive to policy than it actually is. Our device for entertaining the question is to introduce a multiplier which works on the parameter value, making it smaller or larger than the empirical estimate to make a simulated electorate more or less attentive than the actual one.

We let the multiplier (θ) vary over 21 different values, a grid with intervals of size 0.2 from 0.0 to 4.0. That models an even grid of possible parameter values from zero (totally insensitive electorate) through 1.0 (the empirically estimated value) through 4.0 (an electorate four times as sensitive to policy changes as the actual one). Our question is how much does it matter that electorates are only partially sensitive to presidential policy? We answer the question by observing how much difference it makes as we vary sensitivity over a range from totally unaware through actual sensitivity through a hypersensitive electorate reacting four times more than the actual one.

Because actual presidents pursue suboptimal policies (with regard to the re-election goal), we estimate that they have suboptimal re-election outcomes, −1.13 points in the two-party vote.[7] The question then is how much is this effect compounded by making the electorate more sensitive—or reduced by making it less. The estimates, based on a 1,000 repetitions for each parameter value, are given in Figure 46.2.

We learn from Figure 46.2 that attentiveness matters. When the public pays no attention at all ($\theta = 0$) presidential parties do better than expected by about two-thirds

---

[7] We are not asserting, however, that presidents are non-rational. A suboptimal division of the votes might well be compensated by the fruits (e.g. in turnout) of an enthusiastic party base.

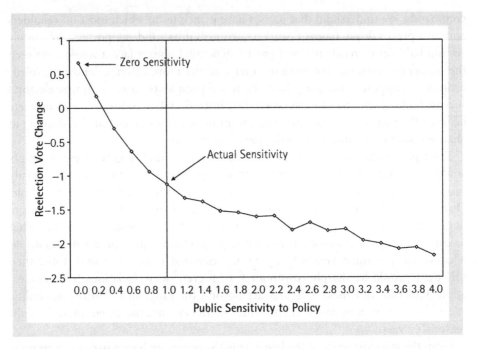

Fig. 46.2 Parameter sensistivity analysis

Note: The estimates show changes in presidential party vote share which result from hypothetical increases or decreases in the public responsiveness parameter in the system model of *the macro polity* (Erikson, Mackuen, and Stimson 2002). Each estimate is the result of 1,000 runs of the system model with different stochastic disturances.

of a point. With each increment in θ party performance drops off. In the range from θ=1.0 (actual) to θ=4.0 the performance penalty doubles. Thus we can surmise that a world of more attentive voters would produce presidents forced to hew closely to the preferences of the median voter. The cost (or benefit, a matter of perspective) of inattention is presidential freedom to pursue party principles and eschew moderation.

4 On the Other Hand

Since *The American Voter* (Campbell et al. 1960) and Converse's "Nature of Belief Systems" (Converse 1964) we have worried that mass electorates lack the ability to play their assigned role in democracy. The other way to view the evidence we have just seen is that things are not so bad. We have demonstrated that attentiveness matters for the quality of citizen-politician interactions over policy. More attentive electorates exercise more control over policy. But the other way to view these results is to point out that absence of attentiveness does not have dire consequences. With the electorate we have— helped out, as always, by the order induced by aggregation—we have about half as much citizen control over policy as in an extreme and unsustainable polity where citizens were full time participants in politics. And half isn't bad.

From this review of our knowledge, a two-word conclusion emrges, "Representation works." The cross-sectional and geographic evidence of congruence suffers from difficulty of interpretation, but we now know that this a less serious difficulty because all other forms of study sustain the strong—that is, responsiveness—interpretation of congruence. The quasi-experimental studies find clear evidence of responsiveness, as do the time-series analyses of either policy domains or global attitudes and policy. And finally analysis at the level of whole systems finds that the responsiveness in both directions—government to citizens and citizens to government—is a necessary part of any model of the polity.

This stands in dramatic contrast to the received wisdom of just a few years ago. Then it was commmonplace to assert that governments were blind to the wishes of ordinary citizens, that democratic forms were empty of real force, overlayed on the absence of real democracy. We have often asked "Is government responsive enough?" The question now seems to have been answered. It might now be useful to return to the normative concern of the eighteenth century, "Is it a good thing that government is so responsive to citizen desires?"

References

ARNOLD, R. D. 1990. *The Logic of Congressional Action*. New Haven: Yale University Press.

BARTELS, L. M. 1991. Constituency opinion and congressional policy making: the Reagan defense buildup. *American Political Science Review*, 85 (2): 457–74.

BUDGE, I., ROBERTSON, D., and HEARL, D. 1987. *Ideology, Strategy and Party Change*. Cambridge: Cambridge University Press.

BURKE, E. [1774] 1889. Speech to the electors of Bristol. In *The Works of the Right Honorable Edmund Burke*, vol. ii. Boston: Little Brown.

CAMPBELL, A., CONVERSE, P. E., MILLER, W. E., and STOKES, D. E. 1960. *The American Voter*. New York: Wiley.

CONVERSE, P. E. 1964. The nature of belief systems in mass publics. Pp. 206–61 in *Ideology and Discontent*, ed. D. E. Apter. Ann Arbor: University of Michigan Press.

—— 2006. Researching electoral politics. *American Political Science Review*, 100: 605–12.

DURR, R. H. 1993. What moves policy sentiment? *American Political Science Review*, 87: 158–70.

ERIKSON, R. S., MACKUEN, M. B., and STIMSON, J. A. 2002. *The Macro Polity*. New York: Cambridge University Press.

—— —— —— 2003. Responsabilité des élus devant l'électorat et efficacité du système politique amèricain: une analyse contrefactuelle. *La Revue française de science politique*, 53: 887–909.

ESAIASSON, P., and HOLMBERG, S. 1996. *Representation from Above: Members of Parliament and Representative Democracy in Sweden*. Aldershot: Dartmouth.

HOLMBERG, S. 1989. Political representation in Sweden. *Scandinavian Political Studies*, 12: 1–36.

KLINGEMANN, H., HOFFERBERT, R., and BUDGE, I. 1994. *Parties, Policy and Democracy*. Boulder, Colo.: Westview.

KUKLINSKI, J. H., and STANGA, J. E. 1979. Political participation and government responsiveness: the behavior of California Superior Courts. *American Political Science Review*, 73: 1090–9.

MacKuen, M. B., Stimson, J. A., and Erikson, R. S. 2002. Preferences, politics, and policy: accountability and efficiency in dynamic representation. Prepared for delivery at the annual meeting of the American Political Science Association, August 28–September 1, 2002.

Mansbridge, J. 2003. Rethinking Representation. *American Political Science Review,* 97: 515–28.

Miller, W. E., and Stokes, D. W. 1963. Constituency influence in Congress. *American Political Science Review,* 57: 45–6.

—— Pierce, R., Thomassen, J., Herrera, R., Holmberg, S., Esaisson, P., and Weßels, B. 1999. *Policy Representation in Western Democracies.* Oxford: Oxford University Press.

Page, B. I., and Shapiro, R. Y. 1983. Effects of public opinion on policy. *American Political Science Review,* 77: 175–90.

—— —— 1992. *The Rational Public: Fifty Years of Trends in Americans' Policy Preferences.* Chicago: University of Chicago Press.

Soroka, S. N., and Wlezien, C. 2004a. Degrees of democracy: public opinion and policy in comparative perspective. Center for Advanced Study in the Social Sciences Working Paper Series. Madrid: Juan March Institute.

—— —— 2004b. Opinion representation and policy feedback: Canada in comparative perspective. *Canadian Journal of Political Science,* 37: 531–59.

—— —— 2005. Opinion-policy dynamics: public preferences and public expenditure in the United Kingdom. *British Journal of Political Science,* 35: 665–89.

Stimson, J. A., MacKuen, M. B., and Erikson, R. S. 1995. Dynamic representation. *American Political Science Review,* 89: 543–65.

Wlezien, C. 1995. The public as thermostat: dynamics of preferences for spending. *American Journal of Political Science,* 39 (4): 981–1000.

—— 1996. Dynamics of representation: the case of U.S. spending on defense. *British Journal of Political Science,* 26: 81–103.

THE METHODOLOGY OF COMPARATIVE POLITICAL BEHAVIOR RESEARCH

PART VIII

THE METHODOLOGY OF COMPARATIVE POLITICAL BEHAVIOR RESEARCH

CHAPTER 47

....

RESEARCH RESOURCES IN COMPARATIVE POLITICAL BEHAVIOR

....

MIKI CAUL KITTILSON

COMPARATIVE survey research projects provide the empirical tools for the systematic study of the political values, attitudes, orientations, skills, and activities of ordinary people living under different political contexts. Indeed, this Handbook would not have been possible without the development of an international network of public opinion surveys and the public sharing of these data. Those scholars who have initiated, coordinated, and sustained these projects are invaluable to the fields of political behavior and comparative politics.

This chapter guides readers to major cross-national survey research projects that address political themes. The first section compares both global and regional surveys along a common set of dimensions. The second section briefly overviews the most extensive national election study series from nations around the world, and gives specific years and data sources. The third section covers some of the major national archives, which store and disseminate these survey data, and displays the contact information. I conclude with a discussion of the importance of standardizing procedures for sharing survey data, and comment on the future of cross-national survey projects.

1 CROSS-NATIONAL SURVEY
RESEARCH PROJECTS

Cross-national survey research is key to developing and testing theories of how individuals perceive and navigate the political world. Rooted in the pioneering cross-national surveys by Almond and Verba (1963) and by Barnes, Kaase et al. (1979), scholars draw upon simultaneous and coordinated surveys of citizens across a variety of political contexts to better understand the most fundamental factors underlying democratic transitions and processes. With a standardized set of questions, general theories can be developed and tested under very different institutional and political contexts. And where scholars find "outliers" in national comparisons, we learn more about the contingencies of our theories.

However, from its inception cross-national survey research encountered many obstacles—both theoretical and practical. Concepts derived from the American context are not always automatically "transportable" across national boundaries. For example, tapping a functionally equivalent conceptualization of party identification requires changes in operationalization in the Netherlands, the Canada context, and in other nations (Thomassen 1976; Clarke and Stewart 1998; Blais et al. 2001; and see Scotto and Singer 2004).

In recent decades, comparative survey research expanded from a limited subset of nations (primarily the US and western Europe) to include new democracies, developing nations, and authoritarian systems (Heath, Fisher, and Smith 2005). The increasingly panoramic lens of survey research largely parallels the expansion of democracy, as scholars struggle to understand the role of citizens in the democratic process. The first waves of cross-national studies were pioneered in advanced industrial nations, for the most part. As many countries shed the research limitations of authoritarian rule, researchers have undertaken surveys in a greater number of new democracies and developing nations. Yet even today established industrial democracies remain over-represented due to the higher start up costs in conducting surveys in remote areas. For example, in rural areas where basic transportation infrastructure and household telephones are lacking, representative samples can be difficult and extremely expensive. At the same time, survey research methods generally grew more sophisticated. Hence, survey projects can be based on very different fundamental procedures, such as sampling methods. As the shape of cross-national projects changed, so have the design and methods.

In this chapter, I compare cross-national survey projects along several key dimensions—origins of the project, research generated, nature of the data collection, substantive themes, scope, potential for cross-national and longitudinal analysis, and accessibility. Table 47.1 summarizes the seventeen large-scale multiple-nation surveys analyzed in this section, and provides contact information for each. I begin by outlining the global surveys, and move on to the regional survey projects.

Table 47.1 Cross-national survey projects

Title	Coordinator	Scope	Funding	Themes	# Nations[a]	Time series	Availability	Information: http://
World Values Survey (WVS)	Ronald Inglehart, ISSR, University of Michigan	Global	Academic	Values, moral issues, political and social trust, protest activity	80	1981; 1990; 1995; 2000	ICPSR—member institutions	www.worldvalues survey.org
International Social Survey Programme (ISSP)	Data merged by ZA, Cologne	Global	Academic	Social, political, and economic attitude items, rotating themes.	39	1983–present (annual)	ZA, Cologne—member institutions	www.issp.org
Comparative Study of Electoral Systems (CSES)	Rotating Planning Committee	Global	Academic	Voting behavior and aggregate contextual data	33 in 1996–2001	1996–2001; 2001–2005	Data available for free download from project website	www.cses.org
Pew Global Attitudes Survey	Madeline Albright, Chair Andrew Kohut, Pew Research Center People, and the Press	Global	Commercial market research companies	Views on other nations around the world, current issues in world politics	49	2002, 2003, 2004, 2005	Data available on website 6 months after the reports issued	peoplepress.org/pgap
Gallup International	Gallup International Association, Zurich	Global	Commercial market research company	Milennium and Voice of the People Surveys, Health of the Planet, Human Needs and Satisfactions	60	2002, 2003, 2004	Electronic data only available for purchase from Gallup.	www.gallup-inter-national.com, www.voice-of-the-people.net

(Continued)

Table 47.1 (*Continued*)

Title	Coordinator	Scope	Funding	Themes	# Nations[a]	Time series	Availability	Information: http://
USIA World Wide Surveys	United States Information Agency	Global/ Regional	USIA	Examples include national concerns, problems, the Cold War, media consumption	varies	Intermittent, Most from 1960s to 1992	Surveys from 1960s and 1970s available from Roper archives, others through US National Archives, Electronic and Special Media Records Service Division	www.ropercenter. uconn.edu and www.archives.gov/ research_room
European Values Study	Coordination Center, Tilburg University, Netherlands	Regional	Academic	Moral and social values underlying European social and political institutions and government	33	1981, 1990, 1999/2000	ZA, University of Cologne	www.european-values.nl
Eurobarometer	European Commission, Public Opinion Analysis Sector	Regional	Academic	Support for European integration, plus rotating themes	25 (EU member states)	1973–present. Biannual	ICPSR; ZA	www.gesis.org/en/ data_service/ eurobarometer
European Social Survey (ESS)	Roger Jowell, National Center for Social Research	Regional	Academic	Core items—attitudes toward Europe's changing institutions, rotating themes	23	2002; 2004 (biennial)	NSD (http://ess. nsd.uib.no)	www.europeansocial survey.org
European Election Studies (EES)	Hermann Schmitt, University of Mannheim	Regional	Academic	EU participation and voting behavior, support for integration and enlargement, performance	25	1979, 1989, 1994, 1999, 2004 (post-EU Parliament Elections)	Steinmetz Amsterdam. 1999, 2004 SPSS portable datasets freely available on website. Pre–1999 studies part of Eurobarometers, ICPSR, ZA Colgne.	www.European electionstudies.Net

Name	Founder/Author	Scope	Type	Themes	No.	Years	Availability	Website
New Democracies Barometer	Paul Lazarsfeld Society of Vienna, with Christian Haerpfer and Richard Rose advising.	Regional	Academic	Focus on themes of democratic transition in central and eastern Europe	14	1991 to present	University of Strathclyde's Center for the Study in Public Policy; not publicly available	www.cspp.strath. ac.uk
New Europe Barometer	Richard Rose	Regional	Academic	Focus on democratic transition in central and eastern Europe	16	1991–present (7 total)	University of Strathclyde's Center fpr the Study in Public Policy; not publicly available	www.cspp.strath. ac.uk
New Baltic Barometer	Richard Rose	Regional	Academic	Focus on democratic transition in Baltic region	3	1993–present (6 total)	University of Strathclyde's Center for the Study in Public Policy; not publicly available	www.cspp.strath. ac.uk
Latinobarometer	Marta Lagos (MORI, Santiago)	Regional	Private project	Social, political, economic attitudes, rotating themes	17	1995–present (annual)	Tables available for fee from Latinobarometer.	www.latinobarome- tro.Org
Latin American Public Opinion Project (LAPOP)	Mitchell A. Seligson, Founder and Director	Regional	Academic	System support, political tolerance, authoritarianism, participation, local government, corruption	14	1994–present	Some data files available for fee. Department of Political Science, Vanderbilt University. Others free through Democracy Survey Database.	www.vanderbilt.- edu/ americas/ English/LAPOP.php
Afrobarometer	Mike Bratton, Bob Mattes, E. Gyimah-Boadi	Regional	Academic	Democratic support, governance, economic evaluations, social capital, identity, participation	15	1999–present (annual)	ICPSR and Afrobarometer website. Survey data files available 2 years after first release of survey's results.	www.afrobarome- ter.org

(Continued)

Table 47.1 (Continued)

Title	Coordinator	Scope	Funding	Themes	# Nations[a]	Time series	Availability	Information: http://
Asian Barometer	Takashi Inoguchi, coordinator	Regional	Academic	Social, and work-place issues in East, Southeast, South and Central Asia	10 Asian countries in 2003	2000, 2003, 2004 (annual)	Institute of Oriental Culture, University of Tokyo	avatoli.ioc.u-tokyo.ac.jp/ ~asiabarometer
East Asian Barometer	Principal Director, Fu Hu, National Taiwan University and core partners	Regional	Academic	Democratic support, reform and political action	9	2001	National Taiwan University. Data slated for public access in August 2005.	eacsurvey.law.ntu. edu.tw

[a]Nations covered in latest survey.

Single-nation studies are not included in the table: there are simply too many for one chapter.[1]

1.1 Global Surveys

In addition to expanding their geographical scope, many cross-national surveys substantially increased the number of countries in the project. The path-breaking *Civic Culture* and *Political Action* studies began with five nations each, and most "global" surveys now boast fifty or more countries. These "large-*n*" studies offer researchers the potential to examine attitudes and behaviors in very different economic and political contexts.

1.1.1 *European Values Study/World Values Surveys*

The World Values Survey (WVS) has grown to capture public opinion and value preferences in sixty countries around the world—comparing a diverse array of societies from wealthy to developing. The WVS and European Values Study (EVS) share a substantive interest in values research, and have in the past coordinated questionnaire development, yet remain organizationally independent.[2] While the EVS explicitly limits its activities to Europe the WVS has a global interest. The effects of the EVS/WVS on scholarship have been profound: 81 books, 157 book sections, and 300 journal articles to date.[3] Major reference works by Ronald Inglehart and his colleagues (2004), and an earlier version covers the 1990–93 surveys (Inglehart et al. 1998). Reference works for the EVS include Halman, Luijkx, and van Zunder 2005.

Each national team in the project aims for representative national samples. In most countries, survey teams employ a form of stratified multi-stage random probability sampling. However, in remote areas where this proves difficult, survey teams may employ cluster or quota sampling. In-person interviews last one hour, and the response rate and sampling methodology ranges considerably. Similarly, the number of cases in each country varies greatly, yet the minimum is 1,000.

The core questions center on basic values, religion, attitudes towards political, social, and economic institutions, membership in a variety of formal and informal organizations, and participation in new forms of political activity. Individuals are asked about new issues such as the environment and human rights, their personal happiness, and trust in others.

The number and list of nations surveyed in the project varies from one round to the next. In order to clearly present changes to the slate, Table 47.2 details the list

---

[1] For a thorough review of the voluminous body of national polls around the world (most by commercial firms), see the edited handbook by John Geer (2004), and the annual volumes in the series by Hastings and Hastings (1989).

[2] In this chapter we often refer to the "European Values Study/World Values Survey" (EVS/WVS) to be more explicit about what is often referred to as the "World Values Survey." The reader should note that that EVS and WVS are now two independent organizations, with separate coordination centers and funding sources. The EVS and WVS contact information are separately listed in Table 47.1.

[3] The number of publications generated by the WVS as reported by the ICPSR website search engine (www.icpsr.umich.edu) in May 2005.

Table 47.2 List of nations included in global surveys

Country	WVS/EVS 1981–3 (N=22)	WVS/EVS 1990 (N=41)	WVS 1995 (N=43)	WVS/EVS 1999–01 (N=60)	ISSP 2004 (N=39)	CSES 1996–2001 (N=33)	CSES 2001–5 (N=35)	Gallup 2004 (N=69)	Pew 2004 (N=50)
Albania				X				X	
Algeria				X					X
Angola									X
Argentina		X	X	X				X	X
Armenia			X						
Australia	X		X		X				X
Austria		X		X	X	X	X		
Azerbaijan			X						
Bangladesh									X
Belarus		X	X	X					
Belgium	X	X		X	X	X	X	X	
Bolivia						X		X	X
Bosnia–Hercegovina				X				X	
Brazil		X	X	X	X	X	X	X	X
Britain	X	X	X	X	X	X	X	X	X
Bulgaria		X		X	X	X	X	X	X
Cameroon								X	
Canada	X	X		X	X	X	X	X	X
Chile		X	X	X	X	X	X		X
China		X	X	X					X

Country								
Colombia		X					X	
Croatia						X	X	
Czechoslovakia								X
Czech Rep.	X	X	X	X	X	X		
Denmark		X	X	X	X			X
Dominican Rep.							X	
Ecuador		X					X	
Egypt	X	X						
El Salvador						X	X	
Estonia						X	X	X
Finland	X	X	X		X	X	X	X
France		X				X	X	
Georgia			X		X	X	X	X
Germany	X	X	X	X	X	X	X	X
Germany (W)		X					X	
Ghana	X					X		
Greece		X					X	
Guatemala	X					X		
Honduras	X		X	X		X		X
Hong Kong		X	X	X	X			
Hungary	X					X		X
Iceland	X		X	X	X			X

(Continued)

Table 47.2 (Continued)

Country	WVS/EVS 1981–3 (N=22)	WVS/EVS 1990 (N=41)	WVS 1995 (N=43)	WVS/EVS 1999–01 (N=60)	ISSP 2004 (N=39)	CSES 1996–2001 (N=33)	CSES 2001–5 (N=35)	Gallup 2004 (N=69)	Pew 2004 (N=50)
India		X	X	X			X		X
Indonesia				X					X
Iran				X					
Ireland	X	X		X	X		X	X	X
Israel				X	X	X	X	X	X
Italy	X	X		X	X			X	X
Ivory Coast									
Japan	X	X	X	X	X	X	X		X
Jordan				X					X
Kenya			X					X	X
Kosovo								X	
Kuwait								X	X
Latvia		X	X	X	X			X	X
Lebanon									X
Lithuania		X	X	X		X		X	
Luxembourg				X				X	
Macedonia				X				X	
Mali									X
Malta				X					
Mexico	X	X	X	X	X	X	X	X	X
Moldova			X	X					

	1	2	3	4	5	6	7	8
Montenegro		X						X
Morocco			X					
The Netherlands	X	X	X	X	X	X	X	X
New Zealand				X	X	X	X	
Nigeria	X	X	X				X	X
N. Ireland			X					
Norway	X	X		X	X	X	X	
Pakistan			X					X
Palestinian Authority								
Panama							X	
Paraguay							X	X
Peru		X	X		X		X	X
Philippines		X	X	X			X	X
Poland	X	X	X	X	X	X	X	X
Portugal	X		X	X	X	X	X	
Puerto Rico			X					
Romania	X	X	X		X	X	X	X
Russia	X	X	X		X	X	X	
Saudi Arabia							X	
Senegal								
Serbia			X				X	X
Singapore			X					
Slovakia		X	X	X			X	
Slovenia	X			X	X	X		X

(Continued)

Table 47.2 (*Continued*)

Country	WVS/EVS 1981–3 (N=22)	WVS/EVS 1990 (N=41)	WVS 1995 (N=43)	WVS/EVS 1999–01 (N=60)	ISSP 2004 (N=39)	CSES 1996–2001 (N=33)	CSES 2001–5 (N=35)	Gallup 2004 (N=69)	Pew 2004 (N=50)
South Africa	X	X	X	X	X			X	X
South Korea	X	X	X	X	X	X	X		X
Soviet Union	X								
Spain	X	X	X	X	X	X	X	X	X
Sweden	X	X	X	X	X	X	X		
Switzerland		X	X		X	X	X	X	
Taiwan						X	X		
Tanzania				X					X
Thailand						X			
Tunisia								X	
Turkey		X	X	X			X	X	X
Uganda				X					X
Ukraine			X	X		X		X	X
United Arab Emirates								X	
United States	X	X	X	X	X	X	X	X	X
Uruguay			X	X	X			X	
Uzbekistan									
Venezuela			X	X	X			X	X
Vietnam				X					X
Zimbabwe				X					X

of nations included in each wave. The first wave (1981–3) began with surveys in twenty-two nations, and was dominated by post-industrial nations. The second wave of the larger project (1990) expanded to forty-one countries, building upon the initial core nations to add several new democracies and developing nations from a diverse array of regions including Latin America, Asia, Africa, and central and eastern Europe. The third wave (1995) consisted of forty-three nations. The fourth wave (1999–2002) offers the greatest geographical coverage to date–sixty nations. A fifth wave entered the field in 2005.

Surveys replicate several items over subsequent waves, making this series ideal for both cross-national and cross-temporal analysis. However, some questions and coding categories change substantially over the course of the waves of the survey. These changes complicate time-series analysis in certain instances, and the researcher must be careful to consult the individual codebooks and surveys for some questions. The WVS team compiled an integrated file covering 1980–95. This cumulative file is freely available to the public at the WVS website, and users can browse the integrated codebook, and run a variety of statistical analyses online.[4]

1.1.2 *The International Social Survey Programme*

Formed in 1983, the founding member organizations of the annual International Social Survey Programme (ISSP) included four established annual national survey projects: the General Social Survey (GSS) of the National Opinion Research Center (NORC) in the United States, the Allgemeine Bevölkerungsumfrage der Sozialwissenschaften (ALLBUS) studies of the Zentrum für Umfragen, Methoden, und Analysen (ZUMA) of Germany, and the British Social Attitudes Survey (BSA) of the Social and Community Planning Research in London, and Research School of Social Sciences, Australian National University. The Central Archive for Empirical Research, Cologne (ZA) merges the data into cross-national files.

Similar to the influential role of the WVS, the ISSP series data generated a considerable amount of scholarly research—the ISSP webpage holds 1,600 listings total in its bibliography.[5] Of these, there are at least seven major collections of ISSP research (Jowell et al. 1989, 1993, 1998; Becker et al. 1990; Frizell and Pammett 1997; Tos et al. 1999). The ISSP collects its data as a ten-minute supplement to pre-existing national survey projects, and as a result the data collection follows rigorous methods derived from national samples. Interviews are conducted in person, by telephone, or mail back.

Sociological themes represent the strength of the ISSP surveys. The core questions focus on attitudes towards the economy, gender, legal system, and a standardized set of demographic variables. In addition, successive waves address special topics: the role of government (1985, 1990, 1996, 2006); the environment (1993 and 2000); social inequality (1987, 1992, 1999); work orientations (1989, 1997, 2005); family and changing gender roles (1988, 1994 and 2002); religion (1991 and 1998); social networks

---

[4] www.worldvaluessurvey.org   [5] www.issp.org

(1986); social relations and support systems (2001); national identity (1995, 2003); citizenship (2004); leisure and sports (2007).

As of the latest survey, thirty-nine countries are members of the ISSP, and they are listed in Table 47.2. Each research organization funds its own data collection. By design, the ISSP facilitates both cross-national and cross-temporal research. The Central Archive for Empirical Social Research (ZA), Cologne, compiled the surveys from 1985 to 2000 to create an integrated data file, and the ZA makes the ISSP data available to all member institutions. Scholars can freely access the files six months after they are archived.

1.1.3 *Comparative Study of Electoral Systems*

Although national election studies often employ some of the highest methodological standards, they are generally not easily compared cross-nationally. To remedy this disadvantage, the Comparative Study of Electoral Systems (CSES) matches up the reliability and rigor of national election studies with a set of standardized cross-national variables. Individual election study teams collaborate on the CSES, adding a standard set of public opinion survey questions in their own national post-election study. The CSES Planning Committee, composed of leading scholars of political behavior from around the world, meets regularly at each stage of the project to coordinate the research agenda, study design, and questionnaire. As supplements to national election studies, CSES data are collected through in-person, telephone, and mail back surveys. The CSES data have already provided the evidential basis for six books, sixteen book chapters, twenty journal articles, and several working papers, as currently indicated on the CSES website.[6] The major reference works for this series include books by Norris (2004) and Klingemann et al. (forthcoming).

The CSES is also distinguished by its potentially powerful marriage of individual-level voting behavior and national institutional context. At the micro-level, the CSES data files offer common core variables concerning demographics, vote choice, economic, candidate, party, and electoral system evaluations. At the macro-level, the CSES compiles district-level data and macro-level data on electoral returns, electoral rules and formulas, and regime characteristics.

The CSES has organized its data collection in three "modules"—1996–2000; 2001–5; and 2006–10 (see Table 47.2). The first module encompasses thirty-three countries and focused on the impact of electoral institutions on citizens' political cognition and behavior; the nature of political alignments; and the evaluation of democratic institutions and processes. The second module includes at least thirty-five nations and centers on the impact of political institutions on attitudes towards government accountability, satisfaction with democracy, and representation in the political process. At present, the third module remains in its planning stages, and the rotating theme will focus on perceptions of meaningful choices in elections. The project is an

---

[6] www.cses.org

exemplar in accessibility: CSES data files can be downloaded freely at the project's website (see Table 47.1).[7]

1.1.4 *Pew Global Attitudes Survey*

Rooted in the 1991 benchmark survey, "The Pulse of Europe," which provides data on thirteen European countries, Pew's series of Global Attitude Surveys began with an elite survey of twenty-four countries in 2001. Since then, the annual Global Attitudes Survey measures public opinion among ordinary citizens, and the most recent release is the 2005 study. To date, the Global Attitudes data have generated several Pew Center reports, and they are available at the project website, and contact information is provided in Table 47.1.

Interviews are conducted in person in some countries, and via the telephone in most. The national samples range from 500 in Canada to over 2000 in China and India. Most samples are representative, with the exception of oversampling of urban populations in China, India, and Pakistan. Further, not all questions were asked in all participating countries simply because they were too sensitive politically (e.g. China).

The Pew Global Attitudes project provides data to compare the viewpoints of people from nations around the world toward a common set of issues: globalization, trade, democracy, current issues in world politics, terrorism and the US response to it, and respondents' assessments of their own lives. The data offer a wide lens on public opinion—surveying 49 countries plus the Palestinian Authority in 2003 (listed in Table 47.2), 44 countries in 2002, and 16 in 2005. The Pew Center offers the Global Attitudes Survey on its website free of charge six months after the reports are issued.[8]

1.1.5 *Gallup International*

Gallup International has conducted several global survey projects. These surveys diverge from academic surveys by describing national and regional patterns in public opinion on global issues. Country or region is the implicit explanatory variable, and few questions are designed to examine the sources of variation in attitudes. In contrast with the academic surveys, global surveys carried out by Gallup International, are commercial public opinion polls. In-depth information on the survey methodology is not published, and so it is not possible to fully evaluate the quality of the sampling and fieldwork. Based upon the limited description of the surveys' methodologies reported on the Gallup International website, I calculate that 42 of the 69 national surveys are conducted in person, and the remaining 27 over the telephone. Of the 69 total national surveys, 46 draw national samples, and the remainder focus on urban centers. Sample sizes range from 250 in countries such as Kuwait and Saudi Arabia to 1,000 in Austria, and to 5,012 in Nigeria.

Gallup affiliates have a long series of end of the year polls. They are described in Hastings and Hastings (1989). In 1974 Gallup commissioned the Human Needs and Satisfactions survey, investigating the fears, aspirations, and life satisfaction of individuals in forty nations. This study was published by Kettering and Gallup

[7] www.cses.org   [8] www.peoplepress.org/pgap

International in 1977, and these data have been utilized by the Pew Center Global Attitudes project for some trend analyses. In 1992 Gallup conducted a twenty-five-nation Health of the Planet survey, in conjunction with the first World Forum on the Global Environment held in Rio de Janeiro, Brazil in January of the same year. Topics include attitudes towards the environment and its relationship with economic development. In addition, Gallup conducted the Survey of Nine Islamic Nations in 2001, immediately after the events of 9/11 in the United States. The project tapped citizen attitudes toward the West.

Gallup International's most recent global series began with sixty countries in 1999 with the Millennium Survey, and the topics include democracy, the environment, human rights, women's rights, religion, crime, the performance of the United Nations, and "What matters most in life."

Following on the success of its first global survey, Gallup International commissioned "Voice of the People" surveys in 2002, 2003, and 2004 in sixty-nine countries from a variety of regions: western Europe; east and central Europe; Mid East; the Americas; and Africa. The countries in the 2004 round are listed in Table 47.2. Designed as an annual survey, the 2002 Voice of the People questionnaire asked respondents to identify the most important problem facing the world today, and to register their attitudes towards elections, government legitimacy, terrorism, globalization, American foreign policy, foreign aid, democracy, and the environment. In addition, the 2002 survey examines both interpersonal trust and trust in political, economic, and social institutions.

Because the survey data are commissioned by a commercial firm, the electronic data are available for purchase from Gallup International. However, a small note on the Millennium Survey internet webpage states that the data are "available pro bono to universities and other relevant institutions for further investigation and study."[9]

1.1.6 *United States Information Agency and Department of State*

The United States Information Agency sponsors multinational surveys. Survey data from the over 1,100 USIA funded projects from 1975 to 1992 (updates continuously) are held at the National Archives, and the inventory can be consulted through the Electronic and Special Media Records Service Division. Although available, these surveys are often scattered, intermittent, and access procedures through the National Archives remain complicated. Assembling questions for longitudinal analysis may prove difficult, yet much of the USIA data remain largely unexplored by academics.

Some of the richest collections of USIA surveys are from Latin America, and one thematic example is the Attitude Surveys of National Concerns/Problems. This survey was also administered in western Europe and Australia, India, the Philippines, and Japan at various points throughout the 1970s and early 1980s. The survey methods vary, and many surveys of developing nations are conducted only in the large cities.

---

[9] www.gallup-international.com/ContentFiles/millennium18.asp (May 9, 2005).

The first in a series "World Surveys" were conducted by USIA in the 1960s. They have continued intermittently, and the data from the 1963, 1964, 1965, 1969, 1972 surveys are catalogued at the Roper Center archives (contact information is provided in Table 47.4). These World Surveys include varying combinations of the following nations: Argentina, Brazil, Britain, Chile, France, Germany, Israel, Italy, Japan, the Philippines, Mexico, Thailand, and Venezuela. Other examples include a Latin American Image Study undertaken by USIA in 1971 in Brazil, and Mexico. USIA also did some comparative European surveys from 1954 on, and some of these data are at Roper, and others at the ZA. Further, the Roper Center archives surveys by the USIA from 1992 for several Middle Eastern nations.

1.2 Regional Surveys

Survey research projects comparing a set of nations within a region were the pioneers of multi-nation studies and continue today. A potential disadvantage to regional surveys is observations from fewer nations, but a potential advantage is a substantive focus on issues particularly relevant to the region. Rather than the "most different systems" research design offered by the global surveys, regional surveys support a "most similar systems" research design, where researchers can hold constant many potentially confounding explanatory variables.

1.2.1 *Eurobarometers*

Among cross-national surveys, the Eurobarometers are the best known, and offer the longest comparable time series. With the Eurobarometer series the European Commission initiated a simultaneously survey of public opinion towards a common market in the European Union (EU) in all member countries. The Eurobarometers are the ideal resource for mapping long-term changes in post-industrial European societies. As a consequence, the Eurobarometer series has provided the evidence for numerous standard and special topic reports and at least 22 books, 20 book sections, and 228 journal articles.[10] Three of the major reference volumes include those by Reif and Inglehart (1991), Niedermayer and Sinnott (1995), and Saris and Kaase (1997).

Carried out biennially, the Eurobarometer draws national multi-stage probability samples of at least 1,000 residents in each member state.[11] Interviews are conducted face-to-face in respondents' home languages. The surveys are carried out in each member state by commercial polling firms.

The 1974 Eurobarometer began with Belgium, Britain, Denmark, France, Ireland, Italy, Luxembourg, Netherlands, West Germany, and subsequently added Greece (1980), Portugal and Spain (1985), the former East Germany (1990), Norway (1991),

---

[10] The number of publications generated by the WVS as reported by the ICPSR website search engine (**www.icpsr.umich.edu**). A search of the ZA bibliography for the term Eurobarometer returns 2,023 entries, some reports and working papers.

[11] Due to its small population size, Luxembourg only has a sample size of 600. Post-reunification Germany draws a sample of 2,000.

Finland (1993), Sweden and Austria (1994), and Iceland (2003). In addition, the Commission launched the smaller scale Flash Eurobarometers, and the Central and Eastern Eurobarometers (1990–8)—subsequently replaced by the Candidate Countries Eurobarometer in 2001, which compares publics of candidate countries with the publics of the candidate states that then became part of the EU after accession.

In addition to expanding its geographical coverage, the Eurobarometers have also widened in substantive focus. The core questions concentrate on attitudes towards European integration, the institutions of the EU, and respondents' perceived quality of life. In addition, each survey in the series gives attention to a special topic. While the breadth of questions and number of surveys may seem overwhelming, the question database integrated text retrieval across all surveys makes cross-national time-series analysis quite manageable. In addition, an integrated file, called the Mannheim Eurobarometer Trend File 1970–2002, is available through ZA, and contact information is provided in Table 47.1.[12]

1.2.2 European Social Survey

Only recently initiated in 2002, the European Social Survey (ESS) may soon form the bases for the rich body of literature associated with its peer survey series. The ESS stands apart from many cross-national surveys for its strict methodological rigor. The ESS aims to translate questionnaires in functionally equivalent ways. The central committee imposes consistent methods of fieldwork, including contacting and coding. For example, the survey standardizes the left–right continuum across all participating nations. The design calls for random sampling design of residents fifteen years and older (no quota sampling), one hour in-person interviews, and a minimum 2,000 respondents per nation. Project coordinators set the target response rate at 70 percent, and most countries achieved this response rate, although some still fought to reach a 60 percent rate. The ability of the ESS to achieve high methodological standards is due in part to its generous funding and large-scale design. Although each national team funds its own fieldwork and operations, the central committee still exerts control at each step in the survey process.

The core questions are repeated in each successive wave: they tap attitudes on Europe's changing institutions, political trust, party affiliation, voting behavior, media consumption, value orientations, social exclusion, and demographics. In addition, each wave includes a rotating theme. In the first wave those supplementary questions included citizenship, immigration, basic value orientations, and additional questions for testing questionnaire reliability and validity (consistent with the project's emphasis on methodological rigor). The second round directed its supplementary focus at "family, work and well-being," "opinions on health and care seeking," and "economic morality."

Conducted in 2001, the first wave of interviews covered twenty-two countries, including fifteen EU member states: Austria, Belgium, Czech Republic, Denmark, Finland, France, Germany, Greece, Hungary, Ireland, Israel, Italy, Luxembourg, the

[12] www.gesis.org/za

Netherlands, Norway, Poland, Portugal, Slovenia, Spain, Sweden, Switzerland, UK. In the second wave in 2003, all twenty-two countries recommitted resources, and Estonia and the Slovak Republic joined the line-up. A third wave of interviews is slated for January 2005.

In addition to optimal methodology, the ESS is also highly accessible to the public. The data for all countries participating in the first wave of interviews are freely available online, and details are given in Table 47.1. The data for the second wave of interviews are slated for public release in August 2005. In addition, the ESS is to be commended for its transparency. Planning documents, technical notes, and response rate reports are all readily available on the project's website. Further, the theme of the rotating supplementary questions is open to competition among European scholars.

1.2.3 *European Election Studies*

Prior to 1999, the European Elections Studies (EES) composed part of the Euro-barometer series, and since then works as an independent project. Organized by the EES workgroup, an international group of scholars, the EES website lists twenty books and edited volumes and sixty-seven articles that have emanated from the survey project, including works by Cees van der Eijk and Mark N. Franklin (1996), and more recent reference work for the 1999 study by Brug and van der Eijk (forthcoming). As an independent project, the EES surveys of the voting age popu-lation are conducted by telephone, with sample sizes in 2004 that range from 500 in the Czech Republic to 2,100 in Sweden.

Carried out after each EU parliamentary election (every five years), the themes of the surveys include participation in EU elections and voting behavior, support for European integration and enlargement, and performance of EU political institutions. The 2004 EES covers twenty-four European member states: Austria, Belgium, Cyprus, the Czech Republic, Denmark, Estonia, Finland, France, Germany, Greece, Hungary, Ireland, Italy, Latvia, Lithuania, Luxembourg, the Netherlands, Poland, Portugal, Slovakia, Slovenia, Spain, Sweden, and the United Kingdom.

The EES not only facilitates regional research, but longitudinal analysis as well. Researchers can compare surveys from 1979, 1989, 1994, 1999, and 2004. Data are freely available at Steinmetz Amsterdam (see Table 47.4 for contact information), and as a portable SPSS file on the project's website.[13]

1.2.4 *New Democracies Barometer (NDB), New Europe Barometer (NEB), New Baltic Barometer (NBB)*

The New Democracies, New Europe, and New Baltic Barometers constitute a series of barometers conducted by the Center for the Study of Public Policy, and Richard Rose coordinates.[14] Table 47.1 provides information on each of these surveys independ-ently. Taken together, these barometer series have generated 211 books and reports, as

[13] www.europeanelectionstudies.net
[14] This Barometer series also includes the New Russia Barometer (1992 to present) and the Korea Barometer, which are not included here because of their single-nation focus.

referenced on the CSPP website, including several reference works by Rose, and Rose and Munro (2003).[15] A similar methodology underpins the three projects: in-person interviews conducted in several languages, and stratified national representative samples of 1,000 respondents.

These surveys of post-communist countries are designed to support research on democratization, development, privatization, parties and elections, social protection, and social capital. The major items common to all three barometers include: attitudes towards the economy, corruption, support for democracy and alternative regimes, enlarging Europe, political trust, and participation in social groups and organizations.

The 1991 NDB included Bulgaria, Czechoslovakia, Hungary, Poland, Romania, Slovenia, Austria. The 1992, 1993/4, 1995 studies include Belarus, Bulgaria, Croatia, Czech Republic, Slovakia, Hungary, Poland, Romania, Slovenia, Ukraine. The 1998 study added Yugoslavia and Austria to that core set of countries.

During the 1990s the New Europe Barometer was part of the New Democracies Barometer. The NEB covers seventeen countries including new EU member states and applicants, and key comparisons in the former Soviet Union and western Europe. The slate consists of: Bulgaria, Czech Republic, Hungary, Estonia, Latvia, Lithuania, Poland, Romania, Russia, Slovakia, Slovenia, Belarus, Ukraine, surveys in Moldova, Croatia, Serbia, and Bosnia-Hercegovina and, for comparison, Austria and Germany.

Initiated in 1993, the New Baltic Barometer surveys Estonia, Latvia, and Lithuania. The 2001 and 2004 New Baltic Barometers joined the New Europe Barometer, allowing for comparison with other transitional democracies in the region.

The data files are not publicly available, and reports utilizing the data are presented to policy making and academic bodies.

1.2.5 *Latinobarometer*

Since 1995, the Latinobarometer surveys individuals regarding their political behaviors and attitudes on political, social, and economic conditions in Latin America. The Latinobarometer was initially funded by the European Commission, and the UNDP. This tie to the Eurobarometer laid the structure for the Latinobarometer, which advertises its comparability with other barometer surveys.

Although the series aims for representative random samples, the Latinobarometer has encountered challenges in its fieldwork. Remote rural have proved especially difficult to sample. Nationwide samples are feasible only in some surveys. Random sampling is utilized in Costa Rica, Ecuador, El Salvador, Guatemala, Honduras, Nicaragua, and Panama. In contrast, the survey team resorts to quota samples in Argentina, Bolivia, Brazil, Chile, Colombia, Mexico, Peru, Paraguay, Uruguay, and Venezuela. The smallest sample size is Paraguay's 600 cases. The remaining nations sample about 1,200 cases, and in Spain the survey samples nearly 2,500.

---

[15] www.cspp.strath.ac.uk

The core questions concern the economy, trade, democracy, politics and institutions, social policies, civic culture and social capital, the environment, and current issues. In addition to the standard battery, each wave concentrates on a new theme. For example, the 1996 survey examined trade, foreign investment, and politics. The 1997 surveys added a focus on political parties, the economy, and confidence between countries. The 1998 wave queried respondents on social capital and corruption. The 1999/2000 survey theme was poverty.

Beginning with eight countries, the Latinobarometer series soon expanded to cover seventeen nations: Argentina, Bolivia, Brazil, Chile, Colombia, Costa Rica, Ecuador, El Salvador, Guatemala, Honduras, Mexico, Nicaragua, Panama, Paraguay, Peru, Uruguay, and Venezuela. In addition, Spain has been added in certain years. Like the Barometers of the former communist nations, the Latinobarometer is restrictive–the data are available for purchase.

1.2.6 *Latin American Public Opinion Project*

From 1994 to 2004, the Latin American Public Opinion Project (LAPOP) commissioned forty-one different surveys to assess citizens' support for the political system, political tolerance, perceptions of local government, corruption, and political activity. The common framework enables comparative analysis. For instance, one set of the most recent surveys contains a common core of questions and provides the evidence for one major reference project, *The Political Culture of Democracy in Central America, Mexico, and Colombia, 2004,* by the LAPOP founder and director, Mitchell A. Seligson.

In the collection of these data, survey teams aimed for the highest standards of academic survey research. Teams constructed multi-stage, stratified, area probability samples with target of 1,500 respondents in each country. LAPOP involves surveys of fourteen countries: Bolivia, Colombia, Costa Rica, the Dominican Republic, Ecuador, El Salvador, Guatemala, Honduras, Mexico, Nicaragua, Panama, Paraguay, Peru, and surveys of Madagascar as well.

The tabular results of surveys funded by USAID are freely available.[16] Other data files are available for a fee from LAPOP at the Department of Political Science at Vanderbilt University, and contact information is provided in Table 47.1.[17]

1.2.7 *Afrobarometer*

The Afrobarometer series began in 1993, and has been repeated in subsets of nations in subsequent waves. This relatively new survey data series has already generated six journal articles, and a book by the project coordinators (Bratton et al. 2004).[18] The Afrobarometer website advertises several recent reports of the results for purchase, and holds nearly fifty downloadable working papers.[19] The surveys are carried out by independent research institutes in each nation, and reflect representative cross-sections of the voting age population, drawn from multi-stage area probability

---

[16] www.millennium-int.com/newdsd   [17] www.vanderbilt.edu/americas/English/LAPOP.php

[18] The number of publications generated by the Afrobarometer as reported by the ICPSR website search engine (www.icpsr.umich.edu) in May 2005.

[19] www.afrobarometer.org

samples. The standard sample size in the second wave of surveys was 1,200 cases, with larger samples in more socially heterogeneous countries. Interviews are conducted face to face.

The Afrobarometer asks a series of standard questions regarding attitudes towards political, economic, and social conditions in Africa. Topics focus on democracy, governance, livelihoods, economic conditions, participation, trust, crime, national identity, and other issues confronting developing nations.

The first round began with twelve countries: Botswana, Ghana, Lesotho, Mali, Namibia, Nigeria, Malawi, South Africa, Tanzania, Uganda, Zambia, and Zimbabwe. The second round added Cape Verde, Kenya, Malawi, Mozambique, and Senegal to the line-up. The third round in 2005 was expected to add Benin and Madagascar to that list.

In contrast to many other regional barometers in transition areas, the Afrobarometer data are made freely available to the public two years after the first release of any survey's results, through the ICPSR, and on the Afrobarometer website.[20]

1.2.8 *Asian Barometer*

Large-scale global surveys have often given short shrift to several regions within Asia. Set to fulfill this need, the recent Asian Barometer (official title: Japan-ASEAN Barometer) is a comparative survey of public opinion in East, Southeast, South, and Central Asia. These data provide the basis for a major reference book, *Values and Life Styles in Urban Asia: A Cross-Cultural Analysis and Sourcebook Based on the AsiaBarometer Survey of 2003*, by Inoguchi et al. (2005).[21]

Although the ideal research methodology is nationwide samples in each country, some rural areas are excluded. Sample sizes average 800 per country, and are drawn from individuals 15–59 years old, based on multi-stage stratified random sampling. Interviewers meet face to face with respondents.

The Asian Barometer covers multiple themes: values, identity, life satisfaction, health, family, work, political activity and evaluations of political, economic, and social institutions. In 2004 the study surveyed Brunei, Cambodia, China, Indonesia, Japan, Laos, Malaysia, Myanmar, Philippines, Singapore, South Korea, Thailand, and Vietnam. The data are slated to be accessible through the ICPSR and the Social Science Japan Archive.

1.2.9 *East Asian Barometer*

A recent project, the East Asian Barometer has already generated two articles and a book, and several working papers, according to the project website.[22] Interviews are conducted in person, drawing upon national samples. The sample sizes vary from 811 in Hong Kong to over 3,100 in mainland China.

Administered in 2001–2, the East Asian Barometer covers China, Hong Kong, Indonesia, Japan, Mongolia, the Philippines, South Korea, Taiwan, Thailand. The

---

[20] www.afrobarometer.org   [21] www.avatoli.ioc.u-tokyo.ac.jp-~asiabarometer
[22] Eacsurvey.law.ntu.edu.tw

survey is designed to tap support for democracy and democratic reform, evaluations of the economy, assess the levels of trust in institutions, degree of membership in associations, and political activity. The survey questions and socioeconomic status variables are standardized across all nine nations. The East Asian Barometer data are slated to be publicly available in August 2005.

1.3 National Election Study Series

Election studies within individual nations are conducted by an independent national research team before and/or after a country's election. The most common questions center on voting behavior in present and past elections, expectations about and interest in the election, party identification, attitudes on current issues and evaluations of political leaders, parties, government performance, and democratic institutions.

Although national election studies lack cross-national comparability in most instances, they often comprise the most methodologically sound surveys available. Generally, sampling procedures are rigorous and interviews are conducted in person as well as some by telephone and mail-back. Certain series can be assembled to examine political behavior over three or more decades. For example, the American National Election Study dates back to 1952, and the cumulative file allows researchers to quickly track trends in Americans' political behavior over nearly six decades.

Not only do questions and coding categories vary across election studies, but they can also vary dramatically within a national series. Yet where similar forms of the same questions are repeated over time within the same series, national election study series are unique in their ability to support powerful longitudinal analyses of citizen attitudes and behaviors. Exemplars in employing several national election study series include the works of Dalton (2004, 2006) and Franklin (2004).

An additional difficulty with national election studies is that the data documentation and codebooks are often written in the study's native language—English translations are only sometimes available. To remedy this barrier, in 1989 the International Committee for Research into Elections and Representative Democracy (ICORE) was founded to promote cross-national research in electoral behavior. One of their major goals is to fund the translations of original questionnaires and documentation into English (Mochmann et al. 1998, 1–2), but this process has been delayed for some series. In addition, to facilitate longitudinal research, many study series have been compiled to produce cumulative files. Still others remain as individual data sets, and assembling trends in the series can be a complex process. The Council of European Social Science Data Archives (CESSDA) represents a step toward holding many European national election studies at a central location.

In this section I cover some of the longest series of national election studies: those from Britain, Canada, Denmark, France, Germany, Israel, the Netherlands, Norway, Sweden, United States. Table 47.3 provides an overview of these studies: the years in the series, the number of studies, and contact information for the data source or archive. Given that cross-national studies are the focus of this chapter, I have limited coverage to series with twenty-five or more years of continuous surveys.[23] For a more detailed listing of European series see the *Inventory of National Election Studies in Europe 1945–1995*, by Mochmann et al. (1998).

The election study series are most extensive in established industrial democracies, and thus these countries form the basis for Table 47.3. From the table, it is apparent that most of these studies began in the 1950s or 1960s and continue through present elections. Although the ICPSR holds some election studies from countries other than

Table 47.3 National Election Study Series

Country	Title	Years	# Surveys	Source/Archives
Britain	British Election Study	1963–2001	11	Data Archive, University of Essex, dawww.essex.ac.uk, and ICPSR pre-1983
Canada	Canadian National Election Study	1965–2004	10	University of Montreal www.fas.montreal.ca/pol/ces-eec/ces.html, and ICPSR pre-1997
Denmark	Danish Election Study	1959–2002	17	Danish Data Archives (DDA) www.sa.dk/dda
France	French Election Study	1958–2002	7	Banque de Données Socio-Politiques (BDSP), solcidsp.upmf-grenoble.fr ICPSR 1958, 68
Germany	German Election Study	1949–1994	13	Zentralarchiv für Empirische Sozialforschung (ZA), www.za.uni-koeln.de
Israel	Israeli Election Study	1969–2001	9	Inter-University Consortium for Political and Social Research (ICPSR), www.icpsr.umich.edu
Netherlands	Dutch Parliamentary Election Study	1967–2003	11	NIWI Steinmetz Archive (STAR), www.swidoc.nl, and ICPSR pre-1982
Norway	Norwegian Election Study	1957–2001	11	Norwegian Social Science Data Services (NSD), www.nsd.uib.no, and ICPSR for 1957, 65
Sweden	Swedish Election Study	1956–2002	15	Swedish Social Science Data Service (SSD), www.ssd.gu.se
United States	American Election Study	1952–2004	14	Inter-University Consortium for Political and Social Research (ICPSR), www.icpsr.umich.edu

[23] For example, the Australian National Election Study was not included here because it dates back to 1987.

the US, the trend is toward national archives holding their own national studies (where they have the resources). The accessibility of these studies varies from one nation (or even principle investigator) to another. Regulations regarding access can be obtained by contacting the relevant archive. Some series are conducted at regular intervals, while others are more intermittent, such as the French election studies. Some of the most extensive series have been compiled into cumulative files, which facilitate longitudinal analysis based upon particular questions or variables. For example, the American, British, Dutch, and German series have released these cumulative files.

2 MAKING SURVEYS ACCESSIBLE: THE ROLE OF THE MAJOR ARCHIVES

Without data archives, many surveys that are so vital to our empirical knowledge of political behavior would be less easily accessed, remaining scattered in the hands of a multitude of principle investigators. Data archives fuel research on comparative political behavior by centralizing, storing, maintaining, and disseminating both cross-national and individual nation surveys. Without archives, many early surveys may be lost, undermining scholars' ability to analyze political behavior over the long term. The following discussion reviews the major survey data archives, and Table 47.4 details the contact information (see also Mochmann 2002).

Established in 1962, the Inter-University Consortium for Political and Social Research (ICPSR) stands out as one of the most prominent data archives in the world. Housed within the Institute for Social Research at the University of Michigan, researchers at ICPSR member institutions can access a diverse range of survey data— from the American national election studies, to various election studies from several national series such as the Canadian, French, German, and Dutch series, to the World Values Survey, to the Afrobarometers and Eurobarometers.

Similarly, the Central Archive for Empirical Social Research (Zentralarchiv für Empirische Sozialforschung, ZA) is a leader among data archives. A major store-house for a voluminous data collection, the ZA headquarters at the University of Cologne. Examples of the ZA's holdings include the ISSP series, and German election study series. The codebooks of this series are available in English language also by the ICPSR which has made them to one of the most frequently used European election surveys in the US and around the world.

Founded just after the Second World War, the Roper Center for Public Opinion Research pioneered survey data archives, and blends both academic and commercial polls. Roper Center data are accessible for a fee, or through paid membership by individuals or institutions. The Center compiled a Catalogue of Holdings, providing

Table 47.4 Major survey data archives around the world

Name	Institution Headquarters	Contact http://
Inter-University Consortium for Political and Social Research (ICPSR)	Institute for Social Research, University of Michigan	www.icpsr.umich.edu
Central Archive for Empirical Social Research (ZA) (Zentralarchiv für Empirische Sozialforschung)	University of Cologne	www.gesis.org/za
The Roper Center	University of Connecticut	www.ropercenter.uconn.edu
UK Data Archive	University of Essex. Data archive for Economic and Social Research Council (ESRC)	www.data-archive.ac.uk
Spanish Social Science Archive (ARCES) Archivo de Estudios Sociales	Center for Sociological Investigations (CIS), Spain	www.cis.es/
Steinmetz Archive (Dutch Social Science Data Archive)	Netherlands Institute of Scientific Information Services	www2.niwi.knaw.nl/en/ maatschappijwetenschappen/ steinmetzarchief/
Norwegian Social Science Data Services (NSSD)	University of Bergen	www.uib.no/nsd
Council of European Social Science Data Archive (CESSDA)	Online, headquarters Norwegian Social Science Data Service	www.nsd.uib.no/cessda/ europe.html
Australian Social Science Data Archive (ASSDA)	Australian Consortium for Social and Political Research, Australian National University	aasda.anu.edu.au
Democracy Survey Database	USAID, Vanderbilt University Center for the Americas	www.millennium-int.com/newdsd
Center for the Study of Public Opinion (CESOP)	University of Campinhas, Brazil	www.cesop.unicamp.br
South African Data Archive (SADA)	National Research Foundation, Pretoria, South Africa	www.nrf.ac.za/sada
Social Science on Japan Data Archive (SSJDA)	Institute of Social Science, University of Tokyo	ssjda.iss.u-tokyo.ac.jp/en
International Federation of Data Organizations (IFDO)	Umbrella organization, 30 members	www.ifdo.org

a searchable description of its 10,000 data sets. While many of its holdings sample the American public, such as the General Social Survey and the Social Capital Community Benchmark Surveys, others poll residents of nations around the world. For example, the Roper Center holds over 1,000 different data sets from Great Britain. In response to the proliferation of independent national data archives in other nations, the Center recently shifted its focus to multinational surveys. In addition, since 1989 the Roper Center offers the Latin American Databank. The databank partners with Latin American regional databanks, institutes, universities, and commercial polling firms to acquire and distribute its 1,000 surveys from sixteen Latin American countries.

Moving down Table 47.4 toward some of the more focused regional archives, the UK Data Archive is located in the University of Essex, and houses over 7,000 social science data sets. The UK Data Archive stores and disseminates data for the Economic and Social Research Council, such as the British National Election Studies, British Census data, and Eurobarometer series. Similar to the ICPSR, the UK Data Archive is a membership-based organization.

Another national organization, ARCES is a social science archive in Spain, sponsored by Spain's Center for Sociological Investigations (CIS). With over 1,600 surveys, ARCES provides access to the Spanish Election Studies, surveys of Spanish youth, and monthly barometer polls. Most of the data are available for a fee three months after the processing is completed. In a similar fashion, since 1962 the Steinmetz Archive houses Dutch social science data, such as the Dutch National Election Study, and multi-nation surveys such as the European Election Study.

The Norwegian Social Science Data Services (NSSD), University of Bergen, stores and disseminates survey data dating back to 1964, surveys such as the Norwegian Election Studies, and census data. The NSSD also sponsors the homepage for the organization of European data archives, the Council of European Social Science Data Archive (CESSDA).

The Australian Social Science Data Archive (ASSDA) works as a unit of the Australian Consortium for Social and Political Research, Research School of Social Sciences at the Australian National University. Since 1981, the ASSDA archives Australian National Election Studies, Australian population and census data and data from other nations in the Asia Pacific Region.

The Democracy Survey Database, supported by the USAID and Vanderbilt University Center for the Americas, provides a web-accessible, centralized source for a series of surveys of Latin and Central American countries, including many of the LAPOP studies described in the previous section. Because many of the surveys were centrally coordinated and have a common framework, the website offers a tool for an organized search of cross-survey topics, and even key question selection.

One of the largest and most accessible archives in Latin America is located at the University of Campinhas in Brazil. The Center for the Study of Public Opinion (CESOP) holds over 2,300 surveys, including a large collection of electoral surveys, publishes a journal about Brazilian public opinion, and is a partner of the ICPSR and Roper Center.

An electronic storehouse for multiple studies of the South African populations, and some comparative surveys, the South African Data Archive (SADA), based in Pretoria, holds academic, government, and commercial surveys. The data catalogue lists a diverse array of surveys—from the annual General Household Surveys, to surveys of political attitudes. Currently there are no costs in ordering data and documentation from SADA.

The Social Science Research of Japan Data Archive (SSJDA) collects, stores, and distributes Japanese survey data. While the collection of such studies as the Japanese Election studies is extensive, and the data freely accessible pending application, the SSJDA website cautions that data sets are provided only in Japanese. The SSJDA, a partner of the ICPSR, is a unit within the Information Center for Social Research on Japan, Institute of Social Science, University of Tokyo, and is sponsored by several other funding agencies. Because the SSJDA is one of the only major Japanese archives, and was only recently established in 1998, many previous empirical data disappeared after its primary analysis. The loss of these data underscores the need for archives to preserve data.

In an effort to centralize information and facilitate the exchange of data across borders, umbrella organizations have been created to connect these national archives. The prominent umbrella organizations include the worldwide International Feder-ation of Data Organizations (IFDO) and the more European-based Council of European Social Science Data Archive (CESSDA). Founded in 1976/7, both organ-izations compile information on a diverse array of data sets from national social science archives such as ZA in Germany and ARCES in Spain. In addition, these organizations work to achieve common standards for documenting and sharing data sets (Mochmann 2002).

3 CONCLUSIONS

Cross-national survey data projects have proliferated in recent years, offering researchers the empirical base to study a variety of different themes and regions. Despite the major advances in survey projects, the opportunity remains to design future surveys with an eye toward teasing out the causal mechanisms behind many of the established relationships. Comparative surveys would be enhanced by the add-ition of more panel studies like the Political Action Study (1973/6, 1979/81), and perhaps even experimental survey designs.

In addition, rather than limiting respondents' options to a predetermined set of responses, greater funding is necessary to allow for more open-ended questions that might allow individuals to more clearly convey the basis for their evaluations of the political world. Likewise, the smaller sample sizes that make contemporary surveys more affordable also limit our ability to draw sufficient cases for in-depth analysis of subsets of the population. The limited number of cases circumscribes our under-standing of what shapes the attitudes and behaviors of groups such as the young, and racial and ethnic minority groups.

Most of the major cross-national surveys primarily tap perceptions, values, and attitudes. Questions addressing actual political behavior are most often found in the national election studies, and CSES is a first step in making these election studies comparable across nations. As it stands, it takes a great deal of effort and time to find questions comparable over time within the same election study series, let alone comparable across nations.

Surveys funded by government organizations are public domain, and accessible to the public. By tradition, most survey data are restricted for a few years after collection. The American National Science Foundation stipulates that investigators share the data they collect "at no more than incremental cost and within a reasonable time" (NSF, GC-1 (07/01/02). However, the "norm" for that interim period of exclusive rights varies across projects, and around the world. Further, many regional surveys are increasingly funded by private sources, and if they provide data to the general public at all, may charge considerable fees. These fees may prove prohibitive for many researchers with limited resources, especially graduate students and junior scholars.

Normatively speaking, what *should be* the obligations to share data? On the one hand, from the perspective of those who invested their efforts in collecting and preparing the data, a brief period is often necessary for in-house analysis. By releasing the data too early, a "free-rider" may achieve the first publication. Usurping the researcher who invested the capital may weaken the future collection of data, reducing the incentive of Principal Investigators to gather the data in the first place. The logic underpinning a brief period of exclusive rights operates much like the market-based logic of research and development for products such as prescrip-tion medications.

On the other hand, some academic surveys remain difficult or expensive to obtain, and/or suffer from an extended delay from collection to public release. The largely pervasive norm of archiving and sharing data within a year or two is essential to the advancement of science. With older data, researchers are often unable to address the most pressing current political issues. Further, survey data that are not shared leave behind gaps in the literature, and a new team must reinvent the wheel. Surveys that merely re-create unreleased data waste precious resources. Limited accessibility to cross-national surveys can impede scholarship in certain areas, especially where there are relatively few surveys conducted at all.

In general, the "large-n" academic studies and surveys of western Europe have been most easily accessed, adding to their visibility, and to the extensive study of individuals in western nations. Specific to emerging democracies and developing nations, the timely release of survey data is especially important, and it is often lacking. Transitions are, by definition, time sensitive. The proliferation of projects in previously undersurveyed regions and countries is only the first step in evening our knowledge of political behavior in a diverse array of political settings. In order to

truly step up research, survey data must be widely shared through established
archives, or online, and advertised to young scholars.

References

ALMOND, G., and VERBA, S. 1963. *The Civic Culture*. Boston: Little Brown.

BARNES, S., KAASE, M., et al. 1979. *Political Action*. London: Sage.

BECKER, J. et al. eds. 1990. *Attitudes to Inequality and the Role of Government*. Rijswijk, The
Netherlands: Sociaal en Cultureel Planbureau.

BLAIS, A. et al. 2001. Measuring party identification: Britain, Canada, and the United States.
Political Behavior, 23: 5–22.

BRATTON, M. et al. 2004. *Public Opinion, Democracy, and Market Reform in Africa*. Cambridge:
Cambridge University Press.

CLARKE, H., and STEWART, M. 1998. The Decline of Parties in the Minds of Citizens. *Annual
Review of Political Science*, 1.

DALTON, R. 2004. *Democratic Challenges, Democratic Choices: The Erosion of Political Support
in Advanced Industrial Democracies*. Oxford: Oxford University Press.

—— *Citizen Politics: Public Opinion and Political Parties in Advanced Industrial Democracies*,
4th edn. Washington, DC: CQ Press.

—— and WATTENBERG, M. eds. 2000. *Parties without Partisans: Political Change in Advanced
Industrial Democracies*. Oxford: Oxford University Press.

EIJK, C. VAN DER, and M. FRANKLIN. 1996. *Choosing Europe? The European Electorate and
National Politics in the Face of Union*. Ann Arbor: University of Michigan Press.

FRANKLIN, M. 2004. *Voter Turnout and the Dynamics of Electoral Competition in Established
Democracies since 1945*. Cambridge: Cambridge University Press.

—— and WLEIZEN, C. eds. 2002. *The Future of Election Studies*. Amsterdam: Pergamon.

FRIZELL, A., and PAMMETT, J. eds. 1996. *Social Inequality in Canada*. Ottowa: Carleton
University Press.

—— —— eds. 1997. *Shades of Green*. Ottowa: Carleton University Press.

GEER, J. ed. 2004. *Public Opinon and Polling around the World: A Historical Encyclopedia*. vols.
i and ii. Santa Barbara, Calif.: ABC-CLIO.

HALMAN, L., LUIJKX, R., and VAN ZUNDER, M. 2005. *Atlas of European Values*. Amsterdam:
Brill Academic Publishers.

HASTINGS, E., and HASTINGS, P. eds. 1989. *Index to International Public Opinion, 1987–1988*.
Westport, Conn.: Greenwood.

HEATH, A. F., FISHER, S., and SMITH, S. 2005 The globalization of public opinion research.
Annual Review of Political Science, 8: 297–333.

INGLEHART, R. et al. 2004. *Human Beliefs and Values: A Cross-Cultural Sourcebook Based on the
1999–2002 Values Survey*. Mexico, D.F.: Siglo Veintiuno Editores.

INOGUCHI, T. et al. 2005. *Values and Life Styles in Urban Asia: A Cross-Cultural Analysis and
Sourcebook Based on the AsiaBarometer Survey of 2003*. Mexico City: Siglo XXI Editores.

JOWELL, R. et al. eds. 1989. *British Social Attitudes: Special International Report*. Aldershot:
Gower.

—— et al. eds. 1993. *International Social Attitudes: the 10th BSA Report*. Aldershot: Dartmouth
Publishing.

—— et al. eds. 1998. *British and European Social Attitudes: The 15th BSA Report.* Aldershot: Ashgate.

KLINGEMANN, H. et al. forthcoming. (CSES) Oxford: Oxford University Press.

MOCHMANN, E. 2002. *International Social Science Data Service: Scope and Accessibility.* Cologne: International Social Science Council.

—— et al. 1998. *Inventory of National Election Studies in Europe 1945–1995.* Bergisch Gladbach: Edwin Ferger Verlag.

NIEDERMAYER, O., and SINNOTT, R. eds. 1995. *Public Opinion and Internationalized Governance: Beliefs in Government,* vol. ii. Oxford: Oxford University Press.

NORRIS, P. 2004. *Electoral Engineering: Voting Rules and Political Behavior.* New York: Cambridge University Press.

REIF, K., and INGLEHART, R. eds. 1991. *Eurobarometer: The Dynamics of European Public Opinion: Essays in Honor of Jacques-Rene Rabier.* London: Macmillan.

ROSE, R., and MUNRO, N. 2003. *Elections and Parties in New European Democracies* Washington, DC: CQ Press.

SARIS, W., and KAASE, M. eds. 1997. *Eurobarometer: Measurement Instruments for Opinions in Europe.* ZUMA Nachrichten Spezial. Vol. ii. Mannheim.

SCOTTO, T., and SINGER, M. 2004. Industrial democracies. Pp. 491–6 in *Public Opinion and Polling around the World: A Historical Encyclopedia,* ed. J. Geer. Santa Barbara, Calif.: ABC-CLIO.

SELIGSON, M. 2004. *The Political Culture of Democracy in Central America, Mexico and Colombia.* Latin American Public Opinion Project (LAPOP), Vanderbilt University, Nashville, Ten.

THOMASSEN, J. 1976. Party identification as a cross-cultural concept: its meaning in the Netherlands. Pp. 63–79 in *Party Identification and Beyond,* ed. I. Budge, I. Crewe, and D. Farlie. London: John Wiley.

TOS, N. et al. eds. 1999. *Modern Society and Values: A Comparative Analysis Based on the ISSP Project.* Ljubljana: FSS, University of Ljubljana; Mannheim: ZUMA.

CHAPTER 48

COMPARATIVE OPINION SURVEYS

JOHN CURTICE

And what should they know of England, who only England know?

(Kipling 1910)

1 WHY DO COMPARATIVE OPINION RESEARCH?

THE study of mass political behavior has a deceptively simple objective—to establish the causes and consequences of the political values and behaviors of the general population.[1] It faces one major obstacle—the sheer size of (most) general populations. Its ability to overcome that obstacle rests heavily on the power of the sample survey. Statistical theory demonstrates that inferences about the characteristics of a large population can in fact be drawn from the evidence of relatively small samples drawn randomly from that population. True, there is some uncertainty associated with those inferences, but its degree is known. Moreover that uncertainty is centered on the true value in the population as a whole. So, for example, if 50 percent of a

---

[1] This chapter focuses on the methods and logic of comparative survey research. The chapter by Kittilson describes the wealth of comparative surveys that are available to researchers.

random sample of 1,000 people has a particular characteristic, there is a 95 percent chance that between 47 and 53 percent actually have that characteristic amongst the population from which the sample was drawn. Armed with that knowledge, the student of political behavior has been able since the advent of the sample survey in the 1930s to make empirically substantiated statements about mass publics on the basis of information gathered from just a thousand people or so.

This approach does, however, beg one important question—what is the population about which we want to make empirically substantiated statements? Sample surveys are commonly conducted within the confines of a particular state. For many purposes this is perfectly acceptable. If, for example, we want to understand why people vote the way that they do in US presidential elections, a survey based on a random sample of the population of the United States is likely to be perfectly adequate. But the study of political behavior has loftier ambitions than simply explaining how people behave in particular countries. It wishes to be able to make statements about behavior in general. Yet we cannot assume that what is true in one country necessarily holds elsewhere. Perhaps, for example, how people vote in US presidential elections is influenced by circumstances that are particular to those elections and thus is different from how people vote in other elections elsewhere.

So survey research that crosses the boundaries of the nation-state is essential to the study of political behavior, as Kipling recognized in the above quotation. At minimum if we are to be able to make statements about how people behave politically that are generally empirically substantiated, they need to be tested in a wide variety of social and political environments. Yet in practice cross-national research has much more to offer than this. If political behavior is influenced by the circumstances in which it takes place, its study needs to be pursued using a research design in which those circumstances vary. This condition is often not fulfilled by research conducted within one country. For example, it is often argued that people are more likely to participate in elections if a system of proportional representation is in place than if a majoritarian system is in use (see chapter by Blais in this volume; Blais and Dobryzynska 1998; Franklin 2002; Norris 2004). Yet, elections within any one country are typically held using either one kind of system or the other, not a mixture of the two. Thus, the study of the impact of electoral systems on turnout at elections almost inevitably requires us to undertake comparative research. Much the same can be said of almost any characteristic that does not usually vary within a country.

Moreover, there is more than one way in which circumstances that vary from one country to another can affect behavior. For example, one way in which the use of proportional representation might increase turnout is simply by increasing the proportion of all kinds of people who vote—young and old, those interested in politics and those less so, strong party identifiers and weak identifiers, etc.—by more or less the same amount. In short, a particular kind of electoral system simply influences the overall level of turnout rather than the kind of person who votes. But an alternative possibility is that the use of proportional representation increases turnout amongst some groups more than others. Perhaps, for example, it has more impact on those belonging to groups who are less likely to vote, such as younger people, the politically uninterested and weak identifiers (Fisher et al., 2006). If that happens, then the electoral system a country uses not only affects the level of participation but its relationship with other variables, such as age, political interest, and strength of identification. The ability of comparative survey research to assess the degree to which relationships may be contingent on national circumstance is at least as important as the opportunities it opens up to assess the impact of national circumstance on the overall incidence of behaviors and attitudes.

Indeed, the ability of comparative research to uncover the impact of circumstances that vary between countries but do not differ within them means that such research should be of interest even to the student whose concern is confined to understanding behavior in one particular country. If, for example, some of the most profound influences upon how people vote in US presidential elections are features that are common across the United States, such as the relative weakness of the country's political parties or the ability of candidates to purchase air time on television, then US presidential elections can only be adequately analyzed and understood if they are compared with elections elsewhere where these circumstances do not pertain. In other words, comparative survey research can enable us better to understand not only the general but the particular as well.

So comparative cross-national mass political research brings three main benefits. First, it enables us to assess the empirical generalizability of claims that we might make about the causes and consequences of political attitudes and behavior. Second, it enables us to widen the range of contextual influences on attitudes and behavior that can be analyzed, in particular making it possible to assess the impact of influences that are largely invariant within countries but do vary between them. Third, it can even contribute to the study of behavior within a particular country by providing points of comparison that make it possible to assess the impact of that country's particular social and political circumstances on behavior within that country.

2 THE PROBLEMS OF COMPARATIVE SURVEYS

The benefits of comparative analyses rest on a crucial assumption—that we can make valid comparisons between the results obtained by surveys conducted in different countries. All forms of survey research are subject to potential sources of bias that mean they fail to provide as reliable a guide to the characteristics of a population as sampling theory would lead us to expect (Groves 1987, 1989). In particular, some parts of a population may be omitted from or under-represented in the coverage of a survey. Meanwhile, the questions asked in a survey may fail to measure accurately what the researcher may have been aiming to measure. The particular difficulty that arises in comparative cross-national research is not that these problems exist, but that their incidence may vary from country to country. As a result we may wonder whether the differences between the results of a survey conducted in two or more countries reflect artifactual differences in how the survey was conducted in the two countries rather than real differences between their populations (Heath, Fisher, and Smith 2005).

Between-country variation in measurement error is perhaps the most obvious pitfall of comparative survey research. Clearly if different questions are asked in different countries, any differences in response may simply reflect differences in question wording. Thus most exercises in comparative survey research are based on a common questionnaire that ideally is administered in an identical manner in every country. But one immediately obvious limitation to the fulfillment of this ideal is that people in different countries speak different languages. Even if a questionnaire is translated faithfully from its internationally agreed original, differences in the structure of different languages and in the connotations associated with different words in different languages may well mean that the cognitive and affective meaning of a question in the minds of respondents varies from country to country. Meanwhile attempts to develop batteries of questions designed to measure adherence to underlying values such as equality or social liberalism may be undermined by the fact that the degree to which any particular question taps adherence to such values varies from country to country. More difficult still is the possibility that a concept may not exist in certain cultures. Previous research on attitudes towards religion, for example, has had to cope with the difficulty that the concept of "God" does not exist in Japanese culture (Jowell 1998).

Less obvious, but no less important however, are differences between countries in survey practice. Survey research is commonly organized on a national basis. That is, while one fieldwork organization will usually be responsible for conducting a comparative survey in its country, a different organization will undertake the survey in another country, etc. In any event, even if this were not the case the way in which a survey is conducted may have to vary from country to country because of national differences of practice and circumstance. For example, the ability to undertake pure random sampling depends on the existence of (and access to) a full (and accurate) population register, or failing that a full list of households or addresses from which a random sample of individuals can be generated. Sampling procedures must inevitably vary depending on the existence and the form of such information. Meanwhile, in some countries securing interviews in rural areas may be difficult either because such populations are geographically widely spread or because of relatively low rates of literacy. Equally, differences of geography may mean that the degree to which samples are geographically clustered in order to keep survey costs down has to vary. Of course, both differences of national circumstance and in the quality of interviewing may produce substantial differences in response rates—and thus different levels of exposure to the possibility that samples may be biased because of differential non-response.

In short—and the above discussion is far from exhaustive—comparative opinion research is exposed to the severe problem that alongside the substantive differences between countries whose impact such research is designed to discern there may well coexist methodological differences that in themselves make countries appear more or less similar to each other than in reality is the case. The comparative researcher's task is already often difficult enough because countries typically do not differ substantively in just one respect, but several, thereby potentially making it difficult to discern which substantive difference might account for any particular difference between the results of surveys conducted in two or more countries. Now it appears that in practice we cannot be sure that any difference we might uncover is not simply an artifact of difference in survey method rather than a real difference. The apparent analytic power of comparative opinion research appears to have crumbled all too readily in our hands.

3 Overcoming the Problems

How might that power possibly be restored? One obvious possibility is to reduce the degree of heterogeneity in survey practice. This is very much the approach that has been adopted by one recently instigated cross-national collaboration, the European Social Survey (European Social Survey n.d.*a*). One of its avowed aims has been to ensure that each participating survey is conducted to more or less the same high standard. Thus, for example, not only are strict guidelines for the implementation of random sampling laid down, but how it is proposed to implement those guidelines in each country has to be agreed by a coordinating methodological committee (Lynn et al. 2004). Amongst the key features of these guidelines are that all interviewing has to take place face to face, with both a minimum target response rate of 70 percent, and a minimum effective sample size (that is after taking into account the impact of any geographical clustering of interviews and any unequal selection probabilities), of 1,500 (European Social Survey n.d.*b*). Meanwhile, questionnaires are independently translated by two native speakers and then any differences are resolved by those with knowledge of survey design and the research topic as well as the languages in question. (For more on translation strategies see Smith 2002.)

Such an approach to comparative survey research places a premium on the quality of the work in those countries that do participate in a survey rather than on ensuring coverage of as many countries as possible—though in the event when the first ESS survey was conducted in 2002 no less than twenty-two European countries endeavored to meet the organizers' exacting standards while twenty-six did so in 2004. (Surveys are being conducted every other year.) In any case, there are other reasons why we might limit the range of countries included in a program of comparative opinion research. First, the more diverse the countries being covered, the greater the difficulty of ensuring that the questions asked have the same meaning to respondents across language and culture. Even if there are attempts to ensure similarity of meaning, when there is a diverse set of countries comparability may only be achieved at the cost of producing questions that are so general and abstract that respondents everywhere may have some difficulty discerning their meaning (Kuechler 1998). Second, the larger the number of countries included, the greater the likelihood that those who attempt to analyze the resulting data do not have sufficient understanding of the social, political, economic, and cultural attributes of each country to be able to interpret the data sensitively and sensibly (Jowell 1998). In short it could be argued that the approach of the first ever major piece of comparative opinion research, Almond and Verba's *Civic Culture* study (Almond and Verba 1963), which confined its attention to five countries chosen for their theoretical interest, provides a model as to how comparative survey research should be conducted.

Indeed, it is interesting to note that many of the more recently instigated programs of comparative survey research have been "regional" rather than "global" in character (also see chapter by Kittilson in this volume). The trend began with the instigation of a range of "barometer" surveys in central and eastern Europe following the collapse of the Berlin Wall (Centre for the Study of Public Policy n.d.). An annual "Latinobarometer" that now covers eighteen countries in Latin America began in 1995 (Latinobarómetro Corporation n.d.), an "Afrobarometer" started in 1999 with twelve countries, with as many as eighteen participating in the third round conducted in 2005–6 (Afrobarometer n.d.*a*), while no less than two collaborations, the East Asia Barometer and the Asia Barometer, have been instigated (in 2001 and annually since 2003 respectively), each covering around a dozen or so countries in overlapping parts of eastern and southern Asia (East Asia Barometer n.d.; Asia Barometer n.d.). These regional collaborations vary in the degree to which they have attempted to impose similarity of methodological rigor across their component countries, with perhaps the most impressive being the attempts of the Afrobarometer to promote the same high standards in countries that often lack a tradition of high-quality survey research or indeed much of the infrastructure required to implement random sampling (Afrobarometer n.d.*b*). Such regional collaborations enable these surveys to focus on those topics that are of common concern in their parts of the world rather than pursuing an agenda that simply reflects the intellectual concerns and assumptions of advanced industrial democracies.

In fact, the ability of the European Social Survey to obtain methodological consistency and rigor is dependent not so much on its regional character as on the organizational structure it has been able to develop. Unlike other collaborations, it has access to funding from cross-national political and scientific institutions such as the European Union and the European Science Foundation.[2] Amongst other things this ensures that it has a comparatively well-funded permanent secretariat and central infrastructure. Meanwhile, funding for the various national surveys typically comes from national scientific funding councils who are willing to support the high standards that ESS demands. In contrast, most comparative research projects are

---

[2] The influence that the existence of the European Union has had on comparative survey research is underlined by the fact that the Union has commissioned, funded, and undertaken the longest-running and most intense program of cross-national research anywhere in the world (European Commission n.d.). While its Eurobarometer surveys (including associated surveys in candidate members of the Union) are primarily concerned with the policy need of the Union to chart public support for its activities and institutions, the series has proved to be an invaluable resource in academic research (e.g. Inglehart 1990; Kaase and Newton 1995). The surveys have been conducted twice a year since 1973. The initial survey covered the nine countries that were members of the EU at that time; it now covers the current twenty-five members.

The introduction of direct elections to the Union's European Parliament in 1979 has also stimulated cross-national survey research on voting behavior and attitudes at those elections, some of which research used the Eurobarometer as its survey platform, under the auspices of the European Election Study (European Elections Study n.d.; van der Eijk and Franklin 1996).

voluntary collaborations between national survey teams and have a relatively limited secretariat that may well be provided by just one country.

Indeed, of the three truly "global" comparative research survey collaborations that currently exist, two do not even attempt to undertake complete whole surveys within each country. Rather, both the International Social Survey Programme (ISSP), a collaboration between general social surveys, and the Comparative Study of Electoral Systems Project (CSES), a collaboration between academic national election studies, are collaborations between national surveys that ask about their own domestic agendas but agree to devote a part of their survey to a module of common questions. Indeed many of the surveys involved in these two collaborations are well-established enterprises. Thus the ISSP was instigated in 1984 by three existing social surveys, the US General Social Survey, the British Social Attitudes survey, and the German ALLBUSS, together with survey researchers from the Australian National University, though it now has as many as forty-one participants who collaborate annually. The CSES, which began in 1996, includes amongst its membership most of the long-running national election studies in the well-established democracies, as well as studies in countries where democratic elections let alone election studies have a much shorter history. Altogether, its first module covered elections in as many as thirty-four countries, the second in over forty.

Collaborations between existing national studies have one key advantage. They are relatively inexpensive, as they do not require the full cost of mounting a survey to be found in every participating country. But they are inevitably limited in the degree of methodological consistency that can be achieved. Faced with the choice between maintaining existing domestic practices and changing those practices to meet international requirements the former pressure will tend to be greater, especially if changing the way an established survey is conducted might compromise the integrity of a domestic time series. Given that constraint the ISSP has relatively strict requirements that a survey must be able to satisfy before it is admitted to its membership (International Social Survey Programme 2003). All surveys are, for example, meant to use random sampling and undertake at least a thousand interviews. Meanwhile, the questions in each annual module (with each module covering a rotating cycle of subjects) are agreed collaboratively by all of the participating members, thereby helping to ensure that they are crafted with sensitivity to cultural and linguistic differences. They are also all asked together in the same order in a block, albeit either face to face or as part of a self-completion supplement. Nevertheless, the program does not have any rules on how questionnaires should be translated while an examination of the methodology actually being employed by its members revealed that not all of them necessarily followed the principles of random sampling that the program was meant to uphold (Park and Jowell 1997).

The CSES is even less rigorous. While it supposedly requires its members to administer the module as whole in a block, not all of them follow this requirement. The module may be administered face to face, by telephone, or by self-completion questionnaire (either as a supplement to a face-to-face survey or as part of a mail-back survey). It does not insist on random sampling nor does it have any rules on translation. This latitude in part reflects the fact that, as we have already noted, the project has had to accept the fact that already well-established national election studies are less willing to compromise their own domestic time series by changing how their surveys are conducted. In part, too, the secretariat lacks either the resources or indeed the authority in what is a voluntary collaboration to insist on greater conformity to a set of common standards. The one crucial requirement that the project does have, however, is that fieldwork should take place in the period immediately after a national parliamentary or presidential election, thereby enabling the project to capture as accurately as possible in each country the attitudes and behavior of the electorate at the occasion of an election. This makes the CSES a unique resource for the comparative study of electoral behavior, though it does mean that the fieldwork for each module has to be spread out over a five-year period in order to ensure that an election has been held in each country that wishes to participate.

The comparative project whose subject matter covers political attitudes and behavior that has the widest reach of all, however, is the World Values Survey. This began life as a solely European survey (the European Values Survey) in the early 1980s, designed to look at social and moral values in the then western Europe. However, it was then promoted by Ronald Inglehart at the University of Michigan and adopted in a dozen non-European countries. Thereafter the collaboration has blossomed (though the European countries continue to have their own organization and secretariat). Now, after four rounds, each around five years apart, it is being conducted in nearly eighty countries. While unlike both CSES and ISSP a whole survey is commissioned especially for the purpose, the project is reliant on teams within each country to raise the necessary funds and in practice the project is not notable for the similarity of methods employed in each country. Thus, while the survey work is nearly always undertaken face to face, it only aspires to follow random sampling "as closely as possible" (World Values Survey n.d.b), while some samples are not fully nationally representative (Inglehart 1997, 346). Meanwhile amongst the thirty-two European countries that fielded the fourth round of the survey in 1999, around half back-translated the questionnaire into English, while the other half did not. Nearly two-thirds added one or more country-specific questions in the middle of the common module. Equally, a third used some form of quota control at some point in the sampling process and around two-thirds allowed some form of substitution for non-contacts, while the remainder did not implement such procedures (European Values Study 1999).

4 MANY COUNTRIES OR FEW?

One feature that these three truly intercontinental projects have in common is that they challenge the earlier notion that in comparative survey research less may be better. They all suffer, even if rather less so in the case of ISSP, from between-country methodological pluralism. They also appear to encourage the user to analyze data from countries about which he or she may know little or nothing. Yet, despite the undoubted disadvantages of their methodological diversity, these exercises are still highly valuable.

To see why this is the case we may perhaps need to remind ourselves as to the analytic purchase that we argued earlier comparative opinion research brings. This is that comparative survey research enables us to examine the links between circumstances that vary between countries (but usually not within them) and both the incidence of various political attitudes and behaviors and the relationships between them. From this perspective our interest in, for example, the United States lies not in the United States per se but in the politically relevant attributes that it has, such as the fact that it is a federal country, has a presidential system of government, uses a single-member plurality electoral system or that health care is primarily funded by private insurance. Equally our interest in, for example, Sweden may lie in the fact that is a unitary state, has a parliamentary system of government, uses a party list electoral system, or that the state funds most health care.

In short, countries may be regarded as cases with theoretically relevant attributes. We can then assess the impact of these attributes by coding each country accordingly and including the resulting variables in our data analyses. While the coding of each attribute needs to be conducted accurately it does not require expert knowledge of the social, economic, political, and cultural attributes of a country. Note further that in such analyses any particular attribute may well be present in more than one country, and indeed will probably be present in several. Thus instead of being reliant on the evidence of just one country to assess the impact of a particular attribute we should have available to us the evidence of a number. This means we can begin to assess whether a *general* relationship exists between the presence of a particular circumstance and a particular attitude or behavior—and it is identifying the existence of such relationships that we have argued is the central task of the study of political behavior.

How does this mitigate the dangers of methodological pluralism? Quite simply because there is safety in numbers. While the results of a survey in any one country with a particular attribute may be more artifact than fact, the probability that this is true of all countries with that attribute is far less. So long as differences of methodological approach are not strongly correlated with the presence or absence of the attribute of interest, then those differences of approach cannot be responsible for any relationship that may be uncovered between that attribute and a particular attitude or behavior. The presence of methodological diversity will probably result in greater error variance between countries and, as a result, real relationships may well be attenuated in the survey data. Nevertheless, the more countries that a program of comparative research covers, the more likely it is to be insulated against the danger that substantive conclusions are drawn on the basis of artifactual differences.

5 THE NEED FOR DATA ABOUT COUNTRIES

One important implication, however, flows from this approach. Comparative opinion research cannot be conducted using survey data alone. Rather it needs to analyze survey data alongside systematically collected and coded data that give details of the attributes of the countries included in the data set. In short, measurement of the (particularly national) context within which the survey data have been collected should be an integral part of any exercise in comparative opinion research. Note indeed that such data could also include information on the key attributes of the methodology deployed in each country, thereby making it possible to include in analyses the possible impact of between-country methodological differences.

In practice, however, only two of the projects referred to so far include in their activities the provision to the wider community of relevant data about the context within which the data have been collected. The Comparative Study of Electoral Systems Project not only provides extensive information on the electoral system and constitutional structure of each country that is surveyed, but also information on the political parties, the issues at each election, and the election outcome, including some data at the level of the electoral district rather than just the country as a whole. Meanwhile the European Social Survey provides some social and economic indicators for each participating country, including some population data at regional level, as well as information on key events that took place in each country during the course of fieldwork. At the same time, the ESS has compiled an impressive set of web links to sources of data and information about individual countries, including data provided by key international organizations such as UNESCO and the OECD (European Social Survey 2003).[3]

6 ANALYZING COMPARATIVE SURVEY DATA

The challenges of comparative survey research are not, however, confined to the conduct of fieldwork or the collection of contextual data. There are also important questions about how best to analyze such data. Note first of all that the data may be regarded as either a sample of individuals or a sample of countries. In the former case, however, a pooled individual level data set from a comparative survey research project cannot be regarded as a simple random sample of individuals. The respondents to the surveys are not independent of each other, but rather are clustered by nation. This has to be allowed for either by using a multi-level model (Snijders and Bosker 1999) or by using statistical routines that take into account the clustered nature of the samples (Seligson 2004). Meanwhile, in the case of the latter approach at least some consideration has to be given as to the weight that each country's sample should have in the analysis. If some countries have included more respondents in their surveys than others, respondents from those countries will have more impact on any estimates derived from the survey

---

[3] The European Election Study has on one or more occasions undertaken content analysis of both media output at the time of European Parliament elections and of party manifestos, thereby making it possible to link survey results to the different national media contexts to which voters were exposed. The 1994 study also undertook surveys of candidates, thereby facilitating a study of political representation in the EU.

data unless this imbalance is altered. One possibility is that the sample sizes should be weighted to be proportionate to population; this might be done if there is a wish to make statements about some coherent geographical entity such as the European Union. Another possibility is to regard each national sample as a separate reading of the phenomena under investigation and to equalize the sample sizes for each country

In addition, comparative survey data can be regarded as a sample of countries. At its simplest this means deriving frequencies and means from the individual-level data for each country. The relationships between these readings across countries may then be analyzed, or analyzed in tandem with data about those countries from other sources. This, for example, is the approach that has been adopted by Inglehart in some of his most striking analyses of data from the World Values surveys, such as examining the relationship between the importance of postmaterialist values and affluence (Inglehart and Abramson 1995), civic norms, and the longevity of democratic institutions (Inglehart 1997), and between the degree of emphasis placed on self-expression and the openness and accountability of a country's political institutions (Inglehart and Welzel 2004). Such analyses may well uncover relationships that do not appear at the individual level—or indeed fail to corroborate relationships that do appear at the individual level. Such instances can tell us a great deal about the nature of the processes that underlie such relationships, and thus both forms of analysis need to be conducted if the full power of comparative opinion research is to be utilized.

Indeed, not only should individual-level and aggregate-level analysis be conducted, but they should also be brought together. Earlier in this chapter we noted that one of the possible roles of comparative opinion research is to identify the degree to which relationships, such as that between interest in politics and turnout, are contingent upon circumstance, such as the kind of electoral system in place. This implies bringing together aggregate data about a country (which may either be derived from the survey itself or from another source) and individual-level data about the strength of the relationship between two or more variables. This may be done in more than one way (Franzese 2005). One is to undertake a pooled individual-level analysis in which interaction terms between aggregate-level national circumstance and one or more independent individual-level variables are included in the modeling. Another is to estimate the individual-level relationship in each country, and then analyze the resulting data alongside other relevant country-level data at the aggregate (country) level (Curtice forthcoming; Lewis and Linzer 2005; Jusko and Shiveley 2005).

7 CONCLUSION

Comparative opinion research is potentially a highly powerful instrument. Indeed it is difficult to see how the aspiration of political science to be able to make empirically sustained generalizations about what influences and structures political behavior can be achieved without it. Thus the substantial increase in the amount of such research that has occurred over the last decade or so represents a significant organizational advance in the study of political behavior.

Yet at the same time it is also methodologically at least a potentially fragile endeavor. Most comparative survey research is a voluntary collaboration between national teams, each of which operates in different circumstances and cultures. As a result there is a tendency for survey research to be undertaken differently in different countries—and even if the same survey instrument is administered in the same manner everywhere there is no guarantee that it has the same meaning for respondents everywhere. Such methodological diversity means that our attempts to study what makes countries different run the risk of being confounded by differences between countries in how surveys are conducted. It certainly means that much comparative opinion research tolerates a degree of methodological inconsistency that would not usually be tolerated on a national survey.

There are two possible responses to this problem. One is to attempt to secure greater consistency of methodological approach—and at a high standard. This is the route that has been taken by the European Social Survey, which is undoubtedly methodologically the most impressive exercise in comparative opinion research that has been undertaken to date. Yet it remains to be seen whether such an exercise can be conducted outside the unique circumstances created in Europe by the existence of a relatively powerful cross-national institution such as the European Union. And if we are to reap fully the benefits of comparative opinion research we need to maximize the variety of countries (and thus of circumstance) that are covered. This suggests that, despite their methodological diversity, there will continue to be an important role for the substantively more diverse global endeavors too.

REFERENCES

AFROBAROMETER. n.d.*a*. Home page at www.afrobarometer.org/index.html
—— n.d.*b* Sampling at www.afrobarometer.org/sampling.html
ALMOND, G., and VERBA, S. 1963. *The Civic Culture: Political Attitudes and Democracy in Five Nations*. Princeton: Princeton University Press.
ASIA BAROMETER. n.d. Home page at http://avatoli.ioc.u-tokyo.ac.jp/~asiabarometer/pages/ english /index.html
BLAIS, A., and CARTY, K. 1990. Does propotional representation foster voter turnout? *European Journal of Political Research*, 18: 167–91.
—— and DOBRZYNSKA, A. 1998. Turnout in electoral democracies. *European Journal of Political Research*, 33: 239–61.
CENTRE FOR THE STUDY OF PUBLIC POLICY. n.d. Barometer Surveys at www.cspp.strath.ac.uk/
Comparative Study of Electoral Systems. n.d. Home page at www.cses.org/
CURTICE, J. Forthcoming. Elections as beauty contests: do the rules matter? In *Political Leaders and Democratic Elections*, ed. K. Aarts, A. Blais, and H. Schmitt. Oxford: Oxford University Press.
EAST ASIA BAROMETER. n.d. Home page at http://eacsurvey.law.ntu.edu.tw/

EIJK, C. VAN DER, and FRANKLIN, M. 1996. *Choosing Europe? The European Electorate and National Politics in the Face of Union.* Ann Arbor: Univ. of Michigan Press.

EUROPEAN COMMISSION. n.d. Public Opinion at **http://europa.eu.int/comm/public_opinion/ index_en.htm**

EUROPEAN ELECTIONS STUDY. n.d. Home page at **www.europeanelectionstudies.net/**

EUROPEAN SOCIAL SURVEY. n.d.*a.* Home page at **www.europeansocialsurvey.org/**

—— n.d.*b.* European Social Survey, Round 2: Specification for participating countries. Available at **http://naticento2.uuhost.uk.uu.net/proj-spec/round_2/r2_spec_participating_countries.doc**

—— 2003. Overview websites with free information on European countries at **www.scp.nl/ users/stoop/ess_events/links_contextual_data2003.htm**

EUROPEAN VALUES STUDY. 1999. Methodological questionnaire. Available at **www.za.uni-koeln. de/data/add_studies/kat50/EVS_1999_2000/ZA3811fb.pdf**

FISHER, S., LESSARD-PHILLIPS, L., HOBOLT, S., and CURTICE, J. 2006. How the effect of political knowledge on turnout differs in plurality electoral systems. Paper presented at the Annual Meeting of the American Political Science Association, 2006.

FRANKLIN, M. 2002. The dynamics of electoral participation. Pp. 148–68 in *Comparing Democracies 2,* ed. L. LeDuc, R. Niemi, and P. Norris. London: Sage.

FRANZESE, R. 2005. Empirical strategies for various manifestations of multilevel data. *Political Analysis,* 13: 430–46.

GROVES, R. 1987. Research on survey data quality. *Public Opinion Quarterly.* 50th anniversary issue: S156–72.

—— 1989. *Survey Errors and Survey Costs.* New York: John Wiley.

HEATH, A., FISHER, S., and SMITH, S. 2005. The globilization of public opinion research. *Annual Review of Political Science,* 8: 297–333.

INGLEHART, R. 1990. *Culture Shift in Advanced Industrial Society.* Princeton: Princeton University Press.

—— 1997. *Modernization and Postmodernization: Cultural, Economic and Political Change in 43 Societies.* Princeton: Princeton University Press.

—— and ABRAMSON, P. 1995. *Value Change in Global Perspective.* Ann Arbor: University of Michigan Press.

—— and WELZEL, C. 2004. What insights can multi-country surveys provide about people and societies? *APSA-CP Newsletter,* 15 (2): 14–18.

INTERNATIONAL SOCIAL SURVEY PROGRAMME n.d. Home page at **www.issp.org/homepage.htm**

—— 2003. Working principles. Available at **www.issp.org/Documents/isspchar.pdf**

JACKMAN, R. 1987. Political institutions and voter turnout in industrialized democracies. *American Political Science Review,* 81: 405–23.

JOWELL, R. 1998. How comparative is comparative research? *American Behavioral Scientist,* 42: 168–77.

JUSKO, K., and SHIVELEY, W. 2005. Applying a two-step strategy to the analysis of cross-national public opinion data. *Political Analysis,* 13: 327–44.

KAASE, M., and NEWTON, K. 1995. *Beliefs in Government.* Oxford: Oxford University Press.

KATZ, R. 1997. *Democracy and Elections.* New York: Oxford University Press.

KIPLING, R. 1910. The English flag. In R. Kipling, *Departmental Ditties and Ballads and Barrack-room Ballads.* New York: Doubleday.

KUECHLER, M. 1998, The survey method: an indispensable tool for social science research everywhere? *American Behavioral Scientist,* 42: 178–200.

LATINOBARÓMETRO CORPORATION. n.d. Home page at **www.latinobarometro.org/ index.php?id=150**

LEWIS, J., and LINZER, D. 2005. Estimating regression models in which the dependent variable is based on estimates. *Political Analysis,* 13: 345–64.

Lynn, P., Häder, S., Gabler, S., and Laaksonen, S. 2004. Methods for achieving equivalence of samples in cross-national surveys: the European Social Survey experience. *Working Papers of the Institute for Social and Economic Research.* Paper 2004-09. Colchester: University of Essex.

Norris, P. 2004. *Electoral Engineering: Voting Rules and Political Behavior.* New York: Cambridge University Press.

Park, A., and Jowell, R. 1997. *Consistencies and Differences in a Cross-National Survey.* London: Social and Community Planning Research.

Powell, G. B. 1986. American voter turnout in comparative perspective. *American Political Science Review,* 80: 17–43.

Seligson, M. 2004. Comparative survey research: is there a problem? *APSA-CP Newsletter,* 15 (2): 11–14.

Smith, T. 2002. Developing comparable questions in cross-national surveys. Pp. 69–91 in *Cross-Cultural Survey Methods,* ed. J. Harkness, F. van de Vijver, and P. Mohler. London: Wiley Europe.

Snijders, T., and Bosker, R. 1999. *Multilevel Modelling: An Introduction to Basic and Advanced Multilevel Modeling.* London: Sage.

World Values Survey. n.d.*a.* Home page at **www.worldvaluessurvey.org/**

—— n.d.*b.* Constitution for the World Values Association. Available at **www.worldvaluessurvey. org/organization/constitution.pdf**

CHAPTER 49

METHODS OF ELITE RESEARCH

URSULA HOFFMANN-LANGE

POWER and elites are universal social phenomena. The distinction between elites and non-elites is therefore an important aspect of social analysis. In the social sciences, elites are customarily defined by their influence on strategic (political) decisions that shape the living conditions in a society.

Elite research studies the characteristics of politicians and other holders of leadership positions in powerful public institutions and private organizations who are distinguished by their regular participation in (political) decision making. This definition comes closest to the phenomenon of power and influence the fathers of elite theory, Vilfredo Pareto and Gaetano Mosca, had in mind (cf. Bottomore 1993).[1]

This elite concept is narrow and broad at the same time. It excludes a large group of individuals whom many people would spontaneously consider as belonging to the *elite*, for example, prominent athletes, artists, scholars, intellectuals, or the owners of large fortunes. Such individuals are distinguished by their exclusive lifestyles or they may be admired for their achievements. However, most of them do not have much influence on important (political) decision making. On the other hand, elites can be found in any social system, for example, in parliaments, political parties, corporations, and labor unions. Similarly, the regional focus may range from a local elite to a national or even transnational elite. Most frequently, however, the elite concept is used for national elites. Even though elite research frequently focuses on political elites, it needs to be emphasized that the elite concept is not limited to

[1] It should be noted that Mosca himself did not use the term "elite," but rather "political class" or "ruling class," which he defined as the minority of influential persons involved in the management of public affairs (1939, 50).

politicians, on the contrary. Its analytical value rests on the assumption that political decision making involves other elites as well.

Since the number of studies of specialized elites is rather large, the present overview will be mostly limited to research on national elites. The methodological and practical problems in choosing an appropriate research design and in conducting an elite study, however, are the same for studying elites in other contexts as well.

The classical elite theories conceptualized power as dichotomous and therefore assumed the existence of a clear distinction between elites and non-elites (or masses). While this crude distinction may be considered as an acceptable simplification of social reality for pre-modern societies in which power was concentrated in the hands of a small hereditary nobility, modern societies are not only characterized by a more or less continuos distribution of power, but also by the lack of a single center of power and by a high degree of horizontal differentiation.

Power and influence may be based on a variety of resources located in different sectors of society, for example, political authority, judicial discretion, economic power, academic or administrative expertise, or influence on public opinion. Moreover, while the assumption of a clearly defined hierarchy of power may be considered as an appropriate approximation of intra-organizational power relations, interorganizational interactions involve multilateral bargaining on a more or less equal footing. This implies a pluralist elite structure and the lack of clearly demarcated vertical boundaries between elites and non-elites, as influence levels off the further we move from the top to the bottom and from more central to more peripheral actors.

1 FIELDS OF ELITE RESEARCH

Elite research may be broadly classified into four substantive areas. *Social background studies* collect data on family background (socioeconomic status of parents), regional background, religious affiliation, and education. This allows us to compare the social backgrounds of elites to those of the general population. It also allows us to determine important prerequisites of elite careers. Such data are of considerable theoretical significance, since they show to what degree the advancement to positions of power and influence is determined by the economic, social, and cultural capital of one's family. The permeability of social barriers to advancement into elite positions is apt to have considerable variation across elite sectors and societies.

Elite recruitment follows the prevailing mobility patterns in a society. In modern societies, a high level of formal qualification is a crucial precondition for achieving positions of higher status. Because of the relationship between social background and educational opportunities, elite studies usually confirm what Putnam has called *the law of increasing disproportion* (Putnam 1976, 33–6). In any organization, there is a close correspondence between the hierarchical status of a position and the representation of members of high-status social groups.

Second, elite research analyzes elite careers: the more or less structured patterns of professional advancement that eventually lead into elite positions. Career patterns vary between sectors and organizations, depending on the qualifications that are considered important by selectorates at crucial career stages. For comparing the elites of different sectors and organizations, the degree of professional specialization is a crucial variable that can show if more emphasis is placed on specialized knowledge or rather on generalist qualifications acquired in different organizational contexts.

Third, elite research makes it possible to study the activities, values, and attitudes and reveal patterns of conflict and consensus among different elite goups. Fourth, questions asking for elite interactions provide crucial information on the access of various elite groups as well as of non-elites to central political decision makers, as well as on the overall degree of elite integration.

The purpose of most elite surveys is the systematic collection of information on the social characteristics, role perceptions, value orientations, and attitudes of the elite respondents, although elites may also be interviewed in their capacity as participants in collective decision making, for example, for reconstructing particular policy decisions or for oral history projects (e.g. Raab 1987). Counting the latter studies as *elite research* would stretch the scope of the present chapter too far, however, because it would imply that any research involving interviews with political actors would qualify as elite research.

2 OPERATIONALIZING THE ELITE CONCEPT: METHODS OF ELITE IDENTIFICATION

The imprecision of the elite concept implies that widely differing strategies are used for identifying elites. The crucial question of how to identify the elite has to be answered at the outset of any empirical elite study. This is not a problem for studies of specialized elites who are defined by their membership in a clearly defined body, for example, a parliament or the executive board of an organization. If an entire elite formation is to be studied, however, both the vertical and horizontal boundaries of the elite have to be specified at the outset.

Three basic methods of elite identification are available, the reputational method, the decisional method, and the positional method (Parry 2005; Putnam 1976, 15 ff.). These methods were originally developed for studying community elites. The *reputational method* relies on experts who are asked to name the most powerful individuals in the community or other political system. A classic example of this method is Hunter's study *Community Power Structure* (1953). Hunter started out by drawing comprehensive lists of leaders who were selected on the basis of their formal positions or were nominated by representatives of local organizations. At the next stage, experts were asked to select the most influential leaders from these lists. It is obvious that the validity of this method depends primarily on the choice of the experts and their knowledge of the actual influence of different elite actors. At the local level, especially in small and medium-sized communities, this is an inexpensive method of identifying community influentials

The reputational method is of limited value, however, in complex settings with a multiplicity of decision-making arenas. Knowledge of who the consequential actors are is here necessarily limited to the participants in the different decision-making arenas. A large number of experts for different policy domains would be needed to produce a comprehensive list of influentials. In a society with a pluralist power structure, such an approach would therefore imply that the identification of relevant actors becomes an elite study in its own right. In his later study *Top Leadership U.S.A.* (1959), Hunter applied the reputational method to the national level. This attempt drew a lot of criticism, however, because of the arbitrary ways of choosing experts and influentials.

Starting out with an analysis of documents and interviews, the *decisional method* identifes elites by studying the decision-making process for important policy issues. It considers the most consequential actors as belonging to the elite. This method was originally developed for studying local elites. Dahl's study *Who Governs?* on the local power structure of New Haven (1961) is a classic example. The validity of this method depends primarily on the choice of the policy issues used for determining the influential actors. If the sample of issues does not cover all important policy domains, this method provides an incomplete picture of the overall elite structure and will miss important actors with specialized influence. Moreover, critics have emphasized that the method tends to ignore influentials who are not actively involved in policy making, but whose preferences are taken into account by the decision makers.

Like the reputational method, the decisional method is primarily useful for identifying local elites. It is obvious that the structural complexity of national policy making cannot be adequately captured by studying who is involved in the decision making on a limited set of issues. It has been successfully applied, however, for studying elites in well-defined policy domains by Laumann and his associates (Laumann and Knoke 1987; Knoke et al. 1996).

The *positional method* of elite identifcation, finally, is customarily used for studying national elites, but it can be equally well applied to smaller settings. It is based on the assumption that in modern societies power and influence are tied to the resources associated with positions of leadership in public institutions and private organizations of national relevance.

The positional method starts out from the formal structure of authority. It implies several steps. In a first step, relevant sectors are defined. Politics, public adminis-tration, business, pressure groups, media, and academia belong to the sectors that are mostly considered as being of primary importance. The next step involves the decision on the most important institutions/organizations within these sectors. They are determined according to sector-specific criteria (e.g. political decision-making authority, organizational membership, capital turnover). The third step involves the identification of top leadership positions within each of these organizations, and the present incumbents of these positions are eventually selected as constituting the elite.

The application of the positional approach is highly formalized and does not require much previous research. Its reliability is rather high, too, as there is a high degree of convergence among scholars on which institutions and organizations are the most powerful. Virtually all major comprehensive studies of national elites have therefore used this method for identifying elites (Australia: Higley, Deacon, and Smart 1979; Germany: Zapf 1965, Hoffmann-Lange 1992 and Bürklin et al. 1997; USA: Barton 1985 and Dye 2002; Denmark: Christiansen, Møller, and Togeby 2001; Russia: Lane and Ross 1999).

This method has one serious drawback, however. It does not provide any guidelines for specifying the boundaries of an elite. The researcher is free to decide on the horizontal (inclusion of sectors and organizations) and the vertical (hierarchical levels within organizations) boundaries. For determining the size of an elite sample, the availability of funding is mostly more important than theoretical considerations.

Regardless of the choice of sample size, the positional method yields a sample of individuals who control important power resources. It allows us to compare the characteristics of different elite subgroups within the overall elite sample. Since it does not provide information on the relative importance of organizations and positions, however, the method does not warrant the aggregation of results across different elite sectors. Inferences about "*the elite*" have to be made with caution, since the marginals for individual variables depend on the composition of the elite sample, especially with respect to characteristics for which substantial differences exist between elite subgroups.

The scholarly dispute over the validity of the different methods of elite identification is closely intertwined with conceptual differences. Scholars claiming that modern societies are characterized by a pluralist power structure tend to use either the decisional or the positional method, while scholars who believe in the existence of a highly integrated *power elite* tend to rely on the reputational method.

Using data from a community power study in a medium-sized West German city, Pappi (1984) demonstrated that these methodological and substantive differences have an empirical basis. He found that perceptions of political influence tend to be highly skewed in favor of a small number of key decision makers, while both the positional and the decisional method yield a more inclusive, pluralist elite structure that reflects the diversity of power resources.

Ultimately, each of these methods focuses on different aspects of the structure of power and influence with respect to two dimensions:

- control of power resources attached to leadership positions and
- active involvement in (political) decision making.

A combination of these two dimensions yields four different possible strategies for identifying elites (Table 49.1). It is obvious that limiting the analysis to individuals with formal political decision-making authority yields the most restrictive definition of positional elites. Elite studies using the positional method usually extend the elite concept with respect to the second dimension and include elites drawn from a broad spectrum of powerful public institutions and private organizations with potential influence on strategic policy decisions. The decisional method, on the other hand, disregards potential influence and limits the analysis to individuals who are actively involved in political decision making, regardless of the resources on which their influence is being based.

The reputational method, finally, is the most inclusive in terms of the power resources and the degree of active involvement considered. At the same time this method is also more exclusive than the other methods and usually yields a much smaller number of powerful individuals. This is due to both methodological and substantive reasons. Methodologically, the size of lists with names of influentials has to be kept manageable and is therefore limited. No single expert will be able to pick influentials from a list of more than about 200 individuals. Theoretically, assuming the existence of one overarching elite whose members are involved in most or all major (political) decisions implies a focus on individuals at the very top of society and disregards individuals with only specialized influence.

Faced with these choices, some scholars have combined different methods. Several studies have started with a positional approach and then complemented the initial list of position-holders by asking respondents for other elites who were either actively involved in political decision making or were considered as influential by the positionally defined elites (e.g. Laumann and Pappi 1976; Pappi 1984). Such a hybrid approach is even possible within the context of large-scale national elite surveys. In a comparative study of US, Australian, and (West) German national elite networks, respondents identified by the positional method were asked to name other actors

Table 49.1 Positional, reputational, and decisional methods of elite identification

	Involvement in political decision-making	
Resources of power and influence	Active involvement in political decision making	Active involvement **plus** (indirect) political influence
Positional power resources: Formal decision-making authority within organizations	Positional Method: Political decision makers only	Positional method: Political decision makers plus incumbents of top leadership positions in influential organizations
Positional power resources plus influence based on personal prestige	Decisional method: Influential political actors, regardless of their formal decision-making authority	Reputational method: all influentials whose preferences are taken into account in political decision making

with whom they regularly interacted (Higley et al. 1991). While most of the actors mentioned by the respondents were themselves holders of top elite positions, this method also yielded the names of additional elites who had not been included in the initial elite sample.

3 METHODS OF DATA COLLECTION

3.1 Studying Elite Circulation and Changes in Elite Backgrounds with Published Data Sources

Collecting data from published sources is relatively inexpensive. Such handbook data are usually the only source for studying historical elites as well as elites in non-democratic settings.[2] However, scholars relying exclusively on published materials are limited to studying elites who are included in elite rosters such as handbooks of political institutions, major economic organizations, academic institutions, or the Who's Who. This is usually the case for government ministers, members of parliaments, board members of large corporations, business associations or labor unions, university professors, etc. Among these, MPs are the elite group for which the most reliable handbook information is available, dating all the way back to the mid-nineteenth century.

Handbooks usually provide basic information on the socio-demographic characteristics of elites such as year and place of birth, family background, education, religion, family status, and careers. However, since these publications list only the information provided by the elites themselves, they are necessarily incomplete with respect to career patterns or membership in private organizations which the elites do not wish to disclose to the public.

The first systematic elite study of historical elites was done by a student of Pareto, Marie Kolabinska (1912), who attempted to corroborate Pareto's theory of elite circulation and his famous dictum that history is a cemetery of elites. Since then, only a few other longitudinal studies have systematically collected information on the historical development of national elites. Among these, the studies of Christiansen, Møller, and Togeby (2001) on Danish elites and by Zapf (1965) on German elites are noteworthy. Both projects studied elites in a variety of sectors, among them politics, public administration, judiciary, military leaders, business associations, major industrial and financial companies, labor unions, churches, media, and universities. They provided comprehensive portrays of continuity and change in the elites of these two

---

[2] A volume edited by Best and Becker (1997) provides an overview of elite research in the Soviet Union and several East European countries. Additionally, two longitudinal studies of the former East German elite should be mentioned (Meyer 1991; Schneider 1994).

countries. The Danish study included a large number of elites at three points in time (1932: n=605; 1963: n=753; 1999: n=1,771). The German study was smaller, including data on some 250 elite positions and it also covered a shorter period (1919 to 1961). It is unique, however, because it combined an analysis of elite circulation in these elite positions over the entire period with a comparison of the social characteristics of the holders of these positions at three different points in time (1925, 1940, and 1955).

Thomas Dye's study of American elites which the author has continuously updated since its first edition in 1976 is another comprehensive study on elite backgrounds, including data on some 7,000 elites from all major sectors of US society.

While these studies were limited to single countries, the comparative *EurElite* project has collected data on parliamentarians in a large number of European countries. Although originally based on individual data, these data have been aggregated for the purpose of analysis into a three-dimensional data set, the so-called *data cube* (see Figure 49.1). This contains background variables (age, gender, education, political and professional background, previous parliamentary experience), organized by party family per country and election year. Even though the data set includes only a small number of variables, it shows that such a data collection may yield major insights into long-term changes in the composition of European parliamentary groups. The first volume, written by a multinational team of scholars and based on data from eleven European countries for the period since the mid-nineteenth century (Best and Cotta 2000) traces the precipitous decline in the parliamentary representation of the traditional nobility and agricultural interests as well as the increasing

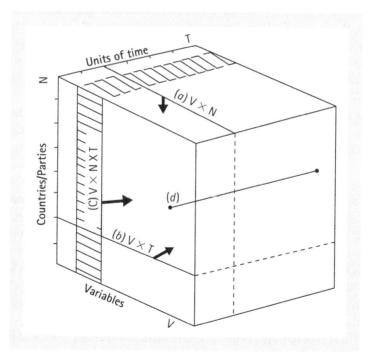

Fig. 49.1 The EURELITE Data Cube

professionalization of parliamentary groups over the last 150 years. Additional volumes are in the making, and more countries have joined the project in recent years, bringing the total number of countries up to seventeen (Best and Edinger 2005, 504).

3.2 Elite Research Based on Surveys

3.2.1 *National and Comparative Elite Surveys*

National parliamentarians are certainly the elite group that has been most widely surveyed. Such surveys provide more detailed information on political recruitment than studies based on published sources alone. They have also considerably enlarged our knowledge about the degrees of consensus and dissensus over policy issues across political parties and countries (e.g. Norris 1997).

Moreover, some studies of parliamentarians also included parallel surveys of the electorate, thus making it possible to study political representation by comparing the political attitudes of parliamentarians and voters. Based on the seminal article by Miller and Stokes on "Constituency influence in Congress" (1963), representation studies following their theoretical and empirical approach were conducted in several European democracies, among them France, Germany, the Netherlands, and Sweden (cf. Miller et al. 1999). These and other representation studies have greatly contributed to enhance our understanding of the theoretical puzzles associated with the comparison of elite and mass attitudes (cf. Klingemann, Stöss, and Weßels 1991).

Candidates and deputies for the European Parliament and the national parliaments were the focus of a large comparative survey in ten EU member countries in 1994. This study also gathered comparable attitudinal data on voters and thus allowed study of elite-voter congruence both at the European and the national level as well as within individual parties and party families (Schmitt and Thomassen 1999; Katz and Weßels 1999).

Limiting the study of political representation to comparisons of parliamentarians and voters, however, ignores the influence of other elites on political decision making. While political elites are certainly of central importance, network analysis has revealed that other public and private sector elites enjoy direct access to political decision making. Middle-level elites and voters play a much lesser role. This is all the more important since the available elite surveys provide ample evidence that the political party affiliations of elites are skewed in favor of conservative parties. By not taking into account the preferences of other elite groups in representation studies, such studies may therefore overestimate the actual influence of ordinary voters and produce an unrealistic portrayal of the process of representation. Only a few studies have studied representation by extending the focus to a broader range of elite groups (Hoffmann-Lange 1992; Bürklin et al. 1997; Verba et al. 1987).

Comprehensive national elite surveys have been relatively rare. Table 49.2 shows the major surveys of national elites that have included elites from at least five sectors (politics, public administration, business, labor unions, media) and interviews with

Table 49.2 Major national elite surveys

Country	Year	Number of Respondents	Reference
Australia	1975	370	Higley, Deacon, and Smart 1979
Brazil	1972–3	259	McDonough 1981
Estonia[a]	1994–2003	271–313	Steen 1997; Steen 2005
European Union[b]	1996	3,778	Spence 1996
Finland	1991	746	Ruostetsaari 1992
Finland	2001	687	Ruostetsaari 2006
(West) Germany	1968	808	Hoffmann-Lange 1992
(West) Germany	1972	1,825	Hoffmann-Lange, Neumann, and Steinkemper 1985
(West) Germany	1981	1,744	Hoffmann-Lange 1992
Germany	1995	2,341	Bürklin et al. 1997; Welzel 2000
Latvia[a]	1993–2003	280–300	Steen 1997
Lithuania[a]	1993	307–333	Steen 1997
Norway	2000	1,710	Gulbrandsen and Engelstad 2005
Russia[c]	1998–2000	605–980	Steen 2003; Gel'man/Steen 2003
South Africa[d]	2002	566	Kotzé/Steyn 2003
Sweden	2001	1,779	Göransson (forthcoming)
United States	1972	545	Barton 1985
United States	1979–85	1,861	Lerner, Nagai, and Rothman 1996
United States	1979		Verba and Orren 1985

[a] The Baltic elite studies included three (Lithuania) and four (Estonia and Latvia) consecutive waves of face-to-face interviews during the period between 1993 and 2003. The number of respondents varied within the range reported in the table.

[b] The EU study of 1996 was conducted in the 15 member states and included from 71 (Luxembourg) to 475 (Germany) respondents. This telephone survey was largely limited to gathering information on the respondents' attitudes towards European integration and world politics. Apart from these questions, only a few demographic and attitudinal indicators (sex, age, age at completing education, left–right orientation) were included in the questionnaire.

[c] The Russian elite study consisted of two waves of face-to-face interviews, 980 in 1998 and 605 in 2000.

[d] This survey was part of a larger comparative elite study in several African countries (South Africa, Nigeria, Senegal, Kenya, Algeria, Uganda, Zimbabwe). However, the elite samples in the other African countries were rather small and included only 97 to 140 respondents.

more than 250 respondents. It is obvious from the table that the number of national elite surveys, while still relatively small, has increased in recent years. Moreover, while the first studies were mostly limited to small sample sizes, some of the more recent studies have included larger numbers of elite respondents. For the purpose of comparing subgroups within the elite samples, studies with larger sample sizes are of course much better suited.

With the exception of the surveys in the three Baltic countries, these studies were limited to single countries, however. Even though they have mostly relied on the positional method for identifying elites, the investigators employed different criteria for the numerical representation of elite sectors and for selecting organizations within the sectors. Some have included small sectors, that is, leaders of protest groups and NGOs, church leaders, military leaders, etc., while others were limited to the above-mentioned major sectors. The comparability of results is also hampered by the fact that the questionnaires included only a few equivalent questions. It is therefore difficult to compare the social characteristics and attitudes of the different national elites even for basic indicators such as social-class background and education, let alone role perceptions, value orientations, and political attitudes.

To date, only three truly comparative elite surveys have been conducted. The TEEPS survey by Lerner and Gorden (1969) encompassed five successive waves of elite interviews in Britain, France, and Germany from 1955 to 1965, with a total of 4,000 interviews. The authors were primarily interested in studying elite perceptions on the role of Europe in the world, foreign policy attitudes, and support for European integration. Unfortunately, the book does not provide much information on the composition of the elite samples, except for listing the number of interviews by year and country and mentioning that the elites were determined by the reputational method. The book focuses on cross-country differences, not on differences between elite groups within countries.

The second comparative elite survey was conducted in the early 1970s. It was limited to elites from just two sectors, politics and public administration (Aberbach, Putnam, and Rockman 1981). Six western European nations (Britain, France, West Germany, Italy, the Netherlands, and Sweden) and the US were included in the study which was conducted by a team of scholars at the University of Michigan. Elites were defined by the positional method. The sample of respondents included parliamentarians, senior bureaucrats, and younger administrators, so-called bureaucratic high-fliers. The book discusses the differences in the social backgrounds, role perceptions, value orientations, and policy attitudes between the two elite groups.

A third comprehensive elite survey sponsored by the European Commission and carried out in 1996 included elite respondents from a variety of sectors in the fifteen EU member countries. This study was based on telephone interviews with altogether 3,778 respondents (Spence 1996). Unfortunately, the questionnaire was mostly limited to asking for the respondents' attitudes towards European integration and world politics, while only a few demographic and attitudinal indicators were included (sex, age, age at completing education, left–right-orientation). The data are therefore of limited use for academic purposes.

3.2.2 *Methodological Problems*

The small number of comparative elite studies and the limited sample sizes of most national elite surveys attest to the difficulties involved in doing such surveys. They entail a lot more work and are more expensive than general population surveys. Identifying an elite sample by using the positional method requires prior collection of information on the organizational structure of the national political system before a list of elite positions can be drawn up and the current incumbents of these positions can be identified. Moreover, contacting the elites, making appointments, and actually conducting the interviews is more difficult. The elites' tight schedules leave little time for interview appointments, and even after appointments have been set up, times are frequently changed due to unforeseen events.

Once one overcomes these difficulties, however, response rates are about the same for elite surveys as for general population surveys. They have been relatively low in Germany and Finland with 55 to 60 percent, while the Norwegian elite survey reached a very high response rate of 87.3 percent (cf. Gulbrandsen and Engelstad 2005, 903).[3] Moreover, response rates are apt to vary considerably across sectors. They are mostly relatively high in the political sector, in the public administration, and in the media, but considerably lower among business elites (cf. Hoffmann-Lange 1987, 36; Ruostetsaari 2006).

Elite respondents are generally cooperative and do not mind answering even highly structured questionnaires. Missing values are mostly lower and the data quality higher than for general population surveys (cf. Lerner and Gorden 1969, 411 ff.).

Most of the national elite surveys conducted so far have used personal interviews. Mail questionnaires are relatively rare for this type of study. The two Finnish elite surveys as well as a survey of EP candidates show, however, that mail surveys of elites can be successfully conducted and may even produce satisfactory response rates. One has to keep in mind, though, that with mail surveys one cannot be absolutely sure if the elite respondents have answered the questionnaire themselves or rather asked one of their staff members to do this. While this is probably not a problem as far as hard facts are concerned (e.g. social backgrounds, career patterns), it cannot be ruled out that this method may produce biased results for attitudinal questions.

With the increasing popularity of telephone interviewing in public opinion research, this approach has to be considered as an additional option for elite surveys. A telephone survey of German parliamentarians conducted in 2003/4 produced a

---

[3] It should be noted that the Finnish elite study used mail questionnaires that normally produce much lower response rates than personal interviewing. All four of the German elite surveys involved personal interviews, instead.

satisfactory response rate of 56 percent (Best and Jahr 2006). However, telephone interviews require a simple question format and set limits for the available interview time. They may thus not be suitable for long and complex interview schedules.

A major problem of elite surveys is the question of protecting the anonymity of respondents. Elites are public figures and it is therefore always possible to identify individual respondents on the basis of just a few variables such as year of birth, family status, sex, type of university degree, organizational sector, and party membership. This is especially true for elite respondens with a rare combination of personal characteristics, for example, female holders of senior positions in the business elite. Even if only broad sector codes are recorded on the data set, later identification of individual respondents cannot be ruled out. Including detailed information about the organization and position of elite respondents in the data set aggravates this problem even further. At the same time, however, it also increases the options for data analysis. Recording information on the exact positions of respondents is ideal since it makes it possible to simultaneously categorize respondents according to different criteria, for example, by (sub)sector, type of position, religion, generation, or party affiliation.

It seems therefore impossible, both out of practical and theoretical reasons, to promise respondents that the data will preclude later identification of individual respondents. Instead, it is advisable to inform the respondents about this dilemma and to promise that the published tables will always be grouped in a way that will not allow such individual identification.

3.3 Studies of Elite Networks

From a theoretical point of view, a central question for elite research is how closely the individual elite members are connected to each other. Since the publication of C. Wright Mills's book on the *Power Elite* (1956), the controversy about the elite structure of developed democracies has never subsided. Following Mills, quite a few scholars from different countries have assumed that even modern democracies are dominated by a small power elite or ruling class (e.g. Bottómore 1993; Domhoff 1998). On the other side, theorists of elite pluralism claim that power is dispersed among a broad set of different elite sectors representing the diversity of interests in these societies (e.g. Dahl 1961; Parry 2005; Keller 1991).

Elite research has tried to come to grips with this fundamental question. However, most of the national elite studies carried out so far have primarily collected information on the individual characteristics of elites and not on relations among them. They have therefore mostly relied on indirect indicators of elite cohesion, by referring to similar backgrounds, positional interlocks, or attitudinal similarities. Based on such results, they have either claimed that the existing similarities supported the existence of a power elite/ruling class, or instead claimed to the contrary, emphasizing the existing differences between elite sectors as indicators of a pluralist elite structure.

It is obvious that background and attitudinal data are inconclusive in this respect. Instead, network data are needed to settle this controversy. Information on elite networks can be collected in elite surveys by asking respondents for their contacts with other elites. Because of the smaller scope of local elites, such questions are easier to ask in local elite studies. Numerous community power studies in different countries provide a wealth of data on local elite networks. They have shown an enormous variation of elite structures across communities even in the same country

One major problem in studying national elite networks is their size. They are simply too large to be covered by a single study. In order to come to grips with the problem of network size, it is necessary to limit the focus of research. Two different strategies are available for achieving such a reduction of complexity. The first strategy relies on limiting the study to ego-centered networks, an approach that has also been successfully employed in public opinion surveys. Questions on ego-centered elite networks were included in three national elite surveys carried out in the 1970s and early 1980s in the US, Australia, and West Germany (Higley et al. 1991). The elite respondents[4] were first asked to name the one national issue on which they had most actively attempted to influence national policy or public opinion during the preceding twelve months. This question was followed by sociometric questions asking for the names of those persons with whom they regularly interacted over this issue. Even though the network information generated by these questions is necessarily incomplete because it is based on interactions over only one issue per respondent, the sociometric analysis revealed the existence of inclusive elite networks of roughly 800 individuals in the three countries.

Within each of these elite networks, it was possible to identify a number of social circles whose members were related to each other either directly or through only a few intermediaries. One of these circles was a relatively large *central circle* made up of 227 persons in the US, 340 in West Germany, and 418 in Australia. These central circles were inclusive in terms of their sector composition, although elites from the various sectors were not equally well represented in the central circles. In all three countries, about half of the central circle members were politicians and civil service elites. Business elites accounted for another 25–30 percent, while other elite groups were less well represented. The density of the central elite circles, albeit considerably higher than the density of the overall elite network, was still less than 5 percent.

Despite the fact that the questions were limited to ego-centered sociometric data, the existence of one overarching elite network in each of the three countries is of particular theoretical relevance. It implies that both competing models of elite structures, that is, the power elite model and the pluralist model, misrepresent the actual structure of power and influence in developed democracies. The elite structures found were more integrated than the pluralist model assumes, but also

---

[4] The original sample sizes were 545 in the US 370 in Australia (see Table 49.2) and 497 in Germany. Since the overall sample of elite respondents had been much larger in Germany ($n=1,744$), only a comparable subset of the German respondents holding the most senior elite positions was used for this comparative analysis.

larger and more heterogeneous than the power elite model warrants. Rather than having the *hollow core* Heinz et al. (1993) found for the network of lobbyists in the US, the center of the elite network was made up of a group of mostly senior leaders from various sectors who were simultaneously active in several policy fields and contributed to the integration of an otherwise highly pluralistic elite.

Laumann and Knoke (1987) took a different approach to studying national elite networks. Rather than limiting their focus to ego-centered sociometric data, they limited the number of relevant actors by studying the relations between collective actors (e.g. parliamentary committees, private corporations, business associations, law firms) in only two policy domains (energy and health). They also used a different network model. The model of *structural equivalence* groups actors on the basis of their ties to other actors in the network (*block-model analysis*). Governmental actors occupied the center of the elite network. They were the main targets of communications initiated by other governmental (congressional committees, White House, etc.) and private (corporations, business associations, law firms etc.) actors (1987, 377). Laumann and Knoke coined the term *organizational state* for designating this type of elite network that does not have any clear boundaries between elites from public institutions and private organizations.

In a later comparative study of labor policies in three post-industrial democracies, the US, Japan, and West Germany, Knoke et al. (1996) used the same approach. This second study confirmed the basic structural characteristics of the previous study, but also showed that the elite networks in these three nations differed in important respects. The elite network in Japan turned out to be much more tightly integrated than the network in the other two countries. The German network structure was more pluralistic and showed a relatively large number of important veto players, while the American network was highly polarized between Republicans and Democrats at the time of the surveys in the mid-1980s.

Despite the difference between the two approaches for data collection and data analysis, these studies of elite networks have confirmed the existence of integrated, yet pluralistic elite structures in highly developed democracies.

4 CONCLUSION

Empirical elite research has been thriving in recent years. The available body of data has accordingly grown as well. Parliamentarians are the elite group about which we know the most, ranging from recruitment and role perceptions to value orientations and policy attitudes. The EURELITE project has collected both longitudinal and comparative data and has thereby greatly enhanced our understanding of long-term changes in the patterns of political recruitment over the past 150 years, especially the impact of gradual democratization in the European countries around the turn of the twentieth century and the effects of the more recent transitions from industrial to post-industrial society.

Several studies on political representation, comparing parliamentary elites and voters, have provided information on the degree of attitudinal congruence across political party families and countries. To date, however, no one has managed to summarize the bewildering complexity of empirical evidence in this field.

The comparative study of entire national elite formations, finally, is still lagging far behind the progress made in other fields of elite research. A couple of studies have provided comparative evidence on the elite changes associated with the regime change in the post-communist countries (e.g. Szelényi and Szelényi 1995; Higley, Kullberg, and Pakulski 1996). Comparative and longitudinal elite surveys are especially needed to refute widespread criticism that elite studies are of only descriptive value and do not contribute much to answering the important theoretical questions associated with elites. Even though the descriptive value of such studies should not be underestimated, single cross-sectional studies of national elites can only provide small mosaic pieces to the puzzle of elite structures and their impact on social and political change that was the fundamental question raised by Pareto and Mosca. This unsatisfactory situation can only be overcome by systematic comparative research and by giving up the search for an overarching elite theory. Instead, it would be more promising if elite research would focus on more limited questions such as identifying the determinants of elite integration or on studying the impact of regime change on elite circulation as well as elite strategies for dealing with potentially divisive issue conflicts. Among the independent variables, prime emphasis should be given to the institutional determinants of patterns of elite interaction and their contribution to moderating conflict between different elite subgroups.

REFERENCES

ABERBACH, J. D., PUTNAM, R. D., and ROCKMAN, B. A. 1981. *Bureaucrats and Politicians in Western Democracies*. Cambridge, Mass.: Harvard University Press.

BARTON, A. 1985. Background, attitudes, and activities of American elites. Pp. 173–218 in *Research in Politics and Society 1*, ed. G. Moore. Greenwich: JAI Press.

BEST, H., and BECKER U. eds. 1997. *Elites in Transition: Elite Research in Central and Eastern Europe*. Opladen: Leske & Budrich.

—— and COTTA, M. eds. 2000. *Parliamentary Representatives in Europe 1848–2000*. Oxford: Oxford University Press.

—— and EDINGER, M. 2005. Converging representative elites in Europe? An introduction to the EurElite project. *Czech Sociological Review*, 41: 499–510.

—— and JAHR, S. 2006. Politik als prekäres Beschäftigungsverhältnis: Mythos und Realität der Sozialfigur des Berufspolitikers im wiedervereinigten Deutschland. *Zeitschrift für Parlamentsfragen*, 37: 63–79.

BOTTOMORE, T. B. 1993. *Elites and Society*, 2nd edn. London: Routledge; originally published 1964.

BÜRKLIN, W. et al. 1997. *Eliten in Deutschland: Rekrutierung und Integration*. Opladen: Leske & Budrich.

CHRISTIANSEN, P. M., MØLLER, B., and TOGEBY, L. 2001. *Den danske elite*. Copenhagen: Hans Reitzels Forlag.

DAHL, R. A. 1961. *Who Governs?* New Haven: Yale University Press.

DOMHOFF, G. W. 1998. *Who Rules America?* Mountain View, Calif.: Mayfield; originally published 1967.

DYE, T. 2002. *Who's Running America? The Bush Restoration*. Englewood Cliffs, NJ: Prentice-Hall; originally published 1976.

GEL'MAN, V., and STEEN, A. eds. 2003. *Elites and Democratic Development in Russia*. London: Routledge.

GÖRANSSON, A. ed. 2007. *Maktens kön*. Nora: Nya Doxa.

GULBRANDSEN, T., and ENGELSTAD, F. 2005. Elite consensus on the Norwegian welfare model. *West European Politics*, 28: 898–918.

HEINZ, J. P., LAUMANN, E. O., NELSON, R. L., and SALISBURY, R. H. 1993. *The Hollow Core: Private Interests in National Policy Making*. Cambridge, Mass.: Harvard University Press.

HIGLEY, J., DEACON, D., and SMART, D. 1979. *Elites in Australia*. London: Routledge & Kegan Paul.

—— KULLBERG, J., and PAKULSKI, J. 1996. The persistence of postcommunist elites. *Journal of Democracy*, 7: 133–47.

HOFFMANN-LANGE, U. 1987. Surveying national elites in the Federal Republic of Germany. Pp. 27–47 in *Research Methods for Elite Studies*, ed. G. Moyser and M. Wagstaffe. London: Allen & Unwin.

—— KADUSHIN, C., and MOORE, G. 1991. Elite integration in stable democracies: a reconsideration. *European Sociological Review*, 7: 35–53.

—— 1992. *Eliten, Macht und Konflikt in der Bundesrepublik*. Opladen: Leske & Budrich.

—— NEUMANN, H., and STEINKEMPER, B. 1985. Conflict and consensus among elites in the Federal Republic of Germany. Pp. 243–83 in *Research in Politics and Society 1*, ed. G. Moore. Greenwich: JAI Press.

HUNTER, F. 1953. *Community Power Structure*. Chapel Hill: University of North Carolina Press.

—— 1959. *Top Leadership, U.S.A.* Chapel Hill: University of North Carolina Press.

KATZ, R. S., and WEßELS, B. eds. 1999. *The European Parliament, the National Parliaments, and European Integration*. Oxford: Oxford University Press.

KELLER, S. 1991. *Beyond the Ruling Class: Strategic Elites in Modern Society*. New Brunswick: Transaction Publishers (originally published in 1963).

KLINGEMANN, H.-D., STÖSS, R., and WEßELS, B. eds. 1991. *Politische Klasse und politische Institutionen*. Opladen: Westdeutscher Verlag.

KNOKE, D., PAPPI, F. U., BROADBENT, J., and TSUJINAKA, Y. 1996. *Comparing Policy Networks*. Cambridge: Cambridge University Press.

KOLABINSKA, M. 1912. *La Circulation des élites en France: étude historique depuis la fin du XIe siècle jusqu'à la Grande Revolution*. Lausanne: Imprimeries Réunies.

KOTZÉ, H., and STEYN, C. 2003: *African Elite Perspectives: AU and NEPAD—A Comparative Study across Seven African Countries*. Johannesburg: Konrad-Adenauer-Stiftung. www.kas.de/db_files/dokumente/7_dokument_dok_pdf_3813_1. pdf

LANE, D., and ROSS, C. 1999. *The Transition from Communism to Capitalism: Ruling Elites from Gorbachev to Yeltsin*. Houndmills: Macmillan.

LAUMANN, E. O., and KNOKE, D. 1987. *The Organizational State: Social Choice in National Policy Domains*. Madison: University of Wisconsin Press.

—— and PAPPI, F. U. 1976. *Networks of Collective Action*. New York: Academic Press.

Lerner, D. and Gorden, M. 1969. *Euratlantica: Changing Perspectives of the European Elites.* Cambridge: MIT Press.

Lerner, R., Nagai, A. K., and Rothman, S. 1996. *American Elites.* New Haven: Yale University Press.

McDonough, P. 1981. *Power and Ideology in Brazil.* Princeton: Princeton University Press.

Meyer, G. 1991. *Die DDR-Machtelite in der Ära Honecker.* Tübingen: A Francke Verlag.

Miller, W. E., and Stokes, D. E. 1963. Constituency influence in Congress. *American Political Science Review,* 57: 45–56.

—— Pierce, R., Thomassen, J., Holmberg, S., Esaiasson, P., and Weßels, B. 1999. *Policy Representation in Western Democracies.* Oxford: Oxford University Press.

Mills, C. W. 1956. *The Power Elite.* New York: Oxford University Press.

Mosca, G. 1939. *The Ruling Class.* New York: McGraw-Hill; originally published 1895.

Norris, P. ed. 1997. *Passages to Power: Legislative Recruitment in Advanced Democracies.* Cambridge: Cambridge University Press.

Pappi, F. U. 1984. Boundary specification and structural models of elite systems: social circles revisited. *Social Networks,* 6: 79–95.

Parry, G. 2005. *Political Elites.* Colchester: ECPR Press; originally published 1969.

Putnam, R. 1976. *The Comparative Study of Political Elites.* Englewood Cliffs, NJ: Prentice-Hall.

Raab, C. 1987. Oral history as an instrument of research into Scottish educational policy-making. Pp. 109–25 in *Research Methods for Elite Studies,* ed. G. Moyser and M. Wagstaffe. London: Allen & Unwin.

Ruostetsaari, I. 1993. The anatomy of the Finnish power elite. *Scandinavian Political Studies,* 16: 305–37.

—— 2006. Social upheaval and transformation of elite structures: the case of Finland. *Political Studies,* 54: 23–42.

Schmitt, H., and Thomassen, J. eds. 1999. *Political Representation and Legitimacy in the European Union.* Oxford: Oxford University Press.

Schneider, E. 1994. *Die politische Funktionselite der DDR.* Opladen: Westdeutscher Verlag.

Spence, J. M. 1996. *The European Union: "A View from the Top."* Wavre: EOS Gallup Europe.

Steen, A. 1997. *Between Past and Future: Elites, Democracy and the State in Post-Communist Countries. A Comparison of Estonia, Latvia and Lithuania.* Aldershot: Ashgate.

—— 2003. *Political Elites and the New Russia: The Power Basis of Yeltsin's and Putin's Regimes.* London: RoutledgeCurzon.

—— 2005. *National Elites in the Post-national Era: Ethno-politics and Internationalisation in the Baltic States.* Oslo: Arena Center, University of Oslo. **www.arena.uio.no/publications/working-papers2005/papers/wp05_06.pdf**

Szelényi, I., and Szelényi, S. 1995. Circulation or reproduction of elites during the postcommunist transformation of eastern Europe. *Theory and Society,* 24: 615–38.

Verba, S., and Orren, G. 1985. *Equality in America: A View from the Top.* Cambridge, Mass.: Harvard University Press.

—— Kelman, S., Orren, G., Miyake, I., Watanuki, J., Kabashima, I., and Ferree, G. 1987. *Elites and the Idea of Equality: A Comparison of Japan, Sweden, and the United States.* Cambridge, Mass.: Harvard University Press.

Welzel, C. 2000. East Germany: elite change and democracy's "instant success." Pp. 103–22 in *Elites after State Socialism,* ed. J. Higley and G. Lengyel. Lanham: Rowman & Littlefield.

Zapf, W. 1965. *Wandlungen der deutschen Elite.* Munich: Piper.

SUBJECT INDEX

Name Index